GREAT LAKES
LIGHTHOUSES
ENCYCLOPEDIA

GREAT LAKES
LIGHTHOUSES
ENCYCLOPEDIA

Larry & Patricia Wright

The BOSTON
MILLS PRESS

In memory of
Steven John (Burt) Ford
1952-2006

A BOSTON MILLS PRESS BOOK

Copyright © 2006 Larry and Patricia Wright

Published by Boston Mills Press, 2006
132 Main Street, Erin, Ontario N0B 1T0
Tel: 519-833-2407 Fax: 519-833-2195

In Canada:
Distributed by Firefly Books Ltd.
66 Leek Crescent
Richmond Hill, Ontario, Canada L4B 1H1

In the United States:
Distributed by Firefly Books (U.S.) Inc.
P.O. Box 1338, Ellicott Station
Buffalo, New York 14205

The publisher gratefully acknowledges the financial support
for our publishing program by the Government of Canada through
the Book Publishing Industry Development Program.

Library and Archives Canada Cataloguing in Publication

Wright, Larry, 1949-
Great Lakes lighthouses encyclopedia / Larry and Patricia Wright.

Includes index.
ISBN-13: 978-1-55046-399-6
ISBN-10: 1-55046-399-3

1. Lighthouses--Great Lakes (North America)--Pictorial works. 2. Lighthouses--
Great Lakes (North America)--History. I. Wright, Patricia, 1949- II. Title.

VK1023.3.W755 2006   386'.8550977   C2006-901324-1

Publisher Cataloging-in-Publication Data (U.S.)

Wright, Larry, 1949-
Great Lakes lighthouses encyclopedia ; Larry and Patricia Wright.
[448] p. : col. photos. ; cm.
Includes index.
ISBN-13: 978-1-55046-399-6
ISBN-10: 1-55046-399-3
1. Lighthouses -- Great Lakes (North America) -- Pictorial works.
2. Lighthouses -- Great Lakes (North America) -- History.
I. Wright, Patricia, 1949- II. Title.
386/.8550977 dc22   VK1023.3.W754 2006

Edited by Jane McWhinney
Designed by Gill Stead

Printed in China

Table of Contents

Lake Erie — USA

Lake Erie — Canada

Lake Huron — USA

Lake Huron — Canada

Lake Michigan — USA

Lake Superior — USA

Lake Superior — Canada

Preface

Created over a span of fifteen years, this book provides a fascinating look at the lighthouses that encircle the Great Lakes, from the St. Lawrence River to Duluth and the Lakehead. While not every light that ever existed is featured, most have been accounted for. We gathered this information from a wide range of resources: national archives, state and provincial archives, county and municipal archives, museums, university and public libraries, special collections, newspapers, periodicals, navigational guides, the internet, historical societies, port authorities, keepers and their families, other lighthouse authors and enthusiasts, the Canadian Coast Guard and the United States Coast Guard.

Although many people and groups have written in greater detail about their favorite lights or those with which they are most familiar, our hope is that this volume will accurately present the whole circle of Great Lakes lights and lend further impetus to their preservation. We traveled the lakes repeatedly to get an understanding of the distinct regions. We visited most of the existing lights on the lakes and are fortunate to have visited and photographed a number of lights that are now gone. Compiling and organizing the materials in this book was a labor of love.

Because so little is known about some of the lights, and because many lights on the lakes have similar names or have had multiple names over the years, it became a researcher's nightmare to sort out the data. Locations were sometimes vague, contradictions were abundant, and dates and names in government agencies and documents varied. It was a constant challenge to fit the available information into a proper timeline for the evolution of construction and to establish an accurate chronology for the lists of lighthouse keepers. What's more, lighthouse groups and museums on every lake seemed to have their own claim to fame for their local lighthouse ("the oldest light," "the tallest light," or perhaps "the last light to have a keeper"). We have done our best to respect shared knowledge and historical accuracy. Our hope is that people who have additional information about these lights will join us in our attempt to preserve the lighthouses and share their histories.

We hope that you enjoy this book.

The Great Lakes

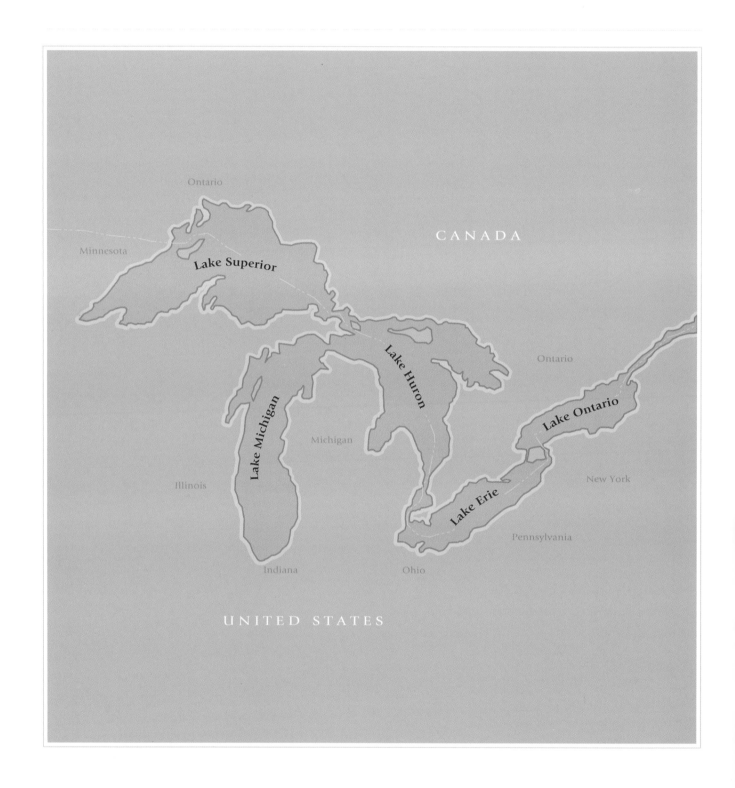

Introduction

Throughout the centuries lighthouses have played a vital role in mariners' spiritual as well as navigational needs. In the words of a French writer quoted in an 1872 *New York Times* article on Great Lakes lighthouses, "A beacon is the sailors' altar…The brilliant flash cheers him as he paces the forecastle of his lonely midnight watch when the weather is clear and the seas are calm. It reminds him of home and its loved surroundings, thousands of miles away. In foul weather, when black darkness reigns and seething waves and howling winds rage around him in a way that might appal the stoutest heart, at the very moment that his gaze is straining to his utmost to detect danger, the lighthouse flashes him a ray which guides his eye to the point of safety…."

Due to the enormous size of the Great Lakes — some 95,000 square miles (153,900 km²) of water surface and 5,872 miles (9,512 km) of coastal and island shoreline on the Canadian side and 5,159 miles (8358 km) on the American side — the distances between ports of call are dramatic. If a ship left the Port of Duluth on Lake Superior and passed Tibbetts Point on Lake Ontario at the entrance to the St. Lawrence River, it would have traveled some 1,160 miles (1879 km) through four of the five Great Lakes, two ship canals, and along three rivers.

The huge size of the lakes makes their weather hard to predict and their destructiveness sometimes devastating. Winds may pick up suddenly, churning shallow waters like those of Lake Erie into a frenzy. (A strong west wind can raise the water level at the east end of the lake by three feet [0.9 m] or more.) The configuration of the lakes makes it difficult for ships to outrun severe storms. Even in better weather, conditions often conspire to produce heavy fog. In the upper lakes, during early spring and late fall, blinding snow and sleet storms can cause heavy icing or "ice devils" on a ship, forcing it to the bottom under the extra weight. Such conditions made early navigation of the lakes perilous and demanding.

Staircase, Gibraltar Point Lighthouse

French immigration along the lower St. Lawrence River in the 1600s, and the push of the British into Upper Canada along the northern shores of the Great Lakes basin, brought the growth of settlement, the expansion of commerce and the need to move goods to market cheaply and quickly. Ships were the most effective means of transport. The first ship built on the Great Lakes was the *Frontenac*. It was constructed by the French at Frontenac (Kingston) and plied its trade up and down Lake Ontario.

The first ship above Niagara Falls, the *Griffon*, was launched in 1679 but was lost shortly thereafter, thought to have sunk in the area of Mackinac or off the west end of Manitoulin Island with a hold full of furs. HMS *Ontario* was sunk off the sandbars and shoals near Golden Hill Creek in Lake Ontario while carrying a payroll of gold and silver. These and countless other stories of loss and damage suggested a need to light the coastlines against its notorious hazards.

The American side of the Great Lakes was settled more slowly than the north side, but as they did settle along the south shores of the lakes, new trade routes were developed to move goods from the continent's interior. The lakes provided a perfect thoroughfare. However, increased shipping in the 1700s brought with it more and more tragedies and loss of life.

Both countries realized the need for safe shipping lanes. Two of the first three lights on the lakes were a combination of landfall and port of destination lights. The identity of first lighthouse is in question. Some historians say it was a light shown from a cupola on top of the barracks at Fort Niagara. The light is sad to have been there before the 1800s, and yet paintings of that time period do not show it. However, it does appear in paintings and sketches done later in the 1800s. The first freestanding lighthouse on the Great Lakes was built by the British at Newark (now Niagara-on-the-Lake) and was lit in 1804. Its first keeper, Dominick Henry, was charged with keeping this lighthouse on Mississauga Point. In the course of a heated battle on May 27, 1813, during the War of 1812, Henry and his wife helped the wounded and gave refreshments to the British troops as the United States squadron bombarded everything around them (the lighthouse being in the line of fire of the American fleet aiming at Fort George).

The second light established on the lakes was on Gibraltar Point at York (Toronto). It was a stone tower 52 feet (16 m) high and was completed in 1808. Today, it is the oldest standing light on the lakes. Although no longer active, it is still viewed by thousands of people each year as they pass by on harbor cruises. The third Upper Canada light was to be built at Isle Forest (Simcoe Island) near Kingston; however, it was delayed until 1833. The first official United States lights on the Great Lakes were established at Buffalo, New York, and Erie, Pennsylvania.

As the United States population expanded west, the demand grew for more illumination along the south shores of the Great Lakes. Goods were transported from all corners of the lakes: wood from the upper lakes, coal from Pennsylvania, copper and iron from Lake Superior, and grain from Ohio and the Midwest. The variety of topography made all sorts of different types of lighthouses necessary. The first were coastal lights or landfall lights, to help mariners locate points of land on the lakes. This was achieved by building lighthouses with a focal point high enough to cast a beam far out to sea. Flash and eclipse patterns, as well as daymarks, also gave mariners a bearing by which to determine their precise location. The next group of lights were distinctive warning lights built on islands, shoals or other hazardous landforms in or near shipping lanes. Another group of lights, such as the light at the entrance to the Welland Canal, marked entrances to harbors, bays, canals and rivers.

Lightships also became an important aid to navigation in the early 1800s. They could easily be moved into place and anchored over shoals, reefs and shifting sandbars where it was impossible to construct lighthouses. They were also used to mark the entrance to such channels as the Long Point Cut, where a lot of "blackbirding" occurred. (By giving false shore signals, "blackbirders" created shipwrecks so they could pillage the cargo. The presence of lightships made it harder for them to operate.) Lightships could also be deployed to mark a wreck in a shipping lane until the wreck could be removed. As well, they were often more economical than lighthouses. The main drawback with lightships was that in high seas or storms they served at their own peril. They were required not to abandon their post for any reason until the end of the shipping season or until they were otherwise relieved. The ships, minimally powered, would sometimes lose their moorings and end up off their stations, or sometimes sink, as in the case of the lightship *Buffalo*, which went down in the severe fall storm of 1913. The last lightship on the Great Lakes was the steel-hulled *Huron*, which was retired in 1970.

Range lights were useful for mariners. They worked in pairs to enable a ship to set a course or make a course correction. Sailors would take a sighting on them, and when they were in line with each other they knew they were on course. These lights were mostly used in rivers and channels, but they were also used in dangerous bay areas to guide mariners safely toward and into port.

The last category of lights are the pierhead lights. Their function was to help guide ships into port. A captain could tell by the type and color of a light whether to approach from the port or the starboard side and where to line up on the sight line. At Grand Haven, on Lake Michigan, for example, the double lights are used as range lights and were painted red so that the navigator knew to keep them to the starboard side.

Until the advent of electricity, the light from a lighthouse always came from some sort of open flame or mantle lamp. The first fishermen sailing home at night would light a lantern so that fishermen returning after dark could line their vessels up with it and sail into harbor safely. Pointe au Baril on the St. Lawrence River got its name from the custom of burning fuel in a barrel to light the shoreline, and Pointe au Baril, on Georgian Bay got its name from a lantern in a barrel placed on a mast at the entrance to the channel.

Even into the early nineteenth century, candles were used as the source of light in lighthouses. However, even though the candleholders had reflectors mounted behind them, they did not emit much light. The next refinement of light was wicked lamps, ranging from solid wicks to circular and flat wicks. Unfortunately, the burning of fuel and wick created a lot of soot and left such a greasy film on the glass and reflectors that it actually obscured the light. Winslow Lewis's oil lamps with parabolic reflectors were an improvement, but they were still not good enough for the task at hand. Experiments with the Fresnel lens began in the 1840s, but it wasn't until the formation of the new Lighthouse Board that serious consideration was given to purchasing this new lens system.

In the mid-nineteenth century, it became a matter of international reputation to establish effective lighthouses: "There is no one of the many hard things which foreigners say about us more than just that in which we are

Old Fort Niagara

accused of criminal disregard of human life … and property … there is no country equal in wealth with the United States… and has done so little to organize means for saving life and property… I have more than once read in the ships-news column of the New York papers notice of this sort in which it was stated that buoys, or beacons, or lightships, had gone missing from their place for a week or fortnight." ("Policemen of the Sea," *Harper's New Monthly Magazine*, 1869.) The voice of public indignation had been growing louder in the United States during the 1850s and 1860s. It required decisive responses.

The organization of lighthouse services had long been in disarray. They were first managed by private interests, shipping organizations, communities or individual states. Then, in turn, the responsibility for American lighthouses was passed to the Secretary of the Treasury, the Commissioner of Revenue in 1792, back to the Secretary of the Treasury in 1802, and then back to the Commissioner of Revenue in 1813. Finally, the Fifth Auditor of the Treasury was put in control in 1820, and responsibility remained in its hands until 1852. Lighthouses were never a high priority with them. They were just another budget to control. In 1852 Congress set up the nine-member Lighthouse Board, mostly made up of military people, to administer the maintenance and oversee development of lighthouses. Under their auspices the network of lights expanded and the lightkeeper's job became more clearly defined.

Under the Lighthouse Board, the system of navigation aid also grew strong. However, in 1910, it was changed again. Congress decided that the Lighthouse Board was not to be controlled by the military, and so the Bureau of Lighthouses (also known as the Lighthouse Establishment) was formed and staffed almost completely by civilians. In 1939 the government (in a logical move) put the control of lighthouses in the care of the United States Coast Guard, which handled all of the aids to navigation, including shore patrol and lifesaving.

Meanwhile, Canadian lighthouses developed under the guidelines of similar institutions. Until 1841 lighthouses on the Great Lakes fell under the jurisdiction of the House of Assembly for Upper Canada. In that year Upper and Lower Canada united into Canada West, and lighthouse maintenance and development became the responsibility of the Department of Public Works for Canada West. When Canada became a country with Confederation in 1867, lighthouses came under the jurisdiction of the newly formed Department of Marine and Fisheries. When the Department of Transport was set up in 1936, lighthouses were thus transferred. This department also controlled the Canadian Coast Guard, which became responsible for transporting lighthouse keepers and managing lighthouse maintenance. Later, the Canadian Coast Guard was placed under the umbrella of the Department of Oceans and Fisheries and lighthouses thus became a part of their jurisdiction, as the Canadian Coast Guard serviced them. With the Coast Guard's involvement in new technologies came the final working phase of lighthouses.

Better equipment meant better lighting. As of the mid-1850s, lights were upgraded, towers had sections added to raise them and give them a better focal plane, and Fresnel lenses of different orders replaced the Lewis lamps. The number of lights along the shores and on the shoals was increased. Towers were constructed of newer designs and sturdier, more weather-resistant materials. Keepers' residences better suited the needs of the keepers and their families.

Tower designs varied widely. There are ten basic styles and numerous other individual or modified styles of towers on the lakes:

- the *conical* tower usually made of stone or brick, like St. Helena;
- the *skeletal* tower made of wood, iron or steel, like Rawley or Whitefish Point;
- the *pyramidal* tower made of wood or iron plate, like Frankfort;
- the *pyramidal style* with dwelling attached made of wood, like Salmon Point (basically a Canadian-style light built because they were inexpensive to erect and could be moved if necessary);
- the *schoolhouse* style made of wood or brick, like Copper Harbor (basically a rectangular building with a square tower up the middle at one end on the outside of the building);
- the *octagonal* brick, stone or wooden tower (some were affixed to a corner of a building, like Eagle Harbor, or just the tower like Port Burwell);
- the *round* or *cylindrical* tower made of brick or stone, like St. James Harbor;
- the *square* tower, usually brick, with a circular brick liner, like Forty Mile Point;
- the *square integral* tower made of wood or steel, like Fairport Harbor or Snug Harbour (basically a building with a square tower going up from the inside of it);
- the *flying buttress* tower made of reinforced concrete, like Caribou Island.

There are a number of exceptions as well, like the style at Toledo Harbor, Point Abino, Sand Hills and Split Rock.

The materials for these lights varied greatly according to the time of construction and the availability of materials. The first towers were made out of wood or rubble-stone, but sandstone was used on many sites in the early 1800s. Granite became a material of choice for a number of curved stone towers and dwellings. At the top of the tower, granite was necessary as a stabilizing floor to support the weight of the lantern rooms that housed the new Fresnel system for the Canadian imperial towers.

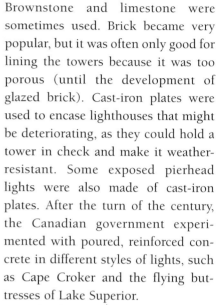
Rawley Lighthouse

Brownstone and limestone were sometimes used. Brick became very popular, but it was often only good for lining the towers because it was too porous (until the development of glazed brick). Cast-iron plates were used to encase lighthouses that might be deteriorating, as they could hold a tower in check and make it weather-resistant. Some exposed pierhead lights were also made of cast-iron plates. After the turn of the century, the Canadian government experimented with poured, reinforced concrete in different styles of lights, such as Cape Croker and the flying buttresses of Lake Superior.

With the new developments in lighthouse design and function came a need for better-trained keepers and a new evaluation of their role. Keepers had always been under-appreciated, but they were a dedicated group who took their job seriously and maintained the lights at all costs. They took it as their solemn duty to get to their stations early in the season so their lights would be lit for the beginning of the shipping season, and they would stay at their station until freeze-up, sometimes having to walk miles across ice at the end of the season. Occasionally they were forced to winter over, and some did not survive.

Although political appointments often played a large part in a lightkeeper's hiring, the keeper's job was not exactly a plum position. Keepers were poorly paid and led a meager existence. A keeper with a family would hope to have his wife appointed assistant keeper so they would have additional income. (That also benefitted the board, as it saved them the expense of building separate quarters for the assistant keeper.) In a number of cases, the government put a family at a station knowing that they would get free labour from members of the keeper's family. Keepers often relied on their wives and daughters to maintain the lighthouse so they and their sons could try to earn additional income from other sources.

Up until the mid-1880s, keepers were also poorly trained. Very few instructions were written down; they

Kincardine Lighthouse

learned the role informally through verbal communications with inspectors or other keepers. After the Lighthouse Board was established and the need for better information was realized, no fewer than ten manuals were written for American lighthouse keepers, spelling out procedures. The instructions were so detailed that a keeper had little room to use his own ingenuity, and the job was frequently routine and monotonous. They were to keep the light and the lantern rooms spotless; they were to maintain the equipment and the grounds in accordance with the board's instructions; during storms they had to do their utmost to keep the light burning at its brightest, even if it meant venturing out on the gallery to clear ice from the lantern. Other duties in the 1881 "Instruction to Employees of the Lighthouse Service" were less routine: "Shipwrecks are to be reported promptly to the inspector. It is the duty of the main-keepers to aid wrecked persons as far as lies in their power."

Although American keepers were uniformed by the government in 1884, they were not made part of the Civil Service until 1896. If they were injured on the job, for whatever reason, there were no benefits owing them or their families, and they were not given any retirement benefits until the act of 1918. All keepers were also made responsible for their own equipment. If something was lost or damaged, the cost of its replacement would be taken out of their pay.

These men and women, who were so important to commercial growth and the preservation of life in our two great countries, were so badly treated, under-acknowledged and poorly rewarded that one can't help thinking of it in terms of the "criminal disregard of human life" complained about in the aforementioned *Harper's* article.

With the development of new navigation aids, radio beacons, radar, DECCA/RACAL, LORAN C — and now GPS, DGPS and electronic maps — the need for functional lighthouses, especially for commercial traffic, is nearing an end. However, the moral and meaningful need continues. Small vessels still rely on visuals to assist them, and mariners still speak of their personal, perhaps even spiritual, need for lighthouses. Also, lighthouses have proven through the years that they continue to work well when GPS signals are not functioning.

It is sincerely to be hoped that the remaining lighthouses in the Circle of Lights around the Great Lakes will continue to shine long into the future. With growing interest in their history and a renewal of restoration efforts, perhaps their numbers may even increase.

LAKE ONTARIO
USA
LIGHTHOUSES

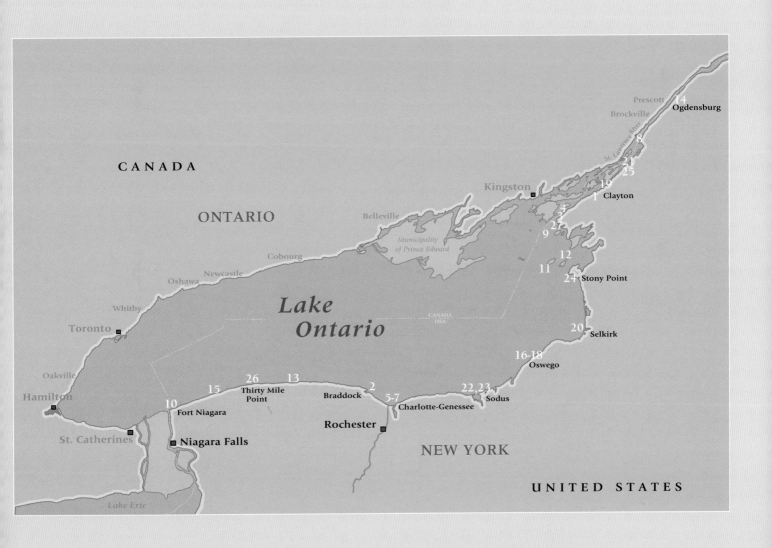

CANADA

ONTARIO

Belleville

Kingston

Prescott
Brockville
Ogdensburg

14

St. Lawrence River

8

21
25

19
1 Clayton

4
27
9

12

11

24 Stony Point

Cobourg

Newcastle
Oshawa

Municipality
of Prince Edward

Whitby

Toronto

Lake
Ontario

CANADA
USA

20
Selkirk

Oakville

16-18
Oswego

Hamilton

15
Thirty Mile
Point

26   13

Braddock   2
5-7
Charlotte-Genessee

22,23
Sodus

10
Fort Niagara

Rochester

St. Catherines

Niagara Falls

NEW YORK

UNITED STATES

Lake Erie

1 Bartlett's Point Light

In June 1838 a report to Congress recommended a lighthouse at Bartlett's Point on the St. Lawrence River where the French Creek emptied into the river. The many hidden shoals in this area, especially on the north side of the river, made night navigation impossible. The site the inspector had chosen was 60 feet (18.5 m) above the river, a spot that could be seen for 14 miles (22.5 km) on three different channels (the upper and lower American channels and the Kingston channel). As traffic on the river increased, this was considered an important location for a light.

The report recommended a 30-foot (9 m) limestone tower and a 1½-story keeper's house. The tower, which was to have an iron lantern with ten lamps and ten stationary reflectors, had an estimated cost of $500, while the proposed total for the whole complex was $1,950. Although Congress approved the building of a lighthouse at Bartlett's Point, it is not known whether this light was ever built.

Braddock Point Lighthouse

2 Braddock Point Lighthouse

In the late nineteenth century the U.S. government planned to build a lighthouse on Lake Ontario at Braddock Point to help mariners navigate between Rochester to the east and the entrance to the Welland Canal to the west. Many vessels had been lost in storms around this area. However, the lighthouse was actually built on Bogus Point, about 3 miles (4.8 km) from Braddock Point. The architect, Lt. Col. Jared A. Smith, designed it after Cleveland's second shore light. In fact, since the Cleveland Light was torn down in 1895, its lantern, Fresnel lens, and ornate metal work were taken to the light at Bogus Point in 1896. Although it was built on the wrong point, it was always called the Braddock Point Light.

The 110-foot (33.8 m) red brick tower was attached to its 2½-story red brick keeper's house. Long narrow windows provided daylight for the 118 steps of the circular tower stairs. The watchroom below the lantern had four ornately framed windows. Scrolled braces supported the octagonal gallery around the circular base of the lantern, and an iron pipe railing surrounded a second, higher gallery that encircled the glass of the polygonal lantern. The tower was capped with a high arched dome with ribbing to join its panels. A ventilator ball and lightning rod topped off the dome. This was to be "the brightest light on Lake Ontario" and its 3½-order Fresnel lens to provide 20,000 candlepower for a beam with an 18-mile (29 km) optimum visibility.

The tower and the ten-room keeper's house were both built in Victorian style. Two small porches on the house faced the water and a larger more ornate veranda ran across the back. A tall chimney extended out of the roof on either side of the front of the house, and a larger one rose out of the roof peak farther back. The station also included a boathouse and a carriage house.

The lighthouse remained in operation until it was extinguished on January 1, 1954. At this time the government placed a light on a 55-foot (16.8 m) skeletal tower. Its visibility was much lower than the old light. Shortly thereafter the government tore down two-thirds of the original tower because of extensive deterioration. The remains were nicknamed "the stump." For a time, government officials lived in the house; for a time it sat empty and was vandalized.

In 1957, and again in 1985, it was sold to private owners.

Its current owners, Bob and Barbara Thulin, have spent ten years renovating the lighthouse, returning it to its original layout and refurbishing or replacing woodwork, according to the original architectural drawings, which they possess. In 1995 they rebuilt the tower to 65 feet (20 m) and on February 28, 1996, the U.S. Coast Guard relit the light. It now had a higher intensity light than the one in the skeletal tower, making it visible for 15 miles (24 km). The redundant skeletal tower was removed. The lighthouse used to sit closer to the water, but erosion has washed away about 30 feet (9.2 m) of the original frontage. To prevent this from continuing, a 175-foot (54 m) breakwall has been put in front of the lighthouse.

The Thulins are very proud of having saved a light for future generations. Since the light is privately owned, their privacy needs to be respected, but they do offer tours of the lighthouse. Was it coincidence or fate that this light was relit exactly 100 years after its original lighting?

Known Keepers: Frank Coleman (1896–1929), Michael Fitzpatrick (1929–35), Claude Jacox (1939–47), R. Millar USCG (1947–50).

Early Braddock Point Lighthouse

Cape Vincent Breakwater Light

3 Cape Vincent Breakwater Lights

In 1900 a pair of lighthouses were built, one at each end of the breakwater at Cape Vincent, New York, on the south side of the head of the St. Lawrence River. Each light was about 20 feet (6 m) from its end of the breakwall, and each was a short square white clapboard tower that flared slightly at the top to support its square gallery and black octagonal lantern. Both lights displayed a fixed red lens-lantern from a 25.5-foot (7.8 m) focal plane. After marking the Cape Vincent Harbor for 50 years, one light was moved to its present location in 1951. No longer on the water, it now sits on a hill and greets visitors as they enter the town of Cape Vincent. The whereabouts of the second light is unknown.

Known Keepers: John Larock (1901–10), Ralph Scobie (1910–10), William Wybrando (1910–12), Halsey Crapo (1912–29), Frank Sellman (1929–32).

Carleton Island Lighthouse, 1911

4 Carleton Island Lighthouse

During the 1700s Carleton Island was known as Buck or Deer Island, and it had a trading post for French merchants and Native Americans. However, by 1774 the island, then under British control, was renamed Carleton Island, in honor of British commander Sir Guy Carleton. Thanks to the island's strategic location 3 miles (4.8 km) northeast of Cape Vincent and between it and Wolfe Island in the St. Lawrence River, the British chose the site for a fort. Gunboats such as the *Ontario* and the *Limeade* were built here. The fort stored food and arms awaiting transport to Fort Oswego and Fort Niagara.

By the late 1700s only a small British contingent remained at the fort. During the War of 1812 the Americans easily took control of the fort and destroyed it. In 1817, as part of a boundary settlement, the island was ceded to the United States. As shipping increased, a lighthouse was built at the head of Carleton Island in 1898 to guide ships entering the St. Lawrence River from Lake Ontario.

The lighthouse first displayed a fixed white lens lantern light, suspended from a white mast on the island's bluff, providing a focal plane of 95 feet (29 m) above the water. Other buildings included a white two-story keeper's house and a white boathouse below the bluff.

Records from 1904 show that a proper lighthouse was then in use. It displayed a fixed white light using a fifth-order lens and a center-draft lamp that used one wick and burned about 8 gallons (32 l) of mineral oil a month. The original keeper, Charles Tucker, transferred the lighthouse property and equipment to Robert Allen on May 28, 1904.

When the light was later automated with a modern system of skeletal range lights just prior to the opening of the St. Lawrence Seaway in April 1959, the light and keeper's house were sold. In June 1966 the Saint Lawrence Seaway Development Corporation dismantled the Carleton Island towers.

Known Keepers: Charles Tucker (1898–1904), Robert Allen (1904–09), Hector De Grasse (1909–13).

5 Charlotte-Genesee Lighthouse

The Port of Genesee on the lower shore of Lake Ontario, was formally established by Congress in 1805. It grew quickly. At first, schooners and other vessels were guided around the sandbar at the river mouth and into the river by lanterns — one in the window of the local hotel and another in a "pilot tree." On arriving at the tree, vessels whistled and rang bells until they reached shore.

In 1820 Congress appropriated $5,000 to build a lighthouse at the mouth of the Genesee River to replace the pilot tree and enable a safer and less noisy entry into the harbor. In 1821 the government purchased 3¼ acres (1.3 hectares) from Mrs. Mehitabel Hincher, whose family had settled the land, for $400. Ashbel Symonds completed the lighthouse by September 1822 at a cost of $3,300.

The octagonal limestone tower was built to last, with foundation walls 4½ feet (1.4 m) thick and tower walls tapering from a base thickness of 3½ feet (1 m) to 2 feet (0.6 m) in the upper levels. The base of the octagonal tower was 22 feet (6.7 m) in diameter, the lantern 11 feet (3.3 m), and the gallery deck 13 feet (4 m). The original lantern was a birdcage style with 18 small "lights" in each of the octagonal sections, making a total of 144 panes. The lantern was equipped with ten Winslow Lewis lamps and reflectors. The lamps were fueled with whale oil. A two-room keeper's house was built adjacent to it and, a well 52 feet (16 m) deep was dug nearby.

This tower, originally on the west bluff close to the lake, is today at least a quarter of a mile farther back. In 1929 Congress

Charlotte-Genesee Lighthouse

appropriated $10,000 to improve the port. Improvements included cutting down trees for harbor visibility, building two piers 360 feet (110 m) apart and extending them 2,500 feet (765 m) into the lake to prevent a sandbar at the river mouth. Sand then began collecting along the piers, and since then the beach has continued to grow, extending the land area out into the water.

In 1838 a secondary light was placed at the end of the west pier. In 1852 Congress appropriated $2,600 to rebuild the pierhead light, install a new lens, and build a catwalk to it for the keeper's protection, adding another $2,000 to renovate the lighthouse on the bluff. In 1853 the original wooden stairs were replaced by a cast-iron stairway supported by a liner of inner bricks; the lamps and reflectors were replaced by a fourth-order Fresnel lens; and a new cast-iron deck and decagonal lantern with large panes replaced the old birdcage-style lantern, whose many astragals would have impeded the new light's beam.

In 1863 the government tore down the small keeper's house and used the stone for the foundation of the new 2½-story red brick keeper's house, which still stands today. The new house was connected to the tower by a brick passageway. It had a slate roof and double chimneys for stoves in several rooms. The front of the house has what looks like bricked-up windows but they were put there for architectural balance. The keeper tended a vegetable garden and small fruit trees on the north side of the lighthouse. Plank sidewalks were used until the early 1900s.

Fourteen keepers had tenure at this light. Giles Holden, the second in line, had a large family and built a wooden addition onto the two-room keeper's house to accommodate them. Then, when he was no longer keeper, he moved the addition across the street as the start of his new home.

In 1881 this lighthouse on the bluff was deactivated, much to the chagrin of many mariners. Its lantern and lens were placed instead on the light at the end of the west pier. Although it was no longer in service itself, keepers lived in it to maintain the pier light. In 1939 the U.S. Coast Guard absorbed the U.S. Lighthouse Service. In 1947, when the pier light was fully automated and the keeper was unnecessary, the brick house became the residence for the local chief of the Coast Guard until 1982.

In 1965 rumor spread that the Coast Guard was going to tear down the lighthouse. Public indignation, led by local high school students, made the Coast Guard maintain the lighthouse.

In 1981 the Coast Guard proposed to vacate the premises and asked the Charlotte Community Association if they wanted to lease the property while they decided what to do with it. The Association agreed, and in September 1982 they leased the two buildings. Almost immediately, the Charlotte-Genesee Lighthouse Historical Society was formed to restore the old tower, lantern and lens, and establish a museum. Students at the Edison Tech High School built a new wooden replica lantern, and the U.S. Coast Guard loaned and installed a fourth-order Fresnel lens in the new location. The lamp was relit in June 1984 as part of the Rochester Sesquicentennial Celebrations.

In the course of a 1983 archaeological dig by St. John Fisher College, the original lightning rod for the lighthouse was unearthed, as well as the original well on the south side of the property. The original windlass, chain and oak bucket had been replaced by a hand-operated force pump.

In 1991 the property was deeded over from the U.S. government to Monroe County. The Lighthouse Society has a 20-year lease to operate the premises as a museum. The Genesee Lighthouse tower is the oldest government structure in Monroe

Early Charlotte-Genesee Lighthouse

County. In 1992 the light was permanently relit to act as a rear range light for the light at the end of the west pier.

Through the action of interested parties, the local lighthouse was saved and today houses a beautiful museum. The buildings remain much as they were, with flourishing flower and vegetable gardens. A rose garden surrounds a boat-mast flagpole, a gift from the great-great-grandchildren of Michael Cook, a stonemason who worked on the lighthouse in 1822. Picnic tables and benches invite visitors to sit and watch the boat traffic on the river.

Known Keepers: David Denman (1822–23?), Giles Holden (1823–35), James Ruggles (1836–37), James O'Maley (1837–38), Roswell Paine (1838–43), Osborn Handford (1843–43), Peter Hillman (1843–47), Martha Warne (1847–49), Erastus Phelps (1849–53), Luther Jeffords (1853–58), Andrew Mulligan (1858–61), John Stephanson (1861–68), D. Budd (1868–68), Rawson Smith (1868–80).

Early Charlotte-Genesee West Pierhead Light

6 Charlotte-Genesee West Pierhead Light

In 1838 a secondary light was placed at the end of the west pier at Charlotte at the mouth of the Genesee River on Lake Ontario to assist vessels into the harbor. Little is known about this light except that it was wooden, built on a pile foundation, and replaced by another wooden lighthouse after a fierce Lake Ontario storm washed it away. The keeper of the main light also tended this pier light.

In 1852 Congress appropriated $2,600 to rebuild the pier light, install a new lens and build a catwalk to the tower for the keeper's safety. It was built on the sturdy pile foundation of the previous light in 1853. The square wooden tower had a base diameter of 15 feet (4.6 m) and supported a dodecagonal lantern with a plate glass panel on each side. The lantern was topped with a zinc-lined dome and housed a sixth-order Fresnel lens (a harbor-sized lens) that came from France at a cost of $400. From a 28-foot (8.5 m) focal plane the light was visible on a clear night for a "considerable distance."

In 1881 this wooden lighthouse was replaced by a new iron beacon, also built at the end of the west pier. A fog signal bell with a striking mechanism was installed with this light. The main lighthouse on the bluff was deactivated at this time, and its more powerful fourth-order Fresnel lens was removed and set in this new pierhead light. While mariners were unhappy with this change, the government stuck to the new plans.

In 1884 this iron tower was relocated to Cleveland Harbor and a new 28-foot (8.5 m) white square gently tapering wooden tower was built to replace it. The new tower was also built on the pile foundation, and the decagonal lantern from the old main light-

house was transferred to it. The new light, housing the fourth-order Fresnel lens from the iron tower, was first lit on April 1, 1884.

More changes occurred as the new century approached. In 1893 a steam fog whistle replaced the fog bell in a building behind the light. In 1896 the west pier was extended 500 feet (150 m) and the light tower and fog signal building were both moved to the end of the pier. In 1902 extensive repairs were made to the west pier, including upgrading the wooden catwalk to a steel one. A diaphone fog signal replaced the fog whistle and a telephone was installed to connect the west pier light with the keeper's home.

Then in 1931 this clapboard lighthouse at the end of the west pier was replaced by a more modern steel skeletal tower that supported a large square gallery, watchroom and lantern. A control station to operate the light was also built onshore near the pier, making light tending much easier for the keepers. This tower served for 64 years, the longest period of time for any of the west pier lights.

In 1939 the U.S. Coast Guard took over the operation of the light from the U.S. Lighthouse Service. During the 1930s and 1940s the lights, fog signal and radio beacon were modernized and automated, so that a full-time keeper was no longer needed. In 1995 the metal tower was dismantled and replaced by a cyclindrical steel one with a modern beacon. While perhaps more durable and functional, it lacks the charm of its wooden predecessors.

Known Keepers: Roswell Paine (1838–43), Osborn Handford (1843–43), Peter Hillman (1843–47), Martha Warne (1847–49), Erastus Phelps (1849–53), Luther Jeffords (1853–58), Andrew Mulligan (1858–61), John Stephanson (1861–68), D. Budd (1868), Smith Rawson (1868–82), Alonzo Corey (1884–99), Richard Tonge (1899–1913), George Codding (1913–40).

7 Charlotte-Genesee East Pier Light

As Charlotte developed as a harbor along Lake Ontario's south shore, it received more maritime traffic. During 1902 harbor improvements, a new beacon was placed at the end of the east pier to facilitate harbor entry. It was a short square two-story wooden tower placed on a raised platform and then raised on block pillars to allow stormy waters to wash beneath the lighthouse. While the bottom half of the tower had straight walls, the tower tapered sharply midway up (almost like a mansard-style roof) and then tapered only slightly to the top. The walls were covered with clapboarding, and a large square gallery overhung the top of the tower.

A large decagonal iron lantern displayed a fixed red light, and it was capped with a segmented and ribbed decagonal dome, a ventilator ball and a lightning rod. Entry was provided by an iron ladder from the pier up to its raised door in the lower level. The keeper for the other Genesee lights also tended this light. It is unknown how long this light serviced the harbor.

Charlotte-Genesee East Pier Light, circa 1910

Crossover Island Lighthouse

8 Crossover Island Lighthouse

Crossover Island Lighthouse is a short white lighthouse that sits on a small island among the Thousand Islands in the St. Lawrence River, near Oak Point, New York. The island got its name because it marked the point where vessels crossed between American waters and the Canadian Channel. While the lighthouse sits on rock at the east end of the island, the 1½-story keeper's house, which resembles an ordinary red farmhouse, nestles on a grassy lawn about mid-island surrounded by mature deciduous trees.

The lighthouse was first built in 1848 but had to be rebuilt in 1882 because of its inferior construction materials. This new lighthouse was built of iron and painted white with a red lantern that housed a sixth-order Fresnel lens. Its illuminant was at first whale oil, later kerosene, and still later batteries that supplied electrical power to light the lens. The keeper's house is similar to the one at Tibbetts Point — red with white trim, six rooms and a cellar. The island constituted an independent complex including the keeper's house, the lighthouse tower, a well, a hen house, a barn, a privy, an oil house and an ash house.

Ralph Hill grew up at Crossover Island, where his father Daniel was keeper from 1909 to 1931. While there, he rescued hundreds of stranded mariners, including occupants of a crashed biplane. Ralph's father rowed the children three quarters of a mile (1.2 km) across the channel to the one-room schoolhouse. The government tender, the *S.S. Crocus*, brought supplies such as coal, kerosene oil, soap, paint, flour and lard twice a year. It left a large box of books for the lighthouse library and picked up others to recycle them at the next lighthouse. The *S.S. Crocus* also doubled as a buoy tender and its crew placed navigation aids and channel markers each spring and collected them at the end of the season.

The Hill family did a lot to supplement government supplies. They raised their own pigs and chickens and, on June nights when the eels surfaced to feed on eel flies,

they speared hundreds of eels. They used the ash house to smoke their own pork, fish and eels. Islanders bought their surplus smoked eel to make hors d'oeuvres for winter parties. Mrs. Hill also earned extra money doing laundry for Oak Point cottagers. She also recycled cloth flour sacks to make undergarments for herself and the girls, or to make a doll or a toy from the pattern prestamped onto the flour sacking.

The seven Hill children entertained themselves swimming, making small sailboats, playing marbles, flying kites and making whistles, and by playing croquet, badminton and mumley-peg (a jackknife-tossing game). Their father made the croquet mallets, and they always had a surplus of croquet balls that had floated down the stream that ran past the island after being knocked into the water. Mr. Hill used some of the extra croquet balls as finials to put on the flagpoles that he made for cottagers.

Water was available from two sources: drinking water from a well, and rainwater from the house eaves stored in a cistern in the cellar for washing. There were two stoves: a large, six-hole, cast-iron stove in the kitchen and a smaller three-burner oil stove in the summer kitchen for hot days. At the end of the navigation season the family moved back to Ogdensburg, where they reveled in running water, indoor plumbing and electric lights.

The lighthouse was decommissioned in April 1941 and today is a privately owned cottage. Viewed from the American shore road, it is most picturesque, with waves lapping at the island's edge, seagulls flying overhead, and river traffic skirting it on either side.

Known Keepers: Ober Robeson (1848–51), Samuel Whitney (1851–56), E. Robertson (1856–61), J. Hill (1861–85), James Hammond (1885–94), John Larock (1894–1901), John Reddy (1901–03), Mial Eggleston (1903–06), Michael Fitzpatrick (1906–08), George Ward (1908–09), Daniel Hill (1909–31), Edward Sweet Jr. (1932–39), Frank Ward (1939–41).

Early Crossover Island Lighthouse

East Charity Shoal Lighthouse

9 East Charity Shoal Lighthouse

Satellite imagery has allowed scientists to determine that the East Charity Shoal is not a shoal but a dished-out crater with a mountain range surrounding it. This underwater landscape in Lake Ontario waters, 7 miles (11.3 km) southwest of Tibbetts Point is a hazard to navigation, and many vessels have rammed into it. In July 1856 the U.S. government appropriated $5,000 to place a day beacon on Charity Shoal. The *Kingston Daily News* of November 22, 1856 carried the following Notice to Mariners: "Charity Shoal, Lake Ontario — The following are the different bearings of the different head lands from the Day Beacon which has just been placed on the shoal by Captain Malcolm, for the U.S. Light House Board. It is 24 feet [7.3 m] high, and can be seen from the deck of a vessel 5 miles [8 km]."

On November 18, 1868, the *Kingston Daily News* reported that despite rescue efforts, the schooner *S. Robinson* still remained on Charity Shoal. A rescue operation was in progress and her sails, anchor, chain cables and about 1,000 bushels of wheat had been removed to lighten the vessel in hopes of pulling her off the shoal. However, the heavy sea was working against the tug trying to free the vessel. Reports of this kind were fairly common.

In 1929 a lighthouse was built to mark the shoal. A square 12-foot (3.7 m) concrete platform was built right where it rose out of the water. A ladder on of the side walls gave access from a boat to the top of the platform. A 10-foot (3 m) black base, which included windows and a door, was placed in the center of this platform to support the lighthouse and to make it higher, since it had been brought from a prior site. This base had a pipe iron railing around the top and a ladder up its side. When the light was placed on its new base, a 5-foot (1.5 m) section was added under it, perhaps for height, or perhaps to patch an entrance area.

The white cast-iron tower tapers gently as it rises, and then flares out at the cornice to support the black gallery, lantern and dome. The octagonal sides have small porthole-style windows to provide interior light. The lantern used to display a gas light using a fifth-order Fresnel lens. Its present lens was installed in 1992. The tower's focal plane is 52 feet (16 m).

This reused tower has an interesting history. It was first used at Vermillion, Ohio, in 1877, but was removed in the 1920s after it was dislodged by moving ice. Ted Wakefield, who had loved it as a boy, searched for it later in his life. Unable to find it, he funded a replica for Vermillion Harbor. After his death, however, Olin Stevens of Columbus, Ohio, a grandson of a former keeper at the Vermillion Light, solved the mystery in 1994, when he discovered from a newspaper clipping he found in his attic that the damaged light had been moved to East Charity Shoal in the 1930s. (See Vermillion Lighthouse.)

In 1997 a Seacoast 20X viewing telescope was installed at Cape Vincent to enable visitors to see the East Charity Shoal Lighthouse from a distance.

Known Keeper: Frank Sellman (1929–32).

10 Fort Niagara Lighthouses

Fort Niagara has seen various lights built in the area, and to this day remains the object of controversy over its claim to be "the first lighthouse to be built and operated on the Great Lakes." Incomplete records, due to a fire in the U.S. Treasury Department in 1920 which destroyed many documents, make it difficult to trace an accurate history.

In the eighteenth century, the Fort Niagara garrison probably used bonfires to guide vessels through fog and darkness. As travel and commerce increased, by the 1770s it was evident that a lighthouse was needed at the mouth of the Niagara River. Late in the American Revolution the British took a major step and established a light at Fort Niagara, which was then called the French Castle. This light was operational by 1782. Some considered it to be the first light on the Great Lakes. However, it was not a true lighthouse; it was a cupola of the "French Castle" that was used as a lighthouse. The cupola was about 40 feet (12.2 m) above the parade ground and was supported by a pedestal constructed on the roof of the "Castle." This light remained in service until 1796 or even a few years later. The old structure had been removed by 1806. (It should be noted that paintings of that period do not show a cupola.) In 1796 the British relinquished Fort Niagara to the United States and they retired to the west side of the river and built Fort George (between 1797 and 1800).

Fort Niagara Lighthouse

Early Fort Niagara Lighthouse

British and American commerce increased, and in 1804 British soldiers from Fort George erected a true lighthouse at the mouth of the Niagara River. This was Mississauga Lighthouse, a 40-foot (12.2 m) hexagonal stone tower built on Mississauga Point (presently the site of Niagara-on-the-Lake Golf Course), directly opposite Fort Niagara. A lightkeeper's home was also built close by. This light survived the War of 1812, as both the British and the Americans valued its service. Then in 1814, the British demolished it to clear a site for Fort Mississauga, and the Niagara River remained unlit for nine years.

In the postwar years steamboats made their debut and Great Lakes commerce and shipping boomed, making the portage around Niagara Falls a busy spot. In 1822 Congress appropriated $1,000 to place a lamp at Fort Niagara. In 1823 a squat, octagonal pedestal was erected on the mess-house roof at the Castle (Fort Niagara) to support a light. Standing 70 feet (21.3 m) above the water, it displayed a fixed white light from its nine lamps and nine reflectors, thus re-establishing a light to mark the mouth of the Niagara River. The assigned keeper, Edward Giddings, made his home where the modern Coast Guard station sits today, and he also operated a ferry and a tavern.

Two years after the completion of the new light, commerce on the Niagara River almost came to a halt due to the completion of the Erie Canal, which diverted cargo from the Niagara Portage. However, enough local traffic remained to justify the continuation of the light at Fort Niagara, and the lower Niagara ports continued to be busy both as ports and shipbuilding centers.

A third light, but the first true lighthouse built on the American side at the mouth of the Niagara River, was started in 1871 and finished in 1872. It was built on the riverbank just south of the fort. It was originally a 45-foot (13.7 m) stone tower but, with its yellow brick extension of 1900, it is now 56 feet (17 m) high and lined with brick. Sixty cast-iron steps ascend its spiral staircase to the decagonal lantern, which once housed a fourth-order Fresnel lens with a 25-mile (40.5 km) visibility from 91 feet (28 m) above the water level. The lens had been moved from the mess-house roof, where it had been installed in 1859. A brick-lined, iron oil house was just behind the lighthouse, and the lightkeeper's house was just to the north.

In 1983 the lighthouse was automated. In the same year, the Old Fort Niagara Association received permission to use the lower part of the lighthouse as an exhibition space, information center and gift shop. In 1993 the light was decommissioned and replaced with a modern beacon to save the mature trees that blocked the path of the light.

Today the lighthouse is part of the Fort Niagara State Park and is on the *National Register of Historic Places*. Visitors immediately notice its unique Queen Anne architectural style. The octagonal gray limestone tower tapers gently up for four stories, and four keystone, arched windows open vertically from the middle. The corners of the tower have offset stone that juts out enough to produce a graceful ascending line that is met at the summit by a circular parapet of decorative stone arches. This has been topped by a circular yellow brick extension with eight arched windows, three of which are still functional. This extension was originally added as a "watch room," and still contains its original built-in desk. The building attached to the tower also has keystone arched windows, an arched doorway and decorative stonework under the eaves. Ornamental, spear-head grill work covers the lower windows. It is definitely a site worth viewing.

Known Keepers: Captain J. Heileman (1823–23), Captain Elijah Boarbman (1823–25), Major Alexander Thompson (1825–26), Ezekiel Jewett (1826–41), William Hamilton (1841–44), H Killifar (1844–46), Alvan Buck (1846–49), Orrin Seeley (1849–50), John Hichcock (1850–53), Charles Robinson (1853–61), Edward Gidding (1861–62), Francis Powley (1862–69), Mrs. Francis Powley (1869–69), Jeremaih Dixon (1869–69), Ebenizer Barker (1869–85), John Taylor (1886–1903), James Matchett (1903-08), Captain Orlo Mason (1908–14), George Ferguson (1914–28).

11 Galloo Island Lighthouse

Galloo Island is a very small island approximately 20 miles (32 km) west of Henderson Harbor at the east end of Lake Ontario. Reefs run into the lake for a half a mile from its southwest tip, and a buoy marks a shoal 1.3 miles (2.1 km) northwest of this point. In 1818 Congress decided to build a lighthouse on Galloo Island to help warn mariners of these hazards. It was built in 1820 on the rocky southwest end of the island, where it also marked the position of Galloo Island. Mariners knew that to the island's northwest side and south of the Real Ducks was the entry into the St. Lawrence River and to its southwest was the entry into the passage for Sackets Harbor.

The tower and 1 1/2-story keeper's house were built from gray limestone that was quarried on the island. A short enclosed walk-

Galloo Island Lighthouse

Early Galloo Island Lighthouse

Known Keepers: Zenas Hastings (1820–37), Goodale Lewis (1837–39), John Pringle (1839–49), Benjamin Henshaw (1849–50), John Gill (1850–51), Benjamin Henshaw (1851–53), Kendall Hursley (1853–61), Theo Stevens (1861–70), William Harris (1870–71), Warren Fuller (1871–76), Philander Tyman (1876–76), F. Johnson (1877–1906), Robert Graves (1906–33), Wiley Koepka (1933–42), Harry Klein (1942–46).

12   Horse Island Lighthouse

Horse Island, is a 28-acre (11.3 hectare) island at the southwest entrance to Black River Bay, an arm of Lake Ontario that runs several miles inland to form a deep natural harbor. This shelter, plus the harbor's proximity to Canada made the village of Sackets Harbor at the end of the bay a natural choice for the U.S. government to set up headquarters for the U.S. Navy on the Great Lakes during the War of 1812. At that time, a third of the U.S. army and a quarter of the navy were stationed here. It was also the most important shipbuilding center for the Americans, making it a prime target for the British. Sackets Harbor successfully fended off two British attacks.

One of these attacks has an interesting story. The British landed at Horse Island and from here shot cannon balls at Sackets Harbor. Most of them hit the stone bluff but one shot over the bluff and furrowed into the ground. An American dug out the cannon ball and put it into "the sow," a huge cannon of theirs. They packed it with whatever they found (petticoats, etc.) and shot it immediately back at the British. It hit the stern of the British ship, killed fourteen and wounded eighteen. Thus repelled, the British high-tailed it for home, with not one single injury to the Americans.

After the war Sackets Harbor remained an important military, shipbuilding and commercial center well into the 1800s. The first American Great Lakes steamship, *Ontario*, was built here. Sackets Harbor also became the main shipping point for exporting lumber, agricultural products and locally manufactured goods. With this increased lake traffic, it was apparent that lights were needed to mark the treacherous entrance to the bay.

In 1831 the first lighthouse was built on Horse Island. Its short octagonal tower rose straight up out of the roof, about midway along the peak of the 1½-story keeper's house. The tower supported an octagonal gallery with a birdcage-style lantern that was topped by a high-arched dome. Its lantern used eight oil lamps and reflectors to provide its fixed light. In 1869 Thompson's *Coast Pilot* reported that the light was fixed and visible for 11 miles (17.8 km).

way attached the house to the 50-foot (15.3 m) conical tower. Narrow limestone steps led up the brick-lined tower to the lantern. The top of the tower flared out slightly to carry the weight of the gallery, which was also supported by carved wooden braces. The circular black lantern had ten large glass panels, and the fixed white light was lit with 15 lamps and 15 reflectors. It later used a Fresnel lens. The lantern was capped with a red, decagonal dome and ventilator stack.

An 1838 inspection showed that the lamps were faulty, the lantern room and deck were leaky, and the exterior needed a coating of Roman cement. By 1867 the tower needed to be rebuilt. It was perhaps also lowered by 11 feet (3.4 m) and had its new fourth-order Fresnel lens installed at this time. It displayed a fixed white light for 14 miles (22.5 km) from its lantern 58 feet (17.7 m) above the water. Other structures at the station included an iron oil house and a red brick fog signal building (1897) about 350 feet (107 m) southwest of the lighthouse situated on a point of land by the water.

Many vessels went down on the nearby hidden reefs and shoals. In 1862 the propeller *Jefferson* picked up a boat off of Galloo Island. After leaving Oswego the boat had tipped over in a storm. Of the three men aboard, two were dead, one barely alive. In 1866 the schooner *N. Ballard*, heading from Detroit to Ogdensburg with a full cargo of wheat, struck the Galloo Island reef and sank. The captain and crew of ten drowned but only a few of their bodies were found.

The light was automated in 1963 and a 190 mm, solar-powered lens replaced the old one. Eventually the light was placed on the *National Register of Historic Places*.

In August 1999 the 2,000-acre (808 hectare) island (which included a mansion, lodge, island manager's house, airplane, yacht, boats, light tower, keeper's house, oil house and fog building) was sold at government auction for $2,472,500 to P.J. Kemper of New York. The island's previous Swiss owners were glad that it sold to an American. Kemper has no plans to develop the island at this time. The Galloo Island light is only visible from the air or the water. Since it is so far out in the lake a daytrip could turn into an overnight trip depending on the whims of Lake Ontario and the size of your boat.

Horse Island Lighthouse

The lighthouse was rebuilt in 1870. This time, a square tower was attached to the front of a 1½-story brick keeper's house. Both were made of red brick and sat on a cut limestone foundation. The tower was entered from outside by stairs up to a side door that has "1870" stamped into the concrete lintel.

About four stories high, the tower arched out at the top to support a decagonal-windowed, circular-based lantern surrounded by a square gallery with iron railings. The dome, made of ten flat sections jointed with ribbing, was topped with a ventilator ball and a lightning rod. The lantern housed a fifth-order Fresnel lens.

While George Ward was keeper from 1909 to 1923 he kept a few farm animals on the island and had a large vegetable garden to help feed his family. In the winter the children only went to school if the water was frozen over and they could walk or use the family horse. Whenever the children went outside they had to wear a life jacket. The logbooks show meticulous record keeping and daily entries for weather and water conditions, work, trips, visitors and notable events.

Since then, at some unknown date, the tower was extended about 10 feet (3 m) to increase its visibility, an addition was added to the back of the house, two dormers were added to the second story, the tower and keeper's house were painted white, and the lantern was painted black. The lighthouse was deactivated in 1957, and a new light was placed on a steel skeletal tower in the same year. In 1963 the lantern was painted red.

Today the island and lighthouse are privately owned, and may be viewed only from the water or the mainland. The island is accessible by boat or a walk through shallow waters to the mainland on its south side (when Lake Ontario waters are low). Well-mown paths surround the island and lighthouse, and a concrete walkway leads from the flagpole to the tower's wide three-panelled red door. The square tower is also red-bricked inside and has been whitewashed. Solid iron steps spiral up to the tower.

Twelve more stairs lead up into the lantern. Its round iron base is lined with tongue and groove oak and it has four vents in its walls. Below one of the windows is a half door providing access to the gallery. From the lantern one can see water on three sides, and directly out over Lake Ontario, a mere 30 miles (48 km) away, is Canada.

At the water's edge limestone steps and a set of wooden steps lead down a short drop to the solid flat rock beach where the Coast Guard's modern white skeletal tower displays its red light from a 57-foot (17.4 m) focal plane.

Known Keepers: John McNitt (1832–41), Jacob Kellogg Jr. (1841–43), Lorenzo Root (1843–44), Samuel McNitt (1844–60), Oris Westcott (1860–61), J. McFarlane (1861–66), Nelson Weeks (1866–83), Horace Holloway (1884–1909), George Ward (1909–23).

First Horse Island Lighthouse

Original Oak Orchard Pierhead Light

13 Oak Orchard Pierhead Light

Oak Orchard is a secure harbor about halfway between Niagara and Rochester on Lake Ontario. A pierhead light was built here in 1871 at the outer end of the harbor's west pier, which extended into the lake to mark and protect the harbor entrance. It stood on four raised block legs to allow heavy waters to wash over the pier and under the light.

The square 27-foot (8.2 m) tower had gently tapering sides and was surmounted by a large square lantern in which three large rectangular panes were set vertically in each of its four sides. The lantern displayed a fixed white light using a fourth-order lens to achieve a visibility of 11.5 miles (18.5 km). It was topped by a plain, hipped dome, ventilator ball and lightning rod. The tower was painted brown below and white above. Sitting part way down from the top edge of the tower was a huge square gallery, unusual in that it was larger than the square base of the tower. The tower was connected to shore by a long wooden catwalk for the keeper's safety. Although this lighthouse was discontinued in 1916 and disappeared after this, the residents of Oak Orchard had a replica of it placed on shore in the early 2000s.

Known Keepers: John Kelly (1871–1901), George Dillon (1901–03), John Safe (1903–05), George Safe (1905–09), Thomas Wilkins (1909–16).

14 Ogdensburg Harbor Lighthouse

First settled in 1794, the site where the Oswegatchie River empties into the St. Lawrence River acquired a lighthouse in 1834. It was built on a low rocky point 200 feet (60 m) above the harbor channel and 100 yards (90 m) from the shore, to mark the flats that extended nearly halfway across the St. Lawrence River. Thus warned, mariners would keep in the deep water closer to the Canadian shore.

The 40-foot (12.2 m) tower and 1½-story keeper's house were built of cut white limestone. The square tower, lit by two large front-facing, four-paned windows, went up the waterside end of the house. In 1870 the lantern was fitted with a fourth-order Fresnel lens, and the keeper's house was modified using wood. In 1900 the tower height was extended to 65 feet (20 m). Scott's 1903 Pilot description of the light included "a fixed white light, 4th order, visible 12¾ miles [20.5 km]. Square tower; white limestone 40 feet [12.2 m]; white brick natural color, balance of height 60 feet [18.5 m] high with dwelling attached, lantern black." Its design is similar to the lighthouses at Stony Point and Horse Island.

Early depiction of Ogdensburg Harbor Lighthouse

Ogdensburg Harbor Lighthouse

Today the point on which this light stands is called Lighthouse Point. The square tower, painted gray below and white on the top, is topped by a red decagonal lantern, from which the Fresnel lens has now disappeared. The second-story roof of the keeper's house lifts on each side, providing a bank of windows that light the interior space. The now privately owned lighthouse sits on a well-kept lawn dotted with deciduous trees — a fitting retirement after more than 125 years of service.

Known Keepers: Amos Wells (1835–51), Luman Newell (1851–54), William Gardner (1854–61), Talman Smith (1861–67), Samuel Sayre (1867–69), James Horton (1869–71), John Ross (1871–71), Lewis Young (1871–88), Samuel Penfold (1888–1913), Amherst Gunn (1913–32), Daniel Hill (1932–33).

Olcott Harbor Pierhead Light

15 Olcott Harbor Pierhead Light

Olcott Harbor is on the south shore of Lake Ontario at the mouth of Eighteen Mile Creek, between the Niagara River and Thirty Mile Point in New York State. A light was built at the outer end of the west pier to mark the harbor entrance. A square pyramidal tower 27 feet (8.3 m) high, painted brown below and white above, it displayed a fixed white light using a sixth-order lens to achieve a visibility of 11.5 miles (18.6 km). It was connected to shore by a catwalk for the keeper's safety in inclement weather. At some time this light was replaced by a flashing red light displayed at a 28-foot (8.6 m) focal plane from a red post also at the end of the west pier.

Known Keepers: Richard Mathews (1873–1910), Joseph Grant (1910–13).

16 Oswego Breakwater Lighthouse

By 1881 an outer west breakwater had just been completed for the harbor of Oswego, New York, on the south shore of Lake Ontario. The iron light previously used at the north end of the west pier, called the beacon light, was moved from the west pier onto a crib at the east end of the new breakwater. In 1889 it was replaced by a new light that served harbor entry until it was removed in May of 1931 by the Great Lakes Dredge and Dock Company as part of harbor reconstruction.

With the completion of new breakwaters, another contract was awarded to the Great Lakes Company in December 1932 to construct a new breakwater light at the end of the western one. Construction was suspended in 1933 due to lack of funds, but the lighthouse was finally completed in 1934 with funds from the *National Industrial Recovery Act (NIRA)*, and it began operation on November 24.

This new lighthouse was built on a concrete foundation that extended up for 10 feet (3 m) above the water and curved out gently to deflect incoming breakers. In the middle of this foundation sat the small square, two-story, white keeper's house, topped with a red pyramidal roof and a tall, thin white chimney extending up from one corner. The square lighthouse tower extended up past the house for two more stories. It was topped by a black iron gallery but had a white polygonal lantern, domed with a red cap and ventilator ball. Both house and tower were encased in metal.

Oswego Breakwater Lighthouse

A black iron railing, mounted to the concrete foundation, surrounded the whole station.

The lantern housed a fourth-order Fresnel lens and its characteristic color was produced by the lens rotating and shining through red panels on the lantern windows. In 1968 the lighthouse was automated, and in 1995 its fourth-order Fresnel lens was removed and given to the H. Lee White Marine Museum at the waterside docks in Oswego. Today the light uses solar power and a modern optic to flash alternately red and white for ten seconds each.

This light was witness to the drowning of six U.S. Coast Guardsmen in 1942. The incident began with an early but harsh three-day blizzard. The lighthouse keeper, trapped by the storm, was lonely and fast running out of provisions. When the winds had abated, he signaled the Coast Guard station five times, apparently panicking to get off the isolated station. A crew of seven men, plus replacement keepers, boarded a Coast Guard picket boat and headed for the lighthouse under Lieutenant Wilson's direction.

The two relief keepers, Bert Egelston and Carl Sprague, were safely exchanged for the stranded keeper, while the extra Coast Guardsmen kept the picket from smashing against the lighthouse's concrete base. The boat was safely backed away, but the engine cut

Early Oswego Breakwater Lighthouse

out when it was put into forward gear, and could not be restarted. The picket crashed onto the eastern breakwater and threw six crewmen into the water. Its bottom was ripped open and it capsized. Two crewmen trapped inside were miraculously able to escape. However, the bodies of the remaining Coast Guardsmen and the lightkeeper, Jackson, were never found.

On December 4, 1996, exactly 54 years after the tragedy, the Coast Guard and the City of Oswego formally held a commemorative service. Survivors, family and city representatives, aboard a lifeboat, placed a memorial wreath in Lake Ontario's waters at the location and time of the disaster. Today, a monument to those who drowned stands in Veterans Park at Oswego.

Before the drownings the lighthouse ran smoothly. After them, unexplained occurrences took place: strange voices and footsteps were heard in the stairwells; malfunctioning lights were found only to be unscrewed lightbulbs; furniture was rearranged; lights illuminated every window in the lighthouse. Even when the lighthouse was empty after its automation in 1968, and though the windows had been sealed over with steel plating, the light was still sometimes seen. Is it coincidence that these unsolved incidents only started after the drowning of the six Coast Guardsmen, or is the lighthouse now haunted by them?

Known Keepers: Orlo Steele (1836–49), Samuel Freeman (1849–53), Jacob M. Jacobs (1853–61), John Pringle (1861–69), John Mason (1869–84), John Budds (1884–96), George Greenfield (1896–1903) George Dillion (1903–04), Charles Tucker (1904–24), Bert Egelston (1928–40), Karl Jackson (1940–42), Olin Stevens (1942–51).

17 Oswego Old Lighthouse

In Iroquois, "Osh-we-geh" means "pouring out place," an apt name for the spot where the Oswego River empties into the east end of Lake Ontario. As early as 1822 a stone lighthouse was built at Oswego to guide vessels into its natural harbor, which became a focal point for settlement. It was built on the east bank overlooking the river mouth, just below Fort Ontario in what was then known as the town of East Oswego. The Oswego *Palladium* of June 15, 1821, carried the details of the proposal for the structures to be built on the east side of the mouth of the Oswego River.

The lighthouse was an octagonal 20-foot (6 m) stone tower built on a stone foundation "as deep as necessary to make the structure perfectly secure." The tower had a base diameter of 14 feet (4.3 m) and a top diameter of 7½ feet (2.3 m), giving it thinner walls as it rose. A stone cornice supported a stone deck, from which an iron-framed copper-covered scuttle door opened into the lantern. Three eight-paned and shuttered windows lit the tower, which was capped by an octagonal iron lantern 4.5 feet (1.3 m) in diameter and 4 feet 10 inches (1.4 m) high. Seven of its eight sides were "glazed with strong double glass, of the first quality, Boston manufacture." The copper-covered dome was formed by "sixteen iron rafters concentrating in an iron loop at the top, forming the funnel for the smoke to pass out of the lantern." A large rotating ball ventilator topped the dome. Finishing touches included an iron balustrade, whitewashing, and the provision of "two complete electrical conductors or rods with points." The lantern used eight Winslow Lewis lamps and reflectors.

The keeper's house was a 1½-story dwelling built of stone in a "simple and utilitarian design" with two rooms downstairs, each with a fireplace. The cellar walls and the house were to be 20 inches (50 cm) thick with "split undressed stone well pointed" and "whitewashed twice over" laid in lime mortar. The roof was covered with "mercantile shingles." A stone well was "to be sunk sufficiently deep to procure good water, at a convenient distance from the Light House." It was "furnished with a curb, windlass, an

Oswego Old Lighthouse

iron chain and a strong iron hooped bucket." A small porch was later built on the south side.

Lake traffic continued to grow with the opening of the Erie Canal in 1825, the Oswego Canal (connecting Lake Ontario to the Erie Canal in 1828), and the Welland Canal in 1828. The harbor at Oswego was improved to serve this increased lake traffic, and in 1836 a pier light was established on the harbor's west pier.

The lighthouse inspector's report of 1838 showed that the old tower was in a dilapidated state but the keeper's house only needed trifling repairs. As a result, the light was discontinued later in 1838. In July 1841 Stephen Pleasonton, the Secretary of the Treasury, recommended that the lighthouse be put up for auction and that the buyer remove it as soon as possible. The tower was sold in August 1841 and was removed in late 1841 or early 1842. The keeper's house still sits on its old location and may be visited just below the walls of Fort Ontario.

18 Oswego West Pierhead Light

With busier lake traffic in the area of Oswego, a new pier was built on the west side of the river and in 1836 a light was built at its east end to mark the harbor entry. The light was a tapering gray stone octagonal structure with an attached oil room. It used 13 lamps and reflectors to display its fixed white light. In 1868 it was raised 25 feet (7.6 m) and a third-order lens was installed to produce a visibility of 15 miles (24.3 km).

The west inner pier was extended to the north in 1869, and a new iron light was built to mark its outer end in 1876. At this time the 1836 light became known as the inner light. It served until it was dismantled in 1929 to accommodate harbor improvements.

19 Rock Island Lighthouse

Rock Island is a small island of rock in the St. Lawrence River about 4.5 miles (7.2 km) northeast of Clayton, New York. A lighthouse was first commissioned for it in 1847 and built in 1848. With its 9-mile (14.4 km) visibility from the center of the island, it helped mark safe passage through the head of the "Narrows" of the Thousand Islands on the south side. Today, all that remains of the original site is the fieldstone smokehouse.

During the Patriot War of 1837–38, Bill Johnston, a river pirate, tried to help the Americans and some British rebels take over Fort Wellington (near Prescott, Ontario) from the British. He boarded a British steamer, the *Sir Robert Peel*, at Wellesley Island, ordered all the passengers ashore, and set fire to the ship. It drifted off, struck a shoal and sank in a blaze of flames and steam. It is supposed that Johnston hid on an island in a small cave called Devil's Oven. He was eventually captured and jailed, but escaped after six months. He was later pardoned and in 1853 became lightkeeper at the Rock Island lighthouse.

In 1882 a new 40-foot (12.2 m) tower, keeper's house, carpenter's house and oil house were built. The tower was moved to the end of a 10-foot (3 m) pier on the island's north shore. The bottom of the tower was concrete and limestone, while the upper portion was iron. Today it is white with a band of black where it changes from concrete to iron. The black gallery and polygonal lantern and are supported by decorative black corbels. The lantern is capped with a black dome and ventilator ball, and a few small, porthole-style windows surround the top of the tower. The original sixth-order lens, which offered a 12-mile (20 km) visibility, has since been removed.

The new keeper's house was a two-story, shingle-style house painted dark red with white trim and fronted with a stone veranda. It has unique multi-paned windows and its roof is steeply pitched. In 1900 a generator house was built and then in 1920 a boathouse was added.

The last keeper, Frank Ward, was appointed in 1938. In 1941 he and his family were transferred to shore to conserve money during World War II. Ward tended several battery-operated lights with generators. Besides lightkeeping he also provided rescue missions. Once, for example, an agitated woman came to ask for his help when her husband failed to return from a day's fishing. Ward found him stranded on an island where his fishing boat had been carried by the wake of a large passing ship. Apparently this was a common occurrence.

Oswego West Pierhead Light, circa 1914

Rock Island Lighthouse

Rock Island Lighthouse

The lighthouse was deactivated in 1958. Once a private residence, it now belongs to New York State and is maintained by the Thousand Islands Region of the Office of Parks and Recreation. The lighthouse is not open to the public. However, the Rock Island Light is a picturesque sight for boaters.

Known Keepers: Chesterfield Pearson (1848–49), John Collins (1849–53), William Johnston (1853–61), Samuel Spaulding (1861–65), Joseph Collins (1865–70), Willard Cook (1870–79), Foster Drake (1880–86), Michael Diepolder (1887–1901), Emma Diepolder (1901–01), Eugene Butler (1901–12), John Belden (1912–40), Frank Ward (1940–52), John Van Ingern USCG (1952–55), Dennis Carroll USCG (1955–56).

20 Selkirk Lighthouse

The Selkirk lighthouse is at the mouth of the Salmon River near Pulaski, New York, on the south side of Lake Ontario in an area first settled by Europeans in the early 1800s. The most plausible source of the name is Thomas Douglas, the Earl of Selkirk, who owned thousands of acres of land on the north side of the Salmon River in the early 1800s. While it was abundant salmon that brought the first settlers, others came to farm nearby. In the 1830s a government engineer determined that the harbor could safely anchor thirty ships, and a lighthouse was built in 1838 to mark the harbor entrance.

The lighthouse, originally called the Salmon Point River Light Station, was a unique specimen of early design. Local contractors Joseph Gibbs and Abner French were awarded the contract for $3,000. They hired local stonemason Jabez Meacham to do most of the actual work. The lighthouse sat close to the water and was built into a slight hill so that it appeared to have 3½ stories on the west side. The stone block structure was typical of the period. Unlike other lighthouses, the octagonal wood-shingled tower, painted red, rose 16 feet (4.8 m) out of the roof on the north side of the house to 32 feet (9.7 m) from the ground. The wooden tower's platform supported an octagonal bird-cage lantern with 15 small glass panes on each side. The wrought-iron railings that supported the lantern and surrounded the gallery were made by blacksmith John Box from Port Ontario. The lantern was furnished with a 14-inch (35 cm) diameter parabolic reflector/lamp system that used eight lamps and reflectors, and from a 49-foot (15 m) focal plane projected a fixed white light for 14 miles (22.4 km).

This system first used whale oil from a 24-hour reservoir. In cold weather a secondary frost lamp warmed the main lamp, aiding combustion in temperatures that would thicken fuel in the reservoir. In 1855 the system was upgraded to a Hains Mineral Oil fountain lamp, a single burner, and a 270-degree sixth-order Fresnel lens about 18 inches (45 cm) high and 12 inches (30 cm) in diameter. However, the beam from this lens was impeded by the lantern's support structure and the astragals that held the small glass panes. It would have been replaced had the lighthouse not been officially decommissioned in 1858, as silting at the river mouth impaired the harbor.

The first of the light's four keepers was Lewis Conant, who activated the light in August 1838. Keepers were paid $350 a year. After the navigation season they went home to Pulaski or Richland for the winter. However, local records show that former keeper Cole lived at the lighthouse from 1852 until his death in 1890. Since he had served honorably in the Civil War and was Pulaski's first tax collector, the lighthouse quarters may have been a government sinecure. He continued to tend the light in an unofficial capacity, maintaining in addition two pier lights, one on each of the (now disappeared) wooden piers of the original breakwater at the river mouth.

In 1895 the lighthouse was auctioned as government surplus to Leopold Joh, a German immigrant and successful Syracuse hotelier. After purchasing adjoining properties, Joh built the prestigious Lighthouse Hotel, immediately attracting vacationers and celebrities. After Joh's death the Heckle family purchased it in 1916, doubled its size and made it famous for German cuisine. During Prohibition it was also very popular with smugglers.

The lighthouse still survives. In 1976 it was named a "Designated Historic Landmark" by the Oswego Heritage Foundation, and in 1979 was placed on the *National Register of Historic Places*. In 1987 it was purchased by Jim Walker, who has worked diligently to restore it. To develop interest and raise funds for restoration, he rents out the lighthouse. This is one of two on the Great Lakes that can be rented, but it is the only one with a birdcage lantern. On August 6, 1989, for the bicentennial celebrations, Walker was able to have the light re-lit as a private aid to navigation. It now uses a photocell-actuated lamp with an automatic bulb changer inside a 190 mm lens, and is once more back on the NOAA charts as a Class II navigational aid.

Selkirk Lighthouse

Selkirk Lighthouse, circa 1910

In 1994 Walker added a website for the Selkirk Lighthouse, initiating a trend that has definitely increased lighthouse awareness, as well as business.

Many interesting guests have stayed at this lighthouse. A caller once declined a booking when she found out the lighthouse's shape, stating that she couldn't *possibly* stay in a lighthouse that was not round. On another occasion guests complained that they had been unable to sleep because the sound of the salmon jumping kept them awake all night. But complaints are few, and many guests return year after year to the lighthouse's quiet beauty.

Very few lighthouses have a birdcage lantern and, according to author Ross Holland, "the Selkirk lighthouse is one of the best examples of its kind and is perhaps in the best condition of its kind to be found anywhere." It is definitely the only lighthouse on the Great Lakes that still has a complete lantern of this type.

Known Keepers: Lewis Conact (1838–49), Lucius B. Cole (1849–54), Charles M. Lewis (1854–57), A.H. Weed (1857–58).

The light used a sixth-order lens to display its fixed white light from a 40-foot (12.2 m) tower for about 13 miles (21 km). It warned mariners of the islands and the hazardous reef in the area. About the same time as the lighthouse was commissioned, it was decided that the river channel would be moved to the American side of the island. This required the blasting of bedrock at the river bottom to deepen the channel. Divers worked from a river barge to place explosives in drilled holes. Nine crewmembers lost their lives when the barge was struck by lightning and blown up during a summer thunderstorm.

The keepers of this lighthouse first watched over oil and then later gas lamps. An annual annoyance was the invasion of shadflies, which were so numerous that they covered the ground. Keepers had to be alert in case the flies blocked the oxygen intake to the lantern and put out the flame, thus causing a dangerous gas leak within the tower.

The light was deactivated sometime in the 1950s, and in 1963 was sold as surplus by a sealed bid in New York City for less than $7,000 to Alfreda and Edward Wolos. They worked hard to restore it from its vandalized condition, turning it back into a well-appointed six-bedroom house with a kitchen that focuses around a large ornate iron and nickel cook stove. The 43 tower stairs wind up from the first floor through the northwest bedroom and the attic to the tower level under the lantern. Twelve ladder stairs lead up to an iron trap door in the floor of the twelve-sided lantern, which retains its lens pedestal but not the lens. The view from the gallery over the river and islands, including the nearby Third Brother Shoal Light, is magnificent.

The well-manicured lawns and the unique limestone and wood architecture make this one of the most attractive lighthouses on the sweetwater route to the interior.

Known Keepers: William Dodge (1870–93), William Dodge (1893–1921), Ralph Scobie (1921–29), Horace Walts (1929–29).

21 Sisters Island Lighthouse

Sisters Island, located in the St. Lawrence River not very far from Lake Ontario, consists of three small islands joined together by bridges of stone and concrete. A lighthouse was built on the island in 1870 to mark a tricky channel on the Canadian side of the island.

The two-story limestone house and tower had walls 18 inches (45 cm) thick. The square tower, built into the center of the north side of the house, extended up one story above the rooftop. The square limestone construction and the stone molding under the gallery gave it a castle-like air. The gallery, surrounded by a black iron railing, was topped with a dodecagonal lantern that had a black dome and a brass-colored ventilator ball. The south side of the slate roof had two twelve-paned dormer windows with ornate wood in the peaks to add space and light to the upstairs bedrooms. The end gables of the house had ornate white braces under the eaves and stick-style white wood in the peaks.

Sisters Island Lighthouse

Sodus Main Lighthouse

22 Sodus Main Lighthouse

In 1824 Congress appropriated $4,500 to construct a lighthouse at Sodus Bay, and land was purchased from the Pultney Estate for $65.75. The light built in 1825, included some of the following specifications: a 40-foot (12.2 m) tower, with a 22-foot (6.7 m) base diameter and a 10½-foot (3.2 m) top diameter, to be built of rough split stone or brick, onto a deep, secure foundation; three tower windows, a stone deck and octagonal iron lantern, made by the Boston Manufactory; lantern dome, of sixteen rafters concentrated into an iron hoop, covered with copper and topped with a traversing ventilator.

The keeper's house, also of split stone, was to be a one-story dwelling finished in a "plain, decent style" using "good seasoned stuff." The finished lighthouse was supplied with eleven patent-lamps and eleven 14-inch (35 cm) reflectors. Ishmael D. Hill, the first lightkeeper, was a veteran of the War of 1812.

Piers were first constructed at the entrance to Sodus Bay in 1834. Congress appropriated $4,000, and another $3,750 the next year, for beacon lights on the piers at the mouth of the Genesee River and Sodus Bay. The stone beacon at Sodus Bay was built on the west pier as a guide for entering the harbor. In 1858 a fourth-order catadioptric revolving illuminating apparatus was put into the lantern.

By 1869 the original tower and keeper's house had so badly deteriorated that Congress appropriated $14,000 to replace them. The limestone for the new 45-foot (13.7 m) square tower and attached two-story dwelling completed in 1871 was quarried in Kingston, Ontario. The stone from the original lighthouse was used to make a jetty to protect the site from erosion, and the new tower was fitted with a fourth-order Fresnel lens.

The station underwent repairs and improvements as needed, but in 1901 the government discontinued the main light on the bluff. In 1984 the U.S. Coast Guard turned the old lighthouse and its outbuildings over to the Town of Sodus Point. Today the old Sodus Lighthouse is on both the state and the national historic registers and is leased and maintained by the Sodus Bay Historical Society. From the tower visitors can see Chimney Bluffs to the east. At the lighthouse there is also a museum, a display of lighthouse artwork and photography, and a gift shop.

Known Keepers: Ishmael Hill (1826–29), Bennet Fitzhugh (1829–44), Lyman Dunning (1844–45), Bennet Fitzhugh (1845–46), Captain Tillitson (1846–49), Charles Hallet (1849–50), George Sergeant (1850–53), Jesse Lyman (1853–62), Elisha Pettit (1862–66), Charles Degan (1866–81), Daniel Phillips (1882–1901).

23 Sodus Range Lights

When the first pier at Sodus Harbor, Lake Ontario, was built in 1834, Congress appropriated $3,000 for a beacon light to be mounted on a stone tower at the end of the west pier to guide mariners entering the harbor. In 1857 a severe storm removed part of the pier and destroyed the lighthouse. When it was rebuilt, range lights were put on the pier. An 1868 inspection report showed that the range light lanterns were broken. They were replaced, but in 1870 a permanent beacon with a new lens was built at the outer end of the pier.

In 1871, when the new Sodus main light was built onshore to replace the deteriorated old one, the stone and debris from the old tower and dwelling were used to build a rough jetty in the lake in front of the lighthouse to prevent erosion. In 1872 a wooden beacon was built on a crib at the head of the west pier in order to move the front range light further into the water for better visibility. The square pyramidal tower housed a sixth-order lens that displayed a fixed white light. An elevated walk 1,150 feet (350 m) long was built between the two range lights. After exposure to the elements, more than half of this walk had to be rebuilt in 1880. Also that year, the front range light received minor repairs and the rear range light was lined with wood and painted.

In 1884 the pier was extended, the front light was moved near its end, and an additional 270 feet (82 m) of elevated walk was built out 28 feet (8.5 m) beyond the light. The elevated walk was continually being repaired or rebuilt due to storm damage. Once, the *Laura* from Windsor, Ontario, damaged the pier and catwalk while being towed out of the harbor.

In 1901–02, with harbor improvements, the front tower was raised 15 feet (4.6 m), making its focal plane 48 feet (14.5 m) and its visibility 14 miles (22.5 km). It was changed from a sixth-order fixed white light to a fourth-order white light varied by a white flash every two minutes (in 1902, every 30 seconds). Concrete piers replaced the former wooden ones. The main light on the bluff was discontinued, and the oil house moved closer to the rear range light. The jetty in front of the lighthouse was extended to 75 feet (23 m).

Sodus First Light, circa 1825

Sodus Front Range Light, circa 1906

Sodus Range Light
Fourth-order Fresnel lens

In 1918 salary changes were made. The head keeper had been receiving $120 a year for fuel and quarters, but when he was lodged in government keeper's quarters, this amount was taken off his salary, dropping it from $672 to $552 a year. Meanwhile, the assistant keeper's salary was raised from $480 to $600 to enable him to rent housing.

In 1925 a fog signal was finally installed — a Strombos marine signal that operated on compressed air (blast 4 s; silence 24 s) and was audible five miles away. In 1938 the front range light was rebuilt and enclosed with ¼-inch steel plates with porthole windows. It was heightened by 9 feet (2.7 m), and electricity for the light was provided via submarine cable from a control house at the shore end of the pier. The light used a fixed fourth-order 300 mm lens that displayed a group-flashing pattern (flash 1.5s; eclipse 2s; flash 1.5s; eclipse 5s.) It had an automatic bulb changer and its focal plane was 51 feet (15.5 m).

A new diaphone fog signal was also installed in 1938 (blast 1.5 s; silence 2 s; blast 1.5 s; silence 25 s — creating a 30-second pattern). The light and fog renovations cost $11,000. While the renovations for the front light were being done, a light was put on a pole 32 feet (9.8 m) above the water.

The Sodus rear range light was also rebuilt in 1938 for $250 to make it more durable and fireproof. The wooden structure was replaced with a 25-foot (7.7 m) steel skeletal tower. It used the illuminating apparatus from the old tower, and its characteristic did not change. In 1939 improvements costing $1,225 were made at the station: two outbuildings torn down near the keeper's house; a laundry/garage building constructed; and a concrete driveway put in. At some point the rear light was discontinued. The keeper's house was used from 1901 to 1984 to house personnel maintaining the pier lights. When the lights were automated in 1984, keepers became redundant.

Known Keepers: Daniel Phillips (1901–17), Wilfred Lewis (1917–39), Edwin Ward (1939–54).

Early Stony Point Lighthouse

24 Stony Point Lighthouse

Stony Point is an anvil-shaped peninsula immediately east of Galloo and Stony Island, and with the mainland it shapes Henderson Bay. Stony Point Passage, a treacherous stretch of water menaced by prevailing westerly winds and by sandbars, shoals and rocks, lies at the north end of an area that nineteenth-century sailors called Mexico Bay and was known as the ship graveyard of Lake Ontario.

The first lighthouse at Stony Point was built in 1830. The light was on the roof of the two-story keeper's dwelling, and consisted of ten lamps with an equal number of bright reflectors. The lantern was said to be high enough for all nautical purposes. Its foundation still remains.

In July 1854 Congress appropriated $800 to build a fog signal at Stony Point Lighthouse, and the new lighthouse and keeper's house were built in 1869. The house is a large 1½-story structure with four dormers, two per side, in its roof. It is white, made of cut limestone blocks, and is trimmed with black shingles and shutters.

The 73-foot (22 m) white square tower is built onto the lakeside end of the house. The top is made of brick, but the bottom is cut limestone like the house. It tapers in slightly about halfway up, and the top half has rounded corners and decorative arches built into the brickwork, an indication that the tower height had been raised. At the summit it widens slightly to support a square, black gallery and decagonal lantern capped by a black dome, ventilator ball and lightning rod.

The lantern originally housed a fourth-order Fresnel lens. In 1869 it had a revolving, flashing light that was visible for 11 miles (17.6 km). In 1903 a 20-foot (6 m) brick extension was added to the tower to increase its focal plane to 58 feet (17.7 m) and thus increase its visibility as well. The tower had also been painted white to create a uniform color. Its flash changed from two minutes to one minute, so it showed a fixed white light varied by a white flash every minute.

The lighthouse was deactivated in 1945, and a new steel skeletal tower with an automated light replaced it.

Sodus Front Range Light

Stony Point Lighthouse at left, rubble remains of original light at centre and modern replacement tower at right.

The lightkeeper lived on shore. Keeper Horace Walts also tended the light at Sisters Island in 1929. Walts rowed a St. Lawrence skiff out each night to light the lantern and back each morning to extinguish it. He also followed the standard procedure of placing a white linen hood over the Fresnel lens every morning. Lenses had to be covered, or the lantern had to have drapes hung around its interior to prevent the lens from getting distorted or acting as a magnifying glass and starting a fire.

Walts's meticulous care of the lights was recognized by the stars he earned. The U.S. Light House Service regularly evaluated the performance of their lighthouse keepers and awarded the best keepers a star, which they kept for one year, in recognition of their excellence. After being honored for nine consecutive years, Walts received a permanent gold star with a diamond in the center.

The old tower and house were sold and are now a private residence. In 2003 the owners gutted the tower and keeper's house to make renovations, which included another dormer window, a summer kitchen on the east side of the house, a solarium on the west, and a new asphalt-shingled roof. The cut block limestone foundation is gray, the buildings are white, and the gallery, lantern and shutters are still black.

Known Keepers: Gilbert N. Wiley (1830–60), Erastus Penny (1869–71), James Dyer (1871), Erastus Penny (1871–76), Newton Smith (1876–1902), Alden Stevens (1903–06), Miles E. Eggeston (1906(?)–42) whose dates are in question but did keep the light for 37 years and was the keeper of the light in 1902, Koepka (1942(?)–45).

25 Sunken Rock Lighthouse

Sunken Rock Island, once known as Bush Island, is a tiny almost submerged island about 20 feet (6 m) in diameter located in the St. Lawrence River just outside Alexandria Bay. In 1847 a short octagonal lighthouse with a brick tower was built on a cut limestone base on the island to mark the east entrance to the narrows between Wellesley Island and the mainland, and to warn mariners of the sunken shoals around the lighthouse. In 1855 this lighthouse was refitted with a sixth-order Fresnel lens. From 28 feet (8.5 m) above water, it displayed a fixed red light that was visible for about 11 miles (18 km).

Today the lighthouse looks different. In 1884 the deteriorating brick was covered over with riveted iron sheets to form a conical shape. Its decagonal lantern and gallery are now painted green and it displays a fixed green light from a modern lens. The gallery is surrounded with a pipe railing attached to spindled posts and is supported from underneath by white braces with spindled ends. These spindles, the ornate grate over the tower's red door, and a decorative pediment over the doorway add touches of elegance to the otherwise plain lighthouse. Small porthole windows provide interior light.

The area has had its share of shipwrecks, among which were the schooner *Catherine* (1890) and the sidewheel steamer *Islander* (1909). The most recent tragedy was on November 20, 1974, when the iron ore freighter *Roy A. Jodrey*, fully loaded, struck the shoal during the night. After foundering for about four hours, the ship finally sank into 250 feet (77 m) of water. Before it sank, the U.S. Coast Guard did manage to rescue all 29 of its crewmembers.

In 1988 the light was converted to solar power. As well as having a new look, this lighthouse now has a new owner, the Saint Lawrence Seaway Development Corporation, which operates the light as a private aid to navigation. Lighthouses owned by this company are readily identifiable by their green-colored lanterns.

Known Keepers: James Merrit (1848–48), Ralph Lasalk (1848–49), Peter Dillenback (1849–53), David Walton (1853–54), Jacob Waggoner (1854–57), John Bolton (1857–61), Henry Campbell (1861–69), Isaac Leonard (1869–71), E. Smith (1871–81), Anson Leonard (1881–1903), Horace Curd (1903–08), John Belden (1908–12), Fredrick Lawson (1912–12), Horace Walts (1912–29), Edward Sweet Jr. (1940–49 USCG).

Sunken Rock Lighthouse

Early Thirty Mile Point Lighthouse

Thirty Mile Point Lighthouse

26 Thirty Mile Point Lighthouse

This lighthouse is so named because it is 30 miles (48.5 km) east of the mouth of the Niagara River on Lake Ontario, near the mouth of Golden Hill Creek. It was built in 1875 to warn vessels of a treacherous sand bar and dangerous shoals that extended out into the lake.

Before this light was placed, many vessels were wrecked in the area. The most notable was the British naval vessel *HMS Ontario*, which was sailing to Niagara, New York, from Oswego with British troops, supplies, military equipment and an army payroll estimated at about $15,000 in gold and silver. The ship left Niagara in a blinding snowstorm and is believed to have gone down near Thirty Mile Point on the night of October 31, 1780. Wreckage from the *Ontario* was found along the south shore of Lake Ontario on November 1. All 88 souls on board were lost, and no bodies were ever found. In 1954 an anchor, which marine experts believe is from the *Ontario*, was recovered off the point. A small cannon, also found near the point but fifty years later, now sits in the lighthouse.

The hill at Thirty Mile Point, where the lighthouse was built, has been called Golden Hill. Two legends offer explanations. The first tells of Daniel Cartwright, an early pioneer farmer who saw men leave an anchored schooner, come ashore, dig up a buried chest from the hillside, and leave. Speculation was that the chest was full of gold. Some even believed it was buried on the hillside by survivors of the *Ontario* who returned to retrieve it. However "Golden Hill" appears on a map that predates this incident. The other legend comes from Wallace Williams, grandson of John Williams, another local pio-

Thirty Mile Point stairwell

neer. He says French explorers were inspired to call the hill "Golden Hill" by its fall blanket of goldenrod flowers that shone like gold.

The Thirty Mile Point lighthouse is made of hand-hewn limestone blocks brought by schooner from Chaumont Bay near Kingston, Ontario. The stone was loaded onto barges and hauled ashore and up a steep bank by horses driven by George B. Hood and William Atwater.

The square 70-foot (21.3 m) tower is attached to the keeper's dwelling. Its third-order Fresnel lens, imported from France at a cost of $15,000, magnified the beam from a kerosene mantle brass lamp to 600,000 candlepower for a visibility range of 16 miles (26 km). It was originally turned by a clockworks that was rewound by hand every few hours. The light's distinctive flash sequence (once every seven seconds) helped ships locate their exact position along the shoreline.

The attached keeper's house, also made of hand-hewn, gray limestone blocks, has a slate roof. Dormers that rise out of and interrupt the eaves of the main roof have decorative braces under them. Later, repairs were made, a yellow brick addition was added to the house, and an assistant keeper was hired. Each keeper had a 24-hour shift. The light was checked every three hours and a weather log recorded every four hours. The engine room was scrubbed and all the brass polished daily.

In 1939 the U.S. Coast Guard took ownership of the lighthouse, and regular inspections became part of the lightkeeper's life. In addition to maintaining and cleaning the light, he now had to maintain the grounds, record lake traffic, and report any distress situations. The light was lit half an hour before sunset and extinguished half an hour after sunrise. Food stocks were increased in the winter so that families could survive being snowed in.

As years passed, the sand bar eroded and the lighthouse was no longer needed. It was decommissioned on December 17, 1958, and its gears were dismantled. It was replaced by an automatic light on a steel tower maintained by the U.S. Coast Guard. Some time after its

Tibbetts Point Lighthouse

closing, the Coast Guard removed the Fresnel lens, with the intention of displaying it at the Coast Guard Station in Buffalo. However, when the lighthouse was refurbished with the idea of returning the original lens, the lens could not be found anywhere.

In 1962 the area was bought by the State of New York and turned into Golden Hill State Park. The park has many campsites for summer and winter camping, hiking trails, small game and pheasant hunting, and fishing. In 1988 a boat launch was constructed for the convenience of fishermen and boaters at a cost of $375,000.

In 1994, to maintain the light's original appearance, $95,000 was spent to refurbish it with a new slate roof, rebuilt chimneys, and all-new lead-coated copper gutters. The grounds retain all adjoining buildings, which include a horse stable (now a garage), two oil houses (one on each side of the lighthouse), a pump house, a privy (roomy two-seater with plastered walls and a side window), and a 1935 fog signal building that has been converted to a campers' recreation building. The keeper's house is open for visits, and shows early life and furnishings of lightkeepers. The panoramic view of the grounds and Lake Ontario from the decagonal lantern is splendid. On a clear day you can even see the Canadian shoreline between Oshawa and Port Hope.

On June 24, 1995, a special celebration was held at Thirty Mile Point Lighthouse to celebrate the commemorative postage stamp that the U.S. Postal Service issued in its honor. This was one of five lighthouses honored in this way.

Known Keepers: Edwin Pratt (1876–78), Samuel Penfield (1878–88), Robert Bannerman (1889–1907), Glenn Seeley (1907–45), Carl Sprague (1945–51), Richard Prange (1958–58).

27 Tibbetts Point Lighthouse

Tibbetts Point received a lighthouse in 1827 to mark the entrance into the St. Lawrence River. The first tower burned whale oil and was in service until 1854. The tower that replaced it is a solid white cylindrical tower with a stucco-like finish. It stands 61 feet (18.6 m) high. It began with a 50 candlepower oil lamp that displayed a fixed beam and had a fourth-order Fresnel lens. The oil lamp was later changed to a 500-watt electric light bulb that gave off a 15,000 candlepower light through the old fourth-order Fresnel lens. This is now the only working Fresnel lens on Lake Ontario.

In 1896 a steam-operated fog whistle was added. In 1927 it was replaced by an air diaphone signal powered by a diesel engine that emitted automatically timed blasts. Today it in turn has been replaced by a radio beacon that guides ships into the river. The buildings on the site include the tower (which has a small room added at the base), a two-story wooden keeper's dwelling (built in 1880), a steam fog building, and an iron oil-house.

The Tibbetts Point Lighthouse remained a U.S. Coast Guard Station until 1981. In 1988 the Tibbetts Point Lighthouse Society was formed, with the purpose of restoring the lighthouse and the grounds as an educational and historical entity. The tower, a State Historic Site, is still an active light maintained by the Coast Guard, while the keeper's dwelling now serves as a Youth Hostel.

Residents and tourists alike walk, bike or drive the 2 1/2-mile (4 km) road from Cape Vincent to the lighthouse, which offers views of sunsets over the lake, ice breaking up in the spring, or ships and boats passing by, heading upbound for the lake or downbound for the river. Depending on the time of year, if you stay overnight on the grounds, you may hear the steady drone of fishing boats through the night.

Many historical landmarks are also visible from the lighthouse: Wolfe Island, named after the British General Wolfe; Grenadier Island, scene of the burning of the *Wisconsin*; Carleton Island, which served as a rendezvous point for the Mohawk Indians and a sentinel during the Revolutionary War. The lighthouse is a good spot to visit.

Known Keepers: Judah Williams (1827–31), Nelson B. Williams (1831–55), Henry Cunningham (1855–61), William Collins (1861–66), A.J. Crastenberg (1878), David K. Montanna (1885–98), William Montanna (1898–1906), J.C. Belden (keeper of fog signal) (1895).

LAKE ONTARIO
CANADA
LIGHTHOUSES

CANADA

ONTARIO

Prescott

Brockville

Ogdensburg

Belleville

Kingston

Clayton

Municipality
of Prince Edward

Port Hope

Cobourg

Oshawa

Whitby

Lake
Ontario

Toronto

Port Credit

Oakville

Hamilton

St. Catherines

Niagara Falls

Thirty Mile
Point

Braddock

Rochester

Stony Point

Selkirk

Oswego

Sodus

NEW YORK

UNITED STATES

Lake Erie

St. Lawrence River

CANADA
USA

1 Barrifield Common (Kingston Range Lights)

Two locomotive headlight lanterns served as the range lights that were established in 1892 on the Barrifield Common at Kingston, Ontario. The front light was placed 370 feet (113 m) east of the end of the bridge to Kingston. It had a focal plane of 48 feet (14.6 m) and displayed a fixed white light visible for 12 miles (19.3 km). The rear light, placed 1,500 feet (457 m) southeast of the front one, was 75 feet (23 m) above the water and displayed a fixed white light from a triangular red skeletal tower with a white beacon. The lights, when aligned, would display a small arc on each side and were used to guide vessels inside the Carruthers and Point Frederick shoals into Kingston Harbour.

Known Keeper: William Murray (1900–).

2 Bay of Quinte Bridge Light

In 1891 the Canadian government placed a lighthouse at the Bay of Quinte Bridge, immediately west of Belleville, Ontario, to assist marine traffic through the area and past the old bridge. At some point this light was removed. Then, when the new modern high bridge over the bay from the mainland to Prince Edward County was constructed, new lights were placed on the bridge to assist boaters.

3 Belleville Lighthouse

Before electricity, oil and natural gas became readily obtainable, residents of Belleville heated their homes with coal and wood. The large freighters that brought in the coal had difficulty navigating the shallow waters of the Bay of Quinte and finding their way into Belleville's small harbor.

To assist them, a lighthouse was built in the water of the harbor in 1881. The short square tapering tower was built on an octagonal concrete pad on a rock-filled timber foundation. The wood frame lighthouse was covered with narrow white clapboarding. A pedimented door gave access to the tower, and large pedimented windows in the tower lit the stairs. The gallery, a minimal board-base platform with pipe iron railing, surrounded the tower about 4 feet (1.2 m) down from the summit. The hexagonal lantern had six large panes of glass and its dome was topped by a curved, rotating ventilator. It displayed a fixed white light that was visible for 11 miles (17.7 km).

Around 1936 it was damaged by ice during a spring flood. In 1941, since lake freighter traffic had dropped significantly and the lighthouse was becoming unsafe, the government removed it. However, the base continued to be a thorn in mariners' sides, since it was above or below the surface of the water, depending on the water table. After numerous complaints by pleasure cruisers and others using the harbor, the base was deemed a hazard to navigation and it was removed in November 1951 by the government dredge. With it gone, boaters usually have a safe 12 feet (3.7 m) depth of water.

Three of the lighthouse keepers are known. In April 1912, H.J. Smith was appointed keeper at a salary of $260 a year. A later keeper was Mathew Weir. Since there was no accommodation at the lighthouse, the keeper had to row out to the lighthouse to illuminate the light and row back in the morning after extinguishing it. With the advent of acetylene, the keeper would row out in the evening to light the light, return to the mainland and then row back out in the morning to extinguish it.

When the light was removed in 1941, it was replaced by a light on the government dock to the east of the old lighthouse. In 1980 the government established a 20-foot (6 m) white circular tower with a green upper portion at Belleville. With its 25-foot (7.6 m) elevation above the water, the fixed green electric light has a visibility of 6 miles (19 kms) .

Known Keepers: John Weir (1901–11), H.J. Smith (1912–), Mathew Weir.

4 Belleville Pier Lighthouse

Very little has been recorded about the Belleville pier light. The only evidence we have of its existence is anecdotal. In August 1887 the keeper forwarded a bill to the Department of Marine and Fisheries for $8.17 for repair of damage to the lighthouse caused by the tug *Bonar*. While towing a raft of saw logs out of the harbor, the *Bonar* had to pass south of the harbor to get to the east channel between the lighthouse and the Grand Pier. The lightkeeper, who had witnessed the events, reported that although the steamer *Alexandria* was coming in at the time, she had given the tug ample room and time to clear the steps of the lighthouse. However, the *Bonar* did not clear the light but snagged the steps and carried them off.

The keeper had presented the bill to the master of the tug, but he had refused payment. In his letter, the keeper "requested to be informed" whether the department could collect the amount on his behalf, and if so what steps should be taken for that purpose. The outcome is not known.

Belleville Lighthouse, circa 1910

5 Brighton Range Lights

The Brighton Range Lights were unusual in that three lights worked together to assist vessels maneuvering into the harbor at Brighton on the north shore of Lake Ontario. They were built in 1891 and known as Brighton Range Lights No.1, No. 2, and No. 3. All three were square white wood towers built onto crib foundations sunk in Presqu'ile Bay. These lights were later replaced by lights on steel poles.

Range Light No. 3, on the north side of the channel, was 30 feet (9 m) high from base to vane, 7,200 feet (2215 m) from the end of the canal piers and 3,920 feet (1206 m) from the wharf. It displayed a fixed white light from a 29-foot (8.8 m) focal plane for a 3-mile (4.9 km) visibility down the canal and in the direction of No. 1 range light. In line with No. 2 range light, it led from the canal up through the center of the channel. After passing it on the starboard side vessels turned and headed directly for No. 1 light.

Range Light No. 2 was 5,360 feet (1649 m) from Light No. 3 and 1,440 feet (443 m) from the wharf. It was 47 feet (14.5 m) high. Its fixed red light, shining from a focal plane of 45 feet (13.7 m), was visible for 6 miles (9.7 m) down the canal and in line with Light No. 3 or, in the wharf direction, aligned with Light No. 1.

Range Light No. 1, the closest light to the wharf, was 1,420 feet (437 m) from Light No. 2 and 1,100 feet (335 m) from the wharf. Its red iron lantern displayed a fixed white light from 28 feet (8.6 m) above the water and was visible for 6 miles (9.7 km), in alignment with Light No. 2 and also toward Light No. 3.

Known Keepers: G.B. Simpson (1873–), H.V. Simpson (1888–) James Grimes (1922–).

Burlington Bay Lakeside Pierhead Light

6 Bronte Pierhead Light

Bronte Harbour was at the mouth of Bronte Creek between Hamilton and Oakville on the shores of western Lake Ontario. Protective wooden piers were built into the lake at the harbor entrance, and the shore on each side of them was formed of shallow rocky flats that extended a quarter of a mile (0.4 km) into the lake.

In 1906 a pierhead light was placed on the north pier. The square white wooden tapering tower with a large cornice supported a large square gallery partway down the tower. It had a pedimented door and a pedimented window for interior light. It was topped with a square lantern with a hipped roof and a straight ventilator stack. It is unknown when this light was removed, but today a modern white circular tower with a red top sits at the outer end of the north pier and flashes a red electric light to mark the harbor entrance.

Known Keeper: C. Osborne (1906–).

7 Burlington Bay Pierhead Lights

Lights at the end of the Burlington Canal piers on Lake Ontario have been modified over time. The first ones, built in 1845, caught fire when sparks from steamers ignited the wooden piers. The steamer *Ranger* caused just such a fire while delivering barrels of whale oil to the lighthouse in July 1856, causing both the pierhead and the main light to burn down. The new lakeside pierhead light was once again rebuilt using wood, but the light was a much shorter white conical tower. Its round gallery supported a round-based lantern that had eight glassed walls, each with four panes of glass. Its octagonal ribbed dome was topped with a ventilator stack and lightning rod. The lantern contained two base-burner fountain lamps on a frame, one with a 20-inch (50 cm) reflector and one with a 16-inch (40 cm) reflector. Both lights were fueled by coal oil (kerosene), whose economic advantages were winning out over

Bronte Pierhead Light

Early Burlington Bay Lakeside Pierhead Light

the disadvantages of its questionable performance in cold weather.

Its main light consisted of six base-burner fountain lamps and six 20-inch (50 cm) reflectors on two iron frames. Five of the lamps faced Lake Ontario for inbound shipping and one lamp faced toward Hamilton to assist outbound traffic through the canal.

In 1870 a storm signal drum was attached to the tower. A series of storms in the late 1890s seriously damaged the pier lighthouse. At first shortened by the removal of rotten timbers, it was later replaced in 1909 by a concrete light. The tapered octagonal tower rose up 25 feet (7.6 m) from the center of the base to support an octagonal gallery trimmed with pipe railing. A double-light window with twelve panes in each section lit the interior. The octagonal lantern that housed the lighting apparatus was capped with an octagonal dome and a ventilator stack.

Today's white reinforced concrete structure took the place of this concrete tower in 1961. This tower swoops gracefully up to a slender peak that supports a square gallery with a pipe railing. The tower has no lantern but is topped by a modern radio beacon light whose yellow isometric light (flash 3 s; eclipse 3 s) shines from 40 feet (12.2 m) above the water.

The lakeside pierhead light worked in conjunction with the 55-foot (17 m) Burlington Main Light until 1961. Industry and boat traffic had increased dramatically by the late 1950s, and pilots complained that the multiplicity of lights in the area caused confusion. As a result, the main light was permanently extinguished in 1961, and a light was placed on top of the new lift bridge (making it perhaps the highest light in the area).

Keepers who tended the Burlington lights were faithful to their job despite personal danger. The main light was relatively accessible from the keeper's house next to the tower, but reaching the lights at the end of the pier was a perilous undertaking when stormy waters made the wooden pier as slick as ice. In May 1892 keeper Campbell was swept into the canal on his way to light the lakeside light in a gale. Fortunately, local residents were able to rescue him with a rope.

Peter Coletti got his job as assistant keeper unexpectedly in 1968 when he went to visit his friend, keeper Mike Gushulak. When Gushulak went to wake up his assistant keeper, old Jack, for his shift, there was no response. After banging on the door and the window of his cottage, the friends broke in and found the assistant dead. Coletti started the very next morning. Later he became head keeper and later sole keeper, and was the last keeper at the Burlington lights when they were decommissioned in 1987.

The other pierhead light was located at the bayside end of the pier around the turn of the century. It was a simple, square white pyramidal wooden tower with a pedimented door and a simple board gallery down from its top. It had a square lantern with a large square hipped oversize dome topped by a ventilator stack.

Burlington Bay Main Light

8 Burlington Bay Main Light

In the early nineteenth century, as shipping increased on the St. Lawrence River, Burlington Bay on the north shore of Lake Ontario was noted as an excellent possibility for a new harbor because it was sheltered, provided good anchorage, and was in a position that could be easily defended against the Americans. However, access to the harbor was impeded by its narrow and shallow entrance.

The government decided to build a canal to join Burlington Bay to Lake Ontario. In 1823, at the urging of Hamilton merchant James Crooks, the House of Assembly authorized the construction. Proposed as one of a series of waterways to provide uninterrupted navigation from Lake Erie to the Atlantic, it was the first public works project undertaken with the financial backing of the Ontario provincial government.

A lighthouse was built at the mouth of the channel to guide ships into the canal entrance. Lieutenant Governor Sir Peregrine Maitland officially opened the waterway on July 1, 1826, even though work had not yet finished. The first schooner to pass

Burlington Bay Main Light

through was the *General Brock*. Unfortunately, it was caught in a cross wind, turned, and ran aground in the canal.

The canal clearly needed to be wider and deeper. Then, winter storms of 1829–30 destroyed the lighthouse and the piers that edged the canal, and blocked the canal with a huge sand bar. Despite delays caused by funding problems and technical difficulties, the Burlington Bay Canal was finally completed in 1832, thereby ensuring Hamilton's rapid growth as a commercial center.

Also in 1832, two new mast lights were built to guide ships into the harbor entrance. The first recorded keeper, M. Homer, earned five shillings a day. People soon realized, however, that these lights were inadequate in storms. So, in 1837, an octagonal, wooden lighthouse was built on

Burlington Bay Main Light and the Royal Hamilton Yacht Club

a stone foundation at the canal by an American, John L. Williams. From the beginning, duties were collected from vessel owners to pay for construction and maintenance of the new lighthouse.

The light burned 213 gallons (970 l) of whale oil annually and went through twelve dozen wicks for its Argand lamps, 20 pounds (9 kg) of soap to clean the glass of the lantern, 2 chamois, and 10 pounds (4.5 kg) of whiting for the exterior. The light's visibility was 15 miles (24.2 km). William Nicholson was appointed the first keeper of the new light in 1837.

Improvements were made to the canal over the years but the canal passage still had problems with silting, cross currents at the entrance, and fires on the wooden piers caused by sparks from steamers. In 1856 sparks from the steamer *Ranger* led to a major fire that burned the pier and destroyed the lighthouse.

To prevent a recurrence, a new limestone lighthouse was built by John Brown of Thorold, Ontario, who was also in the process of constructing the six "imperial tower" lighthouses on Lake Huron and Georgian Bay. The tower had walls 7 feet (2.2 m) thick at the base, a spiral staircase and a copper dome. Its cost was reportedly $10,475, and the salary of its first keeper, George Thompson, was $300 a year. This lighthouse was completed and the lantern lit on October 18, 1858.

The new keeper's house was rebuilt in 1857 by contractor McCallum. It was a 1½-story red brick house and similar in design to the keepers' houses that John Brown built on Lake Huron. Variations in design included the lower ends of the parapet walls being accented by corbels and the ground floor windows being more pronounced with slightly peaked surrounds (a nod to the Gothic Revival style that was just starting at the time). This house first sat across the road from the lighthouse and was later moved to the base of the tower.

This was the first Canadian lighthouse to burn coal oil rather than whale oil. Controversy arose over whalers' loss of jobs and the effectiveness of coal oil lights, as they tended to smoke and choke themselves out, and the oil would freeze in cold weather. However, the price of whale oil was rapidly increasing and its supply was uncertain, so coal oil experiments continued. It became quite successful and by the 1860s many Canadian lighthouses were using it.

Due to land development, industrialization, confusion of lights, and shipping accidents, the Burlington Bay Main Light was decommissioned in 1961, and the main light was placed on top of the new lift bridge.

The light's most colorful keeper was probably its last keeper, Peter Coletti. He was known for his friendly nature and his three parrots. The parrot on his shoulder, coupled with his gray beard and mustache, brought to mind a pirate or an old sea captain, a person out of place in the 1960s. He got his start when he was visiting his friend, keeper Mike Gushulak. When Gushulak's assistant didn't show up for his shift, the friends broke into his room and found him dead. So Coletti started the next morning as the assistant keeper, and took over as keeper when Gushulak left. When the Burlington Station was automated in 1987, Coletti was sent to Long Point and earned a place in history as the last lighthouse keeper for the Burlington lights.

The old stone tower stands abandoned and mostly forgotten below the Burlington Bridge and its original lamp resides in the Joseph Brant Museum in Burlington. Also, the Beach Canal Lighthouse Group of concerned citizens has been formed to undertake restoration of the lighthouse to ensure its continuance.

Known Keepers: M. Homer (1832–36), William Nicholson (1837–46), George Thompson (1846–75), Captain Thomas Campbell (1875–1905), Captain Thomas Lundy (1905–24), Carl Van Cleaf (1941–), Bob Campbell, Harry Dunn, Mike Gushulak, Bill Lamb and Peter Coletti (1968–87).

9 Burnt Island Lighthouse

In 1856 a lighthouse was built on the southeast side of Burnt Island, situated on the north side of the shipping channel through the St. Lawrence River. This light was just a half a mile above Red Horse Rock Light. The tower was 26 feet (8 m) high with an iron lantern 3⅓ feet (1 m) in diameter. It had a fixed white light generated by two No. 1 flat-wicked lamps with two 14-inch (35 cm) reflectors. Its placement high on the island gave it a focal plane of 64 feet (19.5 km) and a visibility of 10 miles (16 km).

Since this lighthouse had been built during the pre-Confederation era, there was no record of the Department of Marine and Fisheries having purchased the required land. When the department inquired about purchasing the whole 14.3-acre (5.8 hectare) island, the Department of Indian Affairs placed a value of $500 on it. The department therefore decided to buy only one acre (0.4 hectares) of land for lighthouse purposes and in 1894 acquired clear title for $35.

Known Keepers: J. Mervin (–1870–78), Collin Turcott (1879–), J.A. Acton (1890–).

Burnt Island Lighthouse

Centre Brother Island Lighthouse

Early Cobourg West Pier Lighthouse

10 Centre Brother Island Lighthouse

Late in the 1880s, the Canadian government decided to build a lighthouse on Centre Brother Island (also called Two Brothers) near Amherst, 7½ miles (12 km) west of Kingston in the Bay of Quinte area. They found that the land, although controlled by the Department of Indian Affairs, had been leased to R.R. Finkle and C.L. Rogers in 1887. In January 1890 these two persons surrendered their interest in the portion required for the lighthouse for a sum of $20. Then the Department of Marine bought the land from the Department of Indian Affairs for $32.

The lighthouse had a white square tower and its lantern displayed a fixed white light with a 10-mile (16 km) visibility. It was built on the north side of the island, ready for use, and its first keeper, Mr. Harty, instructed in its operation by 1890. An inspection report from 1891 declared the "buildings and stores in fair order" and mentioned that Harty supplemented his income by fishing but "did not appear to be making a nuisance of it." Also, since the tower paint was already peeling, being "probably of inferior quality, as in places it [had] turned quite dark," the inspector recommended "a good coat of paint."

The inspector also found, however, that Harty was farming out the keeper's duties to a Mr. Richards, who was living at the station, and that Richards had been running the lighthouse since it opened. Although Richards appeared to be doing a good job, the inspector was concerned at the prospect of having "deputy keepers" and was asked to tell Harty that subcontracting was against regulations; if he did not want to tend the light himself, another keeper would be found.

In November 1900 the keeper of the day, Michael O'Rourke, drowned crossing from Amherst Island to his lighthouse in a small boat. This light no longer exists.

Known Keepers: Mr. Harty (–1891–), Michael O'Rourke (–1900), D. Wemp (1901–13), J. Miller (1913–).

11 Cobourg Pier Lighthouses

Long before the government realized the importance of Cobourg, approximately halfway between Toronto and Kingston on the north shore of Lake Ontario, its residents did. Its long crescent-shaped bay fed by three creeks and edged with sandy beaches provided an excellent resting spot for travelers en route to inland locations. By 1816 a village developed here, and it grew steadily with the area's population. However, large vessels had to anchor offshore and use "jollyboats" to unload people and cargo, and this could be done only in calm weather. By 1828 residents were aware that they needed a harbor.

Local businessmen thus organized the Harbour Company and applied to the Provincial Legislature for a charter to build a harbor. Once granted permission, the company built two rock-filled crib piers out into the lake. By 1832 larger vessels could use them to load and unload passengers and goods. The company introduced tolls from the commerce crossing the Cobourg wharf to offset construction costs and pay dividends to company stockholders. Cobourg also became a landing spot for immigrants. The new harbor's only problem was drifting sand.

Cobourg East Pier Light

In May 1833 the steamboat *Cobourg*, built at Cobourg, was launched. A spacious and elegant vessel propelled by two 50-horsepower engines, it crossed regularly between Cobourg and Oswego, New York. By 1841 the port was booming, bringing in immigrants and manufactured goods and exporting lumber and staples. In that year it received 597 vessels over 50 tons in size as well as many smaller vessels.

In 1842 the Harbour Company gathered materials to extend the western pier to solve the problem of the sand. At that time the new Union Government's Board of Works took over all harbor construction and called for tenders to dredge the harbor and build the piers. The chosen contractor completed the pier extension but never did the dredging — and he pilfered materials for his other contracted jobs.

In 1844 the government built the first lighthouse at Cobourg on its east pier, to assist with navigation. (Although an 1842 period engraving by W. H. Bartlett shows a lighthouse in the harbour). This 16-foot (5 m) square wooden tower stood 20 feet (6 m) above the water. In 1850 the Harbour Company was dissolved and the town of Cobourg purchased the facility by paying the government its existing debt (£10,500). At this time the town dredged the harbor and built an additional wharf between the two piers, continuing to collect tolls on exports and imports.

The new Cobourg-Peterborough Railroad increased the port's value for exports of farm produce, and business thrived, interrupted only by a short depression brought on by the collapse of the railroad bridge bringing produce from the north and the Civil War interfering with business from the south. Harbor traffic escalated once again in the late 1860s, as iron ore from nearby Marmora started passing through Cobourg. This prosperity led to the construction in 1876 of a new west pier 1,550 feet (475 m) directly out into the lake. And a new 20-foot (6 m) lighthouse, which exhibited a flashing white light with a visibility of 8 miles (13 km), was built about halfway along the east pier. Canada's first lifesaving station was established at Cobourg in November 1882.

In 1907 the lighthouse became lit year round, when Cobourg was chosen as the northern terminal for the new ferry, *Ontario 1*, running out of Rochester, New York. The 316-foot (97 m) vessel carried mainly coal-filled railway cars. To accommodate this large vessel, special docks and additions were made, including a southeastern addition to the existing west pier, to make the harbor a safe refuge. In 1916 the *Ontario 2* was added. These ferries ran until 1950, when the advent of diesel locomotives reduced the need for imported coal.

In 1915 the government built a new lighthouse at the end of the east pier. It was a 20-foot (6 m) white concrete tower. Its square base rose about 7 feet (2 m) and then curved and gently tapered upward to support a red metal deck and an electronic beacon. The red flashing light (flash 0.3 s; eclipse 9.7 s) was visible for up to 8 miles (13 km). A radio beacon was also located in the tower.

About halfway along its length, the west pier angled to the southeast into the lake. The pierhead is marked by a much smaller white, cylindrical tower that was built in 1983. This 23-foot (7 m) tower had a green upper portion and a green flashing electrical light (flash 0.55 s; eclipse 3.5 s).

In 1979 a harbor "T" pier light was established. This 12-foot (3.6 m) white circular tower with a red upper portion exhibited a white flashing light with a visibility of 5 miles (8 km). All three pier lights had the same April to December maintenance schedule.

Although Cobourg's harbor no longer sees large lake vessels, it is still an active port for sail and power-driven pleasure craft, and its importance is noted by the continuance of its three harbor lights.

Known Keeper: R. Gordon (1883–1911–).

Cole's Shoal Rear Range Light as seen in 1990

12 Cole's Shoal Lighthouse

Cole's Shoal was named for its proximity to land owned by the Cole family on the St. Lawrence River in Elizabethtown Township of Leeds County just 5 miles (8 km) west of Brockville in the mid-1800s.

In 1860 a site plan was registered for the residence of the Cole's Shoal Lighthouse. In 1877 the tower was a 22-foot (6.7 m) structure with a lantern 6 feet (1.8 m) in diameter with three base-burner lamps, and one 14-inch (35 cm) and two 20-inch (50 cm) reflectors. In 1878 the lighting apparatus became three No. 1 lamps with one 14-inch (35 cm) and two 18-inch (45 cm) reflectors. The wooden light tower was constructed on a 34-foot (10.4 m) pier three quarters of a mile (1.2 km) off the north shore.

At some time a tower with a concrete base and a wooden upper portion with a lantern was built on the shoal in the river, and a wooden light tower was constructed on the bluff to guide downbound vessels. In 1901 the lighthouse was a 33-foot (10 m) white wooden square tower that displayed a fixed white light for 6 miles (9.7 km).

Known Keepers: D. Elliott (1870–), Robert P. Boyd (1884–1915).

Cole's Shoal Front Range, circa 1918

13 De Watteville Range Lights

To assist traffic through the deepwater channel of the St. Lawrence River, the De Watteville Range Lights were first established in 1927 on Canadian shores just below the Cole's Shoal Light.

The front range light was built on the south side of De Watteville Island. It consisted of a 19.8-foot (6 m) white circular tower that had a red upper portion. In 1992 it had a fluorescent orange triangular daymark with a black vertical stripe marking its center, and exhibited an electrical fixed white dioptric light from a 19.5-foot (5.9 m) focal plane.

The rear light was a red steel skeletal pyramidal tower 35 feet (10.7 m) high with an enclosed white wooden service room below its red iron lantern, which once

De Watteville Range Lights

housed a Fresnel lens. In 1992 it also had a fluorescent orange triangular daymark with a black vertical stripe, but the triangle was inverted and the lantern displayed an electrical fixed white dioptric light from a 68-foot (21 m) focal plane. These range lights are visible only when they are in line of the range and can only be viewed from the water.

14 Deseronto Light

Deseronto is located 17 miles (27.5 km) east of Belleville on the north side of the Bay of Quinte along Lake Ontario's northeast shore. In the late 1800s it was one of the main ports between Kingston and Toronto for exporting lumber and other commercial items.

In 1885 a lighthouse was built at Deseronto to assist marine traffic into the small lakeside community. It consisted of a square white wooden tower on the roof of the freight shed of the Bay of Quinte Railway, located near the outer end of the company's wharf. Using gas as its illuminant, it displayed a fixed white light for 11 miles (17.7 km). With the decline in marine transport, this light was eventually discontinued and no longer exists today.

15 Dominion Lighthouse Depot

Along the north shore of the St. Lawrence River is the community of Prescott, Ontario. Today it is a Canadian Coast Guard Base, but in the late 1800s and early 1900s it housed the Dominion of Canada's Department of Marine and Fisheries, the department responsible for maintaining and developing aids to navigation. Their Prescott Depot looked after the department's small fleet of tenders and built and maintained their buoys. Their research and development department tested experimental equipment and sought more efficient lighting apparatus for lighthouses.

This facility had a room referred to as "Room 32," where they tested fuels, wicks, reflectors, designs and combinations of equipment such as burner locations relative to the focal plane to obtain maximum candlepower. They put the materials through intense scrutiny, testing and comparing different products for quality, durability and effectiveness. They were always looking for new materials that would outperform the old ones at lower cost. For example, they tested aluminum for its ability to maintain a polished surface, warpage, cost of production and availability.

The Depot also had a lighthouse lantern constructed on the roof of their storage building to test new or revised lighting devices. A "Notice to Mariners" similar to the following one, would often appear in newspapers and publications.

"River St. Lawrence-Prescott-Dominion lighthouse depot Light for experimental purposes — Caution."

Dominion Lighthouse Depot

Eastern Gap Lighthouse

"*Occasional light* — A large lantern, similar to a lighthouse lantern, has been erected on the roof of the largest building at the Dominion lighthouse depot, Prescott, Ont., for the purpose of testing in it lighthouse illuminating apparatus.

"Lights of varied characteristics, and usually of high candle-power, will occasionally be exhibited without notice given of their characteristic or the time when they will be put in operation. Mariners are warned to pay no attention to this light."

From their rooftop facility, Depot staff measured the efficiency of the test light. By using photometers they could gauge its intensity and candlepower. They would take measurements at various points of the lens from near and far, and they would record the time it took to consume measured amounts of fuels to obtain their burn rates. The data were recorded and photographed with their "Empire State" camera. All apparatus, experiments and equipment sent to any lighthouse were treated this way. Later, as electricity became available, they tested bulbs, transformers and flashing mechanisms as well.

During the 1930s and 1940s, in addition to testing traditional lighthouse equipment, they were responsible for testing and maintaining lighting equipment and beacons for public airports and military airfields, whose lights were also considered lighthouses. The Depot later became part of the Canadian Coast Guard Station at Prescott, and the building and test lantern have now been replaced.

16 Eastern Gap Lighthouses

As the 1858 hurricane moved through the Toronto area, Gibraltar Point, the peninsula on whose point the Gibraltar Point Lighthouse stood, became an island (now Toronto Island) as the storm washed away its marshy connection to the mainland.

The new opening — the Eastern Gap — needed range lights to assist the growing number of vessels that approached Toronto harbor from the east.

The range lights, built in 1895, were taller and shorter white square clapboard pyramidal towers with pedimented doors and windows, and galleries supported by wooden braces. In 1909 a housing for the fog alarm engine was built by local contractor J.D. Young and Sons at a cost of $3,295. These range lights served well until 1973. When the Eastern Gap was widened to 600 feet (185 m) and dredged to 27 feet (8.3 m) deep, they were replaced by more modern equipment. After removal, the lighthouses were stored with the intention of placing them in the Aquatic Park proposed for the area or on the newly developed Leslie Street Spit.

In 1978, while photographing these lighthouses, historian Ken Maxwell thought it would be a great idea if the community of Mimico put in a bid for them. He had a nostalgic relationship with the lights as he had "hoisted a few" with the lightkeeper in the 1940s and had carved his initials somewhere inside one of them. After much negotiation, the lighthouses were loaded onto a barge and floated to their destinations. The shorter one was unloaded first at the Etobicoke Yacht Club. The taller one was unloaded at the Mimico Cruising Club, where fingers of the dock had to be removed to allow the tug and barge passage.

Initially the club wanted to put the light by the bay where it would be more noticeable, but since it was no longer a recognized aid to navigation, the Department of Transport would not allow it. So, the lighthouse was placed on a concrete pad on club land. In 1981–82 club members helped refurbish it as a quaint but small club office.

Known Keeper: Alf Winslow (– 1973)

False Duck Island Lighthouse

17 False Duck Island Lighthouse

Provincial legislation passed in March 1828 granted £1,000 to construct a "good and sufficient lighthouse on False Duck Island" in Prince Edward County, on the northeast shore of Lake Ontario. It was hoped that the light would "tend greatly to the safety and convenience of navigation" on the lake. Built on the island's east point, this lighthouse was one of the earliest in Canada.

The tower and keeper's house were built of limestone. The tower's total height was 73 feet (22.3 m) and its British-manufactured lantern was 8 feet (2.4 m) in diameter and showed a fixed white light with a visibility of 13 miles (21 km) in fair weather. In 1878 the lighthouse had 15 No.1 base-burner lamps and 15 reflectors mounted about 5 feet (1.5 m) off the floor.

By 1898 the lighting apparatus consisted of three, double-wick, duplex burners fitted to a brass fountain enclosed in a third-order Fresnel lens from Paris. Once this light was "properly set going," it did not require constant attention through the night. This is probably why the keeper preferred it to the new apparatus he had been sent, which consisted of a pressure, circular burner lamp that required "constant attention throughout the entire night." During the day the lens was hung with a canvas cover and curtains were drawn across the windows to prevent sun damage. In 1904 a fog building was added to the complex.

In November 1905, lightning ran through the entire tower. It cracked the walls, made holes in the masonry and broke windows and lighting apparatus, and traveled underground to the fog signal plant. Fortunately the lens was not damaged. However, the lightning struck the keeper's house beside the attached storehouse where oil, coal and winter supplies were stored. The oil immediately caught fire and ignited the whole house. Only the keeper and his family — and the stone walls — were saved.

The keeper moved into the fog building for the winter so that he could tend the light to the end of the season. He also stayed on at the island, with emergency provisions, to feed the livestock, but his family moved to the mainland for the winter. Until this disaster he and his family had always wintered on the island but they never did again. After the tower was repaired, the remains of the stone keeper's house were torn down and a new clapboard house was built. A separate oil shed was also added to prevent any such risk in the future. The keeper received $100 to compensate for the loss of his personal effects.

With its long years of service and political appointments, the lighthouse had many keepers. A few led colorful lives, and archival documents relate many disputes over issues such as the keeper's honesty, bribery to obtain and keep the position, political partisanship, neglect of government property, and — most egregious — leaving the light and fog station unattended. One night in December 1902, the steamer *John Hall* was lost in a severe storm close to the False Duck Island Lighthouse when the light was unlit.

Changes occurred with modern times. In 1947 a radiophone was installed. A new fog building was built and ready for use in

False Duck Lighthouse being painted

Old and new False Duck Island Lighthouses, circa 1966

False Duck Lighthouse, circa 1966

October 1952, and the old fog building was remodeled as a keeper's residence. The light was switched from a vapor light to electricity. Then on November 3, 1965, keeper James McConnell extinguished the light for the last time. On Friday, June 3, 1966 the old stone tower was pulled to the ground by the Canadian Coast Guard tender *Simcoe*.

The light was replaced by a 60-foot (18.3 m) hexagonal reinforced concrete tower, painted with 8-foot (2.4 m) red and white horizontal bands. A fog building was attached. The lantern housed an automated, red-colored, flashing, electric beacon that was first lit on November 3, 1966. The iron lantern and light were removed from the old limestone tower and were presented to the Prince Edward Historical Society, which had opened a marine museum in 1966. As a centennial project, the South Marysburgh council had a much shorter (30 feet/9 m) limestone tower built at the museum to support the lantern they were given from the old False Duck Island Lighthouse. On September 17, 1967, this lighthouse was dedicated as a memorial to the sailors of the county who lost their lives under steam and sail. The museum is located at the head of South Bay and is open from Victoria Day to Thanksgiving.

The new light still beams out its warning signal today to help mark safe passage for boaters in the area of Prince Edward County.

Known Keepers: F. Swetman (1863–86), W.H. Lane (1886–91), P.N. Farrington (1891–94), J.M. Hudgins (1894–1903), D. Dulmage (1903–12), J.W. Hudgins (1912–18), G.E. Hudgins (1918–23), K.A. Duette (1923–23), J. Hutchinson (1924–27), E. Bongard (1927–28), K.A. McConnell (1928–57), J. McConnell (1957–65).

Early Gananoque Narrows Lighthouse

18 Gananoque Narrows Lighthouse

In 1856 a lighthouse was established on the northeast end of Little Stave Island on the south side of the old shipping channel, located five miles below Gananoque in the St. Lawrence River. It marked the east entrance to the Gananoque Narrows between that island and Prince Regent Island. It was a square white 44-foot (13.4 m) wooden tower with an iron lantern that displayed a fixed white light generated by three No.1 lamps with three 15-inch (38 cm) reflectors and was visible for 7 miles (11.3 km). Because the light was built on a rocky point, the keeper lived away from the island and traveled by boat to service the light.

In 1887 its keeper, Joshua Legge, wrote to the government from Gananoque requesting permission to use the 27.5 acres (11 hectares) on the island for pasture and a garden as had the previous keeper. In exchange, he was willing to take charge of the island and prevent any person from building a fire

Gananoque Narrows Lighthouse, topped by a modern beacon

on it in the daytime. In dry summers there was a great risk of fires caused by fishing parties who wanted to fry up their catch but did not completely put out their campfires. In 1886 three such fires had been started in the area.

While the lighthouse had been built on the island by the pre-Confederation government, there was no record of the Department of Marine and Fisheries ever having purchased the land from the Department of Indian Affairs. To provide for the necessary and proper title, a half-acre lot was purchased in 1893 for $100. While this light no longer exists today, a modern beacon was established in 1984 to mark the east end of the narrows.

Known Keepers: Cornelius Cook (1870–), Joshua Legge (1887–), Mrs. M. Cross (1908–).

Gibraltar Point Lighthouse

19 Gibraltar Point Lighthouse

The large and easily defended harbor of York (Toronto) was a persuasive factor in Lieutenant-Governor John Graves Simcoe's decision to make the city the naval and military center of Upper Canada. The chosen site for guarding the entrance to the harbor was Gibraltar Point. Fortification began in 1794 and by 1800 two defensible stone houses and a guardhouse had been erected on the site.

Sources vary on the exact date of initial construction of a lighthouse on the point. Some have it as 1798, others as 1800. But by 1803 it was not finished, if it had been started, because in 1803 the Provincial Legislature passed an act for the establishment of lighthouses at Mississauga Point (Niagara-on-the-Lake), Gibraltar Point (Toronto) and Isle de Forest (Kingston, Nine Mile Point of Simcoe Island). Also, according to the act, a toll was to be levied on vessels using the harbors to fund the erection and maintenance of the lighthouses. Although it sounded good on paper and was a practical approach, sailors were outraged to be expected to pay a toll where there were no lighthouses — and refused to do so.

The Gibraltar Point Lighthouse, finished in 1808, is generally agreed to be the second lighthouse built on the Great Lakes, the first being the Mississauga Lighthouse built at Newark (Niagara-on-the-Lake) in 1804. Stone for the lighthouse was quarried at

Queenston and brought to the site on the *Mohawk*. It was a hexagonal, masonry tower with a base diameter of 22 feet (6.7 m) and a base circumference of about 68 feet (20 m). Its walls were 6 feet (1.8 m) thick at the base, tapering to 4 feet (1.2 m) at the top. Eighty wooden stairs wound up the narrow spiral staircase to its cage-like wood lantern and hexagonal gallery.

The tower was 52 feet (16 m) high, including the lantern. It displayed a fixed white light using an oil lamp that burned about 200 gallons (900 l) of sperm whale oil per year. A dumb-waiter, centered within the spiraling stairs, rose up the middle of the tower to haul whale oil up to the lamp. The light's visibility was about 7 miles (11.3 km). Attached to the outside of the lantern room was a signal hoist for raising a flag to inform Fort York of approaching vessels.

The lighthouse at Gibraltar Point freed up lake navigation because vessels could now travel at night. The lighthouse became the best-known landmark in Toronto as, for many years, it was the first building that visitors saw when approaching and the last one they saw when leaving.

Although on a peninsula, the lighthouse site was more like an island because of its isolation and poor accessibility. York residents liked to visit the peninsula to walk or ride, use it as a race ground, to hunt, or to assist recovering convalescents, but to get there they had to travel east along the shoreline, cross the Don River and then travel out the long bottle-neck of land. Crossing the Don River caused most of the problems, as spring runoff would carry away the bridge over it. By 1806 a floating bridge was built to span the Don. In the winter of 1811–12, the skipper of the yacht *Toronto*, confused about the position of the lighthouse, foundered on the southern shore of the peninsula. For many years island visitors went to look at the wreck.

Early Gibraltar Point Lighthouse

Gibraltar Point Keeper's House

During the War of 1812, the Americans destroyed the stone houses built at Gibraltar Point in their second raid on York in 1813, but spared the lighthouse. Also at this time, the Upper Canadian militia retreated to Kingston because they were greatly outnumbered. As a defensive measure, they burned the bridge across the Don River much to the outrage of local residents. By the following May a small blockhouse mounting a gun had been constructed on Gibraltar Point. The building, in ruins by 1823, was dismantled sometime before 1833 and was not replaced.

The keepers and their families were the first civilian residents on the peninsula. The first keeper, John Paul Rademuller, lived in a shuttered pioneer-style frame cottage close to the lighthouse. The house was "built of three-inch [7.5 cm] planks joined by nails from the blacksmith's shop at Fort York." Differing reports speculate on Rademuller's mysterious end. One recounts that on a January night in 1815, soldiers from Fort York visited their friend

Gibraltar Point Lighthouse keeper Captain McSherry, 1907

the lightkeeper and that, becoming drunk and disorderly, beat him to death with their heavy belts because he refused to serve them more liquor. Then they cut his body into pieces buried them around on area islands and escaped along the bay never to be brought to trial.

Another story says that Rademuller simply vanished in 1815. However, part of a human skeleton was found close to the lighthouse in 1893 by George Durnan, the light's keeper at the time. Many believed it to be part of Rademuller's unfound remains. Regardless of how he disappeared, all reports agree that it is Rademuller's ghost who haunts the Gibraltar Point Lighthouse. Some say he haunts it because of his dedication to the light, while others say he is searching for his bones for a proper burial.

Rademuller was followed by keeper William Holloway, who enjoyed the company of the local officers who hunted ducks and snipes nearby. His wife, who kept a cow, gave the hunters bread and cheese. James Durnan became keeper after Holloway. In 1832 he saw another 12 feet (3.7 m) added to the top of the lighthouse tower to increase its visibility. He also lived through many historical events during his stay, including the scourge of the 1832 cholera epidemic, the incorporation of the City of Toronto on March 6, 1834, William Lyon Mackenzie's 1837 Rebellion, Toronto's celebration of Queen Victoria's coronation, and the visit of the Governor-in-Chief, Lord Durham. By 1888 the island had a summer population of a thousand people who made up a complete village.

In 1858 a severe storm washed away the isthmus, and the peninsula became an island (Toronto Island). Other smaller islands were also formed, as well as what became known as the Eastern Gap.

Sometime after 1863, coal oil replaced whale oil as the light's illuminant. While

Keys to Gibraltar Point Lighthouse

cheaper, much more of it was needed — about 900 gallons (4 050 l) a year. In 1877 the light consisted of eleven mammoth flat-wick lamps and nine 15-inch (38 cm) and two 18-inch (45 cm) reflectors mounted on two large copper reservoirs. In 1878 the lighthouse was equipped with a revolving light that turned once every 108 seconds. It was powered by a cable with weights that slowly unwound from a drum and were pulled down by gravity through the old dumb-waiter shaft. The weights needed to be rewound every 14 hours. With its powerful reflectors, this new light was said to be the most powerful in North American waters at that time.

Also in 1878 the wooden gallery and lantern were replaced with new cast-iron ones and topped with a lightning rod. This was most fortunate for the tower because in 1879 lightning struck the rod and removed all the whitewashing as it traveled down the tower sides. If it had still had the wooden topping, it would likely have burned and the tower would be in ruins today.

More changes took place in the twentieth century. In 1916–17 the light was electrified, but continued to display a flashing white light in a 240-degree arc. In 1945 it was changed to a fixed green light so that it could be distinguished from the white lights of Toronto behind it. In 1958 the light was replaced by a small skeletal tower nearby. On May 23, 1958, the lighthouse was transferred to the Municipality of Metropolitan Toronto Parks Department.

Unlike most lighthouses that were built close to the shore, this one has not been threatened with soil erosion but continues to gain distance from the water. When the Gibraltar Point lighthouse was built, it was 25 feet (7.6 m) from the shore, but silt carried on currents originating at Niagara Falls was deposited at the peninsula, and the land area in front of the lighthouse grew a little bit each year. Now, the lighthouse stands some 300 yards (275 m) away from the water.

The stone tower is a grand structure that seems to defy time. To see it you must travel by ferry to Centre Island, and then walk, bike or take a shuttle-tram to the lighthouse. It's worth a visit to see the oldest standing lighthouse on the Great Lakes. The base rises straight up for about 10 feet (3 m) to a row of outcropping stone. From this base the tower tapers to a similar outcropping of stone. Above this, the addition rises straight up again. It supports a twelve-sided lantern with a red dome and hexagonal gallery. The gallery is supported by six ornately carved red wooden corbels. Up the tower, instead of regular windows, there are long, slit openings that may have been rifle windows. The tower is not open to the public, but there are many areas on the island for picnicking and swimming.

Known Keepers: John Paul Rademuller (1809–15), William Hollaway (1816–31), James Durnan (1832–53), George Durnan (1853–1908), Captain P.J. McSherry (1905–12), B. Mathews (1912–17), G.F. Eaton (1917–18), F.C. Allan (1918–44), Mrs. Ladder (1944–55), Mrs. Dodds (1955–58).

20   Graveyard Point Lighthouse

At an unknown date, a light was placed as a steering signal to help mariners with their navigation of the St. Lawrence River east of Iroquois on Graveyard Point. It displayed a fixed red characteristic. In February 1958 the light was changed from electric to acetylene and given a flashing red characteristic for the opening of the 1958 navigation season. Little else is known about it, and this light does not exist today.

21   Grenadier Island Lighthouse

This lighthouse was established in 1856 on Grenadier Island,(also known as Bathurst Island), one of the Thousand Islands. The island is located between Brockville (to the east) and Gananoque (to the west) in the St. Lawrence River and is just 2 miles (3.2 km) below Rockport. The lighthouse reserve was 9.8 acres (3.9 hectares) of land at the southwest point of the island, and the lighthouse was a square white 37-foot (11.3 m) wooden tower that displayed a light from a 55-foot (16.8 m) focal plane.

The fixed white light was generated by three base-burner fountain lamps on a square frame in a lantern 6 feet (1.8 m) in diameter. The lamps were equipped with one 13-inch (33 cm) and two 15-inch (38 cm) reflectors. In 1878 it was generated by three No. 1 lamps with 12-inch (30 cm) reflectors.

A survey from 1905 showed that the frame keeper's house was in good shape and that 3.7 acres (1.5 hectares) of "pine grove" had been cleared for gardening, an orchard and crops. It was adjoined by a National Park that seemed to have encroached on the lighthouse property, thereby creating a rift between the two government agencies. Finally, the lighthouse property had to be fenced. Eventually the lighthouse was discontinued and all physical signs of its existence on the island disappeared.

Known Keepers: Albert Root (1863–), D. Root (1908–16–).

22   Gull Island (Peter's Rock) Lighthouse

Between Cobourg and Port Hope there is a long crescent-shaped submerged reef in Lake Ontario that was a menace to mariners. On April 22, 1835 the *Cobourg Star* reported that the Legislative Council had passed a proposal for the purpose of spending £1,000 to build a lighthouse between the two communities, and that His Excellency had sanctioned it.

On June 21, 1837, the *Cobourg Star* published the detailed specifications for this light, for contractors interested in preparing a sealed bid.

"The Tender to be circular and 28 feet [8.6 m] in diameter at the Base, and 50 feet [15.4 m] high, the foundation to be excavated … into the solid Limestone Rock. The Basement to be solid stone work of 8 feet [2.5 m] in height, the external surface to be worked to an external radius of 70 feet [21.5 m] … All external surface to be set … with prepared Roman or water cement. Backing of Basement. All to be backed with good flat bedded hammer dressed stone, in regular courses, either of one or two thickness, to correspond with the radius and level of front course, no course to be less than 6 inches [15 cm], and none more than 8 inches [20 cm], every stone to be laid flush in well made mortar, and every course properly backed, grouted and leveled with the first course, before another is begun …

"The Platform to be 20 feet [6.2 m] in diameter and 15 feet [4.6 m] thick; composed of sound, well seasoned timber of the most

Gull Island (Peter's Rock) Lighthouse, circa 1903   NAC PA172485

durable nature … Lantern. The top to be 70 feet [21.5 m] above the foundation; the base to be an octagon, 8 feet [2.46 m] in diameter; to be securely rabbited into the upper surface of the platform, and neatly coated with lead, as also the dome, 5 feet [1.5 m] in height.

"The framework and sashes to be composed of clean, well seasoned stuff, Glass to be best plated, run with vermillion, to show a blood light. The interior fitted with an Iron Chandelier, to contain thirteen lights, to have thirteen patent reflectors, each 16 inches [40 cm] in diameter, with fixtures and apparatus; ties and braces corresponding generally with the Lantern at Point Peters, Lake Ontario …

"All the wood, iron and lead work to receive at least two coats of white paint, or McAdam's mineral composition."

Three commissioners were appointed to superintend the work. They received tenders until noon July 1, 1837 at the Exchange Coffee House in Port Hope. The contract was to be completed by October, leaving only four months for construction. This lighthouse was placed on the submerged rock about 1 mile (1.6 km) from shore and about halfway between Cobourg and Port Hope. The light was visible for up to 12 miles (19 km).

Just five years later, the *Cobourg Star* carried another ad "To Experienced Contractors" for making necessary repairs to the Gull Island Light House. Prior to 1877 the lighting apparatus had been changed to nine base-burners and five circular lamps and by 1877 six of the 20-inch (50 cm) reflectors were in need of resilvering. By 1879 the lighting equipment had been upgraded to sixteen lamps, seven mammoth and nine No. 1 base-burners with 17-inch (43 cm) reflectors, for a visibility of 20 miles. The government installed a new oil house and completed extensive pier repairs.

The lighthouse did not, however, meet all of the published specifications, perhaps due to limited funds or the short building time allowed. Scott's *Coastal Pilot* for 1901 described the light as an octagonal 48-foot (14.6 m) tower (not the tendered 70 feet/ 21.5 m), which displayed a fixed white light (not a red one) for 10 miles (16 km).

In 1907 the *Cobourg World* reported that "extensive repairs and enlargements" were being made to the lighthouse by workmen under P.T. Brewel of Ottawa. The work included "practically rebuilding the lighthouse" and enlarging the keeper's accommodations. The light was to run all year "to assist the ferry entering Cobourg Harbour." This may be when the tower became a cylindrical stone one with a slightly conical base, as seen in old photographs.

Sources differ on whether the keeper in 1907 earned $500 a year or $680, as government records show. A few years later the lighthouse was equipped with an automatic light and the keeper was no longer needed. With the demise of commercial shipping to Cobourg, the stone lighthouse was removed and replaced by a much lower platform, equipped with an automatic light, placed on Peter Rock.

Known Keepers: Hales Lupent (–1842), W. Brostorh (1843–), George Roddick (–1860–70–), Robert Roddick (1872 –1907), James Roddick (1907–), Percy Climo (–1924–).

Hamilton Island Lighthouse

23 Hamilton Island Lighthouse

Hamilton Island is a small island in the St. Lawrence River situated between Stonehouse Point and Lancaster Shoal below Cornwall. At an unknown date a lighthouse was built on its southeast side to assist mariners navigating past the island. The lighthouse was a 17-foot (5.2 m) square tapering wooden tower about 27 feet (8.3 m) tall which stood on a small point close to the water's edge. The tower flared slightly to support its square gallery and its wooden lantern 7 feet (2.1 m) in diameter. The lantern contained three mammoth flat-wicked lamps with 20-inch (50 cm) reflectors. The light no longer exists today and was never replaced with a modern beacon.

Known Keepers: John Hamilton (1873–1905), Chas Neaves (1906–14),

24 Jackstraw Shoal Lighthouse

In 1851 the government contracted Joshua Legge of Gananoque to place a beacon light on a 34-foot (10.4 m) mast anchored into a 25-foot (7.6 m) square rock-filled pine crib set into the St. Lawrence River on Jackstraw Shoal on the north side of the channel about two miles east Gananoque.

Then, in 1856, the Legislature of Canada West built a lighthouse at Jackstraw on a crib on the shoal in the river and close to the mast beacon. Its 29-foot (8.8 m) square white wooden

Jackstraw Shoal Lighthouse

tower displayed a fixed white light with a visibility of 10 miles (16.2 km). On April 17, 1858, the following announcement appeared in the *Kingston Daily News:* "$200 Reward — for information on the cut down beacon near Jackstraw lighthouse, below Gananoque." In 1878 a government report recommended that the lighthouse be rebuilt.

The 1966 *St. Lawrence River Pilot* mentions that a light was still shown from Jackstraw Shoal. The tower was described as a white circular tower with a 25-foot (7.7 m) elevation. It was to warn of the shoals that extended for more than half a mile southwest from Jackstraw Island. The lighthouse had been built on the southwest tip of these shoals, which was known at Jackstraw Shoal and was located on the north side of the channel into Gananoque. Its keeper also served as the keeper at Gananoque Narrows.

This light still existed in 1992 but it had been changed. It was a 20-foot (6.1 m) circular white tower with a red upper portion and it displayed a red flashing (flash 0.5 s; eclipse 3.5 s), electric dioptric light from a 25-foot (7.6 m) focal plane.

Known Keeper: Mrs. Manly Cross (1896–1908).

25 Kingston Clock Tower Light

Kingston Harbour, situated at the northeast corner of Lake Ontario just where the lake terminates and the St. Lawrence River begins, is an excellent natural harbor, but the many nearby islands and shoals make its approach very dangerous.

In the mid-nineteenth century, sailors were using the lighted clock tower at Kingston as a lighthouse, according to a report in the *Kingston Daily News* of December 10, 1866: "The lighted dome of the city building has been found to answer a practical and more desirable purpose, to which it was never intended to be applied. Captains of vessels coming down the lake stated that no better beacon light could be devised than that presented by the clock tower during the hours it remains lighted up at night. It can be distinctly seen at a distance of nearly six miles, and by steering directly for it from Four Mile Point or Snake Island the vessel rounds the marine railway point through the channel, and is brought

Kingston Clock Tower Light

into part of the harbour without the least difficulty. The brilliancy of the light, its fine elevation and the great distance at which it can be seen, are spoken of in the highest terms, and its usefulness in this respect during the fall months, and on dark and stormy nights, should be taken into consideration before any steps are taken by the Council to diminishing the light or to cease lighting it altogether."

The light must have been extinguished because in 1871 ship owners, wharfingers and others petitioned the Kingston City Council to illuminate the clock of city hall as a beacon and to request monies for the clock being lit. Some aldermen were instantly in favor of this, as it would enhance shipping into Kingston Harbour. It was estimated that it would cost $4 a night to light the clock. At the same meeting, aldermen reported that buoys marking Point Frederick Shoal were "ridiculous" and "disgraceful to the port." Councilors also discussed the shoal tower being made into a lighthouse or being removed altogether, as it was "a nuisance, and all sailors coming to port considered it as so." The petition was no doubt successful because in 1892 the clock tower was lit and its fixed white light was said to be visible for 9 miles (14.5 km). The light was 96 feet (29.3 m) above the ground, much higher than any other light around.

The 1907 the government's lightkeepers payroll shows that the Corporation of Kingston was paid $100 a year for maintaining this light plus an addition $20 for keeping the clock lit in the winter months.

Knapp Point Lighthouse

26 Kingston Marine Railway Pier Light

It is unknown when this lighthouse was established, but a square white wooden tower was at the end of the pier in 1844. The *Kingston Daily News* reported on November 28, 1859, that during a storm some damage had been done in the harbor and that the abandoned lighthouse on the end of the Marine Railway had been washed away. The date when it had been extinguished is unknown, but it met its end in 1859.

27 Knapp Point Lighthouse

In 1874 the Canadian government placed a light on the north side of Wolfe Island. The tower was 28 feet (8.6 m) tall from base to vane and was topped by an iron lantern 6 feet (1.8 m) in diameter, which displayed a fixed white light created by three flat-wick lamps and three 20-inch (50 cm) reflectors. With its 20-foot (6 m) square white tower, it had a visibility of 10 miles (16 km). The station also had a hand foghorn to answer signals from vessels.

In 1878 keeper Patrick McAvoy was instructed to convert the old oil house into accommodations for the keeper and to buy materials to finish off the interior. In 1879 McAvoy sublet the light to Thomas Sturdy, who was given a vote of confidence by the Superintendent of Lighthouses, Darius Smith.

The light served for many years. In 1947, in a letter to the Chief of Aids to Navigation, the chief's manager reported that several pilots had recently mentioned that this light would be greatly improved by being made stronger. They also wanted a fixed light as it had previously been, and suggested that a green light would be more satisfactory. Pilots were always being helpful, and their suggestions were often implemented. What if any of these suggestions were acted upon is unknown.

In 1992 a white flashing (flash 0.5 s; eclipse 3.5 s) electric dioptric light was being shown from a white 20-foot (6.2 m) tower with a red upper portion. From its 28-foot (8.5 m) focal plane the light was visible for 5 miles (8 km).

Known Keepers: Patrick McAvoy (–1877–), Thomas Sturdy (1879), Allan McLaren (1896–1905), J.J. Brophy (1905–12), W.W. Card (1912–).

28 Lancaster Bar Light

Lancaster Bar is an area of shallow water that extends almost completely across the St. Lawrence River, except for a deep channel, which passes through this bar. It lies southeast of Lancaster on the Canadian side of the river. A light at this location on the St. Lawrence River was the first light to be encountered west of the Quebec-Ontario border in an area referred to as Lake St. Francis. It became known as the Lancaster Bar Leading Light. This bar was originally marked in 1844 with a lightship. When this vessel was found to be rotting and unfit for service in 1869, the government was advised not to replace the lightship but instead to lay down a crib and build a lighthouse there.

The lighthouse and keeper's dwelling was erected on a rock-filled crib in the river during the winter of 1869–70 at a cost of $2,643. The tower was 31 feet (9.5 m) high and exhibited a fixed white catoptric light with a visibility of 8 miles (13 km). After the new light was lit on April 28, 1870, the Department of Public Works removed the lightship. Today this light is one of two known as the Lancaster Range Lights, which continue to mark the area.

Known Keepers: George H. Johnson (–1877–), Thomas Hill II (1878–1906), J.J. Munroe (1906–16–).

29 Lancaster Pier Light

This light was placed on a pier on the north side of the channel 4 miles (6.5 km) southwest of Lancaster for use as a guiding light in conjunction with the Lancaster Bar Light. It was a white square wooden tower 20 feet (6 m) high, and it housed a catoptric lighting system that consisted of three dual-burner fountain lamps, a 15-inch (38 cm) reflector, and a 14-inch (36 cm) reflector. At an unknown date its fixed white light was replaced with a modern beacon to form one of the Lancaster Range Lights, which still mark the area today.

Known Keepers: George Johnston (1877), Thomas Hill (1878–1906), J.J. Munroe (1906–16–).

30 Lindoe Island Lighthouse

Lindoe Island is a small island 5 miles (8 km) northwest of Rockport, on the north side of Wallace Island (also known as Goodman Island) in the Thousand Islands in the St. Lawrence River. In 1856 a lighthouse was built on the northwest point of Lindoe Island. This was one of many lighthouses built to help mariners navigate the Thousand Islands. Because it was a mere 1.4 acres (0.6 hectares), the keeper's house was built on nearby Wallace Island and the keeper had to row to and fro each day.

Lindoe Island Lighthouse

Parliamentary Sessional Papers from 1878 show the tower as a square white wooden one topped with a 3-foot (0.9 m) square iron lantern. It used three No. 1 mammoth flat-wick lamps and two 12-inch (30 cm) reflectors to shine the light from a 40-foot (12.2 m) elevation for 6 miles (9.7 km). The inspector also reported that the lantern was too small and the building needed repairs. The 1879 Sessional Papers show that its illuminating apparatus had changed. It had an iron lantern with a 3.5-foot (1 m) diameter and used three No.1 base-burner lamps with 13-inch (33 cm) reflectors.

In 1890 the Department of Marine and Fisheries bought Wallace Island for $300 from the Department of Indian Affairs. When Indian Affairs asked that it also purchase Lindoe Island, the department responded that it had already bought the island for $100 from John Landers in 1856 when the lighthouse was built. However, Indian Affairs had no record of relinquishing the title and claimed that Landers had no right to sell it, and so the Department of Marine and Fisheries bought clear title to it for $200 in 1893.

In 1897 J.G. Wallace, the Lindoe Island lightkeeper at that time, caused a commotion when he sold 1 1/4 acres (0.5 hectares) of Wallace Island to a W.D. Morris for $250 and Morris built a summer cottage and other buildings on the property. The government, finding the buildings on their property, soon learned of the keeper's doings and how he had told Morris he owned Wallace Island, as his father had occupied it as a squatter and had quit-claimed it in 1886. However, it was quickly ascertained that keeper Wallace had no deed to the land and was not in a position to have sold it.

In the end, Morris was given title for $100, since this acreage was unfit for cultivation, and not required for government use.

However, Wallace continued to claim ownership of the island and continued as lightkeeper until 1904 when the government changed, replaced Wallace as keeper, and tried to expropriate the land. In 1912, reinstated as keeper, Wallace appealed for a fair hearing. He felt the island was his, except Morris's portion, as his family had been in possession of it for over 50 years. Although the Marine Department had bought it for $300, he had paid all improvements and expenses. The representative sent to peruse the island recommended that the buildings and island, except Morris's part and one acre (0.4 hectares), to be kept for future use by the government, be sold to J.G. Wallace for $451. The keeper's house and boathouse, originally built by the government, were given to him free of charge on the condition that while he was keeper he would not be given any other house. By 1913 Wallace finally had a deed of ownership for most of Wallace Island.

Known Keepers: J. Wallace (–1870–), John Wallace (1881–86–), J.G. Wallace (–1897–1904), unknown (1904–12), J.G. Wallace (1912–).

31 Long Sault Rapids Lighthouse

This light has been known by different names — the Dickinson Landing Light, Long Sault Rapids Light, and the Cornwall Light. This light stood at the western entrance to the Cornwall Canal near Dickinson Landing. It exhibited a fixed white light with a visibility of 3 miles (4.8 km) and was maintained by the Department of Railways and Canals. The Cornwall Canal had been built as a bypass around the Long Sault Rapids for ships traveling the St. Lawrence River.

The first light, constructed in 1846, was a white square 20-foot (6 m) pyramidal tower. The second was built in 1865 and was 21 feet (6.4 m) tall. By 1891 that light was so badly rotted it had to be rebuilt again.

Today the light stands in a new home at the west end of the replica canal built at Upper Canada Village. The tower had to be moved from its original location in the 1950s during the construction of the St. Lawrence Seaway. Many structures in the St. Lawrence flood plane had to be moved to higher ground or risk being flooded by the development of the seaway. This light would probably not have survived had it not been moved to the village.

Long Sault Rapids Lighthouse

Main Duck Island Lighthouse

32 Lyndoch Island Lighthouse

This light, near Rockport, Ontario, was established in 1856 on the northwest end of Lyndoch Island at the west end of Fiddler's Elbow, a little over half a mile (0.8 km) west of Wallace Island in the Thousand Islands area of the St. Lawrence River. It was exhibited from a square white wooden tower 26-foot (8 m) from base to vane. It used catoptric illuminating apparatus to display a fixed light from 40 feet (12.2 m) above the water for 7 miles (11.3 km) to mark the south side of the channel. It was one of many such lights provided to assist mariners in navigating the Thousand Islands archipelago.

The 1966 *St. Lawrence River Pilot* describes the light: It "is exhibited, at an elevation of 40 feet [12.2 m], from the roof of a building, situated on the northwest side" of the island. The old tower is long gone, but the spot is still marked today. A modern beacon shines from a circular steel white tower topped with a green band. In 1992 this light showed a green flashing (flash 0.5 s; eclipse 3.5 s) light using an electric dioptric illuminating apparatus.

Main Duck Island Lighthouse, circa 1914

33 Main Duck Island Lighthouse

Main Duck Island Lighthouse, located 12 miles (19.3 km) out in Lake Ontario off Prince Edward Point (Traverse Point), was built in 1913–14 to warn mariners of the hazardous shoals extending from the peninsula and help guide them around it. The 80-foot (24.4 m) octagonal tower was topped by a polygonal red iron lantern equipped with a third-order lens and a 55 mm vapor light of 100,000 candle power. It produced a flashing white light every six seconds and had a visibility of 17 miles (27.4 km) on a clear night. In 1949 the mantle-type burner was replaced by a 400-watt electric, mercury vapor bulb.

In 1915 a fog station was built near the lighthouse. It housed a radio that ships equipped with radio direction apparatus could use to determine their position. In 1965 a concrete block fog building was erected to house the generator powering the fog alarm system.

The islands off Prince Edward Point have been called Isles des Coulages (Shipwreck Islands) because of the many disasters that have occurred in the area; 65 percent of the shipwrecks on Lake Ontario have occurred in a 30-mile (49 km) strand between Point Petre and Main Duck Island. This high mortality led to the legend of graves that line the Duck Island shore. Dying sailors are said to have dug their own graves and buried themselves one by one until the last one died in his own grave. This eerie story certainly bespeaks the island's isolation.

In 1979 the Kingston newspaper ran an interview with Coleman Main, lightkeeper at Main Duck Island. He was quite irate because the government had started enforcing its regulation that two keepers be present at the island's light at all times, nine months of the year, except for occasional absences

Main Duck Island Lighthouse with fog plant, circa 1960s

when supplies were needed the same day. He and his assistant used to share the island's duties, but never to get away in nine months, he said, was "unreasonable even for isolated stations." The government said it was for the lighthouse keeper's safety that no prolonged time be taken ashore and that necessary trips be made in good weather only. Because of this difference of opinion, Main retired nine years early after 28 years of service.

Main had many interesting stories. Once, when he was returning to the island from a visit to another lighthouse one winter's day, he and his two-man crew were caught in the ice and drifted down the lake for a day and a half. Then the boat hit a rock near Chatham, tore out its bottom, and sank. They escaped by throwing a boat hook over the ice wall and climbing out. However, all their possessions were lost.

Another of his tales relates how he, his wife and their three children, having run out of fuel on their way to the island, rigged up some bed sheets to make a sail. However, it was a calm day and it took them a long time to get to the island. His assistant, McConnell, had been keeping watch for them and he thought the sight was the funniest thing he had ever seen. He also tells of being rescued many times from Lake Ontario after the engine of his 16-foot (4.9 m) boat failed. He even remembers fisherman Ron McIntosh rescuing him twice in one day when he ran out of fuel!

If you plan to visit, be sure to go on a calm day since the island is so far out. The public dock in Schoolhouse Bay is available on a first-come, first-served basis.

Known Keepers: J. Clark (1914–15), Fred Bongard (1915–21), Wesley Thomas (1921–53), Harry Dunn (1954–58), Coleman Main (1959–).

34 Makatewis Island Lighthouse

Up until 1966 this island was known as Nigger Island. In December of that year, its objectionable name was changed to Makatewis Island by the Canadian Permanent Committee on Geographical Names. Makatewis is an Ojibway word meaning "island of the black man."

The island is located in the Bay of Quinte, 4 miles (6.4 km) east of Trenton and six miles west of the Bay of Quinte bridge at Belleville. The government erected a 27-foot (8.2 m) square white lighthouse tower there in 1894. It displayed a fixed white light that was visible for 10 miles (16 km). In 1959 the government changed the light to an electric light on a pole on a pier.

Known Keeper: C. Jeffery (1894–).

35 Marine Museum (Old False Duck) Light

On November 3, 1965, after 136 years of service, the old False Duck Island Light was extinguished for the last time. The old tower was torn down and replaced with an automated light. However, the iron lantern and its light were saved and donated to the Prince Edward Historical Society. Since this light and lantern came from Prince Edward County's oldest lighthouse and was an integral part of their heritage, the society had a 30-foot (9 m) limestone tower specially built at the head of Prince Edward Bay for the lantern and light, as a Centennial project. The monument, in the Mariner's Memorial Park, was dedicated in September 1967 as a memorial to the some 125 sailors of Prince Edward County whose lives were lost in boating and shipping disasters.

Main Duck Island Lighthouse, circa 1960s

Marine Museum (Old False Duck) Light

Mississauga Point Lighthouse, circa 1804

Mississauga Point Lighthouse, War of 1812, from battle May 17, 1813

36 Mississauga Point Lighthouse

Upper Canada's border military posts as well as its trade were linked by water routes, so aids to navigation were essential. Three locations were chosen for the first lighthouses: Mississauga Point at the mouth of the Niagara River, Gibraltar Point at York (Toronto) and Isle de Forest (Nine Mile point of Simcoe Island) near Kingston, Ontario. The first was to be built at Mississauga Point because a light there would be of "more general benefit than in any other situation."

To help pay for the construction and upkeep of lighthouses, the Legislature of Upper Canada in 1803 passed an act to collect tariffs on goods shipped into Canadian Great Lakes ports. Dues were set at "three pence a ton on every vessel, boat, raft, or other craft of the burthen of ten tons or upwards entering the port or passing from the lake into the river, to be collected by the collector of duties at the port." The King's vessels were exempt.

Since monies were scarce and tariffs had only started to be collected, the government proposed "the cheapest mode of effecting the purpose," even suggesting that "a mere scaffolding of sufficient strength to support the lantern and give the attendant access thereto, might at first be sufficient." The tariff would later fund a proper lighthouse, they said. While this idea was good in principle, it was not in practice. Mariners who had been paying the tariff started to complain when no lights were built. In response to this unrest, the government built the Mississauga Lighthouse.

The reflecting lamp and the sperm oil for the light were shipped from England and stored at Fort George on the Niagara River. The tariff collector at Port Niagara, John Symington, was hired to oversee the light's construction and execute the government's wishes. He was told, "It is not intended to go to any expense with respect to Ornament this Building — You will principally consult utility and at the same time make it substantial." Also, "the work proposed is to be constructed by Civil Artificers, but that Aid of Labourers will be afforded from the Troops at Fort George."

Detailed plans for a hexagonal 45-foot (13.7 m) stone lighthouse were drawn up, and precise estimates for materials and labor, including civil and military workers, were submitted for government approval. Symington was also warned, "the Lieut.-Governor expects that the estimate for this building is not exceeded." In April, with the realization that the lighthouse had no living quarters, it was decided to build a log house

to accommodate the keeper. The total costs came to £196, 17 shillings, 6 pence for the lighthouse and £53, 10 shillings, 4½ pence for the keeper's dwelling — in Halifax currency.

By June 1804 the tower masonry was ready to receive its reflector and lamp. Tower plans show that the hexagonal walls rose straight for about 6 feet (1.8 m) and then gently tapered to the top. A slightly tapered dome capped the lantern, and a "brief" wooden gallery surrounded the top. Three musket or rifle slit windows ascended the tower above the door. The plans show the lantern to be glassed on just one of its six sides so that the light would shine out in only one direction. The light was lit in June 1804. Dominic Henry of the 4th Battalion of the Royal Artillery from Fort George was assigned the keeper's position, and kept the light for the ten years that it stood.

During the War of 1812 the lighthouse remained in service, as it was of benefit to both sides, warning of the reefs extending into Lake Ontario from the mouth of the Niagara River. On May 27, 1813, when the Americans bombarded Fort George, keeper Henry tended to the wounded while his wife served refreshments to the British troops. However, the paltry defence was soon overcome, and the area was occupied by American troops until they withdrew in December. Before they left, they completely razed the town of Newark (Niagara-on-the-Lake) and some of Fort George, but they left the lighthouse intact.

After the war the British realized that a firm hold was needed at Mississauga Point and so they quickly demolished the lighthouse in early 1814 to erect the new and stronger Fort Riall (Fort Mississauga) on its site. The stone from the lighthouse was used to help build the fort's protective tower. The lighthouse light was transferred to the fort and the fort was garrisoned until the 1840s.

On October 4, 1939, the Historic Sites and Monuments Board of Canada placed a bronze plaque on the wall of the old Fort Mississauga to commemorate the lighthouse. The ceremony was sponsored by the Niagara-on-the-Lake Historical Society. The plaque reads: "Point Mississauga Lighthouse. The first on the Great Lakes, built of stone in 1804 by John Symington under orders from Lieutenant-Governor Peter Hunter, demolished in 1814 to make room for this fort; its materials, with debris from the ruined town of Niagara, were incorporated in this tower. Dated 1939."

Known Keeper: Dominic Henry (1804–14).

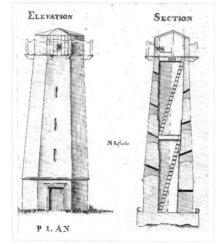

Mississauga Point Lighthouse

37 Murray Canal Lights

In August 1876 two entry lights were placed at what is now the entrance to the Murray Canal near Carrying Place in the Bay of Quinte area. The front light was 29 feet (8.8 m) with a fixed red catoptric light. The rear light was 43 feet (3 m) above the water and also had a fixed red light. These lights were constructed at a cost of $1,450. In 1891 the Canadian government replaced them both to mark the Murray Canal into Presqu'ile Bay. One was placed 30 feet (9 m) from the end of the pier on the north side of the canal at the canal's eastern entrance. The other was placed the same distance from the end of the pier on the north side of the canal at the canal's western entrance.

38 Newcastle Light

While the harbor at Newcastle, 47 miles (76 km) east of Toronto in Lake Ontario, was little used because it could only be entered during fair weather, it did have a light placed in a wooden tower on a storehouse at the outer end of the east pier. Its fixed white light, visible for 10 miles (16 km), helped mark the harbor and warn of hazards. Four miles (6.5 km) to the east was a large boulder in the lake known as the Peach Stone, and four miles east of the Peach Stone was a reef of boulders about 300 yards (275 m) out in the lake in a southerly direction. In 1890 the light was rebuilt and placed on the outer end of the harbor's east breakwater. The light was maintained by the Newcastle Harbour Company.

39 Niagara River Range Lights

During the early spring of 1904 the Canadian government received many letters from mariners requesting a light and foghorn at the mouth of the Niagara River. Their complaints were wide-ranging: visibility in fog was low; the light on the American side behind Fort Niagara was hardly visible and more a menace than an aid; a light could benefit vessels entering the Niagara River, service boats plying up and down the lake to and from the Welland Canal, and create a refuge during storms. They gave reminders of the many disasters at the point — the loss of the *George Foot* (1871), the *I.I. Beard* (1871), the *Allendale* (grounded in 1880 or 1881), and a steam barge from Port Dalhousie (grounded in 1887).

In response to these letters, in June 1904 two locations were sought to place range lights that would properly guide vessels into the river. A fog alarm was also to be established. The lights were lit on October 7, 1904, and the keeper was paid at a rate not to exceed $1 a day until the end of navigation season. The fog signal was ready the next season.

Early Niagara River Range Lights

In November the keeper requested a better burner, as he found the one supplied to be "useless and dangerous." The Dominion Lighthouse Depot replied: "Something is radically wrong with this burner, as it is the first complaint we have against them," adding, "these burners are of English make and the very best that can be got." Although they thought the malfunction was due to the keeper's improper use of the burner, the Depot sent out two more burners, which they had tested and found "to work perfectly satisfactorily." This solved the burner problem. A letter from the Dominion Lighthouse Depot dated December 22, 1904, promised to send the keeper a copy of the instructions for lighthouse keepers.

In September 1906 the lighting apparatus was updated and a fourth-order Holophote (to send light in one direction) complete with lamp and a red shade was sent to the keeper. While most of the keepers names are unknown, it is known that John McKinnie was keeper in October 1906.

Both towers were square white tapering structures covered in narrow clapboarding and arched out at the cornices to support square red lanterns that were topped with domes and ventilator stack. The front tower, placed on the wharf of the Canada Steamship Lines, was 21 feet (6.4 m) tall and displayed a fixed red light from a focal range of 29½ feet (9 m). The rear range tower, placed onshore 685 feet (208 m) from the front range, was 33 feet (10 m) high and also displayed a fixed red light from 42½ feet (13 m) above the water. Over the years these two lights proved to be of immense importance to mariners.

Known Keepers: Edward Wootton (1887–1904), Fred Master (1904–07), John McKinnie (1906), R.J. Allen (1907–16).

Niagara River Front Range Light

Niagara River Rear Range Light

Nine Mile Point Lighthouse

40   Nine Mile Point Lighthouse

Nine Mile Point Lighthouse is situated on the southwest point (Yeo Point) of Simcoe Island (Gage Island or Isle de Forest). It is serviced by one of the world's shortest cable-driven ferry boats from the west side of nearby Wolfe Island. It is also about 3½ miles (5.6 km) southeast of Kingston, Ontario, near the entrance to the St. Lawrence River. The government decided to build a lighthouse here in 1803 to make river entry easier for downbound vessels as well as facilitating entry into Kingston Harbour.

In 1833 the government acquired 5 acres (2 hectares) of land on the stony point from Charles Grant, who turned down any compensation. The National Archives gives the following information about the building of the lighthouse. The total cost was to be £750 sterling. It was to have similar construction to those at False Duck and Point Petre and have eleven lamps and reflectors. No keeper's house was listed at this time. However, a stone berm was put in place to raise the shoreline in front of the lighthouse to fend off waves during high-water cycles.

The area off Nine Mile Point saw many maritime disasters. In August 1856 the steamer propeller *Pinto* lost more than half of its 39 occupants when its small lifeboat capsized, overloaded with passengers attempting to flee the burning vessel. The inquest revealed that the *Pinto* was not intended for carrying passengers, had no life-preservers, and its one lifeboat was insufficient (freight steamers did not usually carry lifeboats at this time). The verdict held the captain and the engineer responsible for putting out to sea without adequate precaution for the passengers' safety.

During a lake storm in 1861 the steamer *Comet* and the schooner *Exchange* collided about 10 miles (16 km) off the lighthouse. The *Exchange* made it safely to port, but the *Comet* did not. When its crew realized it was shipping water, which was putting out the boilers, they headed for the lighthouse. When they lost power, they lowered the lifeboats, but two crewmembers drowned in the process. The rest of the crew and passengers made it safely to the shore and were picked up the next day.

Changes took place at this station. A 1,000-pound (455 kg) fog bell was installed for $1,000 in 1873. In 1874 the fog bell received clockwork machinery and a striking apparatus ($1,274) to semi-automate it. In the 1860s the light was illuminated by six lamps with parabolic reflectors on a catoptric system showing a red light. A twelve-sided iron lantern 7 feet (2.2 m) in diameter was added in 1876, and the lighting system included seven mammoth flat-wick lamps (three with fountains and four with reservoirs) and seven 20-inch (50 cm) reflectors. In 1880 the stone breakwater was repaired.

Nine Mile Point Lighthouse, circa 1914

In 1886 an additional 10 acres (4 hectares) were added to the original land acquisition. In 1892 the fog bell was moved to a more prominent position on the point. In 1893 William Ashe of Ottawa was contracted to establish a steam foghorn to replace the bell. He constructed a building for $1,500 and outfitted it with two boilers and a steam foghorn machine for a total cost of $3,733. The fog signal (blast 8 s; silence 22 s) was sounded from horns pointing southwest out over the lake at an elevation of 16 feet (4.9 m).

In 1894 Stannes Veech was appointed keeper and engineer of the fog alarm at a salary of $450 a year (by 1909, $800 a year). In 1895 he was granted an assistant who was paid $200, but in 1903 when he had no assistant, he was given money to hire help as needed — a situation that continued throughout his tenure.

In 1904 the government considered converting the light from kerosene to the five times more powerful acetylene, but did not do so because better oil lamps were developed. In 1905 the steam foghorn was replaced by a diaphone type that operated on compressed air (blast 7 s; silence 53 s), and an addition was built onto the fog signal building to house the trumpet. Also in 1909 a Robb-Mumford Boiler was installed at the fog signal building as a backup. In the 1930s a stationary engine fueled by kerosene or diesel oil replaced one of the steam boilers, and in the 1940s the lighthouse and the fog signal were converted to electricity.

Although the date of construction is uncertain, some facts are known. The limestone for the stone house foundation and the 2½-foot (0.7 m) walls of the cylindrical tower was picked up or quarried along the shore. A circular staircase (48 steps) wound around a sturdy central newel up the 40-foot (12.2 m) tower to its dodecagonal lantern. From a focal plane of 45 feet (13.8 m) the light shone as far as 15 miles (24 km). The flashing light (0.3 flash, 9.7 eclipse) was accomplished by three flash panels rotating around the light using a gear mechanism driven by a weighted cable that dropped down through the central column of the tower. The weights had to be wound by a hand crank every three hours during the night.

The keeper's home, of frame construction, housed the keeper and his family as well as the assistant when there was one. When the station grew to 15 acres (6 hectares), the keeper was able to keep a cow and a horse. This along with his vegetable garden made him quite self-sufficient. By 1945 a new road made the lighthouse more accessible. During the 1950s the old keeper's house was replaced by two modern ones.

Lightkeepers were independent and tenacious, the substance of legends. During John Cleland's tenure, for example, he and his assistant, George Eves, would row or sail from the island to Kingston. One warm sunny morning, Eves made the trip in the rowboat with a warm south wind at his back. However, on his return, an extremely cold wind blew in from the north. Apparently, in the heat, he had been rowing with his shirt off, and when the weather suddenly turned cold he couldn't put it back on because the ice was forming so quickly that he had to keep on rowing. He did reach the lighthouse before the lake froze over, but his back was severely sunburned and his feet were frozen. The keeper had to radio for a helicopter to airlift him to hospital.

When the last keeper retired in 1990, the light and fog signal were fully automated and controlled by a central command via satellite radio system. In 1991 the fog alarm was discontinued, and the light was extinguished in 1994. Former resident S. Eves sums up the light's history this way: "What has been a familiar beacon to the Simcoe Islanders for 160 years will be just a memory as a new wave of technology eclipses the ways of the past."

Known Keepers: John Dunlop (1867–72), Albert Dunlop (1872–79–), Stannes Veech (1894–1937), George Eves (1937–37), John Cleland (1937–42), Howard Orr and Lewis Orr (1943–73), Bob Corcoran (1973–90).

Oakville Lighthouse

41   Oakville Lighthouse

William Chisholm, an entrepreneur with foresight, moved his family from Nova Scotia in 1794 to take up farming on Burlington Bay. He saw the potential for the mouth of Sixteen Mile Creek to become a safe harbor providing access to the rich farmland to the north. In 1820 he became a member of the House of Assembly and as commissioner supervised the construction of the Burlington Bay Canal and later the Welland Canal. In 1824 he began using his high connections and sizable bank account to purchase land at the river mouth. The Mississauga Indians who hunted, fished and farmed this land were relocated.

In 1827, at a public auction, Chisholm purchased 960 acres (398 hectares) for £1,029 (then $4,116). In 1831, after making his final payment to the Crown, he had the land surveyed and laid out in a grid for streets and building lots for the town site that became Oakville. He even specified the size and type of houses. Among other ventures, Chisholm ran a shipyard at Oakville. His side-wheeler steamers made the run from Oakville to Toronto or Hamilton. The fare was 6 shillings, 3 pence for cabin class, or 3 shillings for deck passengers. When ready to leave port, these steamers fired their cannon as a departing salute. (This practice continued until the mid-1840s, when the steam whistle was invented.)

In April 1836 the steamer *Traveller* en route from Niagara to Oakville, pushed through 15 miles (24 km) of ice 2 inches (5 cm) thick. About mid-lake, she stopped so that the crew could examine her for damage. During the 1½-hour checkup, the passengers and crew walked around on the ice — an unprecedented incident.

By 1836 traffic on Lake Ontario had increased to the point that it was deemed necessary to have a lighthouse at Oakville to warn of the shoal and the large boulders extending out from the shore between Oakville and Port Credit. The House, responding to a petition with 96 signatures, granted Chisholm a loan of £500 for the construction, and in April 1837 Chisholm, George Chalmers, and Merrick Thomas were appointed commissioners for the light at the end of the existing pier at Oakville. To create a solid foundation for the lighthouse, three more cribs were sunk. The lighthouse was completed by November 1837 for a total cost of £852. Chisholm paid the £352 above the government loan out of his own pocket.

The lighthouse was an octagonal wooden structure with gently tapering sides, and was capped with a wooden lantern 5 feet 6 inches (1.7 m) in diameter. It stood 36 feet (11 m) from the pier to its top and was 42 feet (12.8 m) above the water. It had a fixed oil lamp with colorless glass and used a catatropic reflector. Its visibility was supposedly 11 miles (17.7 km), but most mariners found it to be less than 7 miles (11 km).

Government records from 1862 show that Chisholm requested money for supplies and light keeping during the 1860 season. In July 1866, a John Page reported to the government that the lighthouse needed maintenance repairs ($185) and kerosene coal oil, and that the government should pay for it. The government complied and also spent a further $90 to raise the foundation of the lighthouse to make it solid once more. Page also recommended the appointment of a keeper. Thus, R.K. Chisholm was appointed temporary keeper for a salary of $200 without any other allowance. When M. Felan was appointed keeper in April 1894, he earned $260 a year.

By the mid-1870s the light had four dual-burner lamps with 15-inch (38 cm) reflectors on an iron frame. This lighthouse served until April 8, 1886, when a severe storm swept away the old timbers in the east pier, and the lighthouse fell into the channel. The harbor was rebuilt the following year, but the lighthouse was not rebuilt at this time. By 1889 the Hamilton Steamboat Company started using Oakville Harbour for regular passenger service. A new lighthouse was built in the spring of 1889 by Henry George, a contractor from Port Elgin, at a cost of $960, and was was lit on June 4.

The new light was a 25-foot (7.6 m) hexagonal tapering wooden tower covered with cedar shakes and painted white. Its hexagonal lantern had six large rectangular glass panels. The skimpy gallery had a small iron railing and six iron braces for support. The lantern was topped with a curved ventilator reminiscent of a stovepipe. The lantern, dome, ventilator, railing and braces were painted red. Large pedimented windows provided lighting for the interior stairs.

In the early 1960s the lighthouse was removed from service and taken to its present location at the Oakville Yacht Squadron (OYS). Here it sits in a small grassy area as a reminder of its years of diligent service. A plaque on its door reads, "The old lighthouse. Built 1875. Removed from the east pier and preserved in this location 1960 through the interest of the citizens of the town of Oakville."

Oakville Lighthouse, circa 1929

(The date on this plaque does not coincide with data found in research about this light.)

Today Oakville's harbor is marked by a modern light at the end of its east pier. This 20-foot (6 m) white cylinder topped with a red lantern resembles a cigarette, providing a unique day marker. From its position 28.6 feet (8.7 m) above the water, it displays a fixed red electric light that can be seen for 6 miles (9.7 km).

Known Keepers: Robert Chisholm (1860 unofficially; 1861 officially –1877–), M. Felan (1894–).

Onderdonk Point Lighthouse, circa 1925

42 Onderdonk Point Lighthouse

In 1911 the Canadian government built a lighthouse on Onderdonk Point in the Bay of Quinte of Lake Ontario to assist water navigation. It was a square wooden tower and just 20 feet (6.2 m) in height. The only known keeper was William Allison. In 1912 he was paid $140 a year.

Known Keeper: William Alison (–1912–).

43 Pigeon Island Lighthouse

From the air, Pigeon Island is outlined and dotted with white from the guano of the many seagulls on the island. It is said to be named for the once numerous carrier pigeons that lived there. The island is located 5 miles (8 k) west-southwest of the south end of Wolfe Island in Lake Ontario near Kingston.

In November 1870 the *Kingston Daily News* announced that there was a new lighthouse on Pigeon Island. It had been built the previous May by the Canadian Department of Marine. The lighthouse was 41 feet (12 m) high and 46 feet (14 m) above the water, and was furnished with a "powerful revolving" white light that showed at intervals of one minute and ten seconds, giving an expected visibility of 12 miles (19.3 km) in clear weather. The Coast Guard records show it being first lit in 1871. It was reported to be "a revolving white catoptric, containing two mammoth flatwick reservoir lamps with two 21-inch [52.5 cm] reflectors."

Pigeon Island Lighthouse, circa 1880

On September 6, 1871 the Royal Mail Line steamer *Spartan*, on its way from Oswego, New York, to Kingston, Ontario, went ashore at Pigeon Island. About 150 passengers and their luggage were rescued by the steamer *William* and the schooner *Gazelle*. Passengers, crew and lighthouse keeper gave conflicting reports of the incident. Was the lightkeeper careless or the captain of the *Spartan*, as the passengers claimed? Upon investigation the Inland Navigation Company corroborated the explanations of the captain and the keeper that the light was insufficient. The light had never worked properly and sometimes exploded. At the time, the lamp had exploded and the reflectors had been destroyed. However, the light was kept burning.

Aside from disgruntled passengers, no damage occurred: the steamer was pulled off the rock and continued its regular route. Upon arrival in Kingston the passengers were too late to take the afternoon trains and many claimed their hotel expenses from the steamboat company. However, the manager refused, as the steamship line was only insured for fire. The passengers were greatly dissatisfied but could only vent their anger through non-complimentary comments to the steamboat company.

In 1896, J.H. Davis was appointed keeper for an annual salary of $420. He also warned approaching ships of the dangerous shoals using a hand-squeezed foghorn during heavy fog.

In 1909 the old combined lighthouse and dwelling was pulled down and replaced by a specially designed, four-sectioned, skeletal tower and separate dwelling. The new tower was square with sloping sides surmounted by an enclosed wooden service room and a spiral staircase within a cylindrical steel form constructed from the base of the tower to the service room floor. The tower and service room were painted white; the cylinder, octagonal lantern, gallery and dome red. The steel tower, purchased from the Gould, Shapely and Muir Co. of Brantford, Ontario, for $1,677, was 64 feet 4 inches (19.6 m) high and exhibited a white flashing light.

In 1957 the lighthouse was decommissioned. In 1963 the keeper's house and boathouse, being considered surplus, were auctioned to the highest bidder. Although

Pigeon Island Lighthouse, circa 1965

Howard Orr, a former keeper from Nine Mile Point, bid $200, the buildings went to Nelson Eves, conditional on his dismantling and removing them from the island.

Today no human inhabitants live on the island, and it has returned to the gulls and terns. In 1974 the Coast Guard consented to the Canadian Wildlife Service's request not to disturb the bird colonies during nesting season (April to August). The Coast Guard makes regular maintenance runs to the island via helicopter from its base at Prescott.

Known Keepers: James Eccles (1870–71–), Ambrose Davis (–1877–79), Mary Davis (1879–), J.H. Davis (1896–1912–).

44 Pine Tree Point Lighthouse

In 1927 funds were requisitioned from the Canadian government to build a small light on the shore at Pine Tree Point on the St. Lawrence River to act with the light placed at Robertson Point at the same time. These lights were to help mariners navigate the St. Lawrence River upbound, keeping them away from the shore after leaving the head of the Morrisburg Canal. The Pine Tree Point light displayed a fixed red light similar to that at Robertson Point.

45 Point Petre Lighthouse

Built in 1833, the old Point Petre Lighthouse was the second oldest in Prince Edward County, Ontario. It took 2,700 loads of limestone drawn by oxen from Picton to build the 60-foot (18.3 m) tower. Each stone was placed by hand and individually carved to taper in toward the center. This tower, with its few small windows and 87 circular stone steps, was identical in design to the tower at Nine Mile Point.

By 1877 the light's characteristic was a revolving flashing light (flash 3 s; eclipse 97 s) and its illumination was created by ten dual-burner coal oil fountain lamps arranged in three circles with ten 14-inch (35 cm) reflectors. Many years later a mantle-type burner was used in the polygonal lantern. Mantles were 2½–3 inches in diameter and glowed brightly. After filling the fuel tank of the mantle burner, the keeper had to pump up the air tank mechanism to build up pressure. By 1900 the light's flash pattern had changed to a frequency of every 35 seconds. In 1960 the light was electrified using a 1,000-watt bulb.

The keeper also had to wind the clockworks every four hours to make sure the flash panels revolved continually. In 1890 a steam-operated fog house was added (blast 3 s; silence 27 s), and by 1900 the fog signal characteristic had been changed (blast 20 s; silence 35 s). In 1959 a fully automated beacon was installed near Point Petre. It was synchronized with the station's fog signal to assist mariners with distance finding. In thick foggy weather, both signals ran continuously.

A new lighthouse was built at Point Petre in 1967–68 about 200 feet (60 m) northeast of the old lighthouse. Its 63-foot (19.2 m) tower was built with ten tons of reinforced concrete into a somewhat space-age–looking creation by the Ford Construction Co. of Prescott, Ontario.

Point Petre Lighthouse, circa 1909

Point Petre Lighthouse

The tower's narrow base is only 4½ feet (1.4 m) wide. The lantern used a DCB 10-light (250-watt mercury vapor bulb) that rotated once every 30 seconds, 24 hours a day. There was a standby generator in case of emergency. This was the first lighthouse of this style built in Prince Edward County.

An automatic fog signal was also installed at a cost of $35,000, making the manual fog signal obsolete. The radio beacon was moved to the new tower and it transmited the call letter "P". The government also installed Mars II (a Meteorological Automatic Reporting Station), which recorded the temperature and dew point along with visibility, barometric pressure, and wind speed and direction for this area of Lake Ontario. All the data were linked via digital computer and relayed by landline to Belleville and then on to Burlington once every hour. Information gained from about twenty of these Mars II stations positioned around the Great Lakes was used by the Atmospheric Environment Service in Toronto, as well as by the Kingston Marine and provincial airports.

After the new light was activated, the government deemed the old light a hazard and used two and a half cases of dynamite to blow it and the old fog building up. They provided a variety of rationales — the old lighthouse blocked the path of the new light … the old tower was structurally unsafe … public liability … vandalism. While the Prince Edward Historical

Society thought they were in negotiations to acquire the old light and that the government had agreed to a delay demolishing the lighthouse, demolition people had arrived early one Friday morning, advised the keeper, Charles Newman, to remove anything he owned from the structure, and also suggested that he not inform the press.

The Historical Society was incensed at having the county's second-oldest lighthouse destroyed. Although the government did not actually apologize, they issued a public statement that they had erred. Assistant keeper Leonard Goodmurphy salvaged an old brass lamp before the demolition, but only a pile of rubble remained after the explosion. The Historical Society collected a few broken parts to put on display in their Marine Museum at South Bay.

Known Keepers: Anson Palen (1833–70–), James Burlingham (–1877–) Mrs. James Burlingham (?), Guy Scott (1901–11), T.A. Farrington (1911–13), Mrs. Buffer Farrington (1913–27), Howard Lowery (1928–46), Charles Newman (1947–73), Leonard Goodmurphy (1973–)

46 Point Pleasant Lighthouse

In 1864 the government resolved to build a lighthouse on Indian Point (Point Pleasant), the most easterly part of Prince Edward County, where the Bay of Quinte and Lake Ontario are connected by the "Upper Gap," a passage between Point Pleasant and Amherst Island. A light was needed here for two reasons — first, to warn mariners of the shoal that runs out some distance from the shore; and second and more important, to assist vessels coming in from the lake, especially from the direction of Oswego.

To this purpose, a lighthouse was built on the point in 1867, the year of Canadian Confederation, by Thomas Overend of Kingston, Ontario. The 54-foot (6.5 m) octagonal wooden tower tapered gently up to the 5½-foot (1.7 m) lantern and was covered in narrow clapboarding. A plain cornice supported the octagonal gallery and lantern, which used an Aladdin oil lamp to display a fixed white light with a visibility of 12 miles (19.3 km). By 1877 the light had been upgraded to a fixed white catoptric, using nine base-burner fountain lamps on a circle with nine 16-inch (40 cm) reflectors. The light was electrified in 1954.

In 1951 winds and high water washed away one of the lighthouse abutments. Time and weather caused further deterioration until the light was deemed unsafe. Finally, after 89 years of service, it was torn down and burned in July 1956. It was replaced the same year with a 55-foot (17 m) steel tower with an electrically operated light. Although efficient, it lacked the charm of the old lighthouse.

Known Keepers: John Pryner (1867–97), Frank Connors (1898–1912), Mrs. M. Gordon (1914), Sydney Carson (?), Charles Laird (?), Samuel Carson (?), Donley Watkins (1930–54).

Point Pleasant Lighthouse demolition, 1956

47　Port of Britain Lights

Port Britain is located in Lake Ontario about 4 miles (6.5 km) west of Port Hope and 60 miles (97 km) east of Toronto. The harbor constructed here in 1857 was an excellent harbor of refuge, as it was free of boulders and protected on both sides by bluffs. Piers about 700 feet (215 m) long and 300 feet (92 m) apart were built out from the natural harbor basin to form a protected outer harbor. To mark entry to this outer harbor, lights were placed on the piers in 1857.

48　Port Credit Lighthouse

In the early 1800s the Canadian government saw the potential for the mouth of the Credit River to become an important harbor, and the Province of Upper Canada purchased 1,500 acres (607 hectares) of land from the Mississauga tribe for 20 shillings in February 1820. However, as the river mouth silted over and storms shifted sand, the well-protected harbor was left mostly undeveloped.

Then F.C. Capreol, an entrepreneur who wanted to develop Port Credit as an industrial town with his business, the Peel Manufacturing Co., privately built the first lighthouse at the end of the east pier in 1863 to mark the harbor entrance. It was a fixed light with a visibility of 10 miles (16 km). However, lacking financial backing, he abandoned his project, and the lighthouse was taken over by the Ontario government in 1882. The government immediately advertised for tenders to build a new lighthouse in *The Mail*, *The Monetary Times* and *The Irish Canadian*. The contract was awarded to Roderick Cameron of Lancaster, and he completed it for $1350, $150 under budget. Expenses totalled $1,946.

This harbor lighthouse was a white, square wooden tower 36 feet (11 m) from base to vane. It was built on a cribwork block at the outer end of the north breakwater pier and equipped with a sixth-order dioptric illuminating apparatus. It exhibited a fixed white light, 37 feet (11.3 m) above the water and was visible for 11 miles (17.7 km). In December 1897 Captain John Miller was appointed keeper.

The decline in usefulness of the Port Credit Harbour was marked by a reduction in the lighting apparatus from a sixth-order to a seventh-order lens sometime before 1903. In the early 1900s only fishermen, stone hookers, and a few yachtsmen used Port Credit Harbour, because of its silt and sandbar problems. Locals claimed that it was "the safest harbour on the lake, and the only good one between Toronto and Hamilton," but only expert mariners could navigate its shallow waters.

Miller was frequently called upon to aid small craft seeking refuge. In 1904 he rescued the crew of the yachts *Maybelle* and *Fleur de Lys*, who clung to their upturned crafts after capsizing in breakers. Then in 1905, after numerous rescues and pleas for a lifesaving boat, the government finally provided one. The *Brampton Conservator* described this boat as "a good sturdy skiff, not one of the cork lined self-bailing, non-capsizable, non-sinking kind." The skiff came from the W. Watts and Son Boat Company of Collingwood and was put into the care and operation of Captain Miller.

By 1908 the river mouth had filled in so much that only a 20-foot (6 m) channel with water 4 feet (1.2 m) deep was left.

Port Credit Lighthouse

Port Credit Lighthouse, circa 1904

Port Credit Lighthouse, circa 1923

Then spring flooding in 1908 carried away part of the decaying lighthouse pier. The lighthouse was cut off from the mainland and Miller had to use a boat to get out to the light. Severe storms always thwarted attempts to fill the breach with rocks, leaving the lighthouse on an island. In 1909 the government spent $1,500 to dredge the harbor, but it continued to silt up. From then until 1918, when the lighthouse was closed, Port Credit Harbour was used less and less. Its piers rotted, silt clogged the entrance, and the light was frequently unlit when the keeper could not get to the lighthouse. These problems led to the light being discontinued on November 1, 1918. In 1936 the lighthouse site was destroyed by fire allegedly caused by local boys who dropped lit cigarette butts on the wooden floor of the lighthouse.

In 1952 a new unwatched light was established on the south end of the north pier. Its flashing green light was mounted on a steel tower 22 feet (6.7 m) above high water. Then, in 1954 a new fixed green light was mounted on a hydro pole (55 feet/16.7 m above high water) north of the flashing green light. Together these lights formed range lights leading to the entrance of the Port Credit Harbour.

Port Credit now has the hull of an old lake freighter as its unique east pier breakwater, and the entrance light to the harbor is mounted on the bow. The harbor also has a new lighthouse that was constructed in 1991 as a reminder of Port Credit's roots. As well as being a Peel Regional pumping station and tourist information office, it is also a private aid to navigation. The large deck surrounding it offers a good view of the Credit River, the marina and Port Credit.

Known Keeper: Captain John Miller (1897–).

Port Dalhousie Inner Range Light

49 Port Dalhousie Range Lights

The Welland Canal opened officially in 1829. It ran from Port Dalhousie to Port Colborne, connecting Lake Ontario and Lake Erie and bypassing Niagara Falls and the Niagara River. It offered entrepreneurs an alternative route for shipping bulk commodities at competitive prices. In the 1850s, with the development of new industries, Port Dalhousie experienced economic growth, also drawing tourists to its excellent beaches. At one time ferries regularly brought picnickers from Toronto to this crowded paradise known as Lakeside Park. Tourists could participate in a variety of activities — water slides, a merry-go-round, a midway and concession booths — and watch ships passing through the canal, with the lighthouse as the backdrop.

A lighthouse was built in 1852 at Port Dalhousie to mark the northern entrance to the canal. It was a 44-foot (13.4 m) white wooden tower built on a cribwork block attached to the east breakwater and it showed a fixed red light that used a catoptric lighting system. With its six Silber burners and 19-inch (0.5 m) reflectors, it had a visibility of 20 miles (32 km) in fair weather. The first keeper, William Woodall, earned $300 a year and lived in the keeper's house a good distance from the tower.

By 1877 the light, although still a fixed catoptric system, was white, with eight dual-burners and two circular burner lamps with one 20-inch (50 cm) and nine 16-inch (40 cm) reflectors on a three-legged iron frame. In mid-July a fire (the third at this fire-prone light) caused by the explosion of a circular lamp briefly put the light out of commission. In 1878 the lighting apparatus was replaced by six circular Silber burners with six 18-inch (45 cm) reflectors, and in 1879 the light became a revolving light.

The same year, a second lighthouse was built 289 feet (88 m) to the north of the main light at the end of the pier to serve as an outer range light to the existing light. The two worked in conjunction to facilitate entry into the harbor and canal and more efficiently accommodate the heavier water traffic.

The contract for the new range light was awarded to Richard Whiteacre of Allenwood. Far more basic in design than the old light, it consisted of a plain white square tapering tower placed on top of a square wooden cribwork foundation. For the keeper's protection in rough weather, entrance was via a narrow walkway elevated on wooden frames. The tower was capped with a wide frieze and a bracketed gallery surrounded by heavy cross-braced wooden railings. Its octagonal lantern used oil lamps and reflectors to display the light for 12 miles (19.3 km). The tower was 38 feet (11.6 m) from base to vane.

A government inspector in the early 1890s recommended a new inner lighthouse foundation, as the light was sinking. W.H. Noble, foreman of the works, prepared a new foundation, a circular steel casing filled with concrete. However, when the old lighthouse was being moved to its new foundation, it was discovered to also be in bad condition. So, a new tower was built in 1893, and the old lantern and illuminating apparatus were moved to it. In 1897 a new concrete foundation was placed beneath the front range light and the rotten cribwork on the east pier replaced with concrete — also under Noble's direction. In 1898 the elevated wooden walkway between the two lights was replaced with a steel one.

The rear range light was once more set on fire in August 1898 in a morning thunderstorm. A bolt of lightning struck the lantern, smashing the large lamp, splitting the top, and breaking open the oil tank. With the added oil incendiary, the wooden lighthouse burned to the ground very quickly. Fortunately, the keeper had just gone home for breakfast.

A new lighthouse was duly built, but not soon enough for many vessels. Although the tower base was finished and ready to receive the lantern by the end of November, mariners found the single small light at the end of the pier to be a menace. The schooner *Leighton*, for example, was blown ashore at Burlington Beach in December 1898 because the captain did not know until he had

Early Port Dalhousie Inner Range Light

passed it that the small, dim light he had seen marked Port Dalhousie.

The new lighthouse was designed as a coastal light with a greater elevation of 54 feet (16.5 m). To provide for this additional height, an octagonal shape, one of four at the time on the Canadian side of the Great Lakes, was chosen. The other three were at Lonely Island (1870), Port Burwell (1840) and Presqu'ile (1840). Windows on all sides enabled the keeper to track vessels in the harbor and the lake, as well as providing more natural light for improved living conditions. The lighthouse had sleeping accommodations and various control panels to allow the keeper to work within it.

The new tower had a more pleasing appearance than the squat square outer range light. Its wooden frame, set on a stone foundation, was covered with sheathing boards set diagonally and topped with cedar shake shingles. Four ladder-style sets of stairs ascended the gently tapering, four-story tower to its dodecagonal lantern and gallery. The dome was topped with a ventilator ball and a weather vane in the form of a beaver, a familiar Canadian emblem. The light was finally ready to be relit in August 1899.

In 1901 the rear range light was changed from a fixed red to an occulting white light (flash 30 s; eclipse 5 s). It continued to use a catoptric illumination apparatus. However, the illuminating apparatus for the front light was switched from catoptric to dioptric of a seventh order. Both lights acquired electricity for their illuminant at this time. Also in the early twentieth century a fog alarm system,

operated by compressed air, was added to the front light. The compressor and storage tank were stored in the lower level, and the foghorn extended out from the tower's upper north window.

Storms also brought destruction to the area. In April 1908 the vessel *Lakeside* was confined to port because a gale was lifting waters clean over the lighthouse. In September 1923, the steel freighter *Glenarm* struck an uncharted obstruction and sank just past the outer lighthouse. In 1952, after high water levels flooded over the breakwater and surrounded the inner range light, construction was immediately undertaken to extend the beach.

After the Fourth Welland Canal opened in 1932, with a new entrance at Port Weller, most of the industries in the Port Dalhousie area were slowly forced to close down. Then in the 1950s the town also lost its attraction to tourists as a result of publicity about industrial wastes from the former Welland Canal, general concern about Great Lakes pollution, changing vacation preferences, and the upswing in automobile travel. Unable to support itself, the town of Port Dalhousie in 1961 amalgamated with the city of St. Catharines.

The lighthouse underwent still more changes. A 1955 government inspector reported that the front light still used a dioptric illuminating apparatus but that a fourth-order lens and a 100-watt electric bulb were used. The rear range light continued to use a catoptric illuminating apparatus and it had a 200-watt electric bulb. Both lights displayed a fixed red light at this time. After 1965 the eastern pier was extended to 1,500 feet (457 m). In 1968 the range lights were automated, making a keeper no longer necessary. At some time both lights were changed back to white. The front range light to an isophase flash characteristic (flash 2 s; eclipse 2 s) and the front tower was painted white with green upper and lower portions. In 1979 the Local Architectural Conservation Advisory Committee of St. Catharines included both lighthouses in its inventory of local historic buildings.

In 1984 the movie *The Boy in Blue*, the story of world rowing champion Ned Hanlan, was filmed in Port Dalhousie. The inner range light, coated with a special washable paint to make it look aged, was used as a backdrop. Also some time in the 1980s the lighthouses were covered with easy-maintenance aluminum siding, which destroyed many of the pedimented windows. In 1987 the rear lighthouse was surrounded by a chain link and barbed wire fence to deter vandals. Finally, in 1988 the rear range light was extinguished.

In the 1990s the federal government turned the range lights over to the city of St. Catharines and in 1997 the city granted them heritage designation. The local newspaper, the *Standard,* in September 1998 reported that it would cost $136,500 to remove the aluminum siding and return the building to its original exterior style. Friends of the Harbour soon established Friends of the Port Lighthouses and pledged funds toward the restoration of the inner range light. Finally in 2001 the lighthouse was restored to its original state as part of St. Catharines' undertaking to revitalize the Port Dalhousie area as a tourist attraction. With its picturesque harbor, two historic lighthouses, pubs and restored "nickel-a-ride" carousel (the turn-of-the-century price), Port Dalhousie is coming to life again.

Known Keepers: William Woodall (–1870–78), David Hunter (1879–1911), G. Houston (1912–).

Port Dalhousie Outer Range Light

Port Hope Lighthouse

50 Port Hope Lighthouse

A light was built on the wharf at Port Hope, Lake Ontario, at an unknown date. Government records show the light being activated in 1868 at Port Hope. However, the *Kingston Daily News* reported in 1860 that the schooner *Dolphin*, under the command of Captain James, had knocked the lantern of the lighthouse into the lake, so the light must have been built before this date. In 1864 the *Daily News* reported: "Harbour Master at Port Hope has given notice that the white light will hereafter be shown in the lighthouse on the wharf at that place. It is well that shipmasters on the lakes take notice of the change."

In 1870 the *News* reported that the Royal Mail steamer *Corinthian*, on the way from Hamilton to Kingston, had to run into port for shelter at Port Hope, it being the closest safe point between the two cities of its route.

In 1901 Scott's *Coast Pilot* described the light as a square white wooden tower that displayed a fixed white light from a 40-foot (12.2 m) focal plane for a visibility of 4 miles (6.5 km). It was located 110 feet (33.5 m) from the outer end of the breakwater, which protected the east side of the harbor.

The current light, a white circular tower 19.8 feet (6 m) high with a red top, is located on the south end of the east breakwater and is lit by an electric light that flashes red.

51 Port of Liverpool Light

Liverpool (today Pickering) is located 26 miles (42 km) east of Toronto. Its harbor, the first harbor of refuge east of Toronto, was formed by a deep bay that used to be called Frenchman's Bay. Since the bay was landlocked by a gravelly beach separating it from the lake, the Harbour Company cut a 100-foot (30 m) gap in the beach to provide entry to the bay, and built protective piers on either side of the gap. In 1857 there was a lighthouse on the east pier, but it was visible for only 5 miles (8 km).

A new 55-foot (15.7 m) octagonal wooden lighthouse was built at the end of the east pier in 1863, increasing the light's visibility to 10 miles (16 km). It displayed a fixed green light. After new piers were built in 1878–79, the lighthouse was also rebuilt and shortened to 41 feet (12.5 m), decreasing its visibility to 6 miles (9.7 km). This lighthouse became known as the Frenchman's Bay or the Pickering Light.

Known Keepers: William McClellan (1878–), W. O'Brien (1904–).

52 Port of Oshawa Lighthouses

The Oshawa wharf on Lake Ontario, with its surrounding high-banked terrain, created excellent protection for vessels during inclement weather unless it was caused by a storm from the south. The pier stretched out into the lake until there was a depth of 10 feet (3 m) of water for anchorage. From the end of the south pier, reaching 400 yards (365 m) into the lake, there was a dangerous shoal that blocked the approach from the southeast and needed to be avoided. Up until 1857 a large lantern was placed under the gable roof of the red storehouse on the south end of the wharf to help vessels line up and get a safe heading into the harbor. In 1863 a true lighthouse was established on the pierhead.

53 Port Weller Lighthouse

Port Weller is a man-made harbor that provides straight access from Lake Ontario into the fourth building of the Welland Canal, whose locks were big enough to accommodate lake freighters, thus enhancing water commerce on the Great Lakes. It was named after John Laing Weller, its superintending engineer.

Port Weller's two pincer-shaped breakwater piers were built between 1913 and 1931 at the mouth of Ten Mile Creek 1.5 miles (2.4 km) out into Lake Ontario to protect the canal entrance from wind, currents and silting. They were built of concrete made from limestone bedrock that was excavated during the building of the fourth canal. Since the piers were only 400 feet (122 m) apart, a light was needed to guide vessels into the canal entrance, especially in fog. A lighthouse and keeper's house were built on the west pier in 1931, to be ready for the opening of the canal in 1932.

Because these buildings housed essential navigational equipment, and to prevent water and weather damage, they were built of concrete and steel. The lighthouse was a 95-foot (29 m) steel skeletal structure erected about 20 feet (6.1 m) north of the keeper's house. The top of the tower was closed in, and a minimal square gallery surrounded the small square lantern room.

The keeper's house was located about 20 feet (6 m) south of the lighthouse, 20 feet (6 m) back from the canal and 100 yards (90 m) from the Lake Ontario shoreline. A dirt road extending from Lock One to the west pierhead ran in front of the lighthouse. Trees provided a windbreak, but no landscaping was done. The dwelling was a boxy, one-story concrete building featuring art deco, moderne and stylized gothic elements. A date stone indicates that it was built by the Department of the Marine in 1931.

Port Weller Lighthouse

The house was designed to endure the fiercest of storms with poured concrete walls one foot (0.3 m) thick. The interior had 12-foot (3.6 m) ceilings to accommodate navigation equipment, as the house was intended for personal and equipment use. The north section was the keeper's residence, the south for watchroom. It was large enough to house two generators, the foghorn, the radio beacon station, and the switches for remote control of the revolving light on the lighthouse, as well as the east and west pierhead lights and the foghorn. Since the lighthouse was only needed during the shipping season — and to save the cost of a furnace — four portable heaters were installed.

The first keeper, of unknown name, was a one-legged man. Since Port Weller was a lonely and remote place miles from the town of St. Catharines, the keeper's wife (and also his helper) did not stay long, and moved back to town, leaving him needing help. These were the depression years and, as the job paid only room and board, the only helpers he could get were transients. He got by as he could until he died.

The second keeper, as of 1946, was Cyril Williamson, who had been a radar commander in World War II and had owned his own electrical business. When he and his family went to check out the station, he was full of hope for a new future, but his wife, Ethel, was most disappointed. The steel tower looked more like a hydro tower to her than a romantic lighthouse. With no landscaping, the surroundings were desolate and unwelcoming. Despite her despair, however, a week later they picked up the keys and the book *How to Operate a Lighthouse*.

Ethel found the interior just as depressing. The paint was dreary. There was a three-piece bathroom and a hot water tank but no water because the pump house engine was broken. Instead, there were five pails to carry water to the bathroom from the canal. Cyril phoned the Department of Marine and said they couldn't live like that. The pump was repaired and the house repainted. Cyril built a room in the watchroom and put up bunk beds for their teenage sons. Ethel had been hired as Cyril's assistant, receiving her room and board but no other pay. She worked the day shift, Cyril the night shift, and the boys rode their bikes 7 miles (11 km) to high school in St. Catharines.

The isolation was so great that Cyril built a ham radio operation at the station to contact nearby friends. This blossomed into a passion. In 1949 they both received their ham radio operator's license. In their 25-year stay at the lighthouse Ethel contacted over 250 countries on five continents. By the late 1940s she became the Canadian district representative of the Young Ladies' Radio League, a world organization of licensed female operators. This hobby brought visitors — as well as media coverage — to the Port Weller Lighthouse. In 1948 Ethel gave a ten-minute Christmas message over British airwaves about lighthouse life. She was a guest on a TV talk show to discuss the Port Weller lighthouse and later wrote a book, *A Light on the Seaway*. She had many captivating stories to tell.

The exact date of the fog signal building at the end of the west pier is uncertain. However,

Lightkeeper Cyril Williamson and West Pierhead Light, Port Weller

the generators and fog signal equipment were moved into it in 1947. A poured-concrete tower had been added on top of the fog signal building to act as a pedestal for the steel frame of the pierhead light and foghorn. The fog signal had its own characteristic (blast 3 s; silence 3 s; blast 3 s; silence 51 s). The flashing red pierhead light, 48.5 feet (14.8 m) above the water, was visible for 13 miles (21 km). Also in 1947, to upgrade facilities, an aircraft beacon was built beside the fog building at the end of the west pier. Its tower was solid poured concrete. From its square base the sides gently swooped skyward to the summit.

In 1953 a new keeper's house was built as a permanent year-round residence to provide separate living space for the keeper and his family, and lodging for a new assistant keeper. The L-shaped bungalow was typical of 1950s housing for the Niagara Peninsula. It had raised concrete basement walls to ensure that it would always be above the high water table. This house, 30 feet (9 m) south of the former keeper's house, was attached to the first house by a covered breezeway. At this time Transport Canada also pebble-dashed the ham radio room and garage to match the new keeper's house.

The Port Dalhouse lighthouse buildings also proved the durability of the concrete structures. In 1954, when Hurricane Hazel cut its destructive swath through southern Ontario, the station was barely scathed. Only a picnic table was tossed into the canal and an aerial blown down.

Despite their bleak initiation, the Williamsons enjoyed their 25 years at the station. Thanks to their dedication, the Port Weller station achieved international recognition as an important navigation aid on the Welland Canal and later the St. Lawrence Seaway. But in 1970 the lighthouse tower was demolished and keepers were no longer needed. The landscaping was removed, the 1953 keeper's house torn down, and the area returned to its earlier stark appearance. The original 1931 keeper's house became a Search and Rescue Station for the Canadian Coast Guard, and a floating dock was installed in front of the former keeper's house to accommodate search and rescue boats. Navigation aids remain on the pierheads, but the station no longer boasts international recognition.

Known Keeper: Cyril Williamson (1946–70).

Port Weller West Pierhead Light

Prescott Heritage Centre (left) and Prescott Breakwater Light (right)

54 Prescott Breakwater Light

This white tapering tower was about 20 feet (6 m) high and topped by a green lantern and dome. It sat on a rocky breakwater to mark the entrance to the outer harbor at Prescott.

55 Prescott Heritage Visitors' Centre

This fat white, tapering, octagonal lighthouse was originally built as a tourist information center. Its 40-foot (12.2 m) white wooden tower was topped by a red lantern that was originally the test lantern placed on the top of the Coast Guard Depot at Prescott. It was lit in 1989 as a private aid to navigation using a third-order Fresnel lens donated by the Canadian Coast Guard, which is headquartered in Prescott. When it is open, visitors can climb to the top to see the huge lens.

Prescott Breakwater Light

56 Presqu'ile Lighthouse

In the early 1800s Presqu'ile Peninsula in Lake Ontario was chosen as the site for Newcastle, the planned capital for surrounding counties. One of its first planned functions was to host the trial for the murder of a local fur trader. In October 1804 the schooner *Speedy* left the town of York (Toronto) carrying the prisoner and the notables who were to try the case. However, the schooner sank close to Presqu'ile, losing all crew and passengers. This area was soon deemed inappropriate as a capital, and Cobourg was chosen instead. This action severely damaged the area's commercial development, despite its excellent natural harbor where mariners sought shelter before attempting the perilous trip around the Prince Edward Peninsula.

Although risky, ships offered the fastest and cheapest form of transport for trade and commerce in Upper Canada at this time. In 1810 the Provincial Marine's gunboats had a new monopoly on the Great Lakes; only about 26 privately owned sailing vessels were engaged in trade. After the War of 1812 this changed. With the launch of the steamer *Frontenac* from the Kingston shipyards in 1817, a new shipping era began. The opening of the Erie Canal in 1825 and the Welland Canal in 1829 facilitated transport and trade from the upper lakes to the Atlantic, and by the 1830s a steamer could travel from Toronto to Kingston in just 24 hours. As marine traffic increased, navigation aids became necessary.

In 1837 the House of Assembly of Upper Canada passed an Act granting "a sum of money for the erection of certain lighthouses within the province." The sites were to be Oakville, Port Colborne, Port Burwell, Lake St. Clair, and Presqu'ile. Nicol Hugh Baird, a government engineer, drew up plans in 1837 for a new lighthouse to be built at the eastern tip of the Presqu'ile Peninsula, to mark the harbor entrance and the north shore of Lake Ontario.

Construction began in 1838 under the supervision of contractor John McLeod. The lighthouse cost £1,150 and took two years to complete. It was built on a 30-foot (9 m) square, stone foundation, 5 1/4 feet (1.6 m) below grade, bearing on bedrock. On this foundation sat an octagonal cornice from which the tower's gently tapering octagonal limestone block walls ascended 69 feet (21 m), to a 17-foot (5.2 m) diameter below the lantern. The summit flared out to support the gallery. Baird's pointed arch windows and doorway helped create his Gothic design (although the windows are rectangular on the outside today, they remain pointed from the inside). This limestone tower was whitewashed to increase its visibility. The original lantern was an octagonal, birdcage-style with small multi-panes of glass in each panel. It was topped by an "ogee" (a double-curved profile) dome.

Inside, under the first floor, was an oil room — a shallow pit no more than 4 feet (1.2 m) deep that Baird deemed to be of "a sufficient dimension to admit a puncheon [72–120 imperial gallons] of oil." The tower's five stories were connected by five ladder-type sets of stairs with 16 steps each, and the walls were slightly graduated in thickness from the bottom to the top. Windows located above the main entrance lit each landing. The top floor had lathe and plastered walls and a coved ceiling. Otherwise the inner walls, of rubble, were stuccoed. All floors above the first had blind openings, some of which were occupied by cupboards. In 1842 plans were drawn up for a separate keeper's house. It was to be a one-story house, built from cut limestone, with a hipped roof and an 8-foot (2.4 m) basement. It was finally built in 1846, by James Sutherland. Around the turn of the century it was raised to 1½ stories and given a gable roof.

The tower beacon, about 70 feet (21.5 m) above ground level, in 1874 used a catoptric system. While it once burned vegetable or whale oil, it switched to coal oil (kerosene) in 1860. The illumina-

Presqu'ile Lighthouse with an airport beacon replacing its removed lantern

tion was created by ten base-burner fountain lamps on two circles (four on the upper and six on the lower) and it had ten 14-inch (35 cm) reflectors. The light was reportedly visible for 18 miles (29 km). Keeper W. Swetman liked the kerosene: "The oil intended for burning in cold weather is the best oil for burning that has come to the lighthouse during the twenty-one years I have kept it."

By 1896 Presqu'ile had a new seventh-order, dioptric lighting apparatus, but its visibility range was only 13 miles (21 km), perhaps because of the small lens or the visual interference of the lantern astragals. By 1908 the coal oil was vaporized in an incandescent mantle that produced a brighter light, and the lens was changed to a fourth-order lens that also intensified the light.

In 1889 the long-awaited opening of the Murray Canal (connecting Presqu'ile Bay to the Bay of Quinte) took place. Instead of sailing around the Prince Edward Peninsula, vessels could now use a safer route. This made the Presqu'ile Light even more important, as it now marked entry to the bay and the western entrance to the canal. However, the canal was built too late for much commercial use. As it could not accommodate deeper, steel-hulled freighters, they — and passenger steamers — began to avoid Presqu'ile, and the canal promoted the growth of recreational boating instead.

By the early 1890s the lighthouse's exposed storm-washed location had taken its toll. After enduring more than 50 years of fierce storms and frost, its limestone exterior was deteriorating. The government labeled the problem "inadequate stone and workmanship" and in 1894 covered the exterior with protective cedar shingles that were painted white for increased visibility.

In 1906 Presqu'ile received a diaphonic fog alarm to alert mariners during the heavy fog that rolls in off Lake Ontario. It gave a 6-second blast every minute and could be heard over 3 miles (5 km) away. The machine was housed in a wood frame building between the lighthouse and the keeper's house. Its one especially notable feature was its tall brick chimney, which extended from

the roof peak almost as high as the lighthouse itself. This fog alarm building, built by M.J. Egan, cost $3,630. It was discontinued in 1934 due to the lack of commercial traffic.

The first keeper at Presqu'ile, whose tenure lasted from 1840 until his death in 1871 at the age of 86, was William Swetman. His income as an onshore keeper in 1841, when a uniform pay scale was introduced, was £65 a year, which he supplemented by raising cattle on the peninsula. He was appointed before 1844, when the Board of Works assumed control of the lighthouses and passed stricter hiring regulations, giving preference to mariners with lake experience. In 1868, after Confederation, control of the lighthouses passed to the new Dominion Government and its Department of Marine and Fisheries. In 1869, under the new government, Swetman earned $325 a year.

Although the navigation season lasted only from April to December, Swetman remained at the lighthouse year round to maintain and protect it. In 1871 the Government of Ontario transferred the Presqu'ile Peninsula to the Dominion of Canada to help control squatters settling on the peninsula and prevent deforestation, which would destroy the harbor's refuge. Deciding that the

Early Presqu'ile Lighthouse and Fog Signal Building

area's main role was to shelter vessels, the government granted leases to squatters but they were given strict orders not to cut any green timber.

According to an 1871 source, Swetman's grandson, William Swetman III, took over as keeper, while another source states that G.B. Simpson, Swetman's son-in-law and keeper of the Presqu'ile range lights, was given the responsibility of tending the main light as well. When Simpson was appointed keeper of the main light he was also named guardian of the valuable timber. This being too much for one man, Swetman remained keeper of the range lights and Captain William Henry Sherwood was appointed keeper of the main light in 1874. He earned $375 a year to tend the light and guard the timber. During his tenure, more squatters arrived and built permanent cottages. His recommendation that the government remove these cottages was overruled.

In 1898 the new keeper, Herbert E. Smith, inherited the conflict with the squatters. It peaked in 1904 when property-deeded residents complained about the squatters living tax-free. In 1905 the federal government settled the dispute by drawing up leases for the squatters. As well as tending the light and guarding the timber, the keeper now became a government agent, handing out leases, collecting rent, keeping detailed accounts, and approving building plans for cottages. For his time and trouble, he received 10 percent on first-year leases and 5 percent for subsequent years.

In 1927, when the keeper's job was consolidated with that of the fog alarm engineer, Ross Carnite took both roles. He remained keeper until 1935, when the light was electrified. At this time the range lightkeeper, James Grimes, assumed the duties of turning the light on and off. In 1946 he made 75 trips to check the lighthouse during the navigation season. In this period the light had gone out 17 times due to high winds, which broke the lantern's outside glass and its bulbs. A recommendation to remove the lantern was acted on only years later.

By 1921 most of the land of Presqu'ile Peninsula had been transferred back to the Province of Ontario under the authority of the Presqu'ile Park Commission. The 125-acre (50.6 hectare) lighthouse reserve was returned to the province in 1928. In 1935 the keeper's house was sold as a private residence.

In 1947 James Grimes bought the unused fog station building and demolished it to use the wood on his farm in Brighton. Shortly thereafter, the tall chimney was dynamited to eliminate liability. The fog building's foundation is still visible today. In 1952, when the light was automated and the keeper became unnecessary, Grimes was appointed general caretaker. In 1957 the keeper's house was sold back to the Department of Lands and Forests, now the Ministry of Natural Resources. After Grimes died in 1963, his son, John, took over until 1965, when the light was fully automated. The whole lantern was then removed and an airport beacon was mounted on a buoy structure that could withstand fierce winds.

The lighthouse signal, originally a fixed white light, became a fixed red light in 1952. In 1961 it became a flashing red light, but returned to a fixed red in 1980. Due to its reduced role as a guide for pleasure craft, its visibility was lowered to 8 miles (12.8 km).

Today the lighthouse is part of Presqu'ile Provincial Park, where visitors can view its stately, elegant style. The lightkeeper's house has been renovated to show its original stone room, and an addition houses the Visitors' Centre. It remains an impressive lighthouse, being one of the earliest on the Great Lakes and, at one time, the first one east of Toronto on Lake Ontario's north shore.

Known Keepers: William Swetman Sr. (1840–70), G. Simpson (1870), William Swetman III (1871–72), G.B. Simpson (1873), Captain William Henry Sherwood (1874–98), Mr. Smith (?), Fred Cornwall (1912–26), Ross Carnrite (1927–35), James Grimes (1935–52).

57 Presqu'ile Range Lights

After the Presqu'ile Lighthouse was built in 1840 along the north shore of Lake Ontario, marine traffic into Presqu'ile Bay steadily increased. In 1850–51 the Presqu'ile Range Lights were established to assist mariners navigating the area by pointing out underwater shoals and signaling Salt Point, a long spit on the north side of Presqu'ile Point. The range lights were designed by Thomas Dissett, who worked for the Department of Lights, and were built by Thomas Lee, James Newman and James Smith.

An early map of the area (circa 1851–71) shows the location of the range lights. One was on Salt Point and the other was in the vicinity of today's government dock. An 1857 description in Hodder's *The Harbours and Ports of Lake Ontario* outlines harbor entry as follows: "The channel which leads into this fine harbour now becomes difficult, owing to shoals which surround it … Steer … within … the lighthouse [Presqu'ile lighthouse on point] thence N. by E. for a very large and solitary Pine Tree, which stands on the main land … continue this course … until range lights are brought into line … steering directly for them … having passed this point, anchor in the little bay between the two range lights." A photograph of this era clearly shows these range lights bounding the safe bay.

Even with these range lights in place the September 18, 1862, *Kingston Daily News* warned of the area: "The bar at Salt Point now extends 150 feet (45.7 m) from the lighthouse. There is a buoy on the end of the bar but in making the harbour at night it cannot be seen. After ranging the lights and when about 200 yards (183 m) from the lighthouse, it would be well to remember that a 'berth' of at least 200 feet (60 m) should be given the Salt Point lighthouse. Up to this date one steamboat, one propeller, and three schooners, have gone ashore at this point." Perhaps this is why a new channel was dredged into the harbor in 1874.

By 1863 the keeper's house was in poor condition. When the new keeper, James Cummins, arrived at his station in 1863 he wrote to the government: "I found a miserable dwelling, an old log house, a part of it weatherboard, the principal part of it neither lathed or plastered… water and ice is our companion." In the 1871 Sessional Papers the lights were described quite briefly as being two on shore, having a west-southwest by east-southeast alignment, and being visible for 3 to 4 miles (5 to 6.5 km).

An 1873 annual report to the Department of Marine and Fisheries shows W.J. Swetman retiring as keeper from the lighthouse on Presqu'ile Point. His post was awarded to G.B. Simpson, the keeper of the range lights, who became responsible for tending three lighthouses, maintaining the harbour buoys, and safeguarding the timber that sheltered the harbor — all for $700 a year.

The 1877 Papers give more detail. These were square white wooden 14-foot (4.3 m) towers each with a small red iron lantern. Both used a base-burner fountain lamp on a frame with a 15-inch (38 cm) reflector. Their wooden floors were covered with canvas and painted. One of the two had just recently been repaired and the other was in good condition. The inspector recommended a porch to keep the snow off the door of the dwelling.

The 1878 Papers list the lights separately. The front range light was called the Presqu'ile Range Light, Salt Point No 1. It sat on a 42-foot (12.8 m) square pier and used one No.1 base-burner lamp and one 15-inch (38 cm) reflector to produce a fixed white light. The rear range light was called Presqu'ile, range No. 2 and was only described as having a tower similar to No. 1.

The 1879 Papers list the lights as the Presqu'ile Range Lights again but now tell of four range lights, two for the old channel and two leading between buoys for the new channel. Three of the towers were square white wooden ones with their corners painted brown. They had iron lanterns 3.2 feet (1 m) in size that used a No.1 base-burner lamp with a 15-inch (38 cm) reflector. The fourth tower was a triangular gallows, which ranged with Salt Point to make passage into the bay easier.

Lake traffic in the area decreased as the Murray Canal, opened in in 1889, directed traffic away from these range lights. Also, as vessels became larger, they traveled further out in the lake. Ultimately the Presqu'ile Range Lights were discontinued. By 1901 there was only one range light left on Salt Point — a square white tower on the tip of the sand spit that displayed a fixed white light for 4 miles (6.5 km). This light is also referred to as the Salt Point Lighthouse.

When this tower also deteriorated beyond repair, it was replaced in 1964 with a modern beacon. In 1966 it had a circular white tower with a red top and the light was shown from a 30-foot (9 m) elevation. It was placed to mark the northern edge of Salt Reef, which extended north from Salt Point. In 1992 there was still a circular white tower with a red top but it was listed as the Salt Reef light. It used dioptric electric illuminating apparatus to display a red flashing light from an elevation of 34 feet (10.4 m).

Known Keepers: William Swetman Jr. (1850–63), James Cummins (1863–), George B. Simpson (1873–1877–).

58   Prince Edward Point Lighthouse

The Prince Edward Point Lighthouse on Traverse Point marks the entrance to Point Traverse Harbour, which is off Long Point (Prince Edward Point) in Prince Edward County, Ontario. For over half a century Great Lakes mariners referred to the light as the "Red Onion" because of its red, fixed warning light. Since Long Point jutted so far out into Lake Ontario, the lighthouse assisted mariners traveling in all directions. South Bay (north and east of the point) was the only shelter from westerly and southwesterly gales between Kingston and Presqu'ile Point. Because the lighthouse (known to locals as the Traverse Point Lighthouse) marked safe harbor at South Bay, mariners also came to call the light South Bay Point Lighthouse.

The area was dangerous because the point was connected to the False Duck Islands by hidden underwater shoals. Many vessels were either grounded or smashed on the shoals during storms. Among them were the passenger steamer *Ocean Wave* (1853), the two-masted schooner *Red Rover* (1860), the propeller *Banshee* (1861), the schooner *Echo* (1861), the small schooner *Sassy Jack* (1870), the schooner *Minerva Cook* (1886), the tow barge *Condor* (1921), the two-masted schooner *Katie Eccles* (1922), the diesel freighter *Red Cloud* (1942) and the 10,000-ton Greek freighter *Protostatis* (1965).

One incident was of particular interest. In December 1874 the schooner *Star*, heading from Charlotte, New York, to Belleville, Ontario, was blown off course during a snowstorm and grounded just off Main Duck Island.

Prince Edward Point Lighthouse   NAC PA172525

All the crew made it safely to the island but they had insufficient provisions to last the winter there. Fortunately, as it was a bitterly cold winter, the entire east end of Lake Ontario froze over and the crew was rescued to the mainland near Long Point (Prince Edward Point) by sleigh. The *Star*, surrounded by ice, lay safely until the next spring, when she was released from the shoal.

During a particularly fierce four-day storm in the fall of 1878, 64 vessels found shelter at anchor off the end of Point Traverse. Shortly after this, in 1881, a lighthouse was built on the point. Although it did not save all vessels and crew, it did help many. It was a white clapboard combined wooden dwelling and lighthouse with a 36-foot (11 m) tapering tower. John Fagen was the contractor, George Bongard drew gravel for its foundation, and William Smith did the masonry.

Also in the area to assist mariners was the Traverse Bay Lifesaving Station, which opened in 1883. It had only one government lifeboat, which hung in swings when unused. When called out on a rescue mission, the boat was loaded with captain and crew and drawn by horse and wagon down to the bay. Then the wagon and lifeboat were dropped into a railroad-like car that was shot out through the piers into the bay. After its closure in 1942, local fishermen took up the task of lifesaving.

In an early fall storm of 1885 the schooner *Hannah Butler* went ashore east of the Traverse Bay Lifesaving Station. Its cargo of barley was sold to local farmers, and a salvage tug was brought from Kingston to free the stranded schooner. Point Traverse school children were given a holiday so that they could watch the rescue.

In September 1941 the light was automated using an occulting gaslight, and the keeper's job became obsolete. Also at this time, the red light was replaced with a green one — the light was no longer the Red Onion. When the light was deactivated in 1959, its lantern was removed and it was replaced by a white, 40-foot (12.2 m), steel-framed, skeletal tower erected in front of the old lighthouse. Today the tower has an electric, white flashing light (flash 0.5 s; eclipse 3.5 s) to warn of the area's hazards.

Known Keepers: D. McIntosh (1881–1902), M. Vorce (1903–11), Wait Hudgin (1912–27), William J. Ostrander (1927–41).

Prince Edward Point Lighthouse

59 Quebec Head Lighthouse

The Quebec Head Lighthouse was constructed in 1861 on the easternmost point of Wolfe Island at the head of the St. Lawrence River to assist mariners in their easterly approach to Kingston as well as to guide vessels maneuvering from the St. Lawrence River into Lake Ontario. It was a square white wooden lighthouse 20.8 feet (6.3 m) high with a lantern 6 feet (1.8 m) in diameter. Its fixed white light could be seen for 6 miles (9.6 km). The tower lantern was lit with three No.1 flat-wick lamps each with a 15-inch (38 cm) reflector to aim the beam out over the water.

Later in the 1900s the light was electrified and then later demanned. The top has been removed and replaced by a plastic beacon. The keeper's house is now a private residence, and a new summer home, a replica of the Thomas Point Shoal Lighthouse in Chesapeake Bay, has been built on the site.

Known Keepers: Robert Gillespie (1872–85–), Hugh McLaren (–1891–), William Orr (?), James McAvoy (?), John Davis (?).

Quebec Head Lighthouse (the small lighthouse at right)

60 Queen's Wharf Lighthouses

In the nineteenth century, Lake Ontario reached as far north as historic Fort York and, until a severe storm in 1853, what became Toronto Island was connected to the mainland and called Gibraltar Point. Sandbars made navigation into the harbor tricky. Capt. Hugh Richardson saw a need to light the harbor, and placed buoys at his own expense in the early 1800s. He also financed a light at Fort York until the province took control of the harbor.

In 1833 Queen's Wharf Lighthouse was put on the new garrison wharf on the west side of the western gap into Toronto Harbour and situated just southeast of the fort near the foot of Bathurst Street. First lit in 1834, it consisted of an oil lantern erected as a pier light at the end of the wharf. Around 1838–39 a small one-story lighthouse was built.

Then in 1854 the Harbour Trust established a system of range lights, one red and the other white, by building a second light on Queen's Wharf. The iron lantern for this new range light was built and situated on the storehouse on the east side of the wharf in 1856. The lights were both converted to kerosene from sperm whale oil in 1859. Finally, when the building for the Queen's Wharf Lighthouse was ready in 1861, its lantern was moved from the storehouse to the new wooden structure.

This new lighthouse was a two-story square building roughly 10 feet (3 m) square with the corners angled to create an octagonal shape. It was equipped with an iron latch and box keeper on the door (which it still has today). From the roof of the second story there rose a short octagonal section that supported a gallery and an octagonal lantern crowned with an ogee dome. The lantern was unusual. Each side had eight panes and in the second row of two sides there was a single bull's-eye lens. On the southwest corner were two bull's eyes. The rest of the panes were painted red.

In 1867 a new white hexagonal structure was built as the front range light 37 feet (11.3 m) from the end of the pier. The two lights were separated by the harbor master's house.

Considered a harbor light as well as a range light, the Queen's Wharf Lighthouse was relatively short, about 24 feet (7.5 m) and was visible for up to 6 miles (10 km) in clear weather. It was painted red, produced a red light and had a fog bell. Coupled with the white front range light, it helped vessels to maneuver until the red light was lined up behind the white light and the captain could steer through the deepest water of the harbor entrance.

In 1880 locomotive light equipment was installed into these range lights. In 1881 pipes were laid to supply the lights with natural gas. They used an open flame rather than a wick until mantles were installed. In 1885 the Queen's Wharf Lighthouse was moved north onto a new crib to increase its range. Between 1908 and 1912 a new and deeper western channel was cut into the harbor, and it was open for 1912 navigation. New lighthouses were built to mark the new channel, and the Queen's Wharf light was taken out of service at the end of the 1911 season.

In 1929, after harbor improvements had landlocked the old Queen's Wharf Lighthouse, it was moved southwest to its present location at the junction of Fleet Street and Lakeshore Boulevard. This task was achieved by dragging it, using a team of horses, over a series of wooden rollers. In 1961 the Toronto Harbour Board

Queen's Wharf Lighthouse

received jurisdiction of the lighthouse. During the 1988 restoration, the light was repainted brown after the discovery that its original color had been dark, brownish red, not the green it had been for many years. The light was also restored to its 1860s working condition.

Today, surrounded by tall buildings and a streetcar turnaround, it looks out of place. Its quaint nineteenth-century architectural style and its location some blocks from the water's edge make it difficult to discern its purpose at first glance, but it is a unique reminder of Toronto's early maritime history.

In early March, 2006 construction workers digging a foundation for a new condominium at the foot of Bathurst Street at the junction of Lakeshore Boulevard discovered what appears to be a wharf of 11-inch square timbers. Archaeologists belive them to be timbers from the early Queen's Wharf.

Known Keeper: Captain William Hall (?)

Queen's Wharf Lighthouse

61 Queen's Wharf Outer Light

The Queen's Wharf light had been first lit in 1838 on the wharf at Toronto's harbor in Lake Ontario. In 1856 another light was placed on the wharf just 37 feet (11.3 m) from its west or outer end. This light became a front range light for the Queen's Wharf light by also displaying a red light to the west, using a locomotive-style headlamp with a colored lens. This light worked in conjunction with the red rear range light to guide vessels safely into Toronto harbor from a westerly approach. The outer wharf light also had a second locomotive headlight, which showed a white light to vessels approaching the harbor from the south. To enter the harbor, these vessels lined the white light up with the red light from the Queen's Wharf rear light behind it. This outer light does not exist today.

Queen's Wharf Outer Light

62 Red Horse Rock Lighthouse

Red Horse Rock Lighthouse was built in 1856 on a tiny island about 500 yards (450 m) from Bishop Point on the mainland near the west end of Beaurivage Island, now part of the Thousand Islands National Park in the St. Lawrence River. The nearest point on the mainland is the Howe Island Ferry landing at the end of a long peninsula. It is a smooth crossing on a calm day, but a boat can easily be swamped in windy weather.

The 12-foot (3.6 m) square wooden lighthouse was short and plain and its slightly tapered sides were covered with narrow clapboarding. It was built on timber cribbing and connected to the nearest island by a walkway that spanned several wooden cribs. The tower supported a square metal gallery enclosed by a heavy wooden railing. The small, octagonal cast-iron lantern was mounted on a square base that rose from the center of the gallery.

The octagonal lantern was 3½ feet (1 m) in diameter. Five panels had paned windows; the three back panels were blanked out. The lantern was braced and supported by square

Red Horse Rock Lighthouse

iron stays, giving it a birdcage-style appearance. The original light source is unknown, but in 1878 the light contained two No.1 flat-wick lamps with no reflectors. The lantern had an ogee-shaped dome that used ribbed angles and was possibly made of copper. The dome was topped by a rotating ventilator ball with a sheet metal arrow weather vane. From base to vane the tower was 26 feet (8 m) high. Access was provided by a pedimented entry door, which once had a large box lock. Double casement windows provided ample light for both levels. In 1901 the tower displayed a fixed white light that was visible for 9 miles (14.6 km). In 1965 it was lit with a fixed electric light that had a flashing device and a visibility of 9 miles (14.5 km).

In the early 1890s, when the Department of Indian Affairs discovered that the pre-Confederation government had not purchased the island, they suggested that the Department of Marine and Fisheries purchase clear title to the land. After months of correspondence they finally acquired title for $200 in 1893.

With time the island walkway collapsed and the tower's timber cribbing was replaced by four concrete piers. The sills and the floors were also replaced at that time. A hand-painted sign over the north window clearly identified the lighthouse as Red Horse Rock. The lighthouse was replaced in 1984 by a green-topped steel circular tower.

Known Keepers: John Lamdon (1901–11), A. Meggos (1912–).

Salmon Point Lighthouse

Salmon Point Lighthouse

63　Robertson Point Lighthouse

In June 1927 the Department of Marine and Fisheries requested $500 from Ottawa for the construction of a small light on the shore at Robertson Point in the St. Lawrence River to keep vessels offshore as they headed upbound from the head of the Morrisburg Canal. The light, an anchor light hoisted on a mast set in a square 10-foot (3 m) crib, displayed a fixed red light from 25 feet (7.6 m) above high water level and was first lit on October 4, 1927. A galvanized-iron housing and a small oil shed were built on the crib. The lightkeeper was E.H. Robertson.

In the spring and summer of 1947, high water caused the mast, shed and pier to tip over so much that it was impossible to hoist the lantern. Since this light was considered an important and conspicuous marker along the St. Lawrence, $350 was appropriated to replace the old structure with a steel pole sunk into a concrete base. The old structure was entirely removed and the light was changed from a red light to a bright amber one. However, pilots and shipmasters requested that the light revert to its former characteristic, as the bright new light shone in their eyes. In response, the bulbs in the two 7-inch (17.5 cm) pressed lenses were reduced from 100 watts to 50 watts and the light was returned to fixed red.

In July 1952, as Robertson's term as keeper came to an end, the light was automated using a Sangamo Time Clock to turn the electricity on and off. In 1958 the illuminant was changed to acetylene and the fixed red characteristic became a flashing red.

Known Keeper: E.H. Robertson (1927–52).

64　Salmon Point Lighthouse

This was once named Wicked Point Lighthouse, as it warned mariners of some of the most dangerous shoals in the Quinte waters of Lake Ontario. The shoals consist of a spit that extends west southwest for about 2½ miles (4 km) from the point. Salmon Point Lighthouse was erected in 1871 in response to public demand that this point be lit. Up until then the government felt that lights at Point Petre and Egg Island (Scotch Bonnet) were sufficient to light the coast. However, numerous incidents on the shoals of Wicked Point proved that a light was in fact also needed here.

In October 1870 the 121-foot (37 m) schooner *Jessie*, loaded with 13,000 bushels of grain, was stuck in the bay as the winds had shifted and the seas rose. By the force of a gale more ferocious than any had ever seen, the *Jessie* was driven right onto the shoal and engulfed by the waves. While scores of people looked on, locals tried to rescue the four men and a woman seen clinging to the main boom, but their efforts were in vain.

Another disaster was reported in the *Kingston Daily News* in November 1865: "A large American vessel, name unknown, totally dismantled and bulwarks gone, is ashore at Salmon Point, and all hands supposed to be lost. She had a white flag flying from a pole when the steamer *Grecian* passed yesterday but the sea was so high she could render no assistance."

After 30 lives, nine vessels and a cargo valued at $175,000 were lost at Wicked Point between 1860 and 1870, the government finally built a light on land purchased from Peter Huff. The lighthouse was a wooden structure that stood 40 feet (12.2 m) above sea level. It had a white square pyramidal tower with a dwelling attached and was very typical of early Canadian lights — quick, easy and economical to construct. The wooden lantern exhibited a red light using three flat-wick lamps on a cast-iron pedestal and two circular burner lamps with five 20-inch (50 cm) reflectors. The light's first keeper was Peter Huff, the original landowner.

In the winter of 1878–79 the lantern was replaced. The new lantern was 8 feet (2.4 m) in diameter and housed three Silber No. 1 burner lamps, and two mammoth flat-wick lamps with 18-inch (45 cm) reflectors, which exhibited a fixed red light for 12 miles (19.3 km).

Amos MacDonald, the third keeper of this light, wrote: "In 1897 the Federal Government notified me of my appointment as lightkeeper at Salmon Point. My instructions were that I should do everything to assist navigation, and for twelve years and one month, while I remained at my post, I attempted to do so. I believe that the lighthouse was put up at that spot, not so much as a guide to navigation, but to overlook the most dangerous reef in the waters."

The light was decommissioned in 1917, and in 1920 the lighthouse, all the outbuildings and the property were sold to George F. Cummings for $100. He used it as a summer cottage. The property was later sold to the Rankin family, who operated the property as a campground and allowed guests to rent the lighthouse by the week.

Known Keepers: Peter Huff (1871–78–), Lewis Hudgin (1874–91), Amos McDonald (1897–1909), Anson Short (1909–11), James Kavanagh (1911), Alex Clark (1912–17).

65 Salt Point Lighthouse

In 1851 the Canadian government established a lighthouse 150 feet (46 m) from the outer end of the sand spit at Salt Point at the entrance to Presqu'ile Harbour, Lake Ontario, to warn mariners of the natural hazard. It displayed a fixed white light from its square white wooden tower for 4 miles (6.4 km).

Known Keepers: William Swetman Jr. (1850–63), James Cunnims (1863–).

66 Scotch Bonnet Lighthouse

During the 1800s, shipping along the north shore of Lake Ontario was booming, with steamers and schooners carrying cargoes of apples, corn, lumber, pork, cordwood, whiskey, salt, wheat, and coal and bringing in immigrants. Among their hazards was Scotch Bonnet Reef. A Scottish lad who sailed the Great Lakes said the small rock island looked just like a tam o' shanter from back home, and the name Scotch Bonnet stuck. In the early days it was also called Egg Island, in recognition of its shape. The island, 9 miles (14.5 km) out from Presqu'ile, is also about one mile (1.6 km) southwest of Nicholson Island, off Huyck's Point on the north shore of Lake Ontario. Like an iceberg, the barren, rock island rises only 7 feet (2.1 m) above the water, while most of its rocky reef lurks below.

But it was only in 1856 that the government marked this hazard with a lighthouse. The circular, limestone tower was 54 feet (16.5 m) high and housed a fixed white light supplied by ten base-burner fountain lamps on three circles with ten 15-inch (38 cm) reflectors. With its focal plane of 51 feet (15.5 m), the light was visible for up to 12 miles (19.3 km). A keeper's house built of limestone was attached.

Early lists of lights indicate that the keeper would answer vessels' signals by hand on his foghorn. Because of its desolate, storm-swept location, there was a frequent turnover of keepers. Government archives show a battle between keeper Samuel Wilson and the government over his pay, possibly due to neglect of duties, and also record a long debate (1860–67) about obtaining a permanent source of firewood. The deterioration or complete loss of the "boat slide" during storms was also an ongoing problem.

It was once believed that lights at Point Petre and Scotch Bonnet were sufficient to guide marine traffic of the early to mid-1800s. However, many vessels were doomed on nearby rocky shoals, including: the schooner *Northstar*, lost on Scotch Bonnet; the wheat-laden schooner *George Thurston*, which developed a leak off Nicholson Island and was driven ashore by heavy seas in November 1869; the coal-carrying schooner *Blanche*, which disappeared in September 1889, just southwest of Scotch Bonnet; and the schooner *Emerald*, carrying 600 tons of slack coal, which vanished in a westerly gale in November 1903.

Salt Point Lighthouse

Scotch Bonnet Lighthouse

Scotch Bonnet Lighthouse

Around 1912, an acetylene gas burner was installed and the light became an occulting white light with the same visibility. Since the burner required no trimming and the light burned 24 hours a day using compressed gas, the light became "unwatched" or automated. In 1959 a steel skeletal tower 70 feet (21.3 m) high with a white flashing electric light was built.

All that remains today are the crumbling ruins of the tower and the keeper's house, surrounded by the cormorants and herring gulls that make the desolate island their home. During their nesting season, the island is off limits for humans.

Known Keepers: John Giroux (1856–68), Henry Van Dusen and Lafayette Bentley (1868–78), Robert Pye (1878–98) D.O. Spencer, (1898–1903), Cyril Spencer (1903–12), B.Y. Cunningham (1912).

67 Snake Island (Four Mile Point) Lighthouse

In May 1856 the *Kingston Daily News* published a proposition for a lighthouse to be built on Snake Island, Lake Ontario, at a cost of £3,000. This lighthouse was the first to be built in the Four Mile Point area. It was positioned on the north side of the passage between Snake Island and Simcoe Island in the shallow water surrounding the east, south and west sides of the island. The square stone tower was 35 feet (10.7 m) from base to vane. The lantern, 6 feet (1.8 m) in diameter, was lit in 1858 using a catoptric (lamp and metal reflector) lighting system that displayed a fixed red light, visible up to 7 miles (11.7 km) in clear weather. The pier on which it stood was large enough to accommodate a dwelling attached to the tower.

By 1877 the characteristic of the light had changed. It became a fixed catoptric light provided by six base-burner fountain lamps on two circles. The reflectors consisted of two 15-inch (37.5 cm), one 16-inch (40 cm) and three 21-inch (52.5 cm) reflectors that reflected the light through a piece of ruby glass.

The first keeper, L. Wartman, was appointed on April 1, 1858 but in less than a year he left the job and Lawrence Hechemer became the keeper. It was during his tenure (1862) that the schooner *Atlantic* grounded on the shoal around the island twice in the same day. In 1868 the schooner *Defiance* also grounded on these shoals. Apparently the lighthouse was not on the best site to assist mariners. In 1870 a letter to the editor of the *Kingston Daily News* referred insultingly to its placement: "It was evidently the same set of brains that plunked the lighthouse on Snake Island." Nevertheless, it was not moved until several years later.

The keeper's job next went to Nathaniel Orr. Since the few rocky acres around the lighthouse were remote and not very productive, Orr purchased land in 1874 on nearby Simcoe Island to raise his family. Living on Simcoe Island while tending the light on Snake Island required a twice-daily commute of 1½ miles (2.4 km) each way, using a small rowboat or sailboat. If stormy weather came up, the keeper would be forced to stay at the lighthouse. During

Snake Island (Four Mile Point) Lighthouse

such a trip in foul weather, Nathaniel and his wife, Eliza, caught pneumonia and died within a day of each other in November 1887. Their son William then served as keeper until 1899 for a yearly salary of $350.

During William Orr's tenure many changes occurred. Since the pier on which the lighthouse stood was in bad shape and complaints had been received about the placement of the light, it was decided to build a new lighthouse closer to the actual channel, 850 feet (260 m) southeast-by-east of the existing lighthouse. The new lighthouse was also to be built on the shoal and $1,310 was appropriated for its construction. In 1898 steel casing for a concrete pier was built for the foundation of the new lighthouse, but, because the ice was so thin that year, its completion was delayed until spring.

The white octagonal wooden tower was topped with an iron, octagonal lantern painted red. The 39-foot (12 m) lighthouse (from base to ventilator) sat on a steel pier 6 feet (1.9 m) above the water. It used a seventh-order, dioptric illuminating apparatus to display a fixed red light. When it was lit for the 1900 shipping season, the old stone tower was taken down. John Whitmarsh was appointed keeper in July 1900, also at $350. In 1901 timberwork was done on the circular steel pier and a 75-foot (23 m) protective breakwater built around it 4 feet (1.2 m) above the water. The west side was pointed to break stormy waves. A small boathouse was also built on the pier beside the lighthouse. These renovations, supervised by W.B. Lindsay, cost $4,920. Since no accommodation was provided, Whitmarsh bought the house and lot from the Orr family and lived there until he retired.

In March 1912, C.V. (Victor) Sudds was appointed keeper. Interestingly, even though he had more work to do, his salary dropped to $260 a year. For another $25 he also operated the foghorn from Four Mile Point on Simcoe Island. The foghorn, established in 1910, was housed in a small building and was operated by a hand lever that pumped and compressed air to a point that it would push a blast of air through a horn. The foghorn was operated to answer ships' signals whenever fog was heavy.

The Department of Marine and Fisheries purchased 0.97 acres (0.4 hectare) from Richard and Lydia Eve (brother and sister) and moved the lighthouse from the pier to the bluff at Four Mile Point in the winter of 1918. Sudds was contracted to move the lighthouse and place it on concrete butts on the bluff. He used the deep snow and thick ice to his advantage. The lighthouse was loaded onto two round timber skids and drawn across the ice by 24 horses. Undaunted by the steep bluff at the river's edge, Sudds used one horse and a capstan to pull the lighthouse up the slope, which had been prepared by wetting and packing the snow to form a hard, less steep surface.

Sudds continued as keeper until the light was discontinued in 1941. The lighthouse then sat empty until 1958 when it burned to the ground during the winter. Tracks led from the lighthouse but no one knows whether the fire was accidental or deliberate. The land later passed into private hands.

Known Keepers: L. Wartman (1858), Lawrence Hechemer (1859–68), Nathaniel Orr (1869–87), William Breden Orr (1887–99), John Whitmarsh (1900–11), C. Victor Sudds (1912–41).

Stonehouse Point (Glengarry Point) Lighthouse, circa 1902

68 Spectacle Shoal Light

In 1856 a lighthouse was built on Spectacle Shoal on the north side of the channel in the St. Lawrence River into Gananoque. The light sat on a pier in the river and helped mark the safe channel of the river by warning of the shoal. From a square 29-foot (9 m) white wooden tower with an iron lantern 3½ feet (1 m) in diameter, its light was generated by two No.1 flat-wick lamps with no reflectors to achieve a visibility of 9 miles (14.5 km). At the end of the 1878 season the lantern was upgraded with a larger one.

Known Keepers: J. Buck (1870–), John Lamdon (1901–11), A Meggos (1912–).

69 Stonehouse Point Lighthouse

A light was built at Stonehouse Point, also known as Glengarry Point, Lake Ontario, sometime between 1872 and 1877, as we glean from an 1877 report by the inspector for the Department of Marine and Fisheries that mentions the light. It was lit with three mammoth flat-wick lamps with 18-inch (45 cm) reflectors on a cast-iron stand housed in a 6-foot (1.8 m) diameter lantern. The lantern was mounted on a 35-foot (10.6 m) tower with an attached dwelling. Pedimental tower windows provided interior light. The square gallery was supported by wooden corbels and surrounded with a simple wooden railing.

In 1900 the care of the lighthouse and grounds was assigned to Mrs. K. Casgrain, as she owned adjacent land and the light could be accessed through her property. In 1908 she received $50 to settle the account she submitted to the government for remuneration. At this time it was recommended that her son René assume the care of the light, since he already tended the seven automatic gaslights between Cornwall and Hamilton Island, for which he earned $300 a year.

In February 1914 the Lighthouse Board decided to discontinue the light and notified keeper Casgrain in March of their decision. He was to be paid until the end of March. However, the usual practice when discontinuing a light was to give two or three months' notice, and keepers who had served for a long time were given six months' leave of absence with pay before discontinuance of salary. After his mother intervened, the Board reconsidered, and paid Casgrain until the end of June.

With the light discontinued, Mrs. Casgrain was granted permission to rent the lighthouse. However, when she advertised in the local paper to sublet the lighthouse, R.J. Craig, who also had a right-of-way across his property and was concerned about his cattle and crops if cottagers and campers left the gates open, complained to the Department of Marine and Fisheries. The Department in turn told Mrs. Casgrain that subletting was not allowed and that after the season, preference would be given to Craig for the lighthouse's future rental.

Known Keepers: Kenneth McLachlan (1877–), James H. Aitken (1900–03), René Casgrain (1906–14).

Telegraph Island Lighthouse, circa 1900

70   Telegraph Island Lighthouse

Telegraph Island is a very small island on the north side of the Bay of Quinte, Lake Ontario. In 1870 a lighthouse was built on the northwest part of the island to help mariners navigate the bay. Since the island was low to the water, a protective pier was first built, and a combined lighthouse and keeper's dwelling was built on this foundation. The tower extended for two stories up out of the roof at one end of the two-story white clapboard house. The square tower supported a square gallery and a square-bottomed birdcage-style lantern. This 46-foot (14 m) tower exhibited a white occulting light that in 1901 was changed to a fixed white light. The lighthouse and dwelling were demolished in 1950 and replaced by an automatic gas buoy. Then in 1960 a 36-foot (11 m) square steel tower with two white oval-shaped day-marks was erected. This white light produced 15 flashes per minute.

Known Keepers: J. Mason (1870–95), Mrs. Mason (1895), George Rowe (1895–1912), M. Benn (1912–1916–), Mr. Rowes (?).

71   Toronto East Pier Range Lights

Range lights were placed on the east pier of Toronto, Lake Ontario, to make it easier for vessels to dock against the long pier. The front range light was a red steel framework tower with an enclosed upper white section, a white lantern and a red dome. It was 40 feet (12.3 m) from base to vane. Its lantern used a sixth-order lens to display an isophase flashing red light (flash 6 s; eclipse 6 s) from a 43-foot (13 m) focal plane to produce a visibility of 9 miles (14.6 km) over a 180-degree arc. It also had a fog bell raised 25 feet (7.7 m) above the water. It was mechanically struck at three-second intervals or 20 blows a minute.

The back range light was 2,400 feet (732 m) behind the front one. It was a gray iron column placed on a hexagonal shed, and displayed a fixed red light. These range lights no longer exist.

Known Keepers: William Montgomery (1895–1906), G. McKelvie (1907–1915).

72   Toronto Harbour Aquatic Park Lighthouse

A feature of Toronto Harbour's Eastern Gap is the Leslie Street Spit, a peninsula created into Lake Ontario from landfill during the 1950s. The spit was to serve as protection for an outer harbor for the increase in shipping expected as a result of the opening of the St. Lawrence Seaway in 1959. However, since this increase did not take place, the area was slated to become an aquatic park. This park, although planned, has not yet been developed.

The lighthouse, situated at the south end of the park, was built on a man-made knoll of land in 1974 to mark the end of the spit after the widening and deepening of the Eastern Gap in 1973. With its 71-foot (21.6 m) focal plane and its height of 30 feet (9 m), this white hexagonal tower with a red upper portion and lantern displays an electric, red flashing light (flash 0.3 s; eclipse 9.7 s).

Now called the Tommy Thompson Park, the spit attracts bird-watchers and naturalists with its abundant wildlife. The point where the lighthouse stands has been named Vicki Keith Point in recognition of the Canadian swimmer who swam across all five Great Lakes for charity in 1988. Also in 1988 the tower was flood-lit and became listed as an emergency light that is maintained from April to December.

Toronto Harbour Aquatic Park Lighthouse

73   Weller's Bay Range Lights

In the second half of the nineteenth century, as maritime traffic into the Presqu'ile Bay area along Lake Ontario's north shore increased, mariners called to have the area better lit. While they felt the lighthouse on Presqu'ile Point and range lights into Presqu'ile Bay were adequate, they wanted lights at Weller's Bay, just 3½ miles (5.7 km) to the east of Presqu'ile Point, as the northern part of this bay could provide safe harbor and easier access during stormy weather.

While Weller's Bay is 5 miles (8 km) long and about 1 mile (1.6 km) wide, Bald Head Island lies in the entrance to the bay with shallow water surrounding it, and a long low spit of land, known as the Bald Head Spit, extends northwestward from the island to block most of the entrance into the bay. Entry could only be achieved safely through a narrow gap of deep water between the mainland and the tip of the spit. In addition, a bar lay across the mouth of the bay about 2 miles (3.2 km) farther out into the lake. Vessels seeking the shelter of the bay had to maneuver around this bar and then avoid Bald Head Spit before entering the bay. They petitioned the government to light the area.

The government built range lights to assist mariners into Weller's Bay in 1877. Parliamentary Sessional Papers for this same year describe the front range light as being "22 feet [6.7 m] high, covered in, and painted white all the way down," while the rear range light was "35 feet [10.6 m] high … made with open trellis work … painted red." The 1878 Papers describe both lights as red, but this later changed. The 1879 Papers say the lights were respectively 27 feet (8.3 m) and 37 feet (11.4 m) high from base to vane, with the front tower still displaying a fixed red light but the rear tower showing a fixed white light.

Both towers had 4-foot (1.2 m) square iron lanterns, each of which housed a mammoth flat-wick lamp with 18-inch (45 cm) reflectors. A new keeper's house had been built in 1876–77 for the keeper and his family. It had four rooms on the ground floor and three bedrooms upstairs. The station comprised about 6 acres (2.4 hectares), and the house and the vegetable garden were enclosed with "a good board fence."

Mariners found that these simple range lights were misleading and requested that they be moved. A private light was even established for a short period to better light the area. In 1888 or 1889, W.H. Nobel erected a beacon on Bald Head Spit to help sea captains steer clear of it, but during its first winter the beacon was carried away by ice. Also at this time, storms washed away the surface of the gravelly Bald Head Spit, making it even more dangerous because it lay just underwater.

After numerous complaints the government finally sent a ministry official to investigate the situation in May 1892. He traveled the water route himself to ascertain the best new site for the range lights and to make recommendations to the government. He saw the benefit of a light on Bald Head Spit but commented that "it would be difficult and expensive to maintain a beacon there permanently." He recommended two possible solutions. The first would require an additional range light, thereby adding expense and putting one of the lights in a different county. The second was to move both range lights, so as to "clear the Spit and give … a fair crossing, over the bar, while … keeping the front light on property belonging to the Department, and keeping the lights in the same constituency." He recommended $200 for the changes. The government chose to move the lights.

The front range light was to be moved onto Prince Edward's road allowance of the Carrying Place Road, which divided the counties of Prince Edward and Northumberland. The back range light would need to be placed on a road allowance belonging to the Central Ontario Railway. With this aim, the government applied to the Railway for building permission, reminding the Railway that the existence of these lights was important "in allowing vessels to safely reach their wharf in Weller's Bay" and that they were "consequently directly interested in improving approaches." The Railway granted permission.

George Crowe of Trenton placed a tender of $243 to do the work. After being told this was too high, he submitted a second tender of $113.50 to move the two range lights, place them on new foundations and put new joists and flooring under the front range light. His second tender was accepted. During the move it was discovered that both lights required new sills, and an additional $103 was agreed to.

By November 1892 the towers had been moved and their light characteristic altered again. The front light was changed from a fixed red to fixed white, while the rear light was switched from a fixed white to fixed red. The front range light had an elevation of 26 feet (8 m) above lake level, giving it a 10-mile (16 km) visibility. The rear range light was placed 500 feet (155 m) northeast of the front one and had a 37-foot (11.3 m) elevation with visibility of about 7 miles (11 km). With work finally completed, it was reported: "Vessels entering can now pick up the alignment in the deep water of the lake, cross the bar on the alignment, N. E. 3/4 E, and keep it until the extremity of Bald Head Spit is passed at a distance of about 150 feet (46 m), when they will be in deep water of the bay, inside all dangers."

Little is known about the lightkeepers. Wm. H. Orser was dismissed in October 1898, having been found "guilty of offensive political partisanship at or before the General Election." He allegedly made derogatory comments about the Liberal Party and tried to coerce persons into voting his way.

In April 1908 Henry J. Chase was appointed keeper of the range lights for a salary of $150 a year, to be increased by annual increments of $10 to a maximum of $180. Then, in September 1908 Chase was directed to discontinue the rear range light. Since he was now only operating one light, his 1909 salary dropped to $120, with $10 increments until a maximum of $150. In March 1910 the front range light was also discontinued. On February 10, 1921 the lighthouse property was sold to James Harry Orser for $1,025.

Known Keepers: Reuben Young (1878–), William Orser (–1898), Henry J. Chase (1898–1910).

74 Whitby Harbour Lighthouse

Whitby, Ontario, formerly known as Windsor, offered one of the better harbors along the north shore of Lake Ontario. The date for the construction of the Whitby Harbour Lighthouse is uncertain, but reports show it as being there in 1844. In the 1850s the light was reported to be a fixed white light from a 12-foot (3.7 m) tower at the end of the west pier. The light could be seen clearly if approached from the south but was not very visible from the east or west. In the 1880s it came under the management of the Marine Department. At some point the original tower was replaced by a 24-foot (7.3 m) hexagonal tower capped with an octagonal lantern and was placed at the end of the west breakwall. The keeper rowed out to maintain the light.

In 1901 the lighthouse was a square wooden tower that displayed a fixed white light from the west pier. As well as marking Whitby Harbour, the light also helped to mark a dangerous shoal close to shore in the area between Whitby and Liverpool (now Pickering).

Known Keeper: R. Goldring (1911–).

Whitby Harbour Pier Lighthouse

Windmill Point Lighthouse

75 Windmill Point Lighthouse

This unique lighthouse was first built in 1822 by a West Indian merchant named Hughes as a functioning windmill to service the local community of Newport and the surrounding farming community along the Upper Canada shore of the St. Lawrence River. It is famous as the location for the Battle of the Windmill, which was fought around its base in November 1838.

The battle was fought during the Canadian Rebellion or Patriot War. Canadian rebels and American sympathizers fought to liberate Canada from British rule by overthrowing Fort Wellington, while British and British loyalists fought to protect their homes and the established political order of Fort Wellington and the region. The British learned of the rebels' plans and, along with local militia, surrounded them at the windmill area. After four days of bloodshed the rebels were defeated. Thus the battle earned its place in Canadian history.

The windmill, about a mile from Prescott, stands close to the edge of a steep bank 50 feet (15.2 m) above the river and is built into a gently sloping hillside. It was converted to a lighthouse in 1872. Its round irregular coursed-rubblestone tower has six floors but no basement. The base interior diameter is 20 feet (6.2 m), and its walls are 3 feet (0.9 m) thick. While the exterior walls taper upward, a ledge at each floor level inside the tower allows the walls to become thinner as they rise. The flights, each of 15 steps, alternate from north-south to south-north. The stairs from the second floor up were added when the windmill tower was converted to a lighthouse. The stairs and the landings are protected by heavy handrails.

Many window and door openings have been filled in and do not show on the exterior — or perhaps they were always blind to make interior cupboard space. There is a single filled-in opening on the west side of the tower and a pair on the east side. The window openings are about 3 feet (1 m) square and are fitted with wooden louvers. The second, third, fourth, and fifth floors have pairs of widely spaced windows on the east and west sides. In addition, the third floor has filled-in openings for a north and south door. The sixth floor only has one window facing east and one window facing west.

The foundation for the lantern was made of heavy timbers set on top of each other at right angles, plus radial timbers that projected beyond the walls to support the gallery. Beam ends of the radial timbers appear on the outside of the tower beneath the gallery as a decorative feature. The lantern was of standard cast-iron, 7 feet (2.1 m) in diameter. Each of its eight sides had a single large pane of glass. The light stood on a round table with square legs. A mirror was mounted to the north side of the table behind the lens, which had four sections. The lantern was topped with a low-pitched dome that had a central hood with a veined ventilator. By 1878 the 92-foot (28 m) lighthouse exhibited a fixed white light generated by three mammoth flat-wick lamps with 18-inch (45 cm) reflectors.

About 600 feet (185 m) east of the lighthouse are the ruins of a two-story stone house that seems to date from the 1830s or 1840s. It may once have been the miller's house, possibly even an early keeper's house, or just a house in the community of Newport, which once existed close to the windmill. The lighthouse remained in service until 1978. Since then it has been declared one of Canada's National Historic Sites.

A structural inspection in the fall of 2002 confirmed concerns about recent cracking in the masonry and deterioration of the mortar in some areas of the tower. One possible explanation was that it was caused in the spring of 2002 by a slight earthquake that occurred in the area, perhaps moving the bedrock on which the tower sits. Parks Canada secured funds to repair the damage in 2004. The site itself is now maintained and operated by the Friends of Windmill Point in association with Parks Canada. The tower is open to summer visitors, who can climb to an observation level just below the light for an exquisite view of the St. Lawrence River and surrounding area.

Known Keepers: Bernard Kean (–1877–), John Fraser (1901–).

Windmill Point Lighthouse, circa 1905

LAKE ERIE

USA

LIGHTHOUSES

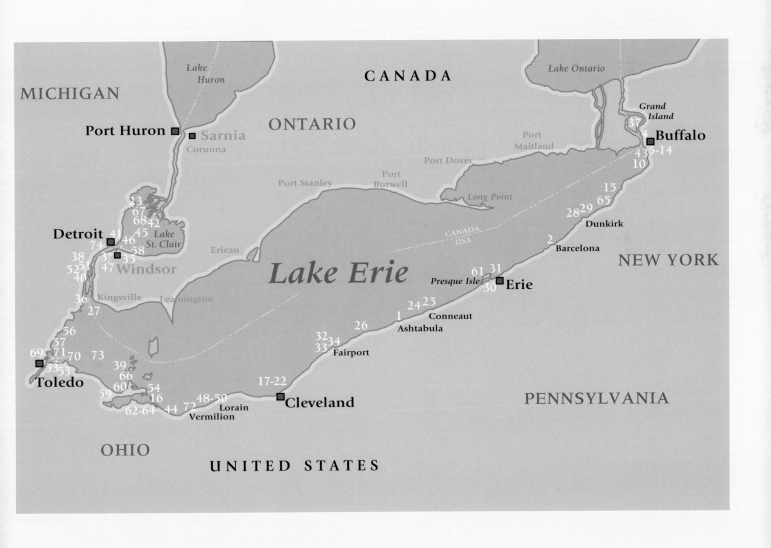

MICHIGAN

CANADA

ONTARIO

Lake Huron

Lake Ontario

Grand Island

Port Huron ■ Sarnia
Corunna

Port Maitland

37
4 ■ Buffalo
43 5-14
10

Port Dover

15

Port Stanley

Port Burwell

Long Point

65
28 29
Dunkirk

23
67
68 42
45 Lake St. Clair
Detroit ■ 41 46
74 37 58
38 37 35
52 51 47 Windsor
40
36 Kingsville
27
Leamington

Erieau

Lake Erie

CANADA USA

2
Barcelona

NEW YORK

61 31
Presque Isle 30 ■ Erie

24 25
1 Conneaut
Ashtabula
26

56
57
69 71 70 73
53 55
Toledo
39
66
60
54
59 16
62-64 44 72 Lorain
Vermilion

32 34
33 Fairport

17-22
■ Cleveland

48-50

PENNSYLVANIA

OHIO

UNITED STATES

Ashtabula Lighthouse

1 Ashtabula Lighthouse

As Ashtabula dock and harbor facilities developed, so did the lighthouses to assist navigation into the harbor. The first form of a light was a lantern hung on a post on the pier. The first actual lighthouse was built in 1836 on the east pier entrance. The light's seven lamps burned sperm oil. The tapering tower, about three stories high, was of a hexagonal board and batten construction with twelve-paned windows at the top of each side, just below the gallery (watch windows). The lantern was of a somewhat unusual bird-cage style construction, with six glass sides, ceiling to floor, each with 24 small panes of glass. In 1876, with the construction of new dock facilities on the east side of the harbor, a new, taller, lighthouse was built on the west pierhead. In 1896 a new fourth-order Fresnel lens was installed.

In 1896 a keeper's house was erected a short distance from the lighthouse on a hilltop. The duplex was of frame construction and housed the keeper, his assistant and their two families. The keepers alternated duties at the lighthouse and made their relief trip by boat. In 1939 the Lighthouse Service was transferred to the U.S. Coast Guard, who maintained the building until it was demanned.

In 1901 the harbor at Ashtabula had range lights. The front light was near the outer end of the west pier. It was a square 27-foot (8.3 m) pyramidal tower painted brown below and white above. Its lantern had a fifth-order lens and displayed a fixed white light varied by white flashes at 2-minute intervals to provide an 11-mile (18 km) visibility in clear weather. It had an elevated walk along the pier to connect it to shore for the keeper's safety during inclement weather. The rear range light was a square brown pyramidal tower that supported an octagonal black lantern and was located near the shore end of the west pier. From a 68-foot (21 m) focal plane it displayed a fixed red lens-lantern light that aligned with the front light to guide vessels into the harbor. The station also had a steam fog whistle at this time (blast 3 s; silence 12 s; blast 3 s; silence 42 s).

In 1905, with the construction of a new dock and the widening of the river, another new lighthouse was built about 2,500 feet (770 m) north of the previous location. It was a large two-story square building erected at the end of a new breakwater, also then under construction. A round tower, lantern and gallery extended up out of the square-based building. This light used the fourth-order Fresnel lens from the preceding lighthouse and had a fixed red light and a first-class siren signal.

In 1916 the old building and tower were moved 1,800 feet (550 m) north-northeast of the 1905 light, to a new crib and foundation where the breakwater was extended. An addition housed equipment for an air-operated diaphone fog signal. In 1959 a new fourth-order Fresnel lens was installed, with a flashing light every five seconds and a 17-mile (27 km) visibility. This station was manned until 1973, when the light was automated and an electric fog signal installed. The light is maintained by the U.S. Coast Guard, accessible by boat only, and not open to the public.

The Coast Guard sold the keeper's house to private owners when they decommissioned the station. After several private owners, the Ashtabula Historical Society purchased the building and converted it into a marine museum that opened in 1984. The museum displays ship and marine information and artefacts, a working miniature model of the Hulett coal-unloading machine, and a wide variety of miniaturized working tools. In 1995 a more modern optic replaced the fourth-order Fresnel lens "to reduce high cost maintenance," reported the Coast Guard. The new light is of a plastic, fiberglass, aluminum construction with a 300-mm lens and is powered by two 12-volt solar batteries. A 35-watt solar panel outside recharges the batteries. The new visibility range is 16 miles (25.6 km). The fourth-order Fresnel lens is now on display in the museum.

One interesting story tells of two keepers who in 1928 were besieged inside the lighthouse for two days during a severe storm. When they tried to escape after the storm, they found they were iced in and had to hack their way free through the ice. Ashtabula Lighthouse is one of ten Ohio Lighthouses on the *National Register of Historic Places*.

Known Keepers: Samuel Miniger (1837–38), Jonathon Johnson (1838–38), Joel Thomas (1838–49), Laban Hill (1849–51), Benjamin Ensign (1851), James Ray (1851–52), Laban Hill (1852–53), Salmon Ashely (1853), Captain Saxton Bigelow (1853–57), Seth Belknap (1857–61), W. Camp (1861–64), M. Brown (1864), Paul Cheney (1864–81), John Oakley (1882–93), Captain Orlo Mason (1893–1900), Enoch Scribner (1900–02), Joseph Crawford (1902–09), Thomas Holtan (1910–15), Ralph Sobie (1915–21), Frank Sellman (1921–29), Francis Comeford (1929–32), John Brophy (1932–37), Eugene Ray (1937–40), Thomas Baker (1940–50).

Early Ashtabula Lighthouse

Barcelona Lighthouse

2 Barcelona Lighthouse

From its rough-cut stone structures and early rustic architecture, it is easy to tell that the Barcelona Lighthouse was one of the earliest built on the Great Lakes. Congress appropriated $5,000 in 1828 for this lighthouse, built in 1829, at Portland Harbor (now Barcelona) on Lake Erie as a port of entry, and to assist navigation for the increased shipping that the opening of the Erie Canal brought.

The 40-foot (12.3 m) conical tower has a base diameter of 22 feet (6.8 m) and a parapet diameter of 10.5 feet (3.3 m). Its stone walls are 3.5 feet (1 m) thick at the bottom and taper to 2 feet (0.6 m) thick at the top. Three tower windows, with twelve lights (panes) each, light the circular plank stairs that wind up to within 6 feet (1.8 m) of the lantern deck. The stone deck is 4 inches (10.2 cm) thick and 12 feet (3.7 m) in diameter, and its joints were originally filled with lead. The scuttle was covered with copper for the keeper's safety.

The octagonal lantern used to have 21 small glass lights and three copper pieces filling the bottom tier of each octagonal panel. The lantern dome was made of 16 iron rafters covered with copper and topped by a ventilator and a 2.5-foot (0.8 m) weather vane. A small iron-framed, copper-covered door led from the lantern to the gallery, which was enclosed by an iron balustrade with two iron bands. A lightning rod fitted on the tower extended 2 feet (0.6 m) above the vane and 2 feet (0.6 m) into the ground.

The lantern was first lit by eleven patent lamps and eleven 14-inch reflectors. The lamps were fueled by oil. Then, in 1831, when residents discovered a natural gas deposit under the local creek bed, an ingenious person ran a pipeline from this gas pocket to the lighthouse through hollowed wooden pipes. When the valve was turned and the jets ignited, the light was visible for miles. When the gas ran out in 1838, oil was once again used.

The keeper's house, also rough-cut stone, was 34 feet (10.5 m) by 20 feet (6.2 m). The basement and walls were 20 inches (50.8 cm) thick. This one-story dwelling had 8-foot (2.5 m) ceilings and was divided into two rooms, each of which had three 16-pane windows. A chimney in the middle of the house was accessible to a fireplace in each room. The interior was lathed and plastered and all inside woodwork was finished in a "plain, decent style." A closed-in porch was also added to the dwelling.

The first lighthouse keeper was Joshua Lane, a local clergyman. The Lighthouse Board decommissioned the lighthouse in 1859 when it discovered that Barcelona did not have a harbor. The lighthouse was sold at auction in 1872 and has remained in private ownership since then.

While the stone has weathered well and the lantern has the iron supports outlining the octagonal panels, the glass, copper panes, and door are gone. The ventilator ball, weather vane and lightning rod are also gone. The dwelling has been made to look like a quaint country cottage. The dome appears to be cedar shakes, and the balustrade now has four tiers. However, a pipe with a light at the top still appears in the center of the lantern. Not only was the Barcelona Lighthouse the only lighthouse ever to be fueled by its own natural gas deposit but it was the first public building to be illuminated using natural gas.

Known Keepers: Joshua Lane (1829–43), Nathanial Bird (1843–45), Joshua Lane (1845–46), Joshua La Due (1846–49), Richard Kenyon (1849–55), Thomas Taylor (1855–56), William Britten (1856–59).

Early Barcelona Lighthouse

Belle Isle Lighthouse

3 Belle Isle Lighthouse

Where the Detroit River meets Lake St. Clair there is an island known as Belle Isle, named after Isabelle Cass, daughter of General Lewis Cass, governor of the Michigan territory. In 1880 the Detroit City Council gave the U.S. government a small piece of land on the southeast tip of Belle Isle to build a lighthouse. In 1881–82 the government (at a cost of $16,000) built a brick lighthouse in ornate Victorian style, with fancy "gingerbread" trim, elaborate brickwork and a wrought-iron fence.

In its 1907 *List of Lights*, the U.S. Lighthouse Board described the Belle Isle station as "a square 5½-foot (17.4 m) tower with dwelling attached, located 2½ miles (4 km) northeast of Windmill Point Lighthouse (Grosse Point). It had a fourth-order fixed red light, visible for 13 miles (21 km). On the southeast point head of Belle Isle, Detroit River, Michigan. A guide for entering and leaving the Detroit River, to and from Lake St. Clair." The lantern, 42 feet (13 m) above water level, was first lit on May 15, 1882.

Because of its location and public visibility, Belle Isle Station had a high social status, as its grand architectural style attests. The island's activities, including picnics, band concerts, hunting, fishing, baseball games in the summer, and ice skating on the canals in the winter, attracted many visitors to the island, many of whom would have visited the light station. With annual salaries of $500 to $800 for the head keeper and $400 to $500 for the assistant keeper — plus the steady stream of visitors — the keepers' positions were probably highly sought after.

Over the years a few changes occurred at the lighthouse. In 1891 a circular iron oil house holding 220 gallons (924 l) was built a safe distance from the house. In 1898 the boathouse was moved 60 feet (18.5 m) inland to a position clear of high water. It is uncertain when the light was extinguished. It was still operating in the early 1920s and was absorbed by the U.S. Coast Guard in 1939. In 1929 the Livingston Memorial Light, America's only marble light, was privately constructed on the northeast tip of Belle Isle. Sometime between the 1920s and the early 1940s the Belle Isle light was extinguished, as it was no longer needed.

4 Black Rock Range Lights

Range lights were built in the Black Rock area just below Buffalo in 1853 to mark the southern entrance to the Niagara River. The front range light was a short rectangular rubble-stone pier light that housed a fifth-order Fresnel lens in a square brick-bottomed masonry lantern. The rear range light was also a crudely built short square rubble-stone tower with a narrow square gallery and a square masonry lantern that also housed a fifth-order Fresnel lens.

These lights were simplistically built to serve as temporary lights until a light could be established on Horseshoe Reef at the entrance to the Niagara River. Considering that the reef light was finished and lit in 1856, it is surprising that these lights continued until 1870, when they were permanently extinguished.

Known Keepers: Folhas Folsam (1856–61), J. Briktel (1861–69), Miss Mary Lee (1869–70).

5 Buffalo Bottle Lights

Around the turn of the twentieth century, as Buffalo developed as a harbor, it acquired new breakwaters, and in 1903 two identical bottle-shaped lights were placed to mark the openings into the harbor. The light on the north side of the new southern entrance displayed a flashing green light visible for 13 miles (21 km). The other, placed opposite the main breakwater light, marked the harbor's northern entrance.

Both consisted of bottle shapes made from boilerplate cast-iron sheets riveted together and painted white. While the 29-foot (8.8 m) towers originally housed sixth-order Fresnel lenses, these were replaced with 300 mm plastic optics when the lights were automated in 1960. The lights were deactivated in 1985.

Both lights have been moved to new locations. One was taken to the entrance of the maritime museum at the Dunkirk Lighthouse, where it can be seen today, and the other was moved close to Buffalo's old 1833 stone lighthouse inside the Buffalo Coast Guard Base, where it can be seen on a tour offered by the Buffalo and Erie Historical Society.

Buffalo Bottle Light

6 Buffalo First Breakwater Light

In 1868 a new, detached 4,000-foot (1230 m) breakwater was built at Buffalo to enlarge its harbor area, and in 1871 a new lighthouse was started. In May a 40-foot (12.3 m) square crib 20 feet (6 m) high was sunk 23 feet (7 m) behind the end of the new breakwater. After settling for a month, the crib was topped with six courses of stone and allowed to settle once again before the lighthouse was built on it. It was a large structure that displayed a fixed red light from a fourth-order Fresnel lens at a 37-foot (11.4 m) focal plane. The fog bell was moved from the old stone tower to this new site so that it could be better heard out over the water. While the light first burned lard oil, its illuminant became kerosene used in oil vapor lamps in 1885.

Buffalo First Breakwater Light

The lighthouse inspector first recommended a switch to a fog whistle in 1890, but the change was not made until 1893 when a 10-inch (25-cm) steam-operated whistle was installed (two 3-second blasts per minute). This characteristic was altered to one blast every minute in 1895, and a large deflector was added behind the horns to send the sound out over the lake but deaden it to the city.

This breakwater light seemed to be a magnet for vessels to collide with it. In 1899 it was struck by a tug; in 1900 by a barge; in 1909 by a freighter; in 1910 by a steamer. As it was weakened with each assault, the government appropriated $60,000 to rebuild and update it between 1912 and 1914. The rebuilt station had a new diaphone fog signal, and upon its completion the third-order Fresnel lens from the old stone tower was moved to the breakwater light, and the stone tower was left unlit.

The huge new structure resembled a large 2½-story house with a short tower and a circular lantern emerging from its roof. A boom extended from one side of the house to take on necessary supplies and equipment. The first level housed supplies and the heavy machinery to operate the fog signal. The clockworks to turn the Fresnel lens were wound from this level every few hours. The second level was living quarters for the keepers, and the third housed the base for the Fresnel lens. The house was surrounded by a concrete walkway with pipe railings. Since the structure sat on its own crib, it was accessible only by water.

In 1918 the light had a head keeper plus four assistants, who rotated on 48-hour shifts. They used the lighthouse's launch, the *102*, to traverse the half mile (0.8 km) across the water with their food and personal supplies. The launch left the pier at 8 a.m. every other morning, weather permitting, to change the watches. The keepers and their families were lodged in the houses on the government's reservation. There were six houses in all, one for each keeper and one for the lighthouse depot keeper.

James Rawson was the head keeper from 1929 until his retirement in 1944 and he ran a "tight" lighthouse. He was awarded the gold star for the most efficient lighthouse in the Tenth District for three straight years in a row. In addition, his station was allowed to fly the lighthouse efficiency pennant for each of the three years so that others could acknowledge its achievement. The head keeper also kept a personal diary where he recorded entries about light upkeep, transmitter stations, facts about his assistants, opening and closing dates for the light, and a list of visitors.

A few changes occurred at the light. In 1925 a radio beacon was added to the station, making it one of the earliest stations on the Great Lakes to have such equipment. By 1930 the keepers alternated 24-hour duties at the lighthouse. Also in the 1930s $5,000

was spent to run an electrical cable from the shore to electrify the light. The oil engines were kept as a backup system for times when power was interrupted. A *Buffalo Evening News* article from August 27, 1930, reported that problems for the keepers included loneliness and storms. One storm even broke the lighthouse windows and washed through the second-floor living quarters, taking the pancakes right off the table!

In 1935 the diaphone fog signal could be heard as far as 25 miles (40 km) away (blast 1 s; silence 1 s; blast 1 s; silence 17 s). The radio beacon gave out four dashes every three minutes. In 1939 the government lighthouse reservation became incorporated into the U.S. Coast Guard Service. By 1954 keepers at the light rotated eight-hour shifts and had two free days ashore each week. Being isolated in the water, their only telephone link to the mainland was the Coast Guard base.

While the keeper only had to flick a switch a half hour before sundown to turn the light on and again after sunrise to turn it off, he did have to continue a daily ritual for operating the Fresnel lens. Each night the keeper lowered its base into the great pot of mercury used to facilitate its constant revolving, and each morning the base was removed. The lens revolved once every 30 seconds when in operation. The keepers changed the 500-watt light bulb regularly and kept the glass prisms of the lens dust-free. With its 65-foot (20 m) focal plane, the light was visible for up to 16 miles (26 km). When visibility deteriorated and the keeper could not see the green flashing light of the Waverly Shoal buoy 5 miles (8 km) away, he started the fog signal and the radio beacon. The keepers were also responsible for the 20 gas buoys from Waverly Shoal to the Peace Bridge and the river lights.

On July 26, 1958, the light station was rammed by the freighter *Frontenac* as it was leaving the harbor. The freighter had swung wider than usual, putting it on a collision course with the station and it hit so hard that it pushed the crib and light station back about 20 feet (6 m), causing the light to tilt at a 15-degree angle. With the light knocked out of service, a temporary light was rigged. Rather than resurrect it, a new automated beacon was built in 1962 on the end of the new west breakwater further out. The contract for demolishing the tilting lighthouse was awarded to the American Demolition Company of Pittsburg, and they tore it down in 1961. The Fresnel lens was saved before the demolition and is on display at the Buffalo and Erie County Historical Society today.

Known Keepers: Howard Winship (1872–74), Myron Woolsey (1874–75), Dudley Rockwell (1875–77), James Stygall (1877–93), Amherst Gunn (1893–1901), James Matchett (1901–03), Edward Ahart (1903–05), Michael Fitzpatrick (1903–06), Howard Stram (1906–10), Captain William Gordon (1910–14), Thomas Holtan (1914–28), James Rawson (1929–44),

7 Buffalo Harbor South Entrance

As Buffalo Harbor continually grew in importance and size it added more breakwaters to protect its harbor. In the early 1900s the new south entrance to the harbor was finished, and a manned light station was placed on the south side of its entrance. Built in 1903, it consisted of a 27-foot (8.3 m) conical tower on a dressed stone and timber foundation. Its lantern was fitted with a smaller fourth-order Fresnel lens that displayed the light from a 40-foot (12.3 m) focal plane. The light was automated in 1935.

Today a modern pole tower displays a blinking red light from a 300 mm plastic optic. The fourth-order Fresnel lens was moved into Buffalo's old stone lighthouse when it was relit in 1988 for the Buffalo–Fort Erie Friendship Festival.

Known Keepers: Delos Hayden (1903–03), Edward Van Natta (1903–04), John Burns (1904–04), George Codding (1904–13).

8 Buffalo Intake Crib Light

In 1908 the Buffalo water intake crib was built in the Emerald Channel of the Niagara River to supply water to the city. Since this round red-roofed structure also marked the entrance to the Niagara River, a light was placed on it to mark its location. By 1920 this light replaced the Horseshoe Reef light to mark the river's entrance, as vessels used the Black Rock channel along the river's east side and no longer used the river to navigate into Buffalo Harbor.

Buffalo Harbor South Entrance Light

Buffalo Harbor South Entrance Light, circa 1945

9 Buffalo Lighthouse Supply Depot

Before the Buffalo Lighthouse Depot was built for the Tenth Lighthouse District, supplies and tools were stored at various lighthouses throughout the district, necessitating a greater supply of materials and tools than was actually needed. To centralize and economize, Congress appropriated $50,000 to built a depot at Buffalo some time before 1900.

Construction began in 1900 under the direction of Major Thomas W. Symons, who was in charge of the Tenth Lighthouse District at the time. The depot was built directly behind the 1833 stone lighthouse. Since the land was under water, the area was first surrounded by a retaining wall and then filled in and built up to an 8-foot (2.5 m) elevation above the water line. A thick concrete floor or pad was laid on this foundation to cover the whole area.

Two main buildings and several sheds were then built on the concrete. The sheds stored buoys and other supplies. One building was used by the district lighthouse inspector and to store supplies. The other served as a lamp and lens repair shop, a tool shop and engineers' quarters. Later, the depot was used to test diaphone foghorns.

The Tenth District encompassed the lights in lower Lake Erie, Lake Ontario and the St. Lawrence River. Three tenders (supply boats) serviced the area — the *Crocus,* the *Sundew* and the *Cherry.*

In 1935, $217,000 worth of improvements were made to the depot. They included adding 3.5 acres (1.4 h) to the reservation, replacing the decayed retaining wall, building a new slip for floating equipment, rebuilding the machine shop, putting an addition on the carpentry shop, adding a new dump scow, and providing adequate mooring for the district's three tenders.

In 1939 another tender, the *Maple,* was added to the station, and the lighthouse reservation was made part of the U.S. Coast Guard service. During the 1950s the depot was the Coast Guard's foghorn repair center. From 1921 until 1947 the Lighthouse Depot keeper was Sam P. Frisbee. He lived in one of the six houses on the reservation supplied for the keepers' use.

Buffalo Intake Crib Light

10 Buffalo Lightship

Although Congress decided to place a lightship off Buffalo in the early 1900s, this didn't happen until 1912. The Buffalo lightship was then positioned southwest of Buffalo Harbor, 13 miles (21 km) from Buffalo, midway between Point Abino on the Canadian side and Sturgeon Point on the American side. It marked the shallows that fingered beneath the lake surface off the tip of Point Abino, and warned of Waverly Shoal, even closer to Buffalo. Three lightships were used from 1912–18: *LV 82*, *LV 96* and *LV 98*.

LV 82 was a brand new ship, built of steel to withstand the harsh Great Lakes storms. About 80 feet (24.6 m) long and 21 feet (6.5 m) wide, it had a "whaleback" foredeck to repel high waves. It was built by the Racine-Truscott-Shell Lake Boat Company of Muskegon, Michigan, and cost $42,910. For the crew's comfort it had such facilities as leather-upholstered oak chairs, French plate-glass mirrors and a small library. The vessel was delivered to the Lighthouse Service on July 22, 1912, and then fitted with light equipment. The beacon consisted of three 300 mm oil lens lanterns grouped together, which were raised and lowered on a sliding band on the 30-foot (9.2 m) foremast. Each lens produced 170 candlepower. The foremast also carried the vessel's daymark, painted a bright "English vermillion."

LV 82 was equipped with two fog signals. A hand-powered fog bell was mounted onto the whaleback foredeck and a 6-inch (15-cm) steam whistle was mounted to the midship funnel or smoke stack. A jigger mast aft carried a steadying sail. It had two lifeboats — a small wooden sailboat and a gasoline powerboat. The vessel itself was powered by an inverted direct-acting high-pressure steam engine that used a 14-inch diameter (35 cm) cylinder to operate a five-foot cast-iron propeller.

It was anchored in position on August 3, 1912, by four 4-ton mushroom anchors fore and aft and a heavy chain secured to her keelson. *LV 82* was intended to serve temporarily until *LV 96* was built to take its place. Its six crewmembers were: Captain Hugh M. Williams, first mate Andrew Leahy, chief engineer Charles Butler, assistant engineer Cornelius Leahy (Andrew Leahy's brother), seaman William Jensen and cook Peter Mackey.

LV 82 had an unusual history. In the November 1913 storm that swept the Great Lakes, close to 250 souls and 19 vessels were lost. But Lake Erie lost only *LV 82* and its crew. While some of the ships belongings, such as life preservers marked "United States LV 82," a ship's galley drawer, and a board from the ship's cupboards with a hand-scrawled message, had washed ashore, it was at first unthinkable that the lightship could have sunk. But the tender *Crocus* and other search vessels could find no trace of it. The station was marked with a large acetylene gas buoy to finish out the season.

After the *Crocus*'s unsuccessful dredging attempts, the search was turned over to the U.S. Lake Survey office in Detroit. The next spring, the search ship *Surveyor* found *LV 82* almost two miles (3.2 km) off station in 62 feet (19 m) of water. After two commercial salvagers had tried to raise the steel hull filled with sand, the Reed Wrecking and Towing Co. finally raised and beached the vessel near Buffalo. After repairs, *LV 82* was refloated, towed to Detroit and refurbished as a relief lightship. It was updated with acetylene lamps, a 10-inch (25-cm) steam whistle and a submarine bell instead of its old fog bell.

Two mysteries arose from the incident. The first was the message on the board, which read, "Good-bye Nellie, ship is breaking

Buffalo Lightship LV 82

up fast. Williams." While *LV 82*'s captain was named Williams, the writing was not his – and his wife's name was Mary. However, since her husband had promised to leave her a message in case of disaster, she believed he had asked a crewmember to write it while he was at the helm, and that the writer had mistaken the name. Mrs. Joseph, wife of keeper Thomas Joseph of the Horseshoe Reef Lighthouse, more or less solved the issue by stating that Williams had called his wife "Nellie" when the couple stayed with the Josephs in 1912.

The second mystery was the disappearance of all six crewmen. While believed drowned with their bodies trapped inside the vessel, no bodies were found when divers searched the vessel in the spring of 1914. Almost a year after the wreck, the body of the chief engineer, Charles Butler, washed ashore on Buffalo's west side. In spite of having been in the water for 50 weeks and having traveled at least 13 miles (21 km), it was quite well preserved, with the upper body petrified. Butler's wife identified him by his coat, a cuff button, and a missing finger. Hope was re-ignited, but no more bodies appeared.

By the end of November 1913, the Tenth District Lighthouse Inspector had written off *LV 82* and recommended to Washington that the crew posts be discontinued. The Secretary of Commerce lined out the jobs and salaries for these crew positions – $900 a year for the captain, $840 for the chief engineer, $660 for the mate and the assistant engineer, $40 a month for the cook and $37.50 a month for the seaman.

Although it had been sunk for almost two years, *LV 82* served for another 28 years. From 1917 to 1925 it was a relief vessel for the Tenth Lighthouse District, and from 1926 to 1935 it marked the Eleven Foot Shoal in Lake Michigan. Declared surplus in 1936, it was sold to the Boston Massachusetts Veterans of Foreign Wars USS Constitution Post 3339 and docked for use as summer quarters for ex-Navy men. However, vandals sank it at dockside and its wreckage was finally raised for scrap.

After *LV 82* the station was marked in 1914 by *LV 96*, a new and larger light vessel also built by the Racine-Truscott-Shell Lake Boat Company. Although originally intended to mark the station permanently, it was in turn replaced by *LV 98* in 1915 and sent to Poe Reef off Michigan. *LV 98*, the sister ship to *LV 96*, marked the station until 1918, when a lightship was no longer necessary because the new Canadian lighthouse at Point Abino marked the shoals as of 1917.

Buffalo Old Main Lighthouse

11 Buffalo Old Main Lighthouse

Having reached a population of 10,000 in 1832, the village of Buffalo was incorporated as a city. In 1826 Congress had ordered the building of a new pier, lighthouse and icebreaker at Buffalo, and appropriated $2,500 for construction in 1827. However, the building took longer than anticipated, Congress had to appropriate another $12,512 in 1830 to finish the construction. When the 1,400-foot (430 m) stone seawall (known as a mole) was finally finished, the lighthouse was built at its lake end in 1832–33.

The new lighthouse was sturdily built. Its 44-foot (13.5 m) octagonal tapering tower was made of hand-hewn, buff-colored Queenston limestone. The walls at the 20-foot (6 m) base were 4 feet (1.2 m) thick. Its upper diameter was 12 feet (3.7 m) and the walls were 2 feet (0.6 m) thick. Fifty stone steps embedded into the walls spiraled up to the iron and glass lantern, supported by a stone cornice. An ornate wind vane and a copper lightning rod topped the lantern. A few narrow windows, each with 20 small panes, lit the staircase. The tower had a 9-foot (2.8 m) foundation of stone that was part of the pier. This basement held an oil vault that was later converted to a coal storage area,and eventually filled with concrete. The first keeper, William Jones, was quartered in the old keeper's house about 1,000 feet (300 m) from the lighthouse.

The lighting apparatus was originally 15 Argand-Lewis lamps that burned sperm whale oil and had 15 parabolic reflectors. In the 1850s, when lard oil was burned, the light was too weak to be a major harbor light, so in 1857 the original lantern was removed and additional stories were added to accommodate a fog bell and a new third-order Fresnel lens that displayed a 216-degree arc of illumination at a focal plane of 76 feet (23 m). The extra stories

consisted of a level of bluish limestone, a round iron pedestal room, and a new decagonal iron lantern. It was finished with a copper-plated, iron-ribbed dome topped with a ventilator ball and a 6-foot (1.2 m) lightning rod. This new tower was 68 feet (21 m) from base to ventilator ball. In 1900 the lighthouse tower was painted white to give it a more visible daymark.

In the 1800s the Buffalo light exhibited a fixed white light. By 1905 its light characteristic was altered to distinguish it from background city lights, and a new revolving lens was ordered from Chance Brothers and Company in England at a cost of $3,387, six times more than the head keeper's annual salary. The new lens flashed a powerful white light every five seconds. It was lit using a kerosene-vapor lamp and was magnified through four bull's-eye lenses surrounded by circles of prisms. Bearings in grooves helped

Chinaman's Light Tower and Buffalo Old Main Lighthouse, circa 1911

the lens turn easily. A weight and chain clockwork mechanism that had to be wound every seven hours powered the rotating lens.

In 1905 an iron oil-house was built nearby, and a pagoda-type tower nicknamed the "Chinaman's Light Tower," which was not a light at all, was built just 150 feet (46 m) from the lighthouse as a watchtower to catch illegal immigrants from Fort Erie, Ontario. When the "Old Stone" watchtower was torn down, its twentieth-century nickname was taken by the lighthouse, which served as a watchtower from 1914 to 1937.

By 1914 Buffalo Harbor was expanding to service the growing lake traffic, and its light was deemed insufficient because of its location. The lens was removed and installed in a massive light-house built behind the harbor breakwater in 1872. This break-water light now became Buffalo's main light. During the 1920s the creek bed was rechanneled to form a deep harbor. Among the tower's uses was the tracking and logging of waterfront activities — including bootlegging — during Prohibition, when it served briefly as a lookout station for rum-runners. In the 1950s it was used to store explosives.

Then in 1958 the Coast Guard decided to demolish it as part of harbor improvements. However public outcry saved it and the Buffalo and Erie Historical Society raised $3,000 to complete needed restoration so that it could host lighthouse tours. In 1961 the Coast Guard officially transferred responsibility and mainte-nance to the society, which soon placed an historical plaque at the lighthouse. In 1984 the lighthouse was included in the *National Register of Historic Places*.

In 1987 the Buffalo Lighthouse Association Incorporated, with the assistance of the U.S. Coast Guard, continued restoration of the lighthouse. A classic fourth-order Fresnel lens was installed, and the lighthouse was lit to help open the first Buffalo–Fort Erie Friendship Festival. In 1988 the open house at the lighthouse drew about six times the population of the Buffalo area when the first Buffalo light was built in 1818.

History has been preserved. This tower is the second-oldest structure in Buffalo and the oldest one still on its original site. It seems highly appropriate that this lighthouse is depicted on Buffalo's city seal.

Known Keepers: John Skaats (1818–27), William Jones (1827–34), Sylvanus Russel (1834–37), Captain Alexander Ramsdell (1837–55), James Anderson (1855–59), Shelton Cady (1859–61), Edward Lee (1861–71), Wallace Hill (1871–76), George Schooter (1876–79), Robert Taggart (1879–84), John Reed (1887–93), George Safe (1893–1905), John Safe (1905–14).

13 Buffalo Range Lights

In 1885 the U.S. government erected range lights to assist lum-ber-carrying vessels navigating the Niagara Channel in the Niagara River. The upper, or higher, range light was located on the shore where Niagara Street and Busti Avenue intersect today. It was an octagonal, slightly tapering tower with a simple gallery and lantern. The lower range light was placed on the Bird Island pier.

The lights were useful until 1929 when the Black Rock Channel, a shortcut between Tonawanda and Buffalo, was opened. Since the range lights were no longer functional — even though they were well-known markers for both mariners and motorists — they were razed in 1931.

14 Buffalo's First Lighthouse

In the late 1700s Joseph Ellicott, a Buffalo-area resident, pro-moted the development of the village of New Amsterdam where the mouth of the Buffalo Creek emptied into the Niagara River, while the village of Black Rock competed for development a short distance downstream on the Niagara River. While Black Rock pro-vided shelter from storms in its leeside, New Amsterdam could not, because of a huge sandbar that blocked the mouth of the creek. New Amsterdam was named Buffalo in 1805. Although it was only a frontier village in Indian territory consisting of a few cabins and people, Congress named it a port of entry in March 1805. By 1811 there was enough water traffic in the area to war-rant a lighthouse, but its erection was delayed due to the War of 1812 and then the burning of Buffalo in December 1813. Eventually, in 1853, Black Rock merged to become part of Buffalo as the waterfront developed.

After Buffalo's renewal, Judge Oliver Forward, collector of the port, was commissioned in 1817 to buy land for Buffalo's first light. He purchased land at the mouth of Buffalo Creek between the creek and the Niagara River for $350. Judge Forward paid for the land out of his own pocket and was later reimbursed. The lighthouse was finished in late 1817 or 1818, making it either the first (or possibly the second) lighthouse to be built on Lake Erie and the first (or second) true lighthouse to be built on the American side of the Great Lakes. (The other lighthouse was built at Erie, Pennsylvania, in 1818. Lack of actual documentation from this early period makes it an ongoing debate which of the two lighthouses was built first. Government reports show the two lights were both built in 1818 for a total cost of $15,500.)

12 Buffalo Outer Breakwater (North Entrance) Light

After the ramming and tilting of the Buffalo breakwater light in 1958, a new breakwater light was built in 1962 at the end of the newly constructed west breakwater. Being an automated light, it needed no keepers. It consisted of a white, 71-foot (21.5 m) steel tower operated by remote control. Its first level, a square base with porthole windows, sat on a steel pier. From this base a smaller octagonal tower rose the rest of the way. This light became Buffalo's main harbor entrance light. Today it supports a modern plastic beacon that operates on solar power.

Buffalo Outer Breakwater (North Entrance) Light

The Buffalo Lighthouse was a plain stone structure consisting of a separate conical 30-foot (9 m) rubble-stone tower topped by a birdcage-style lantern. A simple keeper's house (possibly a log cabin) was built close by. The first keeper was John E. Skoats.

However, the Port of Buffalo had no refuge during storm, and, because of the sandbar that blocked the mouth of Buffalo Creek, vessels had to anchor in the Niagara River and unload their cargo using smaller vessels. To continue its development as a harbor, local residents signed security for a $12,000 bond and mortgage loan from the government in 1819 for harbor improvements. The village wanted and needed a true harbor to be considered a western terminus for the Erie Canal, which was just being built. To this end, a pier was constructed in just 221 days, the sandbar was dredged, and Judge Forward was elected to Congress, where he could promote Buffalo's future. In 1823 the government decided to extend the canal to Buffalo, making it the western terminus, and the canal was finished in 1825.

The 1818 lighthouse was augmented in 1820 by a private light on the new stone pier. It was 46 feet (14 m) high and 20 feet (6 m) in diameter. This pier light assisted one regular user, a steamship the Indians had christened *Walk-in-the-Water*. Built in 1818, it was the first steamship on the Great Lakes and regularly ferried passengers between Buffalo and Detroit. In November 1821, while approaching Buffalo on its last trip of the season, it was beached just above the lighthouse. Its keel broke in two and its hull was shattered, but no lives were lost, thanks to the lighthouse keeper. One survivor, Mrs. Alanson Welton, recounted: "The boat struck the beach in a fortunate spot for the safety of the passengers and crew — near the lighthouse — and all were saved. The warm fireside we gathered around at the lighthouse was comforting to our chilled limbs and our hearts warmed with gratitude to god for deliverance from our peril."

As Buffalo developed, the 1818 lighthouse became obsolete. Some blamed the demise of the *Walk-in-the-Water* on the tower's inadequate light. The light's low height and weak beam, coupled with mists and the wood smoke of the growing population of Buffalo, frequently made it difficult to see. Mariners entering from the lake claimed the light was useless; mariners entering from the newly opened Erie Canal claimed they could not see it at all. A new light was definitely needed.

In 1826 Congress ordered the construction of a new pier, a new lighthouse, and an icebreaker to be built, and all to be finished by 1829. However it took longer than hoped. With the lighting of the new lighthouse in 1833, the old lighthouse was discontinued but the keepers continued to use the old keeper's house. In 1838 Congress decided to sell the 1818 lighthouse and give the proceeds to the Treasury. In the 1850s the structure was torn down to make way for new development.

Known Keeper: John E. Skoats (1818–).

15 Cattaraugus Lighthouse

In April 1884 Congress appropriated $3,000 for a light at the entrance of Cattaraugus Creek, on Lake Erie. In 1838 harbor improvements were advancing so rapidly that an inspector recommended that a temporary light be placed immediately at this location, as increased lake traffic would benefit from a man-made harbor as protection from Lake Erie storms. He estimated $1,000 for a temporary light, with the permanent building in mind.

"This frame may be built as to be converted for use in a second building. It is merely to be rough planked and weather boarded, and the lights to be raised and lowered by pullies. A dwelling for the tender, a story and half in height, built of brick, with out-houses, well of water, fence, etc. may be built under contract for $1,400. A lot may be purchased for $150, making a total of $1,550. This is allowing the dwelling to be 30 feet [9.2 m] by 25 feet [7.7 m]."

This lighthouse must have been built, because a Lighthouse Board Report from June 1858 stated that the beacon at Cattaraugus had been rebuilt. Little else has been uncovered about the history of this light.

Known Keepers: Captain Moses Fuller (1847–52), Josiah Haight (1852–56, 1857–59).

16 Cedar Point Lighthouse

It is unclear exactly when or where the first lighthouse was built at Sandusky. In 1837 Congress appropriated $2,500 to build a light near the entrance to Sandusky Bay. A government inspector surveyed the site and reported that placing a lantern on the keeper's house was a commendable idea. He also recommended that stone-filled cribwork be placed for 150 feet (46 m) along the shoreline in front of the lighthouse to provide permanent protection against erosion. The cribwork was estimated at $500 and was included in the appropriation.

An 1838 report to Congress noted that the materials furnished by the contractor were faultless and that the lighthouse was using 13 of its 15 lamps and reflectors. Also the lighthouse was "an important one, from its favorable location in … the spacious bay of Sandusky." While the exact site of this lighthouse is unknown, it could quite possibly be Cedar Point on the east side of Sandusky Bay. It is known that there was a lighthouse on this point prior to 1862, but its date is unknown.

Another known fact is that a lighthouse was built on the tip of Cedar Point in 1862 near the former Coast Guard station. This was a 1½-story limestone keeper's house from which a square tower ascended for another story in the center of its roof. Its light came from a previous light, removed

Cedar Point Lighthouse

years earlier. In 1901 it used a fifth-order lens that was 21 feet (6.5 m) above ground and produced a 12-mile (19.5 km) visibility. It also had a front range light that was built on a crib 200 yards (180 m) to the northeast. This light was a white shed building with a long paneled front from which its fixed red light was shown using a sixth-order lens. With its 8-mile (13 km) visibility it worked in conjunction with the rear light to provide a range inbound from Lake Erie to the "old Channel," which ran to Johnson's Island and then directly into Sandusky. When the lights were extinguished in 1909, the U.S. Lighthouse Service and then the Coast Guard continued to use the house for storage and maintenance.

In 1998 the lighthouse was recognized for its maritime heritage and placed on the *National Register of Historical Places*. By the new century it had been restored to its original splendor.

Early Cleveland East Breakwater Light

17 Cleveland (Old Land) Lighthouse

In March 1829 Congress appropriated $8,000 for a lighthouse at Cleveland, Lake Erie, between Sandusky and Grand River. This decision aroused controversy over the location for the lighthouse. Lake captains wanted a tower 25–30 feet (7–9 m) high at the end of the existing outer pier. Others wanted the lighthouse on higher elevation to protect it from storms and allow the lightkeeper to reach it in all weather. The latter group won out, and in July 1829 it was announced that the lighthouse would be built on the brow of the hill on old Water (West 9th) Street.

Levi Johnson built the lighthouse, a substantial conical 67-foot (20 m) rubble-stone tower with large twelve-paned rectangular windows ascending it. There was also a small rubble-stone keeper's house. The light was completed and lit in 1830. In 1838 its polygonal lantern used 11 lamps and 13 reflectors.

Inspections in 1837 and 1838 both noted that the pierhead light could adequately mark the harbor. However, the land light continued in service until 1854, when a fourth-order lens was placed in the pierhead light. Although an act of Congress re-established the land light in 1859, by 1867 it was in danger of toppling, as the city had removed ground from around its base to grade the streets. It was torn down in 1872 and replaced with a new lighthouse.

The new lighthouse, much taller, was 83 feet (25 m) high. Its fixed white light shone from a third-order Fresnel lens for a visibility of up to 20 miles (32 km) from a 157-foot (48 m) focal plane. The lamps used about 300 gallons (1200 litres) of mineral oil a year. Since it housed two keepers, the brick keeper's home was built as a duplex with doors on either side of the tower. The keeper was paid $560 a year and his assistant $450.

This new station, surrounded by a decorative black wrought-iron fence, cost $55,775, and its tower was the tallest building anywhere around. Its ornate Victorian-styled octagonal light tower was used until the main harbor light was established on the west pier, at which time the old tower was torn down. The cut sandstone from the old tower base was used in the foundation of the annex built onto the west side of the keeper's house to add space for two more lightkeepers (making the total four). The removed lantern was sent for use at the Braddock Point Lighthouse in Lake Ontario. The renovated keeper's house was used until 1927, when the keepers were lodged in two new dwellings. When the structure did not sell into private hands at auction, it was later razed in 1937 to make way for the Main Avenue High Level Bridge.

18 Cleveland East Breakwater Light

After a 4-mile (6.5 km) breakwater had been completed in 1897 in front of Cleveland's shoreline to form a breakwater on the east side of the city's harbor, lights were built to mark each end. The west end was called the Cleveland East Breakwater Light. Conflicting dates have it being built from in the 1890s to 1911, perhaps because there were at least two different lights. In 1901 it was a brown open-framework pyramidal tower that supported a buff-colored octagonal lantern. It displayed a fixed red-lens lantern from a 35-foot (10.7 m) focal plane. As well as marking the end of the breakwater, it worked with the Cleveland West Breakwater light to mark the entrance to the harbor between them.

At some time this pierhead light was replaced with a 25-foot (7.7 m) conical cast-iron tower that was anchored to the concrete pierhead. It had porthole watchroom windows below its round gallery. Its circular lantern had curved square panes of glass set on the diagonal into metal astragals, and originally housed a fifth-order Fresnel lens to shine its beam from a 31-foot (9.5 m) focal plane. It was automated in 1959. It still operates as an active aid to navigation today, but now has a 300 mm, solar-powered optic instead of its Fresnel lens. It has never had a keeper's house on the pier.

19 Cleveland East Entrance Light

After a 4-mile (6.5 km) breakwater was completed in 1897 in front of Cleveland Harbor's east side to protect it from Lake Erie storms, lights were placed at each of its extremities to mark the harbor entry. The light at the east end of this breakwater was called the Cleveland East Entry Light. It was a short iron skeletal tower with an enclosed top section. Today a modern red beacon it mounted on it.

20 Cleveland East Pierhead Light

Entry to the main harbor at Cleveland, Lake Erie, was protected in 1838 by two parallel piers that ran 600 feet (185 m) into the lake about 180 feet (55 m) apart. While the main light, high on the east shore of the river, marked the harbor and the outlet of the Ohio canal, a pierhead light was constructed at the end of the east pier in 1831 to more clearly mark the entrance into the harbor at night.

It was a 30-foot (9 m) skeletal wooden tower built in three successively smaller tiers. The first two were topped with a square platform area surrounded by a decorative iron railing. The top tier had

Cleveland East Breakwater Light

was moved to the upper position, and the fog bell was moved to the newly established West Breakwater light (which became the main harbor entrance light). Also, a boathouse was built in front of the east pierhead light for the keeper to store the rowboat that had serviced the West Breakwater light, as one keeper and his assistants tended both lights.

In 1901 the 30-foot (9 m) tower was a brown color and its fixed red light was displayed from a 37-foot (11.2 m) focal plane for 8.5 miles (13.8 km). Beyond its arc of illumination to the east, its light showed only dimly to warn vessels that they were too far inshore. This light no longer exists.

Known Keepers: Stephen Woolvertoon (1831–38), George Edwell (1838–41), Philo Tyler (1841–43), Richard Hussey (1843–45), Lewis Dibble (1845–49), James Foster (1849–53), Paul Chase (1853–57), James Farasey (1857–61), William Taylor (1861–65), George Mann (1865–67), Ernest Wilhelmy (1867–70), C. Coulter (1870–73), Oliver Perdue (1873–81), Fred Hatch (1885–1913), Charles Pier (1913–39), Samuel Crozier (1939–49).

a circular gallery that supported a circular lantern with trapezoid-shaped glass panes, of which every other one was inverted. A large three-tiered ventilator stack emerged from the dome on top of the lantern. The stairs to the lantern, which ran up through the center of the tower, were exposed to the elements. In 1838 an additional four lamps were added to the lantern. In 1854 a new lantern with a catadioptric fourth-order illuminating apparatus was installed in this tower to increase its light's candlepower and make it distinguishable from the city lights behind it. In 1860 the east pier was extended another 500 feet (152 m) into the lake, and a new tower was erected to mark its end.

The new pierhead was a tall slender tapering wooden octagonal structure with vertical boarding and large rectangular windows ascending it to provide interior light. It was topped with an octagonal gallery supported from underneath by carved wooden corbels and surrounded with an extremely decorative cast-iron railing. Its light was displayed from a plain decagonal iron lantern.

This tower had to be removed after an 1873 report that it was tilting to the east as a result of settling, and a new lighthouse was built in 1875 to replace it. The new tower was a much shorter square pyramidal one with a simple square gallery and a polygonal lantern. It displayed two sixth-order lenses, one on top of the other. The top one showed a white light and the bottom one a red light. A frame structure in front of this light had a fog bell with a striking mechanism. In 1882 mineral oil became the light's illuminant. In 1886 the white light was discontinued and the red light

21 Cleveland West Breakwater Lighthouse

A shore light marked Cleveland Harbor at the mouth of the Cuyahoga River until a new protective western breakwall was built in front of the harbor in 1884. The eastern end of this breakwater was marked with a temporary light consisting of a simple fixed white lamp and sixth-order optic mounted to its end.

The breakwater lighthouse was started in 1884. A large square timber crib was built at the end of the breakwater and its 29-foot (8.8 m) depth was filled with crushed stone. This foundation was left to settle and the following year it was topped with concrete to a height of 36 feet (11 m). An octagonal "oil cellar" was formed into the concrete pier so that the lighthouse would sit above it. Rather than building a new lighthouse, the octagonal cast-iron tower was moved from Genesee, New York. It had a decagonal lantern that housed a fourth-order lens and from a 36-foot (11 m) focal plane displayed alternating red and white flashes for about 10 miles (16 m).

Its first fog bell was one moved from the pier to the breakwater light. A boathouse was built on the west side of the tower. The keeper had quarters at the main keeper's house on shore, but a bunk was placed in the tower in case he was trapped by bad weather.

In 1889 Congress appropriated $5,200 to add a steam fog signal building to this light. Much controversy arose over its low-pitched sound, as many thought it would be inaudible. However, it was very successful and could be heard about 12 miles (19 km) out on the lake and almost all over Cleveland. In fact people complained so much that a deflector was placed behind the siren to direct the mooing sound of "the cow" to open water.

This light's first keeper was Captain Fred T. Hatch. He noticed that when shore smoke obscured the lighthouse the pier was a magnet for vessels and the rafts of logs being towed into the harbor. Over time their blows affected the crib's stability, and the lighthouse wavered so much in strong winds that the rotating mechanism would stop because the tower was so far off vertical. Hatch used to add extra weights to keep it turning and occasionally even had to rotate the lens by hand. Oak piles were driven into the southeast face of the crib to shore up the pier and fend off collisions.

Before becoming keeper, Hatch had been a crewman for Cleveland's lifesaving station and had been cited the U.S. Gold Medal of Honor for his lifesaving duties. Then in October 1890, as

Cleveland East Pierhead Light, circa 1880

Early Cleveland West Breakwater Lighthouse

stood 67 feet (20.4 m) above the water and had six levels. The main floor was the engine room and the kitchen, the second a bedroom, the third the supply room, and the fourth the watchroom with port-hole windows facing all directions. The fifth floor was the trimming room, where the daily routine included trimming wicks, cleaning the apparatus, and polishing chimneys. From here, a door led to the gallery, which was enclosed with an iron railing. The sixth level, the lantern, housed the lens and the clockworks from the previous light. It too had a door out to an exterior gallery from which windows could be cleaned. It may also have been around 1910 that this light received a diaphone fog signal.

All the Cleveland keepers and their families lived in the original keeper's house, which had been turned into four separate living quarters. Later, two duplexes were built for them. The keepers worked rotational duties except for stormy weather when they could not switch. Their duties included painting and maintaining the appearance of the structure and keeping the diesel engines in pristine condition so they could operate the air foghorns and run the generators to power the light and the radio beacon. The radio beacon had to be activated every half hour for ten minutes at the appropriate interval. In heavy weather it operated at three-minute intervals, dispatching the letter "C" in Morris code.

lightkeeper, he rushed to the aid of the crew of the disabled *Wahnapitie.* Fortunately all eight crewmembers jumped safely to the breakwater just as the vessel smashed on the breakwater rocks about 100 feet (30 m) from the lighthouse. Hatch managed to help the captain and two crewmen who were closest to him get to shelter in the lighthouse. He then tied a rope to himself and the lighthouse pier and rowed for the remaining crew, who were at the mercy of the waves on the breakwater. Before he reached them, three of them were washed into the lake out of his reach. He rescued the other two, one of whom was the captain's wife and ship's cook, Catherine Hazen. A huge wave swamped the small rowboat, and Hatch was only able to drag himself and Mrs. Hazen to the lighthouse. The harbor lifesaving crew rescued the other crewman and two tugs rescued two of the three washed into the lake. Miraculously only one person was lost. In 1891 keeper Hatch was awarded the gold bar from the U.S. Lifesaving Service for his "second service" of heroism.

Changes occurred at the station over time. Around 1910 the old west breakwater tower was demolished and replaced by another tower at the end of an extension built onto the breakwater. It was a wide slightly conical white structure with many large windows up its tower for interior light in the keeper's quarters. The tower

In a newspaper interview in 1949, keeper Crozier said he liked his job because there was no danger whatever of getting hit by an automobile. But he did almost get hit by something else! One stormy November night during a strong northwest wind, noticing that the East Breakwater light was out, he rowed across and hung a lantern to mark the light. Then as he stepped into the boat to return, a wall of water poured over the breakwater. Soaked through, he proceeded back toward the West Breakwater light. When he was out in the channel, he looked over his shoulder through the blinding snow and saw a 600-foot (185 m) outbound freighter about 100 feet (30 m) away, heading straight for him. By

Cleveland West Breakwater and East Breakwater Lighthouses

bearing down on the oars he was narrowly able to get to the life-saving station at the river mouth and out of the freighter's way. He had to wait until morning to return to the lighthouse.

The Cleveland West Breakwater light is automated today, and its alternating red and white light can be seen much further. Its white flash has a visibility of some 24 miles (38 km) and its red flash has a range of about 19 miles (30 km). Although its keepers are long gone, the light remains as a beacon, welcoming mariners into the Cleveland harbor.

Known Keepers: George Tower (1885–88), Fred Hatch (1888–90), Louis Walrose (1891), Charles E Perry (–1920–), Samuel Crozier (1939–49).

22 Cleveland West Pierhead Light

In 1901 a new light was established at the outer end of the newly completed west pier, which had been constructed 65 feet (20 m) west of the old west pier. The light was a cylindrical tower covered in corrugated iron, painted white and topped with a decagonal lantern and a circular gallery. From a 52-foot (16 m) focal plane it used a sixth-order lens to display its fixed white light for 13 miles (21 km). This light no longer exists.

23 Clinton River Light

In 1836 the Committee on Commerce resolved to make appropriation to improve the harbor at the mouth of the Clinton River on Lake St. Clair by removing the sand bar at this location. *Bill 380*, June 29, 1838, indicates that a lighthouse was proposed for the mouth of the Clinton River on Lake St. Clair.

However, Charles T. Platt reported back to Congress in 1838 after an on-site inspection that a light at this location was too far off-route to assist vessels passing through Lake St. Clair to the upper lakes. In his opinion a light here would only benefit local commerce, which was quite limited, and the expense of building a lighthouse at this time at this location could therefore not be justified. He also noted the difficulty of building a lighthouse here because of the marshy land at the river mouth, and so he recommended a floating light. However, since there was only a 6-foot (1.8 m) water depth when the lake level was high, he recommended the smallest class of light vessel if one was to be used. He added that commerce might increase when the State canal united with the Clinton River and that a lighthouse could still be built at the mouth of the river if this happened.

Bill 335, April 12, 1844 stated $3,000 for a lighthouse to be built at Clinton River but then *Bill 636*, Jan 27, 1847 again stated $3,000 for a lighthouse at Clinton River. Whether this lighthouse was ever built is still uncertain. However, there are indications that the light was built in 1847 (charted under the name of Belvidere Light) because older charts do indicate that there was a beacon at this location.

Conneaut West Pier Light

24 Conneaut East Pierhead Light

While the west pierhead light at Conneaut was built in 1835, it is unclear when the east pierhead light was built or removed. It was not there during the 1838 government inspection. However, another source refers to pier lights from 1835 to 1885 and range lights in 1906. The one certain fact is that one did exist for some period of time and it had a continuous line of keepers.

Known Keepers: Walter Woodward (1835–41), Ezra Dibble (1841–46), James Gregg (1846–49), Ephraim Capron (1849–53), Whitney Grant (1853–61), Ephraim Capron (1861–69), George Miller (1869–85), John Starkey (1885–94), Edward Pfister (1894–1936), Joseph Lasko (1936–50), Thomas Baker (1950–65).

Conneaut West Breakwater Light, circa 1918

25 Conneaut West Breakwater and Range Lights

Congress appropriated $2,048 to build a beacon light on the pier at the Conneaut River, Lake Erie, in 1834. In an 1838 report, the inspector recommended that Winslow Lewis lamps be acquired, as the four supplied lamps were insufficient. He also proposed building a keeper's house for $1,000 to save the government $75 a year for renting a house for the keeper. It was to be 1½ stories high, built of stone or brick, have a bedroom and a larder on the first floor — and a good cellar. The inspector added that this was an important and safe harbor, the piers would soon need rebuilding, and stone should be used instead of wood. A keeper's house was finally built in 1873, but it was made of wood; it was remodelled in 1905 to become a duplex for the two keepers and their families.

The first pierhead light, at the end of the west pier, lasted from 1835 to 1885, when a light tower was built adjacent to the keeper's house. In 1897 another pier light was built to form range lights. In 1901 the front range light, 33.5 feet (10.2 m) from the outer end of the west pier, was a white wooden square pyramidal tower that used a fifth-order lens to produce a fixed white light from a 35-foot (10.6 m) focal plane for a visibility of about 12 miles (19 km). The rear light, a dark red square pyramidal wood tower, was 815 feet (248 m) behind the front one, and used a fifth-order lens to display a fixed red light for 10 miles (16 km).

Conneaut West Breakwater Light, circa 1949

Conneaut West Breakwater Light

While the rear range light disappeared, the front one was rebuilt in 1918 and again in 1936, when the existing 60-foot (18.3 m) steel tower was built on a concrete crib at the end of the west breakwater. This light was based on a prototype of a "remote control pierhead station for the Great Lakes," which had been designed in 1934. Its lantern was removed in 1949. The light was automated in 1971–72 and today uses a 375 mm optic from an 80-foot (24.4 m) focal plane. Its daymark is a black mid-band and a black gallery on an otherwise white tower. The light is still an active aid to navigation today, but the keeper's house is privately owned. The light is listed on the *National Register of Historic Places*.

26 Cunningham Creek Lighthouse

During the 1800s the area around the mouth of Cunningham Creek along the lower shores of Lake Erie between Fairport and Ashtabula developed a shipbuilding industry as well as blast furnaces to make iron. Since the creek was too small to provide anchorage, a man-made harbor was planned between parallel piers extending from the shore, with a breakwater parallel to the shore to protect it from lake storms. Only the 475-foot (145 m) west pier was constructed, however. It was made of cribs placed about 30 feet (9 m) apart so that the pier would not block water flow, and then was planked on top to form a pier.

While money for a pierhead light was requested in 1833, it was not appropriated until July 1834, and the light, a simple wooden one without stairs or gallery, was built between August and December. The source of light was a little chandelier from which three bucket lamps were hung; it was hoisted from the bottom of the tower to the lantern by means of a rope and pulley. When a keeper was finally appointed, the light was lit and first displayed its fixed light on October 3, 1835.

The government instructed the keeper to live in the keeper's house and to tend the light himself, but no residence had been built. After some difficulty, he managed to rent one small room for himself and his family in the house closest to the light. In March 1836 the government purchased one acre (0.4 hectares) of land close to the pier from Colonel Robert Harper and Ethan Judson for $200. A building contract for the 1½-story keeper's house was awarded to Samuel D. Rounds and Hubbard A. Smith for $840. Also that year the lamps burned 49 gallons (206 l) of whale oil, the

foundation for the keeper's house was finished and secured, and it was reported that the tower was "deteriorating badly," and the house was finished later.

By 1837 the tower was "leaking and wetting the lamps" every time it rained. The eastern pier was started in this year. However, no appropriations were made to complete the pier or to repair the existing pier or the lighthouse over the next few years.

In 1843 another lamp was added and a simple gallery built around the top of the tower. The lamps burned 67 gallons (281 l) of oil that year and 94 gallons (395 l) in 1844. A recommendation was made to discontinue the light in 1844 and again in 1845, especially since only 22 gallons (92 l) of oil were used for all of 1845, suggesting that the light was seldom lit. Congress finally decided in March 1847 that the light would be discontinued as of the end of that month. The lamps were removed to be used elsewhere but everything else remained.

The government allowed Joel R. Norton Jr., the son of a local shipbuilder, to live in the keeper's house free of charge in exchange for maintaining it. Then the local shipbuilders asked Norton to maintain the old lighthouse on the end of the pier for them. He improvised candle lamps and tended the light on the dock for the next 16 years. After the last ship was built and launched in 1863, the light was no longer maintained. While the pier and tower remained for many years, by the late 1890s Lake Erie had finally claimed them. With no shipbuilding or iron ore, the once flourishing town dwindled.

The 1912 government inspection reported that only wooden piles of the government dock remained, and that the keeper's house, still occupied by Norton, who was then blind, was in poor condition. The document recommended that Norton be allowed to live out his days in the house and the government approved this. After he died in September 1917, his son Frank continued to live in the house. On May 22, 1926, an official government transfer was made to the heirs of Joel Norton. At an unknown date the house was moved about half a mile (0.8 k) west on Lake Shore Blvd. While it still exists today, there is no longer a light to mark the mouth of Cunningham Creek.

Known Keepers: Captain Ephraim Shaler (1835–1841), Dr. Anson Hotchkiss (1841–1843), John Cunningham (1843–1846), Henry Richardson (1846–1847). Joel R. Norton Jr. (1847–1863).

Detroit River (Bar Point) Lighthouse

27 Detroit River (Bar Point) Lighthouse

Vessels traveling to or from Lake Erie and Lake Huron had to negotiate Bar Point Shoal to enter or leave the mouth of the Detroit River. After many vessels were grounded on the shoal in 1872, the Canadian government placed a lightship at the end of it in 1875 to mark the hazardous turning point. However, its light was so dim that it was easily confused with lights from other vessels and with Canadian and American onshore lights. Then, in 1882–83, Congress appropriated $60,000 to build a light to clearly mark the area. The Canadian-American boundary line was even moved to accommodate American jurisdiction.

The U.S. Army Corps of Engineers started construction in 1884. A timber crib, built in Amherstburg, Ontario, was towed to the site and sunk in 22 feet (6.8 m) of water. It took more than two months to fill the huge crib with concrete. Then a cut-granite, stone-block pier was mounted on the crib. Its 15-foot (4.6 m) height included 4 feet (1.2 m) below water level. Its elongated hexagonal shape was pointed at both ends to help deflect water and ice floes. When finished in November 1884, uneven settlement of the crib and pier left the structure more than a foot out of level. In hopes of correcting this, 550 tons (541 T) of rubble stone was set on the pier, mostly on the higher side, and the structure was left until spring. This solution worked, and by spring the pier was level to build on.

A 49-foot (15 m) cast-iron plate, "spark plug" style tower was placed at one end of the pier. It had a base 22 feet (6.8 m) in diameter that tapered to an 18-foot (5.5 m) diameter just under the gallery. A smaller, circular watchroom, with porthole windows, was placed in the center of the gallery and was topped with a decagonal lantern that also had its own small gallery. The lantern housed a fourth-order lens. The light, with a focal plane of 55 feet (17 m) and 62,000 candlepower, had a 25-mile (40 km) visibility when first lit on August 20, 1885. The exterior of the tower was painted white on the bottom and black on the top. This light is similar to the Harbor Beach Light, also built in 1885, except that the Harbor Beach Light is all white.

Attached to the tower and built on the other end of the pier was a fog signal and radio beacon building. The foghorn sounded two long blasts every three minutes. Beyond the fog building was a derrick for loading and unloading supplies at the end of the pier. The original appropriation was too low and it took another $18,000 to complete the station, making a total cost of $78,000.

At one time the station had four keepers, two on and two off. Later, the station had five keepers, with three living in the tower and two on shore. Their two-week tour of duty included eight-hour shifts when they made sure the generators ran smoothly, monitored radio channels, and relayed weather information. As space was limited to the minimal walking area around the building, between shifts they played cards, darts, and bumper pool, read, wrote letters home, or listened to the radio. All keepers agreed that the station, nicknamed "the Rock," was cold in March, hot in July, and lonely all year round.

During Prohibition the keepers had a little more company as the light was a rendezvous point for rum-runners bringing bootlegged booze from Amherstburg on the Canadian side to Toledo, Monroe or Sandusky on the American side.

In fog or inclement weather the lighthouse has frequently had boats collide with it. Its biggest hit was from the M/V *Buffalo*, a 635-foot (195 m) lake freighter, traveling 11–12 mph (17–19 kph), standard river speed, downstream in the Detroit River into Lake Erie on December 12, 1997. Since there was no inclement weather, the *Buffalo* was traveling visually. However, the pilot missed his turning point because of a buildup of ice on the lantern that dimmed the light and made it appear farther away than it was. The *Buffalo* struck the station almost dead-on while trying to maneuver a hard port turn, and tore a 25-foot (7.6 m) gash across the bow. While damage to the freighter was major (about $1.1 million), damage to the station was limited to only cracks in the concrete and granite foundation. The lighthouse survived.

The light was automated in 1979 and given solar panels to power the station. The light has changed characteristics over the years. In 1909 the lens had a single fixed panel of 180 degrees and six bull's-eye panels of 30 degrees, providing a fixed light of 30 seconds followed by six flashes at five-second intervals, with the whole lens rotating once every minute. The present lens has six panels of 60 degrees, with three bull's-eye panels each separated from the other by a 60 degree blind panel. It flashes twice at 6-second intervals and has a 10-mile (16 km) visibility.

The light is still active and is maintained by the U.S. Coast Guard. It is not accessible to the public but may be viewed from the water by boat.

Known Keepers: Charles Northup (1885–86), Richard Oldrey (1887–90), Charles Northup (1893–98), Joseph Crawford (1898–1902), Enoch Scribner (1902–12), Horace Walts (1912–16), Walter Marshall (1916–19), Harry Kcondway (1919–21), John Sweet (1926–33), William Small (1933–38), Eli Martin (1938–39).

Dunkirk Lighthouse

28 **Dunkirk Lighthouse**

This lighthouse, also known as the Point Gratiot Lighthouse, was commissioned in 1826 and built in 1827 at Point Gratiot on a bluff above the harbor. Its light worked with a pierhead beacon to guide vessels safely into Dunkirk Harbor on the south shore of Lake Erie. In 1857 it was refitted with a $10,000 imported, third-order Fresnel lens that had a 17-mile (27 km) visibility and was reportedly the most prominent light on Lake Erie's south shore. The light flashed once every 90 seconds.

Both the tower and the single-story keeper's house were built of bricks made from clay from the shores of Dunkirk Harbor. Old-timers remember the first lighthouse as having a round tapered tower. Its lantern was made by the local blacksmith, Adam Fink. The light had 13 lamps and reflectors and was fueled by whale oil, kerosene, and then acetylene gas. In 1874 the tower was reported to be in precarious condition.

In 1875 a new tower and keeper's house were built. The tower is 61.2 feet tall (18.7 m) from base to ventilator ball. Its focal plane is 82 feet (25 m). Inside is an ornate open-patterned, spiral, cast-iron staircase leads up to the decagonal lantern. All but two of the ten sides are glazed so that the light may be seen on all water surrounding the point. The third-order Fresnel lens was transferred from the old tower to the new one. Today the light is automated, flashing on for 6 seconds and off for 4 seconds.

Early Dunkirk Lighthouse

The newly built tower was circular, made from blocks of local siltstone. Some time later, it was squared on the outside to make it more compatible with the architectural style of the keeper's house. The bottom third of the tower is natural unpainted limestone, while the top two-thirds are painted white. The dome and pedestal room below the lantern are red.

Ten ornate, brass, lion-head gargoyle spouts around the lantern roof once helped drain away any condensation that formed on the inside of the dome of the lantern. Some suggest that they were shaped as gargoyles to ward off evil. (The only other lights on the Great Lakes that have these are the Canadian imperial towers.) The pedestal room is fitted with round brass vents to help ventilation, much like a car defroster, according to curator Harold Lawson. This room also stored sand to douse oil fires, a full water barrel, and pails to douse wood fires, shovels and other maintenance equipment. The keeper would often spend the night on a small cot below this room while on duty to save himself much arduous stair-climbing. Cupboards fitted with curved, wooden doors were built into the corners in spaces between the old round tower and the square one that was built around it. They may be located where windows in the round tower would have been.

A covered passage connects the tower to the keeper's residence, a large two-story, red brick house in "stick" style, a variation of the Gothic Revival

Style that flourished after the Civil War. Given its date, this is the only example of such architecture in Dunkirk. Although it is a brick building, several features definitely mark it as "stick" style: the delicate, ornamental cross-bracing under the eaves; the dormers, which rise out of the brick walls and through the eaves on both sides of the house; and the wooden finials (tiny spires) rising from the house and dormer gables. The small porch on the south side was added sometime after 1892. The doors and windows all have flat stone lintels and sills, and their white trim presents a beautiful contrast to the red brick.

The original fog signal was cannon fire. The army would send a sergeant and two operators to fire the cannon every five minutes during foggy periods. This was found to be very expensive, and electric bells were later installed.

The Dunkirk lighthouse is well maintained. The bluff in front of it is lined with mature trees. The property used to be more extensive, with a road running to the north of the trees but it has eroded into the lake. Erosion continues to eat away at the bluff. The lighthouse is now part of the Dunkirk Historical Lighthouse and Veterans Park Museum. The park entrance is marked by a unique, bottle-shaped light that once was one of the Buffalo Harbor Bottle Lights.

The keeper's house is now a museum. Displays in five of the rooms commemorate the five service branches (Coast Guard, Marine Corp, Navy, Army, and Air Force). The other rooms have displays of maritime history and a lighthouse keeper's kitchen, dining room and parlor. Other displays on the grounds include a 40-foot (12.3 m) lighthouse buoy tender, a rescue boat, assorted anchors, a lightkeeper's rescue boat, lighthouse lenses and a 1923 U.S. Lighthouse Service bell.

A special, annual event is the Victorian Christmas (American Thanksgiving to New Years), when the lighthouse is splendidly decorated in Victorian style. In the "parlor" is a decorated tree with would-be toys and gifts underneath. This Victorian setting can be visited on its own or as part of a bus tour.

Curator Lawson enjoys telling tales of the resident ghost, "Charlie." In the top of the lighthouse is a weather computer maintained by the NOAA Weather Service. Servicemen who came to repair the computer occasionally "slept over" and would hear footsteps at night. Once, when Harold spoke of the resident ghost, one man sank to the floor with his knees up to his chest. He froze in this position and had to be carried down from the top of the lighthouse like a "frozen, human statue."

On another occasion, when visitors were climbing the tower, Lawson called up, "Charlie are you there?" A tourist asked, "Who's Charlie?" When the cura-

Dunkirk Lighthouse's third-order Fresnel lens

tor explained, the tourist hurriedly retraced her footsteps, and exited the building. Is there really a ghost? No one has actually seen it. But every morning, the curator and his wife have to straighten the many pictures in the keeper's house. Do these pictures fall crooked on their own, or is "Charlie" playing practical jokes?

A gift shop is located in the old barn that was built in 1929 to replace the original barn that burnt in 1925.

Known Keepers: Walter Smith (1827–31), Abraham Day (1831–41), Joseph Hall (1841–45), John Cassidy (1845–49), Wilber Gifford (1849–53), John Cassidy (1853–61), Henry Severance (1861–69), Charles Harrison (1869–70), Jefferson Richardson (1870–72), Henry Severance (1872), Byron Rathbun (1872–73), B. Averill (1873–84), Robert Taggart (1884–87), Samuel Penfield (1887), Peter Dempsey (1889–1902), John McDonough (1902–28), Arnold Francis (1928–50), William Gannon (1950–56).

29 Dunkirk Old Pierhead

In 1827 Congress appropriated $3,000 for a breakwater at Dunkirk Harbor and a beacon light to mark the pierhead's lake end. The light was built in 1928–29, and allowed mariners to use the shore and pier lights as range lights to safely come into the harbor. The first pier light was a short octagonal tapering brick tower with a flared brick cornice to support its octagonal gallery. The gallery was surrounded with an iron pipe railing and had a polygonal lantern. The base of the tower had pedimented windows and door, while the watchroom had porthole windows. An elevated wooden catwalk ran from the lighthouse to the shore for the keeper's safety. The keeper at the shore or main light also serviced this pierhead light.

Dunkirk Old Pierhead Light

In 1895 the tower was destroyed by ice. Its replacement was a square pyramidal tower with narrow clapboarding, a square gallery, and a polygonal lantern. At first it burned kerosene. As well as filling the lamps, the keeper had to polish soot off the lens daily and cover it with a large linen sheet by day to keep lint, which might distort the light, off the glass and keep sunlight from magnifying through the prisms. The government sent a new supply of linen cloths each spring, and the old ones were usefully turned into sheets, pillowcases, and clothing by the keeper's wife.

In stormy weather the keeper had to use the catwalk to reach the light, dodging the waves that washed over the breakwater. It served its purpose, for no keeper was ever washed into the lake at this station — although the beacon light was sometimes left unlit. This pierhead light was later replaced with a modern beacon placed on a pole.

30 Erie Land Lighthouse

Lake Erie, the shallowest of the Great Lakes, was often treacherous for early mariners, but Erie Bay was a natural protective harbor. In the early 1800s, recommendations, including one from Commodore Perry, urged Congress to build a lighthouse at Erie to mark the bay entrance. In 1812 the government purchased land for a light from John Kelso. The building contract was given to Beall and Thaxter of Massachusetts for $3,000. The lighthouse sat on a high hill overlooking the narrow channel into the bay. Winslow Lewis outfitted the lantern. While some sources claim the light was operational earlier, government sources show that it was first lit by John Bone, the first keeper, on November 6, 1818. His annual salary was $300.

Erie Land Lighthouse

A lighthouse was also built in Buffalo in 1818. Government records show that the two lighthouses cost $15,500 but do not say which was built first. Therefore both lights are honored as the first true lighthouses on the American side of the Great Lakes.

Little is known about the earliest light because it was razed and no known pictures of it remain. However, between 1997 and 2000 archaeologists uncovered its site about 200 yards (183 m) west of the 1867 Erie Land Light. The lighthouse was likely a square 20-foot (6 m) stone tower built on an elliptical-shaped, 4-foot-thick (1.2 m) foundation of crushed stone, mortar and lime. It was known as the Presque Isle Light. Settling of the foundation necessitated its replacement in 1858.

The fact that the new 56-foot (17 m) round tower was built of "Milwaukee" brick made Erie citizens indignant that imported brick was used instead of supporting the local brick industry. This tower also started to sink and was again replaced in 1867.

However, before the new tower was built, borings were taken. As quicksand was discovered far below the old tower, the third tower was built at a new location 200 feet (61 m) to the east on a substantial 20-foot-thick (6 m) foundation of timbers, limestone, cement and coursed stone. The 49-foot (15 m) circular, unpainted sandstone tower tapers gently as it ascends. There are double galleries: the large one surrounds the base of the lantern and the top of the tower; the small one surrounds the lantern glass. The decagonal lantern is topped with a white fluted dome and ventilator ball. The tower had a brick lining. A work/oil room, also built of sandstone, was attached to the base of the tower. The lantern once housed a third-order Fresnel lens with a visibility of up to 17 miles (27 km). The light burned sperm oil, lard oil, and then mineral oil. A new two-story lightkeeper's house was also built. Described as "salt box" architectural style, the house was separate from the tower.

Around 1870, plans were drawn up to place a lighthouse on the peninsula. As this new light was to be called the Presque Isle Light, the older light was renamed the Erie Light. Today it is known as the Erie Land Light.

In 1881, deeming the Erie Land Light unnecessary since there was a new one, the government discontinued it and sold the property. After much public outcry, they repurchased it and relit it in 1885. On December 26, 1899, the light was extinguished for good. In 1901 its Fresnel lens was transferred to the Marblehead Light in Ohio, and its lantern was removed.

In 1912 the town of Erie assigned the property around the lighthouse for park purposes. Then in 1934 the government gave the lighthouse and property to the town. In 1976, as part of the national bicentennial, funding was acquired to fix up the property and appoint a caretaker. In 1990 the lighthouse was refitted with a wooden replica of its lantern and was dedicated as a Pennsylvania landmark. On December 26, 1999, exactly 100 years to the day after it was extinguished, the lighthouse was symbolically relit to celebrate its history.

In 2003 the replica lantern was severely damaged in a lake storm. Grants of $400,000 for lighthouse restoration were collected from the Pennsylvania Historical and Museum Commission and the Pennsylvania Department of Transport. Fiske and Sons of Erie were contracted to restore the interior stairs and brickwork and clean the outside stone walls. A brand new 6,300-pound (2850 kg) decagonal copper lantern was hoisted to the top of the tower to replace the damaged replica. On June 19, 2004, a relighting ceremony sponsored by the Western Pennsylvania–Erie Port Authority celebrated the rejuvenation of one of America's most historic landmarks.

Known Keepers: Captain John Bone (1819–33), Samuel Foster (1833–33), Robert Kincaid (1833–41), Griffith Hinton (1841–45), Eli Webster (1845–50), Roderick Petlon (1850–50), James Miles (1850–53), Isabel Miles (1853–54), John Graham (1854–58), James Fleming (1858–59), A. Landen (1859–61), John Goalding (1861–64), George Demond (1864–71), A. Fargo (1871–81), George Miller (1885–99).

31 Erie North Pierhead Lighthouse

In 1830 Congress appropriated $2,500 to built a pierhead light to mark the entrance of the harbor into Erie, on Lake Erie. Two subsequent appropriations were made, one in 1832 and a second in 1837, each for $674 to complete the light. In 1830 a square white wooden pierhead light was built at the end of the North Channel pier. A fog bell and a foghorn were later added. The keeper's house was built on shore nearby.

Erie North Pierhead Light

Fairport Harbor East Pierhead Light

A notice to mariners in the *Kingston Daily News* on November 9, 1854, stated that a new illuminating apparatus (sixth-order cata-dioptric with an 11-mile (18 km) visibility) would be in place in the beacon light on the eastern extremity of the North Channel pier at Erie, Pennsylvania, by August 30, 1855.

In 1857 the tower was swept off the pier when a sailing ship ran into it. It was rebuilt in 1858 of wrought iron and later encased in riveted iron plates for added protection from the elements. The 34-foot (10.5 m) tower was square, rising in a pyramidal style for about 20 feet (6 m) and then continuing straight up for another 8 feet (2.5 m). It supported a hexagonal lantern with a ventilator dome and a lightning rod. Originally the lantern housed a new fourth-order Fresnel lens that displayed its light from a 42-foot (13 m) focal plane.

Changes occurred at the light over the years. In 1882 the tower was moved 190 feet (58 m), probably after a pier extension. In 1940 it was moved 509 feet (155 m) and was automated. Then in 1995 the Fresnel lens was replaced with a solar-powered modern lens and put on display at the Erie Maritime Museum. At some point it lost its fog bell and later its foghorn, and the keeper's house was incorporated into a lifesaving station. The light is still an active aid to navigation. Its daymark is a white tower banded with black in the middle and a black gallery and lantern.

Known Keepers: Samuel Foster (1835–37), William Kane (1837–41), Benjamin Fleming (1841–45), Leonard Vaughan (1845–50), Ruben Field (1850), John Hess (1850–53), William Downs (1853–54), Leonard Vaughan (1854–61), George Bona (1861–63), R. Burke (1863–69), Frank Henry (1869–84), Charles Coyle (1885–89), Robert Hunter (1890–1901), Thomas Wilkins (1901–09), Robert Allen (1909–28), Walter Korwek (1928–53).

32 Fairport Harbor East Pierhead Lights

In December 1830 Congress appropriated $1,800 to erect a beacon light on the pier at Grand River, Lake Erie. Then in 1832 and again in 1834 it appropriated another $1,456 to complete that beacon light. It is unclear when the light was actually finished. However, in 1838 there was a white octagonal wooden tower at the end of the east pier, which ran 600 feet (185 m) into the lake. This beacon was used as a front range light at night with the main light as the rear range so that vessels could avoid hitting the end of the west pier, which ran 900 feet (275 m) out into the lake parallel to the east pier and about 200 feet (60 m) from it. The light used four lamps and the harbor accommodated 100 vessels.

In 1875 this light was replaced by a square wooden pyramidal light that also stood at the end of the east pier. It was black below and white above and was surmounted with a black lantern to form a unique daymark.

In 1901 Fairport's east pier had range lights. The front light, located 20 feet (6 m) from the pier's outer end, was a square wooden 28-foot (8.5 m) pyramidal tower that was brown below and white above. It used a sixth-order lens to display a fixed white tower for 12 miles (19.4 km). An elevated walkway along the pier connected it to shore. The rear range light near the inner end of the east pier was a square red pyramidal one built with an open wooden framework and topped with a square lantern. From a 55-foot (16.8 m) focal plane it displayed a fixed red lens-lantern light. These lights later disappeared.

33 Fairport Harbor Old Main Lighthouse

The first lighthouse at Fairport Harbor (formally known as Grand River) on Lake Erie was a conical tower built in 1825 by Jonathan Goldsmith, a well-known Western Reserve architect, at a cost of $5,032 for the tower and the keeper's dwelling. It marked safe entry into Fairport Harbor. This station served as a terminal for the "underground railway" before the Civil War and helped many escaping slaves reach safety in Canada.

A lighthouse commission inspection in 1868 revealed the error of building on an inadequate foundation, which had caused the tower and the keeper's dwelling to be in a hazardous condition. Congress approved $30,000 for the replacement lighthouse in the spring of 1869. A temporary tower was built in late 1869 to allow for removal of the old tower while continuing to supply a beacon. Work on the new tower began in the spring of 1870 on suitable

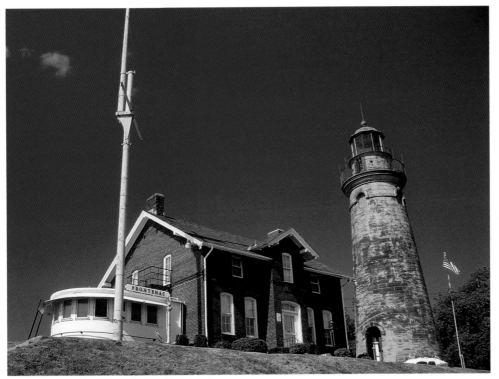

Fairport Harbor Old Main Lighthouse

rific view of village and lake. This room has five round ventilators to control condensation and provide draft for the lamps. Eight ladder steps lead up into the lantern, which is closed to visitors. The original third-order Fresnel lens is displayed in the lighthouse museum. Its lamp burned whale oil (later kerosene) and, with its parabolic reflector (focal point of 102 feet [31 m] above lake level), had a visibility of 17.5 miles (28 km). A passageway once connected the house and tower so that the keeper could stay indoors.

In the early 1900s the light was considered obsolete because it had no fog signal or radio beacon. It was discontinued in June 1925. The new pierhead light on the west breakwater was a light and fog station combined. The government's plan to raze the old tower and use the house for U.S. Coast Guard accommodations aroused such intense public outcry that the government

foundations of timber and dressed stone. Work was suspended when it was half-finished, but resumed in 1871. The light was first lit on August 11, 1871, and the red-brick, two-story keeper's house was completed on October 20, 1871, to a total cost of $28,838.

The conical tower of gray-brown Berea sandstone is 69 feet (21 m) tall, and resembles the Erie Land Lighthouse in both style and materials. It is about five stories high, including two circular galleries with iron railings and a cylindrical pedestal room beneath the lantern. The decagonal lantern, capped by a copper dome and ventilator ball, has long single-glass panels on seven of its ten sides and produced a 216-degree arc of illumination. The tower flares out at the top to support the lower, larger gallery. Beneath this gallery and around the top of the tower is a protruding sandstone ring that connects four arched windows.

The tower walls are 3 feet (0.9 m) thick, as can be seen at the first level window. The 68 open-ironwork steps spiral up to the room below the lantern and the lower gallery, which offers a ter-

reversed its decision and let the tower stand "for the time being."

For 20 years the tower was neglected and the house was used by the Coast Guard. Then in 1941 the village of Fairport was granted a five-year lease for occupancy and use of the property. In 1945 the Fairport Harbor Historical Society was formed with the sole aim of saving the lighthouse. Through diligence and foresight the Society succeeded, making this the first marine museum lighthouse on the Great Lakes and one of ten lighthouses in Ohio to be listed on the *National Register of Historic Places*.

In 1989 the Historical Society received $40,000 in Federal Block Grant funds for repairs to the tower dome. Steel plates covering the lantern windows were removed, seven new panes of glass installed, and the top brickwork was repointed.

Today the museum contains history about shipwrecks, Ohio Indians, and the telegraph, as well as exhibits of marine artifacts, ship-building tools, lumbering tools, ore samples, Indian artifacts, a Coast Guard cannon, large ship models, and nautical equipment, including ship wheels and port lights. It also houses the "Dwight Boyer Wing," a special exhibit of the pilothouse from the *S.S. Frontenac* and equipment from the era. Added in 1968, it gives a view of the lake and the west pierhead lighthouse.

Other items of interest are the clockwork system for the Little Sable Light (Lake Michigan) and the third-order Fresnel lens from the Old Fairport Main Lighthouse. Outdoor exhibits include a U.S. Coast Guard covered rescue-wagon, two Lyle guns used in lifesaving operations, two old stock anchors, a steering apparatus, and the main mast (now a flagpole) of the first U.S.S. *Michigan*, the first iron-hulled ship of the U.S. Navy on the Great Lakes.

Known Keepers: Samuel Butler (1825–33), Elijah Dixon (1833–39), Jeremiah O. Balch (1839), Nehemia Merritt (1839–41), Samuel Butler (1841–45), Thomas Greer (1845–46), Isaac Spear (1846–49), Olmsted Baker (1853–56), Halsey Baker (1856–61), James Adams (1861–65), George Rogers (1865–71), Joseph Babcock (1871–81), George L. Riker (1881–1900), Joseph C. Babcock (1900–19), Daniel Babcock (1919–25).

Early Fairport Harbor Old Main Lighthouse

Fairport Harbor West Breakwater Lighthouse

34 Fairport Harbor West Breakwater Lighthouse

This light was completed in 1925 to replace the Fairport Harbor Main Light on Lake Erie. Located in the Headlands Beach State Park and a long walk from the parking lot along the sandy shore, it stands at the end of a long breakwater of large stones on the west side of the harbor. The lighthouse marks the end of this breakwater as well as the entry to Fairport Harbor at the mouth of the Grand River.

The iron shell and roof for this large square keeper's house and tower, which rises from one corner of the house, was preassembled at the Buffalo Lighthouse Depot and transported on board the steamer *Wotan* to arrive at Fairport Harbor on June 21, 1921. The structure was then hoisted into place and finished both inside and out. The light was lit on June 9, 1925.

The house had many large windows from which the keepers watched the lake, and the windows had storm shutters to close over them when necessary. The 42-foot (12.8 m) tower had a circular lantern that originally housed a fourth-order Fresnel lens and had a 56-foot (17 m) focal plane. The station also had an air diaphone fog signal and a radio beacon. Today it has a 300 mm optic, remains an active aid to navigation, and is listed on the *National Register of Historic Places*. With a good sandy beach along the west side of the breakwater, the lighthouse continues to attract visitors, especially swimmers and fishermen.

Known Keepers: Daniel Babcock (1925), Frank LaRosie (1925–37), John Brophy (1937–40).

Early Fairport Harbor West Breakwater Lighthouse

35 Gas Pipe Line Lightships

Two of these lightships used to mark the location of gas pipelines that ran under the Detroit River at Detroit. One was located at the foot of Chene Street. It was a wooden scow or schooner, built up and painted white with large lettering on the side reading "Gas Pipe Line Lightship — DO NOT ANCHOR." The second was anchored farther downriver near Junction Street. It is not known when they were first placed or removed, but both were in operation in 1902.

36 Gibraltar Lighthouse (Detroit River)

After the opening of the Erie Canal in 1825, settlers poured into the newly accessible area. Their increased boat travel stimulated the U.S. Government to appropriate $5,000 to build a lighthouse in the community of Gibraltar at the mouth and on the western channel of the Detroit River in 1838. This was the first lighthouse built to aid navigation on the Detroit River and also the last in a string of lighthouses built on Lake Erie from Buffalo to the western end of the lake to help mark safe passage.

A yellow brick lighthouse was built at the corner of Grandview and Munro Streets, where it could easily be seen by boats approaching from the lake at the south end of Celeron Island. At the time, all land to the south of it was open farmers' fields.

Reports of the appearance of this first light vary. Although there is disagreement about its style, since it was built in 1838 of yellow brick it was most likely a schoolhouse-style house. All reports agree that it used eleven lamps and eleven reflectors, and that it displayed a fixed light. An inspector's report later in 1838 mentions that the light and the brick dwelling were new and in excellent condition except for the basement and the chimneys.

By the early 1870s it had deteriorated beyond repair, and so in June 1872 the government appropriated $10,000 to build a replacement. It was completed February 1, 1873, for the start of the shipping season. The new tower and keeper's house were also made of brick. The new tower had a 47-foot (14 m) focal plane above the Detroit River. In 1879 the station was discontinued, the lighting apparatus removed, and a custodian put in charge of the property. In 1895 its buildings and grounds were sold at public auction, and the tower's iron lantern and stairway were removed for use in the new lighthouse on South Bass Island. Although the exact location of the second Gibraltar lighthouse is unknown, the house and the tower, minus its lantern are reported to still stand as a private residence.

Known Keepers: William Munger (1838–39), Abraham Lockwood (1839–43), Alanson Parsons (1843–49), Philip Livingston (1849–53), William Noland (1853–61), John Reford (1861–66), William Armstrong (1866–69), M. Vreeland (1869–76), Mary Vreeland (1876–79).

37 Grand Island Range Lights

In 1917 the U.S. government built range lights on Grand Island in the Niagara River to assist mariners moving into the river from Lake Erie. The front range light had a four-story octagonal tower topped with an octagonal gallery. The structure was covered in narrow clapboarding and painted white with black trim. The

Grand Island Front Range Light

ground level rose straight up and then a brief mansard-style roof connected it to the rest of the gently tapering tower. The octagonal gallery was supported underneath by 24 ornately carved wooden braces (three per side) and was surrounded by a black iron pipe railing. The original rear range light was quite similar in style. Being on a higher elevation, it only needed to be two stories high and, although it had the same diameter as the front tower, because it was shorter it appeared to be squatter and wider. After rising for one level the octagonal sides tapered in quickly with the same mansard-style roof and then tapered gently up the rest of the tower. It too was topped with a narrow octagonal gallery supported by 24 ornately carved wooden braces and had an octagonal lantern. At an unknown date this rear range light was replaced with a metal skeletal tower.

Today the front range light is no longer functional but is kept in pristine condition by its private owner, the Buffalo Launch Club and Marina. The rear range light was moved to the Dunkirk Lighthouse Museum at Dunkirk, New York.

Grand Island Rear Range Light, circa 1912

38 Grassy Island Lighthouse (Detroit River)

A lighthouse was built on Grassy Island in the Detroit River in 1848 to assist marine travel by warning of the Grassy Island Shoal. A Lighthouse Board report in January 1858 states that, even though it was only ten years old, the Grassy Island Lighthouse would be rebuilt that year due to evidence of poor construction and materials.

In 1901 the keeper's dwelling was a square 1½-story wooden structure with a sharp roof and dormers. The square wooden tower was built into and projected slightly from the northeasterly side of the house. It had an octagonal lantern that displayed a fixed red lens-lantern from a 30-foot (9 m) focal plane. There was also a boathouse. All buildings were painted a drab yellow. Range lights were later placed at the end of a man-made wooden pier in front of the keeper's house. They were taller and shorter square white tapering wood towers with black cast-iron lanterns and galleries.

This light no longer exists today. In fact, Grassy Island no longer exists today either, as the small low-lying island was washed away over the years by the swiftly flowing currents of the Detroit River. All that remains is the hidden Grassy Shoal, which is marked by a 24-foot (7.3 m) black skeletal tower with a green square daymark which displays a green flash every four seconds from a 26-foot (8 m) focal plane to produce an 8-mile (13 km) visibility.

39 Green Island Lighthouse (Lake Erie)

Green Island is in Lake Erie about 60 miles (97 km) from Detroit and 20 miles (32 km) from Sandusky. It is one of 21 small islands forming the Erie Archipelago in the western part of the lake and is about 1 mile (1.6 k) west of Bass Island. To help mark the Southern Passage through these islands the U.S. government in 1851 appropriated $5,000 to build a light on Green Island, which they purchased from Alfred P. Edwards in December 1851.

However, the lighthouse was not completed until 1855 on the west end of the island. The frame keeper's house, nearly 30 feet (9 m) square, was separated from the tower by a short passage. The tower was 30 feet (9 m) high and had a conical shape, tapering from 11 feet (3.4 m) in diameter at the base to 9 feet (2.8 m) at the top. A 13-foot (4 m) circular cut-stone platform composed of eight stones topped the tower. The octagonal lantern burned seven lamps and used a costly French mirror to reflect the light.

The first keeper, Colonel Charles F. Drake, lived at the light-house on the island with his wife and children. On New Year's Eve, 1863, after unseasonably warm temperatures had plummeted with the arrival of a violent storm, the lighthouse caught fire. The fierce winds made the fire consume the wooden structure quickly, and

Green Island Lighthouse

the family soon saw the futility of their efforts to douse the fire with buckets of lakewater. They were only able to save themselves from the bitterly cold night by nestling between two mattresses in an outbuilding. High waves forced a rescue party from Bass Island to wait until morning before taking the family to Put-in-Bay, where they eventually recovered.

In 1864 a replacement lighthouse was built, a large two-story limestone keeper's house with a square limestone tower at the lakeside end of the dwelling. Its date, 1864, is embedded in the stonework above the door to the tower. Ornamental wooden braces, four per side, helped support the square gallery and its iron pipe railing. The polygonal lantern was given a new fourth-order lens that displayed a fixed white light varied by white flashes at two-minute intervals. This light was displayed from an elevation of 57 feet (17 m) above lake level. During construction, a temporary light displayed a fixed white beam until the new light was lit on July 1, 1865.

One keeper, of unknown name, was said to have a fine team of Italian greyhounds that had been trained to pull a sled. In the winter the dogs made daily trips across the ice to transport the keeper's children to and from school on the mainland.

A small barn housed the keeper's livestock. The animals grazed inside a three-acre partially wooded fenced-in pasture. An inspector visiting in 1916 was impressed because the animals were not allowed to run free on the island as was the case at other light stations. It made things tidier and more orderly, the way the U.S. Lighthouse Service liked them.

In 1889 a boathouse was built at the northeastern end of the small island and connected to the lighthouse by a wooden plank walkway. Around 1920, this plank walk was replaced with a concrete one. Green Island was one of the first stations to receive a boat with an internal combustion engine.

As lake navigation continued to improve, the U.S. Lighthouse Service abandoned the living quarters in 1926 as a cost-saving measure. The keeper at South Bass Island was also put in charge of the Green Island Light at this time. From 1926 until 1939 this keeper was World War I veteran Captain William Gordon. His salary ranged from $1,320 to $1,560. Then in 1939 the U.S. Coast Guard erected a skeletal tower on the southwestern corner of Green Island and installed an automated light. The South Bass keeper no longer had to worry about the Green Island light.

Later, the island was placed under the jurisdiction of the U.S. Fish and Wildlife Department. The department posted the island, making it off-limits to the public. In spite of this, trespassers started a fire in the old keeper's house, which gutted the structure, leaving only a burned-out limestone shell.

Today the ruins are barely visible. The island's high bluffs and the overgrown vegetation have completely hidden them from view on the water. Many vessels boat past the island without knowing this lighthouse ever existed.

Known Keepers: Colonel Charles Drake (1854–71), Nicholas Van Epp (1871–82), Joseph Gibaut (1882–99), John Safe (1899–1903), Robert Waterfield (1903–05), George Ferguson (1905–14), Peter Diffely (1914–17), Captain William Gordon (1917–26).

Grosse Ile North Channel Front Range Light

40 Grosse Ile North Channel Range Lights

To assist navigation along the Detroit River the U.S. government built range lights on a point of Grosse Ile that came to be known as Lighthouse Point. The square wooden pyramidal lights marked the center of the channel and a turning point in the river. The front light was built on an open wooden piling at the end of a short pier right in the Detroit River, and the back one on land. Each had a hexagonal lantern that burned a kerosene lamp until they were electrified in 1929.

The front range light was rebuilt in 1906 and placed on a more durable, poured-concrete pier. The 40-foot (12 m) tower is now a white wooden octagonal one. Its straight sides taper in quickly a third of the way up, and then taper gently to the top. A graceful gallery supported by carved ornamental braces surrounds the octagonal lantern, which is topped by a copper dome and ventilator ball. This lighthouse is similar to the Grand Island Old Front Range Light on the Niagara River at Buffalo, New York. The 2½-story keeper's house, a large Victorian wood home, was a separate structure.

As navigation systems improved, the lights became less necessary. Sometime before 1940 the rear range light was lost, and the front range light was deactivated in 1963. In 1965 the township of Grosse Ile acquired the light from the federal government and turned it over to the Grosse Ile Historical Society. When residents noticed that the crib was in bad shape and the lighthouse in danger of toppling into the Detroit River, the historical society raised money to have the foundation reinforced in the spring of 1985. In 1996 the original wooden siding was replaced with cypress boards, which have a high durability.

Since the light can be accessed only across private property, it is only open by an appointment with the historical society or during a public open house, which the society hosts once a year, usually in October.

41 Grosse Point Light Vessel

In 1882 the U.S. government converted the single-masted 38-foot (11.5 m) wooden scow that had been used as a barge to haul materials for Stannard Rock Lighthouse into a lightship. It was renamed the Grosse Point (*LV 10*) in 1887 and placed at the upper end of the 20-foot (6 m) dredged channel three miles northeast of the Windmill Point Lighthouse at the entrance to the Detroit River. This lightship, which cost just $3,000, helped guide vessels into the Detroit River. In 1888 its position was changed slightly to form a range light with the Belle Isle Light, 5.5 miles (8.9 km) away, making navigation even safer.

The vessel had an 18-foot (5.5 m) beam and a 4-foot (1.2 m) draft. Its single lantern used eight Funck-type oil lamps to display a fixed white light from a 25-foot (7.6 m) focal plane inside a black cage lantern. A hand-operated bell warned mariners of fog. In 1892 it had an extensive overhaul due to "rotten wood in her ends." By 1899 a maintenance check reported that *LV 10* was "old and not worth repair." However, it continued in use at Grosse Point until 1902, when it was dry-docked. After repairs, it served until it was retired later in 1902 and dismantled.

From 1902–11 *LV 75* was used at Grosse Point. This was a brand new lightship, built at Ferrysburg, Michigan, for $14,998. The 85-foot (26 m) vessel was a steel scow with a 23-foot (7 m) beam, an 8-foot (2.4 m) draft, and a large wooden deckhouse. It had a single-lantern mast, oil-burning lamps, and a hand-operated fog bell. It was used at Grosse Point until the end of 1911. In the winter it was removed for maintenance and repairs. In 1912 *LV 75* was renamed the *St. Clair* and moved further northeast where there was a greater need of a lightship. In 1939 this vessel was relieved of lightship duty and sold.

42 Harsen's Island Lights St. Clair Flats

In 1934 the U.S. Lighthouse Service built a 1½-story keeper's house and a set of white steel skeletal range light towers on the south end of Harsen's Island to guide ships into the St. Clair River from Lake St. Clair. These electrical lights were part of the government's depression-era cost-saving measures: one keeper could replace the two previously employed at the two ship canal range lights, reducing personnel and building costs. This keeper was also responsible for other navigation aids up and down the river and could tend to them via a lighthouse service boat. The keeper's house had been designed with this in mind; a boat house was built right onto the end of the house. Some time after this station was lit, the Ship Canal Range Lights were removed and the canal was dredged deeper.

In 1938, when an assistant keeper was added to the station as part of a public works initiative program to help maintain the

river's many navigation aids, a small 1½-story house was built. Also from 1935–1939 the new "robot" lightship *St. Clair*, the first of its kind, was operated from the station.

In the 1970s the Coast Guard purchased a ranch-style house next door to the station to house additional personnel for the now expanding station. In 1985 the station was partially closed. From 1985 until about 1991 it was used as a sub-station and manned only on the weekends by two personnel from the new St. Clair Shores Coast Guard Station. After this, the buildings sat empty and the interiors were damaged by the elements and by vandals.

In 2001 about 30 sealed bids were received in a government auction to dispose of the abandoned station. A Michigan resident, Jeff Shook, was the successful bidder and plans to restore the three houses, storage shed, garage and light towers.

43 Horseshoe Reef Light

To mark Horseshoe Reef, Congress in 1849 appropriated $10,000 for a lightboat or $20,000 for a lighthouse. However, the lighthouse inspector surprised them by recommending $45,000 to build a lighthouse on the reef to mark the entrance to the Niagara River and guide vessels to port at Black Rock and then Buffalo.

While Horseshoe Reef is named in the government reports, the chosen site was actually the submerged Middle Reef, a more central location in the river. As this reef was located in Canadian waters, the U.S. government requested that the British government build the light. While the British saw the advantage of a light at this location for both Americans and Canadians, they did not want to pay for a lighthouse and so they relinquished ownership of one acre of the underwater reef (about a third of the whole reef) to the Americans for the sole purpose of building and maintaining a lighthouse that would sit as an island about 1,150 feet (350 m) within Canadian waters. Britain's actual reply is interesting: "Her Majesty's Government is prepared to advise her Majesty to cede to the United States such portion of the Horseshoe Reef as may be found requisite for the intended lighthouse provided the government of the United States will engage to erect such lighthouse and to maintain a light therein; and provided no fortification be erected on said reef." The British did not want a repeat of the War of 1812, especially since Middle Reef was within cannon shot of Canada.

In March 1851 Congress appropriated another $25,000 to build a lighthouse on the reef instead of placing a light vessel. The building contract was awarded to Isaac S. Smith, a Syracuse contractor. He started work in April 1852, but ran into problems (bad weather, the reef not being solid rock as expected) and could not finish on time. Eventually the government rescinded the contract and the Army Corps of Engineers finished the lighthouse in 1856.

From the wood and stone foundation rose four tapering reinforced-iron columns that created stilt-like legs to support a large square platform with an iron railing. The square white, one-story wood lighthouse stood in the center of the platform, topped by a decagonal iron lantern with a circular base. Its fourth-order lens, first lit on September 1, 1856, stood 50 feet (15.2 m) above the river and had a 10-mile (16 km) visibility. This was considered one of the loneliest stations in the district despite its proximity

Harsen's Island Range Light St. Clair Flats

Horseshoe Reef Light

Huron Harbor Lighthouse

to Buffalo. The two keepers lived on shore but stayed at the light in bad weather. The assistant keeper, Daniel D. Hill, made $490 a year in 1904.

In 1913 a new treaty made a boundary adjustment and the Canadian-American boundary was moved 100 feet (30.5 m) west of the Horseshoe Reef (actually Middle Reef), thus positioning the lighthouse in American waters.

When a light was placed on the water intake crib in the middle of Emerald Channel in 1908, the Horseshoe Reef Light became unnecessary, and it was discontinued in 1920. Abandoned and neglected, it fell into disrepair and its wood rotted away. All that remains is the iron skeleton.

Known Keepers: Brossy Thomas (1857–61), W. Bates (1861–63), George Phillips (1863–73), Myron Woolsey (1873–74), Dudley Rockwell (1874–75), George Schooter (1875–76), Wallace Hill (1876–85), Charles Gilbert (1886–89), George Safe (1890–93), John Safe (1893–98), Fredrick Lawson (1898–1903), Joseph Thomas (1903–20).

44 Huron Harbor Lighthouse

Congress appropriated $2,613 for a beacon light on a proper site for "Huron River" on Lake Erie, in May 1832. The station was established in 1835, and the light tower was built at the end of the west pier to guide vessels into the harbor. However, signs of bad construction and poor materials were soon evident. In 1852, $6,000 was allocated for repairs to "the lighthouse, pier and pierhead in the harbor of Huron, on which the lighthouse was built." But the problem persisted; in July 1856 Congress appropriated $4,580 more to completely rebuild the lighthouse.

The new lighthouse, built at the end of the west pier, was much better constructed. The tower was of plate iron for greater protection against the elements. The lantern was given a fourth-order Fresnel lens, which used a catadioptric illuminating apparatus. First lit on November 12, 1857, it displayed a fixed white light from a 40-foot (12.2 m) focal plane. In clear weather it had a 13-mile (21 km) visibility.

The tower was again rebuilt in the 1900s, this time of steel in an *art moderne* style. The square base sits on a high concrete foundation, from which the sides curve in and up to form a much narrower 72-foot (22 m) tower. The base and tower both have porthole windows for interior illumination, and the tower is painted white for maximum visibility. Instead of a lantern, it is now topped by a 375 mm beacon. The lighthouse was first established in 1936. Also at this time a steel fog signal building was constructed. Its original diaphone fog signal later became an electric horn.

The keeper's house does not exist today. The light is operated by remote control from a small brick-faced building on shore. There is also a radio beacon at this station. This light is listed on the *National Register of Historic Places* and continues to be an active aid to navigation maintained by the U.S. Coast Guard.

Known Keepers: Morris Jackson (1835–37), George Patterson (1837–41), Joseph Barnes (1841–42), M. Ledyard (1842–43), Emmanuel Fisher (1843–44), Alexander Lesley (1844–46), Reuben Smith (1846–49), Zeb Montague (1849–51), Alrathas Strickland (1851–52), Redi Webber (1852–53), Charles Bently (1853), Abel White (1853), Solomon Squire (1853–56), Rosewell Steele (1856–57), Henry Steele (1857), Solomon Squire (1856–61), W. Shirley (1861–63), John Packer (1863–64), Charles Chapman (1864–65), Jacobs Collins (1865–69), William Ryan (1869–70), Richard Mansell (1870–1909), Joseph Crawford (1910–23), Richard Tonge (1923–33), Daniel Hill (1933–42), Robert Siggen (1955–58).

Huron Harbor Lighthouse

Lake St. Clair Crib Lighthouse

45 Lake St. Clair Crib Lighthouse

The St. Clair Crib Light was finished for use in 1939 to replace *LV 75*, which originally marked this location. The 53-foot (16.3 m) structure was placed on a sunken crib in Lake St. Clair. A large circular concrete foundation was placed on top of the crib and rises about 12 feet (3.7) out of the water. This foundation has been reinforced from the elements with steel sheeting. A large but slightly smaller octagonal concrete base rises about 10 feet (3.1 m) up from the foundation and it is topped with a much narrower 30-foot (9.23 m) high straight-sided tower. Rectangular steel panels have been riveted over the tower for additional protection against wind, water and ice. Two small porthole-style windows ascend the tower and four porthole windows surround the watchroom at the top. The watchroom is painted white while the main part of the tower is painted with a green band. The tower is topped with a green beacon and white pipe-iron guardrail.

While the light is modern in style and lacks the "romance" of the older lighthouses in the area, it remains an important aid to navigation for area boaters, especially small pleasure craft.

46 Lake St. Clair Lightship

Prior to a lighthouse being built 3 miles (4.86 km) out in Lake St. Clair, the United States government used a lightship to work in conjunction with the already existing range lights at the St. Clair Flats Ship Canal to help guide the lake's upbound vessels into the canal to the St. Clair River. While there were reports as early as 1838 that suggested the lightship at Mackinaw be moved to quieter waters in the flats of Lake St. Clair, a lightship was not placed at this location until 1912, when the Grosse Point station (*LV 75*) was moved and renamed Lake St. Clair. This new location was about 7 miles (11.34 km) northeast of the old Grosse Point station and on the west side of the dredged channel into the St. Clair River. It was moved here to mark a turn from the lake into the channel.

LV 75 had been built at Ferrysburg, Michigan, at a cost of $14,998. It was an 85-foot (26 m) steel scow with a 23-foot (7 m) beam, an 8-foot (22.4 m) draft, a large wooden deckhouse, a single-lantern mast, oil-burning lamps and a hand-operated fog bell.

Changes occurred with time. In 1922 the illuminating apparatus was converted to use acetylene. In 1926 the vessel was automated for unattended operation, making it a first of its kind in lightships. In 1934 it was fitted with an automatic fog bell system powered by carbon dioxide. In 1935 it was equipped with a radio beacon, the fog

Lake St. Clair Lightship LV 75

bell was switched to an air whistle, and the vessel was outfitted as a remote-control lightship, another first for lightships. Its illuminating and signaling systems were operated from onshore by the keeper's at the Harsen's Island station, thus saving the cost of placing a crew on the lightship. This vessel continued in service until 1939 when it was replaced with the building of the Lake St. Clair Crib Lighthouse. At this time *LV 75* was retired from duty and sold. In 1941 it was registered as a lighter in New York Harbor. It was last heard about in 1983 when it was reportedly still in use.

47 Livingston Memorial Light

This light was privately built in 1929 by the Lake Carriers' Association in memory of William Livingston, a president of the association and prominent Detroit resident. It is situated at the head of Belle Isle, Detroit's island park, in the Detroit River.

The light is a grand monument made of marble. It is 65 feet (20 m) tall but its fluted edges and vertical lines make it appear taller. It is topped with eight pillars and a decorative, octagonal dome over the light. The automated, revolving white light has a 16-mile (26 km) visibility. The monument rests on a wide octagonal marble base with steps leading up to it from all sides. A heavy intricately designed metal door allows entry to the inside, and above the door is a Grecian-style carving in the marble. It is surrounded by a black wrought-iron fence.

This light is recognized as a navigation aid, but has always been privately maintained. It was never operated by the U.S. Light Service or the U.S. Coast Guard. However, it did serve as a guide for ships entering the Detroit River from Lake St. Clair. Age dulled the pristine finish of the marble. By the late 1970s neglect and vandalism had added to its poor state, but in the early 1980s Detroit gave it a "face-lift" to return it to its once-glorious appearance.

Livingston Memorial Light

Lorain East Breakwater Lighthouse

48 Lorain East Breakwater Light

In 1965 it was decided to replace the west breakwater light because its light was difficult to distinguish at night from the background lights of Lorain, Lake Erie. The new light was placed at the end of the east breakwater. It was a two-tiered 60-foot (18 m) steel tower that sat on a steel pile reinforced-concrete pier. The tower had a large square base about one story high and porthole windows. The top of the tower rose another four stories and its square column was uniquely placed on a diagonal to the lower section. Its modern illuminating apparatus magnified the light to 3.5 million candlepower, which would not easily be confused with background lights of the city. When this light was lit in 1966 the keepers were no longer necessary, as this light was automated.

Early Lorain West Breakwater Lighthouse

49 Lorain West Breakwater Lighthouse

While a pierhead light had served Lorain Harbor in Lake Erie from 1837 until 1917, harbor growth boomed in the late 1800s with the Johnson Steel Company moving to Lorain in 1894 and Cleveland Shipbuilding establishing there in 1897. New ships, old ships, ore boats and stone-carrying vessels regularly moved in and out of the Lorain Harbor on the Black River. The harbor was enlarged and improvements were made to accommodate the growth.

In 1917 the Army Corps of Engineers built the Lorain West Breakwater Lighthouse. Its concrete foundation was placed diagonally at the end of the newly constructed stone breakwater. Its poured-concrete and steel walls were over 10 inches (21 cm) thick so as to withstand the fiercest Lake Erie storms. The building was 3½ stories high, including its raised basement. On the first floor was an engine room, housing air compressors for the foghorn and auxiliary power generators; on the second were the living quarters and an office; the third housed the fresh water tank, storage area, and foghorn mechanism. The tower extended one more story out of the roof of the house and supported a circular lantern with curved panes of glass set diagonally into metal astragals. A steel railing surrounded the rectangular gallery. The lantern had a red dome and ventilator ball that matched the red roof shingles, and its fourth-order Fresnel lens magnified the light source to 50,000 candlepower.

By the 1930s the keeper had two assistants, and by the late 1950s the keepers worked six days on and three days off. As this station did not have enough room for the lightkeepers' families, the keepers returned to the mainland for their time off.

The latter half of the twentieth century brought changes to the lighthouse. In 1965 it was decided to replace the light because it was hard to see at night against the background lights of Lorain. So, in 1966 an automated 3.5 million candlepower light was placed on a 60-foot (18 m) steel tower at the end of the east breakwater. The Fresnel lens was removed from the old tower and a small red marker light was added.

Lorain West Breakwater Lighthouse

emerged as a steel and ship building center. It was a wooden structure on the end of a wooden pier. James Connelly, its longest-serving keeper, served with one assistant from shortly after the Civil War until 1903. He walked daily to the end of the pier to light and later extinguish the lard-oil lamps. The new West Breakwater Light replaced this lighthouse in 1917.

Known Keepers: Captain Augusta Jones (1837–41), Patrick Sinnott (1841–43), Thomas Browne (1843–48), David Foote (1848–53), Hugh Sleator (1853–57), Moses Packer (1857–59), Lester Smith (1859–61), Henry Ludnum (1861–65), Alanson Bridges (1865–71), James Connelly (1871–1903), George Ferguson (1903–05), Robert Waterfield (1905–10), Peter Diffley (1910–14).

The U.S. Coast Guard also scheduled the old lighthouse for demolition and gutted the interior in preparation. But concerned citizens formed a "Save the Lighthouse Committee" and persuaded the Coast Guard to delay demolition. Later, when the government "excessed" the light, the Lorain Historical Society purchased it. Then in December 1990 they sold it to the Port of Lorain Foundation Inc., a non-profit group that is restoring it with plans to create a museum. One of their fundraisers included "A Place in Time," at which participants signed a document that was put into a time capsule in the lighthouse base to be opened in 2091. This energetic group is returning the lighthouse to its former beauty, which years ago earned it the nickname "Jewel of the Port."

Known Keepers: Olin Stevens (1920–37), Joe Price (1937–40).

50 Lorain West Pierhead Lighthouse

In 1832 Congress appropriated $2,400 for a beacon at the mouth of the Black River, Lake Erie. This site was chosen because, being 175 feet (54 m) wide and 10 feet (3 m) deep for more than three miles upriver, it provided an excellent harbor that could accommodate at least 50 vessels. The lighthouse, also known as the Black River Light, was built by 1837 on a pier that extended into the lake on the west side of the river mouth.

An 1838 report to Congress described the state of the beacon. Each of the eight fixed lamps had its own bright reflector, but the reflectors needed resilvering. The lantern leaked badly and needed soldering around the frame of the cupola, reputtying around the glass, and "other trifling expenses" to stop the leaking — all for an estimated cost of $25.

The lighthouse stood on the west pier, which extended 680 feet (207 m) into the lake. It was so dangerous for the keeper to go out to the lighthouse in stormy weather that three keepers were washed from the pier in one year, one of whom drowned. It was recommended to raise the pier at least 2 feet (0.6 m).

A recommendation was also made to build a 1½-story, three-bedroom keeper's house in brick or stone. With the inclusion of $200 for outbuildings, a fence, and a well, and still another $200 for a quarter-acre lot, the complete estimate came to $1,400. It is unknown if the keeper's dwelling was actually built.

Congress appropriated $7,300 in 1858 to rebuild the pierhead light at Black River. This lighthouse was built soon after Lorain

51 Mama Juda Front Range Light

At an unknown date a square white pyramidal tower was built on a pile foundation on Mama Juda shoal in 3.5 feet (1 m) of water. It was 600 feet (183 m) from the Mama Juda Lighthouse on the island, which acted as its rear range light. Its octagonal lantern displayed a fixed red lens-lantern light from a 28-foot (8.5 m) focal plane. These range lights marked the line of the best water, which passed about 950 feet (290 m) to the east of the Grassy Island light.

52 Mama Juda Lighthouse

Mama Juda, a marshy, low-lying 3-acre (1.2 hectare) island, was located between Hennepin Point, at the north end of Grosse Isle, and Fighting Island, in the Detroit River downriver from Detroit. The island was named after a North American native woman who set up a fishing camp there every season when the fish were running. Over time three different lighthouses were built on this island to help mark the shoals between the island and Wyandotte, on the American mainland.

The first lighthouse was built in 1849 close to the marshy edge of the island on a wooden platform placed on piles driven into the riverbed. The keeper's house was an L-shaped wooden one-story clapboard dwelling with an octagonal wooden clapboard tower extending up for another story from its one roof-peak end. The tower supported an octagonal birdcage-style iron lantern with a highly arched dome capped with a rotating ventilator stack. Each of the lantern's eight sides comprised 15 small panes of glass set three panes per row. The lantern used a lamp and reflector system to display its light.

One night in 1854 a major marine catastrophe took place near the lighthouse. The *E.K. Collins*, bound from the Sault to Cleveland, caught fire, reportedly from hot smoker's pipe ashes emptied onto the wooden deck. Lifeboats were useless because of the intense heat, and no one thought to use the flotation devices. The wooden vessel was totally burned. Twenty-three persons died either from the fire or by drowning in the swift river currents. Some were rescued by the propeller *Fintry*, which was passing nearby.

In 1865 the fixed light from the lighthouse was visible for 8 miles (13 km). Also in 1865 the lighthouse inspector's report described the structures as "not being thought worthy of the repairs required to make them habitable," and recommended a new lighthouse be built.

Mama Juda Lighthouse

The second lighthouse at Mama Juda Island was again constructed on piles driven into the marshy shore area to create a wooden platform for the house and tower. The keeper's house was a rectangular white wooden 1½-story clapboard house with a pedimented entry at the front. The short square white wooden clapboard tower ascended from the dwelling's roof-peak over the pedimented entry door. The tower's square gallery had chopped-off corners, making it octagonal, and it was enclosed with a pipe iron railing. The tower had an octagonal lantern which in 1901 used a fourth-order lens to display a fixed red light from a 44-foot (13.5 m) focal plane for 13 miles (21 km).

There were only two known lighthouses exactly like this. The other one was built in 1870 at Old Mission Point, Grand Traverse Bay, Lake Michigan. This type of architecture (a square wooden tower built into the roof-peak) was first thought to have appeared in Michigan lighthouses in 1870, but the Mama Juda light put that date back to 1866.

In 1894 a front range light was added to the station. It was a square white wooden pyramidal tower built onto a pile-supported platform in 3.5 feet (1 m) of water on the shoal and 600 feet (185 m) north of the Mama Juda lighthouse, which became its rear range light. It displayed a fixed red lens-lantern light from a 28-foot (8.5 m) focal plane.

The keepers who tended this light lived on the island and had a small farm there to help support themselves. They also tended the Grosse Ile Lighthouse when it was built and maintained all the local channel lights by using a rowboat.

It was rare for a woman to be appointed lighthouse keeper unless her husband had died at the light. Even then, if a man was available, she was often passed over. This almost happened at the Mama Juda Light. When keeper Barney Litogot died in 1873, his assistant applied for the position; however, this assistant was his wife and there were men who wanted the job. The superintendent had to intervene on her behalf with a letter to the Secretary of the Treasury pointing out that she had already been maintaining the light while her husband was alive because, having fought in the Civil War, he had been too disabled to perform his duties. With his backing, Caroline Litogot became the next keeper and she served well until her resignation in 1885.

Orlo J. Mason kept the light for nine years, as of June of 1885. During his tenure he never had a complaint lodged against him, a remarkable feat considering the amount of boat traffic on the river. The lighthouse was a family effort and Mason's wife and daughter, Maebelle, learned to operate the lighthouse and handle boats. When Maebelle went to town she often had to row herself.

In May, 1890, Maebelle, then only 14 years old, performed a heroic rescue. A man in a rowboat was trying to catch a ride by throwing his line to the steamer *C.W. Elphicke*. In the process his boat capsized. The steamer was unable to help and he was left clinging to his overturned boat. When the steamer passed Mama Juda Lighthouse, her captain signaled for help. Since keeper Mason was away in the government rowboat, Maebelle and her mother struggled to put the only other boat, a heavy punt, into the river. Maebelle, the stronger of the two, rowed hard for over a mile to reach the drowning man. They pulled the man aboard, tied his capsized rowboat to their punt and Maebelle rowed them back to safety.

This event was just part of lighthouse life to Maebelle, but the government inspector recommended that her bravery be recognized. Maebelle was presented the silver lifesaving medal by the Tenth Lighthouse District inspector and a gold lifesaving medal from the Shipmasters' Association. It was inscribed: "Presented to Miss Maebelle Mason for heroism in saving life May 11, 1890, by the E.M.B.A. of Cleveland." After this presentation and until she left the lighthouse and island in June 1892 to get married, association vessels saluted Maebelle with a blast from their steam whistles whenever they passed the lighthouse.

In 1901 the keeper was James Story. He was a devoted lighthouse keeper and father. When his daughter, born on the island in 1901, was of school age he rowed her to and from school in Wyandotte every day. Each round trip was two miles of rowing.

The third and last lighthouse at Mama Juda was built around 1910. An old postcard shows a 1½-story keeper's dwelling with a large dormer in its roof and a cylindrical masonry tower extending up about two stories from the house's end roof-peak. The circular tower gallery was supported by a multitude of corbels, surrounded with a pipe iron railing and topped with a polygonal iron lantern.

After the station was automated and abandoned, it disappeared. In 1920 a freighter reportedly struck it and destroyed the lighthouse. Then swift river currents gradually eroded more of the island each year. High waters in 1952 removed most of what was left and high waters in the winter of 1972–73 removed the last of it. Today, all that remains are the underwater Mama Juda Shoals, which are marked by modern beacons.

Known Keepers: David Johnson (1849–53), George Dotey (1853–61), Olison Colbern (1861–66), William Stewart (1866–67), Augustus Clark (1867–73), Barney Litogot (1873), Caroline Litogot (1873–85), Orlo Mason (1885–93), Enoch Scibner (1893–1899), James Story (1899–1911), Thomas Kean (1911).

53 Manhattan Range Lights

In 1895 range lights were built to mark the middle line of the new straight channel into Toledo Harbor, Lake Erie. They were built 3,450 feet (1050 m) apart. The front range light stood on an artificial island 4.9 miles (7.9 km) southwest of the Maumee Bay Range Lights and was connected to shore by a walkway. It had a square white wooden pyramidal tower that used a sixth-order lens to display a fixed red light for about 8.5 miles (14 km). The rear light was built on a pier foundation on the slope of the riverbank at Manhattan Point, North Toledo. It had a square white wooden pyramidal skeletal tower with an enclosed watchroom with green window shutters and an octagonal lantern with a red dome. It used a sixth-order lens to display a fixed red light from a 53-foot (16 m) focal plane for 8.5 miles.

In 1959 the Coast Guard replaced the Fresnel lens from the front range light with a larger lens and a more powerful light. The Fresnel lens was then loaned for a one-month exhibition to the Toledo Museum of Art's Festival of Glass in early 1960.

At an unknown date these range lights were discontinued; today both have been moved. The rear light's top 20 feet (6 m) was taken to the downtown area. It still retains its square metal watchroom, but the lantern is gone and the watchroom has been capped with a roof and a ventilator ball. A metal ladder ascends from the ground up inside the skeletal tower to the floor of the watchroom. The front light's tower top has also been moved. In 1994 parts of the skeletal base were stacked in pieces beside the intact lantern room. Both of these old lights are now on private property.

Known Keepers: Harvey Dayan (1895–1905), Edward Ahart (1905–1926), David Sutherland

54 Marblehead Lighthouse

This lighthouse, built in 1821, was first called Sandusky Bay Lighthouse because it is on the peninsula at the end of Sandusky Bay. As storms come up quickly on Lake Erie and the peninsula is surrounded by offshore islands, this can be one of the lake's roughest areas. The lighthouse warned of this area and guided ships into safe harbor.

Marblehead Lighthouse

The limestone tower was built with stone quarried from Marblehead, Ohio. Its base was 25 feet (7.5 m) in diameter with walls 5 feet (1.5 m) thick; its top was 12 feet (3.6 m) in diameter with walls 2 feet (0.6 m) thick. Its original optics, made by Winslow Lewis, included 13 Argand whale oil lamps, each with its own 16-inch reflector. This tower still stands and operates, making it the oldest lighthouse in Ohio and the oldest operating lighthouse on the Great Lakes.

The first keeper's house was built of fieldstone in 1823. It was 3 miles (4.8 km) from the lighthouse! It is now owned by the Ottawa County Historical Society, which runs programs in the summer and fall to depict early life on the peninsula through re-enactments, demonstrations and other activities.

Many changes occurred at the light. In 1858 the lantern was refitted with a fourth-order Fresnel lens. The new lamp burned lard oil. In 1870 the Sandusky Bay Lighthouse was renamed Marblehead, and in 1876 a lifesaving station was built in the area because of its numerous shipwrecks. From 1897 to 1903 a brick extension was added to the tower, increasing its height by 15 feet (4.6 m), its original wooden stairs were replaced with an 87-step iron spiral staircase, and it received a larger lantern from the Erie Pennsylvania Main Light.

A third-order Fresnel lens from Paris was installed in the lantern after being displayed at the 1904 St. Louis World's Fair, and the light's fuel became kerosene. At this time it probably also used an incandescent oil vapor lamp, which forced kerosene into a vapor chamber where it struck hot walls and instantly vaporized,

giving a cleaner, brighter flame. It's visibility range was now about 16 miles (26 km). In 1902 a new, two-story Victorian keeper's house was built adjacent to the lighthouse, reducing the keeper's travel time. In 1923 the light was electrified, and in 1946 it was demanned. Because of vandalism, the U.S. Coast Guard in 1969 ordered that the house be burned. Concerned citizens protested and saved the house, which is now protected by the Ohio Department of Natural Resources. Also in 1969 the lighthouse was placed on the *National Register of Historic Places*. Its light was changed from ruby red to flashing green, and its third-order Fresnel lens was replaced with a plastic beacon.

The lighthouse had 15 keepers, two of whom were women. The first keeper was Benajah Wolcott, a Revolutionary War veteran and early settler on the peninsula. When he died in 1832 from cholera, his widow, Rachel Miller Wolcott, took over, becoming the first woman lighthouse keeper on the Great Lakes. After tending the light for two years she married Jeremiah Van Benschoten, who served as the light's next keeper.

During World War II the U.S. Coast Guard patrolled in front of the lighthouse, as it had become strategically important for national defense as well as commerce. Today its third-order lens is housed for display at the Marblehead Coast Guard Station nearby. This light has the honor of being the oldest lighthouse in continuous service on the Great Lakes and having the first woman keeper on the Great Lakes. The lighthouse is open to summer visitors. It was one of five lighthouses honored by the U.S. government in 1995 on a commemorative stamp. With its long history, this lighthouse has much to be proud of.

Other historical areas are close by. South of the Marblehead Lighthouse is Johnson's Island, which is connected by a bridge to the mainland. The island displays an area where thousands of Confederate officers who were prisoners of war once camped. Three miles to the north of the lighthouse is Kelley's Island, which visitors may access by ferry to see its glacial rock formations and native petroglyphs.

Known Keepers: Benajah Wolcott (1822–32), Rachel Wolcott (1832–34), Jeremiah Van Benschoten (1834–41), Roderick Williston (1841–43), Charles Drake (1843–49), Lodowick Brown (1849–53), Jared Keyes (1853–58), W. Dayton (1859–61), Thomas Dyer (1861–65), Russell Douglas (1865–72), Thomas Keyes (1872–73), George McGee (1873–96), Johanna McGee (1896–1903), Charles Hunter (1903–33), Edward Herman (1933–43).

Marblehead Lighthouse

Maumee Bay Range Lights

55 Maumee Bay Range Lights

Although the government started appropriating funds as early as 1837 for a light at the western end of Lake Erie, it was not until their 1852 appropriation of $5,000 that a crib light was built 4.5 miles (7.3 km) out in Maumee Bay right in the middle of the shipping channel, to assist mariners into the mouth of Maumee River (Toledo Harbor). It was built on a crib, lit in July of 1855 and destroyed by ice in 1856, but little else is known about this first crib light.

The light was rebuilt by 1884 and then lit by Captain William Jennings, the new light's first keeper but the station's second. He served faithfully for 49 years. Even in the winter when the bay froze over he frequently went out to check on the light's condition. His nephew remembers skating out with him often to check the light.

While it is unknown exactly when a front range light was added to this crib light, Captain Jennings recalled using a rowboat to travel between the two lights to trim the wicks and replenish the oil. The front range light may have been built when the replacement crib light was built in 1884, as Captain Jennings was the first keeper of this light.

During the light's early years, tugboats went out into Toledo Harbor to meet incoming vessels and often tied up at the lighthouse to await their tow. While some of these tugs were alongside, some of their sparks set fire to the lighthouse and almost completely destroyed it. It was replaced with a skeletal steel tower with a simple square gallery and iron-sheeted watchroom topped by an octagonal iron lantern. The front range light was also on a skeletal steel tower but it was much shorter.

In the late 1800s a mammoth dyke, 50 feet (15 m) wide and 1,400 feet (430 m) long, was built to connect the range lights, making it much easier for the keeper to tend them and also providing protection from small sudden Lake Erie storms. The eight-room keeper's house, a 1½-story frame dwelling situated near the base of the rear range light, was also rebuilt after the fire.

In 1901 these two range lights facilitated both eastward and westward maritime traffic. The eastern light had a 42-foot (13 m) focal plane and used a fifth-order lens to create a 13-mile (4 m) visibility. This tower served as both the front range light for vessels heading west and the rear range light for vessels heading east. The western light was equipped with two watchrooms and two octagonal lanterns, both of which displayed a fixed white light using a fifth-order lens. The higher one, with a 64-foot (20 m) focal plane, was the rear range light for vessels heading west and the lower one, with a 25-foot (7.5 m) focal plane, was the front range light for vessels heading east.

As lake vessels became larger, these range lights became more of a navigation hazard than a guiding light. After 1918, their dyke was hit at least four times by ships trying to navigate the channel around them. By the mid-1950s they had outlived their usefulness, and were slated for demolition by the end of the 1956 shipping season.

The last keeper had been Arthur G. Bauman, who had served at this remote post for 15½ years. He lived with only his mother, who served as his unpaid assistant. Although the lighthouse was drafty, it had all the amenities of home, including a gas stove, a refrigerator and, for its last two years, a television to alleviate the loneliness.

The contract for demolition was awarded to the Dunbar and Sullivan Dredging Company of Detroit for $448,750. The buildings were offered free to anyone willing to remove them, but no one claimed them. The steel towers were dismantled and the old steel was shipped to the Toledo Marine Terminals, Inc. On June 30, 1957 about 900 boaters surrounded the lightstation in the mid-afternoon to bid it a watery farewell. Smaller boats anchored in the lee of the crib, while larger vessels formed a triple circle around it. Skippers gave a nautical salute (three long blasts and two short) and dipped their colors in recognition of the lighthouse's years of service.

On August 8, 1957, after the remaining wooden buildings and the crib top had been sprayed with kerosene and doused to ensure a good flame, they were ignited and burned so that the huge crib could be demolished. All remaining materials were removed and loaded onto tugs and hauled to an approved dumping ground 5½ miles (9 km) north of the Toledo Lighthouse in Lake Erie. Crews worked around the clock until the job was completed, weather permitting.

After the crib's removal, the area was dredged to over 20 feet (6 m). The final total removal cost, including dredging, was $526,000. While operators of large lake vessels supported the lighthouse's removal as a safety precaution, smaller boat operators missed its help in safely finding their way to homeport. These range lights have been replaced with modern land-based ones.

Known Keeper: Captain William (Hickory) Jennings (1856–1905).

56 Monroe Lighthouse

The city of Monroe was built at the mouth of Raisin River in western Lake Erie. Because the river mouth was shallow and marshy with shifting sandy shoals, early water traffic docked in nearby La Plaisance Bay and used wagons and horse-drawn railway cars to get to Monroe. A light on Otter Creek Point lit the bay.

Then in 1834 Monroe's city fathers petitioned Congress for a canal to open the mouth of the Raisin River into Lake Erie to facilitate shipping directly into the city. Congress appropriated almost $100,000 to construct the canal. Built in stages from the river into the lake and finished in 1843, it was 100 feet (30 m) wide, 4,000 feet (1.2 km) long, and 12 feet (3.5 m) deep.

Since this new Monroe Harbor was about 4 miles (6.5 km) north of Otter Creek Point and its lighthouse, the inspector in 1838 recommended a beacon light at the end of the newly constructed pier upon its completion, as Monroe Harbor was the only artificial harbor on Lake Erie in the State of Michigan. In 1844 the auditor recommended that the light at Otter Creek be discontinued and replaced by one at Monroe. In March 1847 Congress appropriated $3,000 to build a light at Monroe. Then on August 12, 1848, they approved another $3,522 to complete the construction of the lighthouse. When the light was completed in 1849, the Otter Creek Lighthouse was discontinued.

Monroe Lighthouse

The Monroe Lighthouse was built at the end of one of its two new timber pile piers, which extended 1,135 feet (350 m) into Lake Erie to prevent the harbor entrance from sanding over. The octagonal wooden tower sat at the end of the northern pier and showed a fixed red light to mark the harbor entrance between the piers. The keeper's dwelling, built on land at the other end of the pier, was a white, two-story frame house with green shutters. In 1859 it was moved to the end of the north pier close to the tower.

An 1868 inspector's report showed that the wooden tower needed repainting, the birdcage lantern and the deck leaked, there was no passageway from the tower to the dwelling to protect the keeper, the keeper's house needed extensive repairs and the pier needed replanking. The 1869 report showed that all repairs had been made and that the tower had received a new lantern and deck.

By 1873 the keeper's dwelling was reported "in a ruinous condition," as it stood on a foundation of rotten logs, but not until the 1885 report was it mentioned that the keeper's house and lighthouse were completely replaced along with the rebuilding of the pier in 1884–85. The new 1½-story keeper's dwelling was once again built at the end of the northern pier using a four-gabled design that incorporated the tower right into the house and had a low square tower rising from the lake end of its roof. In 1893, in the course of a severe April storm, the tower and the house were both seriously damaged.

Also in 1893 a circular iron oil house was placed on the north pier about 20 feet (6 m) west of the keeper's house. It had been made in Cleveland and was delivered to Monroe by the lighthouse tender *Haze*. This oil house was indicative of a more combustible illuminant (probably kerosene), which needed to be stored at a safe distance from the keeper's house and the tower to avoid fire damage.

The 1900 *Light List* describes the Monroe Light as using a fourth-order Fresnel lens and having a 13-mile (21 km) visibility. In 1902 the structure received a new concrete foundation to replace the wooden timbers for better protection from Lake Erie storms.

With the advent of the car, water travel decreased and Monroe's harbor traffic gradually declined. In 1916, when an automated gas light was installed on a skeletal steel tower beside the lighthouse on the pier, the lightkeeper was no longer needed and the lighthouse was abandoned. After being sold in 1922 to a Toledo man for $35, it was dismantled and removed. All that remain are a few wooden pilings and a long row of rocks (visible only at low water) as a reminder that a pier with a lighthouse once stood here.

Known Keepers: John Anderson (1848–53), John Paxton (1853–59), Benjamin Sherman (1859–61), Joseph Guyons (1861–65), Israel Noble (1865–72), James McGlenn (1873–88), Peter Gussenbauer (1889–1904), William Haynes (1904–07), August Gramer (1907–08), A. Sanners (1908–16).

57 Otter Creek Lighthouse

In the mid-1820s the U.S. government appropriated money to build a light at the mouth of Otter Creek at the western end of Lake Erie. Then in January 1829 a bill was passed to build it at Otter Creek Point instead of at the creek mouth. The site was a flat marshy area midway between the Detroit River and the Maumee River and about two miles southwest of the mouth of the Raisin River and two miles northeast of the mouth of Otter Creek.

While no picture of this lighthouse is known to exist, the Saturday, July 4, 1829, *Michigan Sentinel*, which was published in Monroe, carried a very precise description. It was to have a 40-foot (12.2 m) conical tower of rough cut stone or brick and taper from a 22-foot (6.7 m) base diameter to a 10.5-foot (3.2 m) top diameter. Its octagonal lantern was to be topped by a copper dome, ventilator and vane. The 1½-story keeper's house was to be made of rough-cut stone. (The lighthouse built at Barcelona in 1829 used these same specs and it is still standing.)

When the lighthouse was built later in 1829 it serviced the community of Monroe at the mouth of the Raisin River about 2 miles (3.2 km) to the northeast. Since the Raisin River mouth was too shallow to allow entry, Monroe used La Plaisance Bay below Otter Creek Point as its harbor, and people and materials were transported from there by wagon and horse-drawn railroad cars into Monroe.

The actual tower was made of rough-cut stone and then whitewashed. The lantern and dome were black and the lantern displayed a fixed light. The lighthouse cost $3,948. By 1838 the tower, though only a few years old, was starting to deteriorate. The gallery was leaking and the outside plaster mortar of the structure was peeling. Meanwhile a canal was dredged through the marshy mouth of the Raisin River, creating a harbor right at Monroe. When this canal was finished in 1843, a pierhead light to mark the harbor entrance was placed at the outer end of the north pier in 1849.

The light at Otter Creek was deteriorating, as Monroe maritime traffic traveled directly into the new harbor, and the light on Otter Creek Point was too far away. The Otter Creek Lighthouse was discontinued when the Monroe Pierhead light was lit. In 1852 the government decided to sell the Otter Creek Lighthouse. John Jacob Luft bought it in 1854 for $10, dismantled it, and used its stones for the foundation of his family home.

Known Keepers: John Whipple (1829–36), Major Lewis Bond (1836–37), John Whipple (1837), Major Lewis Bond (1837–48).

58 Peche Island Light

Peche Island can be found just east of Belle Isle where the Detroit River joins Lake St. Clair. The French originally named it Isle aux Peches (Island of Fish). In 1908 the U.S. government built a lighthouse just off the island to help vessels navigate out of Lake St. Clair into the Detroit River.

The 66-foot (20 m) circular white tower tapers gently up to a ring below the watchroom and then rises with straight sides to the gallery. The watchroom has four windows for monitoring weather and boat traffic, a circular gallery and a circular iron railing. The octagonal lantern has large panes of glass and is topped with a black dome, ventilator ball and lightning rod. The sides of the tower are covered in riveted iron bands to help prevent deterioration. The light was deactivated in 1965.

By the 1980s the tower was tilting and in danger of toppling. However, the Michigan National Corporation of Detroit saved it by purchasing it from the Coast Guard in 1982, and the Coast Guard replaced the light with one on a steel tower.

Peche Island Light

The Michigan National Corporation had ideas for the lighthouse. They planned to turn it into a maritime museum that would attract shoppers to the downtown area, build a closer relationship between business and the community, and increase awareness of maritime history through an outdoor display of Great Lakes maritime artifacts. But first they had to make the light accessible to the public. To do this they moved it to Marine City's downtown Waterworks Park on the Detroit River. The transport was quite an undertaking since the tower was over 60-feet (18 m) high, 44 feet (13.5 m) around at its base, and weighed 35 tons. Once it had been relocated, the new owners had it restored to pristine condition, and it was dedicated to Marine City as part of their Maritime Summer Festival in 1983. A piece of history had been saved. People can now view or admire the lighthouse from the park or from a vessel along the Detroit River.

59 Port Clinton Old Lighthouse

In December 1830 Congress appropriated $5,000 for a lighthouse at or near Port Clinton at the mouth of the Portage River on Lake Erie. The lighthouse was built in 1833 to mark the entrance to the harbor. The lighthouse resembled the Barcelona Light at the east end of Lake Erie, which had been built in 1828.

The tower and the house were both made of stone. The relatively short tower had a wide circular base that tapered gently to a narrower top. Little is known about its lantern. However, it was recorded that it had mirrors on the mainland side of the lantern to reflect the lamplight back out over the harbor, and that its four lamps originally burned whale oil. A lighthouse inspection report shows that by 1838 it used eight lamps and eight bright reflectors arranged in a semicircle behind the lamps. The lighthouse was then working well except that the lamp chimneys were too short as they

did not reach above the scallops of the reflectors. The inspector added his opinion that the lighthouse could be discontinued "without the slightest detriment to the commerce of the lake," adding: "It affords no assistance in making a harbor for there is none in the neighbourhood; the coast is free from rock or shoals, with bold shore, conspicuous to mariners and easily avoided." The light was finally discontinued in 1859. Then it was reactivated in 1869 until it was permanently discontinued in 1870 and the lantern removed from the tower.

The keeper's house was a separate 1½-story house. After the lighthouse was decommissioned different families continued to live in the old keeper's house. One of its keepers, Austin Smith, helped rescue survivors of a shipwrecked Chicago-bound vessel that had drifted onto a sandbar near the Port Clinton Lighthouse. Smith and his wife took in a shipwrecked couple who had immigrated from Scotland and had very bad luck. While sailing for America, the promised land, they had had continuously stormy weather and been robbed of all but ten cents of their money. They stayed and worked in New York until they had saved enough money to continue on to Chicago, their original destination. Since the couple lost all their personal belongings in the shipwreck, they found an empty log cabin and settled in the Port Clinton area.

The original structures were doomed. The circular stone tower was torn down in 1899 and the old stone keeper's house in 1900–01. Very few pictures of this original complex exist today.

Known Keepers: Captain Austin Smith (1833–48), W. Cranfield (1848–49), Benjamin Orcutt (1849–53), George Momeny (1853–59), A. Borden (1859), Leander Porter (1864–70).

60 Port Clinton Pier Light

In 1856 Congress advocated a pierhead light at Port Clinton on Lake Erie, but this light was not built until 1896. Piers had been built out into the lake to protect vessels entering the Portage River, and the lighthouse was placed at the lake end of the west pier to mark the entrance between the piers.

Port Clinton Old Pier Light

Presque Isle Lighthouse (Erie, Pennsylvania)

It was a short square pyramidal tower covered with clapboarding. Two ornamental wooden braces at each corner helped support the square gallery. Its octagonal lantern was topped by an octagonal dome with a ventilator ball. Seven of the lantern's eight sides had large glass windows on the top half. It resembled many Canadian lighthouses. Locals sometimes referred to it as the Portage River Entrance Light.

The light's first keeper, Robert Waterfield, lived in the old stone keeper's house built in 1833, as did Daniel Finn, the second keeper. It was torn down in 1900–01 and replaced with a new one.

At an unknown date a light was placed on a steel tower to replace the Pierhead Light, which was sold to Clair and Eddie Jeremy for $1 once it was no longer needed. It was moved from the pier to the river's edge in Port Clinton. Late in the 1970s the land it stood on was sold to Brands Drydock Marina, which continues to maintain the historic building and has put it on display.

Other buildings were also saved. The second keeper's house was turned into a lighthouse restaurant. Its old boathouse was used by the city of Port Clinton as a storage building at a local baseball diamond.

Known Keepers: Robert Waterfield (1896–1900), George Pope (1900–11), David Sutherland (1912–26).

61 Presque Isle Lighthouse (Erie, Pennsylvania)

This lighthouse, situated on a long 7-mile (11 km) sandy arm of land that curves out into Lake Erie, was built to warn mariners of the Presque Isle Peninsula, which interrupts an otherwise straight coastline. An Erie native legend tells of the Great Spirit putting a protective arm around warriors caught in a storm while fishing on Lake Erie. After the storm, the Great Spirit left a giant sand bar where his arm had lain to act for all ages as a shelter and harbor of refuge for the Great Spirit's favorite children, the Eriez.

During the War of 1812, U.S. Commodore Perry built six of his nine vessels, including the brigs *Niagara* and *Lawrence*, in Misery Bay, which was protected by this peninsula. After fighting in the battle at Put-in-Bay (near Sandusky, Ohio), Perry and his men made Misery Bay their temporary home because of threats of another British uprising. Many of his men were quarantined and later died of smallpox during the winter of 1813–14. Their bodies were buried near what aptly became known as Graveyard Pond.

In 1870 the Lighthouse Board commissioned this new light to replace the Erie Land Lighthouse. Construction began in September 1872. After the loss of a scow carrying 6,000 bricks, the lakeside was deemed too dangerous to bring in materials, and a crude roadway was initiated to connect the station with Misery Bay on the mainland side of the peninsula. This 1.5-mile (2.4 km) road was originally just a sandy path through the swampy interior, but was later planked to improve conditions. In 1925 it was elevated and became a concrete path, today known as the Sidewalk Trail.

The lighthouse was ready for service in July 1873, at a total cost of $15,000. The tower was originally only 40 feet (12.2 m) high to the steel balcony but in 1896 an additional 17 feet (5.2 m) was added. The light is 63 feet (19.2 m) above ground and the tower is now 70 feet (21.3 m) to the top of the ventilator ball. The square tower sits on a limestone foundation and is five courses of brick thick to protect the structure from fierce Lake Erie storms. Inside, 72 iron steps and six landings form the spiral staircase, which was forged in Pittsburgh.

The polygonal lantern has a round bottom. The original light was a fourth-order Fresnel lens that used a whale oil lamp to produce a visibility of 15 miles (24 km). It had a two-red and four-white flash pattern that the locals nicknamed "flashlight." The flashes were created by the lens revolving on a series of ball bearings, with red glass panels affixed to the outside lens. The lens revolved thanks to a clockwork mechanism with chains and weights. Every four hours the keeper had to check the oil supply, clean the lens and rewind the weights.

In the 1920s the light was electrified and a 150-watt bulb served as the light source. The keeper would run diesel generators during the day to charge a bank of batteries that produced electricity for the light and house during the night.

In 1962 the Fresnel lens was removed and an aircraft-type beacon installed. Today the light is completely automated, with a 250-watt bulb in a 300 mm plastic lens. Its keeper is an electronic light sensor. If the main light malfunctions, the sensor switches automatically to a battery-powered backup light attached to the front of the tower.

The keeper's house was a formidable red brick, two-story structure with ten rooms. The "oil room," which stored just enough fuel for one night, was at the bottom of the tower. The interior retains its nineteenth-century French architectural design, including rounded corners and hand-crafted woodwork. Most of this wood was milled from trees near the station. Although now gone, other buildings at the station once included a metal oil house (away from the main house for safer storage of flammable fuels), a barn, a storage building, and privies. Out front, on the lakeside, there was a 300-foot (91.5 m) jetty to receive fuels, new equipment, and food staples twice a year from the Lighthouse Board's supply tenders. For other supplies the keepers had to travel to Erie by land and then by boat. A portion of this jetty, which also helped protect the lighthouse location, is still in place today in front of the lighthouse.

The first keeper was Charles Waldo. His journal included the following entry from July 12, 1873: "This is a new station and a light will be exhibited for the first time to night ... There was no visitors." He was paid $520 a year. His duties included keeping the light, maintaining the tower, equipment, residence, out-buildings, and property, and responding to shipwrecks and other emergencies. His daughter Nellie, born in 1876 to his wife, Mary, was the first child known to be born on Presque Isle. After a seven-year tenure on the peninsula, Waldo described it as "the loneliest place on earth."

Other important dates in the lighthouse's history included: 1921, when the peninsula was established as Presque Isle State Park; 1927, when a main road was opened to the lighthouse on the lakeside (unfortunately storms continually damaged the road and wash-outs were common until the road was moved to its current, more protected location in 1948); 1941, when the U.S. Coast Guard assumed responsibility for the lighthouse from the

Lighthouse Service; 1957, when indoor plumbing was installed; 1983, when the lighthouse was entered into the *National Register of Historic Places*; 1986, when the State signed a 25-year occupancy license agreement; and 1997, when the Lighthouse Exhibit was set up to share historical information with the tourists.

The last true keeper of the light was Frank Huntington. After him, individuals and families lived in the lighthouse as residents, but not as hired keepers. Today the residence is maintained by the Presque Isle State Park and used as employee housing. The light, which now flashes a white light, is maintained by the U.S. Coast Guard. The red-brick tower is painted white with a black lantern, dome, and ventilator ball. Sandy beaches, hiking trails, and protected flora and fauna make Presque Isle State Park a popular destination.

Known Keepers: Charles Waldo (1873–80), George Town (1881–83), Clark McCole (1883–86), Lewis Vannatta (1886–91), Louis Walrose (1891–92), Thomas Wilkins (1894–1901), Andrew Shaw Jr. (1901–27), Frank Huntington (1927–44).

Sandusky Bay Front Range Light

62 Sandusky Bay Lights

Research shows that two different lights marked entry to Sandusky Bay. Sandusky Maritime Museum information reports a lighthouse at the tip of Cedar Point on the east side of Sandusky Bay in 1862. The *Pharos Guide* of 1882 reports "a stationary light, elevated 60 feet (18.5 m) above the lake, on a projecting point of land, about 1.5 miles (2.5 km) west of the entrance to the bay."

It is not documented when a light was first placed at either site. However, a Treasury Department list of 1823 shows that Sandusky's lighthouse used 13 lamps. In 1832 and again in 1834 Congress appropriated $3,500 for a lighthouse near Sandusky. In 1837 Congress appropriated $2,500 for a lighthouse near the entrance to Sandusky Bay. A later report to Congress (1838) for the Sandusky lighthouse states that it had 15 lamps but only 13 were used with 13 bright reflectors, that the materials furnished by the contractor were faultless (indicating a brand new lighthouse that had been built), and that the lighthouse was "an important one, from its favorable location in making the spacious bay of Sandusky."

No mention was made as to exactly where this lighthouse was located. While this information supports the premise of an east and west lighthouse to mark Sandusky Bay, confusion remains as to what was built and where.

Sandusky Bay Rear Range Light

63 Sandusky Bay Straight Channel Range Lights

In August 1895 cribs were sunk in the channel into Sandusky Harbor, Lake Erie, to support concrete foundations for two lighthouses constructed of wood. The square towers ran up one end of both houses, partially in and partially out of the house. Their lanterns, completed in 1896, were one story above the roofs of the houses. They helped guide vessels in and out of the bay until they were removed by controlled fire in 1926 to allow for the construction of "skeletal towers" of steel. These towers have since been replaced by cylindrical steel towers.

64 Sandusky Harbor Pierhead Light

It is unknown when Sandusky Harbor, Lake Erie, received its first pierhead light, and little is known about the light. In 1921–22 it was replaced by a skeletal iron tower constructed on a thick concrete foundation at the end of a rough stone pier that jutted into the lake from Cedar Point. The tower supported a square watchroom with porthole windows. At one time it probably had a cast-iron lantern, which has since been removed. In later years it was topped with a modern beacon style light attached to the roof. In 1967 the beacon exhibited a flashing white light from a 66-foot (20 m) focal plane. This tower was removed in 1996 and replaced by a much shorter, cylindrical tower and horn.

Sandusky Harbor Pierhead Light

65 Silver Creek Lighthouse

The community of Silver Creek, Lake Erie, arose at the mouth of Silver Creek in the early 1800s. Its name came from native folklore, which said there had once been a silver mine nearby. One of its first entrepreneurs, Oliver Lee, stimulated harbor development by instigating the construction of docks to welcome vessels carrying immigrants, ship lumber and farm products. Also, steamers running between Barcelona and Buffalo began to make Silver Creek a regular stop to refuel with needed wood. A shipbuilding business also arose, which in 1837 built the brig *Osceola*, the first vessel to haul grain from Chicago in 1839.

With increased maritime traffic, Lee petitioned the government for a pierhead light and meanwhile personally paid for a light on the pier as needed. The request fell on deaf ears even though an appropriation for $2,000 had been made in 1834. Finally another appropriation was made in 1837 for $4,500 to build a beacon light at the end of the pier at Silver Creek, Lake Erie. However, the Board of Navy Commissioners decided in September 1837 to reject a light at this location. Two months later, the board reversed its decision, and Stephan Pleasonton, the Fifth Auditor of the U.S. Treasury, requested that an engineer draw up plans for the lighthouse. The government accepted engineer Lee's proposal to build the lighthouse and keeper's house and to provide land for the lighthouse use, all inclusive, for the $4,500 appropriation.

The polygonal wooden tapering tower with its birdcage lantern was finished by June 30, 1838. The keeper's house was built onshore and set on blocks. On July 3, 1838, Captain Moses Fuller was hired as keeper for $350 a year. Since Lee was not a practiced lighthouse builder, he had installed several basic whale oil lamps in a circle on a table in the lighthouse's lantern. Captain Fuller replaced Lee's lamps with nine glass-globe whale-oil lamps, which had no chimneys or reflectors and were not standard government issue. In 1838 the lighthouse inspector reported that the contractor's lamps were "deficient" and that the keeper had supplied his own because they were "not fit for use." Further, the tower deck leaked badly; the crib on which the lighthouse stood was good but needed to be filled with stone; and, while the light had great commercial benefit, the harbor was too exposed to provide much safe shelter during storms. Repairs were authorized, and buff-skins and oil were to be supplied by the government. However, the 1839 and 1840 inspections still showed a leaky tower and improper lamps.

In August 1841 the 176-foot (54 m) wooden passenger and freight side-wheeler steamer *Erie* burnt and sank 6 miles (10 km) offshore. It had gone a short way from Buffalo to Chicago when it caught fire. It was carrying Swiss and German immigrants headed for the west and over 200 passengers and crew were lost. Nearby steamers *DeWitt*, *Clinton* and *Lady* were able to rescue only 30 survivors. This was the worst steamer disaster that had occurred up till that time. The *Erie* also carried great wealth on board; when the hulk was raised in 1854, over $200,000 in melted gold and silver was recovered.

The lamps at Silver Creek Lighthouse were finally replaced in 1841. Five Winslow Lewis lamps with 14-inch (35 cm) reflectors were mounted to a chandelier to produce a fixed white light in all directions.

An inspection in May 1842 put the keeper on notice. The lighting apparatus was dirty, although the light was generally good. The report said the keeper was "given to intemperance," "altogether unfit for the responsible station" and "under the influence of liquor" — and recommended his removal. It also noted that the deck of the lighthouse was leaking and the pier had become a "perilous footway to the beacon." The keeper's house also needed repairs. Another inspection two months later found the reflectors had been improperly mounted to the chandelier, impeding the maximum range of brightness of the lamps, as they reflected the light into the sky and the lake instead of to the horizon.

The 1843 inspection found the tower still damp and recommended lining it with wood or plaster and relaying its floors. It also further criticized the 61-year-old keeper: "The keeper is old and imbecile, and scarcely fit to stand the hardships of such a station." The lock was off the door and "people were permitted to stand, during rainy weather, in the beacon, to fish." The inspector "admonished" the keeper about "these improprieties," but went on to note: his duties were "tolerably well attended to. No recent complaints have been made in regard to the light."

In 1844, during a severe November storm, men were trapped at the lighthouse overnight and could only make it safely to shore the next day with the help of a rescue boat, as a good part of the pier had been washed away. Since the keeper could not reach the beacon to light it in stormy weather, the government made repairs to the pier and the lighthouse.

Misfortune again struck the area in November 1846. A heavy storm drove the locally built brig *Osceola* ashore at Silver Creek, and five of its eight-man crew died. In 1847 a beacon light was built at Cattaraugus Creek, 4 miles (6.5 km) away, and for an extra $15 a month the Silver Creek keeper was also put in charge of this new light. Captain Fuller first lit it on November 25, 1847.

The remaining days for the pierhead light at Silver Creek were numbered. In 1851 Congress received a report that the piers at Silver Creek were deteriorating rapidly. Since the railroad arrived at the village in 1851–52, local businessmen were reluctant to spend money on the piers. They preferred to discontinue the pierhead light and move it to the high bluff on the west side of the harbor. The government agreed, provided they were granted a property deed with rights for road access to it. This took place, and the pierhead light was moved at the end of the 1851 season.

The light on the bluff was established by early 1852. When it was realized that the 27-foot (8.2 m) pierhead light (base to focal plane) would be too short when placed on the bluff, an additional 16-foot (4.8 m) rubble-stone base was constructed and the old wooden pierhead light was moved and added to the top of the stone base. This made the bluff light 43 feet (13 m) from the ground to its lantern's focal plane.

The advent of the railroad and new roads led to the light's demise. With poor piers, fewer vessels stopped at Silver Creek. The 1853 inspector's report to Congress viewed the light as "useless" since there was no harbor or shelter. The 1855 report stated

the same. In 1856 the Lighthouse Board requested that Congress discontinue the light, and approval was granted on November 25, 1856. In 1857 all of its equipment was sent for storage at the Buffalo Lighthouse Depot. Although the inspector's 1858 report recommended selling the property, it did not go on sale until the Lighthouse Board advertised it on August 21, 1871. Its sale to Stephen Connors of Silver Creek for $250 officially ended the Silver Creek Lighthouse.

Known Keeper: Moses Fuller (1838–1856).

66 South Bass Island Lighthouse

In June 1838 Congress appropriated $3,000 to build a lighthouse at Gibraltar Point on the northwest side of Bass Island near Put-in-Bay, Lake Erie. Upon inspection of this area in 1838, U.S. Navy Lt. Charles T. Platt reported that this was a bad location for a light to be seen by mariners heading for the South Passage; the light, he said, should be built on the southwest part of the island. So adamant was he that he marked a tree with the letters LH at his chosen spot. However, his recommendation was clearly ignored for many years, as a lighthouse was not built at that site until 1897.

The South Bass Lighthouse sits on the southwest tip of South Bass Island. It is one of several lights that marked the South Passage between the Bass Islands and the Ohio shore, in Lake Erie. Its massive size is impressive; it seems to dwarf the rocky cliffs of the lake in front of it.

With the island's popularity in the 1890s, public and private boating in the area increased. When this was brought to the government's attention, $8,000 was appropriated to build a lighthouse. In 1895, 2½ acres (1.6 hectares) of land on the southwest part of the island were purchased from Margaret and Alfred Parker. Soon, the island's limekiln dock was reconstructed, and the 60-foot (18.5 m) lighthouse and attached keeper's dwelling were built.

The square, red-brick tower has many large windows to light its stairway. The top of the tower flares out gently to help form the gallery. It is topped by a white decagonal lantern with a red dome and ventilator ball. A square, white-painted iron balustrade surrounds the gallery. According to the booklet *Gibraltar, Our Story*, the lantern and circular iron stairway for the lighthouse came from the Gibraltar Lighthouse, which had been taken out of service in 1879 and was sold at public auction in 1895. The lantern was furnished with a fourth-order Fresnel lens that cost $1,500. The light's focal plane was 74 feet (22.5 m).

According to an 1897 report in T. Thorndale's column "Island Jottings" in the *Sandusky Register*, "The principal apartments above the tower are the watch and lamp rooms. The former is amply furnished with everything in the way of lighting supplies and the latter, the keeper courteously unsacks from its canvas covering the lens. It is a beautiful object, catching and holding within its prismatic meshes all colors of the rainbow."

The keeper's house is a 2½-story red-brick structure with a full basement and is built adjoining one side of the tower. Its Queen Anne architectural style with ornately spindled verandas front and back gave it grace and poise. When first built, the house featured many "modern" amenities, as Thorndale articulately

South Bass Island Lighthouse

South Bass Island Lighthouse

to produce 126,000 candlepower with a 15-mile (24 km) visibility. The rotating light flashed, alternating 30 seconds red, 30 seconds white. Another light and aid to navigation on top of the Perry's Victory and International Peace Monument on the island was also placed in his charge. All lights except the South Bass Light were left to operate year-round for the sake of ice fishermen. Keeper Prochnow also received a Distinguished Service award from the U.S. Coast Guard for "devising and installing a superior fire safety system" that the Coast Guard planned to copy at other lighthouses.

describes in her column: "Its numerous apartments are ample and airy. They are handsomely finished with gold tinted wallpaper and gilded mouldings, lovely carpets and richly upholstered furniture. The mantels are beautifully inlaid, bronzed and carved, and everything about the place, above and below, just as nice as it can be … The kitchen is beautifully shellacked, with ceiling painted to match. A massive new range, with a hot water reservoir, is part of the furniture." A separate oil house and a wood framed barn/chicken house were built in 1899.

The first keeper, Harry H. Riley, hired for $560 a year, came to this "dream house" with his bride in 1897 when the light was first lit. But the house turned into a nightmare. Samuel Anderson, taken on as a lighthouse laborer in the summer of 1898, committed suicide after 22 days by jumping from the lighthouse cliff. Some speculated that he had gone crazy from fear of contracting smallpox during a quarantine on the island. Is he perhaps the ghost that allegedly still resides at the lighthouse? Then, just two days after Anderson's death, Riley was arrested in Sandusky and committed to an asylum for mental health problems. Mrs. Riley took over as keeper until Enoch Scribner was appointed in 1899.

Colonel J. (Orlo) Mason's appointment as keeper lasted from 1900 until 1908, when he transferred to the Ashtabula Lighthouse. During this period, the lighthouse tender *U.S. Haze* served the lighthouse. Charles Duggan was keeper from 1908 until 1925, when he fell 30 feet (9 m) from a cliff on the west side of the island and died. He had also owned 20 acres on the island and farmed, growing grapes and peaches to supplement his income. His son Lyle filled in as temporary keeper to finish the season. His annual salary was $1,200 to $1,400.

The next keeper was World War I veteran Captain William Gordon. Economic measures dictated that he was also put in charge of the Green Island and Ballast Island Lighthouses and all the area buoys, for a salary ranging from $1,320 to $1,560. During his term the lighthouse was served by the lighthouse tender *U.S. Crocus*. Historical letters show how the island's lonely isolation was alleviated with the advent of radio.

During the tenure of the last keeper, Paul Prochnow, many changes occurred. The light, powered by the huge iron weight on steel cables, was converted to electricity, allowing a 150-watt bulb

In a newspaper interview, Prochnow told how he almost ended his career in the late fifties when his Model A Ford went through the ice near Green Island. He and a companion had to swim up to the surface from 30 feet (9 m) underwater, where his car had parked. In another interview he related how the pay was not good compared to "city dwellers" but the government supplied the house, heating, and utilities, and transportation was not a problem because he couldn't go out in the evenings anyway. Coupling this with no traffic jams, no noisy neighbors and no door-to-door salesmen, it made for "the good life."

In 1962 the light was automated and moved to a steel skeletal tower with an electronic light, located near the old lighthouse. The lighthouse was rented to Harry Johnson of Williston, Ohio, for the winning bid of $66.50 a month for a five-year period. In 1967 the property transferred ownership to the Ohio State University. In 1983 the National Oceanic and Atmospheric Administration installed a $50,000 meteorological station at the site.

In 1990 the lighthouse was recognized by the *National Register of Historic Places*. Although the lighthouse is not open to the public, it can be viewed from the ferry approach to the island or, for a rear view, from the end of Langram Road on the island. The original lens is on display at the Lake Erie Island Historical Museum at Put-in-Bay, on South Bass Island.

Known Keepers: Harry Riley (1897–98), Mrs. Harry Riley (1898–99), Enoch Scribner (1899–1900), Captain Orlo Mason (1900–08), Charles Duggan (1908–25), William Gordon (1926–39), Frank La Rose (1939–41), Robert Jones (1941–44), Kenneth Nester (1944–47), Paul Prochnow (1947–62).

67 St. Clair Flats Range Lights

During the mid-1800s travel was fastest and cheapest by water. It was Abraham Lincoln, a lawyer and not yet president, who signed the order to build the South Channel Range Lights at the mouth of the St. Clair River, to encourage commerce between Lake Huron and Lake Erie.

The area where the St. Clair River empties into Lake St. Clair is called the "Flats," a delta of shallow water with a network of low-lying islands. Without lighthouses, the South Channel from the lake to the river could be navigated only during the day. One

St. Clair Flats Front Range Light

In July 1871 a new, straighter, shorter channel was opened up for vessel navigation into the St. Clair River. The "Old Twin Sisters" were not as needed as they once were, but they continued to be a help. The front range light sustained more water and ice damage over the years as it had no keeper's house behind it for protection. The limestone foundation gradually eroded and the tower started to tilt. In 1875 it was dismantled and rebuilt on its original stone and timber crib.

By 1907 ships traveling the Great Lakes were too large for the South Channel. They traveled a new deeper channel, so the range lights were deemed obsolete and were removed from service at this time. The abandoned lighthouse sat empty and open to vandalism. Due to its isolation, rumors that it was used by persons engaging in illegal activities (a secret bar?) during Prohibition may be true. The keeper's house was torn down sometime in the 1930s.

At an unknown date the Coast Guard removed the lantern from the front range light and relit it with a solar-powered light as an aid to navigation. By the 1980s the front range light was again tilting as a result of water and ice damage. However, the government would not save it this time. Instead it was rescued by Chuck Brockman, who founded an organization called Save Our South Channel Lights (SOSCL) in 1988. He had boated past them as a child, and as an adult he took action.

The SOSCL group has done much to preserve these lights. Ownership has been transferred from the U.S. Coast Guard to their organization. The Coast Guard will still maintain the light on the front range tower but SOSCL will be responsible for the upkeep of the tower. In 1990 the towers were registered in the *National Register of Historic Places*. The group has stabilized the damaged front range light and built a seawall around it at the cost of $70,000.

account tells of 100 vessels anchoring overnight at Anchor Bay, awaiting daylight to pass through the channel, to prevent a collision or a grounding.

The range lights, built in the water of the South Channel between Gull Island and the southwestern tip of the larger Harsen's Island, allowed boats to travel at night. Mariners leaving Lake St. Clair would line up the range lights to guide them safely into the South Channel of the St. Clair River. Being able to travel 24 hours a day was advantageous, saving both time and money. These lights were called the St. Clair Flats Range Lights or the South Channel Lights and were even nicknamed the "Old Twin Sisters."

A bill was passed in 1854 to build the foundations for the range lights at a cost of $20,000. The towers and keeper's house were finished and the light lit in 1859. They were both built on limestone block foundations placed on top of sunken timber, rock-filled cribs. Both towers were built of yellow brick from Milwaukee. The cornices and the caps and sills for the doors and windows were made of well-dressed limestone from Buffalo quarries. Both towers had cast-iron stairs and were conical in shape.

St. Clair Flats Front Range Light

St. Clair Flats Rear Range Light

In 1995 a dive team from the Macomb County Sheriff's Patrol discovered part of the missing decagonal dome for the front range tower during one of their monthly practice dives. They selected the area around the old

The front range light was the shorter, being 17 feet (5.2 m) with a focal plane of 28 feet (8.5 m). Its fifth-order Fresnel lens displayed a fixed white light that had a 10-mile (16 km) visibility. The rear light, 1,000 feet (305 m) behind the front range light, was 40 feet (12 m) tall and had a 44-foot (13.5 m) focal plane. It had a fourth-order Fresnel lens in its decagonal lantern and also displayed a fixed white light, but it had a 12-mile (19 km) visibility.

The keeper's house, a two-story yellow-brick house with a slate roof, was attached to the rear range light. It also had limestone caps and sills for its doors and windows. There was very little room around the house for the keeper and his family to move around.

St. Clair Flats Rear Range Light

South Channel Lights to help the local historical group in its research and restoration campaign. The lantern piece was recovered and moved to a Harrison Township marina for storage pending restoration. If SOSCL cannot restore it, they will use it to design a replacement dome when they rebuild the lantern room.

The SOSCL has a three-phase plan: first, to jack up the tilting tower and replace its lantern; second, to refurbish the rear range tower, including windows and a new staircase; third, to rebuild the keeper's dwelling. Their dream is to make a maritime museum. While the once-practical function of these range lights has been taken over by modern technological equipment, the towers remain as monuments of an earlier history.

68   St. Clair Flats Ship Canal Lights

As Great Lakes shipping developed, vessels became larger to hold more cargo. For these large ships the South Channel did not provide a deep enough passage between the St. Clair River and Lake St. Clair. A new shipping canal was built and ready for use by 1871. The new channel was much wider, straighter, deeper and a more direct route to the St. Clair River. It was 20 feet (6 m) deep, 300 yards (275 m) wide, and a mile and a half (2.4 km) long. The dredged bottomlands were piled into a long line that created a dyke, which became a man-made tree-lined linear island. Metal seawalls contained the mile-long (1.6 km), 100-foot (30.8 m) wide "dyke."

During the operation the dredging was put on hold for a while until ownership of the area was confirmed. Apparently United States maps showed the canal to be in American waters but British maps showed it was in Canadian territory. Eventually the dispute was solved, American ownership was agreed upon, and construction resumed.

Twin light stations, placed at either end of the mile-long (1.6 km) island, were lit in November 1871 and known as the St. Clair Flats Ship Canal Lights. The 45-foot (13.7 m) towers had a cut limestone foundation and a brick tower, and were built into the corner of the keeper's house. The bottoms of the towers were square with supporting buttresses at the corners, and the tops were octagonal. Octagonal lanterns sat on top of the narrow galleries, which were supported by a multitude of carved wooden braces. The lanterns, topped by domes with ventilator balls, displayed fixed red lights from a fourth-order Fresnel lens. Water for the stations was supplied from Lake St. Clair. Both stations included the lighthouse, a keeper's dwelling, an oil house, a boathouse, indoor plumbing and a hennery.

One known keeper was Andrew (Andy) Rattery. His daughter, Alice, was born in 1896 at the upper lighthouse station, where he was keeper until his retirement after World War 1.

In 1906 a canal was dredged out on the west side of the dyke to allow upbound ship traffic to use the east side and the downbound vessels to use the west side, providing faster, safer passage.

Not long after Rattery's retirement and sometime in the 1930s, both light stations and the man-made islands were leveled and the channel dredged to make way for a larger, deeper waterway, part of the coming St. Lawrence Seaway. This new channel was marked by a lighthouse built on Harsen's Island and a lightship located in the lake at the turning point into the channel.

69   Stoddard Range Lights

During the mid-1800s, when lake travel was on the increase, lights were placed in or around Maumee Bay to help mark the bay's deep water to safe anchorage. One such light was placed on the mainland near Toledo in 1868 on 15 acres of government land under the control of the Rivers and Harbor Bureau.

The lighthouse was most unusual. Built of wood in a board and batten style it looked like a half-a-house, with the high side of the house facing the water and the low side facing inland. It was 60 feet (18.2 m) across the front and 15 feet (4.6 m) wide, just wide enough for one room. The roof was slanted only at the front, leaving the rear of the building a flat expanse where the middle of a normal house would be. The upper level had a bank of 21 windows across the back. It was from here that the keeper shone out the protective light to assist mariners in navigating the old twisting channel of Maumee Bay into Toledo.

Captain George Stoddard lived here and operated and maintained the light until 1905 when the Toledo Harbor Light went into service. Since he was the light's only keeper, it became known as the Stoddard Range Light. After being the lightkeeper for 36 years Stoddard took command of the steamer *Dean Richmond*. This vessel, including all hands, was lost in a fearful storm in October 1883.

This light was considered a rear range light, as it was used in conjunction with another light to line up safe passage. While it is known that a Mr. Fanstock was keeper of the front light, its exact location is a mystery. Both lights were deemed unnecessary once the new deeper and straighter channel was dredged through the bay and the Toledo Harbor Light was built.

Known Keeper: Captain George Stoddard (1868-1905).

70   Toledo Harbor Lighthouse

In 1898 Congress appropriated $75,000 to build this lighthouse, but no one wanted the contract at that price. In 1900 it appropriated $100,000, and the firm of Randolph and Baer was awarded the contract. The lighthouse was planned by Major Symons, a U.S. army engineer. Construction started in February 1901, but the lighthouse was not finished until April 1904, because of delays in iron and steel shipments, a death in the firm and labor strikes.

Toledo Harbor Lighthouse

Upon its completion, the light at Turtle Island, which had previously guided vessels into Maumee Bay, was abandoned.

The Toledo lighthouse stands 12 miles (19.3 km) out in Lake Erie, in about 21 feet (6.5 m) of water, marking the entrance to the deep channel into Toledo Harbor through Maumee Bay. Its first lightkeeper was Dell Hayden and his assistant was Edward Reicherd. At the time it was built it was considered the most modern lighthouse and fog signal station anywhere in the world. Its illuminating apparatus, weighing over a ton cost $5,000 and was a featured exhibit at the 1901 Pan-American Exposition.

Toledo Harbor Lighthouse

The 1901 construction started with the building of the huge crib right in Toledo. The square hemlock timbers were faced with 4-inch (10 cm) oak planking and bolted together with iron screw bolts. In May the crib was launched and towed to the site where it was sunk and filled with stone, sand, and gravel. The crib top was about 2 feet (0.6 m) underwater. It supported the lighthouse's foundation of huge, solid concrete blocks built up to a height of about 12 feet (3.5 m) above lake level. The lighthouse and fog signal station were then built on top of this.

The lightkeeper's house and tower were one unit, complete with basement, three stories, attic, watch room and lantern. Its steel frame was covered by brick. The basement included a furnace room, an oil room and storage spaces. The other floors contained an engine and power room, an office, kitchens, sitting rooms and bedrooms for the two lightkeepers and their families. Above this rose the tower with its watch room and the lantern topped by a dome and a wind gauge that was 90 feet (27 m) above the lake level. The lighthouse has uniquely styled Moorish roofs. The keeper's dwelling was finished with quarter oak and had polished maple floors. It also had polished brass and bronze plumbing fixtures. With its hot air furnace and hot and cold running water, it was considered the best of its time.

The circular lantern with 54 curved panes of glass was surrounded by a circular gallery enclosed by an ornamental railing. Housed inside was a third-order Fresnel lens that revolved on ball-bearings, making one complete revolution every 80 seconds and giving three flashes every revolution. The three flashes included one red and two white of equal duration and intensity. Its focal plane was 72 feet (22 m) above lake level and its visibility was 16 miles (26 km) in all directions. The lens revolved by clockworks operated by weights. This illuminating apparatus was the best available. In 1953 the light became a 500-watt bulb that the lens magnified to 190,000 candlepower. Now it uses a 1,000-watt bulb.

The fog signal building, attached to the keeper's house, was a one-story addition on the northwest side. The fog signal was blasts of 3 seconds duration separated by 17 seconds of silence. They were the first on the Great Lakes to be operated by compressed air produced by compressors attached to a Hornsby-Akroyd oil engine.

In 1966 the U.S. Coast Guard automated the lights and the fog signal. The lighthouse sent out a radio beacon that boats could use to fix their positions.

Its weather bureau equipment was moved ashore. This equipment is the most missed because it used to give wave height at the lighthouse. Now the Coast Guard has to guess the height of the waves.

In 1986 the Coast Guard put a male mannequin, dressed in a lighthouse keeper's uniform, in a second-story window to give the place a "lived-in" look and prevent vandalism. From this, boaters created the rumor of the "Phantom of the Lighthouse." Many people reported seeing the figure, while others said that they couldn't see it at all. Who knows? Perhaps there is more to this haunting than meets the eye.

Known Keepers: Dell Hayden (1903–08), August Gramer (1908–09), Charles Chapman (1909–17), Bert Disset (1917–19), Herman Schroeder (1922–36), Harley Johnson (1936–39), L Jennings (1940), Robert Siggens (1947–55).

Turtle Island Lighthouse

71 Turtle Island Lighthouse

Not far into Lake Erie from the Maumee River mouth and sitting on the Ohio–Michigan border is Turtle Island, a tiny island, mostly clay, gravel and rock, plus overgrown vegetation and one deteriorated light tower. The island was named to show respect for the Miami Chief, Little Turtle, a cunning military strategist and most worthy opponent. While hunting in the area his people would stop at Turtle Island to collect gull eggs.

In 1827 the U.S. government had auctioned off the useless 6 ⅔-acre (2.7 hectare) island to the highest bidder, not foreseeing its future importance. Lake traffic was booming, especially since the opening of the Erie Canal in 1825 and the Welland Canal in 1829. Realizing that navigational improvements were needed for Maumee Bay (Toledo) and the surrounding area, the government decided that Turtle Island was the best spot to build a lighthouse since the main channel ran just south of the island. In 1831 they bought back the island — now only 1½ acres (0.6 hectares) thanks to wind and water erosion — from Edward Bissell for $300 and they appropriated $5,000 to build the light and another $2,000 to "halt the steady erosion of the island." Philo Scovile was contracted to build the Turtle Island Lighthouse.

The lighthouse was on the north end of the island facing south-southeast. Its conical, 44-foot (13.5 m) tower was built of yellow square brick and stone. The black lantern housed eight white fixed lamps with reflectors, which had a 6-mile (9.5 km) visibility. There was a 1½-story, attached wooden keeper's house with four rooms.

By 1836 the island had been further eroded to only one acre (0.4 hectare). In 1837 the Fifth Auditor of the Treasury appropriated $8,000 to "secure and complete the foundation of the lighthouse" and by 1838 another $8,700 had been spent before it was stabilized. In 1857 the lighthouse was given a new fourth-order Fresnel lens with a 14-mile (22.5 km) visibility. By 1865, however, the lighthouse was reported to be in dilapidated condition and a new light was proposed, but no building funds were available until the end of the civil war.

In 1866, $12,000 was appropriated to rebuild the light at Turtle Island. A 1½-story schoolhouse-style keeper's house and tower were constructed of Milwaukee Brick. The 45-foot (13.7 m) tower had a cast-iron circular staircase that led up to its decagonal lantern and three double windows up the front to illuminate the staircase. The relatively new lighting apparatus from the old tower was used in the new one. The gallery was surrounded by an iron railing.

The light was relit on September 12, 1866. Further changes followed: in 1869 a cistern was added to the house; in 1871 a fog bell was installed; in 1876 the pilings and the storm-damaged shore protection were repaired; in 1880 a new well was sunk; in 1881 and 1882, after more storm damage, repairs were twice made to stabilize the lighthouse shore protection. In 1883–84 a 4-foot-thick (1.2 m) concrete wall was built around the lighthouse to protect it from erosion, a storm house was built onto the rear of the keeper's house, storm shutters were added to all the windows and a new boathouse was built.

As shipping continued to increase and boats became larger, the waters around Turtle Island could not accommodate them. When the shipping channel changed, a new light was built at Toledo Harbor and the light at Turtle Island was decommissioned on May 5, 1904.

Turtle Island had 15 main lightkeepers during its 72 years of operation. Although no shipping accidents occurred in its vicinity, the keepers were not so lucky. One of its early keepers, Samuel Choate, and his son Captain Seth Choate both died of cholera on the island in 1834. In 1854 Okey McCormick, the light's tenth keeper, died when he was washed off his sailboat while returning with provisions from Toledo, only 4 miles (6.5 km) away. In February 1869 Nathan Edson, the fourteenth keeper, headed off to Toledo with Martin Goulden to purchase a coffin for Goulden's father-in-law, who had died unexpectedly at the West Sister Island Light. Their boat became trapped in the ice about a mile from the lighthouse and the two men died of exposure. The last keeper was William Haynes, who, more fortunate, converted the upper level of the house to a one-room school where Mrs. Haynes educated all of the children.

Over the years the keepers' payroll gradually increased. In 1847 the keeper made $400 a year. By 1854 an assistant keeper had been added for $100 a year. In 1867 the head keeper made $600 per

Vermillion Lighthouse

year. Perhaps this was a good annual income but it was a most remote, lonely place to spend 365 days a year.

After being decommissioned, the lighthouse was sold at public auction to A.H. Merrill on December 6, 1904 for $1,650. It changed ownership three times from 1905 to 1933. During this time it sat empty and vandals destroyed the tower and the lighthouse, taking pieces for souvenirs. From 1933 to 1937 the Associated Yacht Club of Toledo leased the island as their clubhouse and harbor. They restored the first floor of the lighthouse and the tower but eventually gave up the spot because of its remote location. Since the Ohio-Michigan border runs through the island, owners have paid taxes to both states since 1933. From 1937 the lighthouse stood empty. Then in 1965 the Palm Sunday tornado swept through, ripping the lantern from the tower and flattening the house. Only the tower was left, with the iron rods that once anchored the lantern sticking helplessly into the sky.

In 1997 the island's private owner had hopes of restoring the lighthouse that storms and vandals brought down, but it will take determination for this dream to become a reality.

Known Keepers: William Wilson (1832), Ben Cass (1832–33), Samuel Choate (1833–34), Ebenezer Ward (1834–35), O. Whitmore (1835–37), Ebenezer Ward (1837–39), Gideon Kelsey (1839–47), Alex Cromwell (1847–50), Gordon Wilson (1850–53), Okey McCormick (1853–54), Isaac McCormick (1854–58), John Coonahan (1858–61), Andrew Harrison (1861–67), Nathan Edson (1867–69), Ann Edson (1869–72), Samuel Jacobs (1872–74), Emmet Root (1874–75), William Haynes (1875–1904).

72 Vermillion Lighthouse

Over the years four lighthouses have been built at Vermillion, Ohio, on Lake Erie. In April 1844 Congress appropriated $3,000 to build the first lighthouse at the mouth of the Vermillion River. This lighthouse, of unknown description, was built in 1847. In 1852 Congress appropriated $3,000 for repairs to the pier and for removing the light at Vermillion Harbor. The second light was built at Vermillion in 1859 and its sixth-order lens was upgraded to a fifth-order lens.

The lighthouse was rebuilt for the third time in 1877. The 29-foot (9 m) tapering octagonal tower sat on an octagonal concrete foundation at the end of the wooden pier. Its base was painted reddish-brown while the rest of the tower was white. The octagonal lantern, dome, ventilator stack, and gallery were painted black. A few porthole windows in the tower provided interior light. In 1901 it used a fifth-order lens to display a fixed red light for 9 miles (14.5 km). It had a catwalk out from the shore to help the keeper reach it safely in inclement weather. Around 1919 the light was automated with the change from oil to acetylene, and a keeper was no longer needed.

Then in 1929 this third light disappeared. One morning Ted Wakefield, then a boy fascinated by the Vermillion light, which stood at the end of the pier in the harbor in front of his parents' mansion, looked out at the lighthouse and noticed it was tilting. He told his father, who immediately reported it to the local authorities. Apparently part of the foundation had been swept away by a fierce ice storm and this led to the tower's tilting. However, instead of repairing the lighthouse, a crew from the Lighthouse Service appeared one morning, dismantled the lighthouse, and took it to Buffalo for storage. In its place they erected an 18-foot (5.5 m) steel tower with a beacon on top.

Young Wakefield never forgot the lighthouse. As an adult he tried to find out what happened to it, but Coast Guard records after its removal to Buffalo had gone missing, perhaps in the 1939 turnover from the Lighthouse Service to the Coast Guard. In the 1980s Wakefield spearheaded a program to raise funds to build an exact replica of the third light at Vermillion. He was instrumental in making this dream come true; the replica was built on the shore in front of the Great Lakes Historical Society museum. The replica, Vermillion's fourth lighthouse, was relit in 1991, using a Fresnel lens that displayed a flashing red light. It was not quite the same as there was no catwalk and it was not built on a pier, but it was close to the original location and it was the pride and joy of many Vermillion residents, including Wakefield.

Shortly after Wakefield's death the location of the old, missing Vermillion Lighthouse became known. Olin Stevens was a former lightkeeper at Vermillion sometime prior to 1929. When he died, his grandson went through an old trunk of his grandfather's memorabilia and found a 1937 news clipping that welcomed Olin W. Stevens as the new keeper at Charity Shoal Light. The article went on to say: "Altho this is his first duty on Lake Ontario, Charity Shoal Light, visible from Tibbets [sic] Point Headland, is an old friend. The tower upholding the gas lamp on Charity formerly was under Stevens' charge at Vermillion near Lorain. Victim of an ice shove, it was salvaged and taken to Buffalo, where it was assigned to Charity." Although it had been put on a new, slightly different base, it was in fact the old Vermillion Lighthouse. After 65 years the mystery of the missing light had been solved.

Vermillion was once known as "the city of sea captains" as at one time more than 100 ships' captains called it home. Perhaps this is why it was so important to Ted Wakefield to find or replace the light, or perhaps it was just that he loved the tower so much, having seen it every day until its removal in 1929. As well as being the catalyst for the building of the replica tower, the Wakefield mansion became home to the Great Lakes Historical Society in 1953. Since then, it has been enlarged, giving it space to house a large research library and exhibit many lighthouse and marine artefacts, including the second-order Fresnel lens from Spectacle Reef Lighthouse. When the replica tower was built in 1991 it became part of the complex, and the museum was renamed the Inland Sea Maritime Museum of the Great Lakes Historical Society. The society is the oldest and largest organization devoted exclusively to the maritime history of the Great Lakes. It is conveniently open seven days a week year round.

Known Keepers: William Andrews (1849–51), James Anderson (1851–52), Charles Judson (1852–54), O. Allen (1854–61), William Andrews (1861–69), Burt Parsons (1869–73), Charles Miles (1873–79), Harris Miles (1879–1901), George Codding (1901–04), John Burns (1904–14), John Wetzler (1914–20), Olin Stevens (?).

73 West Sister Island Lighthouse

To help mark the entrance into Maumee Bay at the west end of Lake Erie, Congress appropriated $4,000 in January 1847 for a lighthouse on West Sister Island (also known as Western Sister Island). The lighthouse was built and lit for the 1848 shipping season.

The conical limestone tower was 55 feet (16.7 m) high and painted white for greater visibility. A black iron pipe railing surrounded the gallery. The lantern was originally a birdcage style that used lamps and reflectors. When the tower was refurbished in 1857 its old lantern was replaced with a new cast-iron one so that the astragals would not interfere with the light beam from its new fourth-order Fresnel lens (an upgrade from the reflectors it had previously used). While the lantern was off, the tower was also given an interior brick cylinder, a cast-iron staircase, stone caps and sills, and a cast-iron deck plate for the new lantern. The new lantern's focal plane was 57 feet (17.5 m). The station had no fog signal building but it did have a fog bell.

The 2-story keeper's house was attached to the tower by a covered walkway. Keepers living on this 85-acre (35 hectare) island had to fend for themselves, since they were so far from civilization. They grew their own food and usually home-schooled their children.

West Sister Island Lighthouse with lantern

West Sister Island Lighthouse without lantern

West Sister Island Lighthouse

Today little remains of this once-active station. The last keeper and his family left in 1938 when the light was automated. The keeper's house was removed in 1945 and, although the tower still stands, its lantern has been lopped off. The tower is listed on the *National Register of Historic Places*. There is still an active light on the island, which uses a modern 300 mm lens.

Known Keepers: Alexander Cromwell (1847), Gibeon Kelsey, (1847–50), Dr. Anson Hotchkiss (1850–53), Horatio Winney (1853–60), Charles Whitney (1860–61), Michael Miller ((1861–65), Nathan Edson (1865–69), Cornelius Gilmore (1869–71), Harrison Haynes (1871–85), John Cunningham (1885–89), Delos Hayden (1890–1903), Charles Duggan (1903–08), Horace Curd (1908–09), Chancie Fitzmorris (1909–33), George Gampher (1933–37).

Windmill Point Lighthouse

74 Windmill Point Lighthouse (St. Clair River)

In 1837 the U.S. government appropriated $5,000 to build a light on Windmill Island at the outlet of Lake St. Clair (where the lake empties into the Detroit River). The light was actually built on the shore of the river at Windmill Point in 1838. The original lighthouse was a large elaborate structure. It was rebuilt several times (1866, 1875 and 1891).

The present 35-foot (10.7 m) tower was built in 1933. This gently tapering tower is covered in bands of riveted cast-iron and sits on an octagonal concrete base. Its single tower window, with six small panes of glass, faces toward the river. The cast-iron tower has been painted white and supports a black top section. While the light originally had a sixth-order lens, today it has a 300 mm optic beacon. A pipe iron guardrail stands between the light and the river.

LAKE ERIE
CANADA
LIGHTHOUSES

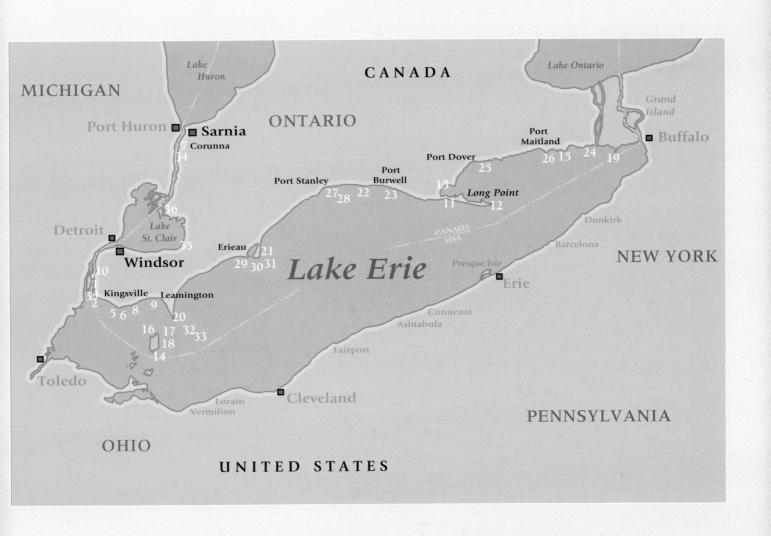

1 Amherstburg Range Lights

The Lake Carriers' Association established range lights at Amherstburg along the east side of the Detroit River in 1889. The front range light stood on the east bank 80 feet (24.5 m) from the river just north of Fraser's dock. The rear light was 475 feet (145 m) south and 1,630 feet (495 m) east of the front one.

In 1901 these lights both displayed a fixed red light using a lens-lantern to guide vessels into the river. The front light was an open-framed 50-foot (15.2 m) white tower, while the rear light was an open-framed 80-foot (24.4 m) red structure. Both towers were slatted on the side facing the range. This station also had a storm signal tower to fly cones to warn mariners of pending weather conditions. While these lights no longer exist today, Amherstburg does still have modern range lights, which were set up in 1959.

2 Bar Point Lightship

The Bar Point Shoals, 3–4 miles (5–6.5 km) from Amherstburg, Ontario, on the north shore of Lake Erie at the mouth of the Detroit River, make entry to or exit from the river quite dangerous. Over the years the area has been marked by a sequence of lightships. The first was the schooner *Louis McLean*, but the date of its placement here is unknown. It may have been 1851 when it was removed from Waugoshance Shoals in northern Lake Michigan, where it had been placed when newly built in 1832. The *Louis McLean* was a 60-ton wooden vessel built in Detroit. It had been badly damaged while serving at Waugoshance Shoals and, in response to a recommendation, the vessel was moved to a calmer position on Bar Point in Lake Erie.

The *Kingston Daily News* of May 4, 1874, reported that the lightship was stationed on the outer shoal, 3 miles (5 km) south and ¼ mile (0.4 km) west of Bar Point in 14 feet (4.3 m) of water. It displayed a green light over its white light to produce a distinctive color to identify its location. Its daymark was a large red ball. In fog, a triangle was sounded at regular intervals to make its presence known.

In July of that first season the captain and his wife were stranded on the lightship. With provisions running low, the captain had sent his assistant to the mainland for supplies. Days later, when the assistant had not returned, the captain started to build a crude raft to escape their floating prison. Fortunately, however, he spotted a passing tug and was able to attract its attention by hammering frantically on the ship's triangle with an axe. The *Douglass* rescued the starving pair and took them safely to Malden, where they discovered that the assistant had spent the grocery money on whiskey and had been enjoying himself getting drunk and fishing. While it is safe to assume that the captain of the lightship resumed his duties, the fate of his assistant is unknown.

During an October storm in 1874, the lightship was ripped from its moorings and washed out into the lake where it sank. Property loss was reported to be $500, the value of its hull.

In June 1875 the Canadian government placed a new lightship at Bar Point, the old government schooner *Dunscombe*, which had formerly been used as a lighthouse tender to supply Canadian lighthouses in the Gulf of St. Lawrence. The vessel, built at Quebec

in the early 1870s, was about 90 feet (27.7 m) long, had a 24-foot (7.4 m) beam and displaced 98 tons. It had two functional anchors, a spare anchor and a fog bell. It was painted red, with "Bar Point Light Ship" painted in large white letters along both sides. After being outfitted with a frame and lights it was placed on the shoal in early July.

In 1893 it was replaced by *LV 59*, which had just been built by the Craig Shipbuilding Company of Toledo, Ohio, for $13,490. Its three sister ships (*LV 60*, *LV 61* and *LV 62*) were also built at the same time and place by the same company. *LV 59* was a wood framed and planked vessel of white oak. It showed a fixed white light using a cluster of three oil-burning lens lanterns hoisted to its foremast. Its 6-inch (15 cm) steam whistle (blast 10 s; silence 30 s) was just ahead of its midship smoke stack. A non-riding sail was rigged to its short aft mast. The vessel was just over 82 feet (25 m) long, with an 18-foot (5.5 m) beam and an 8 foot (2.5 m) draft. Since this lightship was American-owned, the U.S. government first sought permission from Canada to place it in Canadian waters. During the off-season the vessel wintered over for maintenance and repair at the Detroit Depot.

While serving at this station it had some mishaps and underwent some changes. In December 1898 it was carried off-station by ice floes and drifted in the western end of Lake Erie for ten days before being picked up and towed to the Depot. While it was undergoing repairs at the start of the 1902 navigation season, a lighted buoy was used at the station. In October 1906 it was struck by a barge under tow, and so the next March it was equipped with a submarine bell signal. In 1911 it was transferred to Poe Reef, Lake Huron. By the fall of 1914 it was condemned as unseaworthy, retired from lightship duty, and sold for $314 at public auction on October 1, 1914, later to become the tug *Leathan D. Smith*.

Bar Point Lightship LV 59

In 1911 it was replaced at Bar Point by *LV 62*. In fact *LV 59* and *LV 62* simply switched locations. *LV 62* was one of the four sister ships to have been built by the Craig Shipbuilding Company but at a slightly higher cost ($13,900). It had a similar construction to *LV 59*, but its beam was slightly wider — 21.5 feet (6.5 m). Its lighting apparatus was identical to that of *LV 59* but in addition to the 6-inch steam whistle it also had an 800-pound (363 kg) brass fog bell.

LV 62 served at the Bar Point station until the end of the 1919 navigation season, when the Canadian government assumed responsibility for marking the shoals. *LV 62* was relieved from lightship duty at the end of the 1919 season, condemned in 1920, and sold at public auction for $200 on August 8, 1921.

While little is known about the Canadian lightship that marked the shoal, government correspondence reveals that in the 1920s it had a four-man crew: captain, engineer, fireman and cook. Each man had one week of leave out of every four. When the captain was on leave, the engineer was in charge. In 1929 the captain was S.A. McCormick and R.J. Logan was the engineer.

During Prohibition, rum-runner boats, usually speed boats designed to outrun American police patrol boats, plied the river in the area of the lightship. They would often tie up to the lightship or anchor close by, awaiting a shipment of liquor from Amherstburg, Ontario. While lightship crews sometimes did accept fish from rum-runners, they were said to have refused offers

Bois Blanc Island Lighthouse

The land was purchased from Colonel Rankin, and in 1836 the government of Upper Canada called for tenders to construct the lighthouse: "A stone lighthouse and a stone cottage for the keeper on the lower south end of the island of Bois Blanc at the entrance to the Detroit River — plus apparatus — to be 40 feet [12.2 m] tall, 18 feet [5.5 m] circular. Walls to be 5 feet [1.5 m] at the base to 2 feet [0.6 m] at the top. Not to be filled with rubbish but built up throughout with good large stones. An arched door and pine plank stairway. A 5-foot [1.5 m] lantern area for firing and securing the lantern. Twelve good and sufficient 16-inch [40 cm] reflectors and heaters."

The contract went to John Cook of Detroit. Although it cannot be confirmed, it is local belief that the lighthouse was designed by Andrew Kemp, who was attached to the Royal Engineers, Civil Branch, at Amherstburg.

One of the earliest Canadian lights on Lake Erie, this lighthouse was an example of an imperial tower, a common lighthouse style from the 1830–60 period. While the imperial lights varied in height to more than 100 feet (30 m), they all had a circular tapering tower with a rubble-stone core covered with rubble, hammer-dressed stone, or rusticated stone.

The tower at Bois Blanc had a rubble-stone finish and it is thought that the limestone used to build it came from Kingston as ships' ballast. The summit was finished with a cornice of stepped corbelling to support its gallery, and the tower was lit by three windows. It supported a polygonal lantern that first used a catoptric burning apparatus (lamps and reflectors) and likely burned whale oil or lard oil. In 1872 the light was said to have a focal plane of 56 feet (17.2 m) and to be visible up to 18 miles (29 km) in clear weather. In 1877 the fixed white light was provided by six mammoth flat-wick lamps and six 18-inch (45 cm) reflectors on two iron circles. The keeper's house was a limestone cottage. The project was overseen by commissioners appointed by the Assembly of Upper Canada.

The light's first keeper was not actually the person originally hired for the job, and the appointment took place in unusual circumstances. In 1836 Sir Francis Bond Head, the Lieutenant-Governor of Upper Canada, was in Amherstburg making an inspection tour of the new lighthouse and the district, when his carriage passed by the Hackett home. Mrs. Hackett was sitting on the veranda, and the family's Newfoundland dog, Sailor, was nearby. Apparently Sir Francis expressed interest in purchasing the dog, but Mrs. Hackett said he was not for sale. She went on to say her husband was a sailor interested in becoming the lightkeeper at Bois Blanc. After a quick negotiation, Sir Francis acquired Sailor, and Captain James Hackett acquired the position of lightkeeper. The lamps were first lit on November 7, 1836. Captain Hackett was still a ship's pilot on the lakes, however, and so Mrs. Hackett performed all the lighthouse duties for the first five years of the light's operation. The family also farmed on the island to supplement the keeper's income and the family's food supply.

Within a year of their moving to the island, events of the 1837–38

---

of liquor. In the fall of 1929 the lightship was alleged to be acting as "middle-man" in relaying liquor cargoes, but Canadian government officials proved this accusation to be false. However, they did report that American patrols would fire on rum-runner boats in Canadian waters (a "no-no"), that the lightship captain once helped a foundering rum boat in an approaching storm, and that its crew had watched as the Italian rum-runner Tony Armando (a.k.a. "Muzzy") was picked up by the American law when his boat experienced engine trouble. The report reassured the government that the crew of the lightship were neutral — neither aiding nor impeding the rum-runners. It further reported that the captain knew maritime law well, and that any boat was perfectly free to anchor in the area of the lightship without breaking Canadian law.

Known Keepers: *LV 59*: Thomas Cooney (1894–97), William Wybrands (1897–1902), Wedwin J. Wilkinson (1902–   ). *LV 62*: Commanding Officers Walter J. McGuin (1895–   ), Thomas H. Ingersoll (–1920), Canadian *LV* (1929-   ) S. A. McCormick.

3 Bois Blanc Island Lighthouse

With the advent of steamships and the opening of the Erie Canal in 1825 and the Welland Canal in 1829, shipping in the lower Great Lakes grew rapidly. At the west end of Lake Erie where the Detroit River emptied into the lake, the river's navigation channel became very narrow, and dangerous shoals hampered marine traffic. Bois Blanc Island was chosen as the site for a lighthouse to assist mariners.

Bois Blanc was named by French explorers for the "white woods" on the island at the entrance to the Detroit River. The English, finding the name hard to pronounce, settled for "Boblo," and the lighthouse also became known as the Boblo Lighthouse.

The island's location at the river mouth was a useful one. The lighthouse, built on its southern tip, could mark the entrance to the river from Lake Erie, mark the channel for upbound vessels heading to Amherstburg, Windsor, and the upper Great Lakes, and warn of the dangerous shoals in the area.

Bois Blanc Island Lighthouse, circa 1910

Rebellion upturned their lives. On January 8, 1838, a group of 60 Canadian "Patriots" and their American sympathizers landed at the island. They forced the evacuation of the island's small military guard and the lighthouse keeper and his family. As the vessel continued on to Fort Malden, it ran aground near Amherstburg, and the rebels were captured. During the invasion, the keeper and his family stayed in Amherstburg until the rebels were defeated. On their return they found their house plundered and some of their livestock butchered.

The Hacketts lived out their lives on the island and kept the light until 1870. James died in 1872 and Mary in 1873. At the age of 81, James gave the position of lightkeeper to his youngest son, Andrew. After Andrew's death in 1901, his wife, Agnes, kept the light until her son Charles took the position, which he kept until the light was automated in 1927. The position of lightkeeper had remained in the Hackett family for over 90 years and passed through three generations.

During World War I, the island, with the exception of the lighthouse, became an American-owned amusement park. Although American soldiers were not supposed to leave the States on their own, a special bill was passed allowing them to go to Bois Blanc Island, a Canadian island, so they could visit the amusement park with their girlfriends and take romantic evening cruises past the lighthouse.

The lighting apparatus was upgraded with the times. The illuminant probably changed from lard to whale oil to kerosene, and finally to acetylene when the light was automated in 1927. The lamps would have changed from flat wick to round wick to pressurized ones. A 1954 fire, caused by vandals, destroyed the lighthouse, but its limestone walls endured. The Canadian government replaced the lantern with a utilitarian steel frame structure on top of the tower. Sometime in the 1970s this structure was removed and the entrance door and fanlight were restored. When vandals again damaged the site, the entrance was filled in with rubble-stone masonry to prevent further vandalism.

In 1961 the lighthouse was designated a National Historic Site on the basis of being "a point of attack by the American Patriots during the troubles of 1837–1838." Today the lighthouse, which was once such an essential asset to Lake Erie navigation, is owned by Parks Canada and stands lanternless, a solitary reminder to boaters of its previous importance to history.

Known Keepers: James Hackett (1836–70 [Mary Hackett 1836–41]), Andrew Hackett (1870–1910), Agnes Hackett (1910), Charles R. Hackett (1910–27).

Bois Blanc Lighthouse, circa 1907

4 Bois Blanc Island Range Lights

While the Bois Blanc Lighthouse had been established in the Detroit River at the foot, or south end, of Bois Blanc Island in 1837, these range lights were built at the head or the north end of the island in 1875 to assist marine traffic at the opposite end of the island. The front range light stood about 300 feet (90 m) from the island's extreme northern point, and the rear light was 450 feet (138 m) behind it. Both lights needed rebuilding in 1892. These range lights were discontinued and the towers taken down in 1908.

5 Colchester Reef Lighthouse

In 1885 the Canadian government built a lighthouse on the southwestern edge of Colchester Reef in Lake Erie about 4 miles (6.5 km) south of the town of Colchester, Ontario. Built in 14 feet (4.3 m) of water, the circular limestone pier originally held a white hexagonal tapering wooden tower lit by many four-paned, pedimented windows that ascended it. A polygonal lantern surrounded by a hexagonal gallery displayed a red light that was 72 feet (22 m) above the water. A lean-to was attached to the tower's base.

In 1901 the lantern displayed a fixed white light from a third-order lens to produce a 14-mile (22.5 km) visibility. It also had a mechanically operated fog bell in a belfry on the south side of the tower 55 feet (17 m) above the lake. In poor visibility it sounded once every 15 seconds.

In 1954 a 40-foot (12.2 m) steel square skeletal tower was built as a replacement light, and the wooden tower was removed. Today the structure is painted red and displays a red flashing light (flash 0.5 s; eclipse 3.5 s) for a 5-mile (8 km) visibility from a 63-foot (19 m) focal plane. The rest of the old limestone pier is the base for a Canadian Coast Guard helipad.

Known Keepers: John Manson (1886–1911), F. Malott (1911–16).

Colchester Reef Lighthouse

Colchester Reef Lighthouse, circa 1951

6 Colchester Reef Lightship

In the early 1800s vessels traveling up and down Lake Erie to and from the Detroit River had to pass through the narrow Pelee Passage, which, at first, had only a light on Pelee Island to mark the shoal in the middle. Once safely through this danger spot on their way west, pilots then had only their knowledge of the area to help them circumnavigate Colchester Reef, which lay hidden underwater about 4 miles (6.5 km) south of Colchester on the Canadian northern shore and 15 miles (24.3 km) northwest of Pelee Island. Since the reef lay right in the center of the shipping lane, it was a most dangerous hazard. Despite mariners' pleas, the Canadian government was reluctant to light the reef. In the *Kingston Daily News* of March 6, 1863, Captain Thomas McVetty of Buffalo announced his intention to place a "small vessel, with a good light and fog bell, during the season of navigation" on Colchester Reef.

The next mention of a vessel to light the area was made in the September 19, 1864, issue of the *Detroit Free Press*. The captain of the schooner *Wave* had been hired by ship owners and paid in advance to place a vessel at Colchester Reef as a lightship, but after receiving the money he had left the station unattended. The ship owners were outraged when the vessel did not show up as expected.

From 1866 to 1870 a lightship was operated on this shoal by a Mr. Hackett of Amherstburg. Hackett struggled to keep the ship in operation with a meager income of private subscriptions from owners, masters and Underwriters' Associations. But that was not enough to pay for the upkeep and supplies for the vessel, so the government was petitioned for financial assistance. Sessional papers from 1870 show recommendation and payment of $500 for this purpose. Then in 1871 sessional papers again show a request for financial assistance to help maintain the lightship at Colchester Reef but do not mention any remuneration being given. Canada was a fledgling country in the process of undergoing the transition of Confederation, and money was tight. Petitions to permanently light the reef fell on deaf ears. Evidence of a lightship at this reef next appears on an 1881 map published by the Detroit and Cleveland Steam Navigation Company.

Barnet's *Coast Pilot* for the Great Lakes described the lightship as displaying two lights, a red one about 7 feet (2.2 m) above the white one. It produced a visibility of about 3 miles (4.9 km) and was anchored in 18 feet (5.5 m) of water about 600 feet (185 m) due north of the shallowest spot on the reef. To be safe, vessels were advised to pass ¼ mile (0.4 km) south of the lightship.

It is unknown when the Canadian government first contracted the Campbell Brothers and Company to place a lightship on the reef, but it is clear that their service was not reliable. In the latter half of September 1881, with no public notice, the company removed their lightship from the reef — a recipe for disaster.

On September 25 the steamer *Antelope* was making a return trip up the lake in stormy conditions. Just a few days earlier, on the downbound voyage, her captain had seen and passed the lightship marking the Colchester Reef. On the return run, after negotiating Pelee Passage — and unaware that the lightship had been removed — he steered toward a light he assumed was the lightship. Unfortunately, he had headed for another vessel anchored north of the reef. He took a collision course directly toward the reef and struck it hard, causing the almost complete destruction of the vessel. Later that day, while the *Antelope* was still stranded on the reef, the missing lightship returned to its post, but because of faulty equipment, Captain Forrest could only shine the light from the deck level, not the mast. Being so low on the water, the light was insufficiently visible, again causing the reef to be ineffectively lit.

Then, during a fierce Great Lakes storm in November 1883, the lightship and keeper Captain Forrest both disappeared with no trace. The Campbells did not replace the vessel to close out the navigation season because calm water was needed for placing a lightship, and November and December were stormy months on the lake. Ultimately the Canadian government had a lighthouse built on the reef, and the lightship was no longer needed.

Known Keepers: Mr. Hackett (1866–70), Captain Forrest (?).

7 Corunna Range Lights

In 1890 range lights were built at Corunna to help mariners navigate the eastern channel around Stag Island in the St. Clair River. The rear light, a 33-foot (10 m) tapering white wooden tower, stood in the town of Corunna. The front range light, shorter but similarly constructed, was at the edge of the river. Both had a simple square wooden gallery and displayed a fixed red light.

In 1941 the rear range light was removed from service, and the citizens of Corunna bought the lighthouse from the Canadian Coast Guard for $75. Ten years later the Coast Guard bought it back, refurbished it, converted it to electricity and returned it to service. Then 31 years later, in 1982, the Coast Guard decided to replace it with a higher steel tower that would not be hidden by tree growth.

The old rear range light tower was to be demolished, but once again local people saved it. It was moved from its original site to a museum at Mooretown, also on the St. Clair River, 4 miles (6.4 km) south of Corunna. Today the tower supports a diamond-slatted top that displays a small light. This rear range light was replaced with a 50-foot (15.2 m) steel skeletal tower painted white with a fluorescent orange inverted triangular day marker that had a black vertical stripe. It displayed a fixed red electric light.

Corunna Front Range Light, circa 1910   NAC PA148024

The front range light was kept in continual service until 1985, when deterioration and vandalism caused the Coast Guard to replace it with a steel tower. Since the rear range light had been turned over to the Mooretown Museum Board, the Coast Guard looked for an interested party to purchase the front range light. When no one came forward, the Marine Museum at Kingston was contacted. Although very interested, they decided not to take the light for several reasons: they already had a lighthouse; a lot of time, effort, and money would be required to move the front range light; much of the range light tower was rotten; the light apparatus was modern electrical equipment (not original and not historical). Since no one else stepped forward to claim the tower, it was demolished in the summer of 1985.

This front range light was replaced with a 30-foot (9 m) steel skeletal tower that was also painted white and given a fluorescent orange triangular day marker with a black vertical stripe. It too displayed a fixed red electrical light. The only known keeper of these range lights was William Scott, whose annual salary in 1901 was $220.

Known Keepers: William J. Scott (1901–16–).

Corunna Rear Range Light

8 Kingsville Range Lights

Kingsville is in Pigeon Bay about midway between Point Pelee and the mouth of the Detroit River along the north shore of Lake Erie. After improvements to the harbor, two lights were built in 1886 to mark the harbor for local fishermen and to mark the area between Colchester and Leamington for mariners traveling the north shore.

The lights were close together. The front range light was placed on the outer end of the east breakwater pier just 10 feet (3 m) from the water's edge. It was a lantern on a pole that displayed a fixed red light from a 27-foot (8.2 m) focal plane. The rear range light was placed 1,060 feet (325 m) behind it on top of the bank at the head of the east pier. It was a short pyramidal structure with narrow horizontal clapboarding. Its simple wooden gallery, partway down the top of the tower, was supported by eight ornamentally carved

Leamington Lighthouse

wooden corbels (two per side). The tower, painted white with black trim, supported a circular iron lantern with diagonally set astragals forming irregular shapes of glass. It displayed a fixed white light from a 55-foot (16.8 m) focal plane for a 12-mile (19.4 km) visibility. Being visible from all points seaward, these range lights helped to conduct safe navigation throughout the whole area.

The rear range light has been replaced with a modern circular steel light and the old wooden tower has been moved from its original location to a safe-storage area across from the old train station. This light is well on its way to being restored, thus saving another small part of Canadian history.

Known Keepers: Albert Malott (1890–), W.H. Black (1902–).

9 Leamington Lighthouse

The light at Leamington in Lake Erie's Pigeon Bay was built in 1880 primarily to mark the harbor of the blossoming industrial town. It also helped mark the north shore of the lake for mariners crossing the bay to or from Pelee Passage.

The Canadian government had appropriated $1,000 for the light but Peter Williams completed it for just $794. It was built onshore near the pier. The tower was of square pyramidal shape covered in narrow clapboarding, and it had a simple square gallery just below the top, which was surrounded with a pipe iron railing. A polygonal lantern topped the tower and provided a 48-foot (14.6 m) focal plane for the fixed white catoptric light, which had a visibility of 12 miles (19.3 km). Today this light stands near the shore of Lake Erie on private property.

Known Keepers: Joshua Lamarsh (–1883), F.H.C. Conover (1883–).

Kingsville Rear Range Light

10 Livingston Channel Lighthouse

Two light stations first marked this area in the Detroit River, one for the downbound Livingston Channel and one for the upbound Amherstburg Channel. But in 1927 the Canadian government built the Livingston Channel Light mid-river above Amherstburg to mark the division between the two.

The lighthouse was solidly built. A rock-filled crib of 12-inch (30 cm) timbers was sunk in 24 feet (7.5 m) of water, and a square concrete platform 8-foot (2.5 m) thick placed on top of it. Upon this a 40-foot (12.2 m) square reinforced concrete tower rose about 35 feet (10.5 m). The lower level provided keeper's quarters. The tower became much narrower for its second-level watchroom, which had a large pedimented window on each side. A raised concrete band ringed the tower just above the watch windows, and a concrete "stepping-stone" cornice helped support the tower's square gallery. The decagonal lantern was topped with dome, ventilator stack, and lightning rod and was surrounded by a pipe iron railing. The tower was painted white and the top red.

The lantern used a kerosene lamp to display a white and red flashing light (12 s white; 6 s red) visible for 10-miles (16 km). A clockworks that had to be wound every 15 hours, turned the lens to create the flash pattern. In fog a bell warned ships of its location. Although it had to be started manually, once in motion, it too used clockwork weights to keep it ringing every 15 seconds.

When the lighthouse was demanned for the winter, the light displayed a battery-operated flashing white light. It used four rotary-mounted bulbs that were built into the light. If a bulb burned out, this mechanism automatically rotated and started a new one. The light ran all winter to guide a year-round coal carrier.

At some point a marine observation office, the J.W. Westcott Marine Reporters, was added to the base of the tower. Irving Kelly was manager of the reporting station for Westcott. The office operated 24/7, rain or shine. Three keepers each worked an eight-hour shift to keep the logbooks, one for upbound vessels and one for downbound vessels. In 1942 about 120 ships passed each day during the April–December shipping season and the keeper had to record the exact time each ship passed. This information was relayed to a central Detroit office by a battery-operated telephone via underwater cable and sent via direct line teletypes and Western Union telegrams to major newspapers and ports. This service helped companies keep to shipping schedules, port destinations to prepare to unload without delays, families to track the whereabouts of crewmembers, and company owners to track the progress of their vessels.

The service also relayed the information to their mail boat, J.W. Westcott II, a stocky little launch dubbed the "sea-going post office of Detroit" because it met every ship that passed delivering mail, destination orders, parcels, and occasionally a new crewman. Ore-laden freighters often did not know their destination until the mail boat delivered their orders from Detroit. A duplicate copy of the orders was sent to the lighthouse. In the event that the mail boat missed the vessel, the keeper would take the orders out to the vessel, where they were taken aboard via a bucket lowered from the freighter. The mail boat was kept busy.

The light had few keepers; the first was Irving Kelly. By 1952 there were three: Kelly, Miles Miracle, and J.E. McGuire. As well as recording passing vessels and relaying information to Detroit, the keepers recorded the water depth every three hours for the U.S. Lakes survey and Lake Carriers' Association, and relayed wind direction and weather conditions. Occasionally they acted as the mail boat. A less desirable part of the job was the recovery of water-suicide bodies from the Windsor and Detroit area. On such occasions they had to notify the police. With all these tasks, the keep-

ers met their main objective — to keep tonnage of iron ore, coal and all kinds of freight moving on the world's greatest inland waterway.

One morning in September 1952, the E.J. Kulas, a 600-foot (185 m) lake freighter, was steaming down the Detroit River laden with 12,600 tons of iron ore when its radar blanked out. Visibility in the soupy fog was only about 25 feet (7.5 m), and the lighthouse fog bell sounded a long way off. Suddenly the freighter struck the east side of the lighthouse and tore off the thick concrete decking on that side, causing the light to tip over perilously on its crib. At the same time the frame office attached to the lighthouse tower was knocked into the river along with its occupant, keeper J.E. McGuire. He swam away from the accident and hung onto wreckage until he could safely swim to the tilting lighthouse. He clung to the ruined structure while awaiting his rescue.

Meanwhile, Irving Kelly, manager of the Westcott Livingston Light Agency, was waiting to change shifts with McGuire. When he heard on his marine radio that the light had been struck, he and a friend, Grant Duff, left in Duff's fishing tug. The thick fog made it difficult to travel. After hitting a seawall, they eventually found the lighthouse and rescued McGuire. The Kulas sustained underwater damage but was repairable.

Another grounding had also occurred about an hour before the Kulas struck the lighthouse. The Fink, also a 600-foot (185 m) iron-ore carrier, grounded stern first 100 feet (30 m) from the Canadian shore near the lighthouse. Its radar had also cut out, leaving it helpless in the thick fog. These two accidents caused the U.S. Coast Guard to shut down boat travel in the Detroit River until tugs could pull ships into deep water to resume their travels.

This important light was soon replaced. Since the damaged light weighed some 1,600 tons and even the biggest lake derrick could not lift it for repairs, a new light was decided upon. In only a month a 260-ton poured-concrete crib was built at the dry dock in Windsor by the MacNamara Construction Company of Toronto to specifications from the Department of Transport in Ottawa. On October 8, 1952, the new crib, which was 20 feet (6 m) square and 24 feet (7.5 m) high, was towed by the tug Batchawana 18 miles (29 km) to its new site about 30 feet (9 m) from the old lighthouse. RCMP and Canadian Coast Guard escorts signaled traffic to slow down to prevent the crib from being swamped. The wooden crib forms were then filled with water and sunk onto a base of crushed limestone. Six feet (1.8 m) remained above the water.

Once set, the crib was filled with sand and gravel. It also contained an electrical cable conduit from a submerged power line that ran underwater from the Canadian shore. J. Lascomb, an engineer with the Department of Transport, supervised the work. On top of the crib were superimposed a concrete pad, a 20-foot (6 m) square tower base, and then the 24-foot (7.5 m) tower itself, which supported a revolving light. The new lighthouse took about two months to build and cost around $50,000. It was straight and plain, and definitely lacked the elegance of its predecessor.

During construction, a temporary light was constructed. As the leaning tower could not project a useful light and could not be repaired, the Department of Transport blew it up to clear the river. It took a day and a half and 200 pounds (90 kg) of dynamite to completely sink the rubble. The piece of concrete left to hold the temporary light was removed once the new light was ready.

A mere three years later, the new light tower was also tilting. Apparently, river currents and drag created by passing ships were eroding the limestone in the footing. Repairs were estimated at $10,000. Eventually, when GPS systems made it no longer essential, the whole light was removed.

Long Point Cut Lighthouse, circa 1994

Long Point Cut Lighthouse, circa 1900

11 Long Point Cut Lighthouse

When storms washed a deeper, wider new "Cut" through the Long Point peninsula around 1865, the event was marked by moving the lightship from the previous storm-washed channel a short distance to the new cut. Then in 1879 the Canadian government built a lighthouse to mark the eastern entrance to the Cut.

Unlike the lighthouses on Long Point, which had a separate tower and keeper's house, this white wooden tower was built right into the northwest corner of the house. The tower and house were built on a stone foundation 1 foot (0.3 m) thick. The wide-based, square tower tapered up three stories to a 10-foot (3 m) square gallery surrounded by a wooden railing and supported by many ornamental corbels. With its dodecagonal lantern, the tower was almost 65 feet (20 m) high. Within the lantern was a red lamp and below that a white one to identify the Cut. The light had a visibility of 12 miles (19.3 km).

When the government supply boat came it left a year's supply of oil to burn in the light. Because of the isolation, keepers had a long row to Port Rowan if they wanted companionship or local gossip. The government alleviated the problem by installing a telephone in 1908.

The Cut's distinctive red and white light was both a blessing and a nightmare. It was good because it marked the Cut clearly, providing safe access into the Inner Bay for mariners in stormy weather. Its drawback was that pirates — or "blackbirds" as they were known — could copy the light's distinctive symbol on the lakeside shore to lure ships aground on the sandy beach. Once there and realizing their error, the crew would flee for their lives and the pirates would help themselves to the cargo. By the time the authorities arrived, the blackbirds were long gone. American captains complained to the U.S. government, who complained to England and to Upper Canada, but to no avail, since Long Point was far removed from the immediate concerns of nineteenth-century Canadian officials.

By the early twentieth century the lighthouse's days were numbered. Silting was occurring in the passage, shifting sands were reducing the depth of the Inner Bay, new sandy shoals on the lake made a treacherous approach to the Cut, and lake traffic was greatly reduced. As a result, the government decommissioned the light in 1916, and by 1918 its lantern had been removed.

Once decommissioned, the lighthouse was sold to a private owner who turned it into a cottage. In the 1930s it was owned by a Toronto lumberman, T.A. Hancock. In the 1960s it was owned by Donald Carlisle, who rented it out as a cottage for $1,000 a month. In 1968 Ewart Ostrander from Tillsonburg bought the lighthouse

Long Point Cut Lighthouse today

and kept it much as it was when he bought it. When the family came for their summer stay, they discovered snakes — garter snakes, fox snakes, and others — inhabiting the basement, slithering up the basement stairs, and even lurking in the kitchen drawers! But as the lighthouse became more inhabited, the snakes departed.

Much of the original tower and house remained unchanged. It still had original windows and shutters. To accommodate the sloping walls of the tower, the bedroom doorway was off-kilter, and the trap door in the tower was cut on a slant across the bottom to make a "proper fit." The original red brick chimney and fireplace were still in place, as was the cedar shake shingle siding of the tower, and the ornamental braces still supported the gallery.

In 1999 Peter and Brigitte Westaway of Toronto bought the lighthouse with plans to restore it to its original late 1800s style. They stabilized the tower's timber foundation and leveled it by a few inches. The tower, which the wind had corkscrewed out of square over the years, has been resquared. They removed the screened-in porch, which was not original, and replaced the rotting roof with hand-hewn cedar shakes. With the help of a restoration architect, they brought the insides up to modern-day comfort levels, while retaining as much authenticity as possible. They even used a 100-year-old log from the bottom of the St. Lawrence River as a replacement beam in the tower. The lighthouse is fortunate to have been sold to people who have such a concern for its preservation.

Known Keepers: Esley Woodward (?), William Dickson (?), Frank Mason (1901–).

12 Long Point Lighthouse

Long Point in Lake Erie is a 21-mile (32 km) sand spit that juts almost halfway into the lake. The area's ever-changing sands, severe southwesterly storms, and distance into the lake coupled with Lake Erie's fast changing weather have earned it the nickname "the graveyard of the Great Lakes." After four U.S. ships were driven aground and wrecked on the point in the fall of 1828, a report was sent to Washington requesting that the British government be petitioned to establish a lighthouse on Long Point or allow the U.S. Lighthouse Service to build one. The British agreed to appropriate £1,000 in 1829 to build a lighthouse at the end of the point. A 50-foot (15.2 m) stone tower was built, and an additional £400 was appropriated to build a brick keeper's house. The light was first lit on November 3, 1830. Its first keeper, Thomas Price, received $1 a day as long as the light was operational.

Erosion around the foundation caused it to sink and lean badly, and so in 1843 a second lighthouse was built. The new lighthouse, a 60-foot (18.3 m) octagonal wood tower, had an overall height of 75 feet (23 m). Its fixed white light was visible for about 16 miles (25 km). In 1864 the light started burning coal oil (kerosene) instead of sperm oil, as it was more economical, and changed

Long Point Lighthouse painting, circa 1928

to a dioptric lighting system. By 1877 the light had been converted from a fixed light to a revolving white one consisting of six mammoth flat-wick fountain lamps with six 20-inch (50 cm) reflectors on two square frames, three on each side for better visibility.

In 1891 a wooden fog building was added just south of the lighthouse. The horn, which faced southeast 20 feet (6 m) above the lake level, was operated by steam-powered compressed air (blast 7 s; silence 30 s). By 1900 this system was outdated and a new building was erected to the east of the old one. It used coal-fired steam-powered, compressed air, and since it operated year round, an engineer was kept on duty to maintain the steam and operate the horn. Soon, however, cost-cutting measures dictated that the operation of the fog signal become another task for the lightkeeper. In 1941 the foghorn system was converted to oil-burning diesel engines.

By 1915, with this second lighthouse also threatened by shifting sands and wave action, a third tower was started; it was put into use in 1916. The keeper, following government orders, burned the old tower down in 1929, to prevent it from falling into the lake and obstructing lake vessels. The new 102-foot (31 m) tapered octagonal tower of reinforced concrete had a lantern that housed a 100,000 candlepower light with a visibility of 15 miles (24 km). The light burned vaporized petroleum, and a clockwork mechanism, whose weights had to be rewound every six to eight hours, rotated the prisms around the light. Also in 1929 a radio beacon was established at the station.

In 1957 the vapor light was changed to a 1500-watt incandescent lamp and an electric motor was installed to turn the head of the lens. In 1961 a new keeper's house was built for the head keeper and in 1962 the old keeper's house was assigned to assistant keepers Clayton Scofield and Bill Lamb. Another house was built for Lamb in 1963. Also in 1963 a 9 kilowatt generator was installed and a 400-watt mercury vapor light replaced the old light. In 1964–65 a new, concrete block fog alarm building was erected. It also housed the generators and radio room. High waters in the 1980s caused Public Works Canada to invest $500,000 in 1987 to prevent the tower from again falling prey to wind and water erosion. The structure was rebuilt and shored up with concrete pylons reaching all the way down to the bedrock. A helipad was also added at this time. In 1989 the Long Point Light was the last light on Lake Erie to be automated.

During the tenure of Harry Woodward, keeper from 1867 to 1893, his wife, an accomplished taxidermist, preserved many birds that had flown into the lighthouse. Also dating to this period is the story of Long Point's ghost. Apparently, on a November night in the 1880s a coal-laden steamer heading downlake for the Welland Canal was caught in a ship-smashing storm mid-length of Long Point. Knowing the boat was lost, the 14-member crew launched a lifeboat, but in their haste to lower the boat, one of the seamen was decapitated. His head was lost in the lake but his body stayed in the lifeboat. Under the light of the full moon, the survivors searched the beach for the severed head but, unable to find it, they buried the body and left for safety. The story has been told many times through the years. When skeptics question its veracity, they are told to go a mile east of the breakwater under the full moon. There, they will be sure to see the headless seaman walking the beach in search of his missing head.

The next keeper, Walter Stalker, served as both lightkeeper and gameskeeper to the newly formed Long Point Company, a privately owned hunting preserve that owned much of the peninsula.

Sheldon "Shelley" B. Cook was keeper from 1897–1928, except when he took off for the winter of 1911–12 and William Porritt filled in for him. That February, Porritt answered a knock on the door one day to find a 19-year-old American boy, Walter Lick, who had walked 25 miles (40 km) in 12 hours from northern Pennsylvania over the Lake Erie ice. Porritt kept Lick overnight and the youth left for Port Rowan the next day once again across the ice. Close to his destination, he fell through skim ice where ice had recently been harvested, but miraculously, he was rescued. Walter Lick is now a Long Point legend.

After him, Lorne Brown was keeper from 1928 until 1955. During Prohibition in the States, keepers told many tales of smuggling. The most common story was the "old broken engine routine." A boat anchored offshore would tell the keeper they were having engine trouble and ask to use his phone. Being there to "assist," the keeper always said yes. Shortly thereafter, another boat would arrive at the rendezvous, and within a short time the "broken engine" had been fixed and both vessels went on their way. Another common event was to find bottles or crates of whiskey washed ashore, thrown overboard by smugglers afraid of being caught red-handed.

In foggy weather Brown could not tend both the light and the foghorn, so his wife had to fire the fog station boilers. Her memories of the foghorn, she reports, are "less than fond." Keeper Brown loved to roam the point and observe the wildlife, especially the birds. He was knowledgeable about migrating birds and recorded the frequent kills that occurred at the light during migration. He even recorded the number of each species killed.

In 1955 Bill Ansley took over. In March 1963 another ice walker appeared at the light. Gene Heuser, an American, had left Shades Harbor, Pennsylvania, at 8 o'clock one morning. Using a large willow staff to test the ice ahead, and walking 20 miles (32 km) out of his way to avoid stretches of open water and piles of snow and ice, he reached Long Point Lighthouse 24 hours later. Scofield, the assistant, looked after him. The next day he was driven to Port Rowan. For Scofield's generosity, Heuser left him his willow staff. Also during Ansley's tenure, in 1975, a huge solar panel and storage batteries were added to the station.

Ansley, Scofield and Lamb enjoyed occasional company. Al Kendrick, lightkeeper from Port Colborne, and his wife, Isabel, once went to visit. Since there was no road out to the peninsula, the Kendricks drove as far as they could and one of the keepers met them and drove them in the 4x4 along the beach. Isabel Kendrick recalls a "hair-raising" ride — clinging to her glass casserole dish for fear of losing it. Although they spent a lovely day and enjoyed the bird sanctuary, they only visited once.

Long Point Lighthouse

In an interview, Sheryl Lynn Powell, Scofield's daughter, reported similar rides in the 4x4, except she made more than just one visit. She loved going to the lighthouse for a week or two each summer to visit her dad. She described the area as "tranquil," "ever changing" and "nature at its finest." She remembers her dad frequently rescuing boaters for such reasons as sheered cotter pins, being grounded on a sand bar, or running out of gas. One of her pastimes was to look for buried treasure, but she never found any. She remembers being taught that the lake, while being beautiful, had to be respected. She told of a notable airplane crash in June 1964. Although the plane had landed safely at the lighthouse before, this time it developed engine trouble and crashed on the beach south of it. Her dad and his wife, Ruth, went to the crash site to help, but the pilot had died on impact and the pilot's wife died a short time later.

The last head keeper was Bob Nelder. He had three assistants and the job was "two men on, two men off" every two weeks. A helicopter came regularly to rotate the keepers. Although they worked 8-hour shifts, they were always on call. The keepers' job had changed significantly over the years. Now they were responsible for keeping everything in top form and making emergency repairs, but major breakdowns were handled by technicians. They also filed daily weather reports and manned a radio beacon that sent out a Morse code signal to ships. The Long Point signal, dot dash dot dot, stood for the letter "L" in Morse code and signaled to ships that they were in the Long Point area. Nelder was unhappy to see the lighthouse automated because it made his job as the Long Point Lighthouse keeper obsolete.

Today Long Point is designated a World Biosphere Reserve, to help protect the finest example of Canada's remaining Carolinian forest. It is good to know that the lighthouse, also a special part of Canada's history, is at the tip of this biosphere.

Known Keepers: Thomas Proce (1830–), Moses Newkirk (1844–46), Henry (Harry) Clark (1846–67), Harry Woodward (1867–93), Walter Stalker (1893–97), Sheldon (Shelley) Cook (1897–1911), William Porritt (1911–12 winter), Sheldon Cook (1912–28), Lorne Brown (1928–55), Bill Ansley (1955–84), Bob Nelder (1984–89).

13 Long Point Lightship

The many shipwrecks around Long Point, mainly of schooners from the 1800s, easily account for the point's reputation as the "Graveyard of the Great Lakes." As early as 1679, when De La Salle's barque, *Le Griffon*, narrowly escaped the point during a heavy fog, written reports tell of its hazards. The "Ghost Fleet of Long Point" beneath its surface tells of those who did not escape.

To avoid the 25-mile (32 km) voyage around Long Point, small craft in the late 1700s and the early 1800s used to portage over the narrow isthmus. However, schooners and steamers had to circumnavigate the point, risking Lake Erie's water spouts, treacherous shoals and fast-approaching storms. As lake travel increased, the Legislative Assembly for Upper Canada was petitioned in 1829 for funds to build a canal across the peninsula. But Mother Nature took over and cut a 390-foot (120 m) wide passage through the neck of the peninsula, with a depth varying from 11–18 feet (3.5 –5.5 m). The government then constructed piers to keep the channel open. They were finished by 1836, and by 1840 a lightship was stationed on the bay side to mark the channel. The use of a lightship meant that if the channel filled in again or became unusable the government could move the lightship elsewhere.

Around 1865, the effects of numerous storms opened a new cut 20 feet (6 m) deep and ½ mile (0.8 km) wide. This became known as the "Cut." The lightship was moved to mark this new location until a lighthouse was built on the east side of the Cut in 1879, at which time the lightship was moved to the Kingston area.

Since the channel was never dredged or maintained, it did fill in with sand and weeds over time. However, it continued to be used until 1895 when the lake side became completely filled with sand during a storm. Another storm in 1906 filled in the bay side.

14 Middle Island Lighthouse

Between Point Pelee, Ontario, and Sandusky, Ohio, a geological ridge runs along Lake Erie's lakebed, forming islands where it rises above the lake level. Pelee Island is one of the largest of these islands, as is Kelleys Island 8 miles (13 km) to the south of it. Between these two islands, and just south of Pelee Island, lies a small island called Middle Island.

Middle Island Lighthouse, circa 1900 NAC PA172510

Many shipwrecks occurred in the area. In 1847 the schooner *Westchester*, fully laden, ran aground on Middle Island; in 1851 the schooner *Palmyra* grounded on the reef between Kelleys Island and Middle Island; in 1852 the brig *F.C. Clark* was driven onto Middle Island by a fierce storm even though part of its cargo of barley had been thrown overboard in an attempt to save the vessel; in 1854 the brig *Carolina*, laden with rail and road iron, grounded on a reef near Middle Island; in 1868 the schooners *Contest* and *Hyphen* both grounded on a reef near Middle Island, had to be abandoned and were totally lost. Three men from the *Hyphen* were lost. In 1882 the schooner *Gallatin*, loaded with pig iron, struck a reef near Middle Island and sank. Then the schooner *King Sister* ran ashore on a reef near Middle Island in 1884.

The frequency of these shipwrecks prompted the Canadian government in 1871 to authorize the construction of a lighthouse on the island to help guide mariners through the main channel between Kelleys Island and the south side of Middle Island.

In 1872 a 48-foot (14.6 m) square tapering wooden tower built right into a clapboard keeper's house was constructed at the east end of Middle Island at a cost of $5,748. The tower was seven stories high with a stone foundation and an octagonal lantern. It displayed a fixed red light from a catoptric system that used three circular burner lamps with 20-inch (50 cm) reflectors and three mammoth flat-wick lamps with 16-inch (40 cm) reflectors. From about a 70-foot (21.3 m) focal plane the light produced a 12-mile (19.5 km) visibility. By 1877 the light had been upgraded to four mammoth flat-wick lamps and four 20-inch (50 cm) reflectors on cast-iron stands.

Samuel S. Brown, the nephew of abolitionist John Brown of Harper's Ferry fame, first lit the light on September 17, 1872. He was leasing the island at the time, and agreed to tend the light until a permanent keeper could be found.

In September 1889 the crew of the passing schooner *Gulnare* noticed a grass fire near the lighthouse. They immediately dropped anchor, went ashore, and extinguished it, saving the lighthouse with their heroic effort. It was a noteworthy reversal of the lighthouse function of coming to the aid of sailors.

In a 1921 report to the Marine Department, the Superintendent of Lights recommended that the light on Middle Island be discontinued for two reasons. First, the once-busy shipping lane that passed just to the south of the island by then had very little traffic to Canadian ports; second, trees on the heavily wooded island had grown up around the lighthouse, obscuring the light completely in some directions. While it would only cost a little to refurbish the lighthouse, it would cost a lot to trim or cut down the trees. He therefore recommended the most economical solution — to discontinue the lighthouse. Some data say this occurred in 1918, but the light was still functional when this report was filed in 1921.

In 1958 the lighthouse, by then owned by an American, was destroyed by a fire in the structure.

Known Keepers: S.S. Brown (1872–75), William M. Crubb (1876–77), L.S. Brown (1878–86), Horatio Stewart (1886–88), Milo H. Malott (1888–93), Jonathan Case (1893–98), Colin P. Lawson (1898–1905), Frank Lawson (1905–06), J.L. Lidwell (1906–11), J. Lidwell (1911–14), W.K. Wilson (1914–18).

Mohawk Island Lighthouse

15 Mohawk Island Lighthouse

In 1829, after the completion of the first Welland Canal, lake travel on eastern Lake Erie increased considerably. A feeder canal was built to bring water from the Grand River at Port Maitland to ensure supplies for vessels using the Welland Canal. Although this feeder canal had a draft of only 4 feet (1.2 m), many smaller boats used it as an alternative route to the main canal. Because of the rising volume of water traffic at the Port Maitland Harbour and the presence of a dangerous reef nearby, a lighthouse in the area was deemed necessary.

The government contracted John Brown of Thorold in 1846 to build the lighthouse. Brown was a Scottish stonemason who had immigrated to Canada in 1838 where he opened and developed the Queenston Quarry. Brown used the high-quality stone from this quarry to build the 64-foot (19.5 m) conical tower and attached keeper's dwelling on Mohawk Island. Thanks to his meticulous workmanship, including ornate stonework under the tower gallery and special stonework at doors, windows and corners, the project took two years to complete. The tower supported an octagonal lantern that had twelve

Mohawk Island Lighthouse, circa 1950

lights in each side and an ogee dome. The lantern used ten coal oil lamps and eight reflectors to produce a light 65 feet (20 m) above the water with about a 10-mile (16 km) visibility.

During the War of 1812 there had been a naval reserve on the point by Port Maitland, and the government had blueprints drawn up for a lighthouse in the area to mark the reef for their naval vessels. However, after the war, only one naval vessel was allowed to remain on each of the Great Lakes, so the blueprints were not used. When Brown was contracted to build the lighthouse he was given these 1816 blueprints for the lighthouse construction.

The lighthouse was built on Mohawk Island (formerly Gull Island). This small, rocky, barren island, about 2 miles (3.2 km) southeast of Port Maitland offered the only available spot for a lighthouse offshore to mark the dangerous reef. The lighthouse was finished in 1848.

Besides building the Mohawk lighthouse, John Brown later built seven more stone lighthouses for the Canadian government. The next was the Burlington Bay Main Lighthouse in 1856 and then his six famous imperial lighthouses, all finished in 1858–59, on Lake Huron and Georgian Bay.

In 1877 the light at Mohawk Island was a revolving white light furnished by nine base-burners and one circular-burner fountain lamp. In 1901 its lantern displayed a revolving white light that showed three bright flashes at intervals of 30 seconds and then a 75-second eclipse to complete one revolution every 2¼ minutes. It was visible for about 10 miles (16 km).

The first lightkeeper at Mohawk Island was John Burgess, a farmer from Burgess Point. He earned £65 sterling a year. The last keeper was Richard Foster. In returning to the mainland in December 1932 after closing the lighthouse for the season, Foster and his son had their boat caught in the ice floes. Although it was less than two miles to shore, they never made it and were later found dead from exposure.

By 1933, once the entrance to the Welland Canal had been moved to Port Colborne, 12 miles (19.3 km) from the island, there was less lake traffic in this area. This change, coupled with the Fosters' tragic death, made the government decide to leave the lighthouse demanned and convert the light to battery power. Then in 1969, because the lighthouse had been burned by vandals, the lantern was removed and replaced with a floating reef buoy. When the Department of Transport announced plans to raze the lighthouse in 1977, public outcry stopped them.

Restoration efforts (started in 1990) were headed by local marina operator Mike Walker and the Mohawk Lighthouse Preservation Association. A new lantern of welded steel panels rather than cast-iron ones is to recrown the tower. Hopes are to restore the lighthouse as a private aid to navigation using an automated light powered by a solar panel so that local small craft can benefit from its light.

Although the island is almost barren, the lighthouse shares the rock with a variety of birds, including herring gulls, cormorants and rock doves. Now a bird sanctuary overseen by the Canadian Wildlife Society, the island is off limits to visitors during nesting season (April 1 to August 1).

Known Keepers: John Burgess (1848–70), R.H. Smithers (1877–), R.O. Smithers (1896–), Richard Foster (–1932).

16 Pelee Island Lighthouse

Pelee Island is 9 miles (14.4 km) south of Point Pelee on the Canadian shore of Lake Erie, just 8 miles (12.8 km) north of American-owned Kelleys Island. In the early 1800s the reefs and shallow waters of the Pelee Passage (between Pelee Island and Point Pelee) made travel through the passage very dangerous. In 1832 the Legislative Council of Upper Canada appropriated £750 to construct a lighthouse on Pelee Island to help mariners navigate the hazardous waterway.

John Scott of Detroit built the lighthouse in 1833 on a northern point of the island, known as Brushy Marsh Point, a spit of land donated to the government by islander William McCormick. Limestone from McCormick's local quarry was used in the construction. Its round 40-foot (12.2 m) tower had a constant interior diameter of approximately 8 feet (2.4 m), while the outside walls tapered from over 4 feet (1.2 m) thick at the bottom to just over 2 feet (0.6 m) at the top. The stones were held together by a lime and sand mortar. When finished, the tower was whitewashed to protect the mortar from exposure to water. The tower was ascended by a cedar spiral staircase, whose 41 steps were notched and built into the outer wall and toe-nailed to a center post. Six wooden outriggers were placed around the tower at regular intervals. Terminating in the walls of the tower, the ends of the timbers pushed upward against its walls to help support the tower's weight. The tower supported an iron lantern 8 feet (2.4 m) in diameter that had 15 small panes of glass in all but one of its ten sides. The tenth panel was blacked out.

The light was a combination of lamps and reflectors. There were four circular and eight dual-burner fountain lamps and twelve 14–18-inch (35–45 cm) reflectors. It originally displayed a fixed white catoptric light. Its visibility of 9 miles (14.5 km) was sometimes described by mariners as "lacking strength." In 1863 the light was changed from white to red, reducing its visibility to a mere 4 miles (6.5 km). After frequent complaints by mariners, the fixed white light was restored just a few years later.

Shortly after becoming the first keeper in 1834, William McCormick moved his wife and eleven children to live year round on the island. A keeper's house was not built, however, as McCormick had his own house and land on the island. In its first year the lighthouse ran out of oil months early, in September.

In 1835 the future American general Robert E. Lee, while surveying the Ohio-Michigan border, was supposedly in the Pelee Lighthouse because of the "advantage it offered." There he found a most ill-tempered keeper, whom he claimed to have killed in an ensuing fight. Although this information is recorded in a letter of Robert E. Lee's, one must wonder who was killed, if anyone, since William McCormick was the keeper from 1834 until 1840, when he died and passed the job on to his son Alexander.

In the winter of 1838, during the "Patriot" uprising in Upper

Pelee Island Lighthouse

Pelee Island Lighthouse, circa 1918

Canada, patriots invaded Pelee Island from Sandusky, Ohio, and took over the island. The McCormicks left for the safety of the mainland. Soldiers from Fort Malden and a group of natives marched across the ice to drive the patriots from Pelee Island. During the invasion, lamps and reflectors were stolen. Perhaps this is why McCormick did not return to the island until the summer of 1839, leaving mariners without light for a period.

After recommendations in 1845 that a keeper's house be built, Alexander McCormick started to construct his own stone house in 1846. The completion date is unknown. It is said that it was finished for James Cummins, who succeeded McCormick in 1850, but a frame keeper's house was later built around 1856. While keeper, Cummins was awarded a gold watch by the Dominion of Canada for his heroic life-saving service in rescuing crews from the *George Warren* in 1869 and the schooner *Tartar* in 1870.

During the 1870s the light was a fixed white catoptric light furnished by four circular and eight dual-burner fountain lamps on iron circles, and four 14-inch (35 cm), four 15-inch (37.5 cm), and four 18-inch (45 cm) reflectors.

In the 1800s politics was frequently involved in the hiring and firing of lighthouse keepers, and keepers were frequently appointed for their political affiliation. But according to a state-

ment of the Minister of Marine in the House of Commons in July 1899, politics had played no part in the dismissal of James Quick, the lightkeeper and meteorological observer at Pelee Island. Quick had shown himself negligent and disobedient, the minister reported. Ignoring repeated requests, he had refused to send in his reports and complete his duties. Also, he had let the station deteriorate after it had been observed by inspectors over the years to be in top shape.

The light was decommissioned in 1909 during the tenure of John R. Lidwell. With the building of the Pelee Passage Lighthouse in 1902, it had become obsolete, so it was removed from service to save money. Once abandoned, the elements and vandalism took their toll. Reports say the keeper's house was moved after this, but its destination is not specified.

About 1990 a "Relight the Lighthouse" committee was started by 250 permanent island residents to raise the money to restore the crumbling lighthouse. By 1999 they had raised $50,000. Also at this time Ron Tiessen (curator of the Pelee Island Heritage Centre) raised another $175,000 through grant applications. Tiessen oversaw the work by restoration architect Nicholas Hill of Guelph, Ontario. Hill in turn hired Brian Bartlett of Bartlett Restoration in Charing Cross for masonry work, Larry Gervais and Jim Dejong for carpentry work, Jim Wallace as blacksmith, and Steven Rice as painter. Their restoration, aiming for 1833 authenticity, was started in early 2000 and finished in July for the tower's rededication ceremony on August 19, 2000. Newly restored to its former pristine condition, the lighthouse earned its removal from *Lighthouse Digest's* "Doomsday List of Endangered Lighthouses."

Today visitors to the tower can a ferry from Point Pelee to Pelee Island and then drive across the island to Lighthouse Drive. After parking, follow "Ye Olde Lighthouse Trail" for less than 1/2 a mile (0.8 km) to where the trail opens onto a sandy beach just south of the lighthouse. Time and weather brought the tower close to complete ruin, but concerned citizens have saved it. The tower, now part of the Lighthouse Nature Reserve, is one of the island's main tourist attractions.

Known Keepers: William McCormick (1834–39), Alexander McCormick (1840–49), J. McChaplin (1850), James Cummins (1850–60) (1860–88), William Swetman Jr. (1860–66), William Jerome Swetman (1867–68), James E. Quick (1888–99), John R. Lidwell (1899–1909).

Pelee Passage New Lighthouse

17 Pelee Passage New Lighthouse

When the steel tower of the old Pelee Passage light was dismantled in 1976 it was replaced with a new, more up-to-date structure on the existing pier. The whole edifice looks more like a mini-airport than a lighthouse. The keeper's house is on top of the cylinder built high out of the water; its large flat roof serves as a helicopter pad; the light tower rises as a perfect cylinder from one of its corners and is topped by a large gallery with multi-paned lantern windows flaring out as they rise; and the lantern is topped by a radio beacon instead of a dome. The 79-foot (24 m) structure was painted white with green upper and lower portions. With its focal plane of 81 feet (25 m), its white flashing light (flash 0.5 s; eclipse 3.5 s) can be seen for 9 miles (14.5 km). In 1986 it also became a winter light and its intensity was reduced. The light still serves as an important navigation aid for Pelee Passage.

Pelee Passage Old Lighthouse

18 Pelee Passage Old Lighthouse

After the Point Pelee Lighthouse burned down in 1900, the Canadian government decided to replace it with a new one on the dangerous reef in the middle of Pelee Passage to better mark the passage for mariners. They chose to build the light on the shoal at Middle Ground so that it would be visible to vessels traveling in either direction and because the shoal provided a more stable foundation.

In 1900 W.H. Noble was commissioned to supervise the building of the new light. Construction of the cribwork foundation began immediately in Amherstburg, Ontario. The base consisted of grillwork timbers 12 inches (30 cm) square, laid crosswise 6 inches (15 cm) apart, two deep, and bolted firmly together in a platform 65 feet (20 m) in diameter.

In 1901 the base was sunk in 13 feet (4 m) of water. Then the truncated steel cone foundation was placed on the base and a steel cylinder placed inside. The center was filled with stone and gravel that settled down into the spaces of the wooden base, and concrete was poured between the two steel sections to form walls 6 feet (1.8 m) thick. A polygonal cribwork 14-foot (4.3 m) wide was built of 12-inch (30 cm) hardwood timber to surround it and extend 4 feet (1.2 m) above the water level. This cribwork was filled with stone and gravel to support and protect the foundation, which cost $10,429. The top of the foundation was 18 feet (5.5 m) above the water. The next year, a circular, steel plate, tapering tower was built to support a polygonal lantern with a curved decorative iron railing. It extended up for 66 feet (20 m), giving the tower a total height of 84 feet (25.5 m) above water.

The light was white with two brief flashes of 0.58 second's duration separated by an eclipse of 0.85 seconds and followed by an eclipse of 5.48 seconds. The illuminating apparatus was a third-order dioptric lens purchased from Chance Brothers and Co. of Birmingham, England, for $3,216. The illuminant was oil, vaporized and burnt under an incandescent mantle. This air light was manufactured by the Canadian Typographical Company of Windsor. A cluster of three jets formed the main flash and each jet had over 400 candlepower. With its visibility of up to 15 miles (24 km), it was reputed to be one of the best lights on the Great Lakes at that time. It was activated on July 4, 1902.

In October 1902 a steam fog siren was also put into service. The fog signal was placed 28 feet (8.6 m) above the lake and sounded from the north side of the tower (blast 7 s; silence 30 s). In 1910 the steam fog siren was replaced with a diaphone fog signal that had an oil engine to operate the air compressors.

The lighthouse, built at a total cost of $36,793, was intended to be fireproof, and the light and fog alarm were to be in all respects superior to any on the lakes. During construction, two temporary fixed white lights 40 feet (12.2 m) apart were shown from lens lanterns hoisted to the top of the work site. As work progressed, the lights were raised so that they always showed above the completed portion.

By 1976 this once most modern light on the lakes had become obsolete. It was dismantled and replaced with a lighthouse with up-to-date technology. The Dean Construction Company was contracted to tear down the light at the passage, but decided instead, to give the lighthouse to the City of Windsor in honor of their founder, Americo Dean. It was then re-erected on the grounds of the Lakeview Park Marina for the city in 1980. Now, instead of keeping guard and marking hidden shoals, the lighthouse marks the marina. The five-story white tower with its oxide-red domed top was visible for a long way on the Detroit River.

The marina and park are administered by the City of Windsor's Department of Parks and Recreation. The re-erected lighthouse is now a historic site and is also protected as part of the park. It is a tribute to the foresight of a small group of people that this part of history was recognized and has been preserved for future generations.

Known Keepers: P. McIntryre (–1870–), James Edward (–1877–), S. Bottom (1911), Joe Ouellette (1911–45), Cyril Ouellette (1945–)

Pelee Passage Old Lighthouse

Point Abino Lighthouse

19 Point Abino Lighthouse

Point Abino, a popular area for summer residents, juts 2 miles (3.2 km) into Lake Erie about halfway between Fort Erie and Port Colborne on the north shore of the lake. It is named after Father Claude Aveneau, a Jesuit priest who lived there about 1690. It was first called Aveneau, then Abeneau, and finally shortened to Abino. The missionary found solitude in the rolling wooded hills and imposing, fine white sand dunes that characterized the point. Huge quantities of that sand were later excavated and hauled away to supply industries and construction projects in nearby Buffalo, Cleveland and other industrial centers.

Hidden shoals and reefs off the point have caused many shipwrecks. In November 1913 the American Lightship *LV 82*, stationed 6 miles (9.6 km) out and 13 miles (20.8 km) southwest of Buffalo, went down with its six crew members in one of the worst storms to hit the lakes. In 1917 the Canadian government decided to replace navigational beacons in the lake and build a lighthouse on the point to warn ships of the dangerous waters.

The point was owned by Allen Holloway, a Buffalo-area developer who recognized its potential for American cottage residences. He had divided the area into 50 lots and 70 acres (28 hectares) of common land. In 1892 he formed the Point Abino Association to guard the owners' privacy. As a result, the drive to the point is defined by gates and barriers, "No trespassing" signs, and "Private road, members only" signs. These barriers contradicted government policy that all federal buildings should be reachable by ready public access, according to common law. Yet, because of the pre-existing private ownership at the point and its private road, the Canadian government signed an agreement with the Point Abino Association that the lighthouse would be accessed by water only.

Thus, when the Point Abino Lighthouse was built in 1917, it was placed on a rock shelf in Lake Erie. Gravel was hauled from along the west shore of the point by horse and cart, loaded onto barges, and taken to the site to build the concrete structure. This placement of the light also pre-empted residents' concerns about the structure being built on their land.

The lighthouse contained both the light and the fog alarm signal. Normally the fog equipment would have been housed in a separate building, but this was not possible with the light built out in the water. Much attention was paid to this project. The lighthouse was more ornate and detailed than other lighthouses of the period. The keeper's house, built three years later, was also designed to fit in with the nearby residences. It was a two-story Tudor-style house built onshore about 300 feet (90 m) from the lighthouse.

The lighthouse had to be raised well above the water. To this end it was built 98 feet (30 m) high with five levels, each of which had at least four windows, and its lantern was reached by ladder stairs (116 steps). The original lighthouse keeper was Pat Augustine, who started in 1918 and served for 35 years. All supplies were brought to the lighthouse by supply ships until the 1920s, when road access was granted to the lighthouse keepers and their families.

The last lighthouse keeper was Lewis W. Anderson, a native of Cape Breton, who took up the profession after taking early retirement from the Canadian army. He began as assistant keeper in Port Colborne and then agreed to fill in as keeper at the Point Abino Light Station for six months. He and his wife liked it so much that they decided to stay until the end of 1988 — almost 30 years. Anderson is a font of knowledge about the lighthouse. He recalls that the light was originally fueled by kerosene, and the keeper had to climb to the top of the tower every six hours to rewind the chain and weight mechanism that turned the rotating light.

Later the light became electrified, using its own generator and half-horsepower motor to keep the light rotating. In the late 1930s it was converted to hydro-electric power. In Anderson's time as keeper a 500-watt mercury vapor bulb supplied the powerful light, which shone through the original Paris-made, cut-glass Fresnel lens, officially rated with a visibility of 20 miles (32.5 km). The light revolved approximately every twelve seconds.

In his early days, as well as operating the diesel engines that provided the electricity to operate the light, Anderson also ran the compressors that powered the foghorn. Since the foghorn (blast 3 s; silence 48 s) was housed in the same structure as the lighthouse, the sound echoed through the five levels of the lighthouse. "It would reverberate through the whole tower and you'd just have to get out of there," said Anderson. "Even the neighbors came pounding on the door, telling us to shut the damn thing down." The foghorn was later replaced by an electrical one that was barely audible on land.

When the lighthouse was commissioned to service for the 1995 shipping season, the foghorn was removed. During that first season without the foghorn, local small craft owners and yacht clubs were concerned for their members' safety because of the dangerous shoals. Lake freighters and ocean-going vessels kept a safe, respectful distance of 3 miles (5 km) or more from the lighthouse, but pleasure craft frequently ignored it. "There is not a summer goes by that five or six do not crack up," Anderson recalled. Some survivors made it to his door but others were not that lucky.

When Anderson first became a lighthouse keeper he had four main duties: to maintain the operation of the diesel engines that created the electricity to keep the light rotating; to operate the compressor that ran the foghorn; to maintain and repair all the equipment; to keep all the structures in good condition. He described the life as being married to a lighthouse for nine months of the year.

When fierce storms raged on Lake Erie the keeper appreciated his food stores, as the lighthouse became an island, cut off from land for days at a time. Anderson's worst storm was in December 1985. It was more destructive than usual because of the record high water level. The storm smashed the windows and furniture on the lowest level of the lighthouse and filled the engine and watchroom with 4 feet (1.2 m) of water. A lifetime of Point Abino history that Anderson had been collecting was destroyed or washed away. Then the water froze and it took four days for him to chip his way into the structure. "There was 5 feet (1.5 m) of ice. It took three months before it thawed and we had to dry everything with industrial heaters."

Before automation in 1972, Anderson and his assistant worked twelve-hour shifts, seven days a week, during the navigation season. With the arrival of electrical service via underground conduit to the lighthouse in the early 1980s, Anderson said, the job became mainly an eight-hour-a-day maintenance job.

Point Abino Lighthouse, circa 1928

In 1986, after the great storm, the lighthouse's historical value was realized and the government began to restore it, sandblasting, painting, and adding a new roof. In 1987, under a new policy, Point Abino became one of the lighthouses that remained manned because of the harsh weather conditions and its location. It was only partially automated because its old-style light could not be completely converted to a remote-control system.

When Anderson retired at the end of 1988, he was kept on as a caretaker/security guard for the lighthouse and allowed to remain in the keeper's residence. Then in 1989 the light was fully automated, and the automated light transmitter was linked to the Canadian Coast Guard operation's headquarters in Prescott.

By 1991 Anderson was only a seasonal resident who returned each summer to check on the lighthouse, which was then controlled, as it is now, by Transport Canada and the Canadian Coast Guard with its light operations being monitored from Toronto. Also in 1991, new windows were put in and the old delivery doors were bricked over. The light is now operational 24 hours a day and the lighthouse sits empty except for the new equipment and the old air compressor tanks, which were too big to remove.

Anderson's memories also included: the winter of 1977 when a fierce snowstorm left 30-foot (9 m) snow banks; the lake rising 9.5 feet (3 m) in a fall storm and the water being pushed down the lake; boaters crashing into the lighthouse in foggy weather while following the sound of the foghorn and trying to get to safe harbor; a Much Music video being filmed there; and the movie *Lady Killer* being filmed on location there in 1995.

Today, as well as the Point Abino Lighthouse on the point, and the surrounding cottages, there is also a 1,700-acre (680 hectare) bird sanctuary.

Known Keepers: Pat Augustine (1918–53), Lewis Anderson (1962–88).

20 Point Pelee Lighthouse

Two major danger zones imperil water travel along the Lake Erie north shore: Long Point and the Point Pelee area. Both have land spits that jut far out into the lake toward the shipping lanes between Buffalo and Detroit. At Point Pelee there are also many islands, reefs and shoals to maneuver around. The dangerous 9-mile (14.5 km), narrow gap between Pelee Island and Point Pelee was first recorded by French explorers Dollier de Casson and René Brehant de Galinée. They were camped on the beach east of the Point on March 26, 1670, when they witnessed the lake's ferocity. This storm, and the dangerous shoals of Pelee Passage, almost ruined their expedition.

Almost 150 years later, in 1818, a buoy was placed on the tip of the shoal off Point Pelee. In 1828 a shoal, with only 13 feet (4 m) of water above it, was mapped in the middle of Pelee Passage by Lt. Henry Bayfield. In 1833 a light was put on the northeast end of Pelee Island, but the hidden shoal remained unlit.

In 1845 an appeal was sent to the government: "The Passage is becoming of more importance every year; all vessels take it that are bound for the Upper Lakes. To make it navigable at all times a revolving light would be required on the outer end of Pointe aux Pelee not less than 70 feet [21.5 m] high. The improvement of the channel is of the greatest importance and I would beg to call the attention of the Board to it, at as early a day as possible." That same year, two vessels collided head-on in the Pelee Passage because, perhaps for fear of hitting the middle shoal, neither captain would alter course. The collision resulted in the sinking of the *Kent*.

In 1850 the House of Assembly of Upper Canada expended £20,000 on a foundation for a Pelee Passage Light, but in the winter of 1855–56 the foundation was destroyed by ice. Then in July 1856 William Scott, C.E. was appointed to superintend another attempt to build a Pelee Passage Light. The foundation, begun in November 1856 at Amherstburg, Ontario, used 300–400 square oak timbers, designed into an octagonal caisson 30 feet (9 m) high, 64 feet (19.5 m) in diameter at the base, and 50 feet (15.2 m) in diameter at the top. The 30–60-foot (9–18 m) timbers were arranged vertically and bolted together. The 10,000 pounds (4,500 kg) of nuts and bolts needed for the job were admitted duty-free since the contract went to Fulton Ironworks, an American company from Detroit. When calked and completed, the caisson was launched from the work yard in July 1857 and floated into place on the Dummy Reef (today known as Grubb's Reef) about 3 miles (5 km) off Point Pelee, where it was filled with rocks and cement and sunk. This foundation cost £4,500. On August 15, 1857, a temporary red light was placed on the caisson 25 feet (7.6 m) above the water. Mariners reported this light to be visible for about 7 miles (11 km).

By 1861 the permanent wooden tower was completed. It displayed a fixed white light. When mariners complained about not being able to distinguish between the Pelee Island light and this light, the government in 1863 changed the Pelee Island light to a fixed red light. However, since this color reduced the light's visibility from 9 miles (14.5 km) to less than 4 miles (6.5 km) and the Point Pelee light was still confused with a ship's light, the government changed Pelee Island back to a fixed white light and gave Point Pelee a revolving white light.

Being built on Dummy Reef, it was sometimes referred to as the Dummy Lighthouse. More confusion arises, as the light was also referred to as Point Pelee Spit Lighthouse and, in Parliamentary Sessional Papers, as the Point Pelee Reef Lighthouse.

Sessional Papers from 1877 describe the light as a revolving white catoptric one set in a lantern 9 feet (2.7 m) in diameter, which used six mammoth flat-wick lamps with flat reservoirs and six 20-inch (50 cm) reflectors on two iron frames. Three lamps showed in one direction and three in another, so that the light would be visible from two approaches. The tower was an octagonal 54-foot (16.5 m) wooden structure painted white. At that time most equipment was in good order except for the 13-inch (0.3 m) square lamp reservoirs, which were all leaky. Copper ones were recommended in their place.

The 1878 papers mention a white wooden building sheathed in iron. (This shows the exterior must have been covered the previous year, as iron sheathing had not been mentioned previously.) The revolving white light flashed once every minute and had a visibility of about 20 miles (32 km). The wooden caisson needed new timbers to replace rotten ones and boiler plates to replace those torn off by ice. The 1879 papers report a wooden tower 61 feet (18.6 m) from base to vane, with a lantern 10 feet (3 m) in diameter. It displayed a revolving white catoptric light every 90 seconds with an estimated visibility of 18 miles (29 k).

The first keeper, James Edwards, lived with his family in the keeper's house on the mainland of Point Pelee and kept the light until October 1, 1878, when his grandson, W.A. Grubb Jr. took over. In 1886 he received a gold watch from the U.S. President for saving the crews of two American ships, the *Venetta* and the *Star of Hope*.

As the Edwards family had lived on the 29½-acre (12 hectare) lighthouse reserve for many years and since squatters on Point Pelee were obtaining deeds to land they occupied, James Edwards also tried to acquire a deed as of 1882. After his death in 1884 his heirs continued efforts to acquire deeded title even as late as 1910, but they were eventually told they had no justifiable claim to the land, as Edwards had held a government position and lived in a government-supplied house.

On April 17, 1900, in stormy, foggy weather, disaster struck the lighthouse. While keeper W.A. Grubb Jr. was blowing the foghorn, a fire started in the building above him. It may have been caused by a lamp being knocked down by the pounding of waves displacing a wall of the building. Grubb discovered the fire abruptly when the top of the lighthouse fell on him, temporarily pinning him beneath fallen timbers. His clothes were burned off and his back was seriously injured, but he and his assistant both recovered, narrowly escaping the disaster that completely destroyed the lighthouse.

On April 21, 1900, a temporary fixed white light, shown from an anchor light, was hoisted 37 feet (11.3 m) above the lake on a mast placed on the wreck of the lighthouse pier. It was kept lit when weather permitted landing on the pier. Since it was irregularly lit and was so far from the deep water, the government decided not to rebuild the lighthouse, even though the fire had left the concrete pier in fairly good condition. Instead, a new light was planned at Southeast Shoal or Middle Ground, either of which would better mark the dangerous shoal in the middle of Pelee Passage. Middle Ground was finally chosen because a light at that location would be visible to vessels heading in either direction and Middle Ground provided a more stable foundation for a light.

Known Keepers: James Edwards (1861–78), W.A. Grubb Jr. (1878–1900).

21 Pointe aux Pins Light

In 1919 the Canadian government placed a light on a white square skeletal tower at the southernmost tip of Pointe aux Pins, just east of Rondeau Harbour, Lake Erie. Today it displays a fixed red light from a 41.5-foot (12.6 m) focal plane to help guide vessels safely around the point.

22 Port Bruce Light

Port Bruce is at the mouth of Catfish Creek to the east of Port Stanley on the north shore of Lake Erie. A lighthouse was built here in 1876 to mark the harbor. It was known as the Port Bruce Lighthouse as well as Catfish Creek Lighthouse. In 1955 the lighthouse was replaced with a modern 19.8-foot (6 m) white circular tower with a green upper portion that displayed a green electric flashing light (flash 2 s; eclipse 2 s) from a 27.6-foot (8.5 m) focal plane. Today it continues to mark the port for pleasure boats.

Port Bruce Light

Port Burwell Lighthouse

23 Port Burwell Lighthouse

The Port Burwell lighthouse was built in 1840 with financing from the British government. The site was chosen because of the natural harbor formed where Big Otter Creek drained into Lake Erie. Much of the shoreline between Port Burwell and Long Point to the east was clay cliffs with no refuge for vessels in a storm. Being one of few on Lake Erie's north shore in 1840, this light was most important as a beacon either to guide vessels to safety from Lake Erie's violent storms into the Port Burwell Harbour or to warn crafts of their location so they could maneuver their way around the point to the safety of Long Point Bay.

The lighthouse is not the oldest lighthouse on the north shore but it is one of the oldest in Canada. It remained in service for 112 years (1840–1952) without being electrified. Then it operated from 1953 with an electric light until 1963, when it was removed from service.

The octagonal wooden structure used large pine timbers that stretched and tapered in from the ground to the top to make a frame for lapstrake wooden siding. The lighthouse stands some 65 feet (20 m) above the ground on the banks of the Big Otter River and 130 feet (40 m) above Lake Erie.

The original oil lamp required 71 gallons (320 l) of oil and 72 wicks for one year's service — 2,929 hours of burning time. Even after the light was electrified, the original Fresnel lens remained in the lantern to magnify the light beam. This lens is still in the tower today.

The first lightkeeper was believed to have been Thomas Bellairs. However, the Sutherland family were the official lightkeepers for over a century (1852–1952). Their dedicated service earned them the recognition of two monarchs and a place in Great Lakes navigational history. Alexander Sutherland, the first Sutherland lightkeeper, reported that over 50 vessels came to grief in the Port Burwell area during his tenure (1852–73). After his death the position of keeper went to his son John.

John Sutherland left some excellent detailed descriptions of life as a keeper. As well as maintaining the burning of the main light, he had to light the lamps at the end of the short piers as well. This was a most dangerous task in stormy weather. Sutherland was frequently washed off the wooden pier by storm waves smashing over the breakwall. Although he was a strong swimmer, he sustained many injuries — broken legs, arms, ribs, hands and collarbone. In 1935 Sutherland's excellent service was recognized by the King George V Jubilee Medal. After he retired in 1939, a special ceremony was held at Iroquois Beach

Port Burwell Pier Light

in 1940 to honor his long service and courage with the George VI Imperial Service Medal.

In April 1965 the lighthouse received official recognition as an historical site. Public tours began in 1983. In 1986 the lighthouse was restructured, as the foundation and main beams needed replacing. Mennonite craftsman Leroy Eicher was hired because he and his sons used the same type of hand tools as were used to build the original tower. The pine main beams were replaced with Douglas fir, and the original spiral staircase was replaced with a zigzag style for safety. Refurbishing was completed in 1987.

Beside the lighthouse are large anchors from the schooner *Nimrod*, which sank after colliding with another ship in the fog off Port Bruce. Today's visitors can climb to the top and take in the spectacular view of the harbor, lake, and village. Across the road from the lighthouse is a marine museum that displays an excellent collection of lighthouse lenses.

Known Keepers: Thomas Bellairs (1840–52), Alexander Sutherland (1852–73), Alexander Sutherland Jr. (1873–85), William Sutherland (1885–94), John Sutherland (1894–1939), John Sutherland Jr. (1939–47), John Sutherland (1947–52), Jack Hayward (1952–55), John Sutherland (1955–63).

Port Burwell Lighthouse lens

24 Port Colborne Lighthouse

When the first Welland Canal was finished in 1829, arrangements were made to change the entrance name from Gravelly Bay to Port Colborne. The first lighthouse stood on the southeast end of a 1,200-foot (365 m) pier constructed out into the lake from the first lock. The first lightkeeper, Mr. Cochrane, appointed by the Welland Canal Company in 1834, earned $360 a year. The oil lamp in this lighthouse exploded one evening and burned the curtains, but no other damage was done.

After a severe storm in 1844, the piers and the entrance to the canal were moved slightly to the north. The east pier where the lighthouse stood was extended southward, and a new light was built on this extension. This light combined with the first lighthouse to form range lights that guided vessels into the canal. The main light was a white circular 44-foot (13.4 m) wooden tower topped with an iron lantern with an iron floor. It displayed a fixed white catoptric light containing ten dual-burner fountain lamps on three iron frames. The range light was 26 feet (8 m) tall and contained one base-burner and one 15-inch (37.5 cm) reflector. In an 1877 report, and again in 1878, these lights were described as rotten and dangerous for a keeper on windy days.

By 1879 the main light was replaced by a white wooden gallows tower with an enclosed staircase. The tower was 80 feet (24.5 m) high and 100 feet (30.5 m) to the top of the lantern, giving it a new focal plane of 110 feet (33.5 m). At its base it measured 30 feet (9 m) square, and at the gallery 11 feet (3.3 m) square. The lantern was furnished with ten Argand burner lamps with 18-inch (45 cm) reflectors, and the light had a visibility of some 20 miles (32 km) on a clear night. By the end of the century, with rot causing this light and pier to fall into disrepair, funds were appropriated for major harbor improvements: new east and west breakwalls were constructed, the outer harbor was deepened, and new lighthouses and a dwelling for the keeper were built. This house, just south of Sugarloaf Street, was torn down in the early 1930s.

The earliest known fog signal at Port Colborne was a hand-operated horn consisting of a rectangular box with a bellows that blew air into a diaphragm. The bellows was activated by a lever on the side of the box. When it was discarded by the lighthouse, it saw play at the local arena, sounding home-team goals at Saturday night hockey games.

In 1903 the first new lighthouse was built on the east end of the new west breakwall. It came to be known as the inner, or main, light and was the front range light to the new rear range light built onshore in 1904. The main light was a 42-foot (13 m), square white tower made of reinforced concrete. At 50 feet (15.2 m) above the water level, it was visible for some 12 miles (19 km). The gallery and the lantern were painted red. The octagonal lantern room used a kerosene vapor lamp. The flash of its white light was created by the rotation of a metal reflector on a bed of mercury. The bottom of the tower was outfitted to be the keeper's home away from home. A small building, "the engine

Port Colborne Outer Lighthouse

room," also called the watchroom, was attached to the base of the tower. It had a small coal-burning heater and basic furniture, and it housed oil-engine-driven generators to operate a new air horn, which faced the lake through a hole in the south wall of the main lighthouse tower.

In 1927 a south branch was added to the west breakwall. Its shell was built in Port Maitland of box-like concrete compartments that were towed to Port Colborne, where the seacocks were opened, allowing the shells to sink into place. They were then filled with stones and capped with concrete. At the end of the extension, finished in 1928, a beacon was placed to serve as the outer light and front range light for the main light. It showed a fixed red by shining through a red glass placed in front of its reflector. The old rear range light was extinguished when this new range light was lit.

Also at this time the oil-driven engines were replaced by diesel generators that produced electricity for both range lights and the new fog signal. Interestingly, a 200-watt dual-filament bulb was used at the main light to prevent the light from burning out.

The old air foghorn was removed from the main light, and a new type F diaphone was placed in the front range light. This was one of the loudest fog signals on the Canadian side of the Great Lakes. It produced the traditional deep-throated "ooogaaahh" sound and was air-operated from compressors housed in the front range light. The electricity to operate the compressors was transmitted from the main light to the fog alarm building through an armored cable that ran along the breakwall. A tunnel in the new breakwall allowed the keeper to get safely out to the fog alarm building in stormy or icy conditions. An electrically operated fog bell was also installed as an added protective feature at this time. It was activated when visibility was half a mile or less, and worked in conjunction with the diaphone foghorn.

From 1903 until a radio beacon was installed, the only way a lightkeeper could summon help in an emergency was by a flag or a light. Supplies were delivered by the tender *Grenville*, which

Port Colborne Main Lighthouse, circa 1950

served lighthouses from the Ontario–Quebec border on the St. Lawrence River to as far west as Sarnia. Items such as diesel oil, lubricating oils, paint, coal, cleaning equipment, and spare parts were delivered only once a year. Keepers supplied their own food.

In 1943 the radio beacon was added to the station and, to provide larger quarters for the keepers, a two-story frame keeper's house was built to the west side of the tower attached to the engine room. To prevent breakdowns, the radio equipment had two of everything (transmitters, generators, automatic time switches). Twice every hour the time switch would start the generator and keep it running for nine minutes and put the transmitter on air to transmit the signal for Port Colborne — three periods of one minute each with a silent period of two minutes (the letter "Z" repeated three times followed by three long dashes). During the two minutes of silence, two other radio beacons, one from Long Point Lighthouse and one from Southeast Shoal Lighthouse, were each on for one minute with their own special code. All three beacons used the same frequency.

A ship equipped with a radio direction finder could take a bearing on the three stations and determine its position on the lake, or could just use the beacon at the station toward which it was heading. In periods when visibility on the lake was lower than five miles, the radio beacon transmitter was operated during the whole hour following the sequence of "transmit one minute, silent two minutes." The aerial for the radio beacon was a 120-foot (36.5 m) steel tower at the southwest corner of the lighthouse. The radio beacon equipment could also provide communications by radio telegraph with marine Coast Guard stations. Port Colborne made daily contact with the Coast Guard Station VBF Port Burwell, 85 miles (136 km) away. Buffalo and Toronto Coast Guard stations were contacted only when necessary. The radio beacon was automated in 1966.

Besides attending to the range lights, the foghorn and the radio beacon, the keeper also kept an eye on the buoys and a third light on the east breakwall, which showed a green

Port Colborne Main Lighthouse

flashing light operated by batteries. These three lights operated day and night and were usually serviced only once a year.

In 1954 submarine power cables were laid across the outer harbor to the lighthouse, and commercial electricity was used; but the generators were kept in operating condition in case of power failure. In 1959 the inner and outer lights were intensified with higher-wattage bulbs and more modern lighting equipment. The light bulb was increased to 500 watts and an automatic bulb changer installed. The light now had 120,000 candlepower. The metal rotator was also replaced by two 12-inch (30 cm) beehive lenses that rotated to produce a flash once every five seconds.

In 1966 the Canadian Meteorological Service designated the lighthouse as one of its observational locations. Accurate equipment for determining wind speed and direction, temperature, precipitation, humidity and air pressure was installed. The keeper observed and forwarded weather information every six hours to the regional forecast office at Malton, Ontario.

In 1971, to the consternation of many, the foghorn was automated and a new horn (actually four horns electrically run) was installed which produced a high-pitched sound. Local residents complained that it sounded like a rutting bull moose, and mariners said it could not be heard well out on the lake. The horn also had a videograph attached to it to determine how poor visibility was. When fog, rain, or snow reduced visibility to 3 miles (5 km), the horn was triggered to start.

The last keeper left the light in 1986; living quarters were torn down in 1990; in 1997 the radio tower was removed; in 1998 the old lens was replaced with a DB 25 one; the light was fenced to help prevent vandalism.

An interview with Isabelle and Paul Kendrick, wife and son of Port Colborne's keeper Al Kendrick, provided much of this history of the Port Colborne Lighthouse and a good insight into their life as a keeper's family. Kendrick was single when he started as radio beacon operator in 1943, using the newly installed equipment. Because this was a 24-hour job, he stayed at the lighthouse full time. To him the engine room became the "dog house" because that was where he had to be

every night, nine months of the year. He was allowed ashore in the government-issued rowboat only to pick up supplies or to go to church.

In 1946 he took a year off and got married. He returned to the lighthouse as keeper and radio operator combined, when the previous keeper retired. Isabelle acted as assistant keeper from 1947 until 1951 but she did not receive the $35 a month as she was a family member. Her father built a sturdy 16-foot (4.9 m) steel boat nicknamed "Big Bertha" for safer transportation to the lighthouse, and a hoist just outside the engine room to lift the boat easily out of harm's way. Once, when the lighthouse inspector was on his annual visit, Al asked him if the government supplied anything to get rid of the ubiquitous spiders. "Yes," replied the inspector. "We call it a lighthouse keeper."

Shad flies could also be a problem. Once when Kendrick turned the generator on, an upstairs hall light came on, and the shad flies were drawn in through an open window, completely covering the ceiling and walls. He had to sweep the fishy-smelling creatures out of his bedroom before he could retire. Shad flies used to be a danger to early sailors because if too many of them lighted on the sails, they disabled the sailboat.

In 1952 the assistant keeper was George Parker. In 1958 a second assistant was hired and they could finally rotate duties to get time ashore. In 1959 a telephone line was put out to the lighthouse. It had been difficult to find and keep assistant keepers, as they were paid only for the time they worked, but in 1963 the government finally made assistant keepers permanent civil servants with a classification as lightkeepers and an annual salary.

In 1973 the vessel *Vancouver Trader* was grounded between the two sections of the west breakwall during heavy fog. The highlight of Kendrick's years as keeper was a stormy night in 1976 when a sailboat mistakenly got on the wrong side of the west breakwall. He ran out on the breakwall toward the outer light, threw a rope to the stranded people, and rescued all four Americans from the vessel. The next day, when they went back to retrieve their sailboat, nothing was left but a few pieces of floating fiberglass.

The Kendricks retired in 1979 after 35 years of service. Isabelle described their first ten years at the light as the best years. "There's a romance to lighthouses," she said, "especially during storms or during sunsets, but it's gone now." Now, the Port Colborne Lighthouse has no foghorn, no radio tower or transmitter, no engines and no lightkeepers. It's closed up air-tight with no air circulating, and it's rotting from the inside out. Rust can be seen coming out through the walls. The government talks about tearing it down and replacing it with a skeletal tower, but they fear public anger. Paul Kendrick is trying to save it for use as a marine museum.

Known Keepers: Mr. Cochrane (1834–), D. Fortier (1865–78–), Captain George Irwin ( ), Hugh Clarke Jr. (1904–), Jason Sherk (–1947), Al Kendrick (1947–79), Jack Bonisteel (1979–86).

Early Port Colborne Main Lighthouse

Port Dover Front Range Light

25 Port Dover Range Lights

In 1846 the Canadian government established a lighthouse at Port Dover, Lake Erie, to mark the entrance to its harbor at the mouth of the Lynn River. The light was built 110 feet (33.5 m) from the outer end of the west pier, which extended into the lake. The lighthouse was a 13-foot (4 m) square tapering white wooden tower 20 feet (6 m) tall. The lantern, 4 feet (1.2 m) in diameter, housed four No. 1 lamps with 14-inch (35 cm) reflectors, and exhibited a fixed white light for 8 miles (13 km). In 1897 another light was built on the pier behind it to form range lights that made harbor entry easier and safer. In 1927 a foghorn was added to the station (blast 3 s; silence 27 s).

Today the front range light, which shines from the end of the western concrete pier, is a square white pyramidal steel-sided structure; its gallery slightly below the top is surrounded with pipe railing. Standing 28 feet (8.6 m) high, it exhibits a green electric light with a two-second flash followed by a two-second eclipse from a 32.5-foot (10 m) focal plane.

The rear range light is a square white skeletal model, 51.6 feet (15 m) high, which exhibits a green flashing electric light from a 58-foot (18 m) focal plane. It has a fluorescent orange triangular day mark with a black vertical stripe. These range lights continue as active aids to navigation today, serving mainly pleasure craft in the local area.

Known Keepers: Henry Morgan (–1870–), S.L. Butler (1897).

Port Dover Rear Range Light, circa 1920

Port Dover Front Range Light, circa 1900s

26 Port Maitland Lighthouse

A lighthouse was first built at Port Maitland on the north shore of Lake Erie in 1846. It was placed on the west pier to mark the entrance to the Grand River. The harbor offered refuge to mariners in stormy weather — if they could get there. In November 1852 three schooners, *Hamlet*, *Lady Bagot* and *England*, were blown ashore east of the eastern pier while seeking refuge within the harbor.

Changes occurred at the lighthouse over the years. A winter gale on December 19, 1870, blew the old lighthouse into the lake and destroyed it. During the winter the light was reconstructed and readied for operation for the opening of the

Port Maitland Lighthouse

next navigation season. In 1875 the lighthouse was again rebuilt as a white open-frame wooden tower. In 1887 the light was a fixed white catoptric one with four mammoth flat-wick lamps with 20-inch (50 cm) reflectors on an iron table running around the lantern. In 1901 its lantern displayed a fixed white light from a 51-foot (15.5 m) focal plane to produce a visibility of 10 miles (16.2 km). This light is still active.

Known Keepers: F. Schofield (1870–77–), P. Baikie (–1870–), Mrs. J. Grant (1907–).

Early Port Maitland Light

27 Port Stanley Breakwater Light

I n 1901 Port Stanley, Lake Erie, was given a pier light to mark its harbor. It was a square white wooden tower on the west pier and was visible from all lakeside points. The tower displayed a fixed white light to guide mariners into port.

Port Stanley received a new light in 1909. This was a steel-reinforced concrete tower 24.7 feet (7.6 m) high, built in a square pyramidal style at the end of the government's west breakwater by F.R. Miller of Parry Sound at a cost of $3,850. In 1913 a foghorn was added to the station (blast 3 s; silence 27 s).

At some point this light's lantern was replaced with a modern green beacon that flashes for two seconds and is followed by a three-second eclipse from a 28.5-foot (8.8 m) focal plane. A tall radio antenna extends up from the top of the tower. This light still functions today as a guide for local boat traffic.

Known Keeper: J.L. Oliver (1909–).

Port Stanley Breakwater Light

Port Stanley Breakwater Light, circa 1909

28 Port Stanley Lighthouse

The lighthouse at Port Stanley, Lake Erie, was first built on the west pierhead in 1844. A wooden structure with the lantern hoisted on post supports, its light was visible from all points eastward. By the 1870s the light consisted of four flat-wick lamps and four 14-inch (35 cm) reflectors hoisted between two masts. By the late 1870s the supports were rotten and it was recommended that the government replace the decaying structure. The light was rebuilt in 1882.

In 1986 it was replaced with a 15.5-foot (4.8 m) modern circular tower with a green upper portion. It displayed an electric green flashing light from a 20-foot (6 m) focal plane. From its position near the end of the Port Stanley's west pier, it still helps guide vessels into the harbor today.

Known Keepers: C. Ead (–1870–90), Mrs. C. Ead (1890–1908), J.L. Oliver (1908–), Ort Sutherland (?).

Port Stanley Lighthouse

29 Rondeau Harbour (Erieau) East Pier Light

Although the Canadian government resumed ownership of Rondeau Harbour in the late 1850s, they made no major improvements until the 1870s when the harbor opening was dredged and the entrance piers and breakwaters were rebuilt to create a wider entrance.

As part of these improvements, range lights were built in 1876 along the east side of the harbor entrance. The main light was placed on the outer end of the east breakwater pier 70 feet (21.3 m) above the water. The front light was built 780 feet (238 m) away on the east breakwater and exhibited a fixed white light from an elevation of 34 feet (10.5 m) above the water with a visibility of about 10 miles (16 km). On October 19, 1877, a fire damaged the main tower and destroyed its lamps and reflectors.

The 1878 Parliamentary Sessional Papers indicate that the main lighthouse was a white wooden tower with a red iron lantern 10 feet (3 m) in diameter that stood 71 feet (21.8 m) high and housed six circular lamps with 22-inch (55 cm) reflectors. The light exhibited a red and white revolving pattern rotating every three minutes with a visibility of 20 miles (32.4 km). The front range light had a white open framework (trellis design) tower with an iron lantern 4 feet (1.2 m) in diameter. It displayed a fixed white light using one mammoth flat-wick lamp with a 17-inch (42.5 cm) reflector. From base to vane it was 30 feet (9 m) high. The cost of construction for these two lights was $2,692.

These range lights served for many years. At an unknown date, likely in 1912, the shorter range light was removed to avoid confusion when a new light was built on the western pier, making both sides of the harbor entrance lit. Even after a rear range light

Rondeau Harbour (Erieau) East Pier Light

was built to work in conjunction with the west pier light, the east pier light remained in operation. In 1992 it was a square white skeletal tower with a red upper portion, which used a dioptric illuminating apparatus from a 36-foot (11 m) focal plane to display its electric red flashing light (flash 0.5 s; eclipse 3.5 s). This light still operates today to guide vessels (mainly pleasure craft) into Rondeau Harbour.

Known Keepers: Thomas Harrison (1876–), W.R. Fellows (1888–1914), J. Claus (1914–).

30 Rondeau Harbour Old Lighthouse (Erieau)

Between Point Pelee and Port Stanley along the north shore of Lake Erie is a long low sandy ridge that runs about 7 miles (11.3 k) southward into the lake. It ends in an angular point covered in pine trees, the inspiration for its French name, Pointe aux Pins.

Within the point is a natural harbor that became known as Rondeau Harbour. Entry to it was through two openings on the west side of the point, but since the eastern opening of these was the deeper one, harbor protection was built in this opening in 1843–44. Two parallel entrance piers, about 700 feet (215 m) long and 150 feet (46 m) apart, were constructed almost midway in the opening and they were flanked by breakwaters at right angles to them. The western breakwater was 1,000 feet (305 m) long and the eastern 800 feet (244 m) long. A lighthouse was built to mark the entrance between the piers. On July 1, 1851 the the government sold the harbor to the Rondeau Harbour Company for £2,000.

In March 1853, a petition to the Governor–General of British North America sought government aid to establish a steamship line from Rondeau Harbour to the city of Cleveland, almost due south of the point on the American side of Lake Erie. The petitioners also pointed out that the sale of the harbor to a private company had not produced the intended public benefit but had caused disastrous results. They described the light as a "mere decoy," since it had not been lit at all in 1852 and its absence had resulted in several wrecks and loss of life. In 1853 the government sent D. Brown to examine the area and report back. His 1854 report indicated that although the piers, breakwaters, and lighthouse were in good condition, the lighthouse had not been lit in two years. The government did not intervene at this time.

William Scott, C.E. made another report to the Secretary of Public Works in December 1857, stating that the lighthouse, which had not been lit for six years, had been accidentally but

Rondeau Harbour Old Lighthouse (Erieau), circa 1920   NAC PA172545

completely burned down by fishermen seeking shelter. He further reported that Rondeau Harbour "had advantages unequalled by any place on Lake Erie for affording shelter to vessels in distress, and for doing a large trade, if the entrance were permanently improved and a good lighthouse erected." This report resulted in the government resuming possession of the works, but little was done until the early 1870s.

Known Keeper: Thomas Harrison (–1877–1879–).

31 Rondeau West (Erieau) Breakwater Range Lights

To better mark Rondeau Harbour on the north shore of Lake Erie, the Canadian government built a lighthouse on the west side of the harbor entrance in 1912. It was a square white 24-foot (7.3 m) tapered concrete tower constructed at the outer end of the west breakwater pier to work in conjunction with the light at the end of the east breakwater pier, as the harbor entrance lay between these two lights.

While the east light displayed a flashing red light, the new west light displayed a flashing green light. In 1923 a foghorn was added to the station (blast 2 s; silence 18 s). In 1987 this light also began operating as an emergency light. In 1992 the light was powered by electricity and used a dioptric illuminating apparatus from a 28.3-foot (8.7 m) focal plane to display its green flashing light (flash 2 s; eclipse 3 s), but it is unknown when the electricity was first installed.

In 1947 this outer light became the front range light to a new light built 1,240 feet (382 m) behind it, to form range lights. The rear light consisted of a white skeletal tower that used a dioptric illuminating apparatus to display its flashing green electric light from a 55-foot (17 m) focal plane. These range lights made harbor entry easier by providing a straight line of approach. They continue to operate today, but mostly to assist pleasure boaters.

Known Keepers: W.R. Fellows (1888–1914–).

Rondeau West (Erieau) Breakwater Front Range Light

32 Southeast Shoal Lighthouse

When the Canadian government decided to replace the first Point Pelee lighthouse, which had burned in 1900, with a tower on the reef closer to the shipping channel, they almost built it on Southeast Shoal but chose Middle Ground instead for the Pelee Passage Lighthouse. However, all cross-lake vessels still had to navigate around Southeast Shoal before entering or leaving Pelee Passage, and the narrow channel flanked by shallow water had caused many a shipwreck. The government first marked the area with a lightship. Later, they built a lighthouse on the southern tip of the shoal directly behind the deep water channel about 7 miles (11 km) south of Point Pelee and 10 miles (16 km) east of Pelee Island. This was the last lighthouse built to assist mariners through Pelee Passage.

The lighthouse and fog signal station was built in 1927 by the Detroit River Construction Company of Windsor, Ontario, and was considered to be a very modern station. Its timber crib was built in Kingsville, Ontario, floated to the site and sunk onto the shoal in 20 feet (6 m) of water. It was topped with a concrete pier that angled in sharply from the water and rose straight up about 6 feet (1.8 m) and angled out again to support the gallery around the lighthouse. Large boulders were placed around the pier to protect it from Lake Erie's ferocious waves.

The large squat, square building 60 feet (18 m) high was built in the center of the pier. The top story housed the lantern and radio room, the second story the "block house" or living quarters, and the first story the engine room. Below this, built into the concrete pier, was the fuel storage room, which could hold 3,400 gallons (15,300 l) of fuel. There were two large hydraulic cranes on the pier to off-load supplies and equipment from the lighthouse tender.

The 1927 foghorn characteristic (blast 2 s, silence 3 s; blast 2 s) was changed in 1985 to silence 3 s; blast 2 s; silence 48 s. This lighthouse was one of the first to be equipped with a 400-watt valve-equipped radio beacon transmitter and an aerial above the lantern to transmit its signals.

The lantern had a 70-foot (21.3 m) focal plane and displayed a flashing red light (flash 0.3 s; eclipse 9.7 s) with a visibility of about 18 miles (29 km). In 1988 it became an emergency light operating year round. Its flash pattern was changed (flash 0.5 s; eclipse 3.5 s) and its visibility was also reduced at that time.

After the light was electrified a gasoline-powered generator was used to supply the electricity. Gasoline was delivered regularly by the tender *Grenville*. During one such routine stop in 1949, keeper Moore and Dowsley Kingston from the *Grenville* went into the storage room to check on a malfunctioning engine while the gasoline was being pumped into the storage tanks. Suddenly the room exploded, doors were blown off their hinges, thick black smoke rolled from the structure and the two men were severely burned. The *Grenville* rushed them to the Leamington hospital but both later died. Although the inferno caused the light to cease operation, the billowing smoke could be seen for miles and continued to mark the shoal's location for nine days

Being such an important station, it had a

Southeast Shoal Lighthouse

four-man rotating crew. During the 1980s the crew exchanged two men on and two men off every two weeks, weather permitting. In stormy weather the keepers reported that the tower swayed. Keepers' duties included making radio reports of local weather conditions to Sarnia every six hours and maintaining equipment for the foghorn, the radio beacon and the light. In their free time they fished from the rocks around the lighthouse pier or from the station's 14-foot (4.3 m) boat, watched television, played cribbage, read or cooked. One keeper even took daily walks of up to 10 miles (16 km) around the outside of the lighthouse to keep in shape. At this time the keepers also had a private ship-to-shore phone to connect them to the mainland and make their isolated two-week periods in "Little Alcatraz" pass more easily.

The light station underwent major reconstruction after the fire: in 1974 the light was automated; in 1976 a helipad was added on top of the structure; and in 1984 fire-fighting equipment was updated to reach all parts of the station. Today the station is demanned but continues to operate as an active aid to navigation and is monitored by the Canadian Coast Guard.

Known Keepers: William Moore (–1949), Paul Armstrong (?), Norm Mady (?), Lloyd Vickery (?).

33 Southeast Shoal Lightship

Southeast Shoal is in Lake Erie just off Point Pelee, and all cross-lake vessels entering or leaving Pelee Passage had to navigate around it. This narrow channel in the midst of shallow water was the cause of many shipwrecks.

The Lake Carriers' Association first marked the shoal with a lightship. The first one was the schooner *Smith and Post*, a wooden vessel weighing 212 gross tons that had been built in 1862 at Kingsville, Ontario. The association chartered and stationed the vessel on the shoal from 1896 until 1901, when the ship burned and was replaced with another owned and operated by them.

Southeast Shoal Lighthouse burning, 1949

The second lightship stationed at Southeast Shoal was the schooner *Kewaunee*, which stayed in place from 1901 until 1910. This wooden-hulled, steam schooner was built at Kewaunee, Wisconsin, in 1900. It was 90 feet (27.4 m) long, had a 24-foot (7.3 m) beam and a draft of 7 feet (2.1 m), and weighed 133 gross tons. Its illuminating apparatus burned oil, and it had an 8-inch (20 cm) steam fog whistle. Although the vessel was placed on the shoal by the Lake Carriers' Association and was never American-owned, the U.S. government reimbursed the association for the operation and maintenance of the vessel from 1901 until 1910.

In early December 1909, just before removing the *Kewaunee* from the shoal for the winter season, Captain Frank J. Hackett and his crew of three witnessed a gruesome disaster. When a fierce snowstorm hit Lake Erie, temperatures plummeted and winds created waves as high as 20 feet (6 m). In spite of this, the lightship's anchor held and the vessel remained on station. Captain Hackett made sure the oil lantern was kept burning to mark the shoal and to mark his ship so that others did not hit his vessel. Unbeknownst to the *Kewaunee* crew, the storm had already claimed the large car ferry *Marquette and Bessemer No. 2*, with everyone on board (31–36 persons), somewhere east of the lightship's position.

With the falling temperatures, ice formed on the lake — and on the *Kewaunee* — as the storm continued into the next day. In the evening the captain spotted a vessel on fire being blown straight toward the lightship. Knowing he might never get his anchors to rehold if he tried to move his vessel, and knowing that the *Kewaunee*'s slight engine power was no match for the storm, Hackett decided to hold fast. As the fiery vessel passed just 100 feet (30 m) from the *Kewaunee*, they saw it was the package freighter *Clarion*, with her crew on deck screaming for help.

Some of the *Clarion* crew launched a lifeboat, but it was flipped and its occupants drowned. All the *Kewaunee* could do was blow the distress signal with her steam whistles and watch helplessly as the burning inferno passed them by. As luck would have it, two vessels came to the *Clarion*'s aid. When the lake freighter *Josiah G. Munro* attempted to maneuver alongside the *Clarion*, it was grounded on the shoal. However, the freighter *Leonard C. Hanna* traveled around the shoal and let the storm blow the *Clarion* toward her. As the ships scraped hulls, the six remaining crew of the burning vessel jumped to the safety of the *Hanna*.

While no one saw the *Clarion* sink, it was found northeast of the Southeast Shoal Lightship. It was not until the *Kewaunee* docked at Cleveland that the *Clarion*'s survivor's finally learned the fate of her crew. As well as claiming nine crew members of the *Clarion*, this devastating two-day storm also claimed 43 others and $100,000 in losses. While many shipowners vowed to end the navigation seasons on December 1 in the future to prevent such losses, they never did.

In 1910 the Canadian government assumed responsibility for the Southeast Shoal Station and continued to mark the shoal, using *Lightship No. 18*. It had been built in Christiana, Norway, in 1895 as the fishing trawler *Falken*. In 1910 the Canadian government acquired the ship and had it rebuilt as a lightship to be placed at Southeast Shoal, where it served

from 1910 until 1927. The iron-hulled vessel was 86.5 feet (26.3 m) long, had a 17-foot (5.2 m) beam and a 9.1-foot (2.8 m) draft, and weighed 96 gross tons.

In 1912 the Canadian government purchased the *Kewaunee* from the Lake Carriers' Association and continued to use it as a lightship at another location until 1927, when it was retired as a light vessel. When a lighthouse was built on the Southeast Shoal that same year, *Lightship No. 18* was sold into private hands. In about 1928 it was used as the rum-runner *Geronimo* and served for a few successful years until it was captured by the U.S. Coast Guard *C. Cook* while trying to smuggle booze into Green Bay, Wisconsin, in 1931. Next, it was owned by the Filer Fiber Company of Manistee and used as the tug *Tipperary* until it was scrapped in 1947.

Known Keeper: Captain Hackett.

34 Stag Island Lighthouse

In 1900 a light was established on Stag Island but, being just a lens lantern on a pole with a small white shed attached, it was considered inadequate for the increasing volume of ship traffic and the government allocated funds in 1909 to build a lighthouse. The new light, built on the south end of the island, was 22 feet (6.8 m) tall from the base to the tip of the ventilator ball and was a square wooden structure with sloping sides. The tower was surmounted by a square wooden lantern with a fixed white light. The cost of construction was $3,404.

Known Keepers: Ross Taylor (1900–03), Thomas Cowan (1903–16–).

35 Thames River Lighthouse

One of Canada's oldest lighthouses is the Thames River Lighthouse at the mouth of the Thames River, where it empties into Lake St. Clair. Its original date is unknown. Around the time of the War of 1812, the Cartier family settled in the area at the mouth of the Thames River. (These Cartiers are thought to be the direct descendants of French explorer Jacques Cartier.)

The family fished on Lake St. Clair and, to guide them home after dark, they hung a lantern on a post on the shore. Eventually the lantern was replaced by a wood-framed lighthouse. This building was destroyed by fire, and the lower portion of the existing stone lighthouse was built about 1818. (The exact date cannot be verified.) The Cartier family (father, son and two grandsons) manned the light from its inception until 1950, when C.W. Riberdy, an experienced riverman familiar with the area, took over.

The original limestone tower had a constant interior diameter of 8 feet (2.4 m) and tapered from 4 feet (1.2 m) thick at its base to 2 feet (0.6 m) thick at its top, where two rings of stone jutted out from corbeling that supported its original gallery and lantern. The limestone was either quarried at Amherstburg or brought from Fort Malden on windjammer sailing vessels.

The entry door at the base of the tower had a keystone arch and a semi-circular fanlight. Inside the tower, limestone steps were built into the stone wall and onto a center post to spiral up clockwise. The bottom 15 steps went up to a partial landing and 16 more went up to the second one, which had a shallow domed vault with an opening in its top. An eight-step ladder went into the original lantern, which had a paved stone floor. The tower's door and windows had hewn timber lintels.

Thames River Lighthouse

Thames River Lighthouse

Since it is such an early lighthouse, some things about it are unknown — for example, what the first lantern looked like and what its first lighting apparatus was. While it is known that this light became a rear range light for a front range light closer to the lake, it is not known when the front range light was built or what it looked like. In or around 1867 the tower height was raised to 57 feet (17.4 m) by a brick addition that included two stories above the original tower. This increased height was obviously to make the light more visible, but it is unknown if this light was the only one in the area at that time or whether it was raised to become a rear range light if the front range light was built at the same time.

Because of its early inception, the original lantern was probably a bird-cage style one. The lantern topping the brick addition was a decagonal cast-iron lantern. The low-pitched dome was topped by a rotating hood ventilator. The three back panels of the lantern were blanked out as they faced inland. The light was described as "a huge brass affair which when lighted and revolving could be seen for 12 miles [19 km] from shore." It used kerosene lamps until it was electrified in 1963. By 1965 the old lighting apparatus had disappeared and the lantern had two fixed lights. They were mounted one over the other on a stand facing west. The keeper's house was a short distance from the tower. It was a 1½-story dwelling with cross gables and was built on a high brick basement.

In the early days the lighthouse guided large sailing craft and steamships from Lake St. Clair into the Thames River. As land development altered the surrounding area, the lighthouse's main function became guiding pleasure and fishing boats.

In 1872 Thomas Cartier was awarded a $75 inscribed gold watch by the Canadian government for his gallant efforts in saving 13 lives over his years as keeper. In 1895 a new yawl boat was added to the station at a cost of $55 so that the keeper could place and take out buoys.

In 1966 the Department of Transport deemed the lighthouse unsafe, as it was listing slightly to the east and had cracks in its walls. They replaced it with a modern steel tubular lighthouse capped with an automatic light. In 1975 the government once again established simple white circular towers as range lights for the Thames River.

The Lower Thames Valley Conservation Authority acquired the historic site and the old lighthouse through a grant from Her Majesty Queen Elizabeth II on November 6, 1972, to create a conservation and recreation area. In 1973 the conservation authority restored the lighthouse by tearing down the structure stone by stone and brick by brick to rebuild it after repairing the foundation. Thus refurbished, the lighthouse will remain a tribute to the early history of the area for many years to come.

Known Keepers: Cartier Family (1818–50), (Thomas Cartier 1859–), C.W. Riberdy (1950–), Armand Jacobs (–1966).

36 Walpole Island Range Lights

In 1908 the Canadian government decided to erect range lights in the St. Clair River just off Walpole Island to assist navigation in the area. They called for a general council vote from the Walpole Island Indian Reserve in January 1909 to obtain one acre (0.4 hectare) of land on the west side of the island for lighthouse purposes. Although the council voted 95 to 7 against surrendering land, the Department of Marine and Fisheries forged ahead using the Expropriation Act (Chapter 143, R.S., 1906) to obtain the land for public works purposes, and paid $75 (a value set by the Indian Agent) to the Reserve's funds.

Pole lights were erected in the river just offshore from the purchased land later in 1909. White oak timbers for use as the light's poles were purchased from the Indian reserve at the rate of $25 per 1000 cubic feet. The two 30-foot (9 m) poles cost $5.82. Alex Williston, a contractor from Wallaceburg, was hired to pile-drive the poles into the riverbed, and the lights were attached to them. Little else is known about these range lights.

LAKE HURON
USA
LIGHTHOUSES

CANADA

Sudbury

Bruce Mines

Killarney · French River

By, ing Inlet
Pointe au Baril

Manitoulin
Island

CANADA
USA

Georgian
Bay

Parry Sound

16
17
21
33
23
12
34 18 19 7 8
22 32   37
Mackinaw 4-6 2 24 25
City 11
Forty Mile 10

Presque Isle 29-31
20
Alpena 1 40

Lake
Huron

MICHIGAN

Sturgeon Point 38

Collingwood

Southampton
McNab Point

Tawas Point 39

Kincardine
Point Clark

ONTARIO

3
27 26
13
Harbor Beach 14

Goderich

CANADA
USA

35 36
Bay City

Port Sanilac 28

UNITED STATES

Fort Gratiot 9
15
Port Huron Sarnia

Alpena Lighthouse

1   Alpena Lighthouse

The Thunder Bay area along the northwest side of Lake Huron developed a busy milling and lumber-shipping industry in the mid-1800s. Lumber barons petitioned the government to light the mouth of the Thunder Bay River in 1857, but their pleas went unheard until the late 1860s when piers were built at the river-mouth. A pierhead light was planned, but when the piers kept extending farther into the lake a temporary light was set up in 1875.

It was a pole light that extended from a cluster of piles driven into the water 400 feet (122 m) from the north side of the river-mouth. From 25 feet (7.6 m) above the water, a hand lantern displayed a fixed white light for 10 miles (16 km) after it was first lit on October 25, 1875. The first keeper had to find his own accommodations in Alpena, as there was no keeper's dwelling.

With the completion of the piers in 1877, a lighthouse was established. Built onto a timber crib, it was a square, brown, open-bottomed timber-framed tapering tower 44 feet (13.4 m) high, with its top two-thirds enclosed. From its decagonal iron lantern it used a sixth-order Fresnel lens to display a fixed red light for a visibility of 10 miles (16 km). A keeper's house was built onshore.

In the summer of 1888 a fire at one of the sawmills, which destroyed stacks of lumber and more than 200 homes, also burned the pier, the crib and the light-house. The keeper and his wife worked all night carrying water to save their dwelling on shore. When the fire burned out, the keeper erected a temporary light from a 25-foot (7.6 m) pole attached to the base of the burned crib. A construction crew soon arrived with materials to rebuild the light, again a square brown timber-framed tapering tower, now 44.5 feet (13.6 m) high, with an enclosed watchroom below the lantern. To save money its lantern was a refurbished iron

lantern formerly used at the North Point Lighthouse in Milwaukee. Its fourth-order Fresnel lens had been planned for use at Two Rivers but was loaned to Alpena temporarily. The new light was finished and lit on October 1, 1888.

In 1891 a fog bell was installed outside the tower's watchroom. It was mechanically operated to sound once every ten seconds. In 1898 a brick oil house was built to store the light's new illuminant, kerosene. Being much more volatile than whale oil, it needed separate storage but it also provided a brighter light. In 1901 the light had a 13-mile (21 km) visibility.

In 1914 the light had deteriorated beyond repair and was replaced by a new tower. The new, more durable, light was anchored on a new concrete crib. Its tower was a 42-foot (12.8 m) four-legged tapering steel structure that supported a circular service room and an octagonal lantern. The old tower's fog bell and lens were moved to the new tower, this time painted black. An electrical power cable was laid from Alpena to the light. The lens used a 320-candlepower incandescent bulb that was lit on June 26, 1914.

The station underwent a few changes in the coming years. In 1918 the light's characteristic was changed to an isophase occulting white light (flash 1 s; eclipse 1 s) to make it more distinctive. In the 1950s the tower was painted red for greater daytime visibility. It 1957 locals noticed that the tower resembled the newly launched Russian satellite, and nicknamed their light *Sputnik*. At an unknown date the Coast Guard replaced the fourth-order Fresnel lens with a 250 mm Tidelands acrylic optic. Over the years the elements have eroded much of the concrete pier but the light still actively guides vessels into the harbor at Alpena.

Known Keepers: E. Howard (1875–89), John Wallace (1890–1920), George Burzlaff (1920–46).

Alpena Lighthouse, circa 1882

2 Bois Blanc Island Lighthouse

Early explorers named this island Bois Blanc ("white wood") for its mass of white pine and basswood. It is about 9 miles (14.5 km) east of Mackinaw City at the southeast entrance into the Straits of Mackinac, Lake Huron. In December 1855 a group of local merchants from Michilimackinac petitioned Congress for improved navigation aids in the area. Congress assessed the situation and in May 1858 appropriated $5,000 for a lighthouse on Bois Blanc Island.

The light would serve a threefold purpose: to warn of dangerous low water shoals fingering northeasterly into the lake from the peninsula on which it was built; to mark a turning point for vessels entering or leaving the Straits; and to mark the island's location and warn mariners to travel to the north of it to avoid the hazardous shoals between the island and the mainland.

The building contract was awarded to Philo Scoville of Cleveland, Ohio. He built a separated tower and keeper's house on a low gravelly spit of land on the island's northeast side. The 65-foot (20 m) conical masonry tower had 150 steps spiraling to its cast-iron lantern and 13 Winslow Lewis lamps and reflectors which displayed a fixed white light. Scoville completed the light in August 1829 for $4,495, making it the second light to have been built on Lake Huron. (The first was built at Fort Gratiot in 1825.)

The light's first keeper was Eber Ward. His initial annual salary of $350 was augmented to $400 by 1832. Through his letters to the government it is apparent that both house and tower were poorly built and that water leakage was an on-going problem. The lighthouse's low position and the rising lake levels, compounded by shoddy construction, caused Ward to fear the demise of the lighthouse by late 1837. Indeed, on December 9 of that year, when he was visiting on Mackinac Island and his daughter, Emily, and his younger son were tending the light, a vicious east storm battered the tower. Realizing the importance of its equipment, Emily made five trips up and down the tower to retrieve the lamps, reflectors and movable valuables. Shortly thereafter she and her brother watched as two serious cracks rent the tower, making it collapse upon itself.

This event, coupled with a written report from Ward indicating his concern that the same fate awaited the house, convinced the government to appropriate another $5,000 in July 1838 for a new house and tower. District inspector Lt. James T. Homans, in his 1838 report to Congress, stated that the new lighthouse should be placed "some rods farther from the lake than the former site, and on much higher ground." The contract was awarded to William Scott of Detroit.

Scott built the new lighthouse about 150 feet (46 m) behind the old one in 1838. It too was a detached masonry tower and house. However, with its elevation, the tower only needed to be 30 feet (9 m)

high. Its lantern used fewer Winslow Lewis lamps and 14-inch (35 cm) reflectors (nine in total) as a cost-saving measure and it also displayed a fixed white light. In 1857 this light was upgraded with a fourth-order Fresnel lens to increase its visibility.

An 1866 annual report from the Lighthouse Board stated that both structures were severely dilapidated and recommended an appropriation of $14,000 to raze and rebuild them. Congress agreed and appropriated the necessary money in March 1867. By using existing plans (those also used to build the lights at Marquette, Peninsula Point and Grand Island North), the government made some savings.

The third lighthouse on Bois Blanc Island was built in 1867. It was a square 1½-story yellow brick keeper's house with a square 38-foot (11.6 m) yellow brick tower built into the gabled roof of its lake-facing end. House and tower windows were given shutters as storm protection. The tower was bricked to be round inside and had a circular iron staircase to its decagonal lantern. The fourth-order Fresnel lens from the old lantern was reused. From its focal plane of 53 feet (16.2 m) the lantern displayed a fixed white light for 13 miles (21 km) in good visibility. The station now included a frame barn, a dock and a boathouse.

Only two major renovations were made after this. In 1884 the boathouse was moved to the sheltered bay on the south side of the island and a swath was cut through the bush for hauling up supplies. At the same time the work crew installed drains toward the shore to drain off leakage.

The light served until it was deemed no longer useful and decommissioned in 1924. A lightship had been placed on Poe Reef in 1892 and, with the new larger vessels needing deeper water, lake routes into the Straits had moved further east of Bois Blanc Island. With plans to better mark the new route by building permanent lights on Poe Reef and Fourteen Foot Shoal, the government closed the Bois Blanc station. To accommodate local mariners they placed an automated acetylene light on a black skeletal 35-foot (10.6 m) steel tower just to the east of the old lighthouse. In 1941 the U.S. Coast Guard replaced the light with a 17-foot (5.2 m) cylindrical D9 tower that had a focal plane of 32 feet (9.8 m) and used a 200 mm acrylic optic to display its light.

On August 24, 1925, Earl Coffey bought the station for $1,000.

Bois Blanc Lighthouse

Charity Island Lighthouse

was first lit on August 20, 1857. The keeper's house, a duplex for the keeper and his assistant, was completed in 1858. It was a simple 1½-story wood-frame house connected to the tower by a short covered passageway.

Destruction from the elements was an on-going problem. A mere ten years after being built, the keeper's dwelling needed extensive repairs due to seepage. Walls and ceilings were re-plastered and the kitchen given a whole new floor. In the particularly destructive winter of 1881–82, the boat cribs, landing docks and boathouse sustained much damage.

The station also received a few improvements. In 1901 a brick oil house with a capacity of 360 gallons (1,360 l) was built. In 1907 Charity Island became one of the earliest lights on the Great Lakes to use acetylene. The new lamp produced a light with 800 candlepower inside the old fourth-order Fresnel lens. At this time, the light's characteristic was also changed to a fixed white light varied by a flash every ten seconds to enable mariners to better distinguish the station. With the fine-tuning of the acetylene system over the years, it was completely automated by 1916, at which time the last keeper, being redundant, was removed. The building was boarded up and the Lighthouse Service tender stopped periodically to deliver acetylene and check the equipment.

He tried to turn it into a girls' camp, but its remote location made it more suitable for a family cottage. It is currently owned by Chicago-area industrialists Martin and Reinhart Jahn, who have restored the lighthouse. They also registered the building with the Michigan Historical Sites Commission in 1974. Although it has no national status, with owners like these, the lighthouse is in good hands.

Known Keepers: Eber Ward (1829–43), Willard Church (1843–45), Lyman Granger (1845–54), Mrs. Charles O'Malley (1854–55), Henry Granger (1855–57), Mrs. Mary Granger (1857), Peter Therien (1857–59), Charles Syons (1859–61), Charles Louisignau (1861–66), Charles Hamel (1866–67), John Wackter (1867–70), Vetal Bourissau (1870–74), Levi Chapman (1874–81), Lorenzo Holden (1881–94), Henry Metivier (1896–1924).

3 Charity Island Lighthouse

The Charity Islands, basically the above-water portions of a huge limestone shoal, lie on the line of demarcation between Saginaw Bay and Lake Huron. In Lt. J.T. Homans' 1838 report to the government, he recommended a lighthouse be built on the outermost of the Charity Islands to warn of the shallow shoals and thus aid increasing marine traffic to and from Bay City at the mouth of the Saginaw River. However, it was not until 1856 that Congress appropriated $5,000 for a lighthouse on Charity Island.

It served three purposes: to facilitate shipping on the Great Lakes by providing another light in the chain of lights marking Lake Huron; to warn mariners of the shallow rocky shoals in the area around the island; and to notify mariners of the island's location so they could seek refuge within its natural harbors (which had earned it its name).

Construction began in 1856 and was completed in 1857. It was a 40-foot (12.2 m) conical brick tower with a spiral iron staircase that had open-latticed steps. The tower was topped with an octagonal cast-iron lantern that housed a fourth-order Fresnel lens. It used a kerosene lamp to display its fixed white light from a 45-foot (13.7 m) focal plane for a 12-mile (19.3 km) visibility. The light

Then, in October 1939, with the completion of the Gravelly Shoal Light to the southwest of Charity Island, the Charity Island Light was extinguished. Sitting abandoned and empty, the buildings gradually declined, and in 1963 the station was sold into private hands. No changes were made to the island, but the ownership changed several times. Today, most of Charity Island is owned by the federal government and is maintained by the U.S. Fish and Wildlife Service. The Service envisions making a park-like environment with walking paths throughout the island to help protect rare and endangered plant species. They would like to see the lighthouse restored, but have no authority to do so. After a July meeting in 2002 with representatives from the Fish and Wildlife Service, the Michigan State Historic Preservation Office and the Arenac County Historical Society, it was decided that the Historical Society would be the non-profit group to undertake the restoration. They in turn formed the Charity Island Preservation Committee to head up the work.

Once they raise $10,000 seed money they are eligible for state and federal grants to help with the restoration of the tower. However, as long as the house is privately owned, it does not qualify for restoration funds. Unfortunately, the owner had to level the house in the spring of 2003 after most of it had collapsed on itself. The owner has since rebuilt the house following the old blueprints, but has introduced some modifications.

Known Keepers: Colin Graham (1857–65), August Clarke (1865–67), William Stewart (1867–73), Charles Howard (1875–79), Israel Palmer (1880–82), Charles McDonald (1883–1912).

4 Cheboygan Crib Light

With the dredging of a river channel into the Cheboygan River, the Lighthouse Board decided to place a crib light to mark its entrance. In 1884 the wooden crib was built at Cheboygan and then floated into place and sunk by filling it with rock. The surface of the oak pier built on the crib, on which the tapering octagonal cast-iron tower was assembled, was 11 feet (3.3 m) above the water. It provided an oil storage room beneath the tower.

A set of cast-iron spiral stairs gave access to the lantern. The tower was lined with pine boards to insulate it and prevent condensation. Glass prism grates in the lantern floor and four porthole style windows in the watchroom provided interior light. The octagonal cast-iron lantern was topped with a copper dome, an 18-inch (45 cm) ventilator ball, and a lightning rod. It housed a fourth-order Fresnel lens that produced a flashing red light in a 2.5 second cycle (0.5 s flash; 2 s eclipse). From its 36-foot (11 m) focal plane the 159 candlepower kerosene lamp shone a light visible for 10 miles (16 km). After being painted brown as a daymark, the light was lit on November 1, 1884. There being no keeper's house, the keeper had to row the quarter-mile out to the crib light every day to tend it in all weather.

Over the years improvements were made at the station. In 1892 iron davits were added to the pier to enable the keeper to raise his boat above the lake waters and to facilitate the unloading of supplies. In 1897 a small dwelling and a pile protection for the boat were built on the pier, and 3.5 cords of protective riprap were placed around the wooden crib. In 1898 the lantern was upgraded with a new, improved fourth-order lamp that increased the light's

Early Cheboygan Crib Light

visibility to about 12 miles (19 km). In 1899 the wooden pier was replaced because of rot, and 28 more cords of riprap were put around the crib. In 1901 the tower's daymark was changed from brown to white with a red lantern roof to increase its visibility.

In 1903 the rotting wood of the structure was removed down to a foot below water level, where the crib was still sound, and replaced with a concrete pier faced with masonry. At the same time a new oil storage room was put beneath the tower, a cellar under the house, and an iron pipe railing around the pier. In 1906, after a schooner hit the tower in a fog, the railing needed replacing. In 1911 an automated fog bell was installed at the light. Its characteristic was a single stroke every ten seconds. In 1929 the light was automated with an acetylene system that used a sun valve. When the keeper was removed, the unmanned light became known as the "Dummy."

By the 1980s the tower was tilting considerably, and the Coast Guard planned to scrap it, as restoration costs outweighed its aid to navigation. However, public anger influenced the Coast Guard to give it to the City of Cheboygan. The tower was moved in 1984 by a boom barge to a new land location on the breakwall. Glass windows were replaced with plexiglass to prevent vandalism, and it was painted white with red windows and door.

By 2001 the tower was leaking and deteriorating. Two members of the Great Lakes Lighthouse Keepers Association approached the city with a proposal to restore the lighthouse if the city supplied materials. After repairs, the structure was repainted to its historically proper color (all-white tower, gray gallery and red lantern roof) making it weatherproof for the next few decades.

Cheboygan Crib Light

Cheboygan Main Light ruins, 2005

Cheboygan Second Main Lighthouse, United States Coast Guard, circa 1870s

5 Cheboygan Main Light

With the mid-nineteenth-century development of lumbering in northern Michigan, water traffic for lumber export increased greatly. To mark Duncan City, a lumbering town about a mile east of the mouth of the Cheboygan River, a light was placed on the eastern point of Duncan Bay. The light also marked a turning point from Lake Huron at the eastern entrance into the Straits and signaled a nearby shoal.

The lighthouse was built in the early 1850s. After Congress appropriated $4,000 in December 1850, an area of 41 acres (16.5 hectares) on the point was purchased for a lighthouse reservation. The contract went to Rhodes and Warner of Ohio, and construction began in the spring of 1851. The circular tower was 40 feet (12.3 m) high and built of brick on a stone foundation. It was one of the first on the Great Lakes to be equipped with a Fresnel lens, a fifth-order one made by Louis Sautter of Paris. A detached dwelling was also built for the keepers. The first keeper, William Drew, first displayed the light in September 1851.

Just eight years later, high water was undermining the tower's foundation. Fearing its collapse, the Lighthouse Board decided to raze it and build a new light station at a better location. The new station had a combined keeper's dwelling and light tower. The tower rose out of the roof peak and was 36 feet (11 m) above the house foundation. It had an octagonal cast-iron lantern that housed the fifth-order Fresnel lens from the old tower. From a focal plane of 37 feet (11.3 m) the light was visible for 12 miles (19.3 km). The lighthouse was similar in design to the one later built at Port Washington. In 1889 duplicate fog signals were installed at the station. Also, a 225-gallon (850 l) circular iron oil house was built to store the kerosene, a more volatile fuel.

After the Duncan City mill burned down in 1898, the town was abandoned. With better offshore lights to mark the Straits and the Fourteen Foot Shoal Light to mark the Cheboygan River, the Cheboygan Main Light was decommissioned in 1930, locked up, and abandoned.

Over time the buildings were recycled. George Kling, son of the last keeper, Fred Kling, bought the boathouse for $1 and moved it to his home in Cheboygan to become a garage. Bill Singer purchased the lighthouse and sold its material to Bert Toles, who was able to build three small houses from it. The point where the lighthouse had been built gradually became known as Lighthouse Point. Today the land is part of Cheboygan State Park, formed in 1962.

Known Keepers: William Drew (1851–), Fred Kling (1889–1929) (1930–end of light).

6 Cheboygan Range Lights

To facilitate the increased shipping of lumber in northern Michigan, Congress approved dredging the entrance to the Cheboygan River wider and deeper, starting in the early 1870s. In July 1876 Congress then appropriated $10,000 to build range lights to guide vessels into the improved harbor.

The range lights were built in 1880 when the dredging was complete. The front range light was a tower and house combined. The house was a 1½-story clapboard structure, with a 6-foot (1.8 m) square tower ascending up the center of its north, lakeside

Cheboygan Front Range Light

Cheboygan Old Second Light

end. The tower had a square wooden lantern with one large rectangular window facing the water to display its fixed red light through a sixth-order Fresnel lens made by Henri LePaute of Paris. This lighthouse was painted brown as a daymark. The rear range light was a wooden structure with a vertical oval daymark made of wooden horizontal slats. It was lit by a lens lantern that, like the front light, also showed only in one direction. Working as a pair, the range lights were first lit on September 30, 1880.

The light received some improvements over the years. In 1890 the front range light was connected to city water. Also in this year the Lighthouse Board requested $1,500 to purchase adjacent property so as to properly grade and drain the land and prevent stagnant water pools. Congress finally appropriated the money in 1898 but the regrading had to wait until title was obtained in 1909. In 1891 a circular iron oil house that could hold 72 five-gallon (20 l) cans of kerosene was built at the station.

In 1900 the old wooden rear range tower was replaced by a 75-foot (23 m) skeletal one with a small enclosed wooden room under its lantern to store supplies. Also in 1900, the front range light was painted all white to increase its visibility. At an unknown date the Fresnel lens was replaced with locomotive-style lanterns, each with a 10,000 candlepower electric lamp, to increase visibility to 14 miles (22.5 km). Once the light was automated, the keepers were removed in 1928. The front range light is still in use today, mainly serving pleasure craft.

Known Keepers: George Humphrey (1880–82), James Rich (1882–82), Ivory Littlefield (1883–94), Mrs. Ivory Littlefield (1894–94), John Sinclair Jr. (1894–99), John Duffy (1899–1928).

7 Detour Point Lighthouse

Recognizing the need to light the passage between Lake Huron and Lake Superior, the Legislative Council of the Territory of Michigan made the first proposal for a lighthouse at Detour Passage in a petition to Congress in July 1830. However, 17 years passed before the presidential decree that a reservation be set aside for a lighthouse at this location and Congress appropriated $5,000 to build it.

The light was located at a strategic position at the northwestern head of Lake Huron. It had several purposes: to mark the entrance into the St. Mary's River, which connected marine traffic to and from Lake Superior; to indicate the turning point for downbound vessels from Lake Superior headed to Lake Michigan through the Straits of Mackinac and the turning point for downbound vessels heading from the river to Lake Erie; and to point out the rocky shoals that fingered into the lake for about a mile (1.6 km) out from Detour Point on the mainland and warn mariners to "detour" around them.

The first lighthouse, on the mainland shore at Detour Point, was built in 1847 and lit at the start of the 1848 navigation season. It consisted of a white stone tower and a 1½-story dwelling. The tower produced a fixed white light using 13 Argand lamps, each with its own 14-inch (35 cm) reflector, and it was directed in a 270-degree arc. In 1857 the lantern was upgraded to house a fourth-order Fresnel lens that continued to display a fixed white light.

For unknown reasons a new lighthouse complex was built in 1861. It consisted of a 2½-story frame keeper's dwelling attached by an enclosed passage from an upper house level into the above-ground enclosed tower. The tower was similar to that built at Manitou Island and Whitefish Point and had a unique "space-age look." Ladder stairs led up to an enclosed iron cylinder whose spiral staircase in turn led up to the decagonal pedestal room and lantern. This central column was reinforced and supported by an outer square skeletal iron framework with cross braces. The tower stood 70 feet (21.3 m) high, and its lantern continued to display a fixed white light from the fourth-order Fresnel lens, which had been imported from the old tower. The station was completed with a red brick fog signal building.

Over years the lens was changed to improve its visibility. In 1870 it was upgraded to a third-order lens and the old stone tower and dwelling were razed. In 1907 it was changed to a 3½-order bivalve lens but it was replaced shortly after in 1908 with a 3½-order Fresnel lens made by Barbier, Benard and Turenne of Paris. The lens had "USLHE 317" stamped on it. The light's characteristic was also changed at this time to become a flashing white light (flash 1 s; eclipse 9 s). The new light could be seen up to 30 miles (48 km) away on a clear night.

As vessels became larger, lake traffic increased and offshore technology improved, the government decided to place a light right on Detour Reef to better mark the Detour Passage by indicating the actual end of the reef.

Detour Point Lighthouse, circa 1910

Detour Reef Lighthouse

8　Detour Reef Lighthouse

Thanks to improved technology, the government was able in 1931–32 to better mark the Detour Passage into the St. Mary's River by building the lighthouse right on the end of the reef, one mile (1.6 km) offshore. A 60-foot (18.3 m) square concrete and steel crib/pier was placed in 24 feet (7.3 m) of water. It rose 20 feet (6 m) above the water to a wave flare that deflected water. A steel-framed square Art Deco–style tower with three distinct levels rose 63 feet (19.2 m) high to a focal plane of 74 feet (22.8 m). Ever economical, the Lighthouse Service reused the spiral staircase, the Fresnel lens and the iron lantern and pedestal room from the old Detour Point lighthouse. It took 327 working days and $140,000 to build the new lighthouse.

While the light was being moved from the old location, a temporary light was placed on a mast attached to the southeast corner of the concrete crib. It displayed a flashing red light (flash 0.3 s; eclipse 0.7 s) of 10 candlepower. Once lit, the reef light continued to display a flashing white light until 1936, when it was changed to white with a red sector by using a colored screen or shade inside the rotating lens.

The new lighthouse was equipped with a powerful and unique diaphone foghorn. The area was notorious for fog due to cold river water meeting warmer lake water. Keepers kept a close eye on conditions and used two different fog signal blasts to inform mariners. If there was fog on the lake but the river was clear, the fog signal characteristic was three blasts every 60 seconds (blast 2 s; silence 2 s; blast 2 s; silence 2 s; blast 2 s; silence 50 s). If both the lake and river were foggy, the characteristic changed (blast 6 s; silence 54 s). From these signals mariners knew when it safe to enter the river.

Little change occurred at the lighthouse after this. In 1974 the light was automated. In 1988 the Coast Guard disassembled, packed, and removed the Fresnel lens, replacing it with a modern optic. The Fresnel lens was shipped to Mackinaw City for storage, after which its whereabouts became unknown. At some point the 475-pound (215 kg) diaphone foghorn was also removed. Sitting empty, the structure began to deteriorate. In 1996 the Coast Guard installed a new VRB-25 optic in the lantern.

The government excessed the Detour Reef light in the late 1990s, deeming it obsolete in light of modern shipboard navigation systems. As such, its future was bleak — to be torn down or

be allowed to deteriorate until it fell down. To prevent either fate, local residents of Detour Village and Drummond Island banded together and in January 1998 and formed the Detour Reef Light Preservation Society (DRLPS), a non-profit organization, as private individuals could not lease a lighthouse for restoration purposes. DRLPS's main goal was to save and restore the lighthouse. Other goals include preserving lighthouse artefacts and records, educating the public, recruiting volunteers, and eventually providing tours out to the restored lighthouse.

Some of DRLPS's finds were accidental. Its president, Bob Jones, discovered the crated missing Fresnel lens in an unlocked garage in Mackinaw City while searching for something else. The group then obtained Coast Guard permission to display the lens in the Detour Passage Historical Museum, where it can be seen today. Another member of the Society, Jeff Laser of Bellville, Ohio, discovered the old diaphone foghorn sitting on a pallet in a warehouse belonging to the Great Lakes Historical Society in Vermillion, Ohio. DRLPS was able to arrange the foghorn's return, and it is now on display at the Drummond Island Historical Museum.

In 2000 DRLPS negotiated a 20-year lease of the lighthouse from the Coast Guard for restoration purposes. Lighthouse enthusiasts are delighted to see that another lighthouse is being saved for future generations to view.

Known Keepers: John Sweet (1933–40), Charles Jones (1940–63).

9　Fort Gratiot Lighthouse

Along with the opening of the interior, the U.S. government recognized its obligation to protect commerce on the Great Lakes. To this end, Congress appropriated $3,500 for a lighthouse at the head of the St. Clair River near Fort Gratiot in Michigan Territory. Few vessels then traveled Lake Huron, but the government wanted to mark the treacherous approach from Lake Huron into the narrow and swift-flowing St. Clair River. After advertising in the Detroit *Gazette*, they awarded Winslow Lewis the contract to build the lighthouse. He in turn hired Daniel Warren of Rochester, New York, to do the actual work. In April 1825 Congress appropriated another $5,000 to complete the light. Its total cost came to $5,763 and it was first lit on August 8, 1825. Built 12 years before Michigan became a state, it was the first lighthouse on Michigan shores.

The tower was somewhat short — only 32 feet (9.7 m) high. It was conical with an 18-foot (5.5 m) base diameter and a top diameter of 9.5 feet (2.9 m). It had three windows to light its interior, and was capped by a stone deck 4 inches (10 cm) thick and 12 feet (3.6 m) in diameter. An octagonal iron lantern covered by a 3-foot (0.9 m) copper dome with a ventilator and wind vane sat on the stone deck. The lantern housed ten Winslow Lewis lamps, each with its own 14-inch (35 cm) reflector.

The keeper's house was a one-story brick structure with only two rooms. Until an official keeper could be hired, Rufus Hatch acted as temporary keeper, along with Jean B. Desnoyers. While Hatch applied for the position, George McDougall, a Detroit lawyer, was appointed keeper thanks to his friends' political influence. While it was intended as a plum position that could provide comfortably for his retirement with an annual income of $350, this did not prove to be the case.

The tower and keeper's house were not built to government specs. A Fort Gratiot officer described the lighthouse as a "miserable piece of workmanship." While the contract called for the tower and house to be built of quarried stone and Roman cement, the tower was built of beach cobbles and used regular mortar, which gradually crumbled under the onslaught of storms. Rather than being placed on a substantial foundation, the tower was built just on log timbers. The house was built of poorly fired bricks and the interior plaster was applied directly onto the bricks so that rain soaked right through, ruining both plaster and paint. The floors were only single-planked and made of green wood that shrank when it dried. While the contract called for a first and second floor in the tower, they were not built, making the stairs more treacherous. The scuttle door was only 18 by 21.5 inches (45 by 55 cm), a very small opening for a man to pass through. With the ten lamps and reflectors in the lantern, there was barely room for a man to move around. In the house, stagnation from pooled leaking water caused a terrible odor and made the cellar useless for storage.

Fort Gratiot Lighthouse

McDougall arrived to replace Hatch on December 2, 1825. His "plum" lacked many amenities of his Detroit life. There was no stable for his horse or cow, no root house to store vegetables, no garden, no storehouse for supplies, no outhouse, no close neighbors and no regular newspapers. After inspecting the station, McDougall reported how far it fell short of government specifications. He was only 5 foot 9 inches (1.8 m) but weighed about 200 pounds (90 kg) and literally had to squeeze through the small trapdoor into the lantern room. Rumor has it that this was the only time he went into the lantern, as he hired an assistant to do the actual work because of his size and his various ailments.

He was responsible for keeping the lamps clean, lit, and filled with whale oil, which was stored in cisterns at the base of the tower. Every night the oil was carried up to the lantern in a two-gallon (7.5 l) copper measure and a two-quart (1.9 l) feeder was used to fill each lamp. In cold weather the oil was heated before it was carried up so that it did not congeal and cause the lamps to go out. Before being lit, the wicks were trimmed. Each morning the lamps were extinguished and emptied for safekeeping.

McDougall's annual salary of $350 disappeared quickly. He augmented it with another $150 by securing the position of deputy collector to collect revenues and prevent cross-river smuggling. Still, his income was insufficient for his lavish tastes and entertainment. He also had to buy cleaning supplies and pay for repairs from his own pocket, since government supplies or authorization to purchase them often took months. Also, the government was very slow to pay his salary and reimburse him for expenditures. Eventually he had to sell his horse, wagons and furniture to pay his debts.

By the summer of 1828 McDougall reported that the tower walls had cracks, that it was tilting toward the east, and that the river current was eroding the land in front of the lighthouse. Then during a fierce three-day storm in September, the tower was badly damaged and temporarily put out of commission. It fell down in late November.

Acting quickly to replace the light, Congress appropriated $8,000 in March 1829 to construct a new light and keeper's house. The contract was awarded to Lucius Lyon, Deputy Surveyor General of the Northwest Territory and later a U.S. senator from Michigan. Since the old tower had been poorly placed so that vessels could not see it until they were too close to the river mouth, the new tower was built higher and placed further to the north for better visibility. It was a free-standing conical brick structure built solidly on a dressed-stone and timber foundation. Its 8-foot (2.4 m) thick walls were built to last. It rose from a 25-foot (7.7 m) base diameter to a height of 74 feet (22.5 m) at the tip of its vane, and its red brick was whitewashed for greater visibility. An ornate iron spiral staircase with 94 latticed steps circled up to the lantern, which continued to use Winslow Lewis lamps and reflectors. The new keeper's house was a small 1½-story brick cottage to the west of the tower. Costs for the tower and the house totalled $4,445. The new light was finished and ready for use in December 1829.

In the final stages of the tower construction, a hunting party of Chippewa Indians camped to watch the fascinating sight, for they had never seen anything like it. They danced and feasted and marveled at the great structure. They clasped hands around it to measure its base circumference. They were so mesmerized by the light that they tried to creep into the lantern, disassemble the light, and carry it away. The workers managed to keep the light intact, and after three days, discouraged, the Chippewa finally went back up the lake to their Saginaw home.

After the establishment of the U.S. Lighthouse Board and its efforts to improve lights, the light's first Fresnel lens was installed in 1857. It was a fourth-order lens, and when it was replaced by a third-order Fresnel lens in 1861 to provide a brighter light with increased visibility, the fourth-order lens was moved to the Old Saginaw River Lighthouse. To accommodate the larger third-order lens, the tower was raised to an overall height of 86 feet (26.2 m). The tower then had two galleries — one around the new pedestal room and a smaller one around the lantern, which continued to display a fixed white light.

By 1867 railroad use in Port Huron had increased significantly, causing confusion between the lighthouse beacon and locomotive headlamps. The problem was remedied by exchanging the fixed lighthouse lens with the lens from Pointe aux Barques Lighthouse. The new lens used a kerosene lamp to produce a fixed light varied with a flash every 60 seconds for a 16-mile (26 km) visibility.

Although keeper McDougall, who kept the light until his death in 1842, had always hired someone to help him, the government did not officially hire an assistant for this light until June 1870. In 1871 the station acquired its first fog signal. In 1874–75 a substantial two-story red brick keepers' duplex was built to house the keeper and his assistant. It had a hipped gable roof and a pointed Gothic porch. In 1880 a duplicate fog signal was built. Both signals powered 8-inch (20 cm) steam whistles. In 1901 a new red brick fog signal building was built north of the keepers' duplex.

In 1911 a unique fog signal arrangement was also implemented at Fort Gratiot. With the co-operation of the Lake Carriers' Association, a phone system was installed by which river agents could inform the keeper of fog conditions both on the lake above the lighthouse and on the river downstream from it. The keeper would then blow the appropriate whistle to notify mariners. However, during the devastating Great Lakes storm of 1913, 13 vessels in the Fort Gratiot area were unable to hear the fog signal over the roar of the storm. The storm also undermined about a third of the tower's base, and in 1914 steel sheet piling was driven around the base to stabilize the lighthouse and prevent such future damage.

At an unknown date, foghorns were placed on a tower beside the lighthouse. In 1933, when the light was automated, it was changed to a green flashing light to guide mariners entering the St. Clair River to the port (left) side of the lighthouse. This smaller, more powerful electric light, which was installed on the gallery outside the lantern, increased the light's visibility from 16 miles (26 km) to as far as 28 miles (45 km) under optimal conditions. In 1936 a fixed amber 200,000 candlepower fog light was placed on the fog signal tower just below the foghorns. It indicated to vessels approaching from Lake Huron that visibility was low on the St. Clair River. It was one of three such installations on the Great Lakes.

In 1971 the Michigan Historical Commission named the Fort Gratiot Lighthouse an historic site. Since then its history has been celebrated. In 1985 during a 160th celebration of the light's duration, about 450 people toured the lighthouse. In 1995, during its 170th birthday year celebrations, about 5,000 people visited the lighthouse. At that time the light was using a 1,000-watt electric bulb, which was equivalent to a million candlepower. The lens rotated once every 15 seconds (0.5 s flash; 14.5 s eclipse).

In 1990 public pressure saved the light's future when the U.S. Coast Guard announced that it might cease Fort Gratiot's light, as it had now been made obsolete by modern technology. Recreational boaters, commercial carrier pilots, and others notified the Coast Guard that they still used the light as a navigation aid. Acknowledging the help that the light provided vessels with less sophisticated tracking equipment, it was left lit.

The Fort Gratiot light has earned its place in history. It was the first lighthouse on Lake Huron and is the oldest existing structure in Port Huron. In recognition, it is the main symbol of the city and is included on the city seal. The light has provided continual service for almost two centuries and has seen changes in vessels from canoes through sailing ships, steamers and diesel ships. The Coast Guard provides tours through the historical structure, which is situated at one of the world's busiest maritime junctures.

Known Keepers: Rufus Hatch (1825), Jean Desmayer (1825), George McDougall (1825–42), William Church (1842–43), Eber Ward (1843–45), Nathian Wright (1845–49), Elijah Crane (1849–1950), William Taylor (1850–53), Elihu Granger (1853–57), Elijah Burch (1857–59), Peter McMartin (1859–61), Ober Lewis (1861–64), John Van Horn (1864–65), David Cooper (1865), W. Sutherland (1865–66), John Van Horn (1866–69), John Sinclair Sr. (1869–81), Israel Palmer (1882–94), Frank Kimball (1894–1929), John Smith (1929–40), William Wilkinson (1946–50).

10   Forty Mile Point Lighthouse

Once major danger areas along Lake Huron's west shore had been lit, the Lighthouse Board started to recommend lights between existing lights to create a continuous system that would increase marine safety. In 1890 they requested $25,000 to build a light at Forty Mile Point, a location about midway between the lights at Cheboygan and Presque Isle. Congress approved the recommendation in February 1893, and the necessary funding was appropriated in August 1894.

Work on the station began in July 1896. The first task was to construct the wood-framed structure that served as temporary living quarters for the work crew and eventually became a barn for the keeper's animals. The crew used the same plans as those for the Big Bay Point lighthouse on Lake Superior, also built in 1896. It consisted of a rectangular red double-bricked duplex with a tower rising up the middle of the lakeside face of the house. The 52-foot (16 m) tower divided the house into mirror images, each side with its own entry door, cellar, hurricane doors to the cellar, inside entry door to the tower, dormer, kitchen, parlor and upstairs bedrooms. Also, each stairwell had a skylight above it to light the interior and also to allow the keepers to check the light without leaving the comfort of home.

Forty Mile Point Lighthouse

The three-story tower had double windows on its first two levels and a single window on its third level. Fifty-six solid iron steps led up to its octagonal iron lantern, which housed a fourth-order Fresnel lens made by Henri LePaute of Paris. The lens had six bull's-eye flash panels that used a clockwork mechanism wound every four hours to rotate the lens around the oil lamp, creating its characteristic white flash every ten seconds. To increase its daytime visibility, the red tower was painted white on the three sides seen from the lake.

Other structures at the station included a windmill-powered well, a boathouse, an oil house, a red brick fog signal building, which housed equipment to operate duplicate 10-inch (25 cm) steam whistles, board walks to connect all buildings, a T-shaped dock, and a tramway from the dock to the fog signal building and the barn to facilitate hauling supplies. The station was ready in November and the light was inaugurated on May 1, 1897.

Repairs and upgrades were made as needed. In 1900 rotting posts supporting the tramway were replaced by stone-filled timber cribs, and a log retaining wall was built behind the boathouse to prevent sand erosion. In 1905 a 3-foot (0.9 m) square brick chimney was built at the fog signal building to replace the two rusted iron smokestacks. In 1914 an incandescent oil vapor lighting system was installed in the lantern, increasing the candlepower to 55,000 and its visibility to 16 miles (26 km). In 1931 the steam whistles were upgraded to Type F diaphone foghorns. When the station was automated in 1969, the keepers were removed.

Today Presque Isle County owns the lighthouse, while the U.S. Coast Guard maintains access to the still-functioning light. In 1988 Robert Harris, a lighthouse enthusiast and marine surveyor, presented copies of original lighthouse drawings to the Presque Isle County Parks Committee to aid their restoration efforts. The county has made a park around the lighthouse and plans a maritime museum in the keeper's house when it is fully restored. The park also boasts the shipwreck of the *Joseph S. Faye* and a barge it was towing. Their ruins can be seen on the beach by the lighthouse.

Known Keepers: Xavier Rains (1897–1911), John Smith (1911–29), Paul Klebba (1929–36), Clarence Tupper (1936–43).

11 Fourteen Foot Shoal Lighthouse

Long before Lake Huron had a lighthouse at Fourteen Foot Shoal, located just a mile northwest of Cheboygan Point and close to the main entry into Cheboygan Harbor, the area was recognized as a danger to mariners and marked by a can buoy. The shoal was named for the mere 14 feet (4.3 m) of water covering its hard gravelly bottom. As offshore lights were placed at Martin Reef and Poe Reef in the Straits of Mackinac during the 1920s, the Lighthouse Service decided to take advantage of their seasoned work crew and use them to build a lighthouse on Fourteen Foot Shoal. They saved money by making it a radio-controlled light

Fourteen Foot Shoal Lighthouse

operated from the Poe Reef Light, and also by discontinuing the Cheboygan Light once the new light was operational. While awaiting the completion of the Poe Reef Light, Fourteen Foot Shoal was temporarily better lit using an acetylene gas buoy showing a white light of 70 candlepower that flashed every three seconds. The new buoy was placed on April 15, 1925.

Martin Reef and Poe Reef had identical structures, but the lighthouse for Fourteen Foot Shoal, although basically similar underneath, had a new upper design. A wooden crib was constructed at Cheboygan and floated to the site, where it was sunk into place on the leveled shoal by filling it with rocks and gravel. This base was the foundation for a 50-foot (15.2 m) square concrete pier with a wave flare around its top edge to deflect water away from the lighthouse. Its surface was 15 feet (4.6 m) above the water.

The lighthouse consisted of a one-story lower level that supported a tower extending out of its hipped roof. Both structures were framed in steel and had quarter-inch-thick steel plates riveted to their framework. The lower portion housed the machinery to operate the light and the diaphone foghorn. The slightly conical tower, 6 feet (1.8 m) in diameter at the base, emerged from the center of its roof to rise 24 feet (7.3 m). It was topped with an octagonal cast-iron lantern that displayed a fourth-order Fresnel lens and exhibited a flashing white light (flash 1 s; eclipse 2 s) from its 50-foot (15.2 m) focal plane for a visibility of 14 miles (22.5 km). A submarine cable from the lighthouse to Cheboygan supplied the necessary power to run the equipment. The light's illuminant was an 11,000-candlepower incandescent electric light bulb. In the winter, when there were no keepers at Poe Reef to control the light, it was lit by an acetylene light of 130 candlepower and a 200 mm lens.

The Fourteen Foot Shoal light was completed and ready for operation at the beginning of the 1930 navigation season. Once it was lit and running smoothly, the Cheboygan Lighthouse was discontinued as originally planned.

12 Frying Pan Island Lighthouse

Frying Pan Island is two miles (3.2 km) above the mouth of the St. Mary's River, Lake Huron, on the west side of the river and between the mainland and Drummond Island. In 1879 Congress appropriated $2,000 for a light to be placed on the small rocky island to warn of Frying Pan Shoal, which lay just to the southeast of the island. However construction did not commence until the summer of 1882 when title to the island was obtained.

The lighthouse was built on the east side of the island. The tower was merely a prefabricated 15-foot (4.6 m) conical cast-iron structure with a hexagonal lantern and a simple circular gallery braced down from its top. The tower, first painted brown, displayed a fixed red light for 8.5 miles (13.5 km) and was first lit on October 1, 1882. Given the small amount of funding available, the tower had no brick lining to prevent moisture, no shelves or work area for cleaning equipment, no oil storage shed and no keeper's house. The keeper had to find his own accommodation.

When more funding was appropriated in 1884, a small prefabricated storage building was shipped from the Detroit Depot and erected on the island near the light. One end of the building was outfitted with a bunk, shelves and a cleaning table for the keeper, and the other end was used to store oil, probably kerosene, for the light. A boathouse, privy and landing pier were also built at this time.

When a light was later built on Pipe Island, two miles (3.2 km) to the north and also in the river, the two lights worked in conjunction to assist mariners entering or leaving the river and Lake Huron. In 1894 the lighthouse tower was painted white to increase its daytime visibility. After twenty years the government finally appropriated $4,000 in 1902 to build a keeper's house at the station, and in 1903 a two-story four-square frame house was built just northwest of the tower.

Later, the lighthouse was automated and a fog signal was established at the island. In 1955 the fog signal was removed, due to modern onboard ship technology and noise complaints from local residents. Today it is displayed at the Detour Passage Historical Museum on Drummond Island.

In 1956 the tower light was discontinued and replaced by an automatic light on a pole nearby. On August 8, 1988, the U.S. Coast Guard removed the old iron tower and took it back to their station at Sault Ste. Marie. After removing its rust with sandblasting and then repainting and restoring it, they put it on display in front of their main station building where it can be seen today.

Known Keepers: J. Church (1882), Frank Bernard (1884–91), Joseph Riell (1891–96), Herbert Slocum (1896), William Burke (1896–1900), Nelson Abear (1900–17).

Frying Pan Island Lighthouse

13 Gravelly Shoal Light

Gravelly Shoal in Saginaw Bay, Lake Huron, was marked by a gas buoy in 1900, long before it was lit with a lighthouse. The shoal was about halfway between Lookout Point on the bay's west side mainland and Big Charity Island. It extended from the mainland in a southeasterly direction for 2½ miles (4 km). Vessels knew not to pass between the buoy and the point. To better mark the passage between the shoal's tip and Charity Island for larger lake vessels, a crib light was built on the shoal's eastern tip in 1939.

The contract to build the light according to plans previously used on Lake Erie at Huron and Conneaut was awarded to John C. Meagher of Bay City for $75,000. The $24,000 steel tower

Gravelly Shoal Light, circa 1954

was made by the Wickes Boiler Company of Saginaw. Meagher started at the shoal site in April. After driving five wire-wrapped pile clusters deep into the lake bed in 24 feet (7.3 m) of water, he surrounded them with waterproof forms, pumped the water out, and filled the interior with concrete to form a circular 50-foot (15.2 m) pier. With the pier completed in August, he barged the 61-foot (18.6 m) prefabricated steel tower to the site, hoisted it into place and bolted it to the pier.

Instead of a lantern, the tower had a completely automated 375 mm optic equipped with a 15,000-candlepower light. It was powered by a submarine cable laid across the bay to Lookout Point, where it was connected to onshore electricity. From a focal plane of 75 feet (23 m) the light exhibited a white flash every five seconds for 16 miles (26 km). An acetylene backup system, designed to operate automatically when necessary, was installed in case of power failure. The station was also equipped with dual diaphone foghorns for times of poor visibility. They had a 30-second cycle (blast 3 s; silence 27 s). The station, first lit in October 1939, was monitored and maintained by the Coast Guard Base at Tawas. With the lighting of this station, the Charity Island Lighthouse was extinguished and abandoned.

Later, a radio beacon transmitter tower was added to the top of the lighthouse tower. In 1954 Meagher installed another 7-foot (2.1 m) ring of concrete around the pier to protect it from winter ice damage at a cost of $54,000. Today the concrete pier is metal-plated to further ensure against ice damage, and the light is still an active aid to navigation in the area.

14 Harbor Beach Lighthouse

As lake traffic increased in the 1870s, the need for protection from strong currents, dangerous reefs and heavy seas became more apparent. In 1873 the United States conducted an Army Engineer Survey, looking for a "harbor of refuge" between Port Huron and Saginaw Bay. They selected Sand Beach (now called Harbor Beach) because of its natural harbor formation, its easy approach, its freedom from shoals and its better anchorage. The project, comprising three breakwaters and one lighthouse, started in 1873 but was not fully completed until 1894, probably on account of its 8,000 feet (2438 m) of breakwaters. It cost almost a million dollars.

Harbor Beach Lighthouse

The first light at Harbor Beach was located on top of the red and white volunteer lifesaving station and Coast Guard building. The main light, built in 1885, was placed on the north side of the harbor entrance, or main gap, on the angle crib off the breakwater. Its rectangular crib, made of heavy hemlock, was built on land, towed out to the proper location and then sunk in place with large rocks. This crib was then filled with concrete and given a concrete cap that was partially faced with a brick veneer. On top of this base a 45-foot (13.7 m), iron-plated, conical tower was built, tapering from a bottom diameter of 22 feet (6.8 m) to a top diameter of 18 feet (10 m).

The tower was brick-lined. The second and third levels each have four pedimented windows, while the fourth level and the circular watchroom had porthole windows. Above the watchroom and gallery was a smaller, decagonal lantern, which also had a gallery for cleaning the lantern windows. In structure, this light is a twin to the Detroit River light, but was painted all white with some red trim.

The lantern used to house a fourth-order Fresnel lens manufactured by Barbier and Fenestre Constructeurs of Paris. It featured a bull's-eye flash panel and an occulting mechanism that provided a rotational speed of 1.6 revolutions per minute. The signal alternated between a white and a red light. The white light had 70,000 candlepower with a visibility of 25 miles (40 km). The red light had 20,000 candlepower with a 21-mile (33.6 km) visibility. The focal plane was 53 feet (16.3 m) above the lake.

In 1913 the "Big Storm" on the Great Lakes undermined the main breakwater. Winds of 70 miles per hour (112 kph) lashed both water and land, causing the loss of boats, men, buildings and electrical power. Keeper Loren Trescott reported that the lantern's plate glass was coated with 12 inches of solid ice. A sign in Harbor Beach recalls that 178 crewmen and eight ships were lost on Lake Huron during the 16 hours of the cyclone-force winds.

In 1983 the light was listed on the *National Register of Historic Buildings.* In 1986 the Coast Guard removed the original Fresnel lens and donated it to the Harbor Beach Historical Society. Today it is on display in the local Grice Museum. Another artefact, a uniform from a Harbor Beach lighthouse keeper, is in the Huron City Museum, about 10 miles (16 km) north of Harbor Beach. The old lens was replaced with a modern 190 mm plastic lens, thus significantly reducing ongoing maintenance requirements.

In February 1987 another severe storm struck Harbor Beach, leaving much damage and undermining the breakwater in several places. By the end of 1988, at a cost of millions of dollars, all repairs were completed, including the painting of the lighthouse inside and out.

Harbor Beach is also a significant Canadian landmark as 27-year-old Vicki Keith departed from here on July 17, 1988, to complete her epic swim across Lake Huron to Sand Beach, Goderich, Ontario. She swam 48 miles (77 km) and it took her 46 hours and 55 minutes. The American plaque at the Trescott Street Pier on the south side of Harbor Beach reads, "Dedicated to Vicki Keith, 'A Great Canadian,' in commemoration of the first swim across Lake Huron."

Known Keepers: Loren J. Trescott (1880–1912), Archebald Davidson (1920–28), Otto Both (1935–40), Thomas Radcliff (1940).

15 Huron Lightship

Like a lighthouse, a lightship warned mariners of danger, but it could be moved from location to location. The Lighthouse Service used manned lightships instead of lighted buoys because ships were more reliable in areas where frequent groundings occurred, and more practical as offshore lights where the water was too deep, the cost too high or the location too impractical for a permanent lighthouse. Between 1893 and 1940 lightships were placed at 18 locations around the American side of the Great Lakes.

The Huron Lightship marked the Corsica Shoals 6 miles (9.7 km) north of Port Huron and three miles east of the Michigan shoreline, just off the headwaters for the St. Clair River. It also marked the entrance to a man-made channel known as the Lake Huron Cut. From 1893 to 1970, three different lightships served at this station.

The first Huron Lightship, *LV 61*, was used here from September 25, 1893, until the end of 1920. Built at Toledo, Ohio, in 1893 by the Craig Shipbuilding Company, for $13,990, it was one of four sister ships built at the same time by the same company. (The others were *LV 59*, *LV 60*, and *LV 62*.) *LV 61* was framed and planked from white oak fastened with iron bolts and spikes. Its length was 87 feet 2 inches (26.8 m), its beam 21½ feet (6.5 m) and its draft 6 feet 8 inches (2 m). Although it had no self-propulsion and needed to be towed to location, it did have a riding sail on a short aft mast. Its illuminating apparatus consisted of a cluster of three oil-burning lens lanterns hoisted to its foremast, which also carried its black daymark.

Huron Lightship

To warn of fog it had a 6-inch (15 cm) steam whistle (blast 2 s; silence 10 s) placed in front of its smoke stack at midship, as well as a hand-operated 800-pound (363 kg) brass fog bell. It was on station during the navigation season and wintered over at the Detroit Lighthouse Depot.

LV 61 had a relatively uneventful history. In June 1896 a red 35-foot (10.7 m) spar buoy was placed west of the lightship to "more definitely fix the limits of the dredged channel." Then from May to July 1901, *LV 61* left its position at Huron Station (leaving only a buoy until its return) to relieve *LV 62* at Poe Reef Station while *LV 62* underwent repairs. In 1910 the vessel was outfitted with a submarine bell. In 1913 the master chief and engineer launched a lifeboat to rescue a man and woman in a rowboat that was in danger of foundering nearby. At the end of the 1920 season it was condemned, laid up and retired after 27 years of service. It was sold at public auction in August 1921.

The second Huron Lightship was *LV 96*, built in 1914 at Muskegon, Michigan, by the Racine-Truscott-Shell Lake Boat Company for $71,292. It served at the Huron Station from 1921 until May or June 1935. (Its two sister vessels were *LV 98* and *WAL 521*.) Designed with a steel whaleback for its hull to better repel water, it was 101½ feet (31.2 m) long, with a beam 23½ feet (7.2 m) wide and a draft of 9 feet 5 inches (2.9 m).

For reasons of economy, it was given no engines to propel itself and needed to be towed to location. Its light shone from a large tubular lantern mast 42 feet (12.8 m) above water and located at midship. The lantern housing used an electric lamp of 1,000 candlepower and had a revolving parabolic reflector. It had three types of fog apparatus — a 6-inch (15 cm) air siren operated by two 3-cylinder compressors

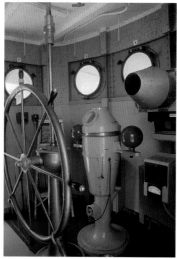

Huron Lightship wheelhouse

driven by kerosene engines, a hand-operated fog bell and a submarine bell.

LV 96 was modified over the years. In 1925 it received a radio beacon that in 1932 was synchronized with its fog signal for distance-finding. In 1933 its submarine bell was discontinued. In 1936 it had a 175 IHP engine installed, which could provide an approximate speed of five knots. In 1936 its cylindrical lantern housing was replaced with a duplex 375 mm electric lens lantern in its masthead gallery. Each lens provided 17,000 candlepower. After *LV 96* had served as the Huron Lightship from 1921 to 1935, it was refurbished and served at Cross Rip, Maine, until it was retired from service in 1955 after 41 years and sold in July 1955.

The third and last vessel to serve as the Huron Lightship was *LV 103*, built in 1920 at Morris Heights, New York, by the Consolidated Shipbuilding Company for $161,074. It was a steam screw steel-hulled vessel 96 feet 5 inches (29.5 m) long, with a 24-foot (7.3 m) beam and a draft of 9.5 feet (2.9 m). Its 175 IEP steam engine was powered by two coal-fired Scotch boilers. It displayed its light from a 300 mm acetylene lens lantern at the top of its tubular 52-foot (16 m) foremast. It also had a 10-inch (25 cm) steam whistle and a hand-operated fog bell.

LV 103 had served at other locations. It first entered the Lighthouse Service as a relief lightship for the Twelfth District, the Lake Michigan District. From 1924 to 1926 and again in 1929 it served at Gray's Reef. In 1926–29 it continued to serve as a relief lightship. In 1934–35 it served at North Manitou Shoal, and from 1935 to 1970 it served as the Huron Lightship.

It too was gradually modified. Its submarine bell, installed in 1924 was removed in 1931. In 1927 its illuminant was changed to electricity. In 1933 the fog signal was changed to a 17-inch

(42.5 cm) steam diaphram horn. It had a radio beacon installed in 1934. In fog it transmitted three dashes for a full minute every three minutes; in clear weather it transmitted six minutes every hour. Also in 1934 its illuminating apparatus reverted back to acetylene. In 1935 its radio beacon was synchronized with its fog signal for finding distance. In 1935 when *LV 103* was moved to Corsica Shoal, Lake Huron, it was repainted from red to black with white lettering, as it marked the port side of the channel and the port side was always marked with black buoys. (This repainting made it the only black lightship on the Great Lakes.) In the late 1930s its illuminating apparatus was converted to a duplex electric 375 mm lens lantern of 15,000 candlepower that could be seen for 14 miles (22.5 km).

Huron Lightship LV 61

LV 103 was renamed *WAL 526* when the Coast Guard assumed responsibility for United States lighthouses in 1939. In 1948 it was repowered using twin diesel engines that could provide a speed of up to nine knots. The vessel could store 6,000 gallons (22,680 l) of diesel fuel, usually enough for one full navigation season. In 1949 it received radar and more modern fog signal equipment. It became nicknamed Old-Bee-Oh, for its "beeeee-ohhhhh" fog signal, which blasted for three seconds every 30 seconds. In 1962 it received an F2T air diaphone foghorn and better radar. From 1940 to 1970 its radio call sign was NMGS. While serving on Corsica Shoals the vessel wintered at Port Huron.

The eleven- to twelve-man crew worked on the lightship for about nine months during the navigation season. Duty was good in fair weather but sleep-challenging in foggy weather when the foghorn was in continual operation, often for 36 hours or more and the vessel vibrated from stem to stern. When not working a shift, the crew could play cards, read, watch television, or study for promotion exams. In 1957, being semi-isolated, they earned one in four compensatory leave days. This meant that after 24 days on duty they got six days off. There were always seven to nine men on board while the rest of the crew was "at liberty" or on shore, which they reached on the small so-called Liberty Boat. In later years the crew worked 21 days and received seven days off. Also the Coast Guard station went to the lightship once a week to deliver mail, supplies and crewmen reporting for duty. The crew averaged a two-year tour of duty on the vessel. The crew of *LV 103* kept a link to the outside world by talking daily to the Coast Guard station and passing ships by radiotelephone. On weekends they even accepted visitors aboard from pleasure craft and gave them a tour of the vessel.

LV 103 earned an honorable place in history. By 1940 it was the only lightship serving on the Great Lakes. During World War II it was the only American lightship to remain on station, as all others were removed to safe harbors to protect them from enemy submarines. After the vessel was decommissioned in August 1970, instead of disappearing as scrap, it was donated to the City of Port Huron, Michigan, in 1971. In 1973 it was listed on the *State Register for Historic Sites*; in 1974 it was dedicated as a historic monument and exhibit; in 1976 it was listed on the National Register; and in 1989 it was listed as a National Historic Landmark, making it the only lightship on the Great Lakes to have this distinction.

In 1972 Port Huron had the lightship dry-berthed on the shore of the St. Clair River as part of Pine Grove Park. From 1973 to 1977 the local naval reserve used the lightship for training purposes. Then after six years of restoration by volunteers it was opened as the Huron Lightship Museum, the only one of its kind on the lakes. During the early 1990s volunteers spent two years restoring the "Old-Bee-Oh" foghorn. Then, after some 25 years of silence, the horn was reblown in September 1994 at an open house at the museum. Now it is only blown on special occasions and holidays. Thanks to the foresight of Port Huron residents, the last lightship on the Great Lakes will continue into the future to mark its role in the maritime history of the Great Lakes.

Known Masters: 1893–1920 LV 61 Charles Calnow (1893–1903), James M. Jones (1903–15), Frank Leimbach (1915–1920). 1921–35 *LV 96* Frank Leimbach (1921–).1935–70 LV 103 Leon DeRosia (1962).

16   Little Rapids Cut Lights (Six Mile Point)

The Six Mile Point Range Lights were located below Little Rapids in the downbound channel on the west side of Sugar Island in the St. Mary's River. At some time, the white, triangular, pyramidal wooden towers that sat upon pilings and grillage piers in the river were replaced by steel circular towers similar in design to the Peche Island range light. They were used until 1974, when winter ice damaged them beyond repair. While only the foundation of the front range light survives today, the rear range light sits in front of the Cedarville Marine Museum in Michigan.

17   Little Rapids Cut North Entrance Lighthouse No. 27

This light was established in the St. Mary's River in 1895 to mark the turn from Bayfield Channel southward into the Little Rapids Cut. It was located about 2 miles (3.2 km) east of the Soo Locks in 20 feet (6 m) of water, and close to the west side of the cut at the north entrance. The lighthouse was built on a 35-foot (10.6 m) square timber rock-filled crib whose deck rose 6 ½ feet (2 m) above the water.

Centered on this crib was the 25-foot (7.6 m), 1½-story keeper's house with a mansard-style roof that had a large dormer protruding from each side. The house was topped with a large square gallery surrounded with a simple pipe-iron railing. It had an octagonal iron lantern that displayed an occulting white light every 5 seconds from a 37-foot (11.3 m) focal plane. As a daytime marker it was painted buff with white trim, and had a black lantern and red roof and crib. The oil house and boathouse were on shore nearby.

The keeper of this station and an assistant keeper also tended range lights in the area. While the head keeper and his family lived on shore, the assistant and his family lived in this lighthouse. In 1911 the light was automated using an acetylene gas lamp. Then in 1929 it was decommissioned at the end of the shipping season and later razed as part of the dredging project to improve the channel for larger vessels.

18 Martin Reef Lighthouse

Realizing that a lighthouse was needed to replace the lightship that marked Martin Reef, the U.S. government had plans drawn up for an offshore lighthouse at this location. A base camp on nearby Government Island at Scammon's Harbor was used to build the 65-foot (20 m) square wooden crib. Meanwhile an area on the southeast end of the reef was leveled in 10 feet (3 m) of water on which to place the crib. The completed crib was floated to the site, centered, and sunk with crushed stone, to serve as a base for a concrete pier. The pier had a wave flare to keep water away from the buildings and prevent ice build-up. A temporary light was attached to its side, and *LV 89* was moved to North Manitou Shoal in Lake Michigan.

Martin Reef Lighthouse

The 52-foot (16 m) Art Deco–style tower, made of reinforced concrete over a steel frame, was centered on the pier. The first three levels were 25 feet (7.7 m) square. The first level housed machinery to operate the station's equipment; the second had an office, a bathroom, and a kitchen; and the third had bedrooms for the keepers. On the top of this section, a smaller 16-foot (4.9 m) square section rose 10 feet (3 m) further to make a watchroom that supported an octagonal cast-iron lantern housing a fourth-order Fresnel lens made by the Louis Sautter Company of Paris. The lens used an 8,000 candlepower lamp to produce its flashing white light, which was visible for 14 miles (22.5 km) from a 65-foot (20 m) focal plane. The station also had a compressed air diaphone fog signal to warn of fog. After finishing the light in the summer of 1927, the crew started building an identical lighthouse on Poe Reef.

Opening the Martin Reef Lighthouse in the spring was a harsh task. Keepers were delivered through and around ice in the spring by a 180-foot (55 m) Coast Guard tender. Before getting the light up and running, the keeper had to chip away the ice around the door to get in, and start up the oil furnace. During the winter the batteries were fully charged to operate a 200 mm optic that was left burning until the spring.

Martin Reef Lighthouse

When the light was automated and the keepers removed, the Fresnel lens was replaced with a solar-powered 200 mm acrylic lens. The Fresnel lens was carefully packed and shipped to the Point Iroquois Light Station Museum, where it can still be seen today. In 2000 the ownership of Martin Reef Light Station was transferred to the Bureau of Indian Affairs, its current custodian.

Known Keepers: Herbert Crittenden (1927–28), Lawrence Clark (1928–30), Frank Davis (1931–40).

19 Martin Reef Lightship

Martin Reef, a reef under very shallow water, is located 12 miles (19 km) north of Spectacle Reef and about 25 miles (40 km) northeast of the Straits of Mackinac in northern Lake Huron. Since the reef posed a maritime hazard to the growing traffic of the late 1800s between the Straits of Mackinac and Detour Passage, the Lighthouse Board petitioned Congress for $15,000 to mark it with a wooden lightship in 1896. The request was reiterated each year by the Lighthouse Board until acted upon in June 1906, when Congress appropriated $25,000 for a steel-hulled lightship that was not to exceed $45,000.

Plans were drawn up by government engineers at the Detroit depot for a vessel that was to have a unique whaleback deck to easily shed water. The contract was awarded to the Racine-Truscott-Shell Boat Company of Muskegon, Michigan. *LV 89* was a steam screw vessel with a steel whaleback forecastle deck, a single lantern mast forward, a jigger aft mast for a riding sail, a large wooden deckhouse, and a smokestack midship. It was 88 feet 3 inches (27 m) long, had a beam of 21 feet (6.4 m) and a draft of 7 feet (2.1 m). It used a one-cylinder reciprocating steam engine of 90 IEP for propelling itself to and from the station. Its light shone from a cluster of three oil lens lanterns raised on the forward mast 35 feet (10.6 m) above the water. For foggy conditions the vessel had a 6-inch (15 cm) steam whistle and a hand-operated fog bell. As a daymark, its hull had been painted bright red to display in large writing, "89 MARTIN REEF 89." Finished in late 1908, the vessel was placed at the beginning of the 1909 navigation season 1 mile (1.6 km) south of the reef to give mariners a wide safe berth. The total cost for this new vessel was $37,500.

During the early 1900s vessels continued to increase in size and the navigation season was gradually extended. *LV 89* was sometimes trapped in ice at the end of the shipping season, and ice frequently delayed its arrival in the spring. Thus, the government drew up plans for a permanent lighthouse to mark the reef. *LV 89* served at Martin Reef until a temporary light was lit, and then it was moved to the North Manitou Shoal in 1927.

Martin Reef Lightship LV 89

20 Middle Island Lighthouse

Middle Island is situated about 2 miles (3.2 km) from the mainland on the west side of Lake Huron and about 8 miles (13 km) north of Alpena. As its name suggests, it is about halfway between Thunder Bay Island and Presque Isle. The Lighthouse Board first recommended a lighthouse on the island in 1896, but Congress approved the request only in March 1902. A lighthouse on the eastern tip of the 275-acre (110 hectare) island was to serve three purposes. It would mark a turning point for mariners traveling the coast and help guide them through a treacherous area known as Shipwreck Alley; it would indicate dangerous low water shoals around the island; and it would mark a shelter from Lake Huron's storms behind the island, although it was a most dangerous area to get to, as proven by the sinking of the brig *James J. Audubon* near the island in 1854.

Congress appropriated $25,000 and construction started in June 1904. The tower, house and fog signal building were all built of brick and placed on dressed stone foundations. Construction was halted during the winter, and the station was completed the following year.

The tower was a completely separate structure on a low rise of ground on the point a short distance from the keeper's house. Its stone foundation was placed on oak pilings driven deep into the sandy soil to create a stable foundation. Its 71-foot (21.6 m) conical tower was 21 feet (6.5 m) in base diameter with walls 2 feet (0.6 m) thick, and it had 100 iron stairs up to its lantern. The diagonal cast-iron lantern housed a fourth-order Fresnel lens that displayed a fixed red light of 3,700 candlepower from a 78-foot (24 m) focal plane. It was visible for 17 miles (27.5 km).

The keeper's dwelling was a 2½-story red brick duplex that housed the keeper and his assistant. Each half had three bedrooms, a kitchen, parlor and dining room, and stoves for cold spring and fall days. A gravity-type coal furnace was later added in the basement. The red brick fog signal building housed duplicate 10-inch (25 cm) steam whistles and equipment to operate them. Its characteristic signal was a 20-second repeated cycle (blast 3 s; silence 17 s).

The station also had a frame boathouse and landing, a tramway system connecting the landing, the fog building and the tower's service room to facilitate the transport of supplies, and concrete walkways to connect all the structures. The light was first lit on June 1, 1905. In 1906 a work crew returned to the station to build a brick oil storage building with a capacity of 500 gallons (2,100 l) to store kerosene.

By 1928 the light had been upgraded to a third-order Fresnel lens with an electrically powered light source of 9000 candlepower and its light had been changed from red to flashing green (flash 5 s; eclipse 5 s). The fog signal had also been updated to a diaphone signal powered by compressed air, with a new characteristic but still a 20-second cycle (blast 2 s; silence 18 s).

Middle Island Lighthouse

In 1939 the Coast Guard assumed operation of the station and changed its daymark to a white tower with a horizontal black mid-band to make it more distinctive. This was later changed to a white tower with an orange-red horizontal mid-band. The island also had a lifesaving station that had been built in 1881 and had quite an active service. It was discontinued in 1969 and all its buildings fell into decay.

In 1961 the light was automated, the keepers removed, and the station's buildings abandoned. They were stripped by vandals during the 1960s and left to further deteriorate. Then, in the 1980s, a group of concerned citizens formed the Middle Island Lighthouse Keepers to preserve and restore the keeper's quarters. In 1988 Marvin and Joy Theut bought Middle Island. In 1990, when they also purchased the lighthouse, the restoration group disbanded. The Theuts then reorganized a restoration group called the Middle Island Lighthouse Keepers Association (MILKA) in February 1992, with the goal of restoring and preserving the light station structures. They leased the keeper's quarters to MILKA for $1 a year and when the restoration is complete they plan to sell the building back to them for $1.

MILKA's first project was to repair and reshingle the roofs of all the buildings. The new tin shingles (identical to the original ones) came from a company in Texas and were individually wrapped in protective plastic covering. With the cost (about $50,000) and time required to bring in the new shingles, remove the old shingles and install the new ones, the reshingling project took over four years to complete. MILKA has also renovated the fog signal building as a B & B to help raise money for restoration. This facility was opened for business in October 2001.

Boy Scout Troop 45 from Farmington Hills, Michigan, has also helped restoration efforts every summer since 1997. Their welcome labor has included rebuilding a log in-ground cold storage cellar in the woods at the edge of the station grounds, cleaning trails, landscaping, repairing the keeper's privy, and helping restore the interior and exterior of the keeper's dwelling.

In 2002 a panel from the light's fourth-order Fresnel lens was returned to the lighthouse. In 1975, on a dare, a teenager had removed the panel when he and some buddies visited the light. After 27 years of guilt he returned it to free his conscience. He has also become a faithful volunteer to restore the light.

MILKA's efforts continue. They also plan a 300-foot (91.5 m) breakwall and docking system at the island's edge to provide better access to the island than their makeshift pontoon dock. Their well-planned goals and dedicated members are a great asset to the cause of lighthouse preservation.

Known Keepers: Patrick Garraty Jr. (1905–17), Michael Nolan (1923–28), Stanley Clark (1934–39).

Middle Island Lighthouse, circa 1930

21 Middle Neebish Island Range Lights

Neebish Island is about 20 miles (32.4 km) south of Sault Ste. Marie, Michigan, in the St. Mary's River. In the late 1800s after the Soo Canal had been opened to connect Lake Superior with Lake Huron via the St. Mary's River, the river was lit to assist navigation. The front range light had been built on the north end of Neebish Island facing downbound traffic.

It was a round tower 40 feet (12.3 m) tall constructed of iron sheeting. When it was discontinued around 1909, it was replaced by steel skeletal towers that flanked the old tower, providing a tower for both upbound and downbound traffic in the river's two channels, each with its own range lights. After the range lights had been replaced by semi-automated acetylene-powered range lights on low maintenance skeletal towers, the Neebish Island Station became a base from which the keeper patrolled and maintained several range lights along the river.

Thomas Brander kept the range lights from about 1932 until 1943. When interviewed, his wife, Jean, described station life as a self-sufficient nineteenth-century lifestyle. They used kerosene lamps, kept a cow and chickens, tended a large fruit and vegetable garden, and gathered fresh wild berries. Jean baked her own bread until her husband was allowed to purchase groceries at the Sault Ste. Marie army base. Their children went to the island's one-room schoolhouse, battling the elements to get there in the winter. In the summer they had plenty of fresh air and space to run, swim, pick berries, and watch passing vessels. The purchases of a gasoline-powered washing machine and a battery-powered radio were family highlights.

While the river provided their livelihood, it also almost caused their demise. After a Christmas party with friends on nearby Sugar Island, Jean and her husband started for home in their outboard motor boat. During the half-mile crossing to the island, their boat became trapped in ice, the motor failed, and they were carried downstream by the current. Thomas told Jean that, with only rowing to save them, they might never see their children again. Whether it was an adrenalin rush, God's will, or just plain luck, said Jean, they managed to row back to the opposite side of the river to their friends' home and return safely to their house on Neebish Island the next day. When the range lights were completely automated, keepers were no longer needed and the Neebish Island station was abandoned.

Known Keeper: Thomas Brander (1932–43).

22 Old Mackinac Lighthouse

As early as 1830 Congress called for the Straits of Mackinac to be lit with a lightship. The ship was placed at Waugoshance Shoal in 1832 to mark the west entrance, but it did not adequately mark the narrow bottleneck where Lake Michigan and Lake Huron meet. In his 1838 report to Congress, Lt. James T. Homans recommended that a beacon light costing $2,660 be built near the town of Mackinaw at the narrowest part of the Straits to mark this hazardous area from both the west and the east. It would also mark entry into the harbor at Mackinaw. While Congress placed lights on other islands and shoals in the Straits, they did not put a light at Mackinaw until the late 1890s.

The fog signal building was built before the lighthouse. In 1888 the Lighthouse Board recommended that Congress appropriate $5,500 for a fog signal building on the higher ground on the west side of Mackinaw to help guide vessels through the narrow spot and into Mackinaw Harbor. They also petitioned for $25,000 for a new light, at a more central location that was visible from both the east and the west, thus replacing the low, poorly placed light at McGulpin's Point. While Congress agreed to both, they only appropriated the money for the fog signal. After land was purchased in 1890, the steam fog signal was completed by October. It was a wood-framed building that had an exterior layer of corrugated iron sheeting and an interior layer of smooth iron sheeting. It had two boilers to operate its twin 10-inch (25 cm) steam whistles, which officially went into operation on November 5, 1890.

In March 1891 Congress appropriated $20,000 for the new lighthouse. The contract went to John Peter Schmitt in early 1892. The attached tower and keeper's dwelling were both built of Cream City brick on an ashlar limestone foundation. The 40-foot (12.2 m) double-bricked cylindrical tower had an outside diameter of 13.2 feet (4 m). Its octagonal cast-iron lantern housed a fourth-order Fresnel lens that displayed a fixed red light varied by a red flash every ten seconds. The light, visible up to 16 miles (26 km), was first displayed on October 25, 1892.

The style of the lighthouse can best be described as a castle. The keeper's house was built in a cross shape. The circular tower had windows resembling arrow-slits. The outcropping of brickwork around the top of the tower had long finger-like protrusions to help support its gallery or parapet. Part of the house looked like a square tower with a crenelated top. The house was built as a duplex for the keeper and his assistant. Downstairs it had two kitchens, dining rooms and parlors; upstairs it had three bedrooms for each family. Its tin roof was painted bright red like the dome of the lantern, to increase its daytime visibility. Other buildings at the station included a storehouse, a barn and a circular iron oil-storage building that could hold 360 gallons (1332 l) of kerosene.

Old Mackinac Lighthouse

While Congress appropriated another $1,000 in 1893 for more land for the station, title was not obtained until 1907. In 1909 the old fog building, which had been too close to the lighthouse, was razed and a new red brick fog signal building was built 55 feet (16.7 m) further to the east.

With the popularity of automobiles, tourists headed to vacation on Michigan's pristine upper peninsula. Regular car ferries crossed the straits, and the lighthouse made it possible for them to operate at night. In 1957, when the well-lit Mackinac Bridge across the straits was opened, the car ferries and the lighthouse both became obsolete and the lighthouse was decommissioned.

The Mackinac State Historic Parks (MSHP) acquired the lighthouse property in 1960, and ran the complex as a maritime museum from 1972 to 1988. In the early 1970s they had the lighthouse added to the *National Register of Historic Places*. With a resurgence of lighthouse interest, MSHP renovated the fog signal building and reopened it in 2000 as a lighthouse information center and gift shop. They plan to use their proceeds to help restore the lighthouse and re-open it to the public.

The original fourth-order Fresnel lens was removed from the lantern after the Coast Guard closed the lighthouse in 1957. With the re-opening of the information center, the old lens was sought and found in Cleveland, Ohio. As of 2003 it is on loan from the Coast Guard to the MSHP for display at their Old Mackinac Point Lighthouse Information Center.

Known Keepers: George Marshall (1890–1919), James Marshall (1919–41), Olsen Henrick (1941–52), John Campbell (1952–58).

Pipe Island Lighthouse, circa 1890

23   Pipe Island Lighthouse

With the opening of the American Soo Locks in 1855 to circumnavigate the Soo Rapids of the St. Mary's River, shipping increased, as exports could now readily be moved from Lake Superior to the lower Great Lakes. This also increased marine traffic on the St. Mary's River, which connected Lake Superior and Lake Huron. During the latter part of the 1800s, sea captains petitioned to have the mouth of the St. Mary's River better lit with the assistance of range lights instead of just the light on Frying Pan Island. When the government did not comply, the Lake Carriers' Association stepped in.

The Association chose Pipe Island as the location for the lighthouse. This 13.4-acre (5.4 hectare) island lies 2 miles (3.2 km) north of Frying Pan Island at the north end of Detour Passage and is about 1.5 miles (2.4 km) from the Michigan shoreline in the middle of the passage between Michigan's mainland and Drummond Island. The site was chosen, as it was close enough and its location would provide proper alignment to work as a front range light in conjunction with the Frying Pan Island light. The Association could therefore respond to the petition for range lights at the river mouth by building only one new light instead of two.

The tower and the house, finished early in 1888, were built on the south side of Pipe Island. The tower was an octagonal, slightly tapering one made of yellow brick. It had recessed windows to provide interior light and a stepped-out brick cornice to support its black iron gallery, which had a pipe iron railing. Its black octagonal cast-iron lantern housed a fifth-order Fresnel lens that displayed a fixed red light with a 10-mile (16 km) visibility when it was first lit on May 12, 1888. The tower's overall height was 33 feet (10 m) and it had a focal plane of 37 feet (11.4 m).

The keeper's house was a 1½-story frame dwelling just slightly northwest of the tower. It was built onto a full basement with a typical stone foundation 24 inches (0.6 m) thick. The interior of the house had rooms with 9-foot (2.7 m) ceilings, solid oak stairs, banisters and railings leading to the second level, a walk-up attic,

wood-burning stoves and an oak icebox. Outbuildings included the privy, a boathouse and a circular cast-iron oil storage house. In 1894 the tower was painted white to increase its daytime visibility. Around 1900 the light was transferred to U.S. government ownership.

In 1937 the lantern was removed and replaced by a steel skeletal extension with a more modern beacon to brighten the light. It was also given an orange and white vertical daymark. These changes made the light's daymark more visible and increased its focal plane to 52 feet (16 m), so that it could be spotted further out in the lake by the larger vessels that now used the river. Also at this time the light was automated through the use of an acetylene gas lamp.

Since a keeper was no longer needed, the island was sold in the 1940s to Deke Dagott, who used it as a fishing and hunting camp. Later, in the 1980s, the island was deeded to the Nature Conservancy for protection and preservation. This institute traded the island to private owners in 2000 to acquire other property they wanted. However, the swap also included a conservation easement to prevent new construction on Pipe Island.

On September 18, 2001, the government excessed the lighthouse. After a cleanup necessitated by contamination from lead paint and spilled battery acid, the lighthouse reservation was sold to the owners of the rest of the island, John and Mary Kostecki of Cedarville, Michigan. The sale was completed on November 16, 2004, for $15,000. The Kosteckis have completely renovated the lighthouse and filled it with period pieces. Today they offer it as a vacation rental destination, a place to "Vacation on a Private Island." In the future the Kosteckis hope to place a lantern back on top of their tower. With such dedicated owners, the future of the Pipe Island lighthouse is secure.

Known Keeper: Norman Powel Hawkins.

24 Poe Reef Lightship

With increased lake traffic in the latter years of the 1800s, the Lighthouse Board called for the marking of dangerous offshore hazards such as Poe Reef, but Congressional funds were increasingly difficult to obtain. The reef was located in the Straits of Mackinac South Channel, which lay between Bois Blanc Island and the Michigan mainland. For reasons of economy, the Board in the early 1890s sought money for a lightship instead of a lighthouse. When this too was denied, the Board redirected an existing $60,000 congressional appropriation for a lighthouse off Peninsula Point to purchase four lightships, one of which was to be placed at Poe Reef.

LV 62 was the vessel assigned to Poe Reef. It was built in 1893 at Toledo by the Craig Shipbuilding Company for $13,990. It was 87 feet 2 inches (26.8 m) long, framed and planked in white oak, had a 21½-foot (6.5 m) beam and an 8-foot (2.5 m) draft. To minimize costs, the vessel was not self-powered and had to be towed into position, but it had a small riding sail on its short aft mast. A cluster of three oil-burning lens lanterns was hoisted to its foremast to display a fixed white light. For fog it had a 6-inch (15 cm) steam whistle (blast 5 s; silence 10 s) and an 800-pound (363 kg) hand-operated brass bell. It carried a red daymark on its foremast and its fire-engine-red hull displayed "POE REEF" in white letters. After sea trials it was towed to the reef by the lighthouse tender *Marigold* and, on September 29, 1893, anchored into position at Poe Reef, where it served until 1910. It was taken to Cheboygan for its winter lay-up and repairs.

In 1911 *LV 62* switched locations with *LV 59*; *LV 59* came to Poe Reef and *LV 62* went to Bar Point. *LV 59* was also one of the four lightships built at Toledo by the Craig Shipbuilding Company in 1893, and so it had almost identical specs to *LV 62*. It served at Poe Reef until it was deemed unseaworthy at the end of the 1914 season.

Its successor, *LV 96*, was repainted and transferred from Buffalo to Poe Reef, where it was used from 1915 until 1920. This vessel had just been built in 1914 by the Racine-Truscott-Shell Lake Boat Company at Muskegon, Michigan, at a cost of $71,292. It was a non-propelled steel vessel built using a whaleback hull design. It was 101½ feet (31 m) long and 23½ feet (7.2 m) wide, and had a draft of 9 feet 5 inches (28.7 m). It was equipped with kerosene engines that operated electrical generators and batteries to power the light and the fog signal. The light was a large cylindrical lantern that housed a 1,000 candlepower electric lamp with a revolving parabolic reflector that produced a flash 42 feet (13 m) above the water. For its fog it had a 6-inch (15 cm) air siren, a submarine bell and a hand-operated bell. When *LV 96* was reassigned to Corsica Shoal in Lake Huron for 1921, *LV 99* took its place at Poe Reef.

Poe Reef Lightship LV 99, circa 1922

Poe Reef Lightship LV 62, circa 1915

LV 99 was brand new, built in 1920 by the Rice Brothers of Boothbay Harbor, Maine, for $97,220. It used a steam screw, steel-hull design and was 91 feet 8 inches (28 m) long and 22 feet (6.7 m) wide, with a draft of 10 feet 7 inches (3.2 m). It was powered by a one-cylinder steam engine with 125 IHP. Its lighting apparatus consisted of a single acetylene lens lantern displayed from its tubular lantern mast, which also had a gallery. It was outfitted with a 10-inch (25 cm) steam whistle and a hand-operated bell for foggy weather. *LV 99* served at the reef until a lighthouse was built to replace it in 1927.

25 Poe Reef Lighthouse

The Lighthouse Service decided to build a lighthouse at Poe Reef in 1927. When work at the Martin Reef Light was completed in the summer of 1927, the whole work crew and base camp moved to the mouth of the Cheboygan River to start the Poe Reef Light. Some of the 80 crew members leveled the reef for the crib placement, while others built the crib at Cheboygan.

The 64-foot (19.5 m) square crib was made of dressed 12-inch (30 cm) square timbers to a height of 45 feet (13.7 m). All timbers were hand-drilled and bolted in place. Iron angles were added at the corners for extra support. The upper portion was covered with exterior steel plates that extended 6 feet (1.8 m) above the sides. Upon completion the crib was launched and floated to the reef between the tenders *Aspen* and *Marigold*. After proper positioning, it was sunk, and filled with concrete poured over limestone and rocks to the upper limit of the steel sheathing. The top was carefully leveled, as it was critical to the upper structure that this base

Poe Reef Lighthouse

be perfectly level. Forms were then used to make a concrete pier, which had built-in ladders on each of its four sides and arch-topped storage areas within. The top of the pier had a wave flare to deflect water.

On the pier a 25-foot (7.6 m) square tower was built 38 feet (11.6 m) high. It consisted of a steel skeletal frame to which steel plates were riveted. Its upper two decks accommodated the keepers and its lower deck housed machinery to operate the lights, fog signal and radio communications. On top of this, a 16-foot (4.9 m) square watchroom was built 10 feet (3 m) high with a window in each side for a lake view in every direction. A polygonal cast-iron lantern was placed on top of the watchroom and equipped with a fifth-order Fresnel lens at a 71-foot (21.6 m) focal plane to produce a visibility of 19 miles (30.8 km). The light was first exhibited on August 15, 1929. Its fog characteristic was a 15-second blast every 60 seconds.

To distinguish this light from the one built on Martin Reef, its main deck, lantern and watchroom were painted black, while the second and third decks remained white. Its lantern dome was red. In 1974, when the light was automated, a 375 mm acrylic optic with an electric light powered by solar panels was installed, and its Fresnel lens was removed. The light continues today as an active aid to navigation.

Known Keepers: Fredrick Kling (1929–30) Lawrence Clark (1930–36), Clarence Land (1936–40).

26 Pointe aux Barques Lighthouse

In response to petitions to light the point into Saginaw Bay, Lake Huron, in the spring of 1838, Congress appropriated $5,000 for a lighthouse in July 1838. Lt. James T. Homans selected the site to be multi-purposed: to mark a very shallow shoal that stretched up to 2 miles (3.2 km) into the lake; to be seen by vessels traveling from the north and/or west across the mouth of Saginaw Bay; and to mark a turning point for vessels traveling north along Lake Huron's west shore and into Saginaw Bay. Homans also reported a considerable quantity of stone nearby, with which the light could be built.

Little is known of the first lighthouse at Pointe aux Barques. It is assumed to have been a short stone conical tower with a separate small stone keeper's dwelling, typical of the time. Although finished in 1847, it was first lit for navigation the next year.

This lighthouse was replaced just ten years later, perhaps because of poor workmanship or because of its inadequate light and short tower. The contract to rebuild it went to Sweet, Ransom and Shinn in 1854. The new tower was 89 feet (27 m) high, built of Cream City brick on a limestone foundation and placed on a 12-foot bluff near the shore. The conical tower had a brick inner lining to prevent condensation and had five windows ascending it to light the 103 open-grillwork cast-iron spiral stairs that led up to its cast-iron lantern.

Its fixed white light, varied by a bright flash of white light every two minutes, was created from the bull's-eye panel in its third-order Fresnel lens, which rotated around the lamp through the use of a clockwork mechanism that needed to be wound every few hours. From its 93-foot (28.3 m) focal plane the light was visible for 16 miles (26 km). The new 1½-story brick keeper's house was attached to the tower by a covered passageway. The new light was first displayed in 1857 and the old tower and keeper's house were razed when the new structures were ready.

Time brought changes to the station. In 1859 an assistant keeper was added and he lived in the keeper's house. In 1860 a breakwall was placed in front of the bluff to stave off lake erosion. In 1867 the flashing third-order lens was exchanged with the fixed

Pointe aux Barques Lighthouse

third-order lens at Fort Gratiot, so that the Fort Gratiot light could be distinguished from locomotive headlights. However mariners disliked Pointe aux Barques' new characteristic and petitioned Congress to have it returned to a flashing light. After some analysis, the light was returned to a flashing pattern, with the white light showing its flash every ten seconds. In 1875 a lifesaving station was built just south of the tower.

In an 1881 forest fire the lifesaving crew rescued the keeper and his family as well as the lighthouse and the lifesaving station. While the keeper went to help save his farm by the water about a mile from the lighthouse, the lifesaving crew remained to guard their station against a possible fire there. When the wind shifted toward the farm, they rowed to the shores of the farm and rescued the keeper and his family, who were unconscious. Upon their return to the station, another wind shift brought the fire to their buildings and they beat back the flames all night long until a morning shift in the wind sent the fire back on itself.

Additions in the upcoming years included: in 1884 a 19-foot (5.8 m) well for the lighthouse water supply; in 1891 a woodshed; in 1893 a circular iron oil storage shed; and in 1899 an automated fog bell. In 1908 a new house was built for the keeper and his family, while the assistant and his family continued to live in the old keeper's house. In June 1914 an incandescent oil vapor lamp was installed in the light, increasing its candlepower to 34,000 and its visibility to 18 miles (29 km). In 1918 a lighted buoy was placed 2.2 miles (3.6 km) offshore to mark the eastern edge of the reef. In 1931 the tower was modernized using an incandescent electric bulb inside the lens. With its new 120,000 candlepower, the light's visibility increased again (flash 3 s; eclipse 7 s). In 1957 the light was automated, the Fresnel lens removed to storage, and twin DCB-224 aero beacons with automatic bulb changers installed. The last keeper was removed in 1958. In 1972 the light was added to the Michigan State inventory of historic sites. It is also on the National Registry.

The old lens was uncrated and for some time displayed at the Grice Museum in Harbor Beach. It is now on display at the Huron City Museum, which also exhibits a fog bell that is possibly the one removed from the Pointe aux Barques Station. Once the station was no longer needed, the Coast Guard sold the reservation to Huron County in 1958.

The traditional lighthouse ghost story surfaced at the Pointe aux Barques light only in 1992 after Huron County hired grounds keepers who lived in the new keeper's house. The couple finally convinced their daughter to visit. One night she awoke and was drawn to the hall, where she saw a specter standing garbed in a high-collared long-sleeved old-fashioned dress. Rather than being frightened, she felt welcomed to the lighthouse. After a time the image simply turned and walked through the closed door towards the lighthouse. When she mentioned the incident the next morning her parents were incredulous. Wes Oleszewski, the author of *Lighthouse Adventures*, however, gladly corroborated the daughter's story. Despite his skepticism, he believes he has the image of the ghost on film and shows the picture in his book.

Today the lighthouse is part of Huron County's Lighthouse Park and the old keeper's house contains a shipwreck museum. The county has thus saved another lighthouse for future generations.

Known Keepers: Peter Shook (1848–49), Catherine Shook (1849–51), Francis Sweet (1851–53), Chauncey Sheldon (1853–57), Amgrad Granger (1857–59), D. Dodge (1859–61), Jacob Groat (1861–63), Andrew Shaw (1863–95), Andrew Mathewson (1895–1905), Peter Richard (1905–39), Daniel McDonald (1949).

27 Port Austin Reef Lighthouse

In March 1873 Congress appropriated $10,000 for a lighthouse to warn mariners of the hazardous shallow shoals extending out from Port Austin Harbor on the northern point of Michigan's "thumb" in Lake Huron. After taking two years to obtain title to suitable land for the lighthouse, the Lighthouse Board was able to convince Congress in 1876 to build the lighthouse offshore instead, to better mark the hazards. It required an additional $75,000 to construct the light, and the keeper's quarters were built on the previously purchased onshore property.

The lighthouse was built in 1878–79. While one crew leveled an area in 4 feet (1.2 m) of water on the northwest end of the reef, the crib was built at Tawas. The huge octagonal crib, built six feet high of oak timbers one-foot (30 cm) square, was 86 feet (26.2 m) in diameter. It was reinforced with inner cross-members secured with 3-foot (0.9 m) long iron bolts. More than 500 5-foot (1.5 m) iron bolts were then used to secure the inner timbers to the outer ones. Upon completion, the crib was floated to Pointe Aux Barques, where 4 feet (1.2 m) was added to the cribwork height. It was then floated to the reef site about 1.5 miles (2.4 km) out from Port Austin Harbor. Once centered on the site, doors were opened in the crib's exterior walls to let water into sealed pockets inside the crib. When the weight of the water overcame the crib's buoyancy, the crib sank into position and was secured to the reef with iron bolts 7 feet (2.1 m) long and 3 inches (7.5 cm) in diameter.

After the crib bottom was sealed, the inner water was pumped out. The crib was covered with a hard brick veneer, extended to 29 feet (8.8 m) in height, and then filled with concrete and crushed stone to form the pier on which the lighthouse was built. In order to stay within the said appropriation, a 57-foot (17.4 m) timber-framed tower was built and its pyramidal sides were covered to store supplies. The tower supported an octagonal cast-iron lantern that housed a fourth-order Fresnel lens made by Henri LePaute of Paris. It rotated around the light to display a red and white characteristic (white light 60 s; a group of 5 red flashes every 12 s). The keeper's house was also completed on shore in 1879.

In 1882 duplicate steam fog sirens were placed on the pier in wooden frame buildings. In 1895 they were upgraded to two 10-inch (25 cm) steam whistles. In 1899 pier and tower, now weather-worn, were rebuilt. During this refurbishing, a boat crane and stairway were added to the landing crib. Also, a new 16-foot (4.9 m) square double-walled brick tower was built, with four, one-room levels, each with four windows.

Keepers continued to use the onshore house as their main residence, and stay at the light during harsh weather. The first level served as a kitchen/dining area, and the other three levels served

Port Austin Reef Lighthouse, circa 1910

Port Austin Reef Lighthouse

28 Port Sanilac Lighthouse

In 1884 Congress appropriated $20,000 for a lighthouse at Port Sanilac to facilitate water traffic in the area. Built in 1886, both the red brick house and the tower were placed on foundations of dressed stone and were given unique architectural features. The octagonal tower tapered from 14 feet (4.3 m) in diameter at the bottom to 9 feet (2.8 m) at the top. Only one window, about halfway up, interrupted the upward brickwork of the tower. When the tapering stopped, an ornamental ring of brick jutted out slightly, and the brickwork started a step-out pattern to create the support for the gallery. This brickwork also extended up, out and over four large windows in the watchroom below the octagonal iron lantern. Recessed windows like these were very unusual in tower design. This shape was listed as an "octagonal hourglass" by the National Park Service. Although painted white now, the tower and lantern were originally whitewashed.

The lantern, with its red dome and ventilator ball, still uses its original fourth-order Fresnel lens made in Paris by Barbier and Fenestre. The lens, once lit by kerosene-burning lamps, has since been electrified and automated. Through the use of panels, it has always shown an arc illumination of 300 degrees. While it used to show a fixed white light, it now flashes once each second for three seconds and is eclipsed for three seconds. The tower is 59 feet (18 m) from base to ventilator ball and has a focal plane of 69 feet (21 m) above low water level. It is visible for up to 15 miles (24 km) in clear weather. In July 1889 the light was changed to a fixed red to better distinguish it from the town lights behind the tower. A ruby-colored glass chimney was placed over its lamp to achieve the red light.

The two-story, red brick, keeper's house with decorative chimneys and diagonally shingled roof was attached to the tower by a covered passage from which a quaint veranda extended out. The station also had a a wooden covered well and a brick oil house, built in 1899, that had stepped brick gables at each end, similar to the house.

In the early twentieth century the light was electrified. With electricity readily available to the town, electricity was used as an illuminant as early as 1924. Its 18,000 candlepower incandescent electric light provided a more intense brightness that could be seen 16 miles (26 km). At the beginning of the 1925 navigation season, the light's characteristic was also changed to become a triple flash every ten seconds. This new system also had an electronic timer and switch mechanism.

All lighthouse keepers were given specific instructions as to how to write their daily log. They were to record daily records of any unusual conditions of wind or weather with any abnormal reading of barometers or thermometers, and were told to write the day's entries carefully on one line. They were also to note visits from inspectors, lamp technicians, or any other authorized persons. They were not to include any personal opinions or remarks on daily duties or family affairs. Port Sanilac only had three lightkeepers, all of whom mostly ignored these government guidelines. They recorded much relevant history for Port Sanilac and the surrounding area. Log books are available for viewing at the Port Sanilac Library.

as bedrooms and office. A square cast-iron gallery surmounted the tower and supported a circular cast-iron watchroom. The watchroom was lined with oak boards to insulate and help prevent condensation, and had four brass porthole windows. It was topped with a circular cast-iron lantern with its own circular iron gallery. The lantern's curved glass was set into diagonal astragals. The old lens was placed in the new lantern and first lit for the start of the 1900 navigation season. With a new focal plane of 76 feet (23.2 m) the light was visible for 16.5 miles (26.5 km).

At some time the fog signal equipment was placed in a new brick fog signal building 34 feet (10.4 m) square with a hipped-roof. The light changed in 1915. Its lamp was upgraded to a 4,000 candlepower incandescent oil vapor unit and its characteristic became a 12-second cycle (red flash 1.4 s; eclipse 10.6 s).

Further changes occurred at the station. When it received Type F diaphone fog horns to replace the steam whistles in 1933, its fog characteristic changed (blast 3 s; silence 3s; blast 3 s; silence 51 s). In 1937 the pier was reinforced using concrete and steel facing. In 1939 the Coast Guard assumed operation and ran a submarine cable to provide electrical power to the station, and the new light source became a 25,000 candlepower incandescent light bulb. In 1942 the Fresnel lens was replaced with a 300 mm glass lens and the light was given a new characteristic (flash 1 s; eclipse 9 s). In 1953, when the light was automated and keepers made redundant, the onshore dwelling was sold into private hands. In 1985 the glass lens was replaced by a solar-powered Tidelands Signal 300 mm acrylic optic, making the submarine cable obsolete.

Weather and vandals attacked the buildings while they sat abandoned. The fog signal roof caved in, windows were broken, and vandals removed anything movable. Pigeons took up lodging and filled the building with 3 feet (0.9 m) of guano. Then, in the 1980s, the Coast Guard made plans to demolish the buildings and put the light on a skeletal tower. However, to save and restore the light, private citizens soon formed the Port Austin Reef Light Association (PARLA), and in 1988 acquired a five-year lease to stabilize and restore the lighthouse. They replaced the collapsed roof and the windows, removed the guano, and began restoration. In 1990 they received an additional 30-year lease to continue their work. PARLA aims to completely restore the lighthouse interior to its original condition and welcomes support in its efforts.

Known Keepers: Charles Kimball (1978–83), Peter Knudsen (1883), Frank Kimball (1883–94), Herbert (1895–1900), Daniel Carrigan (1900–05), Arthur Carter (1905–07), Otto Bufe (1907–10), James Pottinger (1910–28), Frank Marshall (1928–40).

Port Sanilac Lighthouse

Richard Morris was keeper at Port Sanilac from 1886 to 1893. He was an efficient keeper and also an active member of his community. Some of his ledger entries include:

1886
Thanksgiving ... had a splendid turkey dinner 35 cents...

1887
Feb. 11... Roads all blocked ... one of the worst storms in history ... Old Tom Woods and team broke through the ice under the dock and were nearly drowned.
June 24 ... some persons stole Wright Brothers fish boat last night ... Aug ... white washed tower ...

1888
Oct. 2 ... There was a terrible gale during the night from the north ... At 8 a.m. the life saving crew from Harbor Beach with the crew of the barge St. Clair aboard, attempted to make a landing just south of the Port Sanilac dock. The boat capsized in the breakers and five of the St. Clair's crew were drowned...

1890
June ... Mosquitoes unprecedented in number...

William Holmes was appointed keeper in 1893 and kept the position until his death in 1926. He was also an active community member and recorded much more than the required one daily line.

1896
Typhoid Fever prevalent ... received monthly pay ... $44.50 ...

1901
May 25 ... Baltimore floundered and 12 lives lost ...
Sept. 6 ... President McKinley shot at Pan American Exposition ... Chance fair for recovery ...
Sept. 14 ... died

1904
No mail due to roads and railroads being completely snowed in ...

1909
July 4 ... some automobiles in town ... first seen
Dec. 11 ... 52 lives lost and a million dollars worth of property lost on Lake Erie this week ... Steamer *Clarion* burned ... *Richardson* wrecked ... car ferry Marquette *Bessemer No. 2* sunk ...

1913
November 9 ... gale of winds blowing ...
three cribs of steamboat dock are gone
November 10 ... heavy gale continues all night with snow also heavy ... steamboat dock is all gone as also is fish dock and trap nets ... the shore is strewn with wreckage ... worst gale in years ... 12 boats are passing ...
November 14 ... 229 lives lost in Sunday storm ... papers say 272 lives lost on the lake and five million in property damage

1914
August 5 ... report that Great Britain declared war on Germany

1917
October 11 ... keeper buys a Ford touring car ...

Without the meticulous jottings of these keepers, much informal history would have been lost. The Nautical Research Center of California is also helping to record history through a research project with the U.S. Coast Guard Historian's Office. They are indexing 34 reels of microfilmed Coast Guard and lighthouse blueprints from 1850 to 1942. Blueprints in poor condition are being redrawn and prints are being made of all blueprints for towers, dwellings, oil houses, workshops and barns, etc. Included in this collection are the blueprints for Port Sanilac Lighthouse.

After the light was automated, the government sold the house as a private dwelling in 1928 by sealed tender to the highest bidder. The government continues to own the tower and 14 feet (4.3 m) around its base. It also continues to maintain the light, which has served mariners faithfully for over 115 years.

Known Keepers: Richard W. Morris (1886–93), William H. Holmes (1893–1926), Grace Holmes (1926–28).

Presque Isle Old Rear Range Light

29 Presque Isle Harbor Range Lights

When the new coastal light was lit in 1870 on the tip of Presque Isle Peninsula above Alpena on Lake Huron's northwest shore, the old harbor light was extinguished. While traffic into the harbor had decreased, mariners still needed a light to help them navigate into port, so the Presque Isle Harbor Range Lights were also established and lit in 1870, at a cost of $5,000. They stood 1,000 feet (300 m) apart on the west shore of Presque Isle harbor, and their light was visible only on the line of approach.

The front range light was a wooden 16-foot (4.9 m) tower that was square on the bottom and octagonal on its lantern level. It had a front rectangular window to display its fixed white light from oil lamps for 9 miles (2.7 km). A smaller rectangular window in the back allowed the keeper to check the light without walking to the tower.

The rear light was a white wooden schoolhouse-style home with a rectangular wooden lantern room extending up from the front roof peak. Its fixed white light was displayed from an arched window at 25 feet (7.6 m) for 12 miles (19 km). These range lights were almost identical to those at Bailey's Harbor.

The first keeper was Captain William Simms. He was a member of the Masonic Lodge, as was his wife, Adeline. Apparently she had overheard lodge secrets and the only way to silence her was to make her a lodge member — and its first female member. Her story was even featured on Ripley's "Believe It or Not." Disbelievers can check her tombstone, still on lighthouse property, on which the Masonic emblem is inscribed. Simms also built his own schooner to sail the Great Lakes while he was keeper of this light.

Through the years things changed at the light. The last keeper was Anna Garrity, who kept the light for 23 years. In 1908 the structure was one of the few buildings missed by an area forest fire. The light's illuminant changed from whale oil to kerosene to electricity (in 1933). Also that year, the front range light was extinguished and a new taller rear range light was established on a steel tower behind the keeper's house. It became known as the "Dummy Light," and the light in the keeper's house became the front range light. The unused front range light was moved to an inland location near the the Old Presque Isle Lighthouse.

After the harbor range lights were discontinued, the Coast Guard excessed the property and sold it in 1945 to Marshall Spencer. He and his family used it as a cottage for seven years, and in 1952 it became their permanent home. They discovered six layers of brick flooring in the basement with layers of sand every two courses to prevent moisture from seeping in. They also found the letters USLHE (United States Lighthouse Establishment) in various spots. Enclosed steps into the back kitchen, which stored firewood and had a top step that lifted to give access, contained a piece of firewood with "William McKnewley, foreman of this job, July 26, 1870" written on it. The Spencers also operated a summer craft shop on the premises in the 1970s and converted the old keeper's barn into a guesthouse. With such conscientious residents, the lighthouse will remain long into the future.

Known Keepers: Captain William Simms (1870–), Anna Garrity (?).

Presque Isle Old Front Range Light

30 Presque Isle New Lighthouse

This lighthouse, 113 feet (34.4 m) tall, is the tallest of the Great Lakes towers built from the plans of Orlando M. Poe. The group, known as the "Tall Lighthouses of the Great Lakes," also includes: Big Sable, Lake Michigan (1867); South Manitou, Lake Michigan (1872); Grosse Point, Lake Michigan (1873); Little Sable, Lake Michigan (1874); Au Sable, Lake Superior (1874); and Wind Point, Lake Michigan (1880). Each of these lighthouses is exceptionally tall, has four unique, arch-shaped windows beneath the pedestal room, and has windows facing the four compass directions to form a watchroom. Each tower also has a large band of brick around the top just below the windows, and two galleries (a lower gallery around the pedestal room and a smaller upper gallery around the lantern).

The Presque Isle New Lighthouse, built in 1870, replaced a previous one at the harbor. With vessels no longer needing to stop at the harbor for cordwood and the old tower being obscured by the trees on the peninsula, the Lighthouse Board requested $28,000 to build a new light on the peninsula's northern tip to better mark the area for mariners. Congress agreed in 1870, and the light was built the same year.

Its very tall tower was extremely well constructed. It was on a block foundation that extended almost 10 feet (3 m) below ground. Its conical shape tapered in from a base diameter of 19 feet 3 inches (5.9 m) to a top diameter of 12 feet (3.7 m). The tower walls were built using a double-wall style. The outer red brick wall was 5 1/4 feet thick (1.6 m) at the base and tapered as it rose. The inner wall, 1 foot (0.30 m) thick, stayed constant. A spiral iron staircase with 144 open-work steps gave access to the decagonal lantern, which displayed a fixed white light from a third-order Fresnel lens made by Henri LePaute of Paris. The lantern also had five brass air vents to cool the room of the heat generated by the oil-burning lamps. Shining from a 123-foot (37.5 m) focal plane, the light was visible for about 20 miles (32 km).

The small 1½-story red brick keeper's house had a slate roof. It was attached to the tower by a covered passageway, and a room in the cellar provided storage space for lamp oil. Both house and tower were painted white for best visibility. The station was com-

pleted late in 1870 so the keeper, Pat Garraty, and his family moved into the new house and first lit the light to begin the 1871 navigation season. The old light at the harbor was then extinguished, its lantern was removed and it was abandoned.

In 1890 a steam-operated fog signal manufactured by Variety Iron Works of Cleveland was installed. As well, 2,240 feet (683 m) of tramway connected the dock to the fog signal building for easier transportation of the coal to operate the fog signal. The 360-gallon (1360 l) capacity oil house indicates that kerosene was the illuminant at this time as, being more volatile, it needed a separate storage space. Most stations with a fog signal were assigned three keepers, but this did not happen here until 1909.

The station was improved as needed. In 1905 a new two-story keeper's dwelling was built; in 1907 concrete walks were laid to connect the structures; and in 1909 a second assistant keeper was hired. The illuminating apparatus was upgraded to 29,000 candlepower with the installation of an incandescent oil vapor system in 1912. In 1940 electricity and indoor plumbing were installed. During the 1950s the redundant fog signal building and oil house were razed and a large concrete block garage built.

Presque Isle New Lighthouse

Although the light was automated in 1970, the Coast Guard maintained an active station at this site until they moved to St. Ignace in 1972. In 1973 Presque Isle Township leased the 98-acre (40 hectare) Presque Isle Light Station from the Coast Guard to operate it as a park.

In 1981 Dan and Marianne McGee found the rundown lighthouse and Dan was hired to cut the grass. In 1985 he formed the non-profit Presque Isle Lighthouse Historical Society, which signed an agreement with the Coast Guard to lease the station's buildings for maintenance. The group received a $3,000 State grant. In 1998 the Coast Guard transferred the deed to the county. Also in 1998 the Society sent a delegation to Alpena when the Admiral of the Coast Guard was giving a speech there. This resulted in the Coast Guard's authorizing $100,000 for the badly needed rebricking of the tower. The light was placed on the *National Register of Historic Places*.

The Society has spent years renovating the lighthouse to its 1905–15 era. To raise funds, they operate a gift shop/museum at the lighthouse and offer tours up the tower. Being the tallest lighthouse on the Great Lakes, it offers a spectacular view for miles in all directions and one can see the narrow, bottlenecked peninsula for which the lighthouse was named. Just offshore, one can also see the hidden reefs and easily understand why this lighthouse still functions to warn mariners of their danger.

Known Keepers: Patrick Garraty (1871–91), Thomas Garraty (1891–1935), Elmer Byrnes (1935–54).

New Presque Isle third-order lens, circa 1996

31 Presque Isle Old Lighthouse

"Presque Isle" is French, meaning "almost an island." Throughout the Great Lakes, early French explorers found several peninsulas with narrow bases, which made portaging much easier. This resulted in there being a Presque Isle in Lake Erie, Lake Superior, Lake Huron, Georgian Bay, and Lake Ontario. Presque Isle of northern Lake Huron was located between Alpena and Roger's City.

Presque Isle Harbor, a natural, well-protected harbor on the south side of the peninsula, was used in the 1830s both for refuge from storms and as a refueling station for steamships to take on cordwood. By 1840 the harbor was a busy community, with docks, a sawmill, a store, barns and several shanties owned by lumbermen and fishermen.

In July 1838 Congress appropriated $5,000 for a lighthouse at the harbor entrance. The conical tower, 30 feet (9.1 m) high with a base 18 feet (5.5 m) in diameter, was started in 1839 and finished in 1840 by Jeremiah Moors of Detroit. The rubble-stone walls were 4 feet (1.2 m) thick. Hand-hewn stone steps spiraled up the interior to a top diameter of 9 feet (2.7 m). The lighthouse, burning whale oil, was officially lit in September 1840.

The first keeper, Henry Woolsey, served until 1849. In 1857 the light's lens was upgraded to a fourth-order Fresnel. In 1869 the government built range lights across the harbor from the lighthouse as maturing trees were obscuring the old light. Anna Garraty, the daughter of the last keeper, Patrick Garraty, kept watch on these range lights. Then, after 30 years of service, a new, taller, lighthouse was built in 1870 at the end of the peninsula for better visibility to lake traffic. The old lighthouse was abandoned and the Garraty family moved into the new lighthouse for the start of the 1871 navigation season.

In 1897 the lighthouse was sold at public auction to Edward O. Avery of Alpena. Then at the turn of the century, A.C. Stebbins, the owner of a wheelbarrow factory in Lansing who operated a resort on Grand Lake, purchased the old lighthouse at a tax sale for $75 as a picnic area for his hotel guests. The abandoned lighthouse fell to ruins. By the 1920s there remained only a foundation hole outlining the location of the keeper's house, and the circular steps carved out of stone blocks. Stebbins' son Francis acquired the lighthouse in the 1930s. Using pictures, he rebuilt the tower as close as possible to the original.

Francis Stebbins continued restoration. In the 1940s he rebuilt the keeper's dwelling according to its original style, for use as a summer cottage. However, he rebuilt the interior to resemble an English

Presque Isle Old Lighthouse

Round Island Lighthouse

hunting lodge. The slab flagstone floors and wooden roof beams came from the old Lansing Post Office. He used the keeper's dwelling to display marine artefacts he had collected, and in the 1950s he opened a museum at the lighthouse and charged people for what he used to show for free. In the early 1950s he acquired two Fresnel lenses at auction. In the late 1950s he salvaged and moved the hexagonal lantern room from the Fox Island Lighthouse and had it installed on his tower at the Old Presque Isle site. By 1965 restoration to the top of the lighthouse was complete. It was even electrified and in working order. However, the U.S. Coast Guard considered it a non-charted light and, as such, illegal to use.

In 1967 Jim Stebbins, also a lighthouse enthusiast, inherited the lighthouse from his father. By 1994 ticket sales showed that about 26,000 people had traveled through the museum since it opened in the 1950s. The museum is of special interest as it is a "hands-on" museum. Visitors can "shoot the sun" with an old brass sextant, play the pump organ, or rest on the horsehair couch. They can view antique nautical instruments and tools, including a ship's wheel, binnacles and a compass, a barometer, foghorns, marlin-spike tools, capstans and Fresnel lenses. The cottage furnishings are antiques of the 1800s and early 1900s — clocks, ship models, a pump organ, original Currier and Ives prints, pewter and copper kitchenware, wine bottles, and household "appliances."

In front of the lighthouse is an old bronze bell taken from the old Lansing City Hall clock tower when it was being torn down in 1959. Francis Stebbins bought it for $720, its price in scrap metal, and moved it to the lighthouse. The bell, cast in 1896, weighs 3,426 pounds (1551 kg) and is 60 percent heavier than the Liberty Bell. It is a fitting addition to the lighthouse because old lighthouse stations used a bell as a fog warning device.

Besides saving the lighthouse, the Stebbins family also had the old lighthouse listed on the *National Register of Historic Places* in 1973. In 1995 Jim Stebbins sold the lighthouse and museum to the local township, which continues to run it as a museum. Its treed surroundings and spacious lawns make it a great place to visit, picnic, or take part in a time long past.

Known Keepers: Henry Woolsey (1840–47), George Murray (1847–48), Stephen Thornton (1848–53), Louis Metivier (1853–61), Patrick Garraty Sr. (1861–71).

32 Round Island Lighthouse (Straits of Mackinac)

Before the Round Island Lighthouse was built, ships passing from Lake Superior to Lake Michigan usually took a longer but safer route that passed south of Bois Blanc Island. Recognizing that the shorter route would enable swifter navigation, President Ulysses Grant reserved land on Round Island for a lighthouse in 1874. He realized that a light here would help guide commercial vessels through the shoal-infested waters between Mackinac Island and Round Island as well as guide passenger vessels into the harbor at Mackinac Island, a resort area where booming tourism was attracting wealthy vacationers.

It took a long time to get a lighthouse. In 1891 the U.S. Lighthouse Board began to investigate suitable sites. Locals suggested a spot on Mission Point, Mackinac Island. However, this was now costly resort land, and the site would not serve the total needs for a lighthouse in the area. It took three years to finally decide on the spot that President Grant had originally set aside in 1874.

In 1894 Congress appropriated $15,000. The contract was awarded to local builder Frank Rounds, who began building in 1895, the same year the army closed Fort Mackinac and opened the Mackinac Island State Park. The light was lit on May 15, 1896, using a fourth-order Fresnel lens to produce a white light that flashed red every 20 seconds and was visible for 14.5 miles (23.3 km). A clockwork mechanism operated by weights that had to be wound every two and a half hours was used to turn the red flash panels around the lens. The lighthouse also had a foghorn (blast 5 s; silence 55 s).

This large, totally red brick lighthouse, including red shingles, with its three-story house and four-story tower, 53 feet (16.2 m) high, was an excellent daymark. It was built on a 40-foot (12.2 m) square pier that had been shored up 9 feet (2.7 m) with concrete to withstand the elements. It was constructed using three layers of brick with enclosed dead air space to provide insulation. The first floor housed a boiler room for the fog signal, and a coal bin; the second, the living quarters for the assistant keeper; and the third, the head keeper's residence.

The turnover of keepers and assistants at this light was relatively frequent, probably because of the hardships and the confinement. The first keeper, William Marshall, was a former soldier at Fort Mackinac. The keeper's workload included constant cleaning, polishing, or painting of the buildings and equipment to counteract the effects of the weather. Married keepers' families would join them for the full season or just for the summer. However, keepers always spent the winter at their permanent homes.

Many events occurred over the years at the lighthouse. In 1924 the building was painted red and white and the tower received an automated light, but at least one keeper was kept. In 1938 Round Island, except for the lighthouse and land it stood on, reverted back to the federal government from the state of Michigan and became part of the Marquette National Forest, now known as the Hiawatha National Forest. In 1939, when the U.S. Coast Guard took over from the U.S. Lighthouse Service, the whole lighthouse was whitewashed. In 1947, when a light and radio beacon were built near Mackinac Island's west breakwall, the Coast Guard abandoned the Round Island Lighthouse.

In 1955 the Coast Guard recommended that the lighthouse be demolished but instead it was "excessed" or declared surplus. Three years later, they transferred it to the U.S. Forest Service, and the island was classified as a "National Scenic Area," which qualified it to be preserved in its natural condition. However, as the Forest Service had neither time nor means to keep up the lighthouse, it gradually deteriorated through the work of wind, waves, ice, souvenir collectors and vandals. A severe storm in the fall of 1972 opened a large hole in its southwest corner, making its collapse seem imminent.

Since the Hiawatha National Forest could not fund the work in time to save the lighthouse, local citizens formed the Friends of the Round Island Lighthouse. In 1974 the Mackinac Island Historical Society and the Hiawatha National Forest signed a memorandum of understanding agreeing to partial restoration of the lighthouse. In April 1974 the Forest Service informed interested parties that the lighthouse might have to be destroyed for safety reasons. However, since application had already been made for the lighthouse to be declared an historic site, the Forest Service was told that they had to preserve it until a decision was reached. Then in August 1974 the Round Island Lighthouse was added to the *National Register of Historic Places*.

In the fall of 1974, a youth group visiting the island collected scattered bricks for use in rebuilding. Although the light's future now seemed secure, the Forest Service reiterated that no money was available. In 1975, $125,000 that was appropriated for emergency repairs to the lighthouse was vetoed by President Gerald Ford. As a result, it was funding by the Friends of Round Island Lighthouse that allowed the lighthouse to be stabilized and the hole in the wall to be repaired by November 1975. Finally in 1976 the Forest Service allocated funds for restoration and, along with the locals, strove to save the lighthouse.

It became an ongoing battle. In 1986 record high waters tipped the outhouse to a precarious angle. In 1987 Congress changed Round Island from a National Scenic Area classification to a National Wilderness Area as a classification. In 1995 the Great Lakes Lighthouse Keepers Association and Boy Scout Troop 323 joined the restoration efforts. To celebrate its centennial, celebrations took place on nearby Mackinac Island. Boat cruises toured past Round Island for a closer view of the lighthouse, and the

Forest Service offered guided tours for visitors who could get themselves to the island.

Besides its once-practical use and its historical value, the Round Island Lighthouse has other claims to fame. It was the setting for memorable scenes in the movie *Somewhere in Time* and for a photo shoot for the 1993 *Sports Illustrated* swimsuit issue. In addition, it was relit on a temporary basis as a private aid to navigation for Memorial Day, 1996, for the Centennial, and then was granted approval to run permanently on July 12, 1996. Its flash is once every ten seconds from a 300 mm solar-powered optic. This once abandoned lighthouse continues to flash its relit light today.

Although the outside has been restored to its red and white color scheme of 1924, restoration has been slow and arduous and there is still major work to be done, including interior repairs, protection of the outbuildings, and regular maintenance.

Known Keepers: William Marshall (1896–1907), Jacob Gibbs (1907–11), George Smith (1911–14), C. Richardson (1914–18), James Taylor (1924–27), Charles Henry (1927–38), Bert Proctor (1938–47).

33 Round Island Lighthouse (Lower St. Mary's River)

To assist tricky navigation in the lower St. Mary's River a lighthouse was built on the northeast corner of Round Island in 1892. Round island, a small island of about 10 acres, (4 hectares) was just north of Lime Island in the middle of the passage between the Michigan shore and St. Joseph Island. The square 35-foot (10.7 m) wooden tower was built into the center of the lake-facing side of its 1½-story frame keeper's house. The house had been built on a high brick foundation and a concrete breakwall in front of it near the water's edge protected it against erosion. Both structures were originally painted a buff color with white trim and a red roof.

The tower's black hexagonal iron lantern displayed both white and red lights. Using a lens lantern with a 40-foot (12.2 m) focal plane, its white light was visible for 4 miles (6.5 km) through a 180 degree arc of illumination over the shipping channel. This white light was bounded radially by two red sectors. The southerly red sector warned mariners of the shoals that extended south and west of the island. Its northerly red sector marked a turning point in the river. The lights were first lit on September 20, 1892.

The tower light was deactivated in 1923 when an automated light was placed on a skeletal steel tower nearby. This reduced its focal plane to 29 feet (8.9 m). Shortly after its automation, the Lighthouse Board sold the island, except 20 by 40 feet (6 by 12 m) around the active light, into private ownership. For many years its

Round Island Lighthouse, circa 1923

owners only used it briefly during the summer as a camp. Receiving little to no upkeep the buildings gradually deteriorated.

In 1999 a Charlevoix businessman and his wife bought the island. Over a three-year period and many dollars later, they have refurbished and expanded the old light station. They ran a submarine power cable from the mainland to the island for electricity and installed water treatment equipment and a sewage system. While maintaining the original basics of the lighthouse they updated it with large windows, indoor plumbing and a new kitchen. They also added additional living space, but at the back of the house so as to retain most of the lighthouse's original appearance.

A light continues to shine from this location today but it is now displayed from a modern pole placed close to its old pole and uses a modern solar-powered acrylic optic.

Round Island Lighthouse

34   Round Island Passage Light

This light was established in 1948, the year after the Round Island Light (Straits of Mackinac) was discontinued. It stands close to Mackinac Island to assist mariners through the narrow channel. It is an octagonal 60-foot (18.3 m) reinforced concrete tower that rests on a concrete pier over a sunken wooden crib. The corners of the pier have large triangular downward slopes to deflect ice and waves. The structure is completely white except for a square red section at the tower base. The lanternless tower has narrow rectangular horizontally placed windows near the top, and used to have a sealed beam optic to display its light from a 71-foot (21.6 m) focal plane. It also had a foghorn and a radio beacon. It was automated in 1973 and today uses a 190 mm optic to help guide mariners through the passage.

35   Saginaw Bay Lighthouse

As early as 1835, citizens of Lower Saginaw petitioned for a lighthouse at the mouth of the Saginaw River in Lake Huron to assist the growing lake commerce of lumber and other exports. However, their petitions were not acted upon until Congress received a presidential directive in February 1839 to purchase land at that location from the Chippewa. In February 1839 Congress appropriated $5,000 to build the lighthouse, and 40 acres (16.2 hectares) of land was purchased on the west side of the river. Stephen Wolverton arrived in July to build the lighthouse, but Captain Levi Johnson of Cleveland, Ohio, finished the job.

The station was built on the west side of the river mouth into Saginaw Bay. It consisted of a two-story keeper's house with two rooms up and down, and had a separate 65-foot (20 m) tower equipped with eleven Winslow Lewis lamps, each with a 14-inch (35 cm) reflector. By 1848, as a cost-saving measure, the number of lamps and reflectors was reduced to seven.

Round Island Passage Light

Saginaw River Rear Range Lighthouse

Saginaw River Rear Range Lighthouse

In 1851 Congress appropriated $10,000 for harbor improvements. In 1856 the lantern was outfitted with a sixth-order Fresnel lens, and in 1863 the lens was upgraded to a fourth-order one for increased visibility from its 72-foot (22 m) focal plane. This lens had formerly been used at Fort Gratiot and was removed from that station in 1861 when it was upgraded to a third-order Fresnel lens. In 1857 Lower Saginaw had its name officially changed to the more distinctive Bay City to eliminate confusion with other places using Saginaw in their name.

The Saginaw Bay light's best-known keepers were the Brawns. Peter Brawn was appointed in 1864, but soon suffered a crippling injury. His wife, Julia, assumed his duties until he died in 1873, at which time she was officially appointed keeper. During her tenure, their 15-year-old son, Dewitt, devised the first range light system. He loved watching the ships in the bay each morning waiting to get into the river to load and unload their cargo. Dewitt invented a way to help them navigate the tricky shallow waters so that they could reach the docks at night. He built a wooden platform above the water near the river mouth and every night lit two lanterns suspended at two different heights, with one behind the other.

Ship captains soon realized that these two new lights could guide them safely into the harbor. Since time was money, the mariners paid Dewitt $50 a month for his invention and his work. These lights were less powerful than the main light, having only a 5-mile (8 km) visibility, so the main light drew the vessels into the bay and the weaker lights guided them into the docks. In 1876, realizing the value of Dewitt's lights, the government replaced them with towers, one of which was the river's rear range light and keeper's new quarters.

Known Keepers: William Harvey (1841–43), J. Malden (1843–45), F. Simpson (1845–49), William Pomeroy (1849–53), James Terry (1853–54), Levi Clark (1854–59), John Sharpe (1859–66), Peter Brawn (1866–73), Mrs. Julia Brawn (1873–77).

36 Saginaw River Range Lights

After the U.S. Corps of Army Engineers dredged a wider, deeper channel through the bar at the mouth of the Saginaw River, the old lighthouse was no longer properly placed to mark the harbor entry, so the Lighthouse Board requested an appropriation of $12,000 to build a set of range lights designed according to Dewitt Brawn's system (see Saginaw Bay Lighthouse). After delays and a necessarily revised Congressional appropriation of $23,000, clear title of the required land was finally obtained in 1876. Both range lights were built that year.

The front range light, located just off the west riverbank, was basic and utilitarian. It consisted of a square open framework pyramidal tower 34 feet (10.4 m) tall, built on a square timber crib. Its upper portion was enclosed to offer the keeper protection from the elements, as well as a small storage area. Its octagonal cast-iron lantern housed a sixth-order Fresnel lens that displayed a fixed white light from a 37-foot (11.3 m) focal plane for about 8.5 miles (13.7 km). It was painted white for best visibility.

The site chosen for the rear range light was also on the west side of the Saginaw River but about two-thirds of a mile (1 km) from the river mouth and 2,230 feet (680 m) behind the front light. Since the rear light was situated in the marshy shores of the river, it needed a different building style. From architectural plans, one can count over 140 pilings, which were driven deep into the swampy shore. A wide platform placed on them created a base for the 53-foot (16 m) square and slightly tapering tower, which was built into one corner of the two-story Cream City brick house. The front face of the tower had four large house-size windows to light the landings and stairwell, and a circular iron staircase provided access to the lantern and all levels of the house. The tower supported a decagonal cast-iron lantern that housed a fourth-order Fresnel lens with four blacked-out sides. The light had a focal plane of 61 feet (18.6 m).

The cellar of the house, built at ground level, had two rooms, one of which had a brick-look finish and was later used as a recreation room. The main floor kitchen had a walk-in pantry, parlor, large front hallway, oil room, and access to the woodshed and the tower. The second floor had three bedrooms and also had access to the tower. A wooden deck wrapped completely around the main level and provided space under it for boat storage. The whole structure looked somewhat bleak as it rose tall and stark from its surroundings, its only ornamentation being five carved braces under each side of the gallery around the tower and decorative arches around the top of the house chimney.

With the completion of the new range lights, Julia Brawn-Way, with her son, Dewitt, and her new husband, George Way, moved into the new keeper's dwelling at the rear range light. She first lit the range lights on September 15, 1876. Since the old Saginaw Bay Lighthouse was no longer needed, the tower was torn down to prevent confusion with the new range lights. The old keeper's house was left standing as a possible home for an assistant keeper. In September 1877 George Way became keeper and Julia was demoted to assistant. They kept the lights until 1882, when the assistant keeper's position was abolished and George became keeper of both lights. When George died in February 1883, Julia for some reason disappeared from the lighthouse service, and the keeper's roster again indicated an assistant keeper. Later, the assistant kept the front range light and lived in the old brick dwelling that originally served the old Saginaw Bay Light, while the head keeper kept the rear range light and lived in the dwelling attached to it.

Saginaw River Front Range Light, circa 1914

Changes occurred over the years. As Bay City grew, its lights became confused with the rear range light, so the rear light was changed to a fixed red light on June 15, 1891 by placing a red glass chimney over the lamp. In 1886 the front range light's crib was replaced and a 625-foot (190 m) raised plank walkway was built over the swampy ground between the range lights. In 1898 the tower of the rear range light was painted white. Also in 1898 excess land from the old Saginaw Bay Lighthouse reservation was sold at auction for $1,500. In 1901 the west wall of the assistant keeper's dwelling was replaced to prevent moisture seepage, its grounds were regraded and a plank walkway was built from the house to the front light. Further repairs included spreading Portland cement over the entire brick surface to protect it. In 1905 a new two-story assistant keeper's house was built. In 1905–06 the concrete foundation of the rear range light was replaced because of moisture damage. In 1915 a concrete pier replaced the timber crib for the front light and its wooden tower was replaced with a black pyramidal skeleton steel tower with an elliptical white slatted daymark.

Also at this time both range lights were electrified using power from Bay City. The kerosene lamps were replaced with 100-watt incandescent electric lamps equipped with automatic bulb changers. The front range light's sixth-order Fresnel lens was replaced with a 300 mm lens at a 39-foot (12 m) focal plane. With the

reduced workload that electrification brought, the position of the assistant keeper was again eliminated. In 1930 the fourth-order Fresnel lens was removed from the rear light and replaced with a modern apparatus. In 1954 it was changed again, this time to an electrically powered locomotive reflector of 45,000 candlepower that could be seen for 15 miles (24 km) on a clear night.

By 1962 another new channel had been dug from the bay into the river mouth to allow longer freighters into the river. The old rear range light, now obsolete, was discontinued, while the front range light was renamed as a Leading Light. Then, between 1967 and 1971, this Leading Light was discontinued and torn down after the Saginaw Bay Channel Range Lights — modern beacons on steel towers — were established.

The old rear range lighthouse is said to be haunted — was it by a keeper who died at the lighthouse and told his family to keep the light burning and keep a never-ending watch over "his" lighthouse? This fits the description of Peter Brawn, whose wife and son kept the light after him. In 1939, when the Coast Guard took over the Lighthouse Service, loud, echoing footsteps could be heard climbing the circular iron stairway, but when the stairwell was checked, it was always empty. Again, after the light had been deactivated in 1962 but was still used by the U.S. Coast Guard, two guardsmen who were standing a late watch experienced a strange incident. While one dozed, his partner heard pounding footsteps resounding inside the locked tower. He quickly wakened the sleeper, and they both stood listening to heavy footsteps ascend the tower. Then the footsteps stopped as suddenly and inexplicably as they had started.

In 1980 the Coast Guard moved into a newly built station across the river. (Was it to get away from the ghostly sounds?) In 1984 the rear range light was added to the *Federal Register of Historical Places*. The old building was purchased in 1987 for use as a retirement home, but when the Dow Chemical Company refused to grant easement across their land surrounding the lighthouse, the private owner sold the structure and its land-locked property to Dow in 1989 for $100,000. After boarding up the lighthouse to prevent vandalism and more decay, Dow made a study to predict restoration costs.

In the fall of 1999 the Saginaw River Maritime Historical Society (SRMHS) approached Dow Chemical to see if they could help with restoration of the rear range light. This meeting led to a merger of resources. The SRMHS would guide the restoration and provide labor while Dow supplied much of the needed funding. Even local school children have raised money through a school program to help with the restoration of "their" lighthouse. This involvement has become a true community project, with heightened awareness of the local lighthouse. Although it is not yet open to the public, its restoration team envisions a marine museum and possibly a research library in the keeper's quarters, and a maritime park around the structure.

Known Keepers: Julia Brown-Way (1876–1877), George Way (1877–33), Edward Buzzard (1884–86), William Munshaw (1886–88), George Decker (1888–96), Frederick Beland (1896–1900), William Burke (1900–39), George Schinderette (1939).

Spectacle Reef Lighthouse

37 Spectacle Reef Lighthouse

Spectacle Reef, off the east end of the Straits of Mackinac and about 11 miles (17.7 km) east of Bois Blanc Island in northern Lake Huron, is so named because its two limestone shoals resembled spectacles on navigation charts. The least depth of water over the shoal is 7 feet (2.1 m), making it a serious hazard.

In the 1860s and 1870s trade between Cheboygan, on northern Lake Huron, and the Sault flourished. Spectacle Reef lay in a direct line with this marine traffic route. Although several vessels had been lost on the reef, it was not until the loss of two schooners in 1867 that the Lighthouse Board petitioned Congress to mark the reef. While the lighthouse construction was estimated at an exorbitant $300,000, the cargo of the two lost schooners had been worth more, so the lighthouse was considered a good investment. Congress appropriated $100,000 to start the work in 1869 and the same amount for the next two years.

Major Orlando M. Poe of the U.S. Army Corps of Engineers was chosen to design the lighthouse for this reef, a task considered almost impossible for 1869. With the help of fellow Corps staff, W.F. Raynolds (who designed the crib and the cofferdam), a lighthouse was planned. Their chief challenge was to create a structure in open water to withstand the winter ice and the pounding of massive spring ice floes. After a site examination, a site was chosen on the south end of the most northerly shoal. This spot, located in about 11 feet (3.4 m) of water, was covered with the hull of the wrecked schooner *Nightingale* and much of its iron ore cargo, so the debris first had to be cleared.

While this water work was underway, the crib was being constructed at Scammon's Harbor, 16 miles (26 km) northwest of the reef on Government Island. In 1870, after the first two courses of the 92-foot (28 m) square crib were built, it was floated to the site and anchored to a temporary

Spectacle Reef Lighthouse with Tender Marigold, *circa 1915*

pier made of four cribs connected together and decked over to provide protection along the east side of the site. Soundings were then made at 2-foot (0.6 m) intervals along the bottom of the floating raft to obtain accurate contours of the uneven surface of the reef. The raft was then towed back to Scammon's Harbor, hauled out of the water, and its bottom made to conform to the surface of the reef by using wedges of timber. The next summer, after the crib was built up to 12 feet (3.6 m) high, it was floated back to the site, positioned and sunk, using about 1,800 tons of rock to fill its predesigned compartments. The crib stretched over about a quarter of an acre (0.1 hectare).

The next two months were spent building the stone pier on top of the crib to 12 feet above the water. With this complete, the cofferdam, which had been built at the Detroit Depot, was placed inside. It was a hollow cylinder built to 41 feet (12.5 m) in diameter using vertical wooden staves. Braced and trussed internally, it was also hooped with iron rings externally to provide the necessary strength. Once it was lowered into position, the staves were driven down to fit as closely as possible to the irregular rock surface. A diver then filled openings between the rock and the staves with Portland cement, a new invention in 1871, thus making its use at Spectacle Reef Lighthouse one of the first. When waterproofing was complete, the water was pumped out of the cofferdam and the bedrock was leveled with hand tools to prepare for the stonework. Pumps kept the internal area dry from seepage through rock seams.

While the stone lighthouse was originally to have been granite, the contractor was unable to supply it, so limestone from Marblehead, Ohio, was used instead. The bottom 17 courses of the tower were made of solid interlocking stone. The first course was the most important and was bolted to the rock reef with bolts 3 feet (0.9 m) long and anchored 21 inches (0.5 m) into the rock. It was completed by late October, when work halted for the winter. Subsequent courses were bolted together with wrought-iron bolts 2 feet (0.6 m) long and 2.5 inches (6.3 cm) in diameter, and all bolt holes were solidly filled with Portland cement mortar, which became as strong or stronger than the rock of the shoal. After the first course above the solid portion, no more bolts were used.

A vicious September storm hampered work. It destroyed the workmen's quarters, knocked the temporary lens askew, swept away the temporary cribs, and repositioned their revolving derrick from the northeast to the southwest corner of the pier. The only shelter the men found from the devastating storm was on the west side of the tower. When the storm ceased and repairs were made, work resumed.

By the end of the 1872 season the solid courses of the lighthouse had been laid. Before the crew left for the winter they removed the lens and lamp from the temporary light for safe storage. Upon their return in the spring they discovered that the lantern and workmen's quarters had been carried away by the ice, so they were glad the lens and lamps were safe.

The rest of the lighthouse was built in 1873–74. The conical tower had a base diameter of 32 feet (9.7 m) and a top diameter of 18 feet (5.5 m). The bottom 34 feet (10.4 m) of the tower were solid, and the top five stories were hollow, each having one room 14 feet (4.2 m) in diameter. The walls tapered from about 5.5 feet (1.6 m) thick to 1.5 feet (0.5 m) by the fifth story. The brick lining was 4 inches (10 cm) thick and was separated from the stone by a 2-inch (5 cm) air space.

The 93-foot (28.3 m) tower was capped with an iron lantern that housed a second-order Fresnel lens. It displayed alternate flashes of red and white light at 30-second intervals. From its focal plane of 86 feet (26.2 m) it was visible for 16.5 miles (26.5 km) and was first exhibited on June 1, 1874.

In 1883 keeper William Marshal was very eager to get to Spectacle Reef and light it for the opening of the navigation season. When his hired steamboat was out of commission to take him and his assistants there, he acquired a small sailboat, packed it up and headed out in spite of signs of a storm. The storm overturned the boat near Bois Blanc Island and its anchor snagged on the lake bottom. After clinging to the boat for hours the men caught the attention of the Bois Blanc lightkeeper. A fishermen who set out in his small craft to rescue the shipwrecked men had his boat overturned also. Eventually everyone was saved except Marshall's son. In his eagerness to get to the light, Marshall actually started the season late that year and it cost him the death of his son.

When the first keepers arrived at the station in May, ice was piled up over 30 feet (9 m) high around the tower, several feet above the tower entrance. They spent many hours cutting away the ice to get into the tower and display the light.

The total construction cost came in higher than estimated — an unprecedented $406,000. However, the Lighthouse Board was most pleased with their accomplishment and even featured a model of the new light as part of the Aids to Navigation display at the 1893 World's Columbian Exhibition in Chicago.

The lighthouse witnessed tragedy in February 1959. While flying to a new posting, Master Sergeant Frank Wyman's small plane went down about a mile from the lighthouse. He reached it safely and got inside to get dry and warm, but was unable to signal for help. Not having filed a flight plan and having no food, he borrowed supplies and headed across the ice on foot to Bois Blanc Island 11 miles (17.8 km) away. He was never seen again. However, this incident did result in lighthouses being supplied with clothing and non-perishable food during the winter months in case of future emergencies.

Almost a century after being built, the lighthouse was automated in 1972. The keepers were removed and solar panels were installed to power the light. Then in 1973 the Coast Guard declared the second-order Fresnel lens to be excess. The Great Lakes Historical Society raised money to save it. Thanks to their efforts, the huge lens was dismantled, packed into 44 crates, and taken to the Great Lakes Historical Museum in Vermillion, where it was reassembled and is on display today.

In 1995 the lighthouse was one of the five honored by being selected for placement on a commemorative American postage stamp. The original 1869 architectural design for Spectacle Reef lighthouse has also been saved. Hand-drawn and colored on linen drafting cloth, it is one of few such lighthouse drawings to have survived, and can be seen at the Michigan Maritime Museum in South Haven, Michigan.

Today the light continues to flash alternate white and red every 60 seconds but from a modern optic that is solar-powered. Its red light has 80,000 candlepower and its white light has 400,000 candlepower to produce a beacon visible for about 17 miles (27 km). In the winter a new 100-candlepower white light flashes every five seconds. The station also has an air-diaphone fog signal. This light has withstood the test of time and is still considered one of the best monolithic stone masonry constructions ever built.

Known Keepers: Patrick McCann (1874–80), Allen Hulbert (1880–81), William Marshall (1881–96), Frank Bogan (1896), Samuel Roberts (1896–98), Walter Marshall (1898–1910), Edwin Bishop (1910–13), Joseph Metivier (1913–14), George Smith (1914–33), Stanley Clark (1933–34), Wilbert Beloungea (1934–45), Thomas Brander (1945–55).

38 Sturgeon Point Lighthouse

In the mid-nineteenth century two fishermen bought some land and water rights along the west side of Lake Huron. It became known as Davidson's Mill. They sold out to the Harris family, and by 1850 the name had changed to Harrisville. As the population grew and lake traffic increased, a lighthouse was thought necessary at Sturgeon Point, about 4 miles (6.4 km) north of Harrisville, to mark a reef that reaches 1.5 miles (2.4 km) into the lake. Congress appropriated $15,000 in 1868, and land at the point was purchased from John Sabin. The light was built and finished by November 1869, but the late arrival of new keeper Perley Silverthorn made the government postpone the first lighting until the 1870 navigation season.

The conical yellow brick tower rose from a limestone foundation 7.5 feet (2.3 m) high, which was constructed from 4 feet (1.2 m) below ground level. The base was 16 feet (4.8 m) in diameter with walls 4½ feet (1.4 m) thick, and the top was 10 feet (3 m) in diameter with walls 1½ feet (0.5 m) thick. Eighty-four

Sturgeon Point Lighthouse in full sun

Sturgeon Point Lighthouse at dusk

open-grate cast-iron stairs led up to the decagonal lantern, which was topped by a red decagonal dome and a ventilator ball, making the tower 70 feet 9 inches (21.5 m) tall. The tower interior was originally plastered and painted yellow but was later changed to white, perhaps to match the outside of the tower.

The tower lantern was to have originally used a sixth-order Fresnel lens, but in 1869, the year it was completed, it received a 3 1/2-order Fresnel lens that came from the lighthouse in Oswego, New York. Bolted to the lantern floor, it displayed a fixed white light that burned kerosene through a double-wick system. The light was visible for about 16 miles (25 km). In 1892 a separate oil storage shed was built to store the volatile kerosene.

The keeper's house, also made of brick and painted white, had an 11-foot (3.4 m) covered passageway connecting it to the tower to protect the keeper in foul weather. There were only a few keepers at this light. In 1885 the keeper earned $540 a year.

In 1876 the Sturgeon Bay Life Saving Station was added to the point. Volunteer crews operated it at first, remaining on duty until mid-December, when all navigation stopped for the season. The U.S. Coast Guard stationed regular crews at Sturgeon Point after World War I until 1941, when the station was closed.

High lake waters coming to within 40 feet (12.2 m) of the tower in 1886 prompted the government to build five rock-filled cribs into the lake and a 56-foot (17 m) breakwater of driftwood logs along the shoreline. Then in 1889 they built two 60-foot (18.3 m) jetties to further protect the shoreline. Although only remnants of them remain today, these protective constructions served well, keeping the lighthouse from being washed into the lake for more than 100 years.

In 1913 the Lighthouse Service changed the light to acetylene and its characteristic changed to a flashing white light every three seconds. The light used an automated sun valve, and a keeper was no longer necessary. However, the captain of the lifesaving station was given charge of the lighthouse at this time and this senior officer lived with his family in the keeper's house. In 1936 electricity was brought to Sturgeon Point, and in 1939 it was run out to the lighthouse so that the lens could use an incandescent bulb.

When the lifesaving station was closed in 1941, most of the buildings were torn down or vandalized until only the tower and keeper's house remained. They sat empty and unused for many years. In 1961 the U.S. government deeded the Sturgeon Point property to the State of Michigan, except for the tower, which remained under the U.S. Coast Guard, who maintain its active light.

In 1982 Michigan's Department of Natural Resources leased the house and the grounds to the Alcona Historical Society. They have restored the lighthouse and added a small gift shop. The downstairs rooms are refurbished as the keeper's house would have been at the turn of the century, the light's most active period. All items for this purpose were donated. The four upstairs rooms are a maritime museum for ice harvesting, fishing, lake navigation and lake recreational activities. The Sturgeon Point Light Station has been listed on both the *National Register of Historic Places* and the state register (1969).

Known Keepers: Perley Silverthorn (1869–76), John Pasque (1877–81), Louis Cardy (1881–1913), Archibald Davidson (1930–34), George Elmer (1934–41).

Tawas Point Lighthouse

39 Tawas Point Lighthouse

Tawas Point, known as Ottawa Point in the 1800s, marks the northern entry into Saginaw Bay on the west coast of Lake Huron. This point is a hook-shaped peninsula that protects Tawas Bay, making it a natural harbor for vessels seeking refuge from Lake Huron squalls. After a schooner ran aground on the point in the early 1850s, public demand convinced Congress to mark the peninsula and shoals off its point by appropriating money to build a lighthouse. The light, built in 1852–53, was placed at the tip of the peninsula.

The point is continually changing from the shifting of sand from the lakebed and shoreline during storms. As a result, 20 years after the light was built, it sat about three quarters of a mile (1.2 km) from the point's actual tip, making it unhelpful in accurately marking the hazardous spot. This, coupled with the light's dimness, caused the grounding of the schooner *Dolphin*. The captain openly blamed the poor light. More public indignation led Congress to appropriate $30,000 to build another light at the new tip of the point. When the new light was finished in 1876, old light was torn down to prevent visual confusion.

The new 67-foot (20 m) conical tower was made of double brick. It tapered from a 16-foot (4.8 m) diameter at its base to a diameter of 9½ feet (2.9 m) at its top. The base walls were built 6 feet (1.8 m) thick to withstand severe weather. The red brick of the tower was painted white for better visibility. A circular iron staircase led up inside the tower to a decagonal lantern which, along with the dome, gallery and ornamental braces, was painted black. The lantern housed a fourth-order Fresnel lens by Barbier and Fenestre of Paris. It had a focal plane of 70 feet (21.3 m) and a visibility of 16 miles (25.7 km).

The 1½-story keeper's house, also made of red brick, was attached to the tower by an enclosed passageway so that the keeper had easier access to the tower in rough weather. The passageway was also useful in transporting the oil for the lens, as it helped prevent the oil from cooling, which would make it harder to ignite.

While there were numerous keepers at this station, an assistant was added only in 1900. By 1909 the light was busy enough to have a second assistant. At this time a duplex was built beside the main keeper's house for the two assistants.

Lorraine A. Marsh, the daughter of the second assistant keeper, Samuel A. Anderson, who was stationed at Tawas Point from 1939 to 1941, was five to eight years old during her father's tenure. Although she doesn't recall the workings of the light, she remembers living on the second floor of the wooden duplex and her excitement when she was allowed to visit the lantern with her father. She loved to wade in the shallow water and she once got caught in quicksand, which abounded in the area, and was "goggle-eyed" until she was rescued. She also remembers the area being swampy and having an abundance of poison ivy and rattlesnakes.

In 1984 the Tawas Point Lighthouse was added to the *National Register for Historic Places*. Today it is part of the Tawas State Park. The light is still operational and still uses the Fresnel lens. However, an electric motor now turns the lens instead of a clockwork mechanism, and the illuminant is a 200,000 candlepower lightbulb. Its white light, oscillating at four-second intervals has a visibility of about 16-miles (25.7 km). Since the station is still owned and operated by the U.S. Coast Guard, access to the tower is limited. The Coast Guard used to use the keeper's house, but it now sits empty due to its hazardous asbestos insulation and lead paint. Perhaps it will one day be refurbished so that it can be opened to the public.

Known Keepers: Sherman Wheeler (1853–57), John Oliver (1857–61), Joshua Sadler (1861–76), James Harald (1876–80), George Haskin (1880–82), B. Jones (1882–85), Frank Palmer (1885–87), Samuel Palmer (1887–1910), James Brown (1910), Herbert Burrows (1910–14), Oliver St. André (1914–15), unknown (1915–23), John Brooks (1923–28) and Louis Dissett (1928–40).

40 Thunder Bay Island Lighthouse

Thunder Bay Island is a large limestone island that marks the outer edge of a group of islands strung out from and connected to the mainland by a shallow rocky shoal. Located about 3 miles (5 km) northeast of Thunder Bay's northern point and 13 miles (21 km) from Alpena, the island lay directly in the path of vessels traveling from lower Lake Huron to Lake Superior. Mariners nicknamed this major turning point "Shipwreck Alley" because of the many wrecks on its shoals, and called for the island to be lit. Congress appropriated $5,000 for a lighthouse on outer Thunder Bay Island in Lake Huron in December 1830.

The contract for the lighthouse construction went to Jeremiah Moors, a Detroit builder. To make the project cost-effective he used readily available materials — in this case, island limestone rubble — to build both the tower and the keeper's house. The conical tower was 40 feet (12.2 m) high with a base diameter of 21 feet (6.4 m) and a top diameter of 11 feet 4 inches (3.4 m). It was probably capped with a birdcage-style lantern that used an arrangement of Winslow Lewis lamps and reflectors typical of early lighthouses. The house was a detached 1½-story dwelling. The light was first lit in the spring of 1832.

Thunder Bay Island Lighthouse

By 1834 lighthouse reports showed the keeper seeking government reimbursement for personal money that he spent to repair the crumbling tower on their behalf, but the request fell on deaf ears. In Lt. James T. Homans' 1838 annual lighthouse report to Congress, he also mentions the poor state of the tower and recommends protection against the lake's waters lest the tower be undermined. His suggestion of $800 for stone-filled cribs onshore in front of the lighthouse was acted upon, and the lighthouse still stands.

Repairs and improvements were made as needed. In 1853, $2,500 was appropriated for a state-of-the-art mechanical fog bell that rang automatically once started. It was installed in 1855. During the 1850s, with increased marine traffic, the Lighthouse Board decided to heighten the tower and update it with a Fresnel lens. In 1857 the top 14 feet (4.2 m) of the tower was sheathed in brick, which continued above the old tower for another 10 feet (3 m), thus raising the tower height to 50 feet (15.2 m). The whole tower exterior was then reinforced using Cream City brick, making the base walls 6²/₃ feet (2 m) thick and the upper walls 1²/₃ feet (0.5 m) thick. The extended tower supported a decagonal cast-iron lantern that housed a fourth-order Fresnel lens from the Louis Sautter Company of Paris. The lens had six bull's-eye flash panels and a clockwork mechanism that made it rotate around its kerosene lamp to produce a fixed white light varied by flashes. From its 59-foot (18 m) focal plane the light was visible for 14 miles (22.5 km).

Over the years the rubble-stone house kept deteriorating and in 1866 the Lighthouse Board recommended an appropriation of $8,000 to rebuild it. Thus, in 1868 the old house was razed and a new two-story brick house with a hipped roof was built and connected to the tower by an enclosed brick passageway.

In 1870 the fog bell was replaced with duplicate steam whistles, which were louder and carried farther in the fog. A wood frame fog building was constructed in 1871 and it was covered with iron sheeting both inside and out. Locomotive-type boilers powered the 10-inch (25 cm) whistles. The fog signal characteristic was a one minute cycle (blast 8 s; silence 10 s; blast 2 s; silence 40 s).

One whistle was fired whenever visibility was low, in fog, snow squalls or forest fire smoke.

More improvements were introduced as needed. In 1906 the old fog signal building was replaced with a red brick one. In 1907 concrete walkways were laid between the buildings, and the station's wooden underground cistern was replaced with a concrete one to collect rooftop rainwater. In 1913 the lantern lamp was upgraded to an incandescent oil vapor lamp of 5,600 candlepower, increasing the light's visibility to 19 miles (30.5 km). The light's characteristic was also changed to flashing every 30 seconds. In 1921 Type C diaphone fog signals replaced the steam whistle, and the fog characteristic was changed to a 30-second cycle (blast 2 s; silence 2 s; blast 2 s; silence 24 s). In 1932 the Type C horns were upgraded to the more powerful Type F ones. In 1938 the tower's exterior was covered with Portland cement and painted white to help protect it against the elements. Then in 1983 the light was automated with the removal of the Fresnel lens and the installation of a 190 mm solar-powered optic.

With its keepers gone, the abandoned buildings fell victim to the elements and some vandalism. In the 1990s the Thunder Bay Island Preservation Society was formed with the goal of saving and refurbishing the station. In 1997 they signed a ten-year lease with the U.S. Coast Guard allowing them to take responsibility for the station's buildings and grounds. The lease was later extended to 2027. Since signing, the group has refurbished the keeper's house and cleared away brush. They are presently repairing cracks in the outer stucco surface of the tower before chunks begin to fall. With the Society's conscientious adoption of this lighthouse, its future well-being now seems secure.

Known Keepers: Joseph Duchene (1832–32), Jesse Muncey (1832–43), Terry Williams (1843–45), J. Madlen (1845–60), Daniel Carter (1860–61), A. Persons (1861–73), Patrick McGiure (1875–82), John Sinclair Jr. (1882–94), Michael Cooney (1894–1901), William Bennetts (1902–19), Paul Klebba (1919–28), Archebald Davidson (1929–30), William De Rusha (1932–39), Mathew Storback (1939–40).

LAKE HURON
CANADA
LIGHTHOUSES

CANADA

■ Sudbury

91
69 2 87   Bruce Mines
67 66 40 79
77 78

47   3 13 50   Killarney
9   31 36 76   French River
29   1 32   18
48   5
                    19   Bying Inlet
Manitoulin   6   Pointe au Baril
Island   39   59
26   64   37   Georgian   54
44 71   Bay   70   16
                65   Parry Sound
15 17   7   30 74   25
82   88   21
56   89 28 20 4 83
Lake   35   8   45 84 86
38 75   27   12 55 85
Huron   90   46 62
63   42 80 52
53   43 81 51 49
10 68   14
11 41 73   Collingwood
60 61 72   Southampton
McNab Point   ONTARIO
34   Kincardine
57   Point Clark

Mackinaw
City
Forty Mile
Presque Isle
Alpena
MICHIGAN
Sturgeon Point
Tawas Point

Harbor Beach
22-24   Goderich

Bay City
Port Sanilac

UNITED STATES

Fort Gratiot   58
Port Huron   92 Sarnia

Badgeley Island Lighthouse, circa 1978

1 Badgeley Island Lighthouse

Badgeley Island is a small island only 3½ miles (5.2 km) long and 1½ miles (2 km) wide in Georgian Bay. In 1885 it was chosen as a site for one of the eleven "imperial towers"; however, because of the excessive cost of the first six towers, the last five, which included Badgeley Island, were not constructed. Although the island had been recognized early as a strategic spot to light to help marine navigation through the North Channel's east end between Manitoulin Island and the mainland, it was not lit until 1912, when it received two much less expensive range lights. These lights also helped local lumber and fishing traffic between Killarney and Little Current. The rear light was built on a high, southeastern point of the island.

The 51-foot (15.5 m) tower was a square, skeletal tower with a white, boarded, framed-in section at the top. It was 69 feet (21 m) above the water and in 1912 its octagonal lantern displayed a fixed white light with a 13-mile (21km) visibility. The front range light was built on a southern point of the island near the water. It rose up through the center of the roof of the large, square, white clapboard, two-story "plain-Jane" keeper's house. An iron railing surrounded the square gallery. The square lantern had four large rectangular glass panels and was topped with a dome and a ventilator stack. The lantern displayed a fixed white catoptric light with a 10-mile (16 km) visibility. Both lights first burned kerosene and were later switched to electricity.

The station also included a boat dock in a small, protected bay. The third keeper, Frank Fowler, built a sawmill on the island to supplement his income. It produced board lumber and wooden fish crates, both high-demand items in the area, and did well until it was destroyed by fire. Frank Sinclair, the fourth keeper, had a horse and he used the manure to fertilize a garden that he kept in the rocks by the dock.

In the fall of 1946 Ferdinand "Ferdy" Solomon became keeper. He finished this season alone, but the next spring he took his wife, Merle, to her new home. In a personal interview, Merle described the journey as a harrowing sleigh ride across the slush-topped ice. When she first saw the lighthouse she described it as "a haunted house on an iceberg." But after the first year, she loved it because of its solitude.

Keeper F.J. Solomon

One night in 1949 their solitude was interrupted by the lake freighter *Burlington*, which grounded on the shore of Badgeley Island. It scraped right up on the limestone rock on which the lighthouse was built, and stopped with a sound "like an ear-splitting earthquake" a mere 50 feet (15 m) from the house. Ferdy cried out, "My God, Merle, we've got a boat on our veranda!" The stunned keeper immediately checked to make sure his lights were burning because the range lights had never failed before in guiding vessels safely. They were operating just fine. Apparently the captain of the vessel had turned his ship too soon to line up with the range lights.

The station had a hand-operated foghorn, a wooden box that the operator straddled. It had a leather handle and a paddle that was pushed back and forth to compress the bellows. Merle knew nothing about lighthouse tending but she helped out when she could. Once, when it had been foggy for a couple of days and they were running low on groceries, Ferdy boated in the fog to Killarney for supplies. In his absence Merle heard a ship's signal, so she grabbed the foghorn and answered it. The ship kept signaling and she kept replying. Even when the kids were hungry she sent them to fend for themselves while she stayed at her post. When Ferdy returned she was still answering the ship's signal — and getting more and more blisters on her hands. Upon learning that the boat was anchored and was signaling so that no other vessel would collide with *it* in the fog and that she did not have to reply, she felt somewhat foolish. But when the fog lifted and the vessel left, it blew one last signal to salute her for her valiant effort.

The Solomons also experienced personal tragedy at the light. Merle told us how their two-year-old son had fallen into deep water while jumping from the dock to the boat, and drowned. The island then being too strong a reminder of their son's death, Ferdy applied for and received a transfer to another light.

In 1965, when the lights were automated, the rear range light was changed to a flashing white light and given a fourth-order dioptric lighting system (flash 0.5 s, eclipse 3.5 s). It also became the Killarney keeper's duty to check the range lights periodically.

The freighter Burlington *grounded on Badgeley Island, circa 1949*

Badgeley Island Rear Range Light

Bamford Island Lighthouse, circa 1917

It was in the late 1970s that Larry Wright photographed this light for the first time. It was the second lighthouse he had ever photographed. He and a photographer friend, Budd Watson, were on a photographic adventure out of Killarney amongst the islands and pulled up to the Badgeley Island dock to walk to the lighthouse. He remembers it being slightly overgrown and surrounded by wild daisies. He and Watson sat in the screened-in front porch to escape the flies while they ate their lunch. After they shot the lighthouse, they continued on their way.

About ten years later Wright went back to rephotograph the lighthouse, only to discover that it was no longer there! He discovered that the Canadian Coast Guard had blown it up in 1981 to reduce its upkeep and liability — but they had to wait until a Sunday because the dynamite expert they had hired worked for the Badgeley mine and was only free on Sundays. Wright was most disappointed with the 39-foot (12 m) square, white skeletal tower with white daymark that had been built to replace the original range tower. This destruction of a part of Canada's heritage planted the first seed in his mind to do something to record the history of the lights before it was too late. One of the results is this book.

Although the keeper's house is gone, the new range lights still operate today to assist mariners passing in the area. Their white daymark is now made more visible by an orange vertical stripe.

Known Keepers: Patrick Proulx (1912–16), David Mountnay (1919), Frank Fowler (1921–37), F.J. Sinclair (1937–46), F.J. Solomon (1946–50), F.J. Sinclair (1950–57), Peter Tyson (1957–58), Ernst Rogue (1958), Ronald Beaucage (1958–), Lauly Beaucach (1981).

2 Bamford Island Lighthouse

Bamford Island is a half a mile (0.8 km) southwest of the narrow Wilson Channel in the Canadian approach to the St. Mary's River through the North Channel, Lake Huron. A lighthouse was built on the south tip of the island in 1885 to assist marine navigation. It was a square white 32-foot (9.8 m) tapering tower with an attached wooden keeper's house. It had pedimented doors and windows, and a simple gallery dropped down from the top of the tower. Its square lantern displayed a fixed white light for 10 miles (16 km). The station also had a boathouse and other outbuildings. This light, named after long-time keeper Robert Bamford, was also dubbed the Devil's Gap Light after the treacherous area it marked.

The light was first lit by Alexander Brownlee. Later, when Bamford settled in the area about 1880, he became the island lightkeeper. He and his wife lived on the island during the navigation season and wintered at Richard's Landing. When the Wilson Channel Range Lights were established, Bamford finished his season by rowing and tending the new range lights, as the Bamford Lighthouse was extinguished when the range lights were lit. The keeper first had a sailboat and a rowboat, and later a launch as well. During his tenure, Bamford carted soil to the island for a vegetable garden and flowerbeds. He also made most of the lighthouse furniture himself.

After the bridge to the mainland was built, this lighthouse on the small island, just where the St. Joseph Island Bridge touched down en route to the mainland, became almost invisible. It gradually rotted and decayed, and it no longer exists today.

Known Keepers: Alexander Brownlee (1885–89), Robert Bamford (1889–1911).

3 Boyd Island Lighthouse

The Boyd Island Lighthouse, Lake Huron, was built in 1885 on a small rock 240 feet (73 m) southwest of Boyd Island, located between Gore Bay and Kagawong on Manitoulin Island's north shore. It was a square white wooden pyramidal tower that used a seventh-order optic to display a fixed red light for 6 miles (9.7 km) from a focal plane of 41 feet (12.5 m). The light assisted vessels passing through the North Channel as well as those transporting lumber from the area. The white wooden keeper's house was built on Boyd Island and, to facilitate the keeper's job, was connected by a bridge to the rock on which the lighthouse sat.

Keeper William Martin had a narrow escape when the punt he was rowing became wedged between two ice floes in May 1892. His wife sent up a distress signal, which was answered the next morning by a tugboat and crew from the local mill. Fortunately, Martin had meanwhile been able to get the attention of the

Clapperton Island Lighthouse when the ice floes carried him close to it. The Clapperton keeper rescued him and soon had him home safe, except for some frostbite.

The lighthouse was automated about 1916. As lumbering in the area declined and modern on-board vessel navigation improved, the light was extinguished and abandoned in the early 1950s. It was replaced with a modern beacon on a skeletal tower, which displayed a white flashing light.

In the 1960s a Coast Guard crew destroyed the old buildings at the light station before anyone in the community knew what was happening. They filled glass jars with gasoline and set them on windowsills. They then lit a fire at the bottom of the house, and from offshore used a rifle to shoot the glass jars so that the fire below would ignite the spilled gasoline. While no structures remained to cause the government to worry about vandalism and liability, a part of early Canadian history was also lost.

Known Keepers: William Martin (1889–1905), Elizabeth Martin (1905–29).

4 Brebeuf Island Range Lights

Brebeuf Island, a small rocky island with windswept pines typical of Georgian Bay, is about 7 miles (11.3 km) from Midland, Ontario, on Lake Huron. In the late 1800s and early 1900s when there was no road to the area, water travel was the only link to civilization, bringing in new people, vacationers and supplies for loggers. Lighthouses were added around the turn of the century to assist this lake navigation. The light built on Brebeuf Island in 1900 was one of two range lights that marked the entrance to Severn Sound with its communities of Penetang, Midland, Victoria Harbour, Port McNicoll and Port Severn.

The Brebeuf Island Lighthouse was originally built in 1875 on Gin Rock and was moved from there to Brebeuf Island in 1900. Its wood frame structure was placed on a stone foundation. The tapering square tower was built into one end of the 1½-story

house, which also had tapering walls. Both the tower and the house had eight-paned pedimented windows. At the top of the tower, ornamental wood braces supported the square gallery, which was surrounded by an iron railing. A polygonal lantern sat in the center of the gallery. The keeper's house and lighthouse tower, including the lantern, were painted white with red trim. The tower was 36 feet (11 m) high from base to ventilator.

The fixed white light once used coal-oil vapor lamps and reflectors and was visible for 11 miles (17.8 km) from a 40-foot (12.2 m) focal plane. Today the light is electric, with a 10-mile (16 km) visibility.

This lighthouse had only two keepers, both of whom served for over 30 years. The first, William Baxter, came with the light from Gin Rock in 1900. When Cliff Paradis, the second and last keeper of the Brebeuf Range Lights, left in 1962 after the lights were automated, he was presented with a long-service award by the Federal Department of Transport for his 32 years of service.

Because of the light's isolated location and the infrequent services of tender ships, these keepers had to be frugal. Although they could not plant a garden on the rocky island because storms always washed it away, they gathered driftwood to use as firewood and wood to replace their dock, which frequently vanished during a storm. As well as maintaining this light, they also tended the rear range light, on nearby Beausoleil Island. Sometimes this maintenance entailed life-threatening rowboat battles during pelting storms to light the rear range light.

This rear range light, built on the west shore of Beausoleil Island, was at first a square, white, wooden, tapering slatwork tower, 42 feet (12.8 m) from base to ventilator. It displayed a fixed white catoptric light from a 40-foot (12.2 m) focal plane for an 11 mile (18 km) visibility. Now it is a square, white, skeletal tower 86½ feet (26.7 m) high, with a red dome, and a fixed white catoptric electric light. At one time both lights had a vertical orange stripe as a daymark. Today the front light has a vertical red stripe.

With new technology, roads and travel patterns, this waterway

Brebeuf Island Front Range Light, circa 1977

Beausoleil Island Rear Range Light

Bustard Rocks Range Lights, circa 1910 NAC PA

became less used. In the summer months, however, it continues to see much vacation boat travel because it marks the transition from Georgian Bay to the Severn Sound as well as the entrance to the Trent–Severn Waterway.

In 1962, when hydro was cabled to the island, the light was electrified and automated, and needed no keeper. However, Tiny Weiss, once manager of the local hydro office, became the unofficial lightkeeper and was allowed to use the lighthouse as a cottage for 20 years. Then in 1982 the government tendered out the lighthouse to the public for private use as a cottage. These tenders lasted for a five-year period. The first to tender the 1900-vintage lighthouse was Ken Mackey, a marina operator in Honey Harbour.

Mr. Mackey has distinct memories of his tender. When he and his family first went to the lighthouse in the spring, his children excitedly announced the discovery of ducklings under the outhouse seat. The outhouse was built on the rocks and had access under it because of the uneven terrain. Ducks appreciated the shelter and the early spring drying of the high rocky location, and made it their nest every year.

Another memorable event was the annual June visit from Budd Watson, a renowned landscape photographer from Midland, who brought his photography class to the island to photograph the lighthouse. Every year he was given permission to take down the clothesline so that it would not impair their photos. Every year he asked — but was denied — permission to take down the television aerial. And every year, both parties had a good laugh about these negotiations.

Peter Shirriff tendered the lighthouse from 1987 to 1997. Then in 1998, because of heavy water traffic, the Canadian Coast Guard activated a rescue center from the lighthouse. The "Inshore Search and Rescue Centre" was staffed from Victoria Day to Labor Day by three trained university students. The rescue calls were dispatched from RCC Trenton. A hundred years after its inception, the Brebeuf Island light is once again involved in saving mariners.

Known Keepers: William Baxter (1900–31), Clifford Paradis (1931–62).

5 Bustard Rocks Range Lights

The Bustard Islands of Georgian Bay, Lake Huron, are an important group of islands, islets and rocks located 2.5 miles (4 km) south-southwest of the entrance to the French River. Range lights were first built to mark the islands in 1875, and they became known as the Bustard Rocks Range lights because the islands were devoid of vegetation. They were maintained and lit by Edward Borron Jr., the French River lightkeeper, as they were all part of the same station.

During the early 1890s, while making his Georgian Bay survey, Staff Commander J.G. Boulton recommended a third light be added at the Bustards and the temporary structures be made permanent. The work was done in 1893. The main or middle range light was a white wooden tower that tapered from an 18-foot (5.5 m) square base to a 7-foot (2.1 m) square top and was 48 feet (14.6 m) above the water. It used oil wick lamps and a glass lens to produce an 11-mile (17.7 km) visibility. By replacing its blacked-out panel with glass, the light was made visible for 360 degrees.

The inner range light was placed 229 feet (70 m) northeast of the main light. It was a square open-framed wooden tower and used oil lamps to display a fixed white light with a 6-mile (9.6 km) visibility from a 30-foot (9.2 m) focal plane. The outer range light was the new one added in 1893 and was located 193 feet (58.8 m) southwest of the main light. It was an enclosed white square wooden tower with a square red wooden lantern. It also used oil lamps to display a fixed white light that had a 10-mile (16 km) visibility from 27 feet (8.2 m) above the water. The range lights aligned both to and from the French River and also guided vessels past a danger known as Isabel Rock.

When mariners complained about the light's poor visibility from the southeast, the Superintendent of Lights, Hardy, made a trip in 1900 to discover why. He found that the new glass replacing the blanked out panel was too small and the metal frame was partially obscuring the light, so the problem was corrected.

After keeper Edward Borron Jr. died in 1902, the government allowed his wife, Emma, to have the position of keeper, provided her sons would help her. They did, but with the small government boat it was a long trip to the Bustards from their home on Lefroy Island at the mouth of the French River. In rough water she always worried about them boating out to light the range lights, especially when they were trapped on the island and had to spend the night in the lighthouse.

Sometime around 1910 the government built a small 1½-story wooden keeper's house near the main lighthouse. It had cedar shake siding and a beautiful Victorian veranda facing the bay. To insulate it from gale force winds, it was lined with narrow tongue-and-groove cedar called "Philadelphia Fencing."

In 1918 the two sets of range lights were split to form two stations: the French River Station and the Bustard Rocks Station. Emma Borron kept the French River one with a pay cut from $680 to $320 per year, and Thomas Ullman became the keeper at Bustard Rocks for $440 a year. Although Emma seemed to be earning less at this time she was in fact earning more. She had asked the government to split the ranges into two stations or increase her pay. By 1918 she could not afford to hire an assistant keeper any more, since she had to pay him at least $40 per month plus his board. By 1922 keeper David Mountnay earned $720 a year plus an additional $3 a month to operate the hand-operated foghorn. He and his wife had a fine garden and raised chickens to supplement their diet.

During Thomas Flynn's tenure there was a thriving fishing community on the islands and many seasonal fishing shanties. Flynn loved to socialize with the fishermen and other visitors who came to call. He coined many original phrases such as, "Wouldn't that make you jump up and grab your eyelashes." The Flynns added to the island garden by carrying soil from other islands. They too raised chickens and used their bi-products to fertilize their excellent vegetable garden.

In the winter of 1930 Flynn's supervisors called him early to light the range lights. Short of trekking through the snow "up to his armpits" and wading through swamp water so thick you "couldn't drive a squirrel through with a blacksnake whip," Flynn could not imagine how he was to do this. Local pilot Jim McIntosh solved the problem by delivering him to the range lights in his Georgian Bay scoot (snowplane). Being keeper for 24 years, Flynn must have loved the job, but he once described it as the life of a caged lion pacing back and forth.

The range lights used oil wick lamps from 1875 until 1951, when they were converted to electricity using Edison cell batteries. This enabled Flynn to retire and the government hired Reginald McIntosh, a local fisherman, to maintain the batteries and equipment until 1953, when Coast Guard personnel took over the job.

By 1964 the house had deteriorated greatly, so the government decided to sell it. When no buyers came forward, Jim and Gordon McIntosh of French River were contracted to remove it by October 1965. In May 1969 the Parry Sound Coast Guard installed modern electric lights with an automatic bulb changer that used a 55-amp, 12-volt power system. The lights still operate today and are maintained by the Parry Sound Coast Guard Base.

Known Keepers: Edward Borron Sr. (1875–84), Edward Borron Jr. (1885–1902), Emma Borron (1902–18), Thomas Ullman (1918), David Mountnay (1919–28), Thomas Flynn (1928–51), Reginald McIntosh (1951–53).

6   Byng Inlet Range Lights

Byng Inlet is a long, narrow inlet 15 miles (24 km) south of the French River along the northeast shore of Georgian Bay, and it leads to the mouth of the Magnetawan River. The Canadian government, in its project of lighting Georgian Bay's northern shipping route and providing safe harbor, established range lights at the inlet in 1890. The front range light was constructed close to the south side of the channel. The square white wooden tower was 34 feet (10.5 m) high, and displayed a fixed red catoptric light from a focal plane of 37 feet 8 inches (11.6 m) that was visible up to 8 miles (13 km).

The back range light was built 1,505 feet (463 m) behind the front light. It was a square white wooden skeletal tower with only its top enclosed and it was 59 feet 6 inches (18.3 m) tall. To help stabilize it, its four corner posts were anchored in large blocks of concrete. Its lantern also displayed a fixed red catoptric light, but its focal plane was 63 feet (19 m), giving it a greater visibility of 13 miles (21 km). These range lights were tended by the Gereaux Island keepers who were just ¾ of a mile (1.2 km) away.

Byng Inlet Front Range Light

In 1936 a new rear range light was built using a steel skeletal framework instead of wood. Otherwise it was much the same as the first one. At some time a fluorescent orange daymark was added to each of the towers and the lights were electrified. These lights are now automated and continue to assist marine traffic in the area.

Known Keepers: See Gereaux Island

7   Cabot Head Lighthouse

Cabot Head is a bluff peninsula just east of Wingfield Basin on the northeast side of the Bruce Peninsula, which separates Lake Huron from Georgian Bay. Huron and Ojibway Indians had long used the area for its excellent fishing and hunting, but Jesuit priests were likely the first white men in the area, and Cabot Head commemorates John Cabot, the first European to penetrate Canada's eastern seaboard. Nearby Wingfield Basin was named after Lieutenant Wingfield, the first white person to reach it.

In the mid-1800s when the Bruce Peninsula opened up, lake travel, commercial fishing and lumbering in the area boomed. Until the early 1870s, when railways came to remote communities, marine travel was the only link between Georgian Bay settlements. Once Parry Sound had access to the shortest route for shipping local lumber and could forward cargo from the northern Great Lakes to Montreal and the New England coast, grain began to be shipped from the west and trade with large U.S. ports prospered.

Storms took their toll in shipwrecks. Georgian Bay became known as the most dangerous part of the lakes and Cabot Head, one of the most critical areas. It could provide shelter or destruction during storms. Wingfield Basin lent natural shelter, but its shallow entry made it suitable only for small boats. So, Cabot Head was the site of many shipwrecks, both before and after the building of the lighthouse. The wrecks included: the *Beverly* (1856), the *Pioneer* (1863), the *Son and Heir* (1869), the *Shandon* (1884), the *Anne Watt* (1889), the *Bently* (1886), the *Kincardine* (1892), the *Victoria* (1896), the *Thomas R. Scott* (1914), the *N. Ellen M.* (1949) and the *Gargantua* (1951).

The Department of Marine and Fisheries saw the need to place a lighthouse on Cabot Head. When seeking deed to the proposed site in 1894, they discovered that the 23-acre (9.3 hectare) lot was already owned by Thomas Lee. However, the Department of Indian Affairs cancelled Lee's land sale, as Lee had not fulfilled purchase obligations (he had not improved the land, had never occupied it, and was a non-resident). The Department then purchased it for lighthouse purposes on October 19, 1894, for $28.75, the same price Lee had paid.

In 1895 John George of Port Elgin was awarded the contract to build the lighthouse for $3,475, and the station, perched high on a cliff overlooking Georgian Bay, was operational by June 1896. The 1½-story wooden keeper's house was built on a shallow cellar. The main floor had a library/den/office and a parlor on one side and a large kitchen/dining room/family room with an attached pantry/breakfast room and a woodshed on the other. The second floor had four bedrooms. Narrow stairs led to a third-floor tower store room about 10 feet (3 m) square below the lantern. The 49-foot (15 m) tower had a dodecagonal lantern surrounded by an octagonal wooden gallery.

The lantern, made in Montreal, housed a coal-oil Aladdin lamp with a large 3-foot (0.9 m) revolving reflector that used a clockwork weight system to make it turn to produce a flashing white light (flash and eclipse 20 s; flash and eclipse 20 s; flash and eclipse 40 s). From its 80-foot (24.4 m) focal plane the light was visible for 16 miles (26 km). Both tower and house were covered in cedar shingles and painted white for best daytime visibility. The fog signal building was 200 feet (60 m) southeast of the lighthouse on a lower level of the bluff. It was a wooden building housing machinery to operate the steam foghorn, which came from Lévis, Quebec (blast 8 s; silence 40 s). Other structures included an outhouse, an oil storage shed, and a blacksmith shop.

As keepers' positions then depended on the reigning political party, this keeper's position was first awarded to William Campbell, a Conservative. However, before Campbell could even take over his duties, the government changed, and the position was awarded to S.J. Parke in 1896 (he resigned in 1898). Charles Webster Sr. was keeper for the next eight years. His duties included round-the-clock watches, constant tending of the oil lamp, cleaning the 3 foot (0.9 m) reflector behind the lamp, winding the weights twice a day to keep the light flashing, and general maintenance. During his stay, the Wingfield Basin entrance was dredged to 500 feet (150 m) long, 100 feet (30 m) wide, and 19 feet (5.8 m) deep. Since the basin could now provide refuge for larger vessels, it was likely at this time that the first buoy markers and oil range mast lights were also put in place,.

In 1906, with the next change in government, Leslie Martindale became keeper. In 1907 the fog signal building burned down in a

Cabot Head Lighthouse, circa 1897

Cabot Head Lighthouse, circa 1917 NA PA1772462

forest fire that swept the peninsula. It was replaced with another wooden structure built by J.C. Kennedy of Owen Sound for $2,463, just to the north of the old wooden building. The fog signal equipment was upgraded to duplicate diaphone foghorns purchased from the Canadian Fog Signal Company of Toronto for $8,100 installed. The building interior was mainly one room with high ceilings to accommodate the huge engines. Catwalks accessed the upper levels. In 1915 a phone line was put in. As it was strung tree to tree from Gillies Lake, communication was a hit-and-miss venture. The large metal skeletal storm-warning tower northwest of the lighthouse was likely also added at this time. Large conical, wicker baskets would be flown to indicate weather conditions to passing boats. The weather was phoned from Gillies Lake and then the Cabot Head keeper would hoist the appropriate signal.

In 1926 Howard Boyle was awarded the lightkeeper's position because he was a World War I veteran. He was quite fastidious, described by his nephew as a "workaholic" who took his job seriously. His duties included tending the lamps, operating the fog alarm, which had a 20-mile (32 km) range, placing and removing channel markers, lighting and extinguishing range lights daily, raising and lowering storm signal baskets, and general maintenance work. He also made the site look like a park by adding concrete walks, stone walls, fences, lawns and horticulture for all seasons, including lilacs that remain today. He worked a large vegetable garden using "scrapped" fish as fertilizer, and kept a cow, a pig and chickens to vary his family's diet. He worked diligently to create a "show place" that delighted the guests he toured through the station when pleasure boats stopped by on their way from Owen Sound. He also gave the "Big Blast" to greet passing freighters.

In 1951 Harry Hopkins became keeper. His term saw many changes. In the 1950s Hurricane Hazel destroyed the boathouse and dock and covered the marine tracks with boulders, making them unusable. In 1958 a cottage was built for the keeper, and the assistant and his family became the sole occupants of the lighthouse. Until 1963, when the road from Dyer's Bay was opened up, all supplies had come by boat or been packed in from Gillies Lake. The current metal tower was erected and the lantern and tower were removed from the lighthouse in 1968 so as not to obstruct the new light. Renovations occurred inside the lighthouse as well, and indoor plumbing was introduced. Until then water had been hauled up from the lake by lowering a pail with a rope along a wire anchored into the lake. In 1971 hydro arrived, hastening the demise of the manned lighthouse. The fog alarm system was replaced by an automatic one in 1972 (blast 3 s; silence 3 s; blast 3 s; silence 51 s).

In a 1993 interview, Hopkins's wife, Ruby, reflected on her light-

Cabot Head Lighthouse

8 Cape Croker Lighthouse

On the southeast side of the Bruce Peninsula, which separates Lake Huron and Georgian Bay, is quite a large peninsula know as Cape Croker. A lighthouse was first built on the peninsula in 1898 about 1½ miles (2.4 km) southeast of the community of Cape Croker. It marked the turning point into Colpoy's Bay and Wiarton, and warned mariners of Surprise Shoal, a shoal over a mile long northwest of the lighthouse and almost in the direct path of mariners traveling the east shore of the Bruce Peninsula.

The lighthouse was a small one-story wooden rectangular house with a three-sided extension at its lakeside end. Its very short tower was built into the roof over the extension, butting up against the peak of the main house. Its gallery was surrounded by pipe iron railing, and its lantern had large glass panes and was capped with a simple dome and a tall ventilator stack. Weights inside the tower produced the characteristic flashing white light. Both house and tower were covered in narrow clapboarding and painted white for greatest visibility.

In 1902 a white clapboard fog signal building was added. It was a large rectangular building with many 12-paned rectangular windows to give interior light. Its diaphone foghorn pointed northeast from the upper lakeside of the building. Its machinery produced compressed air for the characteristic blast (blast 6 s; silence 54 s). Keeper Adams once saved the structure from fire. Walking toward the tower in a thunder storm, he saw a bolt of lightning hit the spar of a passing sailboat, shoot back into the sky and arc over the water to hit the fog signal building. Adams grabbed the pump he kept hooked up in case of such an emergency, and used a ladder to get to the fog signal attic, where he doused the already-smoking fire.

In 1903 plans were drawn up for a new lighthouse at the station, one of Canada's earliest experiments in lighthouse building with reinforced concrete, a relatively new form of architectural technology. The Forest City Paving and Construction Company of London won the contract for $1,820. A much larger 1½-story white clapboard keeper's house was built behind the old lighthouse, and a separate tower placed just south of the fog signal building. The octagonal tower, about three stories high, was made

house years. The summers meant rattlesnakes and flies, so the screened porch was a great asset. Their children built forts and tree houses, and played on the wreck of the *Gargantua* in Wingfield Basin until a picnicker's hibachi burned it. They also showed tourists around in hopes of earning some tip money. If the tourists did not oblige, the children would wait until their visitors were standing in front of the foghorn to express their disgust!

Harry Hopkins's sister, Minerva Lees of Tobermory, recalled visiting the lighthouse often and enjoying the aroma of Harry's fresh-baked bread. She also recalled having no problems with sleeping arrangements for sixteen children (Harry's nine and her seven). The last keeper, Brent Skippen, who took over in 1982, was more of a caretaker. He maintained the light, the fog alarm and the grounds until 1988, when the light station was completely automated.

In the early 1990s Friends of Cabot Head was formed to ensure that the lighthouse would be restored and the area would remain open to visitors. The group has received several grants but relies also on donations. The tower and lantern have been rebuilt and the lighthouse is now a visitors' center highlighting the area's history and the natural history of Wingfield Basin, now a designated Nature Reserve.

Although the replicated lantern has no light, a white light still flashes from the skeletal tower nearby, producing a flash every 15 seconds from its 42-foot (12.8 m) tower with a 78-foot (24 m) focal plane, to create a visibility of some 14 miles (23 km). In 1991 the light became a year-round emergency light.

A scenic 5-mile (8 km) road winds along the boulder-strewn beach. A short walk leads from the parking area to the lighthouse on the cliff. There is no light in the rebuilt lantern, but those who climb up the four stories are rewarded with binoculars to view all directions. To the west, Middle Bluff, West Bluff, and Wingfield Basin are visible; to the northwest, on a clear day, Bear's Rump and Flower Pot Island, and on an extremely clear day, Lonely Island, a distant isolated island with its own lighthouse.

Known Keepers: William Campbell (1896), S.J. Parke (1896–98), Charles Webster (1898–1906), Leslie Martindale (1906–25), Howard Boyle (1926–51), Harry Hopkins (1951–82), Brent Skippen (1928–88).

Cape Croker Lighthouse, circa 1934,
from left to right: fog signal building, keeper's house and old lighthouse

Cape Croker Lighthouse

of reinforced concrete. The entry door and two rectangular tower windows lit the interior. Its octagonal iron gallery surrounded by a circular pipe iron railing supported a huge circular lantern.

The base of the lantern formed a large room for the pedestal of the lantern's third-order Fresnel lens. A multitude of large curved squares of glass set into iron astragals and placed three rows high formed the glass of the lantern. Using a mercury-vapor lightbulb, its lighting apparatus produced a double white flash every five seconds (flash 0.25 s; eclipse 0.75 s; flash 0.25 s; eclipse 3.75 s) from a focal plane of 66-feet 3 inches (20.1 m), for a 24 mile (38.6 km) visibility. The lantern was capped with a huge circular dome with a cylindrical ventilator and a weather vane. The whole tower from base to vane was 54 feet (16.5 m).

This new lighthouse was finished in 1909 but the old one was kept as a guesthouse. Some time later the old tower and lantern were removed. In 1958 a new bungalow was built for the keeper. Then in 1986 the light was automated and keepers became unnecessary. It may also have been at this time that the light became operational all year round as an emergency light.

While the light still guides mariners today, it sits as part of the Cape Croker Indian Reserve and only the tower and the keeper's bungalow exist, as the Coast Guard has razed all of the other buildings that once formed the station.

Known Keepers: Richard Chapman (1902–10), James Champman (1910–40), Capt. J.D. Chapman (1940), Wesley Morrison (1940–42), Norman Whetton (1942–60), Frederick G. Longe (1960–61), Walter E. Hatt (1961–62), Lionel Cuthbertson (1962–), Charles E. Rouke (?), James Young (1966–69), John Adams (1969–79), Fredric Proulx (1980–86).

9 Cape Robert Lighthouse

Cape Robert is located in the North Channel of Lake Huron on the north side of Manitoulin Island. It divides Bayfield Sound and Vidal Bay. Since this piece of land jutted the farthest of any into the shipping channel, the government contracted John Waddell of Kingston, Ontario, to build a lighthouse on its point in 1883 to warn mariners of its dangers. However the Department of Marine and Fisheries had to assume building and finishing the lighthouse in 1885 when Waddell reneged on his contract.

The lighthouse was built 150 feet (46 m) inside the low northern extremity of the cape and had high white clay banks 400 feet (122 m) behind it, adding to its daytime visibility. Its square white tapering tower was built into the white wooden keeper's house, which had a lean-to added behind it. It stood on a stone foundation, and both house and tower had pedimented doors and windows. Its style was very similar to the lighthouses on Strawberry Island and Clapperton Island. The tower was topped with a square gallery supported by ornately carved wooden corbels and surrounded with wooden cross-braced railing. Its octagonal iron lantern displayed a fixed white light from a 46-foot (14 m) focal plane for a 12-mile (19.3 km) visibility. As this station had no

Cape Robert Lighthouse, circa 1929

protected harbor, a windlass and roller system was provided for the keeper to pull his boat into the boathouse. The station also had a hand-operated foghorn.

Since there was no record of land purchase, the Department of Marine and Fisheries in 1901 formally acquired 101 acres (41 hectares) on the cape from the Department of Indian Affairs for thirty cents an acre ($30 total). They purchased a large reserve to clear land to protect the lighthouse from forest fires and ensure that the keeper had enough land for firewood and farming.

In 1886, in fair June weather, the schooner *Nellie* sprang a leak and sank on the underwater shoal extending out from the cape. In the process, its lifeboat floated away. The captain remained on board, but mostly underwater for more than a week before being rescued. Although he was famished, thirsty, sunburned and swollen, he did recover. With ships passing nearby, many wondered why he had not been rescued sooner.

Instead of living at the lighthouse, keeper Norman Matheson preferred living 15 miles (24 km) away and since there was no road access, he rowed daily to tend the light. When a family member died, his wife had no way of contacting him except through her nine-year-old son. He drove a horse and buggy along a trail to the beach and walked the last four or five miles along the rocky shore, carrying a small lantern. In the early 1900s, a rough buggy path was cut to the lighthouse and the keeper kept back the overgrowth. In the 1940s the road was improved enough for the use of cars.

In the early 1920s a forest fire raged through the area, narrowly missing the lighthouse buildings. A large tract of land south of the lighthouse was burned, and charred stumps remained visible for many years.

Once, after storms had washed clay from the banks behind the lighthouse down into the lake, the water was muddy and drinking water was difficult to get. The keeper's complaints led to the government installing a cistern and collector system to catch diverted rainwater. Unfortunately chemicals from the shingles were also collected, making the water undrinkable, so the keeper went back to using the lake water.

Changes came to the station. Around 1948 a new keeper's bungalow was built to replace the deteriorating old one. During the 1950s a new electric light was erected on a steel skeletal tower measuring 29 1/2 feet (9 m) but its automated flashing white light (flash 0.5 s; eclipse 3.5 s) could be seen for only 3.1 miles (5 km) from a focal plane of 52 feet 8 inches (16 m). After this the old lighthouse was destroyed, the keeper's bungalow was moved to Silver Lake for use as a cottage, and the octagonal iron lantern was placed on the guardhouse at the Parry Sound Coast Guard Base. Nothing remains today to indicate that the light station ever existed.

Known Keepers: A.K. Nesbitt (1885), William Nesbitt (1886–95), Norman Matheson (1896–1922), Mrs. N. Matheson (1922), Frank Sinclair (1923–37), William Rumley (1937–44), Frank Fowler (1945–49).

Chantry Island Lighthouse, circa 1997

10   Chantry Island Lighthouse

Chantry Island is located 1.4 miles (2.3 km) southwest of the mouth of the Saugeen River at Southampton along the east shore of Lake Huron. In 1855, with increased water travel and the development of the Saugeen Peninsula, public calls for navigation aids could no longer be ignored. The Department of Public Works contracted John Brown of Thorold, Ontario, to construct eleven lighthouses to light Lake Huron and Georgian Bay from Point Clark to Christian Island. Due to difficulties and expense in building them, only six, later known as the "imperial towers," were completed: Cove Island, Nottawasaga Island, Griffith Island, Chantry Island, Point Clark and Christian Island.

The light at Chantry Island was multi-purposed. First, it was a coastal light to help mariners pinpoint their location along the east side of Lake Huron. Second, it warned of the many shoals in the area, including those threading underwater for a mile (1.6 km) north and south of this island with as little as 2 feet (0.6 m) of water over them, and the Lambert Shoal north of the island and slightly northwest of the rivermouth. Third, it marked a refuge for mariners on the lee side of the island.

The imperial towers were all built in the same architectural style although their heights varied slightly. Each tower was built of white dolomite limestone, carefully selected to be free of cracks so that moisture could not penetrate. They each had a foundation to stabilize the structure. At Chantry the foundation was blasted out of bedrock and a bed of cement was laid upon a gravel and boulder bottom. The tower's foundation walls were over 7 feet (2. 1 m) thick and its 6-foot (1.8 m) walls at ground level tapered to 2 feet (0.6 m) thick at the top, although its interior diameter remained a constant 10.5 feet (3.2 m). The limestone was topped with granite, flared slightly to support the heavy, red cast-iron, dodecagonal lantern, which had 36 glass panes (three per side) and was 10 feet (3 m) in diameter. This cast-iron lantern was needed to stabilize the Argand lamp and the large second-order Fresnel lens. Both the iron lantern and lens were new, state-of-the-art equipment manufactured by the Louis Sautter Company of Paris. Its assembly was so delicate that a crew of French technicians were sent with the equipment from France.

The lamps were also very important. They used a variety of illuminants over time including sperm whale oil, colza oil, kerosene, acetylene and electricity. To keep the early oil-burning lamps showing a constant bright light, proper ventilation was necessary. This ventilation, which carried combustion wastes, was provided by a trap door into the lantern, a glass chimney and small holes in the ventilator ball on the top of the copper dome. These oil-burning lamps also produced more than their own volume of water vapor in the cold weather, so interior eavestroughs were placed in order to collect this vapor as it condensed on the inside of the dome. They drained the water out through spouts concealed in brass lion's heads located outside at the top of the junction of each glass panel. These spouts spewed the water away from the lantern glass so that it would not impede the light's beam. The oil was brought in by supply ship but, since the shoals made it impossible to get close enough to the island to unload the 50-gallon (225 l) casks of oil, fishing boats ran a ferry service to the island dock.

The copper domes of the imperial towers were of an imperial architectural style. They were higher and more rounded than most domes, perhaps accounting for their being dubbed "imperial" towers. The lantern is also unique in style. With most lanterns the glass sat on a cast-iron base wall called a murette, but the glass for the imperial lanterns sat directly on the granite stone that formed the top of the tower.

These six lighthouses were all built between 1855 and 1859. As their construction progressed, the cost for building them escalated drastically, and John Brown had to petition the Governor General for more funding from the treasury. The lights had been contracted for £3,500 each, but by 1857 Brown had lost £1,500 per light. The final cost was about $37,000 per light or $222,536.91 for the six lights. While more Canadian funds were provided, no British, or Imperial, funds were ever used and Brown lost money building these lights.

The lighthouse on Chantry Island was begun in 1855 and lit on April 1, 1859, the same date that the Point Clark Lighthouse was lit. The light displayed a steady white beam and from its 86-foot (26.2 m) focal plane it had a visibility of 17 miles (27.4 km). It had 115 steps leading to the lantern room, which housed the second-order Fresnel lens. The tower's lower round-headed doorway had a Dutch-style plank door with a semi-circular fanlight window above it. The 105 steep-pitched wooden stairs led through seven levels to the top of the tower and another 10 curved iron stairs accessed the lantern. Six rectangular windows ascended the tower at quarter turns to provide interior light. The windows on the second and third floor were about 5 feet (1.5 m) deep and recessed to the floor. While this design may have been planned to house a fog cannon, no one is sure.

Another small mystery is the origin of its stone. Some locals say the granite came from Europe as ballast on sailing vessels. Even

the limestone's origin is uncertain. Some say it was ship's ballast, was quarried at Kingston by prisoners, or was quarried locally at Owen Sound, Main Station Island and Inverhuron.

The Chantry Island Lighthouse was at first left in its natural stone color, but in 1871 it was changed to white to increase its daytime visibility. Rather than being painted, it was whitewashed with a mixture of lime, salt, ground rice, Spanish whiting, glue and warm water. This surface allowed the limestone walls to breathe and not sweat, as sweating would cause freezing, expansion and unwanted cracks.

The keeper's house was a 1½-story structure with a slate roof and hammer-finished limestone blocks. The south end had a combined living/kitchen area and a dual-purpose fireplace. In the north end were the parlor and the master bedroom; upstairs rooms were loft bedrooms. The pebble-stone floor of the cellar had a large flat rock protruding into it which, as it always remained cold, was used to keep food cool.

The station was finished with other outbuildings. Behind the house was a two-seater double-brick outhouse that was finished inside with lathe and plaster. South of the house was a small limestone building whose use is uncertain. Possibilities include: a powder magazine to store explosive gun cotton that would be needed if there was a fog cannon at the station, a kiln to make lime for lighthouse mortar, an ice house, a

Chantry Island Lighthouse, circa 1997

smokehouse, or a storage shed. A wooden pier and a boathouse were added.

A 540-foot (165 m) breakwall had been built out from the north side of the island heading east toward the mainland to calm the waters and help prevent erosion as well as protect the lighthouse pier. Since prolonged storms could rage for days at a time, isolating the keeper and his family, much thought went into designing the station to make it as self-sufficient as possible for times when boat transportation was futile. A shorter breakwater was also built at an unknown date from the southeast side of the island to prevent storm erosion and protect the lighthouse pier from its south side. The first lightkeeper at Chantry Island was a temporary keeper named Robert Mills. From 1855–1857 he kept a temporary light that was just a seaman's lantern hung from a mast and later from a pole on the lighthouse tower.

The first official permanent keeper was Captain Duncan Lambert, who earned $435 a year. Lambert was keeper for 22 years. He seeded the island for pasture for his dairy cow; he planted fruit trees, herbs and a vegetable garden; and he built storage sheds and additional living quarters, as his family lived on the island year round. To supplement his income he fished and mended nets. Besides tending the light he was the government overseer for repairs. It was a constant battle to maintain the north breakwater. In 1861, 100 feet (30.5 m) of it was washed away and needed to be rebuilt. In 1865 it was strengthened by being raised and then extended to 650 feet (200 m).

Lambert assisted the crews of numerous shipwrecks on the Chantry Shoals. In 1864, after saving the crew of the scow

American Eagle but not being able to assist those on the schooner *Altair*, Lambert pleaded successfully with the Department of Public Works and was granted a small lifeboat. With the completion of the Long Dock and the Southampton Range Lights in 1877, Lambert was also put in charge of maintaining the front range light at the east end of the island's west section, as he could reach it without needing a boat. In 1879 Lambert's son Ross, age 23, drowned while trying to save the crew of the shipwrecked *Mary and Lucy*.

When Lambert retired in April, 1880, his son William became head keeper. He continued island improvements. He built a boardwalk from the lighthouse to the Long Dock at the north end of the island, and used a bicycle to travel to and from the front range light to tend it. He added benches, picnic tables and landscaping to improve the island for picnickers. He even had his own marine museum of artefacts collected from the numerous shipwrecks. Unfortunately, the island became such a popular place to visit that the many visitors wanting tours made it difficult for him to sleep in the daytime — until he posted a sign over the tower door that tours were ten cents. While this first caused some government skirmish (as it was not government policy), he was finally granted permission to do so when he explained why. He put all the money collected from the tours back into island improvements. William received a gold watch from the Canadian government for saving the captain and crew of the sinking schooner *Nettie Woodward* in 1892. In 1906 he was awarded a bronze medal for saving the crew of the schooner *Cavalier*. Then when he retired in 1907 he was presented with the Imperial Service Medal for his 27 years of dedicated service at Chantry Island.

Other keepers kept the light until it was automated in 1954 with electricity and a keeper was no longer necessary. With humans no longer on the island, its population of gulls, herons, terns and cormorants increased, and the Canadian Wildlife Service had Chantry Island declared a Migratory Bird Sanctuary on December 20, 1957. In 1979 the light's characteristic was changed from fixed white to flashing white (flash 0.5 s; eclipse 3.5 s).

With the tower abandoned and empty, vandalism and neglect took their toll. While the tower was maintained by the Canadian Coast Guard, the rest of the buildings fell into ruin. By the early 1990s the roof, inner walls and floors, and some of the stones from the house walls had collapsed into the cellar, and nature was fast reclaiming the interior.

Then in the late 1990s two small groups (the Maritime Heritage Committee and the Propeller Club, both of Southampton) combined to form the non-profit group the Supporters of Chantry Island. Within just a few years they had raised enough money and had attracted enough volunteers to completely rebuild the keeper's house to an 1859 appearance (although they have used recycled-tire shingles, which look like slate and are much cheaper). They held a grand-reopening ceremony on August 11, 2001, to celebrate its completion. Since the island is also a bird sanctuary, they also work closely with the government and the Canadian Wildlife Society in their restoration efforts. Today they offer tours to the lighthouse but must limit visitors so as not to overly disturb the bird population.

Known Keepers: Robert Mills (1855–57), Duncan Lambert (1858–80), William Lambert (1880–1907), Malcolm McIver (1908–16), John Klippert (1917–37), Clayton Knechtel (1937–41), Alfred Huber (1941), Cameron Spencer (1942–54).

11 Chantry Island South Shoal Light

Shoals are a hazard all around Chantry Island on the east side of Lake Huron, and a coastal light had been built on the island (1855–59) to warn of the dangers. In 1870 John Page, chief engineer for the Canadian Department of Public Works, decided to have the eastern area behind Chantry Island made into a harbor of refuge from Lake Huron storms. To help mark this harbor, a light was built in 1874 on the tip of the shoals that stretched underwater to the southwest of the island.

This beacon was placed on an octagonal timber crib constructed in 16 feet (5 m) of water and rose some 40 feet (12 m) above the waterline. The crib, 50 feet (15.5 m) in diameter, had a light on top of it, making it 66 feet (20 m) high from the lakebed to its top. It marked safe entry for vessels passing between it and the mainland, and this channel became the south entrance into Southampton Harbor. In 1900 a barrel buoy replaced the beacon. While evidence of the original light cannot be seen above water today, a local diver did locate its remains underwater, thus verifying its existence.

12 Christian Island Lighthouse

As Georgian Bay opened up for settlement, a string of lighthouses was built between 1855 and 1859 from Point Clark to Christian Island to facilitate marine traffic around the Bruce Peninsula and into Georgian Bay. Their builder was the Scottish stonemason John Brown of Thorold, Ontario. Although contracted to build eleven lights, he only completed six (Point Clark, Chantry Island, Cove Island, Griffith Island, Nottawasaga Island and Christian Island) as each one cost him £1,500 pounds more than expected. The unanticipated costs were due to storm losses, high wages for work in remote locations, downed vessels in uncharted waters, and the need to pay men while awaiting supplies and materials. The final price for the six towers was an astronomical $224,563.91.

The six lights that were finished became known as the "imperial towers" and were built by Brown during the same time period with the same plans (although the tower heights varied according to location). Each one had a small limestone keeper's cottage and a conical limestone tower with walls 6 feet (1.8 m) thick at the base tapering to 2 feet (0.6 m) at the top, keeping a constant interior diameter of 10.5 feet (3.2 m). The top layers were made of granite for durability and support for the heavy cast-iron lantern and its large pedestal-based lens. All lanterns had an arched dome with interior water troughs to collect condensation. Waterspouts hidden inside brass lion heads (painted red) on the outside of the lantern carried the collected water from the troughs to the outside and away from lantern glass. The stairs to the lanterns were wooden, straight and steep, and ascended through several levels of the tower.

In 1857 the government purchased 35 acres (16 hectares) from the Chippewa Indians for a lighthouse reserve. The lighthouse was built on Bar Point, the southeastern spit of Christian Island, on the west side of the harbor, 1.5 miles (2.4 km) from Cedar Point on the mainland and 20 miles (32 km) from Penetanguishene. As well as marking a deep sheltered harbor at Christian Island, it guided vessels traveling through Christian Island Passage into Nottawasaga Bay toward Pentanguishene, Midland, Victoria Harbour and Port McNicoll. In helping to light a much shorter shipping route, the Christian Island Lighthouse minimized time and shipping costs. The passage also had a second light, just a

Christian Island Lighthouse

lantern raised and lowered on a pole on the southwest side of Cedar Point.

Since the spit consisted of gravel and sand, a more sturdy foundation was laid, using two thicknesses of 12-inch (0.3 m) square timbers. They were placed close together with the upper course laid transversely to the lower one, making a surface to support the tower. The 55-foot (16.7 m) tower was the shortest of the imperial six and the first to be finished. By 1857 it was lit with a temporary white light tended by a keeper called Grace. After the installation of its lantern and fourth-order Fresnel lens (from the Louis Sautter Company of Paris), the lantern was officially lit on May 1, 1859 — the last of the six to be lit. It displayed a fixed white light from a 61-foot (18.6 m) focal plane to produce a visibility of up to 15 miles (24 km).

The light's second keeper, John Hoar, was the son of keeper Captain William Hoar. In 1891 he agreed to switch locations with Allen Collins, the keeper of Hope Island, so that Collins' children could go to school on Christian Island. However, when Hoar requested government compensation for the buildings he had erected on Christian Island and for his sailboat, which Collins got, the government turned him down, especially since the sailboat was a government-issued vessel. In turn, Collins accused Hoar of

taking the station's stove. A small feud ensued, and a government official had to be sent out to settle the dispute. He found in favor of Collins, and Hoar became even more irascible, to the point of having to be removed as keeper.

Some changes occurred at the station. A building was placed between and against the house and the tower to provide extra space, but it did not provide tower entry. About 1871 the buildings were whitewashed for increased visibility. The lighthouse was discontinued on April 1, 1922, and Thomas Marchildon, the last keeper, was retired by Order in Council. The light was replaced by a buoy placed 4,800 feet (1.5 km) south of Bar Point at the tip of Campana Shoal. The dock and other buildings gradually disintegrated and the abandoned keeper's house fell into ruins. During World War II the lens was taken away, the iron lantern was cut for use as scrap for the war effort and the tower stairs were removed. Of the six imperial towers, this one is in the worst state. In 1965 a fixed white solar-powered electronic light was mounted on the lanternless tower but in the early 2000s the Canadian Coast Guard put a new red lantern back on top of the tower and moved the beacon into it.

Known Keepers: Captain William Hoar (1857–68), John H. Hoar (1868–91), Allan Collins (1891–1914), Thomas Marchildron (1914–22).

13 Clapperton Island Lighthouse

In 1866 a lighthouse was built on the northern end of Clapperton Island along the north shore of Manitoulin Island in the North Channel of Lake Huron to warn mariners of the Robinson Rock Shoals about a mile (1.6 km) northeast of the lighthouse and to mark the passage between Clapperton Island and the Crocker Islands to the north of it. It was a square white wooden tower that displayed a catoptric fixed white light from a 30-foot (9 m) focal plane for about 10 miles (16 km). The keeper's house was a 1½-story wooden frame structure.

Around 1915 the tower was destroyed by lightning and a new tower was built. It was a short square white wooden tower with a square wooden murette topped by an octagonal glass section with

Christian Island Lighthouse, circa 1941

Clapperton Island Lighthouse, circa 1919 NA PA172467

Clapperton Island Lighthouse and keeper Bill Baker. Courtesy of the Huronia Museum

items found him and took him to the Red Cross Hospital at Mindemoya. Rather than worry about himself, he made sure they contacted Norman Lloyd to replace him at the light. After emergency surgery and a few weeks' hospital rest he resumed his duties. The next winter, while putting up ice at Harbour Island, he was kicked in the back by a horse. He was flown to Little Current and taken again to Mindemoya, where he spent another few weeks recuperating from broken ribs and a punctured lung. Bill again returned to the light and tended it until his retirement in 1962.

When a modern metal beacon was erected at the station, the old wooden tower was rolled into the water and towed to the town of Spanish. It was placed on a sandbar where it stayed until water levels were low enough to retrieve it. The remains of the second lighthouse are said to be lying on the island behind the Baker's old farmhouse.

Known Keepers: Charles Patton (1871–73), Benjamin Baker (1875–94), Henry Baker (1895–1939), William Baker (1940–62), Glenn McFarlene (1963–64).

three rectangular panes of glass set horizontally into each of its eight sides. A gracefully swooping dome capped the tower. Its gallery had a simple one-banister railing around it. When this tower deteriorated from rot, a third tower was constructed in the late 1940s or early 1950s. The third tower was also square. However, it was taller, tapered, had a pedimented door and windows and supported a square wooden lantern with four rectangular windowpanes set horizontally into its astragals.

A number of vessels grounded or sank on Robertson Rock Shoals: in 1915 it was the *Western Star*, in 1926 the *North Wind*. When this ship broke apart, its bridge floated to shore and the Clapperton Island lightkeeper salvaged its pinnacle compass and a hurricane lamp to display at the lighthouse.

The Baker family tended the light for three generations. They also maintained channel buoys, farmed, trapped, fished and worked at lumbering. The first Baker was Benjamin. One day in September 1894, on his return trip from a solo sail to Gore Bay to play cards and drink with friends, only his sailboat, his dog, his wallet and a partly-finished bottle of whiskey arrived. It was believed that he fell overboard and drowned but it is not known whether foul play was involved.

His son Henry was the light's second Baker keeper. As well as looking after the main light, Henry was responsible for the range lights, which had been built on Cartwright Point 1½ miles (2.4 km) to the east. Despite his plea that these lights should be moved back from the shore, as ice from lake spray built up on them and made them treacherous to tend, his request was unheeded. Mariners did not want them moved.

Henry would tie a rope to a tree and around himself for his safety. He used a block and tackle to raise and lower the heavy brass lantern on the 30-foot (9 m) pole. He always feared that the line would break under the weight of the lantern and its coal-oil lamps, and one day his fear came true. While he was hoisting the lantern back into position, the rope snapped and the lantern came crashing down on him. Although seriously injured, he managed to ride his horse back to the lighthouse and was taken to the hospital at Little Current. However, he died of sustained injuries on September 17, 1946, at 82 years old.

William (Bill) Baker took over as the next keeper. After the fatality, the government moved the range lights further inland and also lowered them. Bill also tended the lights faithfully. In September 1950 he was alone at the lighthouse when his appendix ruptured. By the third day he collapsed while trying to make it from the house to the lighthouse to refuel the light, which had gone out. Fortunately, two men who were returning borrowed

14 Collingwood Range Lights

Collingwood, located at the southernmost point of Georgian Bay, became a major link in the northern shipping route in 1855 when the Ontario, Simcoe & Huron Railway (later known as the Northern Railway Co.) came to town. Collingwood's new role as a shipping terminus increased the volume of lake traffic into its artificial harbor, formed by two long breakwaters extending into the bay from the shore. The east one was 3,300 feet (1 km) long, while the west one was 2,400 feet (0.7 km), and there was a 675-foot (208 m) entrance gap between them. A channel 200 feet (61 m) wide and 12 feet (3.7 m) deep was dredged to make the harbor wharves accessible. There was no room for vessels to anchor, but when tied up to the various wharves, they could be safe in any storm.

In 1858 a light was built at the east end of the west breakwater to mark the harbor entrance. It was a tapering white wooden tower that supported a polygonal lantern topped with an ogee dome and a lightning rod. It displayed a fixed red light, and had a hand-cranked foghorn. This lighthouse and breakwater needed to be rebuilt after a storm completely washed them away in 1872.

Reconstruction started in 1873 and was finished the next year at a cost of $57,468. Half this sum was paid by the government, a quarter by the Northern Railway Company and a quarter by the town of Collingwood. The new white-painted wood lighthouse, octagonal this time, was placed in the same position. It tapered up to a wooden lantern 6 feet (1.8 m) in diameter which contained two Silber burners in a dioptic globe of a fourth order. From a 41-foot (12.5 m) focal plane its fixed red light was visible from all approaches for 8 miles (13 km). This light was frequently called the "Dummy" light.

In 1884, to make entry to the Collingwood harbor safer, a light was placed on a crib in the harbor at the turning point of the dredged channel. This was a simple light consisting of a Mississippi lantern hung from a mast rising from a white shed base built on a rock-filled wooden timber crib. It displayed a fixed red light but had poor visibility.

This crib light worked as a rear range light to the front "dummy" light. When entering the harbor, mariners lined up the two lights so that the crib light was slightly to the east of the dummy light. They followed this course until they were past the west pier and about 600 feet (185 m) from the crib light. At this point they swung to the southwest and, after passing the crib light, headed for the elevators, wharves or dry dock. An oil lamp was placed near the granary to help with this last leg of the journey.

In 1885 Georgian Bay's only lifesaving station was established at Collingwood. Local resident Patrick Doherty, its first federally appointed coxswain, handpicked his six-man crew. Since most of them were fishermen, they could easily be notified of an emergency by a flag or gun signal. They used a 25-foot (7.6 m) Dobbins self-righting lifeboat that was so heavy it needed a horse-drawn wagon to haul it to the water's edge. Later they used a marine railway and a winch or tackle to launch it. While their station would have been beside the water, it is not known exactly where it was located or when it was removed from service. Collingwood also had a storm signal tower to fly cones to alert mariners to various weather conditions.

Mariners complained about the crib light's poor visibility. One such report came from Captain Foote in 1890. Once, during a moonlight excursion of his steamer *Atlantic* with 300–400 passengers on board, the weather turned stormy and blew out the range light in the harbor (the crib light). On its return, the steamer narrowly missed hitting the crib. Furious, Foote reported the incident to port authorities in the morning, adding that he had noticed the light out on other occasions as well. Subsequent government correspondence admitted that the crib lantern was "apt to go out after a blow."

The government finally corrected the problem in 1894 by building a brand new lighthouse on the crib. The contract was awarded to D. Peterman and Son of Collingwood. The keeper, Andrew Lockerbie, was to oversee its construction and report weekly to government officials. It was a completely enclosed square wooden pyramidal tower with a pedimented door and window. The exterior, covered in cedar shingles, was painted white, and the small iron lantern, visible in only one direction, was painted red. The simple wooden gallery below the top edge of the tower was surrounded with a pipe iron railing.

The tower's brand new duplex lamp, with a red pressed lens, was placed inside a large iron lamp holder that was fronted with a single pane of glass and topped by a short straight dome-topped ventilator. This lamp holder was suspended by a chain from the top of the lantern and supported by iron rods on either side to prevent it from swiveling on the chain. These rods allowed the keeper to raise and lower the lamp holder to service the lamp through a door in its one side. The rear back surface of the lamp holder was painted red inside, probably to amplify the red color of the light. (This lamp holder and brass oil lamp are presently in the ownership of Larry Wright, co-author of this book).

These range lights served Collingwood as it grew into a renowned ship-building center. In 1902 another tower was built onshore to act as a rear range light to the crib light, so as to help vessels navigate the dredged channel that curved into the harbor. It was a white steel skeletal tower with an enclosed watchroom, and its lantern displayed a fixed red catoptric light.

In 1940 when the harbor was frozen over, lightning rent a huge

Collingwood Breakwater Light, circa 1872

Collingwood Crib Light, circa 1940
NAC PA172470

hole up the side of the crib light's tower, virtually destroying one wall but not setting it on fire. The tower was either rebuilt or replaced and continued in service until it was decommissioned in 1961. Recently it was discovered that the crib tower was not destroyed after it was taken out of service but was stored in a building at a Collingwood-area farm. Mr. Beer of Collingwood has now restored the tower.

Today the harbor is serviced by modern electric range lights. The front one, a circular white tower with a vertical orange daymark, displays a fixed red catoptric light from a 42.5-foot (13 m) focal plane. The rear one is a square white skeletal tower with a rectangular daymark and a vertical orange stripe. Its 49-foot (15 m) tower displays a fixed red catoptric light from a 64-foot (19 m) focal plane.

Known Keepers: Robert Doherty (1878–82), William Bishop (1882–83), Andrew Lockerbie (1883–1903), J.W. Lunan (1904–12), James Wilde (1912–26), Isaac Vankoughnet (1929–32), Herbert Wilde (1934–1946), Barton Vankoughnet (1946–51), Ross White (1952–61), Gertrude White (1961–62), Wilfred Johnston (1962–66).

15 Cove Island Lighthouse

Cove Island is located north of the Bruce Peninsula on the northeast side of Lake Huron. The Cove Island Lighthouse was built on Gig Point, the northeast tip of the island, to mark the dangerous passage between Lake Huron and Georgian Bay. It also warned mariners of Bad Neighbour Rock, just a few feet below the surface, 3 miles (4.8 km) north of Cove Island.

The Niagara Escarpment runs up through the peninsula and continues north, forming Manitoulin Island. Although the escarpment dips between the peninsula and the island to form the entrance to Georgian Bay, islands, hidden reefs and shoals abound. In the mid-1800s lake traffic into Georgian Bay had increased for several reasons: immigrants were flooding in to settle the Bruce Peninsula; the new Soo Canal allowed more east-west shipping; a Canada-U.S. free trade agreement encouraged commerce; and a railroad connecting Collingwood and Toronto led to more vessels traveling in Georgian Bay. The only light to service all this lake traffic was the light built at Goderich in 1847.

By the 1850s the government of Upper Canada had realized the need to light the Bruce Peninsula. John Brown, a Scottish-born stonemason from Thorold, Ontario, was commissioned to build eleven lights. In 1855 he started six lights at the same time: Point Clark, Chantry Island, Cove Island, Nottawasaga Island, Griffith Island and Christian Island. While Cove Island was the first to be finished and lit, the other five were all finished within four years. These lights together became known as Canada's imperial towers. They never received any money from the Imperial coffers. However, their architectural style resembled imperial towers in Europe and the Middle East (as Webster's dictionary suggests). The name also inspired poet Alexander Pope (1688–1744), to write: "Steel could the labor of the gods destroy, / And strike to dust th' imperial towers of Troy"

Brown started work in 1855 by building living quarters for his crew. Seven masons and stone-cutters, ten laborers, one black-smith, a foreman and three horses were engaged. Brown had his own white lime-stone quarries at Owen Sound, Main Station Island and Inverhuron, so the limestone for the station probably came from one of these. The keeper's house, of cut limestone blocks with a hammer-faced finish, was a small 1½-story house with a slate roof and a chimney at each end of the roof peak.

The tower was built of the same lime-stone, chosen to be free of cracks to prevent moisture from getting in and causing dam-age. The base walls 6 feet (1.9 m) thick, tapered gently upward to a thickness of 2 feet (0.6 m). The interior remained a con-stant 10.5 feet (3.2 m) in diameter, and a narrow window gave light to each landing. About halfway up, some initials and the date "1856" have been etched into the stone, probably by a workman. The top of the tower was built of granite and flared slightly to support the gallery and the heavy lantern and lens. An arched doorway, which used to have a fanlight over the door (a trait of the imperial tow-ers on Lake Huron), leads into the tower. The dodecagonal lantern was one of a few on the Great Lakes to receive a second-order Fresnel lens for greater visibility. Its focal point was 90 feet (27.4 m) above the water, and its visibility was listed as 16 miles (26 km), but mariners have reported seeing it as far away as 50 miles (80 km). Instead of being painted white, the tower was white-washed to allow the masonry to breathe and not sweat, as sweat-ing would freeze, expand and crack the walls. The 85-foot (26 m) tower was completed in 1856 but it waited another two years to receive its lantern and lens, both of which were state-of-the-art equipment manufactured by the Louis Sautter Company of Paris. So delicate was the reassembly that a crew of French technicians needed to be sent with the equipment from France. This hand-pre-cision coupled with booming business for Fresnel lenses meant that supply was slow.

The first keeper, George Collins, kept a temporary light, a lantern hanging from a pole on top of the tower, which provided a mere 2-mile (3.2 km) visibility. By October 1858 the lantern had been fitted with its lamp, lens, 36 square windowpanes (three in each of its twelve panels) and a copper dome. It was first lit on October 30, 1858, and produced a white flash every five seconds from its lens and an Argand lamp that burned sperm whale oil. The heavy condensation produced inside the lantern, especially in cold weather, gathered inside the dome top and was fed outside and away from the lantern glass by means of collecting troughs and twelve brass waterspouts hidden inside lion-shaped brass heads.

As technology developed, the lighting of the lens changed. The Argand lamp was followed by a flat-wick coal oil (kerosene) lamp. Around 1900 it used a mantle that

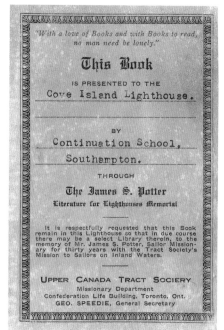

This Book

IS PRESENTED TO THE

Cove Island Lighthouse.

BY

Continuation School,
Southampton.

THROUGH

The James S. Potter
Literature for Lighthouses Memorial

It is respectfully requested that this Book remain in this Lighthouse so that in due course there may be a select Library therein, to the memory of Mr. James S. Potter, Sailor Mission-ary for thirty years with the Tract Society's Mission to Sailors on Inland Waters.

UPPER CANADA TRACT SOCIETY
Missionary Department
Confederation Life Building, Toronto, Ont.
GEO. SPEEDIE, General Secretary

*Cove Island book cover
courtesy of Huronia Museum*

vaporized the kerosene. Electricity was provided by generators in the 1950s, and, in 1971, by submarine power cable laid from the mainland. In October 1999 a large tour boat anchored between Cove Island and Tobermory hoisted its anchor and sheared the cable, putting out the light on Cove Island for the first time. The Coast Guard had to re-lay two miles of new marine cable.

In 1883 a steam-powered fog signal building was added. It subsequently burned down and was rebuilt in 1948. In the mid-1900s cruise ships in the area liked to play a joke on first-trip city dwellers in foggy weather when the fog signal was on. They told them the noise was made by a hungry "sea cow" and proceeded to throw oatmeal into a tub to feed it. One can only wonder about their sense of humor! The Banases, keeper and wife for the year 1946 and also the first and only couple to be married on Cove Island, said June and July were the worst months for fog, but that after hearing the fog signal blaring for almost a week solid they never really noticed it anymore. They also said the wall-shaking signal could be heard as far as 20 miles (32 km) away. In 1971 an automated fog alarm was installed.

As the station grew, additional facilities were added: in 1924 a radio beacon; in 1951 an assistant keeper's house, boathouse and concrete dock; in 1962 a new house for the main keeper and a workshop between the tower and the old keeper's dwelling; and at an unknown date, a helicopter pad. In 1977 the light's status changed to an emergency light and it remained lit year-round.

The lighthouse keepers at Cove Island were a courageous, inde-pendent group. In December 1860 the keeper, David McBeath, had run out of food for his family of seven despite his urgent request for provisions a month earlier. He and his family decided to leave, during stormy seas, in the government-issued 20-foot (6 m) sail-boat, thinking that attempting the 60-mile (96 km) sail to Lion's Head was better than starving. Luckily, the supply vessel arrived just as they were bundling up to get into the sailboat.

Like many good lighthouses, Cove Island has its own ghost story. On September 10, 1881, Captain Amos Tripp had just left Goderich with a cargo of salt in his 75-foot (23 m) schooner, *Regina*, when a gale split the oakum calking of its hull, and water flooded the hold. The crew took to the lifeboats, but the captain tried to save the *Regina* on a sand bar off Cove Island. The schooner sank just short of the sand bar, and Captain Tripp's drowned body was later washed ashore. The keeper, George Currie, recovered the body, wrapped it in sailcloth for lack of a coffin, and buried it on the west side of the island. Perhaps the captain was grateful for a decent burial, perhaps not, but after this, there was a sup-posed "presence" on the island.

After that, as well as being shown how to run the equipment, all new personnel were versed on

Cove Island Lighthouse, circa 1948

the folklore of Captain Tripp's ghost. The captain liked to be helpful, it was said, trimming wicks, polishing mirrors, closing doors, sitting in on a hand of cards, and watching on the beach during specially bad gales. Story has it that on one such November night, in some unremembered year, the light went out for a brief period and then suddenly came back on. The reluctant keeper took credit for relighting it, but years later admitted that not only had he not relit the lamp but he hadn't been at the lighthouse or even on the island. When asked how he thought the light had been relit, he said the ghost of Captain Tripp had done it.

The Missionary Department of the Upper Canada Tract Society had a system whereby people could donate Literature for Lighthouses as memorials. This service led to quite an extensive library at Cove Island. Other recreation included horseshoe pitching — and one of the keepers in the 1930s even had a tennis court put in. The last keeper of this light was Jack Vaughan. By the time he retired in 1991 he was the last of the keepers for the six imperial towers and the last lighthouse keeper on Georgian Bay.

When Cove Island Light was first lit almost a century and a half ago, it was named Isle of Coves Lighthouse, a literal translation from its French original. This later became shortened to Cove Island Lighthouse. Today, the station's buildings are in good shape and well preserved. The original stone keeper's house has survived and could be restored with a little TLC, unlike the keepers' houses at Nottawasaga Island or Christian Island.

The light is still active and maintained by the Coast Guard as an aid to navigation, still using its original Fresnel lens with a 500-watt bulb and rotating flash panels giving a light burst every five seconds. While this light is six miles out from Tobermory, it is easily seen from the car ferry M.S. *Chicheemaun*, which travels between Tobermory and Manitoulin Island. Perhaps its remote location and inaccessibility can account for most of its original buildings and equipment remaining intact. All agree that it is in the best original shape of all the imperial towers, making it the crown jewel of the six lights.

Known Keepers: George Collins (1858–59), David McBeath (1860–172), William McBeath (1873–76), Bryce Millar (1877–78), George Curry (1879–1902), W. Collier (1902–03), Kenneth McLeod (1904–12), W.J. Simpson (1912–15), John A. Leslie (1915–45), William Leslie (1945), Harold Banas (1946), Russel Bothan (1947–48), William Spears (1949–76), Robert Nelder (1977–81), Jack Vaughan (1982–91).

16 Depot Island Lighthouse

The Canadian government placed a light with a square wooden pyramidal tower on the west side of Depot Island along the east shore of Georgian Bay, Lake Huron, to mark the entrance to Depot Harbour. The lighthouse displayed a fixed red light from a 25-foot (7.6 m) focal plane using a seventh-order lens to create a 10-mile (16 km) visibility. Its light was visible for 180 degrees. This light no longer exists today.

17 Flowerpot Island Lighthouse

Flowerpot Island is northeast of Tobermory on the east side of the strait between Lake Huron and Georgian Bay. Its name was derived from huge limestone rock pedestals on the island's east side, which resemble large flowerpots. Face profiles can be seen in the two structures, and a Native legend recounts that they are a

Cove Island Lighthouse

young couple running off to the island to be alone, not knowing the island was haunted. They were instantly turned to stone when they set foot on it as a warning to others, and their profiles are still embedded in the "flowerpots" today.

In 1897, during the height of Great Lakes shipping, a lighthouse was built on Castle Bluff on the northwest side of the island. It was a short white square wooden lantern extending up from the apex of the keeper's house, which had been made from hand-hewn timbers. From an 88-foot (27 m) focal plane it exhibited a fixed white light using a seventh-order lens and a kerosene lamp that was visible for 15 miles (24 km).

To warn of fog, a mechanically struck bell was suspended from the gable on the north side of the house, which faced the water. The bell was 80 feet (24 m) above the water and sounded two strokes in quick succession every minute.

In 1901 a new two-story keeper's house was built on the shore of the cove just west of the bluff. The keeper (who earned $300 a year) moved into it with his family, and the assistant keeper occupied the house at the light. To become more self-sufficient and better provide for his family, the keeper cleared some of the 24 acres (9.7 hectares) of lighthouse reservation on the island behind the lighthouse to plant a garden and pasture a cow. They used a cool cave behind the lighthouse to store their dairy products — but not their meat, as there were too many flies.

Flowerpot Island Lighthouse

In August 1902 the station's fog bell was replaced by a hand horn that responded to ships' signals with a single blast every seven seconds. This was replaced in 1909 by a fog building set on a concrete pad just east of the lighthouse to house a 4 HP standard 1½-diaphone fog signal supplied by the Canadian Fog Signal Company in Toronto. The machinery cost $2,400, and the total, with the building and the installation, came to $4,410.

In 1930 the island became part of the Georgian Bay Islands National Park. At some point a concrete dock was installed. In 1955 the fog signal was silenced. A new keeper's bungalow was built on the beach in 1959 and a boathouse/workshop added in 1963. In 1969 the old lighthouse was destroyed — either by being torn down or being shoved into the lake — and was replaced with a modern beacon on a skeletal steel tower. Some time in the 1960s or 1970s diesel generators were installed for electricity and a new fog building was built where the old lighthouse used to stand.

In the 1980s it was supplied with an automatic videograph with two light beams that measured visibility over the water. When fog came within 2 miles (3.2 km) of shore for more than ten minutes, the alarm sounded once every minute. A sub-marine cable was laid from the Bruce Peninsula to provide electricity to the station, and the old concrete pad of the first fog building was turned into a heli-pad. In 1987 a severe lake storm destroyed the concrete dock on the beach in front of the keeper's house, although its remains can still be seen underwater. Also in 1987 the last keeper was removed from the station at the end of the navigation season, and the light was completely automated for 1988.

The Flowerpot Lighthouse was witness to two marine mishaps. In October 1900 the schooner *Marion L. Breck*, laden with bricks for Blind River, broke up on nearby Bear's Rump Island, and keeper Dan Smith rescued the crew two days later when the storm had subsided enough for safe travel with his small sailboat. The second mishap occurred in October 1909, when the 270-foot (83 m) S.S. *Athabaska* grounded on the rocks below the lighthouse. Fortunately the vessel received only minor damage and could be repaired once it was freed.

A keeper's life was perilous as well as lonely. In the 1920s and 1930s, William Spear and his assistant had to use the 18-foot (5.5 m) rowboat to make their way from Tobermory through the ice-dotted water to get to the lighthouse each spring and repeat the experience each fall. Spear's son, Bill, found it an exciting day when the lighthouse tender brought supplies. If the water was rough, deliveries were made to the beach by punt, and sacks of coal and barrels of oil were hauled by hand up to the station on Castle Bluff. However, when the water

Flowerpot Island Lighthouse with fog signal building, circa 1910

was calm, the tender anchored below the lighthouse and supplies were hauled up to the top of the bluff using an old A-frame and winch at the edge of the cliff.

Once, during keeper Coultis' tenure, lightning struck the water near the dock and, he raced — with a broken leg in a full leg cast — up to the generating station to turn off the power. Unfortunately, lightning struck it before he could get there, and the intense energy charge melted the control panel, the fuse panel, and the distribution panel into one. The building did not burn, but the keepers had to hand-rotate the overheated diesel engines until they cooled down, to prevent them from seizing up.

The last keeper, John Freethy, in an interview for the Owen Sound *Sun Times*, described the island as "somewhere between solitude and tranquillity." Highlights of his career included experiencing waves breaking over the cliff by the light tower, and seeing white caps at Cove Island over 6 miles (9.5 km) away. In 1983 he discovered a body on the beach. An American racing solo in a regatta from Detroit to Mackinaw Island had suffered a heart attack, and his yacht was blown across Lake Huron, into Georgian Bay and onto the shore of Flowerpot Island, where Freethy spotted it. He then waited with the boat and body until the Ontario Provincial Police came and took over.

With the departure of the keepers, no one was left on the island to help mariners or to greet the many tourists. Concerned that the abandoned buildings were deteriorating, the non-profit organization Friends of Fathom Five reached an agreement with the Canadian Coast Guard in 1995 allowing them to maintain and restore the station. Since 1996 they have done general clean-up, repainting, roof re-shingling, garden and lawn care, and trail improvements, created signage, and installed a composting toilet. They even provided laundry flapping from the clothesline, a previously familiar sight to passing vessels (although this wash was shapes cut out of wood and painted).

In 1998 they started a host program that gave Friends of Fathom Five volunteers the chance to live at the light station for several days and perform lighthouse keeper's duties, lead tours and host events at the station for its 10,000 annual tourists. The Friends group has even started a Junior Lightkeepers Program, which runs several times during July and August. One popular event is the annual celebration of Flowerpot Lightstation on the third Saturday in July.

Known Keepers: Dan Smith (1897–1903), John Parker (1903–04), Hector Currie (1904–12), William Spears (1912–37), Bill Spears (1937), Hugh Rumley (1937–49), Audrey Coultis (1950–65), Fredric Jerome Proulx (1966–82), John Freethy (1982–87).

18 French River Range Lights

In 1875 the Canadian government established range lights at the mouth of the French River on the northeast shore of Georgian Bay, Lake Huron. As well as marking the harbor for fishermen and vessels exporting lumber from this booming community, the front range light also served as a coastal light.

The front light was built on the east side of Lefroy Island, a small island on the west side of the rivermouth. It was a square white open-framework tower that displayed a fixed white light from a 16-foot (5 m) focal plane and was visible to the northeast

French River Front Range Light and keeper's house NAC PA195252

and southwest for about 6 miles (10 km). It used a mammoth burner and a lamp with no reflector. The rear range light was built on the mainland on the east side of the river 0.8 miles (1.3 km) behind the front light. It was also a square white open-framework tower but displayed its fixed white light in only one direction for 6 miles (10 km). It used a mammoth burner with only a 6.5-inch (14.3 cm) reflector.

The keeper's house was a simple one-story dwelling also built on Lefroy Island, close to the light. The keeper of these range lights also kept the Bustard Rocks Range lights until the two sets of lights were divided into two stations in 1918.

Between 1882 and 1884 the keeper complained that lumber companies were blocking the rear range light as they were surveying and making plans to build sawmills in front of it. When this was stopped, the lumber companies stacked lumber awaiting shipment on the docks in front of the light. When they denied blocking the light, the keeper clarified that they were blocking the light's daymark, which assisted mariners into the harbor during daylight hours. Eventually the problem was resolved. It may have been at this time that the rear light became a completely enclosed white wooden tapering tower with greater daytime visibility.

In 1900, when sea captains complained of the lights' poor visibility, improvements were made. In September the rear light was given a 16-inch (40 cm) reflector fitted onto a cast-iron stand with a constant level reservoir and an M.F.W. burner and the front range light was outfitted with an anchor lens. As well, both lights were switched from a fixed white to a fixed red characteristic by having red chimneys placed on their lamps. In 1930 the front light received a fourth-order lens that showed for 360 degrees to increase its use as a coastal light.

This light had only four regular keepers. Emma Borron, the third in her family to have the post, was granted the position in 1902 after the sudden death of her husband, who had been keeper for 27 years. She had to plead with the government for the job because local men had also applied for it. The government took her husband's good service record into account, as well as the fact that she had six children to raise, but stipulated that she "hire a good man to stay on the Bustards" and that her "able sons would always help her." She agreed and started at $500 a year. Resentment over her posting led to many complaints, but she was always able to prove her conscientious work, so the government took no action against her.

By 1918, since she was paying her assistant more than she was making herself, Mrs. Borron threatened to resign unless the government increased her salary or divided the two sets of range lights into two stations. The government divided the two stations, but reduced her pay from $680 to $320 a year.

Mrs. Borron had more difficulties. First, the keeper's house on Lefroy Island burned down completely, along with everything she owned, during the winter of 1918. She moved into a deserted house in the lumbering village owned by the Pine Lake Lumber Company, and lived with borrowed furniture. The government neither compensated her nor rebuilt the keeper's house. In 1920 she had to take a six-month unpaid leave of absence from both the light and French River for health reasons. Dean Udy accepted the temporary position on condition that he finish the 1920 season. However, once Mrs. Borron's leave was over on October 26, unaware of the government's agreement with Udy, she wrote to Udy to have him finish out the season. When he did not reply, she sent her son to close out the season for her.

After concern on everyone's part, including the Superintendent of Lights, who suspected Mrs. Borron of trying to make easy money over the winter, the government agreed to let her son close the season and released Udy from the job out of respect for Emma's long service. However, they also made it clear that she must resume her position herself the next spring or another keeper would be hired. When her son went to close out the season he found that her house had been ransacked again, so she did not return to French River that fall. The next spring, unable to find housing and being denied a keeper's house, she resigned.

Robert Young, who became the keeper in 1921, also had more than his share of bad luck. In July 1927 his house was broken into and money, bankbooks, insurance policies, a watch and other articles were taken. The police never found the culprit. Then in November 1927 the keeper was shot through his side and left hand while he was lighting the front range light, and nearly lost his life. Again, no blame was assigned, as the police decided it was a stray hunter's bullet. Since it was already late in the year and there was little boat traffic, Young was put on workman's compensation and the lights closed early. Young resumed his duties the next season, but in early April 1929 his house was broken into again and more items were stolen. Again no culprit was found. Then in June 1929, while rowing across the river to light the front range light, he was swarmed by black flies and bitten so badly that he was blinded by the time he reached shore and had to be hospitalized to treat the infection from the bites. This time, the culprit was known! Instead of granting compensation, however, the board advised him to "plan his trips more carefully" and to "row faster."

When Young's wife died one winter in the early 1930s, he could not bury her body because he had no one to tend the light in his absence. He made a coffin and kept her body in the back room until lumbermen could take it to Parry Sound for burial in the spring. Then for a third time, thieves broke into his house. By now French River was almost a complete ghost town and Young was its last resident. After many mariners complained about the destitute keeper at French River, he was forcibly removed in 1934 and taken to Parry Sound to recuperate — a sad end for a faithful keeper. The light was discontinued April 1, 1934, but was reactivated and converted to electric-battery power in 1939 and Tom Flynn, the Bustard Rocks lightkeeper, was also made caretaker of these lights.

The lights still operate today to serve fishermen and tourists but the front range light is now a circular white mast with a vertical orange stripe. Both lights have also reverted to fixed white catoptric lights and use electricity as their illuminant.

Known Keepers: Edward Borron Sr. (1875–84), Edward Borron Jr. (1885–1902), Emma Borron (1902–20), Dean Udy (1921), Robert Young (1921–34).

19 Gereaux Island Lighthouse

Gereaux Island lies just on the south side of Byng Inlet along the northeast coast of Georgian Bay, Lake Huron. A light partially funded by the Magnetawan Lumber Company was first established on the island in 1870. It was an open gallows tower and displayed a fixed white catoptric light.

In 1885 a light tower with an attached white 1½-story keeper's house was built on a high stone foundation. The large white tapering 48-foot (14.6 m) tower had many large pedimented windows for interior light. A large square gallery surrounded its octagonal lantern, which displayed a fixed white light using a fourth-order lens to create a 12-mile (19 km) visibility from a focal plane of 52 feet (16 m). The station first used a hand-cranked foghorn but when more modern equipment was introduced, its foghorn blasted for two seconds and was silent for 18 seconds. The radio beacon later added had the call letter "G".

The Gereaux keepers also tended the new Byng Inlet Range Lights when they were introduced in 1890. For a while this station had a head keeper and two assistants, but, as modern equipment simplified the job, it reverted to two keepers.

Mariners described the lighthouse as the most conspicuous landmark on the shore, especially when the afternoon sun brought out the contrast between its white walls and the background of rocks, water and wind-swept trees. Perhaps this is why it attracted so many visitors. Tourists were welcomed to tour its facilities as early as 1898, and later entries in the guest book record visits from as far away as Austria, New Zealand and Kenya. Art Niederhumer, the last keeper, felt that, since he was a government employee of a government facility, taxpayers had a right to tour the island. Perhaps this explains why he had up to 200 visitors each summer.

Additions to the station included a boathouse, an oil shed, a keeper's bungalow (1966), a fog signal building, a beacon building (which housed the control panel for the foghorn equipment) and a heli-pad. Once the new keeper's house, including a separate apartment for the assistant keeper, was built, the old keeper's house was reserved for overnight visitors.

Despite its many summer guests, Gereaux Island was still quite remote. Its first direct communication was a phone connection with the Canadian Pacific Railroad coal docks at Britt. Messages received this way governed the hoisting of warning signals at the island for incoming vessels. Sometime after 1963 the station acquired a radiophone, enabling incoming vessels to contact the keeper directly for the latest reports on weather and conditions. With the advent of CB radios, the keeper broadcast daily marine weather reports, which local residents and small craft operators looked forward to and greatly appreciated. In 1980 the light was being shone from a mast alongside the lighthouse.

Gereaux Island Lighthouse NAC PA182839

Gereaux Island Lighthouse

As with many old lighthouses, Gereaux had its resident ghost story. While some keepers have claimed to have heard voices or unaccountable footsteps on the tower stairs — or to have actually seen the ghost — no one has any idea who it is. Could it be the keeper who drowned while making a trip to the mainland for supplies? Another legend connected with the light concerns buried treasure. The tale tells of $36,000 being stolen by the lighthouse keeper and an Ontario Provincial Police officer who supposedly hid the booty, perhaps burying it on the island. Search dogs combed the island for a week but no money was found. Although the keeper and the officer were implicated, they were never convicted as they died soon after, in a manner thought to be suicide.

But the last keeper said his job was not ghosts or legends. It was to keep the light working properly, to paint the installations, to service the generators, to check local buoys, to monitor broadcasts from the boats on the lake, and to assist boaters when possible. Once he was removed in 1989, these services were no longer available.

With the keeper's departure, the Canadian Coast Guard destroyed or removed all the station's buildings except the boathouse, the bungalow, and the original tower and keeper's house. These buildings are now used as a seasonal rescue station, and a light still shines. At some time, perhaps when the keepers were removed, the light was returned from the mast to the tower. Today its white light flashes every five seconds.

Known Keepers: Joseph Lamondin (1877), James Milne (1883), Joseph Lamondin (1885), Louis Lamondin (1901–18), Charles Lamondin (1918–25), Louis Lamondin (1925–46), Joseph Barron (1946–66), John Joiner/Dalton Crawford (1966–70), George Rozel (1967), Herbert Christenson (1968), D.N. Sullivan (1971–72), Bert Hopkins (1973–77), Art Niederhumer (1978–89).

20   Giant's Tomb Lighthouse

This light stands no more, but it once was a proud and important light on the southern tip of the island whose distant profile earned it the name of Giant's Tomb. The citizens of the Midland area petitioned the Canadian government in 1886 to erect lighthouses on Giant's Tomb and Snake Island. The tip of Giant's Tomb was in a strategic location along the shipping lanes for the south-eastern part of Georgian Bay and the ports of Midland and Penetanguishene.

The citizens made a strong case, pointing out that shipowners and captains of passenger steamers and freight vessels regularly complained that the shipping lane was not lit. They also emphasized that whereas in 1884, 320 vessels had used the port of Midland, by 1887 over 1,000 vessels had sailed into the port, three million bushels of grain had been unloaded, and over five million board feet of lumber had crossed the docks. What's more, a string of lights taking in Hope Island, Giant's Tomb, Gin Rock, Whiskey Island and Snake Island would secure the commerce of the region for Canada, and shipments from the 32 mills on Georgian Bay would not go to American ports. With the installation of lights on Snake Island and Giant's Tomb, Midland would become one of the safest ports on the Great Lakes.

Their entreaties were answered and the lighthouse was completed on December 21, 1892. On May 26, 1893, a "Notice to Mariners" was issued by W.M. Smith, the Deputy Minister of Marine and Fisheries, announcing the establishment of the light on Giant's Tomb, and giving its latitude, longitude, and characteristics. Built on the boulder and gravel beach at the island's southern extremity, it was a cedar-shingled wooden tower with keeper's dwelling attached (typical of the Canadian design of the time). It featured a fixed white light with a seventh-order dioptric illuminating device at a height of 40 feet (13 m) above the bay and visible up to 11 miles (17.7 km) on a clear night. The structure was white and the iron lantern red. Its tower was 37 feet (11.3 m) from base to vane.

Alphonsa Tessier from Penetanguishene won the tender to build the lighthouse at a cost of $1,595 (5% of which went to the inspector hired to oversee the job). The first lantern on the tower was made by E. Chanteloup, Iron and Brass Founder, of Montreal for $244. Its design was standard: five glass sides and one blank panel. The roof of the dome was copper, and the glass came from London, Ontario.

Although this light was important in the approach to Midland, its importance seems to have been neglected because its sightline was poorly main-

Giant's Tomb Lighthouse

tained. According to a 1899 report, the light was partially hidden by trees when approached from the west and totally obscured when approached from the east. Archival pictures show a tall skeletal rear light that was built in 1915. It was a metal tower with an enclosed room below the square gallery. Its light was displayed from an octagonal iron lantern. It is unknown when this light was removed.

In 1929 the Giant's Tomb light was changed from a fixed white to an intermittent white light that flashed every 20 seconds. Probably around 1938, when the light was automated, the lantern room was changed and a square top replaced the copper and iron hexagonal one. Years later the lighthouse was blown up by the Coast Guard as a cost-cutting measure and was replaced with the square steel skeletal tower that still stands on the point today. From its 56-foot (17 m) focal plane it exhibits a white flashing light (flash 0.5 s; eclipse 3.5 s) with a visibility of 6 miles (10 km).

Known Keepers: Rowland Little (1893–98), Alfred Griffith (1898–1924), Joseph Martin (1924–37).

21 Gin Rock Light

In 1875 a square white 36-foot (11 m) wooden tower was built on Gin Island to the north of Midland, Georgian Bay, to assist entry into Midland and Penetanguishene harbor. In 1897 the Department of Marine and Fisheries purchased this 3.6-acre (1.5 hectare) island from the Department of Indian Affairs, along with Whiskey Island, for $40. In 1900 this lighthouse was moved from Gin Rock to the north end of Brebeuf Island to become the front range light to the rear range light located on Beausoleil Island.

Known Keepers: Israel Mundy (1875–84), William Baxter (1885–99).

22 Goderich Breakwater Lights

The first mention of any breakwater lights in Goderich appears in the Sessional Papers of 1895: "The Department of Public Work has moved the front range light a distance of 300 feet [9.5 m] west, from its former position, on the block at the previous outer end of the north breakwater, to a block built at an angle, 117 feet [35.5 m] from the outer end of the new addition — the height and characteristics have not been changed."

The first outer north and south breakwaters were started in 1904 at Goderich to protect the inner harbor, but the contractor went bankrupt before their completion and successive storms washed away the fresh concrete pilings. Bill Forest and Bill Birmingham took over the task, completing the north breakwater by 1908 and the south one by 1911. Both walls were later lengthened.

In 1909 a light was placed at the west end of the north breakwater to mark entry into the harbor. It was a 20-foot (6 m) white structure with a 25.5-foot (7.8 m) focal plane, and displayed a green flashing light (flash 0.5s; eclipse 3.5s).

Many years later, in 1945, a light was also placed on the west end of the south breakwater, making two lights through which vessels traveled into the harbor. This light consisted of a tower on a white square building. It displayed a red occulting light (flash 4 s; eclipse 2 s) with a focal plane of 33.5 feet (10.2 m). In 1986 it was lit as an emergency light. In 1952 a foghorn was added to the south breakwater (blast 3 s; silence 25 s). These lights both continue to mark entry into the harbor today.

Known Keepers: See Goderich Lighthouse

Giant's Tomb Lighthouse   NAC PA182838

Goderich Lighthouse

23 Goderich Lighthouse

The town and port of Goderich were founded in 1825 by Canada Company agents William Dunlop and John Galt at the mouth of the Maitland River on the east side of Lake Huron. While the river-mouth tended to silt over, some mariners described the port's natural crescent-shaped bay as "the only Harbour of Refuge on the east coast of Lake Huron." Between 1830 and 1850 the Canada Company spent over £16,000 on harbor improvements, but harbor conditions continued to be quite poor.

Goderich Lighthouse, circa 1916

Goderich's first lighthouse — the first lighthouse on the Canadian side of Lake Huron — was built in 1830–31 by Major Strickland on the high bluff south of the river. It was a log-style lighthouse that displayed a fixed white light. Unfortunately, this lighthouse, further east than the present lighthouse, was wrongly placed, as vessels had to sail past the harbor before they could see the light, and then they had to turn around and come back. To correct this, the government built a new lighthouse in 1847.

The second lighthouse at Goderich was also the second lighthouse built on the Canadian side of Lake Huron. The Charmin Construction Company of Goderich was contracted, and Adam MacViccar, a stone mason from Chatham, was sub-contracted to do the stonework for the 33-foot (10 m) tower and for the small separate keeper's house. Both were made of smooth, even-coursed stone. MacViccar laid a string course of stone between the first and second story of the tower and a second around the top, just below a stone cornice, to support its square gallery, which was topped with a stone deck and a protective iron railing. Both stories had identical large single windows with backmoulds in a flattened Greek ovolo style typical of the 1840s. The interior was finished with lath and plaster. The exterior and the keeper's house were white-washed for best visibility.

In 1878 the light used ten base-burner fountain lamps, each with its own 15-inch (38 cm) reflector, set on two iron circles. The oil lamps

Goderich South Breakwater Light

were Messenger #2 models from the Chance Brothers Company Ltd. Lighthouse Works near Birmingham, England. This apparatus produced a fixed white light visible for 12 miles (19.3 km) from its 150-foot (46 m) focal plane. In 1896 the tower had an octagonal iron lantern with, large rectangular glass panes, and a high ogee dome.

The lighthouse reservation included other structures. Some time before the turn of the century a white clapboard addition was built onto the north side of the house. A board and batten barn and fenced pasture areas provided for the keeper's animals. Near the edge of the bluff, a tall yardarm served as a storm signal tower to warn mariners of weather conditions. Just south of the lighthouse sat the cannon that today stands in the center of the Colbourg Street turn-around.

Goderich Range Light

In 1862 the keeper, Humphrey Fidler, earned $325 a year. By 1911 the annual salary had increased to $540 plus another $50 to operate the range lights. To facilitate rapid access to the range lights, 153 steps were carved into the side of the bluff from the lighthouse to the harbor below.

In 1892 the lighthouse well, near the back of the property, no longer held water, so town water was supplied at $6 per year — plus $55 dollars for it to be piped to the lighthouse. Probably in the late 1800s or very early 1900s, the light's illuminant was switched to kerosene, a cleaner and brighter burning fuel. Its fixed white characteristic also changed to a flashing white one (flash 0.5 s; eclipse 5.5s; flash 0.5 s).

Tragic human loss occurred during the Great Storm of 1913. Ten lake freighters were lost, including the 550-foot (168 m) *James Caruthers*, launched just six months earlier at Collingwood, and the 250-foot (76 m) steamer *Wexford*, downbound from Fort William to Goderich with a load of grain. Since the bulk of the wreckage was cast up on Huron County shores, a Lake Carriers' Association Committee based at Goderich directed the recovery and identification of the bodies. The storm took a record total of 19 vessels and stranded 19 others, with the overall loss of 244 lives. Goderich residents reported that during the three-day storm and fog, although they could hear a ship's whistle (possibly from the *Wexford*), they did not hear the lighthouse's fog signal once.

However, keeper Captain William Robinson insisted that the foghorn had been functioning during the storm. The ensuing inquest found that Goderich's lights were insufficient to effectively light the harbor. Thus, under government supervision, B.C. Munnings raised the lantern of the lighthouse 5 feet (1.5 m) for better visibility.

In 1925, with the changeover to electricity and the installation of a new semi-automatic light, a full-time keeper was no longer necessary. The keeper's house was removed and the materials used to build two cottages. The new electric light had two beams, reflected through two highly polished, mirror-like, concave reflectors that rotated around the light source. The stronger beam flashed at 19-second intervals and the weaker one flashed six seconds later. The new beams were reportedly visible for up to 21 miles (34 km). A local "character," Teeger Wull, tested the new light's accuracy by timing it with his pocket watch.

Other changes also took place. A reinforced concrete slab with coved edges replaced the tower's stone gallery deck. The light's ogee iron lantern was replaced by a plainer octagonal one with a low-pitched octagonal dome that also had an octagonal ventilator with a pointed top (an unusual feature since most domes had a ventilator ball). While the keeper's house is gone today, its foundation outline can be found in the grass. In 1986 the light was fully automated and became operational year round.

This still-functioning lighthouse stands in Lighthouse Park, a favorite attraction for tourists and locals who come to view the lighthouse, picnic or watch the spectacular Lake Huron sunsets. It is maintained by the Canadian Coast Guard out of Parry Sound.

Known Keepers: H. Fidler (–1870–), George McDonald (–1877–), Robert Campbell (1886–), Bert McDonald (1914–?) Captain William Robinson (1911–14, –27), B. McDonald (1927), Captain Robert Mackay (1928–29), Leslie E. Bogie (1929–39), Reginald Robert Needham (1939–59), Norman Cormier (1959–62), Allen K. MacDonald (1962–62), Walter Sheardown (1962–).

Goderich rear Range Light, 1911

24 Goderich Range Lights

In 1873 an initial north river breakwall was built at Goderich to protect the harbor basin and separate it from the mouth of the river. Then piers 1,500 feet (482 m) long and 200 feet (61.5 m) apart were built to flank the harbor entrance and add more protection. In 1879 range lights were added to the north pier: the front light displayed a red light from a square wooden tower and the rear light displayed a green light from an unpainted gallows-style tower with a 36-inch (0.9 m) iron lantern. To enter, vessels would line up the range lights, run up along the pier and then turn into the harbor.

Between 1904 and 1911 north and south breakwalls were built 1,800 feet (554 m) beyond the piers, making the harbor safe to enter under all but the most severe lake and wind conditions. During the construction of the breakwalls, a new rear range light was established on the north pier in 1905 on a white skeletal tower as a daymark. It was 49 feet (15.2 m) high and was changed from green to display a fixed red light that used a catoptric system from a focal plane of 64 feet (19.8 m).

Although notice of the new range lights had been posted, in 1907 the captain of the Ontario Fisheries steamer *Laurine* tried to enter the harbor using the old system. He hadn't checked the latest information, with the result that his vessel struck part of a storm-damaged, submerged breakwall, and was sunk. Only the boiler and the engine could be salvaged. In the end the captain was found at fault and his license was suspended for six months.

In 1909, when the outer breakwalls were completed, a new front range light was built. It was a triangular skeletal tower, whose daymark was also white. It was 35 feet (10.8 m) tall, used a catoptric system to display its red light from a focal plane of 44 feet 9 inches (13.6 m). It was situated on the north pier 590 feet (180 m) in front of the rear range light. In 1984 it was switched to a dioptric illumination system.

Known Keepers: see Goderich Main Light

25 Gordon Rock Light

In 1894 a square white wooden pyramidal tower with a red stripe on its west side was built on the northern part of Gordon Rock to mark this shoal on the east side of Georgian Bay, Lake Huron. Its fixed white light from a seventh-order lens produced a 7-mile (11 km) light from its focal plane of 26 feet (8 m). The light helped guide vessels into Parry Sound. While it is also unknown when the light was deactivated, it may have been when the shoal was marked with a light buoy in 1952. The Coast Guard often refers to this as Jones Island Front Range Light.

Gordon Rock Light

Great Duck Island Lighthouse, first (right) and second (left), circa 1919

26 Great Duck Island Lighthouse

Many vessels were sunk in Northern Lake Huron during the 1870s, but after the loss of the steamer *Asia* with over 100 people, the public demanded more navigation aids in the North Channel. In compliance, the government built a lighthouse in 1877 on the southwest side of Great Duck Island, a tiny isolated island on the shipping lanes of Lake Huron just to the southwest of Manitoulin Island and close to the international border.

The lighthouse was a square white tapering wooden tower attached to a white 1½-story wooden house. The three-story tower had a pedimented door and several large rectangular windows to light its interior. It was capped with a square gallery supported by 20 ornately carved wooden corbels and surrounded by a wooden cross-braced railing. Its decagonal cast-iron lantern used ten Silverburner lamps with 22-inch (55 cm) reflectors to display a red and white light, with one red and two white flashes every two minutes. From a focal plane of 64 feet (19.5 m) the light was visible for 15 miles (24 km).

In 1888 a steam fog signal (blast 8 s; eclipse 35 s) was established. The wooden building southeast of the lighthouse was painted white with a brown roof. The keeper also had a boathouse onshore in front of the lighthouse where he could winch his boat up out of Lake Huron storms.

Inevitably the station underwent change. The fog signal was changed to an air diaphone foghorn (blast 2.5 s; silence 27.5 s). In 1918 a taller tapering octagonal reinforced-concrete tower was built beside the old light. This 84-foot (25.6 m) tower used the old iron lantern from the first lighthouse but it was given a new third-order Fresnel lens that used a coal-oil vapor lamp to produce a group-flashing white light (flash; eclipse 2.5 s; flash; eclipse 2.5 s; flash; eclipse 10 s) that was visible for 17 miles (27.5 km). In the 1920s the station dock was moved to the more protected east side of the island. Two shipwrecks in this area were converted to a dock and a breakwater to form a harbor of sorts. At some time a wooden rail tramway was introduced to facilitate movement of supplies. In 1931 a new two-story wooden keeper's house was added.

Early keepers were brought food supplies by the tender *Lake Erie* but they supplemented their diets with a large garden and a cow. They even had white picket fences to keep animals out. Keepers had to get to and from the station in the government-supplied boat. Opening the season in the early spring and staying until late fall meant that they encountered ice or stormy weather, but their families left before the inclement weather.

In December 1949, in spite of strong winds, keeper Bob Leeson and his assistant, Ray Hughson, headed home to Manitoulin Island 14 miles (22.5 km) away. When they were ¼ mile (0.4 km) from Middle Duck Island, the boat's tail shaft broke and they lost power. The heavy northeast wind blew them onto a submerged rock and pitched them into icy water. In spite of their heavy Mackinaw coats and clothing, they managed to make it to shore, where Leeson became somewhat delirious. Fortunately, Hughson was able to retrieve blankets, sheets, salted pickerel and clothing from the smashed boat when it washed ashore. He stuck their 16 wet matches, head up in a piece of driftwood to dry them in the wind, and by afternoon he had a fire lit. The next day he made a lean-to of sheets as it snowed heavily. For three days they survived on fish and hemlock tea, until Leeson had improved enough for them to retrieve the skiff they had been towing and haul it to quieter water on the island's west side.

When the storm had abated, they rowed back to Great Duck Island, beached the skiff and trekked the 4-mile (6.5 km) length of the island to the lighthouse. They turned the light back on, hoping that someone had noticed it had been off for three days and restarted, and would understand their need for help, since they had no radio-telephone at the station. John Grant of Silver Water *had* noticed, so he called the Coast Guard at Parry Sound and they sent out a float plane. After fearing the worst upon seeing their smashed vessel on Middle Duck Island, the pilot eventually found them alive at the lighthouse and returned them safely to Manitoulin Island. The next year Leeson returned to the island as keeper, but he had a new assistant — and a newly installed radio phone.

In 1981 the station's obsolete diaphone fog signal equipment was removed and placed in the Museum of Science and Technology as an example of this type of historical machinery. The light was next automated by battery-powered electric light. Today all that remains are the tower and a bungalow, since the Coast Guard destroyed all the other buildings. In 1989 the light became lit all year round as an emergency light. It is still operational.

Known Keepers: William Purvis (1877–97), John Purvis (1898–1911), Norman Smith (1912–19), William Boyle (1918–30), William Rumley (1931–36), Frank Fowler (1937–44), William Rumley (1945–47), Bob Leeson (1948–49), John Grant (1949–50), James Howard Noble (1953–56), T.A. Haywood (1956–61), Frank Rourke (1959–65), Jim Rumley (1972), Joe Thibeault (1972).

27 Griffith Island Lighthouse

Griffith Island lies just east of Colpoy's Bay off the east side of the Bruce Peninsula in Georgian Bay, between Cape Croker and Owen Sound. In 1855 the Department of Public Works, Canada West contracted Scottish stone mason John Brown to build eleven lighthouses on Lake Huron and Georgian Bay to light the maritime route from Point Clark to Christian Island. The Griffith Island light was to be multi-purposed: to mark the west coast of Georgian Bay, the turning point to Wiarton at the end of Colpoy's Bay, and a refuge for vessels in foul weather behind White Cloud Island, which lay behind Griffith Island.

The Griffith Island Lighthouse was built in 1857–58 on the northeast side of the island, on a hill with a long slope to the shore. Both the tower and the separate keeper's house were made of first-quality white dolomite limestone believed to have been quarried in the Owen Sound area and ferried over by barge. The limestone was hand-hewn, laid in even courses and left with a rusticated stone finish. The conical tower 54¼ feet (16.5 m) high, was built on a 15-inch (38 cm) bed of concrete on a good clay bottom. Its 5-foot thick (2 m) walls tapered to about 2 feet (0.6 m) at the top, keeping a constant inner diameter of 10.5 feet (3.3 m). The last courses of stone were granite, used for its ability to support the heavy lantern and lens. Metal flooring, supplied by C. Yale of St. Catharines, was installed at the gallery level on I-beams and lengths of railway iron mortared into the stonework. The metal floor provided a fireproof base for the lens pedestal.

Both the octagonal iron lantern and the third-order Fresnel lens were manufactured and installed by the Louis Sautter Company of Paris. The lantern was bolted right to the granite and each of its eight sides had three rows of glass panes set into astragals. Its high-domed copper roof was in the imperial architectural style, segmentally ridged, and topped with a ventilator in the shape of a ball pinnacle. In cold weather, the sperm whale oil that it burned produced more than its own volume of water vapor, which condensed on the inside of the dome and was collected in an inner eave-strough. From here the water was carried outside and spewed away from the lantern glass by spouts hidden inside eight brass lion's heads. The draft to keep the lamp burning brightly was controlled by the lamp chimney, small holes in the ventilator ball and a trap door that could be closed to prevent tower drafts that might extinguish the light.

The lantern displayed a fixed white light that was visible up to 17 miles (27.5 km) on a clear night. The detached 1½-story keeper's house with walls 2 feet (0.6 m) thick had a central entry door and a central boxed-in staircase to the cellar and the second floor. To the left of the door was a large kitchen/family area with a stone fireplace along the end wall. To the right was the parlor with a door to a small master bedroom. The two loft bedrooms were heated by a small pot-bellied stove served by a second chimney at the opposite end of the house. The house was roofed with slate set inside the parapeted end walls. To ensure that rainwater did not penetrate the walls, parapeting of the end gables was achieved with one long stone block per slope, which covered all exposed masonry joints. The interior had circular-sawn lath and plaster covering its walls and wainscoting in the kitchen/family area.

Griffith Island Lighthouse, circa 1908

Griffith Island Lighthouse

While Brown was contracted to build eleven such lighthouses, he only finished six. Unforeseen circumstances — storms, delay in delivery of materials, sunken supply vessels, uncharted waters, the need to pay higher wages for work in remote areas — resulted in his incurring a loss of £1,500 per light and having to approach the government for more money. All six of the finished lighthouses had towers and keeper's houses in the same style, although their heights varied according to location. They were all built between 1855 and 1859 and were placed at Point Clark, Chantry Island, Cove Island, Griffith Island, Nottawasaga Island and Christian Island. These six lighthouses became known as the "imperial" towers. No one is certain why they were called imperial. No British money funded any of their construction, as some believe. As they were pre-Confederation, however, they were built during the Imperial rule of England and they do use an imperial style of dome, which is unique to these towers. Also, the term "imperial" has been used to describe a stone lighthouse style that can endure seemingly forever. Perhaps they are named for a combination of these ideas.

The light's first keeper, John Frame, first lit the light on December 27, 1858. Since he had been hired in October and did not return in 1859 it turned out that he was paid $103.75 for just three months' work. Keeper George Bennett left Thornaleys' dock in a

small motorboat in heavy weather one day in December 1922 during his first season, to go around to the lighthouse about half a mile (0.8 km) away. He was last seen late in the afternoon about a mile south and east of the island, being carried away from the lighthouse. His chance of survival would have been low as it was bitterly cold.

Late nineteenth-century politics were highly partisan, to the extent that the governing Grits allegedly sent 20 voters out to work on the lighthouse to prevent them from voting for the Conservative Party in Gray County in the election of September 3, 1896.

Life at the lighthouse was closely related to the natural world. During the day keepers supplemented their diet with fish from the abundant waters. But at night many birds, attracted by the bright white light, were killed by flying into the lantern glass. It became part of the keeper's daily routine to clean the glass and dispose of the carcasses.

The station changed little over the years. Around 1871 the house and tower, originally of natural limestone, were white-washed to increase their daytime visibility. Between 1883 and 1888 correspondence between the Department of Marine and Fisheries and the Department of Indian Affairs attempted to clarify land ownership. The Department of Marine and Fisheries eventually bought a 16-acre (6.5 hectare) lighthouse reserve from the Department of Indian Affairs for $80 ($5 per acre). A dock, a boathouse and a hand foghorn (1913) were added. In 1924, made surplus by the automation of the light through the use of acetylene, the keeper was removed from the station.

The tower — now solar-powered — displays a flashing white light (flash 0.5 s; eclipse 3.5 s) every four seconds. The house also still stands today, but it is in very bad repair. It is unfortunate that the station is neglected and abandoned, as it is a unique part of the Great Lakes' maritime heritage.

Known Keepers: John Frame (1858), Vesey C. Hill (1859–82), Garrett W. Patterson (1882–84), W.S. Boyd (1889–1922), F.W. Thornley (1922), George Bennett (1922 drowned), F.W. Thornley (1922–23).

28 Hope Island Lighthouse

Hope Island is the northernmost of the three large islands often referred to as the Christian Islands, which lie about 20 miles (32 km) north of Collingwood. The French explorers originally called it Isle au Géant (Giant's Head) referring to the native legend that the islands were footsteps of a giant who made the ground shake when he walked. The name Hope Island was given to it by Lt. Henry Bayfield, its first surveyor.

In 1884 a square tapering white wooden tower and attached keeper's house were built on the northwest side of the island to mark the water route into Nottawasaga Bay from Georgian Bay.

The contract was granted to T.R. Caton of Parry Sound for $2,777, but it cost only $1,864. The tower had 52 steps ascending it and was 57 feet (17.4 m) from ground to vane. Its catoptric lighting system displayed a revolving white light from a 54-foot (16.5 m) focal plane to be visible up to 12 miles (19 km) on a clear night.

Its first keeper, Charles Tizard, earned $450 a year. Lightkeepers had to be "Jacks of all trades" able to handle all problems, as Tizard's first logbook, ending December 31, 1884, illustrates. "I had no instructions to

Hope Island Lighthouse, circa 1907

Hope Island Lighthouse

work the machine so I used my own judgement and found that the reflectors were on upside-down, causing the lamp tubes to ram against the reflectors and when heated, they burst. The light revolves every two minutes and eighteen seconds and flashes every twenty-three seconds. I lighted up the first on the twenty-seventh of October and closed the fifteenth of December."

After Tizard's sudden death in 1886, his wife carried on the job. During her tenure, a fierce storm raised the water levels to within 2 feet (0.6 m) of the lighthouse. Allen Collins was appointed keeper on May 23, 1887, with an annual salary of $450. In August 1888 he assisted the crew of the American schooner *Imperial* when they arrived in a yawl at Hope Island after their three-master had sunk.

On May 15, 1891, so that his children could attend school on Christian Island, Collins switched places with John Hoar, the lightkeeper there. Hoar, who had been appointed keeper in 1868, had built a wooden stable and shed with his own money and asked to bring it with him to Hope Island. The superintendent refused. Hoar had also claimed a small boat as his, but it was a government-issued boat and had to remain at the Christian Island Lighthouse. As a result of the ensuing bickering — in which Hoar complained that Collins had left him a partially paid-for sailboat, Collins claimed Hoar had taken the stove he paid for and Collins received a bill for $70 (due to Hoar) for extensive repairs on Christian Island — the matter was referred to the government for mediation.

Hope Island Lighthouse, circa 1939

Upon investigation in April 1892, the Superintendent of Lighthouses, Mr. Harty, sided with Collins, adding hopefully, "Time will effect a cure between these men and all concerned will be satisfied to remain as they are." Hoar took his case to the Department of Marine and raised the question of pension benefits. His complaint led to the appointment of Thomas Marchildon as lightkeeper at Hope Island for 1894. Furious, and feeling cheated of his job, Hoar refused to leave. As the *Midland Argus* reported on Thursday, December 21, 1893: "Since the announcement that Marchildon had gone to Hope Island, provisioned and equipped for duties of his government job … the report now comes from up the shore that Marchildon has … been compelled to camp a little over gun-shot distance from the lighthouse, because from the moment he set foot on the island, Hoar has maintained a shotgun welcome. What causes the soreness between the old friends is not known here, but people are laughing at the mind picture of Hoar holding Hope Island Lighthouse with a shotgun against Marchildon, and Marchildon being compelled to sit down out of range of the shotgun for a few weeks to await the formation of ice to the mainland so the reinforcements can be secured." Eventually the dispute was resolved and Marchildon took his post.

In the 1890s François Marchildon and William Lacourse mysteriously disappeared near Hope Island. According to local legend, these two fishermen were murdered and buried in the well under the lighthouse. This story was credible enough for Servere and Alfred Marchildon, relatives of the lost François, to tear up the lighthouse floor in 1906. They found nothing, but rumors persisted that the gravesite was elsewhere on the island. Long-time area residents say that Johnny Hoar confessed to these murders on his deathbed, but this has never been substantiated. The purported motive was revenge for having been rescued from an attempted suicide in a barn in Lafontaine.

On October 16, 1891 the *Lottie Wolf*, a two-masted American schooner en route from Chicago to Midland with a cargo of grain, was lost in heavy weather 100 yards (90 m) north of the station on a rock that now bears her name. Arthur Visick, the first cottager at Thunder Bay, retrieved her nameplate in 1916. For years the guests at Thunder Bay Inn were summoned to dinner by the *Lottie Wolf's* ship's bell.

In the spring of 1898 Thomas Marchildon was replaced by Charles Vallée, who continued as keeper until June 1911, when Marchidon returned to the post. This time the change was due to political patronage. The job changes corresponded with the federal government's change from Conservative to Liberal and back to Conservative.

In November 1943 the S.S. *Riverton* fetched up sideways on the Lottie Wolf Shoal off Hardhead Point on the northwest corner of Hope Island during a storm. The steel barge *Michigan* attempted to lighten the stranded *Riverton* by coming alongside and putting pumps into the cargo hold, while the tug *Favourite*, mother ship to the lighter *Michigan*, was on the other side of the *Michigan*. The storm's intensity increased and the ships were pounded together. The *Favourite* maneuvered carefully away from the *Michigan* and dropped anchor to the northeast. She drifted back and secured a line onto the *Michigan*, but in trying to pull her away from the *Riverton*, she pulled the timberheads out of the *Michigan*, which was pounded in two during the night. At daybreak, the *Favourite* dropped "storm oil" to create an oil slick to calm the water. The entire crew was saved and the *Riverton* was successfully refloated.

Over the years the station received new equipment and more buildings. In 1908 a duplicate diaphone fog signal (blast 3 s; silence 3 s; blast 3 s; silence 51 s) was added at a cost of $1647. Sometime after 1915 the light's characteristic was changed from a flashing to a fixed white light. Around 1940 a diesel generating plant was installed for electricity. In 1944 a radio beacon was synchronized with the fog signal to allow vessels to find distance and pinpoint their location. The station was later updated with a radio-telephone, two new bungalows (1962 and 1965), a heli-pad, and a submarine cable for electricity. The light was automated in 1988 and its characteristic again became a flash pattern (flash 1 s; eclipse 4 s). At some point the lantern was removed and a new light was placed on a skeletal tower close to the old light.

In 2002 concerned area residents formed the Huronia Lightstation Preservation Society to assist with the lighthouse's preservation and restoration. The group has a good working relationship with the Canadian Coast Guard and the Christian Island First Nations Band (which now owns the lighthouse reserve), and the three groups are working together to restore the light. In 2004 the contaminated oil and the lead paint were removed from the building and the site. The keeper's house has been reshingled and the lanternless top has been protected from the elements. Steady progress, including the addition of a replica lantern, will eventually make the old lighthouse as good as new.

Known Keepers: Charles Tizard (1884–85), Mrs. Tizard (1885–86), Allan Collins (1887–90), John Hoar (1891–93), Thomas Marchildon (1893–98), Charles Vallee (1899–1910), Thomas Marchildon (1911), P. Leblanc (1911–12), Thomas Marchildon (1912–14), J. Stewart (1915–16), William Ross Wallace (1918–40), Arthur Alexander Herron (1940–62), Dalton Crawford (1963–65), Caleb Donald Graeme Webb (1966), James P. Felon (?), Marvin Graham (1967–72), Ray Dawson (1973–84), Elwood Richardson (1985), Ernie McCombe (1986–87). Also listed: John Archibald McRae (1946?) and Joseph Wallace Hacker (1949?).

29 Janet Head — Gore Bay Lighthouse

In 1855, with the opening of the Soo Locks in Sault Ste. Marie and the arrival of the first railway at Collingwood, the shipping route via the North Channel above Manitoulin Island in Lake Huron and the railway from Collingwood to Lake Ontario became much shorter than the St. Lawrence water system. In the mid- to late 1800s immigrants and supplies were shipped west, and grain and wood products were sent eastward. With the increasing flow of lake traffic in the North Channel, the government saw the need to mark the passage. One of the lights they built on Manitoulin Island was at Gore Bay on a point called Janet Head. "Janet" was said to be a daughter of Lt. Henry Bayfield, who surveyed Lake Huron in his ship, the *Recovery*, between 1822 and 1825.

The lighthouse, also named Janet Head, is a small, white, clapboard tower set on a stone foundation and painted white with red trim. It and the keeper's house were built in 1879. Besides marking the point, the lighthouse also marked the harbor at Gore Bay. The 26-foot (8 m) tapering square tower was built right into the 1½-story keeper's house so that the tower's two stories were living space. A wooden railing with cross supports surrounded the square gallery. The back panel of the octagonal lantern was blacked out. Its original catoptric system of reflectors and oil burning lamps was later changed to a dioptric system, which used a lens with oil burning lamps inside that produced an occulting white light (flash 3 s; eclipse 2 s). With its 43-foot (13 m) focal plane, the light could be seen for 11 miles (17.7 km).

The lighthouse only had five full-time keepers. Their job was to keep the light burning, record weather and events, and answer distress calls, making at least three attempts to reach a ship before abandoning a rescue. Anything noteworthy was to be recorded in a daily log.

Janet Head — Gore Bay Lighthouse

The logbooks of the first keeper, Robert Boyter, give us many details. As Janet Head was a wooden lighthouse on a point surrounded by trees, forest fires were a definite threat. One of Boyter's entries shows, "Paid to Nesbit and Sons for helping to put out and stop a bush fire, $3.00." In December 1879 his log showed that during the last week of operation that season three lamps burning nightly had used five gallons and a half a quart (23.4 l) of oil during 124 hours of operation. (Not all keepers were this precise!)

Boyter even kept the log throughout the winter during the non-shipping season, including a personal tragedy in March 1880. His wife and eldest son left the lighthouse heading to his son's farm on the north shore but the conditions were so bad that they arrived only the next day, severely frost-bitten. Hearing of his wife's condition Boyter arranged for a team of horses and a sleigh to bring her home. On the crossing, he and four other travelers were lost in a snowstorm and could do nothing but return to Gore Bay. One of the travelers, a young girl, died from exposure. Boyter set out on foot to get help, and was found collapsed on the point east of the lighthouse. The whole episode caused an uproar in Gore Bay and an inquiry was held into possible neglect or wrongdoing. Boyter said he had hired the team to leave the lighthouse early in the morning but witnesses saw him in town 1.5 miles (2.4 km) away from the lighthouse at noon. Boyter said they had a drink of whiskey now and then on the trip but none of the men were drunk. Nothing could be proven, however, and no charges were laid.

Other logbook entries recorded a split in the building's foundation in May 1883; that the cellar flooded every spring and fall; and that captains complained in 1885 that there was no foghorn. In 1887 Boyter recorded a request to burn the light year round as there was more winter travel across the ice than summer travel on the water. A later entry, in 1917, shows that by then the light was being lit for ice crossing but it is not known exactly when this started. A hand-cranked foghorn was finally supplied in 1888.

The second keeper, James Kinney, in 1901 recorded the barge *Chamberlain* being grounded at Darch Island on November 11. The log of the third keeper, Captain Angus Matheson, indicated that while the channel usually froze over in December, the last mail boat in 1913 crossed on January 7 and that the first mail over the ice arrived on January 23. The fourth keeper, Robert Lewis, reported that the last trip of the mail boat in 1914 was on January

11, that two days later the temperature dropped to -35°F (-31°C), and that the first mail over the ice was on January 25, only 14 days after the last mail boat. The next winter the channel froze even faster. The last mail boat was December 23, and the first mail over the ice was just six days later. In September 1921 Lewis recorded that high winds and heavy seas had caused a vessel to run aground at Barrie Island.

The fifth and last full-time keeper was George Thorburn. His log recalls five drownings in 1938 and mentions Britain and France going to war with Germany on September 6, 1939. During his last year as keeper, Thorburn lived in the village and rode his bicycle back and forth to the lighthouse to light or extinguish the lamps. If it was foggy he would stay to operate the foghorn.

With automation the lighthouse beacon was extinguished forever and replaced by a battery-operated light mounted on a steel tower. Later the modern beacon was placed in the lantern room of the lighthouse. After automation, Janet Head was privately owned for a number of years. Today the Janet Head Light is a historical site and is open to the public. The second floor is an interpretive center. With a campsite nearby, this is a popular destination for tourists.

Known Keepers: Robert Boyter (1879–90), James Kinney (1895–1903), Captain Angus Matheson (1903–13), Robert Lewis (1913–34), William Johnson (1935–36), George Thorburn (1936–55).

30 Jones Island Range Lights

As part of the Canadian government's lighting of Georgian Bay to prevent major ship catastrophes, range lights were established at Jones Island in 1894. While these lights were to help lead vessels safely through the shoal-infested channel into Parry Sound, sea captains disliked them, as they either vanished into the sun's glare or faded into the backdrop of rugged rock, wind-swept pines and deciduous trees. No matter how the government tried to change the day color characteristic, nothing worked well.

The front range light was a square wooden tower 36 feet 5 inches (11.1 m) high, built on the northernmost summit of Gordon Rock. Its fixed red catoptric light was visible for 7 miles (11.3 km) from a focal plane of 41 feet (12.5 m). The rear range light was a tapering square white tower 50 feet (15.5 m) high,

Jones Island Rear Range Lights

which emerged from the centre of the roof peak of the white 1½-story hip-roofed keeper's house. The tower displayed its fixed white catoptric light from a focal plane of 60 feet 9 inches (18.5 m) for a visibility of 8 miles (13 km). This light was built on the southwest point of Jones Island.

These lights were contracted to and built by Charles Mickler. He finished them in 1894 but they were not lit until 1895. Since Mickler had not built them to government specifications, he was released from the job and W.H. Noble, a public works foreman for the Department of Marine and Fisheries, completed the buildings properly. He had to reshingle the sides and the roofs and rebuild the tower cornices to weatherproof the structures. His refurbishings, which cost $647, were charged against the contract price. Apparently Mickler successfully sued the government for this "hold back" money.

The lanterns of these range lights were designed so that their lights could be viewed only when a vessel was on a direct line of approach and safely aligned in the channel. Around 1913 the lights were automated with the use of acetylene, but the keepers were not removed at this time. Sometime between 1898 and 1929 the front range light was changed from a fixed red to a fixed white light.

In 1929 the front light on Gordon Rock had its characteristic changed from fixed white to occulting white, automatically occulting at short intervals. In 1992 both lights were exhibiting a fixed white light. It is unknown when the last keeper was removed, but the lights continue to operate as aids to navigation today.

Known Keepers: Walter Huff (1897–), Edward Taylor (1901–07), Joseph G. Dixon (1917–19).

31 Kagawong Lighthouse

In 1880 a lighthouse was built at Kagawong on Manitoulin Island's north shore below Clapperton Island in Lake Huron. It was built on the community's first pier at the foot of Mudge Bay to assist mariners in docking. In 1888 a pole light was added on land behind the pier light to make entry even easier. A shed was also built to store the volatile kerosene that was the light's illuminant. In 1892 a forest fire destroyed much of the village, including the oil shed and the pole light.

Kagawong Lighthouse

When contract bids for replacing the pole light seemed unusually high (even the lowest bid was close to $1,000), the government had its own workers do the job for only $294. The new light, built in 1894, was a square white 30-foot (9 m) tapering wooden tower with a red lantern and an ornate circular gallery supported by decorative carved corbels. It was placed 75 feet (22.8 m) back from the shore, 100 feet (30.5 m) west of the dock, and it displayed a fixed white light that was visible for 11 miles (17.8 km). At some point the pier light disappeared, the shore light was changed to a fixed red light, and the tower received a new square, plain-Jane gallery and railing.

During the 1930s Kagawong became a tourist area where passenger steamers stopped on their way to Lake Superior. In 1939, for just $35, vacationers could get a week-long round trip from Owen Sound to Michipicoten. While the steamer refueled at Kagawong, the passengers could take a leisurely stroll to the nearby Bridal Falls. The community's small Anglican Church received many visitors to see its unusual nautical theme. Many years later, in 1970, the prow of the Chris Craft yacht *Rhu*, became the church's pulpit. Today these attractions and the lighthouse continue to draw tourists to the remote village.

Visitors to the light can see 1890s ship arrival and departure times penciled on the wall inside the tower. A ship's arrival was a special event. As soon as the steamship's black, smoky plume was seen trailing across the sky, villagers swarmed to the docks to greet the vessel and hear any news first-hand. Although the light was automated some time in the 1960s with the use of electricity, it still stands serenely on the hillside to watch over its harbor.

Known Keepers: William Boyd (1893–1916), Jacob McPherson (1923–26), William McKenzie (1927–58), Mrs. McKenzie (1958).

32 Killarney East (Red Rock Point) Lighthouse

Along the north shore of Georgian Bay, Lake Huron, and close to the eastern end of Manitoulin Island, is a peninsula that ends in an island known as George Island. The deep waterway between this island and the mainland is called the Killarney Channel, and the community of Killarney along this narrow channel is well protected from fierce lake storms. While it used to be called Shebahaning, meaning "canoe passage" in Ojibway, it was later named Killarney, although no one knows exactly why.

After the lighting of the Bruce Peninsula and some of Georgian Bay with the six imperial towers, lights were placed in the Manitoulin area to support the growing fishing and lumbering industries. In 1866 a lighthouse was built one mile (1.6 km) east of Killarney on Georgian Bay's north shore to mark entry from the east into the Killarney Channel. It was placed on a point known as Red Rock and consisted of a short white wooden square tower with an octagonal birdcage-style lantern and no gallery railing. It used oil lamps and reflectors to display a fixed white light from a 42-foot

(12.8 m) focal plane for a visibility of 11 miles (17.7 km). First lit on July 27, 1867, it was one of the first lights lit for the new Dominion of Canada, which had just been officially formed on July 1, 1867.

The keeper's house was built in 1870 at a cost of $650 in the fishing community of Killarney, a mile away. It was a 1½-story dwelling with large twelve-paned rectangular windows. The Killarney keeper tended both the Killarney East and the Killarney West lights. From his home he could keep an eye on the Killarney East Lighthouse on the rocks, but he had to travel by boat to tend the Killarney West light. While he could travel by land to the east lighthouse it was faster to go by boat unless the lake was stormy.

In 1909 both lighthouses were rebuilt. The east one was of "pepper-pot" design, a 20-foot (6.1 m) square white wooden pyramidal tower topped with a large square gallery with a large curved supporting wooden cornice. It had a pipe iron railing around its gallery and an octagonal cast-iron lantern. At some point its fixed white light was converted to a flashing white light through the use of a lens and a clockwork mechanism that rotated it. It also had a hand-cranked foghorn for the keeper to answer ships' signals.

Killarney's second keeper was Pierre Regis de Lamorandière, a former blacksmith, cooper, gunsmith, sailor, farmer and fiddle player. He had a special kinship to Killarney as his grandfather had started a trading post there in 1820. When he became keeper, locals complained that he collected a keeper's salary ($350 a year) as well as a government Indian annuity (his mother was of Native blood). Further bad feelings arose between the keeper and some local residents in 1893, when the government asked Lamorandière to report illegal fishing to the Department of Marine and Fisheries and his reports led to several convictions of local fishermen. Animosity peaked when fishermen attacked him and his property, shooting his horse, stealing clothing and burning the hay to feed his cattle. The government had to send a constable to Killarney for six weeks to resolve the situation and protect the keeper. Eventually he was given $125 for his losses. In 1923, at age 80 and just two weeks before his death, Lamorandière went to Toronto to petition for a road to Killarney to connect it with the rest of the twentieth century.

Ferdinand (Ferdy) Solomon kept the Killarney lights for almost 20 years. Merle, his wife, came from Providence Bay, Manitoulin Island. In a 2001 interview she spoke about her life as a keeper's wife. She didn't want to come to Killarney because Ferdy had so many relatives living there. (Apparently there was no love lost between residents of Killarney and those of Manitoulin Island. Killarney people were known as "sucker faces" or "fishguts" because they ate a lot of fish. Manitoulin people were known as "haw-eaters" or "hawers" because they ate berries from the hawthorn bush. Each group made fun of the other, and moving to Killarney made Merle feel outnumbered.) However, after she got to know her husband's

Killarney East (Red Rock Point) Lighthouse in summer and winter

relations she found them to be wonderful people. She and Ferdy had seven children.

Ferdy's most harrowing experience was on a windy day in November 1956. He left by boat early in the morning to tend the east light. When he had not returned for breakfast, Merle sent the boys to find him. The next thing she knew, Teddy ran through the back door screaming, "Dad's lying on an island and his boat is going around the island!" Not knowing who to call, Merle rang up the local phone operator and told *her* to call someone. Fortunately Ferdy had grabbed two life jackets as he was pitched into the icy water and wrapped them around his arms. He tried to swim to shore through the 14-foot (4 m) waves, but the water kept dragging him out. He almost gave up, but when he thought about Merle being left alone with all the kids, he got the inner strength to try even harder. Finally, a huge wave floated him up onto the rock "as if it were a Godsend." Onshore, his boys sent Teddy, the fastest runner, to the game warden's house for help. Meanwhile, the operator

Killarney East (Red Rock Point) Lighthouse, circa 1890

found someone from the village willing to try a rescue. Merle called the Coast Guard in Parry Sound but, when they seemed more worried about their boat than Ferdy's rescue, she told them that a coffin would cost more than a boat!

The village rescue boat could not get close enough but the game warden, Tom Houston, tied one end of a rope around himself and, synchronizing his movements with the waves, was able to tie the other end around Ferdy and bring him to shore. They stripped Ferdy and wrapped him in woollen blankets. On their way to the warden's house, they were joined by the priest, so everyone knew it was a life and death situation. Everyone in the small community tried to help. Someone brought a bathtub to give him a warm bath, and almost everyone brought a blanket. There were so many, "they would have touched the ceiling if piled up." Ferdy made a full recovery and continued to tend the light. He later wrote to the Canadian Coast Guard recommending that life jackets have a head support. Perhaps he made a positive contribution to the design of later life-jackets. Ferdy tended the light until 1979, when he died at the age of fifty-nine.

In 1957 the station was given a foghorn (blast 3 s; silence 27 s), and later it received a radio beacon. When the light was electrified, it had an isophase characteristic (flash 2 s; eclipse 2 s) and became operational all year round as an emergency light. In 1965 it became part of the Killarney keeper's job to make periodic trips to check on the range lights on Badgeley Island, which had been automated. At a still later date the Killarney light was also automated, and its exterior was covered with aluminum siding. Today the light still shines, but its keepers and their house are gone.

Known Keepers: see Killarney West Lighthouse.

33   Killarney West Lighthouse

As well as looking after the Killarney East Channel Light the Killarney keeper also looked after the Killarney West Channel Light, which marked the western end of the deep strait into Killarney. This western light was built on the south point of Partridge Island which lay about three quarters of a mile northwest of the channel's western entrance. Built in 1866, it was exactly the same as the East Killarney Light — a square white wooden tower with an octagonal bird-cage style lantern with no gallery railing. It also used oil lamps and reflectors to display a fixed white light from a 30-foot (9 m) focal plane for 10 miles (16 km).

Killarney West Lighthouse

This light was more difficult for the keeper to tend during stormy weather, as it was accessible only by boat. The light's second keeper, Lamorandière, solved the problem by using hermits and creating a win-win situation. He erected a shack in a protected area near the light and furnished it sparsely with a cot, a wood stove, a table, and a bench. The first occupants were Oliver Pilon and Henry Solomen. They got to stay there free of charge in return for lighting the light in foul weather. This worked so well that keepers following Lamorandière adopted the same policy.

In 1909 the lighthouse was replaced with a tower identical to the one erected at Killarney East also in 1909. It was a 20-foot (6 m) square white wooden pyramidal tower topped with a large square gallery with a large curved wooden cornice for support. It had a pipe iron railing around this gallery and an octagonal cast-iron lantern. This style was known as a "pepper-pot" design. It continued to display a fixed white light from a focal plane of 36 feet 8 inches (11.2 m) but had a visibility of only 6 miles (9.7 km). The light was later electrified, given a lens-illuminating optic, and automated. It continues to shine today.

Known Keepers: Philemon Proulx (1866–80), Pierre Regis de Lamorandière (1880–1904), Frank Rogue (1904–12), Joseph Burke (1912–46), F.J. Sinclair (1946–50), F.J. Solomon (1950–60), Basil Roque (1960–61), Ferdinand Solomon (1962–79), Brent Skippen (1979–81), Alfred de Lamorandière (1982–).

34   Kincardine Range Lights

As immigrants settled in Canada West along the eastern shores of Lake Huron, a Scottish settlement grew up at the mouth of the Penatangore River in 1848. First called Penatangore, it was later renamed Kincardine. Originally everything had to be brought in by water and in the 1850s a variety of schooners, steamers and paddle-wheelers stopped here. A breakwater built in an early effort to create a protective harbor was quickly washed away because builders had underestimated the lake's power. In 1856 two parallel piers 97.5 feet (30 m) apart were built to protect the harbor entrance, and in 1866 the harbor basin was excavated to accommodate larger vessels.

With the discovery of salt in the area, the town's primary industry changed from fishing to salt mining and export. The increased marine traffic emphasized the need for a light, and in 1874 a square wooden 32-foot (9.8 m) white skeletal gallows-style tower was placed at the outer end of the north pier 1,185 feet (360 m) from the shore. Below the lantern was an enclosed watchroom/service room. The tower had an open bottom to allow storms to wash beneath it and prevent ice build-up from affecting its stability. The light used a fixed red catoptric illumination system. Five mammoth flat wick lamps, each with an 18-inch (45 cm) reflector, produced the light from a focal plane of 37 feet (11.3 m), making it visible for 8 miles (13 km). Shipping increased still further with the export of grain, lumber, wooden furniture and textiles.

By 1878 the light and wharf were in an advanced state of decay and a new light was recommended. The main lighthouse was provided in 1880 at the inner end of the harbor along the edge of the rivermouth, to act as a rear range light to the pierhead light. The white wooden two-story keeper's house and 62.4-foot (19.2 m) tower were built by William Kay on a stone foundation right into the steep hillside, the former site of the

Kincardine Rear Range Light

However, a wave capsized it with its passengers, and five people drowned. Everyone else was saved by a second rescue boat. Today, the heavy black anchor from the *Ann Maria* is displayed in the front garden of the lighthouse.

When the railroad arrived in Kincardine, the volume of shipping dropped sharply. Rail was safer and more economical for personal travel and the shipping of goods and materials. In the next century the lighthouse underwent changes. On July 9, 1902, the front range light on the north pier burned down and a 28-foot (8.5 m) pole light took its place. In 1922 electricity replaced the kerosene oil lamps and steam foghorn. During the 1950s the lightkeeper was also the harbormaster, maintaining the harbor and collecting mooring fees of two cents per foot. In 1970 the lights were automated through the use of photoelectric cells, and in 1977 the lightkeeper's position was discontinued. In 1980 the Canadian Coast Guard leased the lighthouse to the Kincardine Yacht Club, and that group became responsible for maintaining and operating the lighthouse, the pierhead light and the foghorn. They used the lighthouse as their clubhouse as well as a marine museum.

In the late 1900s the community's Scottish heritage gave the lighthouse a unique attraction. The town's bagpipe band had a piper play from the gallery of the lighthouse for 30 minutes at sunset to honor Donald Sinclair, an early Kincardine piper. Story has it that Sinclair was immigrating to Kincardine with his family in 1856, when a storm approaching at dusk obscured the harbor entrance. Sinclair prayed for safe passage and played a lament on his pipes. Another Scottish settler piped a lament from the shore in response. The captain headed for the drone of the pipes and made it safely to harbor. After this, Sinclair often played his pipes at dusk as a way of recalling his good fortune and reminding people of the power of the pipes. The modern pipers appear daily in July and August, except on Saturday when the band is parading.

Today the rear range illuminant is a 500-watt light bulb. The front range light had its 250-watt light replaced in 1999 with a 35-foot (10.7 m) tri-sector light, and its old lighting apparatus is on display in the museum. The focal plane of the new front range light is 45 feet (13.7 m) and it has an electric foghorn. Today the rear range light has an orange vertical stripe that faces the water as part of its daymark. These range lights still actively draw vessels (mostly pleasure craft) safely into the harbor marina. Its picturesque location in a vacationer's paradise makes the rear range light one of the most photographed lighthouses in Bruce County.

Known Keepers: William Kay (–1877–), William Gordon Temple (1913–28), Donald Martin (1928–29), Oran Westell (1929–), Myron Hall (1955–56), Alonzo Burley (1956–).

Walker and Henry Distillery. Its octagonal wooden tower tapered gently 30 feet (9 m) up from the housetop to a focal plane of 80 feet (24.4 m). Four of its tower walls had large eight-paned windows to light the tower's 69 steps and allow the keeper to survey the harbor. Its dodecagonal iron lantern was blacked out with metal panels on its east side. The light from its kerosene lamps was directed out over the lake by a highly polished metal reflector that, with the high focal plane, allowed a visibility of 21 miles (34 km). Shutters made to rotate around the lamps by a weighted clockworks mechanism created the light's distinctive red flash pattern (flash 1 s; eclipse 5 s). The lantern was surrounded by an octagonal gallery with a protective pipe iron railing and was supported by eight ornately carved, wooden corbels. Both the tower and the house were trimmed in red to complete their daymark.

While built in 1880, as the keystone above its front door proclaims, it was lit in 1881 by Kay, who also became its first keeper. He had a manual outlining the proper procedures for the lamps: 1) light the lamps early enough that they are burning fully before nightfall; 2) turn the wicks down low when first lit, and then very gradually raise them until they reach full flame power; 3) after lighting up, stay for 30 minutes to attend the flames; 4) make sure all lamp chimneys are vertical and truly in position; 5) make sure the glass chimneys are clean; 6) in heavy weather, do not leave the light unattended. The keeper tended both range lights, so that vessels could line up with their beams and safely navigate into the harbor. By 1899 the lighthouse keeper earned $600 a year.

The sandy shallows and rocky beach on either side of the harbor created hazardous conditions for vessels. At least eleven steamers and schooners were shipwrecked in the area between 1864 and 1903. In November 1833 the 214-ton steamer tug *Erie Belle* exploded and sank. Eight of her twelve-man crew were saved. In October 1902 the 242-ton schooner *Ann Maria* sank just south of the harbor while seeking refuge at Kincardine. Hearing the ship's bell and cries for help, the townspeople sent out a lifeboat.

Kincardine Rear Range Light after 1880

35 Lion's Head Lighthouse

Between Cabot Head and Cape Croker along the east side of the Bruce Peninsula, which forms the west side of Georgian Bay, is Lion's Head. While the area had a natural bay with the potential for an excellent harbor, the mouth of the bay was blocked by a sandbar and a channel was not dredged through it until 1883. With accessibility to the bay, the harbor grew, and in 1903 a light was set at the outer end of the north breakwater/pier to mark the harbor entrance.

This simple light consisted of a square lantern with a lamp and reflector that was hoisted nightly to the top of a 15-foot (4.6 m) pole. Its red light was visible for about six miles (9.7 km) and the total cost was only $197. Charles Knapp, a former shoemaker, was appointed its first keeper. When the pier was extended in 1911, the pole light was replaced by a tapering white square frame wooden tower. Within a year this tower was destroyed by a fierce lake storm and had to be replaced.

Another short white wooden tower took its place at the outer end of the pier. Its wooden frame was covered inside with diagonal boarding and outside with vertical boarding. Its tapering sides flared suddenly at the top to create the wooden cornice that supported the simple square gallery and its protective pipe-iron railing. The tower had a pedimented door and two steep flights of ladder stairs. Its square wooden lantern had cast-iron corner posts, four large rectangular windows (set horizontally), and lower outer walls covered in cedar shingles painted white. It was topped with a square dome and ventilator stack. The whole structure stood about 30 feet (9 m) high.

This lighthouse survived both change and disaster. Its first disaster occurred when high winds and pounding 35-foot (10.7 m) waves struck during the Great Storm of 1913 and blew the lighthouse off its pier mooring right onto the harbor's south shore. When the storm had subsided the lighthouse was recovered, repaired, and re-anchored at the end of the pier. In 1919 it was given a more protected position farther back along the pier. Its second disaster came in the form of a fire in 1933. Fortunately it was again repaired and continued as harbor sentry. Sometime during the 1930s a concrete dock was poured and the lighthouse was securely anchored to it. In 1944 the light's fixed red characteristic was changed to green to avoid confusion with the village lights. In 1951 the light was electrified, but the keeper was kept on.

The lighthouse's final fate came extremely early one morning in 1969 when the Canadian Coast Guard arrived and dismantled it, without the prior knowledge of the villagers. Citizens were outraged, but it was too late. By 8:00 a.m. the lighthouse had been dismantled, and its remains were taken to the local landfill site and burned. When the local member of parliament sought an explanation, the Coast Guard said the structure was rotten beyond saving. Local citizens did not agree, and grieved the loss of their beloved landmark. The Coast Guard also automated the light at this time by placing a new light on a 20-foot (6 m) circular steel mast post that used a modern optic to display an isophase flashing red light (flash 2 s; eclipse 2 s) from a focal plane of 29½ feet (9 m). The mast was also given a white rectangular daymark. Locals complained that the town's streetlights were brighter than this new light.

A group of young people finally took action. In September 1980 seven grade-twelve design students at the Bruce Peninsula District School in Lion's Head, chose the project of making a replica of the long-gone lighthouse. By the end of the school year the project was bogged down in red tape and many of the participating students had graduated. But, with perseverance, their teacher's help, and about $4,500 in fundraising, the students' efforts eventually reached fruition. The finished replica was placed on the beach overlooking the harbor in 1983 because the Coast Guard did not permit the replica to be lit or to replace the pole light on the pier for fear of mariners being confused with the change. However, fate intervened. In 2000 during a severe spring storm, the pole light was bent beyond repair and its electrical wiring broken. Instead of making costly repairs or replacing it with another pole light, the Coast Guard moved the replica lighthouse to the original pier location and transferred the flashing red light from the pole to the tower lantern — a win/win situation.

Known Keepers: Charles Knapp (1903–12), P. Webster Brady (1912–27), Ivan Butchart (1927–56), Ed Rouse (1956–69).

Lion's Head Lighthouse

36 Little Current Range Lights

By the mid- to late 1800s steamers made regular stops at Little Current (then known as Shaftesbury), Georgian Bay, as it lay right along the northern shipping route. Ships brought in commodities and shipped out fish. In 1866 the government established range lights identical to those built at Killarney to help vessels into the harbor.

The front range light was built on the east end of Spider Island. It was a 22-foot (6.7 m) square white wooden tower surmounted by a birdcage-style iron lantern and a small gallery with no railing. Using lamps and 16-inch (40 cm) reflectors, it displayed a fixed white light for 6 miles (9.5 km). The rear range light was 450 yards (410 m) south of the front one on the mainland shore between two docks. It was a 24-foot (7.3 m) square white wooden tower with an iron bird-cage lantern and a gallery with no railing. It also used lamps and 16-inch (40 cm) reflectors to display a fixed white light that was visible for 6 miles (9.5 km).

After Canada's confederation in 1867, records were updated. To this end the Department of Marine and Fisheries purchased the land on which the lights were built from the Department of Indian Affairs. Onshore they first bought land at the junction of Robinson and Worthington Streets for $70 on April 22, 1879. When they discovered that the keeper's house, stables and outbuildings sat only partly on the lighthouse reserve, they purchased additional land from William Griffiths for $60 to secure title for all the land on which their buildings stood. One acre (0.4 hectare) at the east end of Spider Island was purchased from the Department of Indian Affairs in August 1886 for $30. The amount finally paid in 1891 was actually $39.40 (the additional $9.40 was for accumulated interest).

It was common for steamers to be trapped at Little Current. Sometimes, when currents shifted log booms, the harbor entrance was blocked and vessels had no choice but to wait until the booms were moved.

In 1907 the range lights were moved: the front light on Spider Island was extinguished; the back lantern was moved to the roof of Byron Turner's warehouse to increase its visibility and it became the front range light; and a new rear range light was erected on a pole behind the new front range light. These lights each used a small lens to display a fixed red light. Since they were used only to guide vessels to the harbor wharves, they just had a one-mile (1.6 km) visibility.

The lights were later changed to fixed green. In 1922 the town of Little Current built a War Memorial at the site of its former onshore rear range light and sometime in the 1950s the light on Spider Island was razed.

Known Keepers: Donald McKenzie (1866–1901), David Boyter (1902–07), William McKenzie (1921–30), Wesley Taylor (1930–37).

Little Current Old Front Range Light, circa 1910

37 Lonely Island Lighthouse

In 1870 the Canadian government built a lighthouse on the high bluff on the north side of Lonely Island off the eastern end of Manitoulin Island in northern Georgian Bay. As well as marking the passage between these two islands, it also marked the northeastern approach to the main strait between Georgian Bay and Lake Huron.

The square wooden tower with two windows rose 42 feet (12.8 m) from the lake end of its 1½-story wooden keeper's house. It supported a simple square gallery with a polygonal iron lantern that displayed a fixed white light using five flat-wick lamps and 15-inch (38 cm) reflectors. Having a 195-foot (60 m) focal plane, the light was visible for 20 miles (32.2 km).

The original lighthouse was set in front of an Indian burial ground. The keepers used to invite passing natives to come and see the lighthouse but were always politely refused, as the natives considered the island sacred ground.

The first fog warning was quite primitive — the keeper would fire a musket. When Captain Foote of the steamer *Pacific* complained that this signal was not satisfactory, a hand foghorn was sent to the station in 1896 for answering signals from passing vessels. However, in response to a petition for a fog alarm on the island, the Department of Marine and Fisheries in 1902 retorted that it was a "perfectly useless" idea because the island was "a large round island and [a fog alarm] could not be so located as to be heard all around [or] be sounded effectively." Furthermore, "a fog alarm is only useful where a vessel can run close up to it. No position on Lonely Island can be found where such conditions would be practicable." No fog alarm was granted.

After this lighthouse burned down, it was replaced in 1907–08 by a new tower and a separate keeper's house. The tower was again perched on the high bluff for best visibility. It was a white octagonal tapering structure covered in narrow clapboarding, with a flared cornice supporting its octagonal gallery. Its door and the windows for interior light were pedimented. The gallery was topped with a large red iron lantern with a circular pedestal room to house its third-order Fresnel lens. Inside the lens, which floated on a bed of mercury, was a coal-oil vapor lamp. The light's characteristic was changed from a fixed white light to a group flashing white light (flash 0.25 s; eclipse 1.25 s; flash 0.25 s; eclipse 4.75 s) with a visibility of 17 miles (27.5 km) from its 193-foot (59 m) focal plane. The lantern was capped with an unusually-shaped circular dome and ventilator that brought the tower height to 54 feet (16.5 m).

The Department of Marine and Fisheries started negotiations in 1891 with the Department of Indian Affairs to purchase the 100-acre (40 hectare) island, since their lighthouse had already been placed on it. After much correspondence, the sale finally took place on June 27, 1913, (22 years later!) at a cost of $172

Lonely Island Lighthouse, circa 1907

(the 1892 price of $84 plus 5% interest on the money since then). In 1944 a fog signal building was constructed on the waterfront; it housed an acetylene gun to be used during thick weather (blast 3 s; silence 27 s).

The new keeper's house, rather than standing on the bluff beside the tower, was on the shore close to fresh drinking water, freeing the keeper from having to carry his water up the 100 wooden steps of the bluff. The frame house was built in a 1½-story four-square design. A boathouse was also built on the beach at this time. In later years (1961–62) a new bungalow for the keeper was also built on the beach.

Life on the island was true to its name. One year the head keeper stayed on after the end of the season to spend the winter at the lighthouse, planning to signal his well-being by showing the light on certain dates. He signaled at Christmas and once more, but the light was not seen again. The mainlanders who checked on him found him dead on the kitchen floor. He had run out of food and smashed his furniture for fuel. He and his faithful dog were buried on the island behind the old oil shed.

In 1872 Henry Solomon was assigned as Lonely Island's keeper. He earned $450 a year and had a large family to support. Although it was about 35 miles (56 km) to Killarney and therefore a dangerous trip, the keeper had to go for supplies in June. However, as he was returning, a sudden squall came up and, although he had almost reached the island, his small boat capsized and Solomon drowned. His son Domonic became keeper after him.

In September 1882, during a hurricane, the steamer *Asia* went down nearby with its 120 passengers. Rescuers who stopped at Lonely Island while searching for bodies and wreckage discovered that Domonic had lied to them. Not only had a body or bodies washed ashore but he had taken their valuables as well as items of wreckage such as life buoys, chains, stools, a trunk and a valise. When questioned further, he did produce the missing jewellery and money. Although the Department of Marine and Fisheries proposed an inquiry into the keeper's alleged conduct, the local newspaper cleared him of all misconduct, as he returned all possessions and his station was so remote and far from civilization.

During John Adams' tenure as keeper from 1959 to 1965, he too ran into problems on one of his supply runs in the 16-foot (4.9 m) government-issued boat. While approaching Yeo Island about 5 miles (8 km) north of Cove Island, he had to change gas tanks. Unable to get the boat running, he flipped up the motor and discovered the entire bottom had fallen off. As he rowed home, he felt he was being watched — but not helped — by the Cove Island keeper, Bill Spears, and plotted his revenge. Spears finally did come to the rescue and offered Adams a swig of whiskey. However, Adams' hands were so blistered that he couldn't even hold the bottle. Adams also remembered carrying lantern oil up the 100 cliff steps using a yoke with a 5-gallon can on each side and having difficulty navigating the steps both in winter when snow piled halfway up the cliff, and in the summer when "rattlesnakes that hell wouldn't have" were coiled beside the steps.

In 1980 the light became an emergency light that operated year around. While the keeper's salary had increased to $880 per year by 1885, just over 100 years later, in 1987, the light had no keepers as it had been converted to solar power. In 1995 the Coast Guard razed all structures on the

beach to lower maintenance costs and avoid vandalism and liability. The tower on the high bluff then became the only reminder of this remote station, and it continues to stand today as a silent sentinel sending its flashing beam over the waters of Georgian Bay.

Known Keepers: John Egan (1870–72), Henry Solomon (1872), Dominic Solomon (1872–85), Jean Haitse (1885–1914), Louis Roque (1914–16), Henry Loosemore (1916–41), Edward Rousseau (1941–58), Thomas John Adams (1959–65), Carroll Fredrick Davey (1967–) Aldon Brethour (–1978), Lorne Gibson (1982–86).

38 Lyal Island Lighthouse

In the late 1800s Stokes Bay on the east side of Lake Huron was a very active fishing and logging community. To assist marine navigation, 6 acres (2.4 hectares) of land were purchased in March 1885 by the Department of Marine from the Department of Indian Affairs for a lighthouse reserve on the northwest side of Lyal Island 6 miles (9.6 km) west of Stokes Bay. As well as easing coastal travel, the light also helped guide vessels past rocky shoals and islands at the entrance into the bay.

It was a simply constructed lighthouse, a square white 51-foot (15.5 m) wooden tower attached to a wooden keeper's house. Its lantern displayed a revolving white light that had 15 seconds between revolutions and was visible for 12 miles (19.3 km).

The first keeper, John McKay, was appointed on October 27, 1884, at an annual salary of $680. He distinguished himself in 1886 by rescuing the crew of the wrecked barge *Iowa*, which had become water-logged and been adrift for a week in November weather. When McKay and James McDonald of Bayfield spotted the vessel off Greenock Point near Stokes Bay, they rescued the entire crew from death by exposure.

As keeper, McKay had to follow strict procedure. When he wished to clear and fence an additional acre or two of land to provide feed for his cow in 1886 he had to seek governmental permission. Even though the land was sitting empty and a fire had burned off its trees a number of years before, his request was denied, as it would effectively confiscate more native lands and potentially create an unwanted situation.

McKay's life on this offshore island was a lonely one. While there, he had to purchase all his provisions at Southampton, almost 40 miles (65 km) away, and bring them to the island by sailboat. He had company for only four months in the summer, when his wife and family joined him. During the stormy spring and fall weather he tended the light alone. Near the end of his 37-year tenure he even worked three seasons all by himself. On his retirement, McKay was awarded the Imperial Service Medal for his faithful duty.

Although this light facilitated entry into Stokes Bay, navigation was still tricky and range lights were later built to give additional help. In 1959 the Lyal Island Lighthouse was automated, a light being placed on a steel navigation tower. The old lighthouse was then assigned to Iver Burley for safekeeping.

Known Keepers: John McKay (1884–), Walter Knight (1919–), John C. Stewart (1946–49), Wilbert Kelly Burley (1949–51), Alonzo Burley (1951–56), John Thomas Adams (1956–59).

Lyal Island Lighthouse, circa 1934 NAC PA172504

39 Manitowaning Lighthouse

Although the harbor at Manitowaning on the northeast side of Manitoulin Island, Lake Huron, offered a safe, deep refuge, it was little used as it was off the main route. With the development of commerce in the village around 1875, large steamers began stopping regularly at the harbor, and sea captains called for it to be lit. On August 26, 1878, for $42, the Department of Marine and Fisheries purchased 84 acres (34 hectares) at Manitowaning to establish a lighthouse reserve. Due to an oversight, the Department of Indian Affairs did not transfer the property to the Marine Department until 1895.

In 1884 the government called for tenders to build the lighthouse, and the contract was awarded to John Waddell of Kingston, Ontario. Although he started the lighthouse in July 1884 and expected to finish by August, Waddell had still not completed it by 1885. Villagers started calling the light "Dawson's Monument," suggesting that its construction was being deliberately delayed so that the position of keeper could be used as political bait during an election. However, the contractor was dismissed for failing to complete the lighthouse as scheduled, and government workers finished the job in 1885.

It was a square white 34-foot (10.4 m) wooden tapering tower that stood on the hill in the village, 150 feet (46 m) from shore and 750 feet (230 m) north of the government dock. Its hexagonal cast-iron red lantern used oil lamps and reflectors to display a fixed white light for 14 miles (22.5 km) from an 80-foot (24.4 m) focal plane. At unknown dates the lighthouse was switched to a green light, given a seventh-order lens and electrified.

The rival steamers *Caribou* and *Manitou* made regular weekly trips to Manitowaning. Every Wednesday for the first few miles after leaving dock, their captains had a friendly race. In preparation, each vessel kept its boilers stoked and ready to go. Even village housewives became involved. They never hung out wash on a Wednesday, knowing it would be covered in soot from the belching smoke of the steamers when they left port. This rivalry existed for many years.

In 1995 the Coast Guard refurbished the rotting tower. Water seepage around its windows had caused the top third of the tower

Manitowaning Lighthouse

to decay. The contractor crane-lifted the iron lantern in order to replace the rotten beams, and the whole tower was stripped and recovered in cedar shingles, which were once again painted white. The renovations were completed in time for Manitowaning's 125th anniversary celebration and also guaranteed the light's well-being for many years into the future. Some townspeople still recall seeing the last keeper (Jack Clarke), who lived in the south part of the town, walking bent over as he carried pails of oil to the lighthouse every day to refuel the lamp.

Known Keepers: Benjamin Jones (1885–86), John Gourley Jr. (1900–06), John J. Morrow (1912–16), John Clarke (1938–64).

40 McKay Island Lighthouse

McKay Island is on the southwest side of Bruce Bay along the North Channel of Lake Huron. A lighthouse was built on the southeast point of the island in 1907 to assist passing ships and to mark the harbor at Bruce Mines 1.2 miles (2 km) away for the shipping of lumber. The harbor's first light was an anchor lens-lantern placed on the government wharf's freight shed in 1902, and it displayed a fixed white light. At a later date it became a red flashing light.

Manitowaning Lighthouse, circa 1900

McKay Island Lighthouse, circa 1904 NAC PA172505

The lighthouse erected on McKay Island was a large square wooden house with a short white square tower, also of wood, extending up from the center of its hipped roof. The lantern had three large rectangular panes of glass set horizontally into three of its four sides, with the back panel being wood. From a height of 34 feet (10 m) the lantern displayed a fixed white light using a kerosene vapor lamp inside a lens to achieve a visibility of 11 miles (17 km). The station also had a hand-operated foghorn to answer ships' signals.

The light's first keeper was Joseph Harvey, son of James and Esther Harvey, who kept the Thessalon light for 43 years, and brother to James Harvey Jr., who became Thessalon's keeper after his mother in 1940. Joseph kept the light for eight years until he died in 1915. His successor was Angus McNeish, who was a bit of a recluse and only left the lighthouse when he was running low on supplies.

McKay Island Lighthouse

When Merritt Strum was keeper he boated to the light each day instead of staying at the lighthouse. He rowed to French Island, walked across the island and then rowed his skiff to McKay Island, tended the light and returned home in the morning. After World War II, when he was permitted to buy a five-horsepower Johnson motor, he traveled straight to the lighthouse.

The last keeper also traveled straight from Bruce Mines to the light. However, when his wife and three children went with him, his wife refused to go the whole way in stormy seas. She insisted on being dropped at French Island, walking across it, and being picked up with the children on the other side of the island to finish the trip.

Today a modern beacon from a 32-foot (9.8 m) skeletal tower has replaced the old light. In 1992 it exhibited an electric isophase white light (flash 2 s; eclipse 2 s) for a 15-mile (24 km) visibility from a focal plane of 44.5 feet (13.5 m).

Known Keepers: Joseph Harvey (1907–15), Angus McNeish (1916–46), Merritt Strum (1946–47), Gordon Inch (1948–53).

41 McNab Point Lighthouse

The McNab Point Lighthouse was originally the rear range light of the Southampton Range lights, built in 1877 to lead mariners through the northern Gap into Southampton harbor. A square white wooden pyramidal tower 28 feet (8.5 m) high from base to vane, it was first placed on the north point of Horseshoe Bay and tended by David Cascaden.

In 1907 the tower was moved to the south point of Horseshoe Bay to form a straight line with the front range light and a gas buoy that had been placed on the tip of a shoal extending underwater north from Chantry Island. These three lights formed a safer line of entry through the local shoals and the Gap into the harbor.

Then in October 1908 the schooner *Erie Stewart* smashed into the long dock and obliterated the front range light. Although that light was never rebuilt, the rear range light continued to shine, displaying a fixed white light, and became known as the McNab Point Lighthouse, probably taking its name from Alexander McNabb, the local land agent for whom the point was named (even though the spelling was changed). In 1988 the Canadian Coast Guard stripped off its wooden exterior and replaced it with aluminum siding. At some point after this, the light was discontinued.

McNab Point Lighthouse

Meaford Pierhead Light, circa 1896

Michael's Bay Lighthouse

42 Meaford Pierhead Light

In 1875 Meaford Harbour was lit by a fixed white light hoisted up a wooden frame. This light, visible for 5 miles (8 km), drew vessels into the harbor to take on fish, grain, and apples from the southwestern side of Georgian Bay. After breakwater piers were built at the rivermouth, a pierhead light was placed at the east end of the western breakwater in 1878 to mark the harbor entrance and replace the post light. It was a short white wooden pyramidal light with a wooden balustrade and a polygonal iron lantern.

By 1906 an extension to the eastern breakwater had been completed, and the old pierhead light was removed and replaced with an automated acetylene light at the west end of the new breakwater extension. It had a large steel cylinder to hold gas and was anchored to the concrete breakwater. Its lantern displayed a white occulting light 20 feet (6 m) above the water and it had an 8-mile (13 km) visibility. This light needed no keeper but was serviced by the vessel *St. Héliers*, which ran out of Midland.

At an early date a foghorn was established on the west pier. In the 1930s it was replaced by a "wildcat" fire siren, which served as a foghorn responding to vessels blasting for its service. By 1955 the white light had been changed to a green flashing light. After long service the light was removed in 1987–88, when the harbor was renovated and new harbor lights were built.

Known Keepers: Samuel Dutcher (1877–1925), H. Hall (Harbor Master 1925–).

43 Meaford Range Lights

Sometime before 1955 the government added a rear range light to work in conjunction with the pierhead light to help guide vessels into Meaford Harbour, Georgian Bay. It was southwest of the pier light and situated on shore. To build it frugally, the government placed a light on the roof of the already existing Waterworks building (now the Meaford Museum). It displayed a fixed red light from a 32-foot (10 m) height. The light was supported by a short skeletal tower anchored to the rooftop. A ladder was attached to one slope of the roof and another ladder to the side of the building below to provide access for maintenance. The range lights were removed in 1987–88 when a new yacht basin was created and modern lights were placed on its east pier.

Meaford Rear Range Light, on roof of shore building MEAFORD MUSEUM

44 Michael's Bay Lighthouse

In 1870 a lighthouse was built on the west point forming Michael's Bay along the south shore of Manitoulin Island, Lake Huron. Its purpose was to mark the bay for shipping lumber. A fixed white light consisting of a mammoth circular burner lamp with no reflector was exhibited from a square white wooden tower with a 4.5 foot (1.4 m) octagonal cast-iron red lantern. It stood 25 feet (7.6 m) from base to vane and had a 40-foot (12.2 m) focal plane. Later it used oil lamps and 33-inch (84 cm) reflectors to display a fixed white light for 11 miles (17.7 m). The station also had a hand foghorn to answer signals from vessels during poor visibility.

The government and local lumbering interests shared the cost of the construction of the lighthouse equally, and the light was maintained by the Mill Company. In 1876 the Department of Marine and Fisheries purchased the land on which the lighthouse stood, paying the Department of Indian Affairs $10 for the 4-acre (1.6 hectare) lighthouse reservation on the point.

The station was discontinued in 1889 but was back in operation in 1901 until it was permanently discontinued in 1909. After a fire destroyed most of the town in 1910, the station was not rebuilt. The lighthouse sat empty and untended until its rotted structure collapsed sometime around 1930.

Known Keepers: John Chisholm (1878–83), H. Bowerman (1901–02), Edward Martin (1902–06), Alexander Chisholm (?).

45 Midland Point Range Lights

The Midland Point Range Lights were established in 1900 on Georgian Bay, Lake Huron, to assist in guiding vessels into Midland Harbour. The old front range light, standing on a cribwork pier 4 feet (1.2 m) high, was a square white wooden tower with sloping sides. It supported a square wooden lantern painted red. The tower was 33 feet (10 m) high from base to ventilator. Its lantern displayed a fixed seventh-order dioptric light from a 31-foot (9.5 m) focal plane and could be seen 10 miles (16 km) away. The back range light was similar to the front one but south of it. It was 43 feet (13.1 m) high, and had a 41-foot (12.5 m) focal plane giving a visibility of 11 miles (17.8 km). Both towers were covered with cedar shake siding.

They were discontinued in 1912 and replaced by white towers with an orange vertical daymark stripe. The front range light was moved in 1915 for use on Turning Rock just off Canary Island.

Known Keepers: Thomas Williams (1912–13), Thomas Williams (caretaker 1913–38), R. VanLuven (1938–), G. Walker, (caretaker until light was electrified, exact dates not recorded).

Midland Range Lights

47 Mississagi Island Lighthouse

In 1884 a lighthouse was built on the south side of Mississagi Island, just above the northwest corner of Manitoulin Island, to help mark the North Channel shipping route. It was a square white tapering tower built into one corner of the 1½-story white wooden keeper's dwelling. The tower's polygonal iron lantern used lamps and reflectors to display a revolving white light from a 53-foot (16 m) focal plane for a visibility of 12 miles (19.4 km). It was later changed to a flashing white light.

Keeper MacDonald used to take a cow to the island with him in his open sailboat so that his family could have fresh milk and butter for the season. In 1948 a fire completely destroyed the lighthouse and it was never rebuilt.

Known Keepers: James MacDonald (1885), Lauchlin MacDonald (1896–1922), Alfred Clark (1922–), Captain Roque (?), Foster Morris (–1948).

48 Mississagi Strait Lighthouse

On brochures this lighthouse is listed as being in Meldrum Bay, but it is over 6 miles (10 km) away, across the peninsula from Meldrum Bay on Mississagi Strait. It was built to protect and guide ships through the perilous, rocky strait that separates Manitoulin Island from Cockburn Island, in Lake Huron.

It is one of eleven lighthouses on Manitoulin Island, the world's largest freshwater island. Built in 1873, it is the oldest standing lighthouse on the island. The 40-foot (12.2 m) tower is linked to the lightkeeper's 1½-story house, making it an actual room of the house. This white board structure with its red roof makes a picturesque scene, from its perch on the rocky cliffs. When established, it had a hand-operated foghorn.

In 1881 a fog alarm plant powered by compressed air (blast 8 s; silence 120 s) was installed at the site to further warn ships of the dangerous coastline. This fog whistle was known as a "wildcat" whistle because it changed tones during the blast, rising from a low tone to a screech, and coming down to another low tone. In

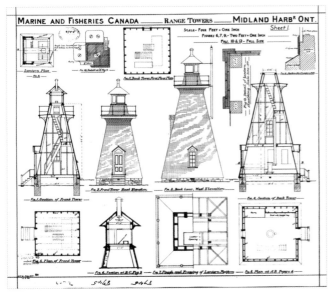
Midland Point Range Lights blueprints, circa 1900 NAC PA162340

46 Midland Range Lights

In 1901 range lights were built in the town of Midland to lead vessels from Midland Point into Midland Harbour on Georgian Bay. They displayed fixed red dioptric lights. With modern improvements in navigational aids, they were discontinued. Midland also had a storm signal tower that flew cones to warn mariners of weather conditions.

Mississagi Strait Lighthouse

1908 this fog system was replaced by a more powerful diaphone-type alarm that reportedly could be heard up to 35 miles (57 km) away. Today there is no fog alarm.

Although the lighthouse was built in 1873, the Department of Marine and Fisheries had no deed. They cleared the record by purchasing the 217-acre (88 hectare) lighthouse reserve from the Department of Indian Affairs on May 11, 1911, at 20 cents an acre for a total cost of $43.40. In 1918 the first telephone was installed at the lighthouse and telephone cables were laid across the strait to Cockburn Island and its residents. A trail was the only way across the island to the lighthouse until 1968, when a road was built.

Other changes took place at the lighthouse. In 1970 hydro was installed and the light was replaced by an automatic light on a skeletal tower that stood in front of the old lighthouse. As keepers were no longer required, the lighthouse was leased, at first privately and then to the Meldrum Bay Historical Society. In 1983 the Society turned the care of the lighthouse over to the Manitoulin Tourist Association.

Today the lighthouse is part of a museum and is furnished as it was by the keeper's family 100 years ago. It is surrounded by a pocked limestone yard containing random vegetation, an iron anchor and an ornate cast-iron hand pump. Its antique barn used to house a cow and chickens. To supplement their twice-yearly supplies the keeper also had a large garden out back.

Entering the summer kitchen is like stepping into another century. Walls and ceiling are tongue and groove wood, furnishings are mostly original, and table settings and other period items have been donated. Of note is an 1873 hand-painted map of the settlements on Manitoulin Island. The walls of two of the three downstairs rooms slope up to the tower. Open stairs lead up to the second floor and two bedrooms, and a trapdoor opens up to the maintenance room on the third level. Another set of open stairs climbs to the octagonal lantern and its square exterior walkway.

The light was originally a coal-oil-fired wick-type lamp that required daily maintenance. It burned inside the original fourth-order Fresnel lens, which is still there, and displayed a fixed white light for 13 miles (21 km) from a 46-foot (14 m) focal plane.

This site had five lightkeepers and families. Little is known about the first keeper except that he was the only white settler in the area during his tenure. The second keeper, William Cullis, had two sons who were educated at home because they had no access to a school. J.H. Ball, the third keeper, had one son, who was educated in boarding schools and boarded in the community while his parents lived at the lighthouse. In the winter they lived on their farm, the "Townsend Farm." One summer, on the island, a great forest fire raged to the south of them. The smoke lasted for so many days that Ball ran out of coal from his constant efforts to keep the fog signal operating in the low visibility.

W.A. Grant, the fourth keeper, had a family of nine and a home in Meldrum Bay, where the children went to school. His son Ken helped operate the light and the fog alarm. In 1915, early in Grant's long stay, the steamer Burlington burned at the dock north of the lighthouse. Its hull is now a diver's dream as it is only 25 feet (7.7 m) from shore.

During Prohibition many Canadians made a fast dollar selling alcohol to their American neighbors, and communities when a liquor store along the north shore also became suppliers. Bootlegged alcohol was delivered to prearranged islands — Green Island in this area — where American boats picked it up and smuggled it into the States. On one occasion the rum-runners ran aground on the magnetic reef and had to unload their cargo. Grant made them a replacement bearing to get them to the mainland and have their vessel properly repaired. In the meantime, he went out to the shoal and found a bag of beer at a buoy. He shared his find

with locals, hiding his cache in an upstairs bedroom wall at the lighthouse. Rumor has it that he made enough money selling beer to the local hotel to buy a car.

Keeper D.N. Sullivan had three children and a home in Meldrum Bay where his daughters went to school. Sullivan opened the road to the lighthouse for car travel, facilitating many visits. During his stay, the Department of Transport hired an assistant keeper and built him a cottage.

The magnetic reef off the east side of Cockburn Island caused many shipwrecks, as its high iron ore content threw off ships' compasses. Among its victims were the Quebec, the Agawa, the Maple Court — and possibly Captain La Salle's Griffon. Over 300 years ago the Griffon went missing in Lake Huron. No one knows its fate. One story is that it became lost in a storm at the Mackinac Straits and that currents pulled it down to the Mississagi Strait, where it floundered on the magnetic reef. Wreckage had been washed ashore just north of the lighthouse, where it lay for years with no identification.

After the hull was stripped of lead for arrowheads and farmers' needs, the remaining pieces were washed out by storms to a still-unknown location. However, a large, human skull was found in an underwater cave just north of the lighthouse, as well as some coins, buttons, and a small cannon of the style that the Griffon would have carried. Some believe the skull is Captain La Salle's, since he was a large man. Unfortunately the coins and buttons cannot be traced. Two wooden beams brought up by divers have been identified as the type of wood the Griffon was built from and dated to the same period (1600s). Since positive identification cannot be made, this theory may remain speculation forever.

Other attractions at the site make it a paradise for hikers, nature lovers, painters, photographers and divers: 30 wilderness campsites, trails along the rugged shoreline, unique rocks, flora and fauna and a nearby shipwreck. The old 1881 fog signal building has been converted into the Fog Station Restaurant/gift shop and, while the menu is limited, the home cooking is excellent. The building has a large central room with silver-painted, pressed-tin walls and a large, old stone fireplace. It still houses the large compressor tanks that operated the foghorn.

Today, the Canadian Coast Guard owns and maintains the new light on the steel tower. The Manitoulin Tourist Association leases the Mississagi Lighthouse and Heritage Park from the LaFarge Construction Company. Since the site and road are privately owned, the lighthouse is only open to the public in the summer season.

Known Keepers: John Miller (1873–76), William Cullis (1877–1900), J.H. Ball (1900–13), William Grant (1913–46), D.N. Sullivan (1947–60), John Oakley Joyce (1960–70).

49 Nancy Island Lighthouse

During the war of 1812 the Americans tried to win the battles against the British on Georgian Bay, Lake Huron, by cutting off their water supply route. On August 14, 1814, they trapped the H.M.S. Nancy, the only remaining British supply ship on the Upper Lakes, which was anchored about two miles (3.2 km) upstream from the mouth of the Nottawasaga River. Lieutenant Worsley, forewarned, had built a small blockhouse with three cannon to defend the Nancy but, despite a courageous battle, the vastly outnumbered British were soon defeated, and the Americans set the schooner on fire and sank her. For the next 114 years her charred hull collected sand and silt, and "Nancy Island" was gradually formed. In 1928 the hull of the Nancy was recovered and today it resides in a museum built on the island.

Nancy Island Lighthouse

Narrow Island Lighthouse, circa 1890

In 1958 a Provincial Park was established at Wasaga Beach, the community that developed at the mouth of the Nottawasaga, to serve the many visitors to the area. Park authorities developed Nancy Island as an historic site. In 1967, as a Canadian centennial project, they had a lighthouse built on Tower Island, which was part of the site.

The lighthouse was a replica of the one that stood on the crib in Collingwood harbor for 65 years. It was a square white tapering wooden 30-foot (9 m) tower with a square lantern and gallery. Covered in cedar shingles over diagonally laid boards, the tower had three pedimented windows for interior light and a pedimented entry door. Three sets of steep wooden interior tower stairs provided access to the lantern. Today this lighthouse helps local boat traffic steer clear of Tower Island, and visitors to the Nancy Island Historic Site may climb the tower to view the area and the town of Wasaga Beach.

50 Narrow Island Lighthouse

Narrow Island (also known as Rabbit Island) is a small island on the north side of Manitoulin Island in Georgian Bay, and about three miles (4.8 km) west of Little Current along the northern shipping route. On October 4, 1889, the Department of Marine and Fisheries purchased the low, flat island from the Department of Indian Affairs for $25. In 1890 a lighthouse was built on its west end to assist eastbound navigation.

The construction of the lighthouse, which was very similar to the Strawberry Island light, was contracted to Charles Mickler, a Collingwood contractor. He built items such as doors, windows, flooring and framework in town and then shipped them to the Narrow Island site. His lighthouse was a square white tapering wooden tower built into a 1½-story wooden keeper's house. It supported a wooden gallery with a cross-braced wood railing, and a red hexagonal iron lantern. From a 34-foot (10.4 m) focal plane it used lamps and reflectors to display a fixed white light for 11 miles (17.7 m). The station also had a hand-operated foghorn.

In 1902 the lighthouse burned down and a temporary light was hung from a pole. The new keeper's dwelling was a large rectangular 1½-story wooden house with cedar shake siding built on a high stone foundation, and its roof peak was flattened to create a foundation for an octagonal wooden lantern. From its 37-foot (11.3 m) height it used a seventh-order lens to display a fixed white light with a red sector, which shone out over the Foster Bank Shoals. The light had a visibility of 11 miles (17.8 m).

A few changes occurred. In 1947 the station's boathouse and oil house burned down. In 1954 a recommendation was made to automate the light. However, out of respect for keeper Carl Dieter's 33 years of dedicated service, the government waited until he retired. In 1958 the hand foghorn was discontinued. The lighthouse was automated in 1962 using photoelectric cells powered by batteries. In 1979 the Department of Transport erected a beacon on a metal pole nearby and in 1982 they tore down the deteriorated lighthouse to eliminate liability and maintenance costs.

Known Keepers: A. Boyter (1898–1916), Roxie Smith (1916–21), Carl Dieter (1921–58), George Squires (1958).

51 Nottawasaga Island Lighthouse

Nottawasaga Island is in Georgian Bay about 3 miles (4.8 km) northwest of the entrance to Collingwood Harbour. The island varied in size from 5 to 13 acres (2 to 5 hectares) according to lake levels and was formed by a low upcropping of shale shelving. After the railroad arrived in 1855, the town of Collingwood boomed, and with this expansion, marine transportation also increased, causing mariners to call for the waterways to be lit. For that purpose, the Department of Public Works for Canada West in 1855 hired John Brown, a Scottish stonemason, to build eleven lighthouses from Point Clark to Christian Island on Georgian Bay. Due to excessive costs, only six of these lights were completed and they became known as the "imperial" towers. They were all built between 1855 and 1859 from similar designs. One of these was constructed on the northwest tip of Nottawasaga Island to mark entry to Collingwood.

Nottawasaga Island Lighthouse

The station consisted of a stone tower with a separate keeper's house, both made of first quality white dolomite limestone quarried at Owen Sound and towed to the island on scows. Because the tower was built on solid rock, the construction of its 6-foot (1.8 m) thick foundation walls was straightforward. The limestone block tower tapered gently to walls 2 feet (0.6 m) thick at the top but maintained a constant interior diameter of 10.5 feet (3.2 m). The last courses of the tower were made of granite to support the weight of the heavy iron lantern and its lens. An iron floor with a trapdoor, supplied by C. Yale of St. Catharines, was set on I-beams and lengths of railroad iron mortared into the stonework. This metal floor provided a stable fireproof base to support the large second-order Fresnel lens and dodecagonal iron lantern.

The lantern and lens were both manufactured and installed by the Louis Sautter Company of Paris. The lantern had 36 panes of glass set into iron astragals (three panes per side) so as not to impede the lightbeam. The lantern was topped with an "imperial" copper dome that was segmentally ridged and topped with a ventilator shaped like a ball pinnacle, the typical "imperial" dome. The tower's lower entry door had an arched top with a semicircular transom. Sets of steep-pitched stairs led up the inside of the tower to the final iron ladder to the lantern. Rectangular windows ascending the tower at quarter turns provided interior light. The completed tower was 80 feet (24.4 m) from the base to the center of the light.

The light's illuminants changed over the years. The first was sperm whale oil burned in a virtually smokeless oil lamp that used a series of round wicks and a glass chimney to create a constant, bright flame of uniform height. In spite of its excellent flame, keepers complained about the oil being too old and thick to burn properly in cold weather. (The government brought the oil supply to the station in 50-gallon [210 l] casks once a year.) In 1862 Colza oil imported from France and Holland was used, but when it was found that twice as much oil was needed to get the same quality of flame, they reverted to using whale oil until 1868 when a new lamp was invented to burn petroleum oils. This lamp was known as Doty's Patent and its use greatly reduced the price of fuel consumption. Kerosene and a pressurized mantle lamp next improved the light. Later still, acetylene was used when the light was semi-automated. Today the light is operated by solar power.

When oil, the light's first illuminant, burned during colder weather it produced much water vapor inside of the lantern (more than a quart of water vapor per quart of oil during colder weather). This water vapor would freeze on the glass, impeding the light's beam so the keeper had to keep the glass free of ice. The lantern had two features to help him with this. One was iron hand holds around the outside of the lantern glass so he could hang on while he scraped ice from the glass. The other was water troughs around the inside base of the dome which collected condensed water vapor from the dome into the troughs. Twelve hidden water spouts inside the brass lion heads around the top of the outside lantern glass removed the water from the inside of the lantern and spewed it away from the outside glass to prevent ice from forming.

Another of the keeper's jobs was to keep the light burning brightly. To achieve proper ventilation the keeper had a trapdoor and removable panels in the lantern floor, the lamp's glass chimney and the ventilator on top of the dome.

The light was visible from all seaward approaches and was first lit on November 30, 1858. To most vessels it displayed a revolving white light every half minute so it could not be mistaken for Collingwood's lights or a fire onshore. The light had a 96-foot 2 inch (29.6 m) focal plane and a visibility of 17 miles (27.5 km). However, it also had one red sector in its lantern so that the light showed red to the southeast between the island and the Collingwood harbor. This area was shallow water because of the reefs that ran along the shore and the red sector warned of this.

The keeper's house was a small detached 1½-story rectangular one made of limestone block walls like the tower. Both ends of the house had a chimney serving a fireplace in the kitchen/living area and an iron stove upstairs. A central door and a central boxed-in staircase divided the house in two. To the one side of the door was a kitchen and general living area while to the other was a parlor and a small master bedroom. Two more loft bedrooms were upstairs. The house had a slate roof.

The pre-Confederation government may have purchased the land on which the lighthouse was built but since there was no record of it, the Department of Marine and Fisheries had to go through negotiations between 1887 and 1888 to acquire title to Nottawasaga Island for lighthouse purposes. The island was 13 acres (5.3 hectares) at this time and a land evaluation put a $2,000 price tag on it, or $154 per acre, when the island consisted only of rock. Since the island had only been used for thirty years, it was suggested that an 1859 price ($500) plus interest would be fair. But that came to $1,670, which was much too high. After considerable haggling, the island was sold for a total of $800.

There were 15 keepers at this station between 1858 and 1983 but its best-known one was George Collins. During his 31-year career he saved 52 lives and received recognition for his efforts. After a harrowing November storm, he and other locals saved the remaining passengers and crew of the steamer *Mary Ward* just before it split apart and sank after being stranded and storm bashed on nearby Milligan's Reef. Each member of the rescue team received $15 for his efforts. Over the years Collins also received a $75 gold watch (1872) and a silver tea service for other rescues. However, his greatest reward was in saving lives.

Besides the illuminants and keepers, some other changes took place at this station. Around 1871 the tower and house were whitewashed to increase their daytime visibility. A hand-operated foghorn was added to the station. In 1959 a fire burned the house and a work shed but there was no damage done to the tower. The light was semi-automated at this time and the keepers no longer lived at the lighthouse. Since they had fewer island lighthouse duties, their job was increased by maintaining other navigational aids for Collingwood Harbour. During the 1970s the government wanted to raze the tower but intervention by the Heritage Foundation stopped it. The island has been declared a bird sanctuary. The last keeper left in 1983 when the light was completely automated and dimmed considerably due to vessels using modern, onboard navigational equipment.

The last keeper, Wilfred Johnston, said the light used to be bright enough to read a newspaper on the shore but after automation it was so dim that he had to hold a match up to see it. The light's visibility had decreased from 17 miles (27.5 km) to just 5 miles (8 km). In 1992 the light flashed twice every ten seconds (flash 1 s; eclipse 1.5 s; flash 1 s; eclipse 6.5 s). Even though the tower had a bulge in it from being struck by lightning, the light continued to shine. Then during the winter of 2004–05, large chunks of stone fell away from the outer wall of the tower, leaving the tower's future well-being "hanging" in the air.

Known Keepers: Captain George Collins (1859–90), Captain A.G. Clark (1890–1902), Fred Burmister (1902–15), Thomas W. Bowie (1915–24), Thomas Foley (1924–32), Samuel Neally Hillen (1932–42), William "Scotty" Hogg (1942–51), Donald Hogg (1951–52), James A. Keith (1953–56), James F. Dineen (1957–59), Ross White (1959–61), Harry Ward (1961–63), Wilfred Neil Johnston (1963–83).

52 Nottawasaga River Range Lights

The mouth of the Nottawasaga River on Georgian Bay did not provide a very good harbor because shifting sand bars changed its entry channel every year. In spite of this, range lights were established at the rivermouth in 1915. In 1922 they were discontinued because of the low volume of boat traffic and the need to reposition them each year.

In 1931 when C. Eberhart of Wasaga Beach petitioned for range lights to accommodate his shipping business from Wasaga Beach to Collingwood, government inspectors invoked the same reasons for recommending against re-establishing range lights. In 1934 Simcoe County maintained lights at each end of the highway bridge across the Nottawasaga River for an annual cost of $7 to $8 each. A harbor here had little commercial use but was helpful to recreational boaters.

Known Keepers: Oscar A. Burnside (1915–21).

Owen Sound Front Range Light, circa 1912
NAC PA 172526

Owen Sound Front Range Light, circa 1900 NAC PA172526

53 Owen Sound Range Lights

The community of Owen Sound developed at the mouth of the Sydenham River along the southwest shore of Georgian Bay. It provided a good harbor for vessels shallow enough to get over the sand bar that blocked its approach. The precise date that the harbor was first lit is unknown, as the harbor records were destroyed by fire in 1874. However, it is known that in 1851 vessels were paying harbor fees to maintain a lighthouse. Little else is known about Owen Sound lights during this period.

After the harbor was dredged to remove the sand bar in the early 1850s, the harbor's accessibility brought rapid growth. In 1883 range lights were built. The front range light was constructed on the east side of the dredged channel. It was a square white wooden tapering tower 21-feet (6.4 m) high. Its lantern displayed a red dioptric light, and with a 39-foot (12 m) focal plane it had a 6-mile (9.6 km) visibility. The rear range light was also a white wooden tapering tower placed 915 feet (278 m) behind the front range light. It was 34 feet (10.4 m) high with a 46-foot focal plane and it exhibited a fixed red dioptric light for 11 mile (17.7 km).

As the harbor developed, the range lights were heightened and moved. In 1895–96 the old rear range light became the front range light and was placed on the east side of the rivermouth. Its fixed red catoptric light had a 7-mile (11.2 km) visibility. The new rear light was placed southwest of the front one. It was a new square wooden building with a square wooden lantern placed on top of the old front range light, which had been set on a new concrete foundation to increase its height to 46 feet (14 m). It displayed a fixed red catoptric light for 8 miles (12.8 km). Both lights were painted white and had a vertical red stripe as part of their daymark.

At some time a storm signal tower was added at Owen Sound to alert mariners to weather conditions. In 1909 newer higher range lights were again built to replace the shorter wooden ones. They were both square skeletal towers with sloping sides and a white wooden enclosed watchroom below the lantern. The rear range light had an octagonal iron lantern and the front light had a square one. Both had white wooden slats and a red vertical stripe as their daymark. The front range light, formerly used at Pointe Au Baril, was 50 feet (15.2 m) high from base to vane. A fog bell was placed on the east pier ahead of it. The rear range light was 82 feet (24.9 m) high and was purchased from the Goold, Shapely and Muir Co. of Brantford, Ontario for $668.50. The towers came at a total cost of $1,638.

By 1992 these range lights had been changed to exhibit fixed green lights, and both used electricity and reflectors as their illuminating apparatus. The focal plane of the front range light was 49 feet (15 m); that of the rear light was 91 feet (28.7 m). For its daymark the front light was white with a vertical orange stripe and two red and white horizontal stripes, and the rear light was white with four horizontal red and white stripes. These lights were visible in line of range only.

Owen Sound lost much of its port significance in 1912 when the Canadian Pacific Railroad moved its headquarters, including its steamships, to Port McNicoll. Instead of continuing to develop as a port of export, Owen Sound developed as a manufacturing center. Today its port facilities are used primarily by pleasure boaters.

Known Keepers: George Scott Miller (1880), Arch McLean (1897–1903), Alex Robertson (1913–42), Earl Clifford Holmes (1942–49), J.W. Hackey (1951), Henry H. Gardner (1953–57), John Angele (1957–59), Robert Campbell (1959–61), Harold Baker (1961–).

54 Parry Sound Lighthouse Depot

The Parry Sound Lighthouse Depot was created in 1905. The depot development was put under the direction of Maurice Brais, a young engineer from Ottawa. Brais was to have returned to Ottawa when the project was finished, but he liked the region so much that he stayed on at the depot for 47 years. Men from the depot serviced a large geographical area extending from southern Lake Huron to the tip of Lake Superior, Lake Winnipeg and the Arctic Circle. The department was the base of operations for the supervision, maintenance and testing of all navigational aids in its district.

The structure to house the depot was an old factory along the north shore of the town. In front of it was a wharf 250 feet (76 m) long by 77 feet (23.5 m) wide for mooring government steamers and storing buoys. The wharf was built by Pratt and McDougall of Midland. A lantern proudly crowns the guard gate at the main entrance of the depot. When the Cape Robert Lighthouse was deactivated and demolished, the Canadian Coast Guard removed the lantern, took it back to their Parry Sound base, and later placed it on their new guard gate, producing a distinctive appearance. This station continues to service the same areas today that it did in the past.

55 Penetanguishene Lighthouse

After the burning and the sinking of the supply ship *Nancy* in the Nottawasaga River, Georgian Bay, in 1814, the British built and manned Fort Nottawasaga at the rivermouth for a short time. However, as shifting sand bars made it a poor choice, they built a fort further north at Penetanguishene, which had a much better natural harbor. As the harbor became busier the need for a lighthouse arose. The land on which a lighthouse was to be built had first been purchased by the province for a penal settlement. However by 1859 it had become a reformatory for boys. In 1877 a lighthouse was built on a block at the end of the reformatory pier on the south side of the harbor. It was a square white wooden 18-foot (5.5 m) tower that displayed a fixed white catoptric light with a 6-mile (9.6 km) visibility.

Known Keepers: Peter Kilgraine (1877–78), P. Gordon (1879), W.A. Thompson (1882–), Christopher Columbus (1893–1924), Andrew J. Bald (1924–46).

56 Pine Tree Harbour Range Lights

It is known that Pine Tree Harbour Range Lights existed on the east side of Lake Huron in 1907, because they were listed in Scott's *New Coast Pilot* for the lakes. While it is unknown when they were established and extinguished, it is believed they were built privately by the owners of the local sawmills as private aids to navigation to facilitate lumber exports.

The front range light was a square white wooden tower with a red top located on the northwest side of the harbor opposite the sawmills. It displayed a fixed white light from a 28-foot (8.5 m) focal plane to produce a 10-mile (16 km) visibility. The rear light was also a square white wooden tower located 350 feet (107 m) behind the front range light. It displayed a fixed white light from a 34-foot (10.5 m) focal plane and had a range of visibility of up to 11 miles (18 km). While these lights provided safe entry over shoals and through narrows, local knowledge was necessary to use them. Today these range lights have vanished.

57 Point Clark Lighthouse

Before lighthouses were built on the Canadian side of Lake Huron after the 1830s, early ship traffic from Goderich to the area north of Point Clark was treacherous. Seamen were warned of the rocky shoals that stretched for 2 miles (3.2 km) into the lake by a lantern hanging from a pine tree. Clark Point, originally called Pine Point, was named for families from Clark Township east of Toronto who settled on the height of land above it.

In the mid-nineteenth century, shipping and water travel on Lake Huron increased for several reasons. Settlers poured into the Upper Lakes region with the opening of the "Queen's Bush" area and the sale of Indian Lands on the Saugeen Peninsula. Canada-U.S. trade was freed up when the United States took duties off fish, furs and lumber in 1854. The new locks at Sault Ste. Marie in 1855 also encouraged shipping between Lake Huron and Lake Superior, as did the new side-wheel steamers.

However, Lake Huron was poorly lit. In 1848 there was only one lighthouse at Goderich. The Department of Public Works for Canada West in 1855 hired John Brown, an experienced contractor with sufficient assets to build lighthouses to light the east side of Lake Huron as well as Georgian Bay from Point Clark to Christian Island. Brown completed six of the eleven planned lighthouses. The original contracted price was £3,500 per tower. However, the building price rose rapidly thanks to factors such as insufficient quantities of readily available limestone; the loss of supply boats due to the location's inaccessibility and the lack of detailed charts and maps; high wages being paid to the laborers for wilderness work; delays in getting men and materials caused by storms; late deliveries of the lighting apparatus. By 1857, having lost £1,500 per lighthouse, Brown petitioned the Governor General, Sir Edmond Walker Head, for more funding. The final cost of the six lighthouses that Brown finished was $222,564, an astronomical amount at the time. These six finished lighthouses became known as the "imperial" towers.

During construction, a settlement arose at the site, with houses for the workmen, workshops, a sawmill, a gristmill, a limekiln, a store and a hotel. However, the community died after the project was completed because the area offered no safe harbor.

The lighthouse was built between 1855 and 1859. Since it was to be built on a sand and gravel bottom, a secure foundation was needed to support and stabilize the heavy tower. Workers created a 30-foot-square (9.2 m^2) surface by driving 12-inch-square (0.3 m^2) hemlock pylons down to bedrock 65 to 70 feet (20 to 21.5 m) by using ox-drawn stone weights suspended from a tripod.

The slightly conical tower was built on this solid foundation. A basement level was built with walls about 7 feet (2.2 m) thick tapering to about 6 feet (1.8 m) thick at ground level, where its diameter was about 27 feet (8.2 m). An underground tunnel provided easy access from the house basement to the tower basement.

Point Clark Lighthouse

master bedroom downstairs and two more bedrooms upstairs. An underground passageway allowed the keeper to service the lamp in the worst weather and permitted relatively quick trips to refill the oil and rewind the weights without having to go outside. The tower and house were whitewashed to increase their visibility and the lantern was painted red. The light was first lit on April 1, 1859, the same date that its sister light on Chantry Island was lit.

There are many interesting stories about this lighthouse. One tells of the lightkeeper's son tying an umbrella to a basket and dropping it from the lighthouse tower to see if a cat could be "parachuted." The cat jumped out, to an unknown end. Another keeper adopted and raised a found fawn, which made a wonderful local attraction for some years, especially after it gave birth to twin fawns. In the early 1950s keeper John C. Campbell reported that a "tidal wave" swept past the lighthouse, uprooting trees and moving cottages hundreds of feet.

The last keeper, Eldon Lowry, lived with his wife at their nearby farm rather than in the keeper's house. Eldon's father had climbed the 114 steps of the tower when he was twenty years old and he repeated the climb on his eightieth birthday, which he celebrated at the lighthouse. Eldon also recalls young men riding horseback out into the lake. One went out too far and fell off his horse. Luckily he grabbed the horse's mane when it turned around to swim back to shore. This rider learned to swim immediately.

In 1947, to check the condition of the pylons, an auger was used to bore a hole down on an angle. Unfortunately, before the test was completed, 18 feet (5.5 m) of water had seeped into the 20-foot (6 m) tower basement. Water has remained in it ever since, and the tunnel to the house had to be closed off. In April of 1953 the light's illuminant, became electricity and the light's characteristic was changed to flash every 20 seconds. The light was automated on September 13, 1962. The lighthouse was closed in 1967 because the light mechanism was damaged by visitors.

Also in 1967, and as part of Canada's Centennial celebration, the Point Clark Lighthouse was acquired by Parks Canada. It became the first lighthouse in the Ontario Region to be declared a National Historic Site to commemorate the importance of the role of lighthouses in early Great Lakes navigation. The refurbished buildings are now part of a National Park with picnic grounds, a boat launch, and a gift shop/marine museum in the keeper's house. The museum, officially opened in 1988, offers tours up the tower. In 1987 the light's characteristic was changed to flash every 3.5 seconds. Today the exterior of the tower is coated with a mixture of paint, whitewash, and salt. The salt binds the paint and whitewash together, and this durable mixture does not peel or come off.

Although all six imperial towers are functional and have automated lights, Point Clark Lighthouse is one of two that have been well preserved. Hopefully more interest in preserving the other four will come in future years.

Known Keepers: John Young (1859–82), Thomas Kilty (assistant 1859–61), William Riggin (1883), David Small (1883), John Ray (1884–93), Murdoch MacDonald (1894–1913), George Ray (1914–24), John Ruttle (1924–38), John A. Campbell (1938–46), John C. Campbell (1947–62), Elmer Mackenzie (1963–64), Eldon Lowry (1964–67).

The walls continued to taper to just 2 feet (0.6 m) thick at the top below the gallery. The tower interior remained a constant 10.5 feet (3.2 m) in diameter.

The blocks of hand-hewn dolomite limestone were mostly quarried at nearby Inverhuron and Main Station Island. Because the relatively thin walls at the top of the tower needed to support the heavy cast-iron base plate and huge second-order Fresnel lens, the top courses were made of granite. The dodecagonal cast-iron lantern that topped the tower sat right on the granite. The light used a weights mechanism to rotate the lens around the Argand lamp to create a white flash every 30 seconds which could be seen up to 15 miles (24 km). This flashing helped distinguish the Point Clark Light from the fixed white lights on either side at Chantry Island to the north and Goderich to the south.

The lamp first burned sperm whale oil. In cold weather, for each quart of oil burned, more than a quart of water vapor was produced. This vapor condensed on the inside of the lantern, and it was the keeper's job to keep the glass clear.

The imperial towers had a unique system to reduce condensation build-up. Collector troughs inside the top of the lantern collected the moisture and directed it out through spouts within brass lion-head gargoyles placed around the top of the lantern on the outside. The lantern was capped with a copper dome, a large ventilator ball and a lightning rod.

The Point Clark Lighthouse had a very tall tower — 80 feet (24.4 m). It had an 87-foot (26.5 m) focal plane over the lake and was 115 feet (35 m) to the top of the lightning rod. Oil was brought in by supply ship but, as ships could not get close to shore because of the shoals, casks of oil were dumped into the water, a big net was put around them, and they were towed to shore by the keeper's smaller boat.

Weights that had to be wound every 3½ to 4 hours made the lens revolve around the lamp. These weights traveled up and down through a shaft in the center of the tower. There was a watch window in the base of the tower, so that when the keeper saw the weights in the window he knew it was time to climb up and rewind them. One keeper used to remove one weight so the weights descended more slowly, giving him 5 to 5½ hours before he had to rewind them — a convenience if he needed to go out.

The keeper's house was a separate 1½-story building also made of limestone blocks. It had a kitchen/living area, a parlor and the

Point Edwards Range Light with Fort Gratiot Light in background)

58   Point Edwards Range Lights

In 1903 the Canadian government established range lights at Point Edwards on lower Lake Huron to help vessels navigate into the St. Clair River. Both were square white wooden pyramidal towers with a pedimented entry door and tower windows. Their lantern windows were set to display the light only when vessels were in a direct line of approach. The rear range light was removed in 1939 and the front range light disappeared in 1959.

59   Pointe au Baril Lighthouse

Many early lights were quite simple, perhaps a mere bonfire on shore or a lantern in a tree. The first lighthouse at Pointe au Baril, however, was unique because it was a lantern set on top of a barrel on a point of land jutting out into the water. This was sufficient to guide local fishermen back in to shore at dusk.

Most lighthouses were named for the land around them. However, here, the land was named for its early light. Pointe au Baril is French, meaning "barrel point." Later, the barrel was placed on its side with the end removed, and a lantern was set inside. This was a great improvement because then the light was visible only from points directly in line. As long as fishermen could see the light they had safe passage into the harbor. This was one of the earliest known types of range light.

Near the end of the nineteenth century, with the rise of the lumbering industry in northern Ontario, many new communities sprang up. In 1881 lumbering companies paid the McIntoshes, a local fishing family living on McIntosh Island in Georgian Bay, to keep lanterns lit at night to guide tugs towing log booms through the channel and into the harbor. The light at Pointe au Baril was one of these.

In 1887 these lumbering companies vigorously petitioned the government to build two simple derrick-style lighthouses as range lights in the channel. The government finally agreed to build the lights but decided to build something more substantial to avoid being petitioned again for better structures in the future. The range lights were erected in 1889 by Collingwood contractor Charles Mickler, who built portable items such as doors and flooring in town and then shipped them to the site. The cost for the lights was $1,515.

The front range light was built on the peninsula known as Pointe au Baril. It was a white, square, tapering tower that stood 33 feet (10 m) from the ground to the vane on the lantern. Built on a solid, stone foundation, it had a 42.5-foot (13 m) focal plane. Today it is a beautiful, well-kept white building. A 1½-story keeper's house has been added to the original building. Its side walls also taper upward, giving the impression that it is bracing itself for Georgian Bay storms. The house and tower are both trimmed in red.

The rear range light was built on Macklin Island inside the channel. It stood 60 feet (18.3 m) above the water and was a 44 foot (13.4 m) square wooden skeletal tower with an upper portion of white slatwork. It showed a fixed red light with a visibility of 10 miles (16.2 km). Mickler installed a dioptric illuminating apparatus from England in the front range light. It had a fixed, white light and a visibility of 10 miles (16 km) over the open water, while the rear light was a fixed red. Sailors used an imaginary line connecting these range lights to guide them through the shoals of the channel into the harbor.

In 1909 the rear range light was replaced by a square white skeletal steel tower with an enclosed watchroom below the gallery. With an overall height of 81 feet (25 m) from base to ventilator, it displayed a fixed red catoptric light from a 93-foot (28.5 m) focal plane for a 10-mile (16 km) visibility. This new tower, built by George W. White of Parry Sound for $570, was placed on higher ground because mariners had complained that the old light was difficult to see when approaching from outside the reefs that lined the channel from Georgian Bay. The steel framework had been

Pointe au Baril Lighthouse

supplied by Goold, Shapely and Muir of Brantford, Ontario, for $668.50, bringing its total cost to $1,238.

While Carl Madigan tended the light from 1949 to 1977, he earned $3 a day as keeper, not enough to feed and raise his six children. He supplemented his salary by building cottages on contract and doing other odd jobs. His wife, Emmaline, developed her own family supplement by establishing a laundry business at the lighthouse. It grew quickly to five washlines and she put her children on storm patrol. Although they notified their mother of black clouds, she occasionally lost an article to the lake or the top of a pine tree. After her husband died in 1977, she took over as keeper until the keeper was removed from the lighthouse in 1983. Fishermen missed her laundry, which had become the local weather forecast for fair weather if clothes were hung out.

As with many lights, Pointe au Baril has its resident ghost who walks the tower stairs and opens doors. Emmaline's family believed it to be Major Evans, a colorful character who had been keeper from 1941 to 1949 and was very fond of the light.

In 1992 these range lights both displayed a fixed red light powered by electricity. However, while the front light used a dioptric illuminating apparatus the rear light continued to use a catoptric system.

Known Keepers: Samuel Edward Oldfield (1889–1907), Ole Hansen (1907–30), James Alexander Vail (1930–40), Kenneth Malcolm Evans (1941–49), Carl Madigan (1949–77), Emmaline Madigan (1978–83).

60 Port Elgin Old Lighthouse

Port Elgin is located on the east side of Lake Huron just 4 miles (6.5 km) below Southampton and 24 miles (38.6 km) above Kincardine. It is formed around a small bay in the shoreline. During harbor improvements of the 1880s a lighthouse was established at the outer end of the government wharf to help guide vessels into port. This lighthouse no longer exists today.

Known Keeper: Robert Lowry (1896–1916–).

61 Port Elgin Range Lights

In 1935 the Canadian government established proper range lights at Port Elgin, a small lakeside town on the eastern shore of Lake Huron, to assist navigation into the harbor. By 1992 these range lights were circular white masts with a vertical orange stripe as their daymark. Both first used reflectors and displayed a fixed green electric light. The front range light was 24 feet (7.4 m) tall and had a focal plane of 28 feet (8.5 m); the rear range light was 40.3 feet (12.4 m) tall with a focal plane of 51.5 feet (15.7 m). In 1982 the front range light received a dioptric illuminating apparatus to magnify its light, and its focal plane was increased to 33 feet (10 m). These lights continue to operate with green lights to guide mariners (mostly pleasure craft) into Port Elgin's small harbor.

62 Port McNicoll Range Lights

Although Owen Sound existed for many years as a shipping terminal for the Canadian Pacific Railway (CPR) trains had to travel over difficult terrain with numerous steep grades. The CPR solved this problem by relocating and establishing their own harbor at Port McNicoll just east of Midland on the Georgian Bay side of Lake Huron. They built docks, freight sheds, grain elevators and range lights. On May 1, 1912, the Canadian Pacific fleet left Owen Sound and headed for their new harbor at Port McNicoll. Very little is known about these range lights except that they guided vessels safely into the harbor to the Canadian Pacific Railway dock.

Known Keeper: Charles W. Beatty (1921–).

63 Presqu'ile Lighthouse (Georgian Bay)

In 1864 John Mackenzie settled in the Presqu'ile area on Georgian Bay. Being on the water, he built a store and a 400-foot (122 m) dock (with some government assistance) in 1865. The port became an important stopover for steamers traveling between Collingwood and Duluth, Minnesota, as it offered deep anchorage for larger steamers to top up on cordwood (which they burned as fuel) and other supplies. As time passed, the steamers also carried hay, grain, and meat for export, and a village grew up to serve them. In 1874 more than 340 vessels stopped at this busy little harbor.

Also in 1874 the steamer *Chicora* brought Governor General Lord Dufferin and Lady Dufferin to Presqu'ile during a summer cruise of the Great Lakes. Since there was no lighthouse at this time, Mackenzie created range lights by hanging a light from a post at the end of the wharf and building a large bonfire onshore behind it. The couple received an enthusiastic reception, and Mackenzie presented Lady Dufferin with a prized local gift, a pot of honey gathered by Grey County bees.

On March 1, 1876, the Department of Marine and Fisheries bought Lot No. 6 of Centre Street in the Village of Presqu'ile at the foot of the dock for $1.00 from Mackenzie and built a lighthouse on it. The light helped guide ships into the dock, and warned them of the rocky reef that extended from the tip of the peninsula to the sand bar at the approach to Owen Sound just 9 miles (14.5 km) away.

The tower was a short square pyramidal structure covered in clapboarding. Its square gallery was enclosed with a wooden railing and supported by 20 wooden corbels (five per side). Its octagonal lantern used three large flat-wick lamps with 16-inch (40 cm) reflectors to produce a fixed white light from a 31-foot (9.4 m) focal plane for a 10-mile (16 km) visibility. The tower was 27 feet (8.2 m) from base to ventilator. As well as being port master, John Mackenzie was appointed the first keeper at $50 a year. He was also the postmaster and operated the general store and a harness shop.

During the 1870s the lit harbor enabled Captain Dunn to offer moonlight excursions on the vessel *O'Connor*. These were an important part of the social life of this isolated community, becoming so popular that excursions ran regularly twice a week.

In 1879 a large wooden oil house was built beside the lighthouse to store the fuel separately from the tower as a safety measure. At some point a storm signal tower was placed nearby. Wicker baskets of varying shapes were hoisted and flown to notify mariners of weather conditions.

Being such an entrepreneur, Mackenzie had two non-paid lighthouse assistants. The first was his youngest daughter, who often lit and extinguished the lamps and cleaned the glass and reflectors. The second was his collie, Buller. Apparently the dog would wake his master if he was sleeping when it was time to light the lamps, and would even have the lighthouse key ready in his mouth. (This key is now on display at the Owen Sound Museum.)

Steamships brought life to the village and steamships took it away. During the 1880s the harbor approaches to Owen Sound were dredged and marine traffic shifted to that port, as it had a harbor that could accommodate larger and more numerous vessels. Also steamers no longer needed to stop at Presqu'ile to pick up cordwood as coal had replaced wood as the fuel of choice. Although Mackenzie tried developing Presqu'ile for tourism in the late 1890s, the area never recovered and eventually became a ghost town.

The government discontinued the light in 1910. In 1918 a farmer wanted to use its wood to repair his barn but did not want to pay the $40 asked for it. In 1922 the government placed tenders in local papers to sell the light, but the only response was from the

Presqu'ile Lighthouse, circa 1910 NAC PA172526

Canadian Wrecking Company in Toronto. They had no time to come and see it, so the light and the property were sold for $10 to J.R. Brown and his wife, Margaret, who built a cottage close to the lighthouse. Cecil Corfe bought both buildings in the early 1950s. The Corfes restored the neglected lighthouse to pristine condition, but could never get rid of its cockroaches. When they sold the property they did not inform the new owners of the occupants but were sure their "repugnance would turn to affection in time." Eventually the Rotary Club bought the property to make a youth camp, but after being used for a number of years the lighthouse was condemned as beyond repair and was torn down. Rumor has it that it was then stacked behind a local barn.

Known Keepers: John Mackenzie (1876–1907), Hugh H. Mackenzie (1907–10).

64 Providence Bay Lighthouse

Providence Bay is located along the southwest coast of Manitoulin Island, Lake Huron. "Manitoulin" is a Native word meaning "Spirit Island," the home of the Great Spirit, Gitche Manitou. Locals claim you might catch sight of a ghostly apparition of a "burning boat," a blazing red ship-like mass, in the Providence Bay area during full moon. But those who do not believe in ghosts, spirits, and apparitions, explain the vision in scientific terms as the result of hot gases and reflections.

A lighthouse was built in 1904 at Providence Point, the east headland of the bay. It was a 42-foot (12.8 m) octagonal white wooden tapering tower with an octagonal cast-iron red lantern that displayed a fixed white dioptric light for 11 miles (17.7 km). In 1955 the light was automated through the use of a cable that provided electricity to the light. Although a keeper was no longer necessary, the government did retain a caretaker to keep an eye on the light. On October 14, 1973, the lighthouse burned down. It is not known if vandals or natural elements were to blame. Instead of rebuilding the tower, the government elected to place a modern beacon on a 20-foot (6 m) skeletal tower. In 1992 it displayed an electric fixed white light visible for 12 miles (19.3 km) from its 46.5-foot (14.2 m) focal plane.

Known Keepers: J.J. Roussain (1904–05), John B. Sinclair (1906–11), Thomas Ellis (1912–30), Milton Buie (1936–49), Jack Cornish (1973).

65 Red Rock Lighthouse

In the late 1800s Parry Sound, Georgian Bay, exported great quantities of lumber, all by ship. Sawmill owners were so eager to have a light to mark the Parry Sound Ship Channel that in 1870 they paid half the cost of building the first lighthouse on Tower Island. It was a 40-foot (12.2 m) square wooden tower on top of a keeper's house. Its fixed white light used flat-wicked lamps and reflectors and was visible for 10 miles (16 km). This light had a short lifespan due to the severe storms on Georgian Bay.

The Red Rock lighthouse keeper's sailboat was built by W. Watts and Sons Boat Builders of Collingwood and provided by the Department of Marine and Fisheries. The 22-foot (6.7 m), double-ended boat was built of cedar planks over a white-oak frame and was outfitted with sails, rigging and oars for a cost of $185. If a keeper wanted an engine for it he was expected to pay for it himself.

In 1881 a second light was built but it was moved to Red Rock Island, so named because of its red granite. It was an octagonal wooden lighthouse with an octagonal wooden tower rising up from it, and it was built on a wooden cribwork pier. The lantern housed a fixed white, catoptric lighting apparatus visible up to 13 miles (21 km) on a clear night. Since the lighthouse was on barren rock, it too was exposed to the full force of punishing storms, which at times washed waves right over the 44-foot (13.5 m) structure. In 1909, in efforts to correct the problem, the cribwork foundation was replaced with a steel cylinder and reinforced inside with stones and concrete. But it was too little too late, and a new light had to be built in 1911.

This third lighthouse was built on the new, refurbished steel and concrete pier. Made of reinforced concrete, it proved to be much more durable. It was also one of two concrete towers ever to be built on Georgian Bay (the other one was at Cape Croker). The 42-foot (13 m) tower had two large oval-shaped levels topped by a polygonal lantern that seemed to be dwarfed by the rest of the tower. Painted with a red base and top, white middle and red trim it was often referred to as the Campbell's soup can. Originally, the lantern showed an oscillating white light that burned acetylene, but it later became an electric fixed white light. The tower entry was at the foundation level, and the first level housed the fog plant and workroom. A spiral staircase led to the second level, which housed the living quarters. It used to have steel shutters to cover the windows to protect them from high waves. A ladder extended from the kitchen to the lantern. Sometime in the 1970s a helicopter pad was built above the lantern to make the station more accessible.

William McGowan was keeper at the first lighthouse on Tower Island (1870–81). Adam Lawson kept the second light on Red Rock from 1881 to 1885. In 1897 Adam Brown, a butcher turned fisherman who knew the waters and the area first-hand, applied for the keeper's position, a more lucrative job at $300–$350 a year than selling fish at three cents a pound. Instead of Brown, John McConachie, who had more political clout, was given the position. However, he was making good money scaling lumber and so he hired Brown to do his lightkeeping job until the government issued an ultimatum and he took over as keeper in the fall and Brown went fishing again. At the end of his season, when storms were most fierce, McConachie's lack of water skill became apparent. Unable to operate the govern-

Red Rock Lighthouse – courtesy Parry Sound Museum

ment-issued sailboat, he tied it to a rowboat and headed toward Parry Sound. Luckily for him, Walter Huff, the keeper at Jones Island, came to his rescue and sailed him to Parry Sound. He had had enough of lightkeeping, and Adam Brown was appointed official keeper the following year.

Brown also had to fight for his position on another occasion. Another would-be keeper, also with political clout, bragged that he would get the job and even went to the light to have Brown show him the ropes. Instead, Brown played a joke on him. He opened an air valve, producing a loud screeching sound, and shouted, "Every man for himself!" Everyone fled the lighthouse and the visitor was eventually found cowering between ice banks cut for the tower's water line. When he finally emerged he decided he did not want to be keeper after all.

One evening Brown saw the deck-heavy *Seattle* heading out to open water with a full load of lumber, and was concerned because the wind was coming up. By midnight it was a fierce gale and the ship's lights had disappeared. In the morning, Brown called for fishing volunteers and they were able to rescue the crew of the wrecked *Seattle*, but the ship sank and lost its load. There is even a rumor that Brown and his fishing buddies confiscated what they could find of the cargo, but it was never proven.

The water was not the only danger. Once, Brown was sitting in a bosun's chair, painting the tower, when an insecure knot, tied by his assistant, let loose, almost pitching him 60 feet (18.5 m) onto the rocks below. Luckily he was able to grab a cable and swing himself through a small window to safety.

Adam Brown was one savvy man. Captain Clark used to tend buoys in the shipping channel and place them every spring when he delivered the keepers to their stations. When delivering Brown one spring, Clark stopped to check and place the Three Star Buoy. Brown used soapsuds, the proper method, and went over the line looking for leaks, but Captain Clark had a more dangerous method — a lit match. Brown admonished him to put it out, and to himself predicted a short lifespan for Clark, who used a match to check for leaks in buoys that were fueled by acetylene. Brown turned down Clark's invitation to help set the rest of the buoys. The very next day, Brown heard an explosion and saw a great cloud of black smoke. Sure enough, Clark had lit one too many matches and blown himself and his boat to smithereens while placing a buoy by Ten Mile Point.

Red Rock Lighthouse, circa 1911

In spite of the station's isolation, Brown often sailed into Parry Sound to visit his friends. He was an important figure in Parry Sound because he was the man who watched the light that guarded the main post of the shipping channel that assisted their livelihood. He was even a member of the Masonic Lodge. Other social events involved partying and dances on the Minks Islands with his fishing cronies.

Besides his conscientious operation of the light, Brown also piloted vessels through the channel when necessary and pumped the hand foghorn to answer ships' signals in foggy weather. With his sense of humor, Brown liked to tell people that was how he "played the organ." He was an excellent, well-respected keeper. For six or seven years he was given an easier job as keeper at Snug Harbour, but his heart was at Red Rock and he returned there as keeper and also head keeper for the shipping channel, with supervision over all the lights and buoys. In 1937, after almost 40 years of lightkeeping, Brown retired at the age of seventy-five. After years of conscientious, dedicated service, he received the Imperial Service Medal from H.M. King George VI in appreciation for his outstanding public service and worthy citizenship.

One of the light's later keepers, Gus Olsen (1966–77), applied for the keeper's job because he wanted steady employment. The advertisement that he answered for keeper asked for men who could operate diesel engines, were handy with boats, and had knowledge of electricity. In 1962 a four-man rotational system had been set in place as a counter-measure to the isolation at Red Rock. Two men were at Red Rock, one was at Snug Harbour, and one was on rotational leave. While there, Olson reported that the Red Rock light used a 250-watt bulb reflected through a huge glass prism and had a 15-mile (24 km) visibility.

The light, still an active aid to navigation today, is difficult for the average person to see since it is 10 miles (16 km) out in Georgian Bay. But one can see the original lamp and reflector from the first lighthouse on Tower Island at the Parry Sound Museum. The reflector is interesting because it is coated in "German Silver," a combination of nickel, copper and zinc.

Known Keepers: William McGowan (1870–81), Adam Lawson (1881–85), Adam Brown (1898–1909; conflicting pay records show Adam Brown taking charge of the light in 1909) (1909–37), Lawrence Tyler (1938–60), Edwin Scott (1961) (1963) (1965), Thomas Flynn (1962), John R. Joinder (1962–65), Roland Sheridan Penrose (1965), Gus Olsen (1966–77).

Red Rock Lighthouse

66 Richard's Landing Light

In 1894 a private light was built on the north side of St. Joseph Island to assist marine travel through the narrow North Channel at this point on Lake Huron. It was a square white wooden 15-foot (4.6 m) tower at the outer end of the wharf at Richard's Landing. It displayed a fixed white light with a 9-mile (14.6 m) visibility. In 1919 the steamers *Manitou* and *Caribou* of the Dominion Transport Company called bi-weekly at Richard's Landing to connect islanders to the mainland as they traveled the North Channel to and from Lake Superior and Georgian Bay. Although this light no longer exists today, the government has established an electric fixed green light shown from a white circular mast, also located on the wharf.

Known Keepers: J. Burnside (?), Herbert Steinburg (1922–27), Karl Johnson (1927–42), Ernest Brownlee (1942–51), John Stanley Tranter (1951).

67 Sailors' Encampment Range Lights

Before the Neebish Channel was widened and deepened in the early 1900s, most vessels traveling between Lake Superior and Lake Huron used a channel to the east of Neebish Island in the St. Mary's River which passed an area on the west side of St. Joseph Island called Sailors' Encampment. Here, the channel was divided by a middle ground of solid limestone. Most vessels passed on the east side of this shoal unless there was a heavy northwest gale, when captains used the deeper but narrower west channel.

The St. Mary's River was treacherous to navigate, and before it was lit captains would hire a river pilot to direct them through its swift currents, hidden rocks and shoals. With the increased shipping of the late 1800s, numerous ship blockades impeded navigation on the river. In November 1871 the steamers *St. Paul* and *Atlantic* were caught in the ice, late in the season and marooned until the next spring at Sailors' Encampment. In September 1899 the downbound steamer *Douglas Houghton* swung across the channel at this area and was then rammed and sunk by the steamer *John Fitz*, causing the channel to be blocked for a week. This blockade affected more than 350 vessels, with an estimated loss to navigation of almost $600,000. Less than three months later, a three-way collision blocked the river in the area again. After the steamer *Ketchum* had blocked the channel for 16 days in 1910, the channel was finally widened to 600 feet (185 m).

Sailors' Encampment was first marked with a light in 1892 so that vessels could travel at night. A crib bearing a red light warned mariners of the middle ground. In 1902 a fixed red tubular lantern light was shown from an upright crib in 8 feet (2.4 m) of water off the south end of Sailors' Encampment to mark the shoal (middle ground) and the east side of the entrance to Sailors' Encampment Passage. In 1909 better light was needed, so the government replaced the early lights with two enclosed square wooden 33-foot (10 m) tapering towers with wooden lanterns that cost $1,687. With the lights being located at different elevations, they were easily lined up to guide vessels. After the deepening of the Neebish Channel, upbound vessels passed to the east of Neebish Island and downbound vessels passed to the west.

Sailors' Encampment Range Light

In 1951 the range lights were electrified, and in 1959 these towers were replaced with white square skeletal towers that displayed a white daymark with an orange vertical stripe. Both lights displayed a fixed white electric dioptic light. The front tower was 49 feet (15 m) high and had a 75-foot (23 m) focal plane. The rear tower was 58 feet (17.7 m) high, with a 103-foot (31.4 m) focal plane. These lights still exist today.

Known Keepers: A.M. Raines (1892–1924), Fred Albert Gilbertson (1924), Harold Raines (1925–46), Murray Ward Smith (1946–52).

68 Saugeen River Range Lights

The Saugeen River's first light was a beacon light placed at the entrance to the river on the east side of Lake Huron to aid fishermen returning at night to Southampton. First lit in 1883, it consisted of a lantern hoisted to a mast erected on a crib 50 feet (15.2 m) from the outer end of the north breakwater pier at the rivermouth. The light burned about 44 gallons (198 l) of oil a year and had a 7-mile (11 km) visibility.

Its keeper, Murdock McLeod, earned $80 a year. In 1886, after buying a house and an outbuilding near the lighthouse, McLeod applied to the government to

Sailors' Encampment Front Range Light

Saugeen River Front Range Light

When the Canadian Coast Guard went to silence the foghorn in 1993 public outcry and the Southampton'-Propeller Club saved it. Today the foghorn operates on a "needs only" basis; boaters use a signal from their marine radios to initiate the foghorn's operation when they need its service. Southampton residents like their heritage and their lighthouses. While these range lights were initiated to assist fishermen returning with their catch of the day, they now function primarily to guide pleasure craft into the harbor.

Known Keepers: Murdock McLeod (1883–99), Donald McAuley (1899–) Big Angus McAuley (1909–28), Joseph Granville (1928–41), Mrs. Lydia Granville (1941–54), John Angus McLean (1954–58), John MacDonald (1958–).

purchase the land on which his buildings sat. After some correspondence the Department of Indian Affairs agreed to sell him the two lots for $25 each.

In 1894 the government supplied a Chance anchor dioptric seventh-order lantern and changed the characteristic from a fixed green to fixed white. The visibility was increased to 10 miles (16 km). In 1900 a privately run light, also a lantern hoisted on a mast, was lit to work as a rear range light to this river entrance light. Its green light had a 45-foot (13.7 m) focal plane.

In 1903 these mast lights were replaced by identical wooden pyramidal towers that were 31 feet (9.5 m) tall from base to ventilator. Both towers had a pedimented door, were covered with cedar shingles and were painted white. Also, each had a square gallery with a matchboard cove supporting it. Both galleries were surrounded with pipe iron railing and supported a square lantern topped with a cornice and then a hipped roof with a ventilator extending from the middle.

These range lights were built by John McAulay for $1,085. They displayed fixed green lights with a 10-mile (16 km) visibility. The front light was placed near the end of the north pier, and the rear light was a short distance behind it on higher ground, also along the north side of the river. In 1906 the rear range light was moved back 1,650 feet (503 m) and placed on a rubble-stone foundation. This provided a higher focal plane of 61 feet (18.6 m) and a straighter line of entry into the river. In 1937 a foghorn was added to the front range light (blast 3 s; silence 17 s).

These range lights today display fixed red electric lights and both have a vertical orange stripe as part of their daymark. The front range light was given a dioptric illuminating apparatus in 1986, and its focal plane was raised to 38.6 feet (11.8 m), but the rear range light continued to use a catoptric system from a 60.5-foot (18.5 m) elevation. The front range light now sits on a concrete base and the rear range light still has its rubblestone foundation.

In 1989 conservationists helped the lighthouse. The Canadian Coast Guard was in the process of removing wooden shingles from the rear range light and replacing them with easy care aluminum siding when public picketing stopped the work. The Coast Guard reversed their decision and replaced the old shingles with new ones and then painted them white, just like the original.

69 Shoal Island Lighthouse

Shoal Island is located off the northwestern tip of St. Joseph Island, in the St. Mary's North Channel of Lake Huron. In the mid-1800s lake travel increased, and mariners were braving the St. Mary's channel with its hazardous swift currents, sunken shoals, rocks, and cross channel currents. Sailing was tricky. As few captains knew the waters well enough to take their vessels through, they would hire river pilots for the stretch from the Sault to Detour, Michigan.

Then about 1861, Philetus Church, a storekeeper at the head of Lake George, supplied the first navigation aid in this area. He employed his captain, David Tate, to stake out the channel of the St. Mary's River each spring and take up the stakes each fall. Later, the Vessel Owners' Association installed and maintained range lights through the St. Mary's Channel.

Finally, the Canadian and American governments assumed the responsibility. In 1885 the Canadian government built a lighthouse on Shoal Island, at the head of St. Joseph Island to help mark the North Channel. As lighthouses around this time were often named after their keepers, this lighthouse was also named Rains Lighthouse, for its first keeper, and sometimes even Mathew Lighthouse (for an island connected to Shoal Island by a small

Shoal Island Lighthouse, circa 1890

Shoal Island Lighthouse

bridge). This was a good time to build this lighthouse because the St. Mary's Canal, started in 1882, was finished and open for traffic September 7, 1895. Now in case of trouble between England and the United States, Canadian boats would not have to rely on American locks.

The Shoal Island Lighthouse was a square white building 32 feet (9.8 m) high. It had a white flashing light (flash 1 s; eclipse 3 s). The duties of the first keeper, Evron (Evan) C. Rains, included lighting and extinguishing the coal-oil lamps, cleaning the glass windows, polishing the reflector behind the lamps, refilling the lamps with coal-oil, trimming the lamp wicks and cleaning the lamp chimneys daily. He and his wife, Mary, raised five children, no small feat on his annual $150 salary. When he asked for a raise, the government's response was that it did not take a wife and five children to operate a lighthouse. He did not get the raise, but he and his wife raised five more children after this! It is amazing that none of them drowned. When Rains died, his wife did the job of keeper until a replacement could be found. Sometime in 1908 or 1909 the lighthouse reportedly burned down and then was rebuilt. Rains' son Roland, like his father, enjoyed writing songs and poetry to help pass the time.

Most other lightkeepers confined their literary efforts to logbooks. The logs of William McKay and Albert Wyatt can be seen at the St. Joseph Island Museum Village on St. Joseph Island. McKay made only two or three brief entries a month, such as, "No fog this month." In Wyatt's books, on the other hand, the entries were recorded religiously every day, although space was limited and point form was necessary. Mrs. Miller, a local resident, recalls that Wyatt did not live at the lighthouse but rowed out to it each day.

The last keeper, Fred Rogers, had a number of lights under his charge including houses, beacons and buoys. At one time he had to visit these daily to fill the oil lamps, trim the wicks, clean the glass, and light and extinguish the lamps. As a result of all this work, he and his wife, Belle, were a familiar part of the channel scene. Rogers saw most of the lights converted to battery power in the 1930s. In the 1950s they were switched to hydroelectric power.

Today Shoal Island Lighthouse may be seen from the northwestern point on St. Joseph Island. From here the

lighthouse is directly opposite. The stately white, clapboard building has twelve-paned windows, a dull-red roof that slopes down from the second story on the west side, tall pillars on the south side and a square lantern that extends up from the roof. The lantern has a square white gallery, a red dome, and at least the west wall as a blacked-out panel. Together, the lantern and dome give the appearance of "a cap on a fancy bottle." The lighthouse stands on smooth rock along with graceful pines and junipers. It is most scenic with its red and white structure set against the grey-green of the island, the blue-green of the lake, and the grey-blue of the cloudy sky.

Known Keepers: Evron (Evan) Rains (1885–), John L. McCluskie (1909–22), Peter J. Brucklebank (1922–24), William McKay (1924–28), Murdock Burnham (1928–29), Albert (Bert) Wyatt (1929–37), Fred Rogers (1937–).

70 Snug Harbour Range Lights

In 1894 the Snug Harbour Range Lights were established on the east side of Georgian Bay, Lake Huron, to mark entry into Snug Harbour as well as to assist vessels heading into Parry Sound. They were built by Charles Mickler of Collingwood, whose trademark was to build as many portable items as possible in Collingwood and then transport them to the site.

The front range light was built on the westernmost point of Walton Island. It was a square white tapering wooden tower with a red stripe on its channel side, and displayed a fixed red light that was visible for about 7 miles (11 km) from a 39-foot (12 m) focal plane. The rear range light was placed on the southern tip of Snug Island on the north side of the entrance to Snug Harbour. Its square white tapering wooden tower rose from the middle of the roof peak of the keeper's house. It also displayed a red stripe on its channel side as well as a fixed white light with a greater visibility of 13 miles (21 km).

Snug Harbour Rear Range Light, circa 1910

After using kerosene oil as an illuminant, the lights were switched to acetylene around 1913. In the mid-1930s the light on the keeper's house malfunctioned and exploded. The damaged lighthouse was rebuilt with a false front. Later on, as freighters became larger, oil tankers frequently became grounded while making their way to the storage tanks in Parry Sound. Among the groundings were the vessels

Glen Eagles, Eastern Shell, Lake Shell and *Imperial St. Clair.* The problem was solved when the storage tanks were removed from Parry Sound.

Although a keeper's life was frequently hard and lonely, keepers often made their work easier using their own ingenuity. During the 1930s, for example, keeper Dan Boterell set up a mirror in the tower to reflect down into his living space so that he could constantly check the light without going up the tower. He also rigged snuffers with a long string so that he could extinguish the flame without going up the tower. With the time he saved he made daily fire patrols along the shore in his canoe.

Snug Harbour Rear Range Light

Today the range lights still shine but they are no longer manned. A tripod tower with a 40-foot (12.2 m) focal plane has taken the place of the front light on Walton Island. In 1992 both lights displayed a fixed electrically powered green catoptric light.

Known Keepers: Charles White (1894–1903), Adam Brown (1909–14), Dan Boterell (1915–31).

71   South Baymouth Range Lights

In 1898 range lights were established at South Baymouth, Lake Huron, to guide vessels between submerged rocks and into the harbor. The front light was a 28-foot (8.5 m) square white tapering wooden tower set on a bare limestone island off the southeast shore of Manitoulin Island. It used a seventh-order lens to display a fixed white light for 10 miles (16 km). The rear light, also a square white tapering wooden tower, was 40 feet (12.2 m) high and placed 770 feet (235 m) behind and to the northeast of the front light in the woods behind the village of South Baymouth. It used reflectors to display a fixed white light for 12 miles (19.3 km). The station also had a hand foghorn.

South Baymouth Range Lights

The village developed as a fishing community and exported its catch. After Michael's Bay, South Baymouth became Manitoulin's main port. In October 1917 the freighter S.S. *George A. Graham* was caught in a heavy storm that shifted her cargo of grain. The ship was heading into South Baymouth for repairs when it struck the east point and buckled. Fishermen rowed the crew safely to shore, and local farmers soon helped themselves to the abandoned grain. The wreck survived for many years and was a playground for local children until it was salvaged for its steel during World War II. At some point the station received a fog whistle and then a foghorn (blast 2.5 s; silence 27 s).

With the decline in fishing, tourism became the village's primary industry. Its range lights then provided a perfect photo opportunity for visitors. While the keeper used to have to row out to the island to tend the lights, low water levels of the 1950s made the front range light part of the main-

land of Manitoulin. The lights were automated in the 1950s and still shine today but they now exhibit fixed green lights and display a vertical orange stripe daymark on their white buildings.

Known Keepers: Jim Ritchie (1898–1902), John Ritchie (1903–06), W. Hudgins (1912–), W.J. Ritchie (1934–35).

South Baymouth Front Range Light

72 Southampton Range Lights

During the 1870s the Canadian government spent $300,000 to make Southampton Harbour behind Chantry Island off the mouth of the Saugeen River on the east side of Lake Huron into a harbor of refuge. Breakwaters, moorings and piers were built over a seven-year period to provide shelter from lake storms.

The biggest undertaking was the construction of the Long Dock, a long, curved dock built in two sections between Chantry Island and the mainland, with a gap between the sections. The section extending from the island was built first. It was a 1,600-foot (488 m) extension onto the breakwater from the north side of the island, and it was built between 1871 and the fall of 1873 by a syndicate of local businessmen. The 1,800-foot (558 m) second section was then constructed out from the mainland to within 450 feet (140 m) of the first section's end. This opening formed the "Gap," the harbor's north entrance. This section was finished in 1877. Both sections consisted of 30-foot (9 m) square wooden, rock-filled cribs that were built up to 7.5 feet (2.3 m) above water and topped with wooden planks to form a boardwalk.

To mark the Gap, range lights were built in 1877. The front light was placed on the eastern end of the Long Dock's island section. The original 1878 front range light was a wooden skeletal tower painted white. The tower was 12 feet (3.7 m) square at the base and had an iron lantern 4 feet (1.2 m) square. The lantern showed a fixed red light created from a mammoth flat-wick lamp with a 17-inch (4 cm) reflector. An 1878 report recommended that the light be enclosed so as to offer protection for the keeper in foul weather. The report also recommended that the lantern be renovated and more glass panels be inserted to assist ships approaching from different directions. Further, a chain railing should be installed the length of the pier for the keeper's safety. At a later date the tower was replaced by a gently tapering square white tower 25 feet (7.6 m) from base to vane.

The rear range light was placed on the mainland, 6,300 feet (1920 m) behind and southwest of the front light just north of Horseshoe Bay. It too was a gently tapering square, white wooden tower but it was 28 feet (8.5 m) from base to vane. Both had a square gallery. The lantern of the rear light was 4 feet (1.2 m) in diameter, had a shingle base and housed one mammoth flat-wick lamp with a 17-inch (43 cm) reflector. While the front light was first tended by the Chantry Island keeper, Duncan Lambert, because he could easily tend it from there, the rear light was first tended by David Cascadin, a keeper who stayed on the mainland.

In 1907 a gas buoy was placed on the tip of Chantry Island's north shoal, and the rear range light was moved to the south side of Horseshoe Bay. The buoy and the range lights worked in conjunction to provide a straighter line of entry between shoals and through the Gap into the harbor.

Even though the range lights marked the Gap, the opening was plagued by strong currents. Several vessels were wrecked at the Gap while trying to enter the harbor. In October 1908 the schooner *Erie Stewart* hit the Long Dock 100 feet (30.5 m) from the Gap while seeking refuge. The schooner broke up and the crew made it safely to the breakwater, from where they watched the schooner's foremast shear off and take out the front range light. After finally securing a small lifeboat from the hut next to the range light, the crew rowed to the safety of the lighthouse.

Unfortunately, the next morning the schooner *Ontario*, which was also seeking harbor refuge, was beached on the gravel bar just south of the Saugeen River. Since the north shoal gas buoy was out, the front range light was missing, and the rear range light was obscured by rain and fog, the vessel had mistakenly headed for the rivermouth.

The front range light was never rebuilt and the Long Dock gradually fell into disrepair. Each year Lake Huron storms and winter ice damaged the boardwalk a little more. By the 1940s the top had been severely damaged and was eventually completely broken apart and washed away. The rear range light continued to shine and became known as the McNab Point Lighthouse. Today, while there are no visible remains of the front range light or the Long Dock and although the Gap opening is marked by red and green navigational markers, area boaters still need to be wary of the hidden danger created by the ruins of the submerged remains of the rock-filled cribs, especially during low water levels.

Known Keepers: (Front) Duncan Lambert (1877), (Rear) David Cascadin (1877–82), John Lee (1882–1904), James Brown (1904–), Andy Brown (?), Jack Buckley (?).

73 Southampton Storm Signal Station

In 1873 a storm signal station was established on the hill on the south side of the Saugeen River mouth at Southampton on the east side of Lake Huron. Wicker baskets of different sizes were hoisted during heavy weather, indicating wind direction and intensity to passing vessels. The keeper at Chantry Island originally tended this signal along with other weather instruments designed to gather information. At some point this storm signal station was moved to the foot of High Street. Also at some point, Johnny Trolford tended the signal for many years. The signal was discontinued in 1951. The Southampton Propeller Club built a replica of the storm signal and today it is displayed in the waterfront Pioneer Park by the river.

74 Spruce Island Shoal Light

To mark Spruce Island Shoal, which extended 2,400 feet (730 m) southwest from Spruce Island along the east side of Georgian Bay, Lake Huron, the Canadian government placed a gas light on a concrete tower and pier in 1907. The contract to build the structure was awarded to Thomas A. White of Parry Sound for $12,875. A 13.5-foot (4.1 m) octagonal crib was sunk on the shoal in 17 feet (5.2 m) of water on August 31, 1907. It was topped with a reinforced concrete pier and a smaller octagonal tower, which was built to 21 feet (6.4 m) above the water. The tower was surmounted by an acetylene gas light with its necessary reservoirs. It displayed a fixed white dioptric light that had a visibility of 11 miles (17.7 m). This shoal light was discontinued in 1949 and was replaced with a more modern buoy.

Spruce Island Shoal Light

75 Stokes Bay Range Lights

While a light on Lyal Island helped to guide mariners into Stokes Bay on the east shore of Lake Huron, it was still tricky for them to navigate the hidden underwater shoals and islands at the bay's entrance. To better mark the bay, range lights were installed in 1904.

The front range light was placed on Knife Island, a tiny island near the middle of the mouth of the bay. It was a square white pyramidal wooden tower that displayed a flashing red light from a 30-foot (9 m) focal plane for about 12 miles (19 km). The rear range light was placed behind the front one on the east side of the Stokes Bay mainland. It was a square steel skeletal tower with an enclosed watchroom and a square lantern. From a 61-foot (18.6 m) focal plane it displayed a fixed red light with a 15-mile (24.2 km) visibility. In 1906 a shelter shed constructed by R.E. Moore of Lion's Head was added at a cost of $165. One of the first keepers, A. Smith, earned $320 a year.

Today the lights are automated and use electricity to produce their red beams. The front light still flashes (flash 0.5 s; eclipse 3.5 s) and the rear still displays a fixed red light. Each tower now has an orange vertical stripe against the white paint as its daymark.

Known Keepers: D.L. McLay (1904–08), A. Smith (1908), J. McIver (1913–), Norman McDonald (1920–56), J.T. Adams (1956–).

Stokes Bay Front Range Light

76 Strawberry Island Lighthouse

Strawberry Island is a small island 7 miles long and about 3 miles east of Little Current on Manitoulin Island's northeast side in northern Georgian Bay. A lighthouse was built on the northernmost point of the island to help mark the Northern Channel shipping route, where the channel's location at the island was narrow, sharply curved, and fast-flowing. This light was most beneficial to mariners during fog.

The light was built in 1881 on a 23-acre (9.3 hectare) lighthouse reservation. It was a square white wooden three-story pyramidal tower with large rectangular pedimented windows ascending each level. Its octagonal iron lantern was surrounded by a square gallery enclosed with a cross-braced wooden railing. From a 40-foot (12.2 m) focal plane its oil lamps and reflectors displayed a fixed white light with an 11-mile (17.7 km) visibility.

The keeper's house was an attached wooden 1½-story frame dwelling, and the tower base made additional living space in the house. Wooden stairs within the tower also led to the upper rooms of the house. The keeper used a portable hand-operated foghorn when vessels signaled their need for assistance. It was housed in a box that looked like a large old-fashioned suitcase. To operate it, the keeper set it facing the water and turned a handle on its side. With the advent of radar and other navigational aids in the 1900s, ships' requests for the horn were less frequent.

Over the years the light changed little. It had few keepers and the only building addition was a lean-to at the back of the house. In 1916 the light received a fourth-order Fresnel lens for its brass kerosene oil lamp to illuminate.

The second keeper, its longest tenant, kept the light for 36 years. His first son was born at the lighthouse with no outside assistance, and he and his wife went on to raise seven children at this location. Interestingly, the small inherited manual of rules and regulations for keepers also included a medical section covering common ailments and cures of the 1800s. It may have been helpful in raising a large family.

When the last keeper retired in 1963 the light was converted to modern electric lamps operated automatically using photoelectric eyes, making a keeper unnecessary. The light still shines today but it displays a flashing white light with a 5-mile (8 km) visibility. In the 1990s the Canadian Coast Guard was leasing the building, and it was used as a summer cottage, with its occupants giving the old structure lots of TLC.

Known Keepers: Bryan McKay (1881–82), William McKenzie (1883–1921), Carl W.D. Deiter (1921–22), Roxie Smith (1922–), Wesley Taylor (?), George Alvin Stewart (1941–64), James Young (1964–66).

New Spruce Island Shoal Light

Strawberry Island Lighthouse

77 Stribling Point Range Lights

During the late 1800s marine traffic on the St. Mary's River, which connected Lake Superior and Lake Huron, increased, especially after the opening of the Soo Locks in 1855. The river was treacherous to navigate because of its swift currents, many twists and turns, and many hazards. With no posted navigation aids captains hired river pilots to safely maneuver them through.

Before either the American or the Canadian government marked the river, a ship captain for merchant Philetus Church placed wooden stakes during the late 1840s and 1850s to mark reefs and sandbars in the river when he first brought supplies to Church's store on Sugar Island each spring. On his last trip each fall he would lift the stakes.

Later, the Coast Guard marked safe passage by placing red stakes along the edge (right side) of the river for upbound vessels and black stakes on the left side for downbound vessels.

However, time was money, and captains wanted the river lit to enable night travel, so range lights were established. Two lights were placed one behind the other in such a way that they were aligned with other range lights on the opposite side of the river. Sometimes these lights were a few miles apart, with one pair being on the American side of the river and the next pair being on the Canadian side (i.e., St. Joseph Island). The wheelsman guided his vessel through the dark river by keeping his ship lined up with one set of lights until the next set was in line and then he would change course to line up the new set of range lights. This system enabled safe nighttime navigation without the aid of a river pilot.

Most of these range lights were first established about 1892. They consisted simply of white-painted boards fastened to taller and shorter poles to reflect light. A coal oil lamp was enclosed in a box with a glass front and slots to permit the air needed to keep the flame burning. The enclosed lamps were fastened to the middle of the white-board background and gave off a yellow glow easily visible to the wheelsmen of passing ships.

The first range lights placed at Stribling Point, the most northwesterly point on St. Joseph Island in the St. Mary's River, were believed to have been of this type, as they were lights shown from mast poles. These temporary range lights had been established and maintained by the Lake Carriers' Association. Other early range lights similar to these were also established in the river at Dark Hole, Hay Point, Six-mile Point and Neebish Island. In 1900 the Canadian government assumed their maintenance.

In 1902 the government built permanent lights to replace the temporary pole lights. The front tower was constructed 190 feet (58 m) from the shoreline. It was a square white tapering wooden tower topped with a white square wooden lantern. From its base to the top of its ventilator the tower was 33 feet (10 m) high. Its lantern used a seventh-order dioptric illuminating apparatus to produce a 3-mile (4.8 km) visibility from a 30-foot (9 m) focal plane. The rear light stood 1,447 feet (440 m) southeast of the front one on a hillside, which increased its focal plane to 53 feet (16.2 m). It too was a square white tapering wooden tower but it had a white octagonal wooden lantern. It was 23 feet (7 m) from base to ventilator and used a catoptric illuminating apparatus to produce a 4-mile (6.5 km) visibility. The lights were only visible when in line of range and they were first lit on August 7, 1902. They were built by H.W. Ross of Sault Ste. Marie for $995.

To prevent trees from blocking the visibility of these range lights the government had a 50-foot (15 m) wide strip on each side of the tower alignment cleared of trees up to the top of the hill behind the rear range light. Besides assisting visibility, the cleared patch also provided a distinctive daymark for mariners. Working together, these range lights led mariners through the middle of the

dredged channel of Middle Neebish Channel from its intersection with the alignment of the lower Hay Lake range lights to its intersection with the alignment of the Harwood Point range lights.

In early days these lights were often referred to as "Humes' Light" after their first keeper, David Humes. In 1912 the keeper, James Hicks, earned $360 a year. However, when the lights were electrified using Edison batteries in the early 1940s, the keeper's job became more of a caretaking job, so the salary dropped to $100 per annum. The modern towers are square steel skeletal ones that are automated, need no keeper, display a white daymark with an orange vertical stripe and show fixed white lights.

Known Keepers: David Humes (1900–12), Thomas (James) Hicks (1912–43), William Rousseau (1943–).

78 Sulphur Island Lighthouse

In 1869 a lighthouse was erected on Sulphur Island, Lake Huron, to help mark the North Channel between Georgian Bay and the St. Mary's River. It was a square white tapering wooden tower with a large square gallery and a simple wood railing. Its lantern had a square bottom with an octagonal glass top. Each panel had three rectangular panes of glass set horizontally one above the other. Its dome was a swooping concave one, rather than being arched. It displayed a fixed white light for 12 miles (19.3 km) using four oil lamps and 15-inch (38 cm) reflectors at a 45-foot (13.7 m) focal plane. The station also had a hand-held foghorn.

In 1906 the lighthouse was rebuilt. The new tower was an octagonal white 43-foot (13 m) tapering wooden one with an octagonal cast-iron lantern that used a fifth-order lens to display a fixed white light for 12 miles (19.4 km).

One January two men took refuge at the lighthouse. George Avis, manager of the Island Cedar Company, and his teamster, George Barry, were caught in a sudden snowstorm while crossing the ice between Cockburn Island and Manitoulin Island. Blinded, they lost their way and let the horses take the lead. When the weather cleared, they discovered they were about a mile from the Sulphur Island Lighthouse, and so they sought shelter there. They broke in, found some food, and after much difficulty, lit the lantern to attract a search party. When found, they were so badly frostbitten that neither of them could walk without assistance.

After the light was automated and there was no longer a keeper at the light, vandals wreaked havoc, and at times the light became unlit. Because of this the government demolished the tower in 1968 and erected instead a skeletal tower with a modern beacon.

Known Keepers: William Shepherd (1869–90), Mrs. Shepherd (1890–1902), J. King (1905–06), William Birch (1910–22), Foster Morris (1923–), W. Thompson (1944), F. Valley (1955), C.P. Edwards (?).

Sulphur Island Lighthouse

79 Thessalon Point Lighthouse

When the Department of Marine and Fisheries inquired about purchasing four acres on the Thessalon Point for lighthouse purposes, they were first told that the land, valued three years earlier at 25 cents an acre, would cost $50 per acre and that if they built a road, the road allowance along the east side of the point would be granted free. After a few more exchanges and discussions about the recent high price for land for lighthouse purposes, an agreement was reached. On October 25, 1897, the Department of Marine and Fisheries bought the four acres of land at the extreme south end of Thessalon Point on the west side of the Thessalon River from the Department of Indian Affairs for $50 total. Also a road right of way was set aside on the east side of the peninsula.

The first light established at Thessalon had not been a government light but a private one built by the Dyment Lumber Company. In 1895 the company had a pier constructed at the mouth of the Thessalon River and upon its completion established a light on the east side of the rivermouth to guide vessels into the harbor. It used oil lamps and reflectors to display a fixed white light for 7 miles (11.3 km). The government lighthouse on the point was a welcome addition to the small harbor light.

The government light on Thessalon Point was supervised by J.M. McGee of Ottawa and built in 1898 for $1,219 to assist navigation through the North Channel of Lake Huron and to mark the harbor at Thessalon. It was located 60 feet (18.3 m) from the point's extremity. The lighthouse was a large square wooden house covered in cedar shingles and painted white. Its brick chimney extended well above the lantern roof in order to carry smoke and sparks safely away from the lantern's wooden dome. The gallery and lantern were centered on the hipped roof of the house. A simple pipe iron railing surrounded the gallery.

The square wooden lantern had a large rectangular pane set horizontally facing south. The east and west sides only had glass in the front half, making the light visible only for an arc of 180 degrees. The lantern dome had a wooden shingled hipped roof with a ventilator stack rising from its centre. From a height of 30 feet (9.1) the lantern used oil lamps and a seventh-order lens to be visible as far as 10 miles (16.2 km). The station was also supplied with a hand-operated foghorn to answer ships' signals. In 1909 an oil storage shed was added at a cost of $212.

By January 1904 the rest of the point, including the road allowance, had been sold for $4 per acre. In 1915 the keeper complained that the private owner was fencing his property's southern boundary across the point and cutting off the roadway to the lighthouse. The government responded quickly and stopped this action.

When the light's first keeper, James Harvey, died his wife, Esther, took his place and kept the light faithfully for 25 years. During her tenure, mariners came to know her as "the brave little lady of the light." Her most notable feat was to save one of two occupants of a gas-powered boat that crashed on nearby rocks by throwing him a clothesline.

Inspection reports showed the lighthouse declining. The 1939 report mentioned a cracked kitchen foundation, a twisted boat-

Thornbury Front Range Light, circa 1910

house and rotting window sills, door frames and wooden floors but nothing was done to correct these problems. By 1950 the report also included a leaky lantern but again no repairs were made.

In 1952 the light became a white flashing light and, as boat traffic decreased and navigational aids became available, the hand foghorn was discontinued. The light was electrified using jar batteries and a caretaker was hired instead of a full-time keeper. In 1960 mariners were notified that the light was temporarily discontinued and then on September 28, 1961, that it was permanently discontinued.

With no one living at the lighthouse vandals destroyed the building. Windows and battery jars were smashed, locks and doors were broken, and by 1969 most moveable parts, including doors, windows and stairs, had been stolen and boards had been ripped from the structure for campfires. Being left no choice, the government razed the structure and in 1970 established a modern beacon on a 29.5-foot (9 m) circular mast. From its 38.5-foot (11.7 m) focal plane its electric white flashing light (flash 0.5 s; eclipse 3.5 s) was visible for 5 miles (8 m). This completely automated the light and made a caretaker no longer necessary. It also ended a small chapter of Canada's marine history.

Known Keepers: James Harvey (1897–1915), Esther Harvey (1915–39), James Harvey Jr. (1940–50), Clyde Lewis (1951–52), William Thompson (1952–55).

80 Thornbury Pierhead Light

Thornbury is located along the south shore of Georgian Bay between Owen Sound and Collingwood. In 1887 its harbor was first marked with a light placed at the end of its west breakwater pier. The lantern was hung from a mast that rose from the roof of a small shed anchored to the pier. It displayed a fixed white light from a 32-foot (9.8 m) focal plane to produce a 7-mile (11.3 km) visibility. Range lights replaced it in 1901.

Known Keepers: Robert Lowe (1887–1925), G.W. Ball (1925–), Harry Pether (1939–).

81 Thornbury Range Lights

In 1901 range lights were built at Thornbury on the south side of Georgian Bay to better mark its harbor entry by guiding vessels through the center of the dredged channel. The front range light was a short white wooden pyramidal tower with a square gallery and lantern. It was placed in the same location at the end of the west breakwater pier where the old pierhead light had sat and displayed a fixed white dioptric light with a 10-mile (16 km) visibility. The back range light was the old pierhead light (both mast and shed), which was moved to an onshore location on the west side of the Beaver River behind the front range light. It too displayed a fixed white dioptric light.

It was possibly at this time that the station received a hand foghorn to answer ships' signals. In 1903 the rear range light was changed from white to red so that vessels could distinguish it from other lights in town.

Tobermory Lighthouse Point Lighthouse

82 Tobermory Lighthouse Point

Tobermory is at the northern tip of the Bruce Peninsula, which divides Lake Huron and Georgian Bay. As trade boomed during the late 1800s, Tobermory's harbor became a busy commercial port for shipping timber, fish and farm produce. The harbor was first lit in 1881 by Charles Earle. The Department of Marine and Fisheries paid him $100 a year as a temporary keeper to keep a temporary light on the west side of the peninsula into Big Tub Harbour to mark the harbor entrance. This light, a makeshift beacon, was likely a lantern hung from a tree or a pole.

In 1885 a permanent lighthouse was built on the same spot to continue marking the harbor entrance. The peninsula it stood on became known as Lighthouse Point and the lighthouse as Lighthouse Point Lighthouse, although most locals refer to it as the "Big Tub" Lighthouse and tourists call it the Tobermory Lighthouse. The light was built by John George and David Currie of Port Elgin for $675. It was a 40.6-foot (12.4 m) white hexagonal wooden tapering tower covered in wooden shingles. A pedimented door provided lower entry into the tower, and rectangular pedimented windows ascending the tower gave interior light. A wooden hexagonal gallery supported by six wooden corbels

Tobermory Lighthouse Point Lighthouse, circa 1910   NAC PA172518

encircled the top of the tower about 3 feet (0.9 m) down from its top edge, making the top of the tower the base of the lantern. There is some discrepancy as to whether its original lantern was wooden or iron, but today it is a hexagonal iron one. Its lantern was outfitted with a seventh-order lens and a duplex-burner lamp that displayed a fixed red light in a 240-degree arc of illumination from a 43-foot (13 m) focal plane for 8 miles (13 km). This station had a storm signal tower to warn mariners of weather conditions.

It is interesting that the lighthouse was built on the peninsula by the Department of Marine and Fisheries while the land was still owned by the Department of Indian Affairs. This did not come to light until keeper Abraham Davis complained to the Deputy Minister of Marine that Charles Earle was putting up a fence across the point on which the lighthouse stood, intending to close the only road by which the lighthouse keeper could reach the light with a team. Earle had been temporary keeper from 1881–85 but was not appointed as the first permanent keeper. His actions suggested jealousy toward the lighthouse keeper. Inquiries resulted in the Department of Marine and Fisheries purchasing lots 40, 41 and 42 for a total of $18 from the Department of

Indian Affairs in 1886, so as to have the land ownership with the correct department and to prevent the closing of the track to the lighthouse. In 1904 a wooden keeper's house was built a little further along from the lighthouse on the inside shoreline.

The first keeper earned $100 a year, the same amount allotted for keeping the temporary light. Perhaps this low salary accounts for the first keepers taking the job and then subcontracting it while they fished or farmed to make a living. To discourage this practice, the government raised the annual wages to $130 in 1898, to $250 in 1903, and to $260 in 1912. By 1925 the salary had increased to $420 (maximum), plus another $36 to operate the hand foghorn. Also that year the Superintendent of Lights, J.N. Arthurs, recommended that much of this money could be saved by converting the lighthouse to an unwatched light when the 81-year-old keeper, J. Smith, retired. He

Tobermory Lighthouse Keeper's House

foresaw the cost of maintaining an unwatched light to be "very small" and advised not worrying about the operation of the hand foghorn as records on file showed that it was never "operated more than four hours in any one year" and that it could be "discontinued without much complaint from Mariners." Smith retired in 1926, but public outcry kept this light from being automated until 1952.

The first permanent keeper, Abraham Davis was appointed on September 25, 1885. According to the *Kingston Daily News* (November 9, 1895) he disappeared on November 6, 1895. At about 10 p.m. he left the lighthouse in a small skiff to look for survivors of two wrecked vessels, the *Owen Sound* and the *Worts,* and did not return. Search parties feared that the prevailing east winds had carried him out into the lake and he had drowned.

During Archibald Currie's tenure as keeper the hand foghorn was established at the station. His extra work to operate it was minimal as he only used it in response to a ship's signal. During the Great Storm of 1913 over half of the shingles were blown off the lighthouse but it remained sound. The light continued to shine and its missing shingles were replaced and painted white, once more presenting an unscathed image. In 1952 the lighthouse was automated through the use of electricity.

In 1985 Friends of Fathom Five and the Township of St. Edmunds started working together to improve and protect the historical lighthouse. They have made the lighthouse accessible by clearing a path, offered to help Transport Canada maintain the lighthouse, and placed a plaque at the lighthouse to tell its history. These groups both wish to attract tourists and scuba divers to the area to see the lighthouse and the many shipwrecks in the underwater Fathom Five National Park. Two of these wrecks are right at the inner tip of Big Tub Harbour. The schooner *Sweepstakes* sank in 1896 and the steamer *City of Grand Rapids* burned and sank in 1907. While the harbor is no longer important for exporting local products, it is very important for pleasure craft. The lighthouse continues to mark the harbor with its fixed red light and its visibility has increased to 12 miles (19.5 km).

Known Keepers: Charles Earl (1881–85), Abraham Davis (1885–95), Henry B. Davis (1895–1901), Daniel Butchart (1901–03), Archibald Currie (1903–12), John Henry Smith (1912–26), T.A. Hopkins (1926–52).

83 Turning Rock (Honey Harbour)

In 1914 a lighthouse was built on the shoal southeast of Robert Island in Severn Sound of Georgian Bay, Lake Huron. As well as assisting increased marine traffic in the area, its flashing white light marked the entrance to Honey Harbour. Little is known of the first tower built here, but today its light shines from a 9.7-foot (3 m) square white skeletal steel tower with a 19-foot (5.8 m) focal plane.

84 Turning Rock (Waubaushene)

A lighthouse was established on Turning Rock to the southeast of Canary Island in Georgian Bay, Lake Huron, to assist lake traffic making the turn into Waubaushene Harbour and the Trent Severn Waterway. In 1914 the Department of Marine and Fisheries purchased the .09 acre (0.02 hectare) rock island for lighthouse purposes from the Department of Indian Affairs for $100. Then in 1915, instead of building a new lighthouse, the government moved the Midland Point front range light to this new location and placed it on a new foundation. It was a square white wooden tower with sloping sides, a square gallery partway down from its top, a square red lantern, and a pedimented entry door and tower windows. The tower was 33 feet (10 m) from base to ventilator and covered with cedar shake siding. Its lantern displayed a flashing white light for a 7-mile (11.3 km) visibility.

In 1992 it displayed a white light flashing (flash 0.5 s; eclipse 3.5 s) at a 33.8-foot (10.4 m) focal plane from a square 30.2-foot (9.3 m) skeletal tower.

Known Keepers: no keepers, as the light was unwatched.

85 Victoria Harbour Range Lights

Lake traffic into Severn Sound of Georgian Bay, Lake Huron, increased greatly during the early 1900s. In 1908, with the opening of the Canadian Pacific Railroad's grain terminal at Port McNicoll, grain shipping in the area increased, as well as lumber export and cruise ship tourism. To facilitate the increased marine traffic, range lights were established at Victoria Harbour in 1910 by the Department of Public Works, with G. Dobson of Victoria Harbour as project foreman. The two lighthouses took about six months to construct and cost $1,767.

Victoria Harbour Rear Range Light

The front range light was built on the shoreline at Bergie's Point. It was a square white wooden tower with sloping sides, cedar shake shingles and pedimented windows and entry door. Its lantern displayed a fixed red light that was visible for 7 miles (11.3 km). In 1960 this lighthouse was torn down and replaced with a 25-foot (7.6 m) steel skeletal tower that continued to display a fixed red light from its 37-foot (11.3 m) focal plane. The rear range light was 31.8 feet (9.7 m) high and similarly constructed, but was located on the hill behind the village. From its 105-foot (32 m) focal plane it also displayed a fixed red light. In 1985 renovations, its entire structure was strengthened and it was covered with low-maintenance aluminum siding.

These lights used different illuminants over the years. Whale oil and seal oil gave way to kerosene. The fuel was supplied once a month by a Dominion steamer to the Georgian Bay lighthouses. For the Victoria Harbour Range Lights all the supplies were delivered to the front light. In 1951 the illuminant became electricity. The lights have undergone continuous service, but in 1968 the last keeper was removed and the Canadian Coast Guard Base out of Parry Sound took over their maintenance.

Known Keepers: Charles Burzie (1910–12), Robert Belcher (1912), Ray Belcher (1912–start of WW I), Clarence Sykes (≠1918), Ray Belcher (1918–51), W.B. Cooke (Caretaker 1951–68).

West Sister Rock Lighthouse on the North Channel, circa 1905

86 Waubaushene Range Lights

During the early 1900s, transportation of lumber and people increased on the Severn Sound of Georgian Bay, Lake Huron. Range lights were established at Waubaushene Harbour in 1910 to facilitate increasing marine traffic, but little else is known about the early lights. Today, fixed red lights are shown from white circular mast towers.

87 West Sister Rock Lighthouse

The Sister Rocks consisted of four small bare rocks lying between the eastern extremity of Campement d'Ours and Portlock Island in the North Channel of Lake Huron. In 1885 the government erected a lighthouse on North Sister Rock to mark the Canadian entrance, a narrow channel along the north side of St. Joseph Island, into the St. Mary's River. It was a white wooden hexagonal 30-foot (9 m) tower that displayed a fixed white light for 11 miles (17.7 km) and had been built on a square crib pier 7 feet (2.1 m) high. The keeper's dwelling was a conspicuous white wooden structure built on nearby Portlock Island, northwest of the tower. Most vessels passed between the lighthouse and West

Sister Rock, but the best water was between West Sister Rock and South Sister Rock, which lay to the southwest.

To mark the preferred route, the government moved the tower to West Sister Rock in 1905. Again, it was placed on a wooden pier. The station also had a hand-operated foghorn.

During the 1885 Northwest Rebellion, mail carriers on their way out west with mail were way-laid, and their mailbags and money were stolen. In 1900 Baptiste Thibault, waiting out a storm on an island near Picture Rock, discovered bags of mail in the sand and gravel of the island. He reported his find to the authorities, and the government, in gratitude for his honesty, prom-ised him and his family employ-ment for the rest of his life. He was appointed keeper at the Sister Rock Lighthouse and his daugh-ter succeeded him.

In 1971 the Sister Rocks almost lost their beloved light.

West Sister Rock Lighthouse

Apparently the tender of the area lights wrote to a friend in the Department of Transport in Southern Ontario that the area lights were in a "terrible state of disrepair." His friend very kindly agreed to have the department remove the lights and replace them with low-maintenance galvanized steel towers like those that had been put up at Sulphur Island. The West Sister Lighthouse was slated for transport to Sault Ste. Marie and a foundation had even been prepared to set it on. When local residents discovered this, the St. Joseph Island Chamber of Commerce immediately complained to the local Member of Parliament, Maurice Foster, who took up the cause. American summer residents also lent their support. This public objection saved the area lights. For a time the West Sister Lighthouse sported a sign that read, "This light was preserved through the efforts of Dr. Maurice Foster and the Courtney Family."

Thus saved, the original tower continues flashing (flash 0.5 s, eclipse 3.5 s) from its 38-foot (11.6 m) focal plane, but it is elec-trically powered now and sits on a concrete base.

Known Keepers: William Weightman (1885–1902), Baptiste Thibault (1905–), Baptise Thibault daughter (?), Thomas Jondreau (1919–51).

88 Western Islands Lighthouse

The Western Islands are located about 20 miles (32 km) north-west of Midland and 27 miles (44 km) southwest of Parry Sound in Georgian Bay, Lake Huron. After three major marine dis-asters on Georgian Bay (S.S. *Waubuno*, 1879; S.S. *Manitoulin*, 1881; S.S. *Asia*, 1882), the Canadian government resurveyed the bay, constructed navigation aids to assist marine traffic, and in 1891 published the *Georgian Bay Pilot*. As part of this development a lighthouse was built on one of the Western Islands to mark the northern approach to Severn Sound, where the communities of Midland, Penetanguishene, Port McNicoll, Victoria Harbour and Waubaushene were situated.

Western Islands Lighthouse, circa 1945 — *Star Weekly* / Huronia Museum

Western Islands Lighthouse

The lighthouse was built on a small 1¹/₂-acre (0.6 hectare) bare granite rock island called Double Top Island, the most southwestern of the Western Islands, a group of outer islands marking the mouth of the Severn Sound. It was built on a solid stone foundation and had an octagonal white tapering wooden tower with pedimented windows and entry door. Topped with a red iron octagonal gallery and decagonal lantern, the tower had an overall height of 60 feet (18.2 m) and wooden interior stairs to reach the lantern.

The illuminating apparatus was furnished by W.H. Noble, the foreman of Public Works for the Department of Marine and Fisheries. He originally supplied the light with a dioptric of the seventh code, which displayed a fixed light from a focal plane of 73.5 feet (22.4 m) to produce a 14-mile (22.5 km) visibility in all directions. The light was first lit on October 24, 1895. Then in 1896 Noble had a more powerful fourth-order drum and lens optic installed on October 12 at a cost of $1,399.

As well as the light, a fog signal building and a two-story keeper's house with a hipped-roof and a central chimney were also built in 1895. In 1896 Noble further improved the station, adding a boathouse, a derrick for landing supplies, and a platform/walkway extending from the landing to the dwelling, lighthouse, and fog signal building for the keeper's safety in inclement weather. These additions cost $508. In 1914 a cableway was installed along the walkways so that the keepers could hang onto the cable in stormy or icy conditions. As ice would often build up to over a foot thick on the cable, keepers were later provided with cleats to help them keep their footing.

Western Islands Lighthouse, circa 1919

Being so isolated, keepers and their families had to be self-sufficient. Each spring they disembarked from the lighthouse tender with their belongings and large supplies of food. They had 100-pound (45 kg) bags of flour and sugar, a 50-pound (22.5 kg) drum of powdered milk, numerous eggs preserved in salt brine, canned fruits and vegetables, and six or seven sides of cured bacon that they hung in the lighthouse shed. They enriched their diet with fish (mostly whitefish and pickerel) and gull eggs, which they collected to use in baking. They had to make all their food from the staples they had. Local fishermen occasionally stopped by and delivered the keeper's mail, but friends rarely visited. Besides working and fishing, the keepers read a lot. During fly season they stayed inside as much as possible to avoid being bitten, and at all times they had to contend with the ubiquitous spiders.

Around 1943–44 lightning struck the station. While it did not start a fire, it did tear a gouge out of the fog signal building and blow the assistant keeper back into the building from the doorway.

During Harry Couling's tenure as keeper (1959–66), Couling's son developed acute appendicitis, but the weather was too stormy for the small government boat to get him to the mainland. A local pilot agreed to attempt the rescue. He successfully landed his pontoon plane, transferred the boy from the lighthouse boat to the plane, and flew him to Midland, where he was immediately hospitalized and treated.

In 1966 the lighthouse was automated, but keepers continued to serve at this station for a while. Although it is not known exactly when the last keeper was removed, there was no keeper in 1970 when the Western Islands Lighthouse became an experimental lighthouse for a pilot program started by Canada's Department of Transport. They tested powering the lighthouse batteries with a wind-driven generator, keeping a standby diesel engine at the ready. If the experiment was successful they planned to use the technique to automate other lighthouses. No written results of this experiment have been found, but the absence of any wind-powered lighthouses leads one to conclude that the system was too costly, too unreliable, or a failure.

At an unknown date the Canadian Coast Guard out of Parry Sound removed all buildings except the lighthouse tower, to prevent maintenance costs and vandalism. Most structures were torn down by hand, but the coastguardsmen could barely dent the house. It took a whole case of dynamite to blow it up, and after the explosion they still had to remove the brick chimney as it had survived the blast. The house had been built to last.

In 1993 Environment Canada set up a permanent weather station at the lighthouse. They installed the needed electrically operated equipment on top of the tower to monitor weather conditions between Wiarton and Parry Sound.

Since the lighthouse is so far out in Georgian Bay and not open to the public, in order to celebrate its 100th birthday, the Huronia Museum of Midland organized a lighthouse tour in conjunction with the Canadian Coast Guard. In preparation, the Coast Guard spruced up the lighthouse with a fresh coat of paint. The 300 or so visitors who came on July 31, 1995, had to supply their own transportation but they could then climb to the top of the tower for a captivating view of the bay. Today the light still shines, but boaters who brave the elements to visit the light can only see it from the outside.

Known Keepers: Richard Smith (1895–1900), Thomas Richardson (1901–06), H. Hewitt (1912–13), E. Smith (1913–18), Joseph Dixon (1919–25), Charles Vassair (1925–31), Lawrence Tyler (1931–38), Arnold Wing (1938–46), P.A. Campbell (1947–50), James Keith (1950–52), Lloyd McAuliffe (1953–55), Frank Rourke (1955–58), Harry Couling (1959–66), Gordon Champion (1965–66), Vladimir Kruglov (1966), George Bishton (1966–67), William Maguire (1967).

89 Whiskey Island Lighthouse

In 1892 a lighthouse was erected on Whiskey Island at the entrance to Penetanguishene Harbour, Georgian Bay, to mark the low 2-acre (0.8 hectare) island and its adjacent shoals. It was a simple but large square white 36-foot (11 m) tapering tower built on a small timber crib. Its fixed white light was displayed using a sixth-order dioptric for an 11-mile (18 km) visibility. The Department of Marine and Fisheries purchased this island, along with Gin Island, from the Department of Indian Affairs in 1897 for $40. The light became unwatched as of the opening of navigation in 1946. At an unknown date it was replaced with an iron pole that had a flashing white light to guide mariners into the harbor.

Known Keepers: Joseph Dions (1882), W.A. Thompson (1882–86), Christopher Columbus (1893–1916). Andrew Bald (1924–46).

90 Wiarton Pierhead Light

The village of Wiarton is located at the west end of Colpoy's Bay along the east shore of the Bruce Peninsula, which divides the main body of Lake Huron from Georgian Bay. The community, known for its lumbering and fishing exports, was a thriving center in the late 1800s. The entrance to the bay was protected by three islands (Hay, White Cloud and Griffith). Griffith Island, lit by an "imperial tower" lighthouse, marked the entrance into Colpoy's Bay. After a vessel had cleared the islands, it had protected sailing all the way to Wiarton. Over time, different lights shone from the outer end of the breakwater at Wiarton, but they were mostly anchor-lens lanterns showing a fixed red seventh-order dioptric light from a focal plane of 19 feet (5.8 m) with a visibility of 6 miles (9.6 km).

The events surrounding the death of keeper Philip Gilbert are noteworthy. In the summer of 1907, Aggie Thomas, a lady of the night from London, Ontario, set up her tent in the park by the water and plied her trade for lumbermen and sailors. As the summer went on, some of her clients developed diseases of a social nature. One warm August evening vigilantes came to the park to confront her and send her packing. The group became aggressive, and Ms. Thomas, fearing for her life as her tent was being raided, reached for her pistol and fired three shots. One bullet struck and killed the unfortunate Gilbert. Thomas was arrested and tried, but was found not guilty because her life had been in jeopardy. After the trial, she returned to London.

Known Keepers: Henry R. Ely (1891–99), Phillip Gilbert (1899–1907), W. Gilbert (1907–13), E. Shackleton (1913–25), Thomas Dargavel (1925–30), Dougal Dargavel (1930–46), John Edward Bennett (1946).

91 Wilson Channel Range Lights

As more lights were placed to mark the northern route from Lake Huron into the St. Mary's River, range lights were established in 1905 on the west side of Wilson Channel (also known as Devil's Gap) to help mariners navigate into the channel from a western approach. This channel had first been staked out and sounded by John Richards in 1876, but was first traveled by Captain Wilson, after whom it is named.

Both lights were placed on the tree-cleared cliffy mainland shore on the north side of the channel, with the rear light to the north and east of the front light. The rear tower was originally of white open slatwork, and the front one was a white cage beacon built on the high ledge at the water's edge. These range lights were later rebuilt as white wooden pyramidal towers with a vertical red

Whiskey Island Lighthouse, circa 1898

Wilson Channel Range Lights

stripe. They displayed fixed red lights, first using oil lamps, then battery-operated lights and finally, in the 1950s, hydro, which had been laid to the lights. The front range light had a white lantern with a red dome and the rear lantern had red from halfway up. The front range light was 27 feet (8.2 m) tall and displayed its light from a 68-foot (20.9 m) elevation, while the 28.6-foot (8.7 m) rear range light had a 116-foot (35.4 m) focal plane. These range lights still operate today.

Known Keepers: Robert Bamford (?), Alfred Clark (1914–22), Archie McIntyre (1922), William Birch (1923–39), James Birch (1940), Daniel McPhail (1941–46), Gordon R. MacDonald (1946–), Fred Rogers (?).

92 Wreck of the Joliet

After the schooner *Kewaunee* was removed from Southeast Shoal in 1910 by the Lake Carriers' Association, it was placed as a lightship to mark the wreck of the freighter *Joliet* in the St. Clair River opposite Sarnia in the early part of the 1912 navigation season. Later that same year it was placed at Vidal Shoals in the St. Mary's River.

LAKE MICHIGAN
USA
LIGHTHOUSES

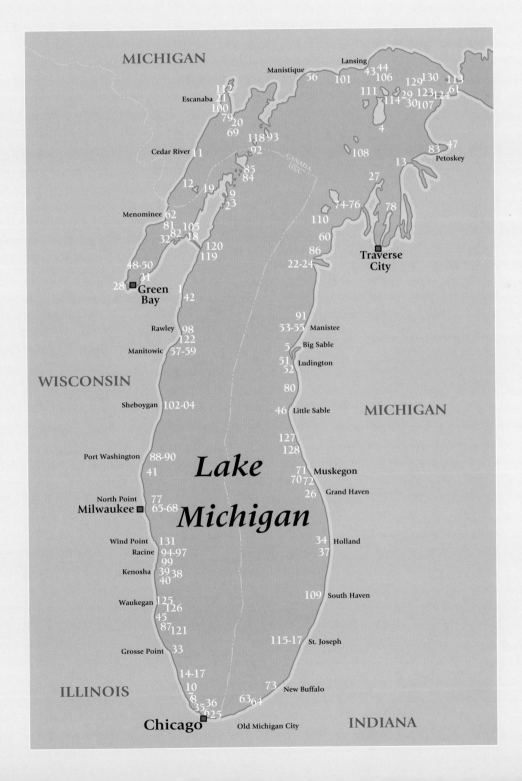

MICHIGAN

Lansing

Manistique
56   101   43 44
106
129 130   113
111   29 123 61
112   114 30 107 124
21   4
Escanaba
100
79 20
69   118 93
92   108   83 47
Cedar River 11   85   13   Petoskey
84
27
12 19   9   74-76   78
23   110
Menominee 62   60
81 105   86
32 82 18   22-24   Traverse
120   City
119
48-50
31   91   Manistee
28 Green   53-55
Bay   1
42   5   Big Sable
51   Ludington
Rawley 98   52
122   80
Manitowic 57-59
46   Little Sable   MICHIGAN
WISCONSIN
Sheboygan 102-04   127
128
Port Washington 88-90   71   Muskegon
41   70 72
26   Grand Haven
North Point 77
Milwaukee 65-68   *Lake Michigan*
Wind Point 131   34   Holland
Racine 94-97   37
99
Kenosha 39 38
40   109   South Haven
Waukegan 125
126
45   115-17   St. Joseph
87 121
Grosse Point 33
14-17
10   73   New Buffalo
8   63 64
ILLINOIS   35-36
6 25
Chicago   Old Michigan City   INDIANA

Algoma Pierhead Light

1 Algoma Pierhead Lights

The Algoma Pierhead light stands at the mouth of the Ahnapee River in Wisconsin, where the town of Ahnapee developed as a fishing community. In 1871 the government began developing the town harbor by building protective piers and dredging the river mouth. These improvements encouraged the growth of the town's commercial fishing fleet so much that by 1879 it had become the largest on Lake Michigan. Also at this time, the town of Ahnapee was formally renamed Algoma.

While locals realized the need to light the harbor entrance, the government did not, so the locals established the first pier lights by placing post lights at the outer ends of the two piers. Finally, in 1891, Congress appropriated $2,500 for range lights on the north pier, and they were built when new piers were completed in 1892. The new north pier had a unique design, as it was split and offset at its midpoint, and a bridge spanned the gap in the pier.

The range lights were basic. The front light, at the end of the north pier, consisted of a single post light. With the lens lantern on top of the 18-foot (5.5 m) pole, it had a 22-foot (6.8 m) focal plane. The rear range light stood 99 feet (30.2 m) behind it. It was a wooden skeletal framework with an open bottom and an enclosed upper service room. It was capped with a square gallery and a decagonal lantern that housed a lens lantern similar to the one on the post. Its 80 candlepower light was visible for 9 miles (14.6 km) from a 34-foot (10.4 m) focal plane. They were first lit at the start of the 1893 navigation season.

Algoma Pierhead Light

Changes gradually occurred at the light. In 1895 the rear range light lens was upgraded to a fifth-order Fresnel lens, increasing its visibility to 11 miles (17.8 km). In 1897 a catwalk 400 feet (122 m) long was placed on the pier so that the keeper could reach it more safely. In 1900 another 338 feet (104 m) were added, to extend from the lighthouse to the shore. In 1908, as the old wooden rear light had deteriorated, it was replaced by a cast-iron tower. The iron bands were riveted together and each band was slightly smaller, so as to sit inside the one below it. The tower's base diameter was 8 feet (2.4 m) and its top diameter 7 feet (2.1 m). A circular gallery surrounded its decagonal cast-iron lantern, which housed the Fresnel lens from the old tower. The new tower stood 26 feet (8 m) to the top of its ventilator ball. This pier light replaced the range lights.

In the early days, keepers had to find and rent their own accommodations. By 1902 the Lighthouse Board started to ask for appropriations to build a keeper's house. When the appropriation was finally made in 1908, a small hip-roofed house was built on the north side of the river overlooking the harbor. In 1910 a compressed-air–powered fog signal was added to the station.

Of the few keepers who tended the light, Gustavus Umberham served the longest. In 1913 Umberham and three others went to Kewaunee with William Anderson on his boat *Reliance*. On their way back in the early evening, the weather had deteriorated quickly, and ice on the windows made it difficult to see. When a large wave struck, the boat rocked and threw Gus against the pilothouse door. The door flew open and Gus was pitched overboard. Algoma residents all grieved for their lost lighthouse keeper.

In 1932, during harbor improvements, the piers were recapped with concrete, a remote-controlled electrically powered diaphone fog signal was installed on the pier, and the lighthouse was raised to increase its visibility. To do this, a cylindrical steel base 12 feet (3.7 m) high was brought from Muskegon, the 1908 tower was lifted, and the base was placed under it. The light's new focal plane was 42 feet (12.9 m). A second gallery was added around the top of the new base.

The light was automated in 1973. Today it still uses its fifth-order Fresnel lens and contains an automatic four-bulb changer. The whole lens is enclosed in an octagonal housing made of ruby-colored glass that creates its red light characteristic. Not only is the light red, the tower, galleries, lantern, dome and ventilator ball are also painted red to form its daymark signature.

Known Keepers: Ole Hansen (1893–95), Charles Young (1895–99), Nelson Knudsen (1899–1901), Gustavus Umberham (1901–13), Eugene Kimball (1913–23), Carl Graan (1930–40).

2 Bailey's Harbor Old Lighthouse

Bailey's Harbor was discovered in 1848 when Captain Justice Bailey sought refuge from a threatening Lake Michigan storm along the west coast of the lake. Shortly thereafter his shipping master, Alison Sweet, brought lumber crews to the area, a town developed, and the busy little harbor became known as Bailey's Harbor. The harbor also became known as the only natural harbor of refuge north of Milwaukee. Thus when Congress was petitioned for money to build a lighthouse, they responded favorably.

The contract was awarded to Sweet, who had helped settle the area. He selected a small island on the northeast side of the bay and built the lighthouse in 1852. The tower was a 52-foot (16 m) conical rubble-stone one with a birdcage-style lantern that housed a fixed white sixth-order Fresnel lens. There was no gallery around the lantern, and a small stone house was built for the keeper. Since the light was found to be too dim, the lens was upgraded to a fifth-order Fresnel lens in 1858.

In 1886, after the light had greatly deteriorated, the Lighthouse Board recommended that it be rebuilt, and Congress appropriated $15,000. However, due to further complaints about the light's dimness and poor location, range lights were built on the west side of the bay and a light on Cana Island was established as a coastal light. With these changes decided, the fate of the Bailey's Harbor light was sealed. On December 1, 1869 the light was exhibited for the last time at the end of the shipping season.

The light was later sold, and it remains privately owned today.

Although much of its original lantern is gone, it retains much of the framework, some of its metal astragals, and its copper dome. This birdcage lantern is one of few still remaining on the Great Lakes, as most were replaced by a polygonal cast-iron lantern to better house a Fresnel lens and not impede its concentrated beam.

Known Keepers; David Ward (1853–54), Albert Barry (1854), David Ward (1854), Michael Green (1854–55), Newton Bacon (1855–62), William Mitchell (1862–63), William Darling (1863–69).

3 Bailey's Harbor Range Lights

In 1868 Congress appropriated $6,000 to build these range lights to help boats maneuver a safe entry into Bailey's Harbor on Lake Michigan. The lights were lit at the start of the 1870 navigation season. Sailors would align the white rear range light with the red front range light and then follow straight through on this course until safely into the harbor. This way they avoided running aground on the hidden reefs near the harbor entrance, which was busy in the early logging days before Bailey's Harbor got road access in 1870.

The lanterns were originally fueled by lard or whale oil, then by kerosene and, in 1923 by acetylene gas. Both range lights were converted to electricity and automatic controls in the early 1930s. These lights were deactivated in 1969 when the single range light across the road was put into service. Fishermen reported that the old lights were much brighter and easier to see than the new one. The lights were unlit from 1969 until they were relit on July 21, 1995 at the dedication of the new boardwalk.

The lower range light sat close to the road and shore. It was a white board building trimmed with dark green. The first level was about 8 feet (2.4 m) square, but became octagonal on the second story. Arched windows lit the first level. A dark green dome, ventilator ball and lightning rod capped the building to make an overall height of 21 feet (6.5 m). A fixed red light from a steamer lantern shone through a window on the south side. The keeper could monitor the light from his house through a small rectangular window opposite this one and facing north. The light's focal plane was 23 feet (7 m).

The rear light, in a white 1½-story house, was 950 feet (290 m) behind the front light. The rectangular tower rose up one level from the roof at the front of the red-roofed seven-room house. A large arched window in its south side displayed a fixed white light from its fifth-order Fresnel lens at a 39-foot (12 m) focal plane. The lighthouse's white color, style and solitary location give it the appearance of a small country church. In fact, it was used as a Lutheran parsonage for 25 years (1930–55), but is now a private residence.

Bailey's Harbor Old Lighthouse

Bailey's Harbor Front Range Light

Bailey's Harbor Rear Range Light

The long boardwalk that now approaches the keeper's house is lined on both sides with a wide border of wild grasses and flowers watched over by an evergreen forest. This tunnel-like entry arouses a feeling of awe in the visitor walking up the natural and man-made aisle.

The first lightkeeper, Fabien Trudell, started on December 1, 1869, although the lights were not lit until 1870. Joseph Harris Jr., son of the editor of the *Door County Advocate*, was the keeper at the range lights from 1875 to 1881. He was there for the occurrence of the great "Alpena Blow" on October 15, 1880, when northwest winds switched suddenly to the south, catching schooners unsuspectingly. The *Lettie May*, loaded with sundries, was washed up onshore near the range lights. Nine schooners were damaged in Bailey's Harbor on that one day.

Henry Gattie started as keeper in 1896 and stayed for 27 years. The year after he began, the front range light's original equipment was replaced with a fifth-order locomotive headlight and a parabolic reflector to provide a stronger light. When the lights were converted to a demanned, acetylene gas system, Gattie was transferred elsewhere and the Cana Island keeper periodically checked the demanned range lights.

In 1934 the Bureau of Lighthouses deeded the land and buildings to the Door County Parks Commission. Their plans to make a trailer park were immediately thwarted by outraged citizens. In 1937 the newly formed Ridge Sanctuary secured leases on the land from the county. Their primary function was to protect the plant and animal wildlife in the area. Their first project was the run-down boardwalk, and in 1939 they hired six men at 35 to 40 cents an hour to do that work. Controversy arose over the wages, as unskilled laborers were usually paid only 25 to 30 cents an hour. The Door County Parks Commission agreed to pay the price for repairs, but the boardwalk was not rebuilt.

Roy Luces was the lighthouse "keeper" from 1964–72. He was the manager and chief naturalist for the Ridge Wildlife Sanctuary from 1964 until he retired in 1990, but he preferred to be called the lightkeeper. He remembers the day in 1969 when the Fresnel lens mysteriously disappeared. On returning home after a brief absence, he smelled smoke. Since he was a non-smoker, he went up to check the light and lens, only to discover that they were gone. He assumed that the U.S. Coast Guard had come and removed them, but to this day they have not been found.

In 1981 the Door County Historical Society took an interest in the range lights' preservation, and they are now listed on the *National Register of Historic Places*. The Society's endeavors have included raising about $75,000, all from private donations, for restoration of the lights and enough funds to build the new boardwalk between the two range lights. On September 1, 1998 ownership of the range lights was formally transferred to the Door County Parks Commission, but the Ridge Sanctuary continues to lease the range lights and some acreage around the lights.

Since the lights are now part of the Ridge Sanctuary, recognized Historic Places, and under the protection of the Door County Historical Society, their future seems secure.

Known Keepers: Fabian Trudell (1869–72), Marcus Shaler (1872–75), Joseph Harris Jr. (1875–81), Hans L. Hanson (1881–82), Burr Caswell (1882), George Larson (1882–88), John Millidge (1888–96), Henry Gattie (1896–1923).

4 Beaver Island Lighthouse

Beaver Island, once known to the French as "Isle du Castor," is the largest island in Lake Michigan and boasts seven lakes of its own. As lake traffic from Chicago to the Straits of Mackinac steadily increased from the early to the mid-1800s, the need to mark treacherous areas of Lake Michigan also increased. In response, President Fillmore in November 1850 designated 158.2 acres (64 hectares) of Cheyenne Point to build a light at the head of Beaver Island.

This light became guardian of the passage between Beaver Island and North Fox Island. It also marked an archipelago of islands off the mainland. It was common practice for northbound vessels to go up the east side of Beaver Island and southbound vessels to come down on the west side. This helped diffuse the congestion caused by the narrow straits at the northeast end of Lake Michigan. The Beaver Island light also offered a beacon of refuge by guiding vessels to safety behind the island, where they could anchor in Sandy Bay.

Along the island's south shore is Iron Ore Bay, so named after an iron-ore-laden ship which sank and lost its cargo there. The lighthouse was intended for Cheyenne Point, and land to the west of this bay was purchased for it. However, the placement of the light was left to the Collector of the District of Michilimackinac, Charles E. Avery, and the building contractor was John McReynolds of Detroit. The lighthouse was built on time, but it was built high on a bluff to the east of Iron Bay instead of on Cheyenne Point. No one knows whether it was the collector's or the contractor's fault. Since the government also owned the new location (Lot 3), it would not have been considered a problem. However, a witness to the building contract, James T. Birchard, seemed to be the first to notice the faux pas, and he thought of making a fast dollar.

Beaver Island land records show that Lorenzo Birchard (a relative of James) sold Lot 3 to James Birchard in 1851, one month after the lighthouse was completed. However, there was no indication of how Lorenzo acquired ownership in the first place. The next year James sold the land back to Lorenzo. In the fall of 1852, Lorenzo told the authorities on Mackinac Island that the lighthouse had been built on his property. He would agree, he said, to release 10 acres (4 hectares) of Lot 3 for $150 to the government

Beaver Island Lighthouse

Beaver Island Lighthouse

Island Lighthouse School, which uses an alternative system for guiding students back to mainstream education. The old fog station has been converted to a laboratory and photography darkroom. Nature trails have been added. Classes focus on conservation, forestry, water quality, geology, astronomy, biology and wilderness survival.

The lighthouse is open to the public from spring until fall. Visitors can even climb the tower, although its Fresnel lens is no longer there. There is a lens on display in the keeper's house, but it is not the one removed from the tower. The tours offer a wealth of information and stories about the lighthouse's history.

Known Keepers: Dennis Chidester (1855–56), Joseph Lobsdell (1856–59), Patrick Loaney (1859–61), Gilman Appleby (1861–63), Harrison Miller (1863–74), William Duclon (1874–83), George Lasley (1884–96), Andrew Bourisseau (1896–97), Charles Butler (1897–1904), Medad Spencer (1904–09), James Wachter (1909–12), Dominick Gallagher (1912–28), Chester Marshall (1928–36), Carl Olson (1938–39), Alex Durette (1939–40), Owen Gallagher (1940).

for the lighthouse, making himself a tidy profit since the whole of Lot 3 was only worth $73.56. No money was exchanged at this time, however, as the transaction had to first be approved by the Attorney General. For the next four years Lorenzo fought to get his money. Since he had no proof of purchase, he finally bought Lot 3 from Washington in 1856 for $73.56 so that he could get his $150. On the books, the Cheyenne Point location of the lighthouse was not clarified in Washington until 1954, when President Eisenhower rescinded the original 1850 land designation.

The tower, lit in 1851, was one of Michigan's earliest lighthouses. However, it must have been poorly constructed because it soon fell over and a new one was built in 1858. The new 46-foot (14 m) yellow brick conical tower tapered slightly as it rose. It was brick-lined, and supported a decagonal cast-iron lantern. Forty-nine self-cleaning (open grillwork) iron steps formed a circular staircase to the lantern. At the top, a solid iron floor with an iron trap door could be closed to control tower drafts. The lantern had three iron panels and seven glass panels, and it housed a fourth-order Fresnel lens. This light had a focal plane of 103 feet (31.4 m) and a visibility of 18 miles (28.8 km).

In 1866 a two-story, yellow brick keeper's house was built and connected to the tower by a covered passageway. As more help became needed at the light, this house accommodated both the keeper and his assistant, but when a second assistant was assigned, a new two-story white clapboard house was attached to the brick house. In 1915 a red brick fog signal building was added near the water. Its original first-class siren was later replaced with powerful, steam-powered foghorns. During the 1930s the light was electrified and the brick tower and keeper's house were painted white. In 1962 the U.S. Coast Guard replaced the light with an automated radio beacon tower.

The abandoned lighthouse was soon vandalized, and in 1967 it was declared surplus government property. Then in 1975 the federal government deeded the lighthouse, outbuildings and approximately 65 acres (26 hectares) of land to the Charlevoix Public School District, making it the only school district to own a lighthouse. With the assistance of government grants and "at-risk" students, lighthouse restoration began in 1978. The white paint was removed from the yellow brick, the grounds cleaned up, and plumbing and electrical systems repaired. By 1980 the lighthouse had been thoroughly refurbished. The station is now the Beaver

5 Big Sable Lighthouse

The initial $6,000 that Congress had approved to survey and buy land for a lighthouse at Grande Pointe au Sable had to be returned to the government coffers to help fund the Civil War. In 1865, when the war was over, Congress appropriated $35,000 for a lighthouse at this location.

The 100-foot (30 m) conical tower was built of yellow brick on a tightly fitted cut stone block foundation that began 6 feet (1.8 m) below ground level and continued for 3 feet (0.9 m) above. The base walls were 5 feet (1.5 m) thick and tapered to 2 feet (0.6 m) thick at the top just below the gallery. Inside the tower a circular inner wall 8 feet (2.4 m) in diameter supported the cast-iron spiral staircase. Two galleries surrounded the summit, one circling the pedestal room and one circling the lantern. For the keeper's safety when he was cleaning the outside lantern glass, handholds were attached to the astragals. Beneath the gallery was a pedestal/watchroom with windows facing all four directions, for the keeper to monitor water traffic and weather conditions. This room had two trap doors, one in the ceiling and one in the floor. When the light

Big Sable Lighthouse, circa 1950

Big Sable Lighthouse

lake. To prevent further erosion, interlocking sheet-steel pilings were driven into the beach in front of the lighthouse in 1943, and more shore protection was added over the years. The fog signal was discontinued in 1970.

Other changes took place in the new century. In 1910 the station's official name was changed from Grande Pointe au Sable to Big Sable to avoid confusion with another lighthouse on Lake Superior. (The Lake Superior light's name was changed from Big Sable to Au Sable.) In 1933 the Department of Natural Resources (DNR) built a road to the station. This was the last American lighthouse on the Great Lakes to receive the modern amenities of electricity (from the mainland) and indoor plumbing, which arrived at Big Sable in 1953. When the light was automated in 1968 the buildings were boarded up. The light was listed on the *National Register of Historic Places* in 1983.

After heavy vandalism, the DNR returned the lighthouse to the Coast Guard, who removed the damaged third-order Fresnel lens for storage in 1985 and replaced it with a 300 mm plastic lens. The Foundation for Behavioral Research leased the station in 1986 for 25 years to restore and maintain it. In 1987 the Big Sable Point Lighthouse Keepers Association was also formed, and the two organizations worked to raise money for lighthouse maintenance and renovations. By November 1987 the Coast Guard had restored the third-order Fresnel lens and put it on display at the Rose Hawley Museum in Ludington; today it is displayed at the Historic White Pine Village just south of Ludington. In 1988 the station was added to the State of Michigan *Register for Historic Sites*. After this, matched grants were obtained to sandblast, repair and paint the tower and provide additional interlocking sheet-steel pilings to prevent shoreline erosion. During the 1990s, restoration of the station continued in earnest.

A unique idea that the Keepers Association has developed to raise money for restoration is their volunteer resident-keepers program. Families, couples or individuals apply for a two-week stay at the lighthouse. If accepted, the person becomes the light's keeper (caretaker), enabling the station to be open to the public seven days a week. It's a win/win situation. The station gets free help and the people get free lodging and a terrific vacation. Overwhelming response to this program has resulted in a waiting list.

Being part of the Ludington State Park, the lighthouse can be reached by a 1½-mile (2.4 km) walk along the sandy beach, a long walk on the road through the park, or a bus ride. Besides the lighthouse, the park offers camping, excellent beaches, and fishing in the Sable River or Hamlin Lake, Michigan's biggest artificial lake. On November 1, 2002 the lighthouse was transferred to State ownership.

Known Keepers: Alonzo Hyde (1867–71), Newton Bird (1871–73), Burr Caswell (1875–82), Hans Hansen (1882–87), James Rich (1887–88), Thomas Bailey (1889–93), George Blake (1899–1905), Samuel Gagnon (1905–22),

was burning, one or both of these trap doors had to be closed at all times to prevent the "chimney effect," a strong updraft that could create havoc with the light's burning lamps.

The decagonal lantern housed a third-order Fresnel lens to display a fixed white light. It had a 216-degree arc of illumination, as the back four panels were blacked out. It was the first of the five "Tall Towers" to be built on the American side of the Great Lakes and was first lit on November 1, 1867 by its first keeper, Alonzo Hyde Sr. With its high focal plane of 106 feet (32.3 m) it was visible up to 19 miles (30.5 km) away.

The original keepers' house was a 1½-story Cape Cod style home with a basement of stone blocks. Its yellow brick was painted white on completion. The house was connected to the tower by a covered passageway that housed the keepers' office. The head keeper's quarters on the first floor comprised an oil storage room, a kitchen, a living room and one bedroom. The assistant keeper's quarters upstairs consisted of a kitchen, a living room, and two bedrooms. Roof gutters collected water for storage in an underground cistern. The gutters had 2-way valves so that the water could be diverted onto the ground until it was clean of roof debris, and then into the cistern for storage.

By the late 1890s the soft yellow brick was crumbling. To bolster the tower, it was encased in bands of iron, each one slightly smaller so as to fit inside the one below it. The bands were made of iron plates riveted together. The space between the iron and the brick was then filled with concrete for additional support. The tower was painted white with a broad black band around the middle as a daymark. Also, in 1900 improved third-order burners were installed inside the lens.

In 1908 a two-story red brick addition was built onto the original house to accommodate the assistant keepers. A second assistant had been hired to help man the fog signal building, which had been built west of the house in 1909 and housed a siren-type compressed-air signal. A new two-tone diaphone fog signal replaced the siren in 1934. In 1941 a fog signal on a skeletal tower took the place of the 1909 fog signal building, which had eroded into the

Buffington Breakwater Light

6 Buffington Breakwater Light

Buffington Harbor, along Lake Michigan's south shore, is a private harbor owned by the Universal Atlas Cement Division of the United States Steel Corporation. The harbor is man-made and was built into the lake in front of the plant. In 1926 it was marked by a reinforced-concrete tower with an octagonal lantern, both of which were painted red. The lantern uses a plastic optic today to shine a light beam from a 48-foot (14.6 m) focal plane.

7 Calumet Harbor Breakwater South End Light

When the gap in the breakwater at Calumet Harbor became too small for larger vessels to use, a channel was dredged around the south end of the breakwater to reach the Calumet outer harbor. A light was built in 1935 on the south end of the breakwater to mark this opening. It was a bottom-open, top-enclosed steel tower painted white and red, and had a 50-foot (15.3 m) focal plane. It has no lantern and displays a modern plastic beacon light from its summit.

8 Calumet Harbor Light

In 1849 Congress appropriated $4,000 to build Calumet Harbor's first lighthouse at the mouth of the Calumet River, Lake Michigan, just south of Chicago. Its rubble-stone tower was built in 1852 on the north bank of the river. However, since the harbor was little used on account of a sandbar blocking its mouth, Congress discontinued the light and sold the lighthouse in 1854.

As industrialization increased in the Chicago area, Congress appropriated funds for harbor improvements, which began at Calumet in 1870. With parallel piers built into the lake and the area between them dredged, access was made for larger freight vessels. The government repurchased the lighthouse and relit it in

1873. However, with further industrial growth, the piers were extended farther into the lake, and the river light was again of little use. Instead, a wooden light was built at the end of the north pier in 1876 to mark the harbor entrance, and the lens and lighting apparatus from the old river light were moved to it. A catwalk along the pier connected the light to shore.

In 1898 this wooden pierhead light was in turn replaced by a more durable cylindrical cast-iron tower. In 1899 a fog signal building was built on the pier behind the lighthouse. It first used a 10-inch (25 cm) steam whistle, but in 1907 an automated fog bell took its place. Also in 1907 the light's fourth-order Fresnel lens was downgraded to a sixth-order one, as a new light on the new breakwater became the main harbor light. When a ship struck the pierhead light in 1976, it was retired from service and razed.

In order to protect the Calumet Harbor by creating an outer harbor, a breakwater was built between 1896 and 1915. In 1906 a new light, known as the Calumet Harbor Light, was built on the breakwater to become the primary entrance light for the harbor.

The station was a combined fog signal building, keeper's house and light tower. The wood frame building was sheeted in iron plates to weather Lake Michigan's storms, and a circular cast-iron tower rose from the lake end of its roof. Its circular lantern with diagonal astragals housed a fourth-order Fresnel lens with a 51-foot (15.7 m) focal plane. To counteract wave and ice damage, the building was jacked up in 1923 and a 13-foot (4 m) reinforced-concrete base was installed under it. However in 1929 during a particularly violent storm, the whole building was moved 18 inches (45 cm) off its concrete base, forcing the government to rebuild it.

While the cast-iron tower was reused, a box-like second level made of reinforced concrete and covered in steel replaced the old structure. Rebuilding was completed in 1930, and this lighthouse marked the gap in the breakwater and entrance to the harbor. Eventually, as ships became even larger to carry more cargo, they could not use this gap safely. The harbor lost importance, the light became neglected, and the Coast Guard had it razed in 1995. A temporary light was displayed until it was replaced in 1998 by a D9 cylinder light.

Calumet Harbor Breakwater South End Light

Cana Island Lighthouse

9 Cana Island Lighthouse

To reach the Cana lighthouse, nestled on its own island along the west side of Lake Michigan, visitors must walk across a low, limestone causeway that has been naturally formed by storms. If lake levels are high, the causeway may be covered. The working tower is not open to the public and the house is now a maritime museum operated by the Door County Maritime Museum. The former oil bunker, which once stored highly flammable kerosene, now houses a mini-museum.

The lighthouse, built in 1869, warned of the rugged shoreline and the treacherous reef offshore. The tower was 18 feet (5.5 m) in diameter at its base and 16 feet (4.9 m) at its top. Originally the same yellow brick as the house, in 1902 it was encased in iron bands with the space between the two filled with concrete to prevent erosion. The base walls are 4 feet (1.2 m) thick and 102 steps spiral up to the lantern. It still has its original third-order Fresnel lens, which stands nearly 5 feet (1.5 m) tall and has a visibility of 18 miles (29 km) from its 89-foot (27 m) focal plane.

The keeper's dwelling housed a keeper, his assistant and their families. The main doors to the 1½-story keeper's house and the tower were on the west side, but in 1940 the U.S. Coast Guard sealed the tower entry. The first floor had four rooms (living room, dining room, bedroom and keeper's office). The bedroom has since been converted to an entry room, and a door to the south has been added. There are four more rooms on the second floor. The original brick lean-to has been divided into a pantry and summer kitchen/entry.

The lantern first used lard or whale oil (when available), then kerosene, acetylene gas and electricity supplied by a generator. The light was automated in 1941. In 1960 power lines were brought in. Today the light is operated by the Coast Guard and maintained by their Aids to Navigation team at Green Bay. The lighthouse is now on both the state and national registers for historic places. The island and buildings are leased and maintained by the Door County Maritime Museum.

In the early days, supplies were brought to the lighthouse by boat. From 1900–20 fill was brought in to make a grassy area around the house and help prevent flooding. A well had been dug, but the water could not be used for drinking. The area is vulnerable to water. In 1985 and 1986 water came to within 18 inches (45 cm) of ground level. Water entered the basement of the house and, at its highest level, covered the causeway by 3 feet (0.9 m). Storms also frequently move rocks from the lakebed onto the causeway and onto the grass around the lighthouse.

Today the station looks much as it did in the early days, with its vegetable garden, its own scarecrow, horseshoe pits, and flowerbeds nestled by the rock fence. The stone fences that frame three sides of the island were built in the 1920s by keeper Oscar Knudsen. In spite of its remote location, the station receives many visitors, and its museum offers a good insight into early lighthouse life. As the Federal government downsizes, it has relinquished its lighthouse ownership. At present the Cana Island Lighthouse is in the keeping of the Federal Bureau of Land Management, an agency that will ultimately decide its future ownership.

Known Keepers: William Jackson (1869–72), Warren Julius (1872–75), Sanderson William (1875–91), Thomas Brown (1891–1913), Conrad Stram (1913–1918), Oscar Knudson (1918–24), Clifford Sanderson (1924–33), Ross Wright (1933–41).

10 Carter Harrison Water Intake Light

The City of Chicago has always taken its drinking water from the lake. When the city built a waterworks plant out in the lake to draw in their water, they marked it with a light. While this light had no function to guide ships into the harbor, it did mark a spot for mariners to avoid so that damage would not result. The light was a simple lantern placed on a skeletal tower. It was quite common for cities to mark their intakes with lights. Some, such as those at Chicago, Buffalo or Detroit, were elaborate and others like the Toledo light were less interesting.

Early Carter Harrison Water Intake Light

Carter Harrison Water Intake Light

Cedar River Range Light, Keeper's House

11 Cedar River Range Lights

A light was first placed at the point where Cedar River empties into Green Bay, Lake Michigan, along its northwest shore in 1889, to mark entrance to the river for lumber shipping. The pierhead light, a white wooden pyramidal structure, was lit on November 20. In 1890 J. Spalding of Chicago donated land for a keeper's dwelling. After much grading to fill in the low, marshy area, the government built a two-story red brick house, a brick oil house, a privy and a barn.

In 1891 a second tower was built in front of the keeper's house as a rear range light to the pierhead light. It was a 40-foot (12.2 m) white skeletal, pyramidal tower that was open below the closed-in watchroom. A drilled well was added to the station in 1895. With the forest area being depleted, the Cedar River Lumber Mill decided not to rebuild after it burned in 1912. This closure resulted in decreased boat traffic to the area, and the government deactivated the lights in 1929. While the two towers are long gone, the keeper's house still exists as a private residence.

Known Keepers: Ole Hansen (1890), Hans Hansen (1890), Jacob Young (1890), Gustavus Umberham (1890–1901), Nelson Knudsen (1901–12).

12 Chambers Island Lighthouse

In the mid-1800s when Green Bay, Lake Michigan, became an important area for exporting fish and lumber, vessels crossing the bay used one of two main shipping channels: Strawberry Channel, a narrow channel east of Chambers Island and close to the mainland, or the deeper and wider main channel on the west side of Chambers Island. Mariners appealed to have both channels lit and Congress appropriated funds in 1866 for two lights. In 1867 the government purchased a 40-acre (16.2 hectare) peninsula on the northwest side of Chambers Island for $250 from Lewis and Anna Williams.

Work on the light station began in the summer of 1868. A sturdy cut-stone cellar was dug into the gravelly island for a 1½-story yellow brick keeper's house. The 10-foot (3 m) square tower incorporated into the northwest corner of the house rose square for two stories and then became octagonal for the third story. For extra support, the tower base also had buttresses. While the same plans were used for the lighthouse on Eagle Bluff, the design of the towers was changed to give them a different daymark and avoid confusion.

The 35-foot (10.7 m) tower was topped with an octagonal gallery and a decagonal iron lantern that housed a fourth-order

Fresnel lens. From its 68-foot (20.8 m) focal plane the lantern displayed a fixed white light varied by a white flash every 60 seconds. It was visible for about 15 miles (24 km). In 1899 the lantern received a new fourth-order Fresnel lens, which rotated on a bed of mercury. Since the mercury allowed the lens to turn with less friction, the characteristic became a fixed white light varied by a 2-second flash every 30 seconds.

The tower interior was bricked round, and 55 self-cleaning iron stairs ascended from the cellar through the house to the lantern. Two small doors, one at the top of the tower and one at the bottom, opened to the chain and weights mechanism that powered the rotation of the lens. When the weights could be seen at the bottom, the keeper knew it was time to climb the tower and rewind them — about every four hours. The square brick chimney of the dwelling, set diagonally into the roof, had four flues to service the four stoves in the house. The station, including dock and boathouse, was completed at a cost of $9,275.

Lewis S. Williams, the light's first appointed keeper (and the original landowner), started at a salary of $600 a year. This compared well to salaries at mainland stations, where keepers only earned $450 a year. Williams first lit the light on October 1, 1868.

Being 8 miles (13 km) out in Green Bay, Chambers Island was almost in the middle of the bay and the only refuge during fierce storms. Its keepers assisted many shipwrecked, windblown or becalmed mariners. In 1869 the *Alvin Clark* went down off the island. In 1870 gale force winds even blew the roof off of the newly built lighthouse. In 1915 the keeper took survivors of the burning *Starlight* to the mainland.

The light's illuminants changed with time. The first change was from whale oil to kerosene (likely in the 1890s). The kerosene was burned under pressure in an asbestos kerosene burner that the Coast Guard called an IOV (incandescent oil vapor) burner. When the correct mix of air and kerosene was forced through a bed of heated asbestos fibres, the fibres would glow with "a brilliance beyond belief." The light had such excellent visibility that mariners claimed to see it 50 miles (80 km) away. In 1910 electric bulbs powered by generators lit the light, and in 1926 an acetylene system was introduced. It was equipped with a sun valve that turned the gas on and off automatically with the setting and rising of the sun. In 1961, long after keepers had been removed, batteries — and later still, solar panels — powered the light.

In 1951 the lantern and lens were removed and a modern beacon was placed on a skeletal tower. In 1958 the fourth-order

Chambers Island Lighthouse

Fresnel lens was sold to Harold Warp of Chicago, ostensibly to be displayed in his Pioneer Village Museum at Minden, Nebraska. However, recent visitors to the museum report that no fourth-order lens is housed there, and so the whereabouts of the lens is unknown. In 1961 the light was moved to a higher 67-foot (20.5 m) steel skeletal tower with a black diamond-shaped daymarker. Its characteristic became a white light that flashed every six seconds and was visible for 12 miles (19.4 km).

When the light was automated the lighthouse was abandoned, and it was heavily vandalized during the 1960s. Local Captain Joel Blahnik, a licensed U.S. Coast Guard skipper for 40 years, was able to interest people in turning the area into parkland, and in 1976 the station was transferred to the Town of Gibraltar for $1.00 for exclusive use as a park. Blahnik and his wife, Mary Ann, became caretakers at the lighthouse and worked on its restoration. In 1977 the park opened to the public. Blahnik spiced up his guided tours with his stories of the lighthouse ghost whose footsteps were heard exiting the building every spring when he opened up the station.

One summer the ghost even became a trickster. As tools kept mysteriously disappearing, the family got to the point of joking, "The ghost did it." Students who came to help with renovations didn't believe the story until they awoke in the middle of the night with their beds shaking with no explanation. While no one ever saw a ghost, Joel felt that a guardian ghost of Lewis Williams was watching over the lighthouse in the off-season while it sat empty and then relinquished its watch when the lighthouse was occupied again. One summer around 1986, when religious sisters were touring the lighthouse, they placed their hands on the house and prayed for the release of its spirit. After that, Joel never heard the ghost again.

While some things at the station have disappeared — like the dock, the barn and the ghost — not all is lost. For example, the keeper's logbooks for the lighthouse are now preserved at the National Archives in Washington, D.C. Also, local people like the Blahniks have managed to save an integral part of the island's history, and have been instrumental in opening it for public visits.

Known Keepers: Lewis S. Williams (1868–89), Peter Knudsen (1889–91), Charles E. Young (1891-95), Soren Christianson (1895–1900), Joseph Napeizinski (1900-06), Jens J. Rollefson (1906–25), Claude Chapman (1925–33), Alfred Cornell (1933–42).

13 Charlevoix Pierhead Lights

Round Lake, on the northeast side of Lake Michigan, provided a perfect natural harbor. Its only drawback was that Pine River, which connected it to the larger lake, was too shallow for most vessels. In the 1860s a 900-foot (275 m) dock was built near the river's opening into Lake Michigan. Ships stopped here to take on their cargo of lumber. However, the elements were hard on the dock. The Pine River was slowly dredged by hand in 1873 to make it 35 feet (10. 8 m) wide and 12 feet (3.7 m) deep, and to prevent the still exposed rivermouth from filling with storm-washed sand, a pier was built to the north side to replace the deteriorating wooden dock. During the winter of 1873–74, nine cribs were built on thick ice, and when the ice was cut through, they sank to the bottom to be filled with rock for strength and stability. Vessels now had access to the harbor in Round Lake, and water traffic in the area increased.

To mark this channel, the government built a common pierhead beacon for the end of the north pier in 1884. It was designed by District Engineer Captain Charles E.L.B. Davis, pre-built at the Lighthouse Depot in Detroit, delivered by the tender *Warrington*,

Charlevoix Pierhead Light

and then assembled and anchored to the end of the pier. Standing 30 feet (9.1 m) tall, it was a simple timber-framed pyramidal structure painted white. The upper half enclosed a service room with a window for a view of the lake and with rear access to the pier or to the wooden catwalk that connected it to the mainland. A square iron gallery and octagonal iron railing topped the tower. An octagonal cast-iron lantern displayed a fixed red light from a fifth-order Fresnel lens. From its 37-foot (11.4 m) focal plane it was visible for 9½ miles (15.4 km). Keeper Wright Ripley first exhibited the light on September 1, 1885.

An oil house was built in 1890 at the inner end of the pier to store kerosene. Also at this time the keeper complained to the district inspector about cargo wagons being driven along the pier to supply vessels whose draft was too deep for them to use the channel to Round Lake. The vibrations from these wagons made the lighthouse lamp flicker wildly and smoke excessively. Since these complaints were not repeated, the channel must soon have been dredged deeper.

In 1904 the Army Corps of Engineers completely rebuilt the deteriorating north timber pier. During construction, the light continued in service. It was placed on blocks while the north pier was rebuilt underneath it, and then lowered back into place and reanchored into position. It was possibly at this time that a south pier was also built. A lifesaving station on shore to the north of the piers was officially opened on July 5, 1900.

Sometime between 1910 and 1914 a fog bell was installed on a timber frame on the lake side of the tower and the light was moved to the end of the south pier. A clockwork mechanism inside the service room operated a striking arm that protruded through a hole in the service room wall to strike the bell. The pierhead light

The steamer Beaver *alongside the Charlevoix Pierhead Light, circa 1908*

Chicago Harbor Light

was painted red when it was moved, as a more effective daymark. A 56-foot (17 m) steel skeletal tower, also painted red, was erected at the end of the north pier as a marker. Its occulting white light (light 3 s; dark 3 s) could be seen for up to 12 miles (19.4 km). With this change, the pierhead light was renamed Charlevoix South Pierhead Light Station. The keeper's work effectively doubled because the channel ran between the two lights.

In 1938 electricity was supplied to the pier and the fog bell was replaced by an electric compressor-powered type C diaphone foghorn (two blasts; silence 20 s). Also, an incandescent electric light bulb with a 1500-watt candlepower replaced the light's kerosene lamp. In 1948 a steel tower manufactured in Milwaukee replaced the decaying timber tower. The new tower had a shorter skeletal section and the top two-thirds of it were covered in steel sheeting. The old lantern and lens were placed on top of the new tower and the structure was painted red.

The Charlevoix Pierhead Light remains active today. Its once red color was returned to white in the early 1980s, and its Fresnel lens was replaced with a 300 mm acrylic optic. It continues to guide water traffic, especially pleasure craft and the Beaver Island Ferry into the channel to Round Lake.

Known Keepers: Wright Ripley (1885–1923), William Shields (1923–24), Everitt Sherritt (1924–34), George Hutzler (1934–40), Peter Gallagher (1940).

14   Chicago Harbor Light

Chicago's Great Fire of 1871 devastated the city, including a number of unfortunate vessels that burned at the docks, unable to get out into safe open water. This disaster, which killed 250 people, left ninety thousand homeless, and destroyed about 4 square miles (10 square km), was said to have started when a cow kicked over a lantern in a backyard shed after an extremely dry spell. The city rapidly recovered and by 1890 its population had surpassed one million.

With their newly rebuilt city, Chicagans hosted the Columbian Exposition or World's Fair in 1893. A number of harbor improvements were undertaken to prepare for this event, including a new lighthouse at the entrance to the Chicago River, close to the site of the 1832 lighthouse (see Chicago's First Lighthouse). This new 48-foot (14.8 m) slightly conical iron-plated tower was lined with bricks and had a spiral staircase up to a decagonal lantern. Living quarters were designed right into the 18-foot (5.5 m) diameter of the tower. This combined tower and keeper's house was intended to showcase the state-of-the-art technology used by the Lighthouse Board. The Lighthouse Board also took advantage of the fair to show a third-order Fresnel lens that had previously won

a first prize in Paris at a glass exhibition. This lens also took a prize at the Chicago World's Fair. The lens was intended for the lighthouse at Point Loma, California, after the fair, but since Chicago residents and city officials loved the lens and since the new Chicago light had just been finished and the Columbian Exhibition was closing in October of the same year, the Lighthouse Board was persuaded to keep the lens in Chicago.

This third-order Fresnel lens featured alternating red and white panels, and the beacon was timed to flash at five-second intervals. This shore light became Chicago's new harbor light and the light on the north pier was extinguished and dismantled at this time.

In 1917 Congress appropriated $88,000 to relocate the shore lighthouse to the south end of the north arm of the outer breakwater to guide vessels around the breakwater. The lighthouse was moved in 1918–19 and placed on a new concrete pier that had been poured over rubble to create a solid base. Hipped-roof buildings were attached: a boathouse to the north, and a square fog signal building to the south. It originally housed a diaphone fog whistle (later changed to a diaphone foghorn). In this new location, the tower had an 82-foot (25 m) focal plane. In 1935 the light was electrified.

Although the tower was only a mile (1.6 km) from shore, it seemed very remote to keepers. In a 1971 interview with the *Chicago Tribune* one keeper testified to its loneliness, telling a story about a keeper who went "nuts" and started eating newspapers and even tried to jump from the tower. The four keepers, called "Coasties," worked two weeks on and one week off. The newest man was assigned the highest bedroom, the one closest to the ear-splitting fog signal, which sounded every 20 seconds around the clock in foggy weather and could be heard 14 miles (22.4 km) away.

The keepers had three main jobs at this station: to maintain and operate the light, to make sure the radio beacon transmitted its signal every six minutes, and to activate the fog signal when visibility was lower than 5 miles (8 km). In 1979 the tower was automated and its keepers were no longer needed. At some point its third-order Fresnel lens was replaced by two quartz bulbs and polished mirrors. This light has been added to the *National Register of Historic Places*.

In 1980 advertising salesman Sterling Bemis rented the lighthouse from the Coast Guard. His rental agreement was a win-win situation: he paid only $1,050 a year for rent, but had to fix and maintain the interior of the lighthouse for the Coast Guard. He lived at the light, except during the winter, and commuted to his day job by boat. The lighthouse exterior was restored in 1997, and this light is off limits to the public.

15 Chicago Harbor Southeast Guidewall Light

In 1938 a square white steel skeleton tower 30 feet (9 m) tall, with its top two levels enclosed, was placed on a guidewall between two smaller piers just south of Chicago's well-known Navy Pier. The light from its black lantern assisted mariners in approaching the piers.

Chicago North Pierhead Light, circa 1995

16 Chicago North Pierhead Light

In 1837 Chicago was incorporated as a city with a population of four thousand. It continued to grow, and in 1847 Congress appropriated $3,500 for another lighthouse at Chicago. Also in 1847 Chicago's north pier was extended to 3,900 feet (1200 m) and a new small lighthouse, made of pine timbers, was placed at its new end to mark the harbor entrance.

With the completion of the Indiana and Michigan Canal in 1848, Chicago was connected to the Mississippi River system and could export goods from the south. By 1849, as the city had become a seaport as well as a lake port thanks to its connection to the St. Lawrence River, Chicago had become the busiest port in the United States.

To better mark this important harbor, the old pierhead light was replaced in 1852 by a more substantial wooden structure just beyond the north end of the pier. It was in turn replaced in 1859 by a 111 foot (34.5 m) cast-iron skeletal tower that used an ultra-modern space-age-style or erector-set design. Its enclosed central tube contained a spiral staircase to access the watchroom below the decagonal lantern. A large circular iron gallery with an ornate iron railing topped the tower and formed the base for the watchroom and a smaller lantern gallery. Eight graceful, skeletal iron legs anchored to the pier helped support the cylindrical tower. A complex network of horizontal struts and diagonal tie rods attached the legs to the tower. The tower was reached from the pier by a straight iron staircase. The two-story wooden keeper's house was built on the pier near the base of the tower. In 1869 a beacon light with a sixth order fresnel lens and costing $2300 was added to the east end of the north pier.

The tall erector-type tower was Chicago's main harbor light but by 1870 it was too dim to be useful because it was obliterated by the smoke from surrounding factories. In 1872 the

Chicago North Pierhead Light, also an exhibit at the 1893 Chicago World's Fair

Lighthouse Board decided to build a new lighthouse at Grosse Point, 13 miles (21 km) away to become Chicago's main entrance light. The north pier light continued to serve the harbor until the Grosse Point light was lit in 1873 and then it became unlit but left standing. Later its modern design became a highlight of the Columbian Exposition of Chicago in 1893. After the exposition it was dismantled and moved to Wisconsin, where it was erected as the Rawley Point Light and still serves today.

Chicago had a new main harbor light onshore at the south side of the river in 1893 and when a new breakwater was built offshore in the early 1900s, the harbor's north pier was shortened to clear the future outer harbor area, and a system of range lights was established on its shortened pierhead. The rear tower was a white conical iron tower that supported a cylindrical lantern with glass panes set diagonally into metal astragals. Its light had a 48-foot (14.6 m) focal plane. A fog bell was also suspended about two-thirds of the way up the outer lake wall of the tower, and a mechanical mechanism was housed inside the tower for striking the bell. The front light had a white iron cylindrical tower and displayed a locomotive head-lamp from a 30-foot (9 m) focal plane. The front light was removed in the 1930s, as range lights were no longer needed. The rear light continued until the 1950s, when it too was discontinued.

Known Keepers: Mark Beaubien (1855–59), Morris Walsh (1859–61), John Lobstine (1861–66), Leonard Miller (1866–69), Charles Boynton (1869–74).

Chicago Pier Light, circa 1880

Early Chicago Pier Light

Chicago's First Lighthouse

17 Chicago's First Lighthouse

French explorers first came to the Chicago area in 1673. As it developed in the 1800s, inbound vessels brought immigrants and building materials, and outbound vessels carried grain and hogs. In 1831 Congress appropriated $5,000 to build a lighthouse at the mouth of the Chicago River on Lake Michigan.

The lighthouse was built in 1831 on the riverbank. Then, either just before it was finished or just after it was completed (conflicting reports), the tower fell over. The builder claimed its collapse was due to the settling of quicksand beneath the tower.

A replacement lighthouse was built in 1832 on the river's south bank near Fort Dearborn. It was a 40-foot (12.2 m) rubble-stone tower with a birdcage-style lantern that housed 13 Argand lamps and 14-inch (35 cm) reflectors. In 1848, to reduce costs, the lamps and reflectors were reduced to five. This tower was either the first or second light to be built on Lake Michigan. There is a discrepancy as to when this light was discontinued. Some say it was when the main light was moved to the north pier. The 1882 *Pharos Light-House Guide* has it still functioning in that year, but it was definitely gone when a new shore light was built in 1893.

Known Keepers: George Snow (1833), Samuel Lasley (1833–34), William Stevens (1835–39), John Gibson (1839–41), William Stevens (1841–42), Silas Meacham (1842–44), James Long (1844–49), Charles Douglass (1849–53), Henry Fuller (1853–55), Mark Beaubien (1855–59).

18 Dunlap Reef Lighthouse

Dunlap Reef is a partially submerged, 700-foot (215 m), limestone reef that lies adjacent to the western edge of the Sturgeon Bay Ship Canal, which had been dredged into Green Bay from Lake Michigan. The canal was finished in 1881, and range lights were also set up that year to mark the reef and guide east-bound ships into the canal.

The southernmost light was the rear range light known as the Dunlap Reef Lighthouse. Built on the reef using a large stone-filled timber crib, it consisted of a 1½-story wood framed keeper's house with a three-story square tower emerging up and out of the northern gable of the house. A boathouse was built on the crib behind the house to store the rowboat in which the keeper rowed to shore and to service the front

Dunlap Reef Lighthouse minus its tower

range light on the northernmost end of the reef. This light was a short, square wooden pyramidal structure with an open lower framework.

After channel improvements, the rear range light became redundant, and the Dunlap Reef light was extinguished in 1924. The Lighthouse Service removed its lantern and lighting apparatus to be used elsewhere. The lighthouse was sold in 1925, dismantled, and moved to the east side of Sturgeon Bay, where it was rebuilt minus its tower, to be used as a private home.

The reef continues to be marked today by a modern light placed on its northwest end and by a number of privately placed and maintained buoys. These aids continue to warn local pleasure boaters of the dangerous reef.

Known Keepers: Graham Henry (1881–82), Joseph Harris Jr. (1882–90), Clifford W. Sanderson (1890–1924).

19 Eagle Bluff Lighthouse

As boat traffic into Green Bay increased in the mid-nineteenth century, mariners called for the narrow shipping passage between Door Peninsula and the Strawberry Islands on the east side of the bay to be lit. The Lighthouse Board responded in 1866 and acquired $12,000 from Congress to build a lighthouse on Eagle Bluff, about 3 miles (4.9 km) north of Fish Creek.

As crews were busy with other lights, construction was delayed until 1868. After clearing the site, the crew hauled the materials up the hill from the bay rather than up the 30-foot (9 m) cliff. They blasted a spot in the rock for the foundation, and then built a 1½-story yellow brick keeper's house. The square brick tower was set diagonally into the northwest corner of the house and was bricked to be circular inside. An ornamental spiral iron staircase connected the basement and the lantern so that the keeper could easily fetch lard oil stored in the cellar.

The 43-foot (13 m) tower supported a square gallery and a decagonal cast-iron lantern that housed a 3½-order Fresnel lens from Paris. The oil-burning lamps of 860 candlepower were visible for 16 miles (26 km) from a 76-foot (23.2 m) focal plane. The chimney of the house was set on a diagonal to match that of the tower and to service stoves in several rooms. The cellar was designed to store lard oil (mineral oil as of 1882) for the light and a year's worth of staples, which came in 50-pound (110 kg) kegs or 100-pound (220 kg) barrels.

On the main floor were a family room/dining room, a parlor, a bedroom/music room, and the kitchen, the most versatile of the rooms, used for sewing, food preparation, Saturday night baths, and laundry. Upstairs was a large bedroom and a small room with the house's only built-in closet to store lighthouse keeping supplies such as chimneys, wicks, linens, cleaning supplies, and hardware for repairs. Steep steps from the lake level ascended the bluff in front of the lighthouse.

The light's first keeper, Henry Stanley, served from 1868 until 1883, when he was transferred to the new light at Sherwood Point. His tenure was remarkable for the arrival of a piano, carried up the steep cliff steps to the lighthouse by 16 men. The 1877 navigational season extended until New Year's Day and the family went for a pleasant boat ride on December 28 — a truly rare event.

Stanley's replacement, William Duclon, who arrived in September 1883, was a Republican and a Civil War veteran, having fought at Gettysburg as a "Yankee." This was in his favor

Eagle Bluff Lighthouse

Mrs. Duclon was famous for her many talents, which included her excellent sewing skills. Besides making all of the clothes for her family, she made crazy quilts and patchwork quilts for which she won many prizes at Door County fairs. In 1899 the station received its first library of books brought to the light by the keeper of Bailey's Harbor.

Being the highest structure in the surrounding area, the lighthouse was frequently hit by lightning. In severe thunderstorms the family often sought the safety of the cellar. Repair crews made regular trips to the lighthouse to make repairs caused by heavy storms. The keepers kept logbooks, but although they were expected to fill two pages a month, all three keepers used only two pages a year. The left page was for recording visitors to the light and the right page the weather. In 1897 an oil house was built to store kerosene, a new more volatile fuel that needed a separate storage area to prevent fires.

as the keeper's position was frequently given to war veterans. He was keeper for 35 years and raised his seven sons at the light, putting them to use with lighthouse tasks. The boys used a wooden yoke to carry water from the lake until a well was drilled in the late 1880s. Other chores were to weed the garden, collect eggs, milk the cow, churn the butter, hunt rabbits, squirrels and deer for fresh meat, fish for food, and gather wild fruits and berries. When being punished, the boys had to paint something at the station, as there was always paint that needed using up. They even had a spyglass to keep a lookout for the lighthouse inspection tender so that everyone could do the last-minute tidying. The system must have worked well since Duclon received many commendations for having the "best looking lighthouse grounds in the Great Lakes area."

In the late 1800s Duclon was earning $30 a month, but spent $50 on a baby grand piano. Each of the boys taught himself to play an instrument. Besides the piano there was a violin, a guitar, and an accordion. Once the community learned of their talents, the family were in great demand to play at dances and weddings. Even in the winter they loaded all of the instruments — including the piano — onto the sleigh to go wherever necessary.

The light underwent changes as technology advanced. In 1918 the 3½-order Fresnel lens was replaced with a fifth-order Fresnel lens, and in 1926 the light was automated through the use of acetylene and the keeper removed. In 1936 lead storage batteries were introduced to power the light. Around 1985, solar-powered batteries were installed to power the light and produce its characteristic flash pattern (flash 1 s; eclipse 6 s) for a 10-mile (16 km) range.

In 1936 the Lighthouse Service leased the dwelling to the State Park. In 1960 the Door County Historical Society became involved in restoring the lighthouse, and had it ready for public tours by 1963. The busy and much-visited lighthouse is listed as a historic site on both National and State lists. To this day it has no electricity.

Known Keepers: Henry Stanley (1868–83), William Duclon (1881–1918), Peter Coughlin (1919–26).

20 Eleven Foot Shoal Lightship

Eleven Foot Shoal is approximately 2 ¼ miles (3.6 km) south of Peninsula Point in northern Green Bay of Lake Michigan. The shoal was a hazard to boat traffic heading to Escanaba, and so it was marked in 1893 by a lightship, a more economical method than building a lighthouse.

The first lightship at this shoal was *LV 60*. It and its sister ships *LV 61* and *LV 62* were each built in 1893 by the Craig Shipbuilding Co. of Toledo, Ohio for $13,990. *LV 60* was 82 feet 2 inches (25.2 m) long, with an 18-foot (5.5 m) beam and a 6½-foot (2 m) draft, and it displaced 160 tons of water. It was a two-masted wooden ship, and the higher foremast displayed the light and its daymark. Its 6-inch (15 cm) steam fog whistle (blast 5 s; silence 10 s) was placed mid-vessel in front the smokestack. It also had an 800-pound (365 kg) brass fog bell that could be operated manually.

Its illuminating apparatus consisted of a cluster of three oil-burning lens lanterns that could be raised and lowered on the fore-

Eagle Bluff Lighthouse's Parlour, circa 2001

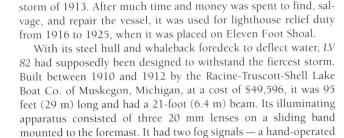

Eleven Foot Shoal Lightship LV 60

It was replaced by *LV 82*, which had first served to mark the Buffalo Harbor for just over a year before it sank during the great storm of 1913. After much time and money was spent to find, salvage, and repair the vessel, it was used for lighthouse relief duty from 1916 to 1925, when it was placed on Eleven Foot Shoal.

With its steel hull and whaleback foredeck to deflect water, *LV 82* had supposedly been designed to withstand the fiercest storm. Built between 1910 and 1912 by the Racine-Truscott-Shell Lake Boat Co. of Muskegon, Michigan, at a cost of $49,596, it was 95 feet (29 m) long and had a 21-foot (6.4 m) beam. Its illuminating apparatus consisted of three 20 mm lenses on a sliding band mounted to the foremast. It had two fog signals — a hand-operated fog bell and a 6-inch (15 cm) steam signal.

LV 82 marked Eleven Foot Shoal until 1935. By then, since vessels were larger and seeking safer passage through deeper water farther south, when a lighthouse was erected to replace the lightship at Eleven Foot Shoal, *LV 82* was placed on nearby Minneapolis Shoal, from which it could more effectively light the area. In 1936 *LV 82* was turned over to the Veterans of Foreign Wars in Boston and anchored at dockside, where it was used as summer living quarters for ex-navy men from 1936 to 1945. Vandals then sank the vessel at dockside, and the wreckage was finally scrapped.

mast. These lanterns displayed a fixed white light from a 40-foot (12.2 m) focal plane for a visibility of 13 miles (21 km). The ship had a black hull with white lettering. It was placed on location and lit on October 6, 1893, and was removed to winter over at Escanaba, as it did every season, except for the winter of 1904 when it underwent extensive repairs at Sturgeon Bay.

Its history was mostly uneventful. In the fall of 1894 faulty equipment caused it to drift off-station, and the tender *Dahlia* had to reposition it. In 1897 modifications were made to its interior to enlarge its coal bunkers. In 1900 its rotten deck planking was replaced. In 1906 it was equipped with a submarine bell signal and in 1917 its fog whistle was upgraded to a 10-inch (25 cm) one. It was retired from duty in 1926 and sold on June 15, 1926. Rumor suggests that it went to Chicago to be used as a floating clubhouse.

Escanaba Crib Lighthouse

21 Escanaba Crib Lighthouse

When harbor improvements at Escanaba on northern Lake Michigan made the old light too far from the water to warn of its hazards, a new crib light was built offshore in 1938 to mark the harbor's low water area. It consisted of a round base with a square steel tower, about 30 feet (9 m) high, placed on top of a concrete pier. The top half is a smaller square. The base is painted black, while the tower is all white and now has a green horizontal band around the middle. Originally operated by remote control from the Coast Guard base onshore at Escanaba, it was automated in 1976, and its modern beacon is today powered by solar panels mounted to one side of the tower.

22 Frankfort North Breakwater Light

By the turn of the century Frankfort Harbor was growing steadily (see Frankfort South Pierhead Light), and the Army Corps of Engineers had to keep improving its piers and lights. In 1924 they started to build two reinforced concrete arrowhead-type breakwaters out into Lake Michigan to create a stilling basin that would further protect the harbor's entrance. When these breakwaters were completed in the early 1930s the twin piers at the entrance to Lake Betsie, no longer needed, were shortened to stubs.

Eleven Foot Shoal Lightship LV 82

In 1932 the North Pierhead light was moved to the end of the north breakwater and placed on a new square steel base that was 25 feet (7.6 m) high, thus making the tower 67 feet (20.5 m) high. With its new 72-foot (22 m) focal plane, its new 17,000 candlepower incandescent electric light, and its old fourth-order Fresnel lens, it had a visibility of 16 miles (26 km).

When rail traffic decreased in the 1960s and 1970s so did the number of car ferries in Frankfort Harbor. The harbor no longer bustles with commercial water traffic as it once did, but it does serve the many pleasure craft that use its facilities today.

Frankfort North Breakwater Light

23 Frankfort North Pierhead Light

As early lake traffic into Frankfort Harbor continued to increase, government improvements kept pace. In 1912 Congress appropriated funds to build a taller, more substantial light at the end of the harbor's north pier to better light the harbor entrance. The structure was 44 feet (13.5 m) high and painted white for best daytime visibility. It consisted of a steel tower sheathed in steel plating and topped with a square gallery that held a decagonal lantern equipped with a fourth-order Fresnel lens. The light's fixed red light was visible for 12 miles (19.4 km) from its 46-foot (14 m) focal plane. The air fog siren (blast 3 s; silence 3 s) was moved from the south fog tower into this structure. This new tower was also connected to the shore by an elevated wooden catwalk for the keeper's safety.

The light from the south rear range pole was moved to the north pier and placed on a 66-foot (20 m) wooden pole 200 feet (60 m) behind the new north pierhead light, to act as its rear range, making entry between the piers easier. When these new lights were completed, the old south pierhead light and fog tower were demolished.

With the arrival of electricity in Frankfort in 1919, the pier lights were electrified. The intensified light in the tower (1,900 candlepower) boosted the light's visibility to 14 miles (22.5 km). The fog signal building was also switched to an electric air-compressor–driven diaphone foghorn (blast 2 s; silence 18 s). The old diesel engine system was left to serve as backup in case of a power outage. This system served the harbor until 1932, when the lights were again improved.

24 Frankfort South Pierhead Light

Captain George Tifft was heading north along the eastern side of Lake Michigan in a violent storm when his schooner was damaged and blown toward shore about 4½ miles (7.2 km) south of Point Betsie. To avoid destruction he rode a wave over a sandbar into a river and thus discovered a lake that later became known as Lake Betsie. This small lake was an ideal refuge from Lake Michigan storms, but Tifft's schooner was trapped until his crew dug an opening through the sandbar large enough for them to sail out.

After Tifft's 1854 discovery became known, the area was quickly logged and settled. In 1859 a private group spent $16,000 to build two short piers at the river mouth and dredge a deeper channel into the river. With water access, the town of Frankfort soon developed along the north shore of Lake Betsie. The town grew steadily and the government was repeatedly asked to improve the harbor. Congress in 1867 appropriated enough funds to build a whole new channel into Lake Betsie about 750 feet (231 m) south of the river. The channel was made 200 feet (60 m) wide and 12 feet (3.6 m) deep. Its entrance at Lake Michigan was protected by two parallel piers and breakwaters.

While the piers were being completed in 1873, plans for a pierhead light were also underway. The first keeper, John H. King, was even hired early, perhaps to help construct the light, which was built at the end of the south pier. It was a square white wooden pyramidal tower with a simple square wooden gallery that held an octagonal iron lantern fitted with a sixth-order Fresnel lens. The fixed red light could be seen for 12 miles (19 km) from its 25-foot (7.7 m) focal plane. The tower had two entrances, one from the pier into the bottom of the tower and one from an elevated catwalk into the service room just below the lantern. The light was first lit on October 15, 1873. Unfortunately, King was forced to rent lodgings in town and it is not certain whether a keeper's house was ever built at this station.

The Army Corps of Engineers returned in 1884 to make more improvements. The south pier was extended 200 feet (60 m) into the lake but not before Lake Michigan wreaked havoc. A violent storm destroyed 90 feet (27 m) of elevated walkway and damaged another 170 feet (52 m) of pier. After repairing and completing the pier, and building a wooden oil house and a boat hoist, the crew then moved the pierhead light 195 feet (59 m) closer to the lake at the end of the newly extended south pier. The schooner *Amsden*, being towed into the harbor during the winter, broke her towline, and her bowsprit damaged 32 feet (9.7 m) of the elevated walkway. Keeper Albert Vorce supervised the repairs.

In 1891 $1,000 was requested for a fog bell, and it was granted. A wooden framed pyramidal tower similar in design to the light tower was built 8 feet (2.4 m) behind the pierhead light. The bell and striking apparatus came from storage at the Detroit Lighthouse Depot. The bell was hung in the top of the tower so that its sound

Gary Breakwater Lighthouse

could travel farther, and the striking apparatus was in a closed section just below the bell. In 1901 an air-operated fog siren replaced the fog bell. Its diesel engine was put in the enclosed section of the fog tower, and the siren and its copper trumpet were installed on the outside. The fog bell and its apparatus remained until 1905, when they were shipped to the St. Joseph Lighthouse Depot.

In 1893 the railroad arrived at Frankfort and the harbor increased in importance as Midwest industries began to rely on it. The Army Engineers again extended the piers, and the pierhead light and fog signal tower were moved closer to the outer end of the south pier. Also, a light was placed on top of a 60-foot (18.3 m) steel post 600 feet (183 m) behind the pierhead light, to act as a rear range light and help vessels locate the opening between the piers.

The south pierhead light and fog signal operated until 1912 when harbor improvements were made once again and a new north pierhead light was built. When it was finished, the south rear range light was moved to the north pier to act as its rear range light and the fog signal was moved into the north pierhead tower. At this time the old south pierhead light and fog tower were demolished as they were no longer needed.

Known Keepers: John King (1873–77), John Brewer (1877–80), S. Brewer (1880–84), Albert Vorce (1884–99), Joseph Wilmat (1899–1911).

25 Gary Breakwater Lighthouse

Gary Harbor, at Lake Michigan's southern end, is a private harbor developed and owned by the United States Steel Corporation. A western breakwater angling to the northeast protects the harbor entrance. The harbor was built in the early 1900s, and in 1911 a light was placed at the east end of the breakwater. Made of cast iron and painted all red, it is somewhat of a squat bottle shape. Its circular lantern originally housed a sixth-order Fresnel lens and used acetylene as a fuel. Today its modern lens is mounted above the lantern and uses electricity. The unlit lantern houses a backup light.

26 Grand Haven Lights

In 1838 the U.S. government bought one acre (0.4 hectare) of land (the "Lighthouse Acre") at the mouth of the Grand River from John Wright. A lighthouse to mark the entrance to the excellent, deep natural harbor was built later that same year on the south side of the river under the bluff. However, when Lt. Homans of the U.S. Navy reported to the Treasury Department that the lighthouse was being built of inferior quality materials, a superintendent, T.H. Lyon, was sent out to dismiss the overseer and make sure the builders, Messrs Rogers and Burnett, used proper materials. His inspection found everything in order and made of quality materials and workmanship, although he recommended a breakwater at the lake edge to prevent erosion, as much of the lot had already disappeared and the lighthouse had been built on the back property line.

The stone for the foundation of the keeper's house came from quarries at Green Bay. Stone for the steps and other hewn stone came from Cleveland, Ohio. Work was often delayed as the crew waited for materials that had mistakenly been shipped to Chicago or Milwaukee. The tower, completed in 1839, was only 30 feet (9 m) tall, and its lantern used eleven Argand lamps and 14-inch (35 cm) reflectors. This light served until a winter storm washed away the wooden breakwater and undermined the keeper's dwelling.

Grand Haven Inner and Outer Lights

Grand Haven Outer Light

In 1855 a new lighthouse was built on top of the bluff on the south side of the harbor. It was a stone dwelling with a tower at its south end. Using a fourth-order Fresnel lens from a 150-foot (46 m) focal plane, it had a general visibility of 18 miles (29 km) and a visibility of 25 miles (40.5 km) in clear weather. The first keeper of this lighthouse was Captain Jebediah Gray.

During major harbor renovations in 1857, breakwaters were built along the river channel to prevent erosion and sand deposits. A short pier extended into the lake from the south side of the harbor entrance. In 1875 a wooden fog signal building was built at the lake end of this pier. In 1881 a 60-foot (18.3 m) beacon light with a 10-mile (16.2 km) visibility was constructed on the pier.

Starting in 1883 the south pier was lengthened. Wooden cribs built onshore were towed into position and sunk by filling them with rocks, and then the pier was built on top of them. With each extension, the fog building was moved to the new end of the pier further out into the lake. By the final extension, the pier was 1,150 feet (350 m) long and the fog signal building was 1,100 (340 m) from shore.

In 1895 a light was added to the lakeward side of the fog signal building. This light worked as a front range light to the inner pier light, which became the rear range light. It used a sixth-order lens to exhibit its light from a 42-foot (12.8 m) focal plane. A wooden catwalk connected the lights on the pier for the keeper's protection.

The current 51-foot (15.5 m) prefabricated cast-iron tower was built in the early 1900s by the American Bridge Company to replace the 1881 rear range light. In 1905 a few major changes took place. The rear light was moved to the inner end of the pier, the lighthouse on the bluff was extinguished, and its fourth-order Fresnel lens was placed in the rear range light. In 1910 the old lighthouse on the bluff was demolished and its masonry walls were recycled in a new 2-story, 13-room keeper's house.

Other changes occurred over the years. In 1921 a cast-iron catwalk replaced the wooden one and the pier was capped with concrete. The pier was given a prow shape to deflect water and ice away from the fog building, and in 1922 the fog building was covered in corrugated metal sheeting to help prevent weather damage. A diaphone fog signal was installed at an unknown date.

At some point the lenses were removed. The rear range light was given a 250 mm optic that displayed a fixed red light for 10 miles (16.2 km) and the front range light received a 190 mm optic. In 1969 the lights were automated. When the Coast Guard planned to remove the catwalk in 1987, Edward J. Zenko and his daughter Terry spearheaded a "Save the Catwalk Committee," which raised $133,000. In 1988 lights were added along the length of the catwalk. The piers and breakwaters at Grand Haven were placed on the *National Register of Historic Places* in 1995. Today the old fourth-order Fresnel Lens can be seen on display in the City of Grand Haven museum.

Known Keepers: Nehemiah Merritt (1839–47), William Haucland (1847–49), George Torrey (1849–53), Peter Vanderberg (1853–58), Jebediah Gray (1858–61), J. Belger (1861), H. Miller (1861–75), Harry Smith (1875–83), Emanuel Davidson (1883–1900).

27 Grand Traverse Lighthouse

The Grand Traverse Lighthouse sits at the end of Leelanau Peninsula and was first built by presidential order to warn passing schooners laden with grain, meat and whiskey of the peninsula. It also marked the entrance to Traverse Bay as well as the entrance into the Manitou Passage and the Straits of Mackinac. Originally it was called Cat's Head Lighthouse. During the last part of the nineteenth century it warned steamships. Today it is part of Leelanau State Park.

The first brick tower, with its separate lightkeeper's quarters, was built in 1852 south of the present site. The square yellow brick tower, now covered with white pressed metal sheeting had an octagonal lantern room that rose about one story above the housetop. The lamp originally burned whale oil. In 1870 it received a fourth-order Fresnel lens to replace its smaller fifth-order lens. The light stood 47 feet (14.5 m) above the lake level and could be seen for 12 to 17 miles (19 to 27 km).

In 1852 the keeper was Deputy U.S. Marshall Phil Beers. He had some interesting times in this remote location. Once, he was invaded by the subjects of "King" Strang, who ruled the Mormon colony 25 miles (40 km) to the north on Beaver Island. He lost his provisions, fishnet and some lighthouse equipment. Fortunately, the imported Fresnel lens was undamaged. After his house burned, the tower was torn down as it was threatened by erosion, and the

Grand Haven Outer Lights and Fog Signal Building, circa 1917

Grand Traverse Lighthouse

General Orlando M. Poe approved plans for range lights to mark the cut through the island.

A timber pier was built along the east side of the cut, and the range lights were placed at the ends of the pier, about 675 feet (200 m) apart. Both range lights were gently tapering pyramidal towers covered with cedar shake shingles. The front, or northern, one was 25 feet (7.6 m) high and topped with an octagonal cast-iron lantern that housed a sixth-order Fresnel lens displaying a fixed white light from a 30 foot (9 m) focal plane to produce an 11-mile (18 km) visibility on a clear night. The rear, or southern, light had a 35-foot (10.7 m) tower, also topped with an octagonal lantern and a sixth-order Fresnel lens. Its fixed white light had a 13-mile (21 km) visibility. About 100 feet (30.5 m) north of the rear range light and just behind the pier, the crew built the 2½-story keeper's dwelling. The lights were first lit on November 15, 1872, by keeper Joseph Wing.

Because of its exposed location, numerous upgrades were needed at the station over the years. In 1880 the house and woodshed roofs were replaced. A breakwater was built in 1889 to stem the erosion on the island's east side, and a landing dock was added. In 1896 the attached kitchen and the boathouse had to be rebuilt due to water damage. In 1901 both lights were reshingled and repainted, and a brick oil storage house was built between the house and the rear range light. As protection against the rising lake level, more stone was added to the east side in 1901, and in 1902 the boathouse had to be raised and a trestle walk added to the landing. In 1907, also to protect against rising waters, 250 feet (76.2 m) of pile and corrugated sheet metal were added to the east side of the island.

Other changes occurred at the station in the twentieth century. In 1901 an assistant keeper was hired. In 1934 the characteristic of both lights was changed to green to make them more visible against the white lights of the city. While the rear range light received a fixed green light with a 10-mile (16 km) visibility, the front range light received a green light that flashed every five seconds. Also in 1934, once the lights were switched to an acetylene system that used a sun valve to turn the lights on and off at sunset and sunrise, keepers became redundant. With the decision to widen the channel in 1966, the lights were slated to be destroyed, but the Green Bay Yacht Club managed to save them and have them relocated onto their property. In 1999 the lights were moved to the piers on either side of the yacht club's entrance, where they remain today.

Known Keepers: Joseph Wing (1872–95), Ole Hansen (1895–1902), Louis Hutzler (1903–33), Lewis Charles (1933–34), Gregory Navarre (1934).

U.S. Lighthouse Board erected the present 2½ story yellow brick house with a rooftop tower and copper-topped lantern in 1858.

The twentieth century brought changes. With the switch to kerosene, a brick oil storage house was built in 1896. In 1899 a fog signal was built for $5,500 and an assistant keeper hired. In 1900 the house was converted to a two-family dwelling. In 1916 a new kitchen was added. In 1933 the steam fog whistle was replaced by a Type F diaphone fog signal. In 1953 the station was modernized and electrified, and porch wings were added. In 1972 the building was closed and an automatic skeletal tower was erected.

In 1986 the old lighthouse was opened to the public as a museum that is maintained by the Grand Traverse Lighthouse Foundation.

Known Keepers: David Moon (1852–53), Philo Beers (1853–57), Gilman Chase (1857–59), Henry Beers (1859–61), Solomon Case (1861–62), Dr. Henry Schetterly (1862–73), Captain Peter Nelson (1875–90), George Buttars (1890–1918), Reynold Johnson (1918–23), James McCormick (1923–38), Paul Walters (1938–39), Ernst Hutzler (1939–46), John Olsen (1948–52), Edwin Johnson (1952–54), John Marken (1957–67).

28 Grassy Island Range Lights

Congress appropriated $4,000 for a lighthouse in Lake Michigan on Grassy Island in 1838, but when Lt. James T. Homans checked the island location, he found Grassy Island to be a most unsuitable location due to its "being nearly under water," and recommended Tail Point instead. Local merchants grumbled about the decision, as vessels entering Green Bay Harbor had to go around Grassy Island to gain entry, and they continued to petition the government to build the lighthouse there, but to no avail.

Much later, in 1866, Congress appropriated $30,000 for dredging and improving the channel entry into the mouth of the Fox River at Green Bay. A channel 200 feet (61.5 m) wide and 13 feet (4 m) deep was dredged right through the middle of Grassy Island for a straight approach into the river. In 1866 Congress also appropriated $11,000 for a lighthouse to guide vessels through the cut in Grassy Island, but its construction was delayed until harbor improvements were finished. In 1871 District Engineer

Grassy Island Range Lights

Gray's Reef Lighthouse

29 Gray's Reef Lighthouse

In 1936 the U.S. government replaced the lightship once used at Gray's Reef with a lighthouse built to mark the dredged channel through the reef, 20 miles (32 km) west of the Straits of Mackinac on the northeast side of Lake Michigan.

A wooden crib was sunk 26 feet (8 m) into the lake onto the reef, and was then filled with stone and concrete. It supported a large concrete deck or pier, 60 feet square (18 by 18 m). A two-story base for the light was built on top of the pier. The lower level included the fuel room, potable water, machinery space with generators, and foghorn engines. One of the two generators always operated to provide electricity and the keepers could not escape this constant noise. Two compressors operated the foghorn when necessary (one engine was always on standby in case of a breakdown).

The foghorn was turned on when visibility was less than 5 miles (8 km) and it frequently stayed on for days at a time. The 8-foot (2.4 m) bronze horn operated on a 20-second cycle (blast 2 s; silence 18 s). Its inescapable vibration made the steel structure vibrate and this went right down to the keepers' bones. The upper level provided the crew with the galley, berthing, and the head (bathroom). The station's radio beacon operated 24 hours a day and each of the three keepers on duty rotated through a six-hour watch. Its "dot, dot, dash" (No. 9 in Morse code) was sent out continuously, and could be picked up as a navigation aid as far as 70 miles (118 km) away.

The 65-foot (20 m) tower was much narrower and swooped up from the base like a rocket on a launch pad. The structure can be identified far away by its art deco style and its brilliant white color. Base and tower were both constructed of steel reinforced concrete. Its 115 stairs led up to the lantern, which originally housed a 3½-order Fresnel lens. In 1966 its 1,000-watt, 9,000 candlepower red light was visible for 17 miles (27.5 m) in good weather. The light's flash pattern (light, 4 s; eclipse, 4 s) was displayed from an 82-foot (25 m) focal plane.

The light had four keepers working at once, one on leave on shore and three on duty at the light. Being so closely confined, they had to work at not going "stir-crazy." Their duties included keeping the machinery operating, radio beacon watch, polishing the main light and putting glycerine on the lens so that it did not fog up. Leisure time included fishing, watching TV, darts, ping pong, weight-lifting or reading. Keepers had to take their own food to the light and they took turns cooking. They were picked up and dropped off from shore leave regularly as long as the lake was calm. Sometimes their two weeks on duty became three or more in stormy weather. Unlike early lighthouse keepers, few of the keepers at this light chose to use the light's 16-foot (4.9 m) boat to go fishing, perhaps because they were so far out in the lake. An underwater phone cable added at some point allowed keepers to call their families occasionally.

In 1965 their mundane routine was interrupted one night by a big "bang" in foggy weather. The lighthouse had been struck by a passing ship and it did not even shake. The vessel did not need assistance, but backed off and continued en route. While only minor damage was done to the lighthouse crib, the bow of the ship was quite battered. Other highlights of duty at this light included finding water snakes on the pier or behind the sea doors of the pier after a storm, being covered by black flies so thick they would have to be hosed off, being confined indoors for days at a time when storms washed over the lighthouse and pier, and trying to get outside when the door was iced over.

In 1976 the Fresnel lens was removed and replaced with a 190 mm lens and the light was automated, making keepers no longer needed. The old Fresnel lens was taken to Charlevoix, Michigan, where it was put on display at the Harsha House Museum.

Known Keepers: Ron Benjamin (1936–39), Harry McRae (1939).

30 Gray's Reef Lightship

Gray's Reef is about 20 miles (32 km) west of the Straits of Mackinac on the north-eastern side of Lake Michigan. This 8½-mile (13.8 km) danger spot for mariners was first marked in 1891 by the lightship LV 57, a wooden vessel built by the Blythe Craig Shipbuilding Company of Toledo, Ohio.

LV 57 was one of three sister ships built in 1891, the other two being LV 55 and LV 56. While Congress had appropriated $60,000 for the three ships, LV 57 cost $14,225. It was 102 ⅔ feet (31.6 m) long, had a 20-foot (6.2 m) beam and an 8 ¾-foot (2.7 m) draft, and displaced 129 tons of water. While it was self-propelled by a steam-screw, one-cylinder, non-condensing engine, it could merely go 8 knots as it was designed only to move to and from location in the spring and late fall. It had two masts, a daymark on the foremast and a riding sail on the aft mast. Its illuminating apparatus consisted of three oil-burning lens lanterns hoisted to each masthead, and it had a 6-inch (15 cm) steam fog whistle. Anchorage was provided at the location by a 5-ton sinker and 15 fathoms of two-inch chain, which had been permanently positioned and buoyed at the reef.

The vessel was designed as an experiment to save money. Instead of building and maintaining a permanent lighthouse for a much higher cost, the government estimated $4,000 a year to operate and maintain the lightship.

LV 57 was delivered to the Detroit Lighthouse Depot in September 1891. After sea trials, which found many defects, the Lighthouse Board made necessary repairs and modifications for the crew's comfort, and had the vessel moved (partly under its own power and partly under tow) by the tender *Dahlia* and anchored onto Gray's Reef on October 24. The vessel served each navigation season at the reef from 1891 to 1923. During the winter it was taken to Cheboygan, where repairs were made if necessary. During the first winter its masts were shortened.

In 1893 a foghorn was added. In 1896 its characteristic was changed (blast,1 s; blast 1 s; silence 20 s). During the 1896 season

Gray's Reef Lightship LV 57

the fog signal operated for a total of 353 hours, using 15 tons (14.2 tonnes) of coal and two cords of firewood. In 1898 its boiler was retubed, its smoke stack replaced, and its deckhouses enlarged and improved. In 1899 its hull was recalked above the water line. In 1900 it received boilers and hull repairs. When extensive rot was found in 1901, the unsound timbers and planking were replaced, the hull was recalked and painted. In 1907 its winter location was changed to Sturgeon Bay, Wisconsin. The vessel served until the end of the 1923 season, when it is assumed to have been sold.

From 1924 to 1926, *LV 103* served at Gray's Reef. Built in 1920 by the Consolidated Shipbuilding Company of Morris Heights, New York, it cost $161,074. It was designed as a steel-hulled steam screw with two masts, a steel pilothouse at the foot of the lantern mast, and its smokestack midship. It was 96 feet 5 inches (29.6 m) long, had a 24-foot (7.4 m) beam, a draft of 9½ feet (2.9 m), and a displacement of 310 tons. It had two coal-fired Scotch boilers to operate its one-compound reciprocating steam engine (175 IHP) and its 10-inch (25 cm) steam whistle. Its illuminating apparatus consisted of one 300 mm acetylene lens lantern that could be raised and lowered on the tubular lantern foremast. The aft mast had a small jigger. A submarine bell was installed in 1924.

From 1927 to 1970, *LV 103* served at other stations as well, as a relief vessel. After 50 years of service it was retired from duty on August 25, 1970 and donated to the town of Port Huron, Michigan, to become Port Huron's Marine Museum known as the *Huron*, where it is dry berthed and on display today. It is the last surviving lightship on the Great Lakes.

In 1927 and 1928, *LV 56* served at Gray's Reef. Being one of *LV 57*'s sister ships, it was built exactly the same. Having served for 37 years, *LV 56* was retired from duty at the end of the 1928 shipping season and was sold on December 20, 1928.

In 1929, *LV 103* resumed duty at Gray's Reef for one year and then *LV 99* served at the station from 1930 until 1935. *LV 99* had been built in 1920 by the Rice Brothers of Boothbay Harbor, Maine, at a cost of $97,220. It was a steel-hulled steam screw with a steel pilothouse that had a bridge. It had a tubular lantern foremast and a short jigger aft mast. It was 91 feet 8 inches (28.2 m) long, had a 22-foot (6.7 m) beam, a 10-foot-7-inch (3.3 m) draft and a displacement of 215 tons. It was powered by a 125 IHP single-cylinder engine. Its singular acetylene lantern was raised and lowered on the lantern foremast and it was outfitted with both a 10-inch (25 cm) steam whistle and a hand-operated fog bell. In 1930 it received a radio beacon and its light was electrified. In 1931 the submarine bell, which had been installed in 1923, was discontinued. With a lighthouse being built on the reef and readied for lighting at the start of the 1936 season, *LV 99* was permanently removed from Gray's Reef at the close of the 1935 shipping season. After serving at other locations it was retired from service in 1956 and sold on November 5, 1956.

Four lightships marked Gray's Reef from 1891 until 1935. While they had been cheaper to operate and maintain, a lighthouse was finally built on the reef to extend the lighting of the shipping season for the larger, stronger vessels that could break through thicker ice. Also, lighthouses remained on station during fierce storms when they were needed the most. When the Gray's Reef Lighthouse was built, the need for a lightship at this location was eliminated.

31 Green Bay Harbor Entrance Light

This lighthouse, almost identical in style to the Peshtigo Reef Lighthouse, was built in 1935 on the west side of the channel into Green Bay, Lake Michigan, 9 miles (14.6 km) north of the river mouth, to mark the approach to the harbor entrance. Resembling a tiered wedding cake, it was constructed on a circular wooden crib that in turn supported a circular concrete pier. At its center the pier housed an equipment room that had porthole windows to light the interior.

A round service room/living quarters was built on the center of the concrete as the base of the lighthouse itself. The smaller tapering tower ascending from the base had an interior spiral staircase to reach the circular lantern. Its fourth-order Fresnel lens beamed the light from a 72-foot (22 km) focal plane. The light's characteristic red color came from the curved squares of red glass that were set diagonally into its astragals. While the light was originally painted all cream except for a black lantern and dome and a rust-red band at water level, today it has a gray bottom, mostly white tower, and a black lantern and dome. Originally it was a manned lighthouse but when it was automated in 1979 the keepers were removed. Today it continues to serve as a light marking the approach to Green Bay.

In 1987 five new navigation aids were designed to further light the Green Bay harbor entrance. The Roen Salvage Company of Sturgeon Bay, Wisconsin, was contracted to build the five automated lights at a cost of $1.9 million. The contract also called for the removal of the steel structure from Long Tail Point. Crews worked around the clock to set pilings, fill them with stones, place a 35-foot (10.7 m) diameter cone on each, fill the cones with rock, inject grout around the rocks to seal them, and place a light on each one.

The five lights consisted of one for the Green Bay Harbor Entrance Channel, range lights for the Green Bay Harbor Entrance Channel, and range lights for the Green Bay Harbor Channel West.

32 Green Island Lighthouse (Green Bay)

During the 1850s increased lumbering at the mouth of the Menominee River in Green Bay, Lake Michigan, caused mariners to request that the area be lit. The Lighthouse Board in 1858 dispatched Captain George Gordon Meade of the Corps of Topographical Engineers to Green Bay to ascertain which lights should be built. Meade recommended a light on Green Island just five miles southeast of the Menominee River to mark the river's entrance. It would also warn of the shoals northwest and southeast of the island, which were on the west side of the main north-south shipping lane of Green Bay. In 1862, 17 acres (6.8 hectares) of land were purchased for the reservation from Samuel Drew. They were on the southeast portion of the 90-acre (36.4 hectare) island.

The lighthouse was finished in 1863. A short square white wooden clapboard tower rose up through the eastern end of the roof peak of the three-course, two-story yellow brick keeper's house. Its tapered corners gave it an octagonal gallery on which an octagonal iron lantern was centered to house a fourth-order Fresnel lens. The 40-foot (12.2 m) tower used oil lamps to display a fixed white light from a 55-foot (16.8 m) focal plane for a visibility of up to14 miles (22.5 km). Each story of the house had four rooms with hardwood floors, white painted wood trim and wainscotting.

The light's first keeper was Samuel Drew, the man who had sold the lighthouse site to the government, and he first lit the light on October 1, 1863. His starting salary was $400 a year. Four years later he was earning $560 a year and his wife, appointed assistant keeper in 1867, earned $400 a year. She was assistant keeper for three years. Since the Drews owned almost half of the island it was easy for them to tend the light as well as their large farm.

Repairs and improvements were made as needed. An 1864 fire at the lighthouse caused extensive damage, but no one was injured. In 1871 a fire at Great Peshtigo, Wisconsin, caused Drew to keep the light lit 24 hours a day to aid navigation through the heavy black smoke that blanketed Green Island. In spite of this, the schooner *George Newman* still ran aground on the reef at the island because the captain could not see the light through the thick smoke. Keeper Drew was able to save the crew and they stayed at the lighthouse for a week while they salvaged all they could from the wrecked schooner.

In 1876 more land was purchased so that a new crib and landing pier could be built in deeper water closer to shore for ease of unloading supplies. Lower lake levels made it necessary to move the boathouse out closer to the water in 1883 and lengthen it by 20 feet (6 m) in 1890. With lower lake levels again in 1893 the well ran dry and had to be deepened. In 1897 a brick oil-storage shed was built, the rear kitchen and woodshed were rebuilt, the piers were extended by 50 feet (15.3 m) into the lake, and a new well was sunk. The year 1902 was also busy. The ice-damaged boathouse was rebuilt, a boat winch was installed on a wooden turntable, boat track was laid, a boat car was placed on the track, cribs and piers were reinforced, some sidewalks and fencing were replaced — and Frank Drew (Samuel's son) became assistant keeper at Green Island.

In 1909 Frank was promoted to head keeper and his younger brother George became his assistant. During their tenure an incandescent oil vapor light was installed in the lens in 1917, and with its 1,700 candlepower it increased visibility to 15 miles (24.3 km). In 1928 car ferries frequently traveled all year across the bay as well as to Green Bay so a 70 candlepower flashing white winter light with an 8-mile (13 km) visibility was installed. In 1933 the light was automated using an acetylene system that used sun valves to automatically turn the light on at sunset and off at sunrise. The keepers were removed and the station was stripped of valuables, boarded-up and left to the elements and vandals.

In 1956 the Coast Guard moved the light to a 65-foot (20 m) steel skeletal tower east of the old light. It used a solar-powered 250 mm acrylic lens to display the light. By 1957 all of Green Island became privately owned by the Roen Steamship Company, but the Coast Guard kept rights to service the light. Today all that remains of the once well-kept lighthouse are partial outside brick walls.

Frank Drew was an interesting lightkeeper. During his tenure, he devised an ingenious array of mirrors to monitor the lantern beam from the keeper's house while he remained cozy inside. He was also known for his heroism in rescuing more than 30 people while he was the Green Island lighthouse keeper. Long after his death in 1931 his heroism was further acknowledged and honored when the Coast Guard introduced a new "Keeper Class" of buoy tenders named after famous keepers. The Coast Guard christened

and launched the cutter USCGC *Frank Drew* on December 5, 1998, at Marinette, Wisconsin. While sailing from Marinette to its assigned duty post at Norfolk, Virginia, the *Frank Drew* made a close pass by Green Island as a last salute to its namesake.

Known Keepers: Samuel Drew (1863–81), Joseph Harris Jr. (1881–82), Benjamin Cane (1882–82), William Wheatley (1883–85), Ole Hansen (1886–90), Soren Christianson (1890–93), Peter Dues (1893–97), William Schroeder (1897–1900), James Wachter (1900–09), Frank Drew (1909–29), Edward Cornell (1929–30), Alfred Cornell (1931–33).

33 Grosse Point Lighthouse

The shoals offshore from Grosse Point, a spit of land in present-day Evanston, Illinois, lie directly in the path of lake travel into and out of the port of Chicago. The history of the area dates back to the days when the French traded with the Indians and the French named it Grosse Point, meaning Great Point.

These treacherous shoals caused many a shipwreck but it was not until the passenger steamer *Lady Elgin*, carrying 350–400 passengers, collided with the schooner *Augusta* with the loss of nearly 300 lives that Evanston citizens were outraged enough to petition Congress for a lighthouse at the point. The project was delayed by the Civil War, but by 1870 over 12,000 ships sailed in and out of the port of Chicago annually. In 1871 Congress appropriated $35,000 for a lighthouse at Grosse Point, and land for the lighthouse was purchased from Hillis M. Hitt for $1,200. The tower, office, passageway and dwelling were finished by June 1873. While the light was first lit on Febuary 11, 1874 by the lampist for the Twelfth Lighthouse District, it was first used for navigation at the start of the 1874 shipping season.

The yellow brick tower and duplex dwelling, designed by Orlando M. Poe, both had a red roof and trim. The conical tower is 113 feet (34.7 m) high and has a focal plane of 120 feet (37 m) over the lake. The double brick walls taper from 7 feet (2.2 m) thick at the base to 32 inches (80 cm) thick at the gallery. While the base has a 22-foot (6.8 m) diameter, the gallery diameter is 13 feet (4 m). Each side of the dodecagonal cast-iron lantern has three square glass plates stacked vertically. With the back four panels being blacked out, the lantern has a 240-degree arc of illumination.

The reflectors and lighting apparatus for the lantern cost an additional $13,000, since it housed a second-order Fresnel lens, the largest used on the Great Lakes. The light source was a three-wick oil lamp and its visibility was 17 miles (27 km). Three panels of red glass mounted in a framework that rotated around the outside of the lens produced its characteristic signal — fixed white light varied by a ten-second red flash every three minutes. The movement of this frame was timed and powered by a 65-pound (29.5 kg) weight that descended 68 feet (21 m) down a drop tube every eight hours, at which time the cable was rewound into the drum by a crank at the top of the tower. This mechanism is still intact today. The light was electrified and automated in 1922.

The first keeper, Captain Boynton, a veteran of 46 years at sea and four years as keeper at the Chicago light, earned $600 a year; his assistant, Robert Seaman, earned $400.

The keeper first opened the light to visitors in April 1874. Over the years they would have seen many changes. In 1878, two cribs were provided for the protection of the shoreline at a cost of $5,000. In 1881 duplicate steam sirens were installed in newly built buildings on the bluff. The next year, 10-inch (25 cm) whistles were substituted for the sirens. In 1901 the fog signal apparatus was provided with 9-foot (2.8 m) sound deflectors for each building. Decreasing lake traffic and increasing shipboard navigation technology led to the steam fog signals being discontinued in 1932.

Grosse Point Lighthouse

The light station was decommissioned by the U.S. Lighthouse Service in 1935, and in 1937 the federal government deeded the property to the City of Evanston, which then leased the area to the Northeast Park District to maintain for year round use. The district has kept the light in operation as an aid to small craft navigation.

Restoration of the lighthouse began in its centennial year, 1973, when several local organizations made significant efforts to preserve it. In 1975 the award-winning film *Lighthouse* focused attention on this historic site and it was soon placed on the state and national registers of historic sites.

This Grosse Point site has evolved into a unique complex of cultural and recreational facilities that include the Evanston Art Center in a mansion just north of the lighthouse, and a public beach managed by the Parks and Recreation Department of the City of Evanston. A portion of the beach east of the lighthouse has been developed by the Evanston Environmental Association as an example of lake shore dunes, and there is a maritime and nature center in the old fog signal buildings and its surrounding property. With so much local support and intergroup cooperation, it is no surprise that this restoration project has been a success.

Known Keepers: Charles Boynton (1874–1880), George Hale (1880-1882), Joseph Harris Jr. (1882–1885), James Rich (1885–1887), Anthony Hagan (1887–1888), Edwin Moore (1888–1924), Oscar Knudsen (1924–1930), John Tucker (1930-1934).

34 Holland Harbor South Pierhead Light

After Duluth settlers put down roots in the Black Lake (Lake Macatawa) area, their leader, Reverend A.C. Van Raalte, lobbied Congress for harbor improvements at the mouth of the Black River. When appropriations were not forthcoming, the work was begun with private funding. The government finally took over harbor improvements in 1867, built a pair of protective piers at the river mouth and in 1870 appropriated $4,000 to build a pierhead light at the end of the south pier to mark entry to the harbor.

This simple light was a 27-foot (8.3 m) white pyramidal beacon with its upper portion enclosed in clapboarding and its lower structure left open so that waves could wash through. The enclosed section acted both as a service room and as a shelter for the keeper during inclement weather. The tower supported a square gallery with a polygonal lantern. The lantern housed a fixed red fifth-order Fresnel lens that had a 32-foot (9.8 m) focal plane and a visibility of 11½ miles (18.6 km). The first keeper, Melgert van Regenmorter, was hired December 3, 1870, for $540 a year, and soon lit the light. He had to find his own accommodations as difficulties arose in getting clear title to the property chosen for building the keeper's house. The dwelling was finally built sometime between 1873 and 1880.

Regenmorter had to carry the lamp oil along the pier from the shore. In foggy weather he used an 18-inch (45 cm) fish-horn to announce the lighthouse's location to incoming vessels. In 1874 a 550-foot (168 m) elevated catwalk was built between the light and the shore. In 1880 it was extended another 260 feet (80 m), and five years later, 600 feet (183 m) of rotted wood had to be replaced.

With only 200 feet (60 m) between the north and south pier, accidents were frequent. In 1887 a vessel seeking harbor refuge smashed into the light's service room. While the maintenance crew was making repairs, they also installed a tin hood above the lantern lens to contain heat. In 1890 a tubular lantern was placed on a 20-foot (6 m) post at the outer end of the south pier to act as a front range light to the pier light, making it easier for vessels to line up harbor entry. In September 1891 this post was destroyed by the scow *Breakwater* when it was entering the harbor, necessitating a temporary light until work crews could arrive. In 1892 the schooner *R. Kanters* damaged the catwalk with her bowsprit while leaving the harbor.

By the twentieth century the nearby Black Lake area had become a favorite vacation spot for residents of Chicago and Milwaukee. In 1900 over 1,095 vessels used the harbor. To accommodate this increased traffic, the Lighthouse Board requested $6,000 for a fog signal but Congress did not comply. In 1901 a pulley system was installed to enable the keeper to more effectively tend the beacon light on the post. Using a pulley and a cable, the keeper hauled the light into the service room of the lighthouse, tended it, and then returned it to its spot on the post by the same means.

In 1902 materials arrived to build a steel tower to replace the deteriorating wooden one. Four concrete piers were set on the top of the old pier to provide a level foundation for the tower, which was bolted to them. Standing 45 feet (13.8 m) high, it also had an open frame construction so that storm waves could pass freely under it. Above this, two levels were enclosed with riveted iron plates. Round porthole windows from the watchroom below the lantern gave the keeper an unimpeded view of the lake. The old fixed red fifth-order Fresnel lens was moved into the new polygonal lantern. Using a 150 candlepower lamp as its illuminant, it was visible for 10 miles (16.2 km). The front range light was discontinued at this time.

Holland Harbor South Pierhead Light

The wooden catwalk was replaced with iron in two equal instalments in 1903 and 1904. During a severe December storm in 1904 the outer crib beneath the steel light was pushed off center and was noticeably leaning. To prevent the light from toppling into the lake it was removed and shipped to the St. Joseph Lighthouse Depot for repairs. Meanwhile, a new wooden foundation pier was built to support the repaired tower when it was returned and again bolted into position.

In November 1905 a fixed red lantern was put on a 60-foot (18.3 m) pole on the pier about 400 feet (123 m) behind the pier light to serve as a rear range light. In 1906 this pole light was replaced by a 61-foot (18.6 m) steel skeletal tower, 795 feet (242 m) behind the pier light, which had now become the front range light. The fixed red light from the pole was moved to the skeletal tower.

Finally, after six years of repeated requests, Congress appropriated $6,000 for a fog signal in 1906. To save costs, the plans were the same as those used at Waukegan and Kewaunee. The fog signal station was built of riveted iron sheets over timber framework about 10 feet (3 m) behind the front range light, and completed by October 1907. Its steam boilers and 10-inch (25 cm) steam whistles, which came from the discontinued station at Calumet, were installed in the lower level. Living quarters for the assistant keepers made up the second level, while the head keeper continued to live onshore.

An arched passageway connected the fog signal building to the front range light, which was upgraded to a fixed red fourth-order Fresnel lens at this time, increasing its visibility to 14 miles (22.5 km). To handle the increased workload of operating the fog signal, two assistant keepers were hired. Both the steel tower and the fog signal building were painted yellow with a deep maroon base as their daymark.

The station was automated in 1932 and electrified in 1934. The use of a 5,000 candlepower incandescent electric bulb increased its visibility to about 15 miles (24 km). An air-operated whistle driven by an electric motor compressor replaced the steam whistles. In 1936, with the light now turning on automatically and the foghorn being activated by remote control, the old lantern was moved onto a new two-level tower on top of the fog signal building between the gable windows, and the old steel tower in front of the fog signal building was removed. In 1956 the station acquired its distinctive red color. This change took place to meet requirements that aids to navigation on the right side of any harbor entrance should be red ("Red Right Return"). From this it gained its nickname "Big Red" and its very distinctive daymark.

More changes took place with advancing technology. In the 1960s the Fresnel lens was removed and replaced with a 250 mm Tidelands Signal acrylic optic. In 1970 the lighthouse was automated and the light and foghorn were moved to the north outer breakwater. In 1971 the old fog signal building was declared surplus, causing concerned citizens to form the Holland Harbor Lighthouse Historical Committee in 1974 with the goal of saving the lighthouse. In 1987 the Coast Guard transferred ownership to this committee, which continued to raise money, mostly from endowment funds, to maintain the lighthouse.

Today the Coast Guard inspects the facility twice a year. While the fog signal has been discontinued, a light was put back into the old pier light. It has a 20-mile (32.4 km) visibility and is maintained by the Coast Guard. The original fourth-order Fresnel lens was donated to the city of Holland and is on display in their museum.

Known Keepers: Melgert Van Regenmorter (1870–1907), Charles Bavry (1907–10), George Cornell (1910), Edward Mallette (1910–11), Joseph Boshka (1911–40), Captain William Robinson (1940).

Indiana Harbor Light, circa 1940's United Stataes Coast Guard

35 Indiana Old Harbor Light

Indiana Harbor is a man-made harbor at East Chicago. Initially, private individuals built two piers into Lake Michigan and dredged the area between them for larger vessels to use. In 1910 the federal government took over the harbor improvements and constructed two rubble breakwaters to protect the harbor entrance. In 1923 the government built a lighthouse at the inner base of the short east breakwater. It was a boxy rectangular structure on a substantial concrete crib that housed storage areas and space for machinery. The steel-framed lighthouse, made of reinforced concrete and red brick walls, sat on the crib, leaving little space around it. Its third level, much smaller but still rectangular, supported a circular lantern with diagonal astragals. An elevated steel catwalk connected the lighthouse to shore. When a new light went into service at the outer end of the newly extended east breakwater in 1935, this old light was given a less intense light. Sometime after 1969 both of these lights were automated. By 1985 the old light had been removed, leaving just the concrete crib.

36 Indiana Harbor East Breakwater Light

With the expansion of the waterfront at Indiana Harbor, the east breakwater was extended farther into the lake, making the old harbor light too far inland to properly mark the harbor entrance. A new light was built in 1935 at the outer end of the east breakwater. The tower, made of riveted steel sheets, swooped up graciously from a square bottom to form a more slender upper portion. Its sides were marked with porthole windows to provide interior light. The tower stands on an arched concrete base that rests on a reinforced stone crib. It has no lantern today, but its modern beacon shines from a 78-foot (24 m) focal plane. The tower was connected to the shore by a long steel catwalk for the keeper's safety. The keeper resided in the old harbor lighthouse keeper's residence until the light was automated in 1969.

Other lights also have steel towers similar to this one. They are located at Port Washington (Lake Michigan), Conneaut (Lake Erie), Huron Harbor (Lake Erie), and Gravelly Shoal (Lake Huron).

Indiana Harbor East Breakwater Light

Kalamazoo River Light

37 Kalamazoo River Light

In 1837 Congress appropriated $5,000 to build a lighthouse at the mouth of the Kalamazoo River, Lake Michigan, to mark the entrance to the river. A plot of land to the north of the river mouth was purchased from Horace M. Comstock for $250. When the contract for the lighthouse's construction was awarded, it was stipulated that the lighthouse was to be finished by October 15, 1838. However, when Lt. James T. Homans did a site inspection in September 1838, the only sign of progress was a pile of stones. A special agent was assigned to superintend the construction, and the lighthouse was completed in 1839.

The lighthouse was built 75 feet (23 m) from the lake and 14 feet (4.3 m) above the lake level. Its 30-foot (9 m) tower was made of rubble stone, and was topped with a birdcage-style lantern that used eleven Argand lamps and 14-inch (35 cm) reflectors. In 1856 the lantern was upgraded and received a fixed white sixth-order Fresnel lens.

When timber at the river mouth was cut down, blowing sand became a problem and the river's entrance continually sanded over. In 1850 a timber protection was built to help prevent sand from eroding around the tower base and undermining its foundation. However, the problem continued and federal funds were requested in February 1858. But action was too slow in coming, and the lighthouse toppled from its foundation later that same year.

The lighthouse was rebuilt 150 feet (46 m) to the northeast of the old tower on a much stronger base. Cast-iron pipe pilings 8 inches (20 cm) in diameter were driven into the sand and filled with concrete and stone, and a foundation of square timbers was bolted to these pilings. Also, to avoid the erosion problems of the first light, limestone slabs brought by barge from Alpena were placed along the dune on which the lighthouse was built. The Lighthouse Board used the same plans they had previously used at Cheboygan. The structure was a 2 1/2-story clapboard keeper's house topped with a square tower that rose 15 feet (4.6 m) up out of its south peak. The tower had an octagonal cast-iron lantern that housed a new fifth-order Fresnel lens to shine from a 45-foot (13.7 m) focal plane. The building was painted white with black trim, which included shutters and the lantern. The station was finished with a well and a barn to house the keeper's horse, and the light was lit in 1859.

Many changes took place in the coming years. In 1876 the light was moved to the south pier as the lighthouse was too far away to clearly mark the river entrance. The Fresnel lens was also moved from the old light to the pierhead light, but the keeper still lived in the old keeper's house and had to row across the river to tend it. The new pierhead light was a 27-foot (8.3 m) white wooden skeletal structure. With its 34-foot (10.4 m) focal plane, it had a visibility of 11.5 miles (18.6 km). In 1883 a small cellar was dug beneath the keeper's house as well as an underground cistern to store rainwater diverted by downspouts attached to the gutter for household use. In 1885 the sand dune was faced with logs to prevent erosion. Iron boat davits were installed at the pierhead light in 1888 to help the keeper lift his boat out of the water.

In 1892 the steamer *Charles McVea* ran bow first straight into the pierhead light damaging it irreparably, so the lens was returned to the shore light and relit there on August 16. In 1894 a conduit light system was built on the south pier. It displayed a fixed red lens lantern and was first lit on May 23, 1894. The shore light continued to serve as a coastal light.

The turn of the century was an active period at the station. The keeper's house was given a cover of cedar shingles, a boathouse and landing pier were built at the riverbank, and a wooden walkway was built from the boat landing to the keeper's dwelling. In 1900 the malfunctioning conduit light system was removed and its light was exhibited from a post near the end of the south pier. In 1904 a new entrance to the river was built less than a mile north of its natural mouth to eliminate a lot of twisting river and minimize dredging. When it was completed in 1906, a simple post lamp was placed at the outer end of its south pier. The keeper of the Kalamazoo light also kept this light. Although the Kalamazoo River light was too far away to mark the new entrance to the river, it was continued as a coastal light and, to help differentiate between the two lights, the new pierhead light was officially named the Saugatuck Harbor South Pierhead Light.

In 1909 the south entrance pier received a concrete foundation on which a square cast-iron base and tower (both painted red) were placed. The base housed acetylene storage tanks to supply fuel to the light atop the 26-foot (8 m) tower. The light was designed to operate for months, as it used an automated sun valve to turn it on and off. Its 300 mm lens exhibited a flashing red light of 35 candlepower for a 7-mile (11.3 km) visibility. The light's characteristic was a single flash every three seconds. When this light was lit, the old Kalamazoo River light on shore was deemed obsolete and was extinguished in October 1914. Its lantern was removed by the Lighthouse Service, and the buildings were leased to Frederick F. Fursman, the director of the Oxbow Summer School of the Arts, for $10 a month.

In 1936 the old station was put up for sale by closed mail bid. Since Arthur F. Deam, an architect and friend of Fursman, put in the only bid, he acquired it for use as a summer cottage and undertook extensive restoration. However, the lighthouse was completely razed by a tornado that ran through the area in April 1956. Undaunted, Deam salvaged bits and pieces from the ruins and used his architectural skills to design a lighthouse-style summer family home that incorporated the salvage from the 1859 lighthouse.

Known Keepers: Stephen Nichols (1839–44), William Scoville (1844–45), William Carley (1845–49), Cephas Field (1849–53), Timothy Coates (1853–60), Stephen Nichols (1860–61), Samuel Underwood (1861–78), George Baker (1878–1909), George Sheridan (1909–14).

38 Kenosha (Southport) Lighthouse

Shortly after settling in Pine Creek, Lake Michigan, in 1835, its residents made their own light to guide vessels into the harbor and around shifting sand bars. It was simply a 10-foot (3 m) high stump from a felled mature oak tree. A platform of rocks was placed on it for fireproofing, and volunteers lit a fire on it every night during the navigation season. In 1837 Pike Creek became Southport because it was the southernmost port in Wisconsin. Then in 1850 it became Kenosha.

In 1840 a better lighting system was set up. It was a 24-foot (7.4 m) four-legged tower topped with a 3-foot (0.9 m) square sash lantern (a box a with window on one side). A private citizen paid its $60 cost, but volunteers continued to keep the light lit.

Congress first approved the building of a government lighthouse at Southport on Lake Michigan in 1838. In 1844 and again in 1847 it appropriated $4,000 to build the lighthouse. In 1847 land was finally purchased on the south side of Simmons Island for the first government lighthouse, which marked the north side of the entrance into the harbor. It was a rubble-stone conical tower that used five Argand lamps and 14-inch (25 cm) reflectors, which were replaced in 1857 by a fifth-order Fresnel lens. Structural defects led to its being torn down in 1858 and replaced with a second conical tower, which still used the fifth-order Fresnel lens. It too was poorly built and in turn had to be replaced in 1866.

The third tower was a gently tapering 55-foot (16.8 m) conical tower built of Milwaukee yellow brick and placed on a stone foundation. Three ascending windows provided interior light. The top of the tower flared out slightly, and bricks were diagonally set to form an ornamental ring and support the gallery. Its decagonal lantern housed a new larger fourth-order Fresnel lens to increase its visibility. It originally exhibited a fixed white light varied by a single flash, but this characteristic was later changed to an isophase flash (same length of light and darkness).

During the twentieth century, changes occurred at the station. In 1903 the Lighthouse Board ordered the light to be lit year round due to the mild winters on Lake Michigan's west coast. In 1906 the light was deactivated and replaced by a new pierhead light but the keeper continued to live in the old house to service the new light. The lighting apparatus and lens were moved from the old tower to the new north pierhead light. In 1913 the lantern was removed from the old, unused tower for service elsewhere,

Kenosha (Southport) Lighthouse

and a storm warning tower was secured on top of it to notify passing mariners of pending weather conditions. This system was used until 1953.

The keeper's house, a separate two-story building, also of yellow brick, had been finished in 1867. At some time a red brick addition was added to the north side of the house to form an L-shaped structure. Also, a second level addition was added to the east side of the house. This addition was made in yellow brick interrupted by a row of red brick every eight rows.

During the 1950s, public reaction scuttled the government's plans to demolish the station. In 1955 the U.S. government provided quit claim of the buildings and property to the City of Kenosha, and the Kenosha County Historical Society, with aid from the Wisconsin State Historical Society, started lighthouse restoration. In 1994 they had a replica gallery and decagonal lantern built and placed on the tower, and a 300 mm plastic lens was installed, giving the light a focal plane of 74 feet (22.8 m). In 1996 the old tower was ceremonially relit as part of the city's Fourth of July celebrations. Today the light is only lit for special occasions, as it is not an active aid to navigation. While the Historical Society hopes to convert the keeper's house into a museum one day, the house is presently rented to raise money for renovations.

Known Keepers: Jeremiah Jordan (1848–49), Charles O'Neal (1849–53), John Duffy (1853–60), Jeremiah Jordan (1860), Edward Morris (1860–61), Otis Colwell (1861), Charles O'Neal (1861–65), Joseph Merrill (1865–71), Mrs. Lorinda Merrill (1871–72), Louis De Diermer (1872–1906).

39 Kenosha Breakwater Light

In 1899–1900 the Corps of Army Engineers built a detached breakwater at the outer entrance to the channel into Kenosha Harbor on Lake Michigan to deter the perennial buildup of shifting sand at the mouth of the channel. In 1900 it was decided to build a light on the southeast end of this breakwater to serve as a front range light for the north pierhead beacon. Until government funds were available to build a permanent structure, a temporary fixed red lens lantern was hung from an iron pole. It was protected from the elements by a V-shaped structure built of square timbers. The light was first lit on October 26, 1900.

Materials for the permanent breakwater light arrived in early 1906. After the crew completed the new north pierhead light, they began work on the breakwater light. Its style resembled an inverted funnel with the top of the tower as a thin octagonal form and the bottom an octagonal pyramid to create room in its base for a service room. The 35-foot (10.7 m) tower was covered in corrugated iron. The lantern was integrated into the thinner octagonal column at the top and was capped with a copper dome supported by sixteen corbels. From a 37-foot (11.3 m) focal plane, the 20 candlepower fixed red lens lantern had a 6-mile (9.7 km) visibility. Four other lights built around this same time used similar plans — Petoskey, Racine, Waukegan and Sheboygan.

In July 1912 the breakwater light was converted to use acetylene as its illuminant and its characteristic was changed from a fixed red to flashing white every three seconds. In 1921 the light was removed from the breakwater and replaced with a 37-foot (11.3 m) red skeletal steel tower. During the 1960s the skeletal tower was replaced by a D9 cylindrical one.

Kenosha North Pierhead Light

40 Kenosha North Pierhead Light

As Kenosha developed as a port on Lake Michigan, its piers were frequently elongated and its entrance dredged of sand. With the first elongation in 1856 a timber-framed pierhead beacon 12-foot (3.7 m) tall was placed on the north pier to mark the channel entrance into the harbor. It housed a sixth-order Fresnel lens that had a 9-mile (14.6 m) visibility from a 16-foot (4.9 m) focal plane. The light was washed away in a severe storm in 1860 and, with the government embroiled in Civil War, a temporary light consisting of a light hung from a pole on the pier was used until replacement funds were available.

In 1865 the Army Corps of Engineers refurbished the wooden piers, dredged the harbor to 16 feet (4.9 m) and finally established a new north pierhead light in 1867. It was a 30-foot (9 m) timber-framed pyramidal beacon that had an enclosed watchroom below the lantern. It used a sixth-order Fresnel lens to display a fixed red light from a 39-foot (12 m) focal plane for a visibility of 12 miles (19.4 km). A wooden catwalk connected it to shore for the keepers' use during intemperate weather.

Each time the pier was extended further into the lake, the pierhead light was moved to its new outer end and the catwalk was lengthened. In 1870 the pier was 1,750 feet (535 m) long with 800 feet (245 m) extending beyond the shoreline. In 1875 it was extended by 320 feet (98 m); in 1880 by 105 feet (32 m); in 1881 by 100 feet (30 m); and in both 1883 and 1884 by 150 feet (45 m). During a November storm in 1891 the schooner *Evelyn* ran into the pierhead light, damaging its watchroom and causing all its contents to be washed out to sea. In 1893 a lens lantern was placed on a post 104 feet (32 m) in front of the pierhead light to serve as its front range light to facilitate entrance to the harbor.

In 1899 the entrance channel was widened, the channel was dredged to 21 feet (6.5 m) and an angled breakwater started in efforts to stem sand deposition. With the completion of the breakwater in 1900, a light was placed on its southeast end to become a front range light to the north pierhead beacon, to which a fog signal was added in 1901. The blower siren powered by two diesel engines was placed in the lower enclosed part of the timber light tower. The wooden catwalk was also replaced with a cast-iron one.

In 1906 work began on a new north pierhead light. The tower was constructed of a series of incrementally smaller concentric cast-iron rings that were riveted together, tapering the tower slightly as they rose. The lantern used the fourth-order Fresnel lens and lighting apparatus from the main light on Simmons Island, which was deactivated at this time. A wood-framed rectangular pyramidal fog signal building was built in front of the iron tower and connected to it by a covered passageway. The tower was painted white and given a new flashing white characteristic. In 1913 its lamp was upgraded to an incandescent oil vapor one. In 1917 it was painted red instead of white, and its light reverted to red but with a new characteristic (flash 2.5 s; eclipse 12.5 s). In 1925 it was electrified and was given an air diaphone fog signal powered by an Ingersoll-Rand air compressor.

Today the fog signal and the catwalk are long gone but the pierhead light continues as an active aid to navigation, using a 250 mm Tidelands Signal optic instead of its Fresnel lens.

Known Keepers: Louis De Diemer (1906–07), Charles Young (1908–32), Edward Knuden (1932–40).

Kevich Lighthouse

41 Kevich Lighthouse

The Kevich light sits on a 120-foot (37 m) bluff above Lake Michigan outside of Grafton, Wisconsin, between Milwaukee and Port Washington, on the site of the nineteenth-century Port Ulao. While the government set aside land to build a lighthouse here, it was never built. It was once a thriving port where lake steamers stopped to load wood for fuel from the wooden pier that extended 1000 feet (308 m) out into the lake, but it had no harbor to offer protection from storms. As the use of steamers and the supply of wood declined, the port became little used.

This light was privately built in 1981 by Yugoslavian immigrants Brana and Neva Kevich. Both the 45-foot (13.7 m) conical tower and the attached house are made of plastered and painted stone and masonry. The tower gallery supports an octagonal lantern topped by a dome and ventilator stack. Two small arched windows provide interior light.

Beside the tower entry door is a plaque that reads: "Kevich Light United States Coast Guard Light List No 19616." The light was certified in 1990 as a Coast Guard Class II Private Aid to Navigation. Its light source consists of 1,000-watt and 400-watt metal halide bulbs, with an eight-second rotating shield to create the light's distinctive characteristic (flash 4 s; eclipse 4 s). The bulbs are controlled automatically by photoelectric cells.

Kevich Light is notable for a few reasons. It is the second highest on Lake Michigan, it is one of few lights privately owned and operated, and it was built in the late twentieth century when most lighthouses were being or had been demanned or abandoned.

42 Kewaunee Pierhead Lighthouse

In 1838 Congress approved a lighthouse at the Kewaunee River on Lake Michigan but it was not built until much later. In the mid-1800s rumors of a gold strike attracted a flood of immigrants to the area. Kewauneee hoped to rival Chicago as a port city and made harbor improvements to accommodate larger vessels.

In 1891 range lights were installed on the new pier, and a catwalk made them accessible during stormy weather. The lights were equipped with fifth-order Fresnel lenses that had an approximate 15-mile (24 km) visibility from their octagonal lanterns.

In response to the frequent fogs in the area, a diaphone fog signal horn was added to the front range light in 1909. To house the steam power plant that operated the foghorn, a large fog signal building was built on the pier behind the front range light. This structure also housed the keepers when their constant presence was needed during long periods of inclement weather. It was attached to the front range light by an elevated closed-in walkway.

In 1931 the station was renovated. The front range light was removed and replaced by a new steel tower built upward from the roof of the fog signal building. The old lantern and the Fresnel lens from the old tower were moved to the new one, which provided a 45-foot (13.7 m) focal plane. At some point after this the catwalk and the rear range light were also removed.

The light is still active today. While it continues to use its Fresnel lens to display its fixed white light, the lens is illuminated with electricity and uses an automated electric four-bulb changer. The fog signal is also still active, but not at Kewaunee. At an unknown date the fog signal was removed for shipment to the Smithsonian Institution, but Duluth's TOOT organization learned of these plans and managed to convince authorities to ship it to Duluth instead. They did. After being rebuilt by Jeff Laser, a fog signal expert, it was placed in Duluth's South Breakwater Light, where it is still functional today.

Known Keepers: Orrin Warner Jr. (1890–92), Charles Peterson (1892–1901), Eugene Kimball (1901–13), Orland Lynd (1913–37), Cecil Scofield (1937–40).

Kewaunee Pierhead Lighthouse

43 Lansing Shoal Lighthouse

Lansing Shoal is located in northern Lake Michigan about 5 miles (8 km) north of Squaw Island, 40 miles (64.8 km) west of the Straits of Mackinac, and 17 miles (27.5 km) south of Seul Choix Point. This hazardous shoal far out in the lake was first marked with a gas buoy and then a lightship to avoid the expense of a permanent lighthouse. As ships became larger and the Davis and Sabin locks were completed in 1919 to accommodate large vessels that could break through thicker ice, the navigation season was extended. However the Lansing Shoal Lightship, a much smaller vessel, had to wait until most of the ice was gone before it could be placed in the spring and had to leave its post before it became trapped in ice at the end of the season. The fact that vessels had to navigate the start and end of each navigation season without the benefit of a light to mark Lansing Shoal prompted Congress to finally give approval in 1926 for a lighthouse on the shoal.

Building the lighthouse was quite an undertaking. In 1927 the chosen site was leveled with the addition of 4 feet (1.2 m) of stone for the foundation. Four very large concrete caissons were placed on the stone leaving a 34-foot (10.5 m) square opening in their center. They were connected at the bottom with steel rods that were then covered with 2 feet (0.6 m) of concrete. The caissons and the center square were filled with stone and capped with 7-foot (2.2 m) thick slabs of steel-reinforced concrete. The basement crib was built on top of the foundation. It had twenty-seven 24-inch (60 cm) porthole windows and was topped with a steel reinforced ceiling that became the deck of the concrete pier.

Unlike the case with other lighthouses, the crib contained the keeper's living quarters as well as engine space. A 37-foot (11.4 m) square tower base of reinforced concrete was placed in the center of the pier. Its large doors allowed the station's boat to be stored inside, as well as the equipment to operate the light and fog signal. The rest of the tower consisted of three smaller cubes that sat on the base, ranging in size from 13 feet (4 m) square at the bottom to 11 feet (3.4 m) at the top. The station's Type F diaphone foghorn was in the top of the tower just below the lantern. The 59-foot (18 m) tower (including its base) was topped with a circular lantern with curved panes set diagonally into metal astragals. It housed a third-order Fresnel lens and a 500-watt incandescent electric lamp to obtain a 16-mile (25.9 km) visibility from a 69-foot (21.2 m) focal plane. It was first lit on October 6, 1928. The following year the interior was finished and the radio beacon added to complete the station for a total cost of $262,000.

The station was built to last. It was given a severe beating during the Armistice Day Storm of 1940, but the light was only minimally out and damage was considered manageable. The Lansing Shoal keeper's logbooks for that day make interesting reading:

"November 11 — Armistice Day. Barometer has been going down all day 4:10 p.m. 28.10. Tightened all portholes and put extra fastening on the south door of the engine room. 6 p.m. both glasses in the storeroom portholes broke out. 6:30 p.m. south door tore away, filling engine with water and put out fire in heating boiler. Pulled all switches on electric and equipment everything out of commission. Called U.S. Coast Guard and told them to report station out of operation. I believe it is now blowing 80 miles (130 km) and cold with some snow. November 12 – 12 midnight, it is blowing just as hard, very steady, about 60 miles (97 km) and getting colder. Crib is icing, ice all over. 8 a.m. What a night we had. This morning everything is washing around in the engine room, and every sea washes across the engine room. The south door is over in the north entrance as near as we dare go is the landing on the stairs and it is awful to see. Every sea coming in and ripping something away and stirring it up with the rest of the wreck.

Lansing Shoal Lighthouse

12 noon. Not blowing as hard as it was but plenty hard, and the wind seems to shift a little from the west, and a heavy sea rolling from SW ... 9:30 p.m. Got the fire going but got all wet and am cold..." While the light was out of commission, the keepers had worked non-stop to get it relit. It took weeks to clean up the rest of the damage while continuing to operate the station.

The Armistice Day Storm, which raged for three days, claimed the lives of 70 sailors, and 13 vessels were either lost or stranded. Captain Bagantz of the *George W. Perkins*, which passed by the Lansing Shoal light during the storm, said it was the worst he had ever encountered, with 50-foot (15.3 m) seas. His vessel had no radar, visibility was poor, the winds were gusting from 100 to 125 mph (160 to 200 kph), and the radio told of other vessels down. He tried to find refuge. He had heard that the lights at both Lansing Shoal and Gray's Reef were out. He spotted a weak light close to Lansing Shoal, barely visible in the gray blur of the snow. Finally, when Baganz realized the light *was* the shoal lighthouse, he called a "hard right." Although only traveling about 12 mph (19 kph) he barely missed hitting the light with the ship's steering pole. When he looked back he saw the stern up in the sky being pushed upward while the bow was in a trough. He thought the stern was about to land right on the lighthouse. Instead, the backwash, which hit the lighthouse, bounced back, hit the ship's stern, and miraculously pushed the vessel safely away from the lighthouse. He then made refuge at Garden Island. That winter the *George W. Perkins* had to have its 175,000 loose or popped rivets re-secured. While Captain Baganz had feared for his life, the Lansing Shoal keepers had been blithely unaware of that near miss; the logbooks mention no vessel sighting.

Very few changes occurred at this light. It was automated in 1976 and the windows, portholes and doors were cemented in, leaving only one access door. In 1985 the Fresnel lens was removed and replaced with a 190 mm solar-powered plastic optic. The Coast Guard made some structural repairs in 1992. In 1995 the *Indiana Harbor*, a 1,000-foot (305 m) freighter, crashed into the lighthouse crib. Incredibly, neither the lighthouse nor the ship was badly damaged. Today the light still shines and is maintained by the U.S. Coast Guard. Its third-order Fresnel lens is on display at the Michigan Historical Museum in Lansing, Michigan.

Known Keepers: Theodore Grosskopf (1933–39), William Keller (1939–47).

Lansing Shoal Lightship LV 55, circa 1906

Lansing Shoal Lightship LV 55, after 1914

44 Lansing Shoal Lightship

Lansing Shoal, a dangerous area for mariners, was far out in Lake Michigan and was not discovered until larger vessels began traveling farther away from shore. It was first lit by LV 55 in 1901.

LV 55 was built in 1891 by the Blythe Craig Shipbuilding Company of Toledo, Ohio, for $14,225. It was 102 feet 8 inches (31.6 m) long, had a 20-foot (6.2 m) beam, and an 8-foot 9-inch (2.7 m) draft, and it displaced 129 tons of water. This wooden lightship had a foremast to hold the illuminating apparatus and its daymark, an aft mast to hold a riding sail, and a smokestack on the deckhouse amid ship. Its illuminating apparatus consisted of three oil-burning lens lanterns. For fog it had a hand-operated fog bell and a 6-inch (15 cm) steam fog whistle. It was propelled by a single cylinder, non-condensing steam screw engine of 100 IHP for a maximum speed of 8 knots. To save costly anchoring equipment, its mooring consisted of a 5-ton sinker and 15 fathoms of 2-inch (5 cm) chain, which were positioned permanently and buoyed on location. The government estimated $4,000 a year for the lightship's maintenance and operating costs. Sister ships to this vessel were *LV 56* and *LV 57*.

After Simmons Reef, where it had served from 1891 to 1900, was discontinued, *LV 55* was moved to mark Lansing Shoal from 1901 to 1920. The vessel wintered over at Cheboygan except for 1906 when it went to Sturgeon Bay. During the 1901 winter, extensive rot was discovered in its frame and planking, so all unsound wood, including one mast, was replaced and the hull was recalked and painted. In 1906 it was equipped with a submarine bell signal. It served at Lansing Shoal uneventfully until September 15, 1920, when it was retired from lightship service. It was sold on February 15, 1922 for $840.

After *LV 55*, the station was marked by *LV 98*. This larger lightship was 101 feet (31 m) long and 23.5 feet (7.2 m) wide, had an 11-foot (3.4 m) draft and a displacement of 195 tons of water. It

was built in 1915 by the Racine-Truscott-Shell Lake Boat Co. in Muskegon, Michigan, at a cost of $87,025. It had a steel whaleback hull design and its 4-foot (1.2 m) propeller, powered by a four-cylinder Mietz and Weiss kerosene engine of 100 IHP, could reach a speed of 6 knots. The vessel had one large diameter tubular lantern mast at midship, which used a revolving parabolic reflector to produce a 1,000 candlepower flash from a 42-foot (12.9 m) focal plane. It had two fog signals, a hand-operated fog bell, and a 6-inch (15 cm) air fog siren that was driven by two kerosene-powered three-cylinder compressors.

LV 98 underwent little change. In 1916 a submarine bell signal was added, and in 1927 it was equipped with a radio beacon. On July 8 and August 4, 1928 it was struck by a passing steamer in heavy fog but it was not seriously damaged. On October 6, 1928, it was removed from the shoal when the newly built lighthouse on Lansing Shoal was lit. *LV 98* went on to serve at other stations until it was retired on January 15, 1955, and sold later that year.

45 Little Fort Lighthouse

Congress appropriated $3,000 in April 1844 for a lighthouse at Little Fort (now Waukegan), Lake Michigan, 35 miles (57 km) north of Chicago. Built in 1849 on a southern bluff near the mouth of the Waukegan Stream it was a small, two-room brick keeper's house with a round brick tower rising from its roof. District superintendent William Snowhook found the brick of the tower to be decaying so badly just three years after it was built that he recommended the building of a pierhead light and the discontinuance of this shore light.

In 1854 Congress made two appropriations of money for Waukegan. One was $1,000 for a beacon-light on the pierhead, and the other was $6,000 for a light on the new breakwater (then being built) upon its completion. However, this did not take place for many years.

In the meantime a new 1½-story clapboard keeper's house with a new square wooden tower emerging from its roof top was built to the north of the old lighthouse. The new lantern housed a fifth-order lens. The old lighthouse was demolished when this one went into service. This new lighthouse served until the end of the 1898 shipping season; and another light was built to replace it in 1899. When the newest light was lit, the old tower was removed and the property was sold to the City of Waukegan.

Known Keepers: Truman Hibbard (1849–53), Sydney Booth (1853–54), William Ladd (1854), Henry Dorsett (1854–55), Edward Dennis (1855–59), Lyman Wilson (1859–61), H. Biddlecom (1861–65), John Williams (1856–92), George Larson (1892–97), Peter Dues (1897–98).

(also known as First Waukegan Light — see Waukegan Harbor Light)

Lansing Shoal Lightship LV 55 and Grays Reef

Little Sable Lighthouse

46 Little Sable Lighthouse

After the grounding of the schooner *Pride* on Little Sable Point, Lake Michigan, in 1871, mariners' appeals for a lighthouse to light this area intensified. In 1872 Congress accordingly appropriated $35,000 to purchase 39 acres (15.8 hectares) and construct the station. It was to be built on the plans of Orlando M. Poe, the Major of Engineers of the Eleventh Lighthouse District. Due to the isolation of the area, the crew first built a lakeside dock to unload materials and then temporary housing for the work crew.

According to the lighthouse specifications, 109 pilings, each 1 foot (30 cm) in diameter, were pile-driven 9 feet (2.8 m) into the sand to form a solid bottom on which 12 feet (3.7 m) of cut stone was laid to form a solid base for the 107-foot (32.7 m) tower. The conical tower's red brick walls were 5 feet (1.5 m) thick at the bottom and tapered to 2 feet (0.6 m) thick at the top. At this point the work had to stop for the winter. It was resumed in the spring of 1874 with the addition of the 139 cast-iron steps for the spiral staircase and the cast-iron gallery and lantern. Lastly the third-order Fresnel lens was installed in the decagonal lantern on its cast-iron clockwork cabinet and raceway. The clockwork mechanism that rotated the lens was powered by a 50-pound (22.7 kg) weight suspended in a vertical housing inside the tower. It had to be wound every few hours to keep the lens rotating.

A 2½-story red brick keeper's duplex was built behind the tower and connected to it by an enclosed passageway. A brick woodshed to the rear of the house kept firewood dry. The station was finally completed with the building of its privy. All structures were left in their natural red brick color. Total construction costs were $28,886, a figure much lower than the initial appropriation.

Although the station was not activated until the start of the 1874 navigation season, its first keeper, James Davenport, was hired in 1873 to maintain it through the winter. His assistant, John Larley, started in 1874 when the light was first lit.

Improvements were made to the station as required. A boat landing and boathouse were constructed (1893), a barn was built (1889), and a 360-gallon (85.7 l) oil storage tank was installed (1892). Since the red brick was not very visible from a distance, it was painted white in 1900 to increase its daytime visibility. When a trail was opened to the area in 1902, wooden boardwalks were installed from the trail to the lighthouse so that supplies could be brought in more easily by land. Also that year, a safer brick oil storage shed was built. In 1911 dormers were added to both sides of the attic roof to create additional living space for the keeper's growing family.

While the light's lens has always been a third-order Fresnel lens, its illuminants have changed with progress. The initial fuel, whale oil, was switched to kerosene around 1892 when the separate oil storage tank was installed. While kerosene was more economical, it was also more combustible and needed to be stored in a separate building to prevent fires. The kerosene light required three large wicks that had to be trimmed and adjusted often. These wicks were next replaced with a mantle lamp in which the kerosene was pressurized to convert it to a gaseous state that allowed it to burn clearer and brighter. These were known as incandescent oil vapor lamps. In 1954, when electricity was extended to the station, a 250-watt electrical lamp was the light source. Also at this time the clockworks mechanism that rotated the lens was removed, and the light's characteristic changed from flashing to fixed.

Assistant keeper Henry Vaurina in an interview recalled the harrowing storm of November 1940. He watched the worst shipwreck he had ever seen. Three ships were involved and two of them, the *Davock* and the *Minch*, sank while the third, the *Novadoc*, was beached. "We lost a lot of men that night," Henry related. "The snow was coming down and the wind was so strong it was peeling the bark from the trees."

The light was automated in 1955 and the U.S. Coast Guard demolished all buildings except the tower. In 1977 the tower, no longer needed by larger ships, was sandblasted and returned to its original red brick to save maintenance costs. In 1984 the light was listed on the *National Register of Historic Places*.

Today the tower is owned by the U.S. Coast Guard as the light still functions, and the grounds of the old station are part of the Silver Lake State Park. A short walk through the sand dunes leads to the tall tower.

Known Keepers: James Davenport (1873–79), Gabriel Bourisseau (1879–85), George Buttars (1887–90), Joseph Hanson (1890–99), J. Hunter (1899–1910), J. A. Hunter (1910–22), Wallace Hall (1922–23), Lewis Allard (1923–24), Charles Lennis (1924–30), Arthur Almquist (1930–35), D. Marin (1935–39), Henry Vaurina (1939–54).

47 Little Traverse Lighthouse

Years went by before Congress responded to the petition of the Michigan Legislature to build a lighthouse at Little Traverse Bay. In 1855 funding was sought to improve the harbor and erect a light to guide vessels around the point that protruded into the northern arm of the bay. Congress ignored the request. In 1871 Orlando M. Poe, Chief Engineer for the Upper Great Lakes Lighthouse District, recommended a lighthouse for the area and the Lighthouse Board petitioned the government for $15,000 in 1873. This request was also ignored. When Indian treaties were "modified" and land around the bay was opened up for settlement, huge tracts were claimed by lumber companies, and moneyed people from southern Michigan's industrial cities flocked to this pristine area to build cottages, mansions and hotels. With this influx of water traffic, Congress could no longer ignore petitions for a lighthouse and appropriated $15,000 in August 1882. It had taken more than a quarter of a century to get the okay.

Little Traverse Lighthouse with fog bell

In 1963 when the light was automated, the lighthouse was closed and a flashing green electric light was placed on a 41-foot (12.5 m) steel skeletal tower. From its position near the old lighthouse, this new light had a focal plane of 72 feet (22 m) and a visibility of 14-miles (22.5 kms).

Being unused, the lighthouse and property were sold to Harbor Springs, an exclusive gated community. The lighthouse is isolated from the general public but is well maintained by its owners and still houses its original Fresnel lens. Because the lighthouse is located right on the point, it is sometimes referred to as the Harbor Point Lighthouse.

Known Keepers: Mrs. William Van Riper (1884–1913), Alfred Erickson (1913–40), Angus Phillips (1943–46), Raymond Buttars (1947–48), Henry Rocheleau (1949–54).

But it still took another two years to get the lighthouse built. In 1882 plans were drawn up and surveyors were sent to find the ideal location. In early 1884 a parcel of land was acquired on Harbor Point in Harbor Springs at the entrance to Little Traverse Bay. The lighthouse foundation was made of cut stone. The 1½-story red brick keeper's house had a 10-foot (3 m) square and 40-foot (12.2 m) high tower attached to its south side where the tower was integrated into house and gable. The tower gallery had a copper floor, iron railings and an octagonal cast-iron lantern. The lantern was equipped with a fourth-order Fresnel lens from Sautter and Lemonnier of Paris, and it displayed a fixed red light. The light was first lit on September 25, 1884 and had a 13-mile (21 km) visibility.

The light's first keeper was Elizabeth Whitney Williams, who had transferred from the St. James Harbor Lighthouse on Beaver Island. Besides tending the light, she welcomed visitors from the area. When tours started to impede her lighthouse duties, she set up a schedule to let visitors know when she would be available. In the off-season, she wrote her memoirs of growing up among Mormons and tending the light on Beaver Island. With encouragement from her friends and relatives, she published her autobiography, *A Child of the Sea*, in 1905.

Ongoing improvements occurred at the lighthouse. In 1887 a 45-foot (13.7 m) well was sunk for fresh water. In 1891 a municipal water supply was established at Harbor Springs and the lighthouse was hooked up to it for protection against fire. In 1896 the station received a fog bell, and a tower was built to house it close to the lake. The 19-foot (5.8 m) structure had an upper open section where the bell was suspended and a lower section to store the Stevens automated bell striking apparatus powered by a clockwork mechanism. The hammer struck two sharp blows every 30 seconds (after 1914, one every 30 seconds). In 1898 the lighthouse's main illuminant became kerosene, requiring that a brick oil house be built to store it at a safe distance from the lighthouse. In 1899 a lightning rod was put on the tower and a beacon placed on the breakwater. The characteristic of the light was changed from fixed red to fixed green in 1939.

48 Long Tail Point (Old) Lighthouse

After strong recommendation that a lighthouse be placed immediately on Grassy Island, Lake Michigan, in July 1838, Congress appropriated $4,000 and sent out Lt. James T. Homans to select a location. With high water levels and Grassy Island almost submerged in the fall of 1838, Homans warned against a lighthouse on this island and proposed a better location on Tail Point, a peninsula a short distance north of the island. Thus steered, Congress approved the building of a lighthouse in this new location in July 1846.

Long Tail Point, as the peninsula is known today, is a long, thin sandy point of land about 3 miles (4.9 km) long that stretches southeast from Suamico into the foot of Green Bay. It is also about 3 miles (4.9 km) north of the Fox River. Depending on the lake level, parts of it are sometimes even submerged, as is the tip of the peninsula. This point and Grassy Island to the south made direct entry into the Fox River impossible. The first lighthouse was placed near the peninsula's southeast end to help guide mariners through the shoals into the Fox River.

The lighthouse was built in the summer and fall of 1847. While the original contractors were from Detroit, they subcontracted to local contractors Edwin and Azael Hart and Daniel W. Hubbard. Edwin Hart did most of the carpentry work and Hubbard had charge of the mason work. While the tower was just built on sand, the workers did place a good foundation about 6 feet (1.8 km) below the surface. Stone for the tower was gathered from the east side of Green Bay and poled around the bay on a scow. Since workers had to stay in water shallow enough to pole (about 6 feet [1.8 m] deep), it took them two days for each load they picked up from across the bay. Lime from Bay Settlement and sand from the point were used to mix the mortar that held the stones of all shapes and sizes in place.

The conical tower, about 25 feet (7.6 m) in diameter at the base and about 9 feet (2.8 m) in diameter at the summit, had base walls that were about 6 feet (1.8 m) thick and tapered to about 2

Long Tail Point (old) Tower, right, and Long Tail Point Second Lighthouse, left

feet (0.6 m) at the top. A horse-driven capstan was used to haul stone and mortar to the top of the wall with a rope. When Hart's truant son skipped school, he would be put to work driving the horse to lift the materials for the rubble-stone tower. The capstones below the gallery were quarried limestone believed to have come by schooner from the Death's Door area. A wooden gallery was placed on the capstone, which supported an iron birdcage-style lantern to complete its overall 84 foot (26 m) height. The oil lamps were first lit by keeper John Dousman at the start of the 1848 season. A small frame keeper's house had been built just north of the lighthouse.

Sometime in the 1850s the light was refitted with a new polygonal cast-iron lantern with a Fresnel lens, and the old lantern was taken to the Fort Howard Museum. Then by 1859, when the lake level had risen and water completely surrounded the base of the lighthouse tower, a new lighthouse was built on higher ground to the north of the old tower, and the lantern and lens were transferred from the old tower.

In the early 1870s the government gave the old stone tower to William Mitchell, a former keeper of the second Long Tail Point Lighthouse, to remove the "eyesore" from the Green Bay area. Mitchell had accepted the offer so he could reuse its stone, but when he tried, he found it "impervious to bar and pick." The tower remained standing.

Sometime after the turn of the century the government again planned to demolish the old tower but a committee headed by Commodore Arthur C. Neville and Judge Carlton Merrill wrote to Washington pleading for its preservation, as it had become a well-known landmark. Once again the tower was spared. It is ironic that this stone tower, replaced by another lighthouse because it risked being undermined by high water, is still standing today, especially since its successor has long since disappeared.

Known Keepers: John P. Dousman (1848–53), Thomas Atkinson (1853–59), William Mitchell (?).

49 Long Tail Point Crib Lighthouse

After the channel through Grassy Island was dredged, creating a straight approach into the mouth of the Fox River on Lake Michigan, complaints arose that the Tail Point Light was too far away to properly mark the hidden, submerged point of the peninsula that bordered the western edge of Green Bay's shipping lane. To solve this, an offshore light was built on the submerged tip of the peninsula and lit in 1899.

A wooden crib was sunk and a square concrete pier was constructed on top of it. A square frame 1½-story structure with a hipped roof stood in the center of the pier. Four dormer windows, one in each side of the hipped roof made a good watchroom from the second story. The top of the roof was flat, creating a square gallery on which a circular iron lantern was placed. The lantern's square curved glass panels were set diagonally into metal astragals and the light displayed a flashing red characteristic. The first floor was used as emergency keeper's quarters in case the keepers were stranded at the light by inclement weather. Otherwise the keepers traveled back and forth daily to the mainland, where they used the house from the Long Tail Point light as their quarters.

In 1936 the Long Tail Crib Lighthouse was automated and the keepers were removed. The light remained active until 1973 when a severe spring storm washed it into the lake. After this a modern pole light was mounted on the old foundation.

50 Long Tail Point Second Lighthouse

In 1859 a new lighthouse was built on higher ground to the northwest of the Old Long Tail Point stone tower because it was believed that rising lake waters, which completely surrounded the old stone tower, would cause it to topple into Lake Michigan. The new frame lighthouse was 27 feet (8.3 m) square and its sills were built on iron piles placed 8 feet (2.4 m) apart. The dwelling was 2½ stories high with a square wooden tower emerging from its roof peak at one end. A square wooden gallery topped the tower. The polygonal iron lantern and Fresnel lens were moved from the old tower to this light, from which they provided a 15-mile (24 km) visibility. The bottom of the house had wide piazzas running its entire length and width. The station was also outfitted with a well, a boathouse that was connected with the lighthouse by a wooden walkway over the marshy shore, and a fog bell, which was later replaced by a compressed-air fog whistle. This station's name was shortened to Tail Point Lighthouse.

Long Tail Point Crib Lighthouse

Long Tail Point Second Lighthouse

From 1870 to 1890 John Dennessen and his sons ran excursion boats on Green Bay and the Fox River. This Long Tail Lighthouse and the old stone tower nearby, with its excellent sandy beach, became a popular spot for people to beat the summer heat. Many bathing and swimming clubs visited in the summer. The tours ended with a splendid supper spread out on the cool stretches of the lighthouse's east piazza. Keeper Mitchell and later keeper Gaylord were both "courteous and delightful gentlemen and great favorites with visitors." The excursions always ended with an evening boat cruise home while crooning well-known favorites such as "Good Night Ladies."

By 1899, after the new channel had been dredged through Grassy Island, the light was deemed to be too far from the shipping channel. In August 1899 it was transferred to the new Long Tail Point Lighthouse, which had been built offshore to mark the submerged tip of the peninsula. The frame lighthouse was retained as living quarters for the keepers of the new light. The house was damaged in a severe storm in the fall of 1929.

In 1936 the Long Tail Point Lighthouse was automated, the keepers were removed, and the house was no longer needed. It was sold to a private individual with the stipulation that it be removed from the area, which had been designated a National Migratory Waterfowl Refuge. While the house was being moved across the winter ice, the trailer wheels broke through the ice and the house had to be dismantled on the spot before it too was lost.

Known Keepers: William Mitchell (?), Captain Gaylord (?), Carl Witzman (–1929–)

Ludington North Breakwater Lighthouse

51 Ludington North Breakwater Lighthouse

Congress first appropriated funds for a light at Ludington, about midway along Lake Michigan's eastern shore, in 1870. After a variety of early lights, its breakwater light was built in 1924 and it still exists today.

It was a formidable structure — a square, white, gently tapering pyramidal tower that stood 57 feet (17.5 m) from base to ventilator and had a focal plane of 55 feet (17 m). The steel-framed tower was encased in riveted steel plates to withstand Lake Michigan storms. The base had a wedge-like protrusion to bear the brunt of fierce waves that lashed the lighthouse. Small porthole windows appeared from all three levels. The square gallery around its polygonal lantern had a black pipe iron railing.

The original optic, a fourth-order Fresnel lens, was manufactured by the Macbeth Evans Company of Pittsburgh, Pennsylvania. It was lit by a two-lamp apparatus that was bolted into the center of the lens and flashed at 4-second intervals to produce a 19-mile (30.8 km) visibility. The light was automated in 1972.

In 1993 the lighthouse received a refurbishing that included: replacement of the lantern and porthole glass with lexan, new wiring, a battery back-up system, a 300 mm back-up light attached to the railing, new sheetrock ceilings, a thorough painting, and a cleaning to make the fourth-order lens sparkle.

In 1994 the Army Corps of Engineers started to place concrete caps on the breakwalls. They also discovered that the base had begun to settle, causing the lighthouse to lean 3 to 4 degrees to the north-northeast, because it had originally been designed for a different lighthouse. On inspection the Corps decided that straightening the lighthouse would be prohibitive but that it could be stabilized. Accordingly, the Gillian Company of Milwaukee, Wisconsin, was contracted to stabilize the lighthouse by means that included installing sheet metal around its base and shoring it up by pouring concrete under the substructure.

In 1995 the Fresnel lens was dismantled and removed from the lighthouse. Today, the U.S. Coast Guard has loaned the lens, estimated at $375,000, to the Mason County Historical Society. It is displayed in the maritime exhibit building at White Pine Village, a historical village south of Ludington.

Today the lighthouse's optic is a 300 mm plastic lens, molded in the Fresnel design. It flashes four seconds on and one second off with a visibility of 19 miles (30.5 km). Although the modern lens is not as "sparkly," it is functional and weighs a lot less than the original Fresnel lens, which probably benefits the leaning tower.

Known Keepers: Fredrick Samuelson (1924–37), John Paetshow (1937–40).

52 Ludington's Early Lights

Early commerce along the shores around Ludington on Lake Michigan's east coast consisted of sawmills and lumber. As the harbor developed, the channel connecting it to Père Marquette Lake was deepened and protective piers were built out into Lake Michigan. Congress appropriated $6,000 in 1870 to build a light at Ludington. This first government light was built on the south pier of the Ludington Harbor Channel in 1871 and included keeper's quarters.

In 1874 the Flint & Père Marquette Railroad started cross-lake railroad car ferry service from Ludington to Sheboygan, Wisconsin, and the harbor was improved to provide better service. A fog building with a 10-inch (25 cm) steam whistle was established. About 1877 the pier light was rebuilt and possibly placed atop the fog signal building. About 1890 range lights were placed on the north pier and connected to shore by a wooden catwalk.

In 1914, along with a million dollars worth of harbor improvements, the lighthouse was moved to the north breakwater and placed on a new crib. It was replaced in 1924. A ferry still runs from Ludington. However it is the *S.S. Badger*, a car ferry service that runs to Manitowoc, Wisconsin. The transport of railroad cars stopped in 1990. Ludington is now lit by a light on its north breakwater.

Known Keepers: William Gerard (1870–78), Edward Dundass (1879), Archibald Hunter (1879–82), Peter Dues (1882–88), Edwin Skyfield (1888–1909), Fredrick Samuelson (1909–24).

Manistee North Pierhead Light

53 Manistee North Pierhead Light

During the late 1800s marine traffic on Lake Michigan steadily increased and in the early 1890s it was decided to better mark the harbor at Manistee. The plan was to reactivate the extinguished shore light, place a pierhead light on the north pier, and move the fog signal from the south pier to the north pier. Having everything on the north side of the river would make it easier for the keeper to tend the equipment.

The crew arrived to do this work in May 1894. The fog signal building was put onto a new foundation 300 feet (92 m) from the end of the north pierhead, but instead of moving the south pierhead light, Major Milton B. Adams decided to use one of his newly designed conduit systems for the north pierhead. A wooden conduit box supported by trestles traveled from the pierhead 290 feet (88 m) into the fog signal building. Inside the conduit a steel trolley sat on two iron rails. This trolley, which held the light, could be moved back and forth between the pierhead and the fog building. The old elevated walkway was moved from the south pier to the north pier and another 460 feet (142 m) were added to it, making an elevated walk of 923 feet (280 m). When the old main light was relit on June 18, 1894, the south pier range lights were discontinued and removed. When completed in 1894 the north pierhead conduit light was also lit.

Affluent people who had moved to Manistee in the 1890s complained about the noise of the fog signal. To appease them the government sent a crew to modify the fog signal equipment. They built a parabolic reflector with a pine frame, covered in iron and packed with sawdust to deaden the sound. The whistles were repiped into the center of the reflector. While the sound still carried out over the water it was much less noticeable to the Manistee residents.

Adams' conduit system was not as successful. It was removed in 1900. The fog signal building was moved to within 42 feet (13 m) of the pierhead, and a gallery and an octagonal cast-iron lantern were mounted to the lakeside gable end of the fog signal building. The lantern used a new sixth-order Fresnel lens to display a fixed red light. Since the lantern blocked the fog whistles and the deflector, they were elevated by 4 feet (1.2 m).

In 1914 the Army Corps of Engineers returned to build a breakwater on the south side of the harbor to work in conjunction with the northern pier to make a stilling basin within the harbor. They placed a red steel skeletal tower on the breakwater 80 feet (24.6 m) from the end. It was equipped with an acetylene powered flashing red light with a 300 mm lens. It stood 45 feet (13.9 m) above the water and had a visibility of 7 miles (11.3 km). The keepers were responsible to maintain this new light also. When hydro came to Manistee in 1925 the lights were switched to electricity, resulting in increased candlepower and thus greater visibility.

During repairs to the piers in 1927, the fog signal building was removed and a 39-foot (12 m) iron tower was built at the end of the north pier. Topped with a circular gallery and a decagonal lantern, it housed a fifth-order Fresnel lens that used an incandescent electric bulb with 5,000 candlepower. The light exhibited a group flashing white light every 30 seconds. With a focal plane of 55 feet (16.9 km), it had a 15-mile (24.3 km) visibility. A Type C diaphone fog signal was also installed in the tower. Its characteristic was similar to that of the light — a group of three blasts every 30 seconds.

Also at this time a new cast-iron walkway replaced the old one. This catwalk is one of only four catwalks remaining on the coast of Lake Michigan and is listed on the *State Register of Historic Sites*. It was repaired in the early 1990s by a "Save the Catwalk" campaign led by the local Chamber of Commerce.

In 1994 the Coast Guard repaired and renovated the tower. Today the tower and catwalk — along with the downtown restoration — lure tourists to Manistee, nicknamed "Lake Michigan's Victorian Port City."

54 Manistee Old Main Lighthouse

During the 1850s lumbermen flocked to the Manistee area to harvest the forests along the river. When lobbying the government for funding to improve the harbor and build a lighthouse brought no results, Manistee businessmen, at their own expense, had a pair of short piers built at the river's mouth to help prevent sand and silt deposits. In 1861 a government survey of the area reported that harbor improvements were valid and necessary, but delayed appropriations until 1867.

This lighthouse was a wooden framed dwelling built in 1870 on a rubble foundation. The tower was integrated into the house and topped with a lantern that held a fifth-order lens. The light's first

Manistee South Pierhead Light, left, and Manistee Old Main Light, right

Manistee Old Main Lighthouse minus its tower and lantern

keeper, Octavius W. Barney, arrived for duty at Manistee in December 1869 and lit the light at the beginning of the 1870 navigation season. When it was discovered that the dwelling was too far back and that the rear of the building was not on lighthouse property, construction halted until an additional portion of land was purchased at the back of the property for $30. The station was finally completed in July 1870.

While it took almost twenty years to get a lighthouse built, just a little over a year later it and the whole town of Manistee were completely destroyed by a forest fire on October 8, 1871. With everything in ruins, the lightkeeper worked resourcefully and erected a temporary light on a pole by the lake to serve until a new one could be erected. Congress appropriated $10,000 for a new lighthouse in May 1872.

The new light was completed by September of the same year. It was also a two-story frame house with a tower built into the house at the front. The new lantern housed a temporary lens until its new fifth-order Fresnel lens arrived in 1873.

Just two years after being built, the main light was extinguished. Part of Manistee's harbor improvements included extending its two piers another 150 feet (46 m) into the lake, but then the shore light was deemed to be too far away to adequately mark the harbor entry. To correct this, a pierhead light was established at the outer end of the longer south pier, using the lens from the shore light, and the shore light was discontinued in October 1875. The keeper continued to use the shore dwelling as his residence.

Then, because lake traffic increased, the main light was reactivated in 1894 to serve as a coast light and to assist mariners into the harbor. It used a new fifth-order Fresnel lens that displayed a fixed white light with a red flash every 45 seconds.

Improvements continued. In 1895 yards of muck and clay were spread on top of the sand around the lighthouse to make a lawn. In 1902 a new pedestal and ball bearings assembly was installed, replacing the old, troublesome rotational mechanism of the lens. The lantern also received new improved fifth-order lamps for its lens. In 1906, 600 feet (184.6 m) of concrete walkway were laid to connect the station's buildings.

By 1939, serving no specific purpose, the main light was permanently extinguished. Its lantern was removed and it was sold to private owners. Years later, in 1993, when the structure was right in the middle of a new development plan, it was moved to a residential area, where it remains today, unrecognizable as once having been a lighthouse.

Known Keepers: Octavius W. Barney (1869–71), John McKee (1871–75), John Roberts (1883–88), Thomas Robinson (1888–1906), Milton McClure (1906–23), Wallace Hall (1923–39).

55 Manistee South Pierhead Light

During the 1870s, renovations at Manistee Harbor on Lake Michigan resulted in both its piers being lengthened by an additional 150 feet (46.2 m) and the channel between them being dredged to 10 feet (3 m). With this improvement, the lighthouse on the shore was deemed to be too far behind the piers to adequately mark the opening to the harbor, so a new pierhead beacon was added at the outer end of the longer south pier. The keeper now had to row across the river to tend this light.

The pierhead light was quite simple. The timber-framed tower was open on the lower half and closed on the upper half to form a service and watchroom for the keeper. A square gallery had an octagonal cast-iron lantern at its center. The lantern displayed a fixed red light using the fifth-order Fresnel lens from the light on shore. The 27-foot (8.3 m) tower had a 35-foot (10.7 m) focal plane that gave the light an 11-mile visibility. When the light was established on October 26, 1875, the old main light on shore was discontinued. However, the keeper did continue to live in the house.

As lake traffic increased, the Eleventh District engineer Major Samuel Mansfield recommended that a fog signal be constructed on the south pier, and Congress appropriated $5,000 in March 1889. It was built in 1890 on the pier just behind the pierhead

Manistee Main Light, circa 1914

Manistee North Pierhead Light and fog signal, circa 1913

Manistee Harbor North Pierhead Light

56 Manistique East Breakwater Lighthouse

The Lighthouse Board recommended a light at Manistique in 1892, but the government did not comply until 1915 when they had completed harbor improvements. These improvements included concrete piers on either side of the river mouth to ensure safer entry for mariners.

A pierhead light was placed at the end of the east pier and lit in 1917. The 35-foot (10.7 m) slightly tapering square tower was constructed of sheet iron plates for durability and painted white for increased visibility. It was topped with a square gallery and a decagonal cast-iron lantern that housed a fourth-order Fresnel lens. Perched on the high concrete pier, it had a 50-foot (15.3 m) focal plane.

Later, to comply with the new "Red Right Return" regulations, the tower was painted red. In 1969 the light was automated and its Fresnel lens removed. Today the Manistique light uses a 300 mm plastic optic to display its red light, and the lens is displayed at the St. Simon's Island Lighthouse in Georgia.

Known Keepers: Charles Corlette (1914–20), Walter Ottesen (1920–40), William Keller (1947–49), Anton Jessen Jr. (1949–51).

57 Manitowoc Lighthouse

Manitowoc" is a Native American word meaning "home of the great spirit." White settlers hoped for a great harbor here, and in 1837 Congress appropriated $5,000 to build a lighthouse on high ground near the mouth of the Manitowoc River. It was finished in 1840 and consisted of a 30-foot (9 m) conical brick tower, a circular gallery, and a lantern that used 11 lamps with 14-inch (35 cm) reflectors to produce the light beam. The keeper's house was a 1½-story detached brick dwelling.

The light was extinguished in 1877, as the north pierhead light was deemed sufficient for the harbor. In 1895 both the tower and the house were razed to make way for a new two-story keepers' duplex, a clapboard building constructed on a brick foundation.

light and was connected to the light by an elevated walkway. The structure was timber-framed and covered with corrugated iron sheeting. It housed two boilers horizontally. These fed the steam up into two 10-inch (25 cm) locomotive whistles installed in the roof. There was also room inside for a coal bin, a water supply tank and a workbench. The crew worked into the winter to have the signal completed for the 1891 season.

Also at this time, a tubular light on a pole was added at the very end of the south pier to act as a front range light for the pierhead light. It consisted of a lantern suspended from a cable that passed around pulleys, one attached to the pole and the other secured to the wall inside the service room of the pierhead light. The idea was to save the keeper work. He could service and light the tubular lantern from inside the service room and then pull it along the cable to transport it to the pole. An assistant keeper was hired in 1890 to help with the increased workload of operating the fog signal and the additional light.

With lake traffic continuing to increase, it was decided to reactivate the extinguished shore light and to establish a pierhead light on the north pier where it would be easier for the keeper to manage the two lights. When the old shore light was relit on June 18, 1894, the south pier lights were discontinued and removed.

58 Manitowoc North Breakwater Light

The harbor at Manitowoc, Lake Michigan, had always had a sandbar that plagued mariners trying to enter its harbor. Larger vessels had to anchor out in the lake and use smaller scows to unload them, costing more time and money. Other boats entering the harbor sometimes had to wait for a large wave to lift them over the sandbar at the river mouth. In 1867 Manitowoc finally raised sufficient money to build a dredge to clean away enough of the sandbar to make harbor entry easier.

However, as the harbor was still exposed to the fury of lake storms, many schooner wrecks took place in the harbor and along the docks. Sand also was continually washed into the river's mouth. To help correct these problems, north and south breakwaters were built during

Manistique East Breakwater Light

Manitowoc North Breakwater Light

the late 1860s to enclose and protect the harbor. In 1895 the first breakwater light was built on the north breakwater. Being a combination light/fog signal building, it was a large rectangular structure covered in corrugated iron to withstand storms. There was a small lantern on the lakeside end of its roof from which a kerosene lamp was shone. The fog building housed a 10-inch (25 cm) steam fog whistle. Since there was no catwalk to this light, the keepers had to row out to it, a daunting task in a severe storm. In fact, a supply of canned goods was always kept at the light for times when foul weather stranded the keeper. The early keepers worked alternate twelve-hour shifts from midnight to noon.

In the early 1900s a severe November storm from the east broke down the door in the east end of the fog signal building. Everything inside was submerged in water. The keeper helplessly clung to a concrete post between two boilers while the storm waters crashed and swirled. By morning the storm had abated and the water left the building, but the keeper had to wait to be rescued, as the boathouse and his rowboat had been washed out to sea. However, the light was well above the water and had continued to shine throughout the storm. In 1902 the lantern received a fifth-order Fresnel lens.

In 1907 the Army Corps of Engineers dredged the harbor deeper and started to install experimental arrowhead-type breakwaters to replace the old ones. When the new concrete breakwaters were completed, a new breakwater light was also built at the end of the north breakwater and the old breakwaters and the light/fog building were removed.

Manitowoc Lighthouse, circa 1880s

This new breakwater light was built in 1918 on a large rectangular reinforced-concrete base 11 feet (3.4 m) high. The upper three levels had a steel frame covered with steel plates for durability. The top level was a circular watchroom topped with a polygonal lantern that originally housed a fourth-order Fresnel lens displaying a fixed red light from a 52-foot (16 m) focal plane to achieve a visibility of 17 miles (27.4 km) on a clear night. The fog signal equipment (a new diaphone Type F) was kept in the two levels below the watchroom. A catwalk connected this light to the shore, and a light cable along the catwalk provided electrical power for the station. A small white acetylene light had also been placed at the end of the south breakwater and the keeper had to row across about once a month to replace the light's acetylene tank. This light flashed 15 beams per minute.

Modernization brought change. The fourth-order Fresnel lens was given a smaller, less intense fifth-order Fresnel lens. In 1927 a radio beacon was installed, and in 1932 the fog signal was synchronized with the radio beacon to more effectively guide vessels into harbor. Manitowoc was one of three stations on the Great Lakes to have this synchronization. The other two were at Muskegon and Ludington. The foghorn (blast 1 s; silence 1 s; blast 1 s; silence 17 s) was turned on when visibility was lower than 5 miles (8 m). Also, a ship's captain could request the fog signal anytime he needed it by issuing three blasts from his whistle.

In 1940 a telephone line and new radio room transmitter were installed. In the 1950s a new power cable replaced the old one, back-up fuel was switched to diesel from kerosene, the light's color changed to white, and the south breakwater light's color changed from white to green. The tower was automated in 1971 and its catwalk and radio beacon disappeared at some point. In 1985 the light was placed on the State's *Register for Historical Sites*. Being central to the west side of Lake Michigan the Manitowoc light operated year round as a terminal point for railroad car ferries crossing the lake. Although these ferries no longer run today, the car ferry S.S. *Badger* still connects Manitowoc to Ludington from May to October.

As harbor and navigation equipment improved, shipwreck numbers declined and keepers seldom had to rescue anyone. Their most hazardous job was getting to the light when the catwalk was sheeted in ice. Sometimes they had to crawl out and chop the ice off the door to get access to tend the light.

Keeper Joseph Napiezinski did make a twentieth-century rescue, but not for a person. A large dog had either been thrown or had fallen off a lake freighter miles out in the lake off Manitowoc. Napiezinski first noticed the dog about half a mile from the breakwater, trying to swim ashore but looking nearly totally exhausted. He rowed out to the rescue. Although he had difficulty getting the dog into his boat, he was able to row safely to shore.

While the tower was originally painted a reddish-brown, it is now white with a black lantern. It is monitored from the Two Rivers Coast Guard Station about 7 miles (11.3 m) away, and repairs and maintenance are done by the Green Bay Coast Guard.

Known Keepers: Christian Anderson (1895–97), Charles Ahlgrin (1897–1911), Joseph Napiezinski (1911–18).

59 Manitowoc North Pierhead Light

As Manitowoc grew as a trading and manufacturing city, it also grew as an important ship-building center. The first Clipper Schooner built on the Great Lakes was built here, and by 1900 over 200 schooners, tugs and steamers had been built in the many shipyards at Manitowoc.

To better serve this development, piers were built into the lake. In 1850 the first pierhead light was built at the end of the north pier. It was a 35-foot (10.7 m) square white pyramidal tower with an open base and an enclosed upper section. A catwalk along the pier connected it to shore. By 1877 this light was deemed sufficient to light the harbor, and so the old main land light was extinguished. A 300-pound (136 kg) fog bell was mounted to the lake side of the tower.

After withstanding numerous abusive storms, the pierhead light was refurbished in 1892. Its main form was retained and the base was closed in. Over time breakwaters were built and then rebuilt. About 1918, after the completion of the new concrete breakwater, the north pier was shortened to make more space within the harbor and the light was moved closer to shore. It continued in service until 1937 when it was destroyed in a severe storm. In 1940 a new steel skeletal tower replaced the old light. In 1947 the skeletal tower was moved to the end of the pier but it was returned to its former location in 1948.

Manning Memorial Lighthouse

60 Manning Memorial Lighthouse

Not many people are honored in death by having a lighthouse built as their memorial but such is the case for Robert H. Manning, who died in 1989 at the age of 62. He had lived and worked in Empire, Michigan, all his life. An avid fisherman, he had often complained about coming in at night off the lake with no light to guide him home. So after his death his family and friends decided to erect a lighthouse for him.

In conception it was a lamppost. In reality it became a 35-foot (10.7 m) cylindrical wooden tower with a white stucco finish and a green lantern that housed a 250 mm Tidelands lantern with an acrylic lens. Built and dedicated in 1991 at Empire Beach near Sleeping Bear Dunes, this light tower stands to guide small craft to the Empire boat ramp after dark.

While the Coast Guard has added the light to their water charts, they have not certified it as an aid to navigation. The dim light is only lit for small craft during the boating season. It is one of just two lights in Michigan that were built as a memorial.

61 McGulpin's Point Old Lighthouse

By the mid-1800s mariners wanted navigation aid in the Straits of Mackinac. Congress appropriated $6,000 to build a lighthouse at McGulpin's Point in August 1854. However, this did not happen and the original appropriation expired unspent. The Lighthouse Board again petitioned Congress in 1866 and $20,000 was appropriated for the McGulpin's Point lighthouse, 3 miles (4.8 km) west of Fort Michilimackinac.

The lighthouse was built in 1869 in the same Norman Gothic style as lights at Chambers Island and Eagle Bluff in Door County, Wisconsin, and White River and Sand Island of the Apostle Islands in Lake Superior. The house and tower were built of Cream City brick on a cut-block limestone foundation. The short tower built into the northwest corner of the house was square at the bottom and octagonal at the top, and it had corner buttresses for extra support. Its octagonal gallery was surrounded with pipe iron railing and supported by 24 short, ornately carved corbels (three per side). Its polygonal lantern housed a 3 1/2-order Fresnel lens. The 1 1/2-story house had stick and spindle decoration in each gable and ornately carved braces under the eaves. The square brick chimney of the house was set into the roof on a diagonal to service more rooms with stoves. This was the first lighthouse built in the Mackinaw area.

McGulpin's Point Old Lighthouse

62 Menominee North Pierhead Light

The Menominee River empties into Green Bay on Lake Michigan. In 1877 a lighthouse was built on the north pierhead at the river mouth to mark the entrance into the river. The 29-foot (8.9 m) slightly tapering octagonal cast-iron tower flared out gently at the top to support its octagonal gallery and lantern, which housed a fourth-order Fresnel lens and displayed a fixed red light. The tower was connected to shore by a wooden catwalk built along the pier. A brick duplex was built onshore to house the keepers.

In the 1890s a fog signal building was built on the pier behind the lighthouse to hold equipment to operate a 10-inch (25 cm) steam fog whistle (blast 5 s; silence 25 s). It was framed in wood and covered in iron sheeting for durability. During the first decade of the new century, a rear range light, built on a steel skeletal tower and placed on the pier between the shore and the lighthouse, operated for a time but was then removed.

During the 1920s vast harbor improvements were made and a new concrete pier was installed with a large circular concrete pad 41 feet (12.6 m) in diameter at its end. A large square concrete base was placed on this pier, and the lighthouse was moved onto it in 1927, increasing its height to 34 feet (10.5 m) and giving it a 46-foot (14 m) focal plane. It was connected to shore by an elevated iron catwalk. The old fog signal building was not moved to the new pier, as a new automated electrically operated fog signal was placed in the new base of the tower. When the light was automated in 1972, the catwalk was removed. At some point the Fresnel lens was replaced with 300 mm optic, and the light is solar-powered today.

Known Keepers: William Holmes (1877–1878), Daniel Andrews (1879–81), Samuel Drew (1881–82), Benjamin Cane (1882–83), Thomas Robinson (1883–88), John Roberts (1888–90), Hans Hansen (1890–99), Charles Young (1899–1905), Hans Hansen (1905–23), Eugene Kimball (1923–28), Henry Anderson (1928–39).

The McGulpin's Point light was discontinued on December 15, 1906 as the light at Mackinaw, built in 1892, was stronger and more visible to mariners navigating the Straits. They found the light at McGulpin's Point of little help as it was too far away from the Straits. The light and lantern were removed from the tower when it was deactivated.

After 1906 the lighthouse sat empty and fell prey to vandals until it was sold at public auction in 1912 or 1913 for use as a private residence. Its first private owners, Mr. and Mrs. Ralph Shaw, restored the structures to their original condition. Since then its private owners have always maintained it well but because it is privately owned and hidden by mature trees its visibility is quite limited.

Known Keepers: Gabriel Alloffe (1869), Charles Louisignau (1869–75), Thomas Dunn (1875–79), Gabriel Bourisseau (1879), James Davenport (1879–1906).

Menominee North Pierhead Light

63 Michigan City (Old) Lighthouse

Michigan City (Old) Lighthouse

Michigan City, located 60 miles (96 km) east of Chicago on Lake Michigan's southeast shore, has had a series of lights to help mark its port. In 1835 Isaac C. Elston, founder of Michigan City, deeded to the U.S. government a tract of land from the bend of Trail Creek to the lake for the purpose of building a lighthouse. The first light was a "post light" — a lantern hung on a tall post. There was also a single-family cottage for the maintainer of the light.

Then in 1837 Jeremy Hixon and his son were contracted to build a lighthouse and keeper's dwelling on the site. The freestanding 40-foot (12.2 m) conical tower had walls 3 feet (0.9 m) thick and was separate from the lightkeeper's dwelling. An early account describes the 1½ story house: ". . . plastered on the outside and dazzling in its whiteness . . . a portico . . . ornamented the front and was covered with trailing vines. The well-kept lawn was dotted with shrubbery, flowers and enclosed by a low, rustic fence, and from a little wicket gate led a white gravel walk to the residence." Its first keeper, Edmund B. Harrison, earned $350 a year.

This lighthouse deteriorated quickly under the constant blasts of sand from the dune across the river. In 1859 the government tore it down and replaced it with a lighthouse that used Joliet stone (a type of granite) for the foundation and Milwaukee brick for the structure. With increases in grain and lumber shipping, came the need to mark the harbor better, so a brighter fifth-order Fresnel lens was placed in the lantern attached to the north side of the house. Fueled by sperm or lard oil, according to availability, the light had a visibility of 15 miles (24 km). John M. Clarkson, the old light's keeper, tended the new light until Harriet Colfax took over.

Miss Colfax, a former music teacher, came from New York to help run her brother's daily newspaper. However, his failing health forced him to sell out, leaving her with no means of support. Not wanting to return to piano teaching in New York, she petitioned her cousin, Congressman Schuyler Colfax, for the position of lightkeeper. Most lighthouse appointments at this time were actually political favors, so Miss Colfax received the position on March 19, 1861. Many questioned her ability but she soon silenced critics with her exemplary performance. Since she was an educated woman, her logbooks were some of the most organized, detailed and legible, and are on display in the National Archives. Her friend, Miss Ann Hartwell, joined her and between the two they kept the light lit in the severest of weather. Colfax often went out of her way to help captains and because of her kindness and friendly nature, they frequently referred to the Michigan City lighthouse as "Miss Harriet's."

In 1871 a second light was added at the end of the east pier and a catwalk was built to assist the keeper in inclement weather. In her logbooks, Colfax frequently mentioned risking her life and the effort it took to crawl out on the 1,100-foot (338.4 m) catwalk in hurricane-force winds and waves. In cold weather the lard oil would sometimes congeal before reaching the light and this meant a return trip after it was reheated. She also recorded the introduction of kerosene in 1880.

In 1874 the pierhead light was moved from the east pier to the end of the west pier 500 feet (154 m) farther out into the lake, to give better protection and guidance into the harbor. An assistant keeper was hired and housed on the west side of the river to prevent his having to cross Trail Creek. In 1886 this new west pier and catwalk were destroyed in a severe storm. In 1887 the light was kept lit all year round rather than just in the shipping season. These keepers had to climb to the lanterns at dusk and at midnight — and again at dawn when the light was extinguished— to trim the wicks, polish the reflectors and replenish the fuel. So diligently did they perform their tasks that the Michigan City lighthouse became known on the Great Lakes as "Old Faithful." Keeper Colfax retired at the age of 80 years old in 1904.

Also in 1904 the west pier light was replaced by a new east pier light with another catwalk out to it and the keeper's quarters, were enlarged into a duplex dwelling for the keeper and his assistant. Since the keeper's house was always bigger or fancier than the assistant's, the keeper's side received an ornately decorated semi-circular veranda with an upper railing enclosing a second-story walkout. The assistant's veranda was rectangular with no top walkout or fancy trim. In spite of the differences, assistant keeper Ralph Moore's daughter believed that their side of the house was better because it looked out over the water.

Also at this time (1904) the fifth-order Fresnel lens was moved from the land lighthouse to the new east pier light where it would be more practical. It was 55 feet (16.9 m) above the water and flashed white every five seconds. The keeper's house was then only used as a residence and the old lantern and short tower were removed from the housetop.

In 1940 the lighthouse was automated and the station de-manned. It sat empty until 1965, during which time it was heavily damaged by water and vandals. In 1960 the Coast Guard declared the old lighthouse surplus and Michigan City purchased it for historical purposes in 1963. In 1965 the Michigan City Historical Society leased it with the agreement to restore it and establish a museum. It took eight years of hard work to refurbish the interior and repair and paint the exterior, and to place a replica of the original lantern and tower on the roof. The society opened the museum to the public in June 1973. In November 1974 the old lighthouse was placed on the *National Register of Historic Places* because of its historically significant architecture and association with lake transportation. The Old Michigan City Lighthouse Museum is well worth a visit.

Known Keepers: Edmund Harrison (1837–41), James Towner (1841–44), Harriet Towner (1844–53), John Clarkson (1853–61), Harriet Colfax (1861–1904).

Michigan City East Pierhead Light

64 Michigan City Pier Lights

The first beacon light was installed at Michigan City in 1871 on the east pier and was maintained by the keeper of the main light on shore. A catwalk was built out to it for the keeper's safety. Even then, the keeper's logbooks show that she frequently risked life and limb to maneuver herself out to the light.

In 1874 the light was moved from the east pier to the west pier, where it was thought to be a better marker for the harbor as the west pier extended 500 feet (150 m) farther out into the lake. This meant more danger for the lightkeeper as she now had to row across the creek in all weathers, walk along the creek, follow the catwalk, and then climb the ladder to the light. While the catwalk was being moved, a Lake Michigan storm carried the mechanical pile driver and its engine away, delaying the move.

Keeper Colfax was concerned that she could not keep both lights lit with the extra difficulty of the pier light being on the other side of the river. In October 1874 she requested an assistant. Her logbook showed that she could not extinguish the pier light on October 29, 1874, as the catwalk had been removed and a storm kept her on shore. Her plea for an assistant keeper was soon granted, and the assistant was housed on the west side of the creek to maintain the west pier light. Even he had difficulty keeping the light lit. Colfax reported the pier light unlit on November 23 due to a severe storm. The storm also removed part of the catwalk, so the light was again unlit the next night.

During a December blizzard in 1885 the catwalk and light were damaged and the light extinguished. When the inspector was informed by telegraph, his reply was to "hang a lantern out." However, the next night this beacon was carried away in the storm. The following two nights a tug was sent out to the light since there was no other way to get out there. When Colfax asked the inspector if she could use the tug for the rest of the season, his reply was to close the lights as soon as possible, so she closed them the next day.

Then, during a severe March storm in 1886, the pier light and much of the catwalk were swept right into the lake. Fortunately, the keeper had just stepped to shore from the catwalk and was not personally harmed. It took until June before a temporary light was erected.

In 1904 after the east pier was extended farther into the lake, a new combined fog signal building and lighthouse tower was built at its end. With its raised concrete base, square fog building with hipped roof, octagonal tower and circular iron lantern with diagonal glass panels, it is identical to the pier light at St. Joseph. A catwalk connected it to shore. The shore light was discontinued and in October 1904 its fifth-order Fresnel lens was put in this new east pierhead light. The fog signal equipment was installed in 1905.

The east pierhead light has undergone some changes. In 1933 the light was electrified and operated from shore and the fog signal was converted to an automated electrically powered air system. In 1960 the station was completely automated and keepers were no longer necessary. At some point the original fifth order-order Fresnel lens was replaced with a modern acrylic optic and the old lens was placed on display in Michigan City's Old Lighthouse Museum (the old 1858 lighthouse) where it can be viewed today.

In 1983, when the Coast Guard announced plans to tear down the deteriorating catwalk, public outcry stopped them. Michigan City residents Patricia Harris and Betty Rinehart persuaded the Coast Guard to deed the catwalk to the city, convinced the city to accept it and then worked to raise funds to restore the catwalk and its lights. In February 1984 the Michigan City East Pier Light Tower and Elevated Walk were placed on the *National Register of Historic Places* because of their historically significant architecture. In 1991 *Historic Landmarks of Indiana* placed the catwalk on its list of the "Ten Most Endangered Structures in Indiana" because of its poor condition. Later that year the city applied for and received a $40,000 grant toward restoration. In 1997 Harris and Rinehart received the Servaas Memorial Award presented by the Historic Landmark Foundation of Indiana for their 14 years of work to save the endangered Michigan City Catwalk.

Known Keepers: Harriet E. Colfax (1861–1904), Thomas Armstrong (1904–19), Phillip Sheridan (1919–30), Walter Donovan (1930–40), Ralph Moore (1940).

65 Milwaukee Breakwater Lighthouse

Construction on Milwaukee breakwaters began in 1881 and, as sections were built, they were lit by minor lights. Sometime during the 1890s an inverted funnel-shaped lighthouse sheathed in iron plating was built on the breakwater. The bottom was used as a service room, and a door through a dormer in one of the six sides provided entry. A window was located above the door for interior daytime light. A simple hexagonal gallery surrounded its small hexagonal lantern, which was topped with an oversized dome. The same style of lighthouse was also used at Kenosha, Racine, Sheboygan, Waukegan and Petoskey.

This first light was replaced in 1926 with a structure 53 feet (16.3 m) high built at the south end of the north breakwater. After a crib had been sunk, it was capped with a concrete pier 23 feet (7 m) high. On this base, a fog signal/lighthouse was built using steel framework covered in steel sheeting and glass for windows ½-inch (1.25 cm) thick. The lower part was a large two-story section 22 feet (6.7 m) high. The first level housed the fog signal equipment and machinery, and the second level was for the keepers' living quarters. The 14-foot (4.3 m) square tower rose 20 feet (6 m) from the center top of the living quarters to the gallery, which held the round cast-iron lantern and fourth-order Fresnel lens that had lens that had been moved from the Milwaukee pierhead light. From its 61-foot (18.8 m) focal plane the red light, which flashed every ten seconds, could be seen for 14 miles (22.5 km). The light was manned by a four-man crew who were responsible for operating and maintaining all harbor lights.

In 1966 the breakwater light was automated and powered by electricity, which was supplied by an underwater cable from the shore. Although its keepers are gone, the light still uses its original fourth-order Fresnel lens.

Known Keepers: William Schroeder (1907–11), Oscar Knudsen (1911–18), Edward Wheaton (1918–1920), Reynold Johnson (1923–24).

Milwaukee Breakwater Lighthouse

First Milwaukee Breakwater Light, circa 1911

66 Milwaukee Lighthouse

In 1837 Congress appropriated $5,000 for a lighthouse at the mouth of the Milwaukee River. When it was near completion in 1838, the inspector's comments caused some controversy about its location. While the 30-foot (9 m) tower and detached house were built of quality bricks and mortar, he was unhappy about the site: "For purpose of practical utility to those engaged in commercial business of the lakes, this site is about the worst that could have been taken in the vicinity of the spot indicated in the law authorizing its construction." Although the light was built on a 56-foot (17 m) bluff overlooking the bay, probably to be seen farther out in the lake, the inspector thought the bluff location was too far from the river mouth (over a mile north of it) to guide mariners accurately.

The keeper also reported a delay in the tower's completion due to the late arrival of its stone platform and cast-iron lantern. The steamship *De Witt Clinton*, which was bringing the lantern to Milwaukee, grounded in September on a shoal near Big Beaver Island in Lake Michigan and had to throw $20,000 worth of cargo — including the lantern for Milwaukee — overboard before it could be pulled off of the shoal.

When finally lit, the lantern used eleven Argand lamps with 14-inch (35 cm) reflectors to produce its beam. This light remained active until 1855, when it was replaced by a taller light that had been built at North Point to the north of the city. When the new light began operation the old one was torn down.

Known Keepers: Eli Bates (1838–48), James Ragan (1848–49), Josiah Sherwood (1849–53), Andrew Sullivan (1853–56).

67 Milwaukee Lightship

The Lighthouse Board had discontinued the Milwaukee North Point light in 1907, but public pressure and the efforts of local businessmen had the light relit while awaiting appropriations to raise the tower for improved visibility. Since a lightship was being built to be anchored offshore Milwaukee in the summer of 1911, the Lighthouse Board stalled on extending the North Point tower upward. However, since the lightship's construction was delayed, plans went forward to raise the existing tower.

LV 95 was to be placed three miles (5 km) offshore to assist lighting the port of Milwaukee. Built by the Racine-Truscott-Shell Lake Boat Co. of Muskegon, Michigan, it was a steel-hulled steam screw with a pilothouse at the foremast, which was a large diameter tubular lantern mast. Its aft mast was a conventional steel one

Milwaukee Lightship LV 95

Milwaukee Lightship LV 95 converted to a relief vessel

by a small deckhouse. The vessel was 108½ feet (33 m) long, had a 23-foot (7 m) beam and an 11½ foot (3.5 m) draft, and displaced 368 tons of water. While it was propelled by a 200 IHP steam engine, it was also rigged for a sail. It was lit using an electrical incandescent lamp and a revolving parabolic reflector inside a large-diameter lantern housing. For fog it had a hand-operated fog bell and a 12-inch (30 cm) steam chime whistle. In December 1911 it sank at the contractor's dock and was raised two months later. It was finally finished in November 1912, at a cost of $74,558, and was then placed off Milwaukee.

The lightship underwent a few technical changes. In 1916 its illuminating apparatus was changed to a duplex 375 mm electric lens lantern that produced 13,200 candlepower. In 1936 it was repowered using a 200 HP Superior six-cylinder four-cycle diesel main engine. With this engine and a 4½-foot (1.4 m) propeller, its maximum speed was six knots (6.9 mile/11 km). In the 1930s it received a diaphone fog signal. From 1940 to 1965 its radio and visual call sign was NNGX.

After serving at Milwaukee from 1912 until 1932, the lightship was removed to do relief work when it was evident that the new Milwaukee breakwater light, built in 1926, was adequately lighting the area and that vessels were familiar with the new light. *LV 95* was retired from lightship duty in 1965.

68 Milwaukee Pierhead Light

During harbor improvements at Milwaukee, a new "Straight Cut" harbor entrance was dredged between 1852 and 1857, to make the new entrance to the river half a mile (0.8 km) north of the natural river mouth. This entrance channel was flanked by parallel piers. By 1868 the channel was dredged deeper and the piers were extended another 600 feet (185 m) into the lake. A pier light to mark the new entrance was first built in 1872. It is believed to have been a square white wooden pyramidal tower with an open base and an enclosed section at the top of the tower.

In 1906 the wooden tower was replaced with a 41-foot (12.6 km) pierhead tower made of cast-iron bands that sat inside each other and were riveted together to form a slightly conical shape. Its circular cast-iron lantern had helical bars and originally housed a fourth-order Fresnel lens made by Henri LePaute of Paris. In 1926 the light was given a fifth-order Fresnel lens and a decagonal

lantern, and the fourth-order lens was moved to the new breakwater light.

At some point after the breakwater light was manned, an underwater cable was installed from the pier light and the keeper assumed responsibility for keeping the light on the pier. Today the pier light still uses its fifth-order Fresnel lens to display its flash every four seconds which can be seen 12 miles (19.4 km) out on the lake.

Known Keepers: Michael Burke (1856–61), William Bruin (1861–71), Charles Lewis (1871), Alonzo Burdick (1871), D. Green (1871–81), Mrs. Georgia Stebbins (1881–1907), Thomas Bailey (1909–17), Martin Knudsen (1917–24), Reynold Johnson (1924–43).

69 Minneapolis Shoal Lighthouse

Minneapolis Shoal lies about 14 miles (22.7 km) southeast of Escanaba and 10 miles (16.2 km) south of Peninsula Point in the northwestern part of Lake Michigan. It was named after the freight steamer *Minneapolis*, which grounded on the shoal during a strong September storm in the late 1890s. After this wreck, a light buoy was placed to mark the shoal.

A lighthouse had been built at Peninsula Point in 1865 to warn of the shoals that ran out from the point into the shipping lane, but as larger ships sailed in deeper water the light was too far from the traveled route to be much help.

In 1934–35 the U.S. government erected the Minneapolis Shoal lighthouse. A square concrete crib was placed on the shoal and capped with a 64-foot (19.7 m) almost square concrete pier. The 30 foot (9 m) square base of the 70-foot (21.5 m) concrete and steel tower was two stories high. From this, a five-story tower, which tapered gently at the bottom, rose straight up. The tower and pier had cut-off corners, making them slightly octagonal. The tower supported a circular lantern with curved glass set diagonally into its astragals, and the lantern used a fourth-order Fresnel lens from an 82-foot (25.2 m) focal plane.

The structure housed a diaphone fog signal, diesel generators, living quarters, storage areas and machinery areas. It was usually manned with a five-man crew who worked four weeks on and two weeks off. It was supplied every two weeks when the crew changed, but when it was automated in 1979 it no longer used a keeper. The light is still operational.

70 Muskegon Breakwater Lights

Around 1916, during more harbor improvements, arrowhead breakwaters were started at Muskegon, Lake Michigan. Upon their completion in the 1920s, lights were placed at their ends to mark the harbor entrance between them. They were tall slender steel pyramidal towers that were fully enclosed.

The breakwaters created an outer harbor and the north and south piers inside them were shortened to provide more space within the harbor. At this time the catwalk and fog signal building were removed. At a later date a modern plastic optic that displayed its warning light from a 70-foot (21.5 m) focal plane replaced the south breakwater light.

Milwaukee Pierhead Light

71 Muskegon Harbor Lighthouse

Congress approved the building of a lighthouse at the mouth of the Muskegon River, Lake Michigan, in 1830. However, it was not until 1849 that they appropriated $3,500 to build a light here, and the station was established only in 1851 or 1852. Although little is known about this first light, it was believed to have been a wooden keeper's house with a short tower on top of it. The polygonal lantern was supplied with a fourth-order Fresnel lens.

Private businessmen started harbor improvements in the early 1860s, and the federal government continued them in the late 1860s when money became available after the Civil War. In 1871 the harbor light was rebuilt. It was a 1½-story wooden schoolhouse-style building with a short square tower extending up from the roof at the front. This style was also used at Old Mission Point (1870), Lake Michigan, and Mama Juda Island (1866) in the Detroit River. This light was discontinued when range lights were placed in the harbor in 1903.

Known Keepers: Alexander Wilson (1851–53), Peter Seaman (1853), Alexander Wilson (1853–56), William Brithain (1856), Alexander Wilson (1856–59), J. Ryan (1859), George Harden (1859), William Monroe (1859–62), Mrs. William Monroe (1862–71), Henry Warren (1871–86), Charles Lindstrem (1886–87), Hans Hansen (1887–88), Charles Lindsterm (1888–1903).

72 Muskegon South Pierhead Light

Along with harbor improvements, Muskegon, Lake Michigan, received its first pierhead light in 1871. In 1899 a frame steam-powered fog signal building was added at the end of the south pier, a lantern room was placed onto the gable end facing the lake, and a catwalk was built to connect it to shore. This new structure replaced the first pierhead light. At a later time, the fog signal was upgraded to a diaphone one.

In 1903 a third light, an iron pier light, was built on the south pier about 700 feet (215 m) behind the fog signal building. The circular tower was 53 feet (16 m) tall and made of riveted bands of iron. The fourth-order Fresnel lens from the Muskegon Harbor lighthouse was moved into the polygonal lantern of this new light. When established, the light became a rear range light for the light on the fog signal building.

When the Muskegon breakwater was built in the 1900s its harbor piers were shortened to provide more space within the harbor. It was at this time that the fog signal building with its front range light became the pierhead light, the south pier having been shortened to end just in front of this lighthouse. At an unknown date the Fresnel lens was removed and replaced with a modern 300 mm optic. While the pierhead light is still active today, the catwalk, like the fog horn, is long gone.

Known Keepers: Thomas Robinson (1906–28), James Burdick (1928–39), Ransom Jakubovsky (1939–40).

73 New Buffalo Lighthouse

In response to local petitioning, Congress appropriated $5,000 in 1838 to build a lighthouse at New Buffalo, Lake Michigan. Land for a lighthouse on the southern 40-foot (12.2 m) bluff above the mouth of the Galien River was purchased from Wessel Whittaker for $200.

Although there is no known picture of the light, the original proposal gives the following specs. A 25-foot (7.7 m) conical stone or brick tower built on a sunken foundation. It was to taper from a base diameter of 18 feet (5.5 m) to a top diameter of 9 feet (2.7 m) with walls 3 feet (0.9 m) thick at the bottom to 20 inches (50 cm) thick at the top. A soapstone deck was to top the tower and a trapdoor to provide entry to the lantern. The whitewashed tower was to have three 12-paned windows ascending it. Circular dressed stone stairs built into the wall were to lead from the ground floor to within 7 feet (2.2 m) of the deck, and an iron ladder to access the lantern. The tower was to be topped with an octagonal wrought iron lantern and seven sides were to contain 18 sections, 15 of glass and the bottom three of copper. The eighth side was to have an iron frame door covered in copper to provide access to the gallery. A copper dome with ventilator stack and a copper vane was to top the lantern, which was to use eleven Winslow Lewis lamps with 14-inch (35 cm) reflectors. A separate stone or brick keeper's house was also planned, a one-story dwelling divided into two rooms and built on a full cellar with an attached kitchen.

The lighthouse was built by Jeremy Hixon, who had built the Michigan City Lighthouse just two years previously. This light was almost identical except that it was shorter. Lime for the whitewashing was made from a large boulder found near the site. Its bricks were made by Isaac O. Adams. Thomas S. Smith, the light's first keeper, was appointed in January 1840 for $350 a year.

Hixon did not have the lighthouse finished in October 1839 as planned, and Smith reported in February 1840, that it leaked badly. The government held off final payment pending repairs. The light was finally lit on June 20, 1840, at a cost of $5,169, but the leaks were not fixed until the fall. By the next summer $30 was spent on repairs and $50 to deepen the well. Smith was relieved as

Muskegon South Pierhead Light

keeper, as he lived 17 miles (27.5 km) away and had subcontracted the keeper's job, a practice the government did not allow.

At the end of 1843 a recommendation was made to discontinue the light, as mariners referred to it as a useless light and the community made up of only 25–30 people did not have a sheltered harbor or enough commerce to warrant a light at this location. However, the light continued to shine.

In 1847 the Michigan Central Railroad finished its line to New Buffalo, their planned western terminus, and started work on piers to make it accessible to steamboats from Chicago. During this time, the New Buffalo lighthouse became very important. In 1849 the light's lamps and reflectors, reduced to four, displayed a fixed light visible for 14-miles (22.5 km), and a light was built on the north pier for $475.

In 1857 the light was refitted with a sixth-order lens that provided a 144-degree arc of illumination. It was not lit again after the close of the 1858 navigational season and was officially discontinued on August 1, 1859. This was due to the railroad being extended to Chicago, to the constantly shifting sands of the river mouth, which reduced boat traffic, and to sand erosion beneath the lighthouse foundation. Bricks and metalwork from the lighthouse were sold at public auction in 1861, as were materials from the keeper's house in 1862. At a later unknown date the remains of the tower and the keeper's house crumbled into the water. The land from the New Buffalo lighthouse reservation was sold at public auction in December 1902 to F.R. Perkins of Chicago for $75.

74 North Manitou Island Lighthouse

By 1892 the port of Chicago was one of the busiest in the world, surpassed only by New York, Hamburg and London. Recognizing this and the importance of safe water passage, the Lighthouse Board acquired land for a light station on the southeast end of North Manitou Island, Lake Michigan, in 1895. This location was chosen to help guide ships through the narrow 2-mile (3.2 km) Manitou Passage by marking the dangerous North Manitou Shoals. The lighthouse was located at one end of the shallow shoals.

Construction began in 1896. Eventually the station included a detached keepers' duplex, a steam-powered fog signal building, a barn, an oil house, and the 50-foot (15.3 m) tapered tower, a simple wooden skeleton covered in clapboarding. The circular lantern housed a fourth-order Fresnel lens and displayed an alternating red and white light through curved square glass panels set diagonally into metal astragals. Finished in 1898, it worked in conjunction with the light on South Manitou Island to guide vessels safely through the narrow passage. When it was found to insufficiently warn of the shoals, a lightship was placed to mark the other end of them in 1910.

The detached red brick keeper's duplex was large and spacious, with two of everything. The main floor rooms had ornamental pressed-tin ceilings, coved mouldings, built-in china cabinets, ceramic tile floors and solid oak woodworking. Numerous windows gave an unimpeded view of the water.

The North Manitou Island light had only a few keepers. Fred Samuelson, the second one, was paid $50 a month (increased in 1908 to $52) plus housing and an allowance for food and uniforms. Samuelson was a photography buff. He took many pictures of life on the island and developed them in his own darkroom in the basement of house. Most of his pictures were on dry glass plates.

The positions of lighthouse keeper and officer in charge of the lifesaving station were respected government positions, and since there was no law enforcement on the island, these two people were called upon to settle disputes. As a reward for his excellent service, Samuelson was chosen to present the lighthouse exhibit at the International Exhibition at Omaha, Nebraska, in 1908, and in 1934 at the Century in Progress exhibition in Chicago. In 1909 Samuelson was transferred to the Ludington lighthouse.

Keepers used to sail the five miles to the nearest island town in the summer. In winter huge snowdrifts blocked the road, isolating them further until the ice was frozen hard enough to them to travel across it in a horse-drawn cutter. Once the ice was thick enough, it served as a road for mail and supplies. The first to cross each season placed cut bushes to mark the trail to the nearest point, Glen Haven. Occasionally the horse broke through the ice. Once, before Samuelson could cut his floundering horse free, it lunged to safety and took off with the cutter wobbling frantically after it.

On one occasion during an early freeze-up, the mail boat became iced-in at Leland. The mailman loaded a sleigh with mail and supplies and headed across the ice to the island. All went well until the horse, sleigh, and cargo fell through open cracks near the lighthouse. Fortunately, the mailman made it safely to the lighthouse, and rescuers saved the horse, sleigh, and mail bags. But before the mail could be delivered, it had to be dried. Newspapers with long-awaited news about World War I were hung carefully on a basement clothesline until they were dry enough to read.

Vivian Langer, daughter of keeper Charles Linsmeir, has some interesting stories. When her parents first arrived at North Manitou Island in the winter by the Ann Arbor car ferry, heavy ice forced the ferry to drop them and their trunks on the ice farther away from the island than expected. As her mother was seven months pregnant, her father walked to the island to borrow a horse and sleigh. One of their first sights was frozen cattle, starved because the extra hay the farmers had ordered had not arrived that year. Even the ferry was stuck in the ice for a week before it could move on.

On another occasion Langer's parents and the other assistant keeper had taken the lighthouse "runabout" to Leland, Michigan, 13 miles (21 km) away to pick up mail and supplies. On the return trip they ran into unexpected foul weather and the engine quit. To keep his seasick wife and the other assistant keeper safe, Charles lashed them to benches in the boat. Eventually Charles found a sparkplug to get the engine working, but in the fog they no longer knew their location. Luckily, Charles heard and recognized the foghorn from South Fox Island and used this knowledge to get them safely home.

In 1935 the lighthouse was deactivated when it became obsolete with the building of a crib light right onto the North Manitou Shoals. The Fresnel lens from this light was moved to the new crib light. Once abandoned, the old lighthouse started to succumb to the work of the elements and shoreline erosion. In 1942 the tower completely collapsed. By 1968 high water eroded the front wall of the house, exposing inner levels of the house. The remainder of the house collapsed sometime in the seventies. Today only a few bricks remain on the shore as a reminder of the buildings that were once there.

Known Keepers: Andrew Bourisseau (1897–98), Fredrick Samuelson (1898–1909), Edward Cornell (1909–11), Reynold Johnson (1911–18), Guy Patterson (1922–28), Charles Linsmier, (?), Paul A. Walters (–1932).

North Manitou Shoal Lighthouse

75 North Manitou Shoal Lighthouse

Before engineering expertise allowed a lighthouse to be built directly onto North Manitou Shoal, the hazardous shoal was marked by a light on the southwest tip of nearby North Manitou Island in 1898. When this light was deemed inadequate, a lightship was also placed at the opposite edge of the shoal. Both the island light and the lightship were deactivated when a crib light was built on the shoal.

The North Manitou Shoal light was built in 1935 right onto the shoal in 26 feet (8 m) of water. It provided reliable, cost-effective protection from the elements and could not be blown off station as a lightship could. Its sunken crib supported a concrete pier and a square steel two-story keeper's house upon which a square steel tower was built. It is similar in design and appearance to the Lansing Shoal light. Its 63-foot (19.8 m) tower has a 79-foot (24.3 m) focal plane and first used the original fourth-order Fresnel lens that had been moved from the North Manitou Island light when it was deactivated.

This station used to house six Coast Guardsmen, five on duty at the light while one was on shore leave for a week. They operated the light, the fog signal and the radio beacon, and maintained the equipment and station in excellent order. Surrounded by water and with little room to walk, it was a most lonely station.

At an unknown date, the Fresnel lens was replaced by a DCB 24 optic. In 1980 the light was automated and the keepers were no longer necessary. Today it still serves as an active aid to navigation and is maintained by the U.S. Coast Guard.

Known Keepers: George Larson (1875–82), Ernst Hutzler (1946–58).

76 North Manitou Shoal Lightship

The North Manitou Shoal in Manitou Passage, on the trade route up the east side of Lake Michigan, was first marked in 1898 by a light on the southeast tip of North Manitou Island. However, when this light was found inadequate, a lightship was placed to mark the other end of the shallow shoals in 1910. Lightships were essential for marking some of the most dangerous areas to navigate but they were frequently blown off station when they were needed most. The North Manitou lightship was blown loose several times. Once it drifted ashore at Leland, where the crew patronized a local bar while the storm howled and their families, seeing the lightship missing, mourned the likely loss of their loved ones.

Three lightships were used at this station. In 1910 *LV 56* was transferred to Manitou Shoals from White Shoal (a station that had been discontinued in 1909) at the Straits of Mackinac. It was one of three sister ships (*LV 55, 56* and *57*) all built to the same specifications by the Blythe Craig Shipbuilding Company of Toledo, Ohio, in 1891. It cost a total of $14,225. *LV 56* was a wooden vessel with a daymark on its foremast, an aft mast for a riding sail, and a smokestack midship on its deckhouse. It used a 100 IEP steam screw engine to achieve a maximum speed of 8 knots. The vessel was 102 feet 8 inches (31.3 m) long, 20 feet (6.1 m) wide, and had a draft of 9 feet 8 inches (3 m) and a displacement of 129 tons.

It was equipped with a cluster of three oil-burning lens lanterns hoisted to each masthead, a 6-inch (15 cm) steam whistle and a hand-operated fog bell. In 1910 a submarine bell signal was added. In the winter of 1913–14 the aft mast was removed and the lettering on the hull was shortened to *Manitou*. The lightship was used for economy, having an estimated annual maintenance and operating cost of $4,000. Also, to avoid costly mushroom anchors and chain, a cheaper 5-ton sinker and 15 fathoms of 2-inch (5 cm) chain were permanently positioned on the shoal to anchor the vessel. *LV 56* served at Manitou Shoal until the end of the 1926 shipping season, when it was moved to Gray's Reef.

The second lightship to mark Manitou Shoal was *LV 89*. It was a steel-hulled boat with a whaleback forecastle deck, a lantern foremast, an aft mast with a riding sail, a large wooden deckhouse and a smokestack midship. It was just over 88 feet (27 m) long, had a beam of 21 feet (6.4 m), a 7-foot (2.1 m) draft, and a displacement of 205 tons. Its 90 IEP one-cylinder reciprocating steam engine propelled it on and off the site. It had a cluster of three oil-burning lens lanterns to light it from a 35-foot (10.7 m) focal plane. Its 6-inch (15 cm) steam whistle or its hand-operated bell warned of fog.

North Manitou Shoal Lightship LV 56, *circa 1910*

Manitou Lightship LV 103, *circa 1934–35*

LV 89 was built for $37,500 by the Racine-Truscott-Shell Lake Boat Co. of Muskegon, Michigan, in 1908. It first marked Martin Reef, but when that station received a lighthouse the lightship was moved to Manitou Shoal to start the 1927 shipping season. In 1930 it was converted to the use of acetylene and in 1933 to electricity. At the end of the 1933 shipping season the lightship was removed from this station. After doing relief duty for two years it was retired from lightship duty in 1936.

The third and last lightship to mark Manitou Shoal was *LV 103*, a sturdy, steel-hulled ship built by the Consolidated Shipbuilding Company of Morris Heights, New York, in 1920 for $161,074. It had a lantern foremast, a small jigger aft mast, a steel pilothouse at the foot of the tubular lantern mast, and a smokestack midship. The vessel was 95 feet 5 inches (29.2 m) long and 24 feet (7.3 m) wide, with a draft of 9½ feet (2.9 m) and a 310-ton displacement. It had a 175 IHP steam engine and two coal-fired Scotch boilers. It used a 300 mm acetylene lens lantern, a 10-inch (25 cm) steam fog whistle and a hand-operated fog bell.

After marking the shoals for 1934–35, it was removed when a crib light was built right on the shoal. From here *LV 103* moved to southern Lake Huron to become the *Huron Lightship*, and marked the entrance to the Huron Cut Channel. It kept vigil there until being retired from service in 1970. Today it stands next to the St. Clair River at Pine Grove Park in Port Huron, where it serves as a marine museum.

77 North Point Lighthouse

In 1852 Congress appropriated $5,000 to relocate the lighthouse at Milwaukee, since the first site had not been ideal. The new site was on top of the 80-foot (24.4 m) bluff between two ravines at the north point of the bay, 3 miles (4.8 km) north of the mouth of the Milwaukee River and 2 miles (3.2 km) north of the existing lighthouse. A light at this spot would be seen by vessels coming from the north as well as those in the bay. Land was purchased in 1853 and construction began in 1855. While little is recorded about this light, it is known that it was a 28-foot (8.5 m) yellow brick tower that used a fourth-order Fresnel lens to display a fixed white light that was varied by a bright flash every 2½ minutes and it had a 14-mile (22.7 km) visibility. The old light was discontinued when this one was lit on November 26, 1855, and Andrew Sullivan, the keeper of the old light, became the first keeper of the new North Point lighthouse.

Shortly after the lighthouse's completion, it was noted that the bluff in front of the tower was eroding. By 1881 the erosion was

North Point Lighthouse

advancing at a pace that caused alarm for the tower's well-being. Congress therefore appropriated $15,000 in 1886 to purchase land and build a new station.

The new station, built just west of the old one, was finished in December 1887. The tower was a 30-foot (9 m) tapering octagonal cast-iron structure with a 14-foot (4.3 m) base diameter and a diameter below the gallery of 9-feet (2.8 m). To prevent inner condensation on the iron walls, it was lined with brick, and lit by ornately pedimented rectangular windows. The watchroom, accessed by cast-iron stairs, was lit by four trimmed porthole windows. The octagonal gallery, trimmed with pipe-iron railing, supported an octagonal lantern that housed the fourth-order Fresnel lens imported from the previous lighthouse.

The keeper's dwelling was a two-story clapboard house in Queen Anne style attached to the tower by an enclosed passageway. It was later converted into a duplex and then a triplex as more keepers were needed at the station. The station also had a brick oil storage house, a 125-foot (38 m) well, concrete walkways, and a surrounding fence. The new light was lit for the first time on January 10, 1888.

As the city developed, a 140-acre (56.7 hectare) park was planned along the crest of the bluff, and in 1892 the city hired celebrated architect Frederick Law Olmsted to plan the park layout. Since this park landlocked the lighthouse reservation, the Lighthouse Board traded land in front of it for property to the west that could connect the lighthouse to the road. Olmsted designed a wide boulevard to pass in front of the lighthouse, with duplicate ornate iron bridges to span the ravines on either side and sculptured sandstone lions to guard each end of the bridges.

Over time the park's maturing trees started to obscure the light, and the lighthouse was being surrounded by a growing number of city lights. Both these factors made it harder to distinguish. Since the light was no longer effective, Congress decommissioned it on June 30, 1907. Mariners and Milwaukee businessmen immediately objected and called to have it relit. Until its relighting was approved by Congress, the light was lit as a private aid to navigation and the Lighthouse Board immediately requested an official relighting as well as $10,000 to elevate the tower. By 1909 the appropriation was approved.

After years of procrastination and indecision, plans to raise the landfall tower finally did proceed. The old tower was set atop a new steel one starting in July 1912, and the lens was moved to a temporary tower while the old tower was dismantled. A new octagonal concrete foundation 21½ feet (6.6 m) in diameter was poured for the new tapering 30-foot (9 m) steel tower base. It was made in an octagonal shape to match the old tower and was given iron porthole windows to match those in the watchroom. When the new base was completed, the old tower was reassembled on top of it, and the fourth-order Fresnel lens repositioned in the old lantern, where it shone from its new 154-foot (47.3 m) focal plane. Using a gas mantle lamp, the Fresnel lens, and such a high focal plane, the light was visible for 21 miles (34 km). The light was finished by April of the 1913 shipping season. The entire refurbishing came in under budget at $9,516.

A few more changes took place at the light. In 1929 it was electrified. The light was automated in 1943, but the keeper's house continued to house Coast Guard personnel until modern navigation systems made the light obsolete and it was discontinued on March 15, 1994. The light had had a four-man crew that was responsible for operating and maintaining all harbor lights.

In 1966 the breakwater light was automated using electricity supplied by an underwater cable from the shore. The keepers were removed at this time but the North Point light continued to use its original fourth-order Fresnel lens. The Fresnel lens was later removed and put on display at the Milwaukee Coast Guard Station. Meanwhile, the station sat empty and neglected.

Then, in the late 1990s a group called the North Point Lighthouse Friends was formed with restoration of the lighthouse as their goal. In 2002 they were awarded a federal grant for $984,000 toward the $1,500,000 needed for total restoration.

Known Keepers: Eli Bates (1838–48), James Ragan(1848–49), Josiah Sherwood (1849–53), Andrew Sullivan (1853–56), Micheal Burke (1856–61), William Bruin (1861–71), Alonzo Burdick (1871), D. Green (1871–81), Mrs. Georgia Stebbins (1881–1907), Thomas Bailey (1909–1917), Martin Knudsen (1917–24), Reynold Johnson (1924–43).

78 Old Mission Point Lighthouse

Grand Traverse Bay of Lake Michigan is split at its bottom into an east and west bay by an 18-mile (29.2 km) peninsula called Old Mission Peninsula. Due to increased trade in the area, the peninsula (with its two miles of underwater rocky outcroppings from its point) needed to be marked to assist mariners. Congress responded by appropriating $6,000 in March 1859 to build a lighthouse on the end of the peninsula known as Old Mission Point. However, with the advent of the Civil War, a site was not selected until 1869.

Old Mission Point Lighthouse

The lighthouse was of a schoolhouse style, identical to the Mama Juda lighthouse (built in the Detroit River in 1866) and the Muskegon Harbor lighthouse (built on Lake Michigan in 1871). The 1½-story clapboard keeper's house had a 36-foot (11 m) tower ascending inside the lakeside end and upward for one story above the housetop. Its square gallery had tapered corners to produce an octagonal shape, and was surrounded by a black iron pipe railing. The decagonal lantern used a fifth-order Fresnel lens to produce a 13-mile (21 km) visibility from its 47-foot (14.5 m) focal plane. It was first exhibited on September 10, 1870.

Time brought changes. In 1889 a 200-foot (61.5 m) timber and rock breakwater was built in front of the lighthouse to prevent erosion. A brick cistern for rainwater was also built into the cellar at this time, and downspouts equipped with diverters to send rainwater directly into the cistern or onto the ground. Before collecting rainwater in the cistern keepers usually let the water run onto the ground for a while to clean the roof first. In 1899 a 360-gallon (1512 l) oil house was built to hold the lamp's new illuminant, kerosene, which was extremely volatile. At the turn of the century many vacationers came to visit Old Mission Point, making it necessary to build fencing around the perimeter of the grounds. Plank walkways improved access for tours. When an automated light was built offshore right on the underwater shoals in 1938, the light on Old Mission Point was deactivated.

The shoal light was constructed almost 2 miles (3.2 km) northwest of Old Mission Point in about 19 feet (5.8 m) of water. A circular steel pier built of interlocking pilings and filled with rocks and concrete supported a concrete base for the 36-foot (11 m) steel skeletal tower. Given a 200 mm lens and a battery-powered electric light of 330 candlepower, the light produced a single white flash every ten seconds to help conserve electricity. From its 52-foot (16 m) focal plane it produced a 13-mile (21 km) visibility. Sometime after its construction, the skeletal tower was replaced with a cylindrical D9 Type tower that used a solar-powered acrylic optic.

A number of keepers kept this light. The first, Pratt kept an unusually meticulous journal of passing ships. On his first day he recorded sighting two schooners, two steamers, 75 sailing ships and five other vessels.

After World War II the State of Michigan purchased the old lighthouse on Old Mission Point as part of a new park. In 1948 its safekeeping was transferred to Peninsula Township. Today the lighthouse can be viewed from the boardwalks in the park, but since park employees live there, it is not open to the public.

Known Keepers: Jerome M. Pratt Sr. (1870–77), John McHaney (1877–81), John Lane (1883–1906), James Davenport (1907–19), William Green (1919–24), Emil Johnson (1924–33).

Peninsula Point Lighthouse tower

79 Peninsula Point Lighthouse

Peninsula Point is the southernmost tip of the Stonington Peninsula, in northern Lake Michigan. By the mid-nineteenth century, lake traffic had increased in the area thanks to iron ore exports from Escanaba. A lighthouse was built on the point in 1865 to mark the peninsula as well as the shoals that divide Little Bay de Noc and Big Bay de Noc in the northern part of Green Bay, and the entry into Escanaba.

By the early 1900s the site included a barn, a woodshed, an oil house, and the tower with attached 1½-story keeper's house. Life at Peninsula Point was hard. The road to the lighthouse was impossible by wagon, so the keeper's children had to walk the 4 miles (6.5 km) to school each day. The family purchased groceries in Escanaba. In the summer they traveled there by boat; in the winter they made the trip by horse-drawn sleigh over the ice. During the fall freeze-up and the spring break-up, travel was not possible, so they had to make sure they had stocked up on provisions.

In 1923 the light was automated with an acetylene system that used a sun valve, but the keepers remained at the station for another two years. Ships still had trouble locating it, and so the Minneapolis Shoal Light was built. When it was activated in 1936, the Peninsula Point Lighthouse was decommissioned.

While it sat empty it became the "playground" for many local teenagers. Then in 1959 a fire gutted the structure. Today, all that is left is the tower and the remains of the cement walkways.

Early Peninsula Point Lighthouse

Although the tower was gutted and is now windowless, visitors can walk up its 41-step, open-cutwork self-cleaning iron stairs to the top for a wonderful view of Escanaba to the west, Minneapolis Shoal Light to the south, and Fayette to the east. A square walkway surrounds the decagonal lantern, and a black iron railing encompasses the outer walkway. The Peninsula Point tower is now part of a beautiful, well-kept picnic area that belongs to the Hiawatha National Forest.

Known Keepers: Ira Buck (1865), Thomas Bearse (1885–67), Charles Beggs (1867–87), Peter Knudsen (1888–89), James Armstrong (1890–1925).

Pentwater Pierhead Lights in the late 1800s

80 Pentwater Pierhead Lights

In 1867 a harbor entrance was dredged into Pentwater Harbor, which is about 20 miles (32.4 km) south of Big Sable Point on Lake Michigan's east shore. It had 610 foot (186 m) piers extending out into the lake on either side of the entrance. In 1873 the south pier was marked with a pierhead light. It was a square wooden pyramidal tower that supported an octagonal cast-iron lantern. A wooden catwalk along the pier connected it to the shore. In 1890 a pole lantern was added in front of the pierhead light to act as a front range light, but it was discontinued when found to be unnecessary. In 1937 a steel skeletal pierhead replaced the wooden one.

In 1987 a pierhead light was added to the north pier. It was a 30-foot (9 m) steel cylindrical tower placed on a concrete base and surmounted by a modern solar-powered plastic beacon. It housed equipment for an automated foghorn signal inside. Although discontinued now, it also housed equipment for a radio beacon transmitter. The tower was modelled after the D9 tower and designed by Jon Kiernan of the Cleveland Coast Guard unit. He planned it with a larger tower than the D9 so that it could hold more equipment than was needed simply for a light.

81 Peshtigo Reef Lighthouse

The shallow waters over Peshtigo Reef, which extends southwest from Peshtigo Point for about 3 miles (4.9 km) under the waters of Green Bay, border the west side of Green Bay's main shipping channel. A lightship first marked this hazard, but a lighthouse was later built on the southeast tip between 1934 and 1936. In the fall of 1934 a wooden crib was placed on the reef. The next spring, sheet piling was put on top of the crib. Inside this, the work crew placed five, 6-foot (1.8 m) diameter steel cylinders, each of which had a group of wooden piles driven into its center. Next they poured concrete into the space left inside the five cylinders, as well as inside the outer piling ring around the cylinders. The piling supported a thick concrete pier.

On this pier, from its 25-foot (7.7 m) diameter base, the lighthouse was built to a height of 14 feet (4.3 m) to provide a service and engine room and temporary emergency living quarters for the keepers. Many eight-paned rectangular windows lit its interior. A tall slightly tapering riveted steel plate tower was centered on this base. Four of its porthole windows looked out from the watchroom below the gallery.

Within, a spiral iron staircase led up to a circular iron lantern that housed a fourth-order Fresnel lens. Curved squares of glass sat diagonally in the metal astragals of the lantern. The electric lightbulb (20,000 candlepower) shone from a 72-foot (22 m) focal plane and was powered by a storage battery that was kept in a constant state of charge by its 110-volt generator and a gasoline engine that operated the generator. The light also had a 200 mm white winter lens (flash 0.55; eclipse 4.5s) activated on December 1 each year. Keepers from nearby Sherwood Point lighthouse tended the semi-automatic station via a small gasoline-driven launch. Part of their job was to ensure that the gas tanks were full. The light's daymark was a cream-color above the black pier except for the black lantern. The light was first lit in June 1936.

Its fog signal was an air diaphone system operated by a compressor also powered by a gasoline engine. It was radio-controlled from the Sherwood Point light and once it was activated, it operated automatically (blast 2s; silences 18s). It also had a solenoid fog bell that rang continuously (one strike every 20 seconds) regardless of weather.

Later, when a submarine power cable was run to the station, the gasoline engines and generators were removed. Once the fog signal was totally automated, the Sherwood Point keepers were no longer responsible for the light.

Other changes included the removal of the Fresnel lens, the installation of a modern optic and a more distinctive painting. While the crib piling and the lantern remained black, the rest of the tower was painted white with a wide red horizontal band around the upper part of the tower to give it a more visible daymark. The light still operates today to warn vessels on Green Bay of the reef's hidden hazards.

82 Peshtigo Reef Lightship

Peshtigo Reef ran dangerously just below the water for 3 miles (4.8 km) out into Green Bay from Peshtigo Point almost directly opposite Sherwood Point. Since it bordered the west side of the main shipping canal through Green Bay, the government responded to the Lighthouse Board in 1866 and appropriated money for lights on Chambers Island, Peshtigo Reef and Grassy Island. However, when it was realized that a larger sum would be needed, the appropriation for the reef light was withdrawn.

Without Congressional funds but realizing the need for a light, the Board constructed a daymark at the outer end of the reef in 1869. It consisted of a 30-foot (9 m) square wooden crib topped with a wooden pyramidal structure that supported an iron cage. It helped, but was useless in fog or darkness. In 1892 the Lighthouse Board again asked for money for a station on the reef. Congress approved a lighthouse, but did not appropriate any money until 1902 and then only to supply a lightship, not a lighthouse.

A contract was awarded in 1902 but was rescinded when work did not start on time. The new contract went to the Johnson Boiler Company of Ferrysburg, Michigan. The vessel, which cost $13,950, was *LV 77*. It was a 75-foot (23 m) "scow style" lightship with a steel hull and a 21½-foot (6.6 m) beam. It drew a draft of 9.2 feet (2.8 m) and displaced 155 tons of water. It contained four staterooms for crew, a head, and a galley. It was equipped with a hollow steel lantern mast on which three oil lens-lanterns could be hoisted and it had a hand-operated fog bell.

Two money-saving measures were incorporated. It had no propulsion system and needed to be towed to and from station by a lighthouse tender (*Dahlia* or *Hyacinth*) each season. Its interior space was used to store food and lantern oil for one season, thus saving the need to resupply it. It was first placed and lit on April 28, 1906 at the opening of the new navigation season. In 1911 it had an 8-inch (20 cm) chime fog signal installed on board.

By the 1930s *LV 77* was showing deterioration and the government decided that it would be cheaper to build a lighthouse right on the reef, as modern technology would allow the light to be mostly unstaffed. When this new light was temporarily lit on August 26, 1935, *LV 77* was removed from the station. It was assigned relief duty on the Great Lakes after this until it was retired from duty in 1940 and sold.

83 Petoskey Pierhead Light

Petoskey Harbor is located along the southeast side of Little Traverse Bay, Lake Michigan, where the Bear River empties into the bay. It is not a harbor of refuge as it offers little to no storm protection, but local commercial and tourist traffic used it in the late 1800s. To provide some protection, a breakwater was built northeast from the mainland into the lake in 1895 and a light was built at the end of the breakwater in 1899.

The lighthouse was one of six built on Lake Michigan in a similar style. The hexagonal base, about 20 feet (6 m) in diameter, tapered to about a 10-foot (3 m) diameter approximately 15 feet (4.6 m) from the base. From here it continued up straight for about another 10 feet (3 m). The gallery was supported by wooden braces and enclosed by a circular iron pipe railing. The hexagonal lantern had six large panes of glass and then another six large panes around the top of the lantern. The lantern housed a sixth-order Fresnel lens and was capped with an ogee copper dome with a hexagonal cupola (for ventilation) and a lightning rod. The tower was sheathed in corrugated iron for protection against the elements. The other lighthouses built on this design were at Kenosha, Milwaukee, Racine, Sheboygan and Waukegan.

At one time the pier and lighthouse were the hub of activity. Since Petoskey was in a tourist area, people gathered around the lighthouse to converse, socialize, view the lake and its boat traffic, and fish from the docks. But this romantic period ended when the lighthouse was replaced by a simple metal skeletal tower after being washed away in 1924. Today a cylindrical steel tower on a concrete base displays a red plastic optic from a 44-foot (13.5 m) focal plane.

84 Pilot Island Lighthouse

Early mariners had to travel around Door Peninsula, a dangerous point on the northwest side of Lake Michigan, to get into Green Bay. If they sailed between the peninsula and Washington Island just north of it, they crossed a hazardous strait called, with reason, Porte des Morts (Death's Door). However, since the strait cut many hours off of a voyage, making it commerce-friendly, mariners called to have it lit. The first light was built on Plum Island, midway through the strait, so that it could be seen when approaching from the east or the west. This was good in theory, but mariners then complained that it was too far west and that a light further east and south would be more beneficial. The Lighthouse Board therefore recommended a change, and in 1858 Porte des Morts Island (officially renamed Pilot Island in 1875), a small 3.5-acre (1.4 hectare) island to the east and south of Plum Island, was reserved for a new lighthouse.

The new station was built on the chosen site in 1858. It was a 2½-story rectangular yellow brick house with a short square wooden tower rising from its west peak. A simple gallery surrounded a decagonal iron lantern that housed a fourth-order Fresnel lens to display the light from a 46-foot (14 m) focal plane.

Frequent fogs necessitated a fog signal. The first, added in 1864, was a trumpet blown by the use of a caloric engine. When mariners complained that it was too weak, the Lighthouse Board installed a more powerful steam signal in 1875 and hired a second assistant to operate it. For security, the Lighthouse Board in 1880 added a duplicate steam siren, in a separate building, as a backup. Other fog signals were tried but none improved over the range of the steam siren. An 1890 visitor reported that the siren's vibration was so intense that the lanterns in the signal house had to be hung by string to prevent them from going out, chickens could not hatch as the vibrations killed them in the shell, and milk curdled within minutes. In 1904 the fog signal was changed to a diaphone system that operated on compressed air.

The island station was renovated as needed. With its exposed location and its orientation toward the east, arrivals and departures depended on the vagaries of the weather. To improve the situation, a new boathouse and pier were added on the west side of the island in 1891. In 1904 the keeper's house was enlarged into a duplex for the head keeper, first assistant and families. Both sides had a separate entrance, stairway, five rooms and a cellar. The unused fog signal building was converted into a dwelling for the

Pilot Island Lighthouse

second assistant keeper. These and the other outbuildings were connected by walkways.

Many shipwrecks and groundings occurred in and around Pilot Island and the keepers saved many lives. One keeper, Martin Knudsen, head keeper at Pilot Island Lighthouse from 1889–97, made a dramatic rescue of a crew in 1892. One very stormy late-October night, Knudsen and his first assistant rescued the whole crew of the schooner *A.P. Nichols*, which had been grounded close to the island's shore. While the *Nichols* rolled side to side in the pounding surf, Knudsen stood on the submerged wreck of the schooner *Forest* and grabbed the crew to safety, one by one, as they jumped toward him when the *Nichols* rolled his way. The keepers housed and fed all 18 crewmembers by for the next two weeks while the storm raged. For his bravery Knudsen was given a gold medal by the Lifesaving Benevolent Association of New York and a silver medal inscribed: "To Martin Knudsen Keeper Porte Des Morts United States Light Station in saving life at Wreck of Schooner A.P. Nichols October 28, 1892."

By 1955 the station's three keepers worked 23 days with seven days off each month, working 12-hour watches, especially alert for fog. The keepers at Plum Island let them know when the light was out as they could see it more easily. They painted, they cleaned and they repaired, and they mowed 2 acres (0.8 hectare) of grass each week with a hand-push mower. They cooked for themselves, ordered food by telephone from Sister Bay, and had the groceries delivered by a passing fisherman. A battery bank was powered by two Kohler generators that provided direct current electricity to operate the light and the water pump.

Once, when a Milwaukee Base technician was checking something at the island, he loaned them an AC power converter, which they used to operate a television. With their homemade-copper-tubing aerial mounted to the lantern, they received channels as far away as Milwaukee. However, passing Lakers complained that the light's characteristic was being altered, and after a visit from the Ninth District's personnel, the aerial was removed from the lantern and placed on a lowly ground pole from which they could only receive Green Bay.

In 1962 the light was automated and the fog signal was discontinued, made obsolete by modern technological equipment onboard vessels. The keepers left the island and cormorants took up residence. At some time the Fresnel lens was replaced by a 300 mm optic and the light was switched to solar-powered panels attached to the gallery railing. The roof on the old fog signal building has collapsed and nature is reclaiming the island, but the light continues to shine.

Known Keepers: William Shurtteffy (1858–59), Mathew Carey (1859–61), E.T. Wells (1861–63), John Kenard (1863–64), D.C. Read (1864–64), Jacob Stahl (1864–65), John Kenard (1865–66), Victor Rohn (1866–76), Emmanuel Davidson (1876–83), Peter Knudsen (1883–88), Nelson Knudsen (1888–89), Martin Knudsen (1889–97), Gottfried Hansen (1897–1902), Charles Bavry (1902–06), Henry Bervy (1907–13), Walter Otteson (1913–23), Robert Young (1923–25), C.I. Haas (1925–28), Clarence Anderson (1939–45).

85 Plum Island Range Lights

When mariners called to have the life-threatening Porte des Morts passage between Door Peninsula and Plum and Pilot islands in northwestern Lake Michigan lit to facilitate shipping into Green Bay, Congress appropriated $3,500 in 1848 for a "lighthouse to guide vessels through the passage from Lake Michigan to Green Bay." The chosen site was on Plum Island, about halfway through the passage, an ideal location as it could help vessels entering from either side of the peninsula. However, mariners complained that it needed to be further east and south to be of good service. Thus, the light was moved from Plum Island to Pilot Island in 1858. Plum Island then remained dark until range lights were lit in 1897.

Although the Lighthouse Board recommended lighting Plum Island in 1890, Congress approved the recommendation only in 1893 and did not appropriate the $21,000 until 1895. In 1896 a work crew arrived, cleared the heavily forested land on the southwest side of the island, and built a barn, boathouse, several piers, the range lights, a fog signal building, the keeper's duplex, a tramway, and 2,500 feet (765 m) of wooden walkways. The keeper's dwelling was a two-story yellow brick house.

The front range light was a short white square-based wooden tower that became an octagonal tower similar to the front range light at Baileys Harbor. Its lantern had a single window to display its fixed red light using a sixth-order lens at a 32-foot (9.8 m) focal plane for a visibility of 8.5 miles (13.8 km).

The more durable rear range light stood about 1,650 feet (500 m) behind it. The tapering, white square skeletal tower enclosed an iron cylinder housing a spiral staircase. The tower supported an 8-foot (2.4 m) cylindrical iron watchroom and an octagonal iron lantern. The watchroom was surrounded by an octagonal iron gallery, while the lantern had its own circular gallery. Its overall height was 65 feet (20 m) but it had an 80-foot (24.4 m) focal plane. A fourth-order Fresnel lens housed in the lantern displayed a fixed red light that was visible up to 13 miles (21 km) away. The light's arc of illumination was 231 degrees. The red-brick fog signal building housed a steam fog siren. With the addition of the light's illumination system in 1897 the station was ready, and its first keeper, Martin Knudsen (former keeper of nearby Pilot

Plum Island Rear Range Light

Island), first lit the light on May 1, 1897.

The station gradually changed. In 1939 when the Coast Guard took over the Lighthouse Service, they merged the light station with the lifesaving station on the island. They removed the piers and the boathouse, and moved the keepers into the lifesaving station's housing on the opposite side of the island. In 1964 they removed the front range light and replaced it with a steel skeletal tower. In 1969 the range lights were automated. In 1975 the fog signal was discontinued. Today the range lights still operate but nature is gradually reclaiming the once cleared land as the remaining buildings deteriorate.

Known Keepers: Martin Knudsen (1897–99), Hans Hanson (1899–1905), Charles E. Young (1905–07), Joseph Boshka (1907–11), Charley Boshka (1911–25), Oscar Johnson (1925–33), Clayton Kinkaide (1933–39).

Point Betsie Lighthouse

86 Point Betsie Lighthouse

Sitting along the east shore of Lake Michigan is the Point Betsie lighthouse. In 1853 Congress appropriated $5,000 for the establishment of a light on this point of land, known to the early French as "Pointe aux Bec Scies." Loosely translated, this means "sawed-beak point," as sawbills, a species of duck, were found in the area. Due to literary deficiencies, Bec Scies became "Betsie." The lighthouse was built in 1858 to mark the entrance to or exit from the Manitou Passage, along the northeast side of Lake Michigan. Sailing ships and steamers, as well as wooden and metal boats, carried lumber, fruit, iron ore and summer vacationers from Chicago, around the point and through the passage.

The cylindrical yellow brick tower, built on a concrete foundation, rises up 37 feet (11.3 m) from the ground. The top extends out with step-ring rows to support the gallery, which holds the red-domed lantern. A simple, black metal railing surrounds the gallery. The lantern housed a fourth-order Fresnel lens that rotated 52 feet (16 m) above the lake, displaying a fixed white light with a flash every 90 seconds for a visibility of 10 miles (16 km) in clear weather.

The keeper's house, a small two-story dwelling also built of yellow brick, stood immediately behind the tower, connected to it by a covered passageway. A cast-iron door into the tower was added as a safety precaution to prevent fire from spreading between the two structures.

The lighthouse, built on a low, sandy rise close to the water was an idyllic setting, but within a year storm erosion had started to undermine the base of the dune and displaced some of the tower's foundation stones. In 1869 a timber protection was built at the base of the dune and the foundation stones were repositioned and reinforced with concrete.

In 1880 the Lighthouse Board recommended a new taller, brighter light for Point Betsie, but the government ignored the recommendation. Thus thwarted, the Board gave its attention to maintaining the present light. While the tower was soundly built, its shallow foundation was continually being undermined by the sand under it. To strengthen the foundation, the tower was blocked, surrounding sand was removed, and a tapering concrete ring was inserted below the tower. This ring was then filled with concrete to lock it to the tower's foundation. Also in 1890, a 240-

foot (74 m) timber and stone breakwater was built at the water's edge to take the brunt of the wave action.

In 1891 Congress appropriated $5,000 to build a fog signal building. This structure was built just north of the lighthouse. Its timber frame was sheathed with corrugated iron sheeting, while the interior was covered with smooth iron sheets. It housed duplicate steam engines that were equipped with 10-inch (25 cm) steam whistles. A well dug beside the building provided water for the engines. The fog signal was put into operation during a snowstorm on December 22, 1891. Due to the increased workload of operating the fog signal, an assistant keeper, Charles W. Butler, was appointed. He moved in with the head keeper and his family. The structure was converted to a duplex in 1895 to give the two keepers more living space.

In April 1892 the district lampist, Mr. Crump, installed a new fourth-order Fresnel lens that had six bull's eyes, and changed the light's characteristic to a white light that flashed every ten seconds. As well, an oil house was built behind the fog signal building, indicating that the light's illuminant was likely switched to kerosene at this time. The work crew also installed 530 feet (162 m) of plank walks to connect the buildings of the complex. A second assistant keeper was added to the station in 1898.

In 1900 both the tower and the keeper's house were painted white with bright red roofs as a more visible daymark. In 1912 the 10-inch (25 cm) steam whistles were replaced with 10-inch chime whistles. In 1913 the lamp was upgraded to an incandescent oil vapor system that had 55,000 candlepower and an increased visibility of 27.5 miles (44.5 km).

With the arrival of electricity to the area in 1921, the lighthouse was switched to using a 110 volt electric bulb as its illuminant. The fog signal was also upgraded to twin Type G diaphones, powered by two electrically driven air compressors. This new system doubled the distance that the fog signal was carried. The fog signal characteristic was also changed at this time to two blasts every 30 seconds.

Around 1940 the boathouse collapsed. The lens clockwork mechanism was removed from the tower in 1944, and an electric motor was installed to rotate the lens.

Little is recorded about the lightkeepers. However, the first keeper was Alonzo Slyfield. He moved here from the South Manitou light. Slyfield and his two sons kept the light at Point

Betsie for 26 years. John Campbell was also a keeper at Point Betsie. Ed Roupe recollects that Edward M. Wheaton was a keeper for about 12 years from 1934 to 1946. Wheaton designed and built the lighthouse porch, using stones he collected along the beach. He transported them from the beach using a light wheelbarrel and planks. Having traveled extensively, Roupe revelled in his appointment: "There is no place with such a distinct peace and tranquillity as can be found along the shores of Lake Michigan, in and around Point Betsie. One has to experience the feeling to fully believe it." Although he had been a keeper at other lights, Point Betsie was definitely his favorite. Point Betsie's last keepers, Neil Martinek and Scott Sandy, were also the last keepers of the last manned lighthouse in the State of Michigan.

The light was also one of the last lighthouses on the Great Lakes to be automated. When first built, it was under the jurisdiction of the U.S. Lighthouse Board. Then on July 1, 1939, the U.S. Coast Guard took over the operation. In 1969 it was placed on the *National Register of Historic Places*.

After it was automated in 1983, the Coast Guard base converted the house to apartments for personnel assigned to the Coast Guard at Frankfort. In 1996, when the rotating mechanism for the Fresnel lens failed, the lens was removed and placed on display at the Sleeping Bear Dunes Maritime Museum. It was replaced with a Vega VRB-25 250 mm acrylic optic. In 1997 the boiler for the heating system quit and the Coast Guard moved the families to alternative quarters. Due to the high cost of maintenance and repairs, the Coast Guard left the building empty. Today the Coast Guard has "excessed" the station and Benzie County, in which the station is located, has assumed stewardship. The group, The Friends of Point Betsie Lighthouse, has also been formed and is working hard to raise funds to restore the station.

Known Keepers: Flury David (1859), Abel Barnes (1859–60), P. Barnes (1860–61), Alonzo Slyfield (1861–82), Edwin Slyfield (1882–88), Peter Dues (1888–93), Soren Christianson (1893–95), Phillip Sheridan (1895–1919), Charles Tesnow (1926–33), Edward Wheaton (1933–46).

87 Port Clinton Light

Port Clinton, on the south shore of Lake Michigan, developed as a stopover for steamers to replenish cordwood for fuel. It had a pier built into the lake but offered no protected bay. A lighthouse was built on a low bluff in 1855 to mark the port. It was a 21-foot (6.5 m) brick tower attached to a square 1½-story keeper's house. When coal became the preferred fuel of steamers and the railway bypassed the village, trade quickly dwindled and the light was discontinued in 1859.

After this a square yellow wooden pyramidal tower with white trim was built on foundation timbers about 20 feet (6 m) from the end of the west pier. It had an octagonal lantern that displayed a fixed red lens-lantern in 1901 to produce an 8-mile (13 km) visibility from a 25-foot (7.7 m) focal plane.

88 Port Washington Breakwater Light

During the early 1930s two breakwaters were built to protect the Port of Washington harbor from storms and to create a stilling basin for the harbor. Upon their completion Congress appropriated $35,000 in 1934 for a lighthouse to mark the south end of the north breakwater.

A modern Art Deco-style light, identical to the one at Indiana Harbor, was constructed on a large concrete foundation with a 20-foot (6 m) square-arched concrete base. From this base a white square steel tower rises about 40 feet (12.2 m). The base of the tower is a much larger square, and the tower above swoops gently and then rises straight up. The tower was originally topped with a square gallery and a circular lantern that housed a fourth-order Fresnel lens. It displayed a red light that flashed every 7.7 seconds and was powered by electricity via an underwater cable that connected with the generator building behind the keeper's house on St. Mary's Hill, as well as to city electricity.

Port Washington Breakwater Lighthouse

Port Washington North Pierhead Light, United States Coast Guard, circa 1914

When this light started to operate at the beginning of the 1935 shipping season, the old north pierhead light was extinguished. The lantern and lens were later removed and the tower was topped with a modern solar-powered red beacon that continues to guide vessels into Port Washington today.

89 Port Washington North Pierhead Light

With the completion of Port Washington harbor piers, the government placed a pierhead light on the north pier in 1889. It was a square wooden pyramidal tower with a simple square gallery and an octagonal cast-iron lantern. The base of the white tower had a skeletal framework for storm waves to wash through, and the top two thirds of the tower was closed in. Small four-paned tower windows looked out over the lake just beneath the gallery. Its lantern housed a fourth-order Fresnel lens that displayed a fixed red light from a 42½-foot (13.2 m) focal plane. A catwalk connected the light to the shore.

To meet the added workload of keeping two lights that were so far from each other, an assistant keeper was soon hired. When the land light was discontinued in 1903, this pierhead light became Port Washington's main harbor light. In 1924 the light was electrified and automated. The light continued until the breakwater light replaced it in 1935.

Known Keeper: Charles Lewis Jr. (1889–1924).

90 Port Washington Old Lighthouse

Congress first appropriated $3,500 to build a lighthouse at Port Washington in 1848. It was built on St. Mary's Hill northwest of the harbor to guide lake craft to port. The station consisted of a 30-foot (9 m) conical yellow brick tower with a birdcage lantern (lit using lamps and reflectors) and a detached brick keeper's house. It was first lit by keeper Cyrus Worth on May 8, 1849. In 1858 the reflectors were replaced by a sixth-order Fresnel lens that displayed a fixed white light.

A new lighthouse, also on St. Mary's Hill and just west of the old one, was built in 1860 to replace the deteriorating old light. It was a 2½-story yellow brick keeper's house with a square clapboard tower rising out of its roof at the south end. An octagonal gallery surrounded its decagonal lantern, which had a copper-lined dome and a sixth-order Fresnel lens imported from the old light. The light was 40 feet (12.2 m) above ground but had a 113-foot (34.4 m) focal plane and could be seen for 9 miles (14.6 km).

Changes were gradually introduced. In 1870 the station received a larger fourth-order Fresnel lens, increasing its visibility to 18 miles (29 km), and the government added piers and dredged the harbor to provide shelter from lake storms. When completed in 1889, the north pier was lit with a wooden pyramidal pierhead light. In 1894 a new brick oil storage house was added, signifying that kerosene became the illuminant at this time. (Kerosene was much more combustible and needed a storage area separate from the keeper's house.) By 1903 the pierhead light was clearly marking the harbor and the hill light was no longer needed so it was discontinued, but the residence still served as the keeper's quarters.

In 1934 the keeper's house was converted to a duplex, and and the barn was torn down and replaced by a fog signal building and a generator. The generator building housed a gas generator in case of an electrical power failure in the city's electricity supply. Once the lights were automated and the fog signal was discontinued in 1972, making the keepers no longer necessary, Coast Guard personnel were housed in the keeper's house until 1992, when the Port of Washington Coast Guard Station was eliminated. At this time the building was leased to the Port of Washington Historical Society, which converted the old house into a museum, with plans for restoration. In 1998 the ownership was transferred to the City of Port Washington. The building is included in both the national and state registers of historical places.

In 2000 the Minister of Sites and Monuments for the government of Luxembourg visited the museum and proposed that his country build, ship, and donate a replica lantern and tower for 2002 as a memorial to the U.S. servicemen who had fought for their freedom during World War II. Inspired by this generosity, the Historical Society increased their efforts and brought local businesses on board to assist with renovations.

Known Keepers: Cyrus Worth (1849–53), David Tuttle (1853–57), Barnard Schoomer (1857–60), Mrs. Bernard Schoomer (1860–61), Fauntleroy Hoyt (1861–66), Patrick Kehoe (1866–74), Charles Lewis (1875–80), Charles Lewis Jr. (1880–1903).

Port Washington (Old) Lighthouse

91 Portage Lake Range Lights

During the late 1800s Portage Lake was developed as a harbor of refuge for vessels traveling along Lake Michigan's eastern coast between Point Betsie and Manistee. Although the small deep lake was landlocked, it was a mere 2,000 feet (615 m) from Lake Michigan, so a channel was dredged, retaining walls were built, and north and south piers were run out into the lake (the north one being longer).

In April 1891 range lights were built on the north pier. The front light was just a six-day lens lantern hung on a pole at the pier's outer end, and the rear light was on the same pier behind it. It was a square wooden tapering skeletal tower with an enclosed room below the lantern to provide protection and storage space. It had a 40-foot (12.2 m) focal plane and was 16 feet (4.9 m) in diameter. The lantern was just over 7 feet (2.2 m) in diameter and housed a fourth-order lens fueled by gas. In 1901 the lights were moved about 700 feet (215 m) farther out on the north pier and a 750-foot (230 m) metal elevated walkway was constructed. Both front and rear lights were fixed and red.

In 1930, when the lights were replaced with new steel skeletal towers and automated acetylene gas lights, John Langland, the keeper since the lights were activated in 1882, was transferred to the Waukegan light station. The new lights were tended once a month by the keeper of the Manistee light. Although Portage Lake never developed into a major port, this small harbor still exists today and its entrance is marked by pole lights to assist pleasure boaters.

Known Keeper: John Langland 1822–1930

Portage Lake Range Lights, circa 1918

92 Pottawatomie Lighthouse

Rock Island, also known as Pottawatomie Island, is just northeast of Washington Island above Door Peninsula, which divides Green Bay from Lake Michigan. In the early 1800s mariners used the Rock Island Passage, which ran north of Rock Island and south of St. Martin Island, to travel safely between the bay and the lake. To accommodate shipping from the Green Bay area to Detroit, 30 Detroit merchants and ship owners petitioned the government to place a light to mark the passage. Congress assented and in 1834 allocated $4,500 to build a light on Pottawatomie Island at the northeast entrance to Green Bay.

Construction began in 1836. The tower was a 30 foot (9 m) rubble-stone conical structure, 18 feet (5.5 m) in diameter at the base and 9 feet (2.8 m) in diameter at the top. It was topped with an iron gallery 11 feet (3.4 m) in diameter, which supported an octagonal iron lantern lit by eleven Winslow Lewis oil lamps and eleven 14-inch (35 cm) reflectors. The 1½-story detached keeper's house was built of rubble-stone. The station, built on a steep cliff on the north side of the island, was nearly ready by October 1837. However, the assigned keeper had turned down his appointment.

By December a suitable replacement was found in David E. Corbin, an 1812 veteran who had once been employed at Fort Howard working for the American Fur Company. Corbin spent an industrious first five years clearing trees from around the lighthouse to improve its visibility. Supplies had to be brought in overland from a dock on the island's south side to avoid the 100-foot (30 m) cliff, and so Corbin also cut a path for a roadway to the dock. The road was over a mile (1.6 km) long but it still made the job of hauling in supplies, which included his drinking water, much easier.

During a lighthouse inspection in 1845, the inspector found all to be well except for the keeper's loneliness, having only his dog and his horse for company. The inspector generously gave Corbin a 20-day holiday to find a wife. Unfortunately, he did not accomplish this task in the allotted time, and remained with only his animals for company until his death at the light in 1852 at age 57. He was buried in the community's small cemetery just south of the lighthouse.

When the lighthouse inspector condemned the tower and house in 1858 because of water damage due to the use of poor mortar, the structures were razed and a more durable 2½-story cut-limestone house with a full basement was erected on the site. A short 8-foot (2.4 m) square wooden tower rose out of the north end of the house peak, to support a nine-sided iron lantern. It housed a fourth-order Fresnel lens that displayed a fixed white light visible for 14 miles (22 km) from a focal plane of about 135 feet (42 m).

From 1872 to 1882 keeper William Betts' assistant keeper was his wife, Emily Betts. As well as being an assistant keeper, Emily looked after the household and their nine children (two of whom were born at the lighthouse), taught school in the lighthouse's basement, nursed the sick on the island, and served as midwife to the island's birthing mothers.

As the island station was further developed, 154 steps were built down the cliffside and a small landing platform provided so that supplies could be carried up the cliff. A red brick oil house was added (likely in the late 1800s when the light's fuel became kerosene a more volatile illuminant that needed a separate storage facility.) In 1904 a telephone was installed at the station. In 1910 a well was drilled on the west side of the house to provide fresh drinking water. The station never received electricity while it was active. From 1910 to 1912 Chester Thordarson, a Chicago inventor who had immigrated from Iceland, bought up all of Rock Island except for the lighthouse reservation. The lighthouse's last civilian keeper, Ernest Lockhart, retired in the early 1940s.

Pottawatomie Lighthouse

Since the Lighthouse Service was absorbed into the Coast Guard in 1939, the next keepers were Coast Guardsmen. In 1964 the island became part of the Wisconsin State park system. In 1966 the light was automated using batteries attached to the lantern deck to power the light. In 1975 the light was added to the state list of historic buildings and in 1979 to the *National Register of Historic Places*. In the 1980s the lantern and lens were removed due to water damage from interior condensation, and a modern beacon was attached to the lantern deck. In 1986 the batteries were replaced by solar panels. In 1988 the light was placed on a steel tower erected just west of the house.

In 1994 a group called The Friends of Rock Island was formed to help the Department of Natural Resources raise the island's historical significance by restoring the lighthouse. They had a replica lantern room built by Tony Hodges of Sturgeon Bay and his son. Hodges drew up plans for the lantern using the remains of the old lantern and by viewing similar lanterns at other sites. After Hodges had built the lantern in his Sturgeon Bay shop, it was disassembled and moved to the lighthouse, where it was reassembled in June 1999. During the reassembly, parts were hoisted to the top of the tower with a homemade crane consisting of an aluminium extension ladder and a battery-powered winch.

By 2004 the Friends of Rock Island were able to furnish their refurbished lighthouse with antiques from the 1858 time period and open the lighthouse to the public with a dedication ceremony. Volunteers take turns living at the lighthouse, a week at a time throughout the summer, to offer interpretive tours. Thanks to this dedicated group the future of another lighthouse has been secured and — better still — shared.

Known Keepers: David Corbin (1837–52), Mr. Cass (1852–53), Captain Allen (1853–55), Jos. LeCuyer Sr. (1855–57), Simon Allaird (1857–59), Frank Sawyer (1859–61), Martin Trobee (1861–65), Abraham Capers (1865–70), William C. Betts (1870–86), Jesse L. Miner (1886–98), Lewis Hutzler (1989–99), Lawrence Brown (1899–1902), Charley Boshka (1902–11), Edward Cornell (1911–28), John Fitzgerald (1928–41), Ernest Lockhart (1941–46).

93 Poverty Island Lighthouse

After the Peninsula Railroad connected iron mines to Escanaba in northern Lake Michigan, ship traffic from Escanaba carrying iron ore to industrial centers on the Great Lakes increased significantly. Since the opening between Green Bay and Lake Michigan was dotted with islands and submerged shoals, vessels had to choose one of four known passages. Vessels heading from Escanaba to the Straits of Mackinaw chose Poverty Island Passage, between Poverty and Gull islands. While this passage was safe for day traffic it was not at night, and vessels had to waste time (and money) if they arrived at the passage around dusk. Heeding mariners' pleas, the Lighthouse Board repeatedly requested an appropriation of $18,000 for a lighthouse on Poverty Island. Congress finally granted the funds in 1873.

With plans from the light at Sturgeon Point, work began at the southwest side of the island in the summer of 1873. However, an October fire halted progress until the following spring. And then the money ran out and, after a temporary light was placed on the finished keeper's house, work halted until a further appropriation of $3,000 came through in March 1875. The work crew built a 1½-story red brick keeper's house attached to a red brick conical tower by an enclosed brick passageway. It sat 100 feet

Poverty Island Lighthouse, circa 1920

(30.5 m) from the shore, and was painted white for best visibility. The tower was 60 feet (18 m) high and topped with a circular gallery and a decagonal cast-iron lantern that housed a fourth-order Fresnel lens. Its red light, flashing from a 65-foot (20 m) focal plane, was visible for 16 miles (26 km). It was first lit on August 10, 1875, and the temporary light was then removed.

Heavy fog in the area necessitated a fog signal building. Added in 1885, it consisted of a dual system of 10-inch (25 cm) steam whistles (one for backup) and was operational by October 1885. In 1894 a circular iron oil house was built, probably to house kerosene, a more volatile illuminant that required separate storage. A new boat landing facilitated the unloading of coal and wood.

In 1957 the light was automated, and the keepers were removed. In 1976 the light was deactivated, the decagonal lantern was removed and left on the ground nearby, the tower was sealed off, and a 300 mm plastic optic was placed on a skeletal tower. In 1982 this light was moved to a pole on top of the tower, which provided it with a higher focal plane.

The Delta County Historical Society discovered the existence of the abandoned Poverty Island lantern sometime in the 1980s and obtained permission from the Coast Guard to install it on top of the refurbished Sand Point Lighthouse near Escanaba. While the lantern has been saved, the Poverty Island Lighthouse falls further into ruin each year, a victim of time, elements and vandalism. The fate of this once vital station hangs in the balance.

Known Keepers: George Larson (1875–82), Charles Hermann (1883–1905), Severin Danielsen (1905–11), James McCormick (1911–15), Niels Jensen (1915–33),

Poverty Island Lighthouse

Racine North Breakwater Light

94 Racine Breakwater Light

With the completion of twin breakwaters at Racine Harbor in 1900, a temporary fixed red lantern was placed at the southerly end. In 1910 iron and steel arrived for a lighthouse at the outer end of the north breakwater. The tower had a hexagonal inverted-funnel shape with a hexagonal gallery around the lantern and an oversized dome capping it. It was covered in corrugated sheet iron and had a larger base to provide space for a service room. The tower's style was similar to those built at Kenosha, Milwaukee, Sheboygan, Waukegan and Petoskey.

The lantern housed a sixth-order Fresnel lens. Sometime between 1916 and 1929 this breakwater light was removed, and the Racine North Pierhead light was brought from the end of the north pier to the outer end of the north breakwater to replace it. This light then became Racine's main light. During the 1920s the tower was equipped with a new air-powered diaphone fog signal that had a 20-second characteristic (blast 1 s; silence 2 s; blast 1 s; silence 16 s).

As harbor improvements continued and the outer harbor basin was enlarged, the north pier and its catwalk up to the front of the keeper's residence were demolished. In 1987 the Racine Breakwater light was discontinued. When the Coast Guard planned to take it down, public indignation saved the structure, and it was moved to become a featured part of the new Reef Point Marina complex. As the harbor expanded yet again, a new light on a modern skeletal tower was placed at the harbor entrance.

Racine South Breakwater Light

Racine North Breakwater Light, circa 1911

Racine Harbor Lighthouse (lantern removed)

95 Racine Harbor Lighthouse

As maritime traffic increased at Racine Harbor, where the Root River emptied into Lake Michigan, the government built wooden piers to protect the harbor entrance. After their completion in 1864, the harbor entrance was 200 feet (61.5 m) farther out in the lake, making the old Root River Light on the shore ineffective to serve mariners as it was too far from the end of the piers. Thus a new light was built on a stone-filled crib at the east end of the north pier in 1865.

It was a 1¹⁄₂-story schoolhouse-style light built of yellow brick and painted white. Its square 36-foot (11 m) tower was built into the east end of the keeper's dwelling. Its polygonal lantern used the fifth-order Fresnel lens from the old Root River Light to display a fixed red light from a 48-foot (14.6 m) focal plane, and produced a 13-mile (21 m) visibility. The onshore light was discontinued when it was first exhibited on September 10, 1866.

Changes accompanied the light into the twentieth century. In 1869 repairs had to be made after a vessel damaged the lighthouse. In 1870 a new and larger fourth-order Fresnel lens with an illumination arc of 270 degrees was placed in the lantern. As the harbor grew, the piers were extended further into the lake and a pierhead light soon marked the end. In the summer of 1872 a wooden beacon light with a catwalk was built at the end of the north pier. This beacon light worked in conjunction with the harbor light to form range lights for mariners entering the harbor. As the pier continued to grow, the pierhead light continued to be moved to the new pier end and the catwalk was extended. By 1889 the north pier jutted 1,150 feet (350 m) into the lake.

The Racine Harbor light was discontinued when a new north pierhead light was activated in 1903. Its lantern room and spiral iron staircase were removed and the tower was capped with a hipped roof. The dwelling was converted into living quarters for the lightkeeper and his assistant. Dormers were added to the second floor for the assistant keeper's quarters, and a wooden staircase replaced the spiral one. In 1939, when the Coast Guard assumed responsibility for the dwelling, they combined it with the U.S. Lifesaving Station (built behind the lighthouse in 1883) to form the Racine Coast Guard Station. When this station closed, the house was sold to the private ownership of the Pugh Marina. The structure is on both the state and national historic registers.

96 Racine North Pierhead Light

As the two piers at Racine were extended into Lake Michigan, a pierhead light was established on the outer end of the north pier. The first one, built in the summer of 1872, consisted of a simple square white wooden pyramidal beacon with an open lower framework that was connected by a catwalk to the harbor light on the pier behind it. Its fixed red light from a 28-foot (8.6 m) focal plane worked as a front range light with the harbor light for guiding vessels into port.

Each time the piers were extended the pierhead light was moved to the new end of the pier and more catwalk was added. By 1889 the north pier extended 1,150 feet (350 m) out into the lake. In 1894 a new conduit system, designed by Major Adams, was installed, whereby the keeper could fuel and maintain the front range light without leaving the harbor light. This system was not very reliable in practice, however, and a regular pierhead light was re-established in 1896.

In the 1890s twin breakwaters were built to better protect the harbor. When they were completed in 1900 it was decided to build a larger and stronger lighthouse at the end of the north pier to replace the Racine Harbor Light. During construction the old wooden pierhead light was moved back 24 feet (7.4 m) on the pier to allow space to build a new concrete crib to support the heavier cast-iron tower.

Built in 1902, the new tower consisted of a square gently tapering riveted cast-iron tower with an open lower framework that allowed storms to wash over the pier and without damaging the tower. It had an overall height of 53 feet (16.2 m), and was originally painted white (but is now red). A fog bell was mounted to its lakeside wall and a few porthole windows lit the interior.

The decagonal lantern housed a sixth-order Fresnel lens and continued to display a red light. After it was first lit in November 1902, the old wooden pierhead light was dismantled. Also the Racine Harbor light was discontinued in 1903 and converted to living space for the keeper and his assistant. The new light was connected to this keeper's residence by means of the previous wooden catwalk. Sometime between 1916 and 1929 this light was moved from the north pierhead to the outer end of the north breakwater.

Known Keepers: James Ginty (1872–83), Lawrence Easson (1883–88), George Larson (1888–99), Martin Knudsen (1899–1917), Edward Knudsen (1917–33).

97 Racine Reef Lighthouse

Racine Reef, Lake Michigan, lay just southeast of Racine and extended over 2¹⁄₂ miles (4 km) to just a half a mile (0.8 km) from the harbor entrance. While the harbor had been lit since 1839, the Lighthouse Board didn't consider lighting the reef until 1868. At this time, since a manned light on the reef was considered too costly, a 108-foot (33 m) coast light was planned at Wind Point, 4 miles (6.4 km) to the north of the reef, and a buoy was to be put on the reef. In 1869 the buoy was placed but the Wind Point lighthouse was not built until 1880. Meanwhile, eleven ships sank on the reef between 1875 and 1895.

Racine Reef Lighthouse

Deeming the reef to be inadequately lit, the government placed a light right on the reef. In 1898 a 9-foot (2.7 m) high, 40-foot (12.2 m) square crib was built onshore, towed to the site and sunk onto the reef using bags of concrete. The crib was then faced with paving brick, topped with a concrete cap and surrounded by 60 cords of riprap to help prevent storm and ice damage. The following spring a Pintsch gas-powered light was placed on the concrete crib. It displayed a red light from the top of a skeletal tower. Pintsch gas, made from oil and the precursor of acetylene gas, provided an automated light, and this light was serviced periodically by the Racine Harbor keepers. It was first lit on August 31, 1899.

It soon became apparent that the Pintsch light was inadequate to mark the reef. It was too low and too dim to be seen at a good distance, it occasionally ran out of fuel and was unlit. The tender *Dahlia* had difficulty filling the fuel tanks because the shallow water prevented it from getting closer than 900 feet (276 m). Finally, in 1903 Congress appropriated $75,000 to build a year-round lighthouse on the reef.

The lighthouse, built under the supervision of Captain James G. Warren, was like no other lighthouse ever built on the Great Lakes. It was started in 1905 at a new location on the reef in 16 feet (4.9 m) of water just northeast of the old Pintsch light. A 60 foot (18.3 m) square timber crib was built onshore at Racine, towed to the reef, and sunk by means of ballast stone placed within pockets built inside the crib. The crib supported an octagonal concrete pier that included a basement engine room at its core. The pier was then surrounded by 76 tons of riprap. The lighthouse was built in a Victorian style with an internal metal frame covered with brick. It was a large octagonal structure placed in the center of the pier in a somewhat cruciform plan.

The lighthouse had five interior levels and stood 66 feet (20 m) from its base to the top of its lantern. The basement engine room had high ceilings that extended into the first level of the lighthouse. Large glass French doors on this level allowed for a large opening to move equipment in and out of the engine room assisted by a hoist above the doors. The date "1906" was carved into the lintel of the entry door, from which stairs led down to the engine room floor or up to the main living level. The third level held the personal quarters; the fourth, much smaller, formed the watch-room, which looked out in all directions. The octagonal gallery surrounded a circular lantern with curved glass set on the diagonal and was capped with an oversized dome. The roof and watch-room were covered with folded-seam copper sheeting. The lantern displayed a fourth-order Fresnel lens that sat on a solid brass pedestal. The rotating lens produced a red and white characteristic (red flash 0.07 s; white flash 4.3 s) from a 72-foot (22 m) focal plane. When this light was lit in 1906, the Pintsch light was taken to be installed on the outer breakwater at Chicago.

The station was equipped with coal-fired twin boilers that produced the steam that heated the structure and operated its 10-inch (25 cm) fog whistles. Between 1924 and 1928 the steam-powered fog whistles were replaced by duplicate air-powered diaphone fog signals and the station's characteristic was modified (blast 3 s; silence 27 s). The steam whistles were left as a backup system.

The light was manned by a four-man crew, of whom two were always on duty, making it one of the few lights on the Great Lakes to be manned in the winter. It was active year round to assist the crosslake railroad car ferries, which had reinforced steel hulls and could break ice.

The station was electrified sometime after 1939 and automated and demanned in 1954. Then, due to advances in radar and radio navigation, the U.S. Coast Guard deemed the light obsolete, extinguished it, removed anything of value, and demolished it in the summer of 1961. The light's fourth-order Fresnel lens was placed in the Racine County Historical Museum where it is presently on display.

To warn of the reef, the concrete pier, and the tons of riprap below the water's surface, the Coast Guard placed a modern acrylic lens on a white skeletal tower on the concrete pier. It exhibits a flashing light every 6 seconds from a 50-foot (15.3 m) focal plane.

Known Keepers: George Cornell (1906–10), Oscar Knudsen (1910–11), Joseph Warren (1911), Edward Knudsen (1911–17), Walter Donovan (1925–30), Edward Wheaton (1930–33), Charles Tesnow (1933–40).

Racine Reef Lighthouse, circa 1935

Rawley Point Lighthouse

98 Rawley Point Lighthouse

Rawley Point is on the west side of Lake Michigan about 5 miles (8 km) north of Two Rivers, Wisconsin. Government survey- ors first named this site "Rowley Point" in 1841, after prominent early settler Peter Rowley. The first light was built north of Two Rivers so the light station was called the Twin Rivers Station. Then, at an unknown time, the point became known as Rawley Point and so did the light station.

In the 1800s mariners discovered a dangerous underwater shoal extending from this point for about 1 mile (1.6 km) into the lake. It caused at least 26 shipwrecks before the point was adequately lit. The most serious of these dis- asters was the 1877 sinking of the steamer *Vernon*, one of the largest steamships on the lakes at the time. During a storm-tossed night, the *Vernon* hit the shoal and sank quickly, taking 52 crew members and passengers with it. Part of its lost cargo was supposed to have been gold coins, but to this day no one has discovered any of this "sunken" treasure.

The first form of light to warn of the shoal was a primitive structure made of four poles erected upright in the air for about 75 feet (23 m). The poles held a rope and a pulley system that served to raise and lower a lantern. This light was replaced in 1853 by a wooden lighthouse that was in turn taken down in 1873 because it had been built 1½ miles (2.4 km) south of the present light and did not adequately mark the point. It was replaced in 1874 by a new round brick tower that was attached to one end of a large, 2½-story keeper's house.

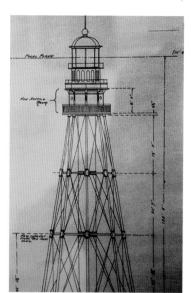

Rawley Point Lighthouse architectural blueprints

The tower and the house were separated by only an interior hallway. The base walls of the tower were 3 feet (0.9 m) thick and the tower rose up about six stories. Its lantern housed a 12 bull's- eye lens set into a frame at the top, and was lit by lard-burning lamps. After the erection of a third light in 1894, this tower's lantern was removed, and the tower was reduced to half its height and given a new hexagonal roof that looked like a castle turret. The remaining three levels were renovated as living space in the house. The lower level became a unique round living room and the two upper levels became round bedrooms.

The erector-style light that replaced this brick tower was origi- nally built as the main Chicago Harbor light and viewed by millions in 1893 at Chicago's world famous Columbian Exposition, as one of the U.S. Lighthouse Service's state-of-the- art exhibits. After the exposition, the structure was dismantled and moved to Rawley Point, where it was reassembled and heightened on a concrete base behind the existing keeper's house. The tower, a riveted, sheet-iron cylin- der, supported three levels, all wider than the 6-foot (1.8 m) cylinder. Since these three lev- els decreased in diameter as they ascended, the whole structure looked like a wedding cake.

Each level also had its own gallery sur- rounded by an iron railing. The lowest was a round watchroom with porthole-style win- dows. The next was the pedestal room, where the light revolved on a steel roller. At the top was the decagonal lantern with nine rectan- gular glass windows and one panel blocked by a metal sheet painted red to match the lantern base and its domed top. The lantern originally housed a third-order Fresnel lens from France lit with a mantle-style lamp that burned kerosene. The clockwork weights that rotated the lens had to be wound every six hours. For added support, eight skeletal legs attached under the lower gallery angled gracefully out to the ground. When complete, the tower was 111 feet (34 m) high, making it the tallest lighthouse of this style, at this time, on the Great Lakes. It had a focal plane of 113 feet (34.4 m) and a 19-mile (30 km) visibility.

In 1893 a fog signal building was built near the water's edge in front of the keeper's house. It first used a 10-inch (25 cm) steam whistle powered by a locomotive boiler. Later, it was switched to a diaphone fog signal that used diesel generators to operate its compressors. It took ten minutes for the compressors to build enough pressure to operate the diaphone. It blasted once every minute for four seconds whenever visibility became lower than 5 miles (8 km) and could be heard 10 miles (16 km) away.

In pre-electricity days, keepers devised a way to check on the equipment without being in the building. The water that was used to cool the compressors was piped outside and fed into a small bucket with holes punched into the bottom. The bucket was on one end of a long pivotal stick, and a wooden flag was attached to the other end. When the water was flowing properly and the compressor was being cooled, the weight of the bucket forced this end down and the flag end up. As long as the keepers could see the wooden flag they knew all was well. If not, they went and checked the equipment.

In 1920 the light was electrified. The original Fresnel lens was used until 1952, when one of its glass prisms was broken. Due to the high cost of repairing it, the lens was replaced with a 36-inch (0.9 m) twin bull's-eye DCB36 aerobeacon. This double-ended, drum-like beacon used a 1,000-watt bulb (250,000 candlepower) and rotated once a minute to produce a double flash pattern (flash 3 s; eclipse 27 s). Its visibility was listed as 20 miles (32 km), but it had sometimes been seen right across the lake at Ludington, Michigan, on a clear night.

A radio monitor was added sometime after it was electrified. The keeper had to monitor 19 beacon stations every three hours to make sure each was sending out accurate signals. If there was an error of more than three seconds in a station's signal, they received a phone call from Rawley Point to correct it and had to make a written report to the district office at Cleveland to explain the malfunction. To make sure that Rawley Point clocks were correct, the station had a radio receiver that received time signals directly from the Bureau of Standards in Washington.

In 1975 the station was added to the *National Register of Historic Places*. The Coast Guard automated the light in 1979. Today it is still used by the Coast Guard as a vacation spot for its personnel, and so it is off limits to the public. However, since it is a part of Point Beach State Forest, it can be easily viewed through the trees from a platform the park has built.

Known Keepers: George Ruggles (1853), Albert Barry (1853–54), David Ward (1854), Albert Berry (1854–59), Samuel Stone (1874–80), Lawrence Easson (1880–81), Peter Danielson (1882–83), Simon Nelson (1883), Andrew Daveport (1884–88), Andrew Allen (1889–95), Gabriel Ariansen (1895–98), James Gallagher (1898–1900), Milton McLure (1900–06), Joseph Napeizinski (1906–11), Otto Schmiling (1911–15), Everitt Sterritt (1915–24), Joseph Kimmes (1925–28), George Haas (1939–40).

99 Root River Lighthouse

The lighthouse at Root River, Lake Michigan, was built in 1839 on the bank overlooking the lake at the river mouth where the community of Racine developed. Congress had appropriated $5,000 for it. The brick for the tower and house was made by Benjamin Pratt, Racine's first brick manufacturer. The tower walls were 2 feet 10 inches (0.8 m) thick at the bottom and tapered to 2 feet (0.6 m) thick at the top. The tower's exterior base diameter was 16 feet 8 inches (5.1 m) and its outside top diameter 9 feet (2.8 m). From the base to the ventilator ball it was 40 feet (12.2 m) high. Three windows ascended the tower walls to light its spiral staircase. Its lantern used eleven (later nine) Argand lamps with 14-inch (35 cm) reflectors to produce the light.

The keeper's house was behind the tower and fronted onto Chatham Street (now Lake Ave.). It was a one-story thick bricked dwelling, with an attached wing. Both it and the tower were kept whitewashed to increase their daytime visibility. Down a steep bank in front of the lighthouse was a short government pier built on rock-filled timber cribs.

In 1858 a 6-foot (1.8 m) addition was added to the top of the tower and the light was upgraded to a fixed white fifth-order Fresnel lens. Since it was so close to the city, its illuminant became city gas, as an experiment, sometime before 1861. With the building of a new north pierhead light, this light was discontinued on September 10, 1866.

In 1870 L.S. Blake and James T. Elliot purchased the old lighthouse and its lot (about one acre/0.4 hectare) from the State of Wisconsin for $1,625. Later, after Elliot became the sole owner, he demolished the lighthouse buildings in 1876 and used the brick to build a new house. It is unfortunate that no known photographs of this lighthouse exist.

Known Keepers: Amaziah Stebbins (1839–46), Captain John T Trowbridge (1846–49), Abner Rouse (1849–53), John Fancher (1857–61), Milton Moore (1861–65).

100 Sand Point (Escanaba) Lighthouse

In July 1856 Congress appropriated $1,000 for "a beacon-light at Sand Point, on the west side of Little Bay du Noquet." However, for an unknown reason, the lighthouse was not built until the next decade, and the funds reverted to government coffers.

After the Peninsula Railroad was completed from the iron ore mines at Negaunee to Escanaba in 1864, there was a significant increase in boat traffic at Escanaba as iron ore was shipped from there to industrial centers on the Great Lakes. The Lighthouse Board's repeated petitions finally led to an appropriation in 1867. The lighthouse was finished in 1868 at a cost of $11,000. It was built on Sand Point, to mark the harbor entrance and warn of the sandy shoals off of the tip of the point.

It was a square yellow brick 1½-story keeper's house with an attached 41-foot (12.5 m) square brick tower. Both were painted white for best visibility. The tower was capped with a square gallery and a decagonal lantern that housed a fourth-order Fresnel lens. The lens used oil lamps to display a fixed red light from a 44-foot (13.5 m) focal plane. Although the lantern was unobstructed because of its height over the house, the construction was unusual in that the tower rose from the end of the house that faced away from the lake. In most lighthouses the tower faced the water.

Improvements came to the lighthouse in 1939. When the contours of the harbor were changed by dredging and filling, the lighthouse stood too far from the water to adequately mark the hazards. The Coast Guard therefore built a crib light offshore and extinguished the Sand Point lighthouse. However, they retained its residence to house Coast Guard personnel at their Escanaba Station, and remodeled the lighthouse into a more comfortable home. By 1985 the Coast Guard had finished their use of the house and wanted to raze it.

Sand Point (Escanaba) Lighthouse

Concerned about its future because this was one of Escanaba's earliest remaining buildings, the Delta County Historical Society negotiated a long-term lease from the Coast Guard, so that they could restore it to its early lighthouse days. They used archival plans of the 1867 lighthouse along with $100,000 to complete the task. They reversed the changes made by Coast Guard, replaced the iron staircase, built a replica gallery, replaced the lantern with a duplicate found sitting on Poverty Island, and borrowed the fourth-order Fresnel lens that had been removed from the Menominee lighthouse. The interior was refinished as a living museum of the lighthouse around the turn of the century. In 1990 a special dedication ceremony was held to open the restored lighthouse as a museum.

Stories are still told — and questions asked — about the suspicious circumstances of the lighthouse fire and the death of keeper Mary Terry in 1886. How could such an efficient keeper have let the wood beside her fireplace get so hot? Was the hired man implicated? Was foul play involved? Why was she not in her bed the night of the fire? Did someone break in to rob her? She was known to be frugal, but why did she have pieces of gold in her kitchen? Does her ghost still wander through the lighthouse? What actually happened was never known, and the inquest ruled her death from "causes and means unknown." Although the fire had gutted the lighthouse and destroyed the woodwork, all the stone, brick and metalwork was still intact, so the structure was repaired and the light was readied for the next season.

More restoration took place in the early 2000s. When the tower lantern was replaced, a fake ventilator ball was used, with detrimental effects. While it looked fine, there was no top ventilation. A proper ball was needed. The Society obtained plans for a decagonal

lantern from the National Archives in Washington, D.C. and found two places that would supply a 200-pound (90 kg) iron ventilator ball — but at a price that exceeded their means. Don Bougie, a local millwright and history buff, learned of their situation and made an even better stainless steel one. He also reinstalled the lantern's lower brass vents to pristine working order. Restoration of the lighthouse has been a huge effort requiring great dedication on the part of the Delta County Historical Association and their friends.

Known Keepers: John Terry (1868), Mary Terry (1868–86), Lewis Rose (1889–1913), Peter Peterson (1913), Mrs. Peter Peterson (1913), Soren Christianson (1913–25), James Armstrong (1925–39), Captain Daniel Garret (1939).

101 Seul Choix Point Lighthouse

Early French fur traders named this peninsula Seul Choix ("sisshwa") — "only choice" — because it was the only safe refuge in the area during a fierce lake storm. In the late 1800s, the Lighthouse Board echoed that in their petition for a light: it was the only place for 100 miles (160 km) along Lake Michigan's north shore to offer protection between the St. Helena lighthouse at the Straits of Mackinac and the Poverty Island lighthouse below the Garden Peninsula. Convinced, Congress appropriated $15,000 in 1886. Late arrivals of materials and excess costs delayed its completion until 1892. The total complex, finished in 1895, included the tower, keeper's dwelling, steam fog building, a stable and other outbuildings, two docks and a tramway for carrying supplies brought in by the lighthouse tender.

The conical brick tower was built on a 12-foot (3.7 m) thick ashlar stone foundation set well into the ground for support. The tower tapered from a base diameter of 18 feet (5.5 m) to a diameter of 12.5 feet (3.8 m) at top, 80 feet (24.5 m) above ground. A circular gallery supported by numerous ornately carved wooden corbels surrounded the pedestal room, which supported the decagonal lantern and the third-order Fresnel lens. Below the gallery was the watchroom, which had four arched windows with beautiful concrete moldings around them. A few rectangular windows with stone sills and lintels dotted the ascent of the tower to provide interior light for its spiral stairs.

The large 1½-story red brick keeper's house was attached to the tower and placed on a high basement wall also made of ashlar stone. The house had a stone chimney and gabled end in each roof peak. The house is architecturally known for the bowed ends of its roof. The assistant keeper's house was a 1½-story clapboard frame dwelling. At some point it was moved to McDonald Lake, northeast of Seul Choix. In 1925 a one-story addition with hipped roof was added to the rear of the main house for additional living quarters. It featured solid copper moldings. The tower was later painted white for best visibility.

In 1972 Congress ordered the U.S. Coast Guard to regulate the lighthouse, so they removed the Fresnel lens and replaced it with a fully automated DCB-24 airport beacon that was visible for 17 miles (27.5 km). Instead of storing the Fresnel lens they donated it to the Smithsonian Institution, where it is now on display.

In 1973 the U.S. Coast Guard discontinued care for the Seul Choix light station. The Gulliver Historical Society fought to save the station from vandalism and neglect. In June 1977 the Coast Guard allowed the Michigan Department of Natural Resources to buy the property. Next, the grounds were leased to Mueller Township for a public park. In 1989 the Gulliver Historical Society took over and started creating the lighthouse park by converting the fog signal building into a museum, restoring the tower and house, and refurbishing the house with furnishings from the 1900–20 period. In 1988 the land and buildings were added to both the state and national historical registers.

The Gulliver Historical Society is continually making improvements toward their overall aim of creating a community park where everyone can be proud to say, "This is part of my heritage." The museum in the fog signal building displays period artefacts and memorabilia. The Historical Society has also found remains of Ottawa and Chippewa villages along the beach, old foundations, rock paintings, a rock inscribed by the French trapper Louis Metty, and a sunken schooner buried in the sand just offshore.

The large rock in front of the lighthouse has an interesting story. Once, unbeknownst to their parents, a few local children built a boat or a raft to sail to Beaver Island. A storm came up, and broken pieces of the boat were discovered on the mainland. Funeral services were held for the children, who were presumed drowned, and their names were carved into the

huge rock in front of the lighthouse. A few weeks later, however, Indians who had rescued the children from Gull Island returned them home, to the joy of all.

This light also has its traditional ghost story. In 1988, when inmates from Camp Manistique Prison were contracted to do repair work for the Gulliver Historical Society, many of them refused to work in the upstairs bedrooms, because they felt "the presence of something supernatural up there." A carpenter, hearing unexplained hammering and footsteps downed tools and vowed never to work alone at the lighthouse again. Sometimes unexplained whiffs of cigar smoke can be smelled. Since the strange incidents had only started with the renovations, they began to wonder if there was some truth to the saying that a house's spiritual occupants become restless when a house is going through major changes.

In an upstairs bedroom a ghostly image of a man with bushy eyebrows, a mustache and a beard sometimes appears in a mirror. An old wives' tale tells that if a mirror is not covered when someone dies in a house, that person's spirit will be trapped in the mirror. Could this have happened at Seul Choix? Using these clues and researching the light's previous residents, Marilyn Fisher, then president of the Gulliver Historical Society, came up with a most likely candidate for the ghost in the person of Captain James Townshend. While visiting his brother Joseph, the keeper at Seul Choix, he suddenly became quite ill and died a painful death in an upstairs bedroom. Fisher learned that he was a heavy cigar smoker. Old pictures show that he had bushy eyebrows, a mustache and a beard, just like the image seen in the mirror.

With its ghost story to provide food for thought, its interesting architectural style, and its willing volunteers who now tend it, Seul Choix and its history will be preserved for many years to come.

Known Keepers: Captain Joseph Fountain (1892–1901), Joseph Townshend (1901–10), William Blanchard (1910–41), William Hanson (1941–45), Ronald Rosie Sr. (1945–64).

Seul Choix Point Lighthouse

102 Sheboygan Lighthouse

Congress appropriated $5,000 in 1837 for a lighthouse at Sheboygan, on the west shore of Lake Michigan. The light was built in 1839 on Sheboygan Point to guide fishing vessels to port. It was a 30-foot (9 m) rubble-stone tower that used lamps and reflectors to produce a light beam. When erosion threatened the structure, the light was razed and a new one was built further back to prevent similar erosion in the future.

This new lighthouse was built in 1860 on a bluff known as North Point, and the lighthouse was often referred to locally as the North Point lighthouse. It was a two-story white clapboard keeper's house with a short square tower extending from one roof end. The tower was capped with an octagonal lantern.

The position of this new lighthouse caused confusion, especially to mariners who were unfamiliar with the area. Their complaints resulted in a pierhead light being built at the end of the north pier in 1873 to better mark the harbor. The old shore light was used until 1904 when it was discontinued because the harbor was well lit by then.

In December 1906 the station was sold to Dr. William Gunther, the local doctor, at public auction for $1,415. Gunther rented the house out for a number of years as an income property and then, in 1916, had it moved into Sheboygan, where he divided it into a duplex and continued to rent it. He then built a new home on the old lighthouse site.

Known Keepers: Stephen Woolverton (1840–45), Elijah Cook (1845–48), Alexander Edwards (1848–49), Thomas Horner (1849–53), Godfrey Stamm (1853), Sylvester Remington (1853–54), Godfrey Stamm (1854–57), Nelson Sticles (1861–65), Santy Brazelton (1865–69), William Mallony (1869), Eva Pape (1869–85), Peter Danielson (1886–1903), Bernhard Pizzalar (1903–04), William Larson (1904).

Sheboygan North Breakwater Light, circa 1910

103 Sheboygan North Breakwater Light

After breakwaters were built to protect the harbor at Sheboygan, on western Lake Michigan, the north breakwater was marked with a pierhead light. It was the short inverted-funnel shape used also at Kenosha, Milwaukee, Racine, Waukegan and Petoskey. The large hexagonal base acted as a service room that was accessible through a door in a dormer on one of its six sides. A simple gallery surrounded the small hexagonal lantern and an over-sized dome capped the structure. The building was covered with sheet metal. This light served from approximately 1899 until 1915, when the cast-iron tower of the north pierhead light was repositioned on the breakwater, making it the harbor's main light.

At some point this light's circular lantern and the old fog signal building on the north pier were removed and replaced by modern equipment placed on the top of the lanternless breakwater light. Today the light is within a plastic lens and has a 9-mile (14.5 km) visibility. An electrically operated fog signal, also on the top of the tower, has replaced the old system. The tower top even has weather equipment that transmits data electronically to the National Data Buoy Center at Fort Worth, Texas, 24 hours a day.

Known Keepers: Amos Carpenter (–1903), Gottfried Hansen (1903–14).

104 Sheboygan North Pierhead Light

With its development as a shipbuilding and fishing community, Sheboygan on western Lake Michigan received pier improvements in the 1870s, and a pierhead light was placed to mark the end of the pier in 1873. It was a wooden pyramidal tower with an open base to allow waves to wash through and an enclosed top to act as a service room and offer protection for the keeper. In March 1880 the tower burned to the pier but fortunately the pier was saved. A similar structure was built to replace the old tower.

Then a fog signal building was built on the pier behind the light, along with a catwalk to connect the buildings to shore. In 1906 the wooden lighthouse was replaced by a tower made of iron bands riveted together to better withstand Lake Michigan's wild storms. The tower had a circular gallery and lantern, and the lantern's curved squares of glass were set into diagonally placed astragals. As the north pier extended farther into the lake, the lighthouse followed it, and the catwalk was lengthened to keep it connected to shore. In 1915 this cast-iron tower was moved to the breakwater to become the main harbor light.

Sheboygan North Breakwater Light

Sherwood Point Lighthouse

105 Sherwood Point Lighthouse

The need for a lighthouse at Sherwood Point tied in directly with shipping and lake travel on Lake Michigan. In the winter Green Bay was landlocked because the northern water routes were frozen. But lower Lake Michigan waters were usually ice-free; so, when the Sturgeon Bay Ship Canal was dug, Green Bay was no longer landlocked and Sturgeon Bay expanded as a port. Additional navigation aids were needed, so a lighthouse was built at Sherwood Point to mark the western entry into Sturgeon Bay and the Sturgeon Bay Ship Canal.

Congress appropriated $12,000 for this lighthouse in March 1881, and the site on Sherwood Point was soon selected. While mariners hoped for the light in 1882, difficulties obtaining a clear title to the land delayed work until 1883. Construction began with extensive blasting to level enough stone to build a rock foundation. The building was a 1½-story, red brick structure with a square tower rising one more level from the lake end of the building. The tower, painted white, supported a square red gallery that held a decagonal white, cast-iron lantern, a red dome and a ventilator ball. Red ornamental wood corbels supported the gallery. The tower was 35 feet (10.7 m) from its base to the top of the lantern. The light's focal plane over the water was 61 feet (18.6 m), due to the height of the limestone bluff it stood upon. This lighthouse was the only one in Door County to be built of red brick. The first lightkeeper at Sherwood Point, Henry Stanley, who was transferred there from the Eagle Bluff lighthouse, officially lit the lamp on the evening of October 10, 1883.

In 1884 Stanley's niece, Minnie Hesh of Brooklyn, New York, came for a short visit after the death of her parents. However, her stay became permanent because she liked the area. She married William Cochems, son of a prominent Sturgeon Bay businessman, in 1889. In 1894 her husband became the assistant keeper and, upon Stanley's death, the main keeper. In 1898 the Lighthouse Board appointed Minnie Cochems assistant, a post she kept until her death in 1928. Her husband commemorated her by placing a small marker northeast of the lighthouse near the road.

Sherwood Point's light characteristic was a white light alternated with a flashing red light. Its visibility was 15 miles (24 km), although people 18 miles (29 km) away in Menominee, Michigan, could see it in clear weather. Since the light's complex mechanism would cease functioning from time to time from unknown causes, this apparatus was discarded in 1892 and replaced with functioning equipment from another lighthouse, which included a fourth-order Fresnel lens. Also in 1892 a square wooden pyramidal fog signal was built in front of the light tower. It originally had a bell that was struck automatically every 12 seconds in foggy weather. This was later changed to a fog horn that used compressed air.

During the 1930s the light was electrified, and in 1933 William Cochems retired and Conrad Stram took over. He was the last civilian keeper at Sherwood Point. In 1941 the Coast Guard began operating the lighthouse and Stram was transferrred to the Coast Guard. From his retirement in 1945 until 1983, Coast Guardsmen manned the light. The light was automated in 1983 and an automatic six-bulb changer installed. At this time the Sherwood Point lighthouse was the last manned lighthouse on the American side of the Great Lakes. Because the lighthouse is on Coast Guard property it is seldom open for viewing.

Although the lighthouse's residents change from year to year, one remains the same and has been reported by a number of different people, says the great nephew of Minnie Cochems, a local storeowner in Door County. He reports that Coast Guard personnel and visitors staying at the lighthouse, especially those who sleep in the bedrooms upstairs, see the same phenomenon — a shadow lady with long grey-white hair in a long white nightgown. All reports confirm that she is friendly and looks exactly like Minnie Cochems, as seen in old pictures of her. It appears that her "short stay" continues.

Known Keepers: Henry Stanley (1883–95), William Cochems (1895–1933), Conrad Stram (1933–45).

106 Simmons Reef Lightship

In 1891 Congress appropriated $60,000 for three sister lightships (*LV 55*, *LV 56* and *LV 57*). They were built by the Blythe Craig Shipbuilding Company of Toledo, Ohio, for a total cost of $42,675.

The vessels were built as an experiment to assist lighting the Great Lakes by avoiding the high initial and recurring costs of a permanent lighthouse. The estimated maintenance and operating costs for each ship were $4,000 a year. To avoid the need (as well as cost) for anchorage, the ships did not carry mushrooms anchors and chain. Instead, a 5-ton sinker and 15 fathoms of 2-inch (15 cm) chain were positioned permanently at each lightship location and were buoyed to mark the site.

Built of wood, these lightships each had two masts, the foremast to hold its daymark and the aft mast to hold a riding sail. Each was 102 foot 8 inches (31.6 m) long, had a 20-foot (6.2 m) beam and an 8-foot-9-inch (2.7 m) draft, and displaced 129 tons. To power them, each also had a single cylinder, non-condensing steam screw engine and a stack on the deckhouse amidship to release smoke. The engines could manage a mere 8 knots at full speed, as they were only designed to ferry to and from their location for the navigation season and to produce steam for the 6-inch (15 cm) fog whistle. The illuminating apparatus consisted of a cluster of three oil-burning lens lanterns hoisted to the masthead.

LV 55, costing $14,225, was delivered to the Detroit Lighthouse Depot in September 1891. In early October the Lighthouse Board conducted sea trials and found many defects. After repairs and interior modifications for the comfort of the crew, the vessel used its own power as well as a tow from the tender *Dahlia* to travel to and be placed on the northerly end of Simmons Shoal on October 24. From November 17–20 the crew sailed the vessel to Cheboygan, Michigan, without any orders, perhaps thinking it was the end of the season. But the Lighthouse Board wanted men who could follow directions so the crew were fired for dereliction of duty and replaced with "more trustworthy" men.

The *Dahlia* assisted in towing the vessel back to the reef and it was anchored for the rest of the season, after which it went to its winter quarters at Cheboygan. During the winter, deficiencies due to missing, incomplete or faulty equipment were made good. Its masts were also shortened, as they had been found to be unnecessarily long. In 1896 a fog bell was added to the vessel and the fog signal characteristic was changed (blast 5 s; silence 55 s). In 1898 the boilers were repaired and the smoke stack was replaced.

LV 55 served at Simmons Reef each navigation season until the reef station was discontinued on December 10, 1900. It then went on to serve at Lansing Shoal until 1920, when it was retired from duty. It was sold in February 1922 for $840. These three sister ships were the first U.S. lightships to be self-propelled by machinery.

107 Skillagalee Lighthouse

Ile aux Galets Island ("Island of Pebbles") was aptly named for its gravel shoal that extends almost 2 miles (3.2 km) to its east and 1.5 miles (2.4 km) to the northwest. The English, finding it tricky to pronounce, anglicized it as Skillagalee. To ships traveling north from Little Traverse Bay, this remote and barren island is the first to be spotted on the horizon. Since it lies just west of the Waugoshance light, it is close to the shipping channel approach to Gray's Reef Passage and the Straits of Mackinac. The government officially recognized the danger of this island after the side-wheel steamer *A.D. Patchin* was grounded on Skillagalee. The crew escaped to the island, but before the *Patchin* could be pulled free, lake storms smashed her to pieces. Congress appropriated $4,000 for a light on the island in 1850.

The island only rises a few feet above water and its size varies according to Lake Michigan water levels. Water and wind erosion have been a constant problem. In 1868 Congress appropriated more funds to build a new lighthouse, as the previous one had deteriorated beyond repair. The Lighthouse Board upgraded the lighting apparatus from the old Lewis lamp array to a third-order Fresnel lens. The station also included a new 1½-story keeper's house and a fog signal building that housed a steam siren. Due to continuous erosion, this lighthouse lasted only 20 years. It was torn down in the spring of 1888 and a third one was built the same year at a cost of $6,875.

This new tower was given a solid stone foundation. Its 58-foot (17.7 m) height tapered from a base diameter of 14 feet (4.3 m) to a 9-foot (2.7 m) diameter at the summit. The octagonal brick tower was painted white for visibility and topped with an octagonal cast-iron lantern outfitted with a fourth-order Fresnel lens manufactured by Barbier and Fenestre of Paris in 1886. The light had a visibility of 15 miles (24 km) from a focal point of 58 feet (17.7 m). This tower was attached to the keeper's dwelling by a covered passageway, and the site included a boathouse and oil house. In 1890 the steam siren was replaced by 10-inch (25 cm) steam whistles.

This station had many keepers: in its first five years it had five, likely because of its inhospitable location. Its receiving an assistant keeper in 1852, a second assistant keeper in 1875, and continuing with three keepers shows the importance of this light. Dates are recorded for keepers up until 1898 but then become unclear.

An 1856 newspaper article tells about the Skillagalee lightkeeper Charles Hale being arrested for stealing a boat. Apparently the Collector at Mackinac wanted the position of keeper for himself, and so he started the rumor about Hale having stolen the boat in his possession. This resulted in "violence and brutality," as boat stealing was highly frowned upon. However, the

Skillagalee Lighthouse

magistrate threw the case out of court, stating that a lighthouse keeper could not be charged with stealing his government-issued boat. But the question arises: "Why would anyone be so desperate to have the job of lightkeeper at such a dismal place?"

There is an interesting tale about pirating by one of the lighthouse keepers. Beaver Island was not too far from Skillagalee, and it was run by Mormon James Jesse Strang, who ruled like a self-appointed king over the island people and was a member of the Michigan House of Representatives. He was influential in the decision that led to the construction of a light on Skillagalee. Some sources say that his surrogate keeper on Skillagalee would turn off his light and display a false light to lure ships onto the shoals where they could be looted. If true, this must have been sometime between 1850, when the light was lit, and 1856, when Strang was mortally wounded.

Although the date when keepers were removed is unsure, the light underwent changes in 1969 when the Coast Guard demolished all buildings except for the tower, and removed the fourth-order lens, replacing it with a 300 mm plastic lens powered from batteries and a solar panel. This third tower has outlived the first two towers and served for well over 100 years. If you wish to view it, you must do so by boat.

Known Keepers: Elijah Pressey (1850–51), Jacob Burk (1851–52), Henry Tucker (1852–53), Ambrose Davenport (1853–54), Alden Hale (1854–55), Ambrose Davenport (1855–61), Jerome Pratt (1861–68), Robert Hume (1868–69), Patrick McCann (1869–74), Vetal Bourisseau (1874–98).

108 South Fox Island Lighthouse

In its undertaking to mark safe passage for vessels plying the eastern shores of Lake Michigan in the later part of the nineteenth century, Congress set aside $18,000 in March 1867 for a lighthouse station on South Fox Island. Situated 17 miles (27.5 km) off Cat's Head Point of the mainland and 18 miles (29 km) south of Beaver Island, the island is on the western edge of the well-used shipping route between the Manitou Passage to the south and Gray's Reef Passage to the north. The lighthouse was to be on the southern tip of the island to warn of underwater shoals that extended as far as 9 miles (14.5 km) to the south.

The lighthouse was built first. The square 45-foot (13.7 m) tower and 1½-story schoolhouse-style attached keeper's house were constructed of yellow Milwaukee brick, which was laid 13 inches (33 cm) thick. A 48-step spiral cast-iron staircase led up to the decagonal iron lantern, which housed a fourth-order Fresnel lens. Revolving on 20 ball bearings at its base and powered by a clockwork mechanism, the lens produced a red light that flashed every two minutes due to the two bull's-eye panels of the lens. During the day the lens was covered with a linen hood to prevent

damage by the sun's rays magnifying through the glass prisms of the lens. The first keeper, Henry J. Roe, first lit the light on November 1, 1867.

The station also included a fog signal building, a frame structure that housed a steam-powered fog whistle. The steam was produced by two boilers that sat on the concrete floor and could be fired with wood or coal. The frame walls were lined with smooth iron sheets to protect them from the heat of the boilers. The outer walls were covered with corrugated iron sheets. The inner wall spaces were filled with a mixture of lime and sawdust, perhaps as an insulator to deaden the fog whistle blasts on shore. The boilers only took one hour at most to make sufficient steam to produce the whistle's three-second blasts. Later this fog whistle was upgraded to a low-toned diaphone foghorn.

The keeper tended the light and kept everything "ship-shape" to satisfy the inspector, who arrived quarterly on unannounced visits aboard the tender *Hyacinth* or *Sumac*. Keepers were even reprimanded for minor infractions such as fingerprints on the brasswork or dirty dishes in the kitchen. However, in colder months the keeper had more significant problems. He had to prevent the lard oil from freezing and keep a stove going in the tower to warm the lantern glass enough to prevent frost from forming and making the lamp useless. For all his efforts he was paid $150 per quarter. Apparently some members of the Lighthouse Board even refused orders to be placed at this light because of its remote location. Others said they had everything they needed to work at the station, except neighbors.

An assistant keeper was assigned to the station in 1871 but it was not until sometime in the 1890s that a frame house was built for him near the lighthouse. The keepers lived at the station only during the shipping season, wintering on the mainland, usually in the Northport area. Their wives and school-age children would stay on the mainland during the school year but live at the light when school was out.

This station was modified over time. In 1880 keeper Warner constructed a high closely boarded fence around the lighthouse to keep out drifting sand and snow. But even this impediment was not high enough at times. Keeper Bourisseau built wood plank walkways and a brick oil house that could store up to 360 gallons (1450 l) of the new and highly volatile illuminant, kerosene. In 1900 the lighthouse's official sailboat was replaced with a steam launch. Around 1910 the frame assistant's dwelling was replaced with a red brick duplex to house the two assistant keepers and their families separately. These quarters even had indoor plumbing, rare even on the mainland. Also at this time, the yellow tower was painted white to slow down the deterioration of its soft brick and provide a more visible daymark.

Around the turn of the century the population on South Fox Island increased enough to warrant a post office being built there

Old South Fox Island Lighthouse

South Fox Island Lighthouse

in March 1906. However, as mail again declined the post office was closed in November 1911. Before and after these years the mail was delivered to the lighthouse by the mail boat, which made bimonthly to monthly drops. Keepers and other island residents sent and received their mail from the lighthouse, as the lighthouse was a government building.

Changes continued at the station. In 1933 the government decided to replace the old yellow brick tower with a taller, more efficient one. The light's old lantern was eventually used during restoration of the Old Presque Isle Lighthouse on Lake Huron, as its lantern had been removed just when the New Presque Isle Lighthouse was built. In 1934 workers reassembled a cast-iron skeletal tower that had been moved from Sapelo Island, Georgia, where it was no longer needed to light Darien Harbor. Concrete foundations 9 feet (2.8 m) deep stabilized the tower's legs. Also at this time, a diesel engine was installed to provide electricity for the light and compressed air for the foghorn. At some point the red light was changed to white.

In 1959 the light was automated, and a spare lantern was moved from South Fox Island for restoration of the old Presque Isle Lighthouse on Lake Huron. The Coast Guard discontinued using the South Fox Island Lighthouse in 1976, as it was made obsolete by modern technology.

Known Keepers: Henry J. Roe (1867–71), William Bruin (1871–76), Willis Warren (1876–82), William Lewis (1883–85), Captain Joseph Fountain (1886–91), Lewis Bourisseau (1891–1915).

109 South Haven South Pier Light

With the rise of lumbering in the area of South Haven, a community developed at the mouth of the Black River, Lake Michigan. In 1861 locals constructed two protective piers into the lake at the river mouth and dredged the opening to a depth of 7 feet (2 m). In 1867 engineers widened the channel between the piers, extended the piers further into the lake, and dredged the channel to 12 feet (3.7 m). Congress appropriated $6,000 for a pierhead light to mark the entrance between the piers. However, before it could be built, Congress then recalled the funds for use elsewhere and plans for the light were put on hold.

In 1871 Congress re-appropriated the money, and the 30-foot (9 m), white wooden pyramidal tower was built. The top half was enclosed with clapboarding, while the bottom half was left open. It had an octagonal cast-iron lantern and was connected to shore by a wooden catwalk. The light was first lit in 1872. The 2½-story white keeper's house with a hipped roof was built on a bluff close the river mouth.

In 1890 the Lighthouse Board chose South Haven as the site to try a Walsbach burner gasoline light, a new illuminating apparatus. The trial was reportedly successful as the apparatus doubled the light's intensity and reduced fuel consumption by half.

The piers were extended farther into the lake in 1900, with the result that the pierhead light and catwalk were moved to the new outer end of the south pier in 1901 and another 250 feet (75 m) of wooden catwalk was built. In 1902 the light received a new fifth-

South Haven South Pier Light

order Fresnel lens made by Barbier and Fenestre of Paris. The station used a hand-operated fog signal. In 1903 the wooden tower was replaced with a prefabricated tower that had riveted bands of iron set inside each other as the tower rose, creating a slightly conical shape. It was 35 feet (10.7 m) in height and painted white. It received the Fresnel lens from the old tower.

After the pier was extended another 425 feet (130 m) into the lake in 1913, the tower was once more moved to the new pierhead and additional catwalk was built. At the same time, a mechanically operated 1,600-pound (725 kg) fog bell was mounted to the lakeward side of the tower. (It was replaced by an air-powered foghorn in 1937.)

In 1916 a 52-foot (16 m) skeletal tower was built on the south pier about 800 feet (250 m) behind the pierhead light to act as a rear range light so that the two lights could guide vessels into the harbor. It displayed a fixed red light of 50 candlepower. Being too dim, the light's intensity was increased to 750 candlepower after just a month. At an unknown date, this skeletal rear range light was removed.

Further changes occurred as well. In 1923 the light was electrified and used a 200-watt bulb. In 1927, 800 feet (250 m) of steel catwalk was moved from the Calumet station and reinstalled at South Haven. The white iron pierhead tower was painted red to comply with new regulations ("Red, Right, Return"). In 1940 the lighthouse was moved to the end of the newly built 1,400-foot (430 m) concrete pier. The light was automated and the keeper's dwelling housed Coast Guard personnel until the late 1980s.

In 1991 the Michigan Maritime Museum in South Haven leased the house as an annex. Public pressure later saved the building from being auctioned, and the property was deeded to the city of South Haven on August 3, 2000. The Michigan Maritime Museum hopes to renovate the dwelling for use as a maritime reference library. Terms in the agreement allow the Museum to lease the property from the city. If the building is not used as a public monument it will revert to Federal ownership. This light, which continues as an active aid to navigation today, is one of few that still maintains its catwalk.

Known Keepers: William Bryan (1871–73), James Donahue (1875–1909), Louis De Diemer (1909–13), Jesse Brown (1913–19), John Langland Jr. (1919–32), Robert Young (1932–40).

110 South Manitou Lighthouse

The islands of North and South Manitou are part of the Beaver Island archipelago and mark the west side of the shipping channel known as the Manitou Passage in Lake Michigan. Lake Michigan storms can be devastating. French naturalist Francis Court De Castlenau's description of an 1838 gale near South Manitou Island gives a taste of their ferocity: "We are a plaything of giant waves … I have seen squalls off the banks of New Foundland and hurricanes off the Gulf of Mexico. No where have I witnessed the fury of the elements comparable to that found on the fresh water sea."

It was a 300-mile (480 km) trip to travel the length of Lake Michigan. By using the Manitou Passage, mariners could save themselves 60 miles (96 km) and avoid exposing themselves to the full-scale storms of the outer passage. To help mark the south entry to the passage and mark the only natural harbor for refuge from storms in this area, Congress appropriated $5,000 in 1838 for a light on the south side of South Manitou Island. The lighthouse was lit by William Burton, its first keeper, in 1840.

The light was the first of three at this location. It was a rubble-stone 1½-story keeper's house with a wooden cupola, or short tower, built on the top of the house. The tower's iron lantern, which was capped with a copper dome, used eleven Argand lamps, each with its own 14-inch (35 cm) silvered reflector, to produce a weak beam of light. Although the light's focal plane was about 75 feet (23 m) because it had been built on high ground, its visibility was only about 8 miles (13 km) due to the poor quality of the lighting apparatus. The heavily treed island had a good lumber trade and also became a source of fuel supply for passing steamers. Apparently keeper Burton, who earned $350 a year as the light's first keeper, found this more lucrative than lighthouse keeping because even after being warned, he still neglected the light to sell wood. Needless to say, he was replaced by another keeper, Zackariah Ward, in 1843.

Recognizing the light's poor visibility, the government took action. In 1857 a new fourth-order Fresnel lens was installed to increase the visibility of the fixed white light. However, the light-house was found to be in such a state of deterioration when the lens was installed that a completely new lighthouse was recommended.

In 1858 the Lighthouse Board replaced the deteriorating light-house with a two-story yellow brick keeper's house. Being built into a sand dune, its foundation was exposed at the north end, making it seem like a three-story house. The year "1858" was bricked right into the west side of the house. This house had a small wooden tower mounted on the roof. The fourth-order Fresnel lens from the old lantern was placed inside the new pre-fabricated iron lantern that topped the tower. The use of the previous poor lamps continued to restrict the light's visibility to just 14 miles (22.5 km). This new lighthouse was virtually a duplicate of two other lighthouses also built that year at Port Washington and Grand Traverse.

Since this light was dim and low, a mainland "blackbird," Joe Perry, would place his own light on the south end of Sleeping Bear Dunes. At night, mariners would see the pirate's light first and mistake it for the South Manitou light. When they ran aground on the shoals and the crew left the distressed ship for safety, Perry and his crew would row out and loot the vessels.

An automated fog bell was also erected at the station. A wooden structure was built to house the 1,000-pound (450 kg) fog bell that hung from the exterior wall. The automated mechanism was powered by a weighted clockworks system. It operated a large mallet that swung through an opening in the outside wall to strike the bell.

Likely in response to complaints about the weak light causing groundings, the Lighthouse Board in 1869 reported that the South Manitou light needed a larger lens, a higher elevation and a light with its own distinct characteristic. A new light was therefore started in 1870. A solid foundation that would support the weight of a tall tower constructed on sandy soil was built by driving 100 white oak beams, each 1-foot (0.3 m) square and 60 feet (18 m) long, deep into the ground and well below the water level to prevent rotting. These pilings were topped with 15 feet (4.6 m) of masonry built up to just one foot (0.3 m) above ground level. The tower was designed by Chief Engineer Orlando M. Poe.

The 104-foot (32 m) double-layered conical red brick tower had an 18-foot (5.5 m) base diameter and ascended to an 11-foot (3.4 m) diameter at its summit. The inner layer of brick ran straight up, while the outer layer, separated by an air space, tapered as the tower rose. The red brick was painted white with black trim for best visibility. A series of open-grate-work iron steps and semi-circular landings were built right into the tower. This technique allowed the spiral stairs to be used as scaffolding during the building of the tower. Also, the open-grate-work stairs were designed as self-cleaning stairs. Vibrations from climbing the stairs made sand and dirt fall between the holes in the steps to the bottom of the landing. The keeper just had to sweep the landings instead of all the steps.

The watchroom and pedestal room had a solid iron floor with a trap door to help prevent tower drafts that would blow out the light. The pedestal room housed the base of the new Fresnel lens. The decagonal lantern had one panel blacked out at the back, and it housed a third-order Fresnel lens manufactured in Paris by Henri LePaute. A clockwork mechanism ,with weights that needed to be wound frequently, rotated the lens. With its triple-wick oil lamp as a light source and a focal plane of 100 feet (30.5 m), the light was visible for up to 18 miles (29 km). The lantern also had a small gallery for window cleaning. When this new light was built in 1872, the old tower on the keeper's house was removed. This new, higher, brighter tower was connected to the old keeper's house by a long passageway in 1858.

This station had 17 keepers and 32 assistant keepers over the years. Starting with the aforementioned Burton, almost all early keepers had a second job such as farming or fishing to supplement their salary, and the government accepted this as long as they also tended the light. The light's fifth keeper, Alonzo Slyfield, was a part-time doctor. He tended the light for six years from 1853. His doctoring skills were put to good use one day when he rescued several men and a woman who clung to their capsized boat. He was also the keeper who moved into the new, two-story brick keeper's house in 1858.

In 1872 when the third tower was lit, an assistant keeper was hired and the brick keeper's house was divided to become a duplex. In 1875, when the second assistant was hired, the house may have been divided into apartments to give each keeper his own space. This second assistant's primary job was to run the new steam-powered diaphone fog signal that was added in 1875. This system was the first of its kind on the Great Lakes. Since it was so efficient, it became the number-one choice for other stations as well.

On March 21, 1878, the *Grand Traverse Herald* of Traverse City Michigan, reported: "A sad accident occurred off the South Manitou Island on Friday, the 15th." The South Manitou light-keeper, Aaron Sheridan, his wife, their youngest child and a friend were returning from the mainland when their small boat capsized about a mile (1.6 km) from the lighthouse. While trying to assist his wife and child, who kept sliding from the overturned boat, he and his family were eventually lost in the cold waters. The friend lived to tell the tale. Mr. Sheridan's attempts to save his family are

South Manitou Lighthouse

the more remarkable since, as his grandson, Stephen Sheridan, told us, his grandfather had lost an arm below the elbow in the Civil War. In 1902 a lifesaving station was added nearby to meet the need created by the increase in shipping accidents in the narrow Manitou Passage.

The light was deactivated in 1958, after the Coast Guard anchored the 15-foot (4.6 m) radar-reflecting South Manitou Shoal Gong Buoy, with its flashing white light that had a 9-mile (14.4 km) visibility. In the 1960s and 1970s the abandoned lighthouse was *the* place to party, which led to vandalism, including the use of the floorboards as bonfire fuel. But the lighthouse endured, if only as a shell. During its inactive years, the South Manitou Passage light acquired a fine store of traditional unexplained phenomena and "ghostly" tales.

Today the lighthouse is part of the Sleeping Bear Dunes National Lakeshore. The tower has been stabilized and restored by the National Park Service, but the keeper's house is still off limits to the general public due to the extensive, interior vandalism. Park rangers affirm that it used to be common practice for unused lenses to be dumped into the lake and that this might have been the fate of the fourth-order Fresnel lens from the old lighthouse.

The park runs interpretive programs in the summer. They include historical lighthouse tours, some even presented in period costume by students from Northern Michigan State University. The third tower, which was built as the South Manitou lighthouse, is one of five American lighthouses on the Great Lakes known as the "Tall Lighthouses." They are distinguished by their great height and their common architectural style, designed by Orlando M. Poe. The other four Tall Lighthouses are located at Wind Point (Wisconsin), New Presque Isle (Michigan), Big Sable Point (Michigan) and Grosse Point (Illinois).

Known Keepers: William N. Burton (1840–43), Zackariah Ward (1843–45), George Clarke (1845–49), Benjamin Ross (1849–53), Alonzo Slyfield (1853–59), Patrick Glenn (1859–61), P Kirkland (1861–66), Aaron Sheridan (1866–78), Lyman Sheridan (1878–82), Martin Knudsen (1882–89), Nelson Knudsen (1889–92), Thomas Kitchen (1892), Thomas Armstrong (1892–1904), William Larson (1904–08), James Burdick (1908–28), Ernest Hutzler (1928–35), John Tobin (1935–41), Ronald Rosie (1941–42).

111 Squaw Island Lighthouse

Squaw Island is the northernmost island in the Beaver Island archipelago of Lake Michigan. Folktales say that its name recalled an Indian woman who came to this particular island because it was supposed to ensure fertility. In 1892 a lighthouse was built on the northern part of this small rocky island to warn of dangerous shoals and mark the western edge of Gray's Reef Passage.

In March 1891 Congress appropriated $2,500 for the light station. The lighthouse tender *Amaranth* delivered the materials and crew in the spring of 1892. The brick tower was built into one corner of the two-story red brick keeper's house. It was square at the bottom with corner buttresses for added support. The top half was octagonal, and a black cast-iron lantern and gallery topped the tower. Two long narrow arched windows graced the front of it and there were four porthole windows in the watchroom below the gallery. Other structures included a fog signal building, an oil house, a frame barn, a wellhead building and a dock. The fog signal was equipped with two 10-inch (25 cm) steam whistles and all equipment in duplicate in case of breakdown.

A tram car connected the dock to the keeper's house and the fog signal building to transport coal, oil and other supplies delivered by the *Amaranth*. After construction was complete the *Amaranth* returned with a lampist to install the lantern's fourth-order Fresnel lens from Paris. The red lens, powered by a clockwork mechanism, revolved around the lamp, and its bull's-eye panels caused the light to flash every 15 seconds.

This station had few keepers. Head keeper William Shields first lit the light on October 10, 1892. His assistant was Joseph Martin. However, when a second assistant was hired in 1893, the house was too small for everyone, so the government converted the barn into a separate residence for the head keeper and his family in 1894. The small chapel by the back of this house may have been built then also.

During the close of the 1900 shipping season, tragedy befell the lighthouse inhabitants. On December 14, Shields, his wife, his two assistants, his niece and his dog left the island in the station's sailboat to winter on nearby Beaver Island. However, shortly after their departure, an unexpected storm capsized their boat. The women were lashed to the floating boat. The dog drowned first, the women and one keeper died of exposure. The next day Shields and the other assistant were rescued by the steamer *Manhattan*, heading for Manitowac with a cargo of coal. Shields was hospitalized with badly frozen hands and feet. After six months and losing one leg at the knee, he was released to resume duty, but was reassigned to "lighter" duty at the newly constructed Charlevoix lighthouse supply depot. Assistant keeper McCauley fared much better, and was promoted to head keeper of Squaw Island, a post he held until the light was closed in 1928, when the Squaw Island lighthouse was made obsolete by the building of the Lansing Shoal Lighthouse offshore.

As with all abandoned buildings, those at this station deteriorated. Luckily there was little vandalism due to their distance offshore but eventually some did occur. Everything transportable disappeared as a souvenir, even the altar, belfry and stained-glass windows of the chapel. The light is in private hands today.

Known Keepers: Captain William H. Shields (1893–1901), Owen McCauley (1901–28),

112 Squaw Point Lighthouse

Squaw Point is on the Little Bay de Noc arm of northern Green Bay on the north shore of Lake Michigan. In 1897 a lighthouse was built on the point to aid mariners traveling to Gladstone and Masonville. As well as being lit as a coast light, it had a red sector to warn of shallow sandy shoals just off the point. The combined tower and 1½-story keeper's house was built with Cream City brick. The octagonal tower, about three stories high, was built into one corner of the house and large rectangular windows provided interior light. An octagonal lantern encircled by an octagonal gallery housed a fifth-order Fresnel lens.

It was first lit in 1897 by keeper Lemeul Marvin. When he died of pneumonia after being keeper for just six months, his wife Katherine (Kate) Marvin, became keeper. With the youngest four of their ten children still to raise, she was glad of the appointment. She was quite isolated as she was 6 miles (9.7 km) from her closest neighbor or a twenty-minute row across the bay to Gladstone.

With the advent of acetylene about 1918, the lighthouse was automated and the keepers removed. On August 9, 1921, the empty structure burned in a forest fire that swept the area, leaving only a charred brick house and tower walls. The Lighthouse Service cleared the ruins and replaced the light with another tower light that served until being transferred to a metal pole in 1964. The pole light was discontinued in 1993 when the point was marked with an offshore buoy. The land was cleared of any light remains and then sold to private ownership.

Known Keepers: Lemeul Marvin (1897), Katherine Marvin (1897–).

113 St. Helena Lighthouse

Before written history, Native Indians called this island "Mish-quo-o-ning," "the beautiful island." In 1744 it appears as St. Hélène on a map by Charlevoix. Fur traders mention the island little, except to say that it provided shelter from Michigan storms on its north side. In 1848 William Belote acquired the island from the U.S. government. In the 1850s St. Hélène became a port of call for steamships taking on fresh supplies and fuel. As fishing in the area increased, families settled and by the 1850s there were 30 year-round residents and 200 seasonal residents.

In 1853 a firm of brothers headed by Archibald Newton bought the island from Belote. The Newtons had the largest house on the island and owned the store, the cooper's shop, and houses that they rented. They gave dinner parties to help pass the long winter nights, and dancing took place in their cooperage.

In 1867 the Lighthouse Board reported: "This island provides an excellent anchorage during westerly gales. It is nothing unusual to see a fleet of fifty sail into the cove at one time and anchor at the island. It is low, and the mainland to the north of it being high, the island when approached from the southwest can be seen but a short distance. A light here would be of much service." A request for funds was made each year. In 1872, after several shipwrecks on nearby shoals, Congress appropriated $14,000 for a lighthouse.

Construction started in 1872, and the lighthouse was finished in 1873. There was a 71-foot (21.6 m) conical brick tower and a 1½-story brick keeper's house with a privy "out back." The house was connected to the tower by a covered archway for the keeper's protection. The lantern housed a 3½-order Fresnel lens and displayed a fixed red light. Its lamp first burned lard oil and then kerosene. As well as marking good anchorage during storms, the light also marked the west entrance to the hazardous Straits of Mackinac and warned of the dangerous shoals off the island's southeast side.

In the 1890s a boathouse, a pier, a boatway and a sidewalk, a double-walled metal oil house and a small barn were added. In 1909 a one-room assistant keeper's house was built next to the privy, but the assistant keeper ate with the keeper's family in the main house. Since the assistant's house was too close to the privy for sanitation standards, a new one was built in 1915 on a site north of the oil house. In 1980 the boathouse and the assistant keeper's house were torn down by the Coast Guard, as they were declared "attractive nuisances."

In 1922, when the St. Helena light was converted to acetylene, it became automated and flashed twelve times a minute. The keeper at Old Mackinac Point lighthouse checked the light twice a year and also when the light

St. Helena Lighthouse

went out. (Once it went out because a fly put out the pilot light.) Sometime during the 1950s–1970s the light was converted to battery power and the Fresnel lens was replaced with a plastic 250 mm lens. Pieces of the old Fresnel lens have been found near the tower. Next, the tower cap was removed to increase the light intensity of the new plastic lens, and the light was switched to operate on solar-powered batteries. In 1985–86 the Great Lakes Lighthouse Keepers' Association (GLLKA) became interested in saving the lighthouse and in 1986 they obtained a 30-year lease from the Coast Guard to restore and use the light station.

It was a huge undertaking because all the buildings had been vandalized and burned. Walls, windows and banisters were gone; there was fire damage in the keeper's house; the oil house was missing 1,400 bricks and its steel door, and holes had been shot in the roof. The flagpole and pump were gone. Sixty years of brush and debris had built up. Area residents woke up and became involved in the restoration.

In 1988 the St. Helena lighthouse was added to the *National Register of Historic Places* and the GLLKA guided the restoration efforts. The association also offered its first educational program at the lighthouse in 1988 to get educators interested in teaching children how to help preserve their heritage. In 1989 the association received a $20,000 grant from the Bicentennial Lighthouse Fund to be matched with labor, goods and donations. Dick Moehl, president of the GLLKA, got the Boy Scouts involved in the restoration work. Since then, the roof has been repaired, the cap returned to the lantern, and the assistant keeper's house reconstructed. Interior restoration continues.

In 1997 the Coast Guard planned to fill in the well because they thought it must be contaminated by batteries left at the lighthouse. However, Moehl had the water tested and it was found to be an excellent 40-foot well, so it was saved. Also in 1997, due to "excessing" the light, ownership of the light-

St. Helena Lighthouse

house was transferred from the Coast Guard to GLLKA, although the Coast Guard still maintains the light. Then, in 1998, the association gained private ownership of the light. The Coast Guard officially turned the light off and it was immediately turned back on as a private aid to navigation.

Of special interest was keeper Marshall. He decided to paint the tower when his wife went to visit on the mainland. While she was gone he got caught in the scaffolding and hung upside down for two days until her return. It was rumored that he was never "right-in-the head" again.

This lighthouse is proof of how people can make a difference. To sum it up as Dick Moehl might: "Our children are the keepers of tomorrow," so we must educate them today.

Known Keepers: Thomas P. Dunn (1873–75), Charles Louisignan (1875–88), Charles Marshall (1888–1900), George R. Leggatt (1900–01), Joseph Fountain (1901–18), Wallace Hall (1919–22).

114 St. James Harbor Lighthouse (Beaver Island)

This light, also known as the Beaver Island Harbor light, was built on Whiskey Point of Beaver Island in Lake Michigan. The point was named for the trading post established there in the 1830s to exchange whiskey for trading goods (especially fish). White settlers developed a community around the post and the natural harbor known as St. James Harbor. As early as 1838, a report to Congress recommended that a lighthouse be built on Beaver Island due to the number of shipwrecks in the area, but it was ignored. By the early 1850s St. James Harbor had supplanted Mackinac Island as the economic center of Michigan's northwest: it offered steamers cordwood for $1 less, it had an excellent natural harbor, and it was more convenient for vessels to stop here between Chicago and Buffalo. With an increase in vessels traveling Lake Michigan as well as increased local boat traffic, more vessels stopped at the island to replenish supplies and the busy harbor needed a lighthouse.

In 1848 Jesse Strang arrived at the island with his Mormon followers. They eventually drove most of the non-Mormon residents off the island and Strang appointed himself "King" of the island in 1850. Perhaps it was Strang's later appointment to the Michigan Legislature, or perhaps it was merely the appointment of a Lighthouse Board in 1852, but in 1856 a lighthouse was built at St. James Harbor to help guide ships into the harbor and mark the harbor as a refuge from lake storms. Also in 1856 Strang was shot by discontented followers and left the island. He later died, and non-Mormons reclaimed their island.

St. James Harbor Lighthouse, circa 1914

Little is known about the first light built here except that it was short and poorly constructed, and had a visibility of only 9 miles (14.5 km). In an 1867 Lighthouse Board annual report, a new, taller light was recommended for Whiskey Point to make the light more effective in guiding lake traffic. This, plus pressure to Congress by Michigan's lumber barons, made Congress appropriate $5,000 to construct a new tower.

The contract was awarded to A.P. Newton, who had led the vigilante group of non-Mormons to roust the Mormons off the island after Strang had been shot in 1856. In 1870 a new, higher cylindrical tower was built of Cream City brick, and connected to the house by a covered passageway. The 41-foot (12.5 m) tower was topped with a decagonal iron lantern that housed a new fourth-order Fresnel lens manufactured by Barbier and Fenestre of Paris. The light, which continued to burn lard oil, was also changed from white to red at this time.

Although unpaid, keeper Van Riper's wife, Elizabeth, loved the light and helped her husband tend it. When he took ill shortly after his appointment, she assumed his duties while he was recovering. Then during a storm one night in 1872, Van Riper rowed out to assist the distressed schooner *Thomas Howland*, which was trying to put into port. The lightkeeper was lost at sea and Elizabeth was appointed keeper in his stead, making her the first woman lightkeeper on Lake Michigan. Three years after her husband's death, Elizabeth married Daniel Williams, who moved into the lighthouse with her but let her continue to keep the light. She received $150 per quarter for tending the light. She remained keeper at this station until she received a transfer to Little Traverse lighthouse in Harbor Springs in 1884.

In 1885 a work party arrived at Beaver Island to make repairs to the lighthouse. The cellar beneath the house was filled in to help stabilize the structure, and an oil house was built to store the highly volatile kerosene, which was now the light's main illuminant.

The last keeper at St. James Harbor was E. Winter. When the light was automated, he and his wife were allowed to continue to live in the keeper's house although

St. James Harbor Lighthouse

his services were no longer required. In the winter of 1941–42 the U.S. Coast Guard demolished the keeper's house and other out buildings, probably for the sake of economy. The remaining tower was left as a lone aid to navigation.

Today, the light is maintained by the Coast Guard but St. James Township of Beaver Island was granted a ten-year renewable Historic Property Lease for the St. James Harbor light in October 2000. The lease allows them to strive to preserve this historic structure, which is an integral part of their community's history.

Known Keepers: Lyman Granger (1857–59), Peter McKinley (1859–69), Clement Van Riper (1869–72), Elizabeth Van Riper (1872–84), Charles Lindstrem (1884–86), Gustavus Umberham (1887–90), John Gallagher (1890–91), Joseph Fountain (1891–92), Nelson Knudsen (1892–99), E. Winter (1899–1914).

115   St. Joseph Lighthouse Depot

The St. Joseph Lighthouse Depot was built in 1891 on the north side of the St. Joseph River just behind the piers, where it was easily accessible to supply boats and lighthouse tenders. It was finished in 1893 at a cost of $35,000. While it was originally a main storehouse and a keeper's house, it was too small to winter the lighthouse tenders, so in 1904 Congress appropriated $75,000 to construct a new depot in Milwaukee. However the St. Joseph Depot grew to a four-building complex. This depot and its tenders supplied all of Lake Michigan's lighthouses, served as a buoy repair station, and also made concrete sinkers for anchoring buoys. The depot remained open until it was terminated in 1917.

In 1918 the depot was transferred to the Navy Department. When government funding was discontinued in 1950 the depot became home to the Army Reserve in 1952. It housed the Michigan National Guard from 1956 to 1993.

During the Guards' occupancy strange happenings were reported from inside the old keeper's house. The house was a two-story, cross-gabled-roof structure, bricked for its first story and shingled above. While still structurally sound, it had been badly

vandalized inside. People entering it reported strange noises, spine-tingling cold spots, and a "feeling" of not being alone, although the house was empty. The National Guard stored supplies on the main floor of the house until things were mysteriously moved. Guardsmen never volunteered to fetch supplies from the house. Twice, a voice from upstairs had said: "Get out. Just leave me alone." Others have seen mysterious lights at night. These oddities were never explained.

In 1993 the depot was placed on the *National Register of Historic Places*. In 1996 three local businessmen purchased it and opened the Lighthouse Depot Brewpub in September 1997.

116   St. Joseph Pier Lights

It is unclear exactly when the first north pierhead light was built at St. Joseph but it may have been in 1846 when a wooden pier was built into the lake. A picture from the 1890s shows the pier light as a white wooden tower with an open skeletal bottom and the top two-thirds enclosed with clapboarding. It was topped with a simple square gallery and iron lantern, which were surrounded with an iron pipe railing. It was connected to a frame fog signal building encased in iron plates. The fog building housed machinery to operate its 10-inch (25 cm) steam-powered fog whistle. The lighthouse and fog signal building were connected to each other and to shore by a catwalk.

In 1907 a local newspaper reported that the lighthouse had been condemned by the government over a year previously and that people were expecting it to topple into the lake as its foundation had been weakend by waves. However, the government first made harbor improvements, extending the piers farther into the lake and placing range lights on the north pier in 1907–08.

The front range light (pierhead light) was a 35-foot (10.7 m) slightly conical prefabricated cast-iron tower with a base diameter of 8 feet (2.5 m) and a top diameter of 7 feet (2.2 m). It supported a decagonal cast-iron lantern that housed a fifth-order Fresnel lens.

St. Joseph Pier Lights

The rear range light, about 900 feet (275 m) behind the front light, was a much larger structure, as it also housed equipment for the new diaphone fog signal. Its steel frame was placed on a raised concrete foundation encased with cast-iron plates and lined with brick. The fog signal building's hipped roof was topped with an octagonal tower and gallery, and a circular lantern that had curved squares of glass set on the diagonal into its astragals. The lantern housed a fourth-order lens (later replaced with a fourth-order Fresnel lens). The structure's overall height was 57 feet (17.5 m) and had a focal plane of 53 feet (16.2 m).

A catwalk connected the range lights to shore for the keeper's safety. In 1928 during a vicious storm the keeper was marooned at the pierhead light by crashing waves. In order to get food out to him, courageous coast guardsmen roped themselves together to make a human chain along which they could pass food. On another occasion, during a 1929 December blizzard, waves froze onto the catwalk so that the keeper and his assistant could only make their way from the fog signal to the light by roping themselves together and then chopping footholds for a distance of over 350 feet (107 m) of ice. Local seaman said it was the thickest ice they had ever seen on the north pier. The ice was 18 feet (5.5 m) high.

These range lights continue to operate today and are one of only three places on the Great Lakes that have pier range lights with the towers and catwalk still intact. The other locations are Grand Haven, and Michigan City, also on Lake Michigan. In 1995 the current north pier lighthouse was featured on a commemorative stamp issued by the U.S. Postal Service.

117 St. Joseph River Lighthouse

Both St. Joseph and Chicago had lights built in 1832, but Chicago boasts of being the first location to have a lighthouse on Lake Michigan, as its lighthouse was built earlier in the year. Congress had approved the lighthouse at the mouth of the St. Joseph River in 1830. It was built on a bluff on the south side of the river mouth overlooking the harbor. It had a 30-foot (9 m) conical, rubble-stone tower and a detached one-story stone keeper's house. The tower's iron birdcage-style lantern used eleven Argand lamps and 14-inch (35 cm) reflectors to produce its beam. It was replaced in 1859 by another lighthouse built on ground with an even higher focal plane.

The second land light at St. Joseph had a combined tower and keeper's dwelling. A short square tower rose from the front roof peak of the two-story clapboard house. The octagonal gallery was supported by eight ornately carved wooden corbels. A utilitarian polygonal iron lantern with large single panes of glass in each of its sides likely housed a Fresnel lens. The house was fronted by an ornate spindled Victorian veranda. Plans for this lighthouse were also used at Cheboygan Point on Lake Huron as well as at lighthouses on Lake Michigan (Sheboygan, Tail Point and Kalamazoo).

With the establishment of the 1907 pier range lights, the government wanted to discontinue this shore light. However, local congressman E.L. Hamilton traveled to Washington with many persuasive letters from lake captains who wished the continuance of the shore light. As a result the light shone until 1924, when it was finally discontinued.

The building then served as headquarters for the American Red Cross, the Cancer Society and the Society for Crippled Children. In April 1954 the house was sold to the town of St. Joseph for $3,000 and shortly thereafter the town announced its demolition to make way for a parking lot. Public outcry arose for the "Lighthouse on the Hill" to be saved as an historic building, but funds to move it were not available so the battle was lost and the structure was torn down by William Kasischke, who had won the bid to remove it. He even paid $169 for the timber in the old structure. With its demolition on September 1, 1955, at the age of 99, a historical link to St. Joseph's former history was also lost.

Known Keepers: Ebinezer Reed (1832), Thomas Fitzgerald (1832–38), James Simpson (1838–41), Daniel Olds (1841–43), Abner Stinson (1843–55), Benjamin Chadwick (1855–61), M. Carlton (1861–61), Mrs. Stutires Carlton (1861), John Enos (1861–76), Mrs. Jane Enos (1878–81), Daniel Platt (1883–85) –(1889–1924).

118 St. Martin Island Lighthouse

When shipping into Green Bay, Lake Michigan, increased in the late 1800s, mariners called to have the western end of the St. Martin Passage into the bay marked with a light to make navigation easier and safer. The Lighthouse Board requested funds for eight years before Congress agreed. Once land was purchased on the northwest part of the island, Congress appropriated funds for the unique iron tower in 1902. But, delayed by an iron shortage and the onset of winter, it was only finished in 1904.

The station consisted of old and new. While the keeper's two-story yellow brick duplex used the same plans as the Plum Island lighthouse and the yellow brick fog signal building used the same plans as Old Mackinac and Beaver Island, the plans for the light tower were of a completely original design never repeated anywhere else on the Great Lakes. It had a hexagonal exoskeleton with six vertical steel posts at its corners. Between these, flat iron panels were riveted to the posts. The tower was attached to its 6-foot (1.8 m) thick concrete pad with lattice-work iron buttresses

St. Martin Island Lighthouse

to help stabilize the tower and reduce wind vibrations. It was 16 feet (4.9 m) in diameter and rose 75 feet (23 m).

The tower was topped with a circular iron watchroom with porthole windows, and a circular iron gallery and lantern, with glass set into diagonal astragals. The lantern housed a fourth-order Fresnel lens with some red panels, so that when it rotated around the light (a 24,000 candlepower incandescent oil vapor lamp) it produced an occulting red and white beam visible for 18 miles (29 km) from its 84-foot (25.8 m) focal plane. The station was completed with an iron tramway to transport supplies and materials, an oil house and a fog signal building that housed twin 10-inch (25 cm) steam whistles.

The station was finished in June 1904. While some sources report that it remained unlit until the 1905 navigation season due to lack of government funds to hire a keeper, others say the first keeper, Christian Christiansen, was hired and started on June 15, 1904.

Another conflicting story is that of its ghostly keeper. One of the keepers is said to have lost his children to the lake in a storm that swamped them when they were rowing across the water to school on Washington Island. Is it his ghost that is seen wandering with a hand lantern searching for his children? Later, when a schooner was shipwrecked on the St. Martin Shoals one stormy night because the light was unlit, the crew followed a faint green light that led them to the safety of the keeper's home. However, although they found the light on the table, the keeper lay dead on the floor (explaining the unlit light) and no one else was there. Was it his ghost that guided them to the house?

This remote station changed little as time went by. The fog whistles were replaced with a diaphone fog signal whose characteristic was a one-second blast followed by a five-second blast. A radio beacon signal was installed and synchronized with the fog signal. The station was electrified and received telephone service. The light was automated. The fourth-order lens was replaced with a 190 mm optic and the old lens was placed on display at the Point

Iroquois Light Station Museum. The light was listed on the *National Register of Historic Places*.

Today the station sits abandoned and boarded up. Communities that once lived on the island are gone. It is to be hoped that with help, the station will not fall victim to nature as other remote lights have done.

Known Keepers: Christian Christiansen ((1904–05), Bernhard Pizzalar (1904–24), David Kincaid (1924–46), Ernest Lockhart (1946).

119 Sturgeon Bay Pierhead Lighthouse

In 1872 local businessmen sponsored the building of the Sturgeon Bay Ship Canal. This canal provided a short-cut entrance to the southern Green Bay area from Lake Michigan, saving the trip around the longer, northern "Death's Door" passage at the top of Door Peninsula. The canal was finished in 1881.

That year, Congress appropriated funds for a lighthouse to mark the eastern entrance of the canal even though the canal was privately owned. The lighthouse was built in 1882. The 29-foot (8.9 m) open-framed, pierhead tower, with its 35-foot (10.7 m) focal plane and its sixth-order lens displayed a fixed red light. The tower was painted white. Since it was at the end of the north pier into the canal, a wooden catwalk was built atop the pier to connect the tower to the shore for the keeper's safety. Even now it is difficult to stand at the end of the pier on a windy day without being blown off, so one can imagine the risks the keepers took in negotiating the catwalk in stormy weather, especially if they were carrying oil or supplies.

Rufus M. Wright, the first keeper, lit the light for the first time on May 15, 1882. He lived on a dredge working on the canal, as no keeper's house was built, due to a lack of funds. In 1884 a steam fog signal building was added and an assistant keeper hired. In 1886 a two-story, white clapboard keeper's house was built

Sturgeon Bay Pierhead Lighthouse

Sturgeon Bay Ship Canal Shore Lighthouse

120 Sturgeon Bay Ship Canal Shore Lighthouse

After the federal government had purchased the Sturgeon Bay Ship Canal into Green Bay from Lake Michigan in 1893, sea captains called for a more powerful, coastal light to mark the entrance, as the pierhead light was too weak. Later in 1893 Congress authorized a new light onshore, but construction did not start until 1898. The lighthouse Board used a new, unique, experimental design. On a concrete foundation they built a double-walled, steel, 8-foot (2.5 cm) cylinder that rose for 78 feet (24 m). It supported a watchroom with four porthole-windows and a circular cast-iron lantern.

The lantern's curved glass panes were set diagonally into iron astragals. The lantern housed a second-order Fresnel lens with a focal plane of 107 feet (32.6 m) and was accessible by a spiral staircase within the steel tower. The tower's only support came from the eight, 16-foot (5 m) buttresses around the base. The new light vibrated so much in windy weather that it affected the light's operation. Guy wires were attached to the tower but it still swayed. Despite this problem it was put into operation in 1899.

In 1903 the Lighthouse Board made changes to stabilize the tower. A skeletal, steel framework was erected around it. It was designed to support the weight of the watchroom and the lantern, leaving the original steel tower to support only the spiral staircase inside. At this time the pierhead light was changed to a combination steel fog signal and light tower, and the keeper's house was enlarged to accommodate the three keepers. The shore light was automated in 1972.

Today the light is operational but it is also an Active Coast Guard base. Its second-order Fresnel lens has been reduced to a less powerful third-order Fresnel lens. Viewing the light gives a sense of majestic splendor as the tower spires up for 98 feet (27 m). With its steel supports that angle out at the bottom, it gives the impression of a futuristic rocketship.

Known Keepers: Rufus M. Wright ((1882–86), Charles Chapman (1899–1910), Charles Bavry (1910–21) (1926–27), Conrad Stram (1927–33), John Tucker (1933–40), John Hahn (1940–42).

onshore, and a second fog signal building and a second assistant keeper were provided. The Federal Government purchased the ship canal in 1893, and in 1896 its navigation aids became the responsibility of the Lighthouse Board.

In 1903 the pierhead light underwent significant changes. A new stone and concrete breakwater was placed farther out in the water, angling out past the end of the north pier and not connected to shore. A new structure was built at the outer end of this breakwater to replace the north pier light and its fog signals. The new 2½-story building had a circular tower that rose up out of the lakeside end of its hipped roof. The light's octagonal lantern used the sixth-order Fresnel lens from the old pierhead light to display a fixed red light from a 40-foot (12.2 m) focal plane. The building was covered with riveted steel sheets. The old catwalk was extended over the gap at the end of the pier and along the breakwater to the new building, and stairs led right up and into the top level. When finished, the building was painted white. The keeper's house on shore was also enlarged at this time to better accommodate the three keepers.

At a later unknown date the lighthouse/fog signal building was painted red for better visibility, and probably to represent "Red, Right, Return" so that ships would know on which side to approach the entrance to the canal. Its sixth-order lens was later replaced by a 300 mm beacon, and the light was automated in 1972.

121 Taylorsport Light

Taylorsport (named after Anson Taylor, the first white settler in the area) developed as a port of call where steamers could replenish their cordwood fuel on the southwest shore of Lake Michigan. Although it did not have a protected bay, a lighthouse was constructed and lit in 1858 to mark the area. It was set on a low bluff along the shoreline and was a 21-foot (6.1 m) tower with a 1½-story attached keeper's dwelling. As vessels changed to a preferred coal fuel, making cordwood no longer necessary, and as the village had been bypassed by the railroad, trade quickly dwindled and the light was discontinued at an unknown date.

122 Two Rivers North Pierhead Light

Two Rivers was named for the East and West Twin Rivers, which flow together as one before emptying into Lake Michigan. During the 1800s a fishing village grew at the river mouth, and north and south piers were built to protect the harbor. To mark the harbor entrance, a light was placed at the end of the north pier in 1886. It was built for the U.S. Lighthouse Board by Mr. Boehmer of Manitowoc.

Two Rivers North Pierhead Light

The lighthouse was a simple wooden one — a square 36-foot (11 m) skeletal tower with its upper portion enclosed to offer the keeper some protection. It supported a decagonal cast-iron lantern and housed a sixth-order Fresnel lens that used an oil wick lamp to display a fixed red light for an arc of 240 degrees. The lighthouse was connected to shore by a long catwalk along the pier. It also had a deep distinctive two-tone diaphone foghorn. The Rawley Point lighthouse keeper also tended this light.

Little happened in the rest of its history. By 1928 the light needed and received extensive repairs. At some time it was electrified. In 1969 it was replaced with an automated light on a modern steel tower and the Coast Guard donated the upper portion of the lighthouse to the Two Rivers Historical Society. In 1974 the lighthouse was moved to the Rogers Street Fishing Village Museum. In 1988 funding to restore the lighthouse was donated by the Wisconsin Coastal Management Program and local benefactors, and the lighthouse is now one of the museum's main attractions.

Known Keepers: Anthony Gauthier (1887–1915), Otto Schmiling (1915–).

123 Waugoshance Shoal Lighthouse

During the 1800s boat traffic on Lake Michigan increased steadily. Ships traveling westward carried lumber, coal, and merchandise to growing towns and ports (like Chicago) along the shores of Lake Michigan. Returning ships carried raw materials like grain and iron ore for processing in Detroit, Cleveland and Buffalo. All these vessels had to pass through the Straits of Mackinac and down the east side of Lake Michigan. The straits were quite narrow, and many islets, reefs and shoals extended from

their southwest side for up to 7 miles (10 km) from a point of land called Waugoshance Point (also known as Little Fox Point). As well, this was the turning point for vessels heading into the straits or along Michigan's east shore and many vessels had been wrecked, grounded, or collided with other ships in this dangerous area. With little water flowing over the shoals, mariners called for the area to be lit in the 1820s.

The U.S. government complied, but not quickly, as lighthouses were under the control of the U.S. Treasury at this time and its members were rather "tight-fisted." Eventually they placed a light vessel at the Waugoshance Shoals in 1832. This was the first "floating lighthouse" ever placed on the Great Lakes. This ship, the *Louis McLean*, served here during the shipping season for almost 20 years. However, the lightship was expensive to maintain, easily blown off position, difficult to position at the start of the shipping season due to ice, and often dangerous to operate. A permanent lighthouse was needed.

In February 1837 Congress appropriated $5,000 to build a lighthouse at Waugoshance, but this did not happen. Further re-appropriations were made, but not until Congress re-appropriated $25,000 in January 1847 did lighthouse construction begin.

While other structures had been built on sunken cribs, this was the first time one had been built on a shoal far out in the water where it would take the full brunt of the lake's storms and ice. First, an accurate model was made of the crest of the reef by the Topographical Bureau (now the Army Corps of Engineers), as the north side of the crib would be in 4 feet (1.2 m) of water while the south side would be in 15 feet (4.6 m) of water. This special crib 32 by 60 feet (10 by 18 m) was built at nearby St. Helena Island and towed to the shoal, where it was positioned and sunk by filling it with huge stones. It was then capped to make an above-water pier on which the tower and the keeper's house were built. The conical, cream-colored brick tower was 76 feet (23 m) from base to ventilator ball. The walls had a base diameter of 20 feet (6 m) and a top diameter of just over 15 feet (4.7 m), and were 5½ feet (1.7 m) thick at the base and 2 feet (0.6 m) thick at the top.

Spiral iron stairs led up into the birdcage-style lantern (one of three such styles remaining on the Great Lakes today). This lantern's fourth-order Fresnel lens may have been the first Fresnel to be installed and lit on the Great Lakes. Its light produced a 16.5-mile (26.7 km) visibility from its 74-foot (22.6 m) focal plane above the lake. While other lights received a new, larger lantern when their lighting apparatus was switched to a Fresnel lens, Waugoshance retained its birdcage copper-domed lantern. The

Waugoshance Shoal Lighthouse, circa 1883

Waugoshance Shoal Lighthouse

keeper's house, also brick, was 2½ stories high and attached to the tower. It had a large dormer window in its roof, also copper-covered like the dome. The station was also equipped with a fog bell and lasted two decades before repairs were necessary.

Waugoshance did not withstand the beating of Lake Michigan. In 1865, funds were appropriated for necessary repairs. A cofferdam was constructed around the crib, water was pumped out, and cement was poured in to make a base on which massive limestone blocks each weighing 12 tons were placed and bolted together. Then a circle of solid concrete was built up around the light extending the crib to 48 by 66 feet (14.5 by 20 m).

By 1883 more repairs were needed. The crib, tower and house were eroding from the effects of wind, water and ice. The tower and the keeper's house were encased with sheets of tank iron, riveted together. The 4-inch (10 cm) space between the iron and the brick was filled with concrete, making the structures much more resilient to the elements. The iron plating was then painted with broad bands of red and white and the lantern painted red to present a distinctive daymark. The stone crib was enlarged to 80 by 90 feet (25 by 28 m) to provide still greater protection for the pier, and a fog signal building was added. Its dual 10-inch (25 cm) steam whistles replaced the inferior fog bell.

In the course of a 1907 lighthouse report and inventory, other things were noted about the station — it had a boathouse; the lantern wall had eight, sliding pattern, iron ventilators; the lens was made by Henri LePaute of Paris; the fixed white light was varied by a flash every 45 seconds; the arc of illumination was 360 degrees; the lens revolved on ball bearings not mercury; the clockwork mechanism to turn the lens had to be wound about every five hours; the lens used a new fourth-order lamp that used one wick to its burner; oil was stored in the boathouse and the basement of the dwelling; the fog whistle blasted for 5 seconds followed by 25 seconds of silence; a well on the southeast side of the of the fog signal building under the rock foundation provided water for the steam whistle; the fog signal building was lined with bricks and covered with iron plates; three keepers manned the station; water for drinking and domestic use was pumped from the lake; the station had two boats.

Most birdcage-style lanterns had many small panes of glass and it was found that their astragals (metal sashes to hold the window panes) interfered with the light rays of the Fresnel lens. This 1907 report shows that Waugoshance had a 16-sided lantern and that each side only had one large pane of glass. Perhaps this light's lantern was never replaced because these large panes of glass had no interfering astragals, or perhaps if it originally had small panes, they had already been replaced with large ones. At any rate it kept its original lantern.

Ships became larger to hold more cargo in the late nineteenth century, and needed deeper water to travel in. As they traveled further out into Lake Michigan they had to watch for White Shoals, located about 4½ miles (7.3 km) northwest of the Waugoshance light. As early as 1878 the Chicago Lumbering Company marked these shoals with a water-logged vessel. In 1891 the U.S. government placed a lightship on the shoals and from 1908 to 1910 they built a lighthouse. When this new lighthouse was completed the Waugoshance lighthouse was less useful, as the White Shoals lighthouse marked deeper water, had a greater visibility — and had no stories about strange happenings.

Some believe that the Waugoshance lighthouse is haunted. While placing the crib, a worker was killed and his cries can supposedly be heard when conditions are right. The other haunting relates to keeper John Herman, who enjoyed drinking and practical jokes. He allegedly returned to the light intoxicated after his leave and locked the assistant in the lantern room, as a joke. The assistant saw him "wobbling" along the pier until he was out of sight behind the buildings but when he finally freed himself he could find Herman nowhere. Did he topple into the lake and drown? (Was this tale the source of the light's nickname "wobbleshanks"?) After this disappearance, keepers complained to inspectors about other strange happenings for which logical explanations were never found. Some even refused to be stationed at this light. The unexplained events only stopped when the light was deactivated on July 1, 1912, and no human keepers remained to report them.

After being abandoned, the lighthouse sat empty and undisturbed until the early 1940s and the advent of World War II. The lighthouse area was placed off limits to civilians as it was used for bombing practice. The lighthouse itself was used for strafing practice and became riddled with bullet and shell marks. Apparently the complex was also hit at this time by a stray missile that set fire to the tower interior and the keeper's house. Vandals, scavengers, souvenir hunters — and possibly government agencies — added to the deterioration. Even the copper dome and the spiral staircase were taken. However, the theft of the stairs did prevent the theft of the birdcage lantern.

Although appearing weak, the lighthouse has continued to stand. Neither the elements nor the target practice have demolished it. While it lost its iron sheeting in the 1980s and 1990s, and the U.S. Coast Guard recommended in 1983 that it be declared surplus and demolished, it still stands. Although it was described as a nautical gravestone in 1994, it has presently been adopted by the Waugoshance Preservation Society, which is raising funds to secure the structure for future restoration.

Known Keepers: John Levaks (1852), Lewis Lasley (1852), Nathanial Johnson (1852–53), Lewis Lasley (1853–55), Augustus Todd (1855–61), Noal Leville (1861–64), Charles Wackler (1864–65), John McHaney (1865–77), John Mulcroone (1877–81), Levi Chapman (1881–82), Thomas Marshall (1883–86), George Marshall (1886–90), John Herman (1892–1900), James Callagher (1900–02), Ingvald Olsen (1902–10), Everitt Sherritt (1911–12).

124 Waugoshance Shoal Lightship

Waugoshance Point was a peninsula that jutted west 2 miles (3.2) from the mainland into Lake Michigan. Beyond the point extended another 6 miles (9.7 km) of islands and shoals, which presented an extreme hazard for early mariners. The area also marked a turning point between southern Lake Michigan and the Straits of Mackinac. As lake traffic increased mariners knew the area needed to be lit. Since the technology for placing a light on the shoal did not yet exist, a lightship was placed on the shoal in 1832.

The schooner *Louis McLean* was placed on the shoal as the Waugoshance Shoal Light Vessel. It was a 60-ton wooden vessel built at Detroit. However, it had difficulty withstanding Lake Michigan conditions. When Lt. James T. Homans made his 1838 report to Congress, he found the lightship in Mackinaw, undergoing extensive repairs after being blown off its mooring and thrown up on the beach the year before. Repairs were slow because mechanics and material had to come from Detroit or farther. It missed almost a whole shipping season. Then, after it was reanchored, heavy storms drove it off the shoal again. Homans' recommendation, based on the vessel's history and seaworthiness, was that it was "very unfit for that location" and could be better employed near the more sheltered flats of Lake St. Clair. "I would strongly recommend that another one be immediately built upon a more approved model for the straits so as to be ready for removal there on the opening of navigation in the spring." However, this recommendation fell on deaf ears and the *Louis McLean* continued

to mark the shoal until 1851 when an offshore lighthouse was built directly on the shoal.

Having been recommended for a more protected area after serving only six years on the shoal and then serving another thirteen years of battering, the vessel must have been well built, even if it did receive extensive repairs from time to time. The *Louis McLean* also earned another honor besides weathering Lake Michigan storms for nineteen years. It was the first lightship ever used on the Great Lakes.

125 Waukegan Breakwater Light

With the harbor breakwater at Waukegan on Lake Michigan nearing completion, a temporary iron post supporting a white lens lantern was built at the outer end of the north breakwater to mark harbor entry. It was lit on August 10, 1898. In October it was changed to a red light, and on December 31, 1889, the Little Fort light on the shore was permanently discontinued.

In 1899 the new breakwater light was built at the end of the north breakwater. Its tower was an inverted-funnel shape, which provided a wider space at the bottom for use as a service room. It was covered in metal sheeting. A dormer built into one of its six sides had a door with a window to light the interior. A simple hexagonal gallery surrounded the small hexagonal lantern, which housed a low-order harbor lens to mark the north side of the harbor entrance. It was capped with an oversized dome.

This same style of pierhead light was also built at Kenosha, Milwaukee, Racine, Sheboygan and Petoskey. None of these early lights have survived.

Known Keepers: Peter Dues (1898–19020, Frederick Raether (1902–07), William Larson (1908–24), Samuel Jacobson (1924–40).

126 Waukegan Harbor Light

When the south pier extension into Lake Michigan at Waukegan was completed, a pierhead light was placed on its lake end to mark entry to the harbor. Known as the Waukegan Harbor light, it was ready for service for the 1899 shipping season. It was a 35-foot (10.7 m) cylindrical cast-iron tower with a round cast-iron lantern that housed a fourth-order Fresnel lens. Its characteristic was fixed white for 20 seconds followed by four red flashes, each at five-second intervals. From a 36-foot (11 m) focal plane it was visible for 13 miles (21 km). It used the same plans as the pierhead light at Calumet.

Waukegan Breakwater Light

Waukegan Harbor Light after 1905

First onshore light at Waukegan also known as the Little Fort Lighthouse (see Little Fort Lighthouse)

In 1905 a fog signal building was added to the pier and connected to the back of the light tower. A catwalk extended along the pier from station to shore for the keeper's safety. The building, covered in protective iron plates, was a two-story structure. The bottom housed the fog signal equipment and the top was the keeper's quarters. The same design was used at Kewaunee (Lake Michigan) and Holland (Lake Michigan).

The old shore light was discontinued when this harbor light began operation. In 1967 a fire destroyed the fog signal building and the tower lantern. Since the fog signal was no longer in use, its remains were removed, as was the tower lantern. The tower was capped with a flat top (leading to its nickname "drum light") and was topped with a green acrylic lens. While it used to be painted all white, today it has a green band around its top.

127 White River Lighthouse

The Muskegon/White Lake area of Michigan was known in the mid-1800s as "The Lumber Queen of the World." Shipping was the most efficient way to transport lumber and as demand increased, so did shipping and the need for navigation aids. Local officials began requesting a light to mark the channel from Lake Michigan to White Lake in the 1850s. Their requests went unheard.

Meanwhile, a seaman, Captain William Robinson, had settled in the area with his family in 1867. Seeing the need for a marker due to his navigation experience he, on his own, often provided a light at the mouth of the old channel to assist incoming ships' captains.

Locals continued their request for a lighthouse and a more direct channel into the lake. Congress finally appropriated $67,000 for a new channel and $10,000 for a new lighthouse in 1866. Channel and harbor improvements went slowly and in 1869 another $45,000 was appropriated to complete the project in 1871. However, since the lighthouse had not even been started, its money reverted to the treasury requiring funds to be reappropriated. Finally, a beacon light costing $1,059 was built on the new south pier. It was only fitting that Captain William Robinson be chosen as the first lightkeeper of this light, since he had been marking the old channel entrance voluntarily for years.

Lake traffic into White Lake continued to increase during the 1870s for several reasons. Lumber was continually shipped to its two main consumers, Milwaukee and Chicago. After the Great Chicago Fire of 1871 a lumber contract for rebuilding the city significantly increased lumber shipping to Chicago. More passenger steamers were traveling Lake Michigan, and White Lake became a major harbor for refueling. More tourists from Chicago and Milwaukee were traveling to the White Lake area to holiday, and its harbor also provided storm shelter. In 1873 the Lighthouse Board noted this heavier traffic and, on their recommendation, Congress appropriated $15,000 in 1874 to build a new lighthouse.

In the 1860s the Lighthouse Board had created several standard designs for lighthouses. The "Norman Gothic" style, a design first used at the Chambers Island lighthouse, was chosen for the White River Light Station. The same design was later used at Eagle Bluff, McGulpin's Point, Eagle Harbor, Passage Island and Sand Island.

Construction of the main lighthouse began in the spring of 1875. Both the tower and the 1½-story keeper's house were given foundations of dressed limestone blocks, the tower being set into the northwest corner of the house. Both were covered with limestone bricks that keeper Robinson even helped to lay. All this limestone came from Michigan and Wisconsin. The square-based, 38-foot (11.7 m) tower had brick buttresses extending about halfway up from its two exposed corners. Above this, its four corners were flattened to create an octagonal tower that supported an octagonal gallery, a decagonal lantern, a copper dome and a ventilator ball. Open-grill-work iron stairs (self-cleaning steps) spiraled from its basement, where oil was first stored, to its lantern, which was outfitted with a fourth-order Fresnel lens and a brass lamp that burned lard oil. In 1879 this lamp was converted to kerosene.

The lens, sitting on chariot wheels on a cast-iron pedestal, revolved once every two minutes. It was powered by a clockwork mechanism that had a 50-pound (22.5 kg) weight attached to a cable wound around a drum in the clockwork mechanism. The weights, which needed to be wound every four hours to keep the lens turning, traveled up and down a special shaft built into the wall of the lighthouse tower. A "weight-watching window" in the tower wall helped the keeper monitor its progress. When the weights reached this window, the keeper only had a short time to rewind the clockworks.

The light's characteristic changed many times over the years in efforts to make it more easily recognizable. It was originally a fixed white light varied by a red flash every 40 seconds. In 1902 the chariot wheels were replaced with ball bearings so that the lens could rotate faster, once every 40 seconds. Its characteristic became a light flashing alternately red and white with 20-second intervals between flashes. Also at this time the old brass lamp was replaced by a new fourth-order lamp that also burned kerosene. In 1912 the characteristic was changed for the last time when the light received a new clockwork and a lens without red panels. The characteristic was now an occulting flashing white light (flash 10 s; eclipse 10 s). In 1918 the lighthouse was converted to electricity and a 1,000-watt incandescent light bulb, equivalent to 9,600 candlepower, provided a 15-mile (24 km) visibility. The kerosene lamp was kept for power outages and the clockwork mechanism was kept for rotating the lens.

Other changes occurred at the station. In the 1880s and 1890s, a storage/woodshed building was provided, a telephone installed (eight years ahead of other residences), a fence built to keep out neighboring cattle, and a flagpole erected. To begin the new century, concrete walks were laid down, a red brick oil house was built, indoor plumbing was installed, and electricity was provided to the tower (to the keeper's house in 1924). In 1945 the light was automated using a special electrical clock to turn the light on and off and an electric motor to rotate the lens. In 1960 the light was decommissioned and the lens and pedestal were removed and stored at the Coast Guard's Detroit depot. At this time the lighthouse was also declared excess by the Coast Guard and turned over to the General Services Administration.

In 1965 Fruitland Township wanted to purchase the property for use as a museum and public park, but was required to pay half

White River Lighthouse

128 White River Pierhead Light

After new piers were built at White River, Lake Michigan, between 1866 and 1871, a beacon light was built at the end of the short south pier. Also finished in 1871, it was a 27-foot (8.3 m) white square wooden pyramidal tower that supported a prefabricated iron lantern and a fifth-order Fresnel lens. From its 33-foot (10 m) focal plane it exhibited a fixed red light with an approximate 11-mile (18 km) visibility. A small oil storage building was also built near it to store the lard oil for burning in the lamp. Its first keeper was William Robinson.

Improvements were made as needed. In 1875 a wooden catwalk was built from shore to the light. In 1876 the south pier was extended into the lake by 100 feet (30 m), the pierhead light was moved out to its end, and the wooden catwalk was extended to the light's new location. In 1902 the light's Fresnel lens was switched to a smaller sixth-order lens, which reduced its visibility to 9 miles (14.5 m). In 1910 the wooden catwalk was replaced with a cast-iron one. In 1917 the pierhead light was painted red, as were many pierhead lights around this time. In 1925 the catwalk was removed because it was continually under repair as vessels frequently struck it when passing. In 1930 a steel skeletal tower replaced the wooden one and the pier was refaced with concrete.

Reusable parts like the lantern and lens from the old light were taken to the Lighthouse Depot at Milwaukee by the lighthouse tender *Hyacinth*. The skeletal tower was equipped with an acetylene lamp, operated automatically by a sun valve. This valve caused continual problems and the light was finally electrified in 1949. In the 1980s the skeletal tower was replaced by a simple steel pole with a flashing red electric light and a triangular red daymark. This simple light continues to function as an aid to navigation.

Known Keepers: See White River Lighthouse.

of the $12,500 appraised value. While this seemed impossible, local citizens chipped in and raised the required amount. The purchase was finalized in 1966 and the museum opened to the public in the summer of 1970. In 1972 its new curator had located the original fourth-order Fresnel lens and convinced the Coast Guard to return the lens and pedestal to the museum for reinstallation in its rightful home, the lighthouse lantern. However, after it was installed it was vandalized, requiring it to be removed from the lantern and put on display in the lighthouse museum.

In its 84 years of operation, the lighthouse only had a handful of head keepers and with reason. The first keeper was Robinson, who had been assigned the pierhead light in 1872. From the time he first lit the main light on May 13, 1876, he kept the two lights, the main light and the pier light. He raised a family of eleven at the light. His oldest son, Tom, was his first assistant keeper in 1877. Since there had never been an official foghorn at the station, Robinson would take a small, hand-carried, brass, pump horn out to the pier and produce a trumpet-like sound to let passing vessels know their proximity to the shore and the piers.

Robinson was keeper for 47 years. When the government said retirement was mandatory at age 70, his reply allegedly was: "If a man is old at seventy then there is a lot of good energy and health left in one old man." He continued to perform his duties for years after his "mandatory" retirement date until he died at the station at the age of 87. At the time of his death, Captain Robinson was the oldest keeper on active duty. His grandson William E. Bush, who had become his assistant keeper in 1911 and had taken over the major responsibilities of keeping the station in 1917 due to his grandfather's advanced age, became the official head keeper of the White River Light Station.

In addition to viewing the original fourth-order lens on its pedestal on the main floor and climbing the tower, visitors can view the ships' museum, installed where two bedrooms once were.

Known Keepers: William Robinson (1876–1919), William E. Bush (1919–43), Leo Wuori (1943–48), Mrs. France Johnson (1949–54), Andrew Newald (1954–59).

129 White Shoal Lighthouse

When mariners headed from Lake Michigan into the Straits of Mackinac, they had to avoid the reefs and shoals in the northern lake. To assist them, the Chicago Lumbering Company stationed a waterlogged vessel over White Shoals in 1878 to mark this dangerous reef, which was over 2 miles (3.2 km) long. This was replaced in 1891 by the U.S. Lightship *LV 56*, making it one of three lightship stations first used on the Great Lakes. Then in 1910 a lighthouse was built on the eastern end of the reef.

This was the second lighthouse to be built on a reef that had formerly been marked by a lightship, the first one being nearby Waugoshance. First a gravel base was put on the shoal to level it. Next, the 72 foot (22 m) square crib was sunk onto this gravel base and filled. The 18-foot (5.5 m) high crib sitting in about 20 feet (6 m) of water was next capped with a concrete pier upon which a 121-foot (37 m) brick-lined steel conical tower was built. The exterior was covered with terra cotta blocks. Many rectangular windows were set into the tower to light the interior. The watchroom had four porthole windows for the keeper to track weather and vessels. Altogether, the tower had eight floors to house equipment, fuel, storage, fog signal, boathouse, living quarters and staff.

The tower supported a circular lantern that had multi-panes of square curved glass set diagonally into metal astragals. The lantern housed a second-order Fresnel lens, one of only five given to lights on the Great Lakes. With its 125-foot (38 m) focal plane and its large clamshell style lens, it had a visibility of about 28 miles (45 km). The lens, which turned on a bed of mercury, was powered by weights that used a clockwork mechanism and had to be wound every two hours and 18 minutes. It had to rotate once every 16 seconds and produce a flash every 8 seconds. The lens weighed about 3,500 pounds (1590 kg), had a diameter over 9 feet (2.8 m), and weighed about seven tons (including its pedestal and support structure). This lens came from Paris, where it had been made by Barbier, Benard and Turenne. The tower dome was highly arched and its multitude of metal sections were joined with raised ribbing. It was topped by a ventilator ball. This tower was originally painted white with a red lantern and dome.

This station had one other special feature. While it had a boat hoist to raise the lighthouse boat from stormy waters, it also had large double doors on the first level that could be opened so that the boat could be put in the boathouse, for even more protection.

Changes were introduced. Possibly in the 1930s, the clockwork mechanism was replaced by an electric motor to rotate the lens. In 1954 it was given a distinctive red and white barber pole striping, making it the only lighthouse on the Great Lakes with this daymark. The lightkeepers were removed from this station when the light was automated in 1976. In 1983 the Fresnel lens was replaced with a 190 mm plastic beacon. This lighthouse has also been placed on the *National Register of Historic Places*.

The White Shoal Fresnel lens can be viewed today in the Shipwreck Memorial Museum owned by the Great Lakes Shipwreck Historical Society at Whitefish Point, where it was installed in 1987 and, after needed repairs, still rotates. Early twentieth-century engineering was amazing. For human technology to build such a large lighthouse on a shoal 20 miles (32.4 km) due west of Mackinac with nothing surrounding it except water, at times calm and at times violently stormy, is a wondrous accomplishment. All materials and equipment had to be taken to the site by boat. No wonder it took almost two years to complete this architectural feat, which is still an active aid to navigation today.

Known Keepers: James Marshal (1910), Ingvald Olsen (1910–14), James Marshall (1914–19), William Barnum (1919–29), Frank Fredrickson (1929–46).

White Shoal Lighthouse

White Shoal Lightship

130 White Shoal Lightship

Northern Lake Michigan was riddled with reefs and shoals, making it difficult for early mariners traveling into or out of the Straits of Mackinac. In 1878 the Chicago Lumbering Company stationed a waterlogged vessel on White Shoal to mark the dangerous reef, which was over 2 miles (3.2 km) long. In 1891 the U.S. government marked the shoal with LV 56.

LV 56 was one of three lightships first used on the Great Lakes. (The other two were *LV 55* at Simmons Reef and *LV 57* at Gray's Reef, both of which were also in northern Lake Michigan.) *LV 56* had been built in 1891 by the Blythe Craig Shipbuilding Company of Toledo, Ohio, at a cost of $14,225. It was a wooden ship with a daymark on its foremast, a Spencer aft mast for a riding sail, and its smokestack was amidship. The vessel was 102 feet 8 inches (31.6 m) long, 20 feet (6.2 m) wide, had a draft of 8 feet 9 inches (2.7 m), and displaced 129 tons of water. Powered by a single cylinder non-condensing steam screw engine of 100 IEP, it was capable of 8 knots. It was also one of the first U.S. lightships to be self-propelled. Its illuminating apparatus consisted of three oil-burning lens lanterns hoisted to each masthead. To warn of fog it had a 6-inch (15 cm) steam whistle and a hand-operated fog bell. Instead of carrying costly anchors and anchor chain, a 5-ton sinker and 15 fathoms of 2-inch (5 cm) chain were permanently pre-positioned on the shoal. The government estimated an annual maintenance and operation cost of $4,000 for the lightship.

LV 56 was turned over to the Detroit Lighthouse Depot in mid-September 1891. Sea trials revealed many defects. After repairs, *LV 56* was placed on the shoal in late October. After the shipping season, it wintered over at Cheboygan. As both masts were found to be unnecessarily long, they were shortened during the winter layover. In 1893 it was equipped with a submarine bell signal. In 1896 its fog signal operated for a total of 371 hours and used 17 tons of coal and 2½ bush cords of wood. Its smokestack was replaced in 1897, and its deckhouses were enlarged and improved. In 1898 interior modifications were made and boilers repaired. Substantial rot caused hull and deck planking to be replaced in 1900 and in 1902, when a stateroom was also built for the ship's master. After weathering Michigan storms for another four years, the vessel needed further repairs in 1906. When it was removed at the end of the 1909 season it was discontinued at this station, since a new lighthouse was built onto the shoal.

After marking White Shoal, *LV 56* went on to mark the North Manitou Shoal (1910–26) and Gray's Reef (1927–28). It was retired from lightship duty at the end of the 1928 shipping season and subsequently sold from government ownership on December 20, 1928.

Wind Point Lighthouse

131 Wind Point Lighthouse

By the 1880s hundreds of ships of all sizes plied the waters of Lake Michigan carrying cargo, local passengers and immigrants. Many Danes settled in the Racine area. Racine Harbor had been marked by a pierhead light since shortly after the Civil War, but it was never satisfactory because Wind Point blocked it from the view of vessels approaching from the north. To correct this and to mark dangerous shoals off the point, Congress appropriated $100,000 to build a "real" lighthouse right on the point.

Orlando M. Poe, Chief Engineer of the Upper Great Lakes Lighthouse District at the time, designed the structure. Construction began in 1877 and took three years to complete. The 108-foot (33.2 m) conical brick tower was placed on a dressed limestone foundation. Its height and style make it one of the five American Great Lakes' "Tall Lighthouses." Inside the tower, 144 open-ironwork, self-cleaning stairs built into the tower wall and attached to a center pole spiraled up to the decagonal lantern, which housed a third-order Fresnel lens with a kerosene Aladdin-style lamp. The revolving lens produced a flashing white characteristic that from its 111-foot (41.6 m) focal plane could be seen for 16 miles (25.6 km). The tower is characterized by its tall slender shape, double galleries, ornately carved corbels and its four arched windows with protruding, decorative lintels around the watchroom.

The 1½-story brick keeper's house also had a dressed limestone foundation, and was attached to the tower by an enclosed passage. Tower and house were both painted white. The light was first lit on November 15, 1880, by its first keeper, Alfred Finch, an experienced keeper who had been transferred from the Pilot Island light. His assistant keeper was his son Asa. Just days after beginning operation, during an early winter storm, the new lens developed a problem with rotation. After notifying the lighthouse superintendent, the two keepers kept the lens rotating manually at a measured speed so that it would flash a 2-second burst every 28 seconds. Incredibly, they did this for five nights, by hand, for 12 hours a night and in below-freezing temperatures, as the lantern room's only heat came from its oil lamp inside the lens.

In 1899 the house had an addition built onto it and was divided into apartments to accommodate the head keeper and his two assistants. The second assistant was hired to help run the fog signal, which was acquired in 1900. The steam whistle could be heard 10 miles (16 km) out on the lake.

As well as the main light, this tower also had a second light that shone from a window in the tower just below the lantern. This light was to warn mariners of Racine Reef to the south. The government installed the light at this location as it was too costly at the time to build a light on the reef. Instead, the reef was marked with a buoy. They believed that the red light, which shone from a sixth-order Fresnel lens at a 105-foot (32 m) focal plane along with the reef buoy, would adequately mark the shoal. In 1897 the Fresnel lens was replaced with a locomotive headlight but it still displayed a red light. When the Racine Reef light was lit in 1906 this secondary light was discontinued.

The station was destined for more changes. In 1924 the light was one of the earliest ones on the Great Lakes to be electrified. In 1964 it was automated and the foghorn was dismantled. The Fresnel lens was replaced by a DCB24 radio beacon that used a 1,000-watt light bulb to produce a 2,000,000 candlepower light visible for a 19 miles (30 km). The light was activated by timers and photo-electric cells, which turned on a half an hour before sunset and off a half an hour after sunrise, or on whenever visibility was lower than 5 miles (8 km). The old Fresnel lens became the property of the Racine Historical Museum and is on display today at the station. Since automation in 1964, the village of Wind Point has leased the buildings and grounds from the Coast Guard, with the exception of the still-functioning tower, to use for municipal offices. In 1975 spotlights began illuminating the tower, accentuating its tall slender form at night.

In 1981 a win-win situation developed. A local fireman was given the job of caretaker and was provided with free accommodation. When he moved in, he said the place was a disaster. All woodwork had been painted over, interior walls had been covered with paneling, the kitchen had been altered, and all mechanical systems (water, electricity and heat) had problems. He and his family fell in love with the lighthouse and worked diligently to maintain and refurbish the buildings and grounds. His son liked to brag that they had the biggest nightlight in Racine at their house. At Christmas they placed a huge wreath on the wall of the caretaker's quarters and strung lights to the top of the tower.

Then in 1997 the ownership for the complex was formally transferred to the Village of Wind Point. While the Coast Guard still maintains the light, the village continues to use the complex to house their police station, a town hall and living quarters for a caretaker. The original third-order Fresnel lens is on display in the village town hall, but unfortunately not open to the public. However, the grounds are open for visits.

Known Keepers: Alfred B. Finch (1881), Lawrence Easson (1882–83), John Sandell (1884–91), Peter Peterson (1891–1913), Henry Bevry (1913–45).

LAKE SUPERIOR

USA

LIGHTHOUSES

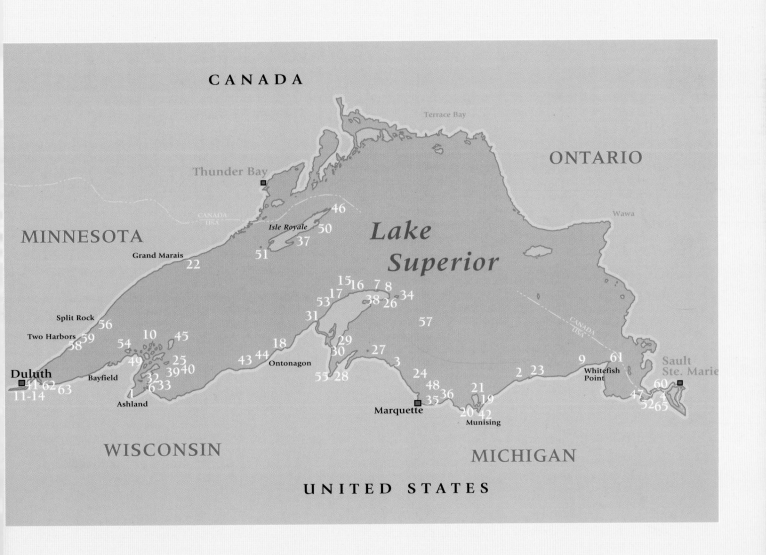

CANADA

Terrace Bay

ONTARIO

Thunder Bay

Wawa

MINNESOTA

CANADA
USA

Isle Royale

Grand Marais

Lake Superior

46
50
37
51
22

Split Rock
56

Two Harbors
59
58

15
16 7 8
17
53   38 26   34
31
57

10   45
54
18
29
43 44   30   27   3
Ontonagon

9   61
2 23

Duluth
41 62   63
11-14

49
25
32 39 40
6 33
1

55 28   24
48
35 36

20 21
19
42

Whitefish
Point

47
52 65

60

Sault
Ste. Marie

Bayfield

Ashland

Marquette

Munising

WISCONSIN

MICHIGAN

UNITED STATES

Ashland Breakwater Lighthouse

1 Ashland Breakwater Lighthouse

The harbor at Ashland first developed for the export of lumber, but in the late 1800s its focus shifted to iron ore. This port in Chequamegon Bay below the Apostle Islands along Lake Superior's south shore was totally unprotected against fierce "nor'easters." To create protection for the harbor, the Army Corps of Engineers in 1889 undertook to build an enormous breakwater. It started about 2,000 feet (610 m) from the bay's southeast side and by 1893 stretched 4,650 feet (1420 m), almost halfway across the bay in a north-northwest direction. In 1900 they started a second, parallel breakwater to protect the southern opening.

While the breakwater served its purpose, mariners had difficulty finding the north entrance to the harbor. As a temporary solution, a fixed red lens-lantern was hung from a pole 10 feet (3 m) above the west end of the breakwater, and was maintained by the Army Corps. When the long breakwater was finished in 1912, the Lighthouse Board requested $25,000 for a pier light. Congress made the appropriation in October 1913.

Unique plans were drawn up for this light. A wooden crib was sunk and capped to form a concrete pier at the end of the breakwater. Next, a reinforced-steel concrete tower was poured on site using sectional forms. Its first-story base was 17 feet (5.2 m) square and its tapered corners made it octagonal. The next two stories, also octagonal, tapered gently to a 14-foot (4.3 m) diameter at the top. The concrete and steel tower was topped with an 8 foot (2.4 m) high cylindrical prefabricated iron watchroom. Above this was a circular gallery and a cylindrical lantern with squares of curved lantern glass set diagonally into metal astragals.

The lantern housed a fourth-order Fresnel lens illuminated by a 1,600 candlepower electric lamp and powered by electricity from the Ashland generating station via submarine cable. While the tower was 58 feet (17.7 m) high, it had a focal plane of 65 feet (20 m). Its flashing light (flash 1s;

Ashland Breakwater Lighthouse, circa 1920

eclipse 2 s) was first lit on October 15, 1915, and could be seen for 16 miles (26 km). Its daymark signature was a white tower with a black lantern.

The station was outfitted with an electrically powered fog siren (blast 4 s; silence 16 s). The compressors and oil tanks to power the siren were in the tower's first level but its horn was on the lake side of the watchroom. Since a keeper needed to stay at the tower in inclement weather or when the siren was in operation, the second and third tower levels were set up as living quarters. In 1916 the keeper's 1½-story dwelling was built onshore, about 2 miles (3.2 m) from the lighthouse, and he boated to and from shore.

By the latter 1900s iron ore export from Ashland had significantly declined. In 1980 the Coast Guard removed the light's Fresnel lens and replaced it with a 12-volt DC solar-powered 250 mm acrylic optic. In this same year the light was listed on the State of Wisconsin *Register of Historic Sites*. Today the once-busy ore docks sit unused and rotting but the light still serves pleasure craft in the area.

Known Keepers: James Bergan (1915–22), Mrs. James Bergan (1922), Roger Campbell (1922–25), Frank Mersy (1925–40).

2 Au Sable Lighthouse

As early as 1622 when French explorers traveled Lake Superior, Pierre Radisson described the area around Grand Sable Dunes as the "most dangerous when there is any storm." The French adopted the Ojibway name "Gitchee Nagow" (Great Sands) as "les Grandes Sables." It became Big Sable Point or Pointe aux Sables. This point was extremely hazardous as it is a shallow, sandstone reef that extends for one mile into the lake. Frequent thick fog caused by the interaction of the cool lake air with warmer air rising from the nearby Grand Sable Dunes was also a hazard. These factors, and the legendary Lake Superior storms, caused the loss of many ships and lives and earned it the mariners' nickname of "shipwreck coast." With just cause, this unlit part of Lake Superior between Grand Island and Whitefish Point inspired fear.

In the 1840s when copper was discovered in the Keweenaw Peninsula and iron near Marquette, people migrated to these areas. With the opening of the Soo Canal in 1855, lake traffic grew significantly as vessels hauled raw materials of ore, lumber and coal down to industrial centers and carried immigrants uplake.

After several wrecks and near wrecks in the area, mariners pressed for a light in the early 1870s. Congress responded by appropriating $40,000 in 1872 to build a light at Au Sable Point. The State of Michigan sold 326 acres (132 hectares) of land to the federal government for the light station at a cost of $407. (It remains unknown why they needed this much land for one station.) Construction was completed in 1874. It was called Big Sable Light until being renamed Au Sable Light in 1910 to avoid confusion with Big Sable Light on Lake Michigan.

The 86-foot (26.5 m) tower, designed by Orlando M. Poe, was on a sturdy foundation of rubble masonry lying on bedrock 23 feet (7 m) below. The double-bricked base walls, over 4 feet (1.2m) thick, tapered up the circular tower to 3 feet (0.9 m) thick just under the lower gallery. A circular watchroom surmounted the tower, topped by a decagonal lantern that held a third-order Fresnel lens manufactured by Louis Sautter and Company of Paris. With its 107-foot (32.6 m) focal point and its lard-oil lamps, the fixed white light was reflected by 90-degree polished mirrors through 270 degrees of lens to 6,750 candlepower, which produced an 11-mile (17.5 km) visibility in clear weather. When the lamp was later switched to more efficient kerosene, it could be seen for up to 18 miles (28.8 km). The tower was painted white for day visibility. This tower used the same plans as Outer Island Light of the Apostle Islands, also built in 1874.

The 2½-story red brick keeper's house was attached to the tower by an enclosed passageway. The "saltbox" style house had a distinctive "Dutch hip" roof construction. In 1875, the house was converted to a "double" with the appointment of an assistant keeper, and a wooden boathouse was built. In 1895 several smaller outbuildings and a brick oil house to store kerosene were added. In 1897, at a cost of $5,500, the station received a substantial brick building to house the new steam-powered fog signal (blast 1.5 s; blast 1.5 s; silence 25.5 s). However, since the water intake crib was "faulty," the fog signal had to wait until the tender *Amaranth* brought a second one in 1898. While keepers no longer had to use the hand-cranked fog signal, the steam-powered signal required many more man-hours for its operation.

A seawall was built in front of the fog building for protection, and the pier was extended eastward to form an L-shape. Also, a well was sunk in one of the pier's cribs, and water piping extended along the pier to the fog signal. An air pump brought water to the cistern and pumped water in an above-ground pipe system to the

Au Sable Lighthouse

Au Sable Lighthouse, circa 1920

cisterns in each building. Around this time the U.S. Lifesaving Service built a telephone line along the lakeshore linking Au Sable, Grand Marais and the stations east to Whitefish Point. In 1899 a 55-foot (16.8 m) tramway was installed, allowing fuel and supplies to be moved more easily between the dock and the fog signal building.

This station was very isolated even though it was on the mainland. The closest civilization was Grand Marais, 12 miles (19.2 km) to the east and the easiest way to get there was by boat. Since supplies could only be brought in by water, on the tender *Amaranth*, the docks were essential to the station. They underwent continual repair and upgrading to counteract the effects of battering waves and ice.

The 1909 the duplex was given separate entrances for the assistant keepers, as a second assistant keeper had been hired to help with the workload, and a new house was built for the main keeper. In 1915 a metal oil house was added. In 1928 a new diaphone fog signal was installed. In 1930 the station acquired a radio, and in 1935 the telephone connected the keepers to the outside world. In the 1940s the keeper's quarters were treated to central heat, gas cooking, electric lights and indoor plumbing. Batteries powered the fog signal and the light, and an electric-powered generator was installed. In 1943 the road built in 1939 was extended to the lighthouse, making a daily drive into Grand Marais quite possible.

The first keepers were cut off from civilization. In summer they walked or boated the twelve miles to Grand Marais; in winter they used snowshoes or dogsleds. Early keepers also wintered at the light, while later keepers went to Grand Marais. To alleviate boredom, Au Sable received its first traveling library from the *Amaranth* in 1878. Besides reading, keepers, who were Jacks-of-all-trades, also followed routines to keep active. Daily they carried kerosene to the lantern, polished the lens and trimmed the wicks; they maintained the station, purchased provisions, kept records and wrote their reports.

In 1958, when the lighthouse was automated and the fog signal removed, keepers were no longer needed. In July 1961 the Coast Guard declared the lighthouse land excess property to the General Services Administration (GSA), and in 1968, the GSA transferred the land to the Department of the Interior, National Park Service, for inclusion in the Pictured Rocks National Lakeshore. In 1972 the Coast Guard removed and stored the Fresnel lens, replacing it with a battery-powered lamp and a 300 mm plastic lens that was attached to the exterior wall on the north side of the tower. This light flashes white for six seconds and is then followed by another one-second flash. The third-order Fresnel lens was later displayed in the Grand Marais Maritime Museum.

Restoration of the station to its 1909–10 period began in 1988. In 1992–93 the exterior and interior of the tower were painted, and work in the lens room completed. Replica linen curtains were hung, a replica chimney installed, and by 1996 the lantern again housed its original Fresnel lens.

In 1998 the Pictured Rocks National Lakeshore started guided tours of the refurbished station to share its wealth of history. The Coast Guard still maintains the replacement light on the tower today, and welcomes visitors who hike the 1.5 miles (2.4 km) from the parking lot at the Hurricane River Campground.

Known Keepers: Casper Kuhn (1875–76), Napoleon Beedon (1876–79), Fred Boesler (1880–84), Gus Gigandet (1884–96), Herbert Weeks (1897–1903), Otto Bufe (1903–05), Thomas Irvine (1905–08), James Kay (1908–15), John Brooks (1915–23), Klass Hamringa (1923–30), Arthur Taylor (1930–36), Edward McGregor (1936–45), Richard Miller (1954–56), A. Mako (1956–58).

3 Big Bay Point Lighthouse

Big Bay Point Lighthouse was built on a high cliff at the east side of Big Bay on the south shore of Lake Superior. Congress appropriated $25,000 in 1894 and the lighthouse was finished in 1896. The light, halfway between the Granite and Huron Islands, which had been lit since 1868, now made sail and steamer travel between Marquette and the Keweenaw Peninsula much safer. It also marked Big Bay for the shipping of lumber when a sawmill was established in 1898.

The keeper's house was an 18-room duplex with a square 60 foot (18.3 m) tower rising up the middle of the north side. Both sides had identical accommodations, except that the main keeper had a direct access to the office at the bottom of the tower and the assistant keepers rooms were slightly smaller. The keeper's privy had a window but the assistant's did not!

The first foghorns were two 10-inch train whistles that protruded from the roof of the signal building and were operated by steam boilers (blast 5s; silence 27s). In 1906 brick cisterns supplied water to the boilers. In 1928 a modern diaphone signal was installed. In cold weather the boiler had to be kept going to prevent the equipment from freezing. A hole had to sometimes be cut in the ice for the water first.

The house was built of five layers of brick to withstand Superior's storms. The outer layers were laid six rows lengthwise and then two courses at right angles to add strength to the structure. Since the interior was plastered directly over the brick, any paint, whitewash and plaster would peel off because of the moisture on the inside of the bricks. The problem was even worse in the lantern. The government agreed to pay for materials if the keeper could find a solution. One creative keeper tried putting oatmeal into the paint but with little success.

The tower had five levels: the first was the head keeper's office, which doubled as a classroom for his children; the second held charts and maps and served as a chapel on Sunday; the third was a storage area; and the fourth and fifth levels housed the third-order Fresnel lens 105 feet (32.3 m) above the lake. This lens, made by Henri LePaute of Paris, was fitted with a three-wick burner. The light was a fixed white light with a brilliant flash of white light every 20 seconds and was visible for 16 miles (25.6 km).

The first keeper, William Prior, was a workaholic and frequently complained of lazy assistants until his son Edward took the job. When the lighthouse tender arrived, all supplies were landed at the water's edge and hauled up to the fog signal building by winch and tramway. From here supplies for the tower and dwelling had to be carried. Coal to operate the foghorn and heat the house arrived in 100-pound (45.5 kg) bags, about 600 of which had to be hauled to the house by hand.

After Edward died in 1901 due to a leg injury that was left unattended, William became despondent. One day in 1901 he left the house with a rifle and some strychnine and went into the woods. He returned safely once, but soon disappeared again and was found seventeen months later by a hunter about 1½ miles (2.4 km) from the lighthouse. He had been hanged. Was it suicide or enemies? He was identified by his uniform and his red hair and was buried at the site of his demise.

In 1941 the light was automated and placed on a metal pole in the yard east of the lighthouse. The assistant keeper's side of the house was leased out as a summer home until the 1950s. In 1951 the U.S. Army moved in and made it home to an anti-aircraft training battalion. During their occupation, an army officer from the unit murdered the owner of the Lumberjack Tavern. From this latter event a novel and then the movie "Anatomy of a Murder" were created.

Big Bay Point Lighthouse

In 1961 the Coast Guard "excessed" the lighthouse, and it was eventually sold by public auction to the highest bidder. Dr. John Pick, a plastic surgeon from Chicago, bought the lighthouse and its parcel of 33 acres (13.3 hectares) for $40,000 and made it into a commodious single dwelling that housed the antiques from his world travels. In 1979 he sold it to Dan Hitchens of Traverse City, who turned it into a conference retreat area. Hitchens moved the Fresnel lens to Traverse City, where it was displayed at his Park Place Motor Inn. In 1986 Norman "Buck" Gotschall and two business partners purchased and turned it into a bed and breakfast. They had the automatic light removed from the pole and placed back in the tower in 1990, made repairs to the fog signal building and had the Fresnel lens retrieved from Traverse City and displayed in the fog signal building where it can be seen today. It has been placed on the *National Register of Historic Places*. In 1992 owners John Gale and Linda and Jeff Gamble, were using it as a bed and breakfast, offering weekly tours of the lighthouse and a special Murder Mystery Weekend. In 1996 the owners sponsored an open house celebrating its centenary, hoping to attract former lighthouse keepers and their descendants and historical miscellanea about the lighthouse. Today, Big Bay Point is one of three bed and breakfasts operating from a lighthouse on Lake Superior. The others are at Sand Hills and Two Harbors.

Known Keepers: William Proir (1896-1901), James Bergan (1901-1915), John A. McDonald (1915-1927), John L. Dufrain (1927-1933), Louis I. Wilks (1933-1936), Charles R. Jones (1936-1940), Vern Matson (1940-1944).

4 Brush Point Range Lights

These range lights were constructed across the river from the Point aux Pins Lighthouse on Brush Point in 1887 to help guide vessels through the cut below Round Island in the upper St. Mary's River. When first built both the front and rear towers were white wood-framed structures. The front tower was only two stories high, sat close to the water's edge and had an overall height of 22 feet (6.76 m). Its bottom half was square; its top half was an octagonal lantern with large vertical panes of glass and it was topped with a simple dome, ventilator ball and lightning rod. Its simple wooden gallery which only surrounded part of the lantern, was supported from beneath by ornately carved wooden corbels and had ornately carved wooden posts to support its simple two-tiered wooden railing. Its lantern housed a sixth order Fresnel lens which displayed a fixed red light from an 18 foot (5.53 m) focal plane to achieve an 8½ mile (13.77km) visibility. The rear range light was located 1430 feet (440 m) behind the front one. It was a square, pyramidal tower that was 13 feet (4 m) square at the base and had a simple wooden gallery, surrounded by an iron pipe railing, and was supported by wooden corbels from underneath. It had a polygonal iron lantern also topped by a simple dome, ventilator ball and lightning rod to produce a 37 foot (11.38 m) overall height. The lantern housed a fifth order Fresnel lens which also displayed a fixed red light from a 33 foot (10.15 m) focal plane to produce a 9½ mile (15.8 km) visibility. The plans used to build these range lights were also used to build the lights at Cedar Point.

The keeper's dwelling, also a wood-frame building, was a 2½-story house painted dark red with a red roof as its daymark. It was located just a short distance from the front tower. The complete station included a wooden boathouse and later a concrete oil house (1906) and the lights were lit in May to start the 1887 navigational season.

During the summer of 1913 these range lights were rebuilt. Both became black pyramidal steel skeletal towers. The front tower was placed in the river in front of the old front tower in 10 feet (3 m) of water and the rear tower was placed 4071 feet (1,252.6 m) behind it. While both towers had a higher focal plane (32 feet (9.84 m) and 55 feet 16.92 m) respectively) and a brighter acetylene light which resulted in increased visibility, they both continued to display a fixed red light. The rear tower also displayed an oval slatted daymark on the front of it. The old 1887 towers were left standing after the new towers were completed.

Since these lights no longer needed a keeper due to their use of acetylene, the keeper's house was moved during the winter of 1915 or 1916 across the ice to Birch Point to replace the keeper's dwelling at this station.

The Brush Point lights were also known as the St. Mary's River Lower Range lights and they changed in style and design as they were rebuilt over the years. The area continues to be lit today by modern steel skeletal towers which display fixed red lights using modern solar-powered optics.

5 Cedar Point Range Lights

The Cedar Point Range Lights were located along the western side of Cedar Point in the upper St. Mary's River and just ½ mile (0.8 km) east of Round Island. They were established to help mariners navigating the river through a channel that had been dredged through the Middle Ground Shoals, which lay between Round Island and Iroquois Point. These range lights were built at the same time as the Brush Point lights ,so the government used the same plans at both locations. The plans used had been drawn up in 1886 by Captain Charles E.L.B. Davis, the Captain of Engineers for the Eleventh Lighthouse District.

After acquiring close to 74 acres (30 hestares), the government had the house, towers and boathouse built and ready for service by the end of February 1887. The front range light, built on pilings and a crib in the river, was a white two story wooden structure that was 21 feet (6.5 m) high. It had a square bottom with an octagonal lantern as its second story. It used a sixth order Fresnel lens to exhibit a fixed white light for 10½ miles (17 km). The rear range light stood 1,180 feet (363 m) behind the front range light and its 13-foot (4 m) square base had been set onto a foundation made of piling and grillage piers. The tower tapered gently for about three stories to its wooden gallery and black iron lantern. This white wooden tower also displayed a fixed white light but used a fifth order Fresnel lens at a 36 foot (11 m) focal plane to achieve a 12-mile (19.4 km) visibility. The lights were first lit in May 1887, to start the navigation season. The keeper's dwelling was a large white wooden 2½-story house located slightly northeast of the front tower. Changes occurred. A concrete oil house was built in 1906.

The lights had their name officially changed in 1909, from the St. Mary's River Upper Range lights to the Cedar Point Range lights. In 1919 the lights were automated through the use of acetylene, and new steel skeletal towers were placed on nearby Round Island. Both towers were painted black with a white slatted oval as its daymark. The front tower had been placed on the northern edge of the island and the rear tower on the southern edge of the island, making them about 615 feet (189.2 m) apart. Since these towers had higher focal planes, 50 and 70 feet (15.4 and 21.5 m), they were visible farther.

In 1926 a red sector was added to the front light to assist mariners in aligning their vessels from the Brush Point lights to the Cedar Point lights. In 1929 the Cedar Point lights were discontinued at the end of the navigation season and removed. The keeper's house was sold to the private sector at an unknown date and the old wooden towers are today long gone.

6 Chequamegon Point Lighthouse

Long Island, Lake Superior, is the southern-most of the Apostle Islands, and it blocks most of the entry into Chequamegon Bay, where Ashland is located. Being a long narrow sand spit, the "island" is often connected to the mainland at its eastern end, depending on how storms move the sand. A light was first built on the island in 1858 to guide vessels into La Pointe on Madeline Island, western Lake Superior's main port at that time. By the late 1800s La Pointe was no longer a significant port but Ashland was, so Congress appropriated $2,500 to build a lighthouse in 1896 at the west end of Long Island to mark the island's end point, and to signal the turning point for vessels heading into Ashland.

Chequamegon Point Lighthouse

The three-story skeletal iron tower was anchored onto four concrete pads. The top section below the lantern was enclosed with iron panels to provide space for storage and equipment to operate its fog bell. It supported a square iron gallery surrounded with a pipe iron railing and an octagonal lantern that housed the fourth-order Fresnel lens from the old La Pointe Lighthouse. Lit on October 11, 1897, its fixed red light could be seen for 13 miles (21 km) from its 42-foot (12.8 m) focal plane. The tower was 39 feet (12 m) high from base to ventilator ball, and its daymark was a white tower with a black lantern and gallery.

A fog bell was suspended from the lake side of the service room and was operated by a Stevens mechanical apparatus housed in the watchroom. A hammer emerged through an opening in the wall to strike the bell once every 20 seconds.

Since the La Pointe lightkeeper tended this light and it was 1½ miles (2 km) from the main La Pointe light, the government in 1903 made a boardwalk by installing large reinforced-steel concrete blocks along the sand dune ridge between the lighthouses. Now the keeper could even ride a bicycle from one to the other. When wave action threatened to erode the sandy shore and topple the light in 1911, a government work crew erected three log stone-filled cribs along the northwest side of the point to stem erosion.

In 1964 the light was automated and maintained by the Devil's Island keepers. When Devil's Island was also automated in 1978, the Coast Guard assumed its maintenance. In 1970 the Apostle Islands, excluding Long Island, became part of the newly formed Apostle Islands National Lakeshore Park. In 1986 the park boundaries were expanded to include Long Island, and the park became part of the National Park Service, thereby practically guaranteeing the well-being of the lights.

When wave action again threatened to erode the lighthouse, the Coast Guard moved the tower back from the shore by helicopter in 1987. They later replaced the tower with a "D9" cylindrical tower close to the shore. It displayed a green light using a 12-volt solar-powered 300 mm acrylic optic. This light still shines today, and although the old tower is also still standing, trees are growing up around it and its lantern railing is gone. As part of a National Park it is also listed on the *National Register of Historic Places.*

Known Keepers: John Haloran (1858–59), John Angus (1859–61), David Cooper (1861–65), Uriah Dawson (1865–67), John Stewart (1867–70), David Cooper (1870–71), John Angus (1871–75), Seth Snow (1876–80), Alexander Davidson (1881–88), Joseph Sexton (1889–1921), Knut Olsen (1921–41).

7 Copper Harbor Lighthouse

In 1841, when Douglas Houghton's geological reports suggested significant copper deposits on the Keweenaw Peninsula along Lake Superior's south shore, miners flooded the area. In 1843 the government established a Mineral Land Agency at Copper Harbor, the focal point for early copper exploration, and in 1844 they established Fort Wilkins at the harbor to maintain order in the region. Since water was the only means of exporting the copper and bringing in men and supplies, mariners called to have the peninsula lit. Congress responded and appropriated $5,000 in April 1847 for a lighthouse to mark the entrance to Copper Harbor. Clear title was obtained to land on the eastern point of the harbor, which became known as Lighthouse Point.

Charles Rude was awarded the contract for $4,800 in 1848. He built a conical split-stone tower and a separate 1½-story stone keeper's dwelling, but he did not adhere to government specs. Instead of erecting a 65-foot (20 m) tower with a 25-foot (7.7 m) base diameter tapering to 12 feet (3.7 m), he built a 44-foot (13.5 m) tower with a 22-foot (6.7 m) base diameter tapering to 13 feet (4 m), and he cut down the number of windows. A wooden spiral staircase ascended to the watchroom where oil was stored, and a short iron ladder led up through the stone deck to its octagonal iron lantern, which had 15 smaller panes of glass and three bottom panes of copper in each of its eight sides.

The lantern housed 13 Argand-Lewis oil lamps with 14-inch (35 cm) reflectors mounted to an iron chandelier, and displayed a fixed white light for 4 to 5 miles (6.5 to 8 km). It was topped by an octagonal copper dome, double ventilator, and lightning rod. Its exterior was double-whitewashed for good visibility. The two-bedroom keeper's dwelling was built on flat land to the south of the tower for easier construction and storm protection. It too was whitewashed and had a shingled roof. Since the interior walls had been plastered and painted right onto the stone, the house was always damp and hard to heat.

The station was completed late in 1848 at a total cost of $4,900 and was lit for the 1849 navigation season. Not wanting it to sit empty for the winter, the government asked the contractor to leave a man to oversee the property until a keeper was hired. Rude's building partner, Ebenezer Warner, wintered over at the light until Henry Clow started in the spring at an annual salary of $350.

Copper Harbor Lighthouse

Copper Harbor Lighthouse

Besides general maintenance and painting, few repairs were needed at the lighthouse. However, in 1856, as part of the Lighthouse Board's upgrading of equipment, which increased its optimum visibility slightly to 6 miles (9.7 km). Its limited visibility required vessels travel close to shore and many were blown onto shoals. After the wrecking and sinking of the fully laden supply vessel *City of Superior* in 1857, the government installed a larger fourth-order Fresnel lens in 1859, increasing the visibility to 14 miles (22.5 km).

Freezing water gradually undermined the stone walls. Since the stone and mortar tower sat in a slight depression, water puddled and leaked into the lower walls. Poor drainage caused it to freeze in cold weather, gradually weakening the walls and causing cracks and decay. A similar process occurred in the keeper's house because moisture froze on the interior walls, which had been plastered but not lathed. By 1863 the inspector recommended significant repairs or new buildings. In 1866 Congress appropriated $13,600 for a new lighthouse at Copper Harbor.

The new lighthouse was built in a schoolhouse style using the same plans as the lights built at Marquette, Gull Island, Grand Island and Eagle Bluff. It was placed 77 feet (23.6 m) east of the original light tower on a higher point of land. Stone from the old tower was reused in the foundations of the new tower, house and privy. A combined yellow brick tower and house was built on the stone foundation. A spiral iron staircase in the square 42-foot (13 m) tower rose both to the decagonal iron lantern and to the second story of the house. The fourth-order Fresnel lens was moved to the new tower to produce a 15-mile (24.3 km) visibility.

The two-story house contained the bedrooms and common spaces. A trapdoor in the woodshed led down to a cellar cistern that collected rainwater for washing and bathing, and a hand pump drew water up to the kitchen. Drinking water was carried from the lake. The first floor rooms were lathed and plastered, and wainscoted. A large chimney provided flues for wood stoves in the kitchen, parlor, master bedroom, and woodshed. The old 1848 lighthouse was now used to store extra oil. The station was also equipped with a hand-operated foghorn to answer ship signals.

In 1870 the army left Fort Wilkins, and the Copper Harbor lighthouse keeper was appointed caretaker of the fort as part of his duties. As compensation he was allowed to use the fort garden and to live in one of the fort buildings during the winter.

In 1873 the Portage Lake Ship Canal was finished, vessels saved 150 miles (24 km) by not having to travel around the Keeweenaw

Peninsula. Also, by 1880 most of the area's copper had been depleted and Copper Harbor's population dropped to a handful. Marine traffic to the harbor had virtually disappeared, so the Lighthouse Board discontinued the light in 1883, thinking that the lights east and west of the harbor could adequately mark the coast. This was true in fair weather but not during autumn storms. After many complaints the light was relit. Since its original fourth-order lens had been removed in 1884, a new 265-degree fourth-order lens was installed and lit on June 1, 1888.

This station's illuminant changed with progress. While it first used sperm whale oil, it changed to lard oil when whale oil doubled in price. In 1879 it was switched to kerosene a brighter, cleaner-burning fuel. Then in 1919 the light was automated with acetylene gas, and the keeper was removed. At this time the keeper of the Copper Harbor Range Lights began checking the acetylene tanks regularly, and the light's characteristic was changed from a fixed white to a flashing white pattern.

Since the keeper's house was no longer used, it was leased in 1927 for five-year intervals at a rate of $85 a year (increased in 1932 to $100 a year). Then in 1933 the government moved the light to a new concrete-anchored 60-foot (18.5 m) steel skeletal tower painted black. Located 77 feet (23.5 m) west of the old tower, it continued to use acetylene gas, but was given a new 375 mm acetylene lantern that displayed the old flash pattern. Its construction cost $1,750. When mariners complained of its poor daytime visibility, the Lighthouse Service painted the front of the house white to contrast with the tower.

In 1937 the light's illuminant became electricity and it received a 300 mm lens. Although it was powered by Edison zinc copper-oxide batteries, the acetylene equipment was retained as a backup system. Since the Copper Harbor Range Lights were also electrified and automated at this time, overseeing these lights became part of the Manitou Island lightkeeper's job.

In 1953–54 a group of landowners built a road to lots they owned at the east end of Copper Harbor. The leaseholder of the lighthouse property gained permission from the Coast Guard to connect a road from the lighthouse to this road, but he had to build it at his own expense.

In December 1953 the Coast Guard excessed the property. In January 1957 the State of Michigan bought the lighthouse reservation and Porter's Island at the harbor entrance for $5,000, but the Coast Guard retained the land around the still-functioning steel tower. The State made the reservation part of their Fort Wilkins State Park. The Department of Natural Resources (DNR) and the Michigan Historical Division worked in diligent partnership to renovate the 1866 lighthouse for the nation's bicentennial celebration. They restored the house to an early-1900s era and finished it with period artefacts. They also created an interpretive trail. It was dedicated and open to visitors in 1975.

Displays list 1860s lighthouse supplies (sperm whale oil, wine to clean the lens, best quality whiting, chamois skins, polishing powder, cleaning towels, glass chimneys, wicking, vials of clerk-marker's oil, and cleaning materials) and keepers' duties (sawing and splitting wood, cleaning the tower and windows, painting the dome and boathouse, whitewashing and oiling woodwork, polishing brass, putting up screens, filing monthly and quarterly reports, and keeping the light functional). In the winter the keeper and his family lived in town where his children could go to school.

One of the area's last shipwrecks occurred in December 1989 when the *Mesquite*, out picking up buoys, drifted and became rockbound. After an overnight storm made a hole in its hull, it was abandoned and sank. It is now a part of an underwater reserve. Since all its equipment was left on board, it makes a most interesting spectacle for divers.

In 1994 archaeologists from the Michigan Technological University found the original tower site. It was their excavation that discovered that the original tower had not been built to the government specs, and that most of the stone from the tower was used to build the foundations for the 1866 lighthouse. Also at this time the DNR reshingled the 1866 keeper's house with replica metal shingles.

In 1997, with the aid of grant money, the DNR started renovating the 1848 keeper's house. They incorporated hands-on activities and computer interactive programs, and restored both dwellings to historically correct colors inside. Both structures were ready to celebrate the 150th anniversary of the lighthouse complex with a rededication on August 6, 1998.

Although there is a road to the lighthouse, the public only has water access, so the lighthouse maintains some of its early isolation. The DNR offers guided tours of the complex. The old 1848 keeper's house was one of the first two built on Lake Superior and is the oldest surviving keeper's dwelling on the lake at this time.

Known Keepers: Henry Clow (1849–53), Henry Shurter (1853–55), Napoleon Bonaparte Beedon (1855–69), John Power (1869–73), Charles Corgan (1873–81), Edward Chambers (1881–83), Henry Corgan (1888–1919).

8 Copper Harbor Range Lights

The lighthouse on Lighthouse Point marked the entry to Copper Harbor on Lake Superior, but navigation into the harbor through submerged rocks was still difficult. A globe lamp set out in a yawl positioned over the channel's submerged rock first marked the area. With the harbor in steady use, the government first appropriated $3,500 in 1860 for lights to assist harbor entry. However, it was not until 1865, when the War Department transferred land from Fort Wilkins, that the government built a pair of wooden towers to provide range lighting into the harbor.

The keeper, who earned $400 a year, lived in one of the fort buildings until 1867, when he took up residence in Copper Harbor village. Having to travel over a mile (1.6 km) to the lighthouse site made it difficult for the keeper to properly tend the lights, so the government built a new rear range light that was combined into a keeper's dwelling. Economy was served by using plans similar to

those for Portage Lake and Grand Island and by importing the experienced work crew from the Portage Lake site. Congress appropriated $5,000 in July 1868 and the building was completed by the end of the season.

Situated along the south shore of Copper Harbor, it was a 1½-story white wooden frame house with a flattened front roofline on which a wooden lantern was placed. Its fixed white light was only visible in a forward direction through a small arched window 26 feet (8 m) above the ground. The front range light was a 16-foot (4.9 m) wooden structure, and its octagonal roof was topped with a ventilator ball. Its fixed white light also shone forward. Since the rear light was set at a higher elevation, the two lights worked in conjunction to form a safe line of entry into the harbor. Vessels could see these lights only from in front of the harbor entrance.

In 1919 the entrance light was automated and the range light-keeper's duties increased. He now had to check the main light regularly, especially the acetylene tanks. For his added work his salary increased from $780 to $840. In 1927 the deteriorating front wooden range tower was replaced with a more modern metal one.

In 1933 the rear range light and dwelling were equipped with a 32-volt electric lighting plant to increase the light's visibility. The front range light continued to use kerosene until it and the main light were electrified in 1937 at a cost of $1,060. Along with the new illuminant came the automation of the range lights and the removal of the keeper at the end of the navigation season. The keeper at Manitou Island was then asked to keep an eye on the lights at Copper Harbor.

With the keeper's house no longer in use, the government leased it for $60 every two years. In 1964 the rear range light was replaced by a modern steel tower with a plastic beacon positioned about 100 feet (30 m) in front of the old rear range light. Eventually the old range light was turned over to the state parks system and its garage was converted to the Fort Wilkins Park Staff Quarters. In 1994 the DNR reshingled the old rear range lighthouse with replica metal shingles. Visitors may photograph the house but are asked to respect the occupants' privacy.

Known Keepers: Charles Davis (1888–1923), Charles Haven (–1937).

9 Crisp Point Lighthouse

One of the most remote lighthouses on the south shore of Lake Superior is the Crisp Point Lighthouse. Although only about 13 miles (21 km) west of Whitefish Point, it was only accessible via poorly marked and maintained roads. These conditions also impeded aid to save the lighthouse from water, wind and soil erosion, since heavy machinery could not easily be brought in. When first built, the lighthouse was some 700 feet (215 m) from the shoreline, but by 1929 it was about 300 feet (92 m) from the shore.

Copper Harbor Rear Range Light

Crisp Point Lighthouse

Crisp Point Lighthouse

In November 1996, after winter storms eroded the brick service building attached to the tower, the water was only 6 feet (1.8 m) from the lighthouse base.

The site was first developed in 1875 and was in action by 1876 for the Crisp Point Lifesaving Station, which operated on the desolate and inaccessible section of Superior shore known as "shipwreck coast" — the 50 miles (80 km) or so between Whitefish Point and Grand Marais. Although it is not a true geographical point, northwest storms and strong currents continually redeposit sand along the shoreline and rearrange sandbars out as far as ³/₄ of a mile (1.2 km) offshore. In heavy storms, ships were blown onto these sandbars and broken up before reaching shore. The point was named after Captain Christopher Crisp, a former shipmaster and the first captain of the lifesaving station.

Trained crews from the lifesaving station patrolled the beaches regularly ("picket patrol") to watch for ships in distress and to retrieve washed-up bodies before wolves got them. After identification, the bodies were often buried near the station because of its isolation. One such cemetery was in front of the Crisp Point Lighthouse and was maintained by keeper Joseph Singleton until, in his words, "the worst storm in over one hundred years hit the shore, took that flagpole, a big pine tree, a tall pump and those graves all back into the lake."

In 1896 the Lighthouse Board recommended a light for Crisp Point to warn ships to "stay clear" of the shifting sandbars. In June 1902 Congress appropriated $18,000 for a lighthouse, and 15 acres (6 hectares) of land was purchased for $30 in May 1903. The light went into service on March 5, 1904. Also in 1903 a fog building was built and its boiler had to be replaced when a storm destroyed the first one. When machinery for the second fog signal was installed in 1903, a new chime whistle replaced the standard whistle. The site included the light tower, a two-story red brick keeper's house, a red brick fog signal building, a two-story lifesaving station, a boathouse, a lookout tower, two cottages for station families and utility buildings. The next year a landing crib was built, but because of the sandbars, service ships still had to unload at least a mile (1.6 km) offshore.

During the navigation season a number of people lived at the isolated station, including the keeper, his two assistants and the lifesaving crew of nine (later reduced to seven). Usually only the lifesaving captain, his number one man and the lighthouse keeper were permitted to have their families at the station. In the winter their families usually remained as there was no nearby center for them to move to. Being so far from civilization meant that keepers and lifesavers, as well as doing their regular jobs, had to be doctors, mechanics and survivalists. Keeper Joseph Singleton earned from $1,500 to $1,860 a year, while the first assistant, Albert Brown, earned $1,320 to $1,680 and the second assistant, Herbert Winfield, earned $1,250 to $1,620.

The keeper and his family lived in one half (six rooms) of the keeper's house and his assistants in the other. A pitcher pump using a drive point well through the cellar floor supplied water. Natural refrigeration was just a few feet underground near the shore where the sand never thawed. Coal stoves were the main source of winter heat, wood in the summer. Later there was a telephone at the station and one at the keeper's quarters.

Crisp Point Lighthouse is 58 feet (17.7 m) from base to ventilator ball. Built on a 10-foot (3 m) thick concrete pad, the double brick conical tower has an outer wall 18 inches (45 cm) thick with a 22-inch (55 cm) air space and an 8-inch (20 cm) thick inner wall. At the gallery, the outer wall narrows to an 8-inch (20 cm) thickness with a 6-inch (15 cm) air space and a 4-inch (10 cm) inner wall. The tower's base diameter is 14 feet (4.3 m) while its upper diameter is 9 feet (2.7 m). An octagonal cast-iron lantern, with an inscribed diameter of 7 feet (2.2 m), tops the tower, and a circular black wrought iron railing surrounds the gallery. The light showed a 360-degree red fourth-order Fresnel lens made by Sautter and Lemonier of Paris.

In 1930, when the light was automated, the property and facilities were appraised at under $20,000. In 1965, after years of vandalism, the Coast Guard destroyed all the buildings except the tower and attached service building.

In July 1997 the Crisp Point Lighthouse, formerly owned by the U.S. Coast Guard, was transferred to Luce County as an historical monument. The Luce County Board of Commissioners leased the lighthouse and a 3.5-acre (1.4 hectare) site to the Crisp Point Light Historical Society. The society raised funds under the leadership of its then president, Nellie Ross, to have rock placed along the shore to reinforce the shoreline in front of the lighthouse to prevent it from toppling into Lake Superior as its service building had. Road improvements and a museum now attract many visitors to the lighthouse.

While the Crisp Point Lighthouse was considered the most endangered lighthouse in America according to *Lighthouse Digest* magazine and was added to their doomsday list in January 1997, it has since been removed from the list thanks to its restoration, making it one of a number of lighthouses in the United States to have achieved a new standing.

Known Keepers: John Smith (1904–06), Herbert Burrows (1906–10), George Smith (1910–11), Jacob Gibbs (1911–13), Daniel Shelson (1915–21), Herbert Crittenden (1921–27), Joseph Singleton (1923–39).

Devil's Island Lighthouse

10 Devil's Island Lighthouse

The Chippewa name for Devil's Island was "Metchimanitou Miniss," Evil Spirit Island. Although unproven, rumors tell how the Ojibway (Chippewa) Indians refused to land on this island because they believed it was home to evil spirits who made the unexplained ghostly, echoing sounds they heard coming from the island. In fact, the island consists of layers of red sandstone rock of different degrees of hardness that have been eaten away by erosion to create caves and rock pedestals. When viewed from the water it resembles worm-eaten wood, and wind and water action moving through these caves and tunnels does create eerie and ghostly sound emissions when the weather is just right.

Devil's Island is the highest, most northern, rugged and inaccessible island of the Apostle Islands, and was the last island in the group to be lit as an aid to navigation. This fact is surprising, because it marks a major turning point for lake travel along Superior's south shore.

In 1888 the Vessel Owners' Association requested a red flashing, third-order Fresnel light and fog signal on the north side of Devil's Island. Congress approved the request in 1888 but appropriated only $5,500, just enough to build a two-story Queen Anne style keeper's house and a steam fog signal building to operate a 10-inch (25 cm) fog whistle. A temporary wood tower had to be built. The lantern was 87 feet (26.5 m) above lake level and housed a fourth-order, red light visible for 13 miles (21 km). It was lit on September 30, 1891.

In 1893 Congress appropriated $22,000 for additions to the station. A red brick house similar to the keeper's house was built for the assistant keeper in 1897, and work began on a permanent 71-foot (21.6 m) cast-iron cylindrical tower. Spiral steps rose from the concrete foundation to the pedestal/watchroom, from which ladder stairs accessed the circular lantern, whose curved glass panels were set on diagonals into metal astragals. The tower was finished in 1898 but had to wait three years for its third-order Fresnel lens to arrive from Henri LePaute in Paris.

The new lens used bull's eyes and red panels to create a red flashing pattern once every 80 seconds. A clockworks mechanism, which had to be wound every four hours, rotated the lens. Since the tower was on such a high site, it was painted white with a black gallery and lantern so as to stand out against the clouds. Finally, 13 years after their original request, the Vessel Owners' Association got the light they wanted in 1901. The lens was first lit using a kerosene-burning lamp and later by a more efficient incandescent oil vapor lamp that used a mantle instead of wicks. The light, with a 100-foot (30.5 m) focal point, had a visibility of 22 miles (35 km).

A tramway was built to the docks, which were one mile away from the light. A steam-powered winch pulled the tramcar up the hill, and then the keepers pushed it by hand along the track. Coal for the houses and the fog signal building was unloaded from the supply boats and loaded into the tramcar by hand. The tramcar still sits today at the end of its unused tracks in front of the keeper's house near the fog signal building, and a chain link fence bordering the property keeps people from the cliffs.

In 1917 bracing "legs" were placed around the outside of the tower to add stability. In 1925 a compressed air diaphone signal and radio fog beacon replaced the steam fog signal. Lake ships determined their distance from the station by timing the delay between the radio and the audible fog signals. A third keeper was added to the station to staff the fog signal plant, and a wooden building at the station was converted to a house for him. In the 1930s the station was the first in the area to receive a radio communications station.

The high cliffs of Devil's Island made landing people and materials a challenging task. During the spring startup, the landing and the rocks were usually still covered in ice, and dynamite was needed to clear the ice from the rocks to land the crew. Even then it was still a treacherous journey to the lighthouse with all the supplies and luggage. Keeper Alexander McLean and his wife spent their honeymoon on the island, but she hated the isolation and the storms. Spray would hit their living room windows even though the house was located about 600 feet (185 m) back from the cliffs.

In November 1919, the tender *Marigold* left Marquette to remove keepers from their stations, but due to the stormy conditions, which iced over the vessel, progress was very slow. By mid-December, the lake was frozen and the Devil's Island keepers made it to shore unaided over the ice, saving the *Marigold* from having to break through the lake ice to remove them. Keepers at these isolated stations were courageous, self-sufficient characters.

From 1925 to 1934 Captain Hans Christensen was the keeper. The highlight of his stay there was August 22, 1928, when President Calvin Coolidge and his entourage picnicked at Devil's Island. Besides viewing the sea caves and local fishermen, the president also toured the lighthouse and signed his name — and thus his approval — in the keeper's logbook. Christensen was most impressed by the visit, declaring it the greatest thing that had happened to him as keeper. However, not all keepers agreed. At least one — unnamed — was infuriated because the president's dinner had cost about $7,000 (more than three times his annual salary) and he felt that the money could have been better spent — to raise his yearly wage, for example.

When other Apostle Island lights were automated, Devil's Island was still staffed by a five-man crew that looked after its light and monitored the other island stations. In 1978 they too were removed when the Coast Guard automated the Devil's Island light. The light was then powered by solar panels and monitored from a switchboard in Duluth. It was to have no more keepers.

In 1989 the Coast Guard removed the third-order lens and replaced it with a plastic beacon that only had a range of 15 miles (24 km). They crated the old lens and put it in storage. The State of Wisconsin had not wanted the lens removed and, after suing the government, they won. They had the lens repaired and put back into the lantern in 1992 for visitors to see. The functioning solar-powered, plastic beacon was moved outside and attached to the gallery of the lantern at this time.

This light is 25 miles (40 km) out of Bayfield, a small village on the mainland, and is open to the public only during the annual Apostle Islands Lighthouse Celebration.

Known Keepers: Henry Baker (1891–93), Charles Brown (1893–98), Alexander McLean (1898–1909), Frank Marshall (1909–21), John Garraty (1921–25), Hans Christensen (1925–34), James Bard (1934–41), ? Simonson (1941–45), Alphonse Gustafson (1945–51).

11 Duluth Buoy Depot

When the Minnesota Point Lighthouse ceased operating, its site was chosen for a U.S. Lighthouse Service Buoy Depot. A $14,000 appropriation from Congress in 1902 was slow in coming, but in March 1903 it was approved. Plans were drawn up to include a buoy shed, an oil house and a wharf, and the necessary surveying was done in 1904. When no bids were received after advertising for contractors, the project work was again advertised in 1905.

When construction finally began, the two separate buildings originally planned were combined into one concrete structure 30 by 97 feet (9 by 30 m), to be used as a combined office, buoy storage, tool room and oil house. A huge wharf, 20 by 96 feet (6 by 29 m), was made of piles driven into the lakebed and topped with thick planking to support heavy traffic. A tramway built right on the wharf connected it to the shed to facilitate the work of moving the buoys. In 1909 a dwelling was added, since the keeper's house from the old Minnesota Point Lighthouse station had been removed after it ceased being used. This depot became unused at some point, and today only the main building and a privy remain.

Duluth Harbor South Breakwater Inner Lighthouse

12 Duluth Harbor South Breakwater Inner Lighthouse

As Duluth developed as a main shipping terminus from the west end of Lake Superior, private businessmen had the Duluth Ship Canal dug at the base of Minnesota Point to provide direct entry into Duluth Harbor. Upon completion in 1872, the canal was flanked by breakwaters and marked by a lighthouse at the outer end of its south breakwater. However, the narrow 300 foot (92 m) opening of the canal made it difficult for vessels to find the correct line of the entry, so a light was also built at the inner end of the south breakwater.

Congress appropriated $2,000 in March 1889 to construct the light to serve two purposes: to mark the inner end of the breakwater, and to form a rear range light to the outer light. The tower was a frame pyramidal structure with an enclosed top section, an octagonal iron lantern, and a fifth-order Fresnel lens. Its six bull's eyes displayed a flashing red light every 6 seconds and had a focal plane higher than the outer light. It was first lit on September 1, 1889. Barely two weeks later, its foundation was damaged when the steamer *India* crashed into the breakwater.

To keep pace with development, plans were made to widen and deepen the entry canal. Mariners were cautioned about the impending changes in an 1899 publication:

"During the next two years dredging and pier building will be going on in the Duluth Ship Canal entrance to the Duluth-Superior harbour ... All vessels ... are required to slow down to 6 miles an hour [9.7 kph] when within 500 feet [153 m] of either entrance of the ship canal, and not to exceed that speed from that point until they have passed 500 feet [153 m] beyond the other entrance. This, irrespective of whether a red flag or lantern be shown or not. Violation of this rule is a misdemeanour punishable by a fine not to exceed $500, or by imprisonment not to exceed six months. Masters of vessels are also specially enjoined to exercise great care in passing through the canal that they do not come in collision with dredges, scows, or mooring piles, or the false work to the new piers."

Then in 1901 Scott's *Coast Pilot* announced that temporary lights and fog signal would be placed on the new south pier at Duluth to serve until permanent structures were built. The temporary front light at the outer end of the new south pier was a fixed red lens lantern, 35 feet (10.7 m) above lake level on a pyramidal frame structure covered with tar paper. Immediately behind it was a frame fog-signal house, also tar-papered. It housed 10-inch (25 cm) steam whistles with the same characteristic as the old signal (blast 5 s; silence 30 s). The temporary rear light was placed near the inner end of the new south pier, where it displayed a fixed red lens lantern from a 52-foot (16 m) focal plane.

Two large concrete blocks within the new breakwater formed the foundation for the permanent light. The tower was a pyramidal iron skeletal frame formed by four main legs with cross-bracing between them. At the center of this was an 8-foot (2.4 m) cylindrical iron column that housed the tower's spiral iron staircase. The tower was topped by a cylindrical iron watchroom with its own octagonal iron gallery and an octagonal iron lantern with its own circular iron gallery. The tower was 70 feet (21.5 m) high from base to ventilator ball. Its lantern, first lit in 1902, housed a fourth-order Fresnel lens with a 68-foot (20.8 m) focal plane.

The three keepers of the outer light also tended this inner light. Housing was provided for the head keeper, but the assistants lodged in Duluth until a duplex was built in 1912. It was a two-story brick dwelling right across from the head keeper's home, and was divided equally into side-by-side two-bedroom houses. A hot water heating system heated the whole house. The light was automated in 1976 when the outer light was also automated.

After a 1995 inspection, the Coast Guard removed the Fresnel lens and replaced it with two plastic optics powered by solar panels because one of the Fresnel's six bull's eyes was damaged. Since the lens had been made by Barbier and Benard in 1896, the Coast Guard donated it to Duluth. Since then, it has been restored and placed on its pedestal and clockwork rotating mechanism, also donated to the city. The lens, pedestal and clockwork mechanism are on display at the Corps of Engineers' Lake Superior Maritime Visitor Center in Duluth, directly opposite its home tower.

Known Keepers: see Duluth North Pierhead Light

13 Duluth Harbor South Breakwater Outer Light

The rise of shipping from the twin ports of Duluth and Superior created their lighthouse history. During the 1850s hundreds of speculators gravitated to its rich copper ore deposits. The natural harbors for the ports, both within Superior Bay, were protected by two long, narrow spits of land, Wisconsin Point to the south and Minnesota Point to the north. Between the two was a narrow, shallow, natural channel called Superior Entry, which led into the harbors.

After the Soo Locks opened in 1855, shipping between Lake Superior and Duluth increased steadily. To support these busier harbors, the federal government built a lighthouse in 1858 on Minnesota Point to mark the Superior Entry. In 1861 the "Topographical Engineers" surveyed the bay area. Their findings led to the first harbor dredging, designed to ensure adequate shipping channels for vessels exporting grain, coal, iron ore and lumber.

In the early 1870s it was determined that a canal from Lake Superior across Minnesota Point and into Superior Bay would offer an excellent shortcut into Duluth Harbor. So from 1870 to 1872 the Duluth Ship Canal, was privately excavated, enabling vessels to enter Superior Bay at Duluth. Breakwaters were also built to

Duluth Harbor South Breakwater Outer Light

flank the canal. To better accommodate ships, the harbor was dredged from its 6–8-foot (1.8–2.5 m) depth to a new 12-foot (3.7 m) depth from 1867 to 1874. In 1881–82 the depth was increased to 16 feet (5 m). To keep up with this busy growth, Congress appropriated $10,000 in 1870 for a lighthouse on the south breakwater to mark the entrance from Lake Superior to the new canal.

The tower was built at the outer end of the pier and the keeper's house was built onshore. The tower was a wooden pyramidal structure with an enclosed upper section. It was topped with an octagonal iron lantern that housed a fifth-order Fresnel lens. From its 40-foot (12.2 m) focal plane it displayed a fixed red light for a 12.5-mile (20.2 km) visibility. A catwalk was constructed from the tower close to the keeper's house. The light was lit on June 2, 1874. In 1877 the light received a larger fourth-order Fresnel lens to respond to marine traffic needs. Expansion moved ahead, and in 1896 Congress combined the Duluth and Superior ports and for the first time provided a joint appropriation of $3 million for harbor improvements. In the next ten years, channels were enlarged and deepened to 20 feet (6 m), large anchorage basins were created within the harbors, and Superior and Duluth entrances were both rebuilt and enlarged.

As a result of these improvements, the Duluth pier was extended and a temporary light was erected until the new permanent Duluth Harbor South Breakwater Outer Light could be built in 1902, making the 1872 light obsolete. This new fog signal and lighthouse was a white brick structure with a red metal roof and black trim. Its gallery and iron railing extended well beyond the 8-foot 4-inch (2.6 m) circular lantern. The green, curved glass panes of the lantern sat in diagonal astragals, and inside the lantern was the fourth-order Fresnel lens from the previous pier light. The 35-foot (10.7 m) tower had a focal plane of 44 feet (13.5 m) above lake level to produce a 12-mile (19.4 m) visibility. This outer light was often used as a front range light in conjunction with the South Breakwater Inner Light (also built in 1901) for entering the channel into the Duluth Harbor. When this light was lit, the old light and fog signal were removed. The two assistant keepers had to rent lodging in town until a new duplex was built for them across from the head keeper's house in 1912.

The original steam whistles were replaced with locomotive whistles. Then in 1923 duplicate type F diaphone foghorns were installed to better warn of the area's thick fog. When local citizens complained about the noise, deflectors were installed to send the sound out over the water, away from Duluth. These foghorns served until 1968, when an electric signal was installed. Surprisingly, the Duluth citizens missed the "Bee-oh" sound of the old foghorns. They formed a group in 1976 to have the government reinstall the old foghorns and were successful. In April 1995 the Type F diaphone foghorns removed from the Keweenaw Pierhead light were refurbished, installed and reactivated at Duluth. The light was automated in 1976.

In 1908 the Lighthouse Board had deemed the approach to the Duluth Harbor to be one of the worst and most dangerous of the whole chain on the Great Lakes. To help rectify this situation another, new, conical tower was built on the north pier. It was completed in 1910 at a cost of $4,000. These lights still shine today to mark the narrow entrance of the Duluth Ship Canal and make entry to the Duluth harbor easier and safer.

Known Keepers: see Duluth North Pierhead Light

Eagle Harbor Lighthouse

14 Duluth North Pierhead Light

The Duluth Ship Canal was cut through the base of Minnesota Point at Lake Superior's western end and marked with a lighthouse in the early 1870s. Then in 1889 a rear range light was added to make the approach into the 300-foot (92 m) wide canal easier. In spite of the range lights, vessels still had difficulty maneuvering into the canal at night or during heavy fog, because they were unsure of the exact position of the northern breakwater.

To correct this, the Lake Carriers' Association repeatedly petitioned the government to light the outer end of the north break-

water. Finally, when no money was thought to be forthcoming, the Association in 1908 placed their own temporary light to light the location. The Lighthouse Board also coincidentally requested $4,000 in the same year for a light at the same location. Congress finally appropriated the money in March 1909. The government engineer revamped the plans for the Peche Island lighthouse for reuse at Duluth. Construction was completed the following spring.

The iron tower was built onto a high concrete pierhead foundation at the outer end of the north breakwater. It was 10.5 feet (3.2 m) in diameter at its base, and tapered slightly to 8 feet (2.4 m) in diameter at the top. Its circular iron gallery was supported by ornamental corbels and it in turn supported an octagonal iron lantern that housed a fifth-order Fresnel lens manufactured by Henri LePaute of Paris. A 210 candlepower electric lamp powered by electricity supplied by the Duluth Electric Utility provided the light's illuminant. When completed, the tower was 37 feet (11.3 m) from base to ventilator ball, and from a 46-foot (14 m) focal plane the light flashed (flash 2 s; eclipse 2 s) to attain an 11-mile (17.8 km) visibility.

When the light started operation on April 7, 1910, the temporary light erected by the Carriers' Association was removed. The new north breakwater light made entry into the narrow Duluth Ship Canal much easier and safer, and it still continues to do so today.

Known Keepers: Ernest Jefferson (1873–88), James Prior (1888–1908), Alexander Shaw (1908–10), Charles Lederle (1910–15), Edwin Bishop (1915–28), John Woods (1928–40).

15 Eagle Harbor Lighthouse

In 1847 U.S. President James Knox Polk reserved 10 acres (4 hectares) for a lighthouse on the site at the west cape of the entrance to Eagle Harbor, Lake Superior. In March 1849 Congress appropriated $4,000 to construct a lighthouse on this land. It was a rubble-stone dwelling with a square white wooden tower built into one end of its roof.

The tower had a birdcage-style lantern and operated a catoptric lighting system that used whale-oil–burning Winslow Lewis lamps and reflectors to display the light from a 47-foot (14.4 m) focal plane. The light was first lit in 1851 to serve two purposes: it was a coastal marker to help mariners find their location; it marked the entrance to Eagle Harbor, which exported copper and logs, and imported immigrants and supplies. Its cost came in just under the appropriated $4,000.

Duluth North Pierhead Light

In 1857 the lantern was modernized and a fourth-order Fresnel lens made by Louis Sautter of Paris was installed. The light's fixed white light characteristic was changed to a white light varied by a white flash every two minutes.

Due to the tower's deterioration, Congress appropriated $14,000 in 1870 to build a new lighthouse. The new one, built in 1871, used the same "Norman Gothic" plans as those used to build the Chambers Island light in 1868. The new 44-foot (13.5 m) tower, with walls 18 inches (45 cm) thick, had a decagonal iron lantern with a 60-foot (18.5 m) focal plane. The tower was built into the northeast corner of the 1½-story keeper's house. The bottom of the tower was squared and two buttresses at its exposed corners helped support it. About halfway up, the squared corners were flattened, making an octagonal tower. The fourth-order Fresnel lens from the old lantern was placed in it.

From inside the four-bedroom house the tower's iron spiral staircase provided access to both the lantern and the upper story of the house. Both the house and tower were made of red brick and placed on a dressed stone foundation. The house also had a few unexplainable bricked-in recessed windows. The house's gable end by the tower had a white crossbeam and an ornate finial that extended well above the peak of the roof and below the crossbeam. The pitch of the roof changed and angled up and well out from the sides of the house just above the eaves. The station also had a brick oil house.

In 1877 the Army Corps of Engineers improved the shallow harbor by cutting a channel 13.5 feet (4.2 m) deep into the harbor to accommodate larger, heavier vessels. Rock-filled cribs on both sides of the entrance marked the channel opening.

Congress appropriated $5,550 in 1892 to build a fog signal at Eagle Harbor. The fog signal added to the light station in 1895 first used a coal boiler to provide steam to operate an 18-inch (45 cm) steam whistle mounted on the hipped roof. The signal had a 44-second cycle (blast 2 s; silence 12 s; blast 6 s; silence 24 s). In 1907 the whistles operated for 544 hours. In 1928 this system was replaced with diesel-powered, air-driven Type F diaphone foghorns whose trumpet-shaped horns protruded through the upper wall facing the lake. The fog signal building was sheathed in metal to repel fire and weather. In 1929 a radio beacon was installed in the fog signal watchroom. Its characteristic was "dot, dash, dash, dash."

The twentieth century brought further changes. In 1907 the woodshed was converted to a summer kitchen, and the kitchen became a dining room. A coal-fired boiler system removed the need for wood to heat the house. In 1912 a lifesaving station was set up across from the lighthouse at the east entrance to the harbor. In 1913 the intensity of the light was increased to 37,000 candlepower by changing the illuminant from oil to incandescent oil vapor.

This light station used a wind signal tower to assist mariners. Upon hearing the weather forecast, the lighthouse keeper would raise an appropriate cone wind signal on this tower as a daytime marker to communicate updated weather conditions to passing mariners.

The light underwent changes. In 1924 red panels were placed over the bull's eyes of its lens to create a fixed white light varied by a bright red flash every two minutes. In 1925 the five sides of the octagonal tower that faced the lake were painted white to increase its daytime visibility.

During a November storm in 1926, the steamer *Thomas Maytham* got hung up on rocks 40 miles (64 km) away. The life-saving rescue crew set out, rescued its 22 crewmembers and headed for home instead of the Mendota Light Station, which was closer. On the return trip they found and rescued 29 more people from the *Bangor*, which had also run aground and become stranded. In 1932, after the lifesaving station was closed, two of its framed houses were moved across the river to be used as housing for assistant keepers.

Winter storms took their toll. *Calumet News* articles dated January 24 and 25, 1938, and titled "Eagle Harbor Left in Ice Storm" and "Icebergs Fill Bay" tell how a gale tore through the area for several days sweeping waves more than 50 feet (15.4 m) high right over the lighthouse and burying it in 8 inches (20 cm) of ice. Windows were broken, the storeroom was filled with water, and the sewer line was damaged. Hydro in the town was knocked out for four days. Damages were soon repaired, but only warmer weather could melt the ice from the lighthouse.

In the early twentieth century the Eagle Harbor "kids" considered the station their own, and paid the keepers daily visits. Then, during World War II, the Coast Guard used the site as a training station. The local children looked forward to watching when the guard held their annual maneuvers.

Sometime in the 1930s the lighthouse was electrified. Its incandescent bulb increased its visibility to 15 miles (24 km). In 1962 its Fresnel lens was replaced by a pair of DCB-224 aerobeacons (red and white aviation beacon lights) which flashed at 20-second intervals (white flash 0.1 s; eclipse 9.9 s; red flash, 0.1 s; eclipse, 9.9 s). The white flash was visible for 29 miles (46.4 km) and the red flash for 22 miles (35.2 km). In 1978 the fog signal was replaced by a bell buoy placed several hundred yards offshore to warn of the nearby reef.

During the 1970s a Coast Guardsman stationed at the lighthouse reported many unexplained happenings, which included heavy footsteps on the stairs, lights turning on and off, the sound of furniture being moved, and a light within a darkened tower. These unnerving incidents happened in the lighthouse and in one of the moved frame houses. Frederick Stonehouse reports, in his

Eagle Harbor Front Range Light

Eagle Harbor Rear Range Light

Eagle Harbor Rear Range Light

16 Eagle Harbor Range Lights

As marine traffic increased on Lake Superior, more and more lights were placed along its south shore to help ensure safe travel. A light had been placed in 1851 to mark Eagle Harbor along the north shore of the Keweenaw Peninsula, but vessels could only seek entry during the day. A long rocky bar extended across the mouth of the harbor and entry was only possible through a narrow area in the bar where the water deepened. To assist entry, private unlit range markers had been placed onshore. However any vessel arriving at night had to wait for daylight or risk hitting the bar.

In 1863 the Lighthouse Board recommended range lights for Eagle Harbor, but all Congressional funding was being diverted to the Civil War. By 1866 the Army Corps of Engineers arrived to cut an entrance 130 feet (40 m) wide and 14 feet (4.3 m) deep into the harbor to create a refuge. In 1873 the supervising engineer recommended range lights to facilitate night entry. To this end Congress appropriated $8,000 in March 1875. Land was selected on low swampy ground behind the entrance and close to the mouth of Cedar Creek. Construction started when title was obtained in 1877.

The plans for these range lights were also used at Copper Harbor (1869), Presque Isle Harbor (1870), and Bailey's Harbor (1870). The rear range light was a 1 1/2-story wood frame house with a small wooden lantern on the roof peak facing the harbor. Wooden stairs connected the levels and extended up to the copper-lined (for fire protection) lantern. It housed a tubular tin lamp that sat on a small cast-iron pedestal. The lantern had one forward window to shine the light in a single direction. The front range light was shorter and on lower ground. It was a 25-foot (7.7 m) wooden tower with a square base and an octagonal upper half, topped with an iron roof, ventilator ball and lightning rod. It also had a tubular tin lamp on a cast-iron pedestal, but had two windows — one to shine the light over the water, and one for the keeper to check the light without leaving his dwelling. Mariners could not see these until they were on a direct line of approach. These range lights were first lit on September 20, 1877. In 1878 the government made it even easier to find the opening in the bar by placing rock-filled cribs on the bar at both sides of the entrance.

The marshy land was a problem. In 1884 the government raised the rear range dwelling to put new foundation walls and a cellar beneath it. In 1885 an elevated wooden catwalk was built to the front range light to save the keeper from slogging through the swamp. In 1901 the rear dwelling was raised another two feet, and a new concrete floor was poured. A two-story barn was built to the rear of the house and the land was regraded to drain water from around the structures. In 1894 the lanterns were improved. The old tin lamps and reflectors were replaced with lens lanterns. At some point a brick oil house was constructed near the front tower and the lights' illuminant was likely switched to kerosene.

With the use of bigger, better vessels, marine traffic in this harbor dwindled after the turn of the twentieth century. The government finally deemed the range lights unnecessary and extinguished them after the 1911 navigation season. While the fate of the front range light is unknown, the rear range light was sold at public auction in 1930 to Gertrude Rowe of Detroit for $4,000. She had it moved across Highway 26 to use as a summer cottage. It has been handed down through her family and is often referred to as the Tower and Lantern cottage. Today range lights once more mark the old location, but they are of a modern steel-pole style. The only hint of structures from long ago is the old brick oil house.

Known Keepers: George Howard (1877–79), Henry Pearce (1879–89), Thomas Thomson (1890–93), James Carson (1894–98), Alexander McLean (1898), Mary Wheatly (1898–1905), Mrs. C. Thomson (1905), Thomas Thomson (1905–08), Norman Smith (1908–12).

---

book *Haunted Lakes*, that the only keeper who died at the light was Stephen Cocking, keeper from 1877 to 1889, and that the "ghostly" occurrences might have been caused by his spirit still remaining at the light, where he dedicated his life.

In 1980, after a long succession of keepers, the light was automated. The light equipment was monitored by the U.S. Coast Guard out of Sault Ste. Marie, Michigan, and serviced by the USCG Portage Station, near Hancock, Michigan.

In January 1982 the Coast Guard began leasing 2.7 acres (1.1 hectares) to the Keweenaw County Historical Society for a museum site. The society restored the keeper's house to an early twentieth-century appearance, including artefacts of that era and mannequins in period costume. The museum opened in July 1983.

The museum also has an exhibit about government-owned lighthouse supply vessels, or tenders, whose history dates from 1789. It was customary to name them after plants and trees until recently, when they started to name them after historic lighthouse keepers. According to the museum, the first tender on the Great Lakes was the *Dahlia*, which was launched in 1874. Other tenders that served in the Keweenaw area included the *Marigold* and the *Amaranth*, which transported keepers, brought supplies like oil, coal, tools, and cleaning and record-keeping materials, tended navigation buoys, and ferried lighthouse inspectors. Another tender, the *Aspen*, was a construction and maintenance vehicle that carried construction supplies and crew. The museum has copies of the keepers' logs from both the Mendota and Portage River Light Stations.

In addition to the lighthouse museum in the keeper's quarters, there is a maritime museum in the fog signal building and a mining museum in the garage. The maritime museum has a scale model of the U.S. tender *Marigold*, which used to bring supplies to this station.

The large, sprawling station is a wonderful spot to visit. The huge rocks of its shoreline suggest some of the hidden underwater dangers for mariners and its white picket fence bordered with marigolds seems a fitting reminder of the supply tender that once served this station. Today this complex is listed on both state and national historic registers.

Known Keepers: John Griswold (1850–59), John Alexander (1859), George Griswold (1859–60), James Bouden (1860–61), R. Latterly (1861–65), Peter Bird (1865–74), George Bird (1876–77), Stephen Cocking (1877–89), Henry Pierce (1889–93), Thomas Thomson (1893–1903), John Nolen (1904–15), Thomas Bennetts (1916–18), Hans Robinson (1918–39), James Brander (1939–40), Edward Byttyla (1940–62).

Eagle River Lighthouse

17 Eagle River Lighthouse

When copper was discovered in 1845 at the Cliff Mine on the Keweenaw Peninsula along southern Lake Superior, the community of Eagle River came into being. It was an important harbor for exporting copper and importing men and supplies. In 1850 Congress appropriated $4,000 to build a lighthouse at the river mouth to mark the harbor entrance.

The light was built after clear title was obtained to land on the west side of the river in 1853. It was a 1½-story yellow brick keeper's house with a 12-foot (3.7 m) square brick tower 24 feet (7.4 m) high built into its northeast corner. The tower was topped with a circular lantern with trapezoid-shaped glass panels of which every second one was inverted. The lantern's sixth-order Fresnel lens displayed a fixed white light for 13 miles (21 km) from a 61-foot (18.8 m) focal plane, thanks to the high sand bluff on which the light was built. When it was finished in 1855 the eleventh district inspector rejected the structure "for non-conformity to the contract." The contractor worked to correct the deficiencies until 1857, when the inspector finally approved the structure.

After the Cliff Mine closed in 1873, the harbor declined rapidly. While the government planned to replace the light with a new one up the coast, since its tower walls had started cracking in 1867 and the harbor was in decline, that did not happen immediately. The Eagle River light was patched and repaired for over 40 years to serve as a coastal light even though its harbor was virtually abandoned. After the light was decommissioned it was sold at public auction in August 1908 for $925. It was replaced when a light was built further along the coast at Sand Hills in 1919.

Known Keepers: John Griswold (1859–61), Mrs. Griswold (1861–65), Henry Feiser (1865–89), Thomas Bennetts (1890–1908).

18 Fourteen Mile Point Lighthouse

In the late 1800s the Lighthouse Board began placing new lighthouses between existing ones to create a continuous string of lights that would ensure safer maritime travel. They chose the Fourteen Mile Point location to build a lighthouse between lights at the Portage Lake Ship Canal, 28 miles (45.4 km) to the east, and Ontonagon, 14 miles (22.7 km) to the west. It was from this second distance that the point got its name.

Congress responded to petitions by appropriating $20,000 in March 1893 to build a first-class lighthouse and fog signal station.

Approximately 50 acres (20 hectares) of land on the point were purchased on July 21, 1893, from the State of Michigan, for $198. Starting in May 1894 the tender *Amaranth* arrived laden with a 30-man work crew and 450 tons of building materials. As soon as temporary quarters were built to house the work crew, they started work on the lighthouse. Under the supervision of R.J. Miller, the Construction Superintendent for the Detroit Lighthouse Depot, the station was finished for fall occupancy.

The lighthouse combined a duplex for the head keeper and first assistant with a central square 55-foot (16.8 m) tower running up the front of the dwelling. The house used double-bricked walls with a 3-inch (7.5 cm) air space between them for insulation. Each side was a mirror image of the other. Brick verandas with graceful symmetrical arches completed the front of the house on either side of the tower.

A short iron spiral staircase connected the workroom to the watchroom that topped the tower. Its porthole windows gave the keeper a good view, as did the square gallery with its iron railing. Above this watchroom sat a decagonal iron lantern that had its own circular gallery and iron railing. It housed a fourth-order Fresnel lens with red flash panels to create its unique flash characteristic as the weight mechanism rotated the lens around its incandescent oil vapor lamp. The lantern was topped with a decagonal dome, ventilator ball and lightning rod. At the base was the keeper's office, well lit by double front windows.

Much attention was given to the brick and stone detailing. The veranda arches and the curved door and window lintels were made of artful brickwork accented with stone sills and base stones. The corners of the house also had stone accenting. The brick outcroppings and tiering at the top of the tower gave it a slightly castle-like appearance. The house had a red metal roof and parapeted end walls that rose to a central chimney. The basement housed two brick and concrete cisterns to collect rainwater and had doors into the tower to give access to the lower cable and weight door of the clock mechanism.

All rooms of the duplexed house were finished with excellent woodworking, which included first-quality oak floors and trim work. The front entryways had intricately designed red tile flooring, most unusual for a lighthouse. Being at such an isolated location, no one really knows why this station was built with such attention to detail, except that it was designed as a first-class station. It was also completely furnished and ready for the keepers' occupancy. They only needed to supply their personal items. The house for the second assistant keeper was behind the duplex. It was a two-story frame board-and-batten house painted yellow and it had a red tin-shingled roof. It is believed that this house was a conversion of the work crew quarters.

The red brick fog signal building was built close to the water just west of the brick keeper's house. It housed a dual steam-driven system that used Fitzgibbon steam engines. Wood was burned to get the fires started and then coal kept the fires going to produce the necessary steam to operate the two 18-inch (45 cm) brass whistles. Water for the steam was pumped from the lake using a windmill and piping beneath a protective crib constructed just offshore. Water for the keepers' houses was then pumped from the fog signal building. The building's smokestack extended well beyond its corrugated iron roof, which was painted red as part of the station's daymark.

Other structures completed the complex: a dock and wooden boathouse, a tramway for hauling supplies, a brick oil house between the house and fog signal building, a barn to house animals and a privy "out back."

The lighthouse was slightly similar in style to those built at Big Bay Point and Forty Mile Point. All three were a large duplex with a central square tower at the front of the house. They also all had separate entries into the tower. But the lighthouse at Fourteen Mile Point was much more ornate.

The station was first lit in the fall of 1894 by the head keeper and his first assistant. The second assistant joined them in 1895. They lived at the station with their families during the navigation season (April to early December) and then closed up for the winter and moved to a populated area until the following spring. The keepers occasionally traveled to Ontonagon for supplies and mail. With the house needing wood for fuel and cooking and the fog signal also using wood, the keepers had to cut wood three to four times a week to keep up the supply. They also supplemented their diet by fishing with gill nets.

In 1901 the light displayed a fixed white light varied by a red flash every twenty seconds for a 15-mile (24.2 km) visibility from a 60-foot (18.5 m) focal plane, and it illuminated a 250-degree arc on the horizon. Its daymark was a red brick house with a red roof and red brick tower with a black cylindrical watchroom carrying a black gallery. Its fog signal produced 5-second blasts with 25 seconds of silence between each blast. The station was so well built that few repairs or changes were needed.

In the late 1920s the keepers encountered many bears. The first assistant could hardly reach the highest scratch marks on the "bear tree" behind the station with his rifle. He once shot a bear from the lantern gallery when it came onto the station lawn. When smoking fish they left the smokehouse door open so that a bear would not bat the building over trying to get at the fish. The keepers liked to rest in hammocks slung between trees, but they always kept a rifle propped by the tree near their head just in case. Once when the keeper's son was sleeping in a hammock, he thought his friend was playfully attacking him. When he realized it was a real bear, he jumped up and ran to the house, only to find that the door had been painted shut. Luckily he had startled the bear as much as it had startled him, and when he looked back he saw it running for the woods.

In 1934 the lighthouse was automated with the use of acetylene gas and put under the supervision of the keeper at Ontonagon, who traveled once a month to check on the station. With keepers no longer on site, furnishings and fog signal equipment were also removed.

As ships became larger and traveled further offshore, the light's usefulness was nearing its end. In 1938 the lighthouse reservation, except for a small piece of land on which the lighthouse sat, was deemed surplus and then turned over to the Department of the Interior in 1940. In 1945 the light was extinguished and its lens and acetylene equipment were removed. Shortly after this, the property, including the buildings, was sold into private hands.

Once it was empty, nature started to reclaim the grounds and vandals took their toll. In July 1984, while vandals were partying, they lit a campfire on one of the wooden floors inside the duplex. The whole building caught fire and everything except its brick walls and the ironwork of the lantern was burned, including its short iron staircase, which dangled high in the tower below the watchroom. The raging flames were reported by a passing boater, but the Ontonagon Fire Department and the Portage Coast Guard Station pumper boats could do little else but contain the flames.

Today the burned-out shell remains with few or no scorch marks on its brick and the heavy iron stoves are in the basement where they landed during the fire. There is no sign of the metal roof. The wooden assistant keeper's house still stands, but is in poor condition, as are the brick oil house and the fog signal building. The boathouse is gone.

While the future of the structure remains uncertain, parts of it have been saved. Its 18-inch (45 m) brass fog whistles are on display at the Ontonagon Fire Department and its original fourth-order Fresnel lens is on display at the Ontonagon County Museum located in the village. As well, the museum also displays one of the keeper's logbooks and photographs of the station when the light was in active operation.

Known Keepers: Thomas Doody (1894–1902), Ralph Heater (1902–11), Henry Noel (1911–12), Ralph Heater (1912–22), Edward McGregor (1924–29), Earl Hand (1934).

19 Grand Island East Channel Lighthouse

Although the Grand Island North lighthouse marked the location of the natural harbor of refuge in Munising Bay along Lake Superior's south shore between Sault Ste. Marie and Marquette, both the eastern and western channels into the bay were difficult to navigate in fair weather let alone in heavy weather or darkness. To assist with the lighting of these channels, U.S. Senator Chandler presented a petition signed by mariners, pilots and vessel owners in the area to Congress in February 1860, and $17,000 was appropriated to construct identical wooden lighthouses to light the two passages.

The eastern passage was deeper and less dangerous to navigate. Its lighthouse was built on a low sandy spit on the southeast side of Grand Island in 1867. Due to the site's low location and proximity to water, cribbing had to be built to combat erosion. To minimize the cost of this lighthouse it was built of timbers and wood siding instead of more durable materials such as brick or stone. However, it was placed on a stone foundation.

The 1½-story house had a square 45-foot (13.7 m) tower attached to its south end, and both were painted white to maximize daytime visibility. Its iron lantern first used an oil-fired steamer lens to display its light from a 49-foot (15 m) focal plane. The light's first keeper, Frederick Giertz, first lit the light on August 15, 1868. In 1869 the steamer lens was replaced by a fifth-order Fresnel lens to increase the light's visibility to 13 ½ miles (21.5 km). It displayed a fixed white light. In 1900 new 8-foot (2.5 m) high cribbing backed by stone replaced the by then badly damaged cribbing.

In 1904 the Lighthouse Board recommended that $13,200 be provided to build range lights to replace the Eastern Channel light for two reasons: the old lighthouse was in poor condition; and the light could not readily be seen until vessels were close to it, by which point new larger ships had difficulty turning into the channel. Range lights on the mainland in Munising would better show vessels a direct approach into the harbor. Congress approved in 1907 and upon completion of the Munising Range Lights in 1908, George Prior, the keeper of the Eastern Channel light, extinguished

Grand Island East Channel Lighthouse

the old light and lit the range lights on October 30, 1908.

The old abandoned lighthouse and land (44 acres/17.8 hectares) was deemed excess and sold to a consortium of 20 people who then divided the reservation into individual parcels, with everyone keeping part ownership in the lighthouse. Sitting abandoned and empty, the lighthouse soon deteriorated to weathered-gray wood. Over time the cribbing eroded and lake water lapped at the building's stone foundation.

In 1999 the Grand Island East Channel Light Rescue Project Committee was formed to attempt to save the lighthouse. Their primary goal was to stabilize the shoreline in front of the structure. After raising sufficient funds they built new cribbing in 2000–01. Since their ultimate goal is to preserve the East Channel Lighthouse, it appears that this famous landmark will survive.

Grand Island East Channel Lighthouse

Known Keepers: Frederick Giertz (1868–69), George Prior (–1909).

20 Grand Island Harbor Range Lights

After receiving petitions from local mariners, Congress granted approval in 1866 to build identical wooden lighthouses to mark the eastern and western channels into the safe natural harbor of Munising Bay, located in the shelter of Grand Island on the south shore of Lake Superior. Then, after consultation they deemed that range lights would be preferable to light and mark the western channel. Construction was started in 1867, but was delayed until 1868 on account of the drowning of the work foreman.

The front range light was a white wooden pyramidal tower that used a sixth-order Fresnel lens to display a fixed white light from a 19-foot (5.8 m) focal plane to provide a visibility of 10 miles (16 km). Five hundred feet (153 m) behind the front light, the rear range light was displayed from a short wooden tower on the top of a frame keeper's house. It also used a sixth-order Fresnel lens to display a fixed white light, but from its higher focal plane of 32 feet (9.8 m) it was visible for 12.5 miles (20 km). These range lights used oil lamps and were first lit on August 15, 1868.

By 1914 the range lights needed rebuilding. The new rear light doubled in height to 64 feet (19.5 m) with the addition of 32 feet (9.8 m) of riveted steel tower that had been moved from Vidal Shoals, a decommissioned light. This reused tower was placed on a new foundation of riveted steel plates. The new front range light was a 23-foot (7 m) iron mast with a slatted white daymark. Both of the old sixth-order Fresnel lenses were transferred to the new towers and were fueled by acetylene. Visibility for the front light was 11 miles (17.8 km) and for the rear light 15 miles (24.2 km). By 1939 both Fresnel lenses were replaced with 350 mm glass ones.

In 1968 the front light was replaced using a D9 design, a tubular steel structure. In 1969 the rear range light was deactivated. At some point a lighted buoy was placed ½ mile (0.8 km) out in the bay to act as a front range light for the still-used tower onshore. The western channel into Munising Bay was never used much because it was shallow.

In 1990 the old abandoned steel rear range tower was refurbished. After it was painted inside and out and its lantern glass was replaced, it looked just like new.

Known Keepers: Frederick Giertz (1869–69), Samuel Barney (1869–73), Napoleon Beedon (1873–76), Casper Kuhn (1876–95), Frank Brannock (1895–1902), Timothy Dee (1902–07).

21 Grand Island North Lighthouse

The completion of the Soo Locks in 1855 linked Lake Superior to the other Great Lakes, and shipping on the lake increased. Most ship captains traveling along the south shore stayed within sight of the shoreline, or "coasted," to maintain their navigational position. The only protection from storms along the south shore between Sault Ste. Marie and Marquette was the natural harbor at

Grand Island Harbor Rear Range Light

Munising Bay in the lee of Grand Island.

Being pressured to light the island, Congress in February 1853 appropriated $5,000 to build a lighthouse on the island's north side to mark the area as a turning point for vessels coasting the south shore and to mark Munising Bay as a harbor of refuge. A site was chosen along the island's north side and the required land was leased from the State of Michigan. The lighthouse was built in 1856 on a 175-foot (53.5 m) cliff, where it was thought to be most visible to both east- and westbound lake traffic.

While little is actually known about this first lighthouse, it was assumed to have been a short wooden tower attached to a small wooden keeper's house. Its lantern used a fourth-order Fresnel lens manufactured by Louis Sautter of Paris to display a fixed white light varied by flashes created from the bull's eyes in the lens revolving around the oil lamp. The system provided a 13-mile (21 km) visibility.

Due to the lighthouse's location on the sheer cliff, its boathouse was in a bay about $^1/_5$ mile (0.4 km) to the southeast, and supplies had to be carried in on a primitive path over rough terrain. In 1860 walkways and a tramline were built from the boathouse to the lighthouse, featuring four trestle bridges across gullies and ravines. Then, during an annual inspection in 1865, the inspector judged the lighthouse and keeper's dwelling to be in such a "wretched condition" that he recommended they be razed and rebuilt. Congress responded in 1866 with $12,000 for rebuilding in 1867.

The new buildings were made of brick to create a more substantial station. All materials had to be shipped in and hauled up to the station site at the top of the cliff. The crew of workers built a schoolhouse-style lighthouse that consisted of a 1 1/2-story keeper's house and a 40-foot (12.2 m) tall square tower attached to one of the gable ends. The Fresnel lens from the old tower was transferred to it.

Few changes occurred at the station over the years. In 1882 the Lighthouse Board recommended a fog signal but Congress never appropriated the funds. In 1885 the walkway was rebuilt and the boatways were extended into the lake. In 1887 funds were appropriated to buy its leased property (almost 400 acres/160 hectares) from the State of Michigan. However, most of the island was auctioned off in 1901 except for the immediate land on which the station sat, as it was deemed surplus.

An interesting mystery evolved during keeper Genry's tenure. In 1908 Genry and his assistant, Edward Morrison, were the only two living at the lighthouse while Genry's family lived in Munising and Morrison's wife in lower Michigan. Apparently Genry had trouble keeping assistants for more than one season and Morrison wrote to his wife that he feared Genry and had difficulty pleasing him. On June 6, Genry returned to the lighthouse in the station sailboat with provisions from Munising. Two days later the keeper of Au Sable Lighthouse, Thomas Irvine, discovered a body in a sailboat off his lighthouse. It was identified as assistant keeper Morrison. An official party was dispatched to the Grand Island North Lighthouse. However, they found no one there, the light untended, no logbook entries for the past several days, and the newly purchased provisions still on the dock. While Genry was never seen again, his sailboat was discovered at the Munising dock.

Speculation has Genry and Morrison arguing and fighting when Genry returned with the supplies and the fight resulting in Morrison's death and his body being placed adrift in the sailboat. Genry then may have returned to Munising, as witnesses are rumored to have seen him drinking at a local bar. However, he never contacted his family or was seen again. Perhaps he hightailed it to safety in Canada, but the truth will never be known.

With the availability of acetylene, the light was automated in

Grand Island North Lighthouse

1927 and a keeper was no longer needed. Unoccupied, the structures deteriorated with time. In 1961 the light was moved to a 25-foot (7.7 m) steel pole at the cliff's edge. It was powered by a 12-volt solar-powered battery and used an automatic bulb changer. The Coast Guard removed the Fresnel lens and shipped it to a destination now unknown.

When the government decided the reserve was no longer of use to them, they sold it to the timber and mining company that owned the rest of the island. As this company was not interested in the lighthouse buildings, they sold them in 1972 to Loren Graham, an MIT professor who had been trying since 1961 to obtain the lighthouse. Graham, along with his wife and family members, spent many years restoring the station's dilapidated buildings.

With no roads to the lighthouse, no boat access, and no electricity to the island, it was a labour of love. Eventually they achieved their dream of creating a private summer home at the lighthouse and saved another part of maritime history. Today the lighthouse remains remote, although the rest of the island is owned by the U.S. Forest Service, and roads have been built around the island making access easier. The owners now dream of making the lighthouse into a museum.

Known Keeper: Genry (–1908)

22 Grand Marais Lighthouse (Minnesota)

The community of Grand Marais developed slowly during the 1800s along the north shore of Lake Superior at its western end. Its French name, meaning "large marsh," may have referred to the edges of its large but shallow bay, which offered early mariners some storm protection. If the storm was from the east, however, there was little protection, as the large mouth of the bay allowed the water to rage in unimpeded.

In the mid-1800s the area started to develop as a rafting point. Logs purchased for pulpwood were made into small pocket rafts within the bay and then towed outside the bay to be made into large booms by enclosing them with a double circle of sitka spruce logs linked together with strong heavy chains. Powerful tugs then towed this floating pulpwood in huge tear-shaped boom rafts of 3,500 to 12,000 cords across Lake Superior to processing cities like Ashland to make pulp paper for newsprint. Each trip was about 80 miles (130 km) and took two to three days to complete, all being well on the trip.

Grand Marais Lighthouse (Minnesota)

To assist this struggling industry, locals petitioned the government for harbor improvements at Grand Marais as early as 1856, but there was no follow-up construction after Congress appropriated $6,000 in August 1856 for a lighthouse at Grand Marais.

In 1876 the schooner *Stranger* was blown back out into the lake from the bay during a storm. Three men went to the rescue but by the time they were alongside to complete their mission, the crew was so exhausted from battling the storm that they couldn't climb into the rescue boat and went down with the vessel. When the schooner *Liberty* also went down at Grand Marais shortly afterward, outraged locals again petitioned for harbor protection.

Breakwater piers were finally built at the bay's mouth to form a protected harbor within, and in 1885 Congress appropriated $9,552 for a light and fog signal at the end of the east pier to mark the harbor entrance. The tower was a 32-foot (9.8 m) square wooden pyramidal structure that was completely enclosed. The materials were delivered to Grand Marais by the tender *Warrington* and the tower was erected and anchored onto the east pierhead.

The tower supported a surplus octagonal lantern from the Detroit depot and displayed a fixed white light using a fifth-order Fresnel lens made by the Louis Sautter Company of Paris. From its 38-foot (11.7 m) focal plane, it had a 13-mile (21 km) visibility. Its fog signal, a 1,500-pound (680 kg) bell formerly used at Passage Island, was mounted to the tower's lakeward side. Its automatic mechanism, which struck a double blow every 30 seconds when in operation, was housed inside the top of the tower below the lantern. Exposed to the full force of Superior's eastern storms, the tower frequently needed work on its battered lower sections over the years.

The first keeper began at Grand Island on February 23, 1886, although the light was finished in 1885. He had to find his own accommodations as a keeper's house was not built until 1896. It was a two-story frame house built on a red brick foundation, located a good distance from the tower. The lower level was covered in clapboard, the upper in painted cedar shake siding, and the roof was shingled in a diagonal pattern. Today it is listed on the *National Register of Historic Places*.

In 1902 the end of the west pier was also marked so that mariners could more easily navigate between the two piers. A fixed red lens lantern was displayed on an iron pole 30 feet (9 m) above the lake. After the keeper had rowed across to tend this light for a year and a half, it was converted to a Pintsch gas light in 1904.

In 1922–23 the Army Corps of Engineers rebuilt the piers as well as lengthening the east pier. Since the light would have to be moved, and since it had been repaired on numerous occasions, the decision was made to build a new lighthouse at the end of the east pier. The prefabricated tower was shipped to the site and anchored in position. It was an open square pyramidal structure made of steel to withstand storms and allow waves to wash beneath it. Its top was an enclosed service room. Its octagonal iron lantern and fifth-order Fresnel lens likely came from the old tower. It used an incandescent electric bulb, and the electricity was supplied by town hydro. As more lights showed in the growing town behind the light, the light's characteristic was changed to a flashing red to avoid confusion (flash 5 s; eclipse 5 s). Its fog bell was replaced with an electric Sireno horn (blast 5 s; silence 30 s).

Few changes occurred after this at the station. On May 9, 1925, the Pinsch gas system used for the light on the west pier was switched to a more reliable acetylene gas system that produced a red flash every three seconds. The lights were automated in 1937 and the keeper was removed. During the 1960s a D9 cylinder light replaced the acetylene one on the west pier. In 1972 the last boom of pulpwood was rafted from Grand Marais. Both pier lights continue to guide mostly pleasure craft today. While the Coast Guard maintains the lights, the Cook County Historical Society maintains the old keeper's house as a museum.

Known Keepers: Joseph Mayhew (1886), John Woods (1909–21), Emmanuel Luick (1921–37).

23 Grand Marais Range Lights

As lumbering came to the fore around Grand Marais area in the latter years of the 1800s, the government developed a harbor of refuge between Whitefish Bay and Grand Island. When it was finished in 1892, Congress approved $15,000 for a pierhead light and a fog bell to mark it.

In 1895 a white 34-foot (10.4 m) skeletal iron pyramidal tower with an enclosed top section, an octagonal lantern and a sixth-order Fresnel lens was bolted to the end of the west pier. It displayed a fixed white light for 15 miles (24.2 km). Rather than acquire a new fog bell, the Lighthouse Board used the fog bell and automated striking mechanism from Point Iroquois, as it was being replaced with a fog whistle. It struck once every 30 seconds. An elevated walkway was built to connect the light to the shore. The keeper had to build himself a temporary shanty at the inner end of the west pier.

In 1898 the government used the rest of the appropriation to build a second skeletal tower for a rear range light to facilitate harbor entry. It was a 48-foot (14.6 m) white skeletal pyramidal tower of iron with an enclosed top section, an octagonal lantern and a fifth-order lens. It also displayed a fixed white light.

Grand Marais Range Lights

24 Granite Island Lighthouse

With the discovery of iron in the Marquette area along Lake Superior's south shore in the early 1840s, marine traffic in the area increased to export the ore to smelters on the lower Great Lakes. Granite Island, known to the Natives as "Na-Be-Quon" ("canoe with a hump") lay almost directly in the path of shipping routes to or from Marquette. It was an especially dangerous area during fog because this 2.5-acre (1 hectare) granite rock island rose almost perpendicularly for 60 feet (18.3 m) above the lake with deep water all around it. This hazard was just 12 miles (19.4 km) north of Marquette and mariners appealed to have it lit.

In 1865 Congress approved lights for Granite Island as well as Huron Island, not far away. The government wanted to build these two lighthouses at the same time with the same plans and the same building materials, in order to save time and money. The title for Huron Island was quickly obtained, but Granite Island had been sold to Henry B. Lathrop in May 1851. In order to obtain title, the Michigan Legislature authorized the governor to seize and procure the condemnation of the island so that it could be used by the U.S. government for lighthouse purposes. This process took place in 1866–67, and clear title to the island was received by the end of the year. Congress appropriated $17,000 for the Huron Island lighthouse in July 1867 and $20,000 for the Granite Island Lighthouse in September 1867, and construction for both began in 1868.

The granite stone for both lighthouses was cut from the Huron Islands and formed to construction size at both sites. The rest of the materials and equipment were brought by the lighthouse tender *Haze* from the Detroit Lighthouse Depot. To meet the challenge of landing materials on the high island, a platform was built 10 feet (3 m) above the water, and materials were moved from the steamer, onto this landing and up the island. A track was laid to the top of the island, a portable steam engine was set up, and materials were hauled up the incline under steam power. The rock at the summit was blasted to make it a level foundation.

The light was a schoolhouse style with a 10-foot (3 m) square tower 39 feet (10 m) high attached to a 1 1/2-story keeper's dwelling and rising above its one end roof peak. Both house and tower were made of hard undressed granite blocks, with coursed ashlar stone used decoratively on the corners and around door and window openings. Stairs in the tower provided entry to the house levels as well as the lantern.

The tower was topped with a square black iron gallery, a black iron decagonal lantern and a black dome to silhouette against the light sky. The lantern housed a fourth-order Fresnel lens made by Henri LePaute of Paris, and displayed its light from a 93-foot (28.4 m) focal plane. The lighthouse was finished in the fall but first lit at the beginning of the 1869 navigation season. Later in its opening year, boat davits were installed to hoist the keeper's boat safely above the lake's waves that surged against the rocks.

When mariners petitioned for a light to mark Granite Island, they also requested a fog signal. However it was not until 1879, ten years later, that one was established on the island. The mechanically struck bell was placed on top of a frame tower behind the lighthouse. Being frugal, the Lighthouse Board reused the bell that had just been removed from the Thunder Bay Island lighthouse when it received a new steam-operated fog system. The oil engine that operated the fog bell was housed in a room built in the tower just below the bell, and the fog bell rang five times a minute when in operation. By 1910 this tower was in an advanced state of decay, so it was replaced by an iron tower supplied by the Champion Iron Company of Kenton, Ohio, for $1,063.

Lake Superior constantly thwarted efforts to keep a safe landing area. In 1891 a new derrick facilitated the landing of supplies. In

Although Congress ignored the need to appropriate money for a keeper's house, a lifesaving station was built at Grand Marais in 1898. In 1904 the west pier was lengthened and its pierhead light was moved to its new outer end in 1905. Finally in 1908 Congress appropriated $5,000 for a keeper's dwelling. To save costs they reused the plans for the Munising keeper's dwelling and built a two-story brick house at Grand Marais. It is odd that it took the government 13 years to provide a house for this keeper.

With the development of larger vessels, the government's Corps of Engineers stopped maintaining the harbor's breakwater in the 1940s, and sand silted the harbor opening, making it useful only to smaller vessels.

Little altered at this station. In 1905 the lights changed from white to red to make them more distinguishable from the town lights behind them. The wooden piers were replaced by concrete ones. When the lights were automated, the lantern was moved from the front range light and replaced with a modern acrylic lens. Today the Coast Guard still maintains the functioning range lights, and the National Park Service, which owns the dwelling, has leased it to the Grand Marais Historical Society. The Society operates a museum out of the dwelling.

Known Keepers: Samuel Rodgers (1898–1904), George Barkley (1904–12), Otto Bufe (1913–25), Roger Campbell (1925–28), William Brooks (1940).

Granite Island Lighthouse

Because access to the island was so difficult, it was automated in the fall of 1939 through the use of acetylene tanks placed in a steel building by the tower. Sun valves automatically turned the light on and off. The fog bell and station furnishings were removed at this time. Sitting empty, the structure was the victim of the elements but not of theft or vandalism thanks to its inaccessibility. In 1990 the Coast Guard stabilized the building with a new roof and sealed the doors and windows. Today the light operates with a modern solar-powered optic from a steel tower.

In 1999, when the station was excessed, the public was allowed to bid on it, and Scott Holman gained ownership with his top bid of $86,000. An avid long-time member of the Great Lakes Shipwreck Historical Society, Holman is the new "keeper" of the Granite Island lighthouse. He has spent much time, effort and money to revitalize the structure. But he too has also found himself in a battle with Lake Superior. He installed a suspended steel dock and stairs on the south side of the island in 2000 and then a fierce nor'easter destroyed it within a year. However, he battles on because he loves the lighthouse. The island is also home to a NOAA weather station that provides a 360-degree view of Lake Superior every hour as well as other weather data. On January 18, 2003, the equipment recorded winds of 143 miles an hour (231 kph). Holman is happy to share his personal retreat in this way. As well as restoring the lighthouse, he has started to delve into its history.

Known Keepers: Isaac Bridges (1868–72), David Campan (1872–73), Samuel Barney (1873), Isaac Wilson (1873–1880), Frank Reuben (1880–85), William Wheatley (1885–93), James Wheatley (1893–1915).

1901 the landing was repaired after an unusually severe storm. In 1902 a new boathouse was placed at the upper end of the north boat landing, a landing built on the old boathouse site on the south side of the island, and walkways laid around the island. In 1906 a concrete sea wall was built on the northeast side of the boat harbor, the boathouse was rebuilt in a more sheltered position, 115 feet (35 m) of new boatways were provided, and a 500-gallon (2100 l) capacity oil house was constructed of concrete blocks. In 1907 a new landing derrick was again installed to replace the now dangerous old one. In 1928 a new concrete and steel landing was supplied, and new steel boatways were placed on the north side of the island. In 1937 the whole boathouse and a 20-foot (6 m) boat were lost during the winter.

The light first used whale or lard oil and then kerosene. In 1901 it was listed as being a fixed white fourth-order light varied by a red flash every 90 seconds and visible for 17 miles (27.5 m). In 1913 it received an incandescent oil vapor lighting system that raised its candlepower significantly — the white light increased from 530 to 4,500 and the red light from 800 to 20,000 candlepower.

Living on such a craggy rock was a lonely life for these keepers. Besides tending the station there was little to do. One keeper planted lilacs, another grew rhubarb. The keepers of the early 1930s grew fresh vegetables and had a flock of chickens. While vegetation was sparse, some wild berries did grow in rocky crevices.

Occasionally a keeper would boat to Marquette for supplies. The trip was always an adventure and, before the days of powerboats, sometimes a deadly one. In 1872 keeper Isaac P. Bridges drowned when his boat capsized while traveling to his home. In 1898 keeper James Wheatley's son, William, died while boating out to visit his father. A sudden squall came up, flipped his small sailboat and he drowned. In October 1903 assistant keeper John McMartin planned a supply run to Marquette while Wheatley remained at the lighthouse. McMartin had just started to move the boat from the north to the south side of the island when a fresh wind picked up from the northeast. The lake waters caught the boat and dashed it and McMartin against the rocks. His body disappeared into the depths of Superior as Wheatley looked on, powerless.

25 Gull Island Light

On the east side of the Apostle Islands along the south shore of Lake Superior can be found a small island called Gull Island, so named for obvious reasons. It is small, rocky, quite flat, island, low to the water, just ¼ mile (0.4 km) from the northeast tip of Michigan Island. It is the only exposed part of the shoal that extends about 3.5 miles (5.7 km) underwater from Michigan Island in a northeasterly direction. This hidden danger lay in the path of shipping routes as vessels became larger and traveled further offshore.

The Lighthouse Board first recommended a light and fog signal for Gull Island in 1906, but Congress balked at the proposed cost of $85,000. Congress sought advice from the Department of Commerce, which, after its own investigation also recommended a lighthouse at Gull Island, since several vessels had grounded on the shoal. Unconvinced, Congress appropriated funds to conduct a survey of the area.

As a result of the survey, District Engineer Major Charles Keller recommended a lighthouse and fog signal at the eastern end of Michigan Island instead of Gull Island in 1909, but at an increased cost of $100,000. Congress approved the plan in June 1910. However, it appropriated no funds because the Lighthouse Board was abolished and its duties were transferred to the newly formed Bureau of Lighthouses (the Lighthouse Service). This new bureau continued to petition for funding to light the area.

In 1928 Congress finally approved $85,000 for a light at the east end of Michigan Island and an automated light on Gull Island. Only $9,495 of the appropriation was for the Gull Island light, however. This light was a black pyramidal 50-foot (15.3 m) skeletal iron tower surmounted by a 375 mm acetylene-powered light. Producing 390 candlepower from a 55-foot (16.8 m) focal plane, the light was visible for 13 miles (21 km). Sun valves turned the light on and off automatically. Since these valves could malfunction, the Michigan Island keepers had the extra daily responsibility of monitoring the Gull Island Light and making necessary repairs if possible.

The light at the eastern end of Michigan Island was built at the same time as the Gull Island light on a recycled tower. When the 112-foot (34.2 m) iron skeletal tower at Schooner Ledge on the Delaware River in Pennsylvania was replaced, the Lighthouse Bureau marked it for use at Michigan Island, since it was still in excellent condition. A radio beacon was also installed instead of a more costly diaphone fog signal.

In the 1950s the Gull Island light was converted from acetylene to electricity. Today it still operates to warn of the shoal, but it uses a 12-volt DC solar-powered 250 mm optic that displays a flashing light for 7 miles (11.3 km).

26 Gull Rock Lighthouse

When Lake Superior storms raged, vessels coasting its south shore often sought refuge behind the Keweenaw Peninsula. If approaching the point from the west they sought the quickest, shortest route between its tip and Manitou Island, rather than take the regular long route around the island. However, Gull Rock and rocky shoals around it lay in the passage about 2.5 miles (4 km) east of the peninsula's tip and 0.5 miles (0.8 km) west of the island, making safe passage almost impossible in stormy weather with the area unlit.

After many complaints, Congress appropriated $15,000 in 1866 for a lighthouse on Gull Rock. For economy, work crews built three lighthouses in the area at the same time, all with the same plans (Gull Rock, Grand Island, and Granite Island). Gull Rock was nothing but exposed rock rising about 12 feet (3.6 m) above

Gull Rock Lighthouse

the water with an area about 250 by 100 feet (76 m by 30.5 m). The lighthouse buildings covered almost all of it. The stone foundation was built right onto the rock to support a 1 1/2-story yellow brick keeper's house with a square 39-foot (12 m) brick tower rising one more story from its front end to form its schoolhouse style. The main level housed the common areas and there were two bedrooms upstairs. Coal and the light's oil illuminant were stored in the basement. Access to all three levels was provided by the tower's circular self-cleaning spiral iron staircase.

The tower was topped with an octagonal iron lantern that housed a fourth-order Fresnel lens and displayed a fixed red light for a 13½-mile (22 km) visibility from a 50-foot (15.3 m) focal plane. First lit on November 1, 1867, this was the first colored light on the Keweenaw Peninsula. The light was intended to be ready earlier, but construction was delayed when William Turnbridge, its foreman, drowned.

Although at a very isolated location that received the brunt of Lake Superior storms, the lighthouse stood up well, needing only minor repairs over the years. However, its dock required constant attention and keepers made sure it was kept serviceable, so that they could "escape" with their small sailboat to Copper Harbor 10 miles (16 km) away or to visit the keeper at Manitou Island. Few changes occurred at this station: in 1896 an oil storage shed was built; in 1898 the light received a fourth-order lamp for its fourth-order lens; in 1901 a rubble and concrete retaining wall was built northeast of the dwelling for storm protection.

Many vessels were damaged seeking passage through this area. They included the schooner barge *G.M. Neelon* (November 1892), the freighter *Spokane* (October 1907), the *E.N. Saunders* (May 1910), the *L.C. Waldo* and the *Taurus* (November 1918), the *Samuel Mather* (October 1923) and the *Charles C. West* (September 1926). It is interesting that none of these vessels sank, and even the damaged ones were retrieved, repaired, and put back into service. The *G.M. Neelon* had been abandoned as a total loss but a year later it was recovered by the wrecker *J.H. Gillett* and reserviced. Another miracle recovery was that of the 312-foot (96 m) freighter *Spokane*, which had been driven onto Gull Rock, and split in two. After being declared a total loss it was recovered and rebuilt, and went on to serve for another 23 years.

There was little work to do at this lighthouse but it always maintained two keepers, probably for companionship. When they

Gull Rock Lighthouse

arrived in the spring from Copper Harbor, they first inspected the station for winter damage, got heat going in the house, and cleaned and lit the lens and lantern. Once the station was up and running, they alternated day and night shifts. The keeper on night shift used the watchroom on the main floor, which had a bed, the keepers' logbook to record, books to read, and letter-writing materials. Daytime duties included a yearly whitewashing inside and out, dock repairs, daily cleaning of the lens, trimming the wicks and filling the oil lamps. This left plenty of time for keepers to become bored — some reports say that a deck of playing cards was the basic staple of this lighthouse. When this station opened, there were no keepers' uniforms and even after their use in 1884, the keepers at this post were so isolated that they wore them only for lighthouse inspections.

The lighthouse witnessed personal tragedy late in the 1896 season. Keeper John Nolen, his wife and assistant keeper Alice, their two young children and a nephew lived at the light. The youngest child became seriously ill and Nolen decided to venture to Copper Harbor to get a tug to take the family to the mainland and medical attention, but a storm was raging and the child died before he could leave. When the storm had abated he rowed to the peninsula and walked the 8 miles (13 km) over rough snowy terrain and through icy water to the keeper's house at Copper Harbor. The tug was made ready to leave the next morning to retrieve his family, and they buried the child in a box Nolen had made on the mainland where there was soil to cover the grave. Despite their tragedy, they returned the next spring to their duties as keepers.

In 1927 the light was automated with acetylene gas and light sensors to turn the light on and off. The keepers were removed and the light was maintained by the Manitou Island keepers. The fourth-order Fresnel lens is now on display in the Great Lakes Shipwreck Museum at Whitefish Point, Michigan. Today the still-functioning light uses a solar-powered 12-volt DC 250 mm acrylic optic and the buildings continue to stand in defiance of Lake Superior. This light is listed on the *National Register of Historic Places* but is not listed on the state register.

Known Keepers: Thomas Jackson (1867–68), Stephen Cocking (1868–77), James Corgan (1878–83), James Rich (1883–85), Norman Guilbault (1887–88), John Nolen (1888–1903), George Peterson (1904–07), George Smith (1907–10), Herbert Crittenden (1910–21).

27 Huron Island Lighthouse

The Huron Islands were a group of seven small islands located offshore below the Keweenaw Peninsula, and they lay in the direct shipping route. Their rocky shores and granite cliffs were especially dangerous when they were surrounded by fog — which was a lot of the time. In the mid-1800s lake traffic along the south shores of Lake Superior increased to meet the needs of the copper and iron ore industry.

Although mariners pleaded to have the area lit, their requests were ignored until the loss of the side-wheeler *Arctic*, the shipwreck that became one too many in this area. In May 1860 the vessel grounded on the easternmost island and although all passengers, crew and cargo, which included cattle, were safely taken ashore, the vessel was storm-battered on the rocks and lost. Press coverage spread the knowledge of this dangerous, unlit area, and the island where the shipwreck occurred became known as Cattle Island.

Finally, in July 1867 Congress appropriated $17,000 for a lighthouse on one of the Huron Islands. A survey crew selected the westernmost island, Huron Island, as the best location. The island had little vegetation, consisting of solid granite rock outcroppings with many deep fissures and chasms, and rose 163 feet (50 m) above the lake level. Clear title was obtained by September 1867.

Huron Island Lighthouse

The Huron Island Lighthouse and the Granite Island Lighthouse were built at the same time to save money by using identical plans and granite rock quarried for both from the Huron Islands. Other needed materials, equipment and men were brought from the Detroit Depot by the tender *Haze*. While a work crew cleared a crude road from the rocky shore to the site atop the island, another crew started to cut blocks of granite. When necessary, the road crew cut trees to build crude bridges over crevices and ravines. This road required an unexpected extra $3,000 so that materials could be hauled to the site where an area was levelled to build the lighthouse.

The lighthouse consisted of a 1½-story granite stone keeper's house with an attached square 34-foot (10.4 m) stone tower built up one end of the house in a schoolhouse style. Its doors, windows and corners were decoratively framed with coursed ashlar stone. The tower was topped with a square gallery and an octagonal lantern that housed a 3½-order Fresnel lens. The lens displayed a fixed white light from a 197-foot (60 m) focal plane for 23 miles (37 m) and was first lit on October 20, 1868. The same lighthouse design was used at Granite Island, Ontonagon, Copper Harbor, Gull Rock, Marquette, and Grand Island, all built from 1866 to 1869.

Mariners had also called for a fog signal but funds were not made available until 1880. Two fog signal buildings were erected in 1881 on a levelled site about a half a mile (0.8 km) from the lighthouse. They were outfitted with duplicate 10-inch (25 cm) steam whistles powered by coal-fired boilers. A separate pump house housed a steam-powered pump to draw lake water up to the fog signal building. In 1883 a tramway was constructed from the dock to the fog signal to facilitate hauling supplies. Also in 1883 a new boathouse and dock were built in a more sheltered location on the southeast side of the island. In 1887 the steam whistles operated for a total of 361 hours.

In June 1890 lightning struck the lighthouse, damaging a side wall and knocking out some of its cornice. In 1898 a larger fog signal building was built and the old structures were removed. In the 1930s a new compressed-air diaphone fog signal system and a ship-to-shore radio were installed. The wick lamp was upgraded to an incandescent oil vapor system in 1912 and the station was electrified through the use of diesel-powered generators after the Coast Guard took over in 1939.

With the Coast Guard takeover, the station was increased to five men. In the 1940s a one-story wooden keeper's house was built adjacent to the lighthouse to accommodate the keepers. By 1961 the existing quarters were considered too cold and uninhabitable, so the Coast Guard had a new barracks-style quarters built near the fog signal building. It had electricity, oil heat, a large kitchen and day room, and separate bedrooms. Also at this time a new solar-powered oscillating light was installed in the lantern. It could be turned on and off at the fog building. This new system increased the light from 20,000 to 45,000 candlepower.

With less work to do, the keepers had more free time to read, play cards, and go fishing and hunting. Local rumors even say the keepers were once seen helping themselves from a fisherman's net. They escaped into the fog and when confronted by local authorities denied ever having been in the vicinity. Other reports tell of keepers hunting wild game against regulations, but while visitors often remarked on how their beef stew tasted like venison, no charges were ever laid.

In 1972 the Coast Guard automated the light at the end of the navigation season. After vandals broke in and destroyed the Fresnel lens in 1973, the Coast Guard removed all unnecessary equipment and usable materials from the site.

Today a modern solar-powered plastic optic still shines on Huron Island. The Huron Islands are owned by the U.S. Department of the Interior's Fish and Wildlife Service, and the islands are part of the Huron Island Wilderness Area, which is administered by the Seney National Wildlife Refuge. Its 147-acre (60 hectare) preserve offers a protected habitat for a variety of wildlife, and remains much as it was in 1800s.

Known Keepers: Abel Hall (1868–79), Duncan Cameron (1881–91), Francis Jacker (1892–97), Charles Schulz (1897–1900)

28 Indian Country Sports Light

In the age of decommissioned and excessed lighthouses, a new one has been constructed as a private aid to navigation. It was built by Steve Koski and is located on the corner of his sporting goods store, Indian Country Sports, in L'Anse along Lake Superior's south shore. The square tower with its octagonal lantern has an overall height of 50 feet (15.3 m). The lantern houses a modern 150 mm optic that uses an electric bulb as its light source. To prevent burnt-out bulbs, it has an automatic bulb changer. The optic displays a flashing white light every 2.5 seconds from a 44-foot (13.5 m) focal plane. When built in 1995 it was made to withstand 100 mph (160 kph) winds. Although Koski had problems getting his lighthouse registered with the Coast Guard as a private aid to navigation, he persevered and eventually achieved his goal.

Jacobsville (Portage River) Lighthouse

29 Jacobsville (Portage River) Lighthouse

After copper was discovered in the 1840s on the Keweenaw Peninsula, lake traffic on Lake Superior significantly increased to transport ingots of copper ore. In 1853 Congress approved the construction of a lighthouse to mark the entrance of the Portage River at the east-side base of the peninsula into the twin cities of Houghton and Hancock, important centers for making and shipping copper ingots.

The lighthouse was completed in 1856 one mile (1.6 km) north of the river mouth. Little else is known. On January 16, 1858, the *Kingston Daily News* ran a report that it was one of three Lake Superior lighthouses that had been rejected by the government for non-conformity to contract. The rejection may have resulted from shoddy workmanship, because the lighthouse was rebuilt in 1869–70, on a 30-foot (9 m) bluff in what is now known as Jacobsville, to direct marine traffic from Lake Superior to the Portage River entrance.

The second lighthouse was a 1½-story red brick keeper's house with stone lintels and sills, built onto a red sandstone foundation. It was attached by covered passageway to a 45-foot (13.7 m) cylindrical stone tower that had a few double windows ascending it for interior light. The tower exterior was mortared and whitewashed to increase its visibility and durability. It was topped by a decagonal red iron lantern that had a recessed church-style-window pattern stamped into its murette walls. The lantern housed a fifth-order Fresnel lens that displayed a fixed white light varied by a red flash every 60 seconds, which had a visibility of 15 miles (24.2 km) from a 65-foot (20 m) focal plane. The station was completed for a total cost of $12,000. Later, when kerosene became the illuminant, a brick oil house was added.

The light's 1873 logbook shows some detailed entries by its keeper J.B. Crebassa. On June 4 he reported: "icebergs aground in 20 feet [6 m] of water." Then on July 9 he wrote: "s.w. gale. Barge St. Clair burnt at 2 o'clock in the morning near 14 Mile Point from Ontongon en route for Portage Lake. Twenty-seven lives lost, fourteen bodies recovered, thirteen not found, five saved." His logbook provides a window to his life as keeper.

In 1883 John H. Jacobs opened quarries to cut the red sandstone around the lighthouse on the peninsula. Stone cutting became the peninsula's third largest industry, as this stone was a popular building material before the days of concrete and steel. The community became known as Jacobsville, so named after its founder.

When the light was discontinued in November 1919, its keeper, Frank Witz, became the first assistant keeper for the new Lower Entry Light. He lived at the Jacobsville keeper's house until the new duplex keeper's house was finished in 1920. He walked back and forth daily along the shoreline to tend the light.

In 1958 the old Jacobsville lighthouse was excessed and sold into private hands and is today a private residence. It now has flowerbeds, lilacs to welcome visitors, and an addition. Its owners have maintained the tower and much of its original décor, so its future seems assured.

Known Keepers: Michael Lyons (1856–57), John Crane (1857), Sam Stevenson (1857–61), Earl Edgerton (1861–65), John Crebassa (1865–78), George Craig (1879–88), B. Gartner (1898–90), Carl John (1891–95), Charles Rosell (1895–1902), Frank Witz (1902–19).

30 Keweenaw Waterway Lower Entrance Lighthouse

Before the winding twisting Portage River at the eastern base of the Keweenaw Peninsula, Lake Superior, was straightened, the Calumet & Hecla Mining Company (C&H) built twelve mini-lighthouses on cribs to mark the river. The lights consisted of a crib base with a small house and an oil lantern. C&H hired local people to light and extinguish them when a vessel was coming or going at night, and supplied materials to operate the lights.

In 1860 the first cut was made to straighten the Portage River, at the river's entrance into Keweenaw Bay. A wooden piling pier

Keweenaw Waterway Lower Entrance Lighthouse

was built along the cut, and its lake end was marked with a wooden tower that housed an oil lamp. In 1869 range lights were built to guide vessels into the Portage River. The front range light was a 19-foot (5.8 m) wooden tower and the rear light, 25 feet (7.7 m) in height, shone from a lantern above a wooden house. These lights were a quarter of a mile inland on the west side of the cut.

About 1916 the rear range dwelling and tower were moved to the east side of the cut during the winter when the water was frozen. Its front range light became a pier light. In 1920 a new tower replaced the range lights. It was a white 31-foot (9.5 m) octagonal steel tower placed on a high pier with a high square building centered on it. The tower's circular black lantern had curved squares of glass set diagonally into its astragals. It housed a fourth-order Fresnel lens that displayed the light from a 68-foot (20.8 m) focal plane. Its foghorn equipment was located in the square building below the tower. Later, the tower also had radio beacon equipment.

A new keeper's house and a brick machinery building were built onshore. The machinery building produced air that was piped out to the lighthouse to operate its fog signals. The old keeper's house was remodeled in 1921 into a duplex for the assistant keepers. Both the station and the tower operated with electricity.

When this new light was lit, the Jacobsville light was extinguished. Its keeper became the first assistant keeper of the new light, but he continued to live at the Jacobsville house until new quarters were ready. These keepers also tended any and all active river lights. This light was automated in 1973 and is still an active aid to navigation. It used to be known as the Portage Lake Lower Entrance Light.

Known Keepers: Oliver St. André (1919–39), Edward Byttyle (1939–40).

31 Keweenaw Waterway Upper Entrance Lighthouse

Marine traffic in the area around the Keweenaw Peninsula, Lake Superior, steadily increased after the discovery of copper on the peninsula in the early 1840s. In 1860–61 private investors dug the Portage River Canal, a channel 10 feet (3 m) deep and 80 feet (24.4 m) wide, through the marshy swampland at the base of the peninsula's west side to provide access to Portage Lake and the Portage River. This passage saved mariners the 150-mile (245 km) distance around the peninsula. The opening was marked with a lighthouse in 1874. It was a two-story brick duplex house with an attached 33-foot (10 m) tower most sat on the bank of the west entrance to the canal. The lantern housed a 3½-order Fresnel lens that displayed a fixed white light.

Since the canal had continual problems with silting, tolls were collected for the necessary frequent dredging. To curb silting, the government built two rock breakwalls that angled to the shore, and two piers at the entrance to the canal. The breakwalls and the east pierhead were marked by fixed red lights on 32-foot (9.8 m) skeletal towers. The west pierhead displayed a fixed red light using a sixth-order Fresnel lens from a 34-foot (10.4 m) open-based skeletal tower. Behind this tower was a fog signal building that housed dual 10-inch (25 cm) steam whistles. Three keepers manned these five lights. Two lived in the keeper's duplex and the third in a separate house.

Changes happened at the station. In the 1920s the fog signal building was moved to shore, just north of the main lighthouse, and was converted to air diaphone foghorns. At the same time a light on a skeletal tower replaced the west pier light. In 1934 the government decided to widen and deepen the canal to accommodate larger vessels. In 1935 the inner piers were removed and the

Keweenaw Waterway Upper Entrance Lighthouse

entrance widened from 100 to 500 feet (30 to 150 m) and dredged to 25 feet (7.6 m). The main lighthouse was removed to complete this construction.

A lighthouse to replace the old main one was built on a hill on the west side of the widened canal. While it was being built, the station's barn was remodeled to house the three keepers until the new triplex house was constructed. Today the converted garage is a private cottage. The government also sold the old fog signal building, and the new owners had it moved about a mile (0.8 km) back. The new light station also had another multi-purpose building used for a workshop or garage, for standing watch, and for housing radio beacon equipment.

In 1950 the light was replaced by a white 50-foot (15 m) steel square tower in an art deco style. It was placed on a high cylindrical red crib made of concrete with a reinforced steel perimeter. The light had an 82-foot (25 m) focal plane and was on the east side of the canal at the end of the rebuilt rubble-rock breakwall. The west breakwall received a flashing red light hoisted on a pole that the keepers could operate remotely. The new lighthouse also housed new fog signal equipment.

In the 1970s, when the lighthouse was finally automated, the keepers were removed. Shortly after this the land and the buildings were sold to private ownership. Today lights still mark the upper entrance of the Portage Lake Ship Canal, now known as the Keweenaw Waterway, but they no longer mark it for lake freight as today's freighters are too large to navigate the waterway.

Known Keepers: Earl Edgerton (1868–72), J. Edgerton (1872–74), Sylvanus Mott (1875–77), Samuel Quinn (1879–97), Arthur Carter (1897–1905), Jean Dimet (1905–17), Klass Hamringa (1918–23), James Collins (1945–56).

32 La Pointe (New) Lighthouse

By the 1890s mariners complained that the La Pointe lighthouse on Long Island was too short and too far west to adequately light their way into Chequamegon Bay and the harbor at Ashland along Lake Superior's south shore. The Lighthouse Board's proposed solution was to build two new lighthouses to replace it. The first was to be a taller one to the east of the existing light. The second was to be built at the west end of the island to mark the island's extremity and to mark the turning point into Chequamegon Bay.

Congress made the proposed appropriation of $10,000 for these two lights in March 1895. Both lights were started in 1896 and finished the next year.

The new La Pointe Lighthouse was built about 3,600 feet (1100 m) to the east of the old lighthouse and adjacent to the fog plant, built in 1890–91. Concrete foundation piers were first poured. Then a central iron cylinder, 8 feet (2.4 m) in diameter, was constructed to enclose the tower's spiral iron staircase. This central column had an additional four iron legs that tapered out from around its top and were cross-braced with iron bars for additional stability. A circular watchroom gallery floor was placed on top of this. Work stopped early for the season as the appropriated money was spent and workers could not be paid.

Construction resumed the next year after Congress appropriated another $1,500 in July 1897. The crew installed the cylindrical iron watchroom, the octagonal lantern, and the iron railings for the tower's two galleries. The lantern was equipped with a new fourth-order Fresnel lens that displayed a fixed white light. Although the tower was just 60 feet (18.4 m) high, it had a 70-foot (21.5 m) focal plane and a visibility of 16 miles (26 km). Its daymark was a white tower with a black lantern and gallery.

Other improvements were also introduced to the station at this time. The old keeper's house was converted to a duplex. A rock and crib dock/boat landing was built close to the boathouse, and a new concrete walkway was laid. In 1925 a diesel-powered genera-

Early La Pointe (New) Lighthouse

La Pointe (New) Lighthouse

tor was installed to provide electricity, and the steam whistle was replaced by type-T diaphone foghorns (blast 3 s; silence 27 s). In 1928 a radio beacon was installed and the light was electrified to use an incandescent electric lamp as its illuminant. At this time its characteristic was again changed to a flashing white light (flash 2 s; eclipse 3 s). For the non-navigation season, when the keepers were absent, a small acetylene-powered winter light was attached to the gallery. In 1938 new triplex keeper's quarters were built close to the tower and fog signal building so that the keepers no longer had to walk so far to tend the light. It was a two-story wooden frame house built in the American four-square style.

In 1964 the light was automated and the keepers were removed. The keepers at Devil's Island checked periodically to maintain the light. At some point the Fresnel lens was removed and replaced with a 300 mm optic. When Devil's Island Light Station was automated in 1978, the light was maintained by the Coast Guard.

With the formation of the Apostle Islands National Lakeshore Park in September 1970, the future of other lighthouses on the Apostle Islands was guaranteed, but Long Island was not yet included at this time. Then in 1986 the Park boundaries were enlarged, Long Island was included, and the park became part of the National Park Service. In 1975 the light was placed on the State of Wisconsin's *Register of Historic Sites* and it is also on the *National Register of Historic Places*.

Today the light still shines, although the fog signal building has been removed, the old keeper's house is in ruins, the boathouse is gone, and the other buildings are deteriorating. The light is well off the "tour" path, so it has few visitors, but this could change in the future.

Known Keepers: Joseph Sexton (1897-1921), Knut Olsen (1921–41).

33 La Pointe (Old) Lighthouse

The community of La Pointe is on the southwest side of Madeline Island, one of the Apostle Islands, which are located along the southern shore of Lake Superior. In the mid-1800s La Pointe was the main port for western Lake Superior, and its commerce centered around fur trading.

In March 1853 Congress appropriated $5,000 to build a lighthouse to assist mariners into La Pointe Harbor. A site was chosen near the west end of Long Island, which lay to the south of Madeline Island, to mark the narrow eastern passage into La Pointe. After clear title was obtained, Sweet, Ransom and Shinn of Milwaukee were contracted for a substantial stone tower and attached stone house. They built the light in 1857. However, there was one huge error! They constructed the light on the wrong island, Michigan Island, located to the northeast of Madeline

Island. No one is absolutely sure how this happened but the government refused to pay the contractors until they built a lighthouse on the correct site.

The contractors did so, but because they had already spent the appropriation to build the light on Michigan Island, they had to dig into their own pockets and therefore erected a much cheaper, less substantial structure to fulfill the contract on Long Island. It was a small 1½-story wooden house built on a foundation of squared timbers about 400 yards (365 m) from the western end of the island on its north shore. Its short square wooden tower was built at one end of the dwelling's roof peak, and topped with a square gallery and an octagonal lantern. It displayed a fixed white light using a fourth-order Fresnel lens that had a 52-foot (16 m) focal plane, and the light was visible for 12 miles (19.4 km).

During storms, high winds shifted the sand from underneath the timber foundation, threatening to undermine the structure. To protect against this, in 1864 pipe supports were installed on stone piers beneath the building for added stability. Then, in 1869 a layer of crushed stone was also added on top of the sand around the house to help hold it in place.

In 1868 the empty lighthouse on Michigan Island was activated and equipped with a fixed white light. To avoid confusion, the La Pointe light was changed to a fixed red. Around 1886, the light was converted from whale oil to kerosene, and a brick oil house was constructed to store the volatile illuminant more safely. Later an iron oil house was also built.

Congress granted approval for a fog signal at the station in 1888 but the $15,000 to build it was not appropriated until March 1889. It was situated ¾ mile (1.2 km) to the east of the lighthouse and construction started in October of the following year after clear title had been obtained. A rectangular frame building covered in corrugated iron was built near the shore. It housed duplicate 10-inch (25 cm) steam whistles and the equipment to run them. Finished in January 1891, it was put into operation starting in March and used 12 tons of coal its first year to blast a total of 189 hours. Its characteristic was: blast 5 s: silence 25 s.

To help cope with the added workload of this fog signal, an assistant keeper was hired in 1891. He lived with the keeper and his family until separate accommodations were provided in 1896. At this time the existing keeper's house was jacked up, a brick level was added below it, and the interior was reconfigured to create a duplex for the two keepers. During this whole process the light was still maintained on top of the house.

In the latter part of the 1800s the port of La Pointe dwindled in significance, but that of Ashland, in Chequamegon Bay to the south of Long Island, continued to grow in importance for the shipping of iron ore. By the 1890s ships were increasing in size and mariners complained that the 34-foot (10.4 m) tower was too short and too far west to give them much assistance. The Lighthouse Board proposed a new 70-foot (21.5 m) tower to the east of the existing one to solve the problem, and a smaller tower at Chequamegon Point to mark the island's western end and the turning point for vessels traveling to Ashland. To this end, Congress appropriated $10,000 in March 1895.

When the new La Pointe tower was lit, the old one was extinguished, the tower was removed, and the roof was boarded over and shingled. The keepers continued to use the residence until new quarters were built in 1938. The old structure soon deteriorated, and all that remains today are the crumbling brick walls of its lower level.

Known Keepers: John Haloran (1857–59), John Angus (1859–61) (1871–75), David Cooper (1861–65) (1870–71), Uriah Dawson (1865–67), John Stewart (1867–70), Seth Snow (1876–80), Alexander Davidson (1881–88), Joseph Sexton (1889–96).

34 Manitou Island Lighthouse

Manitou Island lies about 3 miles (4.8 km) east of the tip of the Keweenaw Peninsula, which juts into Lake Superior along its south shore. As lake traffic increased, a light was placed on the small island in 1849 to help guide vessels safely around the peninsula. It was built in a small inlet along the island's northeast end and marked the turning point for both up- and downbound vessels and warned of underwater shoals that surrounded the island.

The first lighthouse was quite basic. In 1848 Congress appropriated money to build three lighthouses on Lake Superior at Copper Harbor, Whitefish Point and Manitou Island at a cost of $7,500 each. The Manitou Light was the last to be built. It had a small detached rubble-stone keeper's house and a 60-foot (18.5 m) tall rubble-stone tower equipped with a birdcage-style lantern and Winslow Lewis lamps and reflectors. It first shone in September 1849 from its 71-foot (21.7 m) focal plane. In 1856 the lantern was replaced by a cast-iron octagonal one that housed a fourth-order Fresnel lens to increase the light's white signal to a 14-mile (22.5 km) visibility.

The old station deteriorated quickly and soon needed replacing. After a government inspection in 1859, Congress appropriated funds for a new light. The Eleventh District Engineer drew up plans for three lighthouses all to use the same plans — Manitou Island, Whitefish Point and Detour Point. Construction started at Manitou Island in 1861. It was an 80-foot (24.6 m) skeletal tower made of prefabricated iron plates that had been numbered before being shipped to the island. The pieces were reassembled on site like a large puzzle to form one of the first skeletal towers built on the Great Lakes. Its central 6-foot (1.8 m) wide cylindrical column was raised off the ground and lined with wood to prevent condensation. It contained a spiral iron staircase to provide access to the lantern.

A third order Fresnel lens made by Henri LePaute of Paris featured six bull's-eye flash panels that created the light's distinctive characteristic of a fixed white light varied by a white flash every 60 seconds. The light was visible for 17 miles (27.5 km). The central column, lantern and galleries were supported by four tubular iron legs that extended out and down to brace the structure. The legs were bolted to concrete pads at ground level for stability. These legs were in turn braced with horizontal and diagonal iron cross-bracing equipped with turnbuckles. When it was finished the old stone tower and house were razed.

Congress had appropriated $5,000 in March 1871 to build a fog signal building at this station but it was not built until 1875. At that time two wood frame fog signal buildings were constructed, one on each side of the tower. They were lined with sheet iron for fire protection and outfitted with steam engines, boilers and 10-inch (25 cm) locomotive whistles. Another assistant keeper was hired to help with them, and having three keepers changed the Manitou Island station into a first-class one.

Other improvements were introduced through the years. In 1895 a brick oil house was built. The fog signals were updated and both placed in the north fog signal building in 1899. In 1901 the tower's color changed from brown to white. In 1913 the candlepower was increased by a new brighter incandescent oil vapor lamp, and its flash characteristic changed to flashing every 10 seconds. In 1925 a radio beacon was installed. In 1927 the keepers also became responsible for tending the automated light on Gull Rock. In 1928 the light and house received diesel-powered generators and batteries. In 1930 a new compressed-air Type F diaphone fog signal was installed. In the 1930s an electric power cable and a telephone line were laid underwater from Copper Harbor on the Keweenaw Peninsula. The keepers received powerboats to replace the sailboats, and supply runs to Copper Harbor became easier, faster and safer. Once the light was automated (1978) using twin diesel generators and the keepers were removed, the station started to deteriorate.

There was a high turnover of keepers at this light, probably due to its isolated location. Its first three keepers had their wives assigned as assistant keepers to provide income and companionship. In 1875 keeper James Corgan lost his job for an interesting reason. When his wife became pregnant, Corgan tried to get another assistant to replace her, but it did not happen. So when his wife went into labor, he bundled her into the sailboat and headed for Copper Harbor and medical assistance 14 miles (22.5 km) away. Unfortunately, there was little wind and their son was born in the sailboat before they arrived. The Lighthouse Board was aghast that a keeper would leave his light unattended regardless of the situation and they removed him as keeper.

In 1882 two new assistants watched from shore as their head keeper drowned. A short distance from the island the keeper's boat overturned and neither assistant did anything to try and help him. Ironically, James Corgan had been rehired in 1877 as the Gull Rock lighthouse keeper, and he helped search for the missing body. He was also temporarily put in charge of the Manitou station until a replacement could be found.

The Manitou Island light still shines today, but a solar-powered 190 mm acrylic optic has replaced its third-order Fresnel lens, which cannot now be located. The station has also been listed on the *National Register of Historic Places* but not on the state one. While this light and its twin at Whitefish Point still exist, the similar skeletal tower at Detour Point no longer exists.

Known Keepers: Angus Smith (1849–56), Elais Bouchard (1856–59), E. Guilbault (1859–61), Henry Letcher (1861–64), Arnold Bennett (1864–66), Charles Corgan (1866–73), James Corgan (1873–75), Henry Pearce (1875–79), George Howard (1879–81), Henry Guilbault (1881), Fredrick Hanstein (1882–84), Nathaniel Fadden (1884–86), Noah Bennetts (1887–93)

Manitou Island Lighthouse

35 Marquette Breakwater Light

When Marquette, Lake Superior, grew as a port, the government built a 2,000-foot (610 m) breakwater out from Lighthouse Point to help protect the harbor. It was constructed from 1867 to 1875 of rock-filled cribs that were planked over. A beacon light was erected to mark the end of this new breakwater. It was a wooden tower moved from Mendota on the Keweenaw Peninsula. This three-story structure displayed a red lens with a kerosene lamp.

Since the Marquette lightkeeper was also responsible for tending this light, a wooden catwalk was placed on top of the breakwater for his safety — but it stopped 50 feet (15.3 m) short of the lighthouse. In 1886 a fierce three-day November storm washed away the breakwater light and much of the catwalk and blew the tower onto the beach. It was able to be repaired, and returned to service.

Marquette Breakwater Light

In 1890 a new breakwater was built and extended to 3,000 feet (915 m). Its unique construction allowed for a tunnel 6 feet (1.8 m) high to be built inside, making a much safer walk for the keeper. Stone rubble was placed along the seaward side to reduce water impact. A new tower with a sixth-order red lens and gas lantern was placed to mark the end of the breakwater. It had a visibility of 8.5 miles (13.7 m).

When electricity arrived at Marquette, the Detroit Lighthouse Office decided to try electrifying the breakwater light in 1898. A heavy electric cable was run inside a wooden conduit to protect it from moisture. This was laid inside the access tunnel in the breakwater. Despite a month's delay caused by a storm, the light was successfully hooked up by July 17, making this perhaps the first light on the Great Lakes to be electrified. Ironically, early hydro power was poor and during its frequent blackouts the keeper still had to wend his way out to the breakwater light to put the old kerosene lamp inside the lens until the electricity was restored.

In 1908 another breakwater extension was completed. Also on July 8 of that year the keeper's title officially changed from keeper of the Marquette Light Station to keeper of the Marquette Light Station and Marquette Breakwater Light.

Since the old light now sat in the middle of the breakwater, a new light was built to mark the new end. It was a square pyramidal skeletal tower with its upper portion enclosed in steel sheeting to form a service room. It was topped with an octagonal iron lantern and had an overall height of 36 feet (11 m). After a new fourth-order Fresnel lens was installed at the main light, its old lens was moved to the new breakwater light. It was lit on September 12 and shone with a red incandescent electric bulb. An electrically operated fog bell had also been installed at the end of the breakwater, and the Marquette power company ran cables for both the light and the bell up to the keeper's dwelling so that they could be switched on and off easily. With the completion of the new breakwater light, the old one was removed.

In 1985 the Coast Guard removed the breakwater light. Its fourth-order lens and iron lantern are on display at the Marquette Maritime Museum. A white pole with a light inside a modern plastic optic now marks the end of the breakwater.

36 Marquette Harbor Lighthouse

Marquette Harbor, once known as Iron Bay, is a natural harbor along the south shore of Lake Superior. It started to become a shipping center in the mid-1800s after the Marquette Range iron deposits were discovered. Also about this time, shipping on Lake Superior increased significantly due to the opening of the Soo Canal in 1855, making Lake Superior accessible to the other Great Lakes.

A lighthouse was needed at Marquette to guide vessels safely into the harbor and to warn of a rocky reef off the point. Its first lighthouse, a short rubble-stone tower and separate keeper's dwelling, was built in 1853 on a point of land that has since become known as Lighthouse Point. It used seven Winslow Lewis lamps and 14-inch (35 cm) reflectors. This was one of the first lighthouses built on Lake Superior. In 1856 it was given a sixth-order Fresnel lens, displayed a fixed white light, and was visible for 10 miles (16.2 km).

Then in 1865 Congress appropriated $13,000 to build a new lighthouse to replace the old one, which had deteriorated beyond repair. The new light, built in 1866, was a 1½-story dwelling with a center front light tower. Designed by the Army Corps of Engineers, it used the same set of plans as other lighthouses like Grand Island North, Granite Island, Huron Island, Gull Rock, Copper Harbor, and Ontonagon, which were all built from 1866 to 1868. (They were commonly described as schoolhouse-style lights.) As the lighthouse was built on solid rock, space for a foundation had to be blasted.

The stone foundation, with 20-inch (0.5 m) thick walls, was just large enough to provide room for a water storage cistern and a fruit cellar. The outer walls had an air space or cavity in them to keep the cellar's contents from freezing. The brick house walls were 12 inches (0.3 m) thick. The first floor had a small bedroom for the keeper and his wife, a kitchen, an oil room and a woodshed. A cistern under the woodshed collected rainwater from the gutters. Drinking water came from the lake until 1894, when town water became available. The top half-story or attic had a large bedroom for children and a storage area.

The square tower was built 38 feet (11.6 m) high, making it 78 feet (24 m) above the lake. Forty-two iron steps and four landings spiraled up to the white, iron, decagonal lantern, which was topped by a red dome and a ventilator ball. The back six panels of the lantern were blacked out, and five brass ventilators in the lantern regulated the airflow. A fourth-order Fresnel lens made by Barbier, Benard and Turenne of Paris housed a kerosene lamp and produced a light with a visibility up to 19 miles (30.6 km). In 1870 the arc of illumination was deemed too small, so its 144-degree arc was increased to an arc of 216 degrees and only four lantern panels were blacked out.

The main lighthouse was lucky in 1868. When fire swept the town, destroying most of the buildings, the lighthouse survived, perhaps due to its brick and stone construction or its rocky location by the water. At any rate, it is now one of the oldest structures in the city.

There were fog signals 300 feet (92 m) out on the point in front of the lighthouse. Although their date of origin is somewhat

Marquette Harbor Lighthouse

Register for Historic Sites. In 1965 $40,000 was budgeted to refurbish the lighthouse, including painting the outside a bright red, perhaps for the first time in history.

The lighthouse foghorn was removed in 1970, and the radio signal beacon tower was later removed as well. In 1983 the Coast Guard dynamited the fog signal building. In 1994 the lighthouse was placed on the *National Register of Historic Places.* In 1996 the U.S. Coast Guard stopped using the lighthouse to house personnel, and in 1998, with the Coast Guard's permission, the lighthouse was opened for tours given by staff from the nearby Marquette Maritime Museum.

Before 1891 keepers were frequently assigned through political appointments and were often incompetent as a result. In 1859 a Peter White reported on one such keeper to the Secretary of the Lighthouse Board:

"Great complaint is made about the keeper of the light at this place. He is a habitual drunkard, frequently thrashes his wife and throws her out of doors. He has several times failed to light up till near morning — last night he did not light up until midnight – it was a dark stormy night. There are nine steamers coming into this harbour about twice a week each — and upward of twenty sail vessels in the iron ore trade lying in this port — constantly arriving and departing — therefore it is quite important that the light should be kept by a sober man as well as an efficient one. Certain 'Pot House' politicians here have recommended to the collector at MacKinac the appointment of Henry Graveraet — an old man of over seventy years, dissipated and an imbecile, and we protest most earnestly and respectfully against any such appointment." In 1891, McGuire's wife was appointed assistant keeper, but since McGuire had to hire a man to do the work she was supposed to do, he finally requested her "de-appointment." In 1891 the keeper earned $600 a year and his assistant $450.

Many vessels foundered in the area. On October 31, 1911, the steamer *D. Leuty* ran aground one night on a reef directly off the Marquette lighthouse because it took too long to get the steam foghorns operational. The lifesaving station safely removed the crew but the *D. Leuty* broke up on the rocks. The hull sank and the stern was taken to Middle Island Point and converted into a unique summer cabin. White and gray buoys that can be seen from the shore mark the wreck today.

In 2002 the Marquette Maritime Museum obtained a 30-year lease for the lighthouse from the Coast Guard. Then, with help from local high school students, volunteers began lighthouse restoration toward a common goal of returning the lighthouse to its condition at the turn of the twentieth century.

The Marquette Lighthouse is still operational today using a modern 300 mm type acrylic aerobeacon. Marquette is proud of its history and has a history to be proud of.

Known Keepers: Harvey Moore (1853–57), John Roussain (1857–59), R Graverat (1859–61), Nelson Truckey (1861–62), Anastasia Truckey (1862–65), John Cowles (1865–69), Clarke Earle (1869–73), Samuel Barney (1873–77), Phillip Morgan (1877–81), Captain Patrick H. McGuire (1881–93), Captain William Wheatley (1894–98), Robert Carlson (1899–1900), Charles Kimball (1903–25), Frank Sommer (1925–47), Stanley Clark (1947–51).

unclear, the first one was installed about 1873. In 1881 a duplicate fog signal was completed. The two buildings were built side by side on a small crib landing in the lake. The signals were 10-inch (25 cm) steam-powered sirens. To protect these buildings from battering lake storms, a 10-foot (3 m) stone and concrete wall 4 feet (1.2 m) thick was built to the north and northwest. A wooden catwalk connected the keeper's house to the fog signals. In 1901 the whistles gave two 5-second blasts each minute.

In 1886 a fierce, three-day November storm severely damaged the fog signal buildings and the catwalk necessitating repairs and reinforcement. In 1888 the steamer *Arizona*, on fire and carrying barrels of acid, collided with the breakwater but its crew managed to escape safely onto the breakwater. Then a tug pulled the vessel back out into the harbor, where it burned to the waterline.

By now there were two assistant keepers at the light. The main keeper tended the lights while his assistants operated the fog signals. The assistants lived in town until accommodations were provided for them. A one-story assistants' house, added sometime in the 1880s, was built below the hill of the lighthouse. Then in 1896 the barn was converted to a keeper's dwelling. Also prompted by the severe storm of November 1886 was a lifesaving station that was built on site and ready for service in 1891.

The Marquette lighthouse underwent many changes into the twentieth century. In 1902 dormers were added to increase space and light and in 1906 a second story was added. A tramway brought necessary wood and coal up the steep incline behind the lighthouse. In 1908 an incandescent oil vapor lamp replaced the kerosene lamp. In 1915 the breakwater was extended again, and was completed in 1919, along with a new light on a steel tower. In the 1920s a concrete catwalk to the fog signals replaced the old wooden one. In 1927 electricity was brought in from the city, and the light was automated. At some point the two fog signal buildings were replaced by one red brick building that housed a compressed air diaphone fog signal powered by electric motors. In 1928 a radio beacon was installed.

In 1939 the U.S. Coast Guard took over from the U.S. Lighthouse Service. During World War II the Marquette Coast Guard Station became a recruit training station, for about 300 recruits. In 1969 the light was listed on the State of Michigan's

37 Menagerie Island Lighthouse

Thanks to the discovery of copper on Isle Royale and the Keweenaw Peninsula, lake traffic to these areas of Lake Superior increased significantly in the mid-1800s. Also, vessels could seek shelter from unrelenting Superior storms in the lee of Isle Royale, but vessels traveling the south shore risked an encounter with many hidden, jagged reefs, and so mariners called for the area to be lit. Congress responded by appropriating $20,000 to build a light on Menagerie Island in 1873. An 1874 survey chose this island because it was halfway along Isle Royale's south side where it would mark the reef and the entrance to Siskiwit Bay, a major harbor on Isle Royale for shipping copper. The light was planned by the Eleventh District Engineer, Major Godfrey Weitzel, and then built in 1875.

Both the tower and the keeper's house were built of red Jacobsville sandstone quarried from the Keweenaw Peninsula. The 55-foot (16.8 m) octagonal tower had a base diameter of 16 feet (4.9 m) and walls 40 inches (1 m) thick. These decreased gradually in thickness as they ascended the gently tapering tower until they were only 10 inches (25 cm) thick at the top. Inner and outer tower walls had a two-inch air space between them. The open-iron, self-cleaning stairs spiraled up to the decagonal lantern that housed a fourth-order Fresnel lens made in Paris by Henri LePaute. The lens used an oil-burning lamp to create a fixed white light with a focal plane of 72 feet (22 m) and was visible for 15 miles (24.2 m). The tower was whitewashed to increase its visibility. The stone cellar of the keeper's house was built above the rock surface of the island, and the house was attached to the tower by an 8-foot (2.5 m) enclosed passageway. The 1½-story house, with its hipped roof covered in cedar shake shingles, had iron shutters to protect the glass windows from pounding waves. This station never had a fog signal or electricity. The light was first lit on October 19, 1875.

The first keeper was William Stevens (1875–78). His assistant was John Malone, a young Irishman who had helped build the lighthouse. In 1878 Malone became the "principal" keeper at $620 a year. Rumors tell of his superiors preferring married keepers, and that in response, Malone sailed to Hancock in search of a bride. He succeeded and married a young Irish girl, Julia Shea, in 1880. She was 20 years old and he was 35. They raised 13 children at the island. The Malones were noted for naming their children after lighthouse inspectors. One year when there were two inspectors, Julia even had twins so she could use both names.

The keepers were creative in supplementing their government food supplies with fish, fowl, game, and berries, vegetables and potatoes grown in a garden on nearby Wright Island. A family cow was even taken by boat to a neighboring island to graze. Some years their gull egg gathering netted over 1,000 eggs. Logbook entries showed them eating thirty eggs a day. Pictures showing barrels on the dock have led to speculation that they may have pickled gull eggs and sold some of their harvest. Another pastime of Malone's was stuffing the birds and animals he had killed — his prize was a large lynx. He also took parties of excursionists on tours of the area in the Malone family fishing schooner, the *North Belle*, until it sank one winter in Wright Island Cove.

Malone's lightkeeping season usually went from May until November. On October 18, 1878, he logged: "Awful cold — everything freezing, island looks like an iceberg." On November 10,

Menagerie Island Lighthouse

1884 he wrote: "It is most impossible to stop here for we have to cut the ice off the ways everyday or we could not launch our boat." Malone stayed at his station for 34 years, showing his success in dealing with its isolated location. In 1910 he transferred to the Pipe Island Station in the St. Mary's River, near Sault Ste. Marie. Interestingly, his pay dropped to $552 a year from his 1878 salary of $620. While he tended the light at Menagerie Island, Julia was his assistant keeper. When they left the island, his son John Albert Malone took over as keeper until 1912.

The light was automated in 1913 through the use of acetylene and a sun valve, but the keeper was kept on for a time. In 1931 Congress authorized the establishment of Isle Royale as a national park. In 1993 the fourth-order lens was removed, as it had a missing prism, and a modern solar-powered optic replaced it. The Fresnel lens was given to the Isle Royale National Park.

Tour boats for the area will show visitors the light, other lights, and the sunken remains of the excursion steamer *America*, which went down in 1928.

Known Keepers: William Stevens (1876–78), John H. Malone (1878–1910), John A. Malone (1910–12).

38 Mendota (Bête Grise) Lighthouse

The Mendota lighthouse is part of the Keweenaw Peninsula, Lake Superior. It is also called the Bête Grise lighthouse as it sits at the head of a bay by the same name. In French, Bête Grise means "gray beast," which is how the Natives described the fog scuttling in over the water. The Mendota Mining Company mined Mount Bohemia behind Lac La Belle, and to assist the shipping of ingots to the lower lakes areas of Detroit and Chicago for processing, the company cut a canal through the Bête Grise beach for shipping access into Lac La Belle.

In March 1867 Congress approved $14,000 for a white wooden skeletal lighthouse to be built at the end of the south pier in 1868. Its lantern housed a fifth-order Fresnel lens that displayed a fixed white light from a 42-foot (12.8 m) focal plane for 12 miles (19.5 km). A 1½-story brick keeper's dwelling was built onshore. In 1870 this pier light was deemed ineffective because it was sat too low to be a good coastal light. It was decommissioned, dismantled and moved by the tender *Haze* to Marquette, where it was used on the breakwater.

Mendota (Bête Grise) Lighthouse

The light was first lit on November 25, 1895, using an open flame kerosene-burning lamp. Combined with a fourth-order lens it produced a fixed white light, varied by a white flash every 45 seconds, and had a visibility of 13 3/4 miles (22 km). In October 1896 its characteristic was changed to a fixed white light.

William G. Jilbert, the first keeper of this new light, earned $500 a year. His first night of operation involved winding the weights every hour as there was an obstruction in the weight flue. After he fixed the problem, the weights would run for a five-hour stretch.

Jilbert frequently mentioned in his logbook that life at the station was lonely. As he and his family often remained year round and the canal was not used in the winter, they strung a rope/wooden bridge across the canal. However, it was often treacherous due to ice or the risk of flipping over. It was placed to help the children get to school on the mainland because it was not safe to walk across the ice because of the swift current that flowed beneath it. In 1914 the keeper's log reported sadness: "Baby drowned in river this 5 p.m." Today, reminders of his eight children include the four-seater outhouse (two for adults and two smaller ones for children) and a rope swing that still hangs from the rafters in the top of the barn.

Jilbert had a large family to feed. He grew potatoes and other vegetables, and when a barn was built in 1906, he kept a cow and chickens to augment their food supply. One logbook entry even reported that he butchered a cow and used the meat to provide provisions for three ships that were headed for Canadian waters but were running low on supplies. In 1896 he shoveled sand out from below the house to make a cellar, probably to store vegetables and preserves. In 1920, when the supply tender *Amaranth* sank offshore, keeper Jilbert collected the coal that washed up on the beach to use as fuel in his stove. Coal from this ship still washes up onto the beach today.

About 1913 the light was converted to electricity using a 32-volt storage battery and a 100-watt bulb. In 1933 a new asbestos shingled roof was put on the keeper's house and the light was automated using acetylene as fuel. At this time it was also demanned. Jilbert's last log entry reads: "This is the last entry for this station May Be Forever." The light was decommissioned in 1956, when two breakwater walls were built into the lake at the canal entrance and lights were placed on them.

For some years during the period between 1870 and 1890, an unofficial light marked the Bête Grise Bay area. Henrietta Bergh, whose family lived in a small frame house near the entrance to the canal and operated a commercial fishing business, used to place a kerosene lamp in the small east end gable window that faced the lake, for her husband to find his way into the bay when he was returning after dark. Other fishermen noticed and asked if she would also watch for them and place the light when they were late. Henrietta obliged. Even keepers from Gull Rock and Manitou Island told her how helpful the light was when they got caught traveling at night.

Soon Henrietta kept the light all night, every night. Her husband even made a larger-wick lantern with a bigger oil reservoir to hold enough oil to last through the night without refueling. She tended it faithfully for years, expecting no compensation. The government took note when mariners told of the helpful light at Bête Grise Bay, and her light played a large part in the Lighthouse Board's decision to relight the area in the 1890s. Henrietta kept her light burning until the new lighthouse was lit in November 1895. Although she was not on any pay roster, she was well remembered as this area's first female lighthouse keeper.

In 1892, with increased shipping on Lake Superior, Bête Grise Bay was being used as a refuge for vessels to await fair weather before attempting the trip around the Keweenaw Point. However, at night, the bay was almost inaccessible as Henrietta's light was small and weak. In February 1893 the Lighthouse Board authorized $7,500 for a light be placed near the head of the bay to help guide vessels to safe anchorage after dark. The plan was to use the old keeper's house, but in 1894 it was found to be in such ruin that it could only be used for materials. In March 1895 $7,500 was appropriated for the new lighthouse.

The men and equipment arrived at Bête Grise Bay in September courtesy of the tender *Amaranth*. After putting up a cookhouse and crew quarters, they built the light station, keeper's house, boathouse, oil house, outhouse and sidewalks, all that fall. They used as much material from the old keeper's house as possible, building a T-shaped, combined house and tower. The square 44-foot (13.5 m) tower extended up from the middle of the east side of the 1 1/2-story three-bedroom keeper's house. The bottom and tower were built of yellow brick, the top of the house was covered in cedar shake shingles painted yellow.

Mendota (Bête Grise) Lighthouse Fourth-order Fresnel Lens

The lighthouse was then sold at public auction to Heimo (Paddy) and Margaret Jaaskelainen, who worked hard to preserve it. Paddy saved many stranded boaters and once saved two men from drowning. He also insisted that passing boaters have life jackets for all children on board, especially if he thought the boat was overloaded. When Paddy died in 1996, the property went up for sale again. The asking price was $500,000 but the family was willing to sell the property only to someone who would preserve the reservation.

In 1997, Gary Kohs, owner of Fine Art Models in Birmingham, Michigan, purchased the lighthouse and made giant steps in restoring it to its original condition. Among other interventions, he relocated the original fourth-order Fresnel lens from a basement in Sault Ste. Marie and had it refurbished to working order.

Kohs hosted an Open House in July 1998 that attracted 3,000 visitors from 39 states and 23 countries. The weekend highlight was the relighting of the light on July 5, 1998 at 9:45 p.m. as a private aid to navigation. Locals say the relit light with its 2-second white flash and eclipse of 18 seconds is far easier to spot than the breakwater lights because it is higher.

At first sight from across the canal, the tower and the lighthouse's pale yellow walls, high peaked roof, 1½-story construction, small-paned windows and ornamental trim, give it a quaint English-cottage look unlike any other lighthouse on the Great Lakes. A replica flagpole placed on the old base flies a 44-star American flag from 1895, the year when the lighthouse was established. In the interior, baseboards with wooden finials at the corners, transome windows, bedroom ledges and tin ceilings are all original, as is a top-of-the-line Garland coal-burning iron and nickel stove. Many of the "treasures" had been left right in the old buildings he had purchased.

Other of Koh's ideas include developing a conservancy to protect the land of the Keweenaw Peninsula in its pristine state, and registering the lighthouse with the Children's Wish Foundation. In his words: "I don't feel that I own the lighthouse. I'm only the caretaker. I enjoy sharing the lighthouse with others." With visionary men like this, this lighthouse's heritage will remain an integral part of our history.

Known Keepers: Henry Kuchli (1869–70), William Kirby (1870), Henrietta Bergh (1870–95 unofficially), William Jilbert (1895–1933).

39 Michigan Island (New) Lighthouse

Lake traffic changed after the turn of the twentieth century as vessels became longer and traveled further offshore. The Lighthouse Board recommended a taller lighthouse at Michigan Island to mark the eastern area of the Apostle Islands, and to mark a turning point for downbound vessels heading to Ashland.

Many changes occurred at Michigan Island in 1928–29. In 1928 a new brick powerhouse was built to house the diesel-powered electrical generator that supplied electricity for the new light, to operate a winch hoist to haul a tram car along the newly installed tramway, and to operate the radio beacon signal that replaced the fog signal in 1929. A larger red brick keeper's house was built. A 112-foot (34.2 m) white skeletal iron tower, which had been built in 1880 and removed from Schooner's Ledge on the Delaware River near Philadelphia in 1919, was brought to Michigan Island in 1928. The tower was reassembled on new concrete footings to provide a 170-foot (52 m) focal plane for the 3½-order Fresnel lens that was transferred from the old lantern. Using a new electric bulb with the equivalent of 24,000 candlepower, the new light, lit in 1929, was visible for 22 miles (35.5 km).

With less work to be done at the station, the assistant keeper was let go in 1939. Then by 1943 the light was automated and the keeper was also let go. In 1970 the lighthouse became part of the newly formed Apostle Islands National Lakeshore Park. In 1975 the Fresnel lens was removed and replaced by a DCB 224 aero-beacon, which has since been replaced by a 300 mm acrylic optic.

Today the Michigan Island light still shines, the light is listed on the *National Register of Historic Places* and its 3½-order Fresnel lens is on display at the Apostle Islands National Lakeshore Visitor Center. The towers on Michigan Island represent the first and the last lighthouses built on the Apostle Islands.

Known Keepers: Edward Lane (1929–37), Robert Westveld (1937–43).

40 Michigan Island (Old) Lighthouse

In the mid-1800s the busiest port in western Lake Superior was La Pointe on Madeline Island, one of the Apostle Islands along Superior's south shore. In order to light the southern channel leading to La Pointe and its bustling fur-trading community, Congress appropriated $5,000 in March 1853. After title for the site was obtained, the task of building the lighthouse was contracted to Sweet, Ransom and Shinn of Milwaukee. In 1856 a lighthouse was built and finished late in the season. But by mistake it was built on Michigan Island, instead of Long Island where it was supposed to be constructed.

It will likely never be known why this happened, but the upshot was that the government rejected the lighthouse built on Michigan Island for "non-conformity to the contract" and refused to pay the contractor until he built a lighthouse at the proper location on Long Island. The contractor did so, but built a far less substantial tower since he had to pay for it out of his own pocket.

The lighthouse at Michigan Island was a combined tower and keeper's house. It was a small 1½-story dwelling with a gently tapering 44-foot (13.5 m) conical tower attached to the south end of the house. Both house and tower were made of rough stone and masonry, with the exterior walls stuccoed over and whitewashed to increase durability and visibility. The roof of the house had one dormer window on each side and wooden shingles. Three windows ascended the tower for interior light, and the tower was topped with an octagonal iron lantern.

It is debatable whether this light was ever lit after it was first built. If it was, it was only manned for one year and then was extinguished when the proper light was built and lit on Long Island. Then in 1858 the lantern was removed from the Michigan Island lighthouse and moved for use at the Windmill Point light-

Michigan Island New and Old Lighthouses

house on Lake St. Clair. The Michigan Island lighthouse sat empty, neglected and deteriorating for more than ten years.

In 1869 the government decided to light the northeastern area of the Apostle Islands as more lake traffic ventured around them to Duluth and Superior. They chose the already built lighthouse on Michigan Island to light the area. Congress appropriated $6,000 in July 1868 to supply a new lantern and lens, and refurbish the station, including the installation of a 3½-order Fresnel lens, and the light was lit on September 15, 1869. As the tower was built on an 85-foot (26 m) clay bluff, its fixed white light had a focal plane of 129 feet (39.3 m) and a 20-mile (32.4 km) visibility.

It was a very isolated area for keepers to be stationed. Robert Carlson became keeper in 1893 and moved to the island with his wife, Anna, three small children, and his brother. Rather than brave Superior's autumn waters returning to the mainland with the children, they decided to spend the winter on the island at the lighthouse. Early one morning the men went ice-fishing expecting to be back by suppertime. Anna kept their meal warm and the fires banked. The next morning she had to milk the cow, a task she had never done before. She was so afraid that she chopped a hole in the side of the stall big enough for her to reach through and milk the cow. By the third day, on the verge of hysteria, she left the twin nine-month old boys in the care of their two-year-old sister while she ventured out to look for the men. She found nothing. Resigning herself to widowhood, she flew a white sheet from the tower in hopes that someone might see it and come to her rescue. Unfortunately, the navigation season had closed.

The next day, she was astonished to hear her husband's voice calling from outside. Apparently the ice the men were fishing on had broken loose and started drifting. Luckily, the storm winds carried them to Madeline Island instead of out to open water and they were able to jump across the floes to the island, where they found an old fishing camp. They built a fire and survived by making a hot gruel mixture from left-behind flour. The next day they found a leaky old boat onshore and were able to make it usable by patching it with tar and oakum. They then returned to Michigan Island, sometimes rowing on open water and sometimes pushing the boat across frozen ice.

While Anna hated the island's isolation, keeper Ed Lane and his family loved it, and he spent 35 years at the light, making his tenure the longest of any keeper at any of the lighthouses on the Apostle Islands. His daughter, Edna, remembers it as a wonderful place to live. The children's jobs included piling firewood, keeping the woodbox in the kitchen full, grinding coffee beans every morning, and carrying lake water for their mother's gardens.

Edna admired her father's ethic. Once, when a lumber company wanted to cut down a huge pine tree on the edge of the property, her father would not allow it because it was the place where the eagles nested. When he went fishing he always saved a fish to throw in the air for the eagles and the birds never missed catching their free meal.

By the twentieth century marine traffic to the west end of Lake Superior steadily increased and vessels became larger and traveled farther offshore. To better serve these vessels a new, taller light was planned and a fog signal was installed at Michigan Island. When the new light was lit in 1929, the old one was extinguished.

Known Keepers: Roswell Pendergast (1869–74), William Herbert (1870), Pliny Rumill (1875–83), John Pasque (1883–93), Robert Carlson (1893–98), Alexander McLean (1898), Charles Brown (1898–1902), Edward Lane (1902–29).

Minnesota Point Lighthouse

41 Minnesota Point Lighthouse

The opening of the Soo Locks in 1855 finally connected Lake Superior to other shipping routes, and marine traffic on Lake Superior boomed. The St. Louis River emptied into Lake Superior at its western end and divided the states of Minnesota and Wisconsin. Rival ports, Duluth and Superior, developed on either side of the river mouth. In the mid-1800s there was only one way to enter the bay to either port, as the bay had a natural sandbar 9 miles (14.6 km) long blocking its opening to the lake proper. The northern part of the bar was known as Minnesota Point and the southern part as Wisconsin Point. The natural 2,000-foot (610 m) cut between them was called the Superior Entry, and all vessels traveling to Duluth or Superior had to use it. Congress appropriated $15,000 for a lighthouse on Minnesota Point in August 1854.

The contract was awarded to Captain R.G. Coburn of Superior. The lighthouse was built near the tip of Minnesota Point with a cylindrical 45-foot (13.7 m) red brick tower, which was mortared and whitewashed on the outside. It was topped with a decagonal lantern that had five glass panes and five blacked-out rear panels. Housing a fifth-order Fresnel lens, it exhibited a white light from a 50-foot (15.3 m) focal plane for a visibility of 10 miles (16.2 km). For fog, a human-blown tin foghorn was supplied.

The 1½-story keeper's house and attached covered passageway to the tower were also made of red brick but were not whitewashed. This lighthouse was very similar to the one built at Jacobsville in 1870 and the same plans may have been used at both locations. The station's construction cost totalled $13,675. Over the years the light became nicknamed the "Old Standby."

To better service the port of Duluth a private canal was dug at the base of Minnesota Point and completed in 1871. It was 150 feet (46 m) wide and 16 feet (4.8 m) deep, flanked by piers on each side and became known as the Duluth Ship Canal. Superior sued Duluth for building the canal, as it was feared that the canal would divert the river's water, negatively affect the Superior Entry, and thus negatively affect shipping to Superior. The legal decision was to let Duluth keep the canal, but it had to build a dyke through the middle of the bay so that Superior Entry was not affected by the canal. However, since this dyke would cut Superior off from the railroad terminus at Duluth, Superior sued again to have the dyke removed and the canal plugged, but they lost.

The government undertook harbor improvements for the two ports. The Superior Entry was to be deepened and sided with rock breakwaters to protect the passage. Since the cut had moved further south over the years, when the breakwaters were completed, a new pierhead lighthouse (the Superior Entry Lighthouse) was placed on the breakwater that stretched along the tip of Minnesota Point. Being closer to the cut, it better marked the channel, and the old Minnesota Point keeper's house was used as housing for the new light. The government removed the lens, lantern and circular iron staircase from the old tower and installed the old lens in the new pierhead light, which was first lit on September 1, 1878. The old tower was left standing as it marked the "zero-point" as laid out by Lt. Bayfield's 1823 survey of Lake Superior.

In 1895 the Duluth-Superior River and Harbor Commission was formed and the government viewed the two ports as one. After this the rivalry between the two stopped and both concentrated on working together to improve shipping to "their" port. In 1902 the old Minnesota Point reservation was chosen as the government site for its Duluth Buoy Depot. The depot was built in 1903.

Abandoned, stripped and empty, the old Minnesota Point tower gradually deteriorated. In 1974 it was added to the *National Register of Historic Places*. While it still stands today, surrounded by a chain-link fence to protect it from vandals, it has also been listed on *Lighthouse Digest*'s "Doomsday List" for endangered lighthouses. The old tower is crumbling and has lost most of its whitewashed-mortar exterior finish. The tower and its surrounding land are owned by the Army Corps of Engineers–Detroit District, so there are no private plans to restore it.

Known Keepers: R. Barrett (1859–61), S. Palmer (1861–71), Thomas Wilson (1871–73), Horace Saxton (1878–83), Henry Grover (1883–85), Patrick McCann (1886), George Malone (1887–88), Robert Sanborn (1889–1902), Thomas Doody (1902–).

42 Munising Range Lights

In the mid-1800s a light shone from the north side of Grand Island along the southeast shore of Lake Superior to warn mariners of the island as well as to help guide them into the safe harbor of Munising Bay. In 1868 lights were placed to mark the western and eastern ends of a channel between the island and mainland which led more directly into the bay. As larger ships plied the water and the channel became too small for them to use safely, they entered the bay from the east side of Grand Island. However, they had no light to guide them, as they could not see the island light at the east end of the channel until they were almost beside it. In 1905 the Lighthouse Board requested range lights to mark the

eastern approach into Munising Bay, and Congress appropriated funds in 1907. The Lighthouse Board had convinced them it would be cheaper to build the range lights than to refurbish the existing channel light and then built the range lights in a few years anyway.

Congress appropriated $15,000 to build the station. The contract for the metalwork was awarded to the Champion Iron Company of Kenton, Ohio. The front range light was placed on a small parcel of low land close to shore. Its tower was a conical 58-foot (17.7 m) riveted steel plate tower with a circular gallery and an octagonal lantern. The tower was brick-lined. From a 79-foot (24 m) focal plane the lantern displayed an Adams and Westlake 23-inch (58 cm) red reflector light. The rear range light was a 33-foot (10 m) conical riveted steel plate tower with no gallery and only one window to display its twin Adams and Westlake 23-inch (58 cm) red reflector light. It too was brick-lined. While it was a shorter tower, it was built on the much higher ground of the bluffs surrounding the bay, so it had a much higher focal plane of 107 feet (32.7 m). The lights were lit with kerosene and a red brick oil house with a stamped tin roof was built to store the highly flammable fuel.

When these range lights were first lit on October 30, 1908, they made the safety of Munising Bay available to all large vessels during inclement weather. Also, when they were lit, the old east channel light on the southern side of Grand Island was stripped of all valuables and abandoned.

The keeper's dwelling was a detached 1½-story brick house. Plans for this house were also used at Grand Marais and Pointe aux Barques light stations on the west side of Lake Huron. With the arrival of electricity, probably sometime in the 1920s, the lights began using hydro as their illuminant. Electricity supplied by the local Munising utility powered incandescent electric bulbs in the lights to produce 35,000 candlepower with a 19-mile (30 km) visibility. At a later point, the reflectors were switched for locomotive style headlamps. When the lights were automated, the keepers were removed but the U.S. Coast Guard continued to use the keeper's dwelling.

In 2002 ownership of the lights was transferred from the U.S. Coast Guard under the National Historic Lighthouse Preservation Act to the Picture Rocks National Lakeshore. Their primary purpose for acquisition was to continue maintenance and upkeep of the house and the towers. The future of these range lights seems secure. The lights continue to function today as an active aid to navigation.

Known Keepers: George Prior (1909–12), Alfred Evensen (1913–40), Thomas Robinson (1940).

Munising Rear Range Light

Munising Front Range Light

43 Ontonagon Lighthouse

During the 1840s the Ontonagon River area of Lake Superior boomed with the development of copper mining after Michigan State geologist Douglas Houghton reported a huge copper boulder in the vicinity. Eventually this rock was put on display at the Smithsonian Institution in Washington. Miners surged to the river, and the community of Ontonagon developed at the river mouth. As more and more copper was shipped from the river, the government was petitioned to light the port. In April 1847 Congress granted money to purchase land for a lighthouse and then in September 1850 appropriated $5,000 for the lighthouse.

The first lighthouse at the mouth of the Ontonagon River was built by the Detroit contractor C.F. Chittenden. Little is known about this first lighthouse except that it was a nine-room structure, used Winslow Lewis lamps and parabolic reflectors, burned whale oil, and was first lit on August 26, 1853, by the light's first keeper, Samuel Peck. In 1857 the lantern was upgraded with a fifth-order Fresnel lens.

In 1866 the lighthouse was replaced by a schoolhouse style light typical of the times. The 1½-story yellow brick keeper's house and 34-foot (10.4 m) square tower were placed on a high stone foundation to prevent flooding of the keeper's living area, as the structure was situated on low ground close to the west side of the river mouth. The sides of the house had large rectangular windows, each with twelve small panes. The gable roof had a hipped dormer on each side near its west end peak.

The decagonal iron lantern's three rear panels were blacked out. The fifth-order Fresnel lens was imported from the old light. The lantern had five brass wall vents, a top ventilator, and an iron trapdoor in the lantern floor to control the airflow. Its murette, or lower walls, were lined with tongue and groove wainscoting to help prevent condensation. The tower's spiral iron staircase provided entry to the three levels of the house and to the lantern, which displayed a fixed white light visible for 13 miles (21 km). This station cost $14,000.

The first keeper of the new lighthouse, Thomas Stripe, was also the last keeper of the old light. In spite of only having one arm, he kept the light faithfully for nineteen years. He had lost his arm during a Fourth of July celebration in 1859 when he saved another man's life by pushing him out of the line of fire of a cannon being fired as part of the festivities. Even with just one arm he was capable of all lighthouse duties, including cleaning the outside lantern glass. To do this, he stabilized himself with a metal hook attached to a belt around his waist and to metal eyes around the lantern, and then used his one good arm to clean the lantern glass. This also helped give him plenty of upper body and arm strength. He challenged and beat other two-armed men in fights. Local folklore also tells of him organizing a group of dog sleds during the winter of 1855 to rescue Ontonagon's winter provisions, which were stranded on iced in vessels in harbors toward the tip of the Keweenaw Peninsula, when Lake Superior froze over sooner than expected. Residents of Ontonagon would have starved without these supplies. From this exploit keeper Stripe became a legend in his time.

To solve the river mouth's silting problem, the Army Corps of Engineers dredged the entrance and built piers to flank it in 1860.

Ontonagon Lighthouse

The west pier was 650 feet (200 m) long and the east pier 700 feet (215 m). The government decided not to place a light at the end of either pier when they were completed, as the main lighthouse was close enough to mark the entrance. However, sand gradually built up along the west side of the west pier, so that the lighthouse become farther from the shore. The piers needed to be extended into the lake and a pierhead light built.

Further alterations were made at this station. In 1888 a frame woodshed was added along with a 338-gallon (1420 l) brick cistern and a wagon road to connect to the public road nearby. In 1889 an iron gallery was placed around the lantern. In 1890 a brick one-story, 18-foot (5.5 m) square kitchen was added to the back of the east side of the house. At some point the station was outfitted with a hand-operated foghorn (blast 10 s; silence 10 s).

In 1896 the town's wooden sawmill caught fire and high winds quickly spread the fire through the community. While townspeople, including the firemen, ran for their lives, the keeper and his family fervently carried pail after pail of water up to the tower gallery to douse the shingles of their house below to prevent it from burning. They succeeded. The rest of the town was completely gone, however, and never fully recovered. The copper mines had been depleted and the sawmills were not rebuilt.

In 1901 fill was placed to raise the level of the low swampy areas in the road to the lighthouse, and materials were left for an oil house. The lighthouse was now using kerosene, a more volatile fuel, and a 360-gallon (110 l) red brick oil house was built to safely store it. A 1909 picture shows the lighthouse's brick exterior painted avocado green, with shutters and white trim. While the lighthouse was officially electrified in 1938, thanks to its close proximity to the Ontonagon Fiber Company, which already used electricity, it may have been using electricity before this official date.

In 1934 the lighthouse at Fourteen Mile Point had been automated, and looking after its light and equipment became part of the Ontonagon keeper's job. Once a month he would travel to the lighthouse to check it and the fuel level of its acetylene tanks.

The Ontonagon keepers served until automation in 1963 when a new automated foghorn and modern battery-powered light were placed at the end of the east pier. While the old lighthouse officially closed in January 1964, the building was leased to the last keeper, Arnold Huuki, as a residence until he died in 1974.

After its decommissioning, the Fresnel lens was removed, crated, and sent to the Portage Coast Guard Station for safekeeping. However the Coast Guard Commander had it rigged up as a yard light for his residence. Meanwhile, the Ontonagon County Board of Supervisors passed a resolution noting its historical significance and asked the federal government to donate the lens to the county. When their plea was ignored, the official county historian, Fred Dreiss, contacted his congressman to help negotiate the return of the lens. The *Octonagon Herald* as well as a local judge added their influence. Finally their efforts were successful and in October 1965 the Coast Guard notified the Ontonagon County Historical Society that the lens had been declared surplus property and had been donated to the county. Today it is on display at the Ontonagon County Historical Society.

After the lighthouse was decommissioned the Army Corps of Engineers approached the Coast Guard for the land, as they wanted to do work at the river mouth and needed more space. To this end the Coast Guard transferred the land to the Army Corps.

In 1975 archaeological test excavations were made around the lighthouse to determine whether or not the area was ever a prehistoric site. Numerous references to an early historic Chippewa village on the west riverbank led to these test digs. No evidence was found to confirm a prehistoric occupation.

The land around the lighthouse developed as an industrial area and the lighthouse became landlocked by the Smurfit Stone Container Corporation, a brown-paper mill. The east side of the river was owned and operated by Lakeshore Inc., a steel fabrication industry. In 1986 the Department of the Army issued a permit to the U.S. Coast Guard Auxiliary to occupy the lighthouse to serve the navigational interests of the area. They held their meetings, as well as official and public functions, in the lighthouse.

In 1992 the Corps put a new roof on the building and installed a new heating system. The system failed shortly after installation and when the radiators burst the considerable water damage caused the foundation to shift. Local businessmen wanted to tear the lighthouse down and build a replica but the Historical Society became involved and in 1998 the lighthouse permit was modified to allow the Society as co-tenants. They immediately began stabilizing the lighthouse and offered seasonal tours and tours by appointment. In 1999 more than 4,000 people toured the lighthouse.

When the Army decided to relinquish ownership, they approached the village of Ontonagon to see if they would sign a 25-year lease for the lighthouse. The village was interested only if they could move the land-locked lighthouse to a more accessible location. However, since the lighthouse had been placed on the *National Register of Historic Places* in 1995, it could not be moved. At the same time, the Ontonagon County Historical Society did want the historic lighthouse, since it was the oldest remaining building in their village and they fought for years to get it. A new act of Congress, the *National Historic Lighthouse Preservation Act* of 2000 finally helped them by enabling the transfer of a lighthouse to a non-profit historical organization. The Historical Society's Management and Development Plan was accepted, and the lighthouse ownership was transferred to it in December 2000.

With stabilization complete, the Society turned their efforts to restoring and refurbishing the lighthouse to an early 1920s era, which would allow the use of modern amenities such as electricity and indoor plumbing. They also hope to install a walkway along the river to make the land-locked lighthouse more accessible.

Known Keepers: Samuel Peck (1853–59), Michael Spillman (1859–61), Adolphus Schuler (1861–64), Thomas Stripe (1864–83), James Corgan (1883–1919), Charles Henry (1919–22), Earl Hand (1922–25), Frederick Warner (1925–39), James Gagnon (1939–44), Alva Carpenter (1944–45), Arnold Huuki (1945–63).

44 Ontonagon Pierhead Light

The mouth of the Ontonagon River, Lake Superior, was first lit by a shore light in 1853. Later, the mouth was dredged of silt and sand and flanked by wooden piers to help prevent more build-up. Because the west pier was just 650 feet (200 m) long, the east pier 700 feet (215 m) long and the shore light just a shore distance away, the government did not place a pierhead light at this time.

Copper prices fell, copper mining declined, and harbor use dropped significantly until Ontonagon developed sawmills and began to export great quantities of lumber in the late 1870s. To assist harbor entry, the piers were extended into the lake and in 1875 a pierhead light was placed, because the shore light was now too far away. The light was placed on the west pier, although it was the shorter one, to make it easier for the keeper to maintain.

The beacon was a white wooden tower with an open frame bottom and it sat 200 feet (60 m) from the end of the pier. Its iron lantern used a sixth-order Fresnel lens to display a fixed red light from a 27-foot (8.3 m) focal plane for 11 miles (17.8 km).

Sand built up along the west side of the west pier extension just as before, so the piers were again extended and in 1879 the pierhead light was moved out 535 feet (164 m). In 1884 the piers were again extended and the light moved 865 feet (266 m) farther out. A wooden catwalk was built to the light from the end of the old pier because the new extension was 5 feet (1.5 m) lower. In 1893 the light was again moved out by 378 feet (116 m).

In December 1899 a severe storm blasted through the area, ripping the pierhead light from its location and carrying it away in stormy waves. The next navigation season started with a temporary light at the pier end, a square wooden structure with a square lantern that displayed a fixed red lens lantern.

The tender *Amaranth* delivered the new light to Ontonagon in the fall, along with a work crew and materials for installation. It was a square white tapering iron frame tower 26 feet 10 inches (8.2 m) high, which had an enclosed upper section to store materials. The octagonal iron lantern housed a fourth-order Fresnel lens and a kerosene lamp to display a fixed red light from a 31-foot (9.5 m) focal plane for 12 miles (19.4 m).

Ontonagon Pierhead Light

In 1929 electrical cable was laid and connected to Ontonagon's power supply to electrify the light. Its kerosene lamp was replaced by an incandescent light bulb. At an unknown date the tower was equipped with an electrically operated fog siren (blast 3 s; silence 27 s) to replace the hand foghorn. Both light and siren were activated by a switch at the main light.

Commercial fishermen petitioned Congress to also light the end of the east pier in 1948, but this did not happen until the main lighthouse onshore was decommissioned in 1963. At this time a new automated foghorn and modern battery-operated light were installed near the end of the east pier.

Today the wooden piers have been replaced by more durable concrete piers. The east pier is 2,315 feet (710 m) long. The 2,575-foot (790 m) west pier is only 1,300 feet (400 m) beyond the shoreline, due to the build-up of shifting sand along its west side. While the old iron tower still stands near the end of the west pier, its Fresnel lens has been removed and replaced with a 300 mm acrylic optic and it now displays a flashing red light (flash 2 s; eclipse 4 s) for 12 miles (19.4 km).

Known Keepers: See Ontonagon Lighthouse.

Outer Island Lighthouse

45 Outer Island Lighthouse

As east-west traffic increased along Lake Superior's south shore during the mid-1800s in response to the Soo Locks' opening in 1855, more lights were placed to mark the Apostle Islands, an archipelago near Superior's western end. The Lighthouse Board recommended a light on Outer Island for several reasons: it marked the most northeastern part of the islands; it would serve as a coast light for maritime traffic; and it marked a turning point for vessels traveling southward to Ashland. Finally, it marked the submerged Outer Island Shoal, which lay 1½ miles to the north of the island. While a light was first requested for this location in 1869, Congress did not appropriate money until March 1871, at which time they set aside $40,000 for the station.

The lighthouse was designed by Eleventh District Engineer General Orlando M. Poe. Typical of this style, the tower was a tall, gently tapering conical tower set on a solid cut-stone foundation. Its 78-foot (24 m) brick walls rose to support a circular iron gallery that supported a cylindrical iron pedestal room with porthole windows for interior light. The gallery was supported by 16 ornate corbels. The watchroom had four hooded arched windows and extra decorative detailing.

The tower supported a decagonal iron lantern with its own circular gallery for cleaning the glass. The light was outfitted with a third-order Fresnel lens with a band of six bull's eyes around the equator of the lens to produce its characteristic flash pattern of a flash every 90 seconds. The tower's location on a 40-foot (12.2 m) clay bluff gave it a 130-foot (40 m) focal plane and a visibility of 20 miles (32.4 km). This height exposed the tower to storms from the east and keepers reported it swaying.

The keeper's dwelling was a large 2½-story red brick house with hipped roof ends. An enclosed wooden passage provided protected entry to the tower. A spiral iron staircase led up to the lantern. Along its ascent there was a pull-out shelf in the weight pocket of the tower wall to allow the weight to rest during the day and to minimize cable stretch. On the outside the house was left a red brick, but the tower was stuccoed over and whitewashed to increase its daytime visibility. The steam fog signal on the beach completed the station and the light was first lit on October 3, 1874. An identical lighthouse was built in 1874 at Au Sable, which is now part of Pictured Rocks National Lakeshore Park.

By 1875 it was clear that the fog building had to be moved from the beach to the cliff top due to storm damage from Superior's northeast blows. It was now placed about 300 feet (92 m) northwest of the tower. Its 10-inch (25 cm) whistle had a 60-second cycle (blast 8 s; silence 52 s). In 1878 a duplicate fog signal was added in a separate building as a backup. A winch-powered tramway was added in 1884 to move supplies from the boat landing to the fog signal buildings. Then a steam-powered hoisting engine was installed in 1887 to operate the winch. In 1900 the fog signal buildings were combined and the equipment was refurbished. Then in 1929 the whistles were replaced by duplicate Type F diaphone foghorns, powered by diesel engines.

The light's illuminant also changed over time. At first it was whale oil stored in the cellar of the keeper's house. Along with the change to the brighter, cleaner but more volatile kerosene, a brick oil house was built in 1895 to store it away from the station's buildings as a fire precaution. In 1913 an incandescent oil vapor lamp was introduced to vaporize the kerosene and intensify its candlepower from 18,000 to 110,000. Also at this time the light's characteristic was changed to a flashing white light (flash 4.7 s; eclipse 10.3 s). When the station was electrified in 1940, the light's intensity increased to 140,000 candlepower.

Keepers at this light rotated frequently due to its remoteness. During the early 1900s keepers traveled to Bayfield, the closest community, which was 30 miles (48.6 km) away on the mainland, once a month for provisions, mail and newspapers. In between these visits they received no news because telephones, radios and televisions had not yet been invented.

By the 1940s station life had improved. Each keeper received 2–3 days of shore leave per month. Occasionally bad weather extended this a day or two. The two assistant keepers each had two rooms on the second floor for themselves, a bedroom and a kitchen. The rooms were lit with kerosene lamps, although the light for the tower was run by electricity produced by a diesel 110-volt DC generator and a bank of about 50 glass jar storage batteries. Compressed air to operate the foghorn was produced by two, one-cylinder horizontal diesel engines.

The tower was whitewashed every year. The mixture was mixed in a 55-gallon (231 l) drum, and after it cured for a few days all four keepers worked to complete the task. One man handled lines to lower a window-washer-like platform that held the other three men. They used large brushes to quickly whitewash a 5- to 6-foot downward swathe of the tower. Once they had reached the bottom, the platform was moved over and raised to repeat the process until the job was done. It was one day's work.

In 1961 the station was automated, its Fresnel lens was removed, and a modern solar-powered 12-volt DC optic was installed. Keepers from the Devil's Island Station checked the light periodically to maintain the equipment. When this station was also automated in 1978, the Coast Guard maintained the light.

Gradual erosion became a significant problem at Outer Island. By 1987 the lighthouse was 50 feet (15.3 m) from the clay cliff and *Lighthouse Digest* had added the lighthouse to their "Doomsday List" in 2000. After the Department of the Interior did an erosion study in 1999, steps were taken to stem erosion and $600,000 was appropriated for work to start in 2002 after similar work was completed at the Raspberry Island Lighthouse. But at Outer Island the work was postponed until 2008.

Today the light is still an active aid to navigation but it now uses a 190 mm solar-powered optic that was installed in 1992. Its fog signal is no longer active but the fog signal building still houses its diaphone equipment. Being part of the Apostle Islands National Lakeshore Park since 1970 has almost certainly guaranteed the future well-being of this light station, and it has been listed on the *National Register of Historic Places*.

Known Keepers: A. Henry (1876–81), John Armbruster (1881–83, 1884–87), John Leonard (1888–96).

46 Passage Island Lighthouse

Port Arthur and Fort William developed as shipping terminals from the Canadian west during the latter years of the 1800s. To facilitate this increased shipping, mariners called for a light in the narrow 3-mile (4.8 km) channel between Blake Point on Isle Royale's northern tip and Passage Island to the northeast. The Canadian government made application to the American government for the right to build a lighthouse on Passage Island. The Lighthouse Board made its first request for an appropriation for a lighthouse at this location in 1871, but Congress did not respond favorably until 1875, when they agreed to appropriate $18,000 for this lighthouse if the Dominion of Canada built a lighthouse on the dangerous Colchester Reef in Lake Erie.

Because a lighthouse on Passage Island would be so close to Canadian waters, Congress thought it would serve more Canadian vessels than American. On July 17, 1879, the *Thunder Bay Sentinel* reported that William Smith, Canada's Minister of Marine was "strongly impressed with the urgent necessity for a light on Passage Island, for the convenience of steamers plying to and from this port [Port Arthur, now Thunder Bay], and [would] recommend his Department to purchase a piece of land from the U.S. Government and put up a light, if Washington authorities cannot be induced to undertake the duties." While it is not known which government influenced the other the most, the Canadian government did start a

lighthouse on Colchester Reef by 1880 and the American government did release the money for Passage Island Lighthouse in 1880.

The lighthouse was built on the southern tip of Passage Island where it best marked the deepest northern edge of the channel. In 1881 the lighthouse tender *Warrington* delivered the supplies and work crew. The lighthouse was in a Norman Gothic style and followed the same plans as the lighthouses at Chambers Island (1868), Eagle Bluff (1868), McGulpin's Point (1869), Eagle Harbor (1871), White River (1875) and Sand Island (1881). While the light's keystone over its house door was inscribed 1881, the light was not completed and lit until 1882. Both the tower and the 1½-story house were made of coursed fieldstone left in its natural finish. The house had a cellar for storage, a first floor with an office, a kitchen and an equipment room, and two bedrooms upstairs. A circular spiral staircase in the tower gave access to all levels.

The square-based 37-foot (11.38 m) tower was set diagonally into one corner of the dwelling and had stone buttresses at its two exposed corners to provide extra support. Halfway up, the tower transformed and supported an octagonal gallery and a decagonal iron lantern. It used a fourth-order Fresnel lens to display a fixed red light, which was first lit on July 1, 1882. Being high on the island, the light had a focal plane of 98 feet (30 m).

The illuminant and lighting apparatus changed with time. It first used an oil-burning wick lamp and probably kerosene, since the station had an oil house. In September 1897 its characteristic became a white light that flashed every ten seconds through the installation of a fourth-order lens made by Barbier, Benard and Turenne of Paris. The lens was rotated by using a clockwork mechanism that needed winding every few hours. The new light had an increased visibility of 16 miles (26 km). An incandescent oil vapor lamp with a mantle-type burner was supplied in 1913 and this increased the light's intensity to 50,000 candlepower, also increasing its visibility. In 1928 the light was electrified by diesel generators. The station was still manned in the 1950s and it is unknown when the keepers were permanently removed. In December 1978 a solar-powered system was installed to operate the light, and it became fully automated. In 1989 its Fresnel lens was replaced with a 190 mm acrylic optic.

The light's fog equipment also changed over the years. When first built it was outfitted with a 1,500-pound (680 kg) fog bell that had a Stevens clockwork automatic striking mechanism. It had its own separate small building. However, due to the frequency of fog in the area, this system was replaced just two years later with a

Passage Island Lighthouse

steam fog signal. It was housed in a rectangular frame building lined with smooth iron sheets, sheeted on the outside with corrugated iron, and packed with sawdust and lime insulation between the interior and exterior walls. The duplicate 10-inch (25 cm) steam fog whistles (blast 5 s; silence 25 s) sounded from a cupola on the roof. In the first season, the whistle operated for a total of 174 hours. This increased to 755 hours in 1895 and then to 902 hours in 1906. As well as the fog signal building, a tramway from it to the dock was installed and a winch house was built to power the tramcar and make the work easier. At a later unknown date the system was upgraded to compressed air foghorns.

During a sub-zero snowstorm in December 1933 the fog equipment froze and the three keepers had to struggle to somehow keep the foghorns operating. One of them suffered frostbite to his face and ears, but they kept the signal blaring. When the keeper could not contact another lighthouse by radiophone during the first night of the storm, he broadcast a general radio call, as he knew there might be steamers in the area. He asked that someone notify the harbor master at Fort William or the Soo Locks that they were having problems with the fog signal equipment and might have to sound the signal only at intervals. No vessel transferred their request, but it was picked up and rebroadcast by an amateur radio operator in Mackinaw City, nearly 250 miles (400 km) away and in turn picked up by another amateur operator in Indianapolis, almost 500 miles (800 km) from Mackinaw City. He relayed the message by sending a telegram to Detroit. During the storm, the signal was only down for about ten minutes while the keepers switched compressors. For their diligence, they were commended by the Lighthouse Service.

In December 1906 the Canadian passenger ship *Monarch* was driven aground on a reef at Blake Point on Isle Royale's northern tip. A lifeboat was launched to land, but no one could get up the icy cliff of the island to safety. In a second attempt they tied a ladder to the bow of the lifeboat and a crewmember successfully climbed the bluff and tied off a rope. The other 30 passengers then made it to safety by climbing hand over hand along the rope. When the storm was spent, the Passage Island keeper sent his assistant to investigate the smoke he saw coming from the point. Seeing the wreck, the assistant returned and the keeper contacted the passing tug *Whalen*, which rescued the survivors from their four-day ordeal. Although most suffered from frostbite, only one died.

As freighters became larger and better built, they started the navigation season earlier in the spring and ended it later in December because the vessels could handle traveling through some ice. This made it dangerous to deliver and pick up keepers at the start and close of the navigation season. In 1919 the tender *Marigold* left Marquette on November 29 and started its round to remove keepers from the lake's western end (Stannard Rock, Manitou). By December 17, looking like an ice sculpture, the *Marigold* made port at Duluth with just 6 out of 40 tons of coal left. The ice at Duluth was frozen solid for two miles (3.2 km) out and an entrance to the harbor had to be broken. Because the tender had still not picked up the keepers at Passage Island and because of the extreme winter conditions, a Canadian ice-breaking tug out of Port Arthur made its way to Passage Island, collected keeper Gates and his assistants, and docked at Rossport, Ontario, on December 21.

Although the light no longer has keepers today, it continues to shine and it is part of the Isle Royale National Park. Its Fresnel lens (removed in 1989) is on display in the lobby of the Portage Coast Guard Station.

Known Keepers: W. Demant (1882–93), Alexander Shaw (1893–1907), John McDonald (1908–15), Oliver St. André (1915–19), E. Gates (1919–28), Charles Lewis (1928–29), James Gagnon (1929–39), Lawrence Lane (1939–40).

47 Point Iroquois Lighthouse

To assist with lake navigation, the U.S. Lighthouse Board established a contract in 1854 for the building of a lighthouse at Point Iroquois on Lake Superior. The 40-foot (12.2 m) lighthouse, erected in 1857, was built of stone, as was the keeper's dwelling. It used a sixth-order catadioptric Fresnel illuminating apparatus from a 63-foot (19.4 m) focal plane to produce a visibility of 13 miles (21 km). The light was first lit on September 20, 1858.

The purpose of the light was defined by the narrow channel in front of Point Iroquois. To the north, toward Gros Cap on the Canadian side, rocky outcroppings loomed underwater. On the American side of the channel, gravel and sandbars awaited careless navigators. This lighthouse was to guide ships safely between these two dangers (known as the Pillars of Hercules) from the open waters of Lake Superior into the St. Mary's River, which led to the Soo Locks.

Years before, this point of land had been the historic battleground where the westward invasion by the Iroquois Indians was halted by the victorious Chippewa in 1662. Ever since the battle, the native Algonkians called the point Nadouenigoning, combining the words Nadone ("Iroquois") and Arkon ("bone") to signify "the place of the Iroquois bones," and it has been known as Point Iroquois since then. Off the point, the French-Canadian voyageurs, forerunners of Superior's commercial shippers, paddled canoes heavily laden with furs.

By 1870 shipping had become an important industry. In that year, a second lighthouse was built to replace the first one. It was a 65-foot (20 m) conical red brick tower attached by a covered walkway to a 1½-story red brick keeper's house. Both the house and tower were painted white for best visibility. The tower was topped with a circular gallery supported by many ornately carved wooden braces. A spiral cast-iron staircase led up to the polygonal cast-iron lantern, which housed a fourth-order Fresnel lens, whose flashing light (flash every 30 seconds) could be seen for 16 miles (26 km) from its 68-foot (21 m) focal plane. The light first used oil lamps and reflectors and then a kerosene incandescent oil vapor lamp. The fourth-order Fresnel lens had a clockwork mechanism, wound every four hours, to turn the lens that created the flash pattern. Much later the light was electrified.

The station was first equipped with a fog bell but it was updated in the early 1900s to a steam fog whistle (blast 5 s, silence 25 s) powered by coal-fuelled boilers. Since the keepers stayed at the station all year, they could also answer a ship's call during the winter. When the keepers heard a ship's horn in a heavy snowstorm or when it was caught in ice, they replied using a long blast followed by a short blast of the fog signal, which let the ship's captain know he was by Point Iroquois.

The keeper and his assistants were inspected quarterly. Inspections were supposed to be a surprise, but the last-inspected lighthouse keeper informed the next station, if possible, of the coming inspector. In preparation for the inspections, the station was a beehive of activity. The tower was whitewashed in the early summer and any non-moving object was varnished, painted, polished, or shined. Keepers and their families dressed in their finery to meet the inspector, who checked the tower, the fog signal, the quarters, the outbuildings and the keeper's logbook. The inspector also heard any complaints or requests of the keeper. Keepers were scored on their efficiency. The most efficient keeper received the Efficiency Pin and was authorized to fly the "E Flag" during the year. The "E Flag" flew many years at Point Iroquois during keeper Bacon's years of service.

Betty Byrnes Bacon tells of a fascinating life growing up at Point Iroquois in her book *Lighthouse Memories*. She writes of the roast

Point Iroquois Lighthouse

Institution. In 1965 the Coast Guard transferred ownership of the station to the U.S. Forest Service. In 1975 the Point Iroquois lighthouse was placed on the *National Register of Historic Places* and today the lighthouse is part of the Hiawatha National Forest. Renovation of the site began in 1983 by the Bay Mills–Brimley Historical Research Society and the U.S. Forest Service. Since then, they have restored the east part of the lighthouse to make a museum and a caretaker's apartment. In 1989 efforts to replicate the 1944 appearance of the rest of the house began.

Today the station is an interpretive museum that presents the history and technology of the lighthouse, explains its role in Lake Superior navigation and shows aspects of the daily life of the lighthouse keeper at Point Iroquois. The 72 steps of the tower lead to an awesome view out over Lake Superior.

Known Keepers: Charles Caldwell (1856–57), Simon Tuple (1857–62), Edward Fraser (1862–63), M. Hoard (1863–66), John Roussian (1866–69), Hosea Smith (1869–87), Edward Chambers (1887–96), Joseph Bishop (1896–1904), Donald Harrison (1904–05), Robert Sanborn (1905), Otto Bufe (1905–07), Arthur Carter (1907–10), William Campbell (1911–16), Timothy Dee (1916–17), Elmer Byrnes (1917–34), Bacon (?), John Soldenski (1935–39), Stanley Clark (1939–47), J.B. Marshall (1939–40), D.C. McGiverin (?), R.W. Parr (1940), J.E. Ellison (?), H.A. Fay (?).

goose dinner that resulted from Canada geese flying through the lantern glass. She remembers her father using the foghorn in winter storms to guide people and/or vessels to the lighthouse, and tells of collecting snakes and ladybugs as pest control for the family vegetable garden and many more wonderful stories.

Due to their isolated location, the children did not go to school but after a long, hard battle, the keepers finally got their school. The government set up a school right at the station for the six children of the three keepers and three children of a nearby fisherman. The converted storeroom was furnished with blackboards, books, desks and a pot-bellied stove. The Lighthouse Service paid the teacher's salary, and room and board. The children had a one-room school (K to 8) — and received individualized instruction.

In 1919, sixteen crewmen of the steamer *Myron* tragically lost their lives in the freezing waters when the vessel went down in one of the infamous "storms of November." The lightkeeper, Elmer Byrnes, took the bodies, as they washed ashore, to an undertaker in the nearby town of Brimley. The undertaker paid $10 a piece for "floaters." The only survivor of the shipwreck was Captain W.R. Neal.

After 92 years of assisting mariners, this light was extinguished in 1962, when an automated light was placed in the channel. In 1963 its Fresnel lens was removed and sent to the Smithsonian

48 Presque Isle Harbor Breakwater Light

Presque Isle Harbor, just south of Presque Isle Peninsula, was also the upper harbor of Marquette. During the 1900s it developed as a port from which to ship iron ore. Around 1940 the government built a breakwall of riprap stone from the peninsula in a southwesterly direction to protect the harbor from northeast storms. A square concrete pier with a wave flare at its top was built at its outer end in 1941, and a lighthouse was built on that foundation.

The tower consisted of a large base with a much smaller steel tower surmounting it for another three stories. It had porthole windows ascending it for interior light. Instead of a regular lantern it had a modern acrylic optic from which its automated red light shone. This light still functions today to mark the end of the breakwall and the entrance into Marquette's upper harbor.

Presque Isle Harbor Breakwater Light

49 Raspberry Island Lighthouse

The Raspberry Island Lighthouse is on one of the Apostle Islands in western Lake Superior. Before the opening of the Soo Canal in 1855, shipping on Lake Superior was basically local, as most vessels could not be portaged around the dangerous rapids at Sault Ste Marie. However, once the canal was opened, Lake Superior became the last leg of a 1,000-mile (1620 km) water-shipping route, and trans-lake shipping of lumber, brownstone, grain and iron ore increased. One developing port was Bayfield, on the southeast shore of the Bayfield Peninsula, which has the Apostle Islands archipelago just off its tip.

Lake traffic continued to increase and commerce between Bayfield and Duluth, at Superior's west end, flourished. Henry Rice, an influential politician who founded Bayfield, urged Congress to light the western passage to Bayfield. Influenced by the added support of mariners, President Buchanan signed an order in 1859 to reserve all of Raspberry Island for a lighthouse reserve. The island, named by the Ojibway Indians for its abundance of berries, was a small island about 1 mile (1.6 km) long and half a mile (0.8 km) wide, just 1½ miles (2.4 km) north of the mainland on the west side of the Apostle Islands. In March 1859 Congress appropriated $6,000 to build the lighthouse, a moderate amount due to the financing needs of the Civil War effort. The station was finished in 1863.

The lighthouse was built on a 40-foot (12.2 m) high clay cliff on the island's southwest side. It was a house and tower combined. The short square white clapboard tower emerged from the center of the roof peak of the white two-story rectangular clapboard keeper's house. The tower was topped by a square wooden gallery covered in copper and by a decagonal iron lantern. While the structure was complete by the end of 1862, it had to wait until 1863 for the arrival of its fifth-order Fresnel lens from Paris. Once installed, the fixed white light was officially displayed on July 20, 1863. The lens was 27 feet (8.3 m) above the ground but had a 77-foot (23.5 m) focal plane and a visibility of 16 miles (26 m).

Changes soon occurred at the station. In 1869 a dock was built at the base of the cliff, and stairs up the cliffside. Flash panels added around the lens in 1891 created a fixed white light varied by a white flash every 90 seconds. During the late 1890s the dock, boathouse, and cliff steps had to be replaced, the lens was changed to flash every 60 seconds and the light's illuminant became kerosene. In 1902 a red brick steam fog signal plant was built to the east of the lighthouse and equipped with 10-inch (25 cm) fog whistles. A cast-concrete stair and tramway were built to haul supplies up the cliff more easily. A newly built 360-gallon (1512 l) brick oil house stored the volatile kerosene safely.

A second assistant keeper was hired to help with the increased workload and in 1906–07 the keeper's house was remodeled to accommodate three keepers and their families. With developing technology, further changes were introduced. In 1928 diesel engines were installed to operate a generator to produce electricity for the station. In 1933 type T diaphone fog signals were installed to replace the whistles. In 1947 the light was automated and the keepers were removed. In 1952 the fog signal was discontinued and the Fresnel lens was removed. The light was replaced by a battery-operated beacon mounted to a pole in front of the lighthouse. At this time the automated light was checked and maintained periodically by the keepers at Devil's Island, and when their light was automated in 1978 the Coast Guard maintained the Raspberry Island light.

The station was too much work for one person and always had an assistant keeper except for an unexplained lapse of five years from October 1882 until December 1887. During these years, Francis Jacker tended the light by himself, as his wife and family remained on the mainland to look after their farm. He found the required work of tending the light 24/7 exhausting and his log reports no assistance in case of an emergency.

One day in September 1887 Jacker decided to sail the station's sailboat around into the lee of the island for protection from an impending storm. The boat was caught in the wind and smashed on the rocks of nearby Oak Island. He managed to get safely to shore and survive until a passing Indian rescued him three days later and returned him to Raspberry Island. There, much to his surprise, he found his wife. She had come out for a visit after the storm was over. Not finding him there, she lit the light, although she couldn't get the revolving mechanism to work. Instead of being fired for his temporary absence, Jacker was provided an assistant keeper to help him with the workload, once he had explained the circumstances.

Today the lighthouse is under the joint jurisdiction of the U.S. Coast Guard and the National Park Service. The Coast Guard services the light while the Park Service maintains the buildings and the grounds. The Park Service also has a volunteer lighthouse keeper's program. Each year the Apostle Islands National Lakeshore Park chooses "voluntary keepers" to live at the lighthouse, give guided tours, and do small maintenance jobs. Many keepers also get involved with such personal research projects as mapping flora patterns or bird-nesting habits.

The Park Service also has a museum in the keeper's house. Historical photographs, drawings, logbooks and recollections have returned the buildings, gardens and grounds to an original early 1920s appearance. The station's fifth-order Fresnel lens is on display at the Wisconsin State Historical Society Museum on Madeline Island.

Raspberry Island Lighthouse

Raspberry Island Lighthouse is often referred to as the "Showpiece of the Apostle Islands" because it is easy to visit and the station is well kept. However, of concern to the station's future is the erosion caused by "slumping," where clumps of shoreline have fallen into the lake, causing the lighthouse to become closer and closer to the edge of the cliff. In 2000 *Lighthouse Digest* added the light to their "Doomsday List." After a government study in 1999, $1.36 million was set aside for work to stem the erosion and the work began in 2002. It is hoped that this initiative will curb the problem.

Known Keepers: Andrew Cramer (1863), William Herbert (1863–66), Patrick Mulcahy (1866–68), Edward Krense (1868) Lewis Larson (1869–80), Francis Jacker (1888–92), William Pinkerton (1894–95), John Eddy (1895–1900), Charles Hendrickson (1900–09), Alexander McLean (1909–15), Lee Benton (1915–25).

Rock Harbor Lighthouse

50 Rock Harbor Lighthouse

Isle Royale's first inhabitants were Chippewa Indians. In 1837 John Jacob Astor established the first American Fur Company on the island, and shortly after this copper was reportedly found in the area. Then in 1843 the government and the Chippewa Nation signed the Treaty of La Pointe, opening the island for copper mining and exploration. By 1847 more than a dozen companies were mining copper on the island. Commercial fishermen also used it as a base for their operations. Mining companies and fishermen both called for the island to be lit to make water travel safer.

After a survey of the area was completed in 1847, a general location was chosen for a lighthouse near the southwest entrance to Rock Harbor. The anticipated opening of the Soo Locks in 1855 also created pressure for a light at Isle Royale, as the need for increased marine traffic to ship copper from the island to the lower lakes was foreseen. The Superintendent of Lights, Henry B. Miller, recommended the construction of a lighthouse at Rock Harbor in 1852 and Congress appropriated $5,000 for the light in February 1853.

After clear title was obtained, the lighthouse was built in 1855 on the mainland of Isle Royale at the south side of the rock-infested Middle Islands Passage, the south entrance into Rock Harbor, and about 10 miles (16 km) from the east end of Isle Royale along its south shore. It lit the area for local fishermen as well as for vessels bound for Rock Harbor, which served the Smithwick and Ransom Mines (two of the earliest in the area).

The lighthouse was a combined 1½-story keeper's house and 50-foot (15.3 m) tower. The house, 29 feet (8.9 m) square, was set on a stone foundation made of coursed rubble-stone walls. It had a cedar shake shingle roof and two smaller brick chimneys rather than one centrally located chimney. Within, there was an entry, an office, a parlor, a kitchen/living area and a short passageway into the tower on the dwelling's lower floor.

The conical tower was built of stone and brick and had a spiral staircase of pine anchored to a central post which ascended to its iron lantern. The lantern had a cylindrical bottom, eight vertically set rectangular panels (six of glass and two of iron) and a copper arched dome with a ventilator. With the back two panels of the lantern blacked out, the lantern's

Early Rock Harbor Lighthouse

fourth-order Fresnel lens displayed a fixed white light in a 270-degree arc of illumination for 14 miles (22.6 km) from its 70-foot (21 m) focal plane.

The light served for only a short time. With the falling market and the depletion of the initial copper deposits on the island, shipping to the Rock Harbor area fell away to almost nothing, and the light was closed in 1859.

However, when Civil War broke out, more metals were needed. Miners again went to Isle Royale but with newer techniques to more efficiently mine the copper. This renewed mining and the business to support it brought regular shipping back to the island, and the government decided to reactivate the Rock Harbor Light. An inspection in 1873 reported deterioration due to neglect and vandalism. Congress appropriated $5,000 to refurbish and upgrade the station. In 1874 a work crew repaired and renewed the station and the light was relit on August 15, 1874. Its characteristic was switched to fixed red but it continued to use its Fresnel lens.

Its operation was again short-lived. By the end of the Civil War, copper prices had bottomed out and copper mining on Isle Royale ceased. With little boat traffic to Rock Harbor and a more centrally located lighthouse established on Menagerie Island in 1875, the government viewed the Rock Harbor light as redundant. It was permanently extinguished on October 4, 1879.

Although the government abandoned the station, others used its facilities. Around the turn of the century campers drawn to the area used the lighthouse in the summer. Also Louis O. Broadwell occupied the lighthouse for a number of summers in the early twentieth century, making some additions. He kept the lighthouse well while he was there but he left in 1915. From 1928 to 1939 commercial fishermen Arnold and Milford Johnson and their families used the lighthouse as a base of operations. When they left, the lighthouse sat empty again.

In the 1950s the tower started to tilt noticeably so the National Park Service undertook to stabilize it. In 1962 they used 100 bags of cement product to pressure-grout the tower's hollow interior walls and stabilize its foundation. They were able to return it almost to its upright position but it still retains a two-degree tilt.

More restoration was undertaken in 1978 after an inspection showed continued deterioration. In 1980 the dormers and the lean-to room were removed to return the keeper's dwelling to its original appearance. The wayside interpretive exhibit from the 1960s was removed in 1981 after it was damaged by a moose.

This lighthouse, nicknamed the Old Light, has earned a special place in history and is listed on the *National Register of Historic Places*. Although it operated for just a short time, it was the first lighthouse at Isle Royale, the only one on the mainland of the island and the only one of the four Isle Royale lights that has been extinguished. Being such an early part of maritime history it also helps show the development of lighthouse styles. In 1994 the keeper's house became a maritime exhibit featuring all four of Isle Royale's lighthouses and its ten major shipwrecks. Unfortunately, its fourth-order Fresnel lens was removed sometime after the light was extinguished in 1879.

Rock of Ages Lighthouse

Known Keepers: Mark Petty (1856–57), Francis Bomasa (1857–59), A.D. Kruger (1874–76), Martin Benson (1877–79).

51 Rock of Ages Lighthouse

Isle Royale, sometimes referred to as the "Jewel of the Great Lakes," is an archipelago consisting of over 200 islands and jagged rock formations that were created millions of years ago. It lies approximately 50 miles (80 km) northwest of the Keweenaw Peninsula but its northern tip is only 15 miles (24 km) from the Canadian shore. The main island is about 50 miles (80 km) long and varies in width from 4 miles (6.4 km) to 9 miles (14.4 km). It is 1,310 feet (400 m) above sea level, and its large area (some 210 square miles) makes it the biggest island in Lake Superior.

Because of its dangerous reefs and an increase in local and lake traffic, Congress was pressured to build a lighthouse on Isle Royale in the late 1880s. Then as shipping increased between Superior/Duluth and Fort William/Port Arthur, the north channel above Isle Royale became more traveled because it was protected from the full wrath of the lake. A powerful beacon was needed on the southwest side of the island, where reefs abounded. The initial 1895 request for $50,000 for a lighthouse on the Rock of Ages Reef included proof of danger, since the Canadian side-wheeler steamer *Cumberland* had gone down on the reef in 1877. Although the request was declined, it was repeated until 1900 and then rewritten for $125,000, as costs had escalated and another ship, the *Henry Chisholm*, had sunk on the reef in 1898, further illustrating its danger. Congress finally appropriated $25,000. It later appropriated another $100,000 to complete the light.

Major Charles Keller of the Army Corps of Engineers designed the lighthouse but its construction was contracted to Walter F. Beyer of Detroit. Crews first blasted and reshaped the island to make it level for the steel cylindrical base made of riveted steel plate. The base flared gently at the top from a 50- to a 56-foot (15 to 17 m) diameter, to form a wave deflector to keep water and ice away from the tower. In this phase, work crews lived at Washington Harbor on Isle Royale. Once the pier was complete and a large bunkhouse put up, workers lived on site. When the

steel cylinder was ready, the lighthouse tender *Amaranth* anchored offshore and work crews made cement on board and transported it to the island to fill the steel ring. Forms were then built inside it for the two cellar levels, and a steel column was anchored through the very center of the cellars to become the central core for the whole lighthouse, to bear the entire stress load and to stabilize it. The 30-foot (9 m) diameter structural portion of the conical tower was made of a skeletal steel framework, and the tower itself consisted of steel, brick-lined below the watchroom.

Each interior level had a different purpose. The first level was a sub-cellar for storage and the water pump. The second housed the heating plant. The third level, also the entry level, contained the machinery and fog signal equipment, fuel barrels and the lighthouse boat. The fourth level was the office. The fifth level, where the men spent most of their free time, had a kitchen, a mess room and a washroom. The sixth level was the bedroom for the keeper and his first assistant, and the seventh was the bedroom for the second and third assistants. The eighth level was a storage level for supplies and cleaning materials. The ninth level held the pedestal for the lens and a clockwork mechanism to keep the light flashing. (Later, after the light was converted to electricity the mechanism was left because it could be used to operate the light in the event of a power failure.) The tenth level housed the lens.

The Rock of Ages Light was first lit on October 22, 1908, using a temporary third-order lens that displayed a fixed red light. In 1909 Congress appropriated $15,000 for a permanent second-order Fresnel lens from Barbier, Benard and Turenne of Paris. This lens was 8½ feet (2.6 m) tall, 7 feet 9 inches (2.4 m) wide, had four bull's eyes, and floated on a bed of 375 pounds (170 kg) of mercury. The lens and its pedestal base together weighed about 3.5 tons and were more than 17 feet (5.2 m) high. It was first lit on September 15, 1910, and with its incandescent oil-vapor lamp, which burned vaporized kerosene, it produced a white light of 940,000 candlepower. It displayed a double flash every 10 seconds while the lens completed one full revolution every 20 seconds. Because of the light's brilliance and speed it was nicknamed the "lightning light." With a focal plane of 117 feet (36 m) above the lake it had a visibility of 20 miles (32 km) or more.

Due to its isolation, it was supplied with two of almost everything necessary to keep the light functioning and to ensure the keeper's survival. In later years there were two radio transmitters, two timers, two clocks, two diesel generators, two diesel air compressors and two air storage tanks.

Two other ships had mishaps on the Rock of Ages Reef. The first was the steamer *North Queen*, which was grounded on the reef in 1913. The second was the passenger steamer *Cox*, which struck the reef in May 1933. The lightkeepers from Rock of Ages were able to save the 125 passengers and crew before it sank and they all huddled in the lighthouse for about 24 hours until help arrived. Since the steamer still lies where it sank, divers can visit it today.

The light's desolate location 5 miles (8 km) southwest of Isle Royale earned it a reputation as the loneliest lighthouse post on the Great Lakes. In December 1919 storms delayed the *Marigold's* arrival to remove the crew. After waiting for more than a week and with their provisions down to one can of tomatoes, the crew left on their own for the mainland about 20 miles (32 km) away. By the time they reached safety, two of them had sustained frostbite.

In 1929 a radio beacon was added and in 1930 diesel generators were installed to provide electricity. Then in 1931 dual Tyfon fog signals replaced the old fog system. Since the lighthouse was completely surrounded by water and shoals, the two foghorns were placed on the tower facing opposite directions to maximize the area covered by the sound.

In a 1932 letter from Rock of Ages, keeper Melvin Whipple described how he was virtually tied to the lighthouse and how disappointed he was when his leave was cancelled because he would not see his family for another five months. He described living in the round rooms as "living in a brick stove pipe."

John Tregembo, stationed at the light in 1947, referred to the light as a "spark plug" because of its shape. He said paint in the weight flue was still tacky in 1947 but he did not know if it was because of the type of lead paint used, the high humidity in the flue, or something else. He remembered cleaning the lens and brasswork with chamois, numerous trips up and down the stairways to put the curtains up when the light was out and take them down when it was lit, and spending his shore leave at a shack in Washington Harbor if the weather was too harsh to make it to the mainland. He was also glad that the coffee pot was metal because it did not break when it vibrated off the stove when the air compressors were operating the fog signal.

Another of Tregembo's favorite stories about his stay at the Rock of Ages light was about Edward (Ed) Heinsberg, an assistant keeper nicknamed the "mad Russian." Heinsberg had lived in a country bordering Russia at a time when the Russian government would come in, seize residents and relocate them in Russia. He escaped before he could be relocated, eventually traveling the world as a seaman. He later became a civilian lighthouse keeper on the Great Lakes. He started at the Rock of Ages Lighthouse in 1933 as the third assistant and was there when the *Cox* grounded nearby. He worked his way up to first assistant and spent many years at this station. However, he loved indulging in alcohol, a definite no-no at a lighthouse. He had been warned about not drinking while on duty, and since he loved his job he only indulged when away from the light. It was said that he had to be "poured onto the lighthouse tender" for his trip out to start a new season.

Apparently Ed was also a bit reclusive and somewhat eccentric. One day, when Ed wouldn't talk to him, another assistant told him the "Russian" was upset because John was throwing out his lunch. What was the explanation? Every morning, as part of his duties, John would shovel up the dead birds and insects that had flown into the light and throw them into the lake. Apparently Ed, who usually ate alone, was upset by this because he used the bird carcasses to make soup for his lunch. By doing this he could save some of his food rations to take with him during his shore leave away from the lighthouse and save on food costs.

John even got one more laugh about the "mad Russian." While attending a lighthouse function he listened to a guest speaker tell about one of the Rock of Ages keepers being a taxidermist and stuffing birds at the lighthouse. After the talk John politely informed the speaker that the only "stuffing" the assistant keeper did was to stuff the birds, as food, into his stomach.

It took an extraordinary breed of keepers to exist on this tiny island of isolation where the sound of waves crashing against rocks and the lonely cry of gulls could become too monotonous. The crew stationed on "The Rock" as the Coast Guard called it, were usually given one day leave for every two days that they spent at the light and they usually stayed at their post for four to six weeks at a time.

The light was automated at the end of 1977 and the keepers were removed. In 1985 the Fresnel lens and pedestal were removed and put on display in the Windigo Visitors Center five miles away on Isle Royale. The light was replaced with an airport-type beacon, a 300 mm Lucite lens, which runs on solar power. Today Isle Royale is a national park, but the Rock of Ages Lighthouse, still owned by the U.S. Coast Guard, is closed to the public, and the park offers no tours because of its inaccessibility.

Known Keepers: Thomas E. Irvine (1908–14), John Garraty (1914–20), Joseph Metivier (1920–25), Emil Mueller (1925–31), John Soldenski (1931–35), John Kirkendall (1935–39), Charles Miles (1939–40).

52 Round Island Lighthouse (Upper St. Mary's River)

In 1852 Congress appropriated $4,000 to build a beacon light on Round Island, Lake Superior, near the entrance to the St. Mary's River. In June 1855 the schooner *Funny and Flog* passed through the Canal with the Superintendent of Work, A. Smollf, and a crew and materials to build seven lighthouses for Lake Superior, one of them on Round Island. The contractor for these lights was A. Sweet.

Round Island was about 6½ miles (10.5 km) southeast of Gros Cap Reef, halfway between Birch Point to the west and Cedar Point to the east and 0.6 miles (1 km) off Michigan's shore in the Upper St. Mary's River. This light was established in 1855 and reconstructed in 1864. The 35-foot (10.8 m) gray tower emerged from the corner of the stone keeper's house. It was possibly a combined range and turning light as it was here that downbound vessels coming into the river from Lake Superior had to change course from southeast to east to head toward Pointe Louise and Brush Point Range Lights and the narrows of the river, and where upbound vessels heading west rounding Pointe Louise had to head toward Round Island as a turning point to go northwest to Point Iroquois and Gros Cap.

In 1865 the Lighthouse Board ran a notice to mariners in the *Detroit Advertiser and Tribune* on May 16 that the lighthouse at Round Island, near the entrance to the River St. Marie, was to be re-established and given a fifth-order lens to be lit for the first time on June 1, 1866, from a 45-foot (13.7 m) focal plane and showing a fixed red light.

According to the 1901 Scott's *Coast Pilot*, this light had already been discontinued. It was probably replaced by the St. Mary's River Upper and Lower Range Lights (Birch Point ranges and Cedar Point ranges) for the river traffic. Today the stone ruins of the keeper's house are the only indications that a light station had existed on this little island.

Sand Hills Lighthouse

53 Sand Hills Lighthouse

After the harbor at Eagle River, on the west side and near the tip of the Keweenaw Peninsula along Lake Superior's south shore, had declined when copper prices dropped and miners left the area, the Lighthouse Board proposed closing the Eagle River Light in 1892 and replacing it with a lighthouse at Sand Hills further to the south. That location would mark a turning point along the peninsula, act as a coastal light, and also warn of the dangerous Sawtooth Reef, which lay about 1½ miles (2.4 km) offshore. Congress authorized the project in February 1893 but failed to appropriate any money.

The Board reiterated its proposal each year and requested more money as the years passed. Finally, the Eagle River Light was decommissioned in 1908 and, although the northwest coast of the peninsula was left darkened for a great distance, it was not until June 1917 that Congress finally appropriated $70,000 for a lighthouse at Sand Hills, or Five Mile Point as it was sometimes called. A 47-acre (19 hectare) reservation was purchased at the point in October and construction began the next spring.

The first buildings to go up were the barracks to house the work crew, and the fog signal building. After the station was completed, the barracks became a three-car garage. Then during World War II, the building was remodeled as the "Sand Hills Barracks" for up to 200 Coast Guard recruit trainees. The fog signal building was built on a concrete pad at the water's edge to the northwest of the lighthouse. It had hollow tile walls, an exterior stucco finish, and a diagonally placed asbestos-shingled roof. It was outfitted with duplicate Type F diaphone foghorns operated by compressors and oil engines. The second foghorn was to ensure service at all times in case the first one needed repairs. Its cast-iron horns protruded through the top wall of the building's lakeside end so that the signal could be heard for 7 miles (11.3 km). A temporary 300 mm lens lantern was mounted to the northwest corner of the building to display a light during the construction of the lighthouse.

Also during the construction period, a large vegetable garden was planted to the west of the lighthouse site to help feed the workers. As well, the cook and his helpers kept a hennery for fresh eggs and chicken and a few cows for fresh milk.

The building of the lighthouse itself started with a square 70-foot (21 m) concrete and steel tower built at its center. The tower was faced on the exterior with yellow brick and inside with red brick. Its interior levels were each large enough to form a room about 12 feet (3.6 m) square and they were connected by a cast-iron stairway with 100 steps up to its lantern. The second tower level was the keeper's office. The tower rose three stories above the roofline of the house, and the lantern's murette walls were hidden from ground level by a concrete and brick wall and railing that surrounded the gallery.

The tower supported a black cylindrical iron lantern whose curved panes were set diagonally into solid brass astragals. It housed a fourth-order Fresnel lens manufactured by Henri LePaute of Paris. The lens was equipped with a 35 mm incandescent oil vapor lamp and rotated on ball-bearings by the use of a clockwork mechanism to produce the station's fixed light, which was varied by a flash every 10 seconds. From its 91-foot (28 m) focal plane the light was visible for 19 miles (30.5 km).

The keepers' houses were built around and onto three sides of the tower. Connecting walls were made of brick as a form of firewall between the residences. The houses were large, two-storied, flat-roofed, yellow-bricked homes designed as a triplex for the head keeper and his two assistants. The assistant keepers lived in the houses on the east and west sides of the tower, which had an identical but reversed layout. They were a bit smaller than the main house on the north side, which faced the lake and provided a better view for the "principal" keeper.

Each of the dwellings had hardwood trim, doors and floors, its own cellar, a separate door into the tower, separate front porches and entry doors for privacy. They were roofed in copper sheeting, and the flat roofs of the verandas formed second-story balconies with stone balustrades that gave a somewhat Italian appearance. The basement housed the station's central hot water heating and its pneumatic water supply systems. The lighthouse was first lit on June 18, 1918. Its total cost including land, buildings and equipment was about $100,000.

The station, classed as a first class one, operated for 20 years before it was automated with the use of acetylene gas and sun valves in 1939. Then in 1954 it was decommissioned when the government deemed the light unnecessary due to modern navigation aids. The reservation was then turned over to the General Services Administration, declared excess government property, and sold at public auction in 1958 to H.D. Bliss, a Detroit insurance agent, who used it as a private summer cottage. In 1961 it was sold again privately to William Frabotta and his wife, Eve. They converted the fog signal building into a summer cottage that they used for the next 30 years.

Their dream to open a bed and breakfast inn at the lighthouse had to wait until hydro was installed in the area, but was finally realized in 1988. As Frabotta renovated he also collected antiques and memorabilia of earlier days to display in the lighthouse. One of his acquisitions was an almost 6-foot (1.8 m) coffee grinder with its original red paintwork. He also acquired another fourth-order Fresnel lens (not the original) to be placed in the lantern. As well as luxury, the Sand Hills Lighthouse Inn offers solitude and a fantastic view over Lake Superior.

Known Keeper: William Bennetts (1919–30).

Sand Island Lighthouse

54 Sand Island Lighthouse

As the shipping of lumber, iron ore, and grain on Lake Superior increased in the late 1800s, mariners complained that the light on Raspberry Island was insufficient to mark the western passage through the Apostle Islands. In response, a lighthouse was built on Sand Island in 1881. Since this light was primarily to appease mariners, it was built as cheaply as possible (for $18,000) using local materials found on the island. As a result, the structure built in a Norman Gothic style associated with churches and town houses of the period, was made of island brownstone and was unique among Apostle lights. The plans for this lighthouse were also used at Eagle Bluff (1868), Chambers Island (1868), McGulpin's Point (1868), Eagle Harbor (1871), and White River (1875), although these were made of brick.

The 44-foot (13.5 m) tower, built into the northwest corner of the house had a square base that turned into an octagonal top and was circular inside. The tower's corners had a unique "wavy" stonework pattern halfway up where the square became an octagon, and the squared corners also had supporting buttresses at the bottom. Fifty-eight iron spiral steps led to its decagonal lantern, the back two panels of which were solid iron plates. It housed a fourth-order Fresnel lens that produced a fixed white light first lit on September 25, 1881. With its 52-foot (16 m) focal plane it had a visibility up to 20 miles (32 km).

The living quarters of the 1½-story keeper's house were on the main floor with two bedrooms on the second level. A chimney set diagonally into the roof peak allowed for a number of stoves to be hooked up inside of the house. The house also had a red pressed pattern roof, black trim, green shutters, ornamental stonework above the windows, white ornamental trim under the eaves near the lower edges, and a wooden brace and finial in the gable peaks.

Other buildings included the oil house, with a roof designed to explode upwards and not outwards for safety, and a red brick privy with decorative wood trim under the eaves. The boathouse was 300 yards (275 m) to the south but is now gone. Twenty-two wooden steps led down the rise to a large, flat rock boulder-strewn waterfront on the northwest side of the lighthouse.

The first keeper, Charles Lederle, had helped build the lighthouse. In 1885 he saw the *Prussia* on fire during a storm and rowed out 10 miles (16 km) to help the survivors to safety. The second and last keeper, Emmanuel Luick, witnessed the booming population of the island in the early 1900s, including a school, a store, a post office, and a telephone company for the island's farming and fishing residents, who numbered around a hundred. He also witnessed the wreck of the *Sevona* on the Sand Island Shoal during a terrible September storm in 1905. He saw it founder and then recede around the point of the island but could do nothing to help. He later learned that the crew of seven, including the captain, had drowned.

Two volumes from the Sand Island keeper's logs are shelved at the National Archives. They provide insight into life around the turn of the century. Contrary to policy, Emmanuel Luick's wife, Ella, used to write in the logbooks. After ten years of marriage to a lighthouse keeper, she divorced her husband in 1906, a most unheard of thing in these times.

In 1921 an acetylene light (operated by an automated clock) was installed, and the keeper from Raspberry Island checked on it. It displayed a flashing characteristic (flash 1.5 s; eclipse 8.5 s). From 1933–80 a light shone from a steel tower in front of the lighthouse. Then in 1980 the steel tower was removed and the light was returned to the original tower. Today it displays a DCB 24 beacon.

From the lantern you can see waves lapping the shore to the west; Silver Bay, Minnesota 26 miles (41.6 km) to the north; Devil's Island 12 miles (19.2 km) to the northeast; Sand Island Shoal 3 miles (4.8 km) to the northeast; and Bear Island (which has no bears) to the east.

In 1975 the light was added to the State of Wisconsin's *Register of Historic Sites*. It is also listed on the *National Register of Historic Places*. To visit the lighthouse, anchor offshore, kayak in or land at the dock on the south side of the island and hike 2 miles (3.2 km) to the lighthouse. It is an easy walk through island vegetation, which includes some virgin, 240-year-old white pines.

Known Keepers: Charles Lederle (1881–91), Emmanuel Luick (1892–1921).

Sand Island Lighthouse

55 Sand Point Lighthouse

The small town of L'Anse, located in the protected L'Anse Bay along Lake Superior's south shore, developed as an important port from which iron ore could be shipped in the latter part of the 1800s. Residents' 1871 petition for a lighthouse to light the harbor was granted in 1873, but clear title to the chosen site to the north of L'Anse could not be obtained. Meanwhile the financiers behind the Northern Pacific Railroad went bankrupt, and ore shipping from L'Anse stopped. The lighthouse proposal was put on hold. When the ore boom fizzled out, the harbor became important for shipping lumber and therefore still needed to be lit. By 1875, when clear title had still not been procured, a new site was selected at Sand Point across the bay from L'Anse. The lighthouse was again delayed in 1876 by a forest fire. L'Anse, including its docks, was destroyed and needed rebuilding.

In August 1877 the tender *Warrington* arrived with men and materials to build the lighthouse at Sand Point. This lighthouse used plans designed for the Port Austin light. It had a 1½-story red brick keeper's house with an attached 32-foot (9.8 m) square, red brick tower at the lake end of the house. The tower's square gallery had chopped-off corners, giving it an octagonal shape, and it was supported by 16 ornately carved wooden corbels (four per side). It was topped with an octagonal gallery, dome, ventilator ball and lightning rod. The gallery housed a fifth-order Fresnel lens that displayed a fixed red light for 9¾ miles (15.8 km). It was first lit on August 10, 1878. Later the same plans were reused to build lights at Sherwood Point (1883) and Little Traverse (1884).

By 1897 rising lake levels threatened to undermine the lighthouse, which had been built on the sandy point, by eroding the shoreline. To correct this problem, in 1898 the lighthouse was jacked up and placed on a square hemlock crib. The crib had been coated with grease so that the lighthouse could be slid across the timbers and onto a new foundation, built further inland. More hemlock timbers were then used to construct a retaining wall between the shore and the lighthouse to forestall further erosion.

With the advent of acetylene and a decline in the number of vessels in the bay, the lighthouse was automated in 1922. A small brick building was built to house an acetylene tank just to the east of the lighthouse. It was topped by a 35-foot (10.7 m) red iron mast and a 300 mm lantern. The system was equipped with sun valves to automatically turn the light on and off. This new light started on September 25, 1922. This system was later replaced with a modern beacon placed on a steel skeletal tower in front of the lighthouse.

In April 1933 the reservation was excessed and sold into private hands. In 1944 Dr. Louis Guy purchased the lighthouse and the 37 acres (14.9 hectare) surrounding it. At some time a sun porch was added to the full length of the structure. In the 1990s the Keweenaw Bay Indian Community purchased the lighthouse and surrounding area. Their plans for the lighthouse are currently unknown.

Known Keepers: John Crebassa (1878–1908), Thomas Thompson (1908–11), Richard Thompson (1911–22).

Sand Point Lighthouse

Split Rock Lighthouse

56 Split Rock Lighthouse

Split Rock Lighthouse is probably the most frequently visited lighthouse on the Great Lakes. Its majestic location at the top of a 120-foot (37 m) rock cliff along the north shore of Lake Superior offers a splendid view.

The name Split Rock was first recorded on an 1825 map to denote the river 2½ miles (4 km) southwest of the lighthouse. Although theories and speculation abound, its origin is unknown.

In the early twentieth century, Lake Superior's steamship traffic increased substantially thanks to the export of iron ore. However, the ore ranges at Split Rock caused ships' magnetic compasses to perform erratically and made shipping particularly hazardous in the area. In one devastating storm in November 1905, 29 crewmen were endangered on this rocky northern shore known as Split Rock Point, an area already dubbed "the most dangerous piece of water in the world." All aboard except one were rescued, but the vessel *Madeira* smashed and sank. A delegation of steamship owners petitioned the U.S. government for a lighthouse, and in 1907 Congress appropriated $75,000 for a lighthouse and fog signal in the Split Rock vicinity. The 7.6-acre (3 hectare) site was purchased in 1908 for $200 from Mrs. Clara A.H. Smith and the estate of her late brother and governor of New York, Frank Wayland Higgins. (Their father had originally bought it from the government in 1887 for $9.50.)

Ralph Russell Tinkham was commissioned to build the lighthouse, and construction began in the spring of 1909. First, a derrick and a hoisting engine were installed at the top of the sheer rock cliff to hoist up materials, equipment and supplies. (Today only depressions and the ruined foundation of this still exist.) The first summer they built the lighthouse keepers' houses, the oil house and the storage barns. The fog building and light tower were built the next year.

In order to anchor the building foundations, the rock had to be drilled and dynamited. Many workers lived in tents, and during the blasting, pieces of rock would rain down on the camp. Tinkham told of a log from the blasting area becoming airborne one evening and landing between the bunks of one of the tents while the men were inside. Fortunately, no one was ever seriously injured. Once the foundations were completed, a host of other trained workers arrived to complete the buildings. The light station was finished for $72,540 by the next summer and the light was first lit on August 1, 1910.

The keepers lived in three yellow-brick two-story houses built in a row behind the lighthouse. The first principal lightkeeper was Orren "Pete" Young and he lived in the keeper's house closest to the light. His family only visited him at Split Rock and never lived there because of the remoteness. Two months after opening, he sent his two assistants to nearby Beaver Bay to pick up the mail. The last thing he said to his inexperienced helpers was not to tie the sail down so that it could be quickly released in the event of a sudden gust of wind. Sure enough, the sailboat was later found washed ashore with the sail tied down, but the assistants' bodies were never found.

The first assistant, Franklin J. Covell, became the keeper in 1928. His family sometimes stayed with him. Children living in this remote area entertained themselves by walking the tramway tracks, playing on the turntable in front of the hoist house, collecting agates on the beach, building wooden boats, picnicking on little Two Harbors Island, berry picking, befriending wild animals, and fishing. The lightkeeper and assistants supplemented their diet with moose and venison — and occasionally bear.

The tower itself was only 38 feet (11.6 m) tall but it stood 168 feet (50 m) above Lake Superior. The unique octagonal tower of yellow brick and reinforced concrete sat on a concrete foundation topped by an ornate concrete ring.. The yellow brick continued above a second concrete ring to the gallery and lantern, each surrounded by its own low black iron railing. A black dome topped the tower.

Split Rock Lighthouse's circular iron staircase

Three things are noticeable upon entering the base of the tower: the circular iron staircase, the hollow post or "weight-way" in the middle, and the glazed enamel finish on the inner walls. Apparently the tower was bricked both outside and inside and then a glazed enamel finish was installed over the interior bricks for easier cleaning. Although octagonal on the outside, it was circular on the inside. The entry room, also the watchroom, had four windows overlooking the lake, from which the lightkeepers could keep an eye out for ships and changes in the weather. There was also a window known as the watch-window in the "weight-way" where they could see the descending weights that ran the light's clockwork mechanism. When the weights could been seen in the watch window, the lightkeeper had 20 minutes to rewind them before the mechanism would stop. These weights had to be rewound approximately every two hours.

Thirty-two steps ascended to the top. The upper level had interior walkways to aid cleaning and provide accessibility for making repairs. The lens room had 16 panels, each three rows high. The nine panels facing the water had 27 panes of curved, green tinted glass. The seven back panels were steel. Each panel had its own brass vent to regulate airflow and keep the lamp burning well. The main feature of this room is the third-order Fresnel bivalve optic and the gearbox attached to the base of the lens pedestal connected to the clockwork mechanism by a cable whose weights descended in the "weight-way." The vertical descent of these weights was converted by gears into the horizontal turning of the whole lens assembly. The lens floated in 250 pounds (115 kg) of mercury to allow it to turn fast enough that two lens panels could produce the required one flash every ten seconds.

Once, when the light started to slow down, lightkeeper Covell went to Two Harbors to buy more mercury for the bearing surface. Discovering that there was none available, he and his assistant turned the light by hand for two nights, using a marine stopwatch to time the intervals exactly. The next day the mercury arrived from Two Harbors and the light was restored to its normal rotation schedule. Instead of praising him for his ingenuity, Covell's superiors in Detroit held him accountable and asked him to produce a receipt for the £8 ($24) worth of mercury.

The light was produced by an incandescent oil vapor lamp. Its brass fuel tank was supported against the revolving pedestal of the lens. The tank was filled daily with filtered kerosene from the oil house, and the tank was pumped by hand through the night to build up enough air pressure to keep it going. The lamp vaporized the kerosene when it passed over its own Bunsen flame and produced a more powerful light than wick-burning lamps. With the light's bright 1,200,000 candlepower and its 168-foot (51.5 m) focal plane, it was visible for 22 miles (35.5 km), although it was reportedly seen much farther away.

The dock and boathouse were built in 1910. Repairs had to be made regularly to each, depending on the severity of Lake Superior's storms. Supplies were delivered to the station by the tender *Amaranth* or its sister ship *Marigold*. The vessel anchored offshore and used a launch to unload the supplies. They brought bulk quantities of coal, gasoline and kerosene, which took several days to lift by derrick and store away. If the lighthouse inspector was on board, the ship would fly a tiny pennant to indicate this. By 1933 the last lighthouse boat had been burned as worn-out, surplus property. A storm in 1939 destroyed the dock for the last time, and a 1959 storm destroyed the boathouse.

In 1915–16 a tramway had been built from the dock to replace the dangerous derrick for unloading and moving supplies. A gasoline engine drew the car up the tramway by cable to the front of the "hoist" house. From here the car was disconnected and pushed manually to the dwellings and the oil house. In 1934, when the station received a truck to haul its supplies, the tramway was no longer used.

The fog house had two identical gasoline engine air compressors in case of mechanical failure. The loud Type 2-T diaphone foghorns produced loud blasts that scared animals and people up to 5 miles (8 km) away. Within minutes the compressors could build up sufficient pressure to operate the two roof horns, which sounded two seconds out of every 20. Fog tended to distort the sound. On one occasion, keeper Covell, realizing a ship was getting too close to the rocky shore, took a tin whistle, rushed to the end of the dock and blew fiercely on the whistle. The ship heard this additional warning, reversed its engines and moved to safe open water.

To keep pace with the times, further changes were introduced at Split Rock. In 1932 the gasoline fog engines were replaced. (Later, in 1961, the fog signal, no longer needed because vessels had their own navigational devices, was discontinued by the Coast Guard.) In 1924 the North Shore highway was built, opening the area to more tourists. In 1925 a rough road was built from the highway to the lighthouse and boathouse. In 1930 a pump house was added to replace the system of collecting rainwater from the roof in a basement cistern. By the early 1930s about 5,000 people a year visited the light station. Visiting hours had to be established so that tourists would not interfere with the keeper's duties, since he had to accompany visitors on their tour. By 1935 the Lighthouse Service recognized the station as "one of the show places of the district" and built a new access road. In 1939 the U.S. Coast Guard took over the light's operation. When commercial electricity was brought to the area in 1941, the light became electrically lit.

The station was closed in 1969 and listed on the State of Minnesota's *Register of Historic Sites* in 1970. It is also listed on the *National Register of Historic Places*. In 1971 it was deeded to the State of Minnesota and is now part of Split Rock State Park. The Minnesota Historical Society now operates the facilities at the lighthouse. They started renovations in 1981 and are continually improving the site to its early 1920s appearance.

For a small fee, tourists may visit the museum and history cen-ter, the lighthouse, the fog signal building and the keeper's house. They can climb the tower, look at the spectacular view, or camp at the nearby campgrounds and wander the trails. The U.S. government gave special recognition to Split Rock Lighthouse in 1995 by honoring it as one of the five lighthouses on the Great Lakes to be pictured on a commemorative stamp.

Today the light is relit once a year (as it has been since 1985) on November 10 to commemorate the sinking of the *Edmund Fitzgerald*, which sailed out of Duluth Harbor on November 9, 1975 and passed Split Rock. As part of the ceremony, there is a memorial reading of the names of the 29 sailors who died when the vessel sank. This event draws many participants each year. As well as sharing in the memorial, they can glimpse the light operating at night just as it did in earlier years.

Known Keepers: Orrin Young (1910–28), Franklin Covell (1928–44), James Gagnon (1944–46).

57 Stannard Rock Lighthouse

Stannard Rock is really the summit of a submerged underwater mountain well out in the deep water of Lake Superior. The rock, about 1,000 feet (305 m) high, was not discovered until 1835. Early mariners had traveled the lakes by "coasting," staying within sight of the shoreline. As lights were placed, ships could travel farther from land, but in the early 1800s very few lights marked Superior's shores.

Captain Charles C. Stannard, a seasoned navigator and shipmaster, was piloting the brand new 77-foot (23.6 m) schooner *John Jacob Astor*, an American Fur Company vessel, on its maiden voyage from the east end of Superior to Copper Harbor on the Keweenaw Peninsula in August 1835. Traveling slowly with his heavily laden vessel, he was taking a direct route from Whitefish Point, a route he thought to be safe in good weather. He was startled to see waves breaking over a rock in the middle of the lake. He marked his charts. As local mariners learned of its existence, it became known as Stannard's Rock.

This underwater mountain extends about 1/2 to 3/4 of a mile (0.8 to 1.2 km) in a north-south direction, is about 1/4 mile wide, and has water as shallow as 4 feet (1.2 m) flowing over it. It is 45 miles (73 km) north of Marquette, about 35 miles (57 km) southeast of Copper Harbor on the Keweenaw Peninsula, 23 miles (37.2 km) from the nearest land (Manitou Island off the tip of Keweenaw Peninsula) and 32 miles (52 km) northwest of Big Bay Point. It is also just 13 miles (21 km) away from modern shipping lanes and was once almost in the path of shipping routes, when steamers began traveling further offshore.

After the Soo Locks opened in 1855, the Rock was still unknown to mariners further afield — even to the Lighthouse Board. Reports vary on how it was first marked. One is that in 1864 W.H. Hearding, head of a hydrography survey party, anchored on the Rock and set up a temporary tripod of 25-foot (7.7 m) steel rods as a day beacon. On clear days it could be seen for quite a distance but it was useless at night or in a fog. Local folklore tells of a Marquette fisherman who hung stale fish from the rods so that the odor would warn mariners to keep away.

Another report says the Rock was first marked in 1868. In November 1866 General W.F. Raynolds of the Army Corps of Engineers notified the Lighthouse Board of Stannard Rock's existence and proclaimed it "the most dangerous shoal in Lake Superior." Realizing the difficulty of erecting a lighthouse on the exposed rock, he recommended a daymarker. A large wrought-iron shaft was bolted to the south end of the rock to support a frustum of cut stone. An iron cage placed over the structure completed its unique day signal, which was visible for up 5 to 6 miles (8 to 9.5 km). This day beacon also tested the viability of a lighthouse in such an exposed location.

After ten years the Board believed it had passed the test — and mariners were demanding a light. Since the offshore light at Spectacle Reef was just being completed, it seemed economical to import the entire crew, buildings and equipment to use their expertise at Stannard Rock. Knowing it would take years to build a lighthouse, due to the short work season (June–October), the great traveling distance and the exposed offshore location, the government estimated a huge cost of $300,000. The survey crew sent to begin the process in 1873 chose a location northwest of the daymarker.

In March 1877 Congress appropriated $50,000 to start the lighthouse. The Stannard Rock design was similar to that of Spectacle Reef, and John Bailey of the Corps of Engineers was assigned to supervise construction. A base camp was first set up on West Huron Island about 40 miles (65 km) southwest of the Rock. It included a smith's shop, warehouse and tool room, storehouse, icehouse, cookhouse and dining hall, two bunkhouses and an office. With the work town reassembled, attention turned to building four immense timber cribs.

Congress appropriated another $100,000 in June 1878 for the project's continuation. The cribs were towed to the Rock and placed so as to form an 80-foot (24.5 m) square. They were then sunk using about 4,925 tons of stone, a process that itself took about two months. The crib built up about 13 feet (4 m) out of the water. When offshore work stopped for the season, the stone-breaking machines were assembled at West Huron Island. The stone used in the lighthouse may have come from West Huron Island, Marblehead (Lake Erie) or Kelleys Island (Lake Erie). At any rate, the stone was cut and preassembled at West Huron Island and then numbered and dismantled for reassembly at Stannard Rock.

In March 1879 another $50,000 was allocated. That spring the crib was found virtually undamaged, as it had been protected in a casing of thick ice. Waterproof workmen's quarters were built on the crib to house about 25 men so that they could continue work on site even when the tender *Maythem* couldn't get to the light-

Stannard Rock Lighthouse

house. Within the inner square of the pier, the crew assembled a cofferdam made of 12-foot (3.7 m) lengths of small square pine scantlings that were set on end, supported by iron hoops and attached to the cribwork. Oakum-packed piping was placed around the bottom and each scantling was tightly sledge-hammered in to adjust it to the uneven bottom. Water pressure pressed the surrounding canvas close to the wood and curbed the water flow as the cofferdam was pumped empty. Once empty, it was calked and a huge cylinder of boiler iron, which had been made onshore, was placed inside. Loose rocks and boulders were removed from its interior, and the rock was leveled to bedrock.

The first layer of interlocking stone from the base camp was then set into grooved beds to form a circle 64 feet (19.6 m) in diameter. These stones were drilled and anchored 30 inches (0.9 m) into the bedrock with Swede iron drift bolts. These were split at one end, so that when hammered home they spread, forming a riveted head at the bottom. Remaining spaces were filled with Portland cement. From this bottom layer, the crib was built up 30 feet (9 m) with tiers of the numbered stone blocks bolted to the layer below. When the crib was 9 feet (2.7 m) above water, work had to stop for the season.

Congress appropriated another $50,000 in June 1880. Work on completing the crib had resumed in late May after 20 men had spent more than a week removing its winter ice buildup. By August the crib, now 35 feet (10.7 m) high, was complete, including interior spaces laid out like a wheel and reached by spoke-like hallways. They included a pump room, a coalbunker, storage rooms, and a room below water level for refrigerated storage. Since the stonecutters were behind schedule, offshore work was again halted.

A further $73,000 to complete the lighthouse was appropriated in March 1881. The 79-foot (24 m) cut stone tower was built on the crib in 1881 and 1882. It had a base diameter of more than 30 feet (9 m) and walls 10 feet (3 m) thick that tapered to 3 feet (0.9 m) at the top. A circular iron staircase led up to the gallery, dining area and larder, which was well stocked with dried and canned food.

The third and fourth levels were sparsely furnished rooms with bunk beds, and the fifth was a small library. The clockwork power room on the sixth level was only 7 feet (2.1 m) in diameter. The

Stannard Rock Lighthouse

huge lens was rotated using a clockwork mechanism that had a 70-pound (31.8 kg) weight attached to a wire cable descending within a 6-inch (1.8 cm) pipe for 60 feet (18.5 m) inside the tower wall. The keeper had to wind the weights by hand every few hours to keep the lens rotating. While the exterior of the tower was left its natural gray, the interior was whitewashed to allow the stone to breathe and to enhance interior lighting.

The cast-iron pedestal room and dodecagonal lantern housed the light's huge second-order Fresnel lens with twelve bull's eyes. Made by Henri LePaute of Paris, the lens weighed two tons and floated on a bed of mercury. It made one complete revolution every three minutes and, with its 102-foot (32 m) focal plane, was visible for up to 25 miles (40.5 km) on a starry night. Inside the lens a three-wicked oil lamp sat on a stationary platform. The wicks were so close together that their flames united into one blaze. When the light was first lit on July 4, 1882, it flashed once every 15 seconds.

In 1883 a stone engine room was built on the crib beside the tower to house boilers and fog signal equipment for the station's duplicate 10-inch (25 cm) steam whistles. As well, cranes and a boat cradle were also installed on the crib. By October 7 the station was complete. The structure contained an estimated 240,000 tons of rock, cement and steel. Its stonework cost $300,000, and its Fresnel lens $25,000. The grand total was $350,000.

This light was one of the loneliest lights to tend, perhaps even "the loneliest place in America." The keepers could not see land in any direction, even on a clear day, and the station was referred to as "stranded" rock. Some keepers even thought they were sent there as a punishment. Although four men kept the light and rotated duty and shore leave, when they were at the light they were confined there. And no women or children were allowed to stay. While two keepers spent 20 years tending the light, others rotated frequently, one threatened to jump from a tower window, and another had to be removed in a straitjacket. It's understandable that these keepers were paid higher than usual wages: in 1883 the head keeper earned $800 a year, the first assistant $500 and the other assistants $450.

Stannard Rock lighthouse was always at the mercy of nature. In 1882 when the crew arrived to finish the tower, they found ice 18 feet (5.5 m) up the tower walls. In 1926 soundings made in the spring revealed 54 feet (16.6 m) of ice below the water and a 30-foot (9 m) cake of ice above the water, and the entire tower — all 110 feet (34 m) of it — was encased in ice. In 1936 heavy ice kept the keepers from arriving at the station until June 27. The lighthouse had so much ice on it in May that it looked like a massive iceberg and the plate glass lantern windows even had ice a foot (30 cm) thick. Snow has been recorded at the light in every month of the year. Once, during inclement weather when the keepers could not be switched, keeper Louis Wilks spent 99 consecutive days at the light, longer than any modern keeper. Even after the light was automated, the weather wreaked havoc. A maintenance crew was once trapped inside the tower for days. When the storm blew over, it took their rescue party over two days to chop away the 12 feet (3.7 m) of ice to free them.

The most serious accident at the lighthouse was not caused by nature. On June 18, 1961, a serious explosion burst up the tower, killing one man and seriously injuring another. The mysterious blast was blamed on gasoline and propane fumes but no confirmed cause was reported. Three men escaped the inferno through a blown-out galley window to the 8-foot (2.4 m) wide crib below. They were unable to re-enter the tower to look for the last keeper. With no communication to the outside world, they huddled on the ledge on the tower's north side awaiting rescue.

Although the Stannard Rock light was to radio weather reports to Manitou every six hours and contact Marquette twice daily, no one at these stations checked why a report hadn't come through. Also, no vessel had reported that the light was out, and it was two days before the tender *Woodrush*, passing on its regular route, noticed and went to rescue the men. The coal was still burning. Since the light was scheduled for automation the next year, the tower was entirely gutted and the new equipment was installed to finish out the 1961 season.

The light's illuminant changed with developing technology. It was first lit with whale oil, then kerosene and later acetylene. In 1944 it switched to electricity produced by batteries and generators. At this time its light source became a 500-watt lightbulb that was replaced every 30 days to prevent its burning out. The bulb produced 156,000 candlepower. When the light was automated in 1961, it received an automatic bulb changer. Today it uses a solar-powered electric light from inside a 300 mm plastic lens and shines at a reduced 9,000 candlepower.

With the light's automation, the second-order Fresnel lens was crated and removed for storage. At that time no one seemed to care about its whereabouts, and when someone did, it could not be located. Then in 1999 the Marquette Maritime Museum got word that the lens had been found at a Coast Guard curator's warehouse in Forestville, Maryland. It was shipped to Marquette, restored and placed on display in the museum. In 2000 the U.S. Coast Guard removed the lens pedestal from the tower and took it to the museum for restoration and reassembly with the lens. The Marquette Maritime Museum is proud to own this rare duo for public viewing.

After automation the National Oceanic and Atmospheric Administration (NOAA) installed automatic weather reporting equipment. The data were sent by radio to the Marquette Coast Guard Station every three hours and then relayed to the offices at Chicago, Detroit, Cleveland and Buffalo. Weather was updated every six hours to skippers via the Lakes Weather Broadcast.

Today the Stannard Rock Lighthouse has dropped its possessive form and is listed on *the National Register of Historic Places* and on the State of Michigan *Register for Historic Sites* (1971). It is still working to serve maritime travel and has definitely earned its place in the history of the Great Lakes.

Known Keepers: John Pasque (1882–83), John Armbruster (1883), James Prior (1883–88), George Prior (1888–93), William Prior (1893–96), Edward Chambers (1896–1908), Robert Davenport (1908–13), Knut Olsen (1913–21), Lawrence Pederson (1921–21), Louis Wilks (1936–56).

58 Two Harbors East Breakwater Light

As Two Harbors, Lake Superior, developed as a busy port for the shipping of iron ore, breakwaters were built in the late 1880s and early 1890s on both the east and west sides of the harbor to protect it from lake storms. Harbor entry was marked by a fixed red lantern suspended from an iron post at the outer end of the east breakwater.

During the 1940s harbor improvements were made. The east breakwater developed into an "L" shape and its end was marked with a short skeletal pyramidal light. Its four steel legs were anchored to the concrete pier and its upper section was enclosed to form a service room. It was topped by a square gallery and an octagonal lantern. This light still actively guides vessels into port at Two Harbors today.

59 Two Harbors Lighthouse

This lighthouse is 49 ½ feet tall (15 m) from base to ventilator ball but, being located high on the hill, it stands 78 feet (24 m) above the lake to help guide ships into safe harbor at Agate Bay.

The Ojibwa Indians' name for this area — "Wasswewining," "a place to spear fish in the night" — continued to appropriately describe Two Harbors as it developed into a commercial fishing town and went on to export fish. As Superior's fish supply diminished, Two Harbors began exporting taconite pellets, a crude form of iron ore taken from the Mesabi Range. The port also shipped out logs and coal, and provided passenger service to the area. At the turn of the century about 100 boats a week entered the harbor. This busy traffic made it necessary to build a light to mark the harbor. In March 1891 the government purchased one acre (0.4 hectare) of land for the lighthouse reservation from Thomas Feigh for $1 and a warranty deed. Construction began in 1891 and the light was lit on April 4, 1892.

Two Harbors Lighthouse

A narrow staircase of 40 steps winds up through the four tower levels to the lantern. The fourth level has four porthole-style windows in the watchroom for the keeper to watch weather conditions and marine traffic and to help ventilate the lantern. Six sides of the octagonal lantern are glazed and two are closed in so the light shines in a 270-degree arc. A square exterior gallery with a black iron railing surrounds the white lantern, which is topped by a red dome and a ventilator ball.

The wood-frame fog signal building was covered with iron sheeting. Its duplicate 10-inch steam whistles had their own recognizable pattern (blast 5 s; silence 17 s; blast 5 s; silence 33 s). The entire gabled building was painted dark red. At first there were three keepers. The third one was on call and when he worked, he lived in the tiny, first-floor room of the tower.

The original light had a fourth-order Fresnel lens with an oil and wick lamp. It displayed a fixed red light from a 78-foot (24 m) focal plane for 16 miles (26 km). Later a kerosene lamp with about 30,000 candlepower was used and it was changed to a flashing light. Weighted chains that had to be reset every two hours kept the lens rotating to create its distinctive flash pattern. In 1921 the light was electrified, giving it 230,000 candlepower. In 1970 the Fresnel lens was replaced with a two-DCB-224 rotating beacon. Two 1,000-watt light bulbs in each of the 24-inch beacons now rotate in the tower, giving a visibility of 17 miles (27.5 km). The station was automated in 1980 and the light was operated from a station in Duluth, 24 hours a day. Coast Guard personnel continued to use the keeper's house until 1987.

The stately 2 ½-story square red brick house has gable peaks built against two sides of its 12-foot (3.7 m) square tower. The house walls are double-bricked and the tower is triple-bricked. The places where they meet have a thickness of five bricks. As well as providing insulation, these layers of brick helped to provide fire protection. Double windows appear up the sides of the tower and ornate brickwork frames the round windows in the watchroom below the lantern. The nearby assistant keeper's house was a small, white, two-story frame house with a cedar shake roof and gray trim. It was originally a barn but in 1894 it was moved to this site and converted into a home.

Today the light is significant as it is Minnesota's last working lighthouse. The U.S. Coast Guard owns the land and maintains the light, and Lake County Historical Society operates the museum. The Society is gradually restoring the lighthouse and buildings using antiques of the period. Visitors can go up the tower but the four-bedroom lightkeeper's residence is privately occupied.

The original fourth-order Fresnel lens is on display at the Inland Sea Museum in Vermillion, Ohio. The light continues to mark the harbor and the station is listed on both the National and State Register of Historic Places. The light station was decommissioned on August 18, 1982, but the light still shines on, blinking its own distinctive light pattern (flash 0.5 s; eclipse 4.5 s; flash 0.5 s; eclipse 14 s).

Known Keepers: Charles Lederle (1892–1910), Otto Redman (1910–13), Lee Benton (1913–15), Alexander McLean (1919–31), Lawrence Pederson (1931–40).

Two Harbors East Breakwater Light

Vidal Shoals Channel Range Light, circa 1909

60 Vidal Shoals Channel Range Lights

Just before the turn of the twentieth century, range lights were placed near the base of the International Train Bridge on the American side of the St. Mary's River to mark the Vidal Shoals and safe passage into the American Soo Locks and Canal System, which circumnavigated the Soo Rapids and connected Lake Superior to Lake Huron via the St. Mary's River.

The front range light was a white conical tower built on the end of the north pier 1,400 feet (430 m) in front of the rear light. Its fixed red light was exhibited from a fourth-order lens and had a focal plane of 30 feet (9.2 m). The rear range light was an open iron-framed triangular pyramidal tower with its upper half slatted and painted white and its lower half painted brown. It had a fifth-order lens that displayed a fixed white light varied by a red flash every minute. From its location near the railroad embankment it had a 57-foot (17.5 m) focal plane.

In 1902 changes were made at the station. The rear range light's fifth-order lens was changed to a lens-lantern light that displayed a fixed red light. The front range light was switched from a fourth-order lens to a fifth-order lens that displayed a fixed white light varied by a red flash every 40 seconds. Both lights maintained the same focal plane.

These range lights were later modified. The front light was raised about 10 feet (3 m) to increase its focal plane by having another iron section placed beneath it. The rear range light was replaced by a new octagonal white tapering tower with a slightly higher focal plane. These range lights were maintained by the Soo Lock Commission. They no longer exist today and the shoals are now marked by lighted buoys.

61 Whitefish Point Lighthouse

In the 1800s the U.S. government encouraged people to "go west." Some of those who did chose a water route and were lost in wrecks off Whitefish Point, nicknamed the "graveyard of Superior." Reporter Horace Greeley in 1847 accused the federal government of manslaughter for not having erected a lighthouse on the point to assist navigation.

This point is crucial to lake travel because it marks a course change for vessels navigating the treacherous coastline to and from the St. Mary's River and the Soo Canal. During ferocious storms on

Lake Superior, ships would often seek safety in the relatively calm waters of Whitefish Bay behind the point. A lighthouse on the point would help mark the location of the bay as well as warn of the treacherous shoals off the point.

In 1847, 115.5 acres (46.7 hectares) of land were purchased at Whitefish Point for the lighthouse station, and Ebenezer Warner of Sandusky, Ohio, was contracted to build the first light. He built a 65-foot (20 m) stone tower and detached 1½-story stone keeper's house. The stone was hauled from Tahquamenon Island off Emerson by the 52-ton schooner *Fur Trader*, one of three schooners on Lake Superior at that time. The conical tower had a 25-foot (7.7 m) base diameter and a diameter of 12 feet (3.7 m) at the summit. Its walls tapered from 5 feet (1.5 m) thick at the bottom to a top thickness of 2 feet (0.6 m).

It supported a thick stone deck 14½ feet (4.4 m) in diameter. Six 12-paned windows ascended the tower to provide interior light and yellow pine stairs spiraled up the tower to just below the lantern. An iron ladder provided access through the scuttle door in the stone deck. The octagonal birdcage-style lantern was anchored 5 feet (1.5 m) into the tower stonework. Each octagonal panel had 15 lights with a tier of copper panels at the bottom. The illuminating apparatus consisted of thirteen Winslow Lewis lamps that burned sperm whale oil and had 14-inch (35 cm) reflectors. The lantern was lit at the beginning of the 1849 navigation season. This light was one of the two earliest lights on Lake Superior, the other being the Copper Harbor Lighthouse, also built in 1849. While $5,000 had been appropriated to build the light station, its final cost was $8,298.

None of its early keepers stayed at this station very long, perhaps because of its harsh, remote location. The third keeper, Amos Stiles, resigned in August 1853 and was traveling on the *Independence*, the first steamer on Lake Superior, when it exploded later that year. Having survived the explosion, he rode the rapids on a bale of hay, and when he was pulled out of the river at the foot of the rapids he was half dead. After the experience he was known as "the man who never smiled."

By the mid-1800s the newly formed Lighthouse Board (1852) was upgrading technology at lighthouses with the implementation of Fresnel lenses on the Great Lakes. Whitefish Point received its new fourth-order Fresnel lens in 1857, thereby increasing the light's fixed white beam to a 13-mile (21 km) visibility.

While lake traffic boomed after the Soo Locks opened in 1855, Congress was petitioned to improve the light at Whitefish Point. To this end a new, taller lighthouse and keeper's house were built. The new tower was designed as an iron-pile tower to withstand high winds. It had a 6-foot (1.8 m) cylindrical cast-iron center, lined with wood to help prevent condensation. The cylinder was supported by four tubular iron legs bolted to a concrete foundation. The legs were then reinforced with diagonal and horizontal iron cross-braces. The center cylinder was raised 17 feet (5.2 m) above the ground and was met and entered by a covered passageway from the second floor of the two-story clapboard keeper's house.

An octagonal gallery surrounded the pedestal room that housed the base of the huge third-order Fresnel lens. An upper circular gallery provided access for the keeper to clean the 30 exterior glass panels of its lantern. With its 76-foot (23 m) tower and its larger third-order Fresnel lens made by Barbier and Benard of Paris, the light had an 80-foot (24.4 m) focal plane, making it visible for 25 miles (40.5 km). When the station was completed in the spring of 1862, the old tower was torn down but the old keeper's house remained for a number of years. In 1863 an assistant keeper was hired.

In 1869 the lighthouse inspector recommended that a fog signal be added to the station. In 1871 a contract was awarded to

Whitefish Point Lighthouse

build a fog building to house equipment for 10-inch (25 cm) steam fog whistles. The wood-frame structure was covered with corrugated iron sheeting to withstand harsh Lake Superior storms. It was lined with iron sheeting and the space between was packed with sawdust and lime to insulate it and reduce the possibility of fire. In 1896 the steam fog signal building was rebuilt. In 1925 the steam whistles were replaced with more powerful air-powered Type F diaphone foghorns that sounded two short blasts and one long blast every minute. In October 1925 a radio beacon transmitter was installed in the fog signal building. It gave out a single dash every minute during fog. After the fog signal building was destroyed in a 1935 October storm, it was replaced by a new brick building in 1936. In 1983 the diaphone foghorns were changed to an electronic horn mounted on the tower.

The light underwent changes with time. First, its fixed characteristic became a flashing one. Red flash panels were added to the Fresnel lens and in 1893 a ball-bearing mechanism was added to help the lens rotate to produce a fixed white light varied by a red flash every 20 seconds. When the lens pedestal began in 1896 to rotate on a bed of mercury, much friction was eliminated and the lens could rotate faster. The light's characteristic was accordingly changed to a red flash every five seconds. In 1913 the light's lamp was upgraded to an Aladdin incandescent oil vapor system that provided three million candlepower. In 1918 the lens's red panels were removed and the light's characteristic became an occulting white light every two seconds (flash 2 s; eclipse 2 s).

Facilities at the station gradually changed and expanded: circular iron oil house added (1893); second-order kerosene lamp placed inside the lens (1893); second assistant keeper hired (1893); keeper's house remodeled into a duplex for keeper and first assistant (1894); small frame dwelling built for second assistant (1894); tramway installed (1900); submarine fog bell positioned offshore (1912); lifesaving station added (1923); protective piers built in front of the station (1937); light and lifesaving crews amalgamated into one six-man crew to operate light, fog signal, radio beacon and newly added weather bureau station (1947).

In 1968 the Fresnel lens was replaced with a DCB 224 aerobeacon powered by an electric motor. In 1971 the station was fully automated, making the keepers redundant. In 1973 the station was listed on the *National Register of Historic Places*. The Great Lakes Shipwreck Historical Society (GLSHS) was granted a 25-year license from the Coast Guard in 1983 to establish a shipwreck museum, and in 1985 they opened the Great Lakes Shipwreck Museum in the keeper's house. The Coast Guard station at Sault Ste. Marie continued to maintain the light. In 1996 a dedication service was held to open the restored Lightkeeper's Quarters and the government transferred 5 acres (2 hectares) of Whitefish Point and its historic buildings to permanent ownership of the GLSHS. It seems appropriate that the point once nicknamed the "graveyard of Superior" is now home to a museum for shipwrecks, the only one of its kind on the Great Lakes. Besides displaying marine artefacts, which include the second-order Fresnel lens from White Shoal, it also shows films of shipwrecks off the point.

Over 70 major shipwrecks have been recorded in these waters, including the wreck of the famous ore carrier the *Edmund Fitzgerald*, which sank mysteriously in November 1975 during one of Superior's worst storms. The most recent dive to solve the mystery took place in 1995 — a joint effort by the Canadian Navy, the Great Lakes Shipwreck Historical Society and the National Geographic Society. Divers were able to retrieve the ship's bell and it was donated to the Great Lakes Shipwreck Museum in honor of the 29 crew members who lost their lives.

Known Keepers: James Starr (1848–), James B. Van Ranselaer (1848–51), Amos Stiles (1851–53), William Crampton (1853–56), Belloni McGulpin (1856–59), Charles Carland (1859–61), Joseph Kemp (1861–64), Edward Ashman (1868–74), Charles Linke (1875–82), Edward Chambers (1882–83), Charles Kimball (1883–1903), Robert Carlson (1903–31), Harry House (1931–33), Charles Lewis (1933–39).

62 Wisconsin Point (Superior Entry) Lighthouse

The sandbar that crosses the mouth of the bay leading to the ports of Duluth and Superior at Lake Superior's western end is broken by a natural channel known as the Superior Entry, which allows entry to both harbors. The 9-mile (14.6 km) bar is called Minnesota Point on the Minnesota side and Wisconsin Point on the Wisconsin side. To mark the channel the government placed a lighthouse on the tip of Minnesota Point in 1858.

The Duluth Ship Canal was cut through the base of Minnesota Point in 1871 to provide direct, deeper entry to the harbor at Duluth. It was also marked with a lighthouse. As part of its harbor improvements, the government widened and deepened the Superior Entry and built wooden protective piers on either side of it. Because the channel had naturally shifted further to the south before the piers were built, it was deemed better to mark it by placing a new lighthouse right on the northern pier. It was a white skeletal wooden tower. When the new light was lit in 1885, the old Minnesota Point Light was deactivated. However, the keeper's dwelling continued to serve as housing for the new light.

As harbor improvements continued, the government upgraded the piers and decided in 1892 to move the lighthouse to the longer south pier. It was placed near the outer end, stood 44 feet (13.5 m) high, and displayed a fixed white light for 14 miles (22.7 km). At the same time, an elevated walkway was built from lighthouse to shore for the keeper's safety. The keepers continued to use the old housing across the channel until a new duplex was built in 1893 on the Wisconsin side. Work crews also built a boathouse, a 360-gallon (1512 l) oil house, walkways and a fog signal building behind the lighthouse at the end of the south pier. The fog building, a wood-frame structure with corrugated iron exterior walls and smooth iron interior walls, housed equipment to operate duplicate 6-inch (15 cm) steam whistles mounted to the roof. The catwalk was extended to the fog signal building. It was ready for operation on August 27, 1893. In 1895 it blasted its signal (blast 3 s; silence 12 s) for a total of 895 hours.

Range lights were decided on for the south pier in 1898. The original pierhead was to become the front range light and another beacon was to be added behind it to form the rear range light. It was intended to be the temporary skeletal tower used at Devil's Island, but when the arrival of the Devil's Island lens was delayed, a temporary post was erected on the south pier to support a light to act as the rear range light. It was lit on November 30, 1898. Then, when the new lens was installed at Devil's Island in 1901,

the timber-framed skeletal tower of the temporary light was moved and set up on the south pier at Superior Entry. It was equipped with a fourth-order Fresnel lens that shone its fixed white light for the first time on April 1, 1902.

In 1905 a government crew started to build more permanent concrete piers behind the decaying wooden ones. The plan was to move the lighthouses to the new southern pier and to remove the old wooden piers when the new piers were completed. However, a late November storm pounded the area and completely washed away the front range light, part of the catwalk, and the roof and upper portion of the fog signal building. Temporary repairs were made and a temporary wooden lantern was placed on the fog signal building. The signal was repaired the following spring.

By 1910 plans for the harbor had changed. Arrowhead breakwaters were planned for outside the Superior Entry to create a stilling basin for storm protection. A new fog signal building and a new main entry light were planned for the south breakwater. When they were put into service in 1913, the old pier range lights and fog signal were discontinued and the structures removed. Automated acetylene beacons then marked the pier.

63 Wisconsin Point South Breakwater Light

After the completion of the arrowhead breakwaters on the lake side of Superior Entry at Wisconsin Point, Lake Superior, a new combined lighthouse and fog signal building was placed at the north end of the new south breakwater to mark the entrance into the new stilling basin outside Superior Entry.

The lighthouse was built on a concrete foundation 11½ feet (3.5 m) high that had vaulted ceilings for rooms to store paint, oil, and drinking water. A two-story oblong or oval structure was built on the foundation using reinforced concrete. The first level served as a mechanical room for heating and for the duplicate fog sirens. The second level provided the keeper's living quarters.

A short cylindrical tower rose for two stories through the lakeward roof end of the building and was accessed by a spiral iron staircase entered from the main structure's second level. The lower level housed the 6-inch (15 cm) fog sirens with their resonators extending through the tower wall. The upper level was a service room for storing necessary equipment and supplies to operate the light. The tower supported a cylindrical lantern with diagonally set astragals and a copper dome.

The lantern housed a fourth-order Fresnel lens within which there was a rotating screen. This screen was mounted on ball bearings and rotated by a clockwork mechanism to produce a flashing light (flash 5 s; eclipse 5 s) visible for 16 miles (26 km) from its 70-foot (21.5 m) focal plane. When this new light was lit in 1913, the old pier range lights and fog signal were discontinued. Keepers reached the light by a 2,000-foot (610 m) walkway furnished with a steel cable for their safety.

In 1937 the fog siren was replaced with a type F diaphone fog signal and in 1938 a radio beacon was added to the station. The station was automated in 1970 and its lighting apparatus became a DCB 24 aerobeacon that projected a green flashing light every five seconds for 22 miles (35.5 km). This light is still operational today.

Known Keepers: Edwin Bishop (1913–15), Hans Christensen (1834–39), John Kirkendall (1939–40).

Wisconsin Point South Breakwater Light

LAKE SUPERIOR
CANADA
LIGHTHOUSES

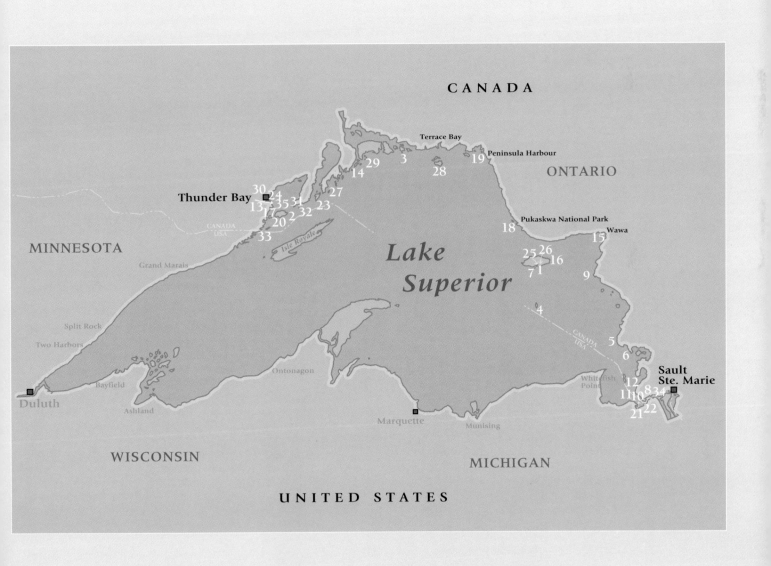

CANADA

Terrace Bay

Peninsula Harbour

ONTARIO

29 3

14 28 19

Thunder Bay

30 24
13 35 31 27
17 2 32 23
20
33

CANADA
USA

Isle Royale

Pukaskwa National Park

18 15 Wawa

MINNESOTA

Grand Marais

25 26
16
7 1 9

Lake
Superior

Split Rock

4

Two Harbors

CANADA
USA

5

Bayfield

6

Duluth

Sault
Ste. Marie

Ontonagon

Whitefish
Point

12
11 8 34
10
21 22

Ashland

Marquette

Munising

WISCONSIN

MICHIGAN

UNITED STATES

Quebec Harbour Lighthouse at left, Agate Island Lighthouse at right

1 Agate Island Lighthouse

Lake traffic along northern Lake Superior steadily increased during the latter part of the 1800s as more wheat, iron ore and lumber were shipped to the lower Great Lakes. To support the "rapidly expanding trade in that direction," the Canadian government in 1872–73 erected three lights. One of them was placed near Superior's west end on Porphyry Island, and the other two at Quebec Harbour on the south side of Michipicoten Island along the lake's northeast coast.

This natural harbor, 2.5 miles (4 km) long and ½ mile (0.8 km) wide, provided deep anchorage for shelter from storms. However, its entrance was tricky to navigate, as it was impeded by many small islands. One light was placed on Chimney Point (see Quebec Harbour) at the east side of the harbor entrance and the other on Agate Island, just inside the harbor. For safe entry mariners traveled between the two lights into the harbor.

The lighthouse on Agate Island, built in 1872, was a simple square 20-foot (6 m) white wooden tower with an iron lantern that displayed a fixed white light produced by two mammoth flat-wick lamps with 16-inch (40 cm) reflectors. From its 32-foot (9.8 m) focal plane the light was visible for 10 miles (16 km).

In 1916 the government decided to better mark the harbor. They built a new light on Davieaux Island just outside the entrance and established range lights at the back of the harbor. In 1917 they moved the Agate Island tower on a scow to the back of the harbor to become the front range light, and built a new tower as the rear range light. When the new lights were lit in 1918, the old lighthouse on Chimney Point was extinguished and abandoned.

Known Keepers: Peter McIntyre (1872–79–), S.C. Gardiner (after 1870s–), Hyancinthe Davieaux (–1910), Charles Davieaux (1910–18).

2 Angus Island Lighthouse

Pie Island is a large island in the entrance to Thunder Bay along Lake Superior's north shore above Isle Royale. Angus Island was basically just a bald-headed rock that rose steeply from the water just east of Pie Island. In 1927 the Canadian government built a lighthouse near the north end of Angus Island to mark the shipping route into the bay where the shipping terminals of Port Arthur and Fort William were located. The first lighthouse, contracted to K. Justin, was almost identical to the last Corbeil lighthouse. It was a large two story, four square frame dwelling with open veranda running almost across the whole front of the house that faced the water. The house was topped with a hipped roof and centered at its summit was a large square gallery surrounded with simple pipe railing. A square wooden lantern with large rectangular windows (one per side) and a hipped roof and ventilator stack finished the lighthouse.

At a later date this lighthouse was replaced with a duplex keeper's house and the light was replaced with a 44.5-foot (13.6 m) square skeletal tower equipped with a catoptric illuminating apparatus that displayed a white flashing light (flash 3.5 s; eclipse 16.5 s) from an 80-foot (24.5 m) focal plane for 16 miles (26 km). The foghorn had a characteristic 30-second repeated pattern (blast 3 s; silence 27 s). A radio beacon was added at a later date.

The keepers were delivered to the lighthouse in the spring, usually late April to early May when the ice was moving out, and were removed at the end of the navigation season in late November or early December, when ice was forming around the shores. In the 1930s the tug *James Whalen* delivered the keepers to Angus Island and to other lighthouses in the area. In 1959 C.G.S. *Nokomis* delivered and picked up the Angus Island Lighthouse keeper.

In 1961 the Department of Transport initiated a higher-tech method for this purpose. The Coast Guard icebreaker *Alexander Henry*, equipped with a helicopter on board, introduced "marine-aerial" service for more efficient delivery and pickup of keepers and supplies. The icebreaker traveled to the lighthouse and then the helicopter lifted the keeper, his family and their supplies to the lighthouse reservation. This method was less labor-intensive, as no supplies had to be hauled across ice or lugged up steep slopes. By the 1980s a Coast Guard helicopter from Thunder Bay transferred keepers directly.

The last keeper, Roger Irvin, reported the island to be "the most beautiful spot alive." Even when he knew it was his last season as keeper, he continued trying to enhance the station with a small reflecting pool and a lawn. Earlier residents, especially keeper Hayward's wife, had tried gathering earth from other islands to build a garden, but had met with little success.

The lighthouse was automated at the end of the 1988 navigation season. The new equipment sent signals to the Coast Guard Base at Thunder Bay to report if the light was working, if the foghorn was sounding, or if someone had broken into the buildings. However, the latter was not anticipated, as the lighthouse was 26.5 miles (43 km) away from Thunder Bay in Lake Superior. This light continues to operate today to guide vessels into Thunder Bay.

Known Keepers: John McClure (1928–37), Charles Merritt (1937–45), Roy McLean (1946), Harry Stevens (1947), Spears (1948–49), Robert Henry Guerard (1950–59), Thomas Hayward (1959–), Walter Stokes (–1981–), Roger Irvin (–1988).

Angus Island Lighthouse, circa 1928

Battle Island Lighthouse

3 Battle Island Lighthouse

During the Riel Rebellion in the Canadian West, troops were brought from Ontario to quell the disturbance. Since the railroad did not yet run through, the soldiers were marched across the ice from Jackfish to the Rossport area. They claimed that local Ojibway fired on them from one of the islands, so they fired back, engaging in a "battle." Although the story may lack validity and the exact island the Ojibway allegedly fired from is unknown, this is the source of Battle Island's name.

Battle Island is about 7 miles (11.2 km) out from Rossport between Simpson Island and Wilson Island along Superior's north shore. The first lighthouse was built on a 60-foot (18.5 m) rock face at the west end of the island because it was close to the east-west shipping channels and could help guide ships through the adjacent Simpson Channel at the eastern entrance to Nipigon Bay. It is said to be the northernmost lighthouse on the Great Lakes.

This first lighthouse, built in 1877 by Joseph White, was a square white wooden 20-foot (6 m) tower with an iron lantern which was 8 feet (2.4 m) in diameter. The station included a boathouse and a keeper's house about 300 feet (92 m) from the tower. The light exhibited a red and white alternating flash pattern, with its brightest light flashing every 90 seconds. From its 85-foot (26 m) focal plane the light was made visible for 16 miles (27 km) by using lamps and reflectors. The station also had a hand-operated foghorn to answer ships' signals during poor visibility.

The present tower, built in 1911, is a white, octagonal, reinforced concrete structure that stands 43 feet (13 m) tall. At 117 feet (36 m) above the water, it has a 13-mile (21 km) visibility. In 1914 oil tanks were installed for a planned fog building. In 1915 the fog building and a new duplex keeper's house were built. Over the years, the Coast Guard made necessary repairs and upgrades: from 1940–42, to the house and the tower; in 1949, to the roof, chimney and veranda following a fire; in 1955, to the tower parapet and the insulation. In 1982 the light's pattern was changed to a flash followed by a 16-second eclipse, a radar reflector and emergency light were added, and the light became operational year round. In 1991 it was automated.

Andrew Dick was temporary keeper when the lighthouse first opened until its first official keeper arrived. He had sailed to the Rossport area in 1862 from Sault Ste. Marie in a small boat. He trapped and fished at Pays Platt until he became keeper. He was at Battle Island for only a few months before being appointed keeper at Point Porphyry.

The first official keeper, Charles McKay, served at Battle Island for 36 years, and received a medal from King George V for his years of dedication. One year he left Battle Island in early December and rowed/sailed to see his family in Sault Ste. Marie. He arrived on Christmas Day but could not get through because of the ice. Another time he rowed/sailed all the way to Thunder Bay (Port Arthur) on business.

Once a summer a supply ship brought food, oil for the light, and boxes of books. In December 1906 the icebreaking tug *James Whalen* picked up the lightkeepers. Keepers were expected to be ready for the pickup and not make the tug wait, because they could see its smoke long before it arrived.

McKay's philosophy was self-reliance. While very lonely and isolated during the week, he often had Sunday visits from summer picnickers. People from Rossport brought baked beans, spaghetti, layer cakes and homemade bread, and it became tradition to boil up a fish chowder when they arrived. Entertainment included playing ball, fishing, dancing, and sing-alongs accompanied by violins, guitars and mouth organs (harmonicas). This camaraderie may have helped McKay stay on as keeper for so long.

In 1899 the *Ontario*, a 181-foot (55 m) CPR-owned supply steamer heading for Rossport, sank in August off Battle Island's eastern tip. While the wreck was scattered in waters offshore, the boiler was washed onto the island's shore. Another mishap was the drowning of keeper Malcolm Sutherland in 1932, after which his wife finished out the season.

Williard Hubelit, assistant keeper at Battle Island from 1960 to 1982, earned $200 a month but had to pay the chief keeper $50 a month for board. His 12-hour shift ran from midnight to noon. He remembers that the coal oil lamps with air mantles had to be filled twice a night, and how carefully the delicate mantles had to be watched because one drop of condensation or the touch of a moth's wing could break them. He guarded against the lamps flaring up because their smoke left black soot on everything and it took a week to clean up. He also kept an eye on the balance weight and tried to never let it wind down completely because it was "awful slow to wind up."

In 1971 Hubelit lost part of a finger in a fierce storm. He was working in the engine room when a mountainous wave washed over the lighthouse, knocked out a window and swept him out the door, while another wave slammed the door on his finger. Only two days later, after the storm had settled, could keeper Joiner take him to the hospital at Terrace Bay. The same storm also washed 500-gallon fuel tanks off their stands on the beach. In 1977 a powerful three-day storm pushed waves up another 100 feet (30 m) to wash right over the lighthouse tower. The 80-mph (130 kmph) winds even blew out windows of the lighthouse lantern.

Another assistant keeper at Battle Island was Bert Saasto, whose claim to fame was that he was the last Coast Guard official to be picked up at the end of the 1991 shipping season. This made him the last lighthouse keeper on the Great Lakes as lighthouses were automated and closed. Saasto remained on as caretaker at the Battle Island Lighthouse for the shipping season even though the light had been automated. This shows a very special love and dedication for the job at this remote lighthouse.

In 1992 the Battle Island Light displayed a triple flash pattern every 24 seconds (flash; eclipse 4 s; flash; eclipse 4 s; flash; eclipse 16 s) for a 13-mile (21 km) visibility. Today the light in the lantern is a modern beacon, but it still uses reflectors brought over from a lighthouse in England, and it still operates as an active aid to navigation.

Known Keepers: Andrew Dick (1877), Charles McKay (1877–1913), Edward McKay (1913–22), Malcolm Sutherland (1920–32), John Sutherland (1932–48), George Brady (1948–61), Willard Hubelit (1961–67), John Joiner (1967–91).

4 Caribou Island Lighthouse

This Lake Superior island is one of the most isolated islands in the Great Lakes, situated 55 miles (88 km) from the mainland, 90 miles (144 km) from Sault Ste. Marie, 28 miles (45 km) southwest of Michipicoten Island, and about midway between Canada and the United States.

The Caribou Island Lighthouse was not on Caribou Island itself, but completely filled a small one-acre (0.4 hectare) island called Lighthouse Island about 1.5 miles (2.4 km) southwest of the main island. This light marked the hazardous Caribou Shoals that stretch finger-like in a direct line along the east-west shipping lanes (which run both north and south of the shoals). Some believe that the big ore freighter *Edmund Fitzgerald* sank during a severe November storm of 1975 after striking an uncharted shoal here.

A light was first built here in 1885 just after the steamer *Spartan* (1883) and the schooner *Lady Dufferin* (1884) were caught on the shoals. A 60-foot (18.3 m) white wooden tower extended up from the 1 ½-story white clapboard keeper's house. The tapering octagonal tower had ascending pedimented windows for interior light and was topped with an octagonal gallery and a polygonal iron lantern. From a focal plane of 76 feet (23 m) the light was visible for 15 miles (24 km) and was first lit in the fall of 1886.

A fog signal building was built 100 feet (30 m) south of the light at the water's edge. The white building with a brown roof housed a steam whistle (blast 5 s; silence 25 s). In 1907 the fog signal was upgraded to a diaphone signal. It housed three large upright internal combustion engines that drove three air compressors via a long flat leather belt. The compressed air was supplied through a timing device to the diaphone (a vibrating cylinder) and then emitted through the foghorn (blast 4 s; silence 56 s).

Realizing the need for a higher, brighter light, the Canadian government in 1911–12 built a new lighthouse beside the old one, which was later removed. It was an example of a new state-of-the-

Caribou Island Lighthouse

art architecture using a reinforced concrete, flying-buttress style, designed by Lt. Colonel William P. Anderson, chief engineer for the Canadian Department of Marine and Fisheries. The lighthouse tower, based on lines of a Gothic cathedral, was centered on a concrete hexagonal tower rising from a round concrete base. On the six sides, flying buttresses angled gently outward from the top toward the base, with horizontal connections to the tower at regular intervals. The reinforced concrete helped stabilize the tower in strong winds by preventing vibrations, so that the lantern would function at optimum accuracy.

Iron ladders rose inside the 82-foot (25.6 m) tower to the polygonal lantern, which had many square glass panes. The dioptric second-order Fresnel lens floated on a bed of mercury and had a flashing white light with a visibility of 20 miles (32.4 km) from its 90-foot (27.5 m) focal plane. The light's flash characteristic had a 10-second pattern (flash 0.5 s; eclipse 1.25 s; flash 0.5 s; eclipse 1.25 s; flash 0.5 s; eclipse 6 s). It used a vaporized kerosene mantle lamp that had pressure tanks (which needed pumping every six hours) and a clockwork mechanism to make its lens revolve and create the flashing light. The mechanism needed to be wound every six hours. The lamp stood on a pedestal inside the lens so as to be in line with the magnifiers of the lens. When the lamp was first lit in cold weather, a small pan filled with alcohol was lit under it, to give it its initial heat. On a very clear night the light was reported to be visible at Gargantua on the mainland 60 miles (97 km) away. A red circular iron gallery surrounded the lantern, which was capped by a red dome.

Other structures at the station included an L-shaped concrete dock, the lightkeeper's house, the assistant keeper's house, an oil house, a boathouse, and concrete walkways connecting them all. The keeper of this new light was paid $1,260 a year, out of which he had to pay his assistant.

Ships could not always avoid the Caribou Shoals, and many seamen were lost in their vicinity over the years. On November 21, 1902, the 245-foot (75 m) grain-carrying *Bannockburn*, belonging to the Montreal Transportation Company, left Port Arthur heading for the Sault. This was the last time the ship was ever seen. It is believed that it may have been stranded on the Caribou Shoals because the Caribou Island Light had already closed on November 15 for the season. Although no one can be sure, sailors have reported that on stormy nights the blink of mysterious lights can be seen while the captain looks vainly for the welcome yellow glow of the Caribou Island light. Could these lights be from the once foundering *Bannockburn*?

Other vessels also foundered in the area. In August 1882 the ore carrier *Western Reserve* disappeared during a storm just 6 miles (10 km) southwest of the island. Late in October 1884 the 380-ton Canadian schooner *Lady Dufferin* was stranded on the rocks near the lighthouse while laden with a cargo of stone. After numerous failed attempts, it was finally released to sail again in July 1885. In November 1895 the steamer *Missoula* ran aground near the south side of the island in a blinding southwest storm. The crew managed to make it to the safety of the island in lifeboats but the ship, valued at $90,000, was lost.

The 536-foot (165 m) steamer *Westmount* ran aground in dense fog on the west side of Caribou Island in July 1917. The Caribou Island keeper heard its distress signal, and upon investigation found the beached freighter with a full load of grain. Although not badly damaged, the vessel could not free itself. The keeper took the captain in the lighthouse boat to Quebec Harbour on Michipicoten Island, where the captain was able to send a message via the Dominion Transport Company's passenger ship to the owners of the *Westmount*. They sent a tug with a lighter barge to the rescue. Once most of the cargo had been unloaded onto the barge,

Caribou Island Lighthouses (new and old), circa 1911

the *Westmount* was successfully refloated and able to make it to drydock under its own power. Just two years later the steamer *John Owen* sank near the island with a full cargo of 100,000 bushels of barley in a northwest gale. Its crew of 22 were all lost. The next spring the keeper found the forward mast with the ship's bell still attached washed ashore on Caribou Island.

Caribou Island keepers had to be hardy and resourceful. When keeper George Johnston broke his leg, for example, he simply put a splint on it, made crutches, and resumed his duties. One spring he forgot his rifle while packing for the lighthouse, but he did remember the cartridges. Being innovative, he carved a stock from driftwood, turned a metal vapor tube into a barrel and fashioned a firing mechanism. Although its aim was poor, it was sufficient to shoot rabbits to supplement his family's fish diet. Johnston also shot one caribou each year on Caribou Island and smoked the meat for his family. The rest of his supplies were ordered for the whole season — bags of flour, sugar and potatoes, boxes of butter, raisins, prunes, currants, dried apples, tea and coffee, pails of candy, ketchup, lard and pickles, wheels of cheese, spices, salt, eggs preserved in waterglass (a preservative), smoked ham and sides of bacon.

Johnston's wife's efforts to keep chickens on the island merely resulted in chicken dinner for the hawks from Caribou Island, even though she guarded the chickens with a 22-caliber rifle and was a good shot. Johnston and his family would don their Sunday best for the annual visit of the government supply boat, which came in July to deliver the light's yearly supply of kerosene, grease, lubricating oil, engine parts and lantern parts. However, it supplied no food or personal items. After the supplies were unloaded, the ship would depart to the lightkeeper's salute and the foghorn's farewell blast. Johnston's sons liked the station foghorn, especially in extended periods of fog, because its engines were thermo-cooled and they could use the run-off water to have a warm bath.

In 1915 the Canadian government stopped providing transport to and from lighthouses. Johnston thought he was doomed, being expected to travel 55 miles (88 km) in a 30-foot (9 m) sailboat in December. In preparation, he fortified his boat with a kerosene engine (at a cost of $400 out of his own pocket), a weather-tight cabin and a coal-fired heater. In 1919 he and his assistant were trapped at Caribou Island by fierce December storms. On Christmas Day, when the weather had cleared, they sailed as far as Michipicoten Island, but could not anchor because of the ice. When another storm came, they headed for open water rather than be smashed onto the ice. Johnson threw out his sea anchor (a cone-shaped affair made of canvas that dragged to slow a vessel's

Coppermine Point Lighthouse, circa 1985

traveling), hoping this would help them just drift slowly. They were able to withstand the storm, including ice floes grating against the boat's exterior. Seven days later they arrived, shaken but alive, at Michipicoten Harbour on the mainland. After being keeper, Johnston became a fog signal inspector.

In 1921 George Penfold took over at Caribou Island. He thought it atrocious that he was expected to reach the mainland in a small boat in December, and he kept writing the government until they rescinded their cost-cutting measure. Thus, in 1921 the C.G.S. *Lambton* was given the job of delivering and picking up lightkeepers. Former keeper Johnston warned about the inappropriateness of this tug for the job because its open steering mechanism was not suited for winter storms on Lake Superior. In the spring of 1922, the *Lambton's* steering mechanism became coated in ice, and the ship sank in a storm about 15 miles (24 km) east of Caribou Island. All perished, including Penfold. Even today some believe that the *Lambton* sails Lake Superior as a ghost ship.

George Rutherford, who became the station's last keeper in 1964, recounted many memories in a 1973 interview. Because of the isolation, he said, he would rather walk away from an argument than argue with his assistant keeper; it was important to use diplomacy while out there as "it might get lonely talking only to Su Ming, the lighthouse cat." They had a small boat to get ashore across 55 miles (88 km) of open water, so they didn't go very often. Once, an American knocked on their door at night. He was making a 127-mile (203 km) voyage to Michipicoten Harbour in a Kentucky swamp-boat that had a paddle, a sail, and a 3-horse-power outboard motor. They later learned that he made it to his destination, checked into customs and headed right back home.

The keeper's job included making weather checks four times a day, maintaining the light, the foghorn, the radio beacon and all the buildings, and assisting when possible in shipwrecks. Although not everyone would crave this isolation, Rutherford would not have traded his job for anything: "If I had known about lighthouses when I was a kid, I would not have gone anywhere else." So, although the Caribou Island Lighthouse is in a rather remote location, perhaps it would be worth a visit. Today it is automated through the use of solar panels and continues its lonely vigil far out in Lake Superior.

Known Keepers: J. May (1886), James Charles Pim (1887–98), Wilbrod Demers (1899–1906) Antoine Boucher (1907–11) George W. Johnston (1912–21), George Penfold (1921–22), George Marshall (1922), John W. Kennedy (1922–28), Charles McDonald (1928–35), Arthur Hurley (1935–62), Alfred Thibeault (1962–64), George Rutherford (1964–).

5 Coppermine Point Lighthouse

Coppermine Point is located at the northeastern entrance into Whitefish Bay across from Whitefish Point on the opposite side of the bay entrance. A light was first placed on the point in 1901 to mark it for fishermen returning with their day's catch, and to mark the entrance and shipping route into Whitefish Bay and the St. Mary's River at the east end of Lake Superior. The first light was exhibited from a lantern on an open-framed wooden pyramidal structure. It was replaced in 1908.

The new lighthouse was a square white wooden pyramidal tower with a pedimented door and window and a red octagonal iron lantern. It angled outward to support its gallery and was 32 feet (9.8 m) high from base to ventilator. It displayed a fixed white light using a fifth-order lens and was visible for 13 miles (21 km) from a 61-foot (18.6 m) focal plane. Constructed by J.C. Kennedy of Owen Sound, it cost $1,200.

Few changes happened at this light. In 1923 the crew of the *Greenville* installed an Aga light. Around 1937 it was automated. When the light was moved to a new skeletal tower in the late 1950s, the old tower was slated for demolition. It once had a female keeper named Blanche Roussain.

To save costs, prevent vandalism, and eliminate liability for the old lighthouse, the Canadian Coast Guard contracted Ernie Demers to demolish it. However, thinking it a shame to lose the historic building to firewood, Demers moved it instead. With the aid of John Helm and a large crane, he removed the iron lantern in one piece and the frame base in a second piece. The lighthouse was then taken 2 miles (3.2 km) north to its destination beside the Lighthouse Tavern on the Trans-Canada Highway (Highway 17 on the old Wawa Trail), 60 miles (100 km) northwest of Sault Ste. Marie, where it became privately owned.

With help from his friends, Demers also saved a propeller from the wreck of the *Charles Hibert*. He had an Ontario Provincial Police diver, Larry Reid, hook a line onto it, had A.B. McChain's barge winch it off the bottom, and then transported it to the lighthouse's new location at the same tavern.

The *Charles Hibert* had sunk in nearby Hibert Bay after striking a rock and breaking up. While it was sinking, the first mate swam ashore in rough seas, pulling a line behind him. He was then able to secure the line to shore, and the rest of the crew made it to safety.

The replacement light at the point was a modern 19-foot-10-inch (6 m) square skeletal steel tower with a red and white rectangular daymark. In 1992 it displayed an isophase (flash 2 s; eclipse 2 s) electric white light from a 48-foot (14.8 m) focal plane.

Coppermine Point Lighthouse. circa 1908

In 1955 A.Y. Jackson, one of Canada's famous Group of Seven painters, used the lighthouse as a subject in a painting. While the painting is listed in an inventory of Jackson's work, there are no known photographs of the piece and the exact location of this painting is presently unknown. Fortunately Jackson and Demers have both helped to preserve this small part of Canadian heritage. While the Lighthouse Tavern no longer operates, the lighthouse continues to stand there, nestled on the shore of Lake Superior.

Known Keepers: F.E. Roussain (1909–23), Blanche Roussain

6 Corbeil Lighthouse

"Batchawana," an Ojibway word meaning "water bubbling like a current" and/or "water swirling around so it never freezes in winter," aptly describes the narrows between Batchawana Island and the mainland, where the current from the Batchawana River flows after emptying into Batchawana Bay. This current passes right out past Corbeil Point at the western entrance to the bay. Corbeil Point was the ideal location for a lighthouse, as it marked the north shore of Lake Superior for vessels heading toward the Sault Ste. Marie locks, and indicated the outer entrance to the fishing village at Batchawana Bay. The Canadian government first confiscated lands from the Batchawana First Nation Reserve, transferring it from the Department of Indian Affairs to the Department of Marine and Fisheries on May 29, 1874.

The first lighthouse at this site was a small, white, one-story, clapboard house with twelve-paned windows, and a summer kitchen. The octagonal, wooden tower loomed right up out of the house, making the house look even smaller. The second floor of the tower was the upper level of the house. The gently tapering tower was 63 feet (19.2 m) high, had three octagonal windows facing north, away from the water, and was topped by an octagonal gallery with wooden railings. The 8-foot (2.4 m) wide octagonal lantern first used two circular and two No. 1 lamps with two 20-inch (50 cm) and two 16-inch (40 cm) reflectors. In 1878 four mammoth flat-wick lamps with 16-inch (40 cm) reflectors were installed, creating a visibility of 20 miles (32 km). Later it acquired a seventh-order lens and kerosene lamps, and exhibited a fixed white light. With its 77-foot (23.5 m) focal plane, this light produced a 16-mile (26 km) visibility in clear weather. The station also had a hand-operated fog signal to answer signals from vessels.

Information about the light and its keepers was gathered from living relatives of the keepers, such as Betsy Sayers (granddaughter of keeper "Billy" Reil), her husband Murray, and her nephew Joe Tom Sayers, who now lives in the lighthouse. The first keeper was remembered for making good moonshine. Local women would tell their husbands that the cows had got out and they had to fetch them. Of course, this was just an excuse to go to the lighthouse and drink the keeper's moonshine. By evening, when their wives had not returned, the husbands had to go and fetch *them*, intoxicated, home from the lighthouse.

In 1879 a boathouse was built at the station but little remains of it today. In 1966 someone checking the battered building found the year 1894 carved into the beams, perhaps indicating the year the boathouse was rebuilt.

William (Billy) Reil, the third keeper of the light, had its longest tenure (1915–46). He raised 14 children. He was most dedicated to his work, and everything was done on time. One of his daughters, Philemon, was still at home in June 1931, when a fierce electrical storm moved in over the lake, with so much lightning that it looked like daylight. "Keeper Billy" was sitting reading by his coal oil lamp when lightning not only struck the lighthouse but also struck his lamp, spreading fuel and fire everywhere. Philemon narrowly escaped with her life. The lighthouse was totally destroyed.

Even after losing everything, Reil built a light of his own making to mark the point and protect mariners until the government rebuilt the light.

The new lighthouse was close to the old one, and salvage from the old lighthouse was used in the concrete basement walls. It was a large, plain, two-story, white clapboard house with eight-paned windows and an open veranda facing the water. The hipped roof supported a square gallery with a pipe iron railing. In the center of the roof was a square wooden lantern with four large windows. Using kerosene lamps and a seventh-order lens, the lantern showed a fixed white light from 43 feet (13 m) above the lake, with an 11-mile (17.8 km) visibility. The keeper's house had three upstairs bedrooms and a small room where the stairs led up to the lantern. The kitchen, parlor, dining room and office were downstairs.

Corbeil Lighthouse, circa 1908

The lighthouse was a strong focus in the community and its lightkeeper was well respected. The nearby church was another strong community influence and Reil sang in its choir. He also managed a large vegetable garden and kept a lawn. The area was plentiful with wild berries like strawberries, raspberries, gooseberries and sugarplum bushes (Saskatoon berries). Apple trees were plentiful too, because it was customary for a young Native couple planning to get married to plant an apple tree on the homestead, and since the lighthouse and church were the main focus for the community, they planted trees near them also. With radio, the lightkeeper's popularity increased again. Locals came every Saturday evening to listen to country music or the "Grand Ole Opry" until 1:00 a.m. Picnics under the big tree in the field next to the lighthouse were also community favorites.

In the lighthouse, Reil trimmed wicks, transferred kerosene from the separate oil house into five-gallon cans, and carried the fuel daily to the lantern for supplying the kerosene lamp, which had "wick all around it." He also kept logbooks. Some winters the water never froze over, but in cold ones the ice would pile up. Spray from late fall storms used to coat the front of the keeper's house, but it was so windy that snow never collected in front of it.

When Reil retired in 1946, Henry D. Nolan, a World War II war veteran, was appointed. The following information was shared with us by his daughter, Ann McLean, and granddaughters Kathy Alish and Karen Francis. Ann remembers that the square lantern was round inside and that double flat wick lamps burned oil

Corbeil Lighthouse, circa 1980

Corbeil Lighthouse, circa 1998

(kerosene). She also remembers reading Keeper Billy's logs; he distinguished the severity of storms by only one word– "big nor'wester," "really big nor'wester," "really really big nor'wester." The Nolans lived at the lighthouse from May to November and wintered in Batchawana. Franny and Henry could both speak Ojibway, French and English, and when visitors came to the light they told stories and laughed a lot.

Bears caused great concern around the lighthouse. Once the Nolans thought they saw a man walking to the lighthouse but discovered it was a bear walking on its hind legs. After this incident, they kept their doors locked. Another time Henry heard a weak "Help, Help" from outside the keeper's house. He responded, "Can I help you?" but the only answer was the feeble "Help, Help." Getting annoyed with this would-be prankster, he retorted, "Well, if you don't want to answer, you can go to hell!" It was a good thing he did not investigate the sound too closely because he later discovered that the "words" were cries from a wounded bear, which could have been extremely dangerous.

One lightkeeping duty that was not needed much was the foghorn. The station had a hand-pumped horn that was kept in the lantern because, when used, the keeper stood on the gallery of the lantern to operate it. Once, when the supply ship brought a new hand-pumped foghorn to replace the old one, Nolan put the old one on his head and clowned around scaring the dogs.

When Henry died in early February 1953, Franny became temporary keeper until Robert Collins was appointed later in 1953. As keeper she reported that the light ran on gas (acetylene) and she did not have to do anything with it. Her duties involved keeping the daily logbook and recording temperatures and weather changes. Without her husband, spring and late fall were lonely, but the summer brought tourists and visitors from Batchawana. She remembers fall as the best and the worst time. Fall brought the "dirtiest blows" from Lake Superior and also the most breathtaking view of colors in the bush around the lighthouse and the rolling mountains of Algoma across the bay.

Collins, the last keeper, kept the light until 1955 when it was automated, using electricity, and a keeper was no longer needed. At this time the light's status changed from watched to unwatched with no fog signal. In 1957 the fixed white light produced by the 100-watt, 110-volt Piper unit, was reported to the Department of Transport in Parry Sound as being "not a very efficient arrangement" as it could not easily be distinguished from other fixed lights in the background. In response, it was changed to a fixed green light by using a green Piper lantern. But the reduced visibility of the green light must have been insufficient, because it was again changed to produce a flashing green light with a visibility of

11 miles (17.6 km). To do this a large barrel lens was moved from Pointe aux Pins and a green shade placed over it. Then in 1962, as modern navigation techniques rendered the light unnecessary, it was extinguished.

In the 1960s the confiscated land was returned to the Batchawana First Nation. After 1962, when the light was no longer used and the lantern was removed, vandals soon scavenged any souvenirs they could find. Each year the lighthouse fell further into disrepair. Finally, in the 1980s, Joe Tom Sayer took an interest in it and started making repairs. In 1995 he moved up to the lighthouse and stayed for the summer and fall. He used a Coleman stove to cook on and covered the windows with plastic and kept moving his bed to avoid leaks. In the fall he asked his uncle, Chief Edward Nebenaigoching of the band, if he could move into the lighthouse to live. "Uncle Eddie" agreed. That was the first time since 1954 that the building had been heated. Joe said the wood cracking from the heat sounded like gunshots. Since then he has put the old cook stove back in, replaced the B.C. fir shingles, replaced windows and doors, fixed the stairs, planed the floors and replaced the siding.

Sayer likes living there despite mysterious events such as footsteps on the staircase, pictures suspiciously falling off walls, and rumors of people being murdered at the lighthouse and buried in the concrete. While restoring the property, however, Sayer did discover eight graves. No one knows anything about them, but in 1997 an archaeologist judged that they were from the late 1800s or early 1900s. To help assist any lingering spirits on their way, Sayer hosted a "feast for the dead."

In the 1970s a restaurant was built near the lighthouse along the roadway, and in the 1980s a lawsuit evolved over road access. The band wanted to make an alternative road around the restaurant to the lighthouse, but because of the found graves the restaurant protested. They also didn't want the natives to have access to the lighthouse, because they used it as a private sightseeing spot for their customers. Chief Nebenaigoching retaliated with blockades to prevent tourists from getting to the restaurant. Eventually all was resolved and the road to the lighthouse was built.

Today the station is somewhat overgrown, trees are reclaiming the land, and weeds vie for growing space between the stones, but the overgrown remains of Franny's rock garden are still visible. While some might question Sayer's technique in acquiring the lighthouse, future generations will appreciate his foresight and preservation efforts.

Known Keepers: David Crawford (1878–), J. Davieaux (1890–1915), William Reil (1915–46), Henry Nolan (1946–53), Franny Nolan (1953), Robert Collins (1953–55).

Davieaux Island Lighthouse

7 Davieaux Island Lighthouse

Michipicoten Island, meaning "floating island," is about 30 miles (48.6 km) from Michipicoten Harbour along Lake Superior's northwest shore. The Indians gave the island this name because it gives the illusion of floating, seeming to be closer or farther away from the mainland according to atmospheric conditions.

Since the island was used for commercial mining and fishing industries as well as providing a refuge for vessels on the east-west shipping route along Superior's north shore, the Canadian government first lit the harbor in 1872. However, by 1916 they decided the system of lights was inadequate. To improve it, the lighthouse on Agate Island, just inside the harbor entrance, was moved to the back of the harbor and was converted into the front tower for the new range lights. A new lighthouse was also built on Long Island just outside the harbor entrance where it was more visible, and then the old lighthouse on Chimney Point was extinguished and abandoned.

The new lighthouse was built on the summit of Long Island in 1917–18 from plans designed by the Department of Marine and Fisheries. It was a slightly tapering 30-foot (9 m) octagonal reinforced-concrete tower with a diameter of about 11 feet (3.4 m) at the base and a top diameter of 9 feet 4 inches (2.8 m). It had a pedimented door, two tower windows facing south out over Lake Superior, and three windows facing Quebec Harbour to the north. The windows were noted for their triangular lintels. A concrete cornice supported an octagonal concrete gallery surrounded by pipe iron railing, and its octagonal iron lantern first used kerosene lamps and reflectors and a clockwork mechanism to produce a flashing light. The whole tower, an overall 44 feet (13.5 m) in height, was painted completely white (later with red accents) to increase visibility.

Davieaux Island Lighthouse, circa 1918

The station had a few other buildings: a white wood frame boathouse on the north side of the island, a shed to store kerosene, and a "shelter shed" to protect the keeper if he was trapped by inclement weather.

The light's first keeper, Charles Davieaux, lit the light in 1918. He and his family lived onshore at the range station and each day he would row the 1 ½ miles (2.4 km) out to Long Island to light the lamps about an hour before sunset. About midnight he went up to the lantern to trim the lamp wicks, check the fuel and wind the clockwork weights. He usually stayed at the island throughout the night, extinguished the lamps in the morning, and then rowed back to the range station, unless the water was too rough. While he tended this light his wife, Charlotte, and his family tended the range lights in the harbor. Davieaux was keeper at this station until 1933 when he died at the age of eighty-four. In honor of his long years of service, and those of his family and his father, Hyacinthe, before him, the government renamed Long Island "Davieaux Island" in their memory.

In October 1917 Davieaux had to perform a grizzly task. He examined and then buried the remains of a French seaman whose body was found by his assistant keeper about 2 miles (3.2 km) west of Quebec Harbour. They marked the grave at Sand Bay with a cross at the head. Davieaux then notified the Department of Marine and Fisheries and included the following description: "Of a sailor officer off some vessel. He had on a blue uniform with a red stripe on each wrist of his coat also, one red anchor marked on each side of his coat collar, brass buttons on which there were marked 'Equipage de la Flotte.' The body was five foot two inches tall red hair turning grey. He had in his left side coat pocket one pipe tobacco tin and watch box." The Consul General for France and the Canadian Commissioner of Lights both commended Davieaux for his actions.

As well as guiding vessels into safe harbor, the light warned mariners of the shoals south and west of the island — but they weren't always successful. Veronica Davieaux, Charles's daughter, remembers that on the day in 1924 when she was leaving the island to go to school in Sault Ste. Marie a large cargo ship carrying flour ran aground on the reef near the harbor. The lake was soon covered with floating flour that she said looked like snow. Later, in 1929, the 325-foot (100 m) *Chicago* grounded and sank on the shoals west of the island, also while carrying flour. The whistle from the *Chicago* was salvaged for use on the vessel *Captain Jim*, and its ship's bell was being used at the cookery in Quebec Harbour in 1932. Although keepers at Davieaux Island were not able to save every ship, they were a brave lot, and saved many crews, such as those from the *Strathmore* in 1906 and the *Chicago* in 1929.

The Davieaux family stayed on the island all year until 1923, when they started wintering at the Sault. Being at such an isolated station, they always enjoyed visitors. The sister ships, the *Caribou* and the *Manitou*, made regular stops at the station — on Mondays and Fridays respectively. On rare occasions the keepers traveled the 30 miles (48 km) into Michipicoten Harbour for supplies and to Caribou Island or East End Michipicoten to visit keepers and their families there. Horst Anderson, a commercial fisherman from Wawa, was always welcomed when he stopped by with mail and supplies.

Some changes occurred at the Davieaux Island station: in 1928 a fog signal building was added; in 1938 a proper keeper's house was built; in 1941 a new boathouse replaced its two predecessors, which had been destroyed in storms in 1939 and 1940. An assistant keeper was hired to run the Davieaux Island light while the main keeper ran the range station. A helicopter landing was established, and in 1963 the lights were converted to electricity using generators and batteries.

The Davieaux Island light used a mercury vapor lightbulb as its illuminant and had four concave mirrors to reflect light out over the lake. The light took 20 minutes to reach full power and its pattern of four flashes every 24 seconds was visible up to 20 miles (32 km) from a 128-foot (39 m) focal plane. The keepers each worked a twelve-hour shift at this time. In 1964 fire destroyed the keeper's "shelter shed" and the assistant keeper, who nearly died, spent the summer in a tent near the helipad. A severe fall storm washed the tent into the lake, leaving him homeless again. In 1965 the government built a new $30,000 duplex to house both keepers, and installed an electric fog signal. At some time the light became a year-round emergency light. The station was demanned in 1991 but continues to operate today.

Known Keepers: Charles Davieaux (1910–33), Joseph Davieaux (1933), Joseph Miron (1934–43), Fred Hurley (1943–44), Normen Gormier (1945–58), Roy Ellis (1959), Gordon Dawson (1960–64), Bob Nelder (1965–67), Milton Hughes (1967–).

8 Foote's Dock Light

While a lighthouse had been built on the south side of Pointe aux Pins in 1873 to assist marine traffic in and out of the St. Mary's River at Lake Superior's eastern end, sea captains petitioned for another light to mark the unlit channel further downriver around the point. Commerce was steadily increasing as more and more freighters shipped iron, copper, lumber and grain to ports on the lower Great Lakes. Also, the Pointe aux Pins area was becoming a popular vacationers' paradise, and the Canadian government was criticized for not lighting the area.

Since the point, with its hotel and camping spots, could only be reached by water or a long, tedious journey over a cart track, there was always a good dock (Foote's Dock) on the southeast side of the point. It was used by a variety of craft, including moonlight excursion boats from the two Saults. A local man, Billy Simms, brought in supplies, and campers would build a large bonfire on the beach to guide his vessel in.

Correspondence shows that in 1887 mariners demanded a light at Foote's Dock to assist with tricky night navigation. Letters mention that Americans were "growling about the Canadian authorities not doing what is needful there." The Pointe aux Pins Lighthouse was helpful to guide mariners from the lake into the river and helpful once it could be seen around the point when heading from the river into the lake, but the unlit part of the narrow channel still caused concern.

In September 1888 investigations showed that Foote's Dock was "falling into decay," as coal-burning steamers no longer needed to stop for cordwood. Also, both upbound and downbound vessels headed for the deepest part of the river channel near the end of the dock. After an inspector recommended placing a Mississippi lantern on a pole under the care of the Pointe aux Pins lightkeeper, a light was established there in 1890 and kept by Henry Wood for $75 a year.

In September 1894, another inspector questioned the need to continue a light at Foote's Dock since range lights had been established on both the Canadian and the American side of the river above the Soo locks. He recommended discontinuing the dock light and taking over the privately operated Canadian range lights from Joseph Rouleau. These lights were pole lights and Rouleau collected $5 from each steamer passing through the locks to cover his expenses and the light maintenance. However, some mariners petitioned to keep the Foote's Dock light. In response, the government decided to retain the light but refused to provide a keeper's house. They agreed to the existing light being moved to the outer end of the new dock, but would not build a new light there and maintain two lights.

Meanwhile, the Algoma Park Summer Resort, which consisted of 2,612 acres (1057 ha), was developed on the point around 1894 by Kirkwood and McKinnon. It had a stone lakeside hotel, a store and parks, and featured a 200-foot (61 m) dock with a 20-foot (6 m) water depth. For the nominal fee of $1, any vessel could dock for up to 24 hours to refuel, buy supplies or seek refuge. The dock was also lit at night and operated a fog bell. Correspondence of March 1895 shows the government was pleased to move the light to the outer end of the new dock and wished it done for the start of the navigation season.

In 1901 the Foote's Dock light displayed a fixed red light for 5 miles (8 km) from a lantern hoisted on a mast. However, it was again exhibited from the shore end of the dock. The point was a busy spot with up to 100 steamers passing it each day. The Foote's Dock light aided their nighttime navigation for a number of years. However, in 1909 it was extinguished and discontinued.

Known Keeper: Henry Wood (–1890–).

9 Gargantua Lighthouse

In the 1870s a fishing village developed at Gargantua Bay along Lake Superior's northeast shore. In 1899 a lighthouse was built on a small island at the bay entrance to mark safe harbor from Lake Superior's western storms and for fishermen returning to the village. It was a 43-foot (13 m) white wooden hexagonal tower with a red iron lantern built on the summit of the island and anchored to the island's rock by four cables. Using a seventh-order lens and a kerosene lamp, it displayed a fixed white light from an 85-foot (26 m) focal plane for 15 miles (24 km). Joseph Ganley of Ainsworth and Ganley supervised the construction of the station. A shack on the island sheltered the keeper when it was too stormy to return to his home on the mainland. The station was also equipped with a hand-operated foghorn to answer signals from vessels.

The light was tended by three generations of the Miron family. The first, Louis Miron, who took charge in November 1889, earned $450 a year. He also fished, scavenged pulp logs from the shore of the island and bay for sale, and charged people who stayed overnight at the lighthouse or stayed for meals. He gardened, raised pigs and chickens for his family and for sale, collected gull eggs from Gull Island, and gathered raspberries and blueberries from the Lizard Islands. He also trapped and snared rabbits and occasionally fishers, martin, mink, weasel, beaver, wolf and bear. He hunted partridges, loons, geese, fox, deer, caribou, moose, wolf and bear.

Gargantua Lighthouse, circa 1930s

Gargantua keeper's house, circa 1943

His duties were to maintain the lighthouse and the keeper's dwelling as well as tend the light. He rowed out to the lighthouse in a small boat except when stormy weather intervened. His log-books also show that he tarpapered the kitchen, painted the house and tower, and moved the stove into the dining room to burn coal instead of wood in the cold weather. He chopped a lot of wood for fuel and kept a horse to haul it. Supplies for the lighthouse (mostly kerosene) were brought in by tender in August. Tenders that Miron recorded included the *Arabian, Golspie, Middle Queen, Neepewaha* and *Simcoe.*

In 1912 Louis Miron's son Charles took over as keeper when his father retired at age seventy-one. He was a kind, cheerful man with great integrity, who raised nine children. Near the end of his tenure, in 1940, a November windstorm blew the tower from its anchoring and carried it away, but the keeper's shack 170 feet (52 m) from the water's edge received little damage. However, storm waters swept over the building and froze, trapping the assistant keeper, who had to be chopped out with an axe. It being late in the season, the lighthouse was not rebuilt until the next spring. In 1942 Thomas (Tom) Miron, Charles' son, became the third keeper of the light, and served until the light converted to propane and was automated in 1948.

One family served continuously at the Gargantua light for three generations, but their transport to and from the light in the spring and fall varied. Louis was usually taken from Sault Ste. Marie by tug or steamer, perhaps on the vessel *Minnie M.* or the *Ossiprage.* In the fall the steamer used to whistle as it passed upbound to indicate that it would stop on the downbound trip the next day to pick up the keeper. However, in 1903 the government notified Louis that he had to find his own way home at the close of the season. When Charles took over, he took the train from the Sault to Agawa Bay and rowed from there to Gargantua, repeating the process in reverse in the fall. In 1921 the government resumed, using tugs — the *Shawanaga, James Reed, Shenick, Booth, Philadelphia, Simcoe* and *Lambton* — to deliver keepers. In spite of the tugs' reliability, the Mirons preferred their own boat and the train, as they feared ending up like the *Reliance,* grounded on the Lizard Islands.

The lighthouse, although closed early for the season, once provided safety to the crew of a 509-ton steamer bound from Port Arthur for the Ogilvies, fully loaded with wheat. A blinding November snowstorm off Michipicoten Island forced the *Acadia* to seek refuge behind Brulé Point on the mainland. When it struck a shoal and took on water, the crew took supplies and headed for shore. The next day the

Gargantua keeper Louis Miron (at right)

captain and four crewmembers went off to the Sault for help in a small boat. Two crewmen were left to keep an eye on the vessel and the remaining ten waited at the Gargantua Lighthouse. After seven grueling days of stormy weather the captain arrived at the Sault and arranged for help to be sent back to his men.

In 1922 the lighthouse tender *Lambton* went down in the spring with the loss of all crew and the Canadian lighthouse keepers it was delivering to their stations. From then on, ghost sightings of the vessel were reported on several occasions around dusk, sometimes just off Gargantua, and were believed to be a ghostship. Mariners feared a marine disaster after each sighting.

Captain McPherson of the tug *Reliance* was one who claimed to have seen the ghostship *Lambton* in December 1922. On the return trip from his last run of the season taking supplies to pulp camps in Puckasaw, foul weather forced him to lay over for two days at each of Michipicoten Harbour, Brulé Harbour, and Gargantua. With food running low, he left Gargantua with twenty passengers and crew. Just 1 ½ hours later the *Reliance* grounded on one of the Lizard Islands and its propeller was torn off. Nine crewmembers were sent to the mainland about 2 to 3 miles (3 to 4.5 km) away in a small lifeboat. The captain and two crew were lost trying to lower another lifeboat to go for help. One man swam the icy 75 yards (68 m) to shore with a rope tied around him. The crew then used this rope and rafts made of wooden ice skids aboard the *Reliance* to safely land the rest of the passengers and crew. The nine who made it to the mainland trekked to Agawa Bay through two feet of snow, subzero temperatures and three waist-deep rivers. They found help at a lumberman's cabin, and then picked up a train to the Sault and sent help for the others. The tug *Gray,* accompanied by the icebreaker *Favorite,* went to rescue the remaining 22 passengers and crew. The tug then dropped the rescued men at Agawa Bay and resumed its duties picking up lightkeepers at Otter Head, Quebec Harbour, East End Michipicoten, Caribou Island and Isle Parisienne.

The light tower was destroyed in a fire in the spring of 1949. Today a light shines at Gargantua from a 16-foot (4.9 m) circular mast with a red and white rectangular daymark. It displays a flashing white light (flash 0.5 s; eclipse 3.5 s) from a 78-foot (24 m) focal plane using an electric light.

Known Keepers: Louis Miron (1889–1912), Charles Miron (1912–42), Thomas Miron (1942–48).

Gros Cap Crib Light, circa 1960

10 Gros Cap Crib Light

A lighthouse was built on Gros Cap Reef in 1952–53 to replace the lightship that had been anchored there. It marked the underwater reef that extended southwest from the mainland, and was built on the reef's southwestern extremity, about 1.7 miles (2.8 km) from the Gros Cap shore.

The Gros Cap Reef lighthouse resembles a very short, cut-off boat. A prow-shaped point is built onto one end of its pier to deflect waves and ice floes. The tower rises two levels from the foundation, just like a layer cake, making the light 59 feet (18 m) above the water. This light was classed as a crib light, and its life preserver reads "Gros Cap Light Crib." Locals called it "The Crib."

Lois See, daughter of keeper Basil Byers, gave much insight into its construction. First, a hollow unit crib was made at McLean's Dock in Sault Ste. Marie. It was towed up through the locks to the site, filled with rocks and sunk in 15–20 feet (4.5–6 m) of water over the reef. The steel hull for the end of the concrete foundation was also towed on a barge up through the canal. The rest of the lighthouse was built on barges at the site. The crib supported a reinforced concrete foundation to which the hull was attached.

A hole was left in the concrete bottom for the large air tank that operated the foghorn, and the engineers were having difficulty figuring out how to lower this tank into the hole without damaging it, when there was not enough room for equipment to move. Byers suggested they fill the hole with water, float the tank into position, and then pump the water out — the perfect solution.

The foundation level also included a basement with a work area, two compressors and two generators. The next level housed the "good-sized rooms" of the residence. The top level contained a third bedroom, the radio equipment and the foghorn, which faced out over the lake. With a double door system muffling the horn's sound, it didn't produce much vibration in the building. Its characteristic was: blast two s; silence 3 s; blast 2 s; silence 3 s; blast 2 s, silence 48 s.

Being built in 1953, the lighthouse did not need a lantern. A rotating electrical beacon flashed red every five seconds from its summit. An ingenious system of mirrors in front of the upper windows angled upwards so that the keepers could check the light's operation from inside without disturbing their cribbage game. Other necessities at the station included steel storm shutters and a lifeboat suspended outside ready for any emergency. The keepers were taken to the station in spring by the icebreaker *Alexander Henry* as soon as the ice broke up. Sometimes they had to pole through floating ice pans and then climb the ladder to the lighthouse.

Byers first came to the Gros Cap lighthouse as an assistant to keeper McAuliffe. Then he was head keeper from 1961 until 1969. His wife, Lois, stayed in town, 2 miles (3.2 km) away. One winter evening, since there were three keepers and no action (no boats) at the lighthouse, Byers surprised his family by walking the two miles across the ice to spend the night at home. On another occasion, Sonny Daygall, who had a license for catching herring, caught six, two-foot herring when he pulled up his nets by the lighthouse. He stopped in at the light, where they filleted the fish, cooked them up and feasted on a fresh fish dinner on the upper deck. On runs to the lighthouse after a hot day in town, the keepers would fill the bottom of the boat with cold water to cool the beer on the ride out. Byers also liked to fish and make models of lighthouses. He even built a playhouse in the form of a lighthouse for his kids at their camp in Goulais Bay.

A helicopter pad added in the 1960s and a power line run out from the mainland in 1969 made the station more accessible. In 1975 Derek Sherlock, son and assistant of keeper Melvin Sherlock at Michipicoten Island East End lighthouse, was transferred to Gros Cap, where he became Gavin McKiggan's assistant. Derek described McKiggan as "the crazy man on the rock." It seemed that Derek could do nothing right and was continually belittled. McKiggan often said he was "stupid" and "useless." He would not even let Derek use the boat to get away from his continual badgering. After just one month of verbal abuse, Derek quit and went to Caribou Island to help a friend stationed there.

The station was later automated and the keepers were removed. In 1989 the light became an emergency light operated year round rather than just in the shipping season. Today the light still stands proud, a reminder of its past and present service.

Known Keepers: Stewart Ewing (1953–56), P.A. Turner (1957–59), Lloyd McAuliffe (1959–60), Basil A. Byers (1960–), Gavin McKiggan (1965–82), Marvin Moreau (1982–), Bryon (Barnie) Nelder (?).

Gros Cap Crib Light visitor

Gros Cap Lightship

11 Gros Cap Lightship

The Gros Cap Peninsula is at the bottom of Whitefish Bay on the Canadian side of Lake Superior about 20 miles (32.4 km) west of Sault Ste. Marie. Dangerous reefs extend southwest from the peninsula into the lake, close to the shipping lanes where vessels enter the St. Mary's River. The reefs were first marked by the Canadian lightship *Gros Cap No. 22*.

This lightship was built in Toronto in 1917 by Polson Iron Works as a navy mine sweeper. It was 130 feet (40 m) long, had a 23-foot (7 m) beam and a 13.5-foot (4 m) draft, and weighed 320 gross tons. When excessed by the navy, it was stationed to mark the reefs just off Gros Cap Peninsula.

This was not a keeper's preferred posting because of the buffeting the ship received from Superior's storms. Byron Nelder stayed for only one year in 1939 before being transferred to Isle Parisienne, where he was keeper for more than 20 years. David Barrett, another keeper at this station, lasted about five years.

In 1953, after many years of Superior's abuse, the lightship was removed from this location when the crib light was lit to replace it. Just four years later, as the ship was being cut up for scrap metal on December 16, it suddenly caught fire and completely burned, leaving only a twisted blackened shell. Somehow this seems an ill-suited fate for a vessel that had saved lives for so many years.

Known Keepers: Captain J. Galloway (1939), Byron Nelder (1939), David Barret (?).

12 Isle Parisienne Lighthouse

Isle Parisienne is a long, narrow, six-mile island located in Lake Superior about halfway between Gros Cap, Ontario, and Whitefish Point, Michigan. A lighthouse and a fog signal station were built on the southwest tip of the island in 1911 to guide east-west lake traffic carrying ore, timber and grain. The lighthouse was built on a narrow peninsula that formed a small, sandy cove on its southeast side.

The gently tapering, hexagonal tower was built of reinforced concrete, and six buttresses extended from the gallery to the ground to support it. The tower's focal plane of about 54 feet (16.5 m) allowed it to be seen for 12 miles (19 km). The tower was lit in 1912 by a white flashing light that had eclipses of two seconds, alternating with illuminations of four seconds. The fog signal building was on the point near the tower. It housed a diaphone fog signal (blast 4s; silence 4s; blast 4s; silence 48s) operated by compressed air produced by an oil engine.

A 75-foot (23 m) concrete dock extended east from the fog building and curved gently toward the bay to shelter the keeper's boat. The square, two-story keeper's house northeast of the tower

was also painted white. The helicopter pad, on which the faded design of a giant old compass (the art work of assistant keeper Ron Watt) is still visible, sat just northeast of the keeper's house.

When Harry Beverly took over as keeper from Basil Byers, he brought his huge German shepherd. The dog guarded the lighthouse and scared away most people. However, he also had an unusual talent. Instead of fetching sticks, he would fetch rocks. Beverly would throw a rock into the bay and the dog would dive right in and bring back the same rock.

Byron ("Barnie") Nelder was keeper at Isle Parisienne from 1942 to 1966. During his tenure, the tower started leaning as nearby sands were washed away. A concrete sea wall was built around the point as a protective counter-measure, but maintaining the tower became a continuous battle. A tunnel used to run between the house and the tower for the keeper's benefit during inclement weather. The station included an oil house, a boathouse, a smokehouse and a log cabin by the sandy bay. Residents of the five-bedroom house used coal oil lamps and burned driftwood in the large old cook stove. The Nelders' bedroom window faced the tower so that they could keep an eye on it. The assistant keeper, Fred Biron, once brought his English wife with him, but she did not get along with the keeper's wife, so she stayed on the mainland after that.

The tower enclosed circular, iron cutwork steps to the lantern. In daytime, canvas was dropped over the lantern glass to keep the sunlight out and at night it was rolled back up when the light was in use. It was painted white with red trim for better daytime visibility and its red iron lantern was topped with a beaver-shaped weathervane. (Was the beaver a reminder of the man who in 1893 tried to raise beaver on the island but failed, or simply a Canadian symbol? In any case, the keepers hated painting it.)

Isle Parisienne Lighthouse, circa 1923

Isle Parisienne Lighthouse

The station also had a battery-operated ham radio that the keepers used to report in every day. To save the batteries, it was used for entertainment just once a week. In the fall everyone crowded around it to listen to the Saturday night hockey games.

An interview with Paula McAulay, Nelder's daughter-in-law, revealed a lot about a keeper's family life. Barnie and his wife, Esther, raised six children, and their son Robert (Bob) also became a keeper. Their oldest son, Graham, once found the body of a drowned sailor along the shore of the island. Another time, some-time in the 1950s, Barnie, his son Bob and Fred Biron had just been dropped off in the spring to open the lighthouse when Fred dropped dead of a heart attack. Having no refrigeration and no way to take the body to the mainland, they stored it in the back room, wrapped up so the mice could not nibble on it while they awaited transport. Bob acted as assistant keeper until a replacement was found.

Barnie used to build boats in his free time. His pride and joy was the *Paula Lee*. The family also tried gardening, but it was too dry and there were too many grasshoppers. Blackflies were a men-ace in the spring but Barnie would kill them off by setting the grass on fire and burning off the swamp — attracting a fire brigade every time. Barnie always pleaded ignorance and no one knew — or acknowledged knowing — that the fire was deliberate. The island was treed but sustained little wildlife. When the boys were sent out to bring home food, they were only given two "22" shells for their rifle and if they didn't bring back game they got in trouble.

Esther tried to home-school the children, but they were too spirited for her, so the school-age children went to school on the mainland, and the younger children stayed at the lighthouse. The Nelders bred beagles on the island, and every year when the light-house tender collected the Nelders it also collected the beagles. The island also had tons of garter snakes. No one was allowed to kill them because they ate the bug population. The kids named them just like any other pets.

Once, while visiting, the grandkids spiffed up the boathouse when the lighthouse inspector was expected. They even ham-mered in nails for him to hang his coat. They painted the drab inside with any and all colors of paint that they could find. But they didn't know that government regulations called for its origi-nal drab color. Instead of helping, they made more work for grandpa because he had to repaint the whole interior.

"Grandpa Barnie" was a noted storyteller and the children never knew if he was telling them the truth or stringing a line. His most famous tall tale was about how he had trained two dogfish to walk with him along the shoreline on their fins. This story spread all the way down to Detroit, where Barnie's sister was a nurse. One day when a patient found out that her nurse's brother was the lightkeeper at Isle Parisienne, she asked if her brother really had trained dogfish to walk on a leash.

Although the keepers were the only island residents, they had lots of visitors. In the fall they had Gros Cap fishermen who had got caught in severe weather and sought refuge in the lighthouse. In the summer they received lots of American visitors in big, fancy boats, on holiday excursions to see the lighthouse.

But since the light has been auto-mated, these visitors are no longer greeted at the dock by friendly keepers. The only sign of welcome is the lilacs that were planted in front of the house long ago. In 1988 the light was classed as an emergency light and put into operation — only at night — twelve months of the year. It is now solar-powered.

Known Keepers: John Wesley Douglas (1912–22), J.D. McKinnon (1922–), Alexander Mitchell (1924–34), C.N. McDonald (1935–42), Byron Nelder (1942–65), William Edward McGuire (1965), Donald Nelder (1965–).

13 Kaministiquia River Range Lights

Fort William was established near the mouth of the Kaministiquia (Kaministikwia) River in Thunder Bay near the west end of Lake Superior. As it developed beside Port Arthur, it also built its own docks and wharves to facilitate shipping. Range lights were set up in 1873 on a 5-acre (2 hectare) lighthouse reser-vation along the river's north shore to guide vessels into the river. One of the lights burned down in 1877.

The inspector's report of 1878 states that the dwelling attached to the tower was much too small and recommended adding a storehouse. The inner white-painted wood tower had a galvanized lantern 4 feet (1.2 m) in diameter that housed one mammoth flat-wick lamp with a 17-inch (43 cm) reflector that produced a visi-bility of 5 miles (8 km). The outer range light was a small square tower with an exterior ladder for the keeper to reach the small lantern, which was illuminated the same way as the inner tower.

Just three years later the rear range light was rebuilt. It became a square white wooden tower with an attached wooden keeper's dwelling on the north shore of the river near Fort William. It now displayed a fixed white light that was visible for 11 miles (17.8 km). In 1895 the front range light was also rebuilt, closer to the river mouth, 879 feet (268 m) east-northeast of the rear range light. From its white open-framed wooden tower it displayed a fixed white light for 10 miles (16.2 km).

While it is unknown exactly when the range lights were extin-guished, they were still operational in 1901 when the Canadian Pacific Railroad applied to build wharves on the riverfront of the reservation. By 1908 they were no longer listed and had apparently been replaced. The new light was a lantern on a white pole mounted on the Empire Elevator Wharf on the north side of the channel. It displayed a fixed red light for 10 miles (16.2 km) from a 25-foot (7.7 m) focal plane using a seventh-order lens. This light was later replaced by light buoys.

Known Keepers: Samuel (Daniel?) Morison (–1877–), John Armstrong (1894–1919).

14 Lamb Island Lighthouse

Lamb Island, a tiny island on the southeast side of Black Bay Peninsula, is located along Lake Superior's north shore to the east of Isle Royale. A lighthouse was built there in 1877 as a coastal light, to warn of nearby shoals, and to mark the narrow western channel into Nipigon Bay. It was a square white 46-foot (14 m) wooden tower attached to a wooden keeper's house. Its lantern displayed a fixed white light generated by four circular No. 1 lamps with 18-inch (45 cm) reflectors and visible from a 90-foot (27.5 m) focal plane for 15 miles (24 km). The station was also equipped with a hand-operated foghorn.

Its keeper, Andrew Alexander, was paid $840 a year plus $3 a month to operate the foghorn. His request for storm windows for the house was still being deliberated two years later, even though the station was regularly pounded by winds. To help feed his family, he gathered together enough soil on the rocky island for a potato patch. Although visitors likened the station to an island jail, Alexander and his family felt differently. They had no luxuries, but they had what they needed, and Andrew found great satisfaction in tending the light and assisting stranded mariners. Once, in response to a visitor's question about the infrequent service of the government tug, he said: "The tugs look after our needs after a fashion. 'We'll take you out in the spring,' they say, 'and if you're still alive in the fall we'll take you off.' But they don't bother us much in between."

In 1928 a fog signal building with a diaphone foghorn was added to the station and an assistant keeper was hired for the additional workload. In 1992 the foghorn had a one-minute signal (blast 2.5 s; silence 3 s; blast 2.5 s; silence 52 s).

By 1960 the tower and house had deteriorated and the contract for rebuilding was awarded to John Anderson of Port Arthur for $37,900. The new tower was a 40-foot (12 m) steel skeletal structure that displayed a flashing white light using an electric catoptric illuminating apparatus. From a focal plane of 102 feet (31 m) the light was visible for about 15 miles (24 km).

The Lamb Island keepers were taken to and from the lighthouse by government transportation. In the 1930s, 1940s and early 1950s it was the tug *James Whalen*. Then the Coast Guard icebreaker *Alexander Henry* took over, and in 1961 a helicopter began working in conjunction with the icebreaker. The vessel provided transportation to the offshore location and the helicopter made the final transfer from ship to shore. In the 1970s transfers were made directly by helicopter out of Thunder Bay.

Even after the light's automation, keepers continued at the station to prevent vandalism and to assist mariners in distress. In 1975 Fred Bronnle, a Lake Superior mariner, had his first occasion

to thank the Lamb Island lightkeeper. The water-pump on his diesel-engine tug *Radville* failed, and his crew managed to cool the engine by pouring buckets of lake water over it, just enough to get to the safety of Lamb Island. With unbelievable ingenuity, the keeper, Charles Gibson, replaced the water-pump with a washing-machine motor. It worked so well that Bronnle used it for the next six months.

Bronnle's second good fortune occurred in September 1988. He and three other crewmembers were aboard his tug, *Annis Lee*, towing two fuel-storage tanks when huge Lake Superior waves began crashing over the tug. In the storm, the tow line to one tank broke and their Zodiak and lifeboat were washed away. The generator was also damaged, causing the loss of the radar and navigation system. Again, Gibson's quick thinking saved the day. When the keeper saw the foundering tug and realized its peril, he had his wife extinguish the tower light while he maneuvered to the northeast tip of the island. He wrapped a white sheet around a rock and shone lights on it to reflect out over the water so that the crew of the tug would know exactly where the tip of the island was. Then, using a radio, he helped them adjust their course safely between shoals and into safe harbor nearby. Bronnle was most glad of this light still being manned.

Two years later the Lamb Island lighthouse was fully automated and the keepers were removed for the last time. The light was switched to solar power and equipped with sensors to alert the Coast Guard to intruders and malfunctioning equipment. This light continues as an active aid to navigation, although its tower and house are now gone.

Known Keepers: John Michelson (–1878–), Andrew Alexander (1897–1931), Donald Alexander (1931–36), A. Newman (1936–51), A. Newman Jr. (1951–), Ralph Miller (1952–56), Lawrence Obrey (1956–58), James Nicholson (1958), (?) MacDonald (1958–59), John Morgan (1960–61), Lloyd Thompson (1961–62), Joseph McIsaac (1962–), Joseph Paquette (1965–), Charles Lorne Gibson (–1989).

15 Michipicoten Harbour Lighthouse

Michipicoten Harbour is located in Michipicoten Bay along the northeast coast of Lake Superior and to the east-northeast of Michipicoten Island. In 1902 a new lighthouse was built on the tip of Perkwakwia Peninsula along the west side of the harbor to mark the entrance to Michipicoten Harbour. Adding to the confusion of a having a bay, harbor, island and lighthouse all named Michipicoten is the fact that the early area was also called Little Gros Cap, and so the lighthouse was also referred to as the Little Gros Cap Lighthouse (not to be confused with the Gros Cap Reef Lighthouse located at the head of the St. Mary's River). The peninsula was first called Little Gros Cap ("Little Big Cape") by the French voyageurs.

An early description of Michipicoten Harbour advertises its advantages: "Affords safe anchorage being surrounded by hills. Here is established a Roman Catholic mission and a Hudson Bay Post from whence diverges the river and the portage route to James Bay some 350 miles (567 km) in distance. The shore of the lake here turns northward towards Otter Head about 50 miles (81 km) distance, presenting a bold and rugged appearance." Being such a natural harbor, it developed quickly as an outlet for the vast mining and pulp cutting endeavors. The steady stream of vessels to the harbor soon earned it the title of "the biggest little port on the Great Lakes."

The Gros Cap Mining Location had mined the peninsula for years without an official deed. In 1900 Arthur C. Ely applied to the government for a confirmatory grant of 27 acres (11 hectares) on the peninsula. The government decided to issue him a quit claim

Lamb Island Lighthouse

Michipicoten Harbour Lighthouse, circa 1900

deed for $200, provided he allow ¼ acre (0.1 hectare) of land on the point for a lighthouse, a boathouse and a right of way to the light. Ely agreed.

The lighthouse station was built in 1902 on the southeast side of the peninsula. It consisted of a large square two-story wood frame house built on a sturdy stone and masonry foundation and covered with white-painted cedar shake siding. The square white wooden lantern rose from the center of the hipped roof, making it 31 feet (9.5 m) above ground level. It had large rectangular panes of glass set vertically, two per side, and was in turn topped with a shingled hip roof and a ventilator stack. Using a seventh-order lens, the lantern exhibited a fixed white light from a 70-foot (21.3 km) focal plane for 14 miles (22.5 km). The light was visible from all points of water approach, but not from the wharves in the harbor. This lighthouse was very similar to the one at Corbeil Point on Batchawana Bay.

In 1912 a white wooden fog signal building was added. The foghorn's characteristic was: blast 3 s; silence 3 s; blast 3 s; silence 51 s. Later, a radio beacon signal was added and a single-story frame keeper's dwelling was built to house extra personnel.

Although the lighthouse was built on the mainland, it was still isolated from the community of Michipicoten Harbour, and the keeper had to travel by water. A 1916 newspaper article by keeper W.D. Reid reported his harrowing ordeal in the wilderness upon closing the lighthouse at the end of this season.

"I left my station, the Little Gros Cap light, on Christmas day and reached the Sault last evening. I set out in my 16-foot [4.9 m] rowboat to row to Michipicoten Harbour to catch the train there, a distance of about 6 to 7 miles [9 to 11 km] ordinarily, but this time I easily travelled a couple of miles extra. The reason I had to do this was the enormous ice fields, which I could not go through, but had to go around. It took me just twenty-four hours to go that distance, and try as I might, to keep out, I was continually getting into a small drifting field. At times I had to get out on the cakes, haul up my boat, and chop the floes apart, so I could proceed. Luckily I had an axe with me or I am afraid I'd be up there yet. The steam that rose off the ice was very dense, and very similar to a heavy fog in summer. I could not see 10 feet [3 m] ahead of me at times. All this time it was about 23° F below zero [−31° C] — at least that was the temperature at the harbour when I got there. I had plenty of food with me all the time, so I did not suffer from

hunger. When I did get to Michipicoten Harbour, the ice prevented me from reaching the shore; and I had to get out, wade through ice and water, a distance of 25 to 30 yards [23 to 27 m]. So you see that when I did finally get to land I was wet through. The intense cold soon froze my clothing to my body, and in a short time I was like a frozen snowman. I tried to get a place at the harbour to get my clothes dried out, but there was not a single house where that could be accomplished. So what did I have to do? Walk back to my light, by land a distance of about 7 miles [11 km] over mountains and hills, as there is no trail to the point from the harbour. I stayed there a day and a night and got dried out, and then came back to the harbour. This time, I profited by my first experience and it did not take me so long to get back to civilization."

In 1967 the original combined tower and keeper's house was demolished and replaced by a modern steel tower, a square skeletal structure almost 40 feet (12 m) high that used a modern electric optic. In 1992 it displayed a white light that flashed every 30 seconds from a 87-foot (26.5 m) focal plane for 16 miles (26 km). The light was later put into service as an emergency light and operated year round. It was manned until 1991, when the last keepers were removed. It is still operational today.

Visitors to the area may also visit the small cemetery outside the village of Michipicoten on the Magpie River by Silver Falls. It is named the Mackenzie Bethune Cemetery, and Louisa (Mackenzie) Bethune, a cousin of Sir Alexander Mackenzie, is buried there. However, there is also a gravestone for one of the Gros Cap Lighthouse keepers. It reads, "Erected to the memory of William T. Richardson, Lighthouse Keeper at Gros Cap for many years. Died at Gargantua February 6, 1915, age 63 years."

Known Keepers: W.T. Richardson (1900–14), William D. Reid (1915–22), Wm Blackington (1922), Joseph Miron (1922–29), Benson Lithgo Whytall (1929–36), Walter Gardner (1937–40), Alex Collins (1940–47), F.W. Pearson (1947–), Lou Brandon (1961–64), George Rutherford (1964–66), Ronald Watt (1966–).

16 Michipicoten Island East End Lighthouse

In Lake Superior, 40 miles (64 km) out from Michipicoten Harbour, is a volcanic island so lush with green trees that it has been called the "emerald isle of Superior." Its name, Michipicoten Island, means "floating island," so named by the First Nations because as lighting changed during the day, the island would appear to be closer or farther away, as if floating on the water. With increased shipping on Superior and mining on the island, the island became lit, but a light at the east end of the island to mark the offshore shoals and reefs was not lit until 1912.

In the early 1900s the Department of Marine designers, under the leadership of the Canadian designer and chief engineer of the Marine and Fisheries Department, Col. William P. Anderson, started to build a completely new style of lighthouses known as "flying" towers. These towers were built of reinforced concrete and, because of their height and their untested style, were supported by additional buttresses. Col. Anderson said the buttresses were not for strength but to add stiffness to the tall towers and help keep them from vibrating and swaying in the high winds, so as to keep the lantern steady and enable the lamp and the Fresnel lens to function at their best. This style was also an economical way to build a strong yet functional lighthouse. These structures were amazing pieces of architecture when one considers that the workers had only pioneer methods and tools, horses or donkeys, and human brawn — no diesel engines, gas-powered cement mixers, chain saws, carbide-tipped saw blades, plywood to build forms or helicopters to transport materials.

The lighthouse at Michipicoten Island East End, was known as E.E. Station and was started in the fall of 1910 at a cost of more than $10,000. The tower, keeper's house and other outbuildings were built the next year. Designed along the lines of a Gothic cathedral, the lantern was centered on a hexagonal tower that rose from a circular concrete base. On the six sides, flying buttress wedges sloped down from the top to the base, with horizontal connections to the tower at regular intervals. Inside, iron ladders connected each floor up to the lantern.

The dodecagonal lantern had three square glass panes in each panel. The second-order Fresnel lens was first lit using a kerosene vapor mantle lamp. The lens rotated on a bed of mercury and was powered by a clockwork mechanism. The 70-foot (21.3 m) tower had a focal plane of 83.2 feet (25.4 m). The white flashing light (flash 0.33 s; eclipse 1 s; flash 0.33 s; eclipse 5 s) had a 20-mile (32 km) visibility and on a clear night could even be seen 40 miles (64 km) away at Michipicoten Harbour on the Ontario mainland.

A lot of the information gathered here about the Sherlock family of keepers came from an interview with the children of Mel Sherlock, whose father, William Sherlock, had been the first keeper at the light. William and his wife, Mary, raised eight children and one (Mel) went on to become a keeper. They would stay up all night to carry oil to the lantern twice a night and wind the weights every six hours. They had an alarm to let them know if the lamp needed attention. Once, during their tenure, the family had a harrowing experience. A forest fire started by lightning burned the whole island except for the tower and the main house, which was only singed. During the event, the family camped out on Gull Rock and ate gull eggs. In 1913 the Sherlocks wintered over at the island lighthouse, a practice the government frowned upon because of the exposed location and the lack of medical aid. But the Sherlocks chose this rather than pay exorbitant rents for winter lodging in Sault Ste. Marie.

In 1915 keepers were informed that, to reduce costs, the government would no longer deliver them to their lighthouse in the spring or pick them up in the fall. Keepers would have to find their own transportation. In December 1916, while William and one of his sons were shipping out at the season's end, in their small government-issue sailboat, they ran into a "nor'easter." At below-zero temperatures, the pump froze. As the boat shipped water they threw everything overboard, including food, in order to stay afloat. Eventually, after a few days and out of food, they reached shore. To survive, they killed and ate their dog. They finally made it to the Sault around Christmas. But the next year William Sherlock was not so lucky. He lost his life returning to the mainland at the close of navigation, 1917. Neither his boat nor his body was ever recovered. His wife, Mary, became keeper after him until 1925. (In 1922 she earned $900 a year.)

In the early 1960s Melvin (Mel) Sherlock, William's third son, became assistant to head keeper Joseph (Joe) Thibeault, also at the E.E. Station. In August 1972 Joe got married in Michipicoten Harbour. He wore full Native regalia and rode his horse bareback up the beach to his wedding. In keeping with tradition, he even paid the preacher in rabbit pelts. (He later paid the legal tender in money.) Thibeault was quite a character. When asked if he was

Michipicoten East End Lighthouse

purebred Indian he would reply, "My mother was ¾ Indian. My father was ¾ Indian. So that makes me an Indian and a half!"

In 1973 Mel went to the Otter Head light until they could find a replacement keeper and then he returned to the E.E. Station. When Thibeault left the station in 1974, Mel Sherlock became head keeper. A small man, only 5 foot 3 inches and about 115 pounds "soaking wet," Mel was a character with a "droll sense of humor." Once he saw a huge beaver heading for the beach by the lighthouse, so he ran out of the house exclaiming, "I'm riding a beaver!" and he did just that. He stood on the beaver's tail and balanced there while the startled beaver high- (or, rather, low-) tailed it to the water. A friend of his made a cartoon sketch of him riding the beaver, complete with reins. Another time Mel took a pig to the lighthouse in the spring to raise and butcher it for meat. However, the pig became a family pet. Mel played hide and seek with him and taught him to dance, making him a star attraction for visitors. When fall came, Mel butchered Arnold as planned, but the kids could not eat their pet. In fact, they couldn't eat pork for two years!

Despite his shenanigans, Mel was a dedicated keeper, and he and his assistants kept everything impeccable and running smoothly. His main job, next to keeping the light, was to help people in distress, so he always left the door unlocked and was on the lookout for "idiots in 16-foot sailboats" miles away from the mainland. Once at 3:00 a.m. in a heavy fog, a man from Sault Ste. Marie knocked on his door. He and his buddies had been guided by the foghorn, with one man positioned at the bow looking for deadheads (floating logs). Mel wondered about the common sense of such people.

Mel rescued mariners whenever possible. He helped in the search for the *Edmund Fitzgerald* in the fall of 1975. Five years in a row, he rescued George Rutherford, his friend and fellow lighthouse keeper at Caribou Island, from a reef near E.E. Station. Every year, Rutherford left his station about 20 miles (32 km) to the south of Michipicoten Island in his small sailboat, to visit Mel and his family. He always left with a 40-pounder of whiskey, started drinking as soon as he was under sail, and inevitably got stuck on the same shoal. When he didn't arrive at the scheduled time, Mel would say, "Well, we better go pull George off the reef." The Sherlocks even named the reef Rutherford's Reef after their friend.

The lighthouse had two boats, the *Blue Goose*, a small rowboat, and the *Tinkerbell*, an old "sow-bellied boat that could go through anything." "Be prepared" was Mel's motto, and he always took a survival kit in two plastic milk crates (one for food and one for boat supplies) whenever he went out on the water. The rations, enough for two days, were put in tins and then the tins were dipped in wax to "waterproof" them. The provisions included "bully" beef (corned beef), Kraft dinner, crackers, tea, sugar and salt, as well as matches dipped in wax, rope, knives and a hatchet. On average, Mel would get stranded four or five times a year.

The keeper also operated the fog signal. At first, it was a hand-pumped foghorn kept in the house. A diaphone fog signal (blast 2 s; silence 18 s) was next, and its generators were put in the old keeper's house. Later, a smaller diaphone foghorn and generators were used and operated out of new, smaller buildings. Later still, the fog signal was automated.

E.E. Station keepers also had to take daily weather readings

Michipicoten Island East End Lighthouse

and radio them in to Quebec Harbour and on to Caribou Island, Isle Parisienne, Gros Cap, and finally to Sault Ste. Marie and Parry Sound. They generally used the MAFOR Code to tell the weather, wind speed and wave height. Mel's children Derek and Sharon described "niners" as bad, "hang-onto-your-butt" storms (9 = 64–71 knot winds and 9- = thunderstorms).

Mel was known to be eccentric. He didn't swear much, but he had unusual sayings. When he "slept" he snored very loudly, but the most he would admit to was that he was "resting his eyes" or that he was "checking his eyelids from the inside for cracks." He carried pails of soil from the bush with a shoulder yoke because his wife, Peggy, wanted a flowerbed and flower boxes. When a damaged rowboat washed ashore, Mel labelled it "Peggy's Garden" and made it into a small vegetable garden. He tried growing tomatoes but the season was too short. However, he still bragged that he could grow bigger, better tomatoes than his cousin in Sault Ste. Marie. To prove it, he blew up red balloons, tied them to his tomato-less plants, took a picture, and then showed off the proof of his "prize" tomatoes.

Another favorite pastime was fishing, especially right in front of the lighthouse. Derek and Mel put the *Blue Goose* into the water as soon as possible each year. They caught whitefish, herring, chub and trout. They fished with a "square hook" (a net) — which was illegal but efficient. What the family could not eat, they froze in their generator-operated freezer. They would swap frozen fish for ice cream, lettuce, fresh vegetables, and "sweets" with sailors from the tender *Alexander Henry*. And they gave frozen fish to tourists who stopped by. For variety, they smoked whitefish, using wild apple, wild cherry or maple wood.

Mel and some friends once introduced squirrels to the island and since they had few predators, the island was soon overrun. He was not supposed to trap, but he snared rabbits and trapped beaver to supplement their food supply. The beaver had a super-strong, gamey taste, so it had to be soaked in milk or salt water for two or three days before being roasted, boiled or stewed. Another of his pastimes was wine making. He had grapes and supplies brought in by the tender ship

but if none were available, he and Joe would make wine out of anything — wild mulberries, blueberries and even onion skins. They put the leftover mash on the beach for the animals to scavenge. The drunken seagulls and squirrels offered great entertainment as they staggered along the rocky beach.

Mel started the season at the lighthouse, and Peggy and the kids joined him for the school holidays. When the two youngest of the five children were about thirteen, they stayed with their older sister on the mainland, and Peggy spent the whole season with Mel. She used to go out in the *Tinkerbell* until one time when Mel took her out during a storm and the soaking trip took several hair-raising hours. After this Peggy insisted on being flown out. Nick Pipoli, an excellent local pilot with his own small "Beaver" pontoon plane, usually flew Peggy and the kids into Quebec Harbour because the updrafts at the end of the island were too strong for most pilots.

The updrafts had to be respected. Once, when the supply helicopter *Amy Bretton* was taking off after bringing in supplies, she got caught in the updraft and flipped right over in mid-air like a child's toy. Upon landing in the cold stormy water, the pilot rubbed himself with axle grease to keep his body heat in, and staved off hypothermia until he was rescued by a fishing tug.

Peggy was also quite a woman. She helped her husband without complaining, but she dealt with things in her own way. To prevent black flies from biting her legs she would wrap her legs in newspaper and then put her stockings over top. Fortunately, she only needed to do this for about two weeks a year. She also hated snakes, so she carried a "snake stick" at all times when outside to "beat the …" out of the ubiquitous garter snakes. Despite these drawbacks, she too loved the lighthouse and served as assistant keeper during Mel's ten pre-retirement years.

The kids would swim in a shallow rock pool in front of the lighthouse, go on picnics, hunt for agates, read, have barbeques, pick blueberries, mulberries, strawberries and choke cherries, gather gull eggs to eat, visit friends at Davieaux Lighthouse, play games or watch TV until it went off (it was powered by their generator). Mel always had something for them to do. Once he had his youngest children and his three granddaughters paint a large maple leaf on the helipad on top of its red dot but he only gave them tiny, oil paint brushes and it took them almost the whole

Michipicoten Island East End Lighthouse keeper' boat, Tinkerbell

summer. Another time, he made the children sit and fan the flies off cleaned fish until it was dry enough to smoke.

One year an infestation of small moths were irresistibly drawn to the light. They got into the lantern through cracks and vents, and got squished in the gear mechanism. They coated the lens and were instantly fried. The next day the children had to help scrape off the prisms of the lens with knives and steel wool.

But in spite of the work Derek and Sharon both loved the lighthouse. Every summer until her father retired, Sharon returned with her own three girls. Mel was keeper (assistant and later head) for 19 years at "his emerald isle" of Superior. In 1987 the light's status changed to an emergency light and it stayed lit all year. But as the light was automated in 1988 and the keepers were removed, the era of lightkeeping at Michipicoten East End Island Lighthouse came to an end.

Known Keepers: William Sherlock (1912–17), Mary Christina Sherlock (1918–25), Charles McDonald (1926–29), M.H. Penno (1929–31), E.W. Gauthier (193133), Albert Green (1933–38), Francis Pearson (1938–47), P.A. Turner (1947–53), J.C. Nagel (1953), P.A. Turner (1954–57), W.E. Trainor (1957), James Fredrick Francis (1957–59), James Ross (1959–60), Everett Marryatt (1960), Alfred Herbert Thibeault (1961–62), Erwin C. Scott (1962–63), Melvin Sherlock (1963–64), Alfred Thibeault (1964–74) Mel Sherlock (1974–81), Lou Brandon (1981–88).

17 Mission Channel Entrance Light

The Mission Channel was dredged and marked with breakwaters to provide a southern entrance into the harbor at Port Arthur. In 1917 a square wooden tower 24 feet 9 inches (7.6 m) high, with a red upper section, was built at the outer corner of the breakwater to mark the channel. In 1939 its fixed white light was changed to a green one. In 1992 it displayed a green flashing light (flash 0.5 s; eclipse 1.5 s) using a lens and electricity, and it was visible for 8 miles (13 km) from a focal plane of 43 1/2 feet (13.4 m).

Known Keeper: Starford (–1950).

18 Otter Island Lighthouse

Otter Island is a small island located along Lake Superior's north shore just west of Otter Head on the mainland, directly north of Michipicoten Island, west of Michipicoten Harbour and 137 miles (220 km) northwest of Sault Ste. Marie. To help mark the northern Superior shipping route, signal a turning point in the lake, and point out the harbor for local miners of iron and tin, a lighthouse was built on the northwest tip of the island in 1903. The separate tower, built on a hilltop, was an octagonal white tapering wooden structure with an overall height from base to vane of 36 feet (11 m), and gently flared to form a graceful cornice to support its octagonal gallery. When first lit, its dodecagonal iron lantern displayed a fixed white light that was visible for 10 miles (16.2 km) from all approaches from its 97-foot (30 m) focal plane. It was later changed to a flashing white light with its seventh-order lens being rotated on a bed of mercury by a clockwork mechanism. This light flashed every eight seconds and shone for about 18 miles (29 km).

Other buildings, a wooden frame keeper's house on the hill, a wooden boathouse, a privy and an oil house, completed the station. A tramway operated by a hand-wound cable helped transport supplies from the bay up the hill. Supplies then had to be carried across a walkway over a crevice to get them to the lighthouse or the keeper's house.

In 1915 the Canadian government informed its keepers they would no longer transport them to and from their stations in the spring and fall. Regardless of distance or the small size of the government-supplied sailboat, keepers were responsible for their own transportation. This proclamation caused the death of the Otter Island lighthouse keeper, Robert McMenemy, in 1916. After closing for the season, he did not make it to civilization but was later found by Indian trappers, sitting frozen against a tree. When a new keeper arrived the next spring, he found McMenemy's note saying that he was quite ill but was leaving for Michipicoten Harbour. It was believed that he landed to warm himself and drifted into unconsciousness.

In 1920 a building was added for a fog signal with a unique characteristic pattern of one-minute repetitions (blast 3 s; silence 3 s; blast 3 s; silence 51 s). By 1923 the keeper earned $1,560 a year plus another $300 for winter allowances. At some point the light was automated and the keepers were removed.

On April 28, 1978 by Order in Council, the lighthouse reservation was transferred to Pukskwa National Park. The light became operational all year round as an emergency light in 1988. Today it is still an active aid to navigation, but it has been automated with solar panels and an electric light produces its signal. A helipad sits close to the tower for the periodic maintenance calls of Coast Guard personnel.

Known Keepers: Robert McMenemy (1903–16), Malcolm Sutherland (1920–22), George Marshall (1922), Gilbert McLachlan (1922–), Albert Murray (1945–), W.E. Trainor (1956–57), Charles MacDonald (1957–58), Robert Collins (1959–).

Otter Island Lighthouse, circa 1935

Otter Island Lighthouse

19 Peninsula Harbour Lighthouse

On November 16, 1891, the Dominion Government of Canada, by Order in Council and approved by the Lieutenant Governor, acquired from the Ontario government an island at the entrance to Peninsula Harbour for lighthouse purposes. The island, about 146 acres (59 hectares) was located along Lake Superior's north shore about 25 miles (40 km) east of the Slate Islands. A lighthouse was established on the south end of the island in 1891 to mark the harbor and to also help mark Superior's north shore.

It was a combined wooden house and tower, with the tower having an overall height of 56 feet (17 m) from base to vane. The square white tower was topped with a red iron lantern that used lamps and reflectors to exhibit a flashing white light every 30 seconds from a 105-foot (32 m) focal plane for 16 miles (26 km). The station also had a hand-operated foghorn to answer signals from ships during poor visibility.

Peninsula Harbour Lighthouse, circa 1914

Known Keepers: J. Blondin (1910–), David Coveney (1920–45), Arden Lewis (1945), A. P. Clark (1946–47), Gerard Smith (1947), C.C. Cress (1948), Harry O'Connor (1949), George Lloyd Dampier (1949), Franklin Ralph Miller (1950–51), Robert Burns (1952), George Duggan (1952–)

20 Pie Island Lighthouse

Pie Island is a large island that lies in the entrance to Thunder Bay along Lake Superior's north shore and just north of Isle Royale. The island is made of basaltic rock, and named for its round flat shape.

In 1895 the government built a lighthouse on a point on the west side of the island to mark the western entrance into Thunder Bay, where the Canadian western shipping termini of Port Arthur and Fort William were located. The square white wooden tower tapered upward to 23 feet (7 m) from base to vane. Its red lantern exhibited a fixed white dioptric light using a seventh-order lens from a 34-foot (10.4 m) focal plane to produce an 11-mile (17.7 km) visibility. The light was visible from all points of approach except the east. The keeper's white wood house was to the northeast of the tower. The station was equipped with a hand-operated foghorn to respond to signals from vessels.

This was a remote lighthouse location. On May 22, 1911, the *Detroit Evening News* reported that Thomas Hamilton, the Pie Island lighthouse keeper, who tended the light alone and had no one to help in case of a mishap, had been found dead. The Native people who discovered his body while taking him provisions thought he had been dead for about ten days. Joseph Vernon took charge of the light in the spring of 1912 and was the keeper until he was transferred in 1921 at the time when the light was changed to an automated Aga light.

In 1982 the light was moved to a 25-foot (7.5 m) square skeletal tower with a red and white rectangular daymark. Its light was changed to an electric white flashing characteristic (flash 0.5 s; eclipse 3.5 s). From a focal plane of almost 30 feet (9 m), it was visible for 5 miles (8 km). This light still operates today.

Known Keepers: Thomas Hamilton (1899–1911), J. Vernon (1912–21).

21 Pointe aux Pins Lighthouse

Pointe aux Pins, as its French name suggests, is a large pine-clad peninsula that juts into the St. Mary's River where the river connects with Lake Superior. It is about 7 miles (11.3 km) above Sault Ste. Marie and on the Canadian, or north, side of the river. Long before locks were built in the river, Pointe aux Pins became a shipbuilding center for Lake Superior vessels, its first ship being launched in 1735. Later, it was the shipbuilding region for the American Fur, the Northwest and the Hudson's Bay companies. During the 1850s Lake Superior was uncharted and mostly unexplored, so mariners traveled mainly by instinct and experience. They carried missionaries, soldiers, miners and prospectors with their supplies, and stopped at many out of the way places.

After the opening of the Soo Locks in 1855, steam barges began operating on the St. Mary's River and on the lake in the 1860s. To enable more cargo to be hauled, old sailing ships, stripped of all except their fore, main and aft sails, were loaded and towed tandem behind the steam barges.

Pointe aux Pins also developed as a pleasure excursion destination and a stop for steamers to take on cordwood. In 1858 by the steamer *Rescue* docked there during its first cruise from Collingwood to Fort William (Thunder Bay). A large elegant resort hotel hosted vacationers from Buffalo and Detroit, but it burned down around 1900.

To facilitate all this increased water traffic in and out of Lake Superior at the St. Mary's River, a light was placed on the southernmost shore of the point. The Canadian government acquired 24 acres (9.7 hectares) of land for a lighthouse reserve by Order in Council from the Ontario government on September 24, 1874. The acreage made up the southeast quarter of Section 24, Park Township, in the District of Algoma.

Although the land had been officially acquired in 1874, the lighthouse was built in 1873. It was a square white 23-foot (7 m) tapering wooden tower with a square gallery supported by carved corbels and surrounded by a simple wooden railing. The 6-foot (1.8 m) octagonal wooden lantern displayed a fixed white light for 8 miles (13 km) using three oil-burning No. 1 base-burner tin

Pointe aux Pins Front Range Light

lanterns with 16-inch (40 cm) reflectors. It was officially lit on September 6, 1873. A fog bell was later added to the station. The hammer to strike the bell was powered by a clockwork mechanism that needed winding every few hours.

On several occasions the government had to deal with persons found removing sand from the reservation. The first perpetrators were Sault Ste. Marie contractors Ryan and Heney in 1889. The firm was reprimanded and ceased for a time. But in 1893 they were again found pumping sand from under the water just 300 feet (92 m) away from the lighthouse and the sand bank was being affected. It was feared this practice threatened the lighthouse. A second letter brought their reluctant agreement to stop. On another occasion, in May 1901, Mrs. E.R. Hughes, the lightkeeper, reported sand again being taken. She was told to advise any vessels within 500 feet (153 m) that they were trespassing and would be prosecuted. In May 1901 the Marine Department received a new copy of the deed clarifying the extent of the reservation, since the original records had been burned in a fire in 1897. Later, in August 1902, sand was again taken by another sand-sucker dredge by D.L. McKinnon. Instead of being prosecuted, McKinnon was charged five cents a yard for the sand he had taken, and he agreed to desist. Fortunately, the removals did not undermine the lighthouse as feared.

Many members of the McKinnon family served as lighthouse keepers. The family owned much of the land around the point, but eventually ran into financial difficulties and had to sell off timber to make ends meet.

Some changes occurred at this station. The catoptric illuminating apparatus was switched to a sixth-order Fresnel lens. In 1944 a road to the lighthouse was opened up. The light was automated in the 1930s, and in 1945, when electricity arrived, it became the illuminant. In 1960 youths celebrating the end of the school year dismantled the fog bell, dropped it to the ground, and tried to remove it. The 300-pound (136 kg) bell was found 200 yards (185 m) from the lighthouse in 4 feet (1.2 m) of water, slightly damaged, but not enough to interfere with its performance. Five years later, vandals caused extensive damage to the lighthouse. Thrown stones had broken its lantern glass and endangered the $3,000 Fresnel lens in what police reported was the fourth night of vandalism in two weeks.

Several keepers at this lighthouse are mentioned here and there. In January 1894 the Attorney General of Canada sent government detectives to the Sault to investigate the disappearance of the keeper, Henry Woods. In April 1900 Captain Joseph Rouleau was put in charge of the light at Pointe aux Pins in addition to tending to his private range lights above the Soo locks. In September 1916 keeper William Rice fell out of a rowboat and drowned in the river while a John Bellow was rowing him out to the light.

Grant McKinnon used to row out to the lights twice a day from his cottage near the Pointe aux Pins store to light and extinguish the main light and the two range lights. Later in his 31-year tenure, he used a powerboat or took the new road. If McKinnon had to be away he hired Don McCloud, a local boy, to row out and extinguish the lights in the morning. Later Jean McCloud performed the task for $7.50 a week. She also cleaned the towers when McKinnon anticipated a visit from the lighthouse inspector.

In 1970 the tower was torn down, burned and replaced with a lanternless cylindrical tower almost 20 feet (6 m) high with a banded daymark and a modern acrylic beacon at its summit. Local Dan Delayer salvaged the old tin lantern and tower door. The Fresnel lens and fog bell were destined for the Parry Sound museum and the keeper's house was sold for use as a cottage.

Today a modern tower continues to exhibit its fixed red light for six miles from a 26.5-foot (8.2 m) focal plane, but the character of the old light is gone.

Known Keepers: Wade G. Foote (1873–), Captain Clark (?), Henry Woods (–1894), Captain Joseph Rouleau (1900–), Mrs. E.R. Hughes (1901–), John Marks (–1904), Alex McKinnon (1904–1934), Frank McKinnon (1934), A.W. Hurley (1934), Bob McKinnon (?), William Rice (?), Grant McKinnon (1935(36)–66), William Chalmers (1966).

22 Pointe aux Pins Range Lights

In 1903 range lights were built at Pointe aux Pins to assist upbound navigation around the point from the St. Mary's River into Lake Superior. They were located just before a bend in the river where the shipping channel navigates around Point Louise, a smaller point on Pointe aux Pins.

The rear light was on shore. It was a three-story square white wooden pyramidal tower surmounted by a square white lantern with just a rectangular glass panel facing the water. It was topped with a hipped red roof and ventilator stack. A simple gallery, supported by two metal braces on each side, was placed partway down from the top of the tower.

The front light was located on the extremity of Point Louise. It was identical in style to the rear range light except that it was only 25 1/2 feet high. These lights used coal oil lamps with 24-inch (60 cm) reflectors to produce their beam, and were visible only when in the direct line of approach.

By 1992 the front range light was still in use, but the rear light was displayed from a 55-foot (16.6 m) tripod skeletal tower. Both lights displayed an orange vertical stripe on white as a daymark, continued to use a catoptric illuminating apparatus (but were powered by electricity), and displayed a fixed green light.

The old rear range light was later sold and a building was added to it. The front range light no longer has its gallery, and the lights now show a fixed red characteristic. They still operate today as an active aid to navigation.

Pointe aux Pins Rear Range Light

Porphyry Point Lighthouse

He and his family lived full time at the lighthouse, which was unusual as most keepers at remote locations wintered on the mainland. He had a large vegetable garden, and stored smoked meat and bags of wheat in the boathouse. His wife died in Port Arthur in 1884, about four months after giving birth to their tenth child. The winters were cold and it was difficult to cut enough firewood to heat the poorly insulated dwelling. The ninth child and the youngest daughter, Emily, did not marry but stayed with her father to help at the lighthouse. As a young adult she worked hard. She cooked, baked, trained dogs to harness, made fishing nets, smoked fish, hunted, cleaned the henhouse, hauled firewood with dog teams, scrubbed wood floors, fed the chickens, gathered eggs, set traps, snared rabbits, buck-sawed wood, and did any other task that might need doing.

The keeper's listing of holiday dinners also gives a glimpse of lighthouse life. In 1899 they had rabbit, caribou steak, eggs, pot barley soup, bacon and apple pie. For the 1900 "guzzle" they had "half-breed" soup (made of cabbage, turnips, vermicelli, pot barley and beef), pie, cake and crumpets. For New Year's Day 1901 they had soup, rabbit, boiled beef, sponge cake, rice pudding and crumpets. Christmas in 1901 was bleak. No mention of food was made. The oldest daughter, Agnes, had died during the year. Emily was not able to kill a chicken and, although it was Christmas, there were no presents. However, they had a good New Year's Day for 1902 with beef, chicken, rabbit, soup, rice pudding, raisin pie and lots of cake. The 1902 Christmas was a very cold (−10°F/−25°C) stormy day. They had rooster, rabbit and pork cakes, soup, and raisin pie. For New Year's Day 1903 they had caribou meat, caribou tongue, beets, soup, pie, cake, butter, tea, sugar and maple syrup. These entries show how they used the foods that were available to them.

Dick also made daily weather entries and often mentioned painting the station — and that he was not fond of whitewashing. An entry at the back of one logbook recorded, "Steal not this book for fear of shame / for under is the owner's name. Andrew Dick. Point Porhyry Lighthouse June 18th, 1890." These logbooks are now at the Thunder Bay Museum.

23 Porphyry Point Lighthouse

As lake commerce increased on Lake Superior after the opening of the Soo Locks in 1855, the Canadian government decided to build lighthouses to mark the north shore of the lake. In 1872–73 they built three lighthouses to assist mariners: two on Michipicoten Island at the east end of the lake and the third on Porphyry Island near the west end. The lights on Chimney Point at Quebec Harbour of Michipicoten Island and Porphyry Island used the same plans.

Porphyry Island is located on the south side of Edward Island, in the mouth of Black Bay about 30 miles (48 km) east of Thunder Bay and just 7 miles (11.3 km) north of the Canada-U.S. border. The Canadian government built the lighthouse on the southwest tip of Porphyry Island in 1873 to serve three purposes: to mark the north shore of the lake; to assist in marking the northern channel above Isle Royale into Thunder Bay; and to light the entrance into Black Bay.

The lighthouse was a combined wooden tower and keeper's house built in a unique style. The tower rose from the roof of the single-story keeper's house like a three-layer wedding cake. A square section rose from one side of the house roof, and it was topped by an octagonal section that rose from a hipped roof on the square section of the tower. The tower was surmounted by an octagonal gallery supported by many corbels, and by an octagonal iron lantern.

The lantern was finished with an octagonal dome and a ventilator stack, making the tower 36 feet (11 m) from base to ventilator. It used a catoptric illuminating apparatus to display a fixed white light produced by four circular-burner lamps and four 20-inch (50 cm) reflectors from a 56-foot (17 m) focal plane for 13 miles (21 km). All three levels of the combined house and tower had large rectangular windows with four-over-four panes of glass and double windows on the first and second levels. The light was first lit on July 1, 1873.

Logbooks from Andrew Dick, one of the early keepers, tell us a lot about his lifestyle.

Porphyry Point Lighthouse, circa 1907

In 1908 a wooden fog signal was added to the station 25 feet (7.6 m) northeast of the lighthouse with its diaphone foghorn projecting from 29 feet (8.8 m) above the water on the southeast end of the building. Powered by two 6-horsepower engines, it emitted a 2 ½ second blast every minute. The system cost $295. Once, when smoke blew over the lighthouse from a large forest fire in Minnesota, the foghorn operated for 75 hours straight. The great November storm of 1913 sent waves of 25 to 30 feet (7.5 to 9 m) crashing onshore and hitting some of the buildings.

An assistant keeper was hired to help with the increased workload of the foghorn. Joseph Bousquet arrived in 1911 for the job and was paid $50 a month. His recollection of keeper Dick was: "He had two suits of long underwear, a heavier suit for winter. After six months he'd change. He'd hang one suit over the woodpile and it would stay there until he changed again." Bousquet became head keeper in 1912 when Dick retired at age 81 and received a long-service medal from King George V. He died five years later in 1917. Along with the keeper's job, Bousquet also inherited 35 years' worth of old Toronto newspapers, and it took him all summer to burn them.

Edward McKay replaced Joseph Bousquet in 1922. He supplemented his salary by selling a few hundred pounds of fish weekly to the Booth Fishing Company in Port Arthur. Booth paid 6 cents a pound for lake trout, 4 cents a pound for whitefish and 1 cent a pound for pickerel.

In 1929 the lake freighter *Thordoc* grounded on Porphyry Point, fully loaded with flour. Its crew tossed hundreds of bags of flour from the vessel to lighten it enough to float. McKay recalled everyone on the north shore having free flour for about ten years.

Changes happened at the station. At some point a radio beacon was erected and a radio operator was added to the crew. In 1961 the old lighthouse was removed and the light was placed on a steel skeletal tower and semi-automated. By the mid-sixties it had only one keeper. Later, the light was moved to a square tower 47 1/2 feet (14.5 m) high at the center of a white steel skeletal framework displayed a white slatwork daymark. This light also changed to a flashing white light (flash 1 s; eclipse 9 s). From an 81-foot (24.7 m) focal plane it was visible for about 15 miles (24 km). In 1972 the fog signal was changed slightly (blast 4 s; silence 56 s). In 1976 the light became operational year round as an emergency light. The keepers were taken to and from the light by the tug *James Whalen*, then by the Coast Guard ice breaker *Alexander Henry*, then by the *Alexander Henry* and a helicopter from it to their station, and finally via helicopter out of Thunder Bay. The light was completely automated at the end of the 1988 season and the keepers were permanently removed.

A win-win situation was created when Maureen Robertson, a mother of four, rented the lighthouse from the Coast Guard in order to have some solitude. As well as providing some income for the upkeep of the property from 1993 to 1996, she reduced the chances of vandalism. The light on Porphyry Island is still maintained as an active aid to navigation.

Known Keepers: Donald Ross (–1878), Andrew Dick (1878–1912) Joseph Bosquet (1912–22), Edward McKay (1922–46), Charles Merritt (1946–58), James Nicholson (1958), Clifford McKay (1959–66), William McKay (1966–).

24 Port Arthur Breakwater Light

Port Arthur was located near the west end of Lake Superior in Thunder Bay. The first steamer to dock there, the *Algoma*, arrived in May 1868 carrying men and mining machinery into the area. That summer a general store, a restaurant and the first business docks were built. The *Algoma* continued bi-weekly supply trips between Collingwood and Thunder Bay. In 1873 the steamer *Erin* exported 10,000 bushels of wheat, the first of many loads to be shipped from western Canada. The Canadian Pacific Railroad (CPR) brought wheat from the prairies to Port Arthur and then transferred it to their lake steamers for transport elsewhere.

Port Arthur Breakwater Light, circa 1909

In 1882 the CPR extended its docks and built the first lighthouse on the southeast corner of one dock. It was a simple square white wooden pyramidal tower with pedimented door and windows. A square gallery surrounded a hexagonal iron lantern capped with a dome and ventilator stack. It had an overall height of 36 feet (11 m) and used a catoptric illuminating apparatus to display a fixed red light for 7 miles (11.3 km) from a 43-foot (13 m) focal plane.

From 1883 to 1887 the 2,600-foot (800 m) northern section of a new breakwater was completed a half a mile (0.8 km) from the shore to protect the harbor at Port Arthur, and harbor dredging deepened the waters for larger vessels. To better light the port, the lighthouse was moved from the CPR wharf in 1887 to 30 feet (9 m) from the westernmost end of the newly completed section of the wooden breakwater, where it was anchored.

The light was equipped with a hand-operated foghorn to answer signals from vessels. From 1888 to 1890 the 500-yard (460 m) southern breakwall section was completed, leaving a 350-foot (107 m) opening between the two sections for vessels to enter the harbor. This light was later removed when newer breakwaters were built and the main entrance light was transferred to them.

Known Keepers: John Cooper (1882), Hugh Jones (–1921), Joseph Vernon (1922), George Brown (1922–).

25 Quebec Harbour (Old) Lighthouse

Michipicoten Island, a volcanic island of knobs or hills, lies 30 miles (48 km) southwest of Michipicoten Harbour in Lake Superior. Sometimes called the gem of Lake Superior, it is about 15 miles (24 km) long and 6 miles (9.6 km) wide. It is most beautiful when approached from the south, where a few picturesque islands grace the entrance to its commodious and readily accessible harbour.

To the early Natives, Michipicoten Island meant "floating island" because it appeared sometimes close and sometimes distant from the mainland. It is now known that this optical illusion is caused by changing atmospheric weather conditions.

The Natives of Michipicoten Harbour told the early explorers of copper on the island, but none were willing to guide them. They refused because many moons before, other Natives who decided to explore the island and stayed overnight had become sick. Those who returned alive told a tale of terror leading to the legend that the island was guarded by spirits who repelled intruders. So the explorers did not go. (This sickness was later scientifically explained by self-poisoning through the use of stones laden with copper that gave off toxic vapors when used to heat cooking water in birch bark containers.) Around 1779, the island was circumnavigated to more accurately determine its resources. The best they could find were colored stones known as "agates."

In continued efforts to exploit the copper, a mineshaft was sunk on the northwest shore of the island. Ore was extracted and transported by road to the large natural harbor on the island's south side. Here, port and dock facilities were built to accommodate the boats that shipped the ore away for processing. The developing harbor, named Quebec Harbour, also supported a commercial fishing station where fish were packed on ice and shipped to the lower Great Lakes.

The island lay along the increasingly active east-west shipping lanes of Superior's northern shoreline. To help light this route the Canadian government built lighthouses, two at Quebec Harbour and one on Porphyry Island at the west end of Lake Superior in 1872 and 1873. The lights at Quebec Harbour marked the harbor for local commerce and signaled a safe refuge from fierce Lake Superior storms, as it was about 2 ½ miles (4 km) long, ½ mile (0.8 km) wide and deep to provide good anchorage to wait out storms. However, small islands impeded its entrance. Two lights were built to allow safe access into the harbor: one was placed on Agate Island; the other at the end of the peninsula known as Chimney Point (Magnetic Point) on the harbour's east side.

The lighthouse on Chimney Point was built by contractor Captain Perry. It was once described as "a squat structure attached to a residence at its west side." One construction worker was miserable there: "[The island is] an exceedingly dreary and desolate place, entirely destitute of any accommodation whatsoever. I had laid over board every night since I came here and have to live in a small shanty 10 feet [3 m] by 12 feet [3.7 m] and 5 feet [1.5 m] high, in which there are twelve men boarding besides myself."

The lighthouse was almost identical to the light that marked the west end of the lake at Porphyry Island. A square tower rose for one story from a side of the roof of the single-story keeper's house. Then an octagonal tower section rose one more story from the hipped roof of the tower. An octagonal iron lantern with large rectangular panes set vertically was surrounded by an octagonal gallery supported by carved wooden corbels and was topped with an octagonal dome with a ventilator stack, to achieve an overall height of 32 feet (9.8 m). Using a catoptric illuminating apparatus consisting of three mammoth flat-wick lamps and three 20-inch (50 cm) reflectors, the lantern displayed a fixed white light from a 56-foot (17 m) focal plane for about 15 miles (24 km). This station was also equipped with a fog bell as the island was frequently shrouded in fog.

In 1916 the government decided to move the lights. A new light was established on Davieaux Island just outside the entrance to the harbor, and the light on Agate Island was moved to become one of the newly formed range lights at the back of harbor. When these lights were completed and lit in 1918, the old lighthouse on Chimney Point was abandoned.

The light on the point eventually fell victim to the elements and was reduced to ruins. Today all that remains are the stone and mortar remnants of the foundation, which have been overgrown with local vegetation.

Known Keepers: Peter McIntyre (–1878–), Hyancinthe Davieaux (–1910).

Quebec Harbour (Old) Lighthouse

26 Quebec Harbour Range Lights

In the late 1800s vessels traversing east-west on Lake Superior coasted the northern and southern shorelines of the lake in order to keep their bearings. To help guide them the Canadian government in 1872 placed two lights at Michipicoten Island, along the northeast shore of Lake Superior. The lights also marked safe entry for vessels seeking refuge in Quebec Harbour, a natural deep harbor on the island's south side. Local vessels also used the harbor to export fish and ore from the island, where there was a mine and a commercial fishing station.

In 1916 the government decided to improve the lights at the harbor. They built a new light on Davieaux Island just outside the harbor entrance and placed range lights at the back of the harbor. Shining in only one direction, these range lights were visible only when a vessel was on-line. Vessels entering the harbor found a safe route by following the line of the two range lights into the harbor.

The front range light was the light formerly on Agate Island. In 1917 this 20-foot (6 m) white slightly tapering square wooden tower and iron lantern were placed on a scow and moved to the shore at the back of the harbor to become the front range light. Its lantern was modified to shine in only one direction. A new tapering white wooden tower was built on the higher elevation behind the front range light. It had a square wooden gallery and a square wooden lantern. Only one window faced the water so that its light also only shone in one direction. Both lights used reflectors and kerosene lamps, and an oil house was built nearby to house the volatile fuel. A white board-and-batten boathouse and a dock were also built slightly to the west of the range lights.

The range lights were first lit by Charles Davieaux, who also, with the help of his family, tended the light on Davieaux Island. Every evening Davieaux rowed out to the island lighthouse to light the lamp about an hour before sunset. He stayed overnight to make sure it burned properly and to wind the weight mechanism that operated the equipment to make the light's characteristic flash

Quebec Harbour Range Lights, circa 1938

pattern. Meanwhile, his family was responsible for lighting and maintaining the two range lights.

The youngest Davieaux girl left the island at age twelve to go to school in Sault Ste. Marie. She said the lake "looked like snow." A freighter had run aground on a nearby reef and had emptied some of its flour cargo in efforts to lighten itself and get off the reef. She remembered, "The sea was covered with white powdered flour." That was her last image of the island, as she never returned.

There are conflicting reports as to where the early keepers lived. In a newspaper interview, Charles Davieaux's daughter described living in "the old range lighthouse, a big double-story building." This might have been the two-story tower at Chimney Point. However, a Federal Heritage Report stated, "The first two keepers at Quebec Harbour occupied very rudimentary houses which they had erected themselves." At any rate, a new combined house and light was built in 1938.

The front tower was moved back to make room for a new building, designed by the Department of Transport. The light had no tower or lantern proper, but shone from a dormer out of the center of the house's south rooftop. The house had a truncated hipped roof, two windows and an open porch at its east end, facing the water. It had no windows on its upper level (except for the dormer) and its second level stored lighthouse supplies and equipment. The main level formed the residence. The privy, as usual, was out back.

The old front range light served as a storage facility but its lantern was removed to avoid confusion for mariners. Henhouses to the east of the house at the edge of the cleared area tell us that the keepers had fresh eggs and chicken, and likely a garden.

To keep up with the times, changes took place at the station. In the 1940s the open porch was enclosed and windows added to the upper level. A larger storage shed replaced the small oil shed in the 1950s, and the original rear wooden range tower was removed and replaced by a modern light on a 42-foot (12.8 m) steel tower. In 1963 the range lights were converted to electricity supplied by batteries and generators. In 1965 a new duplex keeper's house was built on Davieaux Island for the keeper and his assistant. Until then the head keeper had lived at Quebec Harbour and the assistant at Davieaux Island. After the late 1960s, the keepers no longer used the residence at Quebec Harbour. At some time the front range light was moved from the centre dormer window to a higher location on the roof of the dwelling. In the early 1970s a fluorescent orange vertical stripe was added to the front of the house as a daymark after the center and dormer windows of the empty house were closed in. The range lights were demanned in 1991.

While there is no mining or large scale commercial fishing from the island anymore today, the range lights continue to guide the small vessels of cottagers and sport fishermen into the harbor.

Known Keepers: Charles Davieaux (1910–33), Joseph Davieaux (1933), Joseph Miron (1934–43), Fred Hurley (1943–44), Norman Cormier (1945–58), Roy Ellis (1959), Gordon Frederic Dawson (1960–64), Bob Nelder (1965–67), Milton Hughes (1967–).

Shaganash Island Lighthouse

27 Shaganash Island Lighthouse

Lake Superior deserves its reputation as the most fickle of the Great Lakes. A surface as smooth as glass can in minutes transform into mountainous waves. Especially tricky is the inside northern passage between the mainland and Isle Royale. Lights had been placed there to help guide mariners through the narrow passage from an eastern approach into Thunder Bay, the Canadian western shipping terminus on Lake Superior. To further this end, a lighthouse was placed on a smaller island listed as island No. 10 to the west of Shaganash Island in 1910.

Although no known pictures of this island's first light exist, it was a short white wooden tapering tower typical of Canadian lighthouses along the north shore of Superior at this time. It displayed a fixed white light. There was also a house for the keeper and his family.

In November 1921 the station was destroyed by fire, but as it was so late in the season, the light was not replaced until the following year. A temporary pole light was erected, and a temporary keeper took charge of it on May 11, 1922. His annual salary was $500, plus $3 a month to operate the foghorn.

The replacement light, also a short white wooden tapering tower, was almost 24 feet (7.5 m) high and had a pedimented door and windows. The top flared gently to produce a wooden cornice that supported a large square gallery surrounded by a simple pipe iron railing. Its iron lantern produced a fixed white dioptric light from a focal plane of almost 36 feet (11 m). The station also had a hand-operated foghorn to answer signals from ships during times of poor visibility. It is unknown when this light was automated but the keeper was removed at the end of the 1954 season. In 1982 the light was electrified and switched to a flashing white light (flash 0.5 s; eclipse 3.5 s). This solar-power light continues as an active aid to navigation today.

Known Keepers: W. Fairail (1912–22), George Weeks (1922) Andrew McGuinness (1923–28), Samuel Kayes (1929), Arthur Newman (1930–42), Peter Belanger (1943–).

Slate Island Lighthouse

28 Slate Island Lighthouse

The Slate Islands are a group of eight major islands 8 miles (12.8 km) offshore from Terrace Bay, Ontario, on the north shore of Lake Superior. Terrace Bay is about 160 miles (257 km) due north of Marquette, Michigan, and these islands mark the widest point of Lake Superior. The Slates' unusual arctic-type vegetation suggests that a meteor hitting nearby caused the formation of these islands and their unusual flora.

In 1903 the Slate Island Lighthouse was built on 29.6 acres (12 hectares) of land on Patterson Island's southeast side of Sunday Point. Its 36-foot (11 m) octagonal wooden tapering tower is relatively short, but since it stands about 250 feet (77 m) above lake level on a high cliff, it claims to be the highest light on Lake Superior. Its iron lantern used a fourth-order lens to display a fixed white light with a visibility of 10 miles (16 km). Mariners had trouble distinguishing the Slate Island light from the evening stars; only their knowledge of celestial navigation enabled them to tell the difference.

The light served as a navigation point for mariners, as a marker to the entrances into Jackfish Harbour and into Nipigon Bay, along with the Battle Island lighthouse, and as a beacon for refuge from Superior's storms. In 1907 a small beacon light displaying a fixed white light was erected on a red steel skeletal tower on the southwest tip of St. Patrick Island in the entrance to Jackfish Bay. Known as the Jackfish Bay Light, it worked with the Slate Island light to mark Jackfish Harbour.

The location of the keeper's dwelling at the foot of Sunday Bay gave keepers a steep and sometimes dangerous climb up to the light. Its first keeper, Peter King, who had previously made and lost two fortunes in gold through gambling and drinking, carried his high risk tendencies into the job. One winter he and his family decided to winter over at the lighthouse, since the waters froze over and they could walk to Jackfish, 13 miles (21km) away, for supplies if needed. Once his sons Joe and Dolph rowed and sailed on open water for supplies and decided to stop overnight on a small island on their way back. The next morning ice had formed, so one of them had to chop the ice in front of the boat while the

other rowed. On another excursion the brothers walked into Jackfish across the ice. On their return they noticed stars in the ice with every footstep … the next morning the area was all open water. The winter they stayed on the island was especially long and they almost starved. Another year two of the brothers walked out to Battle Island from Rossport to do some illegal trapping, but sparks from their fire caused their tent to burn and they lost all their supplies. Dolph burned his hands badly and laid them on cold tamarack logs. Finding the next morning that his hands were not blistered, he discovered that cold is good for burns.

Charlie Lockwood, one of the next keepers, died while at the light, and his wife kept his body on ice in the back shed until it could be picked up in the fall and buried properly on the mainland.

Keeper Ed Bousquet was glad of his steady income during the Great Depression. He earned $2,520 a year, out of which he had to pay his assistant keeper's salary. The government paid the radio operator. When Bousquet went to the light in 1929, it used a double-wick brass lamp. He later rigged a mantle similar to a Coleman lantern, for the lamp to burn brighter. Before he left in 1944 he remembered the illuminant as a 500-watt bulb. He also reported that the foghorn was audible 30 miles (48 km) away.

Jack (John) Bryson, a radio beacon operator, kept the light for 30 years. His sons recall a root cellar where things were kept cool, an early kerosene refrigerator, and then an electrical fridge run by a kerosene generator. The station had a keeper and two assistants, later reduced to one assistant. In the mid-1960s the station received generators big enough to light the light around the clock.

The icebreaker tug *James Whalen* would take Bryson and his family from Rossport out to the light and pick them up around the close of shipping in mid-December to take them to Thunder Bay. Jack's wife, Flora, remembers that around 1950 the December trip was so rough that all her son's baby bottles were broken. When they finally got to Thunder Bay after a two-day layover at Trowbridge Island, the boat was iced in and a land crew had to chop the ice off the doors to get the passengers out. In the mid-fifties the Coast Guard ship *Alexander Henry* started transporting lighthouse keepers. Then in 1974 helicopters took over the ferrying.

Supplies were either floated in in barrels or brought in by barge and winch, until a dock was put in the mid-1960s. In 1978 the Brysons began to fix up the original keeper's dwelling to save it from ruin. When Jack retired in 1978 the Coast Guard gave him the use of the original lightkeeper's house as a summer house. Hydro was put out to the island in the early 1980s. After Jack's death in 1998, his son Bob leased the old keeper's house, and he and his three brothers now maintain the facility.

In 1989 the last keeper, Orten Rumley, was removed and the lighthouse was demanned. At this time the last operational pneumatic foghorn system on the Great Lakes was dismantled from the Slate Island lighthouse and donated, along with the keeper's logbooks, to the Neys Provincial Park. The clockworks remain in the tower. Although the light has reportedly been seen from Superior Shoal some 30 miles (48 km) away, its usual visibility is 20 miles (32 km).

Memorable moments of Jack Bryson's tenure included: finding an albino caribou on the island one spring; the night in 1974 when son Jim and a buddy let the light go out because they were sipping beer and forgot to check the generators for fuel; Jack's discovery of a lifebuoy from the *Edmund Fitzgerald* in 1977 (two years after the sinking); the Coast Guard bagging sand from the island to make concrete for installation at different locations; the light turning counter-clockwise and then turning clockwise; and Jacques Cousteau's visit to the island in 1982 to interview Jack Bryson and film swimming caribou. Flora recalled assistant keepers Wally Stokes and Gus Olson telling her sons ghost stories about the former keeper Charlie Lockwood walking around in the old keeper's house. The boys got so scared that they wouldn't sleep over in the original keeper's house.

The Bryson boys knew there was no future in lighthouse keeping, as they anticipated automation. The Slate Island lighthouse was fully automated in 1989. However, the brothers love the island dearly and still visit as often as possible. The automated light still operates as an active aid to navigation today exhibiting a double flash pattern (flash; eclipse 3.5 s; flash; eclipse 11.5 s) every 15 seconds.

Known Keepers: Peter King (1896–1908), A.B. Sutherland (1908–18), Charlie Lockwood (1918–28), Ed Bousquet (1929–44), Gerard Smith (1944–47), David Mercer (1947–48), John Bryson (1948–78), Orten Rumley (1979–89).

29 St. Ignace (Talbot Island) Lighthouse

In the mid-1800s, after the Soo Locks were opened in 1855, settlers and fishermen moved into the Lake Superior area. In June 1866 the Canadian government signed contracts to build six new lighthouses to mark the water route from Collingwood to Port Arthur near the west end of Lake Superior. Curiously, only one of these six was built on Lake Superior and was placed more than 200 miles (324 km) west of the Sault on Talbot Island, a small island 2 miles (3.2 km) south of St. Ignace Island, for which it was named. The light served as a coastal light and assisted local fishermen by marking shoals. It was a square white wooden tower built on a stone foundation in a natural clearing of level rock at the southeast corner of the rocky island. It used three kerosene lamps to display a fixed white light. Finished in the summer of 1867 (also the year of Canada's Confederation) at a cost of $605, it became the first Canadian lighthouse on Lake Superior.

This lighthouse was nicknamed the "Lighthouse of Doom" as it had three keepers during the six years that it operated. The island's distance from Sault Ste. Marie made it a problem for the Department of Marine and Fisheries to remove the keeper at the end of the navigational season before freeze-up. Their solution was to have the keeper make his own way to winter quarters. According to instructions, Perry, the first keeper, closed the lighthouse and headed for the Hudson's Bay Company Post at Nipigon in an open boat during November. He never made it. In the spring his body was found on the mainland of Nipigon Bay still 14 miles (22.5 km) from the post.

The second keeper, Thomas Lamphier, had a house built beside the lighthouse on the island so that he and his wife could live there year round. However, he became ill during his first winter and died. Since the island was mostly rock, his wife wrapped his body in canvas, placed it in a rock crevice behind the lighthouse, and kept watch over it for the rest of the winter to keep animals away. In the spring a party of Natives stopped at the lighthouse and took her husband's body to Bowman Island, where they could bury it in a sandy spot. According to the tale handed down, the keeper's wife's dark hair had turned completely white that winter, from dealing with her husband's illness and death all by herself.

The third keeper was Andrew Hynes. After closing and leaving the lighthouse late in the fall of 1872 he endured great fatigue while trying to reach Silver Islet to winter over. He finally arrived after an 18-day trek to cover 50 miles (80 km), but soon died due to the fatigue of his ordeal.

The 1872–73 annual marine report stated: "He [Andrew Hynes] was the second lightkeeper who perished in endeavouring to return from this station; and owing to this fact, and to the light now being of comparatively little importance to navigation in Lake Superior, it has been decided to discontinue it; and to erect other lights of more importance to the present growing trade. It was originally established for the benefit of the fisheries in that district, but … it then became of very little importance." Although many early Canadian lighthouses were moved for use at a new location, this one was simply abandoned.

The lighthouse marked a special spot to fishermen. Folklore even claims that as they returned to port on a moonlit night they often saw a woman with pure white hair walking through the trees of Talbot Island. As a gesture of thanks to the keepers who gave their lives to tend this lighthouse, fishermen George Gerow, his grandson, Bill Schelling, and their families tended the grave of the Thomas Lamphier on Bowman Island, where they had a fishing camp. They maintained a simple white cross to mark the grave, and the children placed wildflowers on it.

The abandoned lighthouse was useful while it still stood. When fog rolled over the lake and fishermen could not find their way, one of them who could make it to the tower would bang the side of the lighthouse with a stout stick. The sound echoed out over the water much like a fog bell and guided boats into safe harbor.

In 1877 the abandoned light was reported to be in good condition, but all that remain today are its overgrown ruins. Since they lie to the west of the foundation, the tower probably came down in a storm from the east. A study of the ruins shows that the tower framework was 6-inch (15 cm) square timbers and that square nails held the lathe work to the keeper's house on the east side of the tower. The dwelling had a brick fireplace and was built as an addition to the tower. Unfortunately, these ruins cannot tell tales of the keepers who once lived within or of the tragic marine events that may have occurred in the area.

Known Keepers: Perry (1867), Thomas Lamphier (1868–69), Andrew Hynes (1870–72).

30 Thunder Bay Main Lighthouse

Beginning in 1936, the Federal Department of Public Works undertook massive harbor improvements at Port Arthur, located at the west end of Lake Superior. The program included a 1,630-foot (500 m) addition to the existing breakwater system, dredging a larger area of deep water within the harbor, reclaiming land within the harbor, constructing a seaplane base, creating a new main harbor entrance and lighting it with a new lighthouse.

The new lighthouse, a combined light and keeper's dwelling, was built at the end of the breakwater on the north side of the new main harbor entrance. Contracted to Thunder Bay Harbour Improvements Ltd., it used a new modern style. It was raised from its concrete foundation pier by four concrete pedestals and foundations to allow stormy waves to wash harmlessly over the pier and under the lighthouse. These pedestals were surmounted by two steel I-beams and a timber platform that formed the base for the two-story frame keeper's house, which housed the diesel machinery for operating its diaphone fog signal, as well as the living quarters.

Thunder Bay Main Lighthouse

A square tower emerged from the center of the dwelling's hipped roof. It supported a square gallery and a polygonal iron lantern with vertically set glass panels. Using an electric catoptric illuminating apparatus, it displayed a flashing red light from a 48-foot (14.5 m) focal plane for 12 miles (19. 4 km). The building was covered in white clapboard siding trimmed with fire-engine red, and its roof was cedar shakes. The seawall corners were reinforced with steel plates, and the first floor windows had steel shutters for storm protection.

The lighthouse emerged in stages. Although first proposed by the Department of Transport in Ottawa in June 1939, its dates are unclear. A 1939 news report stated that the light would be operational for the start of the 1940 season; however, foundation elevations were recorded in 1944. Also the *Canadian List of Lights, Buoys & Fog Signals* lists it being established in 1937.

The lighthouse specifications are of interest. All goods and materials used were to be produced in Canada or, if this was not possible, preference was to be given to products of the British Empire. The framework was to be spruce or fir, boarding and rough flooring of spruce or red pine, and finished flooring of birch or maple hardwood. The shingles were to be of New Brunswick or British Columbia cedar. Its iron lantern and railing were to be supplied by the Department of Transport. Also, this huge undertaking was to be completed within two months of the acceptance of the contract. This was the first lighthouse on the north shore to have a three-piece bathroom and hot and cold running water.

In January 1951, while the keepers were housed onshore for the winter, vandals broke into the lighthouse. Since they came in through a 14-inch (35 cm) porthole window, they were assumed to be boys small enough to enter through such a small opening. They smashed windows, damaged the staircase, lamps and engines, spilled paint, stole tools and mangled a metal fire extinguisher. Tracks found in the snow around the light included footprints, bicycle tire prints and dog prints. Although the Port Arthur Ontario Provincial Police were contacted, the culprits were never apprehended.

In 1952 Bill McLean became keeper of the light. His main job was to keep the machinery working to operate the light and the fog signal. The light flashed every 7.5 seconds. The foghorn, which blasted three times per minute, was operated when the Empire Elevator 3 miles (4.8 m) away at the west end of the harbor could not be clearly seen. It was so loud that, even though the keeper and his wife covered their heads with coats and blankets, it was "ear-splitting." McLean was a Jack-of-all-trades—electrician, radio expert, and first-class mechanic. He kept the light during the day and his assistant keeper tended it at night. Their supply ship was the *St. Heliers*, a Department of Transport vessel operated out of Parry Sound.

In May 1971 the Canada Steamship Lines' *Simcoe* collided with the pier and the lighthouse while leaving the harbor to head downbound fully loaded. In the extensive damage, the pier and lighthouse were moved off their foundation, and the lighthouse was shifted. Submarine cables (electric and telephone) were cut, causing a power outage to the light and all fog signals in the area. The lighthouse had to be shut down, the keepers removed and the harbor entrance closed to marine traffic. By May 20 a temporary battery-powered green flashing light from a 250 mm lantern was erected on the southeast corner of the lighthouse gallery 48 feet (14.6 m) above the water until repairs could be made.

By mid-June power was returned to the power-outed fog signals at the Mission Channel Entrance, the Kam River Entrance and the South Bay Entrance. Instead of replacing the old lead submarine cable, a lighter but just as efficient cable was used. After this, 5,000 feet (1538 m) of cable was run from the fog signal at the main light to the Welcome Island Light so that the keeper at the Welcome Island light could operate it by dial phone until a keeper was returned to the main light. It took four months for repairs to be completed and the station to be manned again.

In 1973 the light became operational year round to guide the icebreaker *Alexander Henry* in keeping the channels open. Since the keepers had already been brought ashore, a submarine cable, installed in the summer of 1972, was used to power the light. The main on/off switch was controlled from the city. Although no commercial vessels would be using the port, maintaining open channels throughout the year was an experiment to see if it could provide better service for the port. In 1979 the light was fully automated and the keepers were removed. This tower still functions as an active aid to navigation today.

Known Keepers: Robert Shaw (1940–47), S.E. Merritt (1948–52), James (Bill ?) McLean (1952–61), Fredrick Solomon (1961), A.F. Kerr (1962–65), Donald Cameron (1965–79).

31 Thunder Cape Lighthouse

Thunder Cape is at the end of a long peninsula on the east side of Thunder Bay along Lake Superior's north shore. A lighthouse was built at the tip of the point in 1874 to mark the entrance to the bay and to indicate underwater shoals to the west and south of the point. It was a square white wooden tower, 28 feet (8.6 m) from base to vane. Its lantern displayed a revolving white light every minute using two flat-wick lamps and two 20-inch (50 cm) reflectors. (Later a fourth-order lens was added.) From a 45-foot (13.7 m) focal plane, the light was visible for 12 miles (19.4 km). The white wooden keeper's house was attached to the tower, and the fog signal building was located 150 feet (46 m) south of the lighthouse. Its whistle was steam-operated (blast 5 s; silence 20 s). This was later changed to a diaphone foghorn that operated using compressed air (blast 3 s; silence 27 s).

In December 1898 the lightkeeper, Captain William Craig, closed the season and crossed to Port Arthur 16 miles (26 km) away. He reported the weather to be "summer-like." However, keepers George Penfold and Malcolm Easton both lost their lives in the spring of 1922 on the way to their new station when the *Lambton* sank off of Caribou Island in a fierce storm.

The lighthouse was dismantled in 1924 and replaced with a steel skeletal tower almost 25 feet (7.5 m) high with an automated light. The keeper, Allan Murray, was transferred to the new lighthouse established about 3 miles (4.8 km) east of the cape on Trowbridge Island to mark the entrance into Thunder Bay. The skeletal tower had a red and white rectangular daymark. In 1992 it displayed a flashing white light (flash 0.5 s; eclipse 3.5 s) using a dioptric electric illuminating apparatus from a focal plane of almost 35 feet (11 m) to produce a visibility of 5 miles (8 km).

Known Keepers: Duncan McEachem (–1877–), Captain William Craig (1892–98–), George Penfold (–1921), Malcolm Easton (1921), Allan Murray (1922–24).

Trowbridge keeper's house

32 Trowbridge Lighthouse

Trowbridge Island is a small rocky island consisting of high cliffs at the shoreline and a mountain of evergreens on its summit. It is 15 miles (24 km) east of Thunder Bay in Lake Superior, along the mainland side of the shipping channel between the mainland and Isle Royale. Mariners hated this northern passage especially in the fall when storms blew up with little warning, but this passage was the only way into Thunder Bay.

The steamer *Theano* ran iron ore from the lake head to the Sault and iron rails back. In November 1906, heavily laden with rails, she was blown a mile (1.6 km) off course by a surprise storm. By the time the captain recognized Trowbridge Island, it was too late. The steamer struck a reef, was held fast and sprang a leak. The crew launched lifeboats and were rescued but the *Theano* went to a watery grave at the bottom of Lake Superior, finally sinking near Marvin Island in 360 feet (110 m) of water.

Eighteen years later, in 1924, the Canadian government built a lighthouse on Trowbridge Island to mark the passage's dangerous reefs and signal the entrance to Thunder Bay. The short 23-foot (7 m) white tower was built on the highest point of the island, giving it a 113-foot (34.5 m) focal plane and a 16-mile (26 km) visibility. The gently tapering octagonal tower, built of reinforced concrete, arched gracefully out at the top to support the red gallery and lantern. The decagonal lantern had ten large, rectangular glass panels set vertically, and it housed a Fresnel lens that produced a flashing white light every 5 seconds. In 1982 it was designated an emergency light and put into operation all year round.

Also in 1924 a fog signal station was built, midway along the island's rocky shore. A space in the cliffs was blasted, and a large concrete base, breakwall, dock and steps to the dock were put in. The fog house, a white clapboard building with red roof and trim, was built on this foundation. Its horn faced southeast (blast 3.25 s; silence 9 s; blast 3.25 s; blast 44.5 s).

Allan Murray was transferred from Thunder Cape to become Trowbridge Island's first keeper in 1924. One can only wonder about his safety during stormy weather. The 175 wooden steps from the fog signal up to the lighthouse had a white handrail for safety, but they snaked perilously up the hillside. A two-story, white clapboard, duplex keeper's house was built for the keeper and his assistant a fair distance from the tower. A hipped red roof topped the structure and half-dormers peeked out from the center

Thunder Cape Lighthouse, circa 1900

Trowbridge Lighthouse

of the roof. A gracious white veranda decorated with a starburst pattern extended the whole length of the house.

The island could be reached by a number of approaches. In front of the house, near the edge of the cliff was a helicopter pad built in the mid-1900s for delivering the keepers in the spring and retrieving them at the season's end. Another path led down to a second dock (also built later) on the opposite side of the island from the fog house. Still one more path led to the spot where the cliff made a shear drop to the water. A small docking area had been set up at its base, and a derrick for hoisting supplies had been secured to a cement foundation at the summit.

An interview with Joyce Kerr helped with some of the light's history. Joyce first lived at Trowbridge when she was seven years old and her stepfather, Simeon "Sim" Merritt, was the lightkeeper there in 1933. She remembered once climbing up and down the 175 steps from the engine room up the hillside to the lighthouse twelve times in one day. She also recalled 24 ladder-type stairs up to the lantern and canvas curtains on a pulley system to raise and lower them over the lantern windows. During warm weather water was pumped into a holding tank in the attic. The lantern used generators to power the electricity for the light but at one time it had a kerosene lamp and weights to wind every four hours.

Joyce's mother had a rock garden full of annuals and perennials, as well as a vegetable garden. Visitors from the camp on Silver Islet who went up to visit her and see the light were told: "Keep your hands in your pockets," to prevent fingerprints on the lens; "Don't turn the table," because if it was accidentally turned backwards, the gear mechanism that rotated the lens would break; and "Don't touch the tub," to prevent spilling the mercury that was essential for the rotation of the lens.

The supply tender brought supplies such as coal, oil, soap, lumber, paint and glass once a year, usually in August. But it brought no food. Keepers had to stock up when they arrived via the *James*

Whalen or occasionally the *Strathmore* in the spring. They brought sacks of potatoes, half a case of eggs, canned milk, full rolls of baloney and roasts of beef, pork and chicken, which were canned in metal tins at the island using a special canning machine. They also had 24 baby chicks to raise for food. Once, when the *James Whalen* dropped them off, there was still so much ice that they had to walk to the lighthouse, hauling all their supplies with them.

During the war, when there were no men to help with lighthouse keeping, Joyce was trained and hired to be her stepfather Sim's assistant. She earned $98 a month and had to pay $60 a month for room and board, while Sim earned $200 a month. One thunderstorm stands out in her memory. Sim was on the hillside stairs between the engine room and the lighthouse when lightning struck. It knocked out the light, traveled through the wires in the lead pipe railing along the hillside stairs, blew the electrical panel and the generator, traveled underground to the oil storage house, and set it on fire. The hit was so powerful that it welded the trap door to the lantern wall. It also paralyzed Sim who was holding on to the metal railing. Sim's brother, Charles Merritt, who was keeper at Angus Island, joined the forces of boatmen who came to help. The light was relit with a "trouble light" (an old kerosene lamp) set inside the lens, and Joyce turned the lens manually for the rest of the night. The spare generator was put into operation the next day, and Sim soon regained his mobility.

Joyce later married Alex Kerr, also a lighthouse keeper. In 1960–61 her husband was stationed at Trowbridge, and she returned to the island with him and their three children. She described the return as difficult because she "felt she hadn't accomplished anything" and the small, isolated island made her feel "cramped." However, there was now a boat dock to land at, and an indoor bathroom. Her husband earned about $400 a month. Besides operating the light, he frequently rescued boats in distress.

The keepers were usually delivered to the lighthouse in the spring and picked up in the fall. For many years this was effected by the tug *James Whalen*. Then the Canadian Coast Guard icebreaker *Alexander Henry* took over the job. In 1961 a helicopter was placed on the deck of the icebreaker to facilitate the transfer of people and supplies. By the 1980s the transfers were made by a Coast Guard helicopter out of Thunder Bay. When the lighthouse was automated at the end of the 1988 season, it retained its Fresnel lens.

Maureen Robertson, who had leased the keeper's house on Porphyry Island from the Canadian Coast Guard as a personal getaway, began leasing at Trowbridge Island in 1996. This location is more isolated but is only an eight-minute trip by helicopter — or a 1 ½-hour boat trip — from Thunder Bay. Looking at the lighthouse today, one sees a strange juxtaposition of rugged, jagged nature and the pristine straight white lines of human construction. One feels a sense of pride at seeing Robertson's Canadian flag flying beside the keeper's house, knowing that while she is there another piece of history is being saved.

Known Keepers: Allan Murray (1924–31), Simeon Merritt (1931–47), Roy McLean (1947–), Alex Kerr (1960–62), Lloyd Thompson (1962–65), Harold Horton (1965–).

33 Victoria Island Lighthouse

Victoria Island lies close to the north shore mainland of Lake Superior about 30 miles (48 km) south-southwest of Thunder Bay. A lighthouse was built here on a high rock that rose abruptly from the low ground near the western tip of the island in 1881. The light helped mark the area's inside channel, a narrow channel between the mainland and a group of offshore islands, which was more protected than the waters between the islands and Isle Royale.

It was a 30-foot (9 m) square white tower that tapered sharply and supported a square gallery. Its square lantern exhibited a fixed white light using a seventh-order lens, and from a 45-foot (13.7 m) focal plane it was visible for 12 miles (19.3 km). The keeper's house was a separate white wooden two-story dwelling built southeast of the tower. The house and a wooden boathouse were both constructed in 1887 by John George, a Port Elgin contractor, at a combined cost of $2,773. The station also had a hand-operated foghorn to answer signals from passing vessels.

In September 1904, while the lighthouse was being moved to a better but more exposed location, it was blown over during a windstorm and smashed beyond repair. As it was late in the season, a new tower was erected the following year. The *Detroit Evening News* carried a warning to mariners using the area: "Boats navigating the dangerous pass in fall storms by night take great chances of going on the rocks."

Victoria Island Lighthouse

Victoria Island Lighthouse

The tower saw other changes. In 1909, $284 worth of repairs were made to the tower. At some time the light was moved to a skeletal tower just short of 30 feet (9 m) tall with two red and white rectangular daymarks. It displayed an electric white flashing light (flash 0.5 s; eclipse 3.5 s) from a 58-foot (18 m) focal plane for 6 miles (9.7 km). This light is still operational today.

Keeper McLean spoke of the isolation of this remote location. Fresh meat, fruits and vegetables were a treat, as most of their food was canned. When passing vessels saluted the keeper with a blast from their horn, as was traditional, McLean assumed this was to relieve their boredom. The keeper made one trip a month to the city, 30 miles (48 km) away for supplies. He and his wife agreed never to argue because they only had each other for help and companionship.

Known Keepers: Francis Levan (–1877–), G. Cosgrave (1889–), James Sutton (1920–27), S.E. Merritt (1928–31), Samuel Kaye (1931–32), James McLean (1932–42), Roy McLean (1942–43), P. Murphy (1943–45), Edward George Hurst (1945–), John McLean (1952).

34 Vidal Shoal Lightship

The Vidal Shoal was located in the St. Mary's River above the Soo Locks between Sault Ste. Marie and Pointe aux Pins. The hazard to marine traffic was named after Vice-Admiral Alexander Thomas Emeric Vidal who, as a young lieutenant, had surveyed the Great Lakes with Henry Bayfield in 1835.

Sometime in the late 1880s or early 1890s the Lake Carriers' Association reportedly placed a lightship at this location to warn of dangerous shoals. In 1910 efforts to have the area lit by a government vessel fell on deaf ears, and in 1912 the Association moved their own vessel, the schooner *Kewaunee*, from marking the sunken wreck of the freighter *Joliet* in the St. Clair River to the Vidal Shoals.

The *Kewaunee* had been built for the Lake Carriers' Association in 1900 at Kewaunee, Wisconsin. This wooden-hulled schooner was 90 feet (27.5 m) long, with a 24-foot (7.3 m) beam, a 7-foot (2.2 m) draft and a weight of 133 gross tons. Its light was produced from oil-burning lamps, and it had an 8-inch (20 cm) steam fog whistle.

The U.S. government never recognized this light station and never reimbursed the Association for operating a lightship at this location, as they had at Southeast Shoal.

Later in 1912, the vessel was purchased by the Canadian government and used as a lightship until it was retired in 1927.

Welcome Island Lighthouse, circa 1907

35 Welcome Island Lighthouse

The Welcome Islands lie just offshore from Fort William and Port Arthur in Thunder Bay along Lake Superior's northern coast. A lighthouse was placed on one of the islands in 1905–06 to better mark the ports and to also mark the shallow water around the islands.

The light station was constructed under the supervision of W.H. Brunell, a government engineer from Ottawa. Started in November 1905, it was completed in April, 1906 and located about 150 feet (46 m) from the water's edge on the northeast extremity of the eastern Welcome Island. The octagonal wooden tower, which rose out of the red roof of the square white wooden keeper's dwelling, was 38 feet (11.6 m) to the top of its ventilator. Its wooden lantern exhibited a fixed white light using a seventh-order lens. From a 112 foot (34 m) focal plane, the light was visible for 16 miles (26 km) in all directions.

In 1908 a fog signal was added to the station. The compressor and other equipment to operate the diaphone foghorn were placed in a rectangular white wooden fog signal building about 50 feet (15 m) northeast of the lighthouse. The foghorn had its own special characteristic of two blasts every 70 seconds (blast 2.5 s; silence 5 s; blast 2.5 s; silence 60 s). The foghorn was located 90 feet (27.5 m) above the water and faced eastward. This fog signal plant cost $402.85.

The weather always affected the opening and closing of the navigation season. It opened in the spring when the ice moved out (usually sometime in April). An April 23, 1907 keeper's log entry for the Welcome Island lighthouse shows that the ice must still have been quite thick at this time, as a car drove over the ice from

Fort William to the tug *James Whalen*, which was out past the lighthouse (a distance of about 5 miles (8 km) over the ice). The actual entry reads "April 23rd — A real spring day. The *James Whalen* has broken her way beyond Welcome Islands. Yesterday Al Sellers, Jas. Whalen and Captain McAllister went out to the Whalen on an automobile."

The delivery and pickup of keepers changed over the years. In 1933 the tug *James Whalen* out of Port Arthur delivered the keepers to the Welcome Island station. In 1936 the tug *Strathmore* from Port Arthur took over. In 1961 keepers and their supplies were delivered out of Port Arthur by a marine-aerial delivery system. The Canadian Coast Guard icebreaker *Alexander Henry* anchored offshore from the lighthouse and then a helicopter flew keepers from the ship to their station, along with their supplies. Later, in the 1980s, a Coast Guard helicopter out of Thunder Bay flew them the whole way. As long as they arrived safely keepers did not mind the means of transportation.

When the light was later automated, it was moved to a steel skeletal tower, and switched to a flashing light that flashed every five seconds. In 1972 the fog signal was automated and changed to a 60-second characteristic (blast 2.5 s; silence 5 s; blast 2.5 s; silence 50 s). The light became used as an emergency light operational 24 hours a day all year round in 1973.

As the work at the station decreased with greater automation, the assistant keeper was removed. In 1979 the keeper was Ray Silver, and his wife Kay stayed with him at the light. She described the life as having "no time to be lonely." In early spring they did painting and necessary maintenance work at the station. Her husband made daily checks of the engine room and the weather station. In the event of a shipping disaster, the keeper notified a rescue unit by marine radio. Her husband was not allowed to climb any higher than 8 feet (2.4 m) up the skeletal tower for his own safety. The bulbs for the automated light were replaced once every five years by specially trained technicians who understood the automatic bulb changer. Its electricity was provided by a diesel engine that never shut off. In the event of a power failure an alternate backup power source automatically took over. The foghorn system was also automatic and started when visibility was poor.

The Silvers loved living at the island. They knew what needed to be done and did it. They had everything they could possibly want — a television, a radio . . . and peace of mind. They never felt lonely because they could just look across the water and see the lights of the city. They always felt pretty lucky to be the keepers of the light.

Complete automation in 1986 removed the keepers from this station so no one was available to manually start the fog signal when it failed to operate in 1988. Apparently, due to the station's height above the lake, when a low-lying fog rolled in, the fog ducked the detector's beam and fooled the foghorn into silence. Fortunately, this rarely occurred. This light continues to shine today as an active aid to navigation.

Known Keepers: A. Perras (1896–), George Cosgrave (–1921), Gilbert McLachlan (1921–22), Joseph Bousquet (1922–30), Joseph Tremblay (1930–31), Allan Murray (1931–42), Fredrick Sikes (1942), Donald Alexander (1943–56), W.J. McLean (1956–60), Albert Wray (1960–62), Norman Cormier (1962), Wesley McLean (1962–63), Harold Mann (1963–), Ray Silver (1979–).

Bibliography

Alles, E. "Rotary Club Camp at Presqu'ile." Presqu'ile: *The Spokesman*, Sept. 10, 1980.

Allwardt, M. "Honeymooning on Outer Island." *Beacon*, Volume 8, Number 3. Dearborn: GLLKA, 1990.

Apostle Islands National Lakeshore. "Raspberry Island Light Station." www.nps.gov/apis/raspberr.htm.

Armstrong-Reynolds, M. *The Port Weller Lighthouse Station*. Ottawa: Federal Heritage Buildings Review Office, 1989.

Badtke, F. "Eagle Lighthouse." Sturgeon Bay: Door County Publishing Co., 1964.

Barry, J. *Georgian Bay: The Sixth Great Lake*. Erin: Boston Mills, 1995.

Beers, D. "Two-Day Stay on Middle Island." Great Lakes Lighthouse Yearbook 2001–2002, October. Rogers City: Dockside Printing.

Berger, T. "The Old Standby Fades Away But Never Dies." *Lighthouse Digest*, Feb. Wells: Lighthouse Digest Inc., 2003.

Biggs, J. "Mission to Mama." *Lighthouse Digest*, Oct. Wells: Lighthouse Digest Inc., 2000.

Biggs, J. "From Here to There on the St. Clair." *Beacon*, Fall. Dearborn: GLLKA, 1999.

Biggs, J. "The Boblo Beacon." *Lighthouse Digest*, March. Wells: Lighthouse Digest Inc., 1998.

Blahnik, J. "110th Anniversary of Lighting of Chambers Island Light." Sturgeon Bay: Door County Advocate, Sept. 26, 1978.

Block, P. "Indian Country Sports Light." www.lightstations.com/home.html.

Bond, S. "Henry Vaurina and the Light of 100 Years." *Beacon*, Volume 14, Number 1. Allen Park: GLLKA, 1996.

Boyer, B. *Victoria Harbour: A Mill-Town Legacy*. Erin: Boston Mills, 1989.

Bruce County Tourist Association. "Lighthouses." www.naturalretreat.com/lighthouses.htm.

Bunn, B. "Marine Band Salutes Lighthouse." *Port Huron Times Herald*, Aug. 19, 1983.

Cameron, E. "Thessalon Landmark." Sault Ste. Marie: *Sault Daily Star*, Dec. 2, 1974.

Campbell, E. "Lighthouses of the Great Lakes." Mackinaw City High School, unpublished, 1974.

Campbell, W. *Northeastern Georgian Bay and Its People*. Sudbury: Journal Printing, undated.

Carnochan, J. *History of Niagara*. Toronto: William Briggs, 1914.

Carroll, P. "Huron Historical Notes." Volume 37. Goderich: Huron County Historical Society, 2001.

Castagnera, J. "A Brief History of the Huron Lightship." *Inland Seas*, Volume 26, Number 3. Cleveland: Davies Wing Inc., 1970

Chronicle-Journal. "Rough Waters." *Thunder Bay Chronicle-Journal*, Oct. 21,1989.

Clifford, C. and M. *Nineteenth-Century Lights: Historic Images of America*. Cypress Communications, Alexandria, Virginia.

Clifford, M. *Women Who Kept the Lights*. Williamsburg: Cypress Communications, 1993.

Climo, P. "Gull Island Lighthouse." *Cobourg Saturday Morning Post*, Aug. 12, 1989.

Coleman, M. "Davieaux Island Light Station Buildings." Ottawa: Architectural History Branch, 1990.

Creamer, M. "Old Bee-Oh." *Port Huron Times Herald*, Sept. 9, 1994.

Cruikshank, F. "Tourist Beacon." *Lighthouse Digest*, April 1997.

DeHut, R. "The Ontonagon Lighthouse." Northern Michigan University, Dec. 1, 2000.

D'Entremont, J. "Rescuing of the Thunder Bay Beacon." *Lighthouse Digest*, July. Wells: Lighthouse Digest Inc., 2004.

Donovan, P. "Lighthouses." *Bruce County Day Trip Companion*. Tobermory: Tobermory Press, 1998.

DRLPS. "History of the Lighthouse." www.drlps.com/page 2.htm.

Eckert, J. "Life on Pilot Island In 1995." *Lighthouse Digest*, August. Wells: Lighthouse Digest Inc., 2003.

Eckert, J. "Life on Pilot Island," unpublished.

Edwards, B. "Windmill Point Repair in Sight." *Lighthouse Digest*, May. Lighthouse Digest Inc., 2004.

Edwards, L. "Lighthouses of Manitoulin Island," unpublished.

Eisner, S. "Manitowoc Breakwater Light." *Lighthouse Digest*, July. Wells: Lighthouse Digest Inc., 1997.

Englund, R. "Saginaw River Rear Range Lighthouse: History." www.geocities.com/saginawriverlight/history.html.

Eves, S. "Simcoe Island: An Eves Perspective." Cobourg: Haynes Printing Co. Ltd., 1994.

Eves, S. "Simcoe Island and Eves Perspective," unpublished.

Fairport Harbor Bicentennial Committee. "A History of Fairport Harbor, Ohio." Painesville: Lake Photo Engraving Inc., 1990.

Fergusson, D. "Petition Aims to Keep Staff at Lighthouse." *Thunder Bay Times-News*, July 15,1989.

Fischer, G. *Sentinels in the Stream*. Erin: Boston Mills, 2001.

Flemming, D. "Fort Mississaga 1814–1972." Manuscript Report No. 122. Ottawa: Parks Canada, 1972.

Francis, B. "Can't Afford Domestic Quarrel." *Port Arthur News-Chronicle*, July 20, 1953.

Frisbee Suggs, M. "Growing Up on the Buffalo Lighthouse Reservation." *Beacon*, Volume 8, Number 2. Allen Park: GLLKA, 1990.

Gertz, J. "New Green Bay Lights." *Beacon*, Volume 5, Number 1. Allen Park: GLLKA, 1987.

Gibson, Mel. "City's First Lighthouse Cost $3300 to Build." Port Credit: Local Archives, unpublished.

Government Document. *Inland Waters – List of Lights, Buoys and Fog Signals*. Ottawa: Marine Navigational Services, 1992.

Graham, L. "A Personal Lighthouse Adventure." *Lighthouse Digest*, October, Wells: Lighthouse Digest Inc., 1998.

Gutsche, A. *Alone in the Night*. Toronto: Lynx Images, 1996.

Harrison, M. "Public Invited to Middle Island Picnic." *The Alpena News*, Aug. 10, 1994.

Harrison, T. "A Forgotten Lighthouse Now Nearly Obscure." *Lighthouse Digest*, June. Wells: Lighthouse Digest Inc., 1998.

Harrison, T. "Galloo Island Goes for 2.47 Million." *Lighthouse Digest*, October. Wells: Lighthouse Digest Inc., 1999.

Harrison, T. "History Made at Erie's Land Light." *Lighthouse Digest*, May. Duluth: Lighthouse Digest Inc., 2004.

Harrison, T. "Lights of the Windy City." *Great Lakes Lighthouse Yearbook 2001–2002*, October. Rogers City: Dockside Printing Inc.

Harrison, T. "Mystery of Middle Island's Missing Lens." *Great Lakes Lighthouse Yearbook 2002–2003*, October. Alpena: Pro Ad, 2003.

Harrison, T. "Sheboygan's Forgotten Lighthouses." *Great Lakes Lighthouse Yearbook 2001–2002*, October. Rogers City: Dockside

Heap, D. *Ancient and Modern Lighthouses*. Boston: Ticknor & Co., 1889.

Henry, A. "The Early History of Sodus Light Station." Sodus Bay: Sodus Bay Historical Society, 2000.

Hodder, E. *Harbours and Ports of Lake Ontario*. Toronto: Maclear and Company, 1857.

Holden, T. "Above and Below." Houghton: Isle Royal Natural History Association, 1985.

Huggins, M. "Monroe's Lighthouses: Lost in the Pages of Time." *Lighthouse Digest*, December. Wells: Lighthouse Digest Inc., 2000.

Hunter, J. "Open House Marks Lighthouse's 100th Birthday." *Midland Observer*, July 15, 1995.

James, B. "Lighting the Way." Copper Harbor: Fort Wilkins Natural History Association, 1999.

Kampschror, B. "Into the Dark." Ontonagon: *Daily Mining Gazette*, July 3, 1998.

Karges, S. "Door County Lighthouses." Sturgeon Bay: Door County Maritime Museum Inc., 1998.

Katzuzin, R. "The Lights of Copper Harbor." *Beacon,* Volume 15, Number 3. Dearborn: GLLKA, 1997.

Kehetian, M. "Saving the South Channel Lights." *Michigan History Magazine,* Nov/Dec, 1997.

Kohane, J. "Unsolved Mystery: Toronto's Gibraltar Point Lighthouse." *Lighthouse Digest,* Jan. 2002 Wells: Lighthouse Digest Inc.

Langer, V. "The Keepers at North Manitou Island." *Beacon,* Volume 7, Number 3: GLLKA, 1989.

Law, W. *Important Light Towers in the Great Water World.* Detroit: Pohl Printing Co., 1898.

Mackinac State Historic Parks. "Old Mackinac Point Lighthouse." www.mackinacparks.com/oldmackinacpoint.htm.

Mansfield, J. *History of the Great Lakes:* Volume 1. Cleveland: Freshwater Press Inc., 1972.

Mansfield, J.B. *History of the Great Lakes.* Cleveland: Freshwater Press Inc., 1972.

Marken, K. "Spectacle Reef Lighthouse: The Engineer and His Plan." *Beacon,* Volume 13, Number 4. Allen Park: GLLKA, 1995.

Mattie, J. *Four Imperial Towers.* Ottawa: Federal Heritage Buildings Review Office, 1991.

McNichol, P. "Demolition of Lion's Head." *Owen Sound Sun Times,* March 17, 1982.

Merkel, J. "Erosion Control Projects Set for Two Apostle Islands' Lighthouses." *Lighthouse Digest,* January. Wells: Lighthouse Digest Inc.

Merkel, J. "Recollections of a Nineteenth Century-style Life at Middle Neebish Island Light Station." *Lighthouse Digest,* November.

Merkel, J. "The Story of One Keeper's Daughter." *Lighthouse Digest,* May. Wells: Lighthouse Digest Inc., 2002.

Metcalfe, W. *Canvas and Steam on Quinte Waters.* Picton: Prince Edward Printing, 1993.

Mosen, C. "Restoring The Ventilation System." *Beacon,* Volume 22, Number 2. Mackinaw City: GLLKA, 2004.

National Archives of Canada. "1914–1921." RG 42, Volume 520, File 22055K.

National Archives of Canada. "1927–1934." RG 42, Volume 521, File 22055K.

National Archives of Canada. "Cape Croker 1886." RG 10, Volume 2338, File 68375.

National Archives of Canada. "Cape Croker." RG 10, Volume 2769, File 154336."

National Archives of Canada. "Charles Davieaux 1917–1919." RG 42, Volume 302, File 49587.

National Archives of Canada. "Collingwood." RG 12, Volume 1503, File 7952-C5.

National Archives of Canada. "Corbeil 1952–1957." RG 12, Volume 1441, File 7952-1735.

National Archives of Canada. "Foote's Dock 1887–1895." RG 12, Volume 1507, File 7958-F1.

National Archives of Canada. "Gore Bay 1883–1902." RG 10,Volume 2213, File 42887.

National Archives of Canada. "Illegal Fishing." RG 23, Volume 100, File 90.

National Archives of Canada. "Lonely Island." RG 12, Volume 1503, File 7952-L2.

National Archives of Canada. "Manitowaning–Little Current (1886–1937)." RG 10, Volume 2344, Reel C-11205.

National Archives of Canada. "Manitowaning 1878–1966." RG 10, Volume 10298, File 468/36-6.

National Archives of Canada. "Manitowaning 1891–1913." RG 10, Volume 2597, File 120488.

National Archives of Canada. "Manitowaning De Lamorandiere (1881–1938)." RG 10, Volume 2143, File 29703.

National Archives of Canada. "Middle Island." RG 42, Volume 369, File 3-5-5.

National Archives of Canada. "Narrow Island (1889–1894)." RG 10, Volume 2470, File 917828.

National Archives of Canada. "Nottawasaga Wasaga." RG 42, Volume 520, File 21998-9K

National Archives of Canada. "Pointe aux Pins." RG13, Volume 124, File 1902-705.

National Archives of Canada. "Series A-1 (1882–1884)." RG 6, Volume 56, File 2983.

National Archives of Canada. "Thessalon Light." RG 10, Volume 8044, File 493/36-6-6-12.

National Archives of Canada. "Tobermory." RG 42. Volume 519, File 21968K.

National Archives of Canada."Gore Bay Missisaugi 1911." RG 10, Volume 3164, File 377673.

National Archives of Canada. "Manitowaning 1876." RG 10, Volume 1977, File 5891.

National Archives of Canada. "McKay 1880." RG 10, Volume 2334, File 67534.

National Archives Washington DC. "Granite Island Light Station Lake Superior." www.graniteisland.com/history.shtml.

National Park Service. "Huron Harbor Light, Inventory of Historic Light Stations: Ohio Lighthouses

National Park Service. "Inventory of Historical Light Stations, Michigan." www.cr.nps.gov/maritime/light.htm.

Nelson, B. "The History of Big Point Sable Light Station." *Beacon,* Volume 13, Number 4. Dearborn: GLLKA, 200/2001.

Nelson, D. "First Woman Light Keeper on the Keweenaw Peninsula." *Lighthouse Digest,* March, 2002 Wells: Lighthouse Digest Inc.

Nelson, D. "Gull Rock and Manitou." *Beacon,* Volume 20, Number 2. Dearborn: GLLKA, 2002.

Nelson, D. "Lansing Shoal Lighthouse." *Beacon,* Volume 14, Number 3. Allen Park: GLLKA, 1996.

Nelson, D. "One of Superior's Little Known Lights." *Lighthouse Digest,* July. Wells: Lighthouse Digest Inc., 1998.

Nelson, D. "Portage Lake Ship Canal Light Station 1874." *Beacon,* Volume 12, Number 3. Dearborn: GLLKA, 1994.

Nelson, D. "Portage River Lower Entry Lighthouses: Part II." *Beacon,* Volume 13, Number 1. Dearborn: GLLKA, 1995.

Nelson, D. "Sand Point Lighthouse Changes Hands." *Beacon,* Volume 12, Number 1. Dearborn: GLLKA, 1994.

Nelson, D. "Update on Sand Hills Lighthouse Bed and Breakfast." *Beacon,* Volume 12, Number 2. Dearborn: GLLKA, 1994.

Niesen, J. "Gibraltar: Its History." Put-In-Bay: South Bass Island Marine Museum, unpublished.

Noble, D. *Lighthouses and Keepers.* Annapolis: Naval Institute Press, 1997.

Nottingham, B."Lake Michigan Lighthouses." *Marquette Mining Journal,* May 18,1966.

Oleszewski, W. "Great Lakes Lighthouses American and Canadian." Gwinn: Avery Colour Studios Inc., 1998.

Pacyon, L. "Sharing Family Memories of Sackets Harbor Light." *Lighthouse Digest,* May. Duluth: Lighthouse Digest Inc., 2004.

Parks Canada. "Bois Blanc Island Lighthouse." http://www.pc.gc.ca/ lhn-nhs/on/boisblanc/natcul/index_e.asp

Penrod, D. "Whitefish Point Light Station." Whitefish: Hiawatha Berrien Center, 1998.

Penrose, L. *A Travel Guide To 100 Eastern Great Lakes Lighthouses.* Davidson: Friede Publishing, 1994.

Penrose, L. *A Travel Guide To 116 Lighthouses of the Western Great Lakes.* Davidson: Friede Publishing, 1995.

Penrose, L. *A Travel Guide To 116 Michigan Lighthouses.* Davidson: Friede Publishing, 1993.

Pepper, T. "A Voice from the Grave at Spectacle Reef." *Beacon,* Volume 21, Number 1. Dearborn: GLLKA, 2003.

Pepper, T. "Lake Huron Lighthouses." www.terrypepper.com/lights/lake huron.htm.

Pepper, T. "Lake Michigan Lighthouses." www.terrypepper.com/lights/lake michigan.htm.

Pepper, T. "Lake Superior Lighthouses." www.terrypepper.com/lights/lake superior.htm.

Pomeroy, J. "The Old Lighthouse at Presque Isle." Back Roads, Sept./Oct. Buchanan: Scarlet Pomeroy, 1993.

Port Credit Library. "Credit Valley Gateway: The Story of Port Credit." Port Credit Public Library Board, 1967.

Potter, R. "Lighthouse: Nancy Island Historical Site." Wasaga Beach, unpublished.

Reutter, J. "South Bass Island Lighthouse." Columbus: Ohio Sea Grant College, 1999.

Richmond, D. "Two Rival Villages." *Buffalo Evening News,* Jan. 18, 1964.

Ripley, J. "Whitefish Point Light." *Inland Seas*, Volume 24, Number 4. Cleveland: Davies Wing Inc., 1968.

Robertson, J. "Landmarks of Toronto." www.hhpl.on.ca/Great Lakes/scripts/page.asp?PageID=121.

Roblee, D. "Historical Society Owns Light." Ontonagon: *Daily Mining Gazette*, Dec. 16, 2000.

Rusco, R. *North Manitou Island*. Book Craftus, 1999

Sanders, C."Despite Outcry Lamb Island Lighthouse Expected to Lose Keeper." *Thunder Bay Chronicle-Journal*, Aug. 30, 1989.

Sapulski, W. *Lighthouses of Lake Michigan*. Manchester: Wilderness Adventure Books, 2001.

Saunders, A. "Old Lighthouse Now Private Home." *Bay City Times*, July 31, 1970.

Saver, E. "Deeds of Valor." *Beacon*, Volume 6, Number 1. Allen Park: GLLKA, 1998.

Scott, G. *Scott's New Coast Pilot for the Lakes*. Detroit: Free Press Printing Company, 1901.

Scott, G. *Scott's New Coast Pilot*. Changes and Additions. Detroit: Free Press Printing Company, 1902.

Selwa, R. "Divers Find Part of Historical Lighthouse." *Beacon*, Volume 13, Number 5. Allen Park: GLLKA, 1995.

Sigurdson, J. "Lighthouse of Doom." Thunder Bay Historical Society Papers to 1967.

Silverwood, T. "The Old Stone Lighthouse." Green Bay Historical Society, unpublished, 1901.

Smith, J. "Background and History of Middle Island." *Beacon*, Volume 12, Number4. Allen Park: GLLKA, 1994.

Smith, K. "Urge to Toot Harbor Foghorn." *Buffalo Courier Express*, July 25, 1954.

Snider, J. "Delivering Lighthouse Keepers Simplified by Helicopter." *Fort William Times Journal*, April 8, 1961.

Snider, J. "Light Keeper's Yuletide Sometimes Bleak in '80s." *Fort William Times Journal*, Dec. 20, 1967.

Snider, J. "Shipping." *Fort William Times Journal*, Jan. 9 and 14, 1963.

Staff. "Equipment in Use 52 Years." *Manitowoc Herald Times*, Sept. 9, 1947.

Staff. "Gull Island Lighthouse." *Cobourg Star*, June 21,1837.

Staff. "Half-a-House Bewilders Motorists." *Toledo Blade*, Aug. 1, 1950.

Staff. "History of Buffalo." *Buffalo Commercial Advertiser*, June 27, 1847.

Staff. "HMS Nancy and Historical Wasaga Beach." Ottawa: Queen's Printer for Ontario, 1990.

Staff. "Lighthouse Proves Model of Housekeeping Artistry." *Buffalo Evening News*, Aug. 27, 1930.

Staff. "Lighthouses." *Kingston Daily News*, Jan. 16, 1858.

Staff. "Lights of the Apostles." Washington: National Park Service, 1989.

Staff. "Old Lighthouse." *Sault Ste. Marie Star*, Aug. 7, 1968.

Staff. "Ontonagon Lighthouse." Ontonagon County Historical Society, unpublished.

Staff. "Port Austin Pigeons and a Dumb Waiter." *Beacon*, Volume 9, Number 2. Allen Park: GLLKA, 1991.

Staff. "Range Light Is Relic of Earlier Times." *Toledo Times*, Aug. 13, 1923.

Staff. "Recalls Exciting Experience with the Lighthouse Service." *Manitowoc Herald Times*, June 30, !941.

Staff. "Rich in City's History." *Toledo Blade*, Feb. 1929.

Staff. "Sand Hills Being Dismantled." Ontonagon: *Daily Mining Gazette*, Dec. 9, 1941.

Staff. "Silver's Job Is a Blessing." *Thunder Bay Chronicle Journal*, July 16, 1979.

Staff. "Site of Old Lighthouse on Bay Sold." *Toledo Blade*, Sept. 1, 1953.

Staff. "Tablet Was Dedicated at Niagara." *St. Catharines Standard*, Oct. 5,1939.

Staff. "The Kaplan Award." *Great Lakes Cruiser*, Volume 8, Issue 2. Royal Oak: Great Lakes Cruiser Ltd., 2001.

Staff. "This Day in Buffalo's History." *Buffalo Times*, May 9, 1923.

Staff. "To Experienced Contractors." *Cobourg Star*, May 25, 1842.

Staff. "Vermillion Progress." *Beacon*, Volume 9, Number 3. Allen Park: GLLKA, 1991.

Staff. "Works for Canal." *Buffalo Commercial Adveriser*, Sept. 7, 1861.

Staff. "Wreck of the Walk-on-the-Water." *Buffalo Courier*, Apr.il 14, 1912.

Staff. Georgian Bay and North Channel Pilot 1899. Ottawa: Government Printing Bureau, 1900.

Staff. Improvements and Changes: 42nd Annual Report. Ottawa: Department of Marine and Fisheries, 1909.

State Historic Preservation Office. "National Historic Landmarks in Michigan"

Stevens, J. "Thames River Lighthouse 1845." Ottawa: Canadian Official Publications, July, 1965.

Stevens, J. "Windmill Point Lighthouse 1873-1965." Ottawa: Canadian Official Publications Collection, unpublished.

Stevens, John. "Lighthouses of the Great Lakes." Ottawa: Canadian Official Publications Collection, Sept. 1965.

Stonehouse, F. *Haunted Lakes*. Duluth: Lake Superior Port Cities Inc., 1997.

Stonehouse, F. *Women and the Lakes*. Guinn: Avery Color Studios Inc., 2001.

Strzok, D. *Exploring Wisconsin's North Coast*. Ashland: Printing Plus, 1992.

Sweet, T. "Pottawatomie Lighthouse Furnished and Dedicated." *Beacon*, Volume 22, Number 2. Mackinaw City: GLLKA, 2004.

Tag, T. "Cunningham Creek, Ohio." Keeper's Log, Volume 15, Number 2. Birmingham: EBSCO Media, 1999.

Tag, T. Great Lakes Lighthouse Research, 2003. *The Lighthouse Keepers of Lake Ontario including the St. Lawrence River*, Revision 2. 6262 Blossom Park Drive, Dayton, Ohio.

Tag, T. "Silver Creek." *Beacon*, Volume 22, Number 2. Mackinaw City: GLLKA, 2004

Thompson. *Thompson's Coast Pilot*. Detroit: Free Press Book and Job Printing House, 1869.

Thorndale, T. "Island Jottings." *Sandusky Register*, July 28 1897.

Tiessen, R. "A Brief History of the Pelee Island Lighthouse." Pelee Island:Pelee Island Heritage Centre, 1999.

Times-Journal."Big Public Works Program Undertaken in 1939. "Fort *William Daily Times Journal*, Dec.16, 1939.

Times-Journal."Lighthouse Is Wrecked by Vandals." Fort William *Times-Journal*, Jan. 10, 1951.

Tinney, J. *Seaway Trail Lighthouses*. Sackets Harbor: Seaway Trail Foundation Inc., 2000.

Turner, G. "Cheboygan Point Memories." *Cheboygan Daily Tribune*, July 28, 1992.

Unknown. "Detour Reef Lighthouse." Detour Reef Light Preservation Society brochure, 2000.

Unknown. "The Lighthouse on Bois Blanc." Amherstburg Bicentennial Committee, unpublished.

Unknown. "The Vermillion Lighthouse." Vermillion: Great Lakes Historical Society, 1999.

United States Government. "USCG Lightships." www.uscg.mil/hq/g-cp/history/weblightships/html.

Vogel, M. *Maritime Buffalo*. Buffalo: Western New York Heritage Institute, 1990.

Wardius, K. "The Forgotten Lighthouse of Green Island." *Beacon*, Volume 18, Number 4. Dearborn: GLLKA, 2000/2001.

Watson, Rod "Lighthouses." http://home.neo.rr.com/rodsphotogallery/index.html

Weber, T. "Lighthouse Losing Its Keeper." *Owen Sound Sun Times*, July 11, 1987.

Weeks, M. *Harbour Lights Burlington Bay*. Erin: Boston Mills, 1988.

Weeks-Mifflin, M. *The Light on Chantry Island*. Erin: Boston Mills Press, 1986.

Wendt, G. "Lights of Sandusky Bay." Sandusky: Sandusky Historical Society, 2000.

West Michigan Tourist Association. "West Michigan Lighthouses." www.wmta.org/lighthouse/html.

Whipple, A. "Notice to Mariners." *Detroit Free Press*, Nov. 5, 1857.

Wilson, M. "Harsen's Island St. Clair Flats." *Beacon*, Volume 19, Number 4. Dearborn: GLLKA, 2001/2002.

Wobser, D. "Pipe Island." www.lighthouse.boatnerd.com/gallery/StMarysRiver/pipeisland.htm.

Wright, L. and P. *Bright Lights, Dark Nights*. Erin: Boston Mills Press, 1999.

Wright, L. and P. *Sweetwater Sentinels*, unpublished.

Wright, Larry and Patricia. *Bonfires and Beacons*. Erin: Boston Mills Press, 1996.

Wyonch, C. *Hewers of the Forests, Fishers of the Lakes*. Owen Sound: Stan Brown Printers Ltd., 1985.

Zafra, D. "Charlotte's Lighthouse and Its River." Charlotte-Genesee: Lighthouse Historical Society, 1993.

Index

Acknowledgments

A book of this magnitude would never have come to fruition had it not been for the magnificent help of many people. During the course of gathering this information over the past 15 years, we have been to virtually every library, museum, archive, and all but a few lighthouses. We have met and interviewed Coast Guard staff from both sides of the lakes, keepers' families, lighthouse owners, other interested lighthouse enthusiasts, writers, ships' captains, pleasure boaters, aviators and, everyone welcomed us with open arms as soon as they knew what we were doing. Many library staff and archivists went out of their way to assist us.

We would like to take this opportunity to thank the families of the keepers who welcomed us to their kitchen tables and shared memories and photos with us. A special warm thanks goes out to the lighthouse enthusiasts who served on the board and as members of the Great Lakes Lighthouse Keepers Association, the many friends of lighthouse groups, and lighthouse restorationists and preservationists.

We would like to also add a special thanks to the National Archives of Canada for their assistance, the Canadian and American Coast Guards, and Phyllis and Thomas Tag for allowing us to include their work on listing the American Lighthouse Keepers from their publication *Great Lakes Lighthouse Research*. Additional gratitude goes to individual friends, researchers and writers Pat and Jerry Biggs, Terry Pepper, Wayne Sapulski, Sandy Planisek and Dick Moehl for exchanging information and allowing us to pick their brains, knowingly or not.

We hope this book captures some of the flavor of the early history of the circle of lights around the Great Lakes. Although we tried desperately to included every light that ever existed on the lakes, I am sure that we have missed a few. There were many lights that were private aids to navigation and were erected and maintained by individuals or companies to service their own needs.

Not all of our research could be used in this book. A lot of material was left "on the cutting room floor" in order to make this book a manageable size.

Once again, a special thanks to all of the people who helped to make this book a reality.